7TH EDITION

Creating Inclusive Classrooms

Effective and Reflective Practices

SPENCER J. SALEND

State University of New York at New Paltz

PEARSON

Boston Columbus Indianapolis New York San Francisco Upper Saddle River
Amsterdam Cape Town Dubai London Madrid Milan Munich Paris Montreal Toronto
Delhi Mexico City Sao Paulo Sydney Hong Kong Seoul Singapore Taipei Tokyo

Library of Congress Cataloging-in-Publication Data

Salend, Spencer J.
  Creating inclusive classrooms : effective and reflective practices / Spencer J. Salend.—7th ed.
    p. cm.
  Includes bibliographical references and index.
  ISBN-13: 978-0-13-703074-3
  ISBN-10: 0-13-703074-6
  1. Inclusive education—United States. 2. Curriculum planning—United States. 3. Classroom
management—United States. 4. Children with disabilities—Education—United States. I. Title.
  LC1201.S24 2010
  371.9'046—dc22

                                                                              2009048020

Vice President and Editor in Chief:
    Jeffery W. Johnston
Executive Editor: Ann Castel Davis
Editorial Assistant: Penny Burleson
Senior Development Editor: Hope Madden
Vice President, Director of Marketing: Quinn Perkson
Marketing Manager: Erica DeLuca
Senior Managing Editor: Pamela D. Bennett
Senior Production Editor: Sheryl Glicker Langner
Senior Operations Supervisor: Matthew Ottenweller

Senior Art Director: Diane C. Lorenzo
Text and Cover Designer: Candace Rowley
Photo Coordinator: Monica Merkel
Cover Art: Fotosearch
Media Producer: Autumn Benson
Media Project Manager: Rebecca Norsic
Composition: S4Carlisle Publishing Services
Printer/Binder: Webcrafters
Cover Printer: Lehigh-Phoenix
Text Font: Garamond

Photo Credits: Jupiter Unlimited, pp. 1, 22, 42, 125, 136, 201, 240, 309, 340; Scott Cunningham/
Merrill, pp. 4, 187, 189, 229, 295, 299, 349, 414, 456, 485; Richard Hutchings/Photo Researchers,
Inc., p. 8; Paul Conklin/PhotoEdit Inc., p. 13; Modern Curriculum Press/Pearson Learning, p. 16;
Bob Daemmrich/PhotoEdit Inc., p. 20; Richard Hutchings/PhotoEdit Inc., p. 33; Lori Whitley/
Merrill, p. 60; Photos to Go, pp. 64, 92, 186, 377; Roy Ramsey/PH College, p. 78; Mary Steinbacher/
PhotoEdit Inc., p. 80; Stockphoto.com, pp. 100, 192, 494; Bruce Ayres/Getty Images Inc.—Stone
Allstock, p. 102; Anthony Magnacca/Merrill, pp. 110, 114, 141 (bottom), 174, 246, 267, 335, 490;
U.S. Census Bureau, pp. 119, 214; Valerie Schultz/Merrill, pp. 135, 324; Laura Bolesta/Merrill,
pp. 141 (top), 212; David Mager/Pearson Learning Photo Studio, pp. 149, 223; Robin L. Sachs/
PhotoEdit Inc., pp. 157, 460; Bold Stock Images by Unlisted Images, p. 164; Ken Karp/PH Photo,
pp. 208, 236; Pearson Learning Photo Studio, p. 253; Larry Hamill/Merrill, pp. 262, 351; Ann Summa
for Silver Burdett Ginn, p. 274; Tom Watson/Merrill, p. 283; Emi DiScuillo, pp. 284, 332, 404;
Liz Moore/Merrill, pp. 305, 479; Silver Burdett Ginn, pp. 358, 421; Lynn Saville/Prentice Hall
School Division, p. 372; Hope Madden/Merrill, pp. 382, 388; Krista Greco/Merrill, p. 432;
David Young-Wolff/PhotoEdit Inc., pp. 439, 446; Superstock, Inc., p. 451; Grantpix/
Photo Researchers, Inc., p. 455; Gabe Palmer/Corbis, All Rights Reserved, p. 502.

Credits and acknowledgments borrowed from other sources and reproduced, with permission,
in this textbook appear on appropriate page within text.

Every effort has been made to provide accurate and current Internet information in this book.
However, the Internet and information posted on it are constantly changing, so it is inevitable
that some of the Internet addresses listed in this textbook will change.

www.pearsonhighered.com

10 9 8 7 6 5 4 3 2
ISBN 10:   0-13-703074-6
ISBN 13: 978-0-13-703074-3

To Suzanne, Jack, and Madison,

All My Loving

Preface

Creating an inclusive classroom means understanding federal legislation as well as national and state standards, but the practical, up-to-date and streamlined seventh edition of *Creating Inclusive Classrooms: Effective and Reflective Practices* recognizes that it means more than that . . .

It means being reflective about your own teaching so you can better differentiate instruction for *all* of your students.

It means collaborating with educators and families to create the most successful educational experience for *all* of your students.

It means using current research related to effective practices in curriculum, instruction, technology, and assessment to foster the learning of *all* your students.

More than anything, it means taking into account the strengths and challenges of each student in today's diverse classroom and implementing practical strategies that address learning ability as well as issues of gender, race, ethnicity, language, socioeconomic status, religion, sexual orientation, and family structure.

This text goes beyond the typical inclusion text, translating current theory and research into practices you can use by illustrating the principles of effective inclusion through classroom scenarios, numerous examples, online video clips, new figures, and successful strategies.

New to This Edition

In this seventh edition you'll find many new teaching strategies, several new boxed features, and the new margin note *Making Connections*, which makes it easier to see connections in content across chapters. You'll also find new, updated, and expanded coverage of:

- Universal design for learning (UDL)
- response to intervention (RTI)
- autism spectrum disorders and students with intellectual disabilities
- positive behavioral supports
- co-teaching arrangements
- instructional and assistive technologies
- differentiating instruction across the curriculum
- student diversity and motivation
- learning strategies
- fostering students' literacy, mathematics, and science learning
- research-based teaching, behavior management, and assessment strategies
- creating accessible teacher-made tests
- teaching, testing, and grading accommodations
- assessment alternatives to testing
- building social relationships among students and positive relationship with students
- implementing IEPs in inclusive classrooms
- teaching study and test-taking skills

A Principled Philosophy

Improving education for *all learners,* effective inclusion educates students together in general education classrooms regardless of their learning ability, race, linguistic ability, economic status, gender, learning style, ethnicity, cultural and religious background, family structure, and sexual orientation. This is an important principle to understand and implement, which is why it's returned to throughout chapters in foundational chapter content as well as in the text's many special features.

These four principles of effective inclusion provide a framework for this book:

- *all learners and equal access*
- *individual strengths and challenges and diversity*
- *reflective practices and differentiated instruction*
- and *community and collaboration*

Each of these principles for inclusive practice is integrated into each chapter of the book, demonstrating that inclusion is not just a government mandate but a principled philosophy of reflective, effective teaching for individualizing the educational system for *all students.*

A Non-Categorical Approach

To serve as a model for creating inclusive classrooms for *all students*, this text takes a non-categorical approach to content coverage. It is meant to facilitate your development of a holistic approach to educating students while focusing on individual strengths and challenges rather than on global disability characteristics. Thus, rather than separating content by disability category or cultural and linguistic background– focusing on the differences that have been used to segregate students from one another–the book approaches inclusion as an ongoing, dynamic process.

New to the Seventh Edition

UDL and YOU Universal design for learning requires flexibility in materials and strategies so they can be used to promote learning for *all students*. This new chapter feature throughout the text guides you in understanding and implementing the principles of universal design to help *all learners* access the general education curriculum and succeed in inclusive classrooms.

- supporting successful transitions
- supporting student learning and behavior
- preparing readable and legible materials
- making large- and small-group instruction accessible to *all students*
- making literacy instruction accessible to *all students*
- making mathematics, science, and social studies instruction accessible to all students
- using technology-based testing and assessment

UDL and YOU
Understanding the Principles of Universal Design for Learning

The movement toward inclusion also was fostered by the application of the principles of **universal design** to educational

different formats and combinations for students to respond and demonstrate and express their mastery such as written, oral, and technology-based projects; role plays; simulations; presentations; tests; and peer-based assignments);

- *engagement*, by which you use classroom practices to prompt and encourage *all* students to perform at their optimal levels and be involved in the learning process (e.g., employ different formats and combinations to foster student engagement such as giving students choices, prompting students to use learning strategies and self-management techniques, and using peer-mediated and technology-based

Using Technology to Promote Inclusion
FOSTERING INCLUSION AND INDEPENDENCE

My name is Robin Smith. I always wanted to be a teacher and was excited when my goal became a reality. I enjoyed my job and looked forward to going to school every day. After several years of teaching, I started to feel exhausted and have recurring body aches. When I wasn't teaching or eating, I was sleeping. After 2 years, I was finally diagnosed as having adult-onset severe rheumatoid arthritis.

My condition got worse, and I had to leave teaching. My fingers were like clay as they seemed to take a different shape every day. Eventually, I moved back home with my family. I could barely move my arms and legs and entered a hospital for several months. Upon leaving the hospital, my life revolved around sleeping, eating, and going to physical therapy five times a week.

tied a string to the directional signal to make it easier for me to use. I used to use a "reacher" to pull tickets out of machines when entering a toll booth. Now that most toll booths have an electronic system, I use the reacher only to enter parking areas.

My success in school was aided by use of a small computer that was like a personal digital assistant with a keyboard. I used it to take notes and as a word processor, calendar, and address book. After school, I transferred the information to a desktop computer. I also tried voice recognition software, but I found it inconsistent. I completed my doctorate and was pleased to be hired as a special education professor. I continue to use many of the same things I did as a student to do the different aspects of my job.

The university I work for is about 200 miles from my family, so I live alone, which is a challenge. However, I use several everyday things to make my life a little easier. I place long sticks with hooks throughout my home so that I can

Using Technology to Promote Inclusion

These features in each chapter present ideas, strategies, and resources for using the latest instructional and assistive technology to help your students succeed in inclusive classrooms. Topics include:

- fostering inclusion and independence
- conducting an individualized technology assessment
- bridging the digital divide
- fostering communication and collaboration
- fostering acceptance and friendships

PEARSON myeducationlab Notes throughout chapters take you to online learning units that help you develop an inclusive classroom that gives all learners equal access to education.

Effective inclusion involves sensitivity to and acceptance of individual strengths and challenges as well as other types of student diversity. To emphasize this second principle of the framework for inclusive education, throughout the text and in important special features in every chapter you'll find clear information on developing this sensitivity and acceptance and using it to inform teaching that benefits *all students*.

Two Complete Chapters

While this principle is discussed as appropriate throughout the text, two chapters look specifically at the individual strengths and challenges and diversity of students in inclusive classrooms, providing comprehensive guidance for understanding, appreciating, and educating *all students*.

- *Chapter 2: Understanding the Diverse Educational Strengths and Challenges of Students with Disabilities* looks closely at the special education identification process, IEPs, and the particular strengths and challenges facing students with high-incidence disabilities, low-incidence disabilities, and those students who are gifted and talented.

- *Chapter 3: Understanding the Diverse Educational Strengths and Challenges of Students Who Challenge Schools* examines recent economic and demographic shifts that affect students and schools, focuses attention on discrimination, family and societal changes, and the specific strengths and challenges associated with cultural and language differences.

IDEAs to Implement Inclusion

Preparing For and Participating In the IEP Meeting

Although he had participated in several family–teacher meetings during his brief time as a teacher, Mr. Myers was nervous about attending his first IEP meeting. He spoke to his mentor teacher about his uncertainty, who suggested that he talk to Ms. Gonzalez, the special education teacher. When Mr. Myers approached her, Ms. Gonzalez was not surprised, as even many experienced teachers were intimidated initially by the IEP process.

Ms. Gonzalez began by explaining to Mr. Myers that his input was extremely important. She showed him a sample IEP, explaining the different components and how they were developed. She told him that he would be asked to talk about the student's progress in the general education curriculum, how the student's disability affected his performance in class, and what services the student and he would need to achieve the goals in the IEP. She noted that other teachers had found it helpful to bring samples of student work to illustrate their comments regarding their students'

- Prepare for the meeting by learning about the issues to be discussed and their relationship to the information you have to share, reviewing current information regarding the student (e.g., current assessment data and IEP), and obtaining an agenda for the meeting.
- Identify and share with other team members your goals for the meeting and the issues you would like to be addressed so those items can be part of the meeting agenda.
- Outline the services you provide to the student and the family and their responses to these services as well as the services and supports you will need to implement the student's IEP.
- Discuss positive aspects of the student's performance first, including the best ways in which the student learns.

IDEAs to Implement Inclusion

These features in every chapter offer practical examples of the application of effective techniques in the book that help you create inclusive classrooms that meet the challenges of the IDEA 2004. Features provide implementation ideas on topics as varied as motivation, gender equality, friendship skills, and self-esteem; content-specific techniques for teaching spelling, and word problem; ideas on facilitating friendships, promoting math and science education; adapting independent assignments, teaching organizational skills, and helping students with oppositional and defiant behaviors, students with ADD, students with expressive language disorders, students with cerebral palsy, and students with TS, and English language learners succeed.

What Would You Do in Today's Diverse Classroom?

★ Marcus, a secondary student, experiences some significant challenges in learning. Because he reads at a fifth-grade level, he struggles with many assignments and does poorly on many exams. Marcus is well liked by peers and participates in several after-school activities. His family expects him to go to college, just like his siblings, and wants him to take all general education classes.

★ Melissa uses a laptop to communicate with others and complete her work. Her classmates and teachers recognize that she is academically capable but are put off by her flapping hands, vocal outbursts, and limited eye contact. Melissa's family and her special education teacher believe that she has done well in school because she receives special attention and services from a trained teacher who understands her needs, and they are worried about other students making fun of her. Therefore, they are not sure that the school's inclusion program is the best educational setting for Melissa.

★ Fourth grader Tyler began school as a kindergartener entirely unable to communicate. He spent his first year of school in a special education classroom,

Updated and Technology-Based
What Would You Do in Today's Diverse Classroom?

These features near the end of every chapter provide descriptions of classroom situations followed by a set of reflective questions. You'll have the opportunity to consider text and video-based case-by-case situations and determine how you would handle each situation yourself in your inclusive classroom.

PEARSON **myeducationlab** New elements in these features integrate interactive online learning experiences from MyEducationLab to take you online to see inclusive classrooms, then ask you to apply what you've learned in the chapter to individual classroom situations. You'll meet students like Bridget, Tyler, and Kevin, learn about their individual strengths and challenges, and find out what inclusive education means for them through authentic and interactive video activities linked to each chapter's feature.

Authentic Classroom Scenes

Throughout the text, classroom-based examples and case studies, MyEducationLab videos and learning activities, as well as chapter opening classroom vignettes, provide examples of teachers implementing effective inclusive educational practices in their classrooms. These regular snapshots of real classrooms show you how to develop and use a sensitivity to and acceptance of individual strengths and challenges as well as other types of student diversity to inform successful inclusive classroom practice.

To accommodate individual challenges and provide *all students* with meaningful access to and progress in the general education curriculum, effective inclusion requires reflective educators who examine their attitudes and differentiate their assessment, teaching, and classroom management practices. This book provides scaffolds throughout its pages to help you become the kind of reflective practitioner who differentiates instruction to benefit *all students*.

Four chapters on differentiated instruction in Part III: *Differentiating Instruction for All Students* provide you with more details and examples on this important subject than any other text in the market.

- *Chapter 8: Differentiating Instruction for Diverse Learners*
- *Chapter 9: Differentiating Large- and Small-Group Instruction*
- *Chapter 10: Differentiating Reading, Writing, and Spelling Instruction*
- *Chapter 11: Differentiating Mathematics, Science, and Social Studies Instruction*

Reflecting on Professional Practices

These features in each chapter look back at the actions of the teacher in the chapter's opening vignette, examining her or his decision making and asking you to reflect on the teacher's actions and their affect on the inclusive classroom.

Reflective Margin Notes

Peppered throughout chapters, these notes pose questions that ask you to reflect on your personal experiences related to the material in the book.

A Guide to Action

This feature in all chapters guides you in creating a plan of action to enhance the effectiveness of your inclusive practices. Topics include:

- Examining disproportionate representation
- Implementing prereferral and RTI systems
- Fostering equity in the classroom
- Enhancing meetings with families
- Selecting books, materials, and web-based information about individual differences
- Promoting students' self-determination
- Creating rules
- Creating readable and legible materials
- Enhancing oral presentations
- Creating a balanced and literacy-rich learning environment
- Selecting textbooks and other text-based materials
- Creating valid and accessible teacher-made tests

Standards Integration in every chapter summary demonstrates where chapter content aligns with national professional standards, helping you make the connections between what you're reading about differentiation and what will be expected of you as an inclusive classroom teacher.

myeducationlab Look for MyEducationLab notes directing you to IRIS, comprehensive online modules offering case studies, videos, learning activities, and guided and reflective questions that lead you to a fuller understanding of reflective practice and differentiated instruction.

Effective inclusion is a group effort. It involves establishing a community based on collaboration among educators, other professionals, students, families, and community agencies. Throughout the text you'll find background information and specific guidance to help you establish a collaborative community to help *all students* succeed.

A Full Chapter

- *Chapter 4: Creating Collaborative Relationships and Fostering Communication* covers the creation and members of a comprehensive planning team, looks at the ways team members can work collaboratively, and discusses opportunities to communicate and collaborate with families.

Integrated Coverage

- MyEducationLab notes take you to IRIS modules and sources of video that help you evaluate and analyze collaborate classroom situations.

- Features throughout the chapters, including chapter opening classroom vignettes, Reflecting on Professional Practices and A Guide to Action often focus on issues of collaboration and community.

MYEDUCATIONLAB

The power of classroom practice.

PEARSON myeducationlab "Teacher educators who are developing pedagogies for the analysis of teaching and learning contend that analyzing teaching artifacts has three advantages: it enables new teachers time for reflection while still using the real materials of practice; it provides new teachers with experience thinking about and approaching the complexity of the classroom; and in some cases, it can help new teachers and teacher educators develop a shared understanding and common language about teaching. . . ."[1]

As Linda Darling-Hammond and her colleagues point out, grounding teacher education in real classrooms—among real teachers and students and among actual examples of students' and teachers' work—is an important and perhaps even an essential, part of training teachers for the complexities of teaching in today's classrooms. For this reason, we have created a valuable, time-saving website – MyEducationLab –that provides the context of real classrooms and artifacts that research on teacher education tells us is so important. The authentic in-class video footage, interactive skill-building exercises and other resources available on MyEducationLab offers a uniquely valuable teacher education tool.

MyEducationLab is easy to use and integrate into assignments and courses. Whenever the MyEducationLab logo appears in the text, follow the simple instructions to access the interactive assignments, activities, and learning units on MyEducationLab. For each topic covered in the course you will find most or all of the following resources:

Connection to National Standards

Now it is easier than ever to see how coursework is connected to national standards. Each topic on MyEducationLab lists intended learning outcomes connected to the appropriate national standards. And all of the Assignments and Activities and all of the Building Teaching Skills and Dispositions in MyEducationLab are mapped to the appropriate national standards and learning outcomes as well.

Assignments and Activities

Designed to save instructors preparation time and enhance student understanding, these assignable exercises show concepts in action (through video, cases, and/or student and teacher artifacts). They help students synthesize and apply concepts and strategies they read about in the book.

Building Teaching Skills and Dispositions

These learning units help students practice and strengthen skills that are essential to quality teaching. They are presented with the core skill or concept and then given an opportunity to practice their understanding of this concept multiple times by watching video footage (or interacting with other media) and then critically analyzing the strategy or skill presented.

IRIS Center Resources

The IRIS Center at Vanderbilt University (http://iris.peabody.vanderbilt.edu—funded by the U.S. Department of Education's Office of Special Education Programs (OSEP) develops training enhancement materials for pre-service and in-service teachers. The Center works with experts from across the country to create challenge-based

---

[1] Darling-Hammond, l., & Bransford, J., Eds.(2005). *Preparing Teachers for a Changing World.* San Francisco: John Wiley & Sons

interactive modules, case study units, and podcasts that provide research-validated information about working with students in inclusive settings. In your MyEducationLab course we have integrated this content where appropriate.

General Resources on Your MyEducationLab Course

The Resources section on MyEducationLab is designed to help students pass their licensure exams, put together effective portfolios and lesson plans, prepare for and navigate the first year of their teaching careers, and understand key educational standards, policies, and laws. This section includes:

- *Licensure Exams:* Contains guidelines for passing the Praxis exam. The *Practice Test Exam* includes practice multiple-choice questions, case study questions, and video case studies with sample questions.
- *Lesson Plan Builder:* Helps students create and share lesson plans.
- *Licensure and Standards:* Provides links to state licensure standards and national standards.
- *Beginning Your Career:* Educate Offers tips, advice, and valuable information on:
  - *Resume Writing and Interviewing:* Expert advice on how to write impressive resumes and prepare for job interviews.
  - *Your First Year of Teaching:* Practical tips on setting up a classroom, managing student behavior, and planning for instruction and assessment.
  - *Law and Public Policies:* Includes specific directives and requirements educators need to understand under the No Child Left Behind Act and the Individuals with Disabilities Education Improvement Act of 2004.

Visit www.myeducationlab.com for a demonstration of this exciting new online teaching resource.

Online Instructor's Manual with Test Items

An expanded and improved online Instructor's Manual includes numerous recommendations for presenting and extending text content. The manual consists of chapter overviews, objectives, outlines, and summaries that cover the essential concepts addressed in each chapter. You'll also find presentation outlines, learning activities, reflective exercises, weblinks, resources, and MyEducationLab activity suggestions. You'll also find a complete, chapter by chapter bank of test items.

The electronic Instructor's Manual is available on the Instructor Resource Center at www.pearsonhighered.com. To access the manual with test items, as well as the online PowerPoint lecture slides, go to www.pearsonhighered.com and click on the Instructor Resource Center button. Here you'll be able to log in or complete a one-time registration for a user name and password.

Online PowerPoint Lecture Slides

The PowerPoint lecture slides are available on the Instructor Resource Center at www.pearsonhighered.com. These lecture slides highlight key concepts and summarize key content from each chapter of the text.

Pearson MyTest

Pearson MyTest is a powerful assessment generation program that helps instructors easily create and print quizzes and exams. Questions and tests are authored online, allowing ultimate flexibility and the ability to efficiently create and print assessments anytime, anywhere! Instructors can access Pearson MyTest and their test bank files by going to www.pearsonmytest.com to log in, register, or request access. Features of Pearson MyTest include:

Premium assessment content

- Draw from a rich library of assessments that complement your Pearson textbook and your course's learning objectives.
- Edit questions or tests to fit your specific teaching needs.

Instructor-friendly resources

- Easily create and store your own questions, including images, diagrams, and charts using simple drag-and-drop and Word-like controls.
- Use additional information provided by Pearson, such as the question's difficulty level or learning objective, to help you quickly build your test.

Time-saving enhancements

- Add headers or footers and easily scramble questions and answer choices—all from one simple toolbar.
- Quickly create multiple versions of your test or answer key, and when ready, simply save to MS-Word or PDF format and print!
- Export your exams for import to Blackboard 6.0, CE (WebCT), or Vista (WebCT)!

Acknowledgments

This book is the result of the collaborative efforts of my students, colleagues, friends, and relatives. The book is an outgrowth of many ideas I learned from students at Woodlawn Junior High School (Buffalo, New York) and Public School 76 (Bronx, New York), colleagues from PS 76—George Bonnici, Nydia Figueroa-Torres, Jean Gee, and Jean Barber—and colleagues at the University of Kentucky, and the State University of New York at New Paltz. Much of the information in this book was learned through interactions with teachers, administrators, and students in the Easton (Pennsylvania) Area School District and other school districts, who both welcomed me and shared their experiences. Many of the examples and vignettes are based on the experiences of my students at the State University of New York at New Paltz. I truly value my colleagues and students, who continue to educate me and add to my appreciation of the remarkable dedication and skill of teachers.

I also want to acknowledge my students, colleagues, and friends who provided support and guidance throughout all stages of the book. I especially want to recognize Deborah Anderson, Lee Bell, John Boyd, Pauline Bynoe, Devon Duhaney, Hala Elhoweris, Meenakshi Gajria, Luis Garrido, Charleen Gottschalk, Margaret Gutierrez, Karen Giek, Mark Metzger, Bob Michael, Winifred Montgomery, Jean Mumper, Helen Musumeci, Kathy Pike, Sarah Ryan, Altagracia Salinas, Robin Smith, Shawna Sylvestre, Lorraine Taylor, Margaret Wade-Lewis, Delinda van Garderen, Halee Vang, and Catharine Whittaker for supporting and inspiring me throughout the process.

My deepest appreciation also goes to Lenore Schulte for coordinating various aspects of the book, Kelly Collins for creating the drawings that appear in many of the figures of the book, Barbara Chorzempa for developing the excellent and innovative materials that support and accompany the book, and Emi DiSciullo for taking some of the photos that appear in the book.

I also want to thank my wonderful and highly skilled colleagues at Pearson Education: Ann Davis, Hope Madden, Sheryl Langner, and Monica Merkel, and to my copyeditor, Laura Larson. I value their guidance, support, and flexibility and their commitment to quality and the field. I am also grateful to the following reviewers: Linda Johnston, University of Tennessee—Chattanooga; Frank Lilly, Sacramento State University; Georgine Steinmiller, Henderson State University; and Sarah Summy, Western Michigan University. Their thoughtful and professional comments helped shape and enhance the book.

This book could not be possible without the love, spirit, intelligence, encouragement, strength, passion, and sense of humor of Suzanne Salend, my collaborator in life. I also want to dedicate this book to Jack Salend, my son, and Madison Salend, my granddaughter.

Brief Contents

Contents

PART III

Differentiating Instruction for All Students   283

Chapter 8
Differentiating Instruction for Diverse Learners   285

Julia and Tom   284

Chapter 9
Differentiating Large- and Small-Group Instruction   333

Ms. Anderson   332

Part

I

Understanding the Foundations and Fundamentals of Inclusion

Part I of this book, which includes Chapters 1, 2, and 3, introduces the concept of inclusion and the benefits and challenges associated with its implementation. The information presented in Part I also is designed to provide a framework for creating learning environments that support the learning and socialization of *all students,* differentiating your instruction to accommodate *all students* and provide them with access to and help them succeed in the general education curriculum; and evaluating the success of your inclusion program for *all students, their families, and professionals.* Throughout this book, *all learners/students* refers to the full range of students who are educated in general education classrooms and includes learners with individual differences related to ethnicity, race, age, socioeconomic status, gender, disability, language, religious and spiritual values, sexual orientation, geographic location, and country of origin (Council for Exceptional Children [CEC], 2008; National Council for the Accreditation of Teacher Education [NCATE], 2009).

Chapter 1 introduces you to the concepts of special education, inclusion, and the least restrictive environment; the philosophical principles that guide this book; the factors that contributed to the growth of inclusion; and the current research on the impact of inclusion on students, teachers, and families. Chapter 2 discusses the Response-to-Intervention (RTI), the prereferral, identification, and placement process for students with disabilities, the Individualized Education Program, and the various special education disability categories. Chapter 3 considers various societal changes and their impact on students and schools, and explains alternative philosophies for structuring schools to address these changes.

MARIE AND MARY

Marie was born in 1949. By the time she turned 3, her parents were sensing that she was developing slowly—speaking little and walking late. Marie's pediatrician told them not to worry; Marie would grow out of it. After another year of no noticeable progress, Marie's parents took her to other doctors. One said she had an iron deficiency, and another thought she had a tumor.

By the time Marie was old enough to start school, she was diagnosed as having mental retardation and was placed in a separate school for children with disabilities. She was doing well at the school when the school district informed her family that the school was being closed and that the district had no place for Marie and the other students. Marie's family protested to school officials and their state legislator, but the school district was not required by law to educate children like Marie.

Concerned about her future, Marie's family sent her to a large state-run program about 200 miles from their home. During visits, they found that Marie was often disheveled, disoriented, and uncommunicative. Once she even had bruises on her arms and legs. After much debate, Marie's family decided to bring her home to live with them. Although now an adult, Marie cannot perform activities of daily living, and her parents are worried about what will happen to her when they are no longer able to care for her.

Mary, born in 1996, also was diagnosed as having intellectual disability. Soon after birth, Mary and her parents enrolled in an early intervention program that included family education sessions and home visits by a professional. Mary's parents joined a group of families that was advocating for services. When Mary was 3, she attended a preschool program with other children from her neighborhood. The school worked with Mary's family to develop an Individualized Family Service Plan to meet Mary's educational needs, coordinate the delivery of services to Mary and her family, and assist her family in planning for the transition to public

Understanding Inclusion

school. After preschool, Mary moved with the other children to the local elementary school. At that time, her family met with the school district's comprehensive planning team to develop an Individualized Education Program (IEP) for Mary. The team recommended that Mary be educated in a self-contained special education class and mainstreamed for special classes like art, music, and physical education. However, Mary's family thought she should be in a setting that fostered her language and literacy skills and allowed her to socialize and interact with her peers who were not disabled. As a result, Mary was placed in an inclusive classroom and received the services of a collaboration teacher and a speech/language therapist, who worked with Mary and her teacher. Over the years, Mary had some teachers who understood her strengths and challenges and others who did not, but she and her family persevered. Occasionally, other students made fun of Mary, but she learned to ignore them and participated in many after-school programs.

When Mary was ready to move to junior high school, the teachers and her family worked together to help Mary make the transition. She learned how to change classes, use a combination lock and locker, and use different textbooks. Her IEP was revised to include instructional and testing accommodations, as well as the use of word processing to help her develop written communication skills. Mary participated in the science and ski clubs and volunteer activities after school and went to the movies with her friends on Saturdays.

Mary graduated from junior high school and entered high school, where her favorite subjects are social studies and science. She also enjoys socializing with her friends during lunch. A classmate helps Mary by sharing notes with her, and Mary's teachers have modified the curriculum for her. She uses a laptop computer with large print, a talking word processor, and a word prediction program. She is also taking a course called "Introduction to Occupations" and participates in a work-study program. Mary hopes to work in a store or office in town when she graduates.

What factors and events led Marie and Mary and their families to have such different experiences in school and society? After reading this chapter, you should have the knowledge, skills, and dispositions to answer that as well as the following questions:

- What is special education?
- What is inclusion?
- What is the least restrictive environment?
- What factors contributed to the movement to educate students in inclusive classrooms?
- What are the laws that affect special education?
- What is the impact of inclusion on students, educators, and families?

As the stories of Marie and Mary indicate, the education and treatment of individuals with disabilities has undergone a change (Duhaney & Salend, in press; Rosenberg, Westling, & McLeskey, 2008). Prior to 1800, individuals with disabilities were feared, ridiculed, abandoned, or simply ignored. As educational methods were developed in the late 1700s that showed the success of various teaching strategies, society began to adopt a more accepting and humane view of individuals with disabilities. However, the 19th century saw the rise of institutions for individuals with disabilities, like the one Marie experienced, that isolated them from society. Although institutional settings played an important role until the 1970s, the early 20th century also saw the rise of special schools and special classes for students with disabilities. The 1960s and 1970s also fostered a period of advocacy and acceptance, which resulted in legislative and judicial actions that provided individuals like Mary and her family with access to society, early intervention programs, and the public schools. In the late 1980s and mid-1990s, individuals with disabilities and their families formed advocacy groups that fostered public policies that allowed individuals with disabilities to become full and equal members of society.

Today, these factors, aided by the technological advances, are transforming our notions of disability and providing individuals with disabilities with full access to the educational, economic, social, cultural, and political mainstream. Thus, whereas Marie's life was characterized by frustration, isolation, and lack of understanding, Mary's experiences were much more positive and inclusive. Although Marie was initially placed in a separate school for students with disabilities, no laws existed that required states to educate students with special needs. When the school closed, Marie's family had few options, and Marie was forced into an even more segregated environment, a state-run institution. Conditioned to live a life fully dependent on others, Marie was limited at the time by society's restrictive perceptions of individuals with disabilities.

Mary, in contrast, benefited from early diagnosis and intervention. She was educated with her peers without disabilities in preschool and included in classes with students from her neighborhood throughout her educational career. Mary's full rights of citizenship, including the right to a free and appropriate education, were ensured by special laws that help protect and empower individuals with disabilities. These laws also recognized that *all students* can learn and granted Mary's family the right to advocate for her when they disagreed with the school's decisions. Mary's teachers had high expectations of what she could accomplish, and they worked together to individualize her instruction and capitalize on her strengths. Upon her graduation from high school, Mary is being prepared to act on her own choices, lead a more independent life, and make positive contributions to her community. Born approximately five decades later than Marie, Mary benefited from a totally changed societal perception of what individuals with disabilities can learn and accomplish when supported by their families, peers, teachers, and community.

SPECIAL EDUCATION

WHAT IS SPECIAL EDUCATION? While Mary benefited from receiving special education services, unfortunately these services were not available for Marie. **Special education** involves delivering and monitoring a specially designed and coordinated set of comprehensive, research-based instructional and assessment practices and related services to students with learning, behavioral, emotional, physical, health, or sensory disabilities. These instructional practices and services are tailored to identify and address the individual and strengths and challenges of students; to enhance their educational, social, behavioral, and physical development; and to foster equity and access to all aspects of schooling, the community and society (Hehir, 2007). Special education, which is an integral part of the educational system, is characterized by the following features:

- *Individualized assessment and planning:* Learning goals and instructional practices are based on individualized assessment data.
- *Specialized instruction:* Instructional practices and materials, curricula, related services, and assistive technology are tailored to the unique strengths and challenges of students.
- *Intensive instruction:* Instructional practices are precisely designed and systematically implemented for a sufficient period of time.
- *Goal-directed instruction:* Instructional practices are guided by learning goals that promote independence and success in current and future settings.
- *Research-based instructional practices:* Instructional practices are chosen based on their research support.
- *Collaborative partnerships:* Professionals, students, family and community members work collaboratively to coordinate their goals and efforts.
- *Student performance evaluation:* Instructional practices are evaluated frequently in terms of outcomes on student performance and revised accordingly (Heward, 2009).

INCLUSION

WHAT IS INCLUSION? While Marie attended schools and institutional settings that segregated students with disabilities, Mary's educational experiences were based on *inclusion,* an important and essential feature of special education. **Inclusion** is a philosophy that brings diverse students, families, educators, and community members together to create schools and other social institutions based on acceptance, belonging, and community (Rose, 2008). Inclusion recognizes that *all students* are capable learners who benefit from a meaningful, challenging, and appropriate curriculum delivered within the general education classroom, and from differentiated instruction techniques that address their diverse and unique strengths, challenges and experiences (Forlin, 2008; Giangreco, 2007; Tomlinson, Brimijoin, & Narvaez, 2008).

Inclusion seeks to provide *all students* with collaborative, supportive, and nurturing communities of learners that are based on giving *all students* the services and accommodations they need to succeed, as well as respecting and learning from each other's individual differences (Hehir, 2007; Swedeen, 2009). Rather than segregating students as in the school Marie briefly attended before being placed in an institution, advocates of inclusion work collaboratively to create a unified educational system

REFLECTIVE

Why is access to the general education curriculum important? Which settings provide students with disabilities the best access to the general education curriculum? Inclusive classrooms? Special education classrooms? A combination of the two?

like the one Mary received (Cushing, Carter, Clark, Wallis, & Kennedy, 2009; Frattura & Capper, 2006; Schwarz, 2007).

The following interrelated principles, which provide a framework for this textbook, summarize the philosophies on which inclusive practices are based.

PRINCIPLES OF EFFECTIVE INCLUSION

Principle 1: All Learners and Equal Access

Effective inclusion improves the educational system for all learners *by placing them together in general education classrooms—regardless of their learning ability, race, linguistic ability, economic status, gender, learning style, ethnicity, cultural and religious background, family structure, and sexual orientation.* Inclusion programs also provide *all students* with equal access to a challenging, engaging, and flexible general education curriculum and the appropriate services that help them to be successful in society (Frattura & Capper, 2006; Hehir, 2007; Rose, 2008). Students are given a multilevel and multimodality curriculum, as well as challenging educational and social experiences that are consistent with their abilities and needs (Giangreco, 2007; Swedeen, 2009). Inclusionary schools welcome, acknowledge, affirm, and celebrate the value of *all students* by educating them together in high-quality, age-appropriate general education classrooms in their neighborhood schools (Ainscow, 2008; Cushing et al., 2009; Sapon-Shevin, 2008).

Principle 2: Individual Strengths and Challenges and Diversity

Effective inclusion involves sensitivity to and acceptance of individual strengths and challenges and diversity. Educators cannot teach students without taking into account the diverse factors that shape their students and make them unique (Taylor & Whittaker, 2009). Factors such as disability, race, linguistic and religious background, gender, sexual orientation and economic status interact and affect academic performance and socialization. Therefore, educators, students, and family members must be sensitive to inclusionary practices, which promote acceptance, equity, and collaboration; are responsive to individual strengths and challenges; and embrace diversity (Forlin, 2008; Sapon-Shevin, 2008; Voltz, Sims, Nelson, & Bivens, 2005). In inclusive classrooms, *all students* are valued as individuals capable of learning and contributing to society. They are taught to appreciate diversity and to value and learn from each other's similarities and differences (Black-Hawkins, Florian, & Rouse, 2007; Swedeen, 2009).

Principle 3: Reflective Practices and Differentiated Instruction

Effective inclusion requires reflective educators to examine their attitudes and differentiate their assessment, teaching, and classroom management practices, to accommodate individual strengths and challenges and provide all students with meaningful access to and progress in the general education curriculum. In inclusive classrooms, teachers are reflective practitioners who are flexible, responsive, and aware of and accommodate students' strengths and challenges (Cushing et al., 2009; Sapon-Shevin, 2008). They think critically about their values and beliefs and routinely examine their own practices for self-improvement and to ensure that *all students'* needs are met (Ainscow, 2008; Regan, 2009). Educators treat students with fairness, not sameness, by individualizing

Implementing Inclusion

7:45 A.M.: Ms. Williams enters the school's office, greets the school secretary, and reviews her mail, which includes a message from one of her student's parents that her son will be late because he has a doctor's appointment.

7:52 A.M.: Ms. Williams enters her classroom. While she sips some tea, she boots up one of the computers in the room and checks her e-mail. She reads a message from a parent whose child will be absent and would like her to send today's homework assignment via e-mail. She starts to review a children's book about the school experiences of a student who does not speak English.

8:01 A.M.: As Ms. Silver enters her classroom, she greets Ms. Williams and thanks her for making tea. She sees Ms. Williams reviewing the book. "What do you think of it?" she asks. "I think it will be a good book to use. We can tie it in to our social studies unit on immigration and our community meetings on friendships." Ms. Williams nods and says, "How's your Spanish? Maybe we can have students work in math by using numbers in Spanish."

8:45 A.M.: Ms. Williams's and Ms. Silver's 23 students start entering the classroom. Amid the chatter, the students organize themselves for the day. While the students socialize, several students perform class jobs. They take the attendance, water the plants, perform the lunch count, and boot up the computers. The class is made up of 12 girls and 11 boys and includes 7 students with disabilities: 4 students with learning disabilities, 1 student with an emotional/behavioral disorder, 1 student with multiple disabilities, and 1 student who has a health impairment. The class also includes 3 African American students, 2 Hispanic students, and 1 who recently arrived from Asia.

9:00 A.M.: Ms. Silver rings a bell and the students go to their desks, which are arranged in groups of five or six. Each group contains a mixture of students by gender, ability, and cultural and linguistic background. One student from each group serves as a homework checker, verifying which students have completed their homework and what help students need. Half of the homework checkers report to Ms. Williams, and half report to Ms. Silver, who record their findings. Before the reading groups assemble, a group of students selects a song and leads the class in singing it.

9:10 A.M.: The students go to their reading groups. Ms. Williams works with one group, while Ms. Silver works with another. As Ms. Williams starts to read a story to her group, several students remind her that Nicole needs her positioning board so that she can see the book. Several students also work independently. James works with Mr. Thomas, the paraeducator. First, James listens to and reads along with a digital recording of a passage from a book; then he reads the section without the recording and answers questions about what he has read and heard. Felicia is using the Internet to find another book written by her favorite author, which her teachers said she could read next.

After each student has had a chance to read, the teachers give them a choice of activities concerning the book. Some students choose to design a book cover reflecting important elements of the book, others choose to write about what they think will happen next, several students work together to role-play the part of the story they just read, and some create a Venn diagram comparing themselves with a character in the book.

9:55 A.M.: While Ms. Williams prepares the materials for science class, Ms. Silver and Mr. Thomas remind the students that they have 5 minutes to finish their work and get ready for science. They show the students some rocks they will be working with in science class. Ms. Silver asks Lewis to help Sandy clean up and get ready for the next activity.

10:05 A.M.: The students go back to their desks and get ready for science class. While Ms. Williams reviews the concepts covered in the previous science class, Ms. Silver moves around the room to make sure that all of the students are ready for science and paying attention. Ms. Williams tells the students, "Today, we are going to learn more about different types of rocks." She shows them the flowchart that they had previously developed to identify and classify rocks. After Ms. Williams reviews the flowchart with the students and demonstrates how to use it to categorize a rock, the teachers place the students in groups. Each group is given six rocks and told to use the flowchart to identify the types of rocks they have and the reasons for their classifications. Ms. Williams, Ms. Silver, and Mr. Thomas circulate to assist the groups, monitor their cooperative skills, and make sure that each group member is participating. Near the end of the time period, each group shares its findings. James and Nicole identify the colors of each rock for their groups. The teachers note the different ways the rocks can be categorized and tell the students that they will continue to work on other rocks tomorrow.

11:10 A.M.: Mr. Thomas announces that it is free time. He shows the students a board game, and several students start playing it. Several other students have brought their yo-yos to school and show each other different tricks they can perform. Other students play with various toys, musical instruments, and computers.

11:30 A.M.: Ms. Williams tells the students that they have 5 minutes left and should start thinking about mathematics.

11:35 A.M.: Ms. Silver asks the students to go to their desks and get ready for math. Several students are still on the floor by the cabinet near the teachers' desks. One student yells, "Geneviere's pen is under the cabinet, and we can't reach it." Ms. Silver again tells the students to go to their desks as Ms. Williams tries to help Geneviere retrieve her pen.

11:38 A.M.: The pen has been retrieved, and the teachers and Mr. Thomas work with the students in math groups. Some students are using Base Ten Blocks to understand place value and count, while others are using them to work on multidigit addition, subtraction, and multiplication. Near the end of the period, the groups come together to play a math game. Throughout the game, students are rotated from team to team, the questions are individualized based on students' skills levels, and the answers to the game's math questions require the input of more than one member of each team.

12:20 P.M.: Ms. Williams asks the students to get ready for lunch, and Ms. Silver takes them to lunch.

12:40 P.M.: The students finish lunch and go outside to play. Milton is playing with a group of students and gets a little too rough. Several of the students call Milton a name.

1:01 P.M.: The students return to class, and Mr. Thomas tells Ms. Williams and Ms. Silver about the name-calling that occurred during recess. The teachers take turns reading aloud while students visit the restroom or get a drink of water.

1:15 P.M.: Ms. Williams and Ms. Silver announce, "We are going to have a community meeting." Without mentioning names, Mr. Thomas describes the name-calling incident. Ms. Williams and Ms. Silver then ask a series of questions. "What does it mean to call someone a name?" "Why does one person call another person a name?" "How does it feel when someone calls you a name?" and "What can be done to prevent name-calling?" Students share their responses and brainstorm solutions to the problem. The teachers summarize the students' responses and end the community meeting by role-playing a conflict between students and asking the students to identify ways in which the conflict could be handled without name-calling.

1:58 P.M.: Ms. Silver asks the students to line up, and Mr. Thomas takes them to music class. Meanwhile, the educators begin assembling a bulletin board. They start discussing the students' reactions to the community meeting, as well as additional activities they could use to counter name-calling and to foster a cooperative spirit in the group. They also discuss potential items related to the unit on rocks that students could include in their portfolios, and they put notes to families in students' homework folders.

2:22 P.M.: Ms. Cameron, the speech and language teacher, stops by to talk with the teachers about tomorrow's Writers'

Workshop activity. She talks about how she plans to work on expanding sentences with her Writers' Workshop group and says that she will need to use the laptop in the classroom. The teachers also discuss the roles family volunteers will play during the Writers' Workshop.

2:40 P.M.: The students return from music class. While one student reads the homework assignment from the chalkboard, Ms. Williams, Ms. Silver, and Mr. Thomas move around the room to make sure that all the students have their colored homework folders and notebooks. The students perform end-of-the-day jobs such as shutting down the computers, washing the chalkboard, and organizing materials.

3:05 P.M.: The teachers praise the students for their good work and remind them of the discussion in the community meeting. While Ms. Silver walks the students to their buses, Ms. Williams sends the day's homework assignment by e-mail to the family that had requested it in the morning.

3:15 P.M.: Ms. Silver and Ms. Williams meet to copy and prepare materials, plan activities, and discuss report grades and testing accommodations for individual students.

4:30 P.M.: Ms. Silver and Ms. Williams wish each other good night and leave the school.

- What aspects of their school day and program make you believe that Ms. Silver, Mr. Thomas, and Ms. Williams work in an inclusion classroom?
- What roles did Ms. Silver, Mr. Thomas, Ms. Williams, and their students play in their classroom?
- How did Ms. Silver, Mr. Thomas, and Ms. Williams address the educational, social, and behavioral challenges of their students?
- What types of support services do Ms. Silver and Ms. Williams receive to help them implement their program?
- What types of support do educators need to implement an inclusion program?
- How does their classroom reflect the four principles of inclusion?

To read an example of how to implement inclusion in secondary-level content-area classrooms, read the Chapter 9 opening vignette.

- How are the four principles of inclusion implemented in secondary-level classrooms?

their expectations for *all students*, and offering differentiated teaching practices to accommodate students' individual differences and to help all students succeed within the general education curriculum (Tomlinson et al., 2008; Swedeen, 2009).

Principle 4: Community and Collaboration

Effective inclusion is a group effort; it involves establishing a community based on collaboration among educators, other professionals, students, families, and community agencies. Inclusion seeks to establish a nurturing community of learners that is based on acceptance and belonging and the delivery of the support and services that students need in the general education classroom (Giangreco, 2007; Sapon-Shevin, 2008). People work cooperatively and reflectively, establishing community, communicating regularly, and sharing resources, responsibilities, skills, decisions, and advocacy for the students' benefit (Ainscow, 2008; Nevin, Cramer, Voigt, & Salazar, 2008; Swedeen, 2009). School districts provide support, professional development, time, and resources to restructure their programs to support individuals in working collaboratively and reflectively to address students' strengths and challenges (Cushing et al., 2009).

Mainstreaming

While the concept of inclusion grew out of and replaced the term *mainstreaming*, it shares many of its philosophical goals and implementation strategies. Therefore, you may hear some people use them interchangeably, while others see them as very different concepts (Mesibov, 2008) (see Figure 1.1). **Mainstreaming** referred to the partial or full-time programs that educated students with disabilities with their general education peers. Often, the decision to place students in mainstreamed settings was based on educators' assessment of their readiness; thus, it was implied that students had to earn the right to be educated full-time in an age-appropriate general

Making Connections
Find out more about how to use differentiated instruction to help all students access and succeed in the general education curriculum in Part III of this book.

FIGURE 1.1 A comparison of inclusion and mainstreaming

Inclusion	Mainstreaming
Who	
• All learners have the right to be educated in general education classrooms.	• Selected learners earn their way into general education classes based on their readiness as determined by educators.
What	
• Full access to the general education curriculum and all instructional and social activities	• Selected access to the general education curriculum and instructional and social activities
Where and When	
• Full-time placement in general education classrooms	• Part-time to full-time placement in general education classrooms
How	
• A full range of services is integrated into the general education setting (e.g., cooperative teaching).	• A full range of services is delivered inside and outside the general education setting (e.g., resource room).
• General and special education are merged into a unified service delivery system.	• General and special education are maintained as separate service delivery systems.
Why	
• To foster the academic, social-emotional, behavioral, and physical development of students and to prepare them to be contributing members of society	• To foster the academic, social-emotional, behavioral, and physical development of students and to prepare them to be contributing members of society

education classroom (McLesky, 2007). The definition and scope of mainstreaming varied greatly, from any interactions between students who did and did not have disabilities to more specific integration of students with disabilities into the social and instructional activities of the general education classroom.

LEAST RESTRICTIVE ENVIRONMENT

WHAT IS THE LEAST RESTRICTIVE ENVIRONMENT? Inclusion is rooted in the concept of the **least restrictive environment (LRE)**, which requires schools to educate students with disabilities as much as possible with their peers who do not have disabilities (Schwarz, 2007). The LRE is determined individually, based on the student's educational strengths and challenges rather than the student's disability (Yell, Katsiyannis, Ryan, McDuffie, & Mattocks, 2008). Although the LRE concept creates a presumption in favor of the placement of students with disabilities in inclusive classrooms (Turnbull, Turnbull, & Wehmeyer, 2010), it also means that students can be shifted to self-contained special education classes, specialized schools, and residential programs only when their school performance indicates that even with supplementary aids and services, they cannot be educated satisfactorily in a general education classroom.

The LRE encourages students to attend school as close as possible to their homes and to interact with other students from their neighborhood. The participation of students with disabilities in all parts of the school program, including nonacademic and extracurricular activities, is another important aspect of the LRE. The LRE also relates to the *principle of natural proportions,* according to which the ratio of students with and without disabilities in a classroom reflects the ratio of the larger population.

Continuum of Educational Placements

To implement the LRE and organize the delivery of special education services, school districts use a continuum of educational placements ranging from the highly *integrated* setting of the general education classroom to the highly *segregated* setting where instruction is delivered in hospitals and institutions. Although variation exists within and among schools and agencies, Figure 1.2 presents the range from most to least restrictive educational placements for students, which vary in the extent to which students have access to the general education curriculum and peers. A student is placed in the LRE based on his or her strengths, challenges, and motivation. A student moves to a less restrictive educational environment as quickly as possible and moves to a more segregated one only when necessary.

> *Option 1. General education classroom placement with few or no supportive services.* The LRE is the general education classroom with few or no supportive services. The student is educated in the general education classroom, with the classroom teacher having the primary responsibility for designing and teaching the instructional program. The instructional program is individualized for the student, and a range of differentiated teaching practices and technologies are used to support the student's learning. Indirect services such as professional development designed to help teachers individualize the instructional program for students with disabilities may be offered.

> *Option 2. General education classroom placement with collaborative teacher assistance.* This placement option is similar to option 1. However, the general education classroom teacher and the student receive collaborative services from ancillary support personnel in the inclusive classroom (Idol, 2006). The collaborative services will vary, depending on the nature and level of the student's strengths and challenges as well as the professional practices of the teacher.

Making Connections
Find out more about working collaboratively with others in Chapter 4.

FIGURE 1.2 Continuum of educational services

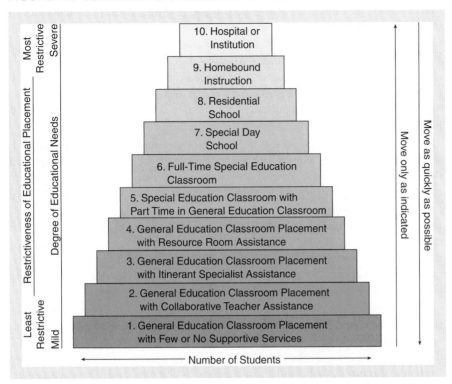

A pyramid diagram showing the continuum of educational services, ordered from most restrictive (top) to least restrictive (bottom):

- 10. Hospital or Institution
- 9. Homebound Instruction
- 8. Residential School
- 7. Special Day School
- 6. Full-Time Special Education Classroom
- 5. Special Education Classroom with Part Time in General Education Classroom
- 4. General Education Classroom Placement with Resource Room Assistance
- 3. General Education Classroom Placement with Itinerant Specialist Assistance
- 2. General Education Classroom Placement with Collaborative Teacher Assistance
- 1. General Education Classroom Placement with Few or No Supportive Services

Left axis (top to bottom): Restrictiveness of Educational Placement / Degree of Educational Needs — Most Restrictive/Severe to Least Restrictive/Mild

Right axis: Move only as indicated / Move as quickly as possible

Bottom axis: Number of Students

Option 3. General education classroom placement with itinerant specialist assistance. Teaching takes place in the general education classroom, and the student also receives supportive services periodically from itinerant teachers, usually within the inclusive classroom (Silverman & Millspaugh, 2006).

Option 4. General education classroom placement with resource room assistance. Students with disabilities educated in inclusive classrooms receive direct services from resource room teachers, usually in a separate **resource room** within the school. Resource room teachers provide individualized remedial instruction related to specific skills (e.g., note taking, study skills, etc.) and provide supplemental instruction that supports and parallels the instruction given in the general education classroom. The resource room teacher also can help general classroom teachers plan and implement instructional accommodations for students. For example, a science teacher and a resource room teacher might meet to identify the vocabulary words that support the key concepts in units of instruction. They would then coordinate their instruction, with the resource room teacher providing supplementary instruction to help students master the key vocabulary terms they identified.

Option 5. Special education classroom placement with part time in the general education classroom. In this option, the student's primary placement is in a

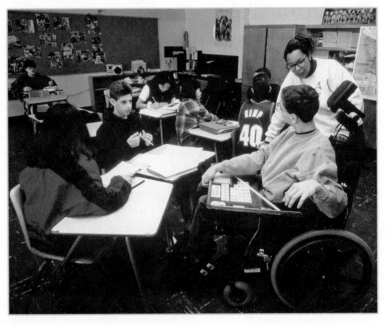

The least restrictive environment (LRE) requires educational agencies to educate students with disabilities as much as possible with their peers who do not have disabilities. How does the least restrictive environment principle work in your school district?

PEARSON
myeducationlab

Go to the Assignments and Activities section of the Topic *Inclusive Practices* in the MyEducationLab for your course and complete the activity entitled *Exploring Inclusion.*

Making Connections
Read more about these societal changes in Chapter 3.

special education classroom within the same school building as peers who are not disabled. The student's academic program is supervised by a special educator. The amount of time spent in the general education setting for academic instruction and socialization varies.

Option 6. Full-time special education classroom. This placement alternative is similar to option 5. However, contact with peers who are not disabled typically is exclusively social; teaching takes place in a separate classroom. Students in option 6 share common experiences with other students on school buses, at lunch or recess, and during schoolwide and after-school activities.

Option 7. Special day school. Students in this placement alternative attend a school different from that of their neighborhood peers. Placement in a **special day school** allows school districts to centralize services. This option is highly restrictive and is sometimes used with students with more severe emotional, physical, and cognitive disabilities.

Option 8. Residential school. Residential programs also are designed to serve students with more severe educational and social challenges. Students attending **residential schools** live at the school and participate in a 24-hour program. In addition to providing education, these programs offer the comprehensive medical and psychological services that students may need.

Option 9. Homebound instruction. Some students, such as those who are recovering from surgery or an illness or who have been suspended from school, may require **homebound instruction**. In this alternative, a teacher teaches the student at home. Technological advances including webcams now allow students who are homebound or in hospitals to interact and take classes with their peers at school.

Option 10. Hospital or institution. Placing individuals with disabilities in hospitals and institutions has been reduced, but it still exists. As with the other placement options, education must be part of any hospital or institutional program. These placements should be viewed as short term, and an emphasis should be placed on moving these individuals to a less restrictive environment.

Judicial decisions have established guidelines that school districts must consider when implementing the LRE concept for students (Hulett, 2009; Murdick, Gartin, & Crabtree, 2007). Taken together, these cases suggest that *all students* have a right to be educated in general education settings and that in placing a student in the LRE, school districts should consider

- the anticipated educational, noneducational, social, and self-concept benefits in the general education setting compared with the benefits of the special education classroom; and
- the impact on the education of classmates without disabilities.

FACTORS CONTRIBUTING TO INCLUSION

WHAT FACTORS CONTRIBUTED TO THE MOVEMENT TO EDUCATE LEARNERS IN INCLUSIVE CLASSROOMS? The number of school districts implementing inclusion for their students with disabilities has increased significantly, and the movement toward educating *all students* in general education classes continues to be an ongoing direction for the field of education. In the following sections, we will look at several factors contributing to this movement. Societal changes have also occurred, and inclusion has proved to be effective for educating diverse learners in general education classrooms.

Normalization

Inclusion is rooted in the principle of **normalization**, which originated in Scandinavia and was later brought to the United States in the 1960s (Wolfensberger, 1972). Normalization seeks to provide opportunities, social interactions, and experiences that parallel those of society to adults and children with disabilities. Thus, the philosophy of educating students with disabilities in inclusive settings rests on the principle that educational, housing, employment, social, and leisure opportunities for individuals with disabilities should resemble as closely as possible the opportunities and activities enjoyed by their peers who are not disabled. Think back to the chapter-opening vignette: Whereas Marie spent some time in an institution, this option was never considered for Mary, in part, because of normalization which also fostered **deinstitutionalization**, the movement of individuals with special needs from institutional settings to community-based settings.

Early Intervention and Early Childhood Programs

The effectiveness of early intervention and early childhood programs (like the one Mary attended) has promoted the placement of students with disabilities in general education settings (Hooper & Umansky, 2009; Raver, 2009). Effective early intervention and early childhood programs offer *all students* and families access to the following:

REFLECTIVE

In what ways has the normalization principle been implemented in your community?

- *Developmentally, individually, and culturally appropriate practices:* instructional practices and a curriculum designed and systematically implemented to address the individual, developmental, and cultural needs of students
- *Natural environments:* the settings where young children commonly learn everyday skills
- *Family-centered service coordination:* the process of forming collaborative partnerships with families to assist them in identifying and obtaining the services, supports, and resources they need to foster learning and development
- *Transition practices:* the planning and delivery of practices that help young children make the transition to general education classrooms (Hooper & Umansky, 2009; Raver, 2009; Winter, 2007)

These programs have increased the physical, motor, cognitive, language, speech, socialization, and self-help skills of many children from birth through age 6 (Hooper & Umansky, 2009; Winter, 2007). They have also reduced the likelihood that children would be in special education, empowered families to promote their child's development, and decreased the probability that children with disabilities will be socially dependent and institutionalized as adults. In a follow-up study comparing adults who received early childhood services with adults who did not, those who received early childhood services were more likely to graduate high school, had better attitudes toward school, made more money, attained a higher level of education, and used fewer social services than those who did not (Raver, 2009).

Technological Advances

Mary's placement in inclusive settings also was fostered by technology that was not available when Marie was growing up. These technological advances have changed the quality of life for many individuals, empowering them by fostering their access, independence, and achievement. Assistive and instructional technology allows individuals with communication, physical, learning, and sensory disabilities to gain more control over their lives and environment, as well as greater access to society and general education classrooms (Dell, Newton, & Petroff, 2008). While these devices were developed for individuals with disabilities, they have consequences and benefits for *all members of society.*

The Individuals with Disabilities Education Act (IDEA; discussed later) and the Improving Access to Assistive Technology for Individuals with Disabilities Act acknowledge the use of assistive technology as a tool for improving the lives of individuals with disabilities and their inclusion in society. These acts delineate two aspects of assistive technology: devices and services. An **assistive technology device** is defined as any item, piece of equipment, or product system—whether

Making Connections
Find out more about assistive and instructional technology in Chapter 8.

Medical and assistive technology devices have promoted the inclusion movement. How have you and your family benefited from medical and assistive technology?

bought, modified, or customized—that is used to increase, maintain, or improve the functional capabilities of an individual with a disability.

Assistive technology is often categorized as being high or low technology. Whereas **high-technology devices** tend to be electronic, costly, and commercially produced and require some education to use effectively, **low-technology devices** are usually inexpensive, nonelectric, easy to use, readily available, and homemade. High-technology devices that are used in classrooms include electronic communication, speech recognition and reading systems, motorized wheelchairs, long canes, adapted keyboards, touch screens, and magnification aids. Low-technology assistive devices that students may use in the classroom include teacher-made communication boards, reading masks, pencil holders, and strings attached to objects to retrieve them if they fall on the floor. An **assistive technology service** is any service that directly assists an individual with a disability to select, acquire, or use an assistive technology device, including physical, occupational, and speech therapy. As a result of these acts, many state education departments have established programs to link individuals with the devices they need.

UDL and YOU
Understanding the Principles of Universal Design for Learning

The movement toward inclusion also was fostered by the application of the principles of **universal design** to educational settings. Universal design (UD), which originated in the field of architecture, is a concept or philosophy that guides the design and delivery of products and services so that they are usable by individuals with a wide range of capabilities and diversities (Dukes & Lamar-Dukes, 2009). Universal design for learning (UDL) applies UD to educational settings to help *all learners* access the general education curriculum and succeed in inclusive classrooms by providing multiple means of

- *representation,* by which you present information and materials in varied ways so that *all* students can access and understand them (e.g., employ visual, graphic, auditory and multilingual formats and combinations for presenting directions and content such as oral statements, text, digital text and pictorials, visual organizers, video- and audio-based materials, peer and adult supports);

- *expression,* by which you offer *all* students a variety of ways to demonstrate their learning (e.g., use

different formats and combinations for students to respond and demonstrate and express their mastery such as written, oral, and technology-based projects; role plays; simulations; presentations; tests; and peer-based assignments);

- *engagement,* by which you use classroom practices to prompt and encourage *all* students to perform at their optimal levels and be involved in the learning process (e.g., employ different formats and combinations to foster student engagement such as giving students choices, prompting students to use learning strategies and self-management techniques, and using peer-mediated and technology-based instruction) (Kurtts, Matthews, & Smallwood, 2009; Sopko, 2008).

The principles of UDL, which often overlap, as well as some examples of them (additional examples are presented throughout each chapter), are presented in Table 1.1.

TABLE 1.1 Universal design for learning principles

Universal Design for Learning Principles	Universal Design for Learning Principle and Inclusive Practices	Examples of the Implementation of Universal Design Principles and Inclusive Practices
Principle 1: Equitable Use	Inclusive practices are designed so that they are useful, appealing, and safe for *all* students, families, and professionals to use. They are respectful of individual differences and are used by *all* in similar or equivalent ways and in different contexts.	• Incorporate universally designed accommodations into students' IEPs (see Chapter 2). • Overcome economic barriers to student performance and family participation (see Chapter 3). • Make the principles of UDL available to all students and address issues of fairness without sameness (Chapter 5). • Employ culturally responsive teaching strategies and multi-lingual and multicultural materials (see Chapters 3 and 8).
Principle 2: Flexible Use	Inclusive practices are designed so that they accommodate the individual preferences and abilities of *all* students, families, and professionals. They are flexible in providing choices in terms of the methods and pace of use.	• Understand and accommodate cross-cultural communication patterns and linguistic factors (see Chapter 4). • Provide students with opportunities to make choices (see Chapters 6 and 9). • Use tiered assignments (see Chapter 8). • Use a range of classroom-based assessment practices (see Chapter 12).
Principle 3: Simple and Intuitive Use	Inclusive practices are designed so that they are easy for *all* students, families, and professionals to use and understand. Their use is not dependent on the experiences, prior knowledge, language, literacy, attention, and cognitive skills, and other learning preferences and abilities of others.	• Establish and teach classroom rules and routines (see Chapter 7). • Present directions clearly and in multiple ways (see Chapter 9). • Use digital textbooks and content enhancements such as graphic organizers (see Chapter 11). • Develop and use instructional rubrics with students (see Chapter 12). • Administer tests via technology (see Chapter 12).
Principle 4: Perceptible Information	Inclusive practices are designed so that they communicate essential information to *all* students, families, and professionals. They present critical information to *all* by using multiple formats (text, oral, visual).	• Enhance the readability and legibility of materials provided to students, families, and other professionals (see Chapters 4 and 8). • Use a range of instructional technologies and assistive devices to support student learning, share information, and communicate with others (see Chapter 8).
Principle 5: Tolerance for Error	Inclusive practices are designed to minimize errors and hazards, adverse consequences, and unintentional actions. They provide safeguards and warnings to assist *all* in using them safely, appropriately, respectfully, and efficiently.	• Teach students to use learning strategies (see Chapter 6). • Teach students to use self-management interventions (see Chapter 7). • Foster student motivation (see Chapter 9). • Use prompting and cuing strategies (see Chapter 10). • Provide students with valid and appropriate testing accommodations and grading alternatives (see Chapter 12).
Principle 6: Low Physical Effort	Inclusive practices are designed to be used comfortably and efficiently, and without much physical effort by *all* students, families, and professionals. They allow *all* to use them with a range of reasonable physical actions, and do not require repetitive actions or sustained physical effort.	• Design classrooms so that they support teaching and learning (see Chapters 4 and 7). • Break lessons and assignments into smaller parts, and allow extra time to work on assignments (see Chapter 9). • Provide personal supports from professionals and peers (see Chapters 4, 8, and 9).

TABLE 1.1 **Continued**

Universal Design for Learning Principles	Universal Design for Learning Principle and Inclusive Practices	Examples of the Implementation of Universal Design Principles and Inclusive Practices
Principle 7: Size and Space for Approach and Use	Inclusive practices are designed for use by *all* students, families, and professionals regardless of their body size, posture, and mobility. They allow *all* to see, reach, and activate important features and information and offer sufficient space for assistive technology devices and personal assistance.	• Use appropriate classroom designs, seating arrangements, and specialized chairs and desks (see Chapter 7). • Use universally designed curriculum and teaching materials (see Chapter 8). • Provide all students with the instructional accommodations and technology they need (see Chapters 8–12).
Principle 8: Community of Learners	Inclusive practices promote socialization and communication for *all* students, families, and professionals.	• Foster collaboration and communication with families and other professionals (see Chapter 4). • Offer social skills instruction (see Chapters 5, 6, and 7). • Have students work in collaborative groups to complete a range of learning and assessment activities (see Chapters 9 and 12).
Principle 9: Inclusive Environment	Inclusive practices foster acceptance and a sense of belonging for *all* students, families, and professionals.	• Help students, families, and other professionals learn about individual differences (see Chapters 3 and 5). • Foster interactions and friendships among students (see Chapter 5). • Use cooperative teaching arrangements and multicultural materials (see Chapters 5, 8, and 9).

The section entitled "UDL and You" in each chapter of this book provides you with ways to apply these principles to help design and implement flexible curriculum and teaching and assessment materials and strategies, and learning environments, as well as your interactions with others so that they are inclusive of *all* of the students, families, and the professionals with whom you work.

Civil Rights Movement and Resulting Litigation

Separate educational facilities are inherently unequal. This inherent inequality stems from the stigma created by purposeful segregation which generates a feeling of inferiority that may affect their hearts and minds in a way unlikely ever to be undone. (Earl Warren, chief justice of the Supreme Court, *Brown v. Board of Education*)

The impetus toward educating students like Mary in inclusive classrooms was also aided by the civil rights movement. The precedent for much special education–related litigation was established by *Brown v. Topeka Board of Education* (1954). The decision in this landmark civil rights case determined that segregating students in schools based on race, even if other educational variables appear to be equal, is unconstitutional. This refutation of the doctrine of "separate but equal" served as the underlying argument in court actions brought by families to ensure that their children with disabilities received a free, appropriate public education.

One example of such a court action is *Pennsylvania Association for Retarded Children v. Commonwealth of Pennsylvania* (1972), which served as a catalyst for change in the way students with disabilities were educated in the public school system. In this case, the families of children like Marie questioned the Pennsylvania School Code that was being used to justify the education of students with disabilities in environments that segregated them from their peers without disabilities. In a consent agreement approved by the court, the Commonwealth of Pennsylvania agreed that all students with mental retardation (the term used at that time) had a right to a free public education. The agreement further stated that placement in a general education public school classroom is preferable to more segregated placements and that families have the right to be informed of any changes in their children's educational program.

Recognizing that language shapes our perceptions, the field of special education has moved away from using the term *mental retardation* because of the stigma associated

REFLECTIVE

What do you think of when you hear or use the term mental retardation? Intellectual disability?

Using Technology to Promote Inclusion
FOSTERING INCLUSION AND INDEPENDENCE

My name is Robin Smith. I always wanted to be a teacher and was excited when my goal became a reality. I enjoyed my job and looked forward to going to school every day. After several years of teaching, I started to feel exhausted and have recurring body aches. When I wasn't teaching or eating, I was sleeping. After 2 years, I was finally diagnosed as having adult-onset severe rheumatoid arthritis.

My condition got worse, and I had to leave teaching. My fingers were like clay as they seemed to take a different shape every day. Eventually, I moved back home with my family. I could barely move my arms and legs and entered a hospital for several months. Upon leaving the hospital, my life revolved around sleeping, eating, and going to physical therapy five times a week.

I took arthritis and anti-inflammatory medications, which over time helped me regain limited use of my hands and feet. With the help of a motorized wheelchair, I started to get involved in the community. I also became active in several groups advocating for individuals with disabilities. I used a tape recorder with dictation and a 1-pound portable computer to write grants for these groups and to prepare materials to lobby legislators.

Although I was feeling better physically and emotionally, I missed teaching. I wanted to combine my love of teaching and my advocacy work and decided to pursue a doctorate in special education. My state's Office of Vocational Rehabilitation helped me in several ways. I needed a vehicle to get to and from my home to school and to participate in other required off-campus activities. After I purchased a vehicle, the Vocational Rehabilitation Office paid to retrofit it so that I could drive it and transport my motorized chair. This involved raising the roof and installing a lift, zero-effort steering, automatic gear shifting, toggle switches, and an electronic seat. While these adaptations helped, I used some homemade materials to more efficiently use the vehicle. I used a long and short dressing stick to reach the radio, fan, temperature controls, and gear-shift buttons and to pick up things from the floor. I also

tied a string to the directional signal to make it easier for me to use. I used to use a "reacher" to pull tickets out of machines when entering a toll booth. Now that most toll booths have an electronic system, I use the reacher only to enter parking areas.

My success in school was aided by use of a small computer that was like a personal digital assistant with a keyboard. I used it to take notes and as a word processor, calendar, and address book. After school, I transferred the information to a desktop computer. I also tried voice recognition software, but I found it inconsistent. I completed my doctorate and was pleased to be hired as a special education professor. I continue to use many of the same things I did as a student to do the different aspects of my job.

The university I work for is about 200 miles from my family, so I live alone, which is a challenge. However, I use several everyday things to make my life a little easier. I place long sticks with hooks throughout my home so that I can reach things and put my clothes on. I tie strings to the doors to help me open and close them, and clip key rings and other small important objects to my clothes so I don't drop them. I tie loops on light objects so that I can pick them up from the floor with my sticks, and I use a dust pan with a handle to pick up heavier items. I use an antiskid mat to get up from chairs and electronic gadgets in the kitchen.

As with many other people, it has been a challenge for me to meet my goals. However, my personal strength and ingenuity, the support of others, and access to technology has helped me reach my goals.

- What high- and low-technology assistive devices were helpful to Robin?
- How did these assistive devices foster Robin's independence and inclusion in society?
- How was Robin able to obtain these assistive devices?
- How would Robin's life be different if she did not have access to these assistive devices?
- What high- and low-technology assistive devices might benefit your students?
- How can you help your students obtain these devices?

with it (Turnbull et al., 2010). Therefore, although the term mental retardation continues to appear in the IDEA, this book will use the term *intellectual disability* to refer to individuals identified previously as having mental retardation (Schalock et al., 2007), which is consistent with the terminology used by organizations throughout the world.

REFLECTIVE
REFLECTIVE

Think of a relative, friend, or neighbor who has a disability. How has that individual affected you and others in your family and neighborhood? How have you advocated for that individual?

Advocacy Groups

Fueled by the momentum of civil rights campaigns, advocacy groups of family members like Mary's and Marie's parents, professionals, and individuals with disabilities banded together to seek civil rights and greater societal acceptance for individuals with disabilities (Duhaney & Salend, in press). Besides alerting the public to issues related to individuals with disabilities, advocacy groups lobbied state and federal legislators, brought lawsuits, and protested polices of exclusion and segregation. The result was greater societal acceptance and rights for individuals with disabilities like Mary.

Various economic, political, and environmental factors have increased the number of individuals with disabilities, adding to the growth of the disability rights movement. Individuals with disabilities have transformed themselves from invisible and passive recipients of sympathy to visible and active advocates of their rights as full members of society. These advocacy groups also have created a disability culture that celebrates and affirms disability, fosters community among individuals with disabilities, promotes disability awareness, and challenges society's conventional notions of disability (Smith, Gallagher, Owen, & Skrtic, 2009).

Segregated Nature of Special Schools and Classes

As the institutionalization of individuals with disabilities declined, the number of special schools and special classes within public schools for students with disabilities rose. However, educators, families, and advocacy groups eventually questioned the segregation of these students.

Studies on the effectiveness of special education programs also revealed that, progress aside, students with disabilities, especially those from culturally and linguistically diverse and low socioeconomic backgrounds, still have high dropout and incarceration rates and low employment rates (Frattura & Capper, 2006; Murray & Naranjo, 2008). In addition, students with disabilities who graduate high school are less likely to attend college than their peers without disabilities (Wagner, Newman, Cameto, Garza, & Levine, 2005).

Making Connections
Find out more about ways you can be an effective advocate for your students, their families, and important educational issues in Chapter 4.

Disproportionate Representation

Advocacy groups also raised concerns about the **disproportionate representation** of students from culturally and linguistically diverse backgrounds, including English language learners, in special education classes that segregated these students, regarding inclusive placements as a way to counter this segregation. For the purposes of this text, *culturally and linguistically diverse students* are defined as those who are not native members of the Euro-Caucasian culture base currently dominant in the United States and/or those whose native or primary language is not English. *English language learners* refer to students "whose native language is a language other than English or who come from an environment where a language other than English is dominant" (Artiles, Rueda, Salazar, & Higareda, 2005, p. 284).

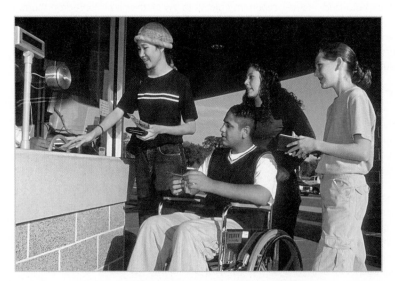

Many individuals become disabled after birth, and anyone can join this group at any time. How are your family members, friends, and neighbors with disabilities included in society?

Disproportionate representation, also referred to as *disproportionality,* is the presence of students from a specific group in an educational program that is higher or lower than one would expect based on their representation in the general population of students. It also includes the **overrepresentation** and **underrepresentation** of students in terms of educational classification and placement, and access to programs, services, resources, curriculum, instruction, and classroom management techniques (Futrell & Gomez, 2008; Lo & Cartledge, 2006).

Unfortunately, concerns about disproportionate representation are a reality for some groups (Artiles & Bal, 2008; Harry & Klingner, 2007; Samson & Lesaux, 2009). African American and Native American students, particularly males, are overrepresented in terms of their classification as students with three types of disabilities: learning disabilities, intellectual disability, and emotional disturbance. Although kindergarten and first grade English language learners are underrepresented in all disability categories, older ELLs are overrepresented (Samson & Lesaux, 2009). Once identified as in need of special education, these students are usually placed in more segregated placements (Skiba et al., 2008). This overrepresentation in special education has raised concerns about tracking students in a separate program that hinders their educational and social performance by limiting their access to the general education curriculum (Brice, Miller, & Brice, 2007; Harry, Arnaiz, Klingner, & Sturges, 2008).

Conversely, when a specific group of students participate at lower rates than their prevalence in the general population of students, underrepresentation is occurring. For example, Hispanic, Native Indian, and African American students are underrepresented in programs designed for gifted and talented students (Ford, Grantham, & Whiting, 2008), and females and Asian American students are underrepresented in special education programs (Doan, 2006; Manwaring, 2008). Underrepresentation also can have a negative impact on students' academic and social performance because it denies them access to services, programs, and resources tailored to address their educational needs.

A variety of educational and sociocultural factors interact to contribute to the disproportionate representation of students from culturally and linguistically diverse backgrounds (Artiles & Bal, 2008; Taylor & Whittaker, 2009). While having a lower socioeconomic status increases the likelihood that students will be placed in special education, the race, ethnicity, and age of students, test bias, the special education identification process, limited access to prereferral and ancillary services, and the unequal funding of schools appear to be major variables that contribute to the disproportionate representation of students from culturally and linguistically diverse backgrounds (Contopidis, LeRoux, & Halpern, 2007; Harry et al., 2008; Skiba et al., 2008).

Because issues of disproportionality are multifaceted and shaped by the cultural experiences of students and professionals, educators need to examine whether their policies, practices, attitudes, and behaviors result in disparate treatment of and disparate impact on students from culturally and linguistically diverse backgrounds (Gollnick & Chinn, 2009; Skiba et al., 2008; Trent, Kea, & Oh, 2008). ***Disparate treatment*** refers to treating students differently because of their characteristics and membership in a group such as their racial and linguistic background. An example would be disciplining such students differently from other students for the same offense. Even when all students are treated similarly, this similar treatment can still have different outcomes, or a **disparate impact** on, members of different groups. For example, sending a letter written in English inviting families to attend a meeting may result in few families who do not speak English attending the meeting.

You can help minimize disproportionate representation by delivering a wide range of effective culturally responsive educational strategies and services within the general education program that support student learning and family involvement (Garcia & Ortiz, 2006; Fielder et al., 2008). These varied services should address students' and their families' unique strengths and challenges, as well as their experiential,

While Caucasian American and Asian American students are underrepresented in terms of their identification as having intellectual disabilities and emotional disturbance, they tend to be overrepresented with respect to being identified as having other health impairments, traumatic brain injuries, and autism (Dyches et al., 2005). Why do you think this is the case?

REFLECTIVE
REFLECTIVE

Can you think of examples of disparate treatment and disparate impact in schools? In society?

Students from culturally and linguistically diverse backgrounds, particularly African American and Native American males, tend to be overrepresented in special education programs and underrepresented in programs for gifted and talented students. Why do you think this is the case?

cultural, and linguistic backgrounds, and therefore help minimize the need for placement in special education.

No Child Left Behind Act

The provisions of the No Child Left Behind Act (NCLB) means that schools must restructure and coordinate their efforts and programs to help *all students*—including those with disabilities— have access to and succeed in the general education curriculum to meet specific learning standards (Turnbull et al., 2010). The NCLB calls on states to establish learning standards and benchmarks that identify the things that learners should know and be able to do at the various grade levels (Ysseldyke, Lehr, & Stodolka Bulygo, 2008). The NCLB also has established that *all students* should be included in **high-stakes assessments** aligned with statewide learning standards.

The NCLB contains accountability provisions mandating that school districts show they are making adequate yearly progress on state tests for *all their students,* including subgroups of students identified in terms of their disability, socioeconomic status, language background, race, and ethnicity (Yell, Katsiyannas, & Shiner, 2006). Schools and school districts that fail to achieve adequate yearly progress are designated as *in need of improvement.* These efforts seek to make schools accountable for educating *all students* and translating assessment results into instructional accommodations that support learning. Thus, rather than segregating students with disabilities, many schools are implementing inclusion programs to unify general and special education into one service delivery system to provide *all students* with a general education.

In addition to the accountability and testing mandates of NCLB, you should be aware of its other important provisions that affect you and your students and their families, including these:

- Requiring school districts to offer families alternatives (i.e., school choice, extra tutoring) if their children attend schools where students do not perform well on state tests.
- Mandating that school districts provide *all students* with highly qualified teachers.
- Fostering the use of scientifically based research educational practices (Vannest, Mahadevan, Mason, & Temple-Harvey, 2009; Ysseldyke et al., 2008).

Although the intent of the NCLB has been applauded, concerns about its impact have been raised (Azzam, 2008). These concerns include the focus on *one-size-fits-all* testing as the sole way to identify student progress, the limited ways in which scientifically based research is conducted, the loss of individualization instruction, and the standardization of the curriculum to match the state tests (which can lead to teaching to the test). Some schools with high numbers of students who struggle to meet the testing performance requirements associated with the NCLB are narrowing the curriculum, which means that more instructional time is spent on reading and math and less time is devoted to other subjects (i.e., science, social studies, art, and music) (Dillon, 2006). Another major concern is that students with disabilities and students from culturally and linguistically diverse backgrounds are being encouraged to leave school so that schools are not identified as in need of improvement. The

Making Connections
Find out more about high-stakes testing in Chapter 12.

A GUIDE TO ACTION
Examining Disproportionate Representation

As specified in the Individuals with Disabilities Education Improvement Act of 2004, school districts and state departments of education must determine whether the problems of overrepresentation and underrepresentation exist, as well as the nature of these problems, which can assist them in adopting policies and practices to address disproportionate representation. You and your colleagues can examine the extent to which students in your school district are disproportionately represented by considering the following questions:

- Are students from culturally and linguistically diverse backgrounds disproportionately referred for and placed in special education? Gifted and talented programs?
- Do the reasons for referrals for special education differ based on the cultural and linguistic background of the students?
- Do patterns of identification by disability category differ by race or ethnicity?
- Do placements within the general education setting vary based on the cultural and linguistic backgrounds of students?
- Do members of the multidisciplinary teams reflect the diversity of the student population they serve, and do they have the preparation and experience to properly and accurately assess the needs of students from diverse backgrounds?
- Do students from culturally and linguistically diverse backgrounds have equal access to the school district's RTI, prereferral, supportive, and transitional services, and extracurricular and community activities?

- Do placement teams consider the impact of cultural, linguistic, and experiential backgrounds and account for assessment bias when assessing students and their educational strengths and challenges?
- Do the curriculum, teaching and classroom management strategies, and instructional materials address the experiences of students from culturally and linguistically diverse backgrounds?
- Are students from culturally and linguistically diverse backgrounds disciplined or treated differently than other students for comparable behaviors?
- Do educators assess the extent to which student behavior is related to cultural, experiential, and linguistic factors?
- Do educators create respectful classrooms that promote acceptance of diversity?
- Are families and community members from culturally and linguistically diverse backgrounds involved in all aspects of the school?
- Do educators employ strategies to interact with family and community members in culturally sensitive ways and adjust their services to the diverse backgrounds of students' families?
- Does the school district maintain a complete database on issues related to disproportionate representation?

How would you rate the extent to which disproportionate representation exists in your school district? ( ) Doesn't Exist ( ) Exists to Some Extent ( ) Exists Extensively

With your colleagues, create a plan of action for addressing disproportionate representation that includes your goals, the actions you will take and the resources you will need to achieve them, and the ways you will evaluate your success.

U.S. Congress is working on making changes to NCLB to address many of these concerns, including the following:

- Measuring student progress by using multiple measures rather than just standardized test scores
- Using a growth model that tracks measures of progress by examining the performance of the same groups of students over time

LAWS AFFECTING SPECIAL EDUCATION

WHAT ARE THE LAWS THAT AFFECT SPECIAL EDUCATION? The factors just discussed helped shape several education and civil rights laws designed primarily to include individuals with disabilities like Marie and Mary in *all* aspects of society. The most important of these laws is the IDEA. Before it was enacted into law in 1975, more than 1 million students with disabilities like Marie were denied a public education, and those who attended public schools were segregated from their peers without disabilities. Since its enactment, students with disabilities have gained greater access to inclusive classrooms and the general education curriculum.

REFLECTIVE
BEFFECTIVE

Based on your experiences as a student or a teacher, how have the provisions of NCLB affected you and your students? Students with special needs? Your curriculum? Your teaching practices? Your work environment?

Making Connections
Find out more about ways
to involve your students and
their families in the IEP
process in Chapters 2 and 4.

REFLECTIVE

By replacing the term *handicapped*
with the term *disabilities* in the
IDEA, Congress recognized the
importance of language. What do
the terms *regular, normal,* and
special imply? How do these
terms affect the ways we view
students with disabilities and the
programs designed to meet their
needs? Do these terms foster
inclusion or segregation?

The Individuals with Disabilities Education Act (IDEA)

Initially known as the Education for All Handicapped Children Act (PL 94-142), this legislation has been amended numerous times since its passage in 1975 and was renamed the Individuals with Disabilities Education Act in 1990 and the Individuals with Disabilities Educational Improvement Act (IDEIA) in 2004. Highlights of these amendments are discussed next. The IDEA mandates that a *free and appropriate education* be provided to all students with disabilities, regardless of the nature and severity of their disability. It affirms that disability is "a natural part of the human experience" and acknowledges the normalization principle by asserting that individuals with disabilities have the right to "enjoy full inclusion and integration into the economic, political, social, cultural, and educational mainstream of society." The IDEA is the culmination of many efforts to ensure the rights of full citizenship and equal access for individuals with disabilities.

The IDEA is based on six fundamental principles that govern the education of students with disabilities (Turnbull, Turnbull, & Wehmeyer, 2010). Under the first principle, *zero reject,* schools cannot exclude any student with a disability, and each state must locate children who may be entitled to special education services. Under the second principle, *nondiscriminatory evaluation,* schools must evaluate students fairly to see whether they have a disability and provide guidelines for identifying the special education and related services they will receive if they do have a disability. The principle of a *free and appropriate education* requires schools to follow individually tailored education for each student defined in an **Individualized Education Program (IEP)**. The principle of the *least restrictive environment* requires schools to educate students with disabilities with their peers who are not disabled to the maximum extent appropriate. The *procedural due process* principle provides safeguards against schools' actions, including the right to sue if schools do not carry out the other principles. The final principle requires *family and student participation* in designing and delivering special education programs and IEPs.

An Overview of IDEA from 1975 to the Present: A Changing IDEA   Since the IDEA was first passed in 1975, it has been amended and changed numerous times.

PL 94-142: Education for All Handicapped Children Act.   Passed in 1975, this act mandates that a free and appropriate education be provided to *all students* with disabilities, regardless of the nature and severity of their disability. It outlines the IEP and states that students with disabilities will be educated in the LRE with their peers who are not disabled to the maximum extent appropriate. It also guarantees that students with disabilities and their families have the right to nondiscriminatory testing, confidentiality, and due process.

PL 99-457: Infants and Toddlers with Disabilities Act of 1986.   PL 99-457 extended many of the rights and safeguards of PL 94-142 to children with disabilities from birth to 5 years of age and encouraged early intervention services and special assistance to students who are at risk. It also included provisions for developing an IFSP for each child. The components of an IFSP are presented in Figure 1.3.

PL 101-476: Individuals with Disabilities Education Act of 1990.   In 1990, PL 101-476 changed the title of PL 94-142 from the Education for All Handicapped Children Act to the Individuals with Disabilities Education Act (IDEA), reflecting "individuals first" language (i.e., using the term *students with learning disabilities* rather than *learning disabled students*) to emphasize the individual rather than disability (Russell, 2008; Snow, 2009). Additionally, all uses of the term *handicapped* were replaced by the term *disabilities*.

Although I have used individuals first language in this book, I also have tried to respect the preferences of some groups regarding what they like to be called. For instance, the National Association of the Deaf's Web site (http://www.nad.org) states, "Overwhelmingly, deaf and hard of hearing people prefer to be called 'deaf' or 'hard

FIGURE 1.3 Components of the IFSP

- A statement of the infant's or toddler's present level of development
- An assessment of the family's strengths and needs for enhancing the child's development, including the resources, priorities, and concerns of the family
- A statement of the outcomes to be achieved for the child and family
- A list of the criteria, techniques, and timelines for evaluating progress
- A statement of the early education services that will be delivered to meet the child's and family's unique needs, including their intensity and frequency
- A statement of the natural environments where the early education services will be delivered, as well as why other environments will be used if necessary
- The dates for starting services and their duration
- The name of the family's service coordinator, who will supervise the implementation of the program
- The procedures for moving the child from early intervention to preschool
- Annual evaluation of the IFSP

of hearing.' Nearly all organizations of the deaf use the term 'deaf and hard of hearing,' and the National Association of the Deaf (NAD) is no exception. The World Federation of the Deaf (WFD) voted in 1991 to use 'deaf and hard of hearing' as an official designation." Therefore, I will use *deaf and hard of hearing students and individuals* to refer to these individuals and students throughout the book.

The IDEA continued the basic provisions outlined in PL 94-142 and made the following changes: the category of children with disabilities was expanded to include autism and traumatic brain injury, related services were expanded to include rehabilitation counseling and social work services, and the commitment to provide services to youth with disabilities from culturally and linguistically diverse backgrounds was increased.

PL 105-17: The IDEA Amendments of 1997. PL 105-17 included several provisions to improve the educational performance of students with disabilities by having high expectations for them, giving them greater access to general education, including them in local and state assessments, and making general and special educators and administrators members of the IEP team. PL 105-17 also sought to strengthen the role of families in their children's education and to prevent the disproportionate representation of students from diverse backgrounds in special education programs.

PL 108-446: The Individuals with Disabilities Education Improvement Act of 2004. With the passage of PL 108-446, Congress made important changes to the IDEA (Hulett, 2009). These changes—which address the IEP; family involvement; the special education identification, prereferral, and disciplinary processes—are presented in the following sections (Murdick et al., 2007; Yell et al., 2008). Other changes of the IDEA of 2004 are the addition of Tourette syndrome to the list of conditions considered under the disability category of "other health impaired" and the targeting of students with disabilities who are also gifted and talented (also called *twice exceptional students*) as a priority group whose needs should be assessed and addressed.

Changes to the IEP and family involvement. In the IDEA of 2004, the Congress eliminated short-term objectives and benchmarks from student IEPs so that annual goals relate to the accountability and testing provisions of the NCLB as well as each state's learning standards. However, IEPs for students with disabilities who take alternate assessments rather than participating in state and federal testing programs still

Making Connections
Find out more about how you can engage in actions and language that are respectful of students' individual differences and focus on their abilities in Chapter 5.

Making Connections
Find out more about twice exceptional students in Chapter 2.

Understanding Inclusion

must include benchmarks and short-term objectives. In addition, other revisions to the IEP and family involvement include the following:

- Allowing families and school districts to agree to exempt any member of the IEP team from attending all or part of an IEP meeting when the team member's area of expertise or related service is not being discussed. When a team member's areas of expertise or related service is being considered by the IEP team, families and school districts also can agree to excuse the team member and obtain written input from the individual prior to the meeting.

- Permitting school districts and families to agree to meet using alternative means, such as video and phone conferences, and to change the IEP after the annual meeting using written documents rather than reconvening the team

- Requiring a description in the IEP of how and when progress in meeting annual goals will be assessed and shared with family members. These descriptions of student progress may be provided via quarterly or periodic communications with families (e.g., report cards).

- Raising the age for all transition requirements, including developing transition plans to age 16, and requiring the IEP to include "postsecondary goals addressing training, education, employment and, where appropriate, living skills"

- Ensuring that a summary of academic and functional performance be provided to students with disabilities who graduate or exceed the age for special education services that also includes suggestions for helping them achieve their postsecondary goals

- Expanding the use of mediation to resolve differences between school districts and families related to the IEP and other procedural disagreements.

Changes in the special education identification, prereferral, and disciplinary processes. Because of concerns about dramatic increases in the number of students with learning disabilities, the IDEA of 2004 provides for the development and use of new ways to identify students with learning disabilities. Previously, school districts used an **IQ-Achievement Discrepancy Model**, which seeks to identify students as having a learning disability if there is a significant gap between their learning potential and academic achievement. Under the IDEA of 2004, districts are not required to use the discrepancy model to identify students with learning disabilities and can use alternatives for or supplements to the IQ-Achievement Discrepancy Model. One such alternative allowed under the IDEA of 2004 is the **Response-to-Intervention (RTI)** method, a multitiered process whereby only students who do not respond to a series of more intensive research-based interventions would be identified as having a learning disability (Fuchs & Fuchs, 2007). To address the overidentification of students with learning and other types of disabilities, Congress also allowed school districts to use IDEA funds to support the establishment of prereferral services for students not identified as needing special education but who need additional academic or behavioral support to succeed in general education classrooms. The IDEA now also requires school districts to implement prereferral programs to reduce high rates of special education placements for their students from culturally and linguistically diverse backgrounds.

Making Connections
Find out more about the RTI method in Chapter 2.

The IDEA amendments of 1997 contained provisions that had a significant impact on disciplinary actions for students with disabilities. Under these provisions, school personnel cannot remove students with disabilities from school for more than 10 days unless the disciplinary action is related to carrying a weapon to school or knowingly possessing, using, or selling illegal drugs at school. In these cases, the IEP team can unilaterally place a student in an interim alternative setting for up to 45 school days. The IDEA of 2004 added "*inflicted serious bodily injury on another person while at school, on school premises, or at a school function*" to the list of disciplinary actions that can result in students with disabilities being removed from school for up to 45 calendar days (under the IDEA of 1997, it was 45 school days). Congress also took actions that prohibit school districts from requiring students to take medications in order to attend school, receive services, or be evaluated for special education.

To assist you in meeting the mandates of the IDEA, each chapter of this book will contain IDEAs to Implement Inclusion, a feature that offers examples and suggestions of the application of techniques for creating inclusive classrooms that meet the challenges of the IDEA.

Other Laws Affecting Special Education

Although your class will include many students who have unique strengths and challenges, many of these students may not be eligible for special education services under the IDEA. However, they may qualify for special and general education services under two civil rights laws whose goals are to provide access to societal opportunities and to prevent discrimination against individuals with disabilities: Section 504 of the Rehabilitation Act (Section 504) and the Americans with Disabilities Act (ADA) (Hughes & Weiss, 2008; Hulett, 2009). Under these acts, individuals qualify for services as having a disability if they

- have a physical or mental impairment that substantially limits one or more major life activities,
- have a record of such an impairment, or
- are regarded as having such an impairment by others.

Major life activities are broadly identified to include walking, seeing, hearing, speaking, breathing, learning, working, caring for self, and performing manual tasks. To be covered against discrimination under these acts, an individual must be **otherwise qualified**, which means the individual must be qualified to do something (e.g, perform a job, sing in the choir, have the entry level scores to be in honors classes), regardless of the presence of a disability.

Section 504 of the Rehabilitation Act   Some of your students may receive special education services under Section 504 of the Rehabilitation Act (PL 93-112), which was passed by Congress in 1973. Section 504 serves as a civil rights law for individuals with disabilities and forbids all institutions receiving federal funds from discriminating against individuals with disabilities in education, employment, housing, and access to public programs and facilities (Murdick et al., 2007; Shaw & Madaus, 2008). It also requires these institutions to make their buildings physically accessible to individuals with disabilities. Section 504 provides students with the right to a general education, extracurricular activities in their local schools, instructional and curriculum accommodations, and equal access to services and programs available to students without disabilities. Students who qualify for services under the IDEA are also entitled to the protections of Section 504.

Section 504 has both similarities to and differences from the IDEA (Hughes & Weiss, 2008; Shaw & Madaus, 2008) (see Figure 1.4). Like the IDEA, Section 504 requires schools to provide eligible students with a free, appropriate public education, which is defined as general or special education that includes related services and reasonable accommodations. Both the IDEA and Section 504 require that students be educated with their peers without disabilities to the maximum extent possible. However, because Section 504 is based on a broader functional definition of disabilities than the IDEA and covers one's life span, far more individuals qualify for special education services under Section 504 than under the IDEA. As a result, potential recipients of services under Section 504 include students with attention deficit disorders, social maladjustments, temporary and long-term health conditions (e.g., arthritis, asthma, diabetes, epilepsy, heart conditions), communicable diseases, AIDS, and eating disorders. Individuals who abuse substances are eligible for services under Section 504 as long as they are in rehabilitation or recovery programs. However,

IDEA	SECTION 504
Type/Purpose/Funding/Enforcement	
• A federal law guaranteeing and guiding the delivery of special education services to eligible children with disabilities.	• A civil rights law forbidding discrimination against individuals with disabilities who are otherwise qualified by programs that receive federal funds.
• Monitored and enforced by the Office of Special Education Programs of the U.S. Department of Education.	• Monitored and enforced by the Office of Civil Rights of the U.S. Department of Education.
• Provides some federal monies to states and school districts.	• Provides no additional federal monies to states and local school districts, and does not allow IDEA funds to be used to provide service to individuals covered only by 504.
Eligibility	
• Covers individuals up to age 21.	• Covers individuals throughout their lives.
• Defines *disability* categorically as having one or more of the disability classifications that have an adverse effect on educational performance.	• Defines *disability* functionally as having a physiological or mental impairment that substantially limits one or more major life activities.
Evaluation	
• Requires that a multifactored and nondiscriminatory evaluation in all areas related to suspected disability be conducted to determine eligibility.	• Requires that a multiple source and nondiscriminatory evaluation in the area(s) of suspected need(s) conducted to determine eligibility.
• Eligibility decision made by a multidisciplinary team of professionals, family members, and the child when appropriate.	• Eligibility decision made by a group of individuals who are knowledgeable with respect to the child, the assessment procedures, and the placement options.
Free Appropriate Public Education	
• Defines appropriate education in terms of its educational benefits.	• Defines an appropriate education in terms of its comparability to the education offered to students without disabilities.
• Requires an individualized education program (IEP).	• Requires an individualized accommodation plan (often called a 504 accommodation plan).
• Requires related aids and services to be delivered to help students benefit from special education.	• Related aids and services are delivered if they are needed to help students access appropriate educational programs.
• Requires that students be educated in the least restrictive environment.	• Requires that students be educated in the least restrictive environment, including having equal access to nonacademic and extracurricular activities.
Due Process Procedure	
• Requires informed and written consent from parents/guardian.	• Requires that notice be given, but not consent.
• Establishes specific due process procedures for notification and impartial hearings.	• Leaves due process procedures up to the discretion of school districts.
• Gives families who disagree with the identification, education or placement of their child the right to an impartial hearing.	• Gives families who disagree with the identification, education or placement of their child the right to an impartial hearing.
• Gives families the right to participate in the hearing and to be represented by counsel.	• Gives families the right to participate in the hearing and to be represented by counsel.

Sources: Bartlett, Etscheidt, and Weisenstein (2007); Hughes and Weiss (2008); Shaw and Madaus (2008); Welner (2006).

if they begin to abuse substances again, they are no longer eligible until they return to a rehabilitation or recovery program. It also covers individuals with disabilities who are not eligible to receive services under the IDEA because they are now older than 21 or because their learning difficulties are not severe enough to warrant classification as an individual with learning disabilities.

Section 504 has fewer specific procedural requirements to guide its implementation than does the IDEA; however, it is suggested that schools employ best practices and follow the policies and procedures that they use to implement the IDEA. Although Section 504 does not require the development of an IEP, you and your colleagues must make accommodations to meet the learning needs of students covered under Section 504. If a student needs special or related services or reasonable accommodations, a planning team that knows the student, the assessment data, and the available services, placements, and accommodations develops a written accommodation plan. A sample Section 504 accommodation plan is presented in Figure 1.5.

Because Section 504 addresses discrimination that denies students equal access to academic, nonacademic, and extracurricular activities, it also covers some situations not addressed in the IDEA that you will probably encounter in your school. Therefore, under 504, you must make sure that all your field trips and after-school programs (e.g., recreational activities, athletic teams) are accessible to *all your students*. However, if an activity is open only to students with certain qualifications, the *otherwise qualified* principle applies. Here, students with disabilities may not be selected to participate in a specific activity as long as they are given the same opportunity as other students to demonstrate whether they have the qualifications. For example, students with disabilities should be provided with an equal opportunity to try out for the school's soccer team, and the decision regarding their selection for the team should be based on their ability to demonstrate their skills at playing soccer. Section 504 also affects the grading of students and their access to honors and awards.

Americans with Disabilities Act In 1990, Congress enacted PL 101-336, the Americans with Disabilities Act (ADA), a civil rights act designed to integrate individuals with disabilities into the social and economic mainstream of society (Hulett, 2009; Price, Gerber, & Mulligan, 2007). The ADA extends the civil rights of individuals with disabilities by providing them with access to public facilities including postsecondary education, restaurants, shops, state and local government activities and programs, telecommunications, and transportation (Hughes & Weiss, 2008). Employers and service providers in the public and private sectors cannot discriminate against them. The ADA requires employers to make reasonable accommodations for individuals with disabilities to allow them to perform essential job functions unless the accommodations would present an undue hardship. To comply with the ADA, schools must make their facilities accessible and offer reasonable accommodations to students with disabilities.

IMPACT OF INCLUSION

WHAT IS THE IMPACT ON INCLUSION ON STUDENTS, EDUCATORS, AND FAMILIES? Researchers have conducted studies with different groups to assess the extent to which inclusion is achieving its intended benefits and to identify issues that need to be addressed to improve inclusion programs. Because inclusion is a relatively recent movement, these studies are not longitudinal, and studies that examine the long-term impact on a wide range of students, families, and educators are needed to help us learn more about inclusion (Sindelar, Shearer, Yendol-Hoppey, & Liebert, 2006). The lack of experimental research involving random selection and assignment of students and the relatively small sample sizes also limit the findings of these studies (Begeny & Martens, 2007). Thus, it is difficult to compare the impact of inclusion and noninclusion programs because students with disabilities placed in inclusive classrooms tend to be more academically and socially skilled than students with disabilities placed in noninclusive settings. It also is important to keep in mind that inclusion programs are multifaceted and varied in their implementation and the services provided (Ainscow, 2008; Idol, 2006), which can explain the differing results reported in studies.

Impact of Inclusion on Students with Disabilities

Several studies have examined the effect of general education placement on students with disabilities. These findings, which are summarized in Figure 1.6, reveal a varied impact on students' academic and social performance and on their reactions to

REFLECTIVE

Whereas the IDEA provides funding to schools for eligible students, money for students eligible under Section 504 comes from the school district's general education funds. As a school administrator, would you prefer a student to be eligible under the IDEA or Section 504? As a parent of a child with special needs, what would you prefer?

REFLECTIVE

The ADA appears to be underutilized as individuals with disabilities may conceal their disabilities from their employers (Madaus, 2008; Price et al., 2007). Why do you think this occurs?

myeducationlab

Go to the Assignments and Activities section of the Topic *Inclusive Practices* in the MyEducationLab for your course and complete the activity entitled *Special Education Characteristics, Attitudes, and Impacts.*

FIGURE 1.5 Sample Section 504 accommodation plan

Name: John Jones

School: Porter High School   **Grade:** 10th

Date: 10/6/2011   **Age:** 15

Follow-up Date(s): John's plan will be reviewed and evaluated at the end of each semester.

Teachers: Mr. J. McKenzie (Social Studies), Mr. W. Dumont (English), Ms. M. Tinsley (Biology), Mr. S. Labiosa (Spanish), Ms. R. Shankar (Mathematics)

1. **General Strengths:** Individualized standardized testing indicates that John is a capable student who is performing at or near grade level. His favorite subjects in school are mathematics and science. He wants to succeed in school and is very interested in going to college.

2. **General Concerns:** John's performance in school is erratic. He completes approximately 70% of his assignments and does poorly on tests. Observation of John in his classes shows that he often calls out and frequently fidgets in his seat or leaves it without permission. His teachers also report that he rarely pays attention to directions and is often distracted by events in the classroom. They also note that John rarely interacts with his peers.

3. **Nature and Impact of Disability:** John has been diagnosed as having Attention Deficit Disorder with Hyperactivity (ADHD) by his family physician. Behavior rating scales and observations by educators and family members suggest that John's activity level is significant and interferes with his educational and social performance in school and at home.

Goal	Accommodations	Person(s) responsible for accommodations
1. To increase John's work completion	A. Step-by-step written and verbal directions for assignments, including examples, will be given to John. B. Assignments will be broken into several shorter parts and John will receive a break of 5 minutes between assignments. C. A daily homework notebook system will be implemented. D. Learning strategy instruction will be provided to John.	A. John's teachers B. John's teachers C. John, John's family, and John's teachers D. Special education teacher
2. To increase John's performance on tests	A. Study and test-taking skills instruction will be provided to John. B. John will receive the following testing accommodations: extended time, breaks, and testing in a separate location.	A. Special education teacher B. John's teachers
3. To increase John's on-task behavior	A. A self-monitoring system will be used by John to keep track of his on-task behavior. B. A daily behavior report card system will be implemented. C. John's work area will be located at front of the room.	A. John and John's teachers B. John, John's teachers, and John's family C. John's teachers
4. To increase John's socialization with peers	A. Social skills and attribution training instruction will be provided to John. B. John will be taught about and encouraged to participate in extracurricular and community-based activities.	A. Special education teacher B. John, John's family, John's teachers, and John's school counselor

Participants:

Mr. John Jones, Student

Ms. Janice Jones, Parent

Ms. Roberta Shankar, Mathematics teacher

Mr. Jose Garcia, Special education teacher

Mr. William Dumont, English teacher

Ms. Freda Hargrove, School Counselor

Mr. Carl Rogan, District 504 Coordinator

Dr. Loren Phillips, Family physician

_____

(Parent/guardian)

I agree with the 504 accommodation plan outlined above

_____

(Parent/guardian)

I do not agree with the 504 accommodation plan outlined above

Impact of Inclusive Placements on the Academic Performance of Elementary Students with Disabilities

- Students with mild disabilities educated in inclusive classrooms had improved standardized test scores, mathematics and reading performance, grades, on-task behavior, motivation to learn, and more positive attitudes toward school and learning as well as mastery of IEP goals (Hang & Rabren, 2009; Hunt et al., 2000; Idol, 2006; Nevin et al., 2008; Peetsma, 2001).
- Students with intellectual disabilities and more severe disabilities in inclusion programs had greater access to the general education curriculum and instructional accommodations, learned targeted skills, had more engaged and instructional time, and had greater exposure to academic activities than students with severe disabilities educated in special education settings (Cushing et al., 2009; Hunt, Soto, Maier, & Doering, 2003; Soukup, Wehmeyer, Bashinski, & Bovaird, 2007).
- Students with disabilities taught in inclusive classrooms are not given "specially designed instruction" to meet their academic needs in inclusion programs (Dymond & Russell, 2004; Fabel, 2009; Simpson, 2004; Zigmond, 2003, 2006) and perform better academically in pull-out resource programs (Manset & Semmel, 1997; Marston, 1996).
- Observations of inclusive classrooms indicated that teachers rarely made specialized curriculum accommodations for students with disabilities (Dymond & Russell, 2004).
- Higher-functioning preschoolers and elementary students with disabilities benefit more from placement in inclusion programs than their lower-functioning counterparts (Klingner et al., 1998; Mills, Cole, Jenkins, & Dale, 1998; Rafferty, Piscitelli, & Boettcher, 2003).

Impact of Inclusive Placements on the Social and Behavioral Performance and Attitude Toward Placement of Elementary Students with Disabilities

- Students with mild disabilities in inclusion classes develop friendships with other students, feel a part of their classes' social networks, have self-concept scores similar to those of their classmates without disabilities, and are rated as equal to their general education peers in terms of disruptive behavior (Estell et al., 2008; Lee, Yoo, & Bak, 2003).
- Students with learning disabilities educated in inclusive classrooms had more positive social and emotional functioning and satisfying friendships with best friends, were less lonely, and exhibited fewer inappropriate behaviors than their peers who were educated in self-contained classrooms (Wiener & Tardif, 2004).
- Students with autism spectrum disorders educated in inclusive classrooms experienced increased social interactions with classmates (Owen-DeSchryver et al., 2008), and had social acceptance and peer group membership that was similar to their classmates without disabilities (Boutot & Bryant, 2005).
- Students with intellectual disabilities in inclusive classrooms achieve social acceptance ratings that are higher than those of their counterparts who are educated in noninclusive settings and lower than their classmates without disabilities (Freeman & Alkin, 2000).
- Students with moderate or severe disabilities in inclusion programs interact with others more often, receive and offer increased social support, and develop more long-lasting and richer friendships with their general education peers (Hunt et al., 2003). However, interactions between these students and those without disabilities are often initiated by the latter, are often assistive, and tend to decline over the school year (Coster & Haltiwanger, 2004; Lee et al., 2003).
- Students with learning disabilities in inclusive classrooms are less often accepted and more often rejected by those without disabilities; have lower social status, self-perceptions, and self-concepts than their general education peers; fewer best friend nominations; are more likely to have friendships with classmates with disabilities (Estell et al., 2008, 2009); and report that they experience school-related loneliness (Estell et al., 2008; Lloyd, Wilton, & Townsend, 2000; Pavri & Luftig, 2000; Pavri & Monda-Amaya, 2001).
- Students with disabilities prefer to leave the general education classroom to receive individualized services that help them academically and believe that the general education classroom is best for meeting their academic and social needs (Elbaum, 2002).
- Students with disabilities in inclusive classrooms are concerned about the recreational and academic activities they are missing when they are being pulled out of their general education classrooms (Ferri et al., 2001).
- Students with disabilities report that leaving the general education classroom for specialized services was embarrassing and provoked name-calling and ridicule from their peers (Reid & Button, 1995).

Impact of Inclusive Placements on the Academic Performance of Secondary Students with Disabilities

- Students with mild disabilities educated in inclusive settings make academic gains and transitions, and achieve academic engagement and passing rates that are comparable to those of their peers without disabilities (Brigharm, Morocco, Clay, & Zigmond, 2006; Cawley et al., 2002; Idol, 2006; Wallace et al., 2002; Wilson & Michaels, 2006).
- Students with learning disabilities educated in inclusive settings tend to receive higher grades in all content areas, earn higher or comparable standardized test scores, and attend school more frequently than their peers who were served in pull-out programs (Rea, McLaughlin, & Walther-Thomas, 2002; Wilson & Michaels, 2006).
- Students with moderate and severe disabilities improved in reading and classroom work skills when they received instruction in inclusive settings (Dore et al., 2002; McDonnell, Johnson, Polychronis, & Risen, 2002).
- Students with disabilities in inclusive placements are more likely to take and pass statewide assessments, complete high school, attend college, obtain a job, earn a higher salary, and live independently (Wyatt, 2000).
- Students with disabilities may not be receiving differentiated and individualized instruction in inclusion programs (Fabel, 2009; Harbort et al., 2007; Murawski, 2006; Paterson, 2007; Zigmond, 2006).

(Continued)

FIGURE 1.6 **Continued**

- Students with significant learning disabilities in inclusive classrooms performed poorly on statewide exams (Fabel, 2009).
- Students with intellectual disabilities taught in general education classrooms had a decrease in their graduation rates (Katsiyannis, Landrum, & Reid, 2002).
- Students with significant intellectual disabilities educated in inclusive classrooms may not be learning the functional skills they need for success in school and community settings (Billingsley & Albertson, 1999).

Impact of Inclusive Placements on the Social and Behavioral Performance and Attitude Toward Placement of Secondary Students with Disabilities

- Students with learning disabilities or emotional disorders educated in general education classrooms had higher levels of social acceptance, and comparable levels of behavioral incidents as their peers educated in pull-out programs (Cawley et al., 2002; Rea, McLaughlin, & Walther-Thomas, 2002).
- Students with learning disabilities did not cause a significant number of behavior problems, and had friendship ratings and self-concept scores that were comparable to those of their classmates without disabilities (DeSimone & Parmar, 2006; Forgan & Vaughn, 2000).
- Students with moderate or severe disabilities have increased social interactions in inclusive educational placements (Hughes, Carter, Hughes, Bradford, & Copeland, 2002). However, they engage in fewer social interactions with classmates and spend more time as passive participants in interactions (Mu, Siegel, & Allinder, 2000).
- Students with moderate or severe disabilities taught in general education classrooms experienced brief, assistive, and superficial social interactions with their peers without disabilities (Dore et al., 2002), and demonstrated more self-determined behaviors in resource room programs than in general education classrooms (Zhang, 2001).
- Students with disabilities prefer placement in general education because their friends were in those classes, and they were treated like other students. Students also worried that their special education placement would cause them to lose their friends and to feel stigmatized and deficient (Eisenman & Tascione, 2002; Lovitt, Plavins, & Cushing, 1999).
- Students with disabilities preferred special education classes academically because they received more help, liked the smaller class size, and believed the work was easier. However, students also viewed special education as low-level, irrelevant, and repetitive and not helping them learn very much. Although some students preferred the general education setting because it was more challenging and "cooler" and resulted in more learning, others reported that it was not reasonable for their general education teachers to accommodate their learning needs and that such accommodations would lead to increased academic stigma (Eisenman & Tascione, 2002; Lovitt et al., 1999).

and attitudes toward inclusion. Note that like many other educational programs, inclusion may impact students in different ways as they age and based on their nature of their disability. Thus, the impact of inclusion on elementary- and secondary-level students and students with varying disability conditions may differ as well as their reactions to inclusion.

Academic Performance Several studies and school reports on the impact of inclusion on the academic performance of elementary and secondary students with disabilities are presented in Figure 1.6. In general, the findings suggest that the academic performance of students with disabilities can be enhanced when they receive appropriate curricular and instructional accommodations within the general education setting (Black-Hawkins, Florian, & Rouse, 2007; Cushing et al., 2009; Hang & Rabren, 2007; Hehir, 2007).

Social and Behavioral Performance and Attitudes Toward Placement

Like most people, I don't remember much about my first years in school. Most of my memories are from the last 2 years in special education. I remember becoming unhappy about school then. I think I was at the age when I began to realize I was separated from the "regular kids." I can remember that during lunch the special ed kids and the "regular" kids ate at separate tables, and all the special ed kids were herded onto the G–12 bus. The incident that sticks out in my mind involved a kid named Jimmy, who was in another special education classroom but lived in my neighborhood. One morning at the bus stop, Jimmy told me that he was going to start going to the neighborhood school with the "regular" kids. I can remember the sadness I felt that it was not me. (A student with a disability)

I hated high school. Whether I was in the regular or special education class, it was bad. I was often lost in the regular class, and sometimes other kids would tease me. It was terrible for me when I had to read out loud. Sometimes, I made like I was sick or had to go to the bathroom. Anything to avoid having to read in front of my classmates. I blamed the teachers. If they spent more time with me, I could have learned more. But they didn't have the time, and it was embarrassing to be helped by the teacher in front of the other kids. Nobody wanted that.

Then, it got worse. I was placed in a special education class. I didn't want anyone to know I was in that class. I knew eventually they would find out, and my friends would not like me anymore, and think I was stupid. No one would date me. Even the kids in the special education class avoided each other and made a special effort to be seen with their friends in the regular classes.

I know I was supposed to learn more in the special education class and I think I did. But I still didn't learn anything important. We kept learning this easy, boring stuff over and over again. You just sit there and get bored, and angry. (A high school student with a learning disability)

REFLECTIVE

If you were a student with a disability, would you prefer a general or a special education setting?

Studies examining the social, behavioral, and self-concept outcomes for students with disabilities educated in inclusive settings are summarized in Figure 1.6. In general, the social, behavioral, and self-concept outcomes for students with disabilities educated in inclusive settings are better than those of students educated in noninclusive settings (Salend & Garrick Duhaney, 2007). However, these outcomes tend to lag behind those of their classmates without disabilities (Estell et al., 2008), because their friendships are more likely to be with other students with disabilities and less likely to be long lasting (Estell, Jones, Pearl, & Van Acker, 2009).

The personal accounts of students with disabilities about their experiences in general education settings present a mixed picture (Rose, 2008). Some students reported that life in the general education classroom was characterized by fear, frustration, ridicule, and isolation, whereas others saw placement in general education as the defining moment in their lives in terms of friendships, intellectual challenges, self-esteem, and success in their careers. Some students felt that they benefited from receiving special education services; others noted that receiving these services in separate locations placed them at risk for disclosure, stigma, shame, dependence, and lowered expectations (Eisenman & Tascione, 2002; Hehir, 2007; Ferri, Keefe, & Gregg, 2001). Students with mobility related disabilities reported that the barriers they encountered in inclusive settings included difficulties with the physical environment of their schools, isolation and bullying from their classmates, and a lack of understanding from their teachers (Pivik, McComas, & Laflamme, 2002).

Research indicates that inclusion can result in students without disabilities developing positive attitudes toward, meaningful friendships with, and sensitivity to the needs of students with disabilities. Have you observed these benefits in your students?

Impact of Inclusion on Students Without Disabilities

Academic Performance Studies have also examined the impact of inclusion on the academic performance of students without disabilities. In general, these findings suggest that placement in an inclusive classroom does not interfere with, and may enhance, the academic performance of students without disabilities (Salend & Garrick Duhaney, 2007). Researchers also have suggested that the academic performance of students without disabilities may be enhanced by receiving a range of individualized teaching strategies and supports from teachers (Ainscow, 2008; Burstein et al., 2004; Salisbury, Brookfield, & Odom, 2005; Wilson & Michaels, 2006) and by providing peer support to students with moderate or severe disabilities (Copeland et al., 2004).

Elementary Students. Studies on the academic performance of elementary students without disabilities educated in inclusive classrooms reveal that their academic performance tends to be equal to or better than that of general education students educated in noninclusive classrooms (Idol, 2006; Salisbury et al., 2005); these positive academic outcomes were also reported for high-achieving students (Klingner, Vaughn, Hughes, et al., 1998). In addition, although students with disabilities often receive more attention from general education teachers, their peers without disabilities did not experience a significant reduction in the instructional time they received from their teachers and maintained high levels of academic participation (Salisbury et al., 2005).

Salisbury and colleagues (2005) studied the impact of inclusion by examining changes in the classroom environment and teacher behaviors, and reported mixed results. They found that as the percentage of students with disabilities in a class increased, there were increases in instructional time devoted to whole-class instruction and reading as well as in the extent to which teachers showed approval and used nonverbal prompts. They also observed a decrease in the time students spent working independently, and they found no relationship between the presence of students with disabilities and the level of difficulty of the assignments given to students.

Secondary Students. Similar results have been found with respect to the academic impact on secondary students without disabilities. Idol (2006) reports that secondary teachers felt that the academic performance of students without disabilities educated in inclusive settings was either unaffected or enhanced; only 10% of the teachers indicated that the academic performance of their students without disabilities was hindered. Cawley, Hayden, Cade, and Baker-Kroczynski (2002) note that the presence of learners with disabilities did not have a negative effect on the educational performance of their general education peers without disabilities. Wilson and Michaels (2006) and Wallace, Anderson, Bartholomay, and Hupp (2002) found that although students with disabilities received more attention from general education teachers, their classmates without disabilities benefited from individualized assistance and demonstrated high levels of academic engagement.

> Maybe (inclusive education) serves much more the other children rather than the disabled child. I know that it serves both; but in fact the lesson learned by the rest of the school population is so important, and it is this sort of respect for everybody, for all people, no matter what. (A teacher working in an inclusive school, cited in Hunt, Hirose-Hatae, Doering, Karasoff, & Goetz, 2000, p. 315)

Social Performance Research has also addressed the social impact of inclusion programs on students without disabilities. These studies reveal that students without disabilities have predominately positive views of inclusion and can benefit socially in several ways from being educated in inclusive settings (Owen-DeSchryver, Carr, Cale, & Blakely-Smith, 2008; Schwartz, Staub, Peck, & Gallucci, 2006; Siperstein, Parker, Bardon, & Widaman, 2007). For example, Bunch and Valeo (2004) found that elementary and secondary students in inclusive schools had positive views of inclusion, made friends with and advocated for students with disabilities, and felt that students with disabilities were less likely to be ridiculed.

Elementary Students. Idol (2006) and Burstein et al. (2004) note that inclusion programs benefited *all students* by making them more accepting of each other and helping them to be familiar with and adjust to individual differences. Salisbury et al. (2005) found that inclusion did not have a negative impact on the behavior and social competence of students without disabilities. Increased social interactions and friendships between elementary students without disabilities and students with moderate and severe disabilities can develop in inclusive classrooms (Owen-DeSchryver et al., 2008), but you need to make sure that students without disabilities do not assume a caretaking role.

REFLECTIVE

Have you ever been a student in an inclusive classroom? How did that experience impact you?

Secondary Students. Research suggests that the attitudes of secondary students toward individuals with disabilities and inclusion are varied (Krajewski & Hyde, 2000; Siperstein et al., 2007). Some studies report that middle and high school students in inclusive classrooms tend to have positive views of inclusion and believed that it helped them understand individual differences, the needs of others, their ability to deal with disability in their own lives, and their ability to make friends with students with disabilities (Burstein et al., 2004; Cook-Sather, 2003; Copeland et al., 2004). However, although secondary students without disabilities also report that they have made friends with classmates with disabilities, these friendships may decline as students age (Gun Han & Chadsey, 2004).

Siperstein et al. (2007) surveyed middle school students concerning their attitudes toward the inclusion of their classmates with intellectual disabilities and found that they (a) believe that inclusion has positive and negative impacts; (b) feel students with intellectual disabilities can be participate in nonacademic classes rather than academic classes; and (c) have limited interactions with students with intellectual disabilities in school and prefer not to socialize with them after school. Idol (2006) noted that some secondary-level teachers reported that placement in inclusion classrooms resulted in an increase in behavioral problems among their students without disabilities.

Impact of Inclusion on Educators

Because the cooperation of educators is critical to the success of inclusion programs, studies have investigated the attitudes of general and special educators toward inclusive education, their experiences, and their concerns about program implementation. These studies and their findings, which are summarized next, reveal that teachers have complex, varying attitudes and reactions to and experiences with inclusion (Ainscow, 2008; Black-Hawkins et al., 2007; Salend & Garrick Duhaney, 2007).

> **Making Connections**
> Find out more about the experiences of general and special education teachers working collaboratively to implement inclusion in Chapter 4.

Attitudes Toward Inclusion

I'm a fourth-grade "Regular Ed" teacher who was very reluctantly drafted to have a child with severe disabilities in my room. It didn't take me long to be genuinely glad to have Sandy in my class. I can support inclusion. But please tell me who is going to watch out for people like me? Who will make sure administrators give us smaller class loads to compensate? Who will keep the curriculum people off my back when I don't cover the already overwhelming amount the state expects us to cover? After all, to properly achieve inclusion my time will now be more pressed than ever. Who will ensure that I receive the time I need to meet with the rest of the team (special educator, physical therapist, occupational therapist, etc.)? Who will watch over us? (Giangreco, Baumgart, & Doyle, 1995, p. 23)

Educators tend to agree with the principle of placing students with disabilities in general education classrooms, although some controversy still exists (Ainscow, 2008; Elhoweris & Alshiekh, 2006; Silverman, 2007). Although most teachers and administrators support inclusion, some support it only when it requires them to make minimal accommodations and others view included students with disabilities with concern, indifference and rejection (Cook, Cameron, & Tankersley, 2007; Dore, Dion, Wagner, & Brunet 2002).

Educators working effectively in inclusive classrooms tend to have more positive views of inclusion than those who teach in noninclusive settings (Ainscow, 2008; Roll-Pettersson, 2008; Silverman, 2007; Waldron, 2007). In general, elementary teachers appear to favor inclusion more than secondary teachers (Idol, 2006), and special educators appear to have more positive views of inclusion than general educators (Cameron & Cook, 2007; Elhoweris & Alshiekh, 2006). Educators also tend to support inclusion for students who demonstrate the academic and behavioral skills to fit into the general education setting (Praisner, 2003; Roll-Pettersson, 2008). The factors affecting their attitudes include the effectiveness of the program for students with disabilities and their general education classmates, the development of a school community, the availability

REFLECTIVE

Why do you think there are differences in the attitudes of elementary and secondary teachers toward inclusion? Special educators and general educators? Teachers who work in inclusive settings and those who do not? What factors affect your attitude toward inclusion?

FIGURE 1.7 Questions educators have about inclusion

Based on research, the following are some questions that you and other teachers may have about inclusion. As you read this book, you will be able to answer these questions.

- What is inclusion? What are the goals of the inclusion program?
- Is inclusion for all students with disabilities or just for certain ones?
- Do students with disabilities want to be in my class? Do they have the skills to be successful?
- What instructional and ancillary support services will students with disabilities receive? Can these services be used to help other students?
- Will my class size be adjusted?
- Will the education of my students without disabilities suffer?
- What do I tell the students without disabilities about the students with disabilities?
- How do I handle name calling?
- What do I tell families about the inclusion program? What do I do if families complain about the program or don't want their child to be in my class?
- What roles will families play to assist me and their child?
- Do I decide whether I work in an inclusion program?
- Am I expected to teach the general education curriculum to everyone? How can I do that?
- What instructional accomodations, technologies, and classroom management strategies do I need to use?
- How am I supposed to evaluate and grade my students with disabilities?
- What instructional and ancillary support services will I receive?
- How can I address the health, medical, and behavioral needs of students with disabilities?
- What does it mean to work collaboratively with other professionals in my classroom? Will I be able to work collaboratively with others?
- Will I receive enough time to collaborate and communicate with others?
- What type of training and administrative support will I receive to help me implement inclusion successfully?
- Who will monitor the program? How do I know if the inclusion program is working? How will I be evaluated?

of collaborative teaching arrangements and administrative and family support, and the adequacy of the support services and training they receive (DeSimone & Parmar, 2006; Nevin et al., 2008; Rice, Drame, Owens, & Frattura, 2007; Silverman, 2007).

Outcomes for General Educators   Positive outcomes for general educators include increased confidence in their teaching efficacy, more favorable attitudes toward students with disabilities, greater awareness of themselves as positive role models for *all students,* more skill in meeting the needs of *all students*, and acquaintance with new colleagues (Ainscow, 2008; Burstein et al., 2004; Nevin et al., 2008; Rice et al., 2007). Concerns include the insufficient support, training, and time to collaborate with others; the large size of their classes; and the difficulty in meeting the medical needs and behavioral challenges of students with disabilities, and in designing and implementing appropriate instructional accommodations (DeSimone & Parmar, 2006; Harbort et al., 2007; Idol, 2006). In light of these concerns, educators frequently have questions regarding the implementation of inclusion (see Figure 1.7).

Outcomes for Special Educators   Special educators working in inclusion programs report having a greater sense of being an important part of the school community, an enriched view of education, greater knowledge of the general education system, and greater enjoyment of teaching that was related to working with *all students* and observing the successful functioning of their students with disabilities (Burstein et al., 2004; Nevin et al., 2008). For example, Cawley and his colleagues (2002) report that being an integral part of general education program increased the status of special education teachers with respect to students without disabilities; these students viewed the special educators as their teachers and introduced them to their families in that way.

Special educators, especially those at the beginning of their careers, also report experiencing challenges in implementing inclusion (Otis-Wilborn, Winn, Griffin, & Kilgore, 2005; Westling, Herzog, Cooper-Duffy, Prohn, & Ray, 2006). These challenges include increasing their familiarity with the general education curriculum, accessing appropriate curriculum materials, collaborating with general educators, and overcoming negative attitudes toward and low expectations for students with disabilities.

Special educators have expressed concerns related to their fear that inclusion would result in the loss of specialized services to students with disabilities and their jobs (Burstein et al., 2004). Teachers working in cooperative teaching arrangements also report disagreements related to delineating responsibilities for instructing and disciplining students with disabilities, which can result in inequitable responsibilities that limit the instructional roles of special educators in the classroom and limited use of the specialized teaching practices suggested by special educators (Scruggs, Mastropieri, & McDuffie, 2007; Simmons & Magiera, 2007). This lack of parity may particularly occur at the secondary level, where the general educator is trained in the content area and therefore may assume the major responsibilities for teaching (Harbort et al., 2007). Some special education teachers also were worried that their subordinate role in the general education classroom would cause students to view them as a teacher's aide or visitor rather than a teacher.

Impact of Inclusion on Families

Like students and their teachers, family members have different views of and experiences with inclusion (de Vise, 2008; Moreno, Aguilera, & Saldana, 2008). These reactions can affect the important roles that family members perform in the implementation of successful inclusion programs and the establishment of meaningful and reciprocal family–school collaborations (Yssel, Engelbrecht, Oswald, Eloff, & Swart, 2007).

In general, studies suggest that while the attitudes and reactions of families of children with and without disabilities appear to be generally positive, family members also have important concerns that need to be addressed (Yssel et al., 2007). Their varied, multidimensional perspectives seem to be affected by a variety of interacting variables related to the impact of the inclusion program on their children (Leyser & Kirk, 2004; Salend & Garrick Duhaney, 2007).

Families of Children with Disabilities

I wanted my child to have the same experiences as other kids and to learn to live in the real world with its joys and frustrations, and the inclusion program has allowed her to do that. She has learned to be more independent, which will be helpful for preparation for later life. I don't believe that isolating her from other children is better for her or for her classmates. I want my child to learn from other kids and they can learn from her.

My child has done well in the special education class. He receives special attention from a trained teacher who understands his needs, and I don't have to worry about other kids making fun of him. Some students can be included, but many of our students need special attention and individualized instruction, which only special education teachers can provide.

The parents quoted here represent some of the various views of families of children with disabilities. Some families believe that inclusive education has benefited their children, providing them with increased friendships and access to positive role models, a more challenging curriculum, a positive and caring learning environment, higher expectations and academic achievement, and better preparation for the real world, as well as an improved self-concept and better language and motor skills (Burstein et al., 2004; Downing & Peckham-Hardin, 2007; Yssel et al., 2007). Family members note that inclusive placements benefit students without disabilities by helping them be sensitive to individuals with disabilities, and allowing them to experience firsthand how others deal with adversity, and appreciate their own abilities (Downing & Peckham-Hardin, 2007;

REFLECTIVE

Some educators propose that teachers should be allowed to decide whether to work in a setting that includes students with disabilities. Do you think teachers should have this choice? Should they be allowed to choose the students in terms of the academic levels, ethnic, linguistic, and religious backgrounds, socioeconomic status, gender, and sexual orientation they want to teach? If you were given such a choice, what types of students would you include?

REFLECTIVE

Research suggests that families of younger children with disabilities tend to have more positive views of inclusion than families of older children (Leyser & Kirk, 2004). Why do you think this may be the case?

PEARSON
myeducationlab

Go to the Building Teaching Skills and Dispositions section of the Topic *Inclusive Practices* in the MyEducationLab for your course and complete the activity entitled *Creating a Supportive Classroom Climate*. As you work through the learning unit, consider what you've read in this chapter about inclusive practice.

Palmer, Fuller, Aurora, & Nelson, 2001; Yssel et al., 2007). Family members also have concerns about inclusive education, including the loss of individualized special education services, a functional curriculum, instructional accommodations, and community-based instruction delivered by specially trained professionals, as well as the fear that their children will be isolated from classmates and targets of verbal abuse and ridicule, which will lower their self-esteem (de Vise, 2008; Moreno et al., 2008; Pivik et al., 2002).

Families of Children Without Disabilities

I'm all for having a variety of students in the class, but won't these students take time away from the other kids and slow things down? We don't have enough money in the district to implement it. Classes are too big as it is, and the teachers are not trained to teach those students. And the regular students will make fun of the special education students.

While I didn't know much about the inclusion program, when I was notified that my child would be in it, it has had a positive impact on my child. He has grown academically and has become more sensitive others. I am very pleased and hope that he will be in a similar program next year.

What Would You Do in Today's Diverse Classroom?

★ Marcus, a secondary student, experiences some significant challenges in learning. Because he reads at a fifth-grade level, he struggles with many assignments and does poorly on many exams. Marcus is well liked by peers and participates in several after-school activities. His family expects him to go to college, just like his siblings, and wants him to take all general education classes.

★ Melissa uses a laptop to communicate with others and complete her work. Her classmates and teachers recognize that she is academically capable but are put off by her flapping hands, vocal outbursts, and limited eye contact. Melissa's family and her special education teacher believe that she has done well in school because she receives special attention and services from a trained teacher who understands her needs, and they are worried about other students making fun of her. Therefore, they are not sure that the school's inclusion program is the best educational setting for Melissa.

★ Fourth grader Tyler began school as a kindergartener entirely unable to communicate. He spent his first year of school in a special education classroom, but each year after, spent more and more time in an inclusive general education classroom. His father supports Tyler's inclusion in the general education classroom and is thrilled with his progress.

1. What legal, philosophical, historical, and social factors impact the educational placement for these learners?
2. Why do you think these families feel the way they do about inclusion?
3. How do you think inclusion might affect these students? Their families? Their peers? Their teachers?
4. What challenges do these students and their families, peers, and teachers face in making inclusion a successful experience for all?
5. What knowledge, skills, dispositions, resources, and supports do you need to address these feelings and challenges?

myeducationlab Watch the video of Tyler talking about his experiences in an inclusive classroom by visiting the MyEducationLab for this course. Go to the Assignments and Activities section under the topic *Inclusive Practices*, and complete the activity entitled *Benefits of the Inclusion Classroom for Students* to answer questions about how Tyler's experiences with inclusive education have helped him blossom.

Although their attitudes toward inclusion are not as positive as family members of children with disabilities, family members of children without disabilities—like the parents just quoted—also appear to have favorable views of inclusion and important concerns (Salisbury et al., 2005). While some family members initially may have concerns about whether their children would receive less teacher attention and acquire inappropriate behaviors, many report that an inclusive classroom did not prevent their children from receiving a good education, appropriate services, and teacher attention. Family members also note that inclusive programs fostered a greater tolerance of human differences in their children (Schwartz et al., 2006) and benefited children with disabilities by promoting their acceptance, self-esteem, and adjustment to the real world (Burstein et al., 2004).

REFLECTIVE

If your child had a disability, would you prefer a general or special education setting? If your child did not have a disability, which class would you prefer?

SUMMARY

This chapter has presented some of the foundations of inclusion as a philosophy for educating students with disabilities in general education settings. Research indicates that inclusion is a complex undertaking that can have a positive impact on students, their teachers, and their families. However, this impact appears to be related to educators' willingness to accommodate the diverse needs of students and their families. This, in turn, depends on the administrative support, resources, and education that teachers receive to implement effective inclusion programs. Given these findings and the continued commitment to educating students with disabilities in general education classrooms, this book is intended to provide you with the knowledge, skills, and dispositions to develop and implement effective inclusion programs and create learning environments that promote the academic and behavioral/social performance of *all students*. Toward these ends, it offers strategies to aid you in providing *all of your students* with access to the general education curriculum; to promote the sensitivity to and acceptance of your students' individual challenges and differences; to help you work collaboratively with your colleagues, families, students, and community agencies; and to assist you in reflecting on and differentiating your teaching and curriculum to so that *all students* benefit academically, behaviorally, and socially.

As you review the chapter, consider the following topics, and remember the following points.

What Is Special Education?
CEC 1; PRAXIS 1

Special education involves delivering and monitoring a specially designed and coordinated set of comprehensive, research-based instructional and assessment practices and related services. These instructional practices and services are tailored to identify and address the individual strengths and challenges of students; to enhance their educational, social, behavioral, and physical development; and to foster equity and access to all aspects of society.

What Is Inclusion?
CEC 1, 9; PRAXIS 1, 3; INTASC 3, 5, 9

Inclusion is a philosophy that brings students, families, educators, and community members together to create schools based on acceptance, belonging, and community. Inclusionary schools welcome, acknowledge, affirm, and celebrate the value of all learners by educating them together in high-quality, age-appropriate general education classrooms in their neighborhood schools. Whereas mainstreaming can be viewed as either part-time or full-time placement based on a student's readiness for placement in the general education setting, inclusion is thought of as full-time placement in the general education setting based on the belief that all students have the right to be educated in general education classrooms.

What Is the Least Restrictive Environment?
CEC 1, 9; PRAXIS 1, 2, 3; INTASC 3, 9, 10

The LRE requires that students with disabilities be educated as much as possible with their peers without disabilities. The LRE tells us to look at and consider the general education setting as the first option, not the last, and to move to a more restrictive setting cautiously and only as needed.

What Factors Contributed to the Movement to Educate Students in Inclusive Classrooms?
CEC 1, 2, 3, 9; PRAXIS 2, 3; INTASC 3, 9, 10

Contributing factors include normalization, early intervention and early childhood programs, technological advances, the principles of universal design, the civil rights movement and its resulting litigation, advocacy groups, the segregated nature of special schools and classes, disproportionate representation, and the provisions of the No Child Left Behind Act, and the laws that affect special education.

What Are the Laws That Affect Special Education?
CEC 1, 9; PRAXIS 2; INTASC 2, 9, 10

In addition to the No Child Left Behind Act, several laws have had a significant impact on students with disabilities, including PL 94-142, the Education for All Handicapped Children Act; PL 99-457, the Education for All Handicapped Children Act Amendments of 1986; PL 101-476, the Individuals with Disabilities Education Act; PL 105-17, the IDEA Amendments of 1997; PL 108-446, the Individuals with Disabilities Education Improvement Act of 2004; PL 93-112, the Rehabilitation Act and Section 504; and PL 101-336, the Americans with Disabilities Act. These laws contain a variety of provisions that promote the inclusion of individuals with disabilities in schools and all aspects of society.

What Is the Impact of Inclusion on Students, Educators and Families?
CEC 1, 9, 10; PRAXIS 1, 3; INTASC 3, 9, 10

Research on the impact of inclusion is inconclusive and offers a variety of perspectives. Some studies suggest that inclusion results in positive academic and social outcomes for students with disabilities; other studies indicate that some students with disabilities do not receive the instructional accommodations they need to benefit from inclusion. Studies suggest that students without disabilities are not harmed academically by an inclusive education and that they benefit socially.

General and special educators have mixed reactions to inclusion. Their attitudes are related to their efficacy in implementing inclusion, which in turn depends on the administrative support, resources, time, and training they receive to implement effective inclusion programs. The attitudes and reactions of families of children with and without disabilities to inclusion are complex and multidimensional, affected by many interacting variables.

MARTY

Ms. Tupper was concerned about Marty's inconsistent performance in school. He knew a lot about many topics and liked to share his knowledge with others. He picked things up quickly when he heard them explained or watched them demonstrated. He loved it when the class did science activities and experiments. However, Marty's performance in reading and math was poor. Despite having highly developed verbal skills, he also had difficulties with writing assignments.

Ms. Tupper noticed that Marty had trouble starting and completing his assignments. Sometimes he began a task before receiving all the directions; at other times, he ignored the directions and played with objects in the room or at his desk. He frequently worked on an assignment for only a short period of time and then switched to another assignment. When he completed assignments, his work was usually of high quality. Marty's parents were concerned.

They thought he was smart but lazy and capable of doing much better work, and they indicated that they were considering putting Marty on medication to help him focus and pay attention.

Marty also worried about his difficulties in school. He wondered why he was not like others. He thought he was "not smart" and that reading, writing, and math would always be hard. Sometimes, out of frustration, he acted like the class clown. At other times, he was quiet and withdrawn to avoid drawing attention to his difficulties. Marty loved to talk and joke with others. He was fun to be with, but sometimes he got carried away, which bothered some of his friends. Marty was the best student in the class at fixing things. When other students needed assistance with mechanical things, they came to Marty. He enjoyed taking things apart and putting them back together. In his neighborhood, he was famous for fixing bicycles.

Understanding the Diverse Educational Strengths and Challenges of Students with Disabilities

Ms. Tupper liked Marty and felt frustrated by her inability to help him learn. She decided that she needed assistance to help Marty succeed and contacted the school's Student Study Team. The team met with Ms. Tupper and Marty's family to discuss Marty, including his strengths, challenges, interests, and hobbies, as well as effective instructional techniques to use. They also gathered information by observing Marty in several school settings and talking with him. The team then met with Ms. Tupper and Marty's parents to plan some interventions to address Marty's challenges. They talked about and agreed to try several environmental and curricular accommodations. To improve Marty's on-task behavior and the communication between Ms. Tupper and Marty's parents, a daily report card system was used. Ms. Tupper also moved Marty's seat closer to the front of the room to improve her monitoring of his ability to pay attention and understand directions. Members of the Student Study Team worked with Ms. Tupper to implement and evaluate the effectiveness of these interventions.

In addition, Ms. Tupper implemented a Response-to-Intervention process to monitor Marty's progress in reading and writing. First, Ms. Tupper tried several interventions, which she found were effective with many of her students. Since these strategies did not improve Marty's reading and writing, Ms. Tupper collaborated with a special educator and a literacy educator to plan and deliver more intensive, individualized, and supplementary instruction to Marty. As part of this process, Ms. Tupper and her colleagues regularly collected data on Marty's reading and writing. Although the interventions improved Marty's ability to complete his work, Marty failed to make significant progress in reading and writing.

As a result, the Student Study Team referred Marty to the school district's Comprehensive Planning Team to determine whether he would benefit from special education and related services. With the consent of Marty's family, the Comprehensive Planning Team conducted a comprehensive assessment of Marty's performance in a variety of areas. The school psychologist gave him an intelligence test and concluded that Marty had above-average intelligence and strong verbal skills. The special education teacher assessed Marty's skills in reading, writing, and math and identified his strengths and challenges in these areas. Tests of fine motor and gross motor abilities as part of a physical exam conducted by the school physician also revealed Marty's strengths in these areas. An interview with Marty and the observations of his family also led the team to believe that Marty's learning difficulties were lowering his self-esteem.

After all the data were collected, the team met to determine Marty's eligibility for special education. They reviewed the data and listened to the views of the various team members. Some members thought Marty had a learning disability. Others thought he had an attention deficit disorder and should be served under Section 504. Several members also believed that Marty needed a program for gifted and talented students. After some discussion and debate, the team concluded that Marty's inability to perform academic tasks at a level in line with his potential showed that he had a learning disability. The team also decided that Marty should remain in Ms. Tupper's class and that an IEP to meet his needs there should be developed. They also agreed to recommend Marty for inclusion in the district's gifted and talented program.

What factors should educators consider in designing an appropriate educational program for Marty? Does Marty qualify for special education services? After reading this chapter, you should have the knowledge, skills, and dispositions to answer these as well as the following questions.

- How does the special education process work?
- How can IEPs be implemented in general education settings?
- What are the educational strengths and challenges of students with high-incidence disabilities?
- What are the educational strengths and challenges of students with low-incidence disabilities?
- What are the educational strengths and challenges of students who are gifted and talented?

SPECIAL EDUCATION PROCESS

HOW DOES THE SPECIAL EDUCATION PROCESS WORK? A **comprehensive planning team** composed of professionals and family members, with the student when appropriate, makes important decisions concerning the education of students like Marty. The special education identification process that the comprehensive team follows for students who are experiencing difficulties in school is outlined in Figure 2.1. As we saw in the chapter-opening vignette, prereferral and RTI systems were implemented by Ms. Tupper and her colleagues to address Marty's challenges in her class. Once they determined that Marty needed additional services, the team assessed his eligibility for special education via the IDEA or Section 504.

For students like Marty who are found to be eligible for special education under the IDEA, the team develops an IEP based on his strengths and challenges, current assessment data, and the concerns of Marty's family. Although Marty's family actively participated in the decision-making process and agreed with the team's recommendations, when disagreements between families and schools arise, **mediation** services

FIGURE 2.1 Special education process

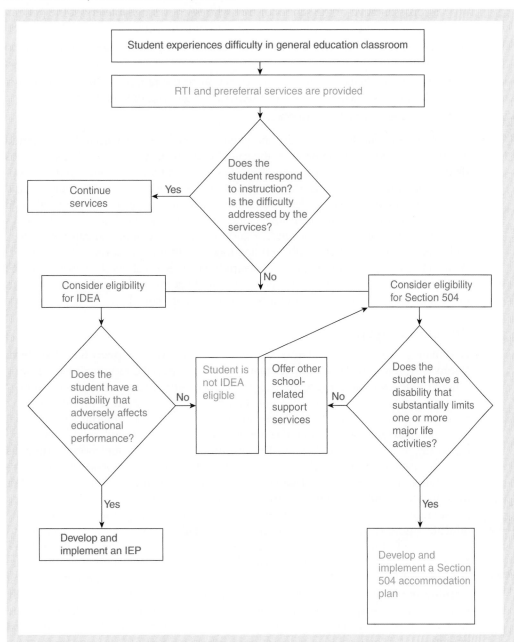

are offered to resolve differences. If an agreement still cannot be reached after mediation, a due process hearing conducted by an **impartial hearing officer** is scheduled (Hulett, 2009; Murdick et al., 2007). Mueller (2009) offers guidelines that you and your colleagues can use to try to resolve IEP-related conflicts between families and schools so that expensive and potentially divisive due process hearings are avoided.

Members of the Comprehensive Planning Team

As the student's teacher, you are an important member of the team. The other members of the team are

- the family members of the child,
- at least one general education teacher (if the student is participating in the general education classroom),

REFLECTIVE

In Chapter 1, we learned about the differences between the IDEA and Section 504. How are they different?

Making Connections
Find out more about the diverse perspectives, experiences, and roles of the members of the comprehensive planning team and the ways in which the team functions to make decisions collaboratively in Chapter 4.

Making Connections
Find out more about the strengths and challenges of students from culturally and linguistically diverse backgrounds in Chapter 3.

- at least one special education teacher/provider,
- a representative of the school district who is knowledgeable about the general education curriculum and the availability of resources,
- an individual who can determine the instructional implications of the evaluation results,
- other individuals selected at the discretion of the family or the school district who have knowledge or special expertise regarding the child, and
- the student, when appropriate.

When students from culturally and linguistically diverse backgrounds are referred to the comprehensive planning team, the team frequently faces many challenges such as differentiating linguistic and cultural differences from learning difficulties, and developing an appropriate educational program that addresses students' linguistic, cultural, and experiential backgrounds (Fielder et al., 2008). Therefore, it is recommended, although not mandated, that the planning team include individuals who are fluent in the student's native language, understand the student and the family's culture, and can help collect and interpret the data in culturally and linguistically appropriate ways (García & Ortiz, 2006). The inclusion of these individuals helps the team learn about the family's and the student's cultural perspective and experiential and linguistic background, and assists in the determination of the origins of the student's learning difficulties.

Prereferral System

Like many school districts, Marty's school district employed a **prereferral system**. Because the term *prereferral* implies that a referral to special education is likely, many school districts refer to these teams as a *teacher assistance team, instructional support team,* or *child or student study team*. Prereferral is a preventive problem-solving process assisting classroom teachers like Ms. Tupper before referral for a special education placement is considered (Bahr & Kovaleski, 2006). Prereferral strategies are especially important in addressing the disproportionate representation of students from diverse backgrounds (García & Ortiz, 2006; Gravois & Rosenfeld, 2006).

Once a request for assistance is received, the team helps teachers gather information about students and the difficulties they are experiencing. Goals to assist students and teachers are then generated, and interventions to successfully educate students like Marty in the general education classroom are selected and implemented. Interventions are determined based on the individual student's strengths and challenges; educational, social, and medical history; and language and cultural background, as well as the teacher's concerns and the nature of the learning environment. The team works collaboratively with teachers and family members to develop a plan that includes a range of methods for addressing the student's strengths and challenges (a sample prereferral planning form is presented in Figure 2.2). The implementation and the effectiveness of these interventions are then assessed for a sufficient period of time. If the interventions are successful, they are continued or gradually faded out as students succeed in their classrooms. If the interventions are not successful, the team considers other interventions and whether students should be formally evaluated for placement in special education.

Eligibility Determination

Response-to-Intervention   In addition to using prereferral systems, schools are implementing a **Response-to-Intervention (RTI)** model prior to considering whether students are eligible for special education. An alternative or supplement to the special education identification process allowed under the IDEA of 2004, RTI is a multitiered identification and instructional model for assessing the extent to which your students respond to and need more intensive and individualized research-based interventions to succeed in your inclusive classroom (Fuchs & Fuchs, 2007; Kavale & Spaulding, 2008). (See Figure 2.3 for the steps in the RTI process. Note that many

PEARSON
myeducationlab

To enhance your understanding of the prereferral system, go to the IRIS Center Resources section of Topic: Prereferrals, Placement, and IEP Process in the MyEducationLab for your course, and complete the module entitled, *The Prereferral Process: Procedures for Supporting Students with Academic and Behavioral Concerns.*

Making Connections
This discussion of RTI builds on what we covered earlier on this topic, in Chapter 1.

FIGURE 2.2 **Sample prereferral planning form**

Student:_____ Age:_____ Grade:_____

Teacher:_____ Subjects Taught:_____

Difficulties and Concerns: *What are the difficulties and concerns associated with the student? What factors appear to be contributing to the difficulties and concerns?*

Prior Interventions: *What intervention strategies have been tried? How successful have these interventions been?*

Student Characteristics: *What are the student's strengths and challenges? What other student characteristics do we need to consider in understanding the difficulties and concerns and planning the intervention(s)?*

Home, Language, Cultural, and Other Considerations: *What experiential, language, cultural, and other factors should we consider in understanding the difficulties and concerns and designing interventions?*

Goal(s): *What outcomes do we want for the student? The teacher(s)? Families? Others (please specify)?*

Instructional Interventions	**Intervention Plan**	**Behavioral/Social Interventions**
	What intervention(s) will we implement?	
	Who will be responsible for implementing the intervention(s)?	
	Where, when, and how will we implement the intervention(s)?`	
	What resources, materials, technology, staff and education do we need to implement the intervention(s)?	

Family and Community-Based Interventions	**Other Interventions** (e.g., peer-based, nonacademic activities)

Assessing the Intervention(s) Effectiveness	**Follow-up Activities**
How will we know if the interventions are working? *How will we collect data regarding the success of the interventions?* *Who is responsible for gathering the data?* *How frequently will we gather and analyze the data?*	*When will we meet again?* *What will we discuss at our next meeting?* *What roles and responsibilities will individuals assume to report to us at our next meeting?*

Additional Comments:

Source: Ormsbee (2001).

FIGURE 2.3 Sample response-to-intervention process

Tier 1: Primary Prevention: Universal Screening by General Education

Goal: To keep learning difficulties from developing

- Deliver a high-quality general education curriculum to all students.
- Assess all students.
- Identify students not performing at a specific level on norm-referenced tests, or not meeting benchmarks via state assessments/achievement tests or district/teacher identification via curriculum-based measurement.

Tier 2: Secondary Prevention: Implement More Intensive General Education Classroom Instruction

Goal: To provide early identification and correction of learning difficulties

- Deliver research-based instructional practices in small groups within the general education setting to students having difficulty (Tier 1–based instructional practices are also provided).
- Regularly assess student progress (e.g., tests, curriculum-based assessments).
- Identify students not progressing.

Tier 3: Tertiary Prevention: Implement More Intensive Effective Supplementary Instruction

Goal: To offer aggressive treatment to limit the negative consequences of learning difficulties

- Deliver more intensive research-based supplementary instruction (e.g., special education, literacy, bilingual education, ESL, and speech/language professionals) (Tier 1– and 2–based instructional practices are also provided).
- Ensure that instruction is collaboratively planned and delivered by general, special, bilingual, ESL, speech and language and literacy educators.
- Implement Tier 3–based instruction in smaller groups.
- Assess student progress and identify students not progressing.

Tier 3 interventions

- focus on individualized goals, which may or may not be on grade level;
- entail more frequent sessions and smaller group sizes; and
- are individualized based on each student's progress monitoring data.

Tier 4: Assessment to Determine Eligibility for Special Education

Goal: To determine if special education services are needed

- Students not progressing receive individualized evaluation by the comprehensive planning team.
- Follow legal guidelines and due process procedures. (For English language learners, rule out lack of instruction and limited English proficiency.)
- Consider data collected during the RTI process.
- Continue effective interventions.
- Individualize instruction via IEP.

Sources: Berkeley et al. (2009); Council for Exceptional Children (2007); Fuchs and Fuchs (2007); Stecker (2007).

states and school districts use a three-tier model that combines elements of tiers 3 and 4.) The RTI process attempts to minimize the number of students receiving special education by ruling out poor instruction or lack of instruction as reasons for poor academic performance. The RTI model incorporates the following components:

- *Universal screening:* All students are initially assessed.
- *Identification of students:* Students having difficulty are identified to determine those needing more intensive instruction.
- *Tiered instruction:* A series of more intensive, high-quality classroom, group, and individualized instruction and interventions are delivered to identified students. While the number of tiers varies, there are usually three or four tiers that

differ in terms of the interventions, size of student groups, length of instructional sessions, frequency of progress monitoring, and the types of educators involved (e.g., special, literacy, bilingual, ESL, speech/language, etc.).

- *Fidelity of effective interventions:* Research-based instruction and interventions are delivered as intended.
- *Collaboration:* Educators work together and share expertise.
- *Progress monitoring:* Measure students' response to interventions. **Progress monitoring** refers to your conducting ongoing assessments to determine your students' learning progress and the effectiveness of your instructional program (Stecker, 2007; Yell, Busch, & Rogers, 2007). Thus, assessment data are continuously collected over time and promptly analyzed to identify students who are progressing and ready for new instruction as well as those students who have not yet demonstrated mastery and need additional or revised instruction.
- *Consideration for special education:* Students who do not respond to the series of effective interventions may be considered for identification as a student with a disability (Berkeley, Bender, Peaster, & Saunders, 2009; CEC, 2007; Fuchs & Fuchs, 2007). Although the RTI model has been initially used primarily at the elementary level and focused on literacy skills, models to implement it at the secondary level and across the curriculum, including behavior, have been developed (Fuchs, Fuchs, & Hollebeck, 2007; Johnson & Smith, 2008; Lechtenberger, Mullins, & Greenwood, 2008).

When using RTI with your students from culturally and linguistically diverse backgrounds, it is important for you to tailor it to their individual strengths, challenges, and experiences. This means that the interventions, assessments, and points of reference for judging their responses you use should be culturally responsive, consider their experiential, educational, cultural, and linguistic backgrounds, address home and community factors, and be consistent with research-based practices for working with these students (see Esparza Brown & Doolittle [2008], García & Ortiz [2008], Rinaldi & Samson [2008], and Klingner & Edwards [2006] for guidelines for using a cultural, linguistic, and ecological RTI process).

When the RTI or prereferral processes are not effective, as in the case of Marty, the planning team, with the consent of the student's family, determines whether a student is eligible for special education. To determine eligibility for special education services under the IDEA, the team uses standardized and informal assessment procedures including interviews and observations to determine whether the student has a disability that adversely affects educational performance. If the student is not IDEA eligible, the team may consider the student for special education services under Section 504. As we saw in Chapter 1, if a student is eligible for 504, an accommodation plan must be developed.

Cautions About Labeling Students

State and federal funding formulas require the use of labeling of students in order for them to receive special education services. However, you need to be aware of the problems associated with labeling students. Labels tend to locate problems within students rather than within the educational system. These labels can also limit the way you and others interact with students, thereby disabling these students academically and socially and hindering the development of their self-esteem. Therefore, it is important for you to recognize that no two students are alike and that each educational program must be based on individual strengths and challenges rather than on a label.

Individualized Education Program

If the comprehensive planning team determines that a student's needs require special education services, an **Individualized Education Program (IEP)** is developed for the student. The IEP is a written, individualized education plan listing the special

Making Connections
Find out more about assessment strategies for monitoring the learning progress of your students in Chapter 12.

Making Connections
Find out more how RTI is being extended to provide a continuum of tiered schoolwide positive behavioral interventions and supports in Chapter 7.

PEARSON
myeducationlab

To enhance your understanding of the Response-to-Intervention model applied to reading, go to the IRIS Center Resources section of Topic: Learning Disabilities in the MyEducationLab for your course, and complete the modules entitled *RTI (Part 1): An Overview, RTI (Part 2): Assessment, RTI (Part 3): Reading Instruction, RTI (Part 4): Putting It All Together,* and *RTI (Part 5): A Closer Look at Tier 1.*

PEARSON
myeducationlab

To hear an expert discuss RTI and cultural considerations, go to the IRIS Center Resource section of Topic: Learning Disabilities in the MyEducationLab for your course, and listen to the podcast entitled "Episode 5: Leonard Baca on RTI and Cultural Considerations."

A GUIDE TO ACTION

Implementing Prereferral and RTI Systems

Prereferral and RTI systems are important aspects of creating inclusive schools and have reduced the number of students inappropriately placed in special education. To ensure successful prereferral and RTI systems in your school, you and your colleagues can consider the following questions:

- Are administrators, educators, and family members committed to implementing and promoting the prereferral and RTI systems?
- Are criteria and procedures for the selection of educators to be members of the prereferral and RTI teams appropriate?
- Do the prereferral and RTI teams include educators who have a range of backgrounds, experiences, expertise, and education and who perform a variety of functions?
- Are family members and community agencies involved in the prereferral and RTI processes?
- Do the prereferral and RTI teams have the resources, professional development, and time to perform their activities?
- Is there a system to help teachers, students, and families access and use the services of the prereferral and RTI processes?
- Do the policies, practices, forms, procedures and technologies employed in the prereferral and RTI systems facilitate the process?
- Do prereferral and RTI teams have adequate and flexible procedures for determining the goals, types of interventions, tiers, services, assessments, and decision-making criteria based on students' strengths; challenges; educational, social, and medical history; and experiential, language, and cultural background, as well as the teacher's concerns and the learning environment?
- Do the prereferral and RTI teams consider a range of reasonable, effective instructional and family involvement strategies, curricular and classroom design accommodations, assessment procedures, culturally relevant instructional and classroom management techniques, instructional and assistive technologies, professional development and collaboration activities, and school- and community-based supportive services to address students' learning, behavior, and socialization?
- Are interventions that are part of the prereferral and RTI systems implemented as intended and for a sufficient period of time?
- Are valid data collected and analyzed on an ongoing basis to monitor the progress of students and to examine the effectiveness of the interventions?
- Are data collected and analyzed on an ongoing basis to evaluate the effectiveness of the prereferral and RTI processes and to make revisions based on these data?

How would you rate your school's prereferral and RTI systems? ( ) Excellent ( ) Good ( ) Needs Improvement ( ) Needs Much Improvement

With your colleagues, create a plan of action for improving your school's prereferral and RTI systems that includes your goals, the actions you will take, and the resources you will need to achieve them, and the ways you will evaluate your success.

education and related services students with disabilities will receive to address their unique academic, social, behavioral, communication, functional, and physical strengths and challenges. It contains several components that seek to provide students with disabilities with greater access to the general education curriculum, which are outlined next. Gibb and Taylor Dyches (2007) also offer guidelines that you and your colleagues can use to develop IEPs for your students with disabilities. (Later in this chapter, you will learn about specific disabilities and the educational strengths and challenges of students with these disabilities.)

IEP Components The IEP developed by the team must include the following components:

- A statement of the student's present levels of performance (PLP) in terms of academic, socialization, behavioral, communication, and functional skills. This statement should address how the disability affects the student's involvement and progress in the general education curriculum. For preschoolers, the statement should discuss how the disability impacts participation in appropriate activities. In developing the IEP, the team also should assess the strengths of the student and address the student's family's concerns for enhancing their child's education.

- A list of measurable annual goals, including academic and functional goals, relating to students' progress in the general education curriculum, as well as other educational needs. However, IEPs for students with disabilities who take alternate assessments rather than participating in state and federal testing programs also must include benchmarks and short-term objectives. Capizzi (2008) offers recommendations and resources that can assist the IEP team in writing measurable annual goals and short-term objectives, and Lynch and Adams (2008) provide strategies for developing standards-based IEP objectives for students with significant cognitive disabilities.

- A statement of the special education and related services, as well as supplementary aids and services and other supports, to help the student reach the annual goals, be involved and progress in the general education curriculum, and participate in extracurricular and nonacademic activities with other students (Yell et al., 2008). Where possible, it is suggested that these services, aids, and supports be based on peer-reviewed research findings. These services and aids include transportation, speech and language therapy, psychological services, counseling, school health and social work services, physical and occupational training, interpreters, hearing and vision services, therapeutic recreation, and family education as well as others that help students benefit from a special education program. Another service and aid that the IEP team may consider is the need for a paraeducator including selection, qualifications, job functions, education, and supervision of the paraeducator. This statement also should address the program modifications and support for school personnel, such as general educators receiving consultation and collaboration services or professional development related to specific issues.

Making Connections
Find out more about working collaboratively with paraeducators in Chapters 4 and 8.

- An explanation of the extent, if any, to which the student will *not* participate in the general education classroom and in other activities with students without disabilities.

- A statement of any testing accommodations that the student will need to participate in state, districtwide, and classroom-based assessments (Salend, 2009). Keep in mind that testing accommodations related to high-stakes testing should be consistent with statewide and districtwide policies on approved testing accommodations and should be provided under certain testing situations. Therefore, it is important for the IEP to differentiate between testing accommodations that are used during the administration of classroom-based, districtwide, and state assessments and to make this distinction explicit when identifying testing accommodations on students' IEPs and 504 accommodation plans. You can obtain information about your state's testing accommodations policies by contacting your State Education Department or visiting its Web site.

- If the IEP team determines that a student will not participate in a particular assessment, the IEP must include an explanation of why the test is not appropriate and why the alternate assessment is appropriate for the student. The IEP also should address the alternative methods that will be used to assess the student's learning and progress. Alternate assessments based on modified learning standards addressing challenging but less difficult grade-level content from the general education curriculum can be used for your students with disabilities who
  - do not have a significant cognitive disability;
  - have access to grade-level content instruction;
  - have IEPs that include goals addressing grade-level content standards;
  - are not likely to reach grade-level proficiency in the same time frame as their classmates without disabilities.

For example, these students might take less rigorous grade-level content tests that have multiple-choice items with fewer choices or reading tests that ask them to read fewer passages.

Understanding the Diverse Educational Strengths and Challenges   51

Making Connections

Find out more about testing accommodations and alternative assessment techniques in Chapter 12.

PEARSON
myeducationlab

Go to the Assignments and Activities section of the Topic *Prereferrals, Placement and IEP Process* in the MyEducationLab for your course and complete the activity entitled *Understanding the IEP Document*. As you watch the video and answer the accompanying questions, consider the special considerations in developing IEPs.

Making Connections

Find out more about positive behavioral supports, functional behavioral assessment, and individualized behavior plans in Chapter 7.

REFLECTIVE

In *Schaffer v. Weast*, the Supreme Court ruled that when families and school districts disagree regarding a student's IEP, the burden of proof lies with the party challenging the IEP to prove that it is ineffective (Yell, Katsiyannis, Ryan, & McDuffie, 2009). How do you think this decision will affect the IEP process? Families? School districts?

Your students with more severe cognitive disabilities who are not able to participate in testing may take modified assessments that relate to *alternate achievement standards* that are not as complex as the state's grade-level achievement standards (Towles-Reeves, Kleinert, & Muhomba, 2009). In most states, these collections of student work are linked to statewide standards and evaluated via performance-based assessment, portfolios, or checklist or an instructional rubric.

- A description of how the student's progress toward the annual goals in the IEP will be measured and how and when progress in meeting annual goals will be assessed and shared with the student's family (Hessler & Konrad, 2008; Yell et al., 2007). These descriptions of student progress may be provided via quarterly or periodic communications with families, such as report cards.
- A projected date for the initiation of services and accommodations, as well as their anticipated frequency, location, and duration.

A sample IEP for Marty, the student we met at the beginning of this chapter, is presented in Figure 2.4.

Computer programs are available that can assist teams in and save time when developing IEPs and updating records (Serfass & Peterson, 2007). These software programs can help IEP teams link IEPs to statewide learning standards and ensure compliance with legal guidelines by prompting teams to complete all aspects of students' IEPs. For instance, these programs can remind teams that a student is turning a certain age and that the team must now update the student's IEP to address transitional services. When using these programs, you and your colleagues need to be careful not to develop "canned" or "boilerplate" IEPs that fail to address the individualized and diverse strengths and challenges of your students. Therefore, when selecting and using these programs, it is important to choose ones that are secure, easy to use, contain the features you and your colleagues need, interface with other districtwide programs, protect confidentiality, and allow teams to personalize all aspects of the IEP (Serfass & Peterson, 2007).

Special Considerations in Developing IEPs   In addition to the components of the IEP just outlined, the IEP team also can consider several special factors related to the unique challenges of students.

- For a student whose behavior interferes with his or her learning or that of others, the IEP team should consider behavioral strategies, including positive behavior interventions, strategies, and supports. To address behaviors that interfere with learning and socialization, some teams perform a functional behavioral assessment and develop an individualized behavioral plan.
- For a student who is developing English proficiency, the IEP team should consider the student's language needs as they relate to the IEP.
- For a student who is blind or visually impaired, the IEP should provide for instruction in Braille and the use of Braille unless the IEP team determines otherwise.
- For a deaf or hard of hearing student, the IEP team should consider the language and communication needs of the student, the student's academic level, the full range of needs (including the student's social, emotional, and cultural needs), and the student's opportunities for direct communication with peers and professionals in his or her language and communication mode.

Assistive Technology   The IEP team also should determine whether the student needs assistive technology devices and services and include a written statement regarding the selection of the appropriate technology on the student's IEP (Bausch & Ault, 2008; Dell et al., 2008). These determinations are made based on an **individualized technology assessment**, which usually includes the following:

- Student-related information including an identification of the student's strengths; challenges; preferences; age; gender; cultural perspectives; linguistic

FIGURE 2.4 Sample IEP

Unified School District
Individualized Education Program

Student: Marty Glick

School: Hudson Elementary

Placement: General Education Classroom

Date of IEP Meeting: 12/17/2011

Date of Initiation of Services: 1/3/2012

Dominant Language of Student: English

DOB: 8/5/2001

Grade: 5

Disability Classification: Learning Disability

Notification to Family: 11/3/2011

Review date: 1/3/2013

Medical Alerts: Takes medications

CURRENT LEVEL OF PERFORMANCE IN THE GENERAL EDUCATION CURRICULUM
ACADEMIC/EDUCATIONAL ACHIEVEMENT

Mathematics

Marty's strongest areas include geometry, measurement, time, and money. He has difficulty with multiplication, division, fractions, and word problems. He especially had difficulty solving problems that contained nonessential information.

Reading

Marty's reading is characterized by weaknesses in word recognition, oral reading, and comprehension. Marty had difficulty with the passages that were written at a third-grade level. His oral reading of the passages revealed difficulties sounding out words and a reliance on contextual cues. He had particular problems with comprehension questions related to large amounts of information and interpreting abstractions.

Written Language

Marty's writing portfolio reveals that he has many ideas to write about in a broad range of genres. However, Marty avoids using prewriting tools such as semantic webs or outlines to organize his thoughts. Consequently, his stories don't usually follow a chronological sequence, and his reports do not fully develop the topic. He uses a variety of sentence patterns but frequently ignores the need for punctuation. Marty has difficulty editing his own work but will make mechanical changes pointed out by the teacher. He rarely revises the content or organization of his writing in a substantial manner. Marty's teacher has observed that Marty enjoys working on the computer and performs better on writing tasks when he uses a talking word processor.

SOCIAL DEVELOPMENT

Level of Social Development

Marty shows attention difficulties when attempting some academic tasks. He has a good sense of humor and seems to relate fairly well to his peers.

Interest Inventory

Marty likes working with peers and using computers. He prefers projects to tests. He likes working with his hands and fixing things.

PHYSICAL DEVELOPMENT

Marty is physically healthy and has no difficulties with his hearing and vision. He has had no major illnesses or surgeries, and his parents recently made the decision to place him on medications.

BEHAVIORAL DEVELOPMENT

A functional assessment of Marty's classroom behavior indicates that Marty is frequently off-task and has difficulty completing his assignments. He often works on assignments for a short period of time and then works on another assignment, engages in an off-task activity such as playing with objects, leaves his work area, or seeks attention from his teacher or his peers. His behavior also appears to be affected by other activities in the classroom, the placement of his work area near certain students, and the type and difficulty of the activity.

(Continued)

FIGURE 2.4 **Continued**

RELATED SERVICES

Service	*Frequency*	*Location*
Group counseling	Once/week	Social worker's office

SUPPLEMENTARY AIDS AND SERVICES

Service	*Frequency*	*Location*
Collaboration teacher	2 hours/day	General education classroom
Paraeducator	3 hours/day	General education classroom

PROGRAM MODIFICATION AND SUPPORT FOR SCHOOL PERSONNEL

Marty and his teacher will receive the services of a collaborative teacher and a paraeducator. Marty's teacher will be given time to meet with the collaboration teacher, who also will modify materials, locate resources, administer assessments, and coteach lessons. Marty's teacher also will receive professional development related to differentiated instruction, classroom management, and assessment alternatives and accommodations.

EXTENT OF PARTICIPATION IN GENERAL EDUCATION PROGRAMS AND WITH PEERS WITHOUT DISABILITIES

Marty will remain in his fifth-grade classroom full-time. The collaboration teacher and the paraeducator will provide direct service to Marty in the general education classroom.

RATIONALE FOR PLACEMENT

It is anticipated that Marty's educational needs can best be met in the general education classroom. He will benefit from being exposed to the general education curriculum with the additional assistance of the collaboration teacher and the paraeducator. The use of testing accommodations and computers with talking word processors also should help Marty benefit from his general education program. Marty's social skills and self-concept also will be improved by exposure to his general education peers. Counseling will provide him with the prosocial skills necessary to interact with his peers and complete his work.

INSTRUCTIONAL PROGRAM

Annual Goal: Marty will read, write, listen, and speak for information and understanding. (State Learning Standard 1 for English Language Arts)

Evaluation Procedures

1. Given the choice of a narrative trade book at his instructional level, Marty will be able to retell the story, including major characters, the setting, and major events of the plot sequence.

   Teacher-made story grammar checklist

2. Given a passage from his social studies or science textbook, Marty will develop three questions that require inferential or critical thinking.

   Teacher evaluation of student response

3. Using a prewriting structure to organize his ideas, Marty will write a paragraph describing a process that shows logical development and has a minimum of five sentences.

   Writing rubric

Annual Goal: Marty will read, write, listen, and speak for literary response and expression. (State Learning Standard 2 for English Language Arts)

Evaluation Procedures

1. After choosing a favorite poem to read to his peers, Marty will memorize it and recite it with fluency and intonation.

   Peer and teacher feedback

2. Given the choice of texts with multisyllabic words, Marty will read with 90% accuracy.

   Teacher analysis of running record

3. Given a choice of biographies, Marty will reflect upon the events and experiences which relate to his own life.

   Teacher evaluation of dialogue journal

FIGURE 2.4 **Continued**

Annual Goal: Marty will understand mathematics and become mathematically confident by communicating and reasoning mathematically. (State Learning Standard 3 for Mathematics, Science, and Technology)

Evaluation Procedures

1. Given a one-step word problem with a distractor, Marty will write the relevant information and operation needed to solve it 90% of the time.

   Teacher-made test

2. Given the task of writing five one-step word problems with a distractor, Marty will write four that are clear enough for his classmates to solve.

   Teacher evaluation of student response

Annual Goal: Marty will demonstrate mastery of the foundation skills and competencies essential for success in the workplace. (State Learning Standard 3a for Career Development and Occupational Studies)

Evaluation Procedures

1. When working independently on an academic task, Marty will improve his time on task by 100%.

   Self-recording

2. When working in small groups, Marty will listen to peers and take turns speaking 80% of the time.

   Teacher observation or group evaluation

TRANSITION PROGRAM

Marty is very interested in and skilled at working with his hands to make and fix things. In addition to using these skills as part of the educational program, Marty will participate in a career awareness program designed to explore his career interests.

This program will expose Marty to a variety of careers and allow him to experience work settings and meet professionals who are involved in careers related to Marty's interests. This program also will aid Marty in understanding his learning style, strengths and weaknesses, interests, and preferences.

Annual Goal: Marty will be knowledgeable about the world of work, explore career options, and relate personal skills, aptitudes, and abilities to future career decisions. (State Learning Standard 1 for Career Development and Occupational Studies)

Evaluation Procedures

1. Marty will identify three careers in which he may be interested and explain why he is interested in each one.

   Self-report

2. Marty will research and explain the training and experiential requirements for the three careers he has identified.

   Interview

3. Marty will evaluate his skills and characteristics with respect to these careers by identifying his related strengths and needs.

   Self-report

4. Marty will follow and observe individuals involved in these three careers as they perform their jobs.

   Student-maintained log

ASSISTIVE TECHNOLOGY AND COMMUNICATION NEEDS

Marty will be given a computer and talking word processing system with word prediction capabilities and a talking calculator (with headphones) to assist him with classroom activities and tests.

PARTICIPATION IN STATEWIDE, DISTRICTWIDE, AND CLASSROOM-BASED ASSESSMENTS, AS WELL AS TESTING ACCOMMODATIONS AND ALTERNATIVES

Participation in and testing accommodations during the administration of statewide and districtwide assessments: Marty will participate in all statewide and districtwide assessments and receive all statewide and districtwide approved testing accommodations. Where the district does not limit the use of testing accommodations, Marty will be provided with appropriate testing accommodations that are used during classroom-based assessments.

Participation in and testing accommodations during classroom-based assessments: Marty will participate in all classroom-based assessments. Teacher-made tests will be individually administered by the collaboration teacher in a separate location, with extended time and breaks every 30 minutes. Marty will be allowed to use a talking word processing program with word prediction capabilities. For math tests that do not assess mental computation, he will be allowed to use a talking calculator. When possible and appropriate, Marty will demonstrate his mastery of classroom content through projects and cooperative learning activities.

(Continued)

FIGURE 2.4 **Continued**

METHOD AND FREQUENCY OF COMMUNICATION WITH FAMILY

Marty's family will be regularly informed through IEP progress reports, curriculum-based assessments, and Marty's general education report cards. In addition, feedback on Marty's performance and progress will be shared with his family through quarterly scheduled family-teacher meetings, results of state and district assessments, and portfolio reviews.

Committee Participants	Relationship/Role
Ms. Rachel Tupper	5th grade teacher
Mr. Terry Feaster	Special Ed. teacher
Mr. Kris Brady	Sp. Ed. administrator
Ms. Jessica Amatura	Educational evaluator

Signature(s)

If family members were not members of the committee, please indicate:

I agree with the Individualized Education Program _____✓_____
I disagree with the Individualized Education Program _____

Harry Glick Agnes Glick
Parent/Guardian Signature

I participated in this meeting. I agree with the goals and services of the Individualized Educational Program.

Marty Glick
Student's Signature

---

background; motor skills, level of and desire for independence; educational, social, and community-based goals; and ability, motivation, and training needed to use the device (Heller, Mezei, & Thompson Avant, 2008)

- Family-related information including the strengths, challenges, views of independence, linguistic background, and cultural values of the family, such as the sociocultural and linguistic factors that affect the family as well as the impact (Fitzpatrick & Brown, 2008)
- Information related to customary environments including the various activities and needs of the student in his or her environments, such as the classroom, school, home, and work setting (King-Sears & Evmenova, 2007)
- Technology-related information including the nature of the technology, its potential effectiveness, ease of use, features, obtrusiveness, effect on peers, noticeability, comfort level, dependability, adaptability, durability, transportability, safety, cost, and comparability to other devices, as well as a statement addressing the advantages and disadvantages of the alternative strategies and technologies for meeting the student's identified technology needs and the training and administrative support that students, families, and educators need to use the device (Bausch & Ault, 2008; Boone & Higgins, 2007; Newton & Dell, 2009). In addition, the IEP team should consider whether the device allows the student to function at a higher level or more efficiently within inclusive classrooms and the general curriculum, as well as its ability to foster social acceptance from classmates.

UDL and You

Incorporating Universally Designed Accommodations into IEPs

The IEP also includes information related to the accommodations your students will need to succeed in your inclusive classroom (Ketterlin-Geller, Alonzo, Braun-Monegan, & Tindal, 2007). *Accommodations* refer to changes in curriculum, instruction, and assessment that allow students to participate in and access all aspects of inclusive classrooms and schools without significantly altering the nature of the activity. You and your colleagues on the IEP team can use the following steps to incorporate universally designed accommodations into your students' IEPs. Keep in mind that the principles of UDL relate to *all* of your students, and you can use these guidelines to ensure that *all* of your students receive the individual accommodations that help them to access and succeed in your inclusive classroom.

Step 1: Identify the Student's Strengths and Challenges. The team identifies the student's individual characteristics, cultural, linguistic, and experiential backgrounds; and academic, behavioral, and socialization strengths and challenges and examines how these variables impact the student's performance and interactions.

Step 2: Examine Aspects of Your Inclusive Classroom That Affect Student Performance. The team examines all aspects of your inclusive classroom to determine those that affect student performance such as your curricular expectations, teaching and assessment strategies, classroom routines and rules, and your students' social interaction patterns.

Step 3: Identify Barriers Related to Access and Success. The team discusses the information collected in steps 1 and 2 to identify the classroom related factors that might prevent the student from having access to and success in your inclusive classroom.

Step 4: Consider a Range of Possible Accommodations: The IEP team considers a range of possible accommodations addressing the barriers to the student's access and success in inclusive classrooms.

Step 5: Use the Principles of UDL to Select Accommodations That Address the Student's Individual Characteristics and Barriers Related to Access and Success. The team uses the principles of UDL we learned about in Chapter 1 to guide the selection of accommodations that address the student's strengths and challenges and the barriers that hinder the student's access and success in your inclusive classroom.

Step 6: Incorporate Explicit Universally Designed Accommodations into the Student's IEPs. The team explicitly lists the selected universally designed accommodations on the student's IEP so that everyone knows the specific actions to be taken to overcome the barriers to access and success. To foster understanding and implementation of the accommodations, the IEP contains concise statements related to the conditions associated with the accommodations, including (a) when the accommodations will be needed; (b) which individuals will be responsible for implementing the accommodations; (c) what materials, resources, technology, locations, and equipment will be needed to implement the accommodations; and (d) what preparation and education the student and educators will need to learn to implement the accommodations.

Step 7: Evaluate Impact and Implementation. The team evaluates the selected accommodations to assess their impact on access and success by examining the student's learning, behavior, and socialization. The evaluation also includes information to determine the extent to which the accommodations are being implemented as specified in the student's IEP. Effective accommodations are continued or, if possible, gradually faded out so that the student performs in the same ways as classmates. Accommodations that are not achieving their intended outcomes should be revised to make them more effective or replaced by others if they continue to be unsuccessful.

Sources: Byrnes (2008); Ketterlin-Geller et al. (2007); Salend (2009).

Important factors that IEP teams also should consider when selecting and evaluating the impact of assistive technology include abandonment and stigma. **Abandonment** refers to students choosing not to use technology. Abandonment may be related to several factors, including the extent to which students and their families view the technology as effective, efficient, functional, easy to use, and culturally appropriate. Another factor that impacts abandonment is the stigmatization associated with a technological device. If students and their families feel that a device results in stigmatization, they are not likely to use it. For example, although a device may be very effective in helping a student communicate, the student and the family may not use it in social settings in order to avoid attention from others. Therefore, in conducting an individualized technology assessment, the IEP team also should consider the device's aesthetics, age and gender appropriateness, and social and cultural acceptability (Fitzpatrick & Brown, 2008).

Once appropriate technology has been selected, IEP teams should establish a plan of implementation and examine the impact of the technology on students' performance in school and at home and include ways to prevent abandonment. Bausch and Ault (2008) offer guidelines and forms to assist IEP teams in creating an assistive technology implementation plan; and Parette, Peterson-Karlan, Wojcik, and Bardi (2007) provide strategies for evaluating the effectiveness of assistive technology.

Making Connections
Find out more about appropriate technologies for your students in Chapter 8.

Transition Services   The **transition services** component of the IEP addresses natural transition points and includes a set of coordinated activities within a results-oriented process that is designed to improve the students' academic and functional achievement and to address postsecondary goals in the areas of training, education, employment, community participation, and, where appropriate, independent living

Using Technology to Promote Inclusion
CONDUCTING AN INDIVIDUALIZED TECHNOLOGY ASSESSMENT

As part of the IEP for Elisa Sanchez, a student with a significant communication disorder, the IEP team met with her family to discuss her needs in terms of assistive technology devices and services. Because of Elisa's expressive language difficulties, the team was considering recommending that Elisa use some type of augmentative or alternative communication system. While some members proposed that Elisa continue to use a communication board, others thought that her ability to communicate with others in a variety of environments would be enhanced by her use of an electronic device with digitized speech.

Recognizing the importance of Elisa and her family's feelings regarding these choices, the team solicited information from them regarding their perspectives on these technologies. Convinced that Elisa had the skills to effectively use either system, they spoke with her and her family about their preferences. Elisa indicated that she was eager to use the electronic system as "it would make communicating with others easier, and faster for everyone, and allow me to say more." Because the system was programmed in English and Spanish, she liked that she could select the language in which she needed to communicate depending on the person with whom she was speaking.

Although her family agreed with Elisa, they also had some concerns. They worried about paying for the device and using, transporting, and maintaining it. They also were concerned that it would draw attention to Elisa in public settings and make them feel different.

The team found this information very helpful and used it to determine the assistive technology devices and services that would be incorporated into Elisa's IEP. The team decided that Elisa could benefit from using both types of communication systems and that she and her family could determine when to use each system. They discussed the need for tailoring the system to Elisa and her family so that the symbols, photographs, and voices used matched those of the family's culture. They also agreed that the school district would purchase a lightweight system, and work with Elisa and her family to help them learn how to use and care for and transport it. It also was arranged that the company that sold the system would provide technical support to Elisa's family in Spanish.

- How would Elisa's use of technology affect her access to your inclusive classroom and to society?
- Why are the preferences and goals of students and their families important in determining assistive technology devices and services?
- How would you solicit information from students and families about their perspectives on assistive technology devices and services?
- What preferences and perspectives toward the technology did the IEP team need to consider for Elisa and her family?
- How were these preferences and perspectives addressed by the IEP team?
- What other factors should the IEP team consider when conducting an individualized technology assessment?

skills (Test, Aspel, & Everson, 2006; Trainor, 2008). These goals and services are based on students' challenges and should consider students' strengths, preferences, and interests. For example, for students who will go to college after graduation, the transition services component may relate to learning study skills and advocating for one's needs. For students who will go to work, the transition services component may focus on assessing employment interests and preferences, developing important job-seeking and job performance skills, finding recreational opportunities, and preparing for independent living. Konrad, Walker, Fowler, Test, and Wood (2008) offer a model for teaching transitional skills and aligning them to the general educational curriculum.

Once students with disabilities graduate or exceed the age for receiving special education services, the school must develop a **Summary of Performance (SOP)** that addresses students' academic achievement and functional performance and includes suggestions for achieving their postsecondary goals. Some schools meet the transition services requirement by developing an Individualized Transition Plan (ITP) as part of the IEP.

Making Connections
Find out more about transitional planning and creating SOPs in Chapter 6, which also includes a sample ITP.

Student Involvement

When I started working on the student-led IEP, I was very excited because I could tell the teachers what I needed instead of them telling me what I need (Hapner & Imel, 2002, p. 123).

I made note cards to read during my IEP. I looked in books to find examples of what we can say during the meeting. I filled out papers that asked how I was benefiting from my IEP and what I was learning. I felt really ready to do my IEP (Hapner & Imel, 2002, p. 123).

The IDEA supports the involvement of students in the IEP and ITP process, which can in turn promote the implementation and success of the instructional program and the planning and delivery of transition services (Danneker & Bottge, 2009; Konrad, 2008). As the previous comments indicate, students can offer a unique perspective on their own strengths and challenges, preferences, interests, hobbies, talents, and career goals, as well as successful teaching strategies and materials (see Figure 2.5 for sample student questions you can use to solicit information from your students).

FIGURE 2.5 **Sample student questions**

- How do you feel about school?
- What do you like about school?
- How could school be improved for you?
- What are your greatest strengths and talents in school? What do you do well in school?
- In what areas do you think you need to improve at school?
- How would you describe your behavior in school?
- How do you get along with other students in your class/school?
- Who are you? How would you describe yourself?
- What are your strengths? What are your needs/challenges?
- What are your successes? Dreams/hopes for the future?
- What things would you like to learn about yourself?
- What things would you like to learn in school?
- In what ways do you learn best?
- What things could your teacher(s) do to help you learn or be more successful in school?
- Are you completing your classwork, homework, and assigned projects? If not, why not?
- Briefly describe your study skills and work habits.
- In what school and community activities do you participate? If none, why?
- What do you like to do after school? What are your hobbies?
- What careers interest you?
- What are your goals after you graduate from this school?

FIGURE 2.6 Strategies for involving students in the IEP process

Before the IEP Meeting

- Discuss with students the purpose and agenda of the meeting, including who will attend, and what will go on.
- Teach students the social, communication, etiquette (including how to dress), and self-advocacy skills they need to participate.
- Give students an overview of appropriate aspects of special education laws, the components of the IEP, and relevant vocabulary.
- Review copies of their current IEPs with students. For example, you can have students complete an IEP scavenger hunt to locate specific information on their IEPs.
- Give students inventories and checklists to help them identify their strengths, challenges, goals, learning styles, study skills, transition and career goals, interests, preferences, concerns, and feelings about the issues to be discussed, including the need for and effectiveness of various instructional and testing accommodations. (See Figure 2.5 for a listing of questions for students.)
- Ask students to write about their strengths, challenges, and goals. Use prompts to guide students who have difficulty writing such as "I am very good at _____; I want to work on improving my skills at _____; and after I graduate, I want to _____."
- Provide students with opportunities to talk with other students who have successfully participated in the IEP process and to view videos of simulated student-led IEP meetings.
- Guide students in creating a draft of their IEPs and portfolios of their work, and in creating templates, PowerPoint slides, and note cards to present their comments.
- Conduct simulated meetings, and help students develop and rehearse their comments before the meeting.
- Solicit help from students in preparing for the meetings such as writing letters inviting others to attend their IEP meeting, making name tags and agendas, and serving refreshments.

At the Meeting

- Ask students to introduce themselves; explain their strengths and challenges; describe effective instructional accommodations; discuss their past and future goals, and opinions.
- Encourage all participants to limit their use of professional jargon and acronyms, to use language students understand, to provide examples, and to speak directly to students rather than speaking about students to others.
- Give students time to formulate and present their responses, listen and pay attention to their comments, ask them for input and opinions, and incorporate their comments into the decision-making process.

Following the Meeting

- Ask students to provide feedback on the meeting and their participation.
- Give students a copy of their IEP, and encourage them to review it periodically and to work toward meeting the goals and objectives listed there.
- Collaborate with students to create a guide summarizing important information from their IEPs to share with others (see Figure 2.7).
- Teach students how to remind others of the accommodations and services they should receive, to self-monitor their progress, and to periodically develop a progress report related to their IEP goals.

Sources: Danneker and Bottge (2009); Hawbaker (2007); Konrad (2008); Myers and Eisenman (2005); Uphold et al. (2007); Van Dycke, Martin, and Lovett (2006).

The comprehensive planning team works with students and their family members to design an IEP. What have been your experiences in collaborating with students, their families, and other educators to develop IEPs?

Involving students in the IEP process can help incorporate the principles of UDL into the IEP by guiding the team to focus on positive aspects of the student's performance and ensuring that practical, functional, and meaningful goals are included in the IEP. Because student involvement in instructional planning can be empowering, it also can foster students' motivation, self-reflection, independence, self-advocacy, and self-determination.

You and your colleagues and family members can use various strategies to help students participate in the team process. These strategies, which also can be modified to assist family members in learning about and participating in the IEP process, are presented in Figure 2.6. Konrad (2008), Uphold, Walker, and Test (2007), and Hawbaker (2007) offer resources to help you involve your students in the IEP process.

IMPLEMENTING IEPS IN GENERAL EDUCATION SETTINGS

HOW CAN IEPS BE IMPLEMENTED IN GENERAL EDUCATION SETTINGS? The IEP can provide students with disabilities with access to the general education curriculum. This section provides you with ways you can work with others to implement the IEP in the general education classroom.

Involve Teachers in the IEP Process

The inclusion of general and special educators in the IEP planning process can foster the link between the IEP and the general education setting. The involvement of general educators provides the team with important information about the general education curriculum as well as their perceptions of the student's progress within it. Their direct involvement in the IEP process also provides a basis for general educators receiving the supportive services to help students access and succeed in the general education curriculum.

Special educators can give the team relevant information about the student's academic, behavioral, and social strengths and challenges, which is essential to determining and implementing the instructional and testing accommodations that also help students access and succeed in the general education curriculum. The inclusion of special educators also can help ensure that instructional goals and strategies address student needs related to a functional or specialized curriculum.

Align the IEP to the General Education Curriculum

General and special education teachers also can assist the team in aligning the IEP to the general education curriculum by converting curriculum standards into measurable learning objectives that can be addressed instructionally (Parrish & Stodden, 2009). In the case of Marty, Ms. Tupper's involvement helped the IEP team translate the state standards into more specific objectives that Ms. Tupper could teach in her classroom. This process begins with collecting assessment data to determine students' current levels of performance within the curriculum. Curriculum-related annual goals and differentiated instructional and classroom management strategies are then identified and implemented.

Differentiate Instruction to Address IEP Goals

The successful implementation of the IEP in the general education setting is related to the use of differentiated instruction to address IEP goals. Therefore, you and the team can work collaboratively to identify and employ a range of curricular, instructional, technological, and testing accommodations and supports to provide *all students* with access to the general education curriculum.

Establish an IEP Implementation Plan

Once the IEP has been developed, a plan to implement it in the general setting can be established (Jung, Gomez, Baird, & Galyon Keramidas, 2008). You can work with the IEP team to create a matrix that links the student's IEP goals and services with the student's general education program. In creating the matrix, you need to integrate the objectives, statewide learning standards, related services, technology, instructional and testing accommodations, and alternative assessments outlined in the student's IEP with the critical components of the classroom schedule, curriculum, and routines (Parrish & Stodden, 2009). The goals and objectives of the IEP are then implemented by all professionals in the general education classroom as part of the class's ongoing instructional activities.

The success of the plan can be fostered by highlighting and communicating meaningful IEP information to those who will be responsible for implementing it. This is particularly important at the secondary level when students have several

Go to the Assignments and Activities section of the Topic *Prereferrals, Placement and IEP Process* in the MyEducationLab for your course and complete the activity entitled *Convening the Multidisciplinary IEP Team*. As you watch the video, think about how to involve teachers and other stakeholders in the IEP process.

REFLECTIVE

Have you participated in the development of an IEP? What factors hindered and fostered your involvement and involvement of others? How could the IEP process be improved?

Go to the Building Teaching Skills and Dispositions section of the Topic *Prereferrals, Placement and IEP Process* in the MyEducationLab for your course and complete the activity entitled *Conducting or Participating in an IEP Meeting*. As you work through the learning unit, consider what you've read in this chapter about IEPs.

Preparing For and Participating In the IEP Meeting

Although he had participated in several family–teacher meetings during his brief time as a teacher, Mr. Myers was nervous about attending his first IEP meeting. He spoke to his mentor teacher about his uncertainty, who suggested that he talk to Ms. Gonzalez, the special education teacher. When Mr. Myers approached her, Ms. Gonzalez was not surprised, as even many experienced teachers were intimidated initially by the IEP process.

Ms. Gonzalez began by explaining to Mr. Myers that his input was extremely important. She showed him a sample IEP, explaining the different components and how they were developed. She told him that he would be asked to talk about the student's progress in the general education curriculum, how the student's disability affected his performance in class, and what services the student and he would need to achieve the goals in the IEP. She noted that other teachers had found it helpful to bring samples of student work to illustrate their comments regarding their students' strengths and challenges. She also gave him a handout from the state that summarized laws and information related to special education and the IEP process and a list of relevant websites.

At the meeting, Mr. Myers, although still nervous, actively participated and benefited from hearing the perspectives of others. As a group, they developed an IEP that addressed the student's varied strengths and challenges and offered the supports that Mr. Myers needed to implement it.

Here are some other strategies you can use to implement the IDEA in your inclusive classroom and foster your participation at IEP meetings:

- Prepare for the meeting by learning about the issues to be discussed and their relationship to the information you have to share, reviewing current information regarding the student (e.g., current assessment data and IEP), and obtaining an agenda for the meeting.

- Identify and share with other team members your goals for the meeting and the issues you would like to be addressed so those items can be part of the meeting agenda.

- Outline the services you provide to the student and the family and their responses to these services as well as the services and supports you will need to implement the student's IEP.

- Discuss positive aspects of the student's performance first, including the best ways in which the student learns. Support your statements by citing examples and sharing work samples and anecdotal records.

- Avoid using professional jargon, and seek clarification when you don't understand terms or information presented by others.

- Ask questions to obtain more information and to clarify and reflect on the impact and feasibility of major decisions, responsibilities, and dates.

- Be prepared to compromise and mend fences when you disagree with families or other participants.

teachers. For example, you can develop a form that gives the student's teachers and supportive service personnel a summary of essential aspects of the student's IEP that lists the student's educational strengths, challenges, and goals, and accommodations for addressing them (Sayeski, 2009) (see Figure 2.7).

STUDENTS WITH HIGH-INCIDENCE DISABILITIES

WHAT ARE THE EDUCATIONAL STRENGTHS AND CHALLENGES OF STUDENTS WITH HIGH-INCIDENCE DISABILITIES? Students like Marty are referred to as having **high-incidence disabilities** or mild disabilities that include such disability categories as learning disabilities, mild intellectual disabilities, mild emotional/behavioral disorders, and speech/language impairments (Raymond, 2008). Students with high-incidence disabilities make up between 90% and 95% of the students with disabilities and have many things in common. (Later in the chapter, we will learn about students with **low-incidence disabilities**, which include students with physical, sensory, and more significant cognitive disabilities.)

The factors that contribute to the development of high-incidence disability categories appear to be multifaceted and are the focus of ongoing research. Several biological and sociocultural factors appear to interact to affect an individual's learning and behavioral abilities and styles. Biological factors such as one's temperament and neurological development are thought to play an important role in making individuals more predisposed to certain behaviors. Environmental factors also may make some individuals more likely to engage in specific behaviors. Experiential factors such as the nature of an individual's interactions with family members and

FIGURE 2.7 Sample IEP summary form

Student's Name: Marty Glick   **Age**: 10 1/2   **Grade**: 5

Educators: Ms. Rachel Tupper (5th grade teacher), Mr. Terry Feaster (Special education teacher), Ms. Stephanie Brown (paraeducator), Ms. Pennee Gee (school counselor), Mr. Kris Brady (administrator and service coordinator)

Family: Harry and Agnes Glick

Marty's Strengths

- Geometry, measurement, time and money
- Enjoys working with technology and classmates
- Creative
- Likes working with hands and fixing things
- Friendly and sociable
- Relates well to others
- Good sense of humor

Marty's Challenges and Goals

- Work on word recognition, oral reading fluency and comprehension
- Work on computation skills and solving word problems
- Work on prewriting skills, sequencing, and punctuation
- Enhance work completion
- Increase on-task behavior
- Foster self-esteem
- Explore career interests

Instructional Strategies

- Give clear, concise, step-by-step directions.
- Break assignments into smaller chunks.
- Use a talking word processor with word prediction and a talking calculator (with headphones so as not to distract others).
- Use cooperative learning groups.
- Give choices concerning instructional activities and how to complete them.
- Use hands-on learning activities and active instructional games.
- Post homework and other assignments online.
- Teach and monitor use of learning strategies.

Behavioral and Social Strategies

- Teach and encourage use of self-management techniques.
- Provide frequent praise.
- Allow free time with a peer after work is completed.
- Assign class job related to his mechanical skills.

Assessment Considerations

- Participation in statewide and districtwide assessments with approved testing accommodations (separate location, extended time).
- Individually administered teacher-made tests.
- Use performance assessment and progress monitoring.

Communication and Collaboration Considerations

- Monitor side effects of medications.
- Meet with and coordinate with Ms. Brown, Mr. Feaster, and Ms. Gee.
- Complete daily report card.

educators, family life, and cultural, linguistic, and economic background also influence students' behaviors.

The developmental nature of the high-incidence disability categories affect individuals in different ways as they age (Raymond, 2008). In early childhood, although children with these conditions may exhibit learning difficulties and high levels of activity, they may not be viewed as different from other young children who typically engage in similar behaviors, albeit at lower rates. However, as they enter elementary school and the academic and behavioral demands increase, their learning and behavioral difficulties impact their school performance and may start to cause frustration, social rejection, low self-esteem, and a dislike of school. Some learners may outgrow their condition or some of the symptoms associated with it when they reach adolescence. However, many do not, and the interaction with the typical adolescent desire for independence, peer acceptance, and conformity intensifies their academic, organizational, and social difficulties.

As we saw in the case of Marty, educators often have trouble differentiating among students with these disability categories because their behaviors tend to interfere with their learning and academic performance, their social interactions and

Students with disabilities have a variety of strengths and challenges, and no two students are alike. How are your students similar to and different from each other?

friendships with others, and their emotional development (Raymond, 2008). As a result, the teaching strategies you will use to promote their learning also overlap. These students also challenge you to be knowledgeable of their unique characteristics so that an educational program that addresses their strengths and challenges is planned and implemented.

Students with Learning Disabilities

Your class will include students like Marty, whose school performance and behavior may not live up to their potential and your expectations. While they may do some things well, they lag behind their classmates in many areas. You may view them as unmotivated or not trying hard enough; however, like Marty, they may have some type of learning disability.

Students with *learning disabilities* make up 5% of the total school population. Slightly more than half of the students receiving special education services have learning disabilities, making them the largest and fastest-growing group of students with disabilities (Mercer & Pullen, 2009). This growing prevalence rate is due to several factors, including the social acceptability of the learning disabilities label. In most cases, the cause of a student's learning disability is not known.

The federal government defines a **specific learning disability** as a disorder in one or more of the basic psychological processes involved in understanding or using spoken or written language, which may appear as an impaired ability to listen, think, speak, read, write, spell, or do mathematical calculations. The term *learning disability* includes such conditions as perceptual handicaps, brain injury, minimal brain dysfunction, dyslexia, and developmental aphasia. It does not include learning problems that are primarily the result of visual, hearing, or motor handicaps; mental retardation; emotional disturbance; or environmental, cultural, or economic disadvantage.

Like Marty, many students with learning disabilities have average or above-average intelligence, although they often fail to perform academically in line with their potential as well as their peers (Bender, 2008). Therefore, many of these students show a discrepancy between their ability and their actual performance in your classroom. The characteristics and behaviors of these students vary; some have difficulties in only one area, while others have difficulties in a variety of areas, such as learning, language, perceptual, motor, social, and behavioral difficulties.

Learning and Academic Difficulties   Many students with learning disabilities have memory, attention, motivational, and organizational difficulties that hinder their ability to learn and master academic content (Bender, 2008). Students with learning disabilities experience difficulties perceiving, processing, remembering, and expressing information. Their learning profiles also are characterized by their tendency to use inefficient and ineffective learning strategies and lower self-perceptions of self-efficacy, mood, effort, and hope than their classmates (Lackaye, Margalit, Ziv, & Ziman, 2006). As a result, they often exhibit difficulties across the curriculum.

Many of these students also experience reading difficulties (Mercer & Pullen, 2009). These difficulties appear as the failure to recall letters, their sounds, and words; overreliance on whole-word, phonological, and contextual reading strategies; a slow reading rate; and poor listening and reading comprehension ability. When reading, they may lose their place and/or read in a choppy way. As they enter the secondary grades, these reading difficulties may result in misreading of directions, an avoidance of reading and writing, and trouble accessing and comprehending information in content-area textbooks.

Many students with learning disabilities who have reading difficulties also may have trouble writing (Bender, 2008). An examination of their writing may reveal problems in the areas of idea generation, text organization, sentence structure, vocabulary usage, spelling, and grammar (Dockrell, Lindsay, & Connelly, 2009; Graham & Harris, 2009). These writing difficulties can affect their performance across the curriculum.

Although most students with learning disabilities have reading problems, they may be proficient in some content areas and below average in others (Heward, 2009). However, students with learning disabilities also may experience difficulty with mathematics (Fuchs & Fuchs, 2008; Mabbot & Bisanz, 2008). You may observe this in their lack of knowledge of basic facts and difficulties in discriminating numbers, symbols, and signs; understanding math terms and vocabulary; performing calculations; solving problems; making comparisons; and performing more complex procedures (Rousselle & Noel, 2008).

Language and Communication Difficulties Language difficulties are a common characteristic of many students with learning disabilities (Mercer & Pullen, 2009). As a result, some of these students may use immature speech patterns, experience language comprehension difficulties, and have trouble expressing themselves. In the classroom, they may have difficulty learning new vocabulary, following directions, understanding questions, pronouncing and rhyming words, and expressing their needs.

Increased attention has focused on students with **nonverbal learning disabilities** who have a hard time processing nonverbal, visual-spatial information and communications such as body language, gestures, and the context of linguistic interactions (Antshel & Joseph, 2006; Schiff, Bauminger, & Toledo, 2009). Although these students may talk a lot, their language tends to be repetitive, which results in a rigid communication style and narrow word selection. They rely on spoken language to communicate, speaking in a flat tone of voice and often interpreting language literally. When interacting with others, they frequently fail to identify and understand nonverbal social cues, and assess the reactions of others. Because students with nonverbal learning disabilities tend to focus on details rather than the whole, they often experience difficulties understanding and remembering information that is presented visually, completing novel and complex tasks, establishing priorities, identifying main ideas, taking notes, and organizing and connecting their written products.

You can aid these students by helping them understand part–whole relationships, establishing and following routines, giving specific sequenced verbal directions that help them set priorities for completing multitask activities, beginning lessons with familiar content prior to introducing more novel and complex material, and providing them with social skills instruction. You also can assist them in developing accurate and flexible interpretations of words, verbal analogies, body language, and facial expressions; by fostering their verbal expressive and reasoning skills; and by teaching them to decrease their use of irrelevant verbiage.

Perceptual and Motor Difficulties Even though it appears that their senses are not impaired, many students with learning disabilities may have difficulty recognizing, discriminating, and interpreting visual and auditory stimuli. For example, some of these students may have trouble discriminating shapes and letters, copying from the blackboard, following multiple-step directions, associating sounds with letters, paying attention to relevant stimuli, and working on a task for a sustained period of time.

Students with learning disabilities also may have gross and fine motor difficulties. Gross motor deficits include awkward gaits; clumsiness; poor balance; and an inability to catch or kick balls, skip, and follow a rhythmic sequence of movements. Fine motor problems include difficulty cutting, pasting, drawing, tracing, holding a pencil, writing, and copying and aligning columns. Another motor problem found in some students with learning disabilities is hyperactivity, which results in constant movement and difficulty staying seated.

Social-Emotional and Behavioral Difficulties Students with learning disabilities may have social and behavioral difficulties and may show signs of a poor socialization, self-concept, confidence, and motivation and social withdrawal, loneliness, frustration, and anxiety (Murray & Greenberg, 2006; Sideridis, 2007). They may engage in classroom behaviors that interfere with their learning and fail to predict the consequences of their behaviors. Because of their poor social skills, they may fail to interpret social cues and adjust their behaviors accordingly, which can result in difficulties relating to and being accepted by their peers (Estell et al., 2009). For example, some students with learning disabilities may have difficulties understanding the subtle cues that guide social relationships, which can hinder their development of friendships. As students age, their lack of social skill can result in difficulties accepting feedback, advocating for oneself, understanding the perspectives of others, and resisting peer pressure.

Students with Emotional and Behavioral Disorders

Several terms are used to refer to students with emotional and behavioral disorders (Austin & Sciarra, 2010). Although an estimated 3% to 5% of students have emotional and behavioral disorders, only 1% are identified as such, with boys significantly outnumbering girls (Yell, Shriner, Meadows, & Drasgow, 2009).

Students with emotional disturbance exhibit one or more of the following characteristics over a long period of time and to a marked degree, which adversely affects their educational performance:

- Inability to learn that cannot be explained by intellectual, sensory, or health factors
- Inability to build or maintain good relationships with peers and teachers
- Inappropriate behaviors or feelings under normal circumstances
- A general, pervasive mood of unhappiness or depression
- A tendency to develop physical symptoms or fears associated with personal or school problems

The term *emotional and behavioral disorders* includes children who have schizophrenia. It does not include children who are socially maladjusted unless they are emotionally disturbed.

Students with emotional and behavioral disorders are often categorized as mildly or severely disturbed, depending on their behaviors and the nature of their condition (Yell, Shriner, et al., 2009). Like students with learning disabilities, many of these students experience learning, behavioral, and motivational difficulties that cause them to underachieve in reading, writing, mathematics, and other content areas (Mattison, 2008; Sutherland, Lewis-Palmer, Stichter, & Morgan, 2008). They also exhibit challenges related to self-control, anger, and impulsivity, little on-task behavior, reduced frustration tolerance, and poor self-concept and social skills (Cullinan, 2007; Deming & Lochman, 2008). Although inappropriate behaviors may mark all students to some degree, those with emotional disturbances may often use inappropriate, avoidance, and noncompliant behavior (Kauffman & Landrum, 2009). They thus run the risk of performing poorly in all academic areas; being rejected by their teachers and classmates; and having high dropout, absenteeism, and suspension rates (Crews et al., 2008). Consequently, their placement in inclusive settings and their rates of success in graduating, enrolling in postsecondary education, obtaining competitive employment, and living independently are lower than other students with high-incidence disabilities (Mihalas, Morse, Allsopp, & Alvarez McHatton, 2009).

However, with teaching strategies tailored to their strengths and challenges, their academic work and behavior can improve significantly through use of positive behavioral supports, social skills instruction, behaviorally based interventions, peer-based techniques, and differentiated instruction (Austin & Sciarra, 2010; Ryan, Pierce, & Mooney, 2008). They also can benefit from **wraparound planning**, a multidisciplinary process for collaboratively designing and delivering student- and family-centered educational, counseling, medical, vocational, and mental health services to address their unique strengths, challenges, and behaviors (Eber, Breen, Rose, Unizycki, & London, 2008; Lechtenberger et al., 2008).

Some of these students also may exhibit oppositional and defiant behaviors or have conduct disorders (Austin & Sciarra, 2010). These **students with oppositional and defiant behaviors** exhibit a variety of behaviors designed to resist the requests of authority figures, which often interfere with their school performance. As a result, they tend to seek attention; bother, blame, or argue with others; or express their anger and frustration indirectly by engaging in manipulative, vindictive, and/or non-compliant behavior. **Students with conduct disorders** engage in aggressive and disruptive behaviors in "a repetitive and persistent pattern of behavior in which the basic rights of others or major age-appropriate societal norms or rules are violated" (American Psychiatric Association, 2000, p. 93).

Students with emotional and behavior disorders also include those with obsessions, compulsions, and anxiety disorders (Austin & Sciarra, 2010; Schoenfeld & Konopasek, 2007). You can help students with obsessions and anxiety disorders by working with their families and mental health professionals in your school, helping students avoid situations that trigger their conditions, and giving them choices. You also can support them by being aware of their conditions and empathetic and sensitive to their unique challenges.

Many of us exhibit some type of compulsive behavior, but **students with obsessive-compulsive disorders (OCD)** feel compelled to think about or perform repeatedly an action that appears to be meaningless and irrational and is against their own will. Students with anxiety disorders include those with **generalized anxiety disorder**, **separation anxiety disorder**, **social phobia**, **panic disorders**, or a combination of these conditions (Kauffman & Landrum, 2009; Schoenfeld & Konopasek, 2007). Students with generalized anxiety disorder chronically worry, have difficulty relaxing, and frequently complain of stomachaches and headaches. Students whose anxiety is triggered by their separation from their primary caregivers also may complain of physical ailments when they are expected to be away from their caregivers. Students with social phobias experience anxiety related to interactions in public settings and therefore may avoid speaking in front of the class, trying out for clubs or teams, and establishing close friendships. When confronted with specific types of events, students with panic disorders become fearful and may experience emotional discomfort and a variety of physical symptoms such as shortness of breath, heart palpitations, and excessive sweating and fainting.

One group of students whose anxiety disorder affects their communication with others is **students with selective mutism** (Berger, Bartley, Armstrong, Kaatz, & Benson, 2007; Crundwell & Marc, 2006). Despite possessing the ability to speak, students with selective mutism fail to communicate in selective social situations or environments. For example, although they may verbally interact with others in their home, they may refrain from using verbal and nonverbal communication to avoid social interactions when they are in school. You can help these students by identifying the factors that may be contributing to their behavior, limiting their anxiety by not focusing on their need to speak, fostering their use of nonverbal communication systems such as use of gestures and symbols, providing them with opportunities to engage in activities that do not involve speaking, and using buddy systems and small-group instruction (Kern, Starosta, Bambara, Cook, & Gresham, 2007). As students feel more comfortable in your inclusive classroom, you also can gradually encourage them to move from using gestures and symbols to one-word and then multiple-word responses. You also can help these students by collaborating with their families and other professionals, learning more about the condition, and sharing this information with others who work and interact with them (Berger et al., 2007). A good resource for learning about students with selective mutism is the Selective Mutism Foundation (*http://selectivemutismfoundation.org*).

Making Connections
Find out more about wraparound planning and working collaboratively with other professionals and families in Chapter 4.

Making Connections
Find out more about how you can foster the prosocial behaviors of your students in Chapter 7.

Making Connections
Find out more about students with eating disorders in Chapter 3.

Helping Students Who Exhibit Oppositional and Defiant Behaviors Succeed

Justin seemed to delight in irritating Mr. Howe, and it was working. Even the simplest request from Mr. Howe resulted in resistance from Justin. Mr. Howe initially dealt with Justin's resistance by trying to cajole, convince, or bribe him to comply, but he had started to lose his patience with Justin. Now, when Justin refused to do something, Mr. Howe got angry and quickly threatened him in front of the class, which Justin seemed to enjoy even more.

Realizing he was playing into Justin's hands, Mr. Howe contacted the school's prereferral team, which included Ms. Douglas, a special educator who had worked with Justin and his family. The team collected information about Justin and his behavior. They analyzed several recent incidents to identify the actions of Justin and Mr. Howe that precipitated and maintained their power struggles. Justin's family also discussed how they use routines and structure transitions to avoid these confrontations with him at home. Based on this information, the team concluded that Justin enjoyed his confrontations with Mr. Howe. The team then collaborated with Mr. Howe to create a plan to try to reduce Justin's power struggles. They determined which classroom rules were nonnegotiable and what the consequences would be for violating them. They used these rules to establish a home–school contract with Justin's family. They also discussed instructional changes Mr. Howe could make to motivate Justin and involve him in the learning process and in monitoring his own behavior.

Mr. Howe also tried to change his demeanor and facial expressions with Justin, made sure that he calmly gave brief, easy-to-follow directions, and provided Justin with some choices. If Justin resisted, Mr. Howe briefly listened to Justin's explanation, and either discussed it privately with him or quickly exited the situation. When Justin complied with Mr. Howe's request, Mr. Howe occasionally and privately acknowledged it by employing a quick walk-by reinforcement such as a gesture, whisper, or a pat on the back or by leaving a note for Justin to find later in the day.

Here are some other strategies you can use to implement the IDEA in your inclusive classroom and help students who exhibit oppositional and defiant behaviors and students with other behavioral disorders succeed in your inclusive classroom:

- Minimize resistance behaviors that are related to learning difficulties by implementing appropriate instructional accommodations and curricular enhancements and adjustments.
- Identify and try to minimize the events that trigger students' oppositional and defiant behaviors.
- Establish and follow routines, help students make transitions, and structure activities so that students work with their classmates.
- Use learning activities that are motivating and instructionally appropriate for students, and celebrate their successes.
- Build positive and caring relationships with students inside and outside the classroom. For example, you can attend an extracurricular activity in which your students participate, and connect classroom activities to students' interests and hobbies.
- Provide students with opportunities to make choices, problem solve, and offer feedback. For example, you can solicit their input into the rules for the classroom and the consequences for following and not following them.
- Look for opportunities to enhance students' self-esteem.
- Try to avoid escalating the situation, making threats, using body language that communicates disapproval, and responding emotionally during confrontations.

Sources: Austin and Sciarra (2010); Mihalas et al. (2009); Salend and Sylvestre (2005); Yell, Shriner et al. (2009).

REFLECTIVE

Although elementary-level girls and boys experience depression at the same rate, adolescent females are twice as likely to be depressed than their male classmates. Girls and boys also experience different depressive symptoms, with boys being four times more likely to succeed at committing suicide. Why do you think this is the case?

As part of their adjustment to a new culture, many students who are immigrants also may show signs of anxiety, fears, and depression. However, their conditions may not be identified because they may show up via culture-bound syndromes such as a fear of wind and cold or an uncontrollable mimicking of others (Kershaw, 2003). Because many mental health professionals do not recognize these culture-bound syndromes, and because these students may not feel comfortable seeking help from others, these conditions often go untreated. Therefore, it is important for you to collaborate with culturally sensitive professionals who can help you and your students and their families understand and address these conditions.

Depression and Suicide A significant percentage of all adolescents experience symptoms of **depression** and consider committing suicide, with adolescent females having higher rates of depressive symptoms than their male counterparts (Montague, Enders, Dietz, Dixon, & Cavendish, 2008; Wachter & Bouck, 2008). Unfortunately, many of these students are not diagnosed and treated for depression. Students with emotional and behavioral disorders and learning disabilities may be particularly vulnerable to depression and suicide, as are students who suffer a significant loss via death or divorce, are victims of abuse, or witness violent acts (Kauffman & Landrum, 2009; Maag & Reid, 2006).

Although most individuals who are depressed do not attempt or commit suicide, there is a high correlation between depression and suicide. Therefore, you should be aware of the following warning signs of depression, a mood disorder that can occur in childhood and adolescence:

- Overwhelming sadness, apathy, irritability, and hopelessness, along with a persistent loss of interest and enjoyment in everyday pleasurable activities
- A change in appetite, weight, sleep pattern, body movements, or participation and energy levels
- Pervasive difficulty in concentrating, remembering, or making decisions
- Anger, rage, and overreaction to criticism
- A sense of inappropriate guilt, worthlessness, or helplessness and a decrease in self-esteem
- Recurrent thoughts of death or suicide
- Inability to get over the death of a relative or friend and the breakup of friendships
- Noticeable neglect of personal hygiene, dress, and health care and/or self-mutilation
- An increase in giving valued items to others or engaging in risky behaviors
- A dramatic change in school performance characterized by a drop in grades and an increase in inappropriate behaviors
- A radical change in personality or increased use of drugs or alcohol (Crundwell & Killu, 2007; Wachter & Bouck, 2008).

Some students also may have a **bipolar disorder**, which results in them having fluctuating moods that vary from depression to a mania. Manic episodes may be characterized by grandiose, provocative, or aggressive thoughts and actions, recklessness, increased energy, creativity, distractability, and activity levels, and a reduced need for sleep (Egan, 2008). These fluctuations—which may be triggered by such environmental events as conflicts with family members, friends, and teachers, personal and academic stress, and poor health and sleeping habits—can interfere with one's learning, behavior, and friendships (Killu & Crundwell, 2008).

You can take several actions to help students who are experiencing mood disorders (Austin & Sciarra, 2010; Killu & Crundwell, 2008). First, you need to be aware of important events in students' lives such as breakups, family conflicts, substance abuse, alcohol consumption, recent humiliations, social isolation, and impending legal or disciplinary actions. Second, speak to and collaborate with family members and other professionals such as school counselors, social workers, and school psychologists to help the student receive the services of mental health professionals. It is also important that you work extrahard to establish and maintain a personal connection with the student and facilitate the student's interactions with you and peers (Mihalas et al., 2009). Finally, because some students may be reluctant to share their feelings with others, reading about literary and historical figures who triumphed over depression can be used as a way to prompt them to discuss their feelings.

You also should be aware of school policies dealing with depressed, suicidal, or violent students; make appropriate referrals; provide adequate supervision; and document and report your specific observations and changes in students' behavior. You also can work with others to establish a schoolwide suicide prevention program. (Information about such programs can be from the American Foundation's Suicide Prevention Resource Center). If you encounter a student who is considering suicide, violence, or in trauma, you can respond in the following manner:

- Introduce yourself to the student (if you are not known), telling him or her that you are there to help.
- Stay with the student, remaining calm and speaking in a clear, gentle, empathetic, and nonthreatening manner.

- Show concern for the student and use the student's name.
- Maintain a positive body posture, with the hands open and in view, and eye contact without staring.
- Remain close to the student while respecting the student's personal space.
- Consider the cultural, linguistic, and experiential background of the student.
- Ask the student to give up any objects or substances that can cause harm.
- Encourage the student to talk, listen carefully, and acknowledge the student's comments.
- Help the student clarify the issues.
- Avoid being judgmental, offering alternatives that are not available, arguing about the value of life and suicide, pressuring the student, and promising complete confidentiality.
- Help the student identify options, and reinforce positive statements and comments on alternatives.
- Remind the student that others care and are available to help.
- Contact the student's family, your principal, and the mental health and public safety professionals in your school to alert them of your concerns and what has happened.
- Seek counseling and support for yourself (Wachter & Bouck, 2008).

Students with Attention Deficit Disorders

Steven has difficulty completing assignments. Sometimes he starts an assignment before his teachers finish giving the directions. At other times, he squirms in his seat, and calls out answers to questions. Observations of Steven in his classes reveal that he often leaves his seat without permission to interact with his peers, or to hang out by the window. When he works on an assignment, he focuses on it for a short time period and then switches to another activity.

Nicole, a quiet student, is described by her teachers as disorganized, unmotivated, and a bit lazy. Her teachers notice that she spends a lot of time in her own world and frequently seems to daydream. As a result, Nicole often asks them to repeat directions. However, even after they explained the assignment to her, she dawdles at her desk, stares into space, and fails to complete her work.

Although Steven and Nicole differ in many ways, they both exhibit behavioral patterns that are characterized by difficulty identifying and maintaining attention to relevant classroom directions, information, and stimuli, which affect their school performance and indicate that they may have some type of **attention deficit disorder (ADD)** (Zentall, 2006). ADD is the most common childhood psychiatric condition, affecting between 3% and 7% of the students in the United States. There is no definitive cause of ADD. While the factors that contribute to the development of attention difficulties appear to be multifaceted and are the focus of ongoing research, there is a growing recognition of it as a neurological condition (Schuck & Crinella, 2005). Although ADD tends to occur at the same rate in all types of student groups regardless of socioeconomic status and ethnicity, boys like Steven are three to nine times more likely to be diagnosed than girls like Nicole, in part because ADD is more likely not to be detected or treated in female students (Lee, Oakland, Jackson, & Glutting, 2008; Zambo, 2008).

Because ADD is a psychiatric diagnosis rather than a separate disability category recognized in the IDEA, it is defined by the American Psychiatric Association (2000) as "a persistent pattern of inattention, impulsivity, and/or hyperactivity-impulsivity that is more frequently displayed and more severe than is typically observed in individuals at a comparable level of development" (p. 85). The persistent pattern must

- occur for at least 6 months;
- be evident before age 7;
- interfere with the individual's social, educational, and occupational performance in two or more settings (e.g., home, school, work); and
- not be related to other medical or psychiatric conditions such as schizophrenia, or anxiety and mood disorders.

Types of ADD There are three types of students with ADD based on the unique characteristics that accompany their high levels of inattention (McKinley & Stormont, 2008). The first type includes students like Steven, whose attention deficit disorder is associated with constant motion. These students are referred to as students whose inattentiveness is accompanied by hyperactivity (ADHD-HI or ADDH), impulsivity, distractibility, and disorganization. In the classroom, their high level of activity and impulsivity may lead them to engage in such high-activity behaviors as fidgeting with hands and feet and objects, squirming, calling out, being out of seat, talking excessively, and interrupting others, which result in their failing to follow directions and to complete their work (Mulrine, Prater, & Jenkins, 2008). Socially, these students often engage in aggressive, intrusive, immature, impulsive, uncooperative, and bossy behaviors that may lead them to be rejected by their peers and adults. For example, they may fail to wait their turn during social activities or share with others, which can result in their classmates avoiding or rejecting them.

Nicole is an example of the second type of students with attention deficit disorders. These students are referred to as having an attention deficit disorder that is predominately of the inattentive type (ADD/I), without hyperactivity (ADD/WO), or undifferentiated attention deficit disorder (UADD) (Zambo, 2008). Like students with ADD with hyperactivity and impulsivity, these students engage in a variety of behaviors that reveal their inattention, distractibility, and disorganization. However, their inattentiveness appears to be related to their distractibility and preference for internal events rather than their frequent movements. Although these students tend not to be viewed as behavior problems, their classroom behavior may be characterized by their paying attention to extraneous information and stimuli; daydreaming; and appearing to be lethargic, shy, disorganized, and forgetful. Socially, while these students are less likely to exhibit behaviors that alienate their peers, they are often neglected and overlooked by peers. Students with the third type of attention deficit disorder exhibit multiple behaviors that are similar to both Steven and Nicole. These students, who make up the largest group of students with ADD, are referred to as students with a combination of hyperactivity and distractibility (ADHD-C).

All three types of students with ADD have several things in common. Their inattentiveness, disorganization, and poor motivation interfere with their learning, memory and academic performance, their social interactions and friendships with others, and their emotional development (Preston, Heaton, McCann, Watson, & Selke, 2009; Skowronek, Leichtman, & Pillemer, 2008). Because students with all three types of ADD also exhibit learning, behavioral, and social-emotional profiles that resemble other students with high-incidence disabilities and other health impairments, it is very difficult to differentiate the presence of ADD from one of these other conditions. Students who are gifted and talented also may exhibit behaviors that are similar to students with ADD. Educators also encounter difficulty in distinguishing the existence of ADD from the behavioral patterns found in children suffering from depression, residing in chaotic living conditions, and experiencing health and nutrition problems and auditory processing problems. Because of the differing cultural values and expectations of teachers and students, and because of acculturation issues, many students from culturally and linguistically diverse backgrounds are overidentified or underidentified as having ADD.

Although ADD is a psychiatric diagnosis and is not recognized as a separate disability under the IDEA, school districts must provide special education and related services to students with ADD under the IDEA if these students are otherwise health impaired, learning disabled, or emotionally disturbed (McKinley & Stormont, 2008). As we saw in Chapter 1, students with ADD who do not qualify for services under the IDEA can be eligible for services under Section 504. Whether students with ADD qualify for services under Section 504 or the IDEA, they will probably be educated in the general education classroom, requiring you to use a variety of effective educational interventions (Trout, Lienemann, Reid, & Epstein, 2007; Zentall, 2006). Because these students may be taking medication, you must also collaborate with their family members, their physician, and the school nurse to manage, monitor, and evaluate their response to these medications.

Students with Intellectual Disabilities

Making Connections
This change in terminology relates to our earlier discussion of the importance of language in Chapter 1. Find out more about how you can engage in respectful and positive actions and language that focus on students' abilities in Chapter 5.

The significant increase in students with learning disabilities has been paralleled by a decrease in students with intellectual disabilities to approximately 1%. The federal government still uses the term *students with **mental retardation*** to refer to students who demonstrate "significantly subaverage general intellectual functioning, existing concurrently with deficits in adaptive behavior and manifested during the developmental period, which adversely affects educational performance." However, because of the stigma associated with the term *mental retardation*, these individuals are now referred to as having an *intellectual disability,* which is defined as "significant limitations both in intellectual functioning and in adaptive behavior as expressed in conceptual, social, and practical adaptive skills. This disability originates before age 18" (Schalock et al., 2007, p. 118).

Learners with intellectual disabilities have traditionally been classified as having mild, moderate, or severe/profound conditions. They also have been classified in terms of the intensities of the supports they need: intermittent, limited, extensive, and pervasive (Turnbull et al., 2010). A growing number of students with intellectual disabilities are being educated in inclusive classrooms.

Students with *mild intellectual disabilities* have IQs that range from above 50 to below 75 and need intermittent and/or limited supports to foster their learning. Like their counterparts with other high-incidence disabilities, these students exhibit similar behaviors, are often now taught in general education classrooms, and benefit from your use of many of the same teaching practices.

However, whereas students with other high-incidence disabilities may have an uneven learning profile, with strengths and challenges in different areas, students with mild intellectual disabilities typically show a steady learning profile in all areas. In addition to memory, attention, and motivational difficulties, their learning profile also is characterized by their difficulties in learning and generalizing and applying their learning to other situations (Heward, 2009). These cognitive difficulties can result in the frustration of repeated school failure, which in turn may lead to low self-esteem, an inability to work independently, a mistrust of their own judgments, and an expectancy of failure. Many students with mild intellectual disabilities may also have poor social and behavioral skills, making it hard to interact with their peers (Rosenberg et al., 2008).

Students with *moderate intellectual disabilities* have IQ scores that range from 30 to 50, and they often need consistent and long-term supports to enhance their learning (Drew & Hardman, 2007). Learners with moderate intellectual disabilities also include several genetically based syndromes:

- **Down syndrome:** a condition associated with difficulties in learning and expressive and receptive language development and relative strengths in visual short-term memory
- **Fragile X syndrome:** a condition associated with learning, speech, mathematics, and language difficulties, and autistic-like behaviors

Helping Students with ADD Succeed

Ms. Postell liked Lewis but found him difficult to teach. No matter how hard Lewis tried, he was never able to pay attention and complete his work. He was frequently out of his seat asking her for help, looking out of the window, or bothering another student.

To help Lewis, Ms. Postell varied the types of activities, as well as the locations where students performed them. She followed a teacher-directed activity with a learning game or instructional activity that involved movement. She also adapted assignments by breaking them into smaller chunks, having students work for shorter periods of time and on one assignment at a time, and providing short breaks between activities so that they could move around. When she noticed that Lewis was getting restless, she gave him an excuse to leave his seat for a short time, such as taking a message to the office or sharpening a pencil for her.

Here are some other strategies you can use to implement the IDEA in your inclusive classroom and help students with ADD succeed:

- Vary the types of learning activities, minimize schedule changes, and limit distractions.
- Place students in work areas with no distracting features and clutter; away from stimulating areas such as doors, bulletin boards, and windows; and near positive role models and the teacher.
- Offer a structured program; set reasonable limits and boundaries; establish, post, and review schedules and rules; follow classroom routines; help students make transitions; and inform students in advance of deviations from the classroom routines and schedule.

- Give clear, concise, step-by-step written and verbal directions for assignments that include examples. Provide students with daily assignment sheets and encourage them to show all their work when completing assignments.
- Increase the motivational aspects of the curriculum and lessons and the attentional value of the materials as part of the lesson. For example, you can add novelty to lessons and tasks by using color, variation in size, movement, music, and games. You can also structure learning activities so that students are active and learn by doing.
- Give students choices concerning instructional activities and how they complete them. For example, offer students two or three activities and allow them to select one of them or give them choices about completing assignments with classmates or by standing when doing independent work.
- Incorporate outlets for students' energy within the classroom schedule such as hands-on learning activities, active instructional games, class jobs, movement oriented transitions, or the opportunity to squeeze a ball and to exercise.
- Help students organize their classwork and homework assignments. For example, you can encourage and prompt students to use daily assignment notebooks, different-colored folders and notebooks for each class, and daily and weekly schedules. You can also suggest that they wear a hip- or backpack to carry important information and items.

Sources: Austin and Sciarra (2010); Lerner and Johns (2007); McKinley and Stormont (2008); Mulrine et al. (2008); Zentall (2006).

- **Prader-Willi syndrome:** a condition associated with cognitive and sequential processing difficulties, obsessive-compulsive behaviors, and relative strengths in integrating stimuli into a unified whole
- **Williams syndrome:** a condition associated with anxieties and fears; heart and health problems; hypersensitivity to sound; difficulty with visual-spatial tasks; and relative strengths and talents in terms of language, sociability, verbal processing, and music (Murphy & Mazzocco, 2008; Taylor, Smiley, & Richards, 2009).

These students also have adaptive behavior needs that affect their daily functioning (Turnbull et al., 2010). Therefore, educational programs for these students often focus on the development of communication and on vocational, daily living, leisure, work, health and safety, and functional academic skills.

Students with *severe and profound intellectual disabilities* have IQ scores below 30 and may have significant cognitive, communication, behavioral, physical, speech/language, perceptual, and medical needs (Snell & Brown, 2006). Educational programs for these students help them live independently, contribute to and participate in society, and develop functional living and communication skills. While these students have traditionally been educated in self-contained classrooms or specialized schools, successful programs and instructional methods exist to integrate them into the mainstream of the school. Later in this chapter, we will learn more about students with significant cognitive disabilities.

Students with Speech and Language Disorders

Your class also will include students with speech and language disorders, who have difficulties receiving or sending information, ideas, and feelings (Owens, 2010). In the classroom they may experience difficulty following your directions, understanding and responding to your questions, expressing their thoughts, pronouncing words, learning new vocabulary, and being understood by others. Although the impact of speech and language disorders on students' behaviors varies, these communication difficulties can interfere with their learning, their literacy and writing skills, and their interactions with their classmates (Dockrell, Lindsay, & Connelly, 2009).

A student with a **speech and language impairment** has "a communication disorder such as stuttering, impaired articulation, a language impairment, or a voice impairment, that adversely affects educational performance." Although the cause of most communication disorders is difficult to identify, environmental factors such as vocal misuse, inappropriate language models, lack of language stimulation, and emotional trauma may contribute to a speech or language impairment. Also, students from various ethnic backgrounds and geographic regions may have limited experience with English or speak with a different dialect, so you should be careful in identifying these students as having a communication disorder (Roseberry-McKibbin, 2007).

Making Connections
Find out more about how to distinguish between learning and communication disorders and language differences in Chapter 3.

Students with speech and language disorders have receptive and expressive language difficulties that affect their communication and make it difficult for them to receive, understand, and express verbal messages in the classroom (Kuder, 2008). Whereas **speech-related disorders** refer to the verbal aspects of communicating and conveying meaning, **language-related disorders** address one's ability to understand and communicate meaning (Owens, 2010).

Speech and language disorders fall into two different types: receptive and expressive. **Receptive language** refers to the ability to understand spoken language. Students with receptive language problems may have difficulty following directions and understanding content presented orally.

Expressive language refers to the ability to express one's ideas in words and sentences. Students with expressive language disorders may be reluctant to join in verbal activities. This can impair both their academic performance and their social-emotional development. Expressive language problems may be due to speech disorders that include articulation, phonology, voice, and fluency disorders. **Articulation disorders** are motoric difficulties that result in omissions (e.g., the student says *ird* instead of *bird*), substitutions (the student says *wove* instead of *love*), distortions (the student may distort a sound so that it sounds like another sound), and additions (the student says *ruhace* for *race*). Phonological difficulties include students failing to use final consonants (the student says *ca* for *cat*) and unstressed syllables (the student says *bove* for *above*), or engaging in cluster reductions (the student says *tore* for *store*), and fronting (the student says *took* for *cook*). While articulation problems tend to consistently occur with a few sounds and have a limited impact on intelligibility, phonology-based disorders typically have an inconsistent impact on many sounds and have a significant impact on intelligibility.

Voice disorders relate to deviations in the pitch, volume, and quality of sounds produced. Breathiness, hoarseness, and harshness, as well as problems in resonance, are all indications of possible voice quality disorders. **Fluency disorders** relate to the rate and rhythm of an individual's speech. Stuttering is the most prevalent fluency disorder.

Some students with language disorders also may have **pragmatic** difficulties, which cause them to have problems understanding and following the rules that guide communication and language usage (Brice et al., 2007). As a result, they may have difficulty adjusting to different conversational contexts. For example, they may interrupt others or give the impression that they are not listening, which can affect their ability to initiate and maintain social relationships with others.

You can help students with speech and language disorders by creating a classroom that fosters language learning (Brice et al., 2007; Wegner & Edmister, 2007). You can create this type of environment by giving students opportunities to hear language and to speak; creating functional situations that encourage students to communicate; using concrete materials and hands-on learning activities that promote language; offering students academic and social activities that allow them to work, interact, and communicate with other students; asking students to relate classroom material to their lives; and designing the classroom to promote interactions and language (e.g., posting photographs and other visuals that promote discussion, and placing students' desks in groups rather than in rows).

STUDENTS WITH LOW-INCIDENCE DISABILITIES

WHAT ARE THE EDUCATIONAL STRENGTHS AND CHALLENGES OF STUDENTS WITH LOW-INCIDENCE DISABILITIES? Students with physical, sensory, and multiple and significant cognitive disabilities are sometimes referred to as having *low-incidence disabilities* because they make up approximately 6% of the students with disabilities. These students demonstrate a wide range of behaviors and are sometimes categorized based on the functional impact of their disabilities and the level of support that they need: mild, moderate, and severe. Because there is a great deal of variation in the characteristics of students with low-incidence disabilities, designing and implementing programs to meet the needs of these students is a challenge. However, you will find that teaching these students can be a rewarding, enjoyable, and fulfilling experience, and that they can succeed in your inclusive classroom.

Help Students Access the General Education Curriculum

Students with low-incidence disabilities can learn and participate in the general education curriculum (Lee, Soukup, Little, & Wehmeyer, 2009; Parrish & Stodden, 2009). You can help *all learners*, including those with low-incidence disabilities, gain access to the general education curriculum by doing the following:

- Analyzing the general education curriculum to identify the goals of the lesson/activity/assignment, link the goals to the learning standards and IEPs, and determine the extent to which students can participate in the lesson/activity/assignment without the use of instructional accommodations
- Delineating the rationale for the instructional goals and format(s), and the teaching strategies to be employed
- Enhancing the general education curriculum by incorporating IEP goals into the curriculum, adding content to the curriculum to foster success (e.g., learning strategies instruction), and identifying ways in which the content can be taught to students with a range of learning abilities and styles
- Making the general education curriculum more accessible by using universal design and instructional and assistive technology; adjusting the presentation and response modes, the instructional objectives, arrangement, and materials, and the pace, complexity, or size of the activity or assignment; and providing additional supports from peers and other adults
- Assessing student performance within the general education curriculum via use of formal and informal assessment strategies, and revising or continuing the educational program based on these data (Browder et al., 2007; Clayton, Burdge, Denham, Kleinert, & Kearns, 2006; Parrish & Stodden, 2009; Downing & Peckham-Hardin, 2007).

Some learners with low-incidence disabilities also may benefit from access to a **functional curriculum** that teaches them the skills they need to function independently in inclusive schools, their homes, and community settings; provides them with the social and communication skills to access the general education curriculum;

Helping Students with Expressive Language Disorders Succeed

Mr. Lombardi's class includes Jessie, a student who stutters. Mr. Lombardi finds it uncomfortable to watch Jessie struggle to express his thoughts, and he avoids asking him to respond. When Jessie does speak, Mr. Lombardi occasionally interrupts him and completes his sentences.

Mr. Lombardi approached Ms. Goldsmith, the speech and language teacher who works with Jessie in his class, for some suggestions. Ms. Goldsmith said, "Why don't you start by asking Jessie to respond to questions that can be answered with relatively few words, such as yes or no questions? Once he adjusts to that, you can ask him to respond to questions that require a more in-depth response. This way, you control the difficulty of the response, and you can help Jessie succeed and develop his confidence.

"If he struggles with a word or a sentence, telling him to relax, slow down, or to take a deep breath is not going to help him and he may even find comments like that demeaning. Be patient, and don't speak for him or interrupt him. In this way, you will serve as a model for the other students, who also will benefit from your teaching them how to respond to Jessie and other students who have difficulty expressing themselves. Let's make some time to talk about how we can teach the other students how to respond to Jessie."

Here are some strategies you can use to implement the IDEA in your inclusive classroom and help students who have difficulty responding orally succeed:

- Respond to what the students say rather than how they say it. Use your body language and facial expressions to show students that you are focused on the content of the communication.
- Make typical eye contact with students, and pause a few seconds before responding to show them how to relax, and to slow down the pace of the conversation.
- Stay calm, do not hurry students when they speak, criticize or correct their speech, or force them to speak in front of others.
- Teach all students how to respond to classmates who have expressive language difficulties.
- Have students read in unison with their classmates if they tend to stutter when reading aloud.

Sources: Brice et al. (2007); Kuder (2008); Owens (2010); Wegner and Edmister (2007).

---

and prepares them for successful transitions upon graduation from school (Downing, 2008; Rosenberg et al., 2008). Because these skills are best taught in natural and community-based settings, you can teach them to your students in real-life and inclusive environments such as your classroom or community settings (Westling & Fox, 2009).

Collaborate with Related Service Providers, Paraeducators, and Peers

Making Connections
Find out more about collaborating with other professionals in Chapter 4.

Because of their unique challenges and chronic conditions, some students with low-incidence disabilities may need the services of related service providers such as physical therapists; vision, hearing, orientation, and mobility specialists; speech and language professionals; paraeducators; and peers to access and succeed in inclusive settings (Taylor et al., 2009). You can also increase the effectiveness of the services these individuals provide by collaborating with them to establish goals, integrate these services throughout the school day, plan instruction, share responsibilities, reinforce and support each other's efforts, and evaluate student progress.

Use Assistive and Instructional Technology

Making Connections
Find out more about assistive and instructional technology in Chapter 8.

The educational, social, and behavioral performance of these students also can be fostered by providing them with the assistive and instructional technology they need to succeed in the general education classroom (Dell et al., 2008). These technologies—which can assist students with low-incidence disabilities in learning; accessing information; communicating; performing daily living skills; supporting, stabilizing, and protecting body parts; moving from one location to another; and participating in leisure activities—are discussed in subsequent chapters of this book.

Adopt a Competency-Oriented Approach

Learners with low-incidence disabilities are often thought of in terms of what they cannot do, and their relatively visible disabilities may affect how others perceive and interact with them (Best, 2005a). However, like their classmates, these learners display a full range of individual characteristics that include many positive traits that affect and enhance their learning, motivation, and ability to get along with others, and have a positive impact on their classmates.

In teaching these students, it is important for you to adopt a **competency-oriented approach** (Smith et al., 2009). Rather than seeing students in terms of what they cannot do, educators with a competency-oriented approach focus on what students *can* do, using these strengths to create a learning environment that supports their integration, participation, and growth, and maximizes their abilities.

You can implement a competency-oriented approach in your classroom by

Making Connections
Find out more about how to engage in behaviors that support a competency-oriented approach in Chapter 5.

- learning about students and what they can do,
- referring to students in terms of their strengths,
- recognizing and building on students' strengths,
- encouraging and acknowledging their positive contributions,
- being patient and taking the time to establish trusting relationships,
- building community in your classroom and promoting friendships among all students,
- having challenging expectations for them,
- treating them fairly and in age-appropriate ways,
- providing them with the same opportunities and choices as your other students,
- offering instructional activities that focus on their strengths and preferred methods of learning,
- using a variety of ways to assess their progress,
- meeting regularly with and coordinating your activities with their families, and
- taking risks and learning from them (Smith, 2009; Smith et al., 2009; Turnbull et al., 2010).

Understand and Address Students' Unique Abilities, Challenges, and Preferences

Learners with low-incidence disabilities vary greatly in terms of their abilities, challenges, and preferences. Some students with low-incidence disabilities will need access accommodations such as the use of Braille to succeed in your classroom, whereas others will have more significant cognitive needs, which will mean that you have to make significant adjustments in what and how you teach them. Therefore, you also can support their learning and access to appropriate general education and functional curricula by understanding their unique abilities and needs and using effective teaching practices that address these characteristics (Downing, 2008), which are discussed in the following sections.

Students with Physical and Health Needs Students with physical disabilities are identified as students with orthopedic impairments or students with other health impairments. **Students with orthopedic impairments** are defined as having a

> severe orthopedic impairment which adversely affects a child's educational performance. The term includes impairments caused by congenital anomaly (e.g., clubfoot, absence of some member, etc.), impairments caused by disease (e.g., poliomyelitis, bone tuberculosis, etc.), and impairments from other causes (e.g., cerebral palsy, amputations, and fractures or burns which cause contractures).

Students with other health impairments are defined as having

Students with special physical and health needs can learn to perform their routine health care procedures independently, like this student who is testing his blood sugar levels. How can you and your colleagues support students in developing their independence?

limited strength, vitality, or alertness, including a heightened alertness to environmental stimuli, that results in limited alertness with respect to the educational environment, that is due to chronic or acute health problems such as attention deficit disorder, a heart condition, tuberculosis, rheumatic fever, nephritis, asthma, sickle-cell anemia, epilepsy, lead poisoning, leukemia, diabetes, or Tourette syndrome which adversely affects educational performance.

The term *other health impaired* can also include students who are medically fragile or those who may be dependent on technological devices for ventilation, oxygen, and tube feeding.

Because of the many conditions included in this category, its specific characteristics are hard to define and vary greatly from student to student. Students with physical and health conditions tend to have IQ scores within the normal range and have numerous educational, social, technological, and health care needs.

When developing inclusive education programs for these students, you need to be aware of several factors (Heller, Forney, Alberto, Best, & Schwartzman, 2009). Although many of these conditions are stable, some are progressive, and others are terminal (Best, 2005a). Some of these conditions are **congenital**, which means they are present at birth; others are **acquired**, which means they are due to an illness or accident. Because of their conditions, these students may be absent frequently or may have limited exposure to certain experiences that we take for granted. It also is important to remember that these students and their families have mobility, physical, medical, and social-emotional needs that you should address. Be aware of the importance of your communication and collaboration with the student's family and medical providers, as well as the educational rights of students with special health care needs (Heller, Forney, 2009). Finally, professional organizations can provide information, resources, and support groups for students and their families.

The progress of some students, particularly those with physical and sensory disabilities, also depends on the use of adaptive and prosthetic devices. The failure of these devices to work properly can limit the likelihood of success for students who need them; therefore, monitor their working condition. If there are problems, you should contact students' families or appropriate educational and medical personnel.

Students with Cerebral Palsy **Cerebral palsy**, which affects voluntary motor functions and muscle tension or tone, is caused by damage to the central nervous system before birth or during one's early years (Heller & Garrett, 2009). It is not hereditary, contagious, progressive, or curable (Best & Bigge, 2005). Although there is no typical student with cerebral palsy, students with cerebral palsy may have seizures; perceptual difficulties; and motor, sensory, and speech impairments. There are four primary types of cerebral palsy—hypertonia, hypotonia, athetosis, and ataxia—and some students have a combination of these conditions:

- **Hypertonia:** movements that are jerky, exaggerated, and poorly coordinated
- **Hypotonia:** loose, flaccid musculature and sometimes difficulty maintaining balance
- **Athetosis** (also referred to as *dyskinetic*): uncontrolled and irregular movements usually occurring in the arms, hands, or face
- **Ataxia:** difficulties in balancing and using the hands

Because their educational program will need to address their motor and physical needs, you will need to collaborate with physical and occupational therapists,

Helping Students with Cerebral Palsy Succeed

As the school year was coming to an end, Mr. Lewis thought about his first interactions with Linda, a student with cerebral palsy. At first he was too protective; he underestimated her abilities and limited her participation in certain activities. He remembered that the turning point for him was seeing Linda during physical education class with the other students. Although her movements were limited, she was every bit as competitive as the other students. From that moment on, he began to treat Linda like other students. He assigned her classroom jobs, reprimanded her when she misbehaved, and encouraged her to participate in all classroom and school activities. Rather than excusing her from assignments, he gave her more time to complete them, reduced the amount of board work and textbook copying she had to do, placed rubber bands or plastic tubing around the shaft of her writing utensil, and gave her felt-tipped pens and soft lead pencils so that she could write with less pressure.

Here are some other strategies you can use to implement the IDEA in your inclusive classroom and help students with cerebral palsy succeed:

- Do not hesitate to ask students to repeat themselves if others do not understand their comments.
- Learn how to lift, position, reposition, and transfer students who use wheelchairs; teach students to reposition themselves; and learn how to push wheelchairs (see Campbell, 2006; Peck, 2004).
- Give students two copies of books: one set for use in school and the other set for use at home.
- Give students copies of class notes and assignments and easy access to personal and classroom supplies.
- Plan students' schedules so that they move from class to class when the hallways are less crowded.

medical personnel, and family members to foster their learning, socialization, independence, and physical, communication, and emotional development. Best and Bigge (2005) offer information, strategies, and resources that can help you create an inclusive classroom that addresses the needs of students with cerebral palsy.

Students with Spina Bifida   Another group of students with unique physical, medical, and learning needs are those with **spina bifida** (Heller, 2009c). Spina bifida is caused by the failure of the vertebrae of the spinal cord to close properly, which usually results in paralysis of the lower limbs, as well as loss of control over bladder function. Students with spina bifida often have good control over the upper body but may need to use a prosthetic device for mobility such as a walker, braces, or crutches. They also may need a catheter or bag to minimize bladder control difficulty and a shunt for hydrocephalus. Spina bifida can affect students' cognitive, physical, social-emotional, and language development and many of these students may have nonverbal learning disorders.

In addition to designing and implementing programs that meet their academic and social needs, you can help these students by working with the school nurse to address their medical challenges (Heller, 2009c). Because students with spina bifida may be dependent on others to assist them with their physical needs, it is very important for you to foster their independence and socialization with others (Best, 2005c).

Students with Asthma and Allergies   **Asthma** is a treatable respiratory ailment causing difficulty in breathing due to constriction and inflammation of the airways (Heller, Schwartzman, & Fowler, 2009). It is the most common childhood chronic illness and the leading cause of absence from school. The symptoms of asthma, which can occur at any age, vary and include repeated episodes of wheezing, sneezing, coughing, shortness of breath, and tightness in the chest. The conditions that trigger an asthma or allergy attack also vary and include stress; respiratory viruses; exertion and exercise; certain weather conditions; strong emotions; pollens; pet dander; and airborne irritants such as smoke, strong odors, and chemical sprays (Dozor, 2009).

By being aware of the stimuli that trigger students' asthma and allergies, you can create learning conditions and activities that minimize the likelihood of an attack (Heller, Schwartzman, & Fowler, 2009). In working with these students, you may need to observe their unique reactions and warning signs, and learn about each student's

Asthma is the most common childhood chronic illness. How do you minimize the likelihood that students with asthma and allergies will experience an attack?

asthma and allergy management plan and your school's policies for dealing with asthma and emergency medical treatments (Best, 2005b; Dozor, 2009). You also may need to deal with frequent absences, collaborate with families and medical personnel, help make sure that students who use inhalers carry them at all times, and understand the side effects of medications on behavior and learning. Also, keep the classroom free of dust, plants, perfumes, strong smells, cold or dry air, and other materials and situations that trigger reactions; and understand the students' capacity for physical activities. You can try to keep your classroom and school as germ-free as possible by teaching your students to wash their hands using soap and water for at least 15 seconds (about the time to sing "Happy Birthday"); to cover their mouths while coughing or sneezing by using disposable tissues (it is good for idea for you to make them available to your students) or their clothing rather than their hands; and to avoid sharing food, drinks, and utensils. You also can teach *all students* about asthma and allergies using the American Lung Association's Open Airways for Schools curriculum (www.lungusa.org).

Some of your students may have food allergies, which can affect their well-being (Parker-Pope, 2009). While the types and severity of food allergies vary, you need to be aware of the foods that your students must avoid and ways to keep them safe. Therefore, it is important for you to collaborate with your students' families and medical and nutritional personnel to learn about your students' conditions and the foods they must avoid. When necessary, it is also important for you to

- be especially vigilant during holidays, special events, and birthday celebrations;
- establish policies that prevent food sharing;
- refrain from reusing food containers;
- maintain jars of family-provided foods that are safe for students;
- use and label eating and serving utensils for use with different foods;
- clean tables using different rags;
- share information about food allergies with other professionals including substitute teachers; and
- understand and follow procedures in case of an emergency.

Students with Tourette's Syndrome Your classroom also may include students with **Tourette's syndrome (TS)**, an inherited neurological condition whose symptoms appear in childhood (Christner & Dieker, 2008). These symptoms may include involuntary multiple muscle movements and tics, and uncontrolled, repeated verbal responses such as noises (laughing, coughing, throat clearing), words, or phrases. These symptoms vary greatly from individual to individual in terms of their frequency, type, and level of severity, but most students with TS are males and exhibit relatively mild symptoms. The symptoms—which are affected by stress, fatigue, and environmental factors such as noises, words, and pictorials—appear and disappear at various times, change over time, and may result in others being scared, annoyed, or amused. Although many students with TS perform well academically, others may have learning disabilities, language disorders, obsessive-compulsive behaviors, anxiety attacks, and difficulty paying attention and controlling impulses, which may result in academic, behavioral, social, and self-esteem difficulties (Christner & Dieker, 2008; Prestia, 2003).

Students with Diabetes At some point, you will have a student with **diabetes**, a chronic metabolic condition (Getch, Bhukhanwala, & Neuharth-Pritchett, 2007). These students lack enough insulin and therefore have trouble gaining energy from food. Be aware of the symptoms of diabetes, including fatigue, hunger, frequent requests for liquids, repeated trips to the bathroom, unhealthy skin color, headaches, vomiting and nausea, failure of cuts and sores to heal, loss of weight despite adequate food intake, poor circulation as indicated by complaints about cold hands and feet, and abdominal pain (Scruggs, 2008). When a student has some of these symptoms, contact the student's family, the school nurse, or another medical professional (Getch et al., 2007).

For diabetic students, be aware of the signs of **hyperglycemia** (high blood sugar) and **hypoglycemia** (low blood sugar) and be able to act in an emergency (Heller, 2009a). Students with hyperglycemia are thirsty, tired, and lethargic and have dry, hot skin, loss of appetite, difficulty breathing, and breath that has a sweet, fruity odor. Those with hypoglycemia are confused, drowsy, inattentive, irritable and dizzy, perspiring, shaking, and hungry, with headaches and a pale complexion. When these conditions occur, you must be prepared to act and contact medical personnel immediately. In the case of hyperglycemia, it may be appropriate to have the student drink water or diet soda. For hypoglycemia, it may be appropriate to give the student a source of sugar immediately, such as a half cup of fruit juice, two large sugar cubes, or a can of regular soda. Therefore, you should keep these supplies in your classroom so that they are readily available in case of an emergency.

You can take certain actions to help students with diabetes succeed in school (Getch et al., 2007; Heller, 2009a). You can limit hyperglycemia or hypoglycemia by making sure that students eat at the right times. Observe students after physical education class and recess and make sure that their blood sugar levels are measured at appropriate times. You may need to modify your rules so that students with diabetes can eat snacks and leave the classroom as needed, as well as refrain from penalizing them for frequent absences and lateness. It may be necessary to reschedule tests or other activities for students with diabetes if their performance is affected by their condition. Finally, you can work with the school nurse, family members, certified diabetes educators, and students with diabetes, if they are willing, to develop an

IDEAs to Implement Inclusion

Helping Students with TS Succeed

You could see the signs of anguish on Ms. Dean's face as her principal told her that Frank, a student with Tourette's syndrome (TS), would be joining her class next week. Ms. Dean prided herself on how well behaved her students were, and as she read about Frank's periodic episodes of uncontrolled verbal responses, she was worried about how they would affect her students and her ability to manage their behavior.

Ms. Dean's principal suggested that she talk to Mr. Lopez, a special education teacher who had worked with Frank in the past. Mr. Lopez told her, "Frank is really a neat kid. He works hard, and he's got a wonderful sense of humor. You're going to like him."

Ms. Dean said, "I'm sure he's a nice kid. But what do you do when he starts having his episodes?" Mr. Lopez said, "I spoke to Frank and his family about my concerns. They were worried about it as well. We came up with the following system. Before Frank's verbalizations became uncontrollable and distracting, we created a situation that allowed him to leave the room for short periods of time. I would ask him to take a message to the office or return a book to the library and he would go to a private location like the nurse's office. Sometimes, when Frank sensed an episode coming on, he signaled me and he left the room. It worked pretty well.

"I also helped the other students learn about and understand the needs of students with TS. I showed the class the video

I Have Tourette's but Tourette's Doesn't Have Me (Kent & Aala, 2005), which showed several students with TS in social and school settings and sharing information about TS. The students were very supportive and understanding of Frank."

Here are some other strategies you can use to implement the IDEA in your inclusive classroom and help students with TS succeed:

- Be patient, and react to students' involuntary inappropriate behavior with tolerance rather than anger.
- Seat students near the front of the class and the teacher's desk so that they can be subtly redirected to pay attention.
- Offer students with vocal tics the opportunity to drink water throughout the day to avoid throat dryness.
- Use alternative assignments to minimize the stress on students with TS such as having students create a video of a presentation rather than doing a live presentation in front of the class.
- Offer activities to develop students' social and friendship making skills.

Sources: Bronheim (n.d.); Christner and Dieker (2008); Prestia (2003).

individualized health care plan and to educate *all students* about diabetes. For example, you can conduct health science lessons about diabetes and introduce diabetes to students via books.

Students with Seizure Disorders   Some students, including those with physical disabilities and other health impairments, may have seizures. When these seizures occur on a regular basis, the individual is said to be suffering from a *convulsive disorder* or **epilepsy** (Heller & Cohen, 2009). There are several types of seizures: tonic-clonic, tonic, absence, and complex and simple partial seizures.

- *Tonic-clonic seizure*. Formerly referred to as *grand mal,* this type of seizure is marked by loss of consciousness and bladder control, stiff muscles, saliva drooling out of the mouth, and violent body shaking. After a brief period, the individual may fall asleep or regain consciousness and experience confusion.

- *Tonic seizure*. A tonic seizure involves sudden stiffening of the muscles. Because the individual becomes rigid and may fall to the ground, these seizures often cause injuries.

- *Absence seizure*. Also referred to as *petit mal,* this type of seizure is characterized by a brief period in which the individual loses consciousness, appears to be daydreaming, looks pale, and drops any objects he or she is holding.

- *Complex and simple partial seizures.* When a seizure affects only a limited part of the brain, it is called a *partial seizure*. Also referred to as a *psychomotor seizure*, a complex partial seizure is characterized by a short period in which the individual remains conscious but engages in inappropriate and bizarre behaviors. After 2 to 5 minutes, the individual regains control and often does not remember what happened. During a partial seizure, the individual also remains conscious and may twitch and experience a feeling of déjà vu. Prior to these seizures, students may experience an *aura* or a *prodrome,* a sensation and a symptom indicating that a seizure is imminent.

Suggestions for dealing with seizures in your classroom are presented in Figure 2.8.

Students Treated for Cancer   Many students treated for cancer are attending school, which can provide a normalizing experience for them and enhance their quality of life (Frenette, 2006). The type and length of cancer therapy vary. However, while many treatments are effective in treating the cancer, they are toxic and can affect the student's cognitive, gross and fine motor, language, sensory, neurological, and social-emotional development, as well as resulting in life-threatening chronic health problems (Hall, 2008). Frequent or lengthy hospitalizations resulting in erratic school attendance also can hinder learning, self-esteem, and socialization. While returning to school can be educationally and emotionally important to these students in resuming and gaining control over their lives, they may experience physical and psychological challenges, including dealing with depression, social anxiety, fatigue, pain, sensory loss, poor self-concepts, and school phobia (Heller, 2009a). You can work with others to facilitate their readjustment to school by developing and implementing a transition plan, learning about the student's condition and treatment including possible side effects, establishing close communication with the student's family, and maintaining contact when the student is in the hospital or receiving homebound instruction (Frenette, 2006).

Students with cancer may also be embarrassed by their appearance and worried about losing their friends and being teased by their peers. Therefore, although you need to be sensitive to their unique needs, it is also important for you to treat them in ways that acknowledge what they can do and make them feel like their classmates (Spinelli, 2004). You also can collaborate with the student, family members, other educators, and medical professionals to address these concerns by using interactive activities that help the student's peers understand the student's illness, including the fact that cancer is not contagious and that radiation treatments don't

FIGURE 2.8 Guidelines for dealing with seizures

Students who have seizures need few accommodations in the general education setting, but you can minimize the potentially harmful effects of a seizure by carefully structuring the classroom environment and considering the following guidelines before, during, and after a seizure occurs.

BEFORE THE SEIZURE

- Be aware of the warning signs that indicate an impending seizure, and encourage the student to speak to you immediately if he or she is able to recognize the aura or prodrome. In these cases, if time allows, remove the student to a private and safe location.
- Encourage the student with epilepsy to wear a Medic-Alert bracelet or necklace or carry a wallet card.
- Teach students about epilepsy and what to do when a classmate has a seizure. With the student's permission, you, the school nurse, the student, and family members can talk with the class about epilepsy and how to respond to seizures. Books such as *Taking Seizure Disorders to School* (Gosselin, 1996) can be used to introduce students to these issues.

DURING THE SEIZURE

- Prevent the student from being injured during a seizure by staying composed and keeping the other students calm (it often helps to remind the class that the seizure is painless).
- Do not restrain the student, place fingers or objects in the student's mouth, or give the student anything to eat or drink.
- Make the student as comfortable as possible by helping him or her to lie down and loosening tight clothing.
- Protect the student by placing a soft, cushioned object under the head, ensuring that the space around the student's work area is large enough to thrash around in, and keeping the area around the student's desk free of objects that could harm the student during the seizure.

AFTER THE SEIZURE

- Help the student by positioning the student's head to one side to allow the discharge of saliva that may have built up in the mouth; briefly discussing the seizure with the class, encouraging acceptance rather than fear or pity; providing the student with a rest area in which to sleep; and documenting the seizure.
- Contact other necessary school and medical personnel and the student's family.
- Document and share with others relevant information regarding a student's seizure. Kuhn, Allen, and Shriver (1995) and Michael (1992) have developed a Seizure Observation Form that can help you record the student's behavior before the seizure, initial seizure behavior, behavior during the seizure, behavior after the seizure, actions taken by you, the student's reaction to the seizure, peer reactions to the seizure, and your comments.

Sources: Heller and Cohen (2009); Michael (1995); Spiegel, Cutler, and Yetter (1996).

make the individual "radioactive" (Frenette, 2006). Peers also may benefit from understanding treatments and their side effects. In addition, you may need to handle issues related to dying and death (Heath et al., 2008). Guidelines and resources to help you deal with these issues with students, families, and colleagues and understand the grieving process are available (Frenette, 2009; Heath et al., 2008; Jellinek, Bostic, & Schlozman, 2007; Spinelli, 2004).

Medically Fragile Students School districts are serving an increasing number of students who are **medically fragile** (Rues, Graff, Ault, & Holvoet, 2006). While not all students who are medically fragile require special education services, these students do require the use of specialized technological health care procedures to maintain their health and/or provide life support.

Medically fragile students have a variety of chronic and progressive conditions, including congenital malformations; loss of limbs; and neurological, infectious, or muscular diseases such as cystic fibrosis and muscular dystrophy (Best & Heller, 2009a, 2009b; Heller, Mezei, & Schwartzman, 2009; Heller & Schwarzman, 2009). While the developmental needs and academic performance of these students and the extent and nature of their disabilities may vary, these students have comprehensive medical needs and important socialization needs. In classroom situations, these students may have limited vitality and mobility, fatigue, attention and learning problems. Heller (2009b) and Rues, Graff, Ault, and Holvoet (2006) offer information, strategies, sample forms and resources regarding the delivery of special health care procedures and services.

Decisions on their educational program and placement should be based on their medical and educational needs and should be made in conjunction with families and support personnel such as physical, occupational, and respiratory therapists, doctors, and nurses who can work with you to develop health care plans for these students and make instructional accommodations to address their needs (Best, 2005b; Heller, 2009b). The health plan may need to address such issues as giving students rest periods, help in the lunchroom (e.g., carrying their trays, special dietary considerations), assistive technology, electric devices (e.g., electric pencil sharpener), locker assistance, modified physical activity, early release to help them move from class to class, and schedule adjustments (e.g., shortened day, periods, and bus routes). You can help these students by allowing them to use assistive and instructional technology to obtain, retain, and present information and have an extra set of books for use at home (Heller et al., 2008). They may benefit from use of a desk podium to raise their papers or use of a marker instead of a pencil. You can also minimize their fatigue by limiting the number of motor responses you ask them to make. For example, you can limit boardwork and textbook copying by providing them with peer note takers, as well as written copies of directions and other important information.

The social and emotional needs of the student must also be considered. Their needs include embarrassment related to the symptoms associated with their conditions, the side effects of treatment on their appearance and behavior, dependence on medical devices, difficulty in accepting their illness, withdrawal and depression, and the need for friendships. Create opportunities for these students to participate in social activities with peers. For example, you can encourage social interactions with others by teaching adults and other students to talk directly to the student rather than to the student's aide or nurse.

When working with these students, become familiar with their equipment, ventilation management, cardiopulmonary resuscitation, universal precautions, and other necessary procedures (Best, 2009; Heller, 2009b). It is necessary to understand the warning signs indicating that equipment needs repair; make sure that replacement equipment is readily available; and establish procedures for dealing with health emergencies, equipment problems, and power failures, as well as minimizing interruptions due to medical interventions that the student may need.

Students with Traumatic Brain Injury   Another group of students who have diverse learning, physical and medical needs are those with **traumatic brain injury (TBI)** (Arroyos-Jurado & Savage, 2008; Grandinette & Best, 2009). TBI is defined as

> an acquired injury to the brain caused by an external physical force, resulting in total or partial functional disability or psychosocial impairment, or both, that adversely affects educational performance. The term applies to open or closed head injuries resulting in impairments in one or more areas, such as cognition; language; memory; attention; reasoning; abstract thinking; judgment; problem-solving; sensory, perceptual, and motor abilities; psychosocial behavior; physical functions; information processing; and speech. The term does not apply to brain injuries that are congenital or degenerative, or brain injuries induced by birth trauma.

TBI may be categorized as mild, moderate, or severe, depending on how long one loses consciousness, whether there is a skull fracture, and the extent and nature of the after effects. The characteristics of students with TBI depend on their level of functioning prior to the injury, the nature and location of the injury, their recovery time, and the age at which it occurred (Arroyos-Jurado & Savage, 2008). Table 2.1 describes the effects of TBI on students and strategies for helping them in your classroom. In addition, you can help students recognize what they can do rather than only what they are no longer able to do. It also is helpful to remain calm and redirect students when their behavior is inappropriate.

It is important to be aware of the differences between students with TBI and those with learning and behavioral problems. The performance and behavior of students with TBI tend to be more variable than those of students with learning

Making Connections
Find out more about ways to poster acceptance and friendships in Chapter 5.

TABLE 2.1 **Characteristics of and strategies for accommodating students with Traumatic Brain Injury (TBI)**

Effects of TBI:	Provide Student with:	Teach by:
Cognitive and Academic Skill Impacts • Memory • Problem-solving and planning • Attention and concentration • Reading recognition and comprehension • Mathematics calculation and reasoning	• Diagrams, maps, charts, or other graphic cues • Cognitive organizers • Opportunities for problem-solving in functional settings • Preferential seating, proximity to visual or auditory aids and instructional assistance • Personal work space free from distracting stimuli • Individual peer tutor or opportunities to participate in structured collaborative groups	• Using strategies for problem-solving and copying (self-talk, verbal rehearsal, self-questioning, reflection) • Memory aids (visualization, mnemonic devices, paraphrasing, and retelling) • Using survey and preview techniques • Providing practice in guided reading activities • Task analyzing academic requirements • Using a variety of prompts and fading as self-regulation improves
Language Impacts • Expressive • Receptive • Written language	• Support from related services personnel • Assistive technology to communicate and process information and to accommodate motor and sensory deficits • Age-appropriate language models • Opportunities for structured and unstructured communication exchange • Visual aids in conjunction with auditory input • Functional materials and experiential learning opportunities	• Modeling questioning techniques • Providing appropriate wait time to formulate and respond to questions • Teaching note-taking formats and practicing during guided lectures • Stressing previewing, active listening, brainstorming, and reviewing from notes and graphic aids • Checking comprehension regularly • Conducting frequent cumulative review • Teaching specific spelling and production strategies • Matching complexity of instructional language to student's PLP (Present Level of Performance) • Modifying writing requirements based on PLP
Social Impacts • Peer/adult interactions • Labile mood • Self-concept • Verbal outbursts or aggressive episodes • Response to stress/demands • Pragmatic language	• Support from related services personnel having expertise in social communication skill development • Support from peer, buddy, and cooperative learning partners • Strategies and skills for dealing with anger and frustration • Systems for self-monitoring behavior and charting progress • Varied schedules of reinforcement • Structured environment • External cues (charts, contracts, graphs, posted rules, timers, etc.)	• Conducting ecological analysis prior to programming • Identifying TBI-related behaviors and collaboratively developing consistent, positive support plans • Conducting an analysis of the communicative intent of behaviors and teaching skills appropriate to individual needs • Targeting behaviors of greatest concern and implementing behavioral changes gradually

(Continued)

TABLE 2.1 **Continued**

Effects of TBI:	Provide Student with:	Teach by:
	• Opportunity to remove self and place to go when overwhelmed by stimuli and demands of environment • Opportunities for success with activities appropriate to PLP • System to alert student to problems and cues for redirection to desired target behaviors	• Using direct instruction, modeling, role playing, and scripting to teach specific social and communication skills • Encouraging practice across natural environments • Teaching skills in small group & structured settings • Generalizing skills to larger, less structured contexts
Organizational Skill Impacts • Assignment completion • Arrangement and retrieval of materials • Organization of personal work space • Time management • Orientation and direction	• Group, class, or individual schedule • Daily or weekly calendar and materials checklist corresponding to schedule demands • Individual work area with provision for materials and completed tasks • Notebooks with dividers, colored folders, plastic bins, or portfolio containers • Reduced assignments and/or additional time • Opportunities to practice transition routes (e.g., classroom to cafeteria)	• Using consistent routine, introducing gradual changes in routine • Teaching organizational skills directly related to planning, material organization, and schedule completion • Implementing schedule systems and other organizational cues that transfer across settings and individuals (e.g., resource room to general education settings) • Clearly delineating areas of the classroom by purpose (personal space, leisure areas, centers for instruction) • Collaborating with personnel to consistently provide organizational cues

Source: From "What are multidisciplinary and ecobehavioral approaches?" by J. Doelling, S. Bryde, and H.P. Parette, 1997, *Teaching Exceptional Children, 30*, pp. 58–59. Copyright 1997 by The Council for Exceptional Children. Reprinted by permission.

PEARSON
myeducationlab

To enhance your understanding of students with health needs and the individuals you can collaborate with to help them succeed in your inclusive classroom, go to the IRIS Center Resources section of Topic: Physical Disabilities and Health Impairments in the MyEducationLab for your course, and complete the module entitled *Working with Your School Nurse: What General Education Teachers Should Do to Promote Educational Success for Students with Health Needs.*

and behavioral disabilities. Thus, they may be able to perform algebra and fail to remember monetary values. In the 6 months to a year following their injury, students with TBI also may make accelerated gains in their academic skills, which can be followed by subsequent plateaus and advances in learning.

Students with TBI also are more likely to tire easily, have headaches, and feel overwhelmed and frustrated. Therefore, you may need to provide them with periodic breaks, schedule important classes when students are most alert, adjust their workloads and deadlines, and divide assignments into smaller units (Arroyos-Jurado & Savage, 2008). It also is important to keep in mind that students with TBI and their family members, friends, and teachers remember successful experiences before the trauma occurred, which can cause psychosocial problems for everyone involved. In particular, adolescents with a brain injury may have trouble coping with the reality of their new condition (Parker Adams & Adams, 2008). Because these students have probably been treated in hospitals, they may need help in making the transition back to school (Turnbull et al., 2010). It is important to (a) establish and maintain communication with families, (b) obtain information about the student's injuries and their consequences from families and medical personnel, and (c) be sensitive to families and understand the pressures associated with having a child with TBI.

Students with Autism Spectrum Disorder Your classroom also will include students with **autism spectrum disorder (ASD)**, a broad continuum of cognitive and neurobehavioral conditions that typically include sensory impairments and difficulties in socialization and communication coupled with repetitive patterns of behavior (Ben-Arieh & Miller, 2009; Owen-DeSchryver et al., 2008). Because autism is viewed as a *spectrum* disorder, students with autism vary greatly with some students having relatively mild symptoms and others having more severe symptoms (Hall, 2009). Thus, some students with ASD may have intellectual disabilities; others may be selected for participation in programs for students who are gifted and talented.

In addition to students with autism and Asperger syndrome (which is discussed next), ASD also includes students with the following interrelated conditions:

- **Childhood disintegrative disorder**: a condition associated with a loss of speech and other previously learned skills and the presence of other autistic like behaviors following an initial period of normal development.
- ***Rett syndrome***: a progressive genetic disorder affecting girls which affects one's neurological development and often includes a loss of previously learned skills, repetitive hand movements, and a loss of functional use of one's hands (Katsiyannis, Ellenburg, Acton, & Torrey, 2001).
- ***Pervasive developmental disorder—not otherwise specified (PDD-NOS)*** *or atypical autism:* a condition that resembles autism but is usually not as severe or extensive.

Autism, also referred to as *pervasive developmental disorder* (*PDD*), is a complex developmental neurological condition. It usually involves severe disorders in verbal and nonverbal communication, socialization, and behavior that typically occur at birth or within the first 3 years of life. Students with autism may have trouble staying engaged, responding to verbal cues and interacting with others, displaying affect, showing affection, and forming attachments with others. They may engage in repetitive and perseverative movements and stereotypic behavior, exhibit various inappropriate behaviors, and have challenges learning and understanding and using language and engaging in prosocial behaviors (Hall, 2009). They also may be resistant to playing with others or to changes in routines, and be over- or undersensitive to some types of sensory stimuli (Westling & Fox, 2009).

One form of ASD is known as **Asperger syndrome**, which some people call *high-functioning autism* (Smith Myles, 2006). While their academic performance and IQ usually varies from average to exceptional, students with Asperger syndrome tend to have social skill challenges, be very literal and fact oriented, have good but rigid verbal skills, and adhere strictly to routines, which can hinder their learning, communication, social interactions, and postschool outcomes (Bianco, Carothers, & Smiley, 2009; Smith Myles et al., 2007). These individuals also may have a narrow range of interests and fascinations, resulting in their displaying great interest in and talking a lot about esoteric subjects (e.g., train schedules, ceiling fans) (Winter-Messiers, 2007). They also make have an increased sensitivity to noise and light and experience difficulties with fine and gross motor skills (Wexler, 2009). As a result, they may have difficulty completing assignments, paying and maintaining attention, processing information, following classroom routines, making transitions, communicating and establishing friendships with others, and responding to traditional consequence-based classroom management systems (Marks, Hudson, Schrader, Longaker, & Levine, 2006). Because these students also may exhibit obsessive-compulsive behaviors, misinterpret social, facial, and nonverbal cues, they may be socially awkward, anxious, or intrusive and therefore may not make friends of the same age or may appear to be rude, nervous, or aggressive.

Because they display a wide range of characteristics depending on the nature and severity of their ASD, these students also vary greatly in ability and personality (Hall, 2009). While some may have cognitive disabilities, others may benefit from participation in your school's program for students who are identified as gifted and talented (see Bianco et al. [2009] for suggestions and resources for working with gifted students with Asperger syndrome). Socially, some may prefer to be alone and others may develop an enjoyment in socializing with others.

Many teaching and classroom management strategies can be used to promote the learning and prosocial behaviors of students with ASD in general education classrooms. You can

- recognize and value students' individualized strengths, interests, and talents and use them to motivate and help them learn (Mancil & Pearl [2008] offer guidelines and examples of ways you can incorporate students' interests into your instruction);
- provide students with alternative ways to complete assignments;
- minimize their sensory overstimulation by using visual supports that help them understand verbal information, and social and environmental demands (e.g., presenting directions via black and white pictures, using icons to represent locations and actions and pictorials to present choices, schedules, and rules, placing masking tape on floors to mark areas), providing tactile cueing (e.g., prompting students to pay attention via a tap on their shoulders) and auditory cues (e.g., using verbal reminders or finger snaps to sustain attention), and making environmental changes (e.g., adjusting the lighting, eliminating distracting noises, or using colored transparencies);
- help students maintain their self-esteem and find mentors, heroes, and friends with and without disabilities;
- establish and follow routines, help students make transitions to activities, and make instructions and expectations brief, concrete, explicit, and clear;
- use positive behavioral supports, students' interests, and structure in the classroom to increase their appropriate behaviors and decrease their inappropriate behaviors;
- create a learning environment that is respectful of individual differences and does not tolerate teasing and bullying;

Making Connections
Find out more about ways to prevent bullying in Chapter 7.

- highlight key concepts and use graphic organizers, word and symbol cards, posters, photographs, and visual activity schedules that prompt these students to understand language and the sequence of activities, and to use prosocial behaviors;
- use **priming**, which involves familiarizing students with new activities, information, routines, and materials prior to introducing them in class;
- provide students with alternatives to stressful situations or overstimulating environments (e.g., noisy lunchroom), such as a home base where they can go to escape stress, prevent behavioral incidents, regain control of their behavior, and organize themselves;
- teach students to use visualize information and events and learning strategies that guide them in performing academic and social activities and remembering important information (a personal digital assistant [PDA] can offer reminders to guide these students to engage in specific prosocial and learning behaviors);

Making Connections
Find out more about how to teach social skills in Chapter 5.

- use social skill training programs and strategies such as social stories and comic strip conversations to help them learn to read social cues, take turns, initiate interactions with others, ask for help from others, comply with rules, and work and play cooperatively with others;
- work with families and related service providers to learn more about the students' strengths, skills, interests, and communication patterns and to make sure that students continue to use prosocial behaviors in a variety of situations (Banda, Grimmett, & Hart, 2009; Bianco et al., 2009; Cafiero, 2008; Denning, 2007; Goodman & Williams, 2007; Hart & Whalon, 2008; Jaime & Knowlton, 2007; Koenig, Bleiweiss, Brenan, Cohen, & Siegel, 2009; Leach & Daffy, 2009; Rao & Gagie, 2006; Roberts, Keane, & Clark, 2008; Smith Myles, 2006).

You can also encourage your students to support and interact with each other and to serve as good role models by teaching them about autism, the importance and value of making friends with all types of students, and other ways to communicate (Hall, 2009). For example, videos, children's books, and/or guest speakers can be used to teach students about autism and communicating in different ways, responding to attention seeking and unusual behaviors, beginning and maintaining interactions, including others in social and learning activities, and using appropriate behaviors (McCracken, 2006).

Students with Severe, Significant, or Multiple Disabilities   The term *individuals with severe, significant, or multiple disabilities* often refers to individuals with extensive and pervasive intellectual and sensory, communication, medical, motor, behavioral, and emotional disabilities. Because of the significant medical, cognitive, language, physical, and social needs of students with severe and multiple disabilities, no one set of traits characterizes this group of individuals (Westling & Fox, 2009). As a result, they also need many different levels of ongoing support to perform life activities and to participate in integrated educational and community settings (Snell & Brown, 2006; Turnbull et al., 2010). However, students with severe and multiple disabilities may have some of the following: (a) impaired cognitive functioning and memory, which causes them to learn at a slower rate, and have difficulty maintaining new skills and using them in other situations; (b) delayed use of receptive and expressive language; (c) impaired physical and motor abilities; and (d) limited repertoire of socialization, daily living, vocational, and behavioral skills (Rosenberg et al., 2008). These students also can be a joy to have in your classroom, as many of them display and model warmth, self-determination, humor, and other positive traits (Heward, 2009).

Inclusive educational programs for students with severe and multiple disabilities have increased their cognitive functioning and social interaction skills. You can help them learn in your inclusive classroom by providing them with an educational program tailored to their unique needs by

- giving them a developmentally appropriate, community-based curriculum that teaches them in natural settings the functional and academic and communication skills they need to be more independent and socialize and succeed in inclusive settings (e.g., include functional skills such as coin identification and making purchases in your mathematics curriculum);
- embedding instructional goals for students within the general education curriculum;
- task analyzing instructional goals to break them into discrete and multiple-stepped skills;
- using positive behavioral supports;
- encouraging them to use a range of communication strategies such as verbalizations, gestures, and pictorial symbols;
- using age-appropriate activities and materials with them;
- giving them opportunities to socialize with others and to work in cooperative learning groups;
- encouraging them to make choices and to develop their self-determination;
- giving them useful technology and assistive devices;
- working collaboratively with families and other professionals;
- using gestural, physical, pictorial, model, and oral prompts as necessary;
- making sure that you promote the maintenance and generalization of skills taught to students; and
- monitoring their progress in learning and socializing with others (Giangreco, 2006; Heward, 2009; Snell & Brown, 2006; Taylor et al., 2009; Westling & Fox, 2009).

Medication Monitoring

REFLECTIVE

The use of drugs with students is very controversial. How do you feel about the use of medications with students?

A significant and growing number of students, particularly those with medical and mental health needs, epilepsy, or ADD, are taking prescription medications to improve their school experience and performance (CEC, 2009; Ryan, Reid, & Ellis, 2008). Some believe that medications can improve academic, behavioral, and social performance; others believe that they are ineffective or have only short-term benefits and can have adverse side effects. There are concerns about the long-term impact of medications that have not been tested on children, including their impact on subsequent substance abuse problems, and the pressures on students who use medications to sell or trade them to others.

The question of whether to use medications should be considered after appropriate teaching and classroom management techniques have been used correctly, for a reasonable amount of time, and proved ineffective (Austin & Sciarra, 2010). Ultimately, the decision to use drugs is made by the families in consultation with physicians. In recognition of this, the IDEA of 2004 prohibits school districts from requiring students to take medications in order to attend school, receive services or be evaluated for special education.

Once that decision is made, it is important for you to (a) know the school district's policies on drug management, including the steps to take if a medication-related emergency occurs; (b) learn about and help others learn about the type of medication: dosage, frequency, administration schedule, duration, instructions for storage, benefits, symptoms, and side effects (e.g., changes in appetite and energy level, aches and pains, irritability, repetitive movements or sounds); (c) understand and provide for any accommodations students need as a result of taking medications (e.g., dietary, hydration, and environmental needs and restrictions, rest periods); (d) use a multi-model approach that includes academic, behavioral/social, and family-based methods; and (e) work collaboratively with families, medical personnel, and other professionals to develop a plan to monitor students' progress and behavior while taking the drug and maintain communication with families and medical professionals (CEC, 2009; Ryan et al., 2008; Schoenfeld & Konopasek, 2007). Because many medications have side effects, you should keep a record of students' behavior in school, including their academic performance, social skills, notable changes in behavior, and possible drug symptoms. This record should be shared with families and medical personnel to assist them in evaluating the efficacy of and need for continued use of the medication.

Students with Sensory Disabilities

Deaf and Hard of Hearing According to the federal definition, students are considered **deaf** when they have a hearing loss that is so severe (70 to 90 decibels or greater) that the student is not able to process linguistic information through hearing, with or without amplification, which adversely affects educational performance. **Hard of hearing** students have mild or severe hearing losses (20 to 70 decibels) and often use some spoken language to communicate (Heller, Eastbrooks, McJannet, & Swinehart-Jones, 2009).

Some hearing losses may not be detected before the student goes to school. This may especially be the case when students have a **noise-induced hearing loss**, which is a gradual condition resulting from repeated exposure to loud noises (Haller & Montgomery, 2004). Therefore, many students with hearing losses are identified by teachers. Figure 2.9 on page 92 presents some of the warning signs of a possible hearing loss. If you suspect that a student may have a hearing loss, contact the family and refer the student to the school nurse or physician for an **audiometric test** that determines the degree of hearing loss by measuring the intensity and frequency of sound that the student can hear (Roberts, 2010).

The intellectual abilities of deaf and hard of hearing students parallel those of students with hearing. However, deaf and hard of hearing students may experience communication problems in learning an oral language system. These difficulties can

Supporting Students on Medications

Ms. Tupper wasn't surprised when Ms. Glick, Marty's mother, notified her that the family had decided to place Marty on medication. Although Ms. Tupper had tried several teaching and classroom management strategies with Marty, she knew that the Glick family was not happy with his progress and considering the use of drugs.

Ms. Tupper realized that regardless of her beliefs about medications, it was now her job to work with the family and the medical staff to manage and evaluate the use of drugs with Marty. Ms. Tupper researched her district's policies, which included a statement on who can give drugs to students; forms for obtaining the physician's approval, including the name of the drug, dosage, frequency, duration, and possible side effects; a format for maintaining records of drugs given to students; procedures for receiving, labeling, storing, dispensing, and disposing of drugs; and guidelines for students administering drugs to themselves.

Next, Ms. Tupper met with the Glicks, their physician, the IEP team, and the school nurse. First, they discussed the potential benefits and adverse side effects of the medication, and the school nurse gave everyone information and a list of references about the medication. They also reviewed procedures on who would administer the drug, when, how, and where. It was agreed that Mr. Schubert, the school nurse, would be the only one to handle the drug, and would give it to Marty in his office.

Mr. Schubert explained that he stored all medications in a secured location, clearly labeled each student's medication and made sure it had the student's name and photograph on it, and maintained an electronic log of the medications dispensed. He also discussed the importance of maintaining confidentiality, and of not attributing the student's good or bad behavior to

the drug, such as asking "Have you taken your medication yet?" after a student misbehaves. He also planned to talk with Marty about the drug's possible side effects, and how Marty could handle comments from other students about taking it.

Finally, the group developed a plan for monitoring the drug's effect on Marty. They agreed that Ms. Tupper and the other professionals would use observations and checklists, and interview Marty to collect data on the drug's effects and side effects on Marty's academic skills, classroom behavior, and social interactions. The family also agreed to talk with him and keep a diary on Marty at home and on their feelings about his behavior, friendships, and schoolwork. Ms. Tupper was happy that they also talked about the importance of individualized teaching and classroom management techniques for Marty, as well as a plan and criteria for phasing out the use of the drug. They ended the meeting by setting up procedures for communicating with each other and setting a date and a time for their next meeting. While still concerned, Ms. Tupper left the meeting feeling somewhat better.

- As a teacher, how do you feel about the decision to place a student on a drug?
- How do you think the Glick family felt about their decision? What do you think about the school district's response to their decision?
- What are the roles of families, teachers, doctors, school nurses, and students in drug use with students?
- How did Ms. Tupper feel at the end of the meeting? Why did she feel that way?
- What makes this a good example of a process for using medications with students?

create barriers in gaining experience and information that hinder the academic and literacy performance and social-emotional development of these students (Howell, 2008). Depending on their hearing levels, these students may use assistive technology and the following methods to communicate:

- *Oral/aural:* use of speaking, speech reading, and residual hearing to communicate with others
- *Manual:* use of some form of visual-gestural language to communicate with others
- *Bilingual-bicultural:* use of some form of visual-gestural language such as American Sign Language (which is not based on English) and the written form of English, with no use of spoken English
- *Total communication:* use of a combination of approaches, including manual and oral/aural methods (Roberts, 2010)

Some individuals also use cued speech, which involves dividing words into syllables and then communicating them via hand movements and lip reading (Narr, 2006).

An estimated 80% of the deaf and hard of hearing students are served in public schools, with more than a third of them in general education classrooms. As their

FIGURE 2.9 Warning signs of a possible hearing loss

Students with a hearing loss may do some or all of the following:

- Have trouble following directions and paying attention to messages presented orally
- Speak poorly and have a limited vocabulary
- Ask the speaker or peers to repeat statements or instructions
- Avoid oral activities and withdraw from those that require listening
- Respond inconsistently and inappropriately to verbal statements from others
- Mimic the behavior of others
- Rely heavily on gestures and appear to be confused
- Turn up the volume when listening to audiovisual aids such as televisions, radios, cds, and recorders
- Speak with a loud voice
- Cock the head to one side
- Complain of earaches, head noise, and stuffiness in the ears

Deaf and hard of hearing students may have difficulty following directions or remaining engaged in activities requiring listening. How do you help your deaf and hard of hearing students understand your directions?

Making Connections

Find out more about specific teaching, technological, and classroom design factors in differentiating instruction for deaf and hard of hearing students in Chapters 7 and 8.

teacher, you can collaborate with other professionals to develop and implement an educational program that addresses their unique communication, learning, and socialization needs (Howell, 2008; Taylor et al., 2009). To minimize their auditory difficulties, you can create a visually rich learning environment and use written materials, visual aids such as graphic organizers to present content and summarize the main points of lessons, and cues to support instruction (Haller & Montgomery, 2004; Williams & Finnegan, 2003). Use experiential and hands-on learning to allow these students to experience a concept; provide a context for understanding language, reading, and writing; and act out and role-play important principles, concepts, and information (Roberts, 2010). You also can promote learning by linking words with pictures or graphics that students will recognize, using gestures and facial expressions, restating and paraphrasing statements, speaking in shorter sentences, teaching new vocabulary, checking for understanding, connecting new learning to students' prior knowledge about the topic, using cooperative learning, and adapting the classroom environment (Wurst, Jones, & Luckner, 2005). Socially, these students should be encouraged to take part in all school and community activities, and these activities should be adapted to help them participate.

In designing educational programs for deaf and hard of hearing students, you should also be aware of the Deaf culture movement (Howell, 2008; Taylor et al., 2009). This movement views deaf individuals as a distinct cultural group whose language, needs, values, behaviors, customs, social interaction patterns, folklore, and arts are quite different from those of hearing individuals who communicate through spoken language (Johnson & McIntosh, 2009). Thus, deaf students need to be exposed to the Deaf culture, and you should view deafness as a cultural issue and explore ways of promoting the bilingual and bicultural abilities of these students.

Students with Visual Disabilities   Your classroom also may include students with visual disabilities (Heller, Eastbrooks et al., 2009). A **student with a visual disability** has "an impairment in vision that, even with correction, adversely affects educational performance. The term includes both partial sight and blindness." Students with visual disabilities may have difficulty with their

- **visual acuity:** the ability to see details;
- **visual field:** the area one sees when viewing something straight ahead;
- **ocular motility**: their ability to track stationary and moving visual stimuli (Howell, 2008; Swift, Davidson, & Weems, 2008).

Students with visual disabilities are classified into three types based on their ability to use their vision: low vision, functionally blind, and totally blind (Lewis, 2010). **Students who have low vision** can see nearby objects but have trouble seeing them at a distance. Although they may work slowly with visual stimuli, they usually can read print using some type of optical aid or by having access to enlarged and or contrast enhanced print. **Students who are functionally blind** usually need Braille for effective reading and writing; they can use their vision to move through the classroom and classify objects by color. **Students who are totally blind** have no vision or limited light perception and do not respond to visual input. Like students who are functionally blind, these students need tactile and auditory teaching activities.

Because visual disabilities can hinder a student's cognitive, language, motor, and social development, early detection is important. Figure 2.10 presents some of the warning signs that a student may be experiencing visual difficulties. If you suspect that a student may have a visual problem, refer the student to the school nurse or physician for an evaluation and contact the family.

Students with visual disabilities are a varied group and their characteristics are affected by the degree and age of onset of their visual impairment (Taylor et al., 2009). Most of these students have IQ scores within the normal range. However, their cognitive, language, and social development may be affected because of their limited ability to obtain, experience, and understand visual information, move around their environments, and learn by observing others (Heward, 2009; Lewis, 2010). For example, these students may have problems learning spatial concepts or vocabulary that describes objects. Their language may rely on **verbalisms**, or words or phrases that are inconsistent with sensory experiences. Also, because of limited mobility, some students with visual disabilities may have delayed motor development.

Approximately 85% of the students with visual disabilities are served in public schools, and about two-thirds of them are taught in general education classrooms. As their teacher, you can work with vision specialists to learn about appropriate instructional and curricular accommodations, materials, assistive technology, and resources (Taylor et al., 2009). You also will need to adapt your teaching materials by pairing visually presented information with tactile/kinesthetic- and auditory-based learning activities and physical prompts, using Braille, technology, and digitized materials, as well as

REFLECTIVE

In Chapter 1, we learned that deaf and hard of hearing people prefer to be called "deaf" or "hard of hearing rather than people with hearing" impairments. How do you think the Deaf culture movement has impacted the terms that are used to refer to deaf people? The inclusion of deaf individuals into society?

FIGURE 2.10 **Warning signs of a possible visual difficulty**

Visual problems are indicated when the student does any or all of the following:

- Holds reading material close to the eyes
- Has trouble seeing things from a distance and/or performing close-up tasks
- Reads slowly and has immature handwriting
- Rests the head on the desk when writing or coloring
- Has poorly organized notebooks
- Frequently skips lines, loses place, needs breaks, uses a finger as a guide, and uses head movements when reading
- Blinks, squints, rubs the eyes, or tilts the head frequently
- Takes unusual head postures to try to view things with the "good part of the eye"
- Covers or closes one eye
- Frequently has swollen eyelids and inflamed or watery eyes
- Complains of seeing double or seeing halos around lights and having headaches
- Exhibits irregular eye movements
- Appears clumsy, trips over and bumps into things, walks hesitantly, and has difficulty negotiating stairs and drop-offs

Making Connections
Find out more about specific teaching, technological, and classroom design factors in differentiating instruction for students with visual disabilities in Chapters 7 and 8.

an enlarging machine to prepare large-print materials (Li, 2004; Howell, 2008; Spungin & Ferrell, 2007; Swift et al., 2008). For example, outlining a chart with string can help students with visual disabilities tactilely access visual information. You also can foster learning by letting students work with real objects and manipulatives, linking new material to students' prior knowledge, providing students with opportunities to use materials prior to beginning the lesson, checking for comprehension regularly and allowing them a sufficient amount of time to respond, using cooperative learning arrangements, and giving students many activities to practice new skills in natural environments.

In addition to the general education curriculum, you may need to work with an orientation and mobility specialist to help these students learn how to move around your classroom and school (Li, 2009; Taylor et al., 2009). They and their classmates also need to be taught how to interact with each other. They also should be encouraged to participate in all school and community activities, and these activities should be adapted to help them take part.

STUDENTS WHO ARE GIFTED AND TALENTED

WHAT ARE THE EDUCATIONAL STRENGTHS AND CHALLENGES OF STUDENTS WHO ARE GIFTED AND TALENTED? The federal government defines gifted and talented students as those "who give evidence of high performance capability in areas such as intellectual, creative, artistic, or leadership capacity, or in specific academic fields, and who require special services or activities not ordinarily provided by the school." These students, whose special needs are often overlooked, may differ from their peers in terms of their creativity, the speed and level at which they learn, the depth of their mastery, and the topics that interest them (Turnbull et al., 2010; VanTassel-Baska & Stambaugh, 2006). Like all students, **students who are gifted and talented** differ in their strengths, interests, motivation, learning styles, and needs (Clark, 2008; Karnes & Stephens, 2008). Some of them might be advanced in all academic areas, while others might excel in only one area or struggle in some areas.

Traditional methods used to identify students who are gifted and talented have relied primarily on teacher referrals and intelligence testing, which have limited the participation of students from culturally and linguistically diverse backgrounds in these programs (Ford et al., 2008). As a result, many educators are now broadening the concepts of intelligence and talent. For example, many school districts use the framework of *multiple intelligences* to outline at least eight areas in which individuals may exhibit their intelligence and talent:

- *Verbal-linguistic:* sensitivity to the sounds and functions of language and an ability to use language and express oneself verbally or in writing
- *Logical-mathematical:* ability to organize and solve numerical patterns, use logic, understand the principles of causal systems, and deal with the abstract
- *Visual-spatial:* ability to perceive the visual-spatial world accurately and to create and interpret visual experiences
- *Musical:* ability to produce, recognize, remember, and appreciate various forms of musical expression and a sense of rhythm, pitch, and melody
- *Bodily-kinesthetic:* ability to control one's physical movements and work skillfully with objects to solve problems, make something, or participate in a production
- *Interpersonal:* ability to understand and respond to the feelings, moods, and behaviors of others and to get along and work with others
- *Intrapersonal:* ability to understand one's own feelings, reactions, needs, and motivations, as well as one's strengths and weaknesses
- *Naturalistic:* ability to understand the environment and other parts of the natural environment (Armstrong, 2009; Gardner, 2006)

Educators also are examining the concept of *emotional intelligence,* which involves understanding one's feelings and the feelings of others as well as the ability

PEARSON
myeducationlab

To enhance your understanding of students with visual impairments and the individuals you can collaborate with to help them succeed in your inclusive classroom, go to the IRIS Center Resources section of Topic: Visual Impairments in the MyEducationLab for your course, and complete the module entitled *Serving Students with Visual Impairments: The Importance of Collaboration.*

REFLECTIVE

Students identified as gifted and talented are not covered under the IDEA. Why do you think this is the case? Do you think they should be included in the IDEA?

to use one's social and collaborative skills to establish and maintain relationships with others (Beland, 2007; Pellitteri, Dealy, Fasano, & Kugler, 2006).

Although educators tend to focus more often on the academic needs of students who are gifted and talented, these students often have unique social and emotional needs that should be addressed (Clark, 2008; Karnes & Stephens, 2008). Some of these students experience difficulties such as uneven development, resentment from peers, perfectionism and self-criticism, pressure to conform, avoidance of risks, and difficulty making friends or finding peers who have similar interests and abilities. Currently, the vast majority of students identified as gifted and talented are educated in general education classrooms. Like *all students*, these students can benefit from the use of the strategies and principles for creating inclusive classrooms presented in this book.

You can accommodate gifted and talented students in your classroom by providing *all students* with varied learning activities and multiple ways of demonstrating their understanding and mastery (Armstrong, 2009; Mulrine, 2008; Turnbull et al., 2010). You can adapt your teaching program for them by presenting activities that actively engage students in directing their learning. To do this, give students opportunities to select what they want to learn, the ways in which they want to learn it, and how they will demonstrate their learning. For example, students can be asked to select their own topics for cooperative learning groups, papers, presentations, and independent study assignments. You also can employ **curriculum compacting**, which involves allowing students who demonstrate mastery at the beginning of a unit of study to work on new and more challenging material or student-selected topics via alternate learning activities. They also can be given choices about whether to present their learning by telling a story; participating in a debate; writing a poem, story, or play; creating a video, song, artwork, or photo album; teaching another student; or reporting on a community-based project. You also can use online learning activities and games, thematic units, independent studies, questioning and learning centers to enrich the curriculum and extend the learning of these students (Mulrine, 2008).

In addition, you can create a learning environment that encourages students to be creative, develop their strengths, take risks, and extend their learning (Clark, 2008; Karnes & Stephens, 2008; VanTassel-Baska & Stambaugh, 2006). For example, when learning to solve word problems, you can ask students to create their own word problems and to explain their reasoning. In social studies, students can write journal entries from individuals who have opposite points of view on a specific issue or event. You also can ask students to respond to higher-level questions that allow them to justify and discuss their responses. Discovery and **problem-based learning** approaches can allow students to work on complex open-ended problems and issues that have multifaceted solutions. Participation in leadership, mentoring, and service learning programs can be used to motivate students and extend their learning and leadership skills. It also is important for you to work with students and their families to help them understand and commit to talent development, to set challenging learning goals, and to access school and community resources that foster students' talents and interests.

REFLECTIVE

How do you think inclusion impacts students identified as gifted and talented?

Students with Special Needs Who Are Gifted and Talented

Although we often think of students with disabilities in terms of their learning difficulties, students with special needs, like Marty, the student we met at the beginning of the chapter, may also be identified as being gifted and talented. We often refer to these students as *twice exceptional* (Bianco et al., 2009; Rizza & Morrison, 2007). Although twice exceptional students resemble other students who are gifted and talented in terms of their intelligence, creativity, critical thinking skills, and expressive language, they tend to have learning and behavioral difficulties that affect their academic performance, self-concept, and socialization (King, 2005; Nielsen & Higgins, 2005). For example, Soenksen and Alper (2006) and Murdick, Gartin, and Rao (2005) provide information and strategies addressing students with **hyperlexia**, a condition characterized by advanced reading abilities and significant difficulties in comprehending what they have read, using expressive language and socializing with others. Unfortunately, like other students who are gifted and talented, twice exceptional students are often overlooked and underserved.

The traditional method of identifying students who are gifted and talented underidentifies and underserves gifted and talented students who are from culturally and linguistically diverse or lower socioeconomic backgrounds, disabled, and female (Ford et al., 2008). To counter this potential bias, you can work with others in your school district to adopt an inclusive and culturally relevant concept of giftedness, use many different forms of assessment, consider multiple perspectives when identifying the unique talents and learning strengths of *all students* and help your students and their families understand the benefits of these types of programs (Henfield, Moore, & Wood, 2008; Rizza & Morrison, 2007). For example, indicators of giftedness can be expanded to include coping with living in poverty, assuming adult roles in one's home, having a strong sense of self, speaking more than one language, and understanding one's cultural identity. The process for identifying students as gifted

What Would You Do in Today's Diverse Classroom?

As a member of your school district's comprehensive planning team, you are asked to address the educational strengths and challenges of the following students:

★ Ethel was recently in a serious car accident. Although she was wearing a seat belt, her skull was cracked, and there was considerable swelling of her brain. She lapsed into a coma for several days and had surgery to repair the damage to her skull. She has had several seizures since the accident and is taking medication to control them. Since she returned to school several months ago, her academic performance has slipped and she seems to be a different person. She has trouble controlling her impulses, organizing her work, socializing with others, and maintaining attention.

★ Tony has significant learning and communication difficulties. He knows his name, basic colors, and some functional words, and he can follow simple commands. Although he can say single words, only a few of his words are understandable. He likes being with others and attempts to participate in all activities.

★ Kevin's educational achievement is far below what would be expected considering his abilities. He has no physical, visual, hearing, health, or mental difficulties. He's shown minor emotional and behavior difficulties, but the source of Kevin's struggles has been hard to pinpoint.

1. Do you think that these students qualify for special education services? If so, under which disability category do they qualify? If not, why not?

2. What goals should their IEPs address, and what services should they receive to meet those goals?

3. How might placement in a general education classroom benefit these students?

4. How would you feel about having them in your class?

5. What knowledge, skills, dispositions, resources, and supports do you need to address their strengths and challenges?

PEARSON myeducationlab Watch Kevin's comprehensive planning team comb through data to determine whether he is eligible for special education services by visiting the MyEducationLab for this course. Go to the Assignments and Activities section under the *Prereferral, Placement, and IEP Process* topic and complete the activity entitled *The Multidisciplinary IEP Team Meeting* to answer questions about the referral process.

and talented also can be expanded by involving family and community members and peers in the assessment process, and using observations, interviews, self-identification, and portfolios.

In addition to broadening the identification process, educators can use a variety of strategies to differentiate instruction for students with special needs who are also gifted and talented (Bianco et al, 2009; Clark, 2008; King, 2005; Nielsen & Higgins, 2005; Karnes & Stephens, 2008). These strategies include

- helping them recognize their areas of giftedness and understand and accept their disabilities;
- employing differentiated instruction and assistive and instructional technology to allow students to perform based on their strengths;
- using a challenging interdisciplinary curriculum and infusing multicultural content into the curriculum;
- providing mentors and opportunities to assume leadership roles;
- offering instruction in the use of learning strategies, and coping and self-management skills;
- using flexible learning arrangements that allow *all students* to work in different groups;
- working with students to develop learning contracts that specify individualized learning goals, activities, time lines, and evaluation criteria;
- providing students with choices and opportunities to work on assignments that require different learning styles; and
- using authentic assessment activities that allow students to demonstrate their learning in real-world contexts.

SUMMARY

This chapter has provided information to help you understand the educational strengths and challenges of students with disabilities and how you can effectively educate them in inclusive classrooms. Other strategies to foster their success are presented in later chapters. As you review the questions asked in this chapter, consider the following questions and remember the following points.

How Does the Special Education Process Work?
CEC 1, 2, 3, 9, 10; PRAXIS 1, 2, 3; INTASC 2, 3, 9, 10
A planning team composed of professionals and family members, and the student when appropriate, makes important decisions about the education of the student with disabilities. Before considering a student for special education placement, the planning team uses a *prereferral system* and the Response-to-Intervention method. That is, a team of educators works together to help classroom teachers develop and use effective strategies and interventions methods that help students succeed in the general education classroom. If the prereferral and RTI systems are not successful, the planning team determines whether a student needs special education and related services. If the team determines that a student is eligible for special education, an IEP is developed.

How Can IEPs Be Implemented in General Education Settings?
CEC 1, 4, 5, 6, 7, 9, 10; PRAXIS 2, 3; INTASC 2, 3, 4, 5, 6, 7, 9, 10
The IEP serves as a tool for providing students with disabilities with access to the general education curriculum. The implementation of the IEP in the general education setting can be facilitated by involving teachers in the IEP process, aligning the IEP goals to the general education curriculum, differentiating instruction to address IEP goals, and establishing an implementation plan.

What Are the Educational Strengths and Challenges of Students with High-Incidence Disabilities?

CEC 1, 2, 3, 4, 5, 6, 7, 9; PRAXIS 1, 3; INTASC 2, 3, 4, 5, 6, 7, 9, 10

Students with high-incidence or mild disabilities include those with learning disabilities, mild emotional and behavioral disorders, mild intellectual disabilities, speech/language impairments, and ADD. Their characteristics, behaviors, strengths, and challenges vary; some have difficulties in only one area, and others in several areas. These challenges may occur as learning, language and communication, perceptual, motor, social, and behavioral difficulties.

What Are the Educational Strengths and Challenges of Students with Low-Incidence Disabilities?

CEC 1, 2, 3, 4, 5, 6, 7, 9; PRAXIS 1, 3; INTASC 2, 3, 4, 5, 6, 7, 9, 10

Students with physical, sensory, and significant disabilities are sometimes referred to as having low-incidence disabilities. These students have a range of characteristics. No two students are alike, and each educational program must be based on individual strengths and challenges rather than disability categories.

What Are the Educational Strengths and Challenges of Students Who Are Gifted and Talented?

CEC 7; PRAXIS 3; INTASC 2, 3

In addition to focusing on the academic strengths of students who are gifted and talented, you also need to recognize that these students often have unique social and emotional challenges as well. You can address these challenges by using Gardner's framework of multiple intelligences and by creating a learning environment that encourages students to be creative, develop their strengths, take risks, and direct their learning.

HALEE

My mother told me that I was born during the war, which continued for the first 10 years of my life. Between ages 2 and 10, I lived on and off with my grandmother so that I could provide her with some companionship. No matter where I lived, the bombing seemed to follow me. Several times a week, the bombing would start, and we would have to leave our homes and hide in the forest.

Finally, when I was 10, the bombing stopped and the war ended. My family was airlifted to an internment camp in a neighboring country, but I was left behind with my grandmother. Three months later, my father returned to get me and smuggled me into the camp. While I was happy to be reunited with my family, I missed my grandmother, who did not come with us.

Although we moved several times from one camp to another, each of the camps was the same. We lived in a small area surrounded by barbed wire, and we had no privacy or toilet facilities. Our camp was frequently raided by the locals, and we were often targets of burglary, rape, and murder.

I didn't get to go to school because I was a girl. My responsibilities were to help my mother take care of my brothers and sisters. However, I did hear about how life would be wonderful and full of riches for us if we could get to the United States. After living in the camps for 3 years, we came to the United States. When our plane landed at the airport, I saw a man putting garbage in a clean and shiny plastic bag and thought that the United States really was a wealthy country. However, this view was short-lived, as we were placed in a small apartment in the poorest section of the city. Soon after settling in, I started school. When I got off the bus with my sister, the teachers were pointing here and there, and I went wherever they pointed. Although I was old enough to be in a higher-grade class,

Understanding the Diverse Educational Strengths and Challenges of Students Who Challenge Schools

I was assigned to a lower-grade class. I was scared and very cautious.

I really felt confused by the social interactions and the behaviors of my classmates. At home, I was supposed to be passive and obedient. However, in school, all the other kids were very verbal and physically expressive. One time, we went to a swimming pool, and I didn't know that I was supposed to bring a bathing suit. In fact, I didn't know what a bathing suit was. When we arrived at the pool, someone gave me a bathing suit. I put it on over my underwear and was very embarrassed when everyone laughed at me.

I struggled academically, and my teachers thought I had a learning problem and referred me for special education or something. However, I knew my academic struggles were due to the fact that I didn't understand or speak much English. When teachers and students spoke to me, I looked around to see what my classmates were doing and then mimicked them. I felt overwhelmed, as I didn't understand what they were saying. They would repeat themselves over and over again or talk very slowly, as if that would make me understand them. I wanted to run away to escape their bombarding me, but there was no forest to run to for safety.

What factors led to some of the difficulties that Halee had in school? Should Halee have been placed in special education classes? How does inclusion affect students like Halee? After reading this chapter, you should have the knowledge, skills, and dispositions to answer these as well as the following questions.

- How have economic changes affected students and schools?

- How have demographic shifts affected students and schools?

- What are the educational strengths and challenges of students from culturally and linguistically diverse backgrounds?

- How can I differentiate cultural and language differences from learning difficulties?

- What is the effect of discrimination and bias on students and schools?

- How have family changes affected students and schools?

- What are some alternative philosophies for structuring schools to address societal changes?

The United States continues to undergo major changes that have a tremendous effect on schools and the students they seek to educate. Society has been reshaped as a result of changing economic conditions, demographic shifts, racism and sexism, changes in the structure of families, and increases in substance abuse and child abuse. These factors have contributed to a society that jeopardizes the physical and mental health and educational performance of many of its children. These factors also make it more likely that students like Halee and the other students you will meet in this chapter—who do not have disabilities—may experience difficulties and an achievement gap in school, be referred to and placed in special education settings, and drop out of school. For students with identified disabilities, these factors often interact with their disability to place students in double jeopardy.

Schools need to respond to these societal changes and meet the needs of increasingly diverse groups of students who challenge the school structure (Baca & Cervantes, 2004; Gollnick & Chinn, 2009; Taylor & Whittaker, 2009). Inclusive educational practices have focused on students with disabilities, but it is important to remember that inclusion programs seek to restructure schools so that they address the needs of and benefit *all students*.

Children represent the fastest-growing poverty group in the United States. Why do you think this is occurring?

ECONOMIC CHANGES

HOW HAVE ECONOMIC CHANGES AFFECTED STUDENTS AND SCHOOLS? In the United States, economic changes have had a profound effect on children and the urban, rural, and suburban schools they attend. Sadly, children represent the fastest-growing poverty group, with poverty affecting nearly 20% of U.S. children. These rates are higher for children with disabilities (Parish, Rose, Grinstein-Weiss, Richman, & Andrews, 2008) and children from culturally and linguistically diverse backgrounds (Chau & Douglas-Hall, 2008).

Poverty

The harmful effects of poverty often interact to affect all aspects of a child's life, including health, cognitive development, school performance (Rothstein, 2009; Walker Tileston & Darling, 2009), and the likelihood that children will develop disabilities (Parish et al., 2008). The mothers of children from lower socioeconomic backgrounds often do not receive early prenatal care. From birth through adolescence, these children also are more likely to suffer from illnesses and diseases and less likely to receive appropriate medical care. Children from lower socioeconomic backgrounds often live in substandard housing; lack health insurance; are more likely to be victims of hunger, poor diets, and lead poisoning usually enter school with fewer skills than their peers; and often attend schools that have limited funds and high teacher turnover rates. As a result, they are more likely to be recommended for and placed in remedial and special education programs, and to drop out of school than their middle- and upper-income peers (Howard, Grogan Dresser, & Dunklee, 2009). Once identified, the families of poor children with disabilities also face financial burdens that can impact the family's economic well-being (Parish et al., 2008).

The effects of the depth, timing, and duration of poverty on students are also important factors (Walker Tileston & Darling, 2009). Students who live in extreme poverty for a long time and students with disabilities are particularly likely to suffer. Students who experience poverty earlier in their lives are more likely to be harmed than students who experience poverty only in their later years.

Urban Poverty Poverty is especially prevalent in U.S. cities, where about 30% of all students live in poverty. Urban poor children may live in crowded, rundown apartments; are more likely to have lead poisoning, which can cause learning and behavioral difficulties, stunted growth, and hearing loss; encounter violence and crime; have limited access to health care; suffer malnutrition; and attend underfunded schools.

Homelessness. There has been a dramatic increase in homelessness, particularly among families with children (Israel, 2009; National Law Center on Homelessness and Poverty, 2009). **Homeless children** do not have a regular residence and may be living with others, in cars, motels, bus or train stations, campgrounds, or shelters. Sadly, approximately 1.4 million children, or 2% of the students in the United States, are likely to become homeless during the school year. This group of students also includes adolescents who leave their homes for a variety of reasons.

The McKinney-Vento Homeless Assistance Act is a federal law that guarantees homeless children the right to a free, appropriate public education in a mainstream school environment and seeks to eliminate barriers to their school attendance (Hartman, 2006; National Law Center on Homelessness and Poverty, 2009). For example, it requires school districts to employ a homeless education liaison, to enroll students even if they do not have their records, and to provide students who are homeless with transportation to attend the same school even if they change residences. But in spite of this law, many homeless students in this country are not attending school. Many of these students do not attend school because of transportation needs, inappropriate class placement, lack of school supplies and clothes, poor health, hunger, and residency and immunization requirements. In addition, many of them may not produce birth certificates, school files, and other important records and forms. Homeless students also may have few recreational opportunities; little privacy; and limited access to meals, books, school materials, and toys.

Students who are homeless may perform poorly in school and be in need of special education services, may be separated from their families for extended periods of time, and are often held over. Because they may lack washing facilities and adequate clothing, homeless students may have health care needs and may be ridiculed by peers (Israel, 2009). However, because of their frequent movement from place to place and their high absenteeism rates, many homeless students who are eligible for supportive services do not receive them. Some students also may be embarrassed by their homelessness or fearful that they will be separated from their families; thus, they may attempt to hide it from their teachers and peers.

Rural Poverty Rural school districts serve a greater percentage of students living in poverty than do nonrural school districts and for longer periods of time. Rural school districts also serve more students with disabilities in general education classrooms than do nonrural school districts, as well as a growing number of students from culturally and linguistically diverse backgrounds (Roberts, 2008b).

Children of Migrant Workers.

> *My name is Erika Garcia. My parents work very hard in the pickles. Sometimes my sister and I go to help my parents. We have seen my parents work many times, and just by looking, we see it is hard. First, you have to wake up at 5:45 A.M. because everyone goes to the field at 6:00 A.M. Picking pickles is like cracking your back. Some people hang the basket on their waist, and some drag it along.*
>
> *After work we go home, and my mom and dad take a shower, and my mom makes a lot of tortillas. Then we take a nap, and then we go back to the fields at 6:00 P.M. and do more rows of pickles to get a good start in the morning. My parents sent me to summer school, but then they needed some help, and so I only went to school for 3 weeks because I needed to help them by working in the fields or watching my brothers and sisters. When I work picking pickles, my back hurts, and my fingers bleed and sting from the pesticides.*
>
> *Then when the pickles finished, my mom and dad worked in the tomatoes. When the tomatoes are done, my dad works in the sugarbeets. My mom stays home, and my sisters and I go to school. My dad works at 5:00 A.M. and comes home at 1:00 A.M. Sometimes I don't get to see him for up to 4 days. Then when the sugarbeets finish, we go back to Texas and return to Ohio around May 1, and start the season all over again. It's very hard work.*

Students like Erika, whose family members travel from state to state to pick the ripening crops, make up one group of culturally and linguistically diverse students who live in rural areas—the children of migrant workers (McGrath, 2008; Taylor & Whittaker, 2009). Because of the migrant lifestyle, these students experience many challenges in school. Entering new schools, learning a new language, making new friends, adjusting to new cultural and school expectations, being taught with different instructional techniques and materials, and meeting different graduation requirements are some of these difficulties. Poor sanitation in the fields and work camp facilities; overcrowded, substandard housing and poor diets; exposure to pesticides and other hazards of agricultural work (particularly harmful to pregnant women and young children); limited health care; and low wages make migrant youth particularly vulnerable to health conditions and poor performance in schools. As we saw in the case of Erika, migrant students often work in the fields to help support their families, watch their younger siblings while their parents are working, and serve as the link between their families and societal institutions such as schools.

You can help improve the school adjustment and performance of mobile, homeless, and migrant students in a variety of ways (Smith, Fien, & Paine, 2008). You can welcome and orient them to your class and assign classroom buddies and mentors to help them. Acknowledge their strengths and unique experiences, promote their self-esteem, reach out to their families, and involve them in extracurricular activities. Provide these students with a personal study space in the classroom that is labeled with the student's name, decorated by the student, or personalized by a special symbol selected by the student.

When they are getting ready to move, you can provide their families with a portfolio of their children's work and a checklist of school-related documents they should bring with them so that they can facilitate their child's adjustment to their new school. You and your class also can periodically send letters or e-mails to them. Educationally, you can collaborate with school counselors and migrant and bilingual educators to assess and address their academic, health, and social adjustment needs. Include their experiences and cultural backgrounds in the curriculum. For example, some teachers incorporate the experiences of migrant workers into their math and English classes by using word problems that ask students to calculate the miles traveled by migrant families or to estimate a fair wage based on the number of buckets of produce they have picked (Makkonen, 2004), and by giving reading and writing assignments about their lives and family members.

Because migrant families travel within and between states, you also need to be aware of the programs available to address the challenges of migrant students and their families and promote cooperation among teachers (Graves, Leiva, & Sparaco, 2005; Hartman, 2006). You can obtain more information about these and other programs for migrant students by contacting your local migrant education center or your state director of migrant education.

Native Americans   Many of the more than 1.5 million Native Americans reside in remote rural areas. Because of their high unemployment and poverty rates, language differences, and limited access to health care, Native American youth often experience challenges that affect their educational performance and school completion and result in high rates of referral for special education (Demmert, 2005; Pewewardy & Fitzpatrick, 2009).

As you do with other students, you can promote their school success by holding high expectations for them and using culturally sensitive strategies to collaborate and communicate with their families (Banks, 2008). Diversifying your curriculum to address their cultural, experiential, and linguistic backgrounds and to counter negative and stereotypical portrayals of Native Americans can help them succeed in your classroom and enhance the education of *all students* (Banks, 2009). You can also assist these students by learning about and respecting their cultural, historical, and language backgrounds and understanding how they affect their learning and your educational goals for them. For example:

- Use modeling, demonstration, and hands-on learning techniques.
- Supplement oral instruction with use of visuals including Native American images.
- Employ flexible timing for completing assignments.
- Offer activities that ask students to work cooperatively.
- Understand that some students may not feel comfortable being "spotlighted" in front of the class.
- Provide real-life examples to explain key points.
- Allow students time to practice a task, skill, or activity.
- Involve family, elders, and community groups.
- Offer a range of ways for students to demonstrate mastery (Banks, 2004; Demmert, 2005; Pewewardy & Fitzpatrick, 2009; Sparks, 2000a).

Suburban Poverty   Even though we often think that the suburbs are affluent, many people from lower socioeconomic backgrounds also live there. Therefore, if you teach in the suburbs, you also are likely to teach students struggling to deal with poverty. You also will have many students from culturally and linguistically diverse backgrounds in your classroom (Roberts, 2009), and you may encounter communities that are dealing with increased poverty, crime, segregation, racial divisions, acquired immunodeficiency syndrome (AIDS), homelessness, and unemployment.

Wealthy Children

Affluence also has an impact on the educational, social, and behavioral development of children. Wealth can produce psychological and emotional challenges such as a sense of entitlement, a perception of one's self-esteem in terms of wealth, and a desire to have the newest and the best of everything. Wealthy children can grow up to expect the best and the most expensive, and fail to develop personal accountability

Making Connections
Find out more about bringing the experiences of migrant students into your classroom and helping others learn about them in Chapter 5.

REFLECTIVE

Moving from school to school is a common occurrence for many students, especially those from lower socioeconomic backgrounds, which can hinder their educational performance (Smith et al., 2008). How does student mobility affect your school? What strategies do you use to help these students?

REFLECTIVE

What activities in your school require students and their families to pay to participate? How could these activities be restructured so that students can participate without paying a fee?

Making Connections
Find out more how you can address the diverse needs, backgrounds, and experiences of families in Chapter 4.

and a motivation to achieve. As a result, they may demand constant stimulation, have difficulty completing projects, form superficial relationships, fail to develop a sense of compassion for others, take little responsibility for personal property, mislead others when confronted with a demanding situation, and be present and pleasure oriented. They may feel insulated from challenge, risk, and consequence, which can result in underachievement in school; boredom, low self-esteem, and a lack of motivation; and susceptibility to teenage sex and substance abuse.

UDL and YOU
Overcoming Economic Barriers and Providing Equitable Opportunities

As we have discussed in this chapter, poor students encounter many factors that have a significant impact on their school performance. Rather than assuming that all students have equal access to the same learning experiences and sufficient financial resources, you can apply the principles of UDL so that your school and inclusive classroom are respectful of individual differences related to economic factors. This means that you and your colleagues need to avoid activities that require students and their families to pay and raise monies to participate and find ways to make these activities available to *all* students (Huguelet, 2007). Therefore, when planning activities, make sure participation does not require students and their families to spend money. If a fee must be charged, provide families with no-cost options such as allowing them to volunteer to perform a task in lieu of paying a fee. Similarly, consider using school resources to address students' economic needs. For example, showers, clothes, snacks, supplies and fees for school activities and trips can be made discreetly available to students who need them.

Here are some effective practices that others have used to apply the principles of UDL to create equitable inclusive classrooms that overcome economic barriers to student performance and family participation:

- Learn about poverty; your students' strengths, struggles, communities, and home lives; as well as school and community resources addressing students and families living in poverty.
- Be aware of signs of economic difficulties such as wearing the same clothes; being chronically tired and/or hungry; having hygiene needs; wanting to stay in school rather than go home; not having school supplies; not completing homework; experiencing tardiness, attendance, and transportation problems; and not having notes signed by family members.

- Make your curriculum relevant to students by teaching about and using materials related to issues of class, poverty, antipoverty work, and ways to counter stereotypes, and by taking students on field trips to historical, artistic, and recreational sites within their communities.
- Foster resiliency in students by encouraging them to participate in extracurricular activities and by providing them with opportunities to perform activities that allow them to display their abilities, work with and assist others, hear speakers from their communities, and interact with mentors.
- Help students and their families complete forms, such as those necessary for the student to receive school breakfast and school lunch and to participate in extracurricular activities and to go on field trips.
- Collaborate and communicate with others in your school and personnel from community agencies to offer a range of integrated, comprehensive services addressing the holistic needs of students and families at school buildings and within community settings.
- Understand that students may have particular difficulties completing homework and assignments that require economic resources, and offer help and alternatives.
- Encourage family participation by
  - conducting activities and meetings at locations in the community and
  - providing transportation to meetings and child care during meetings.

Dryfoos (2008); Gorski (2008); Howard et al. (2009); Landsman (2006); San Antonio (2008); Sober (2009); Walker Tileston and Darling (2009).

DEMOGRAPHIC SHIFTS

HOW HAVE DEMOGRAHPIC SHIFTS AFFECTED STUDENTS AND SCHOOLS? A variety of demographic factors have led to dramatic changes in the population of the United States, which has become a far more culturally and linguistically diverse country, with a significant increase in the Hispanic, Asian and Pacific Islander, Latino/a, Native American, and multiracial populations in urban, suburban, and rural areas (Roberts, 2008a, 2008b; Thompson, 2009). Although many of these groups share common traits, variety characterizes the U.S. population (Gollnick & Chinn, 2009; Lee, Turnbull, & Zan, 2009). For instance, there are more than 300 independent Native American groups, with different beliefs, customs, traditions, and languages. Although some Asian and Pacific Islander groups may hold some common beliefs, they come from more than 25 different countries with unique languages, religions, and customs. Latino/a groups speak different dialects of a common language, and each group's identity is based on separate beliefs, traditions, histories, and social institutions. Similarly, although Caribbean groups share a history that is characterized by conquest and colonization, these groups differ in their ethnic, language, and religious backgrounds (Roopnarine, Bynoe, Singh, & Simon, 2005).

Currently, students from culturally and linguistically diverse backgrounds either make up or approach the majority of students in many urban school districts. Furthermore, census data show that almost half of the children under the age of 5 in the United States are from culturally and linguistically diverse backgrounds (Roberts, 2009).

English language learners, who come from families that speak over 400 different languages, make up the fastest-growing group of students in schools (García, Jensen, & Scribner, 2009; Goldenberg, 2008). It important for you to be aware that many English language learners are not from immigrant families; it is estimated that approximately 60% of English language learners are second- or third-generation Americans who were born in the United States (Thompson, 2009). Thus, although these students may have some oral proficiency in English, they may still struggle with English literacy and content knowledge (Rance-Roney, 2009).

To hear an expert discuss the variations in the backgrounds of English language learners and ways to support their learning in inclusive classrooms, go to the IRIS Center Resource section of Topic: Cultural and Linguistic Diversity in the MyEducationLab for your course, and listen to the podcast entitled "Episode 2: Diane Torres-Velásquez" on diverse learners.

Immigration

A significant factor in the U.S. population changes and the makeup of schools is immigration, with children of immigrants making up approximately 20% of the children in the United States (García et al., 2009). Depending on their economic, educational, cultural, experiential, and language backgrounds, immigrants may go through a series of stages as they acculturate and adjust to their new country (Igoa, 1995; Thompson, 2009). Initially, they may be curious as they encounter a new language and culture. Afterward, however, many immigrants may experience shock, depression, and confusion. They also may show signs of anxiety, withdrawal, fatigue, distractibility, and disorientation, which may reveal itself through culture-bound syndromes (Kershaw, 2003). In the final stage, either they assimilate and give up some of the cultural values of their homeland to become part of the mainstream culture, or they become part of the dominant culture while maintaining their own cultural values and traditions.

Students Who Are Immigrants A growing number of students are like Halee, the student we met at the beginning of this chapter, who left their countries to escape political, religious, or racial repression or to have better economic opportunities. Like Halee, to reach their new country, many of these students may endure a long, difficult, and life-threatening journey characterized by malnutrition, disease, torture, and fear, and it is important for you to learn about and try to understand their immigration experiences. Once they arrive, they must cope with a type of stress disorder as a result of witnessing atrocities and torture, experiencing losses, and attempting to adjust to a new society. In school, they may encounter racial tension and rejection from peers. Immigrant youth also may fear authority figures such as the principal because they or a family member have an undocumented status. As a result, these youth may be reluctant to make friends with others, to seek help from and interactions with professionals, to attempt to gain recognition or excel in programs, or to draw attention to themselves.

Like Halee, some immigrant students may be **students with interrupted formal education (SIFE)**, which means they have encountered circumstances that caused them to have limited, erratic, or nonexistent access to schooling (Cloud, 2008; DeCapua, Smathers, Tang, 2007). These students usually enter school in the United States after grade 2, perform at least 2 years below their expected grade levels in reading and math, and may not be literate in their native language, which can hinder their content knowledge and their ability to learn English.

Regardless of the conditions of their immigration, students who are immigrants face many difficulties as they enter and progress through school (García & Cuéllar, 2006; Lang Rong & Preissle, 2009) (see Figure 3.1). As a result, they may be placed in special education by mistake or not promoted (Hoover, Baca, Smith-Davis, & Wexler Love, 2007). You can enhance the education of students who are immigrants in a variety of ways, which also benefit *all* of your students (Hoover, Klingner, Baca, & Patton, 2008). Learn about their strengths, past experiences, interests, and concerns by giving them opportunities to tell their stories through narratives, digital storytelling, role playing, journals, and bibliotherapy (Campano, 2007; Dong, 2009). Campano (2007) offers suggestions for fostering student storytelling and a list of stories about the experiences of immigrant children and families.

You can bring their culture, language, and experiences into your classroom by using materials in their native language and encouraging them to do projects related to their prior experiences and interests (Dong, 2009; Lang Rong & Preissle, 2009; Villegas & Lucas, 2007). Allowing students who are literate in their native language to read materials in that language also can strengthen their background knowledge and understanding of the content and topics being discussed in your class. You can try to learn some vocabulary from their native language so that you can communicate with them and show them that you value them and their language

FIGURE 3.1 **Difficulties facing students who are immigrants**

Students who are immigrants are likely to encounter several problems, including the following:

- Learning a new language that differs from their native language in terms of articulation, syntax, and graphic features
- Adjusting to a new culture that values and interprets behavior in different ways
- Obtaining access to health care that addresses their needs, such as mental health services to help them deal with their experiences of being tortured or seeing their relatives and friends tortured, raped, and executed
- Experiencing guilt as a result of their survival and concern about leaving others behind
- Facing economic pressures to work to support their family in the United States and family members in their native country
- Coping with sociocultural and peer expectations, such as self-hatred and youth gangs
- Dealing with cross-cultural and intergenerational conflicts and posttraumatic stress disorder
- Being targets of racism, violence, and harassment
- Developing a positive identity and self-concept
- Entering school with little, occasional, or no schooling in their native countries
- Being unfamiliar with schools in the United States
- Lacking school records and hiding relevant facts in order to avoid embarrassment, seek peer acceptance, and promote self-esteem
- Having to serve as cultural and language interpreters for their families

Sources: García & Cuéllar, (2006); Harris, (1991); Hoover et al., (2007).

(Agirdag, 2009). You also can provide them with multilingual visual glossaries that include a pictorial representation of the key term or concept and its definition in English and the other languages that your students speak (Dong, 2009). You can also help these students adjust to their new culture and language by offering them intensive English language and literacy programs; using nonverbal teaching methods such as music, dance, and art; and teaching them about their new culture (Rance-Roney, 2009).

Socially, you can assist these students by using peers and community members as a resource, encouraging these students to participate in culturally sensitive in-school and extracurricular activities, and inviting them to join peer discussion and support groups related to their interests and experiences. It is also important to involve parents, extended family members, and knowledgeable community members in ELLs' educational program (Araujo, 2009; Lang Rong & Preissle, 2009). Finally, you can provide students and their families with materials containing information about the school and about their rights written in their own language.

Educational Rights of Students Who Are Immigrants

It is also important for you to be aware of the educational rights of students who are immigrants. As a result of the Supreme Court decision in *Plyler v. Doe* (1982), all undocumented students have the same right as U.S. citizens to attend public schools (Rance-Roney, 2009). School personnel cannot take actions or establish policies that deny students access to public schools, and they have no legal obligation to implement immigration laws. Schools cannot prevent these students from attending school based on their undocumented status, nor can they treat these students in a different way when identifying their residency. School personnel cannot engage in activities that may intimidate or threaten students and their families based on their immigration status, such as allowing Immigration and Naturalization Service (INS) personnel to enter or remain near the school or requiring students or their families to identify their immigration status. They may not inquire about the immigration status of students or their families; ask students to provide Social Security numbers, which may indicate their immigration status; or give the immigration status information contained in a student's school file to outside agencies without the family's permission.

Bilingual Education

Effective **bilingual education** programs employ both the native and the new language and culture of students to teach them (García & Jensen, 2007). As students acquire English language skills, more and more of the curriculum is taught in English. In addition to teaching English, bilingual education programs help students maintain their first language and pride in their cultural backgrounds. Many students who are immigrants may be eligible for bilingual education services under the Bilingual Education Act. This act established guidelines and funding to encourage school districts to employ bilingual education practices to teach students who speak languages other than English.

Research indicates that many English language learners improve their cognitive and sociocultural development, academic progress, self-esteem, and learning of English in bilingual education programs (Goldenberg, 2008; Rolstad, Mahoney, & Glass, 2005; Slavin & Cheung, 2005). When students are taught in their first language, they develop essential background knowledge. This makes it easier for them to learn a second language and read, write, and perform academically in English (García & Jensen, 2007; Krashen, 2005). Bilingual education also allows English language learners to keep up with their English-speaking peers in learning the content of the general education curriculum (science, social studies, mathematics, etc.). Studies also show that students who received English-only instruction lag behind their peers who attend a bilingual education program (Rolstad et al., 2005). Finally, with bilingual education, these students have higher levels of self-esteem and academic aspirations.

Making Connections
Find out more about effective teaching strategies and instructional and assistive technology for fostering the learning of ELLs in Chapter 8.

PEARSON
myeducationlab

Go to the Assignments and Activities section of the Topic *Cultural and Linguistic Diversity* in the MyEducationLab for your course and complete the activity entitled *Culturally Responsive Environment*. As you watch the video, think about how immigrants and other English learners may feel uncomfortable in the classroom and how creating a comfortable environment can increase their confidence and educational opprtunities.

REFLECTIVE

Rosibel and her family arrived in the United States several months ago. After Rosibel applied to participate in the free lunch program, the principal asked you to obtain her Social Security number. As Rosibel's teacher, what would you do? (Developed by Elizabeth Sealey.)

Second language learning also has personal, cognitive, cultural, and societal benefits (Cutshall, 2005; Lopez Estrada, Gomez, & Ruiz-Escalante, 2009). Personally, second language learning offers students greater access to other individuals, resources, and employment opportunities, as well as a greater understanding of their heritage and cultural diversity. It also can promote greater family cohesion as children still retain their first language and use it to communicate with their families. Cognitively, learning a second language helps students improve their reading and problem-solving skills and promotes their creativity. In terms of societal benefits, individuals who speak more than one language can increase the economic competitiveness of the United States.

Research indicates that many English language learners will benefit in terms of academic progress and acquisition of English skills from bilingual education programs. How could all students benefit from a two-way bilingual education program?

Two-Way Bilingual Education Programs. One integrated example of a bilingual education program is a **two-way program** or *dual language program* that mixes students who speak languages other than English with students who speak English (García & Jensen, 2007; Lopez Estrada et al., 2009). Research indicates that these dual language programs help *all students* develop proficiency in both languages, as well as an understanding of different cultures (August, Calderón, Carlo, & Nuttall, 2006; Thomas & Collier, 2004). While both languages are used to deliver instruction, content is taught in each language approximately 50% of the time. Faltis (2006), the Center for Applied Linguistics (2005), and Calderón and Minaya-Rowe (2003) offer principles, guidelines, and resources for implementing two-way bilingual education programs.

English as a Second Language. A program that can be a component of or an alternative to a bilingual education program is instruction in **English as a Second Language (ESL)**, sometimes referred to as *English to Speakers of Other Languages* (ESOL) (Levine & McCloskey, 2009). ESL is usually a pull-out program that uses the students' native culture and language to develop their skills in understanding, speaking, reading, and writing English. In ESL programs, content instruction and communication occur only in English.

Making Connections
Find out more about effective ESL practices in Chapter 8.

PEARSON
myeducationlab

Go to the Building Teaching Skills and Dispositions section of the Topic *Cultural and Linguistic Diversity* in the MyEducationLab for your course and complete the activity entitled *Culturally Responsive Instruction*. As you work through the learning unit, consider what you've read in this chapter about the strengths and challenges of students from culturally and linguistically diverse backgrounds.

REFLECTIVE
ВЕЕГЕСІІХЕ

How have your cultural, linguistic, and ethnic identities affected you? Advantaged and disadvantaged you in society?

EDUCATIONAL STRENGTHS AND CHALLENGES OF STUDENTS FROM CULTURALLY AND LINGUISTICALLY DIVERSE BACKGROUNDS

WHAT ARE THE EDUCATIONAL STRENGTHS AND CHALLENGES OF STUDENTS FROM CULTURALLY AND LINGUISTICALLY DIVERSE BACKGROUNDS? As we learned earlier in this chapter, a growing number of students attending schools in the United States are students from culturally and linguistically diverse backgrounds. Data indicate that although their educational performance is improving, they are achieving below their potential and at a level that is not commensurate with their peers (Goldenberg, 2008; Taylor & Whittaker, 2009). However, it is also important to recognize that variety also characterizes these students and their school performance with many of them performing above grade level, being highly motivated to succeed in school, and coming from varied class backgrounds. Therefore, when designing programs targeting the academic, social, and behavioral needs of students from culturally and linguistically diverse backgrounds, you need to build on students' strengths and be aware of the cultural, religious, linguistic, experiential, and economic factors that affect these students (Obiakor, 2007; Villegas & Lucas, 2007).

Cultural Considerations

Our schools—and therefore the academic and social expectations for our students—are based on mainstream, middle-class culture. For many students from diverse backgrounds, it is important to be aware of this potential cultural mismatch and bias and its effects on your students' academic performance and cultural identities (Gollnick & Chinn, 2009; Rueda, Jin Lim, & Velasco, 2007). In addition, it is important for you to maintain and communicate high expectations for *all* of your students and understand their different backgrounds, and respect and accommodate their similarities and differences. You can do this by using culturally responsive teaching so that your instructional strategies and curricula reflect the different cultures, experiences, and languages of your students (Araujo, 2009; Obiakor, 2007). You also need to reflect on how cultural assumptions and values influence your own expectations, beliefs, and behaviors, as well as those of your students, other professionals, families, and community members (Cartledge & Kourea, 2008; Taylor & Whittaker, 2009). It is also important to develop cultural competence and intercultural communication skills so that you can support your students' cultural identities and establish collaborative partnerships with them and with family and community members (Harry et al., 2008; Sheehey, Ornelles, & Noonan, 2009).

Learning Style Because cultural differences also affect the way individuals process, organize, and learn material, you need to observe students and adjust your teaching behaviors to identify and match their diverse learning styles (Daniels, 2007). Irvine (1991) notes that many students from nondominant cultures use a learning style based on variation, movement, divergent thinking, inductive reasoning, and an emphasis on people.

Another factor that affects how classrooms are structured and how students function is the way activities and classroom interactions are ordered (Cloud & Landurand, n.d.). In *polychronic* cultures, individuals engage in many different activities at the same time. For example, students from polychronic cultures may talk with others while doing seatwork, whereas those from *monochronic* cultures may prefer to work without talking.

Researchers also have found cross-cultural differences in movement (Cloud & Landurand, n.d.). Students who are used to being active may have difficulties in classrooms where movement is limited. These differences also can influence the teacher's perception of a student's academic and behavioral performance.

Religious Diversity

Today's schools include a diverse group of students including those from a variety of religious backgrounds (Taylor & Whittaker, 2009). Religious beliefs and traditions can affect students' attendance, participation in activities, diet, dress, learning, or behavior in school. Although these differences can be a rich source of learning for *all students*, they can create divisions and conflicts among students, and challenges that educators need to address (Whittaker, Salend, & Elhoweris, 2009).

DIFFERENTIATING CULTURAL AND LANGUAGE DIFFERENCES FROM LEARNING DIFFICULTIES

HOW CAN I DIFFERENTIATE CULTURAL AND LANGUAGE DIFFERENCES FROM LEARNING DIFFICULTIES? Students' abilities to use language and adjust to the culture have a great effect on their educational, social, and behavioral performance. Students who are learning English like Halee often have the usual difficulties associated with learning a second language, such as poor understanding, limited vocabulary, grammatical and syntactical mistakes, and articulation difficulties. They often may exhibit similar learning, attention, social, behavioral, and emotional difficulties as students with high incidence disabilities (Baca, 2008; Klingner, Artiles, & Mendez Barletta, 2006). However, if they are placed in special education classes, these students often receive little support in their native language, which can hurt their linguistic and

Making Connections
Find out more about effective culturally responsive practices in Chapter 8.

PEARSON myeducationlab

Go to the Assignments and Activities section of the Topic *Cultural and Linguistic Diversity* in the MyEducationLab for your course and complete the activity entitled *Cultural, Linguistic, and Other Factors that Influence Participation.*

REFLECTIVE

How has your cultural background affected your learning, teaching and communication style?

Making Connections
Find out more about guidelines and strategies to teach students about religious diversity in Chapter 5.

BEELECIIΛE

If you moved to another country that had a different language and culture when you were in school, what aspects of school would be difficult for you? Would you want to receive your academic instruction in English or the language of your new country? Would you want to receive special education services?

Making Connections

This discussion about diversifying the planning team builds on what we covered earlier on the role of the comprehensive planning team in the special education process, in Chapter 2.

academic development. Therefore, you and other members of the comprehensive planning team must be able to understand the behaviors of English language learners that resemble those of students with learning, speech, and language disabilities so that English language learners are not inappropriately placed in special education (Klingner et al., 2008; Spinelli, 2008). These behaviors are presented in Table 3.1.

In assessing English language learners, it is also important to recognize that the IDEA mandates that students should not be identified as having a disability if their eligibility and school-related difficulties are related to their cultural and experiential backgrounds, their proficiency in English, or their lack of opportunity to receive instruction in reading or mathematics. The following sections offer guidelines for more accurately and fairly assessing English language learners to differentiate learning difficulties from language differences.

Diversify the Comprehensive Planning Team

The composition and training of the comprehensive planning team are critical factors in determining the educational strengths and challenges of English language learners. Therefore, the team should include family and community members, as well as professionals who are fluent in the student's native language (e.g., bilingual educators), understand the student and the family's culture, and can help collect and interpret the data in culturally and linguistically appropriate ways (Figueroa & Newsome, 2006).

Compare Student Performance in Both the Primary and Secondary Languages

The assessment plan for English language learners should collect data to compare student performance in both the primary and secondary languages (Esparza Brown & Doolittle, 2008). Data relating to students' performance in both languages can be

TABLE 3.1 Characteristics of English language learners resembling those of students with learning disabilities

Characteristics of Students with Learning Disabilities	Characteristics of English Language Learners
Significant difference between the student's performance on verbal and nonverbal tasks and test items	May have more success in completing nonverbal tasks than verbal tasks
Difficulty mastering academic material	May have difficulty learning academic material that is abstract or taken out of context
Language difficulties	May have language difficulties that are a normal part of second language learning, such as poor comprehension, limited vocabulary, articulation problems, and grammatical and syntactical errors
Perceptual difficulties	May have perceptual difficulties related to learning a new language and adjusting to a new culture
Social, behavioral, and emotional difficulties	May experience social, behavioral, and emotional difficulties as part of the frustration of learning a new language and adjusting to a new culture
Attention and memory difficulties	May have attention and memory problems because it is difficult to concentrate for long periods of time when teaching is done in a new language

Sources: Fradd and Weismantel (1989); Klingner et al. (2008); Mercer and Pullen (2009).

collected through the use of standardized tests, language samples, observations, questionnaires, and interviews. These methods can be employed to examine students' language proficiency, language dominance, language preference, and code switching. **Language proficiency** relates to the degree of skill in speaking the language(s) and includes receptive and expressive language skills. While proficiency in one language does not necessarily mean lack of proficiency in another language, **language dominance** refers to the language in which the student is most fluent and implies a comparison of the student's abilities in two or more languages. **Language preference** identifies the language in which the student prefers to communicate, which can vary depending on the setting. **Code switching**, a phenomenon commonly observed in individuals learning a second language, relates to using words, phrases, expressions, and sentences from one language while speaking another language (Reyes, 2004).

Making Connections
This discussion of student's language performance builds on what we covered earlier on speech and language disorders, in Chapter 2.

Consider the Processes and Factors Associated with Second Language Acquisition

The assessment process for English language learners like Halee should recognize that learning a second language is a long-term, complex, and dynamic process that involves different types of language skills and various stages of development (Goldenberg, 2008). Therefore, when assessing English language learners, the team needs to consider the factors that affect second language acquisition and understand the stages students go through in learning a second language (Esparza Brown & Doolittle, 2008).

Gaining proficiency in a second language involves the acquisition of two distinct types of language skills (Lopez Estrada et al., 2009). ***Basic interpersonal communication skills (BICS)*** are the social language skills that guide students in developing of social relationships and engaging in casual face-to-face conversations (e.g., "Good morning. How are you?"). These social conversations tend to involve use of shorter sentences that contain simpler vocabulary and syntactical and grammatical structures and relate to familiar and repetitive topics (e.g., daily events, the weather). Even though they are relatively repetitive, are paired with gestures, occur within a specific and clearly defined context, and are not cognitively demanding, research indicates that they typically take up to 2 years to develop in a second language (Cummins, 2000).

Cognitive/academic language proficiency (CALP) refers to the language skills that relate to literacy, cognitive development, and academic development in the classroom (Goldenberg, 2008). It includes understanding such complex and technical academic terms as *photosynthesis, onomatopoeia,* and *least common denominator.* Because CALP does not have an easily understood context and tends to be cognitively demanding, it can take up to 7 years to develop and use these language skills (Cummins, 2000). CALP skills developed in one's first language foster the development of CALP in one's second language; therefore, it is important to gather information on students' proficiency and educational training in their native language.

In learning a second language, students go through developmental stages (see Figure 3.2) that should be considered when evaluating their learning (Goldenberg, 2008; Levine & McCloskey, 2009; Rubinstein-Avila, 2006). Initially, English language learners' understanding of the new language is usually greater than their production. Many English language learners go through a **silent period** in which they process what they hear and focus on processing language but refrain from verbalizing. This is often misinterpreted as indicating a lack of cognitive abilities, disinterest in school, or shyness.

When students are ready to attempt to speak a new language, their verbalizations are usually single words such as *yes* or *no* or recurring phrases such as "How are you?" and "Thank you." Once students are ready to speak their new language, their verbalizations gradually increase in terms of their semantic and syntactic complexity. You can help students who are ready to speak by creating a risk-free environment,

REFLECTIVE

What was it like for you to learn a second language? What stages did you go through in learning a second language?

FIGURE 3.2 Stages of second language learning

In learning a second language, some students may go through the following stages:

- *Preproduction or Silent period.* Students focus on processing and understanding what they hear but avoid verbal responses. They often rely on modeling, visual stimuli, context clues, and key words, and use listening strategies to understand meaning. They often communicate by pointing and physical gestures. They may benefit from classroom activities that allow them to respond by imitating, drawing, pointing, and matching.
- *Telegraphic or Early Production period.* Students begin to use two- or three-word sentences and show limited comprehension. They usually have a receptive vocabulary of approximately 1,000 words and an expressive vocabulary of approximately 100 words. They may benefit from classroom activities that employ language they can understand; require them to name, label, and group objects; ask them to respond to simple questions and use vocabulary they already understand; and offer praise and encouragement for their attempts to use their new language.
- *Interlanguage and Intermediate Fluency period.* Students use longer phrases and start to use complete sentences. They often mix basic phrases and sentences in both languages. They may benefit from classroom activities that encourage them to experiment with language and develop and expand their vocabulary.
- *Extensions and Expansions period.* Students expand on their basic sentences and extend their language abilities to synonyms and synonymous expressions. At this stage, they are developing good comprehension skills, using more complex sentence structures, and making fewer errors when speaking. They may benefit from classroom reading and writing activities, as well as from instruction that expands on their vocabulary and knowledge of grammar.
- *Enrichment period.* Students are taught learning strategies to assist them in making the transition to the new language.
- *Independent Learning period.* Students begin to work on activities at various levels of difficulty with different groups.

Source: Goldenberg (2008); Gutierrez (2007); Maldonado-Colón (1995).

Students go through several stages in learning a second language and adjusting to a new culture. Why is it important for you to understand these stages?

simplifying your language, focusing on communication rather than grammar, providing visual cues and physical gestures that offer students a context for understanding verbal comments, and acknowledging and responding to their attempts to communicate (Al Otaiba & Pappamihiel, 2005).

It also is important for the team to be aware of other factors that may affect students and their developmental progress in maintaining their native language and learning their new language (Rance-Roney, 2009). Therefore, keep the following points in mind:

- Students who have been educated in their native language often progress faster in learning a new language than those who have not had a formal education (Goldenberg, 2008; Lopez Estrada et al., 2009).
- Students who speak languages that are similar to English tend to learn English faster than those whose first language is very different from English (Dong, 2009). It also is very common for students to attempt to apply the rules of and cognates

from their first language to their second language, which can affect students' comprehension (in French, *angles congruents* is *congruent angles*), pronunciation (e.g., students say *share* for *chair*), syntax (e.g., in Spanish, adjectives follow the noun and agree with the gender and number of the noun), and spelling.

- As some students learn a second language, they may experience language loss or arrested language development in their native language (Wrigley, 2004).
- Children who simultaneously learn two languages from birth may initially experience some temporary language delays in achieving developmental language milestones and some language mixing, which tends to disappear over time (Rodriguez & Higgins, 2005).

Employ Alternatives to Traditional Standardized Testing

Rather than relying solely on potentially biased, standardized tests, the team can employ a variety of alternative assessment procedures to assess students from culturally and linguistically diverse backgrounds accurately (Rinaldi & Samson, 2008; Spinelli, 2008). These assessment alternatives can provide the team with more complete profiles of students like Halee including their academic strengths and challenges, learning styles, and the impact of the school environment on their learning.

Making connections
Find out more about assessment alternatives to standardized testing in Chapter 12.

Identify Diverse Life and Home Experiences That Might Affect Learning and Language Development

Many English language learners have diverse life experiences that can have a significant impact on their learning and language development, such as being separated from family members for extended periods of time (Esparza Brown & Doolittle, 2008; Fielder et al., 2008). Students' home environments also can affect their language acquisition, including the language(s) that students are exposed to in their homes and communities (Rinaldi & Samson, 2008). Identifying these experiences and factors can help determine whether students' learning and language difficulties are related to the existence of a disability or other experiential factors (Klingner et al., 2008). Therefore, you and other professionals can use the guidelines in Figure 3.3 to collect information to help determine whether a student's difficulties in learning are due to language, cultural, and experiential factors or lack of exposure to effective instruction. The team also should consider the effect of the student's motivation, personality, and social skills on school performance.

Analyze the Data, and Develop an Appropriate Educational Plan

After the data have been collected, the team analyzes the information and makes decisions about students' educational programs (Fielder et al., 2008; Rinaldi & Samson, 2008). For English language learners, the analysis should focus on examining the factors that affect learning and language development, determining whether learning and language difficulties occur in both languages, and developing an educational plan to promote learning and language acquisition (Esparza Brown & Doolittle, 2008; Figueroa & Newsome, 2006). Damico (1991) offers the following questions that can guide you and others in examining the data to identify the factors and conditions that may explain the student's learning and/or language difficulties:

- Do the student's difficulties occur in both the student's primary and secondary (new) language?
- Are the student's difficulties due to normal second language acquisition, dialectical differences, or cultural factors?
- Are the student's difficulties related to lack of or limited opportunities to receive instruction?

FIGURE 3.3 Life experience factors and questions to consider in assessing second language learners

Length of Residence in the United States
- How long and for what periods of time has the student lived in the United States?
- What were the conditions and events associated with the student's migration?
- If the student was born in the United States, what has been the student's exposure to English?

Students may have limited or interrupted exposure to English, resulting in poor vocabulary, slow naming speed, and minimal verbal participation. Being born and raised in the United States does not guarantee that students have developed English skills and have had significant exposure to English and the U.S. culture.

School Attendance Patterns
- How long has the student been in school?
- What is the student's attendance pattern? Have there been any disruptions in school?

Students may fail to learn language skills because they do not attend school.

School Instructional History
- How many years of schooling did the student complete in the native country?
- What language(s) were used to guide teaching in the native country?
- What types of classrooms has the student attended (bilingual education, English as a second language, general education, speech/language therapy services, special education)?
- What has been the language of instruction in these classes?
- How proficient is the student in reading, writing, and speaking in the native language?
- What strategies and teaching materials have been successful?
- What were the outcomes of these educational placements?
- What language does the student prefer to use in informal situations with adults? In formal situations with adults?

Students may not have had access to appropriate instruction and curricula, resulting in problems in language learning, reading, and mathematics.

Cultural Background
- How does the student's cultural background affect second language learning?
- Has the student had enough time to adjust to the new culture?
- What is the student's acculturation level?
- Does the student want to learn English?

Since culture and language are closely linked, lack of progress in learning a second language can be due to cultural and communication differences and/or lack of exposure to the new culture. For example, some cultures rely on body language as a substitute for verbal communication. Various cultures also have different perspectives on color, time, gender, distance, and space, which can affect language.

Performance in Comparison with Peers
- Does the student's language skill, learning rate, and learning style differ from those of other students from similar experiential, cultural, and language backgrounds?
- Does the student interact with peers in the primary language and/or English?
- Does the student have difficulty following directions, understanding language, and expressing thoughts in the primary language? In the second language?

The student's performance can be compared with that of students who have similar traits rather than with that of students whose experiences in learning a second language are very different.

Home Life
- What language(s) or dialect(s) are spoken at home by each of the family members?
- What language(s) are spoken by the student's siblings?
- When did the student start to speak?
- Is the student's performance at home different from that of siblings?
- What language(s) or dialect(s) are spoken in the family's community?
- Is a distinction made among the uses of the primary language or dialect and English? If so, how is that distinction made? (For example, the non-English language is used at home, but children speak English when playing with peers.)
- What are the attitudes of the family and the community toward schooling, learning English, and bilingual education?
- In what language(s) does the family watch television, listen to the radio, and read newspapers, books, and magazines?
- What language does the student prefer to use at home and in the community?
- To what extent does the family interact with the dominant culture and in what ways?
- How comfortable are the student and the family in interacting with the dominant culture?

Important information on the student's language proficiency, dominance, and preference can be obtained by getting data from family members. The student's language learning can be improved by involving family members in the educational program.

Health and Developmental History
- What health, medical, sensory, and developmental factors have affected the student's learning and language development?

A student's difficulty in learning may be related to various health and developmental problems.

Source: Langdon (1989).

- Are the student's difficulties linked to
  - Experiential background and migration?
  - Cultural factors and acculturation?
  - Educational, home, and community factors?
  - Stressful life events and health?
- Were the student's cultural, linguistic, dialectic, and experiential backgrounds considered in collecting and analyzing the assessment data (e.g., selection, administration, and interpretation of the test's results; RTI and prereferral strategies; learning styles; family involvement)?

These questions also can guide the team in differentiating between two types of English language learners and planning appropriate educational programs for these students (Baca, 2008). One type is like Halee. These students tend to have some proficiency in their native language. However, their skills in and difficulty in learning their new language are consistent with the typical stages of second language acquisition, and they need help to develop their skills in their new language. These students may benefit from an academically rich curriculum and appropriate instructional strategies that recognize and support their primary and secondary languages and cultural identity (Hoover et al., 2008).

The other type of English language learner has language, academic, and social behaviors in the first and second languages that are significantly below those of peers who have similar linguistic, cultural, and experiential backgrounds (Baca, 2008; Klingner et al., 2008). In addition, these students may show some of the behaviors listed in Figure 3.4 both in school and at home. Furthermore, assessment may show that they have not made satisfactory progress even with an appropriate curriculum and teaching provided by qualified educators for a long period of time. These students may have a disability and may benefit from a special education program and IEP that addresses their unique linguistic, cultural, and experiential backgrounds and learning strengths and challenges.

To enhance your understanding of how culture and language can influence performance in your inclusive classroom, go to the IRIS Center Resources section of Topic: Cultural and Linguistic Diversity in the MyEducationLab for your course, and complete the module entitled *Cultural and Linguistic Differences: What Teachers Should Know.*

FIGURE 3.4 **Student behaviors to observe when distinguishing a language difference from a learning difficulty**

Teachers can tell when a student from a linguistically and culturally diverse background might need special education services for a language-learning disability when some of the following behaviors are manifested in comparison with similar peers:

1. Nonverbal aspects of language are culturally inappropriate.
2. Student does not express basic needs adequately.
3. Student rarely initiates verbal interaction with peers.
4. When peers initiate interaction, student responds sporadically/inappropriately.
5. Student replaces speech with gestures, communicates nonverbally when talking would be appropriate and expected.
6. Peers give indications that they have difficulty understanding the student.
7. Student often gives inappropriate responses.
8. Student has difficulty conveying thoughts in an organized, sequential manner that is understandable to listeners.
9. Student shows poor topic maintenance ("skips around").
10. Student has word-finding difficulties that go beyond normal second language acquisition patterns.
11. Student fails to provide significant information to the listener, leaving the listener confused.
12. Student has difficulty with conversational turn-taking skills (may be too passive or may interrupt inappropriately).
13. Student perseverates (remains too long) on a topic even after the topic has changed.
14. Student fails to ask and answer questions appropriately.
15. Student needs to hear things repeated, even when they are stated simply and comprehensibly.
16. Student often echoes what she or he hears.

Source: From C. Roseberry-McKibbin, *Multicultural Education*, Summer 1995, p.14. Reprinted by permission.

DISCRIMINATION AND BIAS

WHAT IS THE EFFECT OF DISCRIMINATION AND BIAS ON STUDENTS AND SCHOOLS? Students from specific racial, linguistic, and religious backgrounds face discrimination in society and school (Nieto & Bode, 2008; Thompson, 2009). While this discrimination is displayed openly in verbal harassment and physical violence in society, it is more subtle in institutions such as schools, which are becoming more segregated. In addition to almost complete segregation, severe inequalities in funding, preschool opportunities, class sizes, physical facilities, resources, remedial services, instructional materials, textbooks, certified teachers, technology, and expectations of student performance serve as the basis for different treatment and expectations in the classroom based on socioeconomic status, race, and language background (Kozol, 2001; Nieto & Bode, 2008).

REFLECTING ON PROFESSIONAL PRACTICES

Assessing English Language Learners

Halee was placed in Ms. Ruger's class and started to struggle academically. She sat quietly in the back of the room and kept to herself. Whenever directions were given, she seemed lost and had difficulty completing tasks and participating in class discussions. During teacher-directed activities, Halee often looked around at other students or played with materials at her desk.

Ms. Ruger was concerned about Halee's inability to pay attention and complete her work. She would watch Halee talk "a lot" (for Halee) at recess with the other students but be quiet in class during academic instruction. Ms. Ruger felt that as a teacher she was doing something wrong, that she was intimidating Halee.

She thought Halee might have a learning problem and referred Halee to the school's Student Study team. The team, which included Ms. Vang, a bilingual educator, began to work with other members of the team to gather information about Halee. Ms. Vang assessed Halee's skills in her native language. She reported that Halee grasped concepts quickly when they were explained in her native language and figured out grammatical patterns in English exercises when directions were explained to her. Although Halee told Ms. Vang that she hadn't learned to read in her native language, Ms. Vang realized that Halee could use her native language to retell stories in her own words, predict sequences, and answer questions accurately. Ms. Vang was also able to obtain information about Halee's past by speaking to Halee's mother in her native language. Halee's mother told Ms. Vang that she finds it difficult to help Halee with her schoolwork and relies on Halee to help take care of the younger sister and to cook and clean. Halee's mother also told Ms. Vang that although her children watch television in English, the interactions in the home are in their language. Interactions with the family also revealed that the family has few links to and interactions with the community and that their lifestyle parallels the traditions of her native country.

Other members of the team collected data on Halee's English skills. One team member observed Halee in her classroom, in the cafeteria, and during recess. The team met to share their findings and concluded that Halee was beginning to learn English. They noted that Halee was a capable student who was having many of the difficulties English language learners experience in learning a new language and adjusting to a new culture.

The team also discussed and identified ways to assist Ms. Ruger in understanding and meeting Halee's needs. They helped Ms. Ruger understand that it is not uncommon for students like Halee to appear to lose their concentration after about 10 minutes of instruction. They explained to Ms. Ruger that instruction delivered in the student's second language requires intense concentration, which is difficult for an English language learner to sustain for long periods of time. They said that Halee's behavior was not a disability but rather an indication that her "system was shutting down" and that she needed a break. They also talked about learning a second language and how social language develops first, as well as the difficulties in learning the academic language used in the classroom.

Ms. Ruger seemed to understand and to feel better. Knowledge of Halee's past gave her insights into the emotional side of Halee. She worked with Ms. Vang and others on the team to make instructional, content, and testing accommodations to address Halee's strengths and challenges.

- Why did Ms. Ruger refer Halee for assessment?
- What strategies did the team use to collect information about Halee?
- Why did the team conclude that Halee did not qualify for special education services?
- What role did Ms. Vang play?
- Why was it important for the team to include her?
- If you had a student like Halee, what services do you think she would need to succeed in your class?
- What services would you need to help Halee?

Through subtle experiences at school, students and their families can internalize perceptions of themselves held by educators and other members of society (Brandon & Brown, 2009; Thompson, 2008). Positive perceptions about an individual's race and identity can promote increased self-esteem and success in school, whereas negative attitudes can achieve the opposite results. Unfortunately, school curricula, teacher behaviors, assessment instruments, teaching materials and textbooks, family involvement procedures, and peer relationships usually address the academic and socialization needs of white middle-class students only (Nieto & Bode, 2008). As a result, students from lower socioeconomic backgrounds and students from nondominant groups suffer both hidden and overt discrimination in schools. This can cause underachievement and loss of cultural identity, leading eventually to placement in special education classes. Schools and teachers need to challenge racism and offer education programs that promote the identity and academic performance of *all students*.

Multiracial/Ethnic Students

Because of the changing demographics in the United States, teachers will be serving an increasing number of students from multiracial/ethnic families (Taylor & Whittaker, 2009). Multiracial/ethnic students who grow up appreciating their rich multiracial/ethnic identity are able to function well in many cultures and to understand and adjust to a variety of perspectives. However, these students and their families face racial discrimination and many challenges, such as being forced to choose one racial identity over the other, describing themselves to others ("What are you?"), and making friends and participating in social groups that are generally based on racial and ethnic similarities (Davis, 2009). The result can be cultural and racial identification problems, self-concept difficulties, the feeling of being an outsider in two or more cultures, and pressures to cope with conflicting cultural perspectives and demands. Brown (2009) and Davis (2009) offers information and resources that can help you understand these students and their families and help them succeed in your inclusive classroom.

Gender Bias

Educators also have been exploring differences in the way schools respond to female and male students and the outcomes of this different treatment (Murray & Taylor, 2009; Reasoner Jones, 2008; Sadker, Sadker, & Zittleman, 2009). Schools tend to treat girls differently from boys and inadvertently reinforce stereotyped views of girls in terms of behavior, personality, aspirations, and achievement, which may hinder their academic and social development (Manwaring, 2008). For instance, in many elementary and secondary classrooms,

- boys talk and are called on more, are listened to more carefully, and are interrupted less than girls; and
- boys are given more feedback, asked to respond to higher-level questions, and take more intellectual risks than girls (Sadker et al., 2009; Sanders & Cotton Nelson, 2004).

Boys and girls generally enter school with equal academic abilities and self-concepts, but girls usually lag behind boys in both areas when they graduate from high school. Although the gap has narrowed in most areas recently, girls' access to technology and training in computer sciences and underrepresentation in high-paying and high-status careers are still troubling issues.

Gender and race interact, making girls from culturally and linguistically diverse backgrounds even more susceptible to bias in society and in school (Rollock, 2007).

REFLECTIVE

Because mainstream schools do not educate African American students effectively, several urban school districts have proposed separate schools for African American boys. Do you think this separation by gender and race is appropriate?

PEARSON
myeducationlab

To hear an expert discuss how cultural and linguistic differences can affect you and your students go to the IRIS Center Resource section of Topic: Cultural and Linguistic Diversity in the MyEducationLab for your course, and listen to the podcast entitled "Episode 1: Donna Ford on Cultural and Linguistic Differences."

Because girls generally don't act out and attract as much attention as boys, their unique and special needs are sometimes overlooked. What are some of the unique needs of your female students?

Using Technology to Promote Inclusion
BRIDGING THE DIGITAL DIVIDE

Technology has become an essential tool for accessing information and the general education curriculum, and an important teaching tool for differentiating instruction to support student learning. However, despite the growing availability of technology, a **digital divide** still exists, which means that your students from culturally and linguistically diverse backgrounds, students living in poverty, students with disabilities, and female students may encounter barriers that limit their access to and use of technology in their homes and schools. Because web-based information can reinforce existing societal inequities and stereotypical views, bridging the digital divide also means that students need to learn how to evaluate web-based information and sites in terms of the accuracy of the content of the site as well as the impact of the content on visitors to the site.

Although providing *all students* with access to technology and the training they need to use it effectively is a challenge, here are some strategies that others have used to bridge the digital divide:

- Collect information to determine which students have access to and use technology, and which students do not.
- Teach *all students* the skills they need to access information via technology.
- Establish partnerships with community-based organizations such as libraries, colleges, and community centers to make technology available to students and their families after school.

- Create a technology lending library so that students and their families can borrow technology, and provide students and their families with a list of free or low-cost resources that can help them get online (e.g., local libraries, community centers).
- Conduct technology events that relate to students' interests and special themes, and activities that counter stereotypical views associated with technology use.
- Motivate students to use technology by providing them with opportunities to use a wide range of hardware, applications, educational games, and simulations and to apply their technology skills to benefit and connect with their families, communities, and other students.
- Use a multifaceted approach to instruction and grading so that students are not penalized for their lack of access to technology. For example, provide students with alternatives when giving them assignments that require them to use technology to which they do not have access.
- Communicate with students and their families so that hard copies of products available online are also available for students and families who cannot access the material online.
- Choose software programs and digital materials that are challenging, interactive, and motivating, allow choices in terms of levels of difficulty, are sensitive to diversity, avoid negative stereotypes, and can be used in several languages.

Sources: Prensky (2008); Salpeter (2006).

Making Connections
Find out more about how to teach your students to evaluate web-based information and sites in Chapter 8.

REFLECTIVE

How would you describe the level of access you and your students have to technology? What does your school do to foster access to technology for students and educators?

In addition, many female students from nondominant cultural backgrounds face conflicts between the cultural values of mainstream U.S. society, which emphasize independence and ambition, and their own culture, which may promote traditional roles for women. Females from culturally and linguistically diverse and from lower socioeconomic backgrounds also may have to assume responsibilities at home or work to help support their families.

There also appears to be a self-esteem gap in the ways society and schools respond to girls and boys. Girls are taught by society to base their self-esteem on physical appearance and popularity, while boys are encouraged to do so in relation to school and sports. Girls, particularly in adolescence, may be vulnerable to peer pressure that encourages social success at the expense of high grades. This fear of rejection and of being smart but not popular can cause girls to underachieve, to attempt to hide their success, to not enroll in advanced and challenging courses, and to select careers that are not commensurate with their skills. Because girls generally don't act out and attract as much attention as boys, their unique and specialized needs are often overlooked (Manwaring, 2008), and therefore programs to address these needs are not funded. As these students leave school and start to work, they continue to encounter different treatment. As a result, they become overrepresented in low-paying and low-status occupations that offer fewer benefits and less job security.

Gender stereotypes also affect boys, albeit in different ways. For example, data indicate that

- girls score higher on reading and writing standardized tests than boys;
- girls are less likely to be placed in special education than boys; and
- girls complete school, take advance placement courses, and go on to college in higher rates than boys (Coutinho & Oswald, 2005; Murray & Taylor, 2009).

In particular, African American males experience an achievement gap in comparison with their male and female peers. They also are more likely to be placed in special education and suspended or expelled from school and less likely to enroll in college preparation courses (Perkins-Gough, 2006; Varlas, 2005). Like girls, the education of boys, including African American males, can be enhanced by providing them with positive role models, helping them learn to identify and challenge stereotypes, offering them a challenging and motivating curriculum that addresses their needs and interests, and using cooperative and active learning strategies (Brozo, 2006; King & Gurian, 2006; Murray & Taylor, 2009; Varlas, 2005).

Eating Disorders and Obesity   The pressures placed on girls in terms of their appearance via advertising, fashion, and entertainment that promote an idealized view of the female body and the need to be the "perfect girl" contribute to the likelihood that some of your female students may have eating problems such as disordered eating, binge eating, bulimia, and anorexia (Botti, 2009). Students who participate in your school's sports programs, who are perfectionists, and who experience loss of personal relationships (e.g., family deaths or breakups) are particularly susceptible to developing some type of eating disorder.

Disordered eating is a generalized condition that refers to individuals who are preoccupied by the size and/or shape of their bodies and limit their eating and/or engage in compulsive exercise (Austin, & Sciarra, 2010; Botti, 2009). Whereas **binge eating disorders** typically involve repeated instances of secretive binge eating that lead to feelings of guilt, **bulimia** (or *bulimia nervosa*) involves binging on food followed by repeated attempts to purge oneself of the excess calories by vomiting, taking medications or laxatives, fasting, or exercising. Less prevalent than bulimia, **anorexia** (or *anorexia nervosa*) involves refusal to eat and a disturbed sense of one's body shape or size, which results in a skeletal thinness and loss of weight that is denied by the individual. Both conditions affect one's health, emotional development, and school performance and can be life-threatening.

Helping these students involves being aware of the warning signs of these conditions, which you may observe via their frequent requests to go to the bathroom, dental problems, bad breath, and hair loss (see Table 3.2). In addition, collaborate with medical and psychological professionals (e.g., family physician, dietitian, school counselors, nurse, social worker, etc.) and family members to implement a comprehensive program to address related issues and support healthy eating habits, and observe and document student behaviors. You also can reflect on your comments, behaviors, and attitudes regarding body image; model healthy attitudes and behaviors; teach students how to critique messages from the society and the media; and make sure that students are not ridiculed because of their appearance. Additional information and resources related to eating disorders is available from the National Eating Disorders Association's Web site (www.nationaleatingdisorders.org).

Unfortunately, a growing number of children and youth in the United States are overweight (Lapkoff & Li, 2007). These children may experience a variety of health problems, including a lack of energy, and teasing and discrimination, which can affect their learning, socialization, and self-esteem. Some of these children have medical conditions that make them prone to being overweight, but a poor diet and a sedentary lifestyle also are culprits (i.e., spending significant amounts of time watching TV or on a computer). Rather than focusing on a student's size, weight loss, or diets, you can promote the acceptance of different body types, and emphasize

Making Connections
This discussion of eating disorders builds on what we covered earlier on obsessive-compulsive disorders, in Chapter 2.

TABLE 3.2 Symptoms of individuals with anorexia nervosa and bulimia nervosa

	Anorexia Nervosa	Bulimia Nervosa
Behavioral	May establish goals that are often not attainable Severe weight loss Excessive dieting May engage in ongoing purging and bingeing Compulsive exercising Socially withdrawn and isolated from others Avoids events that involve eating Complains of abdominal pain and constipation	May establish goals that are often not attainable Frequent variations in weight Excessive dieting May engage in ongoing purging and bingeing Compulsive exercising Very social and extroverted Has bad breath, mouth sores, and sore throat Frequent trips to the bathroom after eating Complains of abdominal pain, constipation, diarrhea, and nausea Swollen cheeks and broken blood vessels in the eyes and loss of tooth enamel
Psychological	Experiences concentration and attention difficulties that are often related to obsessions about caloric intake, weight, body image and shape, food or eating rituals Adopt strong positions and view things and situations as either right or wrong Struggles to remember content and information Has difficulty making decisions	Experiences concentration and attention difficulties that are often related to obsessions about caloric intake, weight, body image and shape, food or eating rituals Adopt strong positions and view things and situations as either right or wrong
Social-Emotional	Constantly strive for perfection, which results in ongoing feelings of failure Shows signs of being depressed Appears anxious and irritable Easily upset and frequent mood swings Exhibits a low self-image and esteem Feels ashamed and guilty about eating behaviors May be overly compliant and eager to please others	Constantly seeks perfection, which results in ongoing feelings of failure Shows signs of being depressed Appears anxious and irritable Easily upset and frequent mood swings Exhibits a low self-image and esteem Feels ashamed and guilty about eating behaviors

Sources: Manley, Rickson, and Standeven (2000); Medicinenet.com (2009).

Making Connections
Find out more about how to teach students to understand and confront stereotypes and bias in Chapter 5.

Making Connections
Find out more about ways to swiftly and consistently deal with insensitive and intolerant acts in Chapter 5.

and model healthful lifestyles, eating, and exercise as ways to feel better and have more energy (Lapkoff & Li, 2007; Simpson, Swicegood, & Gaus, 2006).

Gay, Lesbian, Bisexual, and Transgendered (GLBT) Youth

Gay, lesbian, bisexual, and **transgendered** (i.e., individuals who do not identify themselves as either of the two sexes) (GLBT) youth and youth who are questioning and exploring their sexual identity face homophobia and discrimination in schools and society (Quart, 2008; Sileo & Whittaker, 2009). This discrimination often takes the form of ridicule or bias-related physical assaults, which hinder the students' educational performance, emotional development, and participation in school-related programs (Byrnes, 2005a). Furthermore, when these events occur, very few teachers intervene. As a result, many GLBT youth attempt to hide their sexual orientation, whereas others are disciplined and referred for placement in special education programs for students with emotional and behavioral disorders (Denizet-Lewis, 2009; Raymond, 1997).

Because of the pressure to grow up "differently" and because of the homophobia in society, GLBT youth are at greater risk for poor school performance, substance abuse, leaving school, and suicide (Sileo & Whittaker, 2009). They frequently

A GUIDE TO ACTION
Fostering Equity in the Classroom

A very important part of your inclusive classroom is creating a classroom that fosters equity for *all students*. To create a classroom that fosters equity for *all students*, consider the following points:

- Avoid grouping students based on gender, race, language background and ethnicity, such as by forming separate lines, separate teams, separate seating arrangements, and separate academic learning groups, and comparing students across gender and racial variables.
- Hold high expectations for all of your students.
- Learn about the beliefs, traditions, customs, and experiences of all students in your classroom.
- Assign students of both sexes and *all races* to class and school jobs on a rotating basis.
- Use lessons and teaching materials that include the contributions of both sexes and *all races and groups*.
- Use gender-race-inclusive and gender-neutral language.
- Provide *all students* with models and mentors who represent a variety of perspectives and professions.

- Encourage *all students* to explore various careers, as well as academic, extracurricular, and recreational activities.
- Display pictures of males and females from *all races, religions, sexual orientations, and economic backgrounds* performing a variety of activities.
- Use cooperative learning groups and cross-sex and cross-race seating arrangements.
- Identify, confront and eliminate gender, racial, and other forms of bias in your classroom, school, assessment strategies and curriculum.
- Encourage female and male students of *all races* and *language backgrounds* to take risks, make decisions, assume leadership positions, and seek challenges.
- Affirm efforts and attributes that contribute to success in *all students*.

How would you rate how well you create a classroom environment that promotes equity for *all students*? ( ) Excellent ( ) Good ( ) Needs Improvement ( ) Needs Much Improvement

Create a plan of action for fostering equity in your classroom and school that includes your goals, the actions you will take and the resources you will need to achieve them, and the ways you will evaluate your success.

encounter rejection and abuse from their families, which affects their decision to reveal their sexual preference to others and results in high rates of homelessness.

Students with HIV/AIDS

Another group of students who have encountered bias are those with **acquired immune deficiency syndrome (AIDS)**, a viral condition that destroys an individual's defenses against infections (Spears, 2006). **Human immunodeficiency virus (HIV)**, which causes AIDS, is passed from one person to another through the exchange of infected body fluids (Best & Heller, 2009). Most children with HIV acquire the disease at birth. It is growing most rapidly among heterosexual men and women, infants, and teenagers. Some of the characteristics associated with adolescents make teenagers, especially those with disabilities, particularly susceptible to being exposed to HIV/AIDS (Sileo, 2005).

Even though there are no known incidents of the transmission of AIDS in school, issues related to teaching students with AIDS continue to be debated. Students with infectious diseases, including AIDS, are covered under Section 504 of the Rehabilitation Act. While special education is not required for all students with AIDS, such students who also have special educational needs are eligible for services under the IDEA. Thus, students with AIDS should have the same rights, privileges, and services as other students and should not be excluded from school unless they represent a direct health danger to others (e.g., engage in biting or scratching others, practice self-abuse, have open sores). Decisions on how to educate students with AIDS should be made by an interdisciplinary team based on the students' educational needs and social behaviors, as well as the judgments of medical personnel (Best & Heller, 2009). Teachers must also obtain written, informed consent before disclosing HIV-related information.

Supporting GLBT Students

As a junior high school teacher for 5 years, Mr. Rivers had witnessed his share of homophobic comments and actions from students and colleagues, and it bothered him that he had not confronted these biased individuals. Therefore, he was looking forward to the professional development session related to gay, lesbian, bisexual, and transgendered students.

At the session, he heard others talk about how they implemented antibias activities in their schools. One educator noted that "invisibility was a major issue" for their school. "We all assume everyone is heterosexual, and it's as if these kids don't exist. We decided to make GLBT issues visible and used our language, the school environment, and the curriculum to achieve that goal. We started by using the terms *gay, lesbian, transgendered,* and *bisexual* in school and in positive ways. We also tried to use gender-neutral language such as *partner or significant other* rather than *boyfriend* or *girlfriend*. We sought to promote visibility and support by displaying books, posters, and stickers that are sensitive to GLBT issues and by wearing GLBT-positive symbols. We got other teachers to put a pink or rainbow triangle on their classroom doors to indicate that everyone is safe in their rooms. We also placed books, magazines, and newspapers dealing with issues of sexual orientation on our bookshelves, offices, and common areas. We used the curriculum to make GLBT issues more visible. To counter the bias and exclusion in the curriculum regarding GLBT issues and individuals, we expanded the curriculum to include these issues and individuals in positive ways. For instance, some teachers mention the sexual orientation of famous GLBT historical figures, authors, musicians, scientists, and poets, which helps establish positive role models for students. We also promoted a discussion of GLBT issues by inviting speakers to talk to classes, assemblies, and faculty and family meetings and by structuring class projects around these issues. It has really helped."

Another group of teachers spoke about their efforts to respond immediately and sincerely to incidents of homophobia, heterosexism, and stereotyping in school. They talked about the legal requirement and need to establish and enforce sexual harassment, antiviolence, and antidiscrimination policies in the schools. They told the audience that "you need to make it clear that language has power and that abusive language has harmful effects and will not be tolerated. Persons who make derogatory comments and jokes, and use harassment focusing on an individual's sexuality or other personal characteristics, should be quickly informed that the school community considers their behavior inappropriate and that it will not be tolerated."

Mr. Rivers left the meeting determined to counter homophobic behavior in his school. He spoke to his principal, and to several teachers and students, and shared some materials and resources with them. Here are some other strategies you can use to implement the IDEA in your inclusive classroom and support GLBT youth and youth who are questioning and exploring their sexual identity:

- Use teaching materials that address issues related to sexual orientation and provide accurate information.
- Learn more about GLBT issues and speak to students about the terms they prefer to use to define and describe themselves.
- Include GLBT issues in the school district's plan to address student diversity.
- Refrain from advising students to reveal their sexual orientation to others, and help them understand the factors they should consider in sharing their sexuality with others.
- Help students and their families obtain appropriate services from agencies and professionals who are sensitive and trained to deal with GLBT issues.
- Acknowledge the achievements and concerns of GLBT students publicly.
- Collaborate with others to form a GLBT/Straight School Alliance, an after-school club welcoming all members of the school and community members who were interested in learning more about issues of sexual orientation in a safe environment, and promoting an accepting, safe, nondiscriminatory, and supportive environment in which all students are valued.

Sources: Adams and Carson (2006); Daniel (2007); Denizet-Lewis, 2009; Gay, Lesbian, Straight Education Network (GLSEN; 2002a, 2002b); National Education Association (2006); Schniedewind and Davidson (2006); Raymond (1997); Young et al., (2008).

FAMILY CHANGES

HOW HAVE FAMILY CHANGES AFFECTED STUDENTS AND SCHOOLS? During the last two decades, the structure of the U.S. family has undergone compelling changes. High divorce rates, economic pressures requiring both parents to work, and welfare reform have brought dramatic changes in the composition, structure, and function of families (Parish et al., 2008; Smith, Gartin, Murdick, & Hilton, 2006). As a result, the definition of *family* in the United States has changed dramatically, and you are likely to have students who live with both parents, one parent, other family members, friends, two mothers, two fathers, or foster families. Regardless of the family's composition, it is important for you to recognize that although these families may have unique challenges, they also want their children to succeed in school and share the same strengths, joys, and frustrations as other families (Dettmer et al., 2009; Wadsworth & Remaley, 2007).

Making Connections
Find out more about the strategies you can use to encourage families with a range of configurations to be partners with you in their children's education in Chapter 4.

Supporting Students Who Have AIDS

Mr. Ball was recently informed that Mary, one of his students, had AIDS. Not knowing much about AIDS, Mr. Ball decided that he needed to learn more. He used the Internet and found websites that provided information about students with AIDS. Through the Internet, he "spoke" with other teachers who had taught students like Mary. They told him that he needed to follow and maintain the legal guidelines for confidentiality contained in the Family Educational Rights and Privacy Act, which meant that he could not share information about Mary's medical condition with others. They also encouraged him to remember that Mary's social needs might be greater than her academic needs. With that advice, Mr. Ball was determined to encourage and assist Mary in participating in as many classroom and extracurricular activities as possible. Only if necessary would he limit Mary's participation in sports or other activities.

Here are some other strategies you can use to implement the IDEA in your inclusive classroom and support students with AIDS:

- Collaborate with others to deliver sensitive, nonjudgmental, and compassionate services to students and their families and work closely with medical personnel.

- Learn more about HIV/AIDS and prevention education programs.

- Pay attention to quality-of-life issues including relationships with friends and families, enjoying learning, broadening perspectives, and achieving independence and self-determination.

- Take universal precautions to protect one's health and safety, as well as the health and safety of the student with AIDS and other students. Methods include using protective barriers such as disposable surgical gloves, masks, aprons and eyewear when providing personal or health care to the student, covering wounds, using puncture-proof containers, cleaning surfaces with blood spills using a disinfectant, washing hands, and having access to facilities for washing and properly disposing of all items (e.g., gloves, bandages) that may be exposed (see Best, 2009, and Edens, Murdick, and Gartin, 2003, to learn more about universal precautions).

- Educate *all students* and families about the school district's policies and procedures regarding HIV/AIDS and about the use of universal precautions that protect *all students*.

- Include information about HIV/AIDS and its prevention as an important part of the curriculum.

Sources: Best and Heller (2009); Johnson, Johnson, and Jefferson-Aker (2001); Prater and Sileo (2001); Spears (2006).

Single-Parent Families

One result of the changes in families is the growing number of children living in single-parent homes, especially children with disabilities (Barton, 2004; Parish et al., 2008). It is estimated that fewer than 50% of the children in the United States live with both biological parents, and that 59% of all children will live in a single-parent household before they reach the age of 18. The growing number of children born to single mothers also has increased the number of single-parent families, with about a fourth of children younger than 18 living with a single parent who has never married.

Divorce

Divorce means that you are likely to have many students who live with one parent in your class. Approximately 90% of these children live with their mothers, who face many burdens as they assume many of the economic and social roles necessary to sustain the family. Divorce also can be hard for nonresidential parents, frequently fathers, who may find that their role in the child's life is decreased.

The effects of divorce tend to vary from child to child; however, the effects on boys seem to be more profound and persistent. Initially, children whose parents have divorced may exhibit anger, anxiety, depression, loneliness, noncompliance,

A growing number of students live in single-parent families. What can you do to help these students?

confusion, behavior and health problems, difficulty establishing close relationships, and poor school performance (Wallerstein, Lewis, & Blakeslee, 2000). Children who experience divorce, particularly girls, frequently feel torn between their parents, assume roles of caretakers for other family members, and may feel pressured to grow up too fast (Marquardt, 2005). Some researchers note that the negative effects of divorce are short-lived (Hetherington & Kelly, 2000); others believe that they are long lasting (Marquardt, 2005; Wallerstein et al., 2000). For some children, divorce may have positive effects. Children raised in two-parent families where the parents are in conflict have more difficulty adjusting than children raised in supportive, conflict-free, single-parent homes. The effects of a single divorce or multiple divorces on children depend on several factors, including the amount and nature of the conflict between the parents, the continuity parents provide for their children after the divorce, how much help parents can give their children, and the need to move.

As a result of conflicts between divorced parents, you may be put in a difficult situation. Some teachers deal with these conflicts by sending copies of all communications and assignments to both parents, as well as giving both parents the opportunity to attend conferences, either jointly or separately, depending on their preferences (Smith et al., 2006). School districts may have different policies regarding communication with family members, and the legal situations between family members may be complex, so consult your principal regarding contacts with both parents. For example, at the beginning of the school year, you can request a list of adults who may interact with your students at school. Many children live in blended families, in which one of their parents has married someone who also has children, so you should also seek clarification regarding the roles of these parents.

Extended Families

There also has been a dramatic increase in the number of children who live in **extended families** or in households headed by family members other than their parents (Green, 2009). Because approximately 5 million children live with their grandparents, you will probably also have children in your class who live in such a family. In addition to adapting your family involvement strategies to address their needs, you can help grandparent-headed households by linking them to groups that offer services to them.

Families Headed by Gay, Lesbian, Bisexual, and Transgendered Parents

An estimated 6 million to 12 million children live in families headed by gay, lesbian, bisexual, or transgendered family members (Lamme & Lamme, 2002). Like other families, these families are structured in a variety of ways, including two-adult families, single-parent families, joint parenting arrangements, and extended families. Although some studies suggest that children raised by gay and lesbian parents are well adjusted, these children also may have unique difficulties. Because their families may attract prejudice, these children may try to hide their family relationships from others. You can work with these families by learning more about them and the issues they face, and create a friendly and welcoming environment for *all families*.

Adopted Children

Between 1% and 2% of the children in the United States have been adopted. Many adoptions are intercountry or international adoptions, which involve the adoption of children born in other countries, many of whom were initially raised in orphanages (Meese, 2005). While the quality of care children receive in orphanages in other countries varies, these children may have learning, language, behavioral, social, and medical needs.

Whether children are adopted soon after birth or later, they and their families may face numerous adjustments and challenges (Meese, 1999). Early on, children must adjust to their new family and environment and deal with the separation from former caregivers, relatives, and friends, which can result in difficulties making emotional attachments with others or feeling pressure to be perfect in order to stay with their new family. They may believe that they caused others to "give them away because they are bad," which can make them depressed or afraid that they may be abandoned again. As they reach adolescence, adopted children may again experience grief as they seek to develop their identities and try to understand their biological past. Their behavior also may be shaped by the extent to which they were victims of abuse and neglect, and by whether they have lived with many families.

It is important to be sensitive to the unique needs of the child and the child's family. You can help *all children* appreciate the various ways families are formed and model positive attitudes toward adoption. For example, rather than using the terms *real* or *natural* parent and *adoptive* parent, you can use the terms *birth* or *biological parent* and *parent,* respectively. You also can give students alternatives to assignments that assume that students live with their biological parents or family members, and incorporate representations of adoptive families in classroom activities and discussions. For instance, rather than asking students to create a family tree or share baby pictures with the class, you can allow students to chronicle an important time in their lives or share a favorite picture of themselves. When working with students who were adopted after infancy, be aware of anniversaries (e.g., birthdays of relatives and the date they were removed from their birth home) that may cause unexplained or unusual behaviors. In addition, be sensitive to the feelings of adoptive parents, understand your role in the telling process, and become aware of adoption services and agencies that can assist you in working with students and their families.

Foster Families

An estimated 550,000 children and youth live with foster families (Lovitt, Emerson, & Sorensen, 2005). For a variety of reasons, many of these students experience school- and postschool-related difficulties (Zetlin, Weinberg, & Shea, 2006). They might blame themselves for their removal from their families and might move from one household to another. Thus, they might be secretive about their home life, be picked on by other students, and need special services.

Child Abuse

Unfortunately, a growing number of families are engaging in child abuse. Your female students and students with disabilities are particularly prone to being victims of abuse. Victims of abuse are vulnerable for runaway behavior; see Rafferty and Raimondi, (2009) for guidelines, strategies, and resources for understanding and preventing runaway behavior. Because of the rise of child abuse and its harmful effects on children, states have passed laws that require you and other professionals who work with children to identify (see Figure 3.5 for the physical and behavioral indicators of child abuse) and report suspected cases of child abuse (Lowenthal, 2001). Therefore, it is essential that you be well versed in the laws addressing abuse in your state.

When reporting child abuse, familiarize yourself with your school's policies and document the data that led you to suspect child abuse. It may be helpful to talk with other professionals concerning their views and knowledge of the child and the family, and with your principal to discuss the components of a complete report, how to deal with the family's reactions to the report, and the administrative support you will receive. Because it is an emotionally upsetting experience, you should also seek out educators, family members, and community members who can provide emotional support.

Supporting Students Whose Families Are Undergoing Changes

As Ms. Doney's students were writing in their journals, Felicia started to cry. Ms. Doney took her aside and asked, "What's the matter?"

Felicia said, "Last night, my parents told me that my father was going to move."

Ms. Doney asked, "How does it make you feel?" "Sad," Felicia said. "I miss my dad. I want him back."

Ms. Doney said, "I know it's hard for you. Would you like to talk more with me about this?"

"No, not now," Felicia said. "Can I work on the computer now and do my work later? I just want to be alone." Ms. Doney agreed and reminded Felicia that she was available to talk with her.

As she had done with many of her other students who were having family difficulties, Ms. Doney also referred Felicia to the school's counseling service, which offered students an opportunity to talk with a counselor and peers about their feelings.

Here are some other strategies you can use to implement the IDEA in your inclusive classroom and support students whose families are undergoing changes:

- Encourage students to attend and participate in counseling, and teach them how to express their feelings in appropriate ways.

- Communicate with the student's family concerning the child's social, behavioral, and academic adjustment.

- Implement strategies for enhancing self-esteem and making friends, try to lessen sources of stress in school, and make exceptions where possible.

- Encourage students to differentiate between events that they can control (e.g., working hard in school, performing a class job) and events that are beyond their control.

- Provide alternatives to projects that are based on traditional assumptions of families.

- Use books and teaching materials that deal with children in a wider range of family arrangements.

- Work collaboratively with other professionals such as the social worker and school counselor and with community agencies.

REFLECTIVE

Kevin has been misbehaving. Your principal tells you to talk to his family. You are concerned about their reaction, as they frequently use physical punishment to discipline Kevin. What would you do? What professionals might assist you?

In cases of suspected abuse of children from culturally and linguistically diverse backgrounds, you also may need to consider the family's cultural background. In many cultures, medical and spiritual cures may require marking the child's body, leaving bruises, and creating other marks that may be considered abuse. In some cases, confronting family members with information or concerns about their treatment of their child can lead to further difficulties for the child. Although it is important to understand the family's cultural perspective and select the most beneficial outcomes for students, your course of action must comply with laws on child abuse.

In addition to reporting suspected cases of abuse, you can give students choices and other opportunities that allow them to experience some sense of control, and provide them with a safe and supportive learning environment. You also can use positive techniques to help them learn to manage their behavior and understand their emotional responses.

Substance Abuse

Many families from all economic backgrounds, ethnic backgrounds, and geographic regions are dealing with the problem of substance abuse by adolescents or other family members (Buckley, 2009; Schroeder & Johnson, 2009). Substance abuse rates are roughly equal for boys and girls, but this abuse is more widespread among whites than among African Americans or Hispanics and more widespread among suburban and rural students than among urban students. Students with disabilities also are at risk for substance abuse problems (Almodovar, Tomaka, Thompson, Mckinnon, & O'Rourke, 2006), especially those who are not educated in inclusive settings (McCrystal, Higgins, & Percy, 2006). Substance abuse can hinder student

FIGURE 3.5 Physical and behavioral indicators of different forms of child abuse

Physical Abuse

Physical Indicators

- Frequent unexplained
  - bruises, scrapes, burns, welts, and wounds;
  - head injuries and fractures.
- Fabricated and family-induced illnesses

Behavioral Indicators

- Avoids interactions with and situations involving family members and other adults
- Appears to be overly anxious when others are injured
- Fears family members
- Regularly avoids going home or runs away
- Frequently refers to physical punishment from adults
- Exhibits self-injurious behavior, phobias, and a range of anxiety disorders
- Attempts to conceal injuries (e.g., wears inappropriate clothing)
- Demonstrates poor self-esteem and blames self for the inappropriate behavior of others
- Talks about or attempts harming self

Sexual Abuse

Physical Indicators

- Has unexplained difficulties walking, sitting, or standing
- Wears blood-stained or torn clothing
- Experiences pain, bruising, scratching, or bleeding in genital area
- Shows evidence of sexually transmitted diseases, repeated urinary infections, discharges, or extraneous materials in the body
- Becomes pregnant

Behavioral Indicators

- Refers frequently to sexual acts
- Engages in shy or childlike behaviors or flights of fantasy
- Exhibits difficulties socializing with others
- Refers to running away
- Acts in a sexually seductive way
- Pressures others to perform sexual acts
- Fears being touched by others
- Avoids coming to school
- Talks about or attempts harming self
- Demonstrates poor self-esteem and blames self

Neglect

Physical Indicators

- Demonstrates ongoing physical, health, and emotional needs
- Hindered physical, cognitive, speech, language and social-emotional development
- Comes to school hungry and tired
- Exhibits poor hygiene and ongoing medical conditions that are not addressed
- Shows signs of substance abuse or withdrawal

Behavioral Indicators

- Engages in begging and stealing from others
- Comes to school before school begins and leaves late
- Regularly avoids going home or runs away
- Falls asleep in class
- Engages in repetitive behaviors (e.g., rocking, sucking fingers, etc.)
- Wears inappropriate clothing for the weather
- Wears dirty or the same clothing for several days in a row
- Experiences and talks about limited supervision after school or at home
- Talks about experiences and topics that are inappropriate or not age-appropriate
- Often absent from and late to school
- Avoids social interactions with others
- Exhibits extreme changes in behavior
- Talks about or attempts harming self

Source: New York State Department of Education (n.d.)

learning and can result in high rates of inappropriate and aggressive behavior and attendance problems.

Because of the harmful effects of substance abuse, you should be aware of some of the signs of possible substance abuse (see Figure 3.6). You also can help prevent problems by learning more about substance abuse, including its effects,

FIGURE 3.6 Common indicators of alcohol/drug use

Performance Indicators	Behavioral Indicators	Physical Indicators
Memory difficulties	Inability to sleep, awake at unusual times, unusual laziness	Clumsy
Noticeable drop in grades, motivation and participation in school events	Reluctance to discuss possible alcohol or drug use	A marked change in physical appearance and personal habits and hygiene
Assignments missing or not complete	Mood changes, irritability, unwarranted anger	A new curiosity for the drug culture (related posters, clothes, etc.)
Inattentiveness, sleeping in class, aggression	Noticeable change in social circle and increased secrecy regarding new friends and avoidance of old friends	Persistent use of eye drops, mints, gum
Loss of interest	Evasive about activities (lying, omissions)	Constant hacking cough and runny nose
Unexplained absences and lateness	Marked change in taste in music	Appetite changes, increased thirst, hurried speech
Problems with school, work, or police	Increased need for money and efforts to borrow money, stealing money or items	Weight gain or loss
Increased evidence of discipline problems	Defensive or aggressive attitude, very negative, lack of motivation and enthusiasm	Bloodshot and watery eyes
Change in activities or hobbies	Persistent deceitfulness, stealing	Odor of tobacco, marijuana, alcohol
	Overly private	Puffy face, blushing, or paleness
		Tired and sleepy

Common alcohol or drug paraphernalia

Rolling paper	Plastic bags, balloons	Spray cans
Pipes	Vials	Household glue
Cigarettes	Syringes	Cleaning rags
Cigars (blunts)	Spoons	False ID card
Roach clips	Lighters, matches	Empty alcohol containers
Razor blades	Tin foil	Paper packets
Straws	Pill bottles	Needles

Sources: American Council for Drug Education (2009); Elmquist (1991).

prevention strategies, and treatment programs (Schroeder & Johnson, 2009). In addition, work to increase your students' attachment to school by interacting with them in a respectful and caring manner and encouraging them to be involved in extracurricular activities and schoolwide programs. It also is important to work collaboratively with family and community members, agencies, students, and other professionals to design and implement substance abuse prevention programs.

ALTERNATE PHILOSOPHIES FOR STRUCTURING SCHOOLS

WHAT ARE SOME ALTERNATE PHILOSOPHIES FOR STRUCTURING SCHOOL TO ADDRESS SOCIETAL CHANGES? Changes in U.S. society have significantly increased the number of students like those discussed in this chapter, whose needs challenge schools and whose academic profiles resemble those of students with high-incidence disabilities; however, these students frequently do not have disabilities. Unfortunately, the vague definitions of disabilities, imprecise and discriminatory identification methods, and limited funding resulting in a lack of appropriate services all increase the chances that these students will be identified incorrectly as needing special education. Several alternative viewpoints, such as multicultural education and inclusion, have been proposed for structuring schools to meet the needs of *all students* without labeling and separating them. These philosophies challenge schools to reorganize their curricula, teaching, staff allocation, and resources into a unified system that pursues both equity and excellence by asserting that *all students* have strengths and can learn at high levels in general education programs.

Multicultural Education

One important educational philosophy for restructuring schools is **multicultural education** (Banks, 2008; Gollnick & Chinn, 2009). This term originated in the post–civil rights efforts of various ethnic and language groups to have their previously neglected experiences included in the structures and curricula of schools (Nieto & Bode, 2008). Multicultural education seeks to help teachers acknowledge and understand the increasing diversity in society and in the classroom, and to see their students' diverse backgrounds as assets that can support student learning and the learning of others. For many, multicultural education has expanded to include concerns about socioeconomic status, disability, gender, national origin, language background, religion, and sexual orientation (CEC, 2008; National Council for the Accreditation of Teacher Education, 2009).

Definitions of *multicultural education* range from an emphasis on human relations and harmony to a focus on social democracy, justice, and empowerment for *all students*. These definitions focus on the development of students' academic skills, and help students understand their backgrounds and perspectives as well as those of other groups that make up society. Multicultural education also includes students taking actions that transform society and make it more democratic and equitable for *all*.

Proponents of multicultural education also try to change the language of schools. Terms such as *culturally disadvantaged, linguistically limited, at risk, slow learners, handicapped,* and *dropouts* locate problems within students rather than within the educational system (Freire, 1970). These labels present a view of students that often contradicts the way these students regard themselves. These conflicting perspectives can disable students academically and prevent the development of self-esteem.

Multicultural Education and Inclusion

Multicultural education and inclusion are inextricably linked. Many of the challenges confronting advocates for multicultural education are also faced by those who support inclusion. As seekers of educational reform, the multicultural education and inclusion movements share many of the same principles and educational goals. Both movements

- seek to provide access, equity, and excellence for *all students,*
- focus on students' individual strengths and challenges and diversity,
- involve the use of effective and reflective practices and differentiated instruction and assessment to support and document student learning, and
- recognize the importance of community, collaboration and acceptance of individual differences.

By recognizing their commonalities, those who support inclusion and multicultural education seek to create a unified school system in which *all students* are welcomed and affirmed in the general education classrooms.

REFLECTIVE

We refer to students who have needs that challenge the school system as *at risk, handicapped, culturally disadvantaged,* or *linguistically limited.* How might things be different if we referred to schools as *risky, disabling, disadvantaging,* and *limiting*?

To reflect on and enhance your understanding of how diversity can impact your teaching and your students' learning, go to the IRIS Center Resources section of Topic: Cultural and Linguistic Diversity in the MyEducationLab for your course, and complete the module entitled *Teaching and Learning in New Mexico: Considerations for Diverse Student.*

SUMMARY

This chapter offered information on how societal changes have helped to make inclusive education necessary to meet the strengths and challenges of increasingly diverse groups of students who challenge the existing school structure. As you review the chapter, consider the following questions and remember the following points.

How Have Economic Changes Affected Students and Schools?
CEC 2, 3, 9; PRAXIS 2; INTASC 2, 9, 10

The United States has experienced dramatic economic changes marked by a growing gulf between wealthy and poor, as well as a shrinking middle class. As a result of these changes, schools are being challenged to meet the educational strengths and challenges of a growing number of students who live in urban, rural, and suburban poverty.

How Have Demographic Shifts Affected Students and Schools?
CEC 1, 2, 3, 6, 9; PRAXIS 2; INTASC 2, 3, 9, 10

The makeup of the U.S. population has also changed dramatically, making the United States a more linguistically and culturally diverse country. As a result, schools will need to structure their programs and services to address a more diverse student population.

What Are the Educational Strengths and Challenges of Students from Culturally and Linguistically Diverse Backgrounds?

CEC 1, 2, 3, 5, 6, 9; PRAXIS 2; INTASC 2, 3, 6, 9, 10

In addressing the educational strengths and challenges of your students from culturally and linguistically diverse backgrounds, be sensitive to and adapt your services to take into account the cultural, linguistic, religious, and economic factors that affect you, your students, and their families. It is important to develop cultural competence and intercultural communication skills, and to support your students' cultural identities. You must also adjust your teaching behaviors and curricula to reflect your students' differing cultural and religious backgrounds, learning styles, economic and experiential backgrounds, and linguistic abilities.

How Can I Differentiate Cultural and Language Differences from Learning Difficulties?

CEC 1, 2, 3, 6, 8, 9, 10; PRAXIS 1, 3; INTASC 2, 3, 6, 8, 9, 10

You can work with a diverse team of professionals and family members to assess your students' performance in both their primary and secondary languages, understand the processes and factors associated with learning a second language, employ alternatives to traditional testing, and identify your students' diverse life and home experiences. You and the team can then analyze this information to try to differentiate cultural and language differences from learning difficulties and to develop an appropriate educational plan. Students whose linguistic, academic, and social behaviors in both languages are well below those of peers who have similar linguistic, cultural, and experiential backgrounds may have a learning difficulty.

What Is the Effect of Discrimination and Bias on Students and Schools?

CEC 1, 2, 3, 5, 9; PRAXIS 2; INTASC 2, 3, 6, 9, 10

Students from specific racial, linguistic, and religious backgrounds; female students; gay, lesbian, and transgender students; and students with HIV/AIDS can be victims of discrimination in society and schools. This discrimination harms their school performance, socialization, self-esteem, and outcome in later life. You must use a variety of strategies to foster the academic performance and self-esteem of these students.

How Have Family Changes Affected Students and Schools?

CEC 1, 2, 3, 9, 10; PRAXIS 2; INTASC 2, 3, 9, 10

Because of the dramatic changes in the composition, structure, and function of families, you will probably have students who live with both parents, one parent, family members, friends, two mothers, two fathers, or foster parents. You also may be called on to help families deal with child abuse or substance abuse. Regardless of the family's composition, it is important to recognize that while these families may have unique needs, they also have many of the same joys, frustrations, and strengths as other families.

What Are Some Alternative Philosophies for Structuring Schools to Address Societal Changes?

CEC 1, 5, 9; PRAXIS 3; INTASC 3

Inclusion and multicultural education are philosophical movements that challenge schools to restructure their services and resources into a unified system that addresses societal changes. Multicultural education and inclusion share similar goals and principles and seek to provide access, equity, and excellence for *all students*.

Part II

Creating an Inclusive Environment That Supports Learning for All Students

Part II provides strategies for creating an inclusive environment that supports learning for *all students*. Chapter 4 introduces the members of the comprehensive planning team and provides strategies for establishing collaborative relationships and fostering communication with professionals and family members. Chapter 5 offers strategies that support learning by fostering acceptance of individual differences related to disability, culture, language, gender, religion, sexual orientation, and socioeconomic status and promoting friendships among your students. Chapter 6 provides a framework for helping students make the transition to inclusive learning environments and from school to adulthood. It also offers strategies for helping your students develop self-determination. Chapter 7 discusses ways in which you can plan and implement strategies to promote positive behaviors that foster learning and prevent students from harming each other. It also provides guidelines for designing your classroom to accommodate students' learning, behavioral, social, and physical needs.

MS. CARR AND MS. STEVENS

Ms. Cathy Carr, a general education teacher, and Ms. Sarah Stevens, a special education teacher, had worked as a co-teaching team in an inclusion program for several years. Things had gone well over the years, and the teachers tried to make improvements to their program each year. This year they decided to focus on family involvement. Because many families in the past did not know much about inclusion and their program, the teachers decided to have a meeting to explain their inclusion program to families.

There was a good turnout of family members. Ms. Carr and Ms. Stevens asked all in attendance to introduce themselves and then started talking about their program. They explained inclusion and discussed the philosophy and goals of the program, the day's schedule, communications with families, and various other aspects of the program. They also asked the paraeducators to explain their responsibilities, noting how fortunate the class was to

have their assistance for all the students in the class. They briefly explained the research on inclusion in language that families could understand and cited examples of how their students had grown academically and socially. They invited family members of a former student to speak about the program and its impact on their child.

Next the teachers solicited questions from family members. Family members asked questions like "Does the class have computers?" and "How does the teaming work?" One family member asked, "If there are two teachers in a class, which one is my child's 'real' teacher?" Ms. Carr and Ms. Stevens explained, "We both teach all the students. Sometimes one of us leads a lesson while the other helps students to participate, and sometimes we both work with groups at the same time." They concluded the meeting by thanking families for attending and participating, and inviting them to visit and volunteer in the class.

4

Creating Collaborative Relationships and Fostering Communication

To provide families with additional information about inclusion, they gave family members a handout that gave them resources about inclusion, and a handout of relevant Web sites that offered information and activities that families could use to support their children's learning.

At the end of the meeting, Ms. Carr and Ms. Stevens asked the family members to complete a survey that asked them to rate their satisfaction with the content, activities, organization, and scheduling of the meeting, and to identify the things they would like future meetings to address. Several family members indicated that they would like to learn more about how they could support the inclusion program. Others suggested that the teachers provide them with updates on the inclusion program, which they decided to do via a monthly newsletter and a weblog of the class's activities maintained with the assistance of the students.

Following the meeting, the professionals met to discuss it. They talked about how it went, what was successful,

and what they would do differently. They also reviewed the feedback from family members and started to plan the next meeting.

What factors made this meeting successful? What strategies could professionals and families employ to collaborate and communicate to help students learn better and develop the support of their students' families for inclusion? After reading this chapter, you should have the knowledge, skills, and dispositions to answer these as well as the following questions:

- Who are the members of the comprehensive planning team?

- How can members of the comprehensive planning team work collaboratively?

- How can I foster communication and collaboration with families?

As teachers like Ms. Carr and Ms. Stevens recognize, an essential principle of effective inclusion programs is good collaboration and communication among teachers, other professionals, families, and community members and resources (Dettmer, Thurston, Knackendoffel, & Dyck, 2009). Good collaboration and communication can strengthen the connection between school and home, create a shared commitment to learning, support student learning, and build support for your inclusive classroom (Swedeen, 2009). Stivers, Francis-Cropper, and Straus (2008) provide guidelines for implementing activities throughout the school year to communicate with your students' families about your inclusive classroom. This chapter offers strategies for creating collaborative relationships and fostering communication with other professionals, families, and community members to support the development and implementation of inclusive classrooms that promote the learning of *all students*.

MEMBERS OF THE COMPREHENSIVE PLANNING TEAM

WHO ARE THE MEMBERS OF THE COMPREHENSIVE PLANNING TEAM? The comprehensive planning team (which has different names in different states and school districts), including students and their families, makes collaborative decisions about the strengths and challenges of students, and provides appropriate services to students and their families. Effective teams engage in a **wraparound process**, a multidisciplinary, interagency, strength-based, and student- and family-focused process for collaboratively designing and delivering individualized, culturally sensitive, school- and community-based educational, counseling, medical, and vocational services to address the unique strengths, challenges and behaviors of students and their families (Eber et al., 2008; Lechtenberger et al., 2008). The wraparound process guides the team in solving problems; coordinating a full range of services available to students, families, educators, and schools; and sharing the responsibility for implementing inclusion.

In addition to students, the team consists of general and special educators, administrators, support personnel, family members, peers, local community resources, and professional and family-based organizations, as shown in Figure 4.1. The members of the team and their roles vary, depending on the strengths and challenges of students, families, and educators. The roles and responsibilities of the different team members are described in the following sections.

Family Members

Relatives are key members of the planning team, and communication and collaboration with them are essential. They can provide various types of information on the student's adaptive behavior and medical, social, and psychological history. Family members also can help the team design and implement educational programs and determine appropriate related services.

School Administrators

A school administrator who supervises the districtwide services usually serves as the chairperson of the team. The chairperson is responsible for coordinating meetings and delivering services to students and their families. He or she also ensures that all legal guidelines for due process, family involvement, assessment, and confidentiality have been followed. Through their leadership and support, school administrators also can foster acceptance of and commitment to the concept of inclusion and encourage educators and families to collaborate.

General Educators

The team should include a general education teacher who has worked with the student and who can offer information on the student's strengths and challenges, as well as data on the effectiveness of specific teaching methods. General educators can provide a perspective on the academic and social rigors of the general education curriculum and classroom.

Making Connections
The wraparound planning process is defined in Chapter 2.

Making Connections
This discussion of the roles of the members of the comprehensive planning teams builds on what we covered earlier, in Chapter 2.

Making Connections
Strategies for involving general educators in the IEP team process are discussed in Chapter 2.

FIGURE 4.1 Members of the comprehensive planning team

Special Educators

The special educator provides information on the student's academic, behavioral, and social skills and the student's responses to different teaching techniques and materials. When a student is to be placed in an inclusive setting, the special educator can collaborate with general education classroom teachers on curricular and teaching accommodations, learning strategies, classroom management strategies, testing accommodations, grading alternatives, assistive devices, and peer acceptance. At the secondary level, special educators also play important roles in teaching study, independence, functional, and vocational skills, and working with community agencies.

Paraeducators

Because paraeducators can perform many important roles to help you promote the educational, social, and behavioral performance of *all students* in inclusive settings, it is important for them to be part of the planning team and have a shared vision for the inclusion of students (Carnahan, Williamson, Clarke, & Sorensen, 2009; Causton-Theoharis, 2009; Suter & Giangreco, 2009). Including paraeducators on the planning team also can help them understand students' strengths and challenges, effective instructional strategies, and the goals of students' educational programs. Their participation also can clarify their roles and responsibilities in supporting you—and not replacing you—in implementing and assessing students' educational programs effectively (Giangreco & Broer, 2007; Liston, Nevin, & Malian, 2009) and in fostering the social, behavioral, and academic development of students. See Figure 4.2 for a delineation of the roles of paraeducators so that they are not asked to assume responsibilities that teachers should perform. It is important to note that the activities of paraeducators should be identified by IEP teams and must be supervised by and performed under the direction of licensed professionals (Devlin, 2008; Etscheidt, 2005; Maggin, Wehby, Moore-Partin, Robertson, & Oliver, 2009).

FIGURE 4.2 Delineating the roles and responsibilities of paraeducators in inclusive settings

Roles and Responsibilities of Paraeducators

Paraeducators can support teachers and students by
- assisting students with daily living skills and health and physical needs (e.g., toileting and feeding).
- performing clerical duties and custodial tasks (e.g., insuring proper positioning).
- supervising students during activities outside the classroom.
- recording behavior and helping manage students' behavior.
- reading to students and playing educational games with them.
- serving as a translator.
- preparing, individualizing, and adapting materials.
- providing individualized and small-group instruction and reinforcing concepts/skills taught previously.
- helping students with motor and mobility difficulties, and providing emotional support.
- observing students.
- facilitating social interactions with peers.
- modeling appropriate skills.
- ensuring student safety.
- prompting students.
- assisting with follow-up instructional activities (e.g., homework, studying for tests).

Roles and Responsibilities Outside the Scope of Paraeducators

Paraeducators should not be asked to replace teachers by
- being solely responsible for planning, delivering, and monitoring instruction to specific students.
- administering and interpreting formal and informal assessment instruments unless trained to do so or monitored by a trained professional.
- signing formal documents such as IEPs.
- assigning grades.
- disclosing confidential information.
- serving as a substitute teacher or substitute for teachers at meetings.

Sources: Carnahan et al. (2009); Causton-Theoharis (2009); Etscheidt (2005); Giangreco, Yuan, Mckenzie, Cameron, & Fialka (2005); Liston et al., (2009)

Because paraeducators often reside in the community, they may also provide valuable information regarding links to community-based services (Villa, Thousand, & Nevin, 2008). In particular, paraeducators who are educated in or have experience with students' languages and cultures can play an important role in educating students who are English language learners. Therefore, it is important that you and other members of the team treat them with respect, and appreciate and acknowledge them for the meaningful contributions they make (Causton-Theoharis, 2009; Liston et al., 2009). It is also important to communicate regularly and share information with them; solicit their perspectives; address their concerns and suggestions; and offer them support, professional development, and feedback to improve their performance (Carnahan et al., 2009; Devlin, 2008).

School Psychologists

The school psychologist is trained in the administration and interpretation of standardized tests. In addition to testing, school psychologists collect data on students by observing them in their classrooms and by interviewing other professionals who work with the students. School psychologists also sometimes counsel students and family members and assist classroom teachers in designing teaching and classroom management strategies.

Speech and Language Clinicians

Information on students' communication abilities can be provided by the speech and language clinician. To rule out or confirm a language disability, these clinicians are often the first persons to whom students learning English are referred. They can also

Making Connections
Find out more about how you can work effectively with paraeducators to differentiate your instruction in Chapter 8.

Making Connections
Information about students with speech and language disorders is presented in Chapter 2.

help you improve the communication skills and academic success of students in the classroom (Kuder, 2008; Owens, 2010).

Social Workers

The social worker serves as a liaison between the home and the school and community agencies. The social worker counsels students and families, assesses the effect of the student's home life on school performance, and assists families during emergencies. In addition, the social worker can help families obtain services from community agencies, contact agencies concerning the needs of students and their families, and evaluate the impact of services on the family. Social workers also may offer counseling and support groups for students and their families.

Paraeducators serve important roles in inclusive classrooms. What roles do paraeducators perform to promote the success of students in inclusive classrooms?

School Counselors

The school counselor can provide information on the student's social and emotional development, including self-concept, attitude toward school, and social interactions with others. In schools that don't have a social worker, the counselor may assume that role. Frequently, counselors coordinate, assess, and monitor the student's program, as well as counsel students and their families. For example, during the transition period, the student may need counseling to adjust socially and emotionally to the general education classroom.

Vocational Educators

Vocational educators offer valuable information on the student's work experiences and career goals. They can help the team develop the transitional services component of students' IEPs. Vocational educators also provide students with vocational and career education experiences. This involves collaboration with families and employers in the community.

School Physicians and Nurses

School physicians and nurses can aid the team by performing diagnostic tests to assess the student's physical development, sensory abilities, medical problems, and central nervous system functioning (Heller, 2009a). They can provide information on nutrition, allergies, chronic illnesses, and somatic symptoms. In addition, they can plan and monitor medical interventions and discuss the potential side effects of any drugs used. Since physicians' services are costly, many medically related services may be provided by school nurses.

Speech and language clinicians develop students' communication skills. How can you collaborate with them?

Physical and Occupational Therapists and Adapted Physical Educators

Students with fine and gross motor challenges may need the services of **physical** and **occupational therapists** and adapted physical educators (Heller, Forney, et al., 2009; Menear & Smith, 2008). These therapists can recommend various types of adaptive

Making Connections
Find out more about helping students make transitions from school to adulthood in Chapter 6.

Creating Collaborative Relationships and Fostering Communication

Making Connections
This discussion of professionals who work with students who are English language learners builds on what we covered earlier, in Chapter 3.

equipment and suggest how to adapt teaching materials and classroom environments. The physical therapist usually focuses on the assessment and training of the lower extremities and large muscles; the occupational therapist deals with the upper extremities and fine motor abilities. The physical therapist helps students strengthen muscles, improve posture, and increase motor function and range. The occupational therapist works with students to prevent, restore, or adapt to impaired or lost motor functions. This therapist also helps students develop the necessary fine motor skills to perform everyday actions independently. Adapted physical educators offer a range of services and strategies to foster students' gross and fine motor skills and participation in physical activities.

Staff from Community Agencies

For many students, the team will need to work collaboratively with staff from community agencies. For example, if a student with a visual impairment must have an assistive device, a community agency can be contacted to help purchase it. In working with community organizations, the team should consider the unique medical, behavioral, and social needs of each student, as well as the financial resources of the student's family. Because many students may require similar services from agencies, teams can maintain a file of community agencies and the services they provide.

Professionals for Students Who Are English Language Learners

In addition to the professionals just described, teams for students who are learning English and who are referred for special education services should include personnel who are fluent in the student's native language and bicultural in the student's home culture. Therefore, planning teams working with these students should include such professionals as ESL teachers, bilingual educators, and migrant educators.

ESL Teachers ESL teachers instruct students in English. They build on students' existing language skills and experiences to enhance their learning of English. In addition, they can help the team address students' language and learning strengths and challenges, as well as offer many effective strategies for teaching English language learners.

Bilingual Educators Many students come from backgrounds where English is not spoken and need the help of a bilingual educator. This educator performs a variety of roles. These include assessing and teaching students in their native language and in English, involving families and community members in the educational program, helping students maintain their native culture and language and adjust to their new culture, and working with general educators.

Migrant Educators To help educate **migrant students**, the federal government funds migrant education programs through the states. Typically, when a migrant family moves to a new area, it is certified as being eligible for migrant status and services by a recruiter from a local migrant education agency. Then a migrant educator helps the family enroll the children in school. The migrant educator also contacts local agencies, organizations, businesses, and other community resources that can assist migrant families. Once the migrant students are in school, the migrant educator often gives them supplementary individualized instruction in small groups.

COLLABORATIVE TEAMING

HOW CAN MEMBERS OF THE COMPREHENSIVE PLANNING TEAM WORK COLLABORATIVELY? Successful comprehensive planning teams are collaborative and interactive. All members work together to achieve a common goal, are accountable to the team, share their diverse expertise and perceptions with others, and respect the code of ethics for educators (Arthaud, Aram, Breck, Doelling, & Bushrow, 2007; Bucholz, Keller, & Brady, 2007; Skinner, Garganis, & Watson, 2009). They are interdependent and empathetic, understanding their roles and roles of others. A key member of the team is the case manager, service coordinator, or support facilitator. This person promotes the team process, coordinates the services for students and their families, and provides follow-up to ensure that goals are being met (Dettmer et al., 2009).

Successful collaborative teams also develop good interpersonal and communication skills. Fleming and Monda-Amaya (2001) and Garmston and Wellman (1998) summarize the roles that team members can perform to help the team function efficiently and establish a caring, positive, trusting working environment:

- *Initiating:* All members identify problems and issues to be considered by the team.
- *Information gathering and sharing:* All members collect and share relevant information.
- *Clarifying and elaborating:* All members seek clarification, probe for specific facts and details, and provide elaboration.
- *Summarizing:* All members review and paraphrase key points discussed by the team.
- *Consensus building:* All members participate in decision making.
- *Encouraging:* All members encourage others to participate in the process and pay attention to the contributions of others.
- *Harmonizing and compromising:* All members assume that others have good intentions and seek to resolve conflict and compromise.
- *Reflecting:* All members reflect on their own feelings, comments, and behaviors, as well as those of others.
- *Balancing:* All members try to balance advocacy and inquiry.

To help the team develop these skills, the team can establish ground rules to guide their interactions and the decision-making process. Individual team members can also be assigned roles such as facilitator, recorder, timekeeper, observer, and summarizer. You can use effective communication skills to support the success of the team by (a) listening carefully and empathetically to others; (b) being tolerant of differing points of view; (c) presenting your positions, feelings, and perspectives using "I" statements, examples to support your statements, and graphics when appropriate; (d) using paraphrasing to check to make sure that you understand the comments of others; (e) understanding culturally based differences in verbal and nonverbal communication; (f) respecting the confidentiality of others; (g) disagreeing respectfully; and (h) being willing to compromise (Cancio & Conderman, 2008).

Use Person-/Student-Centered Planning

Effective teams use *person-/student-centered planning* to guide the delivery of services to students and their families (Bambara, Browder, & Koger, 2006; Dettmer et al., 2009). Person-/student-centered planning recognizes the importance of the roles that students and their families play as advocates in identifying meaningful goals and appropriate strategies and services for meeting them. It employs a variety of assessment procedures to identify the strengths, preferences, personal characteristics, cultural, linguistic, and experiential backgrounds and challenges of students and their families. These variables are then examined to develop a comprehensive and holistic plan to coordinate the students' inclusion programs.

Map Action Planning System   One person-centered planning strategy that many teams use is the **Map Action Planning System (MAPS)** (Sheehey et al., 2009). MAPS also can be used to help the team develop IEPs. In MAPS, team members, including students with disabilities, their families, and peers, meet to develop an inclusion plan by first answering the following questions:

- *What is a map?* This question allows participants to think about the characteristics of a map.
- *What is [the student's name] history?* This question helps the team understand the events that have shaped the student's life and family.

Go to the Assignments and Activities section of the Topic *Collaboration, Consultation, and Co-Teaching* in the MyEducationLab for your course and complete the activity entitled *Related Service Providers*. As you watch the video and answer the accompanying questions, consider the full team approach to inclusive teaching.

REFLECTIVE

How would you describe your communication style? What communication skills do you use that support the success of teams? What communication skills would you like to improve?

Making Connections
Find out more about using person-/student-centered planning to develop individualized transition plans in Chapter 6.

- *What is your (our) dream for [the student's name]?* This question allows team members to share their visions and goals for the student's future.
- *What is your (our) nightmare?* This question helps the team understand the student's and family's fears.
- *Who is [the student's name]?* This question gives all team members the opportunity to describe their perceptions of the student.
- *What are [the student's name] strengths, gifts, and talents?* This question helps the team focus on and identify the student's positive attributes.
- *What are [the student's name] challenges? What can we do to meet these challenges?* These questions help the team define the student's challenges in a variety of areas.
- *What would be an ideal day for [the student's name]? What do we need to do to make this ideal real?* These questions help the team plan the student's program by listing the goals and activities for the student, services and accommodations needed to achieve the goals and foster participation in these activities, and individuals responsible for delivering the services and accommodations.

Work in Co-Teaching Arrangements

Many school districts are using **co-teaching**, also called *cooperative* or *collaborative teaching*, whereby teachers like Ms. Carr and Stevens work together to educate *all students* in inclusive classrooms (Friend & Cook, 2010; Stang & Lyons, 2008). Teachers involved in co-teaching share responsibility and accountability for planning and delivering instruction, evaluating, grading, and disciplining students (Villa et al., 2008). Students are not removed from the classroom for supportive services. Instead, academic instruction and supportive services are provided where the need exists: in the general education classroom (Hines, 2008).

Co-teaching teams can use many different instructional arrangements based on the purpose of the lesson, the nature of the material covered, and the needs of students (Stivers, 2008; Villa et al., 2008). Examples of these instructional arrangements are described here and in Figure 4.3.

PEARSON
myeducationlab

Go to the Assignments and Activities section of the Topic *Collaboration, Consultation, and Co-Teaching* in the MyEducationLab for your course and complete the activity entitled *Teacher Collaboration*. As you watch the video and complete the accompanying questions, consider the different types of co-teaching arrangements and their affect on inclusive classroom teaching.

- **One teaching/one helping**: One teacher instructs the whole class while the other teacher circulates to collect information on students' performance or to offer help to students (see Figure 4.3a). This arrangement is also used to take advantage of the expertise of one teacher in a specific subject area, and allow the other teacher to monitor and assist students.
- **Parallel teaching**: When it is necessary to lower the student–teacher ratio to teach new material, to review and practice material previously taught, or to encourage student discussions and participation, both teachers can teach the same material at the same time to two equal groups of students (see Figure 4.3b).
- **Station teaching**: When teaching material that is difficult but not sequential, when several different topics are important or when reviewing material is an important objective of the lesson, both teachers can teach different or review content at the same time to two equal groups of students, and then switch groups and repeat the lesson (see Figure 4.3c).
- **Alternative teaching**: When teachers need to individualize instruction, remediate skills, promote mastery, or offer enrichment based on students' needs, one teacher can work with a smaller group or individual students while the other teacher works with a larger group (see Figure 4.3d).
- **Team teaching**: When it is important to blend the talents and expertise of teachers or to foster interactions with students, both teachers can plan and teach a lesson together (see Figure 4.3e).

Co-teaching is designed to minimize some of the problems of pull-out programs, such as students missing academic instruction, insufficient communication

FIGURE 4.3 Cooperative teaching arrangements

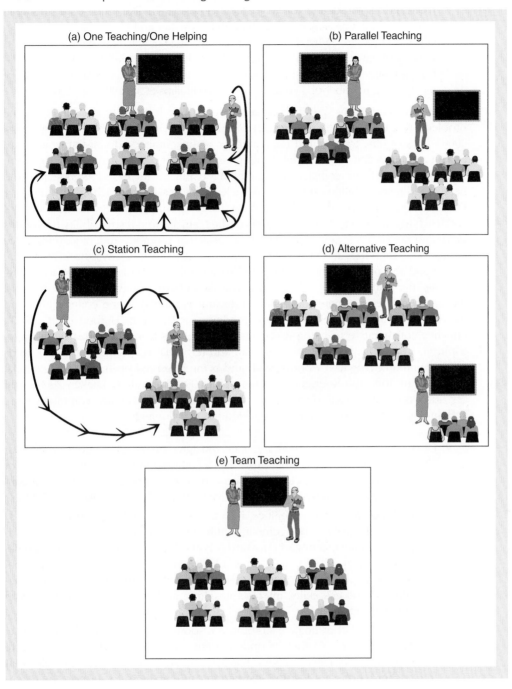

(a) One Teaching/One Helping

(b) Parallel Teaching

(c) Station Teaching

(d) Alternative Teaching

(e) Team Teaching

and coordination between professionals, scheduling problems, and fragmentation of the curriculum. It also allows supportive services and modified teaching for students with academic and behavioral difficulties without labeling them. In addition to helping students with disabilities, co-teaching gives *all students* the assistance and expertise of at least two professionals rather than just one (Hang & Rabren, 2009; Tannock, 2009). Teachers working in cooperative teams also note that these programs help make teaching more enjoyable and stimulating, give them new insights and experiences regarding teaching strategies, and prevent the isolation that sometimes occurs when teachers work alone (Kamens, 2007; Nevin et al., 2008).

At first, I was nervous, because you're not used to having another teacher in the classroom and all of a sudden you've got another person. I'm like, "Am I doing this right? Does she think this is okay?" Even though I knew her and I really liked her personally, I still thought, "What if she doesn't like my style of teaching? What if she thinks I'm lazy? What if she doesn't like this or that?" That sounds terrible, but the most difficult adjustment wasn't really pointed towards the kids, it was what she thought of me. (From a member of a co-teaching team) (Phillips et al., 1995, pp. 266–267)

Co-teaching teams, particularly at the secondary level, may encounter several problems that can limit their effectiveness (Alvarez McHatton & Daniel, 2008; Hines, 2008). Lack of time to plan and implement programs, limited administrative support, lack of resources and professional development, unclear roles of teaching team members, resistance from colleagues, scheduling conflicts, increased workloads, and heightened responsibilities are major obstacles to successful co-teaching (Murawski & Dieker, 2008; Scruggs et al., 2007). Teachers also report that they need to learn to work and teach together so that both members of the team assume responsibility for *all students* and perform relevant and meaningful tasks that promote student learning (Rice et al., 2007; Tannock, 2009). For instance, if one teacher is always the instructional leader and the other teacher is relegated to the role of assistant or aide for a few students, the team may not be effective. This lack of parity may particularly occur at the secondary level, where the general educator is trained in the content area and therefore may assume the major responsibilities for teaching (Harbort et al., 2007). Effective collaborative teaching takes time and requires teachers to deal with philosophical, pedagogical, historical, logistical, and territorial issues, as well as concerns about communicating and working with and being observed by another professional (Conderman, Johnston-Rodriguez, & Hartman, 2009; Murawski & Dieker, 2008). You can address these issues and work toward establishing compatibility, communication, and an equal status relationship by considering the following:

- Discuss why you want to work together, and agree on the goals you have for your classroom. It is also important to establish a common vision and ground rules for your collaboration and discuss what you expect of each other, as well as your concerns and fears about working cooperatively (Tannock, 2009; Villa et al., 2008).

- Learn about each other's abilities, beliefs, routines, teaching and communication styles, classroom management, family involvement approaches, and grading and assessment strategies (Howard & Potts, 2009; Murawski & Dieker, 2008). Conderman et al. (2009), Villa et al. (2008), and Keefe et al. (2004) present forms, surveys, and questions that co-teaching teams can use to become familiar with each other's skills, interests, teaching and communication styles, and educational philosophies.

- Understand and coordinate each other's responsibilities and areas of expertise, as well as the roles of others (Conderman et al., 2009; Linz, Heater, & Howard, 2009; Murawski & Dieker, 2008). Lodato Wilson (2008) outlines the roles that the teacher who is not leading instruction can engage in to support the teaching and learning processes.

- Consider using a variety of scheduling arrangements to coordinate the scheduling needs of teachers and students (Friend & Cook, 2010).

- Be sensitive to cross-cultural perspectives and interactions. Understand and accept multiple perspectives, and work toward accepting and responding appropriately to each other's cultural beliefs and communication styles (Taylor & Whittaker, 2009; Villa et al., 2008).

- Arrange the classroom to support collaboration. Agree on the placement of your work areas, students, and materials, and the scheduling of routines and activities (Stivers, 2008). Make sure both teacher's desks are adult-size and in prominent locations in the room, and that both of you share materials and classroom spaces and have easy access to them. Also, use a flexible layout so that your classroom can be easily adapted to the different types of collaborative teaching arrangements used.

- Establish and agree on a common set of expectations for judging and grading students' academic, behavioral, and social performance (Howard & Potts, 2009; Stivers, 2008).

- Develop communication, problem-solving, and team-building skills (Linz et al., 2009; Murawski & Dieker, 2008). Work toward honestly, respectfully, and reflectively talking to and listening to others, expressing opinions without taking a value position, and understanding each other's verbal and nonverbal communication styles (Conderman et al., 2009; Council for Exceptional Children, 2008; Tannock, 2009). Hoerr (2009) suggests that co-teaching relationships can be enhanced by striving to use *the rule of six*, which means trying to give the other person a minimum of six positive comments for each negative comment. It is also important to use self-disclosure and perspective taking, to think and communicate in terms of "we" and "our" rather than "I" and "my," and to make decisions by consensus. Consider establishing nonverbal cues to communicate such as hand signals to indicate that a break or communication is needed (Conderman et al., 2009).

- Understand that co-teaching is a developmental process, and be prepared to encounter problems at first (Cramer & Stivers, 2007; Villa et al., 2008). Successful co-teaching goes through stages and therefore involves taking time to adjust to working with another person to resolve logistical and territorial issues, to determine roles and responsibilities, and to blend skills (Dettmer et al., 2009; Murawski & Dieker, 2008).

- Share the workload and instructional materials, vary responsibilities, and don't relegate one person to a lesser role (Linz et al., 2009; Murawski & Dieker, 2008). Make sure that the contributions of all team members are recognized and valued by students, students' families, and other professionals (Stivers, 2008). For instance, place both teachers' names in prominent locations in the classroom, on communications with others, and on all teaching materials and official documents (e.g., report cards, class rosters, IEPs, etc.). At the secondary level, special education co-teachers can become members of the content area departments (Simmons & Magiera, 2007).

- Vary the arrangements used to teach students based on the purpose of the lesson, the nature of the content covered, and the strengths and challenges of students (Linz, Heater, & Howard, 2009; Sayeski, 2009). Use a range of activities that allows both team members to take a leadership role and to feel comfortable. A template to guide the planning and evaluation of co-teaching lessons is presented in Figure 4.4.

- As we saw in the chapter-opening vignette, meet periodically with families to explain the program and to share information on students' progress. It is important that both teachers attend all meetings with families and present information about their program (Howard & Potts, 2009).

- Communicate regularly to reevaluate short- and long-term goals, solve problems, plan instruction, divide responsibilities, share instructional roles and administrative tasks, brainstorm new ideas and approaches, and talk about students' progress (Conderman et al., 2009; Linz et al., 2009; Murawski & Dieker, 2008; Rice et al., 2007). In addition to addressing problems, remember to also discuss the things that are working. Howard and Potts (2009) provide a sample agenda of a co-planning meeting.

- Seek support and feedback from families and other professionals. Observe other co-teaching teams, and meet with them to discuss effective strategies and ways to improve your co-teaching (Simmons & Magiera, 2007). Solicit the support of your administrators, who can be instrumental in providing the time, professional development opportunities, and resources to facilitate the success of your

Making Connections
Find out more about ways to grade students in inclusive classrooms in Chapter 12.

FIGURE 4.4 Cooperative teaching lesson planning template

What are our objectives, and how are they linked to our learning standards?	What individualized objectives do we have for our students with special needs?	What instructional and assessment accommodations will we use?	What co-teaching arrangements will we use?	What roles will we perform?	How can we establish an equal-status relationship?	What materials and technology will we use?	How will we arrange the classroom to support our collaboration and student learning?	How will we assess student learning and our success at working collaboratively?
Objectives 1. 2. 3. Learning Standards 1. 2. 3.	Individualized Academic Objectives 1. 2. Individualized Behavior Objectives 1. 2. Individualized Social Objectives 1. 2. Other Individualized Objectives 1. 2.	Instructional Accommodations 1. 2. 3. Assessment Accommodations 1. 2. 3. Other Accommodations 1. 2. 3.	☐ One teaching/one helping ☐ Parallel teaching ☐ Station teaching ☐ Alternative teaching ☐ Team teaching	Teacher A 1. 2. Teacher B 1. 2. Paraeducator 1. 2. Other Professionals 1. 2.	1. 2. 3. 4. 5.	Materials 1. 2. 3. Technology 1. 2. 3.	1. 2. 3. 4. 5.	Assessment of student learning during the lesson 1. Assessment of student learning at the end of the lesson 1. Ways we collaborated successfully 1. Ways we can improve our collaboration 1.

Sources: Magiera & Simmons (2007); Vaughn, Schumm, & Arguelles (1997); Villa et al. (2008).

collaborative efforts (Friend & Cook, 2010; Simmons & Magiera, 2007). Linz et al. (2009), Villa et al. (2008), and Hines (2008) provide ways administrators can foster collaborative teaching arrangements and how you can encourage your administrators to support and become engaged in your co-teaching inclusive classroom.

- Address philosophical, pedagogical, logistical, and interpersonal conflicts directly and immediately (Conderman et al., 2009; Hines, 2008). Be aware of the signs of these conflicts, such as team members (a) speaking and contributing less during conversations, (b) avoiding certain topics, (c) discussing problems with others outside the collaborative classroom, and (d) failing to complete agreed-on activities (Council for Exceptional Children, 2008). Don't let conflicts escalate; resolve them by listening to each other without blame, trying to understand the other person's perspective, discussing the situation and possible solutions from your perspective, identifying the sources of the problem, examining existing roles and responsibilities, negotiating, compromising, problem solving and taking actions to address the difficulties, and scheduling future meetings to evaluate success and plan additional activities (Bradley & Monda-Amaya, 2005; Conderman et al., 2009).

A challenge for many co-teaching teams is to establish an equal status relationship. How can co-teaching teams make sure both teachers perform meaningful roles that facilitate student learning?

- Use a range of strategies to assess the impact of the program on *all students and teachers*, and revise the program based on these data (Conderman et al., 2009; Linz et al., 2009; Murawski & Dieker, 2008; Rice et al., 2007).

- Engage in self-evaluation and reflection to examine the team's success and the ways the team can improve (Linz et al., 2009; Tannock, 2009). Continually examine shared values and goals, as well as concerns, problems, misunderstandings, expectations, and plans for the future (Conderman et al., 2009; Murawski & Dieker, 2008; Villa et al., 2008). Interviews (see Figure 4.5) and surveys (see Figure 4.6 on p. 152) can be used to help you reflect on aspects of your co-teaching team. Other formats for examining a team's collaboration are available (Simmons & Magiera, 2007; Villa et al., 2008; Wiggins & Damore, 2006; Wilson, 2005).

Making Connections
Find out more about strategies you can use to examine the effectiveness of your inclusion program in Chapter 12.

- Acknowledge, celebrate, and share your success. Enjoy, share, attribute, and reflect on your accomplishments as a team, and share them with others (Magiera, Simmons, & Crandall, 2005; Murawski & Dieker, 2008).

Employ Collaborative Consultation/Problem Solving

Teachers may also use **collaborative consultation**, sometimes referred to as *collaborative problem solving*, to facilitate the success of their inclusion programs (Dettmer et al., 2009; Santangelo, 2009). This involves working together to problem solve and implement mutually agreed-on solutions to prevent and address learning and behavioral difficulties and to coordinate instructional programs for *all students*. Collaborative consultation is designed to address students' strengths and challenges and to give general education teachers improved knowledge and skills to deal with similar situations in the future (Bahr & Kovaleski, 2006).

The "consultant," usually a special, bilingual, or multicultural educator or an ancillary staff member (a school psychologist, speech/language therapist, or physical therapist), works collaboratively with the general education teacher, who has primary responsibility (Paulsen, 2008). Figure 4.7 (p. 153), a diary of the experiences of a collaborative consultation teacher, presents some of the services provided.

REFLECTIVE

Think about a situation in which you worked collaboratively with a team. How was the outcome affected by the collaboration? What problems and successes did the team have in working collaboratively? How did the team resolve the problems?

Working as a Co-teaching Team

Ms. Cathy Carr and Ms. Sarah Stevens remembered their first year working together as a co-teaching team. Although they had worked together before to reintegrate students with disabilities into Cathy's general education classroom for specific subject areas and activities, they were both anxious and excited about working as a co-teaching team. Initially, they had experienced some difficulties. Sarah felt out of place in Cathy's classroom. She was frustrated because she didn't know where the supplies and materials were located and frequently had to ask Cathy. She also worried that Cathy would have all the responsibilities and be the "real" teacher and that she would function as a teacher's aide.

Cathy sensed Sarah's concern and was also worried about their differences in terms of roles, teaching style, and philosophy. Sometimes she wondered whether Sarah thought she was too controlling and disapproved of her concern about getting students ready for the statewide tests. Both Cathy and Sarah were also concerned that the students and their families viewed one of them as the teacher and the other one as a teacher's assistant.

At first, Sarah and Cathy had some difficulty determining their responsibilities and blending their skills. They struggled as they attempted to teach lessons together and coordinate their instructional activities. Sometimes, while Cathy led a lesson, Sarah seemed lost and felt like a helper rather than a teacher. They also had different opinions about the abilities of the students with disabilities. Sarah worried that "her" students would not be able to keep up with Cathy's plans for all the students, and that they were not receiving the services they needed. At the first family meeting, their roles were clearly delineated, with Sarah speaking to the classified students' families separately. They quickly realized that this was a mistake and were determined to work on blending their skills.

As they worked together, they began to notice and respect each other's skills, perspectives, experiences, and areas of expertise. Cathy was impressed with Sarah's effectiveness in dealing with behavior problems, and Sarah was excited about the way Cathy made instructional activities come alive. They both wanted to learn from each other. They also started to improve in planning and teaching lessons together and performing administrative tasks. In teaching together, they began to anticipate each other's styles. Their principal observed them teaching a lesson and noticed that they were starting to teach together in a natural way even though their perspectives were different. When they completed the students' report cards together, they were amazed at how close they were in assessing students' needs and progress.

As they got to know each other, Cathy and Sarah began to experiment with new teaching methods, and both seemed to have a renewed enjoyment of teaching. They used role plays, puppets, and sometimes spontaneously acted out stories and lessons. Both teachers were surprised by how much more fun they and their students were having in class.

Although things were going well, Cathy and Sarah's concerns about teaming and their philosophical differences surfaced periodically. Sarah, who was trained in a skills-based approach, was concerned that Cathy's approach was not effective with some of the students. Sarah discussed this with Cathy, who was very understanding, and they decided to do skills work, too.

Their commitment to teaming was sustained by the positive changes they saw in their students. Sarah and Cathy were pleased that all the students had progressed developmentally, academically, and socially. They were particularly surprised and motivated by the influence of their collaboration on the sense of community in the classroom, which was seen in the students' unusual sensitivity to their peers.

Cathy and Sarah also were pleased with the support they received from their principal. The principal met periodically with them to discuss problems and solutions; to acknowledge their efforts and growth; and to offer assistance, support, and resources. The principal also rearranged their schedules to give them planning time together and encouraged them to visit schools with model programs.

Looking back on their experiences as a co-teaching team, Sarah and Cathy agreed that it was a successful year. Sarah noted, "What an incredible year! After so many years as a special education teacher, it was refreshing to interact with a greater variety of students. It was a great learning year for me. I don't think teachers know how enjoyable teaching can be when you share it." Cathy said, "This is the end of a wonderful year. The students and we as teachers became a close-knit community of learners. We all did learn and grow this year. It was like dancing with someone; sometimes you lead and sometimes you follow. We began with a lot of apprehension and ended with much enthusiasm."

- Why do you think Cathy and Sarah were initially both anxious and excited about working together as a co-teaching team?

- What problems and concerns did they have? How can these problems and concerns be addressed?

- How did working together benefit Cathy and Sarah and their students?

- What factors helped make this a successful school year?

- How would you feel if you were asked to be part of a co-teaching team?

- What resources, knowledge, skills, and dispositions do you need to teach effectively in a co-teaching team?

FIGURE 4.5 Sample cooperative teaching interview

- How is cooperative teaching working in your class?
- What components and practices of your cooperative teaching team appear to be effective?
- What difficulties have you encountered working as a cooperative teaching team?
- What do you enjoy the most about working in a cooperative teaching team?
- What are your biggest concerns about working in a cooperative teaching team?
- What support from others, resources, and training have you received to work successfully as a cooperative teaching team? What support from others, resources, and professional development have been most helpful? Least helpful? What additional support from others, resources, and training would be helpful?
- How has your cooperative teaching team affected the academic, social, and behavioral development of your students, and your interactions with their families? Describe the positive and negative outcomes you have observed in your students and their families.
- How do your students' families and other professionals feel about your cooperative teaching team?
- How has working in a cooperative teaching team affected you as a professional and a person? Describe the positive and negative effects for you.
- In what ways have your roles changed as a result of working in a cooperative teaching team? How do you feel about your new roles?
- How did the collaboration process change throughout the school year?
- What did you learn from working as a cooperative teaching team?
- How do you work through conflicts?
- What suggestions would you have for others interested in working in cooperative teaching teams?
- What schoolwide and districtwide practices have supported your efforts to work as a cooperative teaching team? Hindered your efforts? In what ways should these practices be revised?

Steps in Collaborative Consultation   The steps in effective collaborative consultation are (a) goal and problem clarification and identification, (b) goal and problem analysis, (c) plan implementation, and (d) plan evaluation (Dettmer et al., 2009; Santangelo, 2009).

Goal and Problem Clarification and Identification.   The first step in the consultation process is to identify goals and problems, using who, what, and where questions that help teachers clarify and agree on their goals and concerns. For example, consultation teams can address questions like these: What are the student's strengths and interests? What challenges does the student have in class? What goals do we have for the student? What can we do to address these challenges and help the student achieve our goals? Goals and problems also can be identified by examining students' IEPs and observing students in their classrooms.

Often it is best for the consultation to focus on one situation at a time. If several goals and problem areas must be handled simultaneously, it is advisable to set priorities and deal with the most important ones first. A consultation assistance request form that can be used to identify goals and problems is presented in Figure 4.8 (p. 154).

Goal and Problem Analysis.   In the second phase of the consultation process, educators analyze the features that appear to be related to the identified goals and problems. These may include the curriculum, the physical environment of the room, teaching strategies, grouping arrangements, teaching and learning styles, peer relationships, student ability levels, family, and the school's policies and procedures. This analysis helps educators plan appropriate intervention strategies.

Making Connections
This discussion of collaborative consultation is based on what we covered earlier, in Chapter 2, and you can use Figure 2.2 to guide the collaborative consultation process.

FIGURE 4.6 Sample cooperative teaching survey

Directions: Please indicate your feeling about the following statements using this scale:

Strongly Disagree (1)	Disagree (2)	Neutral (3)	Agree (4)	Strongly Agree (5)

1. I like working in a cooperative teaching team.   1 2 3 4 5
2. Students benefit from being taught by a cooperative teaching team.   1 2 3 4 5
3. I feel like this is our classroom.   1 2 3 4 5
4. Students with disabilities receive fewer specialized services as a result of cooperative teaching.   1 2 3 4 5
5. My students' families are satisfied with our cooperative teaching arrangement.   1 2 3 4 5
6. Other professionals are supportive of our cooperative teaching arrangement.   1 2 3 4 5
7. Our cooperative teaching team has sufficient time to communicate effectively.   1 2 3 4 5
8. Our cooperative teaching team shares responsibility for all instructional and noninstructional activities.   1 2 3 4 5
9. Our cooperative teaching team blends the teaching styles, philosophies, talents, and expertise of both teachers.   1 2 3 4 5
10. Working in a cooperative teaching team has encouraged me to try new instructional strategies.   1 2 3 4 5
11. Our school district provides the necessary support from others, resources, and professional development to implement cooperative teaching effectively.   1 2 3 4 5
12. I enjoy teaching more because I work in a cooperative teaching team.   1 2 3 4 5
13. I like having another adult in the classroom.   1 2 3 4 5
14. It is easy to communicate with my cooperative teaching partner.   1 2 3 4 5
15. I perform a subordinate role in our cooperative teaching team.   1 2 3 4 5
16. I have benefited professionally and personally from working as a cooperative teaching team.   1 2 3 4 5
17. My workload has increased as a result of working in a cooperative teaching team.   1 2 3 4 5
18. I am satisfied with the schoolwide and districtwide policies regarding cooperative teaching teams.   1 2 3 4 5
19. I would like to continue to work in a cooperative teaching team.   1 2 3 4 5

Plan Implementation. During this phase, educators plan which interventions to use to address the identified goals and difficulties. They brainstorm and share their expertise, considering factors such as practicality, effectiveness, resources needed, and effects on others. Once the preferred interventions have been selected, they can be outlined in detail, and responsibilities and time lines can be determined.

Plan Evaluation. Once the intervention has been implemented, its effectiveness should be checked periodically. This can be done by direct observation, curriculum-based assessments, analysis of student work samples, and other techniques that assess student progress.

Follow-up evaluation can also examine how the intervention has been implemented, whether it needs to be revised, and what additional problem areas need to be solved. Feedback should be an ongoing, interactive process focused on the intervention plan rather than on the individuals involved.

Even though consultation is effective, professionals may resist its use. This attitude is often associated with frustration, professional pride, and different views of the process. Other major barriers include insufficient time for team members to

FIGURE 4.7 Diary of a collaborative consultation teacher

September 7: *I can only be in one place at a time! Juggling teacher schedules and getting to students for assistance in their academic areas of need will be a feat worthy of a gold medal. And on top of that, time has to be set aside to conference with classroom teachers. I'm frustrated!!*

September 8: *I've worried about how junior high students would accept my presence in the classroom. . . . I discussed this with Mr. T, the building principal. During the grade level orientations, Mr. T introduced me as a teacher who would be in several different classes to assist students.*

September 13: *I did it! Schedules typed, all academic areas covered. I even managed to schedule time to conference with teachers (and it's not during lunch!). Mrs. C is not too keen on meeting with me on a regular basis and voiced a great concern about how much work this would add to her already overloaded schedule. Copies of all schedules have been sent to teachers, administrators, and parents. I have contacted every parent by phone and explained the service.*

September 14: *Mrs. M came to see me. She blurted out to me that she didn't know if she could go through with having me work in her room. She indicated to me that she felt extremely intimidated and was worried about what I would think. My first reaction was, "Don't be silly." Thank goodness I didn't say that. It really wasn't silly, because, I, too, was very nervous. I told Mrs. M that I understood what she meant, and explained my own nervousness.*

September 18: *A pleasant surprise. Mr. K introduced me as a co-teacher. He told his students that if they had any questions they could ask either himself or me. . . . I was wondering exactly how this would work out, when several different students raised their hands for assistance. In the end, I put together a small group of children to work with at the back table. How nice to see that the students I expected to work with, along with other students, accepted my presence and wanted my help.*

September 20: *I met with Mrs. E today. Together we worked on J's IEP, reviewed her entire curriculum, and decided on goals which should be included. It was wonderful having her input.*

October 12: *Mrs. C asked me if I would be willing to take a group of students for the social studies lesson and work on latitude and longitude. . . . We discussed the format and objectives of the lesson. During the class, we divided the room into groups and each taught a group. After the lesson, we were able to meet and discuss the results.*

November 16: *Ms. D, a first grade teacher, approached me and asked if I could speak with her about one of her students. I do not have a student in her room. We met after school and discussed the difficulties this child was having. Ms. D then asked if I would sit in on a parent conference. I guess there is a lot more to this job than just working with my assigned students.*

November 20: *Today's consultation with Mrs. K centered on getting her feedback on a study guide I created. We went over all the points, and at the end of the conversation she asked me if I would mind if she duplicated the guide and gave it to all her students.*

December 5: *Mrs. M indicated that the whole class was having difficulty getting the concept of contractions. We discussed some strategies, and she asked if I would like to teach the lesson the following morning. At the end of the consultation session, she turned to me and said, "You know, I am still a little nervous, but I really do like this collaborative consultation."*

Source: From "Diary of a Consulting Teacher," by K. Giek, 1990, *The Forum, 16*(1), pp 5–6. Copyright 1990 by New York State Federation of Chapters of the Council for Exceptional Children. Reprinted by permission.

meet and overwhelming caseloads. Successful consultation programs have administrative support and adequate resources so the classroom teachers and support staff have time to consult with one another, and offer educators reasonable caseloads and schedules (Santangelo, 2009; Villa et al., 2008).

FIGURE 4.8 Consultation assistance request form

ASSISTANCE NEEDED

Teacher _____   Today's Date

Student _____   _____

Other _____

☐ There's a problem. Let's put our heads together.
☐ I need your help in the classroom.
☐ Develop alternative assignment or activity.
☐ Arrange cooperative learning groups & activities.
☐ Implement peer tutoring or peer partners.
☐ Produce alternative materials or locate resources.
☐ Develop a modified grading system.

☐ Create a study guide.   ☐ Plan a lesson.
☐ Modify materials.   ☐ Team teaching.
☐ Modify a test.   ☐ Classroom management.
☐ Develop guided notes.   ☐ Instructional strategies.

When? _____

Additional information:

_____
_____
_____
_____

Source: From "Collaborative Teaching in the Secondary School," by E. A. Knackendoffel, 1996, in D. D. Deshler, E. S. Ellis, & B. K. Lenz (Eds.), *Teaching Adolescents with Learning Disabilities* (2nd ed.), p. 585. Copyright 1996 by Love. Reprinted with permission.

Promote Congruence

Successful collaboration and communication requires **congruence**, a logical relationship among the curriculum, learning goals, teaching materials, strategies used in the general education classroom, and supportive services programs. A congruent program is one based on common assessment results, goals and objectives, teaching strategies, and materials.

Ideally, supplemental and remedial teaching should parallel the general education curriculum. Unfortunately, many of these programs are fragmented, based on different—and conflicting—curricula and teaching approaches. These incompatible and conflicting programs can confuse students rather than help them learn. For instance, confusion can occur when you and your school's literacy educator use different approaches to teach reading.

You can use two models for coordinating teaching so that the ancillary program supplements learning in the general education classroom: an a priori model and a post hoc model. In the **a priori model**, supportive services educators teach new content that supports the content to be learned in the general education classroom. This instruction lays the foundation for instruction in the general education classroom. For example, the ESL educator might introduce on Monday the spelling words that will be introduced on Friday in the general education classroom.

In the **post hoc model**, supportive instruction reinforces skills previously introduced in the general education classroom. Thus, rather than introducing new content, the supportive services educator reviews and reteaches content previously covered in the general education classroom. For example, while a student is learning how to add fractions in the general education classroom, the resource teacher helps the student understand the process and develop automatic methods of responding to similar items.

Meetings   Meetings such as IEP conferences also can be used to establish congruence by involving general and supportive services educators in planning and implementing teaching programs. They can agree on common objectives, teaching methods and materials, lesson plans, and evaluation procedures to assess student learning. As students master the objectives, additional meetings can be held to revise the instructional program and evaluate congruence. Meetings also can promote congruence by having teachers share lesson plans.

Student-Led Conferences and Interviews   You also can use student-led conferences and interviews to ensure and evaluate congruence (Cullotta, 2008). Specifically, students can lead conferences or complete interviews addressing, "What things are you learning in (class)?" "What type of activities do you do in (class)?" "What materials do you use in (class)?" "Does (class) help you in other classes?" and "What strategies help you learn?"

Note Card Systems   Congruence and communication between professionals can be fostered by the use of a note card system. Each professional working with the student completes a note card or technology-based file that serves as an ongoing record of the student's performance in that class for a specified period of time. The information on the card could include a rating of the student's progress, a list of the skills mastered and not mastered, upcoming assignments and tests, successful strategies, teaching materials being used, and skills other teachers can attempt to foster. One educator can be asked to categorize the information and share it with others to ensure the continuity of instruction.

Engage in Professional Development

Your ability to collaborate and communicate with others and create inclusive classrooms also can be enhanced by engaging in professional development activities to improve your teaching (Leko & Brownell, 2009). These professional development activities include attending workshops, faculty meetings, and professional conferences, reading journal articles and books, viewing Web sites and videos, joining professional organizations and learning groups, and taking classes. For example, many teachers work in collaborative learning and teaching groups to experiment and reflect on teaching strategies and programs designed to enhance student learning and inclusion (Darling-Hammond & Richardson, 2009; Herner-Patnode, 2009).

One form of professional development that is particularly helpful for beginning teachers is **teacher mentoring** (Bay & Parker-Katz, 2009; McCabe, 2008). Mentoring programs involve frequent collaborative interactions between experienced, effective teachers and new teachers to address the challenges that new teachers encounter. Mentoring dyads observe each other's classrooms, discuss their teaching, assessment, and classroom management practices, curricula, and instructional materials, and develop plans to facilitate the teaching, learning, and collaboration process. Mentors also provide information related to the field and the school district, as well as emotional support. In addition to helping mentees adjust to the profession and their jobs, mentoring programs also benefit mentors.

Facing the Challenges of Being a Beginning Teacher

Ms. Salinas had always wanted to be a teacher and was looking forward to her first teaching position in an inclusion program. Before the school year began, she went into her classroom to get it ready and worked on reviewing student records, preparing lessons, and creating a newsletter for families. When school began, she was confident that she could apply what she had learned in her teacher education program. Although things got off to a good start, Ms. Salinas started feeling stressed out. Even though she arrived early and stayed late, she found herself overwhelmed by the paperwork and her unfamiliarity with the district policies. When some lessons didn't go as planned, and when she had conflicts with one of the paraeducators and a family member, Ms. Salinas started questioning her decision to be a teacher. Sensing Ms. Salinas's frustration, her principal spoke to her about being mentored by Mr. O'Connor, an experienced teacher with an excellent reputation in the school district. Ms. Salinas was reluctant, but her principal explained that what she was experiencing was typical and that mentoring is provided to all beginning teachers.

A week later Ms. Salinas and Mr. O'Connor met after school. They talked about the challenges facing a beginning teacher, and Mr. O'Connor shared some of his first-year teaching experiences, which were very similar to what Ms. Salinas was experiencing. He also told her that he wished he had the help of someone when he started teaching and that she should try not to be too hard on herself.

They made a plan to observe each other's classrooms so that they could both learn from one another. After Mr. O'Connor's first observation, he told her that she was doing fine and made some suggestions about teaching strategies she might want to try, which he modeled for her when she came to see his classroom. They also spent time talking about the district's policies, inclusion programs, the curriculum and discipline, and how to handle conflicts with other professionals and family members. Mr. O'Connor liked being helpful to Ms. Salinas, and he also learned some things from her. Ms. Salinas appreciated the support and felt better about her decision to be a teacher.

Here are some other strategies you can use to implement the IDEA in your inclusive classroom and face the challenges of being a beginning teacher:

- Recognize that teaching is a difficult and challenging job, and give yourself permission to experiment and learn from your experiences.

- Take care of your emotional and physical health. Remember your personal and family needs. Find time to socialize with friends, family, and colleagues, to do things you like to do, and to keep your life as balanced as possible.

- Learn organizational and time management strategies that help make you more effective and efficient.

- Get to know the other professionals (e.g., other teachers and service providers, paraeducators, school secretaries, janitors, cafeteria workers, and administrators) in your school and school district, and establish a good working relationship with them. Ask them about schoolwide policies and procedures, and about ways to help you and your students and their families.

- Reflect on your teaching practices. For example, maintain a journal where you reflect on your experiences as a teacher and the outcomes of your actions in specific situations.

- Take advantage of whatever professional development activities you can fit into your schedule.

- Use materials and resources (e.g., lesson plans, assessment activities, classroom management plans) that you developed or acquired as part of your participation in your teacher education program.

- Work in teacher learning cohort groups with other teachers and university professionals to establish a collaborative resource network.

- Keep in touch with your former classmates and even your professors. Use them as a resource and as a sounding board.

Sources: Bay & Parker-Katz, 2009; Cancio & Conderman, 2008; Cramer & Stivers, 2007; Nieto, 2009.

COMMUNICATION AND COLLABORATION WITH FAMILIES

HOW CAN I FOSTER COMMUNICATION AND COLLABORATION WITH FAMILIES?
As Ms. Carr and Ms. Stevens recognized in the chapter-opening vignette, a key component of effective inclusion programs is communication and collaboration with the student's family. As well as being educationally sound and in accord with the IDEA, involving family members in the education of their children can help you build support for your inclusion program (Yssel et al., 2007). You can view them as a valuable resource and partner in the educational process by (a) using a variety of ways to share information with them about your inclusion program; (b) engaging families in curriculum planning; (c) holding meetings with them to develop students' IEPs; (d) inviting them to volunteer and attend school and classroom events; (e) providing them with information and resources so that they can help their children learn and complete their

REFLECTIVE

Research indicates that family involvement in school declines significantly as students age. Why do you think this is the case? What could you and schools do to counter this pattern?

homework; and (f) soliciting information from them about their children's strengths, challenges, and progress (Floyd & Vernon-Dotson, 2008; Van Haren & Fieldler, 2008).

Gain the Trust of Families

Family involvement and empowerment are based largely on the trust established between families and educators (Angell, Stoner, & Shelden, 2009; Sebald & Luckner, 2007). If families and school personnel distrust or feel uncomfortable with each other, the family's involvement and therefore the student's performance may be harmed. You can involve and empower families by working with them using methods that are based on collaboration, empathy, understanding, honesty, and respect and that recognize the strengths of each family (Angell et al., 2009; Van Haren & Fieldler, 2008). Trust can be established when schools serve as a resource for families and collaborate with them to offer and coordinate a broad range of flexible, usable, and understandable services that support the many changing needs of families (Angell et al., 2009). You also can gain the trust of your students' families by interacting with them in many settings and by attending after-school activities and community events.

Family involvement and empowerment can be fostered by establishing trust between families and educators. How do you promote mutual trust with and gain the respect of your students' families?

When the experiences and expertise of family and community members are incorporated into school programs, the result is mutual respect and trust among schools, families, and the community (Checkley, 2008). Students see their families and community actively engaged in schools and classrooms. In the process, families and the community become empowered, positive partners in the educational process. Families and community members can be part of an ongoing program that allows them to share their experiences and knowledge in schools (Matuszny, Banda, & Coleman, 2007).

Learn about the strengths, experiences, cultures, communities, and attitudes of families and students, and then interact with them in ways that acknowledge their strengths and respect their values (Ramirez & Soto-Hinman, 2009; Rothstein-Fisch & Trumbull, 2008). For example, some families may have cultural beliefs that view the teacher as a highly respected person and that it is not their role to disagree with you, interfere in their children's education, or ask questions. Therefore, rather than viewing them as disinterested in their children's education, it is important for you to understand their positive beliefs about education and adjust your interactions with them accordingly (San Antonio, 2008).

In addition to understanding the cultural perspectives of your students' families, you can examine your own viewpoints, attitudes, and behaviors related to your cultural background and diversity (Nieto, 2009; Rothstein-Fisch & Trumbull, 2008). It is important to recognize how your cultural beliefs may be different from those of your students and their families and to interact with students and families in culturally sensitive ways (Dettmer et al., 2009; Harry et al., 2008). Ramirez and Soto-Hinman (2009), Rothstein-Fisch and Trumbull (2008), Richards, Brown, and Forde (2007), and Ginsberg (2007) present activities you can use to learn more about your students and their families and to increase your cultural awareness.

Advocate for Students and Their Families

You can gain the trust of families by advocating for them, their children, and your inclusive classroom, which is part of your professional responsibility (Mihalis et al., 2009; Stivers et al., 2008). In school, you can engage in advocacy informally via conversations with others and formally via your participation in comprehensive planning team meetings and other committees that influence decision making (Smith et al., 2006). You also can post articles or relevant materials in prominent locations in your school or community, and lead discussions about the issues discussed. Outside school, you can advocate by

- joining professional organizations, and other groups that offer support for advocacy efforts;
- contacting legislators and policymakers and writing letters to the editor regarding issues that affect your students and families and your profession;
- challenging myths and inaccurate and stereotypical statements made by others;
- making presentations to community groups and school boards;
- inviting community members and influential decision makers to visit your classroom and other effective programs in your school and community (Stivers et al., 2008).

You can enhance the success of your advocacy efforts by being aware of the law and related issues; developing your communication, collaboration, and conflict resolution skills; and helping students and their families learn to be effective advocates for themselves and all students (Checkley, 2008).

When advocating for students and families, you also need to be aware of the personal and professional risks. At times, your views on issues affecting your students and their families may put you in the difficult position of opposing your school district or others with whom you work. Thus, you need to comply with ethical standards for educators and be able to deal with indirect and direct pressure to conform with school district requests, and possible reprisals (Bucholz et al., 2007; Skinner et al., 2009).

Ensure Confidentiality

Ensuring students and families their right to *confidentiality*, which is specified in the Family Educational Rights and Privacy Act (FERPA) and the IDEA, is essential to establishing a trusting and collaborative relationship with families and students (Devlin, 2008; Smith et al., 2006). Educators directly involved in teaching a student may have access to his or her records, but before a school district can allow other persons to review these records, it must obtain consent from the family.

Confidentiality also guarantees the family the opportunity to obtain, review, and challenge their child's educational records. The family can obtain their child's records by requesting a copy, which the school district must provide. However, the family may have to pay the expenses incurred in duplicating the records. If the family disagrees with these records, the family can challenge them by asking school officials to correct or delete the information or by writing a response to be included in the records.

In addition to addressing protecting records, confidentiality means that professionals should refrain from

- revealing personally identifying information about students (e.g., their disability or immigration status, medical conditions and needs, test scores, etc.) and families to others; and
- speaking about students in public ways and places (e.g., teacher's room, meetings with other families, college classes and in-service sessions, etc.) that allow specific students to be identified.

Meet Regularly with Families

We knew it would be another rough year. After only 2 months, Paul's new teacher, Mr. Rodl, called and said, "Paul is falling behind, and we need to do something." Mr. Rodl asked us to come to a meeting with a team of professionals to discuss Paul's progress. He said we could schedule the meeting at a time that was convenient for us.

Making Connections
Find out more about how you can help your students learn advocacy skills in Chapter 6.

REFLECTIVE

What are some issues for which you would advocate for students and families? How could you advocate for your students and their families? What factors would affect your ability to advocate for them?

REFLECTIVE

Given families' and students' right to confidentiality, what would you do in the following situations? Teachers are discussing students and their families during lunch in the teachers' lounge. You notice that the students' records in your school are kept in an unsupervised area.

Going into the meeting was scary. There sat Paul's teacher, the principal, the school psychologist, and several other people we didn't know. Mr. Rodl started the meeting by introducing us to the others in the room. Then he said, "Since I work closely with Paul, I'll lead the meeting and coordinate the decisions we'll make about Paul's program. We call that being the service coordinator."

He asked each person in the room to talk about Paul. As different people spoke, others asked questions. When several people used words we didn't understand, Mr. Rodl asked them to explain the words to us. When our turn came, Mr. Rodl asked us to talk about what was happening with Paul at home, what we thought was happening with him at school, and what we would like to see happen at school.

At first, we felt very nervous. As people in the room listened to and discussed our comments, we became more relaxed. The group discussed several ways to help Paul. In the end, we all came up with a plan to help Paul learn better. Mr. Rodl summarized the plan and the roles each person would play to make it successful. We also discussed how we would continue to communicate and collaborate to help Paul, and agreed to set up a home–school contract to share information about and support Paul's progress. We left the meeting feeling really good about being part of a team that was trying to help our son.

As this vignette of Paul's family suggests, you can foster collaboration and communication with families and increase their involvement in and commitment to your inclusive classroom by improving the quality of family–educators meetings (Dettmer et al., 2009; Mueller, 2009; Sheehey & Sheehey, 2007; Whitbread, Bruder, Fleming & Park, 2007). Many educators are encouraging students to attend and take an active role in these conferences (Cullotta, 2008; Konrad, 2008).

Making Connections
Strategies for involving students and families in IEP conferences were presented earlier, in Chapter 2.

Plan the Meeting   Plan carefully for the meeting by identifying the reasons for the meeting and developing an appropriate agenda. The agenda should allow enough time to discuss and resolve issues and address concerns of families and other educators. These issues and concerns can be determined by contacting others *before* the meeting so that they understand what will be discussed at the meeting. Share the agenda with families and other participants, encourage them to bring useful records and materials to the meeting, and give them the necessary background information to take part in the meeting. Important documents and materials such as copies of legal rights, IEPs, work samples, test results, and other teachers' comments related to agenda items and student performance can be organized and sent to participants beforehand. Some families may appreciate it if you give them a list of questions or suggestions to help them participate in the meeting, and tell them which school personnel will also be there. For example, before the meeting, you can ask family members to be prepared to discuss their goals for their child's educational programs, their perceptions of their child's feelings about school, interests, hobbies, strengths and challenges, their suggestions for effective strategies, and any questions and concerns they have. You also may want to invite family members to observe in the classroom as a way to prepare for the meeting.

Good planning also ensures that the meeting time is convenient for families and professionals (Stoner et al., 2005). Families can be contacted early in their preferred method of communication (i.e., written communication, telephone, face-to-face meetings, e-mail) to determine what times and dates are best for them, to encourage them to invite persons who are important to them, and to determine whether they need help with transportation, child care, or other special needs or circumstances. Once the meeting has been scheduled, you can contact families and professionals in advance to give them the time, place, purpose, and duration of the meeting and to confirm that they will be there. Follow-up reminders to families via mail, e-mail, or telephone will make them more likely to attend.

Structure the Environment to Promote Communication   The setting for the conference can be organized for collaborating and sharing information (Mueller, 2009). Comfortable, same-size furniture can be arranged to promote communication among all participants. Barriers such as desks and chairs should not be placed between families and teachers. Chairs and tables can be positioned so that all persons can see each other.

Welcome family members and other participants, engage in pleasant, informal conversation before the meeting starts; and offer refreshments. This will help participants feel comfortable and establish rapport. To improve participation and follow-up, you can ask the participants if they would like pads and pencils to take notes, and give them name tags.

To make sure that the meeting is not interrupted, post a note on the door indicating that a conference is in session. Distractions caused by phones and cell phones should be minimized.

Conduct the Conference   As Mr. Rodl did in the vignette with Paul's family at the beginning of this section, you should conduct the conference in a positive way that encourages understanding, participation, and collaboration (Mueller, 2009; Sheehey & Sheehey, 2007). Welcome and introduce participants or ask them to introduce themselves, review the agenda and the purpose of the meeting, and establish ground rules (Whitbread et al., 2007). One ground rule that many groups find helpful is the use of a "parking lot" for comments and questions that are important but not related to the meeting's agenda. You can establish a parking lot by having a flip chart in the room and using it to list comments and questions that can be discussed later in the meeting or during a future meeting.

The meeting can start on a positive note, with participants discussing the strong points of the student's performance. Next, participants can review any concerns they have about the student. They should present information in a way that is understandable to all and share materials such as work samples, test results, and anecdotal records to support and illustrate their comments. Some professionals find it helpful to supplement their presentations by using video, PowerPoint, and the Internet to access and share information and easels or chalkboards to record ideas and highlight important points.

You can ask families to discuss the issues or situations from their perspective or to respond to open-ended questions. Family sharing at meetings can be increased by listening attentively; by being empathetic; by acknowledging and reinforcing participation ("That's a good point"; "I'll try to incorporate that"); by avoiding asking questions that have yes/no or implied answers; by asking questions that encourage family members to respond rather than waiting for them to ask questions or spontaneously speak their minds; by informing them that there may be several solutions to a problem; by not criticizing family members; by using language that is understandable but not condescending; by explaining unfamiliar terminology; by checking periodically for understanding; by paraphrasing and summarizing the comments of family members; by using humor; and by showing respect for cultural differences and families and their feelings (Montgomery, 2005). Interpreters and translators can be used to promote the understanding of families who have difficulties with spoken or written English.

You can adjust the structure of the meeting, depending on how the family prefers to communicate. For families that value personal relationships, you can sit close by, and use self-disclosure, humor, and casual conversation. Other families may be goal oriented and respond to professionals they perceive as competent and organized. These families may expect you to structure the meeting, set goals, define roles, and ask questions of family members.

End the meeting on a positive note by summarizing the issues discussed, points of agreement and disagreement, strategies to be used to resolve problems, and roles to be played by family members and educators. At the end of the meeting, participants can agree on a plan of action, establish ongoing communications systems, and set a date for the next meeting. It is also important to share with

FIGURE 4.9 Sample schedule for a family–educators conference

- ❏ Greet, welcome, and thank all participants.
- ❏ Ask participants to introduce themselves and briefly describe their roles and the services they provide.
- ❏ Review the meeting's agenda, purpose(s), and ground rules.
- ❏ Discuss relevant information from prior meetings.
- ❏ Start with positive aspects of the student's performance. Ask family members and then professionals to discuss their view of the student's strengths and challenges and the issues on the agenda. Educators should be encouraged to support their statements with examples, work samples, anecdotal records, and assessment results.
- ❏ Discuss the comments of family members and professionals attempting to achieve a consensus.
- ❏ Determine a plan of action.
- ❏ Summarize discussions and the results of the meeting and review the future plans.
- ❏ Determine an appropriate date for the next meeting.
- ❏ Adjourn the meeting.
- ❏ Evaluate the meeting.

families the best ways and times to contact you and the other professionals. Feedback from families and professionals concerning various aspects of the meeting also can be solicited to identify successful factors as well as to pinpoint aspects in need of revision. A sample schedule of activities for a family–educators conference is presented in Figure 4.9.

Resolve Conflicts Constructively

Your ability to establish a trusting and collaborative relationship with families also will be affected by how you and your students' families resolve the conflicts that may occur during meetings and the school year (Mueller, 2009). These disputes often are the result of miscommunication and different views concerning academic performance and grades, student behavior and disciplinary actions, educational placement, and the availability and delivery of educational and related services. It is important that you also recognize that these conflicts may be related to families' past experiences with schools.

In addition to regularly communicating and collaborating with families using the strategies presented in this chapter, you can do several things to limit the potential negative consequences of conflicts with families and develop constructive solutions that address the concerns and issues that are at the center of conflicts (Smith et al., 2006). Recognize that families are knowledgeable about their children, and show that you care about and respect them and their children. Rather than viewing family members negatively as "overprotective," "troublemakers," "uncaring," or "uncooperative," try to identify the factors that might explain their perspectives and behavior. It also is important to understand the family's emotional reactions to their child's difficulties, which may include a combination of disappointment, fear, anger and avoidance (Smith et al., 2006).

When interacting with the family, maintain an attitude of communication, collaboration, and conciliation, and a commitment to what is best for the student (Mueller, 2009). Establish ground rules and an agenda, and serve as a neutral facilitator. Listen carefully and reflectively as family members share their concerns and perspectives without interrupting them, seeking clarification only when necessary. Avoid

A GUIDE TO ACTION
Enhancing Meetings with Families

Although a variety of techniques are possible to collaborate and communicate with families, one important strategy is meeting with families. To enhance your meetings with families, consider the following points:

- Be prepared for the meeting, and help others prepare for the meeting.
- Schedule the meeting at a time and place that is convenient for the family members and other participants.
- Address the special circumstances of families that might prevent their attendance or participation in the meeting.
- Ask for suggestions from family members and other participants about the agenda.
- Make the purpose of the meeting clear to all.
- Allow enough time for the meeting.
- Create a welcoming, positive, respectful, and comfortable environment that encourages participants to share their perspectives and work collaboratively.
- Ensure that the meeting occurs without interruptions.
- Address the issues, questions, and concerns participants want to discuss.

- Provide all participants with enough opportunities and time to present their opinions, to ask questions, and to receive feedback from others.
- Make sure that the participants discuss the strong points of the student's performance.
- Use student work samples to support your comments.
- Use technology to enhance the meeting's effectiveness.
- Listen attentively, and acknowledge and encourage participation from others.
- Communicate in a clear, nonthreatening manner using language that others can understand.
- Adjust the content, structure, tone, and interaction patterns of the meeting to be consistent with the family's cultural, linguistic, and experiential background.
- End the meeting effectively.
- Protect the family's confidentiality.
- Evaluate and reflect on the meeting.
- Take follow-up actions based on the decisions made at the meeting.

How would you rate your meetings with families? ( ) Excellent ( ) Good ( ) Needs Improvement ( ) Needs Much Improvement

Create a plan of action for enhancing your meetings with families that includes your goals, the actions you will take and the resources you will need to achieve them, and the ways you will evaluate your success.

---

acting emotionally, taking things personally, making assumptions or promises that you cannot keep, and rebutting each point brought up by the family (Montgomery, 2005). While you don't have to agree with families, it is important that you refrain from dismissing or diminishing their comments, recognize their role in making decisions about their children, and avoid using language that might escalate the situation. Be constructive by calmly, directly, and honestly discussing your viewpoint and the reasons for it, and citing and displaying documentation to support your statements (Smith et al., 2006). Convey your message with a respectful tone of voice and appropriate body language. Emphasize points of agreement, propose choices and options, and seek solutions that are acceptable to all parties. If conflicts cannot be resolved constructively by you and the family, seek the assistance of others who can help mediate disputes. Ultimately, it is important for you to mend fences with families.

Address the Diverse Strengths, Challenges, Beliefs, Backgrounds, Resources, and Experiences of Families

Families, like students, have diverse strengths, challenges, backgrounds, beliefs, resources, and experiences, and they are structured in different ways. In communicating and collaborating with families, be aware of these factors and how they affect families, and adjust your style and services accordingly to promote family involvement (Dettmer et al., 2009; Harry et al., 2008; Lo, 2005; Ramirez & Soto-Hinman, 2009). You can learn about your students and their families' preferences by meeting with them to discuss their daily rituals at home; their important values and customs; their feelings about their child's strengths and challenges; and their expectations of their child's behavior, their roles, the school, and you (West, Leon-Guerrero, & Stevens, 2007).

Cultural Factors   Families are interested in their children's education, but different cultural perspectives can make it hard to establish traditional school–family interactions (Araujo, 2009; Brandon & Brown, 2009; Lee et al., 2009). In designing culturally sensitive programs to involve and empower families, you should adjust to the family's level of acculturation, feelings about and knowledge of schooling, prior experience with discrimination, structure, beliefs, child-rearing practices, developmental expectations, perceptions of disability, emotional responses, and communication patterns (Harry et al., 2008).

Level of Acculturation.   The level of **acculturation**, the extent to which members of one culture adapt to a new culture, will affect a family's cultural perspective and school involvement (Olivos, 2009). Because children tend to acculturate faster than adults, children may perform some roles in the new culture that adults assumed in their native country, such as interacting with social institutions like schools. These roles involve time and stress and the dependence of adult family members on children. This can have a significant impact on adult–child relationships and the student's academic performance.

Feelings about and Knowledge of Educational System.   Family members' feelings about and knowledge of the educational system and their prior experiences with schools also can affect their involvement in school (Angell et al., 2009; Kozleski et al., 2008). Family members with limited knowledge of the educational system or negative experiences as students may not feel comfortable participating in family–school activities (Olivos, 2009). These understandings, feelings, and experiences also can influence what they expect of you and the schools their children attend. Family members who are immigrants may also have different perceptions of schooling.

Prior Experience with Discrimination.   Many families may have suffered discrimination, which can influence their behavior and attitudes (Alvarez McHatton, 2007). These families may not want to attend meetings at the school if they or others have been discriminated against or treated with disrespect there. You can increase the family's comfort in attending school-related events and establish trust and a welcoming environment by doing the following:

- Invite important extended family members to school events.
- Address elders first.
- Refer to family members by their titles, such as Mr., Mrs., Ms., Dr., or Reverend (or ask them how they like to be addressed).
- Make school facilities available for community activities.
- Speak to families in a respectful and sincere manner.
- Respond in a warm and caring way.
- Decorate the school and classrooms with icons from various cultures (Angell et al., 2009; Brandon & Brown, 2009).

Family Structure.   Most school-based strategies for involving families focus on the needs of the nuclear family. However, many cultures emphasize the value of the extended family (Pewewardy & Fitzpatrick, 2009). For example, many families live in a framework of collective interdependence and kinship interactions. They share resources and services, and offer emotional and social support. Rather than asking for help from schools in dealing with educational issues, these families may feel more comfortable relying on community members or agencies. Therefore, you need to identify and involve the informal systems that support families.

In many families, roles are hierarchical, and elders may play an important role in decision making and child care (Roopnarine et al., 2005). When working with families that value and rely on extended family members, you can involve all family members in the school program. For example, in writing to families, you could say that all family members are welcome at educational meetings.

REFLECTIVE

What are the values and perspectives that make up your family's belief system? How do these belief affect your family's views, priorities and decisions?

Belief Systems and Child-Rearing Practices, Developmental Expectations, and Perceptions of Disability. It is essential that you understand the beliefs of your students' families and use this information to address their strengths, concerns, challenges, and goals, and adjust your interactions with them. **Belief systems** refer to the values and perspectives that inform the family's world view, way of life, priorities, and decision making (King et al., 2009).

The family's belief system impacts their views on child rearing, appropriate behavior, disability, and developmental milestones (Harry, 2008; Kozleski et al., 2008; Sheehey et al., 2009). These different perspectives also can affect how they view their children's educational program. For example, some families may stress the importance of children reaching developmental milestones at appropriate ages, but other families may not. Similarly, for some families, independence is a goal for their child, but others may view it as interfering with their preference that their child remain a part of the family. Because the behavioral and developmental expectations of schools and families may conflict, you must work cooperatively with families to develop a culturally sensitive and relevant teaching program. The program should include agreed-on bicultural behaviors, appropriate cultural settings for these behaviors, and cross-cultural criteria for measuring progress.

Families also may have different views of *disability* and its impact on the family (Harry, 2008; Kozleski et al., 2008). For example, some use a broader idea of disability that is often related to the child's ability to function at home and the family's beliefs about the child's future. As a result, they may also resist, resent, or misunderstand the labeling of their child as having a disability, which can cause them to not trust the school.

You also need to recognize that the family's belief system also has a cultural, spiritual, and religious basis (Ault & Collins, 2009; Blanks & Smith, 2009). Religious and spiritual beliefs may provide guidance, support, and strength to some families of children with disabilities (Elhoweris, Whittaker, & Salend, 2007). Some families may believe that disabilities are positive signs for the family or that a child's difficulties are caused by reprisals for rule violations by family members, spirits, failure to avoid taboos, fate, choice, and lifestyle imbalances (Masood, Turner, & Baxter, 2007). Families also may have perspectives that cause them to prefer home remedies and alternative practices, and to reject Western views of medicine and technology. Therefore, you may have to address these issues before families accept and respond to traditional educational strategies.

Emotional Adjustments The family's beliefs also shape their emotional adjustment to having a child with a disability (Dettmer et al., 2009; Smith et al., 2006). Families may go through several transformative stages as they learn to adjust to and accept their child's disability (Singer, 2002). These stages, which vary from family to family based on beliefs, experience, culture, socioeconomic level, spirituality, religious beliefs, the nature of the child's disability, and the support they receive from others, may include the following:

Many families report experiencing positive effects as a result of having a child with a disability in the family. What might be some ways in which having a child with a disability affects the whole family?

Stage 1: Families may be shocked and dejected, and experience grief and fear.

Stage 2: Families may be confused, deny their child's disability, reject their child, or avoid dealing with the issue/situation by looking for other explanations.

Stage 3: Families may experience anger, self-pity, disappointment, guilt, and a sense of powerlessness that may be expressed as rage or withdrawal.

Stage 4: Families may start to understand and accept their child's disability and its impact on the family.

Stage 5: Families may accept, love, and appreciate their child unconditionally.

Stage 6: Families may begin to focus on living, on the benefits accrued, on the future, and on working with others to teach and provide support services to their child.

In addition to helping families as they go through these stages, be aware of the varied belief systems and culturally appropriate coping strategies that families have, and consider these values strategies when designing and delivering services (Harry, 2008; King et al., 2009). You also can aid families by being honest with them, showing genuine care and compassion, being empathetic rather than sympathetic, and encouraging them to obtain supportive services. You can also encourage them to communicate with other family members and other important persons in their lives, join family support groups, ask questions, and express their emotions.

It also is important for you to understand and help others recognize that many families report experiencing positive effects as a result of raising a child with a disability (Ferguson, 2002; Taunt & Hastings, 2002). These benefits for parents and siblings include developing coping skills and family cohesiveness; facilitating shared values and parenting; increasing one's perspective on life, sense of purpose/responsibility, and sensitivity to others and assertiveness; improving communication within the family; and expanding the family's social network.

Socioeconomic Factors   Many socioeconomic factors also can affect the family's participation in their child's education (Brandon & Brown, 2009; San Antonio, 2008). Although many families face increased financial pressures related to raising and providing for their children with disabilities, these economic hardships can particularly affect families living in poverty. Long work schedules, time conflicts, transportation problems, and child care needs can be serious barriers that you and your colleagues need to address. These barriers can be reduced by the use of home visits (see Ginsberg [2007] for guidelines for conducting home visits). However, many families may consider a home visit intrusive, so you should ask for the family's permission before visiting their home.

Use Written Communication

You can use written communication such as letters and notes and other documents such as handbooks, orientation manuals, and homework guidelines to establish ongoing communication with families (Brandon & Brown, 2009; Smith et al., 2006). Written communication is often used to share information on students, schedule meetings, and build support for your inclusion program. For example, you can periodically ask your students' families to complete short questionnaires to obtain feedback about your inclusion program and their children (Muscott, Szczesiul, Berk, Staub, Hoover, & Perry-Chisholm, 2008).

It is important that you evaluate written documents sent to families in terms of readability, legibility, tone, and the use of clear, respectful, welcoming, and jargon-free language (Fitzgerald & Watkins, 2006). Look at Figure 4.10, and note how the letters to family members are different. Which letter is more likely to result in family members attending the meeting? Letter A is impersonal, uses technical terms, places the school's needs above the needs of family members, can intimidate the family, and does little to encourage family participation. Letter B is welcoming and less formal, tries to establish rapport, and respects the family, their scheduling needs, and their contributions to the education of their child. It also avoids professional jargon, encourages participation and collaboration, and gives the family positive suggestions for preparing for the meeting.

You also can increase the effectiveness of your written communication with families by sharing affective and factual information; using familiar language and avoiding using acronymns; examining its readability; emphasizing positive aspects of students and their families; using examples, visuals, icons, and cultural referents; and monitoring the response rate from family members (Fitzgerald &

REFLECTIVE

Research indicates that families of children with low-incidence disabilities are more involved in school than families of children with high-incidence disabilities. Why do you think this is the case?

Making Connections
Strategies for overcoming economic barriers to student performance and family participation are discussed earlier, in Chapter 2.

To enhance your understanding of how culture and language can have an impact on family involvement, go to the IRIS Center Resources section of Topic: Cultural and Linguistic Diversity in the MyEducationLab for your course, and complete the module entitled *Cultural and Linguistic Differences: What Teachers Should Know.*

UDL and YOU

Understanding and Accommodating
Cross-Cultural Communication Patterns and Linguistic Factors

Rather than assuming that all of your students' families communicate in the same ways, you can apply the principles of UDL to your interactions with families by understanding and accommodating the communication patterns and linguistic factors that differ from one culture to another (Harry, 2008; Lee et al., 2009). This means that you are sensitive to linguistic and communication style differences, and interpret verbal and nonverbal behaviors within a social and cultural context (Gollnick & Chinn, 2009). For example, eye contact, wait time, word meanings, body language, facial gestures, voice quality and tone, personal space, and physical contact have different meanings and purposes in various cultures (Matuszny et al., 2007). You also need to understand that communications between cultures are affected by turn taking, by physical closeness or distance, and by spoken and unspoken rules of conversation. For example, in some cultures *yes* connotes "I heard you" or "I am listening to you" rather than agreement. Similarly, individuals from some cultures may interpret laughter as a sign of embarrassment rather than enjoyment.

Cross-cultural communication patterns also may affect communication, the discussion of certain issues, and the ways in which families view, seek, and receive assistance (Harry, 2008; Kozleski et al., 2008; Lo, 2005). Some families may not feel comfortable discussing personal problems and concerns, viewing that behavior as being self-centered or disgracing the family, while others may be reluctant to disagree in order to maintain harmony (Banks, 2004). Some families may not want to interact with the school staff because they believe that teachers know what is best for their children and that it is not appropriate for them to question the authority of teachers (Ramirez & Soto-Hinman, 2009). Community members who understand the family's needs, emotional responses, and culture can help break down these communication barriers by helping you understand and interpret the family's communication behaviors; serving as liaisons among schools, families, and communities; and orienting new families to the school.

Language factors also may block communication between schools and families (Harry, 2008; Lo, 2005). Communication difficulties may be compounded by problems in understanding educational jargon and practices that may not exist in the families' language and culture (Ramirez & Soto-Hinman, 2009). For example, some families from different cultural and language backgrounds believe that special education implies a program that is better than general education. You can correct this misconception by giving these families forms, lists of key educational terms, and information about their rights in their native languages. Learning greetings and words in the family's native language also can create a positive environment that promotes communication and respect.

Interpreters and translators can be used to promote communication between English-speaking educators and families who speak other languages (Olivos, 2009). Whereas interpreters foster oral communications during face-to-face meetings, translators focus on rewriting correspondence and documents in the family's primary language. (We will discuss the roles of translators later in this chapter.) Interpreters should speak the same dialect as the family; maintain confidentiality; avoid giving personal opinions; seek clarification from families and professionals when they have problems communicating certain information; use reverse translation when exact translations are not possible; and show respect for families and professionals. The interpreter will be more effective if you discuss the topics and terminology with the interpreter before the meeting, use nonverbal communication as well as speech, are aware of the nonverbal behaviors of family members, and ask for the interpreter's feedback about the meeting. It is also important that family members and professionals speak to each other rather than directing their comments to interpreters.

Although many families may rely on their child to interpret for them in general, the child or other students should not interpret during meetings. A child serving as an interpreter for the family can have a negative impact on the family, as this situation reverses the traditional adult–child relationship. For children, interpreting places them in the adult role in the family, which can make them anxious and frightened. For adults, being dependent on their child as their interpreter can be considered demeaning. It also may be awkward for family members to share information about their child when the child is interpreting.

Watkins, 2006). Since some family members may have difficulty accessing written information, it is always a good idea to ask families how and what they wish to communicate, and to find alternatives to written communication, and offer some form of oral communication to clarify written communications and documents (Davern, 2004).

FIGURE 4.10 Samples of written correspondence to families

LETTER A

To Whom It May Concern:

The school district has scheduled a meeting to review your child's educational program. The meeting will be held on March 15, 2008, in the conference room at the administrative offices.

The following members of the school district will be in attendance:

Mrs. Lorraine Hamilton	School Social Worker
Mrs. Constance Franks	Special Education Teacher
Mr. Patrick Hardees	General Education Teacher
Mr. Donald Fein	School Psychologist
Mrs. Joanne Frederick	Principal

If you would like the school physician to be at the meeting, please contact my office at least three days prior to the meeting.

Please contact my office if you plan to attend the meeting. My office will be able to tell you approximately what time your child will be discussed. If you are unable to attend the meeting in person, you may participate by telephone.

The meeting will take place as scheduled unless you request otherwise. I will send the results in writing after the meeting is over. Feel free to contact me with any questions or concerns related to your child's education.

Yours truly,

Donald Smith,

Director of Pupil Personnel Services

LETTER B

Dear Truman Family:

Hello. My name is Donald Smith, and I am the Director of Pupil Personnel Services for the Bellville School District. It is my job to assist you in understanding the educational system and to work with you in creating an educational program that meets the needs of your child.

Your child's teachers would like to schedule a meeting with you to discuss your child's educational program. It is important that you attend this meeting. You know your child better than anyone and can provide important information concerning your child's school performance. You may also wish to bring others with you to attend the meeting. It is also possible for you to request that the school physician attend this meeting.

If you have time, you can do several things to prepare for the meeting. You can talk to your child and his/her teachers about his/her performance in school and the ways to improve his/her learning. You also can visit your child's classroom. It also will be helpful if you bring materials to the meeting such as your child's schoolwork, school records, and reports, as well as medical information. At the meeting, we will talk about the goals for your child's education, the way your child learns best, and his/her favorite activities and interests.

I will be calling you to schedule the meeting at a time that is most convenient for your family to discuss who you would like to attend the meeting, and to answer any questions you may have. We also can assist you in attending the meeting by providing you with transportation, child care, and the services of an interpreter. I look forward to speaking with you and working with you to meet the educational needs of your child.

Yours truly,

Donald Smith,

Director of Pupil Personnel Services

Translators who help prepare written communications and community members can help you develop culturally relevant and sensitively written documents that are rewritten into the native languages of your families (Araujo, 2009). You can collaborate with translators to produce quality translated materials by using examples and activities that are culturally appropriate, including visuals and photographs that appeal to and depict the intended audience, and avoiding technical terms and jargon or including an explanation when you must use them. Software and Web-based translation programs are available to provide quick translation of material, but you should exercise caution in using them because they often fail to capture the cultural, syntactical, and linguistic meanings of the communication and address dialectical and word differences, which can result in confusing or offensive communications.

Creating Collaborative Relationships and Fostering Communication

REFLECTIVE

Think about several people you interact with regularly. How do their communication styles differ in terms of eye contact, wait time, word meanings, facial and physical gestures, voice quality, personal space, and physical contact? How do these differences affect you? How do you adjust your communication style to accommodate these differences?

Informative Notice   You can share information with families by using an *informative notice*. This is a brief written communication that alerts families to various school and classroom activities, student progress, and the materials students will need to complete their assignments. At the beginning of the school year, the informative notice can take two forms: (a) personalized postcards to students welcoming them to your class and (b) letters to families to introduce yourself and various aspects of your inclusive classroom, to explain your expectations, invite them to various school and class-related events, and to ask for their support and collaboration (Brandon, 2007; Ramirez & Soto-Hinman, 2009).

Newsletters   A form of written communication that teachers like Ms. Carr and Ms. Stevens used with families is a *newsletter*, which can tell them about school and classroom events, useful resources and community services, extracurricular activities, meetings, school policies, and menus, and offer family education (Brandon, 2007; Ramirez & Soto-Hinman, 2009). Consider the following when creating newsletters:

- Create a title for the newsletter.
- Make them brief (no more than three pages).
- Present information in a clear, focused, and interesting manner.
- Consider using bulleted or numbered lists.
- Make them attractive by using graphics, columns, and colors.
- Involve students in creating them.
- Post them on the Internet.
- Focus them on information, resources, and topics that are useful to students and their families.
- Solicit feedback on their value and suggestions for future issues (Dardig, 2008).

Daily/Weekly Note   The **daily/weekly note** is a brief note that alerts families to the accomplishments and improvements in their children and other issues of interest or concern (e.g., behavior, socialization, health, participation, work completion). The value of daily/weekly notes can be increased by providing a space for family members to write their messages to you. These notes can be made more effective by pairing them with praise from family members. Therefore, when family members receive these positive notes from you, they should be encouraged to read the notes promptly, praise their child in the presence of others, put the note in a prominent location (e.g., on the refrigerator door) where their child and others are likely to see it, and share their desire to receive additional notes of praise.

Two-Way Notebooks   You also can communicate with families by using **two-way notebooks** and assignment folders (Sebald & Luckner, 2007). Two-way notebooks, carried to and from school by students, allow you and family members to exchange comments and information, ask questions, and brainstorm solutions. The notebook can have the student's name on it, as well as a place for family members' signatures, the date, and the number of assignments included.

Daily/Weekly Progress Reports   A **daily/weekly progress report**, a written record of the student's performance in school, is effective in communicating with families. Its content and format will vary, and could include information on academic performance, preparedness for class, effort, behavior, peer relationships, and homework completion. The format should be easy for you to complete and easy for families to interpret. As students demonstrate success over a period of time, the progress report can be shared with families weekly, biweekly, and then monthly. A sample weekly progress report is presented in Figure 4.11.

FIGURE 4.11 Sample weekly progress report

Student:

Teachers:

Classes: **Rating**

    __English/Language Arts (ELA)   1 = Unsatisfactory
    __Mathematics (M)   2 = Needs Improvement
    __Social Studies (SS)   3 = Good
    __Science (S)   4 = Excellent
    __Other (please list)

	Monday	Tuesday	Wednesday	Thursday	Friday
Academic performance	1 2 3 4	1 2 3 4	1 2 3 4	1 2 3 4	1 2 3 4
Class work completion	1 2 3 4	1 2 3 4	1 2 3 4	1 2 3 4	1 2 3 4
Direction following	1 2 3 4	1 2 3 4	1 2 3 4	1 2 3 4	1 2 3 4
Class participation	1 2 3 4	1 2 3 4	1 2 3 4	1 2 3 4	1 2 3 4
Motivation and effort	1 2 3 4	1 2 3 4	1 2 3 4	1 2 3 4	1 2 3 4
Homework completion	1 2 3 4	1 2 3 4	1 2 3 4	1 2 3 4	1 2 3 4
Classroom behavior	1 2 3 4	1 2 3 4	1 2 3 4	1 2 3 4	1 2 3 4
Socialization with peers	1 2 3 4	1 2 3 4	1 2 3 4	1 2 3 4	1 2 3 4
Cooperation with adults	1 2 3 4	1 2 3 4	1 2 3 4	1 2 3 4	1 2 3 4

Teacher Comments:
                                             Signature: Date:

Family Comments:
                                             Signature: Date:

Student Comments:
                                             Signature: Date:

Sources: Battle, Dickens-Wright, & Murphy (1998); Dardig (2008).

Home–School Contracts The daily/weekly progress report system also has been used as part of a home–school contract. *Home–school contracts* allow families to learn about their children's progress in school and reinforce their children's improved academic performance or behavior in school. You observe students in school and report your observations to families, who then deliver reinforcers to their children. These reinforcers take many forms.

Before using a home–school contract, you can discuss the specifics of the program with the family. This discussion gives both parties an understanding of the behavior to be changed, details of the communication system between home and school, potential reinforcers, and when and how to deliver the reinforcers. Once the system is in place, follow-up communication is critical to talk about the implementation and impact of the system.

Encourage and Facilitate Family Observations

Communication between the home and the school and support for your inclusion program can be fostered by encouraging family members to observe in the classroom. This experience allows family members to see and understand different aspects of the school environment and student behavior. It gives families the background information needed to discuss school-related issues with you.

Family members can be prepared for the observation if you review ways to enter the room unobtrusively, locations in the room to sit, suitable times to observe, appropriate reactions to their child and other students, and the need to maintain confidentiality. Before the observation, you can discuss with family members the purpose of the observation and the unique aspects of the educational setting. After the observation, you can meet with family members again to discuss what they saw.

Using Technology to Promote Inclusion
FOSTERING COMMUNICATION AND COLLABORATION

Technological innovations are changing the ways in which teachers, schools, students, and families interact and communicate (Ramirez & Soto-Hinman, 2009; White Englund, 2009). Many schools and families use Web sites, e-mail, multilingual hotlines, Twitter, interactive videoconferencing, automated notification systems, and telephone answering machines to communicate (Meadan et al., 2009). For example, families can use these technologies to view their children's work and grades online, see what the school is serving for lunch, check on their child's attendance record, or find out what homework has been assigned. Like Ms. Carr and Ms. Stevens did in the chapter-opening vignette, you and your students can communicate with families by maintaining a **weblog**, a journal of the class's activities and related Web links that is posted on the Internet. You can also use technology to provide families with suggestions for teaching specific skills to their children, report on student performance in school, give families information on their rights and specific programs, offer information on educational opportunities and local events of interest to students and their families, and recommend resources and other learning materials to families. Online communication also can be used by families to support, communicate, and share information with you and each other (Margalit & Raskind, 2009; Meadan et al., 2009).

If family members cannot arrange to come to school, you can use video to introduce them to various aspects of your inclusive classroom, to provide them with another opportunity to view important school and classroom activities, and to increase their awareness of their children's progress. In using video observations, you need to determine what will be recorded, as well as when, how often, and by whom will it be recorded. You also must obtain permission from your students' families to record them and share the recordings with others. It is also helpful to provide families with a format to guide them in viewing the videos such as an introduction to the activities recorded, a summary of the video, and questions they can answer as they view the video.

You also can conduct meetings via telephones and interactive videoconferencing that allow families to participate without leaving work or their homes (Patterson, Petit, & Williams, 2007). When using these technologies, you should ensure that all participants have immediate access to all the information presented and can interact directly and actively throughout the meeting. Before the meeting, all participants should receive copies of the materials that will be discussed and referred to at the meeting. As with any meeting, you also need to be sensitive to cultural and linguistic factors, and protect the confidentiality of students and their families. A telephone relay service and a TeleTYpewriter/Telecommunications Device for the Deaf (TTY/TDD) can be employed to facilitate the involvement of deaf or hard-of-hearing family members.

In addition to communicating with families, technology can be used to help you obtain information and collaborate and communicate with others and to facilitate your professional development (Frey, 2009; Walker, 2009). E-mail, blogs, Twitter, podcasts, wikis, Really Simple Syndication (RSS) feed readers, discussion groups, streaming video, and listservs allow you to obtain information, and to "talk to" and distribute communications to others (Ferriter, 2009; Kingsley, 2007; Robinson & Kelley, 2007). They can be used to share ideas and concerns, learn about model strategies and programs, develop lessons, and brainstorm solutions to problems. Online services give professionals, families, and students access to a wide range of professional development activities, resources from around the world, and opportunities to receive and exchange information and ideas with colleagues. Most professional organizations and clearinghouses offer professional development and maintain a list of online networks and resources, including discussion and support groups.

When communicating with families and colleagues via technology, remember that many individuals may not feel comfortable interacting with you in that way or may not have access to technology. Therefore, rather than assuming access, it is best for you to ask families and colleagues to identify the best ways to contact and communicate with them at the beginning of the school year.

Offer Educational Programs to Families

Because family members may need education to understand model programs like inclusion and to perform various roles in the educational process, many schools and teachers like Ms. Carr and Ms. Stevens offer family education as part of their delivery of services to students and their families (Dettmer et al., 2009; Stivers et al., 2008; Van Haren & Fieldler, 2008). Some schools have family education committees that offer schoolwide programs and activities. Other schools collaborate with national and local family-based organizations such as the Parent Teacher Association (PTA) to conduct a range of family education sessions and programs. When setting up and evaluating family education programs, you, your colleagues, and your students' families can consider the following issues.

Offer Educational Programs to All Family Members   Although most programs educate mothers, education should be available to all family members, including fathers, grandparents, and siblings. For example, education and support can address the special issues of siblings and help them understand inclusion and the nature of their brother's or sister's disability and deal with the impact of having a brother or sister with special needs (Cook, 2006; Diament, 2009). Education for siblings can focus on helping them understand the causes of various disabilities, fostering the learning of their siblings, dispelling myths and misconceptions about disabilities, discussing ways of interacting with and assisting their sibling, dealing with unequal treatment and excessive demands, responding to the reactions and questions of their friends and other persons, and understanding human differences.

Focus the Content of the Educational Program on Families' Needs   Generally, education should give family members the skills to understand and support your inclusion program, the skills to teach their child at home, the ability to communicate and collaborate with professionals, the ability to serve as advocates for their child, the information they need to obtain services for their child and their family, and ways to plan for their child's future (Checkley, 2008). Family members who speak languages other than English may benefit from family-based ESL and literacy programs.

Conduct the Educational Program in a Range of Settings   Education can occur in the home or in the school at times that are most convenient for families. In some cases, it may be important to conduct the educational programs in nonintimidating, community-based locations (Matuszny et al., 2007).

Use a Variety of Strategies to Educate Families   As Ms. Carr and Ms. Stevens did in the chapter-opening vignette, you can use a variety of strategies to educate families, including multimedia, the Internet, group discussion, role playing, simulations, presentations by professionals and other family members, and demonstrations. Print materials and education programs for families are also available from state education departments, as well as from local groups serving families and professional organizations. Experienced, skilled, and highly respected family members can be a valuable resource for educating other families (Stivers et al., 2008).

REFLECTIVE

What have been your experiences using technology to communicate with others and to engage in professional learning? What were the advantages and disadvantages? How do these systems affect the communications and the information shared? What skills do teachers, students, and family members need to use these systems effectively and efficiently?

REFLECTIVE

Do you have a family member with a disability? How has this individual affected other family members? What types of educational programs would benefit your family?

myeducationlab

To reflect on and enhance your understanding of families of children with disabilities and ways to build positive relationships with them, go to the IRIS Center Resources section under the Topic: *Parents and Families* in the MyEducationLab for your course, and complete the module entitled *Collaborating with Families*.

What Would You Do in Today's Diverse Classroom?

★ When you volunteered to work in a co-teaching team, you and your partner were excited about the possibility of using a variety of teaching arrangements. However, you find that your team continually has the same teacher taking the lead while the other teacher monitors individual students.

★ One of your students has been acting as the class clown and fails to complete his schoolwork. His family is concerned and believes that he should receive special education services. Although you are also concerned about the student, you do not believe he needs special education services.

★ You work with a paraeducator who has developed a close and positive working relationship with Josh, one of your students. You notice that that her presence and assistance sometimes interferes with Josh's interactions with you and other classmates.

1. What challenges(s) might you encounter in each situation?
2. What factors do you need to consider in addressing them?
3. How would you address these situations?
4. What knowledge, skills, dispositions, resources, and support do you need to address these situations?

Watch Josh work with his paraeducator in his inclusive classroom by visiting the MyEducationLab for this course. Go to the *Assignments and Activities* section under the Topic *Autism Spectrum Disorders* and complete the activity entitled *Classroom Aides* to answer questions about their relationship in an inclusive classroom.

SUMMARY

This chapter provided guidelines for establishing an inclusive environment that supports the learning of *all students* by creating collaborative relationships and fostering communication among students, professionals, families, and community members. As you review the questions posed in this chapter, remember the following points:

Who Are the Members of the Comprehensive Planning Team?
CEC 1, 7, 9, 10; PRAXIS 2, 3; INTASC 10

The comprehensive planning team may consist of students, general and special educators, administrators, support personnel such as speech/language therapists, bilingual educators, paraeducators, family members, peers, local community resources, and professional and family-based organizations. The members of the team vary, depending on the strengths and challenges of students, families, and educators.

How Can Members of the Comprehensive Planning Team Work Collaboratively?
CEC 1, 7, 9, 10; PRAXIS 2, 3; INTASC 1, 3, 9, 10

Members of the comprehensive planning team can work collaboratively by using collaborative teaming, person-/student-centered planning, co-teaching, and collaborative consultation, as well as by promoting congruence and engaging in professional development.

How Can I Foster Communication and Collaboration with Families?

CEC 1, 2, 3, 7, 9, 10; PRAXIS 2, 3; INTASC 3, 10

You can foster communication and collaboration with families by gaining their trust, advocating for them and their children, ensuring confidentiality, meeting regularly with families, resolving conflicts constructively, using written and technology-based communication, encouraging and facilitating observations at the school or via technology, and offering educational programs to families. Families, like students, have diverse strengths, challenges, backgrounds, belief systems, resources, and experiences, and they are structured in different ways. In communicating and collaborating with families, be aware of these factors, adjusting your style and services accordingly to promote family involvement.

MR. MONROIG

One of Mr. Monroig's goals is to teach his students how to interact with, understand, and accept others. Mr. Monroig asks students to identify aloud two things they think are easy and two things that are hard to do. He notes the similarities and differences between the students' responses and records them on a "same/different" chart. He then discusses with the class some of the factors that affect the ease with which one can perform a task. He asks them to identify things that would be easy or hard to do if they

> had difficulty reading,
>
> used a wheelchair,
>
> didn't understand English,
>
> couldn't hold a pencil,
>
> had difficulty seeing, or
>
> had difficulty hearing.

Mr. Monroig then has the students perform various tasks with and without a simulated difficulty. He has students watch a television show in Spanish, attempt to go to the bathroom using a wheelchair, and walk around the classroom blindfolded. He videos them performing these activities, and as students view the video, he asks, "What was easy or hard for you?" and "How did it feel?" As a follow-up activity, he has students complete an online learning experience that allowed students to use a virtual wheelchair to maneuver to several locations in a virtual school, and he gives students opportunities to simulate reaching for out-of-reach objects, and hearing and responding to inappropriate comments from others.

He asks the students to think about something they would like to improve that is hard for them. He also asks his students to respond to the question "If you knew someone who found something hard to do in our class, what could

5

Creating an Environment That Fosters Acceptance and Friendship

you do to show that person that you understand that some things are hard?" After presenting classroom scenarios related to some of the difficulties that the students have mentioned, he leads the students in brainstorming the ways students can help each other. He guides the class in examining each suggestion by asking students to evaluate it in terms of its impact on the student and the class.

Mr. Monroig concludes the activity by having students complete a contract that lists their goals for improving their area of difficulty, the ways that they will work to improve it, and the things that their classmates could do to assist them. He then asks each student to share their contract with the class and to maintain a reflective journal of their experiences. At the end of each week, he selects different students to discuss their journal, their progress, and what others have done to assist them.

What other strategies can Mr. Monroig use to help his students understand and accept individual differences and develop friendships? After reading this chapter, you will have the knowledge, skills, and dispositions to answer these as well as the following questions:

- How can I assess attitudes toward individual differences?

- How can I teach acceptance of individual differences related to disability?

- How can I teach acceptance of individual differences related to culture, language, gender, religion, and socioeconomic status?

- How can I facilitate friendships among my students?

REFLECTIVE
REFLECTIVE

How are persons with disabilities
and those from various cultural
and linguistic backgrounds
presented in books, television
shows, movies, cartoons and
online? How do these portrayals
affect you and your students'
understanding and acceptance of
individual differences?

Like Mr. Monroig's classroom, today's classrooms include students with a variety of individual differences. Unfortunately, due to societal influences, many students enter school holding misconceptions and stereotypical views about persons they perceive as different, which can affect students' self-identities and friendships (Siperstein et al., 2007; Zambo, 2009). Societal factors also may limit interactions between students based on disability, race, gender, sexual orientation, socioeconomic status, and language abilities.

Attitudes toward persons who have disabilities, speak different languages, and have different cultural backgrounds are shaped by the media, literature, and visual images and representations in society, which unfortunately tend to portray these groups negatively and in stereotypical ways (Black & Pretes, 2007; Zambo, 2009). For example, fairy tales, comic books, cartoons, and children's books, which are used to introduce children to the culture, often inaccurately present persons with individual differences as bumbling (e.g., Mr. Magoo), evil (e.g., Captain Hook), deformed (e.g., Rumpelstiltskin), and comical (e.g., Porky Pig and Elmer Fudd) (Dyches, Prater, & Jenson, 2006). As a result, many students learn that individual differences have low-status and negative connotations, and they often react to these individuals with disabilities with fear, pity, fascination, and ridicule.

Individual differences can be a rich source of learning for *all students*, but they also can create divisions and conflicts among students that you will need to address. Therefore, rather than assuming that your students respect and accept one another, an important goal of your inclusive classroom is to teach *all students* to appreciate diversity and to value and learn from each other's similarities and differences. Teaching students to accept and appreciate the value of individual differences can be integrated into your curriculum and reinforced by making your classroom reflect *all students*. This approach will facilitate the acceptance of *all students*, establish a sense of community in the classroom, and prepare students to be citizens in a diverse world (Meadan & Monda-Amaya, 2008; Price & Nelson, 2007). It can also help your students understand that they are more similar to each other than different and can identify their unique strengths and challenges, likes, and dislikes. Finally, it can help reduce name-calling, staring, and the formation of exclusive cliques and make it easier for students to develop friendships.

ASSESSING ATTITUDES TOWARD INDIVIDUAL DIFFERENCES

REFLECTIVE
REFLECTIVE

When you were growing up, did
you have opportunities to interact
with children and adults with
disabilities? How did these
experiences help you understand
and accept individual differences?

HOW CAN I ASSESS ATTITUDES TOWARD INDIVIDUAL DIFFERENCES? It is important to understand your students' attitudes toward and knowledge of individual differences as well as their social interactions and friendships as a starting point to help you plan appropriate activities. You can use the techniques described here to do this.

Attitude Assessment Instruments

Several instruments have been developed to assess attitudes toward individuals with disabilities (Campbell, 2007; Siperstein et al., 2007). Many of these instruments ask students to indicate their agreement with ("Yes, I agree"), disagreement with ("No, I disagree"), or uncertainty about ("Maybe; I'm not sure") items that are phrased either positively ("I could become close friends with a student with a disability") or negatively ("I wouldn't spend my recess with a kid with a disability").

These instruments can be adapted to assess attitudes toward persons with other types of individual differences by modifying the directions and items. For example, they can be adapted by asking students to complete each item with respect to individuals who speak a language other than English. You also can adapt these instruments by simplifying the language, phrasing items in a true/false format, and using pictorials.

Knowledge of Individual Differences Probes

You can use individual differences probes to assess your students' feelings about differences and factual knowledge about various groups ("What does it mean to have a learning disability?"); stereotypical views of others ("True or false: 'Homeless people are adults who don't work and choose to be homeless'"); challenges of other individuals ("What are three things that you would have difficulty doing in this classroom if you were learning to speak English?"); ways to interact with others ("If you were deaf, how would you want others to interact with you?"); and devices and aids designed to help individuals ("What is a device that a student with one arm could use?").

You also can assess your students' knowledge of and feelings about individual differences by using sentence completion items (Shapiro, 1999). For example, you can ask your students to respond to the following:

If I used a wheelchair, I would want others to _____.

When I hear someone speak another language, I feel _____.

Student Drawings

Having students draw a picture of a scene depicting other individuals can be a valuable way of assessing their attitudes. To assess students' feelings accurately, you can also ask them to tell or write a story explaining their picture. For example, examine the picture in Figure 5.1. How would you rate the attitude toward individuals with disabilities of the student who drew this picture? At first, the drawing may suggest that the student has a negative attitude. However, the accompanying story shows the student's attitude much more clearly. The student explained the picture by stating, "People with disabilities are almost always made fun of. This picture shows a person with a disability crying because of the way other people laugh at him. Put yourself in his position."

Observational Techniques

Through direct observations of interactions between students, you can gain insights into their attitudes toward others and their interaction patterns, as well as the factors that can foster their friendships (Peterson Nelson, Caldarella, Young, & Webb, 2008;

FIGURE 5.1 **Student drawing depicting an individual with a disability**

Swedeen, 2009). You can examine the interactions of your students by observing them during various learning and social activities. This information can then be analyzed by considering the following questions:

- How often and for how long are students with and without disabilities interacting with each other?
- What are the nature of these interactions (e.g., spontaneous, assistive, reciprocal, instructional, disciplinary, attention seeking, playful) and the outcomes of these interactions?
- Who is beginning and ending the interactions?
- What events, activities, individuals, objects, and other stimuli seem to promote interactions? Limit interactions?
- What roles, if any, do race, gender, language, religion, sexual orientation, and socioeconomic factors play in the interactions among students?
- Do the students with and without disabilities have the skills needed to interact with their peers?

These observations can be supplemented by interviews with students, peers, family members, and other professionals to learn about student interactions and the social skills they use effectively.

Sociometric Techniques

Data on the social relationships students prefer and their friendships can be collected using **sociometric techniques** (Estell et al., 2009). *A peer nomination sociogram* involves asking students to respond confidentially to a series of questions that reveal classmates with whom they would like to perform a social or classroom activity. Because it is important to obtain information on both popular and unpopular students in the class, sociograms should include both acceptance (i.e., "Which five students from this class would you most like to invite to your birthday party?") and rejection ("Which five students from this class would you least like to sit next to during lunch?") questions. In addition to providing data on the acceptance or rejection of students, sociograms can help you identify students who need to improve their socialization skills.

Several structured sociometric rating procedures have been developed for teachers (Meadan & Halle, 2004). They provide specific questions to ask students and standardized procedures to follow when administering the rating scale.

TEACHING ABOUT INDIVIDUAL DIFFERENCES RELATED TO DISABILITY

HOW CAN I TEACH ACCEPTANCE OF INDIVIDUAL DIFFERENCES RELATED TO DISABILITY? When students have negative attitudes toward individuals they view as different, you can foster positive attitudes by using a variety of *attitude change* and *information-sharing strategies*. These strategies also can help you confront **ableism**, the belief that individuals with disabilities are in need of assistance, fixing, and pity (Hehir, 2007; Smith et al., 2009) and replace negative labels and stereotypes with meaningful information related to individuals and the supports that enhance their learning and inclusion (Smith, 2009). Key factors in the success of these strategies are as follows:

- Viewing *all* persons as capable individuals with unique personalities, qualities, likes, dislikes, strengths, and challenges
- Promoting the view that similarities and differences are natural and positive and that we *all* benefit from diversity and appreciating individual differences
- Fostering sensitivity rather than sympathy

- Emphasizing that we *all* have more similarities than differences and that our differences make us unique and our similarities unite us
- Understanding that we *all* need some types of supports and that supports for individuals with specialized challenges are useful and appropriate for *all*
- Establishing frequent collaborative interactions and ongoing *equal-status relationships*, in which both parties view each other as equal in social, educational, or vocational status
- Sharing meaningful and credible information and addressing issues and questions openly, honestly, accurately, and objectively
- Fostering an understanding of the importance of one's individuality, independence, dignity, and self-determination, and avoiding pitying and protective responses
- Providing information, direct contact, and experiences that share important information about and counter stereotyped views of others perceived as different
- Engaging in actions that support others (Flower, Burns, & Bottsford-Miller, 2007; Hehir, 2007; Meadan & Monda-Amaya, 2008; Smith, 2009; Smith et al., 2009)

Many different strategies to change attitudes, share information, and teach students about individual differences are described in this chapter. Figure 5.2 is a checklist for selecting a strategy that works in your own classroom situation. In using these strategies to teach about invisible disabilities, those conditions that are not obvious and apparent to others, you need to be careful that you teach about them in ways that your students can understand and that you do not highlight behaviors and individual differences that your students are not experiencing. The guidelines and strategies used to teach acceptance of individual differences related to disability also can be adapted to teach students about individual differences related to culture, language, gender, religion, family structure, socioeconomic status, and sexual orientation as well.

You also can get help from students, their families, and other educators in planning and implementing these strategies. For example, your school's nurse and occupational and physical therapists can collaborate with you to teach your students about physical disabilities and the assistive devices these individuals use. You also can collaborate with school counselors, who can use their training to lead role plays and group discussions. Other professionals also can help you identify resources such as curriculum materials, guest speakers, and community organizations that can be used to educate your students about individual differences. In collaborating with

REFLECTIVE

What are your attitudes and behaviors in regard to individual differences? Are there individual differences with which you feel comfortable? Uncomfortable? How do you reveal these attitudes to others? How did you develop these attitudes and behaviors?

FIGURE 5.2 **Attitude change strategy checklist**

Several attitude change strategies exist. You can determine which strategy to use in your classroom by answering the following questions:

- Is the strategy appropriate for my students?
- What skills do I need to implement the strategy? Do I have these skills?
- What resources do I need to implement the strategy? Do I have these resources?
- Does the strategy teach critical information about the group and the acceptance of individual differences?
- Does the strategy present positive, nonstereotypical examples of the group?
- Does the strategy establish an equal-status relationship?
- Does the strategy offer students activities in which to learn about the group and individual similarities and differences?
- Does the strategy promote follow-up activities?

PEARSON
myeducationlab

Go to the Assignments and Activities section of the Topic *Cultural and Linguistic Diversity* in the MyEducationLab for your course and complete the activity entitled *Impact of Teachers' Attitudes on Students in the Inclusive Classroom.*

Making Connections
Find out more about ways to establish caring and respectful relationships with your students in Chapter 7.

REFLECTIVE

What individual differences do you have? How do they define you, your experiences, and how others view and describe you?

REFLECTIVE

Snow (2009) notes that the word *handicapped* evokes negative and stereotypical images and derives from an Old English term that refers to the loser of a bartering game as being left with "hand in his cap." Which term do you prefer to use? Why?

Making Connections
This discussion of individuals-first language builds on what we discussed earlier in Chapter 1.

families and other professionals, you may need to discuss and resolve different perspectives toward individual differences and attitude-change strategies.

Reflect on Your Attitudes, Behaviors, and Language.   Because students look up to and are influenced by their teachers, you can serve as a role model by reflecting on your attitudes, behaviors, and language (Russell, 2008). You also can interact with your students in ways that show you are comfortable with individual differences and respect and care about *all of them*, which affects their identities and your relationships with them (Fink Chorzempa & Lapidus, 2009; Mihalis et al., 2009; Sapon-Shevin, 2008). It is especially important for you to watch your language because it communicates how you think, feel, and act regarding individual differences and the inclusion of various types of learners (Russell, 2008; Snow, 2009). Here are some ways your behaviors, language, and interactions can focus on students' competence, strengths, and similarities rather than their deficits and differences, and how you can create a classroom environment that models acceptance of diversity and *all your students*, fostering friendships and motivation among your students (Learned, Dowd, & Jenkins, 2009; Meadan & Monda-Amaya, 2008; Smith et al., 2009; Swedeen, 2009; Tomlinson, 2008a).

Learn about all of your students, and view all of them as competent and multidimensional.   Learn about *all your students'* backgrounds, strengths, interests, hobbies, and talents so that you and others can view them as competent and capable, and understand their multiple dimensions. Share this information with others, and incorporate it into your classroom in varied ways.

Highlight students' abilities rather than their challenges, and describe them in positive and meaningful ways.   Focus on and emphasize *all students'* strengths and positive attributes rather than their limitations, and offer positive descriptions related to their abilities and progress. For example, describe students in terms of what they can do or who they are (e.g., an excellent speaker of Spanish who is also learning English), rather than what they cannot do (e.g., limited English proficient) or who they are not (e.g., non–English speaking). Avoid referring to students using terms such as *dropouts* or *disadvantaged*, which focus on their difficulties.

Use individuals-first language, and refer to students by their names.   Show respect for your students by calling them by their names and using individuals-first language that focuses on the person rather than the individual differences. For example, saying, "The inclusion kids will work with Mr. Josephs, and everyone else will work with me" sets students apart and objectifies them. When you must refer to students in reference to their disabilities, rather than calling them disabled, refer to the person first and then the disability (e.g., "students with learning disabilities" rather than "learning disabled students"). Remember that organizations for the deaf note that deaf people prefer to be called deaf. Similarly, using nicknames for students with unusual names also can make students feel different.

You also should avoid using such terms as *handicapped, cripple, invalid, victim of, birth defect, midget, normal,* or *able-bodied,* as these terms are associated with sympathy and suffering or being different or having bodies that are abnormal (Russell, 2008; Snow, 2009). For example, rather than saying that John is confined to a wheelchair, you can say that John uses a wheelchair. Russell (2008) offers a self-assessment to evaluate your use of individuals-first language. Guidelines for communicating with individuals with disabilities that you can use and teach to your students are presented in Figure 5.3.

Acknowledge individual differences when they are relevant to the situation.   It is important to acknowledge the individual differences of your students when these differences are relevant to the situation. Ignoring individual differences may mean not acknowledging important aspects of who students are, how they define themselves, and how they experience the world. For example, rather than ignoring students' use of

Communicating with Individuals with Disabilities

- View the individual as a person, not as a disability.
- Direct comments and questions to the individual.
- Refrain from "talking down" or speaking in a condescending way.
- Be yourself, relax, be considerate, and treat the individual with respect.
- Talk using language and about topics that are age appropriate.
- Don't apologize for using common expressions that may relate to the individual's disability such as "I've got to run" or "Have you seen Mary?"
- Greet the individual as you would others. If the individual cannot shake your hand, he or she will make you aware of that.
- Understand that the environment can affect communication. An overly noisy or dark room can make communication difficult for individuals with speech and sensory disabilities.
- Don't assume that the individual needs your assistance.
- Ask for permission prior to touching the individual's possessions, equipment, and assistive devices.

Communicating with Individuals Who Use Wheelchairs

- Respect the individual's space by refraining from hanging on the wheelchair.
- Sit or kneel at the individual's eye level when the conversation is going to continue for a long period of time.
- Don't assume that the individual wants you to push the wheelchair.
- Allow the individual to guide you in providing assistance if nonaccessible areas are encountered.

Communicating with Individuals with Speech/Language Difficulties

- Focus your attention on the individual.
- Avoid correcting or speaking for the individual.
- Be encouraging and patient.
- Seek clarification when you don't understand by repeating what you did understand or asking the individual to write it down.

Communicating with Individuals with Visual Disabilities

- Introduce and identify yourself and any companions when encountering the individual.
- Speak directly to the individual in a normal voice.
- Direct communications to the individual by using the individual's name.
- Provide an explanation of visual events, cues, or body language, when they are important aspects of the conversation or interaction.
- Remember that a guide dog is responsible for the individual's safety and should not be distracted. Therefore, walk on the opposite side of the dog, and ask for permission before interacting with the dog.
- Tell the individual when you are leaving or ending the conversation.

Communicating with Deaf and Hard of Hearing Individuals

- Make sure that you have the individual's attention before speaking.
- Speak clearly and in short sentences.
- Avoid raising your voice or exaggerating your mouth movements.
- Use appropriate facial expressions, physical gestures, and body movements.
- Refrain from repeating yourself. If the individual doesn't understand, rephrase your message, use synonyms to convey it, or write it out.
- Talk directly to the individual even if the individual uses an interpreter.
- Remember that it is harder to understand when walking and talking at the same time.

Sources: Russell (2008); Shapiro (1999); Snow (2009).

a wheelchair or cultural or racial identity, it is important to acknowledge them as an aspect of how they experience the world.

Note the similarities among students.   Take opportunities to acknowledge the ways in which *all your students* are similar. For example when students are interacting academically or socially, you can make their similarities explicit by commenting on them (e.g., "You both like using computers to complete your work").

Establish high and appropriate expectations for students.   Articulate challenging and reasonable expectations for *all your students*, and expect all of them to participate academically and socially and to complete their work.

Affirm students and their achievements.   Use verbal and nonverbal communication to acknowledge *all your students* and their contributions, and note how the presence of *all your students* benefits the class. However, be careful not to patronize your students with individual differences by praising them excessively or for behaviors that are not necessarily praiseworthy.

Use humor carefully and strategically.   Your use of humor can be a double-edged sword as it can create bonds between students or foster stereotypes and conflicts. Therefore, you need to use it strategically and carefully; make sure that it is respectful and warranted and that it fosters empathy, understanding, and relationships (Smith & Sapon-Shevin, 2009). Also make sure that it is not misinterpreted and viewed as ridicule or sarcasm and is free of disability, racial, ethnic, religious, sexual, and gender bias stereotypes and connotations. Smith and Sapon-Shevin (2009) offer guidelines and resources for using humor and cartoons to teach about disabilities.

Listen to students, give them choices, and solicit their preferences.   Show *all your students* that you view them as independent, active, and competent learners by listening to them to learn about their perspectives, offering them choices, and asking them about their preferences.

Provide opportunities for students to assume leadership positions.   Allow *all your students* to perform important classroom positions and jobs and to assume roles that offer them opportunities to show their strengths and assist others. For example, develop a chart of classroom jobs and a system for rotating them among all students, and introduce it by telling the class, "These are important jobs, and everyone can do them and will have a chance to do them." It also is important to give students classroom jobs that foster interactions with their peers. Smith (2009) provides a listing of classroom leadership roles that students can perform.

Use language and talk about topics that are age-appropriate.   Speak to *all your students* in age-appropriate language and about age-appropriate topics.

Speak directly to students.   Discourage talking about students as if they were not there, and talk to *all your students*, even those who benefit from the services of interpreters and paraeducators. If others speak to students through you or other professionals, redirect them to speak directly to the students.

Respect your students and their independence.   Demonstrate respect for *all your students*, offer them assistance only when necessary, and refrain from placing them in embarrassing situations. It is important that other professionals, including paraeducators, do not engage in "caregiving/parenting behaviors" such as hovering around them; doing so can prevent students from interacting with classmates and developing a positive and independent self-identity (Causton-Theoharis, 2009; Giangreco & Broer, 2007).

Teach your students to show mutual respect for each other.   Teach your students to show respect for their classmates and to appreciate the varying viewpoints, strengths, and challenges they have. Also, help your students learn to share their

UDL and YOU

Addressing Issues of Fairness Without Sameness

As you use UDL in your classroom, your students may initially fail to understand the difference between fairness and sameness. Thus, as you implement UDL, your students may ask, "Why does Johnny get to do it that way, and I don't?" Through your language and actions, you can help your students understand that it is not necessarily fair to treat everyone in the same way, as it does not acknowledge and respect individual differences (Murawski & Dieker, 2008). You can address fairness issues in your classroom by doing the following:

- Help *all students* understand the complexities associated with fairness and sameness (i.e., fairness does not mean that everyone receives the same things), the differences between equality and equity, and that treating everyone in the same way is not always fair. For example, you can ask students to role-play and discuss various scenarios that depict situations when it is fair and appropriate to treat everyone in similar ways and situations when it is fair and appropriate to treat individuals differently.

- Explain the principles of UDL to your students. Many teachers do this by describing the various people who use the ramp to get into their schools—not only people who use wheelchairs but parents pushing strollers or delivery people, too.

- Establish an equity threshold with your students that includes classroom expectations and rules and guidelines for making exceptions and accommodations for *all students*.

- Create a system such as an exceptions/accommodations/supports box that allows *all students* to request the exceptions and accommodations they need and why they need them.

- Make your use of UDL and differentiated instruction to provide *all students* with varied learning activities and multiple ways of demonstrating their understanding

and mastery of learning standards explicit to *all students and their families*.

- Teach *all students* to understand how they are unique and to view themselves in terms of their own strengths, challenges, performance, and progress and the supports they need to succeed rather than defining themselves in relation to others.

- Use classroom meetings to explain and discuss issues of fairness. As Mr. Monroig did in the chapter-opening vignette, you can use collaborative problem solving to present scenarios related to some of the classroom difficulties that students are experiencing. Students can then discuss them collaboratively and brainstorm possible solutions. You can promote the discussion by helping students identify the issues, providing additional information when necessary, and sharing your own beliefs about fairness. Once potential solutions are generated, the class can evaluate their completeness; fairness; feasibility; ability to solve the problem; and impact on peers, teachers, and the targeted student(s). Pavri and Monda-Amaya (2001) have developed vignettes that address classroom-based social situations that involve peer support, including dealing with rejection, jealousy, peer conflicts, different personality traits, and different physical appearances that you can use or adapt to your classroom.

- Ask *all students* to identify the things that are difficult for them and the special things that they need to help them succeed (as Mr. Monroig did in the chapter-opening vignette).

- Explain that *all students* in your classroom get what they need to succeed and the reasons for treating students in different ways (without violating confidentiality or placing students in awkward situations)

Sources: Bartholomew, 2008; Bucalos & Lingo, 2005; Smith, 2009; Tomlinson, 2008a; Welch, 2000.

perspectives, disagree respectfully, and provide their peers with feedback and praise (Fink Chorzempa & Lapidus, 2009).

Use Disability Simulations

A method that Mr. Monroig and many other teachers employ to teach their students about individuals with disabilities is the use of **disability simulations**, in which students experience how it feels to have a disability (Cerve, 2008; Jordan, 2008; Killeen, 2009). In addition to demonstrating the challenges encountered by individuals with

REFLECTIVE

Think about how you would address issues of fairness and sameness in the following situation: In class, your students are required to take notes, and some of the students have trouble doing this.

Empowering Language

As part of her teacher education program, Ms. Ryan performed fieldwork in Mr. Monroig's class. By observing Mr. Monroig and other professionals, she was learning about assessment, curriculum, teaching, and working with students and their families. Several incidents forced her to reflect on the issues of teacher behavior as well as the language used in special education and its effects on students, families, and professionals.

The first incident occurred during an observation in another teacher's class. While the students were working nearby, the teacher nodded toward a student who was struggling with his work and said, "Can you believe he was supposed to be mainstreamed?" The second incident occurred later that same day in another class. As a teacher prepared materials for a math assessment, the paraeducator approached her and asked, "They get to use calculators?" In front of the whole class, the teacher responded, "Well, they are special education students."

During the third incident, Ms. Ryan observed Mr. Monroig who approached his students' differences in a very different way. One student asked Mr. Monroig why another student received extra time to complete an assignment, saying, "That's not fair." Mr. Monroig responded, "Just like you, all the students in the class are learning new things in their own ways. In this class, we do not expect everyone to learn, look, sound, and act the same." Later, Mr. Monroig told the students, "In your lives, you are going to meet a lot of people who are different from you,

and it is these differences that make life special. Think about how boring it would be if we were all the same."

The final incident occurred when Ms. Ryan attended a planning team meeting that included a student and the student's family. The team discussed the student's strengths and challenges and strategies to enhance learning, rather than the student's disability category. Team members and the student noted that "he was good at some things and had difficulty with other things." The educators listened carefully to the comments made by the student and the family and said that they believed that the student could succeed in their classroom. They told the student that "trying is one of the stepping stones to learning."

- How did the behaviors and language of the educators in the first two incidents differ from the behaviors and language of the educators in the second two incidents?
- How were the students, educators, and family members affected by the language associated with special education and individual differences?
- How would you categorize your language, behaviors, and interactions with students, family members, and other professionals?
- How can you use language and behaviors that show your acceptance of individual differences?
- How can you help students discuss their individual differences in empowering ways?

disabilities, simulations expose students to the accommodations that individuals with disabilities find helpful. Simulations of varying disabilities and sample follow-up questions are presented in Figure 5.4.

When using simulations, you need to be aware of some limitations (Flower et al., 2007). Attitude changes related to simulations tend to be brief and may result in a feeling of sympathy. You also need to make sure that students don't trivialize the experience and think that having a disability is fun and games (e.g., wheeling around in a wheelchair). You can counter these limited reactions and make the simulations more effective by using several guidelines. For example, select simulations that are as realistic as possible, and tell the students that they must take the activities seriously and not quit until they are complete. During the simulations, assign an observer to watch and, if necessary, help students who are participating in the activities.

As Mr. Monroig did in his class, it is important that you follow up simulations by having students reflect on the experience (Flower et al., 2007). For instance, they can maintain a journal of how they felt, the barriers they encountered, and their reflections on what they have learned about individual differences, themselves, and others. They also can use the experience as a springboard to identify and work on something that is difficult for them. You also may want to make video recordings of them, which can be used to have students reflect on the simulations by conducting group discussions and by asking students to write about their experiences.

REFLECTIVE

Simulate several disabilities for part or all of a day. How did the simulations make you feel? How did others treat you? What problems did you experience? What did you learn? How did you adapt to the various disabilities?

FIGURE 5.4 Sample disability simulations and follow-up questions

VISUAL IMPAIRMENT SIMULATIONS

Activity

Have students wear blindfolds during part of the school day. Blindfold one student and assign another student as a helper to follow the blindfolded student around the room and building. Periodically, have the helper and the blindfolded student change roles. Structure the activity so that students must move around in the classroom, eat a meal, go to the bathroom, and move to other classes. Have the blindfolded student complete a form, with the helper providing verbal assistance only.

Follow-up Questions

1. What difficulties did you have during the activity? What difficulties did you observe as a helper?
2. What did you do that helped you perform the activities without seeing?
3. What did the helper do to help you perform the activities?
4. What changes could be made in school to assist students who can't see? At home?

DEAF AND HARD OF HEARING SIMULATIONS

Activity

Show a movie or video without the sound. Ask students questions that can be answered only after having heard the sound. Show the same film or video again with the sound and have students respond to the same questions.

Follow-up Questions

1. How did your answers differ?
2. What information did you use to answer the questions after the first viewing?

PHYSICAL DISABILITIES SIMULATIONS

Activity

Put a dowel rod in the joints of the students' elbows while their arms are positioned behind their backs. Ask students to try to comb their hair, tie their shoes, write a story, draw, and eat.

Follow-up Questions

1. Were you successful at combing your hair? Tying your shoes? Writing the story? Drawing? Eating?
2. What other activities would you have difficulty doing if you had limited use of your hands?
3. Are there any strategies or devices that you could use to perform the tasks?

Activity

Have students use wheelchairs to maneuver around the classroom and the school. Structure the activity so that students attempt to drink from a water fountain, write on the blackboard, make a phone call, go to the bathroom, and transfer themselves onto a toilet. Because of the potential architectural barriers in the school, have a same-sex peer assist and observe the student in the wheelchair.

Follow-up Questions

1. What difficulties did you encounter in maneuvering around the school?
2. What were the reactions of other students who saw you in the wheelchair? How did their reactions make you feel?
3. What are some barriers that would make it hard for a person who uses a wheelchair to move around on a street? In a store?
4. What modifications can make it easier for individuals who use wheelchairs to maneuver in schools? In streets, stores, or homes?

SPEECH IMPAIRMENT SIMULATIONS

Activity

Assign students in pairs. Have one student try to communicate messages to the other by using physical gestures only, by talking without moving the tongue, and by using a communication board.

Follow-up Questions

1. What strategies did you use to communicate the message?
2. How did you understand your partner's message?
3. If you had difficulty talking, how would you want others to talk to you?

LEARNING DISABILITIES SIMULATIONS

Activity

Place a mirror and a sheet of paper on the students' desks so that students can see the reflection of the paper in the mirror. Have the students write a sentence and read a paragraph while looking in the mirror. Then have the students do the same tasks without looking in the mirror. Compare their ability to do the tasks under the two different conditions.

Follow-up Questions

1. What difficulties did you experience in writing and reading while looking in the mirror?
2. How did it feel to have difficulty writing and reading?
3. What other tasks would be hard if you saw this way all the time?

Sources: Cerve (2008); Horne (1998); Jordan (2008); Killeen (2009); Shapiro (1999).

Study About Disabilities and Individuals with Disabilities

Many individuals have some type of disability. Lessons, games, and assignments on the experiences and achievements of individuals with disabilities can help present disabilities in a positive light and foster the self-awareness of your students with disabilities (Lindstrom et al., 2008; Merlone & Moran, 2008). You can have students write about a friend or relative who has a disability, read an autobiography of an individual with disabilities, complete a research report on the topics related to disability, or search Internet sites addressing disability (Eisenman & Tascione, 2002; Lava & Lehman, 2007). In doing these assignments, remind your students to focus on the person first and to use individuals-first language when writing about people with disabilities (Russell, 2008; Snow, 2009).

Invite Guest Speakers

One of the most effective attitude change strategies is to provide your students with opportunities to interact with individuals with disabilities (Flower et al., 2007). You can expose students directly to individuals with disabilities by inviting guest speakers who have disabilities (Chadsey & Gun Han, 2005). When using guest speakers, it is important that you carefully identify, select, and prepare them, and determine whether you want to have several speakers at the same time (Shapiro, 1999). You can find potential guest speakers by contacting local community agencies, professional and advocacy organizations, and special education teachers. Meet with any potential speakers to determine how relevant and appropriate it would be to invite them. Determine whether speakers can speak in an open, honest way and in language that your students can understand. It is also important to consider whether they can use short anecdotes and humorous and meaningful examples that present their independent lives in a positive light and foster positive attitudes.

Once you have selected a speaker, meet with this individual to discuss the goals of the presentation and possible topics to be covered. Speakers may want

An effective way to teach about disability is to provide your students with opportunities to interact with individuals with disabilities. What challenges would you encounter having individuals with disabilities speak to your class?

to address such topics as the difficulties they encounter now, as well as those they experienced when they were the students' age; school and childhood experiences; hobbies and interests; family; jobs; a typical day; future plans; causes of their disability; ways to prevent their disability, if possible (e.g., wearing a bicycle helmet can help prevent traumatic brain injury if you fall off your bike); accommodations they need; ways of interacting with others; and assistive devices they use. Remember also to ask speakers about what materials, accommodations, and assistive devices they require, so that your school and classroom are accessible and set up appropriately. It is also important for you to confirm dates and times and to ensure that speakers have appropriate parking and transportation to and from your school.

To help speakers tailor their remarks to students, provide background information about the class (age level, grade level, exposure to and understanding of disabilities) and possible questions students may ask. Before the speaker comes to class, you can have students identify the questions they have about the disability to be discussed. You also can prepare students by providing them with information about disabilities and the speaker beforehand. Schedule time during the presentation to welcome and introduce speakers and to allow students to ask questions and share their feelings and experiences. Because some students may hesitate to ask questions, you can help overcome their reluctance by initially asking the speaker some of the questions the students previously identified. As a follow-up activity, have students write thank-you notes or create projects that express their appreciation.

Students with disabilities and their family members (with the permission of the student) can also share information about the characteristics of the disability (Campbell-Whatley, 2006; Chadsey & Gun Han, 2005). They can use home videos, photographs, and items that reveal important information about one's strengths, interests, hobbies, and challenges. They also can address the accommodations and assistive devices used, as well as questions and concerns raised by classmates. For example, students who use a wheelchair can explain to the class that they will ask others to push them if they need assistance, how the chair works, and how to push someone in the chair.

Use Films/Videos and Books

Many films, television shows, documentaries, and videos depict the lives of persons with disabilities or present disability-related issues (Black & Pretes, 2007; Connor & Bejoian, 2006; Dole & McMahan, 2005; Safran, 2000; Shepherd, 2007). Your class can view them and analyze and discuss their portrayal of disability related issues. Videos of news segments, commentaries, and documentaries from professional organizations, individuals with disabilities, advocacy groups, and television stations can also be accessed via video sharing websites (Bromley, 2008). In addition to teaching about disabilities, videos can be used to teach students about overcoming challenges, friendships, teamwork, and cultural, gender, family and socioeconomic differences, and stereotypes (Dole & McMahan, 2005; Wilson, 2004).

A variety of fiction and nonfiction children's and young adult literature and picture books about individuals with a range of disabilities and related issues can help counter stereotypical views and teach students about individual differences and disabilities (Altieri 2008; Dyches, Prater, & Leininger, 2009; Kurtts & Gavigan, 2008; Prater & Dyches, 2008; Prater, Dyches, & Johnstun, 2006; Sotto & Ball, 2006; Zambo, 2006). Autobiographies are particularly good resources, especially for older students, as they allow students to learn about disabilities from the perspective of authors with disabilities (Lava & Lehman, 2007). However, because many of these books can inadvertently reinforce negative stereotypes, it is important for you to identify appropriate, accurate, and realistic books that focus on inclusive settings, acceptance, and similarities; then use them to counter negative stereotypes and misconceptions about individuals with disabilities (Altieri, 2008; Prater & Dyches, 2008).

Books about individuals with disabilities also can serve as a springboard for helping students reflect on their beliefs about individual differences and disabilities, and what strategies they can employ to support persons with individual differences. You also can use them to help your students with disabilities understand their own disabilities more clearly and develop their self-awareness and self-advocacy skills (Konrad, Helf, & Itoi, 2007). You can increase the effectiveness of these books with guided discussions and activities related to the story's plot, information about disabilities, the characteristics and abilities of the characters, the stereotypes that are depicted and challenged, and the similarities between the characters and your students.

Teachers can use a variety of materials and strategies to teach students about disabilities and individual differences. What materials and strategies have you found to be most helpful and effective?

Use Curriculum Guides and Instructional Materials Many curriculum guides and instructional materials to teach students about individual differences are available (Shevin, 2005). These materials can be used to infuse content about individual

A GUIDE TO ACTION
Selecting Books, Materials, and Web-Based Information About Individual Differences

You can use books, materials, and Web-based information to teach about and foster acceptance of individual differences. To choose appropriate books, materials, and Web-based information to teach your students about individual differences, consider the following questions:

- Does the author have the background to accurately depict and present information about the group(s) discussed?
- Are the language, plot, readability, content, and style of the materials appropriate for your students?
- Does the material have a bias or a hidden agenda?
- Is the content factually correct, current, realistic, and presented in a culturally appropriate and understandable manner?
- Is the material written using updated, accurate, inclusive, and appropriate content, language and terminology?
- Is the content motivating, thoughtful, relevant, and properly organized?
- Are sources of the information provided?
- Are individuals depicted in a variety of situations and settings that represent their own cultural norms?
- Are individuals portrayed in a positive, well-rounded, capable, independent, complex, and nonstereotypical way?
- Are individuals presented as having unique personalities and qualities, likes and dislikes, and strengths and challenges?
- Does the content address important issues and recognize and include the varied experiences, perceptions, and contributions of individuals from diverse groups?
- Does the material introduce students to the accommodations and devices that individuals with differences find helpful?
- Does the material allow the students to develop an equal-status relationship with others and learn about the things they share with others?
- Does the material help students understand subtle stereotypes and present diversity within and across groups?
- In what proportion are individuals from different groups shown in the illustrations and graphics?
- Are the illustrations and graphics accurate, current, and nonstereotypical?
- Will the material and the illustrations stimulate questions and discussions about individuals with differences?
- Does the material promote sensitivity and inclusion, and avoid pitying and protective responses?
- Does the material suggest ways to take actions to challenge inequities and stereotypic perspectives and to support individuals with individual differences?

How would you rate your selection of books, materials, and Web-based information about individual differences? ( ) Excellent ( ) Good ( ) Needs Improvement ( ) Needs Much Improvement

Create a plan of action for improving your selection of books, materials and Web-based information to teach students about individual differences that includes your goals, the actions you will take and the resources you will need to achieve them, and the ways you will evaluate your success.

What are some goals and steps you could adopt to improve your selection of books, materials, and Web-based information about individual differences?

To reflect on your perceptions of disability and enhance your understanding of individual differences related to disability, go to the IRIS Center Resources section of the Topic: Autism Spectrum Disorders in the MyEducationLab for your course, and complete the module entitled *What Do You See? Perceptions of Disability.*

differences related to disability into your classroom or as part of a separate unit of study. They usually include a variety of goals, learning activities, materials to implement the activities, multimedia materials, and a teacher's guide.

You also can promote acceptance by creating a classroom environment that supports the acceptance of individual differences through the use of teaching materials and games (Lindstrom et al., 2008; Prater et al., 2005; Shapiro, 1999). For example, you can introduce materials that stimulate discussions, such as wall art, photographs and posters of individuals with disabilities, multiracial dolls, dolls with differing abilities and assistive devices, and stuffed animals that depict individuals with disabilities (Midgley, 2008).

Teach About Assistive Devices Because many students with disabilities may use assistive devices, teaching others about these devices can be beneficial. Wherever possible, it is best for the students with disabilities to introduce and explain the aids and devices they use. It is also important to help students learn that these devices are important tools that help people and not toys and to refrain from touching or playing with them without permission. If students do not feel comfortable showing and explaining the aids they use, a professional or family member can do so.

PEARSON

Go to the Assignments and Activities section of the Topic *Cultural and Linguistic Diversity* in the MyEducationLab for your course and complete the activity entitled *Self Esteem and Cultural Diversity*. As you watch the video and complete the accompanying questions, consider the importance of teaching about individual differences.

TEACHING ABOUT INDIVIDUAL DIFFERENCES RELATED TO CULTURE, LANGUAGE, GENDER, RELIGION, AND SOCIOECONOMIC STATUS

HOW CAN I TEACH ACCEPTANCE OF INDIVIDUAL DIFFERENCES RELATED TO CULTURE, LANGUAGE, GENDER, RELIGION, AND SOCIOECONOMIC STATUS? In addition to considering the guidelines and adapting the strategies we just discussed, you can use a variety of learning activities to teach students about individual differences related to culture, language, gender, religion, and socioeconomic status. These activities can be integrated into your curriculum to foster your students' empathy, understanding, and commitment to social justice and to create a classroom that welcomes, acknowledges, and celebrates the value and experiences of *all students* (Nieto & Bode, 2008).

Reflect on Your Knowledge, Experiences, and Beliefs Related to Diversity

As we discussed earlier in this chapter, your attitudes, behaviors, and language related to diversity will affect your students' views and behaviors with respect to diversity. Therefore, it is important for you to reflect on your knowledge, experiences, and beliefs related to your students' diversity and use your reflections to create an inclusive learning environment that fosters an understanding and acceptance of diversity (Cartledge & Kourea, 2008; Obiakor, Algozzine, & Bakken, 2007; Richards et al., 2007).

Promote Acceptance of Cultural Diversity

Many students may view peers who come from other cultures and speak other languages as different, and they may seldom interact with them because of their unique language, clothes, and customs. You can help students overcome these attitudes by teaching them about different cultures and the value of cultural diversity (Banks, 2009; Gollnick & Chinn, 2009; Taylor & Whittaker, 2009). With these activities, students gain a multicultural perspective that allows them to identify underlying and obvious similarities and differences among various groups (Hanc, 2008). An environment that accepts other cultures can enhance the self-esteem and learning performance of *all students* by affirming their cultures, languages, religions, and experiences (Cartledge & Kourea, 2008; Nieto & Bode, 2008).

You can use antibias curricula to foster your students' understanding and appreciation of differences related to race, language, gender, religion, socioeconomic status, and disability. Antibias curricula often include a variety of activities to teach students to be sensitive to the needs of others, think critically, interact with others, and develop a positive self-identity based on one's own strengths rather than on the weaknesses of others. When teaching students about cultural diversity, consider the following guidelines:

- Examine cultural diversity with the belief that *all students* have a culture that is to be valued and affirmed.

Students can be resources for helping their peers learn about cultural diversity. How do you use your students' diversity as a resource?

- Teach initially about cultural diversity by noting the variety of students and adults in the classroom and then extending the discussion beyond the classroom.
- Collect information about your students' cultural backgrounds.
- Help students view the similarities among groups through their differences.
- Tailor the curriculum and activities to your students' developmental levels and interests.
- Make cultural diversity activities an ongoing and integral part of the curriculum rather than a one-day "visit" to a culture during holidays or other special occasions.
- Relate experiences of cultural diversity to real life, giving students hands-on experiences that address their interests.
- Teach students about the various types of individual behavior within all cultures, and emphasize the idea that families and individuals experience and live their culture in personal ways and have multiple identities (Banks, 2008; D. A. Brynes, 2005a; Taylor & Whittaker, 2009).

Incorporate Cultural Diversity into the Classroom   You can incorporate acceptance of cultural diversity into your curriculum and classroom in a variety of ways (Nieto & Bode, 2008; Sloan, 2008) (see Figure 5.5). Incorporate multicultural literature, storytelling, poems, folktales, films, periodicals, and magazines on multicultural issues into the curriculum (Campano, 2007; Manning & Baruth, 2009). Students can then respond to questions that help them discuss and review the plot and identify the issues presented from multiple perspectives. They also can work in cross-cultural literature circles and develop character study journals in which they think about, write about, and maintain connections with the characters'

FIGURE 5.5 **Activities to promote acceptance of cultural diversity**

- Share information about your own cultural background, and ask students and their family members to do likewise.
- Discuss the similarities and differences among cultures including music, foods, customs, holidays, and languages.
- Make artifacts from different cultures.
- Read ethnic stories to and with students.
- Listen to music from different cultures and learn ethnic songs. A variety of music examples, lesson plans, recordings, videos, and practical strategies for teaching music from a multicultural perspective are available from the Music Educators National Conference Publication Sales (www.menc.org).
- Decorate the room, bulletin boards, and hallways with artwork, symbols, and murals that reflect a multicultural perspective.
- Make a class calendar that recognizes the holidays and customs of all cultures, and celebrate holidays that are common to several cultures in a way that recognizes each culture's customs.
- Plan multicultural lunches in which students and their families work together to cook multiethnic dishes. Have students interview family members about their dishes and write about their findings, which can be posted next to each dish.
- Take field trips that introduce students to the lifestyles of persons from different cultures.
- Show multimedia that highlight aspects of different cultures.
- Teach students ethnic games, and encourage them to use cross-cultural and cross-gender toys and other objects.
- Give students multicolored paints, paper, other art materials, and skin-tone crayons.
- Have students maintain an ethnic feelings book that summarizes their reactions to multicultural awareness activities and their experiences with their culture and other cultures.

Sources: Gollnick and Chinn (2009); Manning and Baruth (2009); Nieto and Bode (2008); Schniedewind and Davidson (2006); Sloan (2008).

feelings and situations, as well as their similarities to and differences from the characters and conflict resolutions depicted. You can enhance the effectiveness of these books and stories by helping your students clarify the issues, concepts, and events depicted; make connections to them; and identify and engage in behaviors that are supportive of diversity.

Your classroom environment can be organized so that it acknowledges cultural diversity (Cartledge & Kourea, 2008; Manning & Baruth, 2009). Create bulletin boards, for instance, that showcase newspaper events and/or photographs of diverse community members, or display student work around the theme of cultural diversity. In addition, incorporate cultural diversity into your classroom by using folklore and recognizing that your students and their families can be resources for helping their peers learn about cultural diversity (Nieto & Bode, 2008). For example, you can structure classroom activities and assignments so that students share information about their cultural and experiential backgrounds. Similarly, you can diversify your students' learning by inviting family members and community members to share culturally relevant information about topics your class is studying, or by taking students on field trips to interact with diverse members of the community.

You also can use multicultural teaching materials and multimedia and include the contributions of members of different groups in the content areas (Manning & Baruth, 2009). For example, discussing the work of African American and Russian scientists in science classes or Hispanic and Irish poets in English classes can teach students about the contributions of those ethnic groups (Sloan, 2008). Students can also be assigned to read books about different cultures and biographies of women who have made significant contributions to society.

Making Connections
Find out more about creating a multicultural curriculum and using culturally responsive teaching practices in Chapter 8.

Teach About Language Diversity   Acceptance of language diversity can increase the self-esteem and school performance of students who are learning English and students who speak dialects of English (Dong, 2009; Nieto & Bode, 2008). Acceptance also demonstrates a positive attitude toward students' language abilities and cultural backgrounds. Rather than viewing language diversity as a barrier to success in school, schools need to regard it as an educational resource (Agirdag, 2009). This diversity offers teachers and students many opportunities to learn about the nature and power of language and to function successfully in our multicultural world.

Many strategies can promote acceptance of language diversity (Agirdag, 2009; Dong, 2009). When teaching, you can use diverse cultural and language referents, teach and offer support in students' native languages, encourage and teach students to use multilingual picture dictionaries, allow students to ask and answer questions in their native languages, and use peers to tutor and help students in their native languages. For example, during instruction, introduce *all students* to *cognates*, words in different languages that have similar definitions and sounds (e.g., *triangle* and *triangulo*). You can also establish social and work areas in the classroom and give students opportunities to work and interact with peers from diverse backgrounds.

Technology also can foster communication among your students and language diversity (Berlin, 2009; Cutshall, 2009). Via the Internet, students can access text, audio, and video in various languages and "talk" with others in various languages via e-mail, chat rooms, and online translators. For example, the Internet provides links to newspapers and radio and television stations from around the world. In addition, language diversity also can be incorporated into the classroom by providing students with access to online language learning resources and activities and translation software (Lowdermilk, Fielding, Mendoza, Garcia de Alba, & Simpson, 2008). (When using translation software, it is important for you and your students to consider selecting a software that provides audio pronunciation and to exercise caution—appropriate and grammatically correct translations are not always possible across languages.) Students also can use software programs that teach different languages.

Teach About Dialect Differences

You know, it's funny. I speak English and Black English. Outside of school I hear a lot of white kids trying to speak like I do. They listen to rap music and try to speak like they are black. But when I'm in school, the same students make faces when I sometimes use Black English in class. It's like they don't respect our language or are afraid of it.

Because all English-speaking students speak a dialect, you also will work with students who speak various dialects of English (Adger, Wolfram, & Christian, 2007; Bomer, Dworin, May, & Semingson, 2008; Pransky, 2009). Rather than making students who speak other dialects of English feel deficient by interrupting and correcting them in midsentence, you can create a classroom that acknowledges and affirms the use of standard and other dialects of English as appropriate in various school and societal contexts (Christensen, 2008; Lessow-Hurley, 2009). One effective approach for creating such a classroom is the **bridge system**, which encourages students to be bidialectical and to understand that different dialects are used in different situations. In this approach, you help students understand when to use standard English and when it is appropriate to use other dialects. For example, when you need to prompt students to use standard English, you can ask, "How can you say that in school language?" In addition, you can help students become bidialectal by showing respect for students' dialects and the cultures they reflect; acknowledging the oral traditions of some students' cultures; exposing students to and discussing with them other English dialects through literature, books, songs, poetry, and films; and discussing and role-playing situations in which standard English and other dialects of English would be appropriate (Adger et al., 2007; Christensen, 2008; Pransky, 2009; Wheeler, 2008).

You also can help students discover and understand the connections among different languages and dialects, as well as the differences among languages (Dong, 2009; Lessow-Hurley, 2009; Wheeler, 2008). Students can study various aspects of languages and dialects and examine how sentences, words, sayings, riddles, and stories in different languages may share the same derivations and have different grammatical structures and meanings (Goldenberg, 2008). For example, students can experiment with Spanish words ending in *-cia* (e.g., *distancia*) and English words ending in *-ce* (e.g., *distance*) to begin to understand the commonalities of Spanish and English. Students and teachers can learn and use parallel sayings in English and other languages, and attempt to create their own sayings in many languages and dialects.

Students speak different dialects. What are the dialects that your students use? What dialects do you speak?

Help Your Students Develop a Global Perspective Your students' cross-cultural understanding also can be fostered by helping them develop a global perspective (Sloan, 2009). An understanding of other cultures and global issues can provide *all students* with cross-cultural learning experiences that teach them about the similarities, differences, and interdependence among people and countries from throughout the world (Suarez-Orozco & Sattin, 2007; Zhao, 2009). You can do this by

- incorporating literature, films, history, music, cultural experiences, news, and other resources from around the world into your classroom and curriculum;

Affirming Acceptance of Linguistic Diversity

Ms. White's school has had an increase in the number of students who are learning English. Several of these students were ridiculed because of their accents and their difficulties in understanding and talking with others. Ms. White was asked to serve on a school-wide committee to counter this teasing and help all students feel comfortable in their new school. At the first meeting, she suggested that community members who speak the students' native languages should be invited to join the committee.

The committee decided to start by creating a school environment that welcomed students and their families and reflected the different languages spoken in the community. They posted signs, bulletin board notices, and greetings in several languages in classrooms and throughout the school. They also displayed books and materials written in several languages in classrooms, the school's office, and the school library, and they posted students' work in several languages. Occasionally, the school played music in different languages over the loudspeaker and invited speakers and storytellers who spoke various languages to address different classes. The changes appeared to work. Several teachers noted that the new students seemed to feel more comfortable in school and that many of the English-speaking students were attempting to speak to them by using the new students' native language.

Here are some other strategies you can use to implement the IDEA in your inclusive classroom and affirm acceptance of linguistic diversity:

- Encourage students to use their native language in school, and teach some words from their language to others.

- Teach lessons about languages other than English. For example, you can teach lessons that compare the English alphabet with the alphabets of other languages.
- Stock the classroom with bilingual books.
- Ask students to explain words, customs, games, folktales, songs, or objects from their culture in their native language, and show videos and play music in various languages.
- Label classroom items in multiple languages, and use various languages in school newsletters and other written communications.
- Have students write journal entries and poems, contribute pieces to school publications, sing songs, and perform plays in their native languages.
- Learn to pronounce students' names correctly, and learn greetings and words in the students' languages. When students speak to you in their native language, ask them the meaning of words and phrases you don't understand.
- Give awards and recognition for excellence in speaking languages that may not be part of typical foreign language courses offered at the school.

Sources: Adger et al. (2007); Agirdag (2009); Dong (2009); Jik Bae and Clark (2005); Lessow-Hurley, (2009); Nieto and Bode (2008).

- infusing international content, issues, perspectives, and challenges across the curriculum (e.g., global food shortages can be studied in science and social studies classes)
- using your immigrant students and their families as well as community members and international visitors as resources for helping students learn about other cultures;
- providing students with accurate information related to global cultures, conflicts, and issues that allows them to understand their complexity and challenge stereotypes and misconceptions.

You can use technology to identify international resources and to collaborate with others from around the world (Jackson, 2007; Sloan, 2009). The Internet also can provide your students with cross-cultural, collaborative, equal-status experiences and opportunities to practice a foreign language and learn about other cultures. For example, via such sites as the International Education Resource Network (www .iearn.org) and E-pals (www.epals.com), your students can interact with students from different parts of the world by working on collaborative online projects across the curriculum; communicating via videoconferencing, blogging, discussion groups, and Twitter; or using e-mail to establish electronic pen pals.

Teach Gender Equity An effective program to teach students about cultural diversity should include activities that promote an understanding of gender equity (Murray & Taylor, 2009). These activities can be integrated into all content areas to help female and male students expand their options in terms of behaviors, feelings, interests, career aspirations, and abilities. Gender equity activities also make *all students* aware of the negative effects of gender bias and of ways to combat sexism. For example, as part of your math class, have students graph the number of male and female athletes mentioned in their local newspaper. A variety of curriculum activities, media, books for students and adults, photographs, posters, toys, games, and professional organizations are available to use as resources for teaching students about gender equity and sexual harassment (Koch, 2005; Sadker et al., 2009; Schniedewind & Davidson, 2006).

Foster Acceptance of Religious Diversity

Your inclusive classroom will be made up of students from a variety of religious and spiritual backgrounds. Fostering religious and spiritual diversity can help your students understand and respect each other (G. R. Carter, 2008; Whittaker et al., 2009). In doing this, educators need be aware of legal and legislative mandates so that they teach respect for *all* religions and religious figures by presenting them in a factual, respectful, neutral, and balanced manner and establishing a context that does not endorse, promote, distort, or denigrate any religion (Haynes, 2005). You also need to be aware of the impact of these activities on your students and be sensitive to and prepared to address the misinterpretations, disagreements, and discomfort that might occur.

One of the best ways to teach about religious and spiritual diversity is through the curriculum (Haynes, 2005; Whittaker, Salend, & Elhoweris, 2009). Many state

IDEAs to Implement Inclusion

Promoting Gender Equity

After taking a workshop on gender bias in the classroom, Ms. Stillwell tried to assess its extent in her classroom. She observed that her students appeared to segregate themselves during recess and lunch. Boys sat and played with boys, and girls sat and played with girls. She also noted that she and her students frequently used male-based metaphors such as telling the class that "you guys can tackle that problem."

Ms. Stillwell decided to change her behavior and the behavior of her students. She used self-recording to keep track of her interactions with her male and female students. She also introduced several vignettes showing positive and negative interactions in schools between male and female students. Students acted out these vignettes and then discussed them in small mixed-sex groups. Each group then shared its reactions to the vignettes with the class. Ms. Stillwell continued to observe her own and her students' behaviors, noticing many improvements that made her feel better. However, she knew that she needed to continue to confront this issue and other issues in her classroom.

Here are some other strategies you can use to implement the IDEA in your inclusive classroom and promote gender equity:

- Help students recognize when they are responding in a sexist manner, and challenge and teach them how to challenge sex-role stereotyping in school and society.
- Use gender-neutral language and language that includes both genders.

- Teach students how their attitudes and behavior relating to sex roles are affected by television, movies, music, books, advertisements, and the behavior of others.
- Avoid grouping students on the basis of gender, such as by forming separate lines, teams, seating arrangements, and academic learning groups and by comparing students by gender. Consider grouping your students based on what they are learning. For example, if you are teaching calendar skills, group them by the months in which they were born.
- Assign students of both sexes to class and school jobs on a rotating basis.
- Establish a classroom and school environment that encourages female and male students to play and work together. For example, decorate the classroom with pictures of males and females performing a variety of activities, and use cooperative learning.
- Use nonsexist teaching materials that challenge stereotypical roles and, when possible, modify sexist teaching materials.
- Provide all students with access to same-sex mentors.
- Encourage male and female students to participate in a variety of physical education and extracurricular activities.

Sources: Murray and Taylor (2009); Reasoner Jones (2008); Sadker et al. (2009); Schniedewind and Davidson (2006).

standards include instruction about religion as part of the social studies curriculum, literature, and fine arts, but the study of various religions can be incorporated into other subject areas as well. For instance, in social studies studies, teachers can teach students about how religious beliefs are manifested in the everyday life of people around the world. The ODIHR Advisory Council on Freedom of Religion or Belief (2007) offer guidelines and resources for teaching about religions and beliefs and Whittaker et al. (2009) and Greer and Oldendorf (2005) provide listings of children's and young adult literature addressing a variety of religious and spiritual traditions.

Acknowledging religious holidays can provide schools with an effective opportunity to teach about religious diversity. However, because schools cannot celebrate holidays as religious events or take actions to encourage or discourage observance by students, educators need to address religious holidays carefully. Therefore, when making the decision to acknowledge religious holidays and display religious or seasonal symbols, educators should make sure that they are used for a variety of religious groups, are employed as teaching aids and for academic purposes, and are temporary in nature.

In acknowledging religious holidays, you need to identify the academic and social goals and roles of holidays in the educational program, determine which holidays will be acknowledged, and plan how they will be presented (Haynes, 2005). You need to acknowledge religious holidays in a balanced and inclusive manner so that they reflect the traditions of students' families, and introduce students to traditions of others. Holidays should be presented in culturally relevant, nonstereotypical, respectful, and factual ways so that none of the students' religious backgrounds are excluded, trivialized, or portrayed as exotic. Therefore, it is important to research and solicit information from families and community-based religious leaders to understand the authentic and different ways that families celebrate holidays. As part of these learning experiences, you can include lessons that address the origin and religious and social meaning of various religious holidays, and avoid role plays and other activities that may be viewed as stereotyping a group or violating or trivializing the sacred nature of rituals and other important aspects associated with a group's religious beliefs. You also can use the Internet to connect your students to students from around the world to share information about their holiday traditions. The acknowledgment of holidays should include plans for students whose families do not want them to participate in these activities.

An inclusive way to acknowledge holidays is to organize them across a range of religions and around common themes (Jones, 2005). For instance, you can use the theme of light to teach students about different religious holidays that are related to light such as Hanukkah (Jewish), Christmas (Christian), and Diwali (Hindu). Other possible common themes for holidays could include the life cycle, liberation, cooperation, fasting, seasons, harvests, and planting. You also can use themes to refer to holidays and schoolwide activities in an inclusive manner. For example, rather than referring to events or activities by linking them to a specific holiday (e.g., Christmas break, cards, music, parties), you can refer to them by using themes (e.g., winter/holiday break, cards, music, parties).

You also need to be aware and respectful of aspects of your students' religions that may affect their school performance and require you to make accommodations (Whittaker et al., 2009). These aspects include medical and dietary restrictions, clothing, rituals and observances, and absences during holidays. For example, during some holidays, students from some religious backgrounds may be required to fast or pray during school hours or miss school for extended periods of time. Similarly, some students may wear religious garb or may not be able to participate in certain school activities because of their religious beliefs.

Teach About Family Differences   In light of the different kinds of families that students live in, accepting cultural diversity also can include teaching about family differences. By teaching about family differences, you can acknowledge the different family arrangements of your students (Sapon-Shevin, 2008). You also can use the stories of students' families as the basis for interdisciplinary lessons (Nieto & Bode, 2008). Because students have a variety of family arrangements, it is important to be careful when assigning projects (e.g., family trees) or holding events (e.g., mother–daughter activities) that relate to or assume that students live in traditional nuclear families; instead, frame these assignments in a more inclusive manner.

Making Connections
This discussion of socioeconomic differences and AIDS builds on what we discussed earlier, in Chapter 3.

Teach About Socioeconomic Differences, Homelessness, the Migrant Lifestyle, and AIDS   Students from lower socioeconomic backgrounds, homeless and migrant students, and students with HIV/AIDS may be targets of ridicule by peers. To counteract this problem, you can use a range of activities and resources to teach about these circumstances carefully so as to avoid stigmatizing these students (Davidson & Schniedewind, 2005; Gorski, 2008; Hershey & Reilly, 2009; San Antonio, 2008; Seider, 2009). You also can take actions to limit the extent to which monies and other resources are required for students to participate in school activities (Huguelet, 2007). The homeless and migrant lifestyles can be presented by guest speakers and through multimedia materials, books and service learning projects. Photographs and videos depicting the migrant lifestyle or homelessness can give students direct, real-life experiences with issues related to these individuals.

Students often learn about conditions such as AIDS through television and other media. As a result, they often have misconceptions about AIDS and are afraid to be in classrooms with students who have AIDS. Several culturally appropriate instructional strategies can help to overcome these negative attitudes and misconceptions. A trained professional or an individual with AIDS can be invited to speak about the social and medical aspects of the disease (Sileo, 2005). Many curriculum materials and resources for teachers, and books for students, are available (Prater & Sileo, 2001; Sileo, 2005). In using these materials, be sure that they present current, accurate information and are consistent with school district policy.

Teach About Stereotyping   Many students gain negative perceptions of others through stereotypes. It is important to help students understand and challenge the process of stereotyping, in addition to learning about a group's experiences and history (Gorski, 2008; Richards et al., 2007). You can counter the harmful effects of stereotyping by doing the following:

- Invite individuals who challenge stereotypes to speak to the class.
- Have students read books and view videos that challenge stereotypes and address discrimination.
- Display pictures and materials that challenge stereotypes.
- Discuss and critique how language, books, television shows, commercials, cartoons, jokes, toys, and common everyday items (e.g., lunch boxes) create and foster stereotypes.
- Compare items, images, and words and expressions that portray various groups.
- List and discuss stereotypes that students have about others, as well as the stereotypes that others have about them (Sapon-Shevin, 2008).

Teach About Discrimination   Issues of diversity are related to issues of power in schools and society. Therefore, it is important to teach your students to recognize and confront discrimination and its harmful effects (Banks, 2009; Nieto & Bode, 2008; Sapon-Shevin, 2008). Case studies and short books and stories on various cultures and instances of discrimination can stimulate group discussions that introduce students to a variety of perspectives, experiences, and ideas. The purpose of such discussions is to help them reach conclusions, as well as question and

REFLECTIVE

Think about a situation in which you were stereotyped. What factors contributed to that stereotype? How did it make you feel? How did it affect the outcome of the situation? Think about a situation in which you stereotyped someone. What factors contributed to that stereotype? How did it make you feel? What would you do differently?

affirm their own viewpoints. Facilitate the discussion of these issues by engaging in the following:

- Respond to all questions and comments respectfully and seriously.
- Ask students, when necessary, to clarify comments and questions.
- Address students' questions and comments and confront their misrepresentations honestly using age-appropriate language and examples.
- Seek additional information to address questions you cannot answer or to correct inaccurate or incomplete answers.
- Be aware of students' emotional responses.

Students can learn about these issues by experiencing them (San Antonio, 2008). For example, you can group students according to some arbitrary trait (e.g., hair color, eye color, type of clothing) and then treat the groups in different ways in terms of rules, assignments, compliments, grading procedures, privileges, homework, and class jobs. You can also show students what it means to be discriminated against by assigning several groups the same task while varying the resources each group is given to complete the task, so that the different performance of the groups is related to resources rather than ability. After these activities, you and your students can discuss their reactions and the effects of discrimination. You also can discuss with them how they treat others and would like to be treated by others.

Teach Visual and Media Literacy

Help your students develop their visual and media literacy skills so that they are better able to critically analyze and examine the various images and forms of media they encounter in their lives (Sapon-Shevin, 2008; Zambo, 2009). Zambo (2009) outlines the following steps for teaching visual literacy:

Step 1: Identify the issue and choose the image. Issues and images can be related to exclusion or bias related to appearance, ability, race, ethnicity, gender, sexual orientation, socioeconomic status, and family structure.

Step 2: Guide students in examining the image's details. Provide students with time to examine the images and then use questioning to guide them in examining the details depicted.

Step 3: Provide additional related information. Use a range of formats to educate students about the issues presented in the image.

Step 4: Facilitate a thoughtful and open discussion. Use questioning to lead a discussion about the image and the issues, encouraging students to support their statements and opinions.

Step 5: Foster student reflection. Have students reflect on the image, issues, and their viewpoints and learning via personal journals.

Step 6: Assess student learning. Assess student learning and what additional information and activities you need to provide to address misconceptions and to extent their understanding of the issues.

You also can teach your students how to act and unite to challenge discrimination and stereotyping. *All students* may form a media watch to identify and share examples of bias and unbiased presentations in the media. Students can then work to take actions that

- acknowledge constructive and complex presentations of individual differences;
- counter negative, inaccurate, and stereotypical portrayals of persons with individual differences and related issues, and the use of incorrect terminology; and
- call for more presentations addressing persons with individual differences and related issues.

REFLECTIVE

Look at the images presented to you via the media you use. How do they present issues and images related to individuals with individual differences?

Teach Others to Respond to Stereotyping and Discrimination

Once students learn about the negative effects of prejudice, they can be taught how to respond to stereotyping and discrimination (Nieto & Bode, 2008; Wessler, 2008). Learning how to respond appropriately is especially important for students who are the targets of stereotyping and discrimination. In doing this, it is important for you to help your students learn to differentiate legitimate dislikes (e.g., disliking foods) from discrimination and stereotyping (e.g., disliking individuals with differences) (Shapiro, 1999).

You can establish an inclusive classroom environment by modeling acceptance of *all students* and by establishing the rule that gender, race, ethnicity, language skills, ability, religion, physical appearance, sexual orientation, or socioeconomic status is not a reason for excluding or teasing someone. Books and films depicting individuals and communities acting interdependently to confront prejudice also can be used to help students learn how to take positive actions to challenge acts of intolerance (Schmidt, 2009).

Role playing and group discussions also help students learn how to respond to discrimination and stereotyping (Sapon-Shevin, 2008; Wessler, 2008). For example, present a bias-related incident, and ask students to role-play their responses. Afterward, the students can discuss their experiences and reactions.

Sometimes students express a desire to change their physical appearance or identity. When this happens, tell students immediately that they are fine; assure them that others like them the way they are; explain to them that others who do not like them that way are wrong; point out that many people have the same traits; and confront others who made negative statements that triggered the students' reactions.

Address Insensitive and Intolerant Acts   Just as with any learning experience, students will come to school with gaps and inaccuracies in their knowledge of individual differences. As a result, sometimes students will, intentionally or unintentionally, engage in insensitive and intolerant acts toward others. Responses to such acts will vary depending on the school's policies; the nature of the act and its time and place; and the history, age, and intent of the individuals involved. For example, if the intent of the act was not to hurt others, you might want to deal with students privately or present the situation confidentially at a class meeting to discuss ways to avoid similar insensitive acts. You also can use class meetings and peer mediation to address and discuss misunderstandings and answer students' questions.

However, you also are likely to encounter students being intentionally intolerant of others. When this occurs, you can act promptly and decisively to help students learn that discriminatory degrading, and hurtful language, jokes, and behaviors are unacceptable (Gorski, 2008; Sapon-Shevin, 2008). Prompt, consistent, and firm responses to all acts of intolerance, harassment, and exclusion can minimize their negative effects and serve as a model for how students can react to them (Wessler, 2008).

In addition to using the strategies presented in this chapter to establish a learning community that is respectful of all its members, you can respond decisively when intolerant behaviors occur in your school by doing the following:

- Establishing and communicating policies and rules against all acts of intolerance and exclusion, and procedures for making complaints about their occurrence
- Identifying the act of intolerance and why it is unacceptable: "You just insulted a religious group and our school. Why was it hurtful?"
- Making it clear to students that these behaviors will not be tolerated and making sure that all individuals in the area are aware of your comments and actions: "That was a stereotype. What you did was wrong and hurtful. We respect everyone in this school, and comments like that are not welcome here."
- Responding immediately to all incidents of intolerance by addressing their impact on the community, providing direct consequences, and informing students

Making Connections
Find out more about strategies for responding to bullying in Chapter 7.

REFLECTIVE

Think about how you would respond to your students teasing a male student who likes to sew.

Using Technology to Promote Inclusion
FOSTERING ACCEPTANCE AND FRIENDSHIPS

The Internet and technology can be good resources for fostering acceptance and friendships. Via the Internet, you can provide students with opportunities to engage in online and technology-based disability awareness activities. For example, online simulations and virtual reality experiences related to various disability conditions are available. The American Foundation for the Blind has created Braille Bug (www.afb.org/braillebug), a Web site that offers a variety of online activities to teach sighted students about Braille and your students also can learn some key words in sign language by visiting Web sites. Prior to using sites addressing individual differences, carefully evaluate them and the Web-based information they present.

Here are some other ways you can use technology to teach students about individual differences and promote interactions and friendships among students.

- Have your students learn about a variety of disabilities by visiting online disability awareness sites, which provide access to a wide range of information and resources about disabilities, as well as many exploratory and discovery-based learning and communication experiences.
- Have your students perform online simulations by visiting such websites as these:

  Misunderstood Minds (www.pbs.org/wgbh/misunderstoodminds)—offers simulations addressing learning differences and disabilities related to attention, reading, writing and mathematics difficulties

  National Eye Institute (www.nei.nih.gov/photo/keyword.asp?narrow=Animation)—offers simulations related to various visual related disability conditions

- Have your students make online visits to disability-related virtual museums—for example:

  Disability Rights Movement Virtual Museum (www.americanhistory.si.edu/disabilityrights/welcome.html)—offers online access to a virtual exhibition developed by the Smithsonian Natural Museum of American History on the Disability Rights Movement

  Disability History Museum (www.disabilitymuseum.org)—provides online access to exhibits, a library, and teacher resources and course packets designed to teach about the historical experiences of individuals with disabilities

- Have your students learn about individual differences related to disability via use of online games (Levy, 2006).
- Have your students use streaming audio and video technology to watch or hear live or prerecorded audio and video broadcasts of disability-related topics and video sharing Web sites that present respectful information about individual differences (Bromley, 2008).
- Use online learning activities to incorporate content about disability into the curriculum. The Center on Human Policy at Syracuse University's Disabilities Studies for Teachers Web site (www.disabilitystudiesforteachers.org/lessons.php) and the Education for Disability and Gender Equity (EDGE) (www.disabilityhistory.org/dwa/edge/curriculum) offer lessons and varied resources for teaching about disabilities and integrating disability awareness and issues into the curriculum. A historical perspective of disabilities including current resources can be integrated into the social studies curriculum through use of such Web sites as the Disability Social History Project (www.disabilityhistory.org), and the Disability Resources' History of Disabilities (www.disabilityresources.org/HISTORY.html).
- Obtain and use curriculum guides and learning materials related to individual differences and friendships online. For example, via the website of the Boston Children's Museum (www.bostonkids.org/educators/disability_awareness.html), you can access *Some Ways the Same, Some Ways Different*, a disability awareness curriculum. Information about additional disability awareness resources for use with your students is available via the website of the National Information Center for Children and Youth with Disabilities (www.nichcy.org) and the Disability Resources website (www.disabilityresources.org/DIS-AWARE.html).
- Use software programs that teach about individual differences, social skills, and friendships (Goodwin, 2008). For example, Mind Reading: The Interactive Guide to Emotions is a software package containing video and audio clips of different emotions that can be varied and presented to students as interactive games to teach students how to interpret a range of emotions (Lacava, Golan, Baron-Cohen, & Smith Myles, 2007).
- Teach social skills via use of video modeling and self-modeling (Bernad-Ripoll, 2007; Cummings et al., 2008), technology-based social stories and power cards (Parette, Crowley, & Wojcik, 2007), and PDAs that prompt students to engage in appropriate social skills (Wexler, 2009).
- Carefully consider whether it is appropriate for your students to use safe virtual reality, online social networks and social support groups, and websites to guide them in learning about and practicing social skills and interacting with others (Ayres & Langone, 2008; Wexler, 2009). When using these sites, it is important to make sure they are safe and appropriate for your students, and that you teach them to use the

(Continued)

Creating an Environment That Fosters Acceptance and Friendship

technology in a safe, responsible, respectful and appropriate manner (Mustacchi, 2009; November, 2008). Also, you need to work with your students to help them learn to apply the skills they have learned in online environments to face-to-face social situations.

- Use collaborative, technology-based academic and social activities. For example, students can work in groups to use computers to produce newsletters, fliers, invitations, banners, and illustrations for the classroom. They also can work in groups to maintain blogs and to use the Internet to gather information about acts of tolerance or intolerance and then create a web page to disseminate their findings to others.

- Have students work together on a webquest, an inquiry-oriented, cooperatively structured group activity in which some or all of the information that students use comes from resources on the Internet or videoconferencing. For example,

you can have students work in collaborative groups to complete webquests that ask them to use teacher-approved websites to gather and present information on various religions, disabilities, or cultural groups. Each group can study a different religion/disability/culture, and each group's project can be used to explore the similarities and differences among the various religions/disabilities/cultures studied.

- Obtain information about films and documentaries about individuals with disabilities by visiting the website Films Involving Disabilities (www.disabilityfilms.co.uk).

- Provide students with access to safe, effective, and universally designed toys and adapted play materials such as toys with Velcro, magnets, handles or switches (e.g., switch-activated switches), visual sensory input (e.g., flashing and blinking lights), auditory sensory input (e.g., sounds, recordings, music such as balls with bells,), tactile input (e.g., Braille playing cards), and aids to operate electronic devices (Bouck, Okolo, & Courtad, 2007; Wolfe Poel, 2007). Goetz Ruffino, Mistrett, Tomita, and Hajare (2006) offer guidelines for evaluating the extent to which toys and play materials are universally designed.

Making Connections
Find out more about how you can teach your students to be good digital citizens who use technology safely and appropriately in Chapter 8.

that they must change their behavior in the future: "This school is a community, and we do not say hurtful things. We want everyone in school to feel welcome and safe. In the future, you need to think before you speak or act. What are you going to do to make sure it doesn't happen again?"

- Following up incidents by checking with the target of the intolerance: "How are you feeling? I'm sorry this happened to you and our school. It was wrong and unfair. You and everyone else in this school should feel welcome and safe. I will speak to the student(s) who said (did) this. If this happens again, please let me know and I will take additional action."

- Reporting incidents to school administrators and other professionals and enlisting their support in addressing these issues

FACILITATING FRIENDSHIPS

HOW CAN I FACILITATE FRIENDSHIPS AMONG MY STUDENTS? Friendships in and outside school are important for everyone and are one of the desired benefits of inclusion programs for *all students* (Smith, 2009). In addition to promoting students' self-esteem, friendships also can foster students' learning, language development, and acceptance of individual differences (Meadan & Monda-Amaya, 2008). However, because some of your students may have few friends and limited peer support, you may need to use a variety of strategies to promote the development of friendships and peer support systems (Estell et al., 2009; Swedeen, 2009).

Engage in Professional Behaviors That Support Friendships

Several professional behaviors support friendships (Chadsey & Gun Han, 2005; Meadan & Monda-Amaya, 2008). You can make sure that all students have easy access to their classmates, interact in meaningful ways and everyday situations, and understand the things in common they share with their peers (Swedeen, 2009). Also, use rewards that encourage students to interact. For example, you can reward students by giving them extra time to socialize and work with classmates.

Talk with students about their friendships and friendship-making skills (Meadan & Monda-Amaya, 2008). You might initially assist students in interacting with classmates by leading social activities, modeling social interaction skills, and prompting students to interact, and then gradually reducing your assistance as students socialize on their own (Angell, Bailey, & Larson, 2008).

Be careful that students don't inadvertently reinforce caregiving and "parenting" actions rather than reciprocal friendships, and make sure your policies and procedures do not prevent students from having opportunities to socialize and make friends. You also can make sure that the proximity of adults doesn't interfere with the social interactions of your students (Giangreco & Broer, 2007). For example, try to foster friendships among *all students* by having them spend time and eat meals with other students rather than with their paraeducators or other adults (Church, Gottschalk, & Leddy, 2003).

Mutual friendships in and outside school are important for all students and are one of the benefits of inclusion. How would you describe your students' friendships?

Teach About Friendships

You can help promote friendships by integrating teaching about friendships into the curriculum (Gordon, Feldman, & Chiriboga, 2005; Meadan & Monda-Amaya, 2008). This can include exploring the meaning and importance of friendship, the qualities of good friendship, and the problems that some students have in trying to make friends. Students can then explore their own friendships by developing a friendship chart that includes the names of several of their friends, the activities they do with their friends, the qualities they like in their friends, and how they met each friend; writing a friendship poem; or creating a wall with each block indicating a barrier to friendships (Froschl & Gropper, 1999).

Offer Social Skills Instruction

Teaching about friendships also should include teaching *social skills*, the cognitive, verbal, and nonverbal skills that guide interactions with others (Cartledge & Kourea, 2008; Swedeen, 2009). *All students* can learn how to initiate, respond to, and maintain positive, equal-status social interactions with their peers; show empathy; and deal with frustration, conflict, rejection, and refusal (Angell et al., 2008; Kuhn, Bodkin, Devlin, & Doggett, 2008; Owen-DeSchryver et al., 2008). For example, you can model and have students role-play responses to various friendship-making situations, and prompt and praise them when they demonstrate prosocial skills during interactions with others.

You can also use learning strategies and social skills curricula that teach students friendship skills such as sharing and turn taking; listening and talking to friends; and complimenting, encouraging, respecting, and helping others (McIntosh & MacKay, 2008; Meadan & Monda-Amaya, 2008). Bock (2007) developed SODA, a learning strategy that guides social interactions by prompting students to

Stop: Determine the room arrangement, activity, schedule, or routine and where to observe.

Observe: Note what people are doing and saying as well as how long they speak and what they do after interacting, and what happens after they speak.

Deliberate: Think about what to do and say and why and how I feel.

Act: Approach others, greet them with "Hello" and "How are you?" Listen to others and ask appropriate questions, and look for cues related to whether to continue or end the interaction.

Students also can be asked to perform a *social autopsy* to reflect on their social skills by responding to the following: (a) What happened? (b) What did you do to get along with others? (c) How well did it work? (d) How do you think the others felt about what you did? (e) What did you learn from this experience? and (f) What could you do next time to get along better with others? (Linn & Smith Myles, 2004).

Another effective technique for teaching social skills to your students is the use of social stories (Okada, Ohtake, & Yanagihara, 2008; Reynhout & Carter, 2007; Wang & Spillane, 2009). **Social stories** involve the use of individualized, brief, predictable, easy-to-follow stories written from the viewpoint of students that describe social situations, the perspectives of others, relevant social cues, appropriate social behaviors, and ways to engage in and the consequences for demonstrating appropriate behaviors (Spencer, Simpson, & Lynch, 2008). Social stories often include the following elements:

- *Descriptive sentences*, which provide students with an overview of the setting and the social rules and events occurring in the setting ("At our school, students play together on the playground.")
- *Directive sentences*, which offer students prosocial ways to behave and interact with others ("When I'm on the playground, I need to choose the playground equipment I want to use, stay in line, and wait my turn. If others are using the equipment together, I look at them and ask them if I can play.")
- *Perspective sentences*, which present the feelings of others regarding the event and/or the students' behaviors ("Waiting for my turn is not easy. It gives everyone a fair chance and makes them feel better.")
- *Affirmative sentences*, which highlight important information and facts ("This is working. I like it and it's OK for me to keep doing") (Delano & Stone, 2008)

They also may include control sentences that guide students in focusing on important aspects of the event, and cooperative sentences that identify who will aid the student and how to be successful in the situation (Okada et al., 2008).

Effective social stories are written in language students can understand, contain repetition of key words, pair pictorial cues with text, and avoid use of literal and complex words (e.g., *usually*). They can include an introduction, the story, and the ending presented in the first person, and with a positive tone presented in two to five sentences (Delano & Stone, 2008). You introduce students to social stories by reading them to students and asking them to respond to questions about the stories. As students become more comfortable using social stories, they can then read the stories to themselves or aloud to others, listen to a reading or recording of the story, view a video presentation, and create digital social stories (Bernad-Ripoll, 2007; Schleibaum, 2007). More (2008) offers suggestions and resources you can use to guide your students in creating digital social stories.

You also can use variations of social stories such as comic strip conversations, power cards, and I WILL cards. Whereas social stories are depicted using text and pictorials, **comic strip conversations** use only comic strip pictorials to depict social events and prosocial behavioral responses (Pierson & Glaeser, 2007). Students and teachers can compose and draw individualized comic strip conversations by using simple figures, comic strip symbols and speech bubbles, and conversation symbols and personal symbols dictionaries. **Power cards** are adaptations of social stories that link the prosocial behaviors to the student's special interests (Spencer, Simpson, Day, & Buster, 2008). **I WILL cards** are usually index cards containing first-person statements that prompt students to engage in appropriate behavior (e.g., "When someone says hello, I will. . . .") (Boutot, 2009).

You also can use literature and picture books to teach social skills (Forgan & Gonzalez-DeHass, 2004; Zambo, 2007). Students also can work in groups to read, discuss, and role-play the use of social skills in juvenile literature (Gut & Safran, 2002).

Foster Communication Among Students

Because students' sensory, speech, and cognitive abilities can affect their social interactions, you also may need to teach your students how to interact and communicate with classmates (Angell et al., 2008; Meadan & Monda-Amaya, 2008). For

Making Connections
Find out more about teaching social skills in Chapter 6. Also, an example of an I WILL card is presented in Figure 6.6.

Facilitating Friendship Skills

Ms. Rollings and Ms. Kieck noticed that their students were having many disagreements. These disagreements frequently escalated, causing one of the teachers to intervene. Frustrated by their students' inability to work through these situations, they decided to implement a series of activities to help their students learn how to compromise. They began by having their students observe them as they role-played a situation of two people disagreeing about where to go to dinner, and then compromising on their choice of a restaurant. Following the role play, the teachers asked:

- "What did we do?"
- "What steps did we follow?"
- "What was the purpose of compromising?"
- "Were we satisfied with our compromise?"

As the class responded to these questions, the teachers discussed how they compromised, highlighted the steps they followed to achieve their compromise, and discussed why they were satisfied with their compromise.

Next, the teachers told the class, "We demonstrated how to compromise, and now you are going to work in pairs to learn how to compromise when you have a disagreement." They reviewed the steps the students needed to perform to arrive at their compromises, and the guidelines they should follow to achieve a compromise that both parties felt good about. The teachers then gave each pair a situation that had resulted in a disagreement in their class and required a compromise. They also gave each pair a sheet that asked them to list their disagreement and possible choices as well as their compromise, how they reached it, and

their level of satisfaction with it. When the students finished, the teachers asked the pairs to share their situations and explain their compromises. At the end of the activity, the teachers reminded the students to use the skills they had learned to compromise with their classmates when they had a disagreement. Later that day, the teachers were pleased when two students negotiated a compromise to a disagreement that occurred in the hallway.

Here are some other strategies you can use to implement the IDEA in your inclusive classroom and facilitate friendships among your students:

- Discuss how it is important to treat everyone in a respectful way and what that means.
- Offer students insights about friendships by talking about the importance of your friendships and the things you like to do with friends.
- Structure activities so that students work and socialize in groups or pairs and in a variety of settings.
- Highlight the strengths, interests, and hobbies of *all your students* as well as their similarities.
- Share information about after-school and community-based activities and encourage *all your students* to participate in them.
- Help students and other adults understand the differences between supporting others and helping them too much.

Sources: Meadan and Monda-Amaya (2008); Sapon-Shevin (2008); Swedeen (2009).

instance, you can teach them to talk to and socialize with their classmates with disabilities in the same ways that they interact with their other friends. As we discussed earlier, you can help students understand the communication needs of others by teaching and modeling appropriate terminology and ways of interacting with others such as using individuals first language and the guidelines presented in Figure 5.3. Russell (2008) provides a listing of resources that you can use to teach your students about individuals first language and friendships.

Alternative communication systems that students with disabilities use, such as Braille and sign language, can be introduced in a variety of ways that also promote academic skills. You can teach students the manual alphabet and then have them practice their spelling by spelling the words manually. Similarly, rather than writing the numbers for a math problem on the chalkboard, you can present them using numerical hand signs. Basic signs can be introduced to students and used for assignments. Students who have learned Braille can be asked to read and write in Braille.

Use Circles of Friends

You also can use circles of friends to help *all students* understand support systems and friendships and expand their social networks (Causton-Theoharis & Malmgren, 2005). To do this, give students a sheet with four concentric circles, each larger and farther away from the center of the sheet, which contains a drawing of a stick figure representing a student. First, ask students to fill in the first circle (the one closest to the stick figure) by listing the people whom they love and who are closest to them.

REFLECTIVE

Make a circle of friends for yourself. How have your friends and support group assisted you during stressful times?

The second circle contains a list of the people they like, such as their best friends. The third circle contains a list of groups that they like and do things with, like members of their teams or community organizations. Finally, the fourth circle contains a list of individuals who are paid to be part of their lives, such as a doctor or teacher. Students' circles are then shared with their peers, and the meaning and importance of friendships are discussed, including strategies for helping students make friends and expand their circle of friends.

You may need to address several potential concerns associated with using circles of friends (Frederickson & Turner, 2003). These issues include the perception that the targeted student is in need of help, the participation of classmates who are not part of the circle, and the importance of teaching social skills. You can address these issues by using this technique with *all students* and ensuring that *all students* are included in the process and that they develop the social skills they need to support friendships with others and expand their own social networks.

Create a Friendly Classroom Environment

You also can support the development of friendships by creating a friendly classroom environment that promotes social interactions among students (Meadan & Monda-Amaya, 2008). To do this, use friendship activities including books, cooperative academic and nonacademic games, and learning centers to establish an environment that supports friendships (Sapon-Shevin, 2008). Have students do activities such as creating friendship murals, bulletin boards, posters, and books with illustrations, and teach them songs with the theme of friendship. An environment that supports friendships also can be created by providing your students with access to culturally diverse, age-appropriate materials, toys, and games that they like to use with others.

A friendly school environment also results from cooperative grouping in which students work and play together in groups (Chadsey & Gun Han, 2005; Sapon-Shevin, 2008; Swedeen, 2009). For example, make sure all students are in close proximity to their classmates during academic and social activities. You also can teach students simple noncompetitive and enjoyable games that don't require a lot of skill or language abilities. When using these games, consider how they can be adapted by modifying the rules, using assistive devices, and employing personal assistance strategies such as playing as a team.

A friendly and caring classroom environment can be fostered by activities that promote a sense of community, shared interests, reciprocity, and class cohesiveness (Collins, 2009; Meadan & Monda-Amaya, 2008). Such community-building group activities promote friendships and acceptance by creating a class identity and connectedness that recognizes the similarities and differences among students and the unique contributions of each class member (Fink Chorzempa & Lapidus, 2009; Sapon-Shevin, 2008). For example, students can create a class book, video, mural, newsletter, or tree that includes and recognizes the work and participation of everyone in the class. Throughout the school year, students can use many different getting-acquainted activities such as playing name recognition games, developing a class directory, and interviewing each other and reflect on their efforts to build a classroom community. Collins (2009), Jones and Jones (2007), Morrison and Blackburn (2008), and Schniedewind and Davidson (2006) provide activities to introduce new students to the group and promote class cohesiveness, giving all students a common experience on which to build future interactions and friendships. Figure 5.6 offers examples of community building activities.

Use Peer-Based Strategies

Peer-based strategies increasing the social and academic interactions among your students also can foster friendships and acceptance (Meadan & Monda-Amaya, 2008; Sapon-Shevin, 2008). Academic interactions can be promoted through use of peer-mediated instruction and cooperative learning groups, which allow *all students* to learn and to be social together. Socially, you can offer *all students* numerous

FIGURE 5.6 Activities to promote a sense of class cohesiveness

- Create a class history or class photo album that is updated periodically and includes a summary of the year's activities, as well as work produced by and information about each student.
- Create special class days, such as T-Shirt Day, when all students wear their favorite T-shirts.
- Create a class web page.
- Publish a class newspaper/newsletter, to which each student contributes a piece or drawing during the school year.
- Have students work in groups to complete a "Classmates Scavenger Hunt" by giving each group a list of feelings (e.g., "A classmate who makes others feel good"), interests (e.g., "A classmate who likes to draw"), and skills (e.g., "A classmate who is good at math") that is completed by placing the names of classmates who have those feelings, interests, or skills on a poster.
- Make a class mural and have each student complete part of it.
- Construct a class tree. Each branch of the tree can contain a picture of a student or a work produced by that student.
- Compile a *Who's Who* book of the class, with each student having a page devoted to his or her interests, achievements, and so on.
- Have a "class applause" in which the whole class acknowledges the accomplishments of classmates.

opportunities to interact, including playing cooperative games and using interactive technology with their peers.

Positive Peer Reporting (PPR)   Some teachers promote social interactions among their students by using **positive peer reporting**, which involves students publicly praising their classmates for engaging in prosocial behaviors (Fenty, Miller, & Lampi, 2008). One way to do this is to teach your students to write peer praise notes to their classmates to acknowledge helpful and friendly classroom behaviors (Peterson Nelson et al., 2008). After you teach students how to write a peer praise note, you can foster their use by collaborating with your students to design a peer praise template that includes the date, the prosocial behavior (e.g., "I liked how you . . ."), and the names of the receiving and sending student. You also can encourage their use by sharing them with the class and rewarding the class for achieving a specified goal related to the number of notes written.

Some teachers also have a positive-comment box in the classroom. Class members who see another student performing a kind act that supports others record the action on a slip of paper that is placed in the comment box. At the end of the day, positive actions are shared with the class. Other teachers use an appreciation circle by asking students to identify things that their classmates did well during an activity or the school day.

Peer Support Committees and Class Meetings   Peer support committees and class meetings can be used to address classroom social interaction problems, promote friendships and community, and ensure that *all students* are valued members of the class. The peer support committee identifies problems that students or the class as a whole are experiencing and creates strategies to address them, such as establishing buddy systems, peer helpers, and study partners. The committee also brainstorms strategies for promoting friendships in the classroom and involving students in all academic and social aspects of the school, including extracurricular activities. Typically, membership on the committee is rotated so that each member of the class has an opportunity to serve.

Peer Mentoring, Buddy, and Partner Systems   Friendships also can be promoted through the use of peer mentoring, buddy, or partner systems (Chadsey & Gun Han, 2005; Gordon et al., 2005). Because peer-based systems during noninstructional activities lead to more high-quality interactions between dyads of students with and without disabilities, you can try to structure classroom activities so that students have numerous opportunities to interact with their peer mentors and partners in social

Making Connections
Find out more about how to use cooperative learning arrangements effectively in Chapter 9.

settings. Peers, particularly those who are valued and respected, also can interact by introducing their classmates to various academic and social features of the school, and classroom routines (Carter, Clark, Cushing, & Kennedy, 2005). For example, peer partners and mentors can help students learn the school's locker system and encourage classmates to attend extracurricular activities. Three to five students also can be paired to be buddy groups to facilitate interactions during lunch or recess or to work on community-based projects. You can support the success of these peer-based systems by meeting periodically with peer partners to examine their success in supporting each other, offering education about individual differences, and rotating partners.

Encourage Participation in Extracurricular and Community-Based Activities

Many friendships begin outside the classroom and school, so students should be encouraged to meet and make new friends through extracurricular and community-based activities (Kleinert, Miracle, & Sheppard-Jones, 2007; Swedeen, 2009). Because these activities provide opportunities to share mutually enjoyable activities, similarities among students are highlighted. You can work with other professionals, family members, students, and community groups to offer and adapt after-school activities that allow various groups of students to participate and interact socially.

Making Connections
Find out more about involving students in community-based activities in Chapter 6.

What Would You Do in Today's Diverse Classroom?

★ You are concerned about your students' social interaction patterns. You observe your students' interactions inside and outside the class and notice that they are mimicking a student's accent, segregating themselves by gender, and teasing others for being overweight or because they wear old clothes.

★ Robert does well in school, is kind to others, and has a good sense of humor. Although he desperately wants to have friends, he is awkward around others and avoids his classmates. When he is around peers, he fidgets and fails to look at them and speaks in a low monotone.

1. Why is it important for you and your colleagues to address these situations?

2. What are some strategies you could use to encourage your students to accept one another's individual differences, and develop friendships?

3. What knowledge, skills, dispositions, resources, and support do you need to address situations like these?

★ Ms. Heward spends time teaching her students in American Sign Language. She begins by having students run quickly through the alphabet, then asks them as a group to suggest some common phrases to review. After, individual students create sentences for the class to guess.

1. Why do teachers like Ms. Heward teach this type of lesson?

2. What makes this a successful activity to teach students about individual differences?

3. How does this lesson help create an inclusive classroom that supports acceptance of individual differences and friendships?

4. What other activities could Ms. Heward use to teach her students about individual differences?

myeducationlab Watch one of Ms. Heward's lessons by visiting the MyEducationLab for this course. Go to the *Assignments and Activities* section under the topic *Hearing Loss and Deafness* and complete the activity entitled *Use of American Sign Language as an Inclusive Practice* to answer questions about why it is important to teach about individual differences in inclusive classrooms.

Involve Family Members

Family members can work with you to support budding friendships, develop friendship goals and plans, and problem-solve ways to facilitate friendships (Boutot, 2006). Family members can create interactions outside school (e.g., encourage their children to invite friends home or to attend a community event with the family), get to know other families with children, encourage and assist their children and others in attending extracurricular and community-based activities activities (e.g., learn about after-school and community activities and provide transportation), and volunteer to lead or attend these activities. They also can make their home a safe, accessible, and enjoyable place for *all* to gather, and supervise peer interactions when appropriate and necessary. To help family members do these things, you can offer them information and resources, and suggest games and activities that promote friendships among children.

Making Connections
This discussion of the roles of families in fostering friendships builds on the family involvement issues we discussed in Chapter 4.

Summary

This chapter offered many strategies for teaching students to accept individual differences and develop friendships. As you review the chapter, consider the following questions and remember the following points.

How Can I Assess Attitudes Toward Individual Differences?
CEC 2, 3, 5, 8, 9; PRAXIS 3; INTASC 2, 5, 8, 9
You can assess attitudes toward individual differences by using attitude change assessment instruments, knowledge of individual differences probes, observations, sociograms, and student drawings.

How Can I Teach Acceptance of Individual Differences Related to Disability?
CEC 2, 3, 5, 9; PRAXIS 3; INTASC 2, 3, 5, 9, 10
You can teach students about individual differences by reflecting on and modeling desired attitudes, language, and behaviors, addressing issues of fairness without sameness, and using simulations. You can also have your students study about disabilities and the lives of individuals with disabilities; invite guest speakers; and use films, videos, literature, and curriculum guides and teaching materials about disabilities. Other methods include teaching about assistive devices and using technology.

How Can I Teach Acceptance of Individual Differences Related to Culture, Language, Gender, Religion, and Socioeconomic Status?
CEC 1, 2, 3, 5, 6, 7, 9; PRAXIS 3; INTASC 2, 3, 5, 6, 9, 10
You can reflect on your knowledge, experiences, and beliefs related to diversity, and integrate (into your curriculum and classroom learning) activities and materials that promote acceptance of cultural, linguistic, and religious diversity and gender equity. These activities and materials can also be used to teach students about global perspectives, family differences, homelessness, the migrant lifestyle, AIDS, stereotyping and discrimination, media and visual literacy, and to help you and your students respond to acts of insensitivity and intolerance.

How Can I Facilitate Friendships Among My Students?
CEC 2, 3, 5, 9; PRAXIS 3; INTASC 2, 3, 5, 9, 10
You can facilitate friendships among students by engaging in professional behaviors that support friendships, teaching about friendships, teaching social skills, using activities that develop social skills and encourage communication among students, using circles of friends, creating a friendly classroom environment, and using peer-based strategies. Other methods include encouraging students to participate in extracurricular and community-based activities, and involving families.

NICK

Nick is about to be placed full-time in general education classes. Nick's special education teacher, Ms. Thomas, collaborates with Nick's new teachers to plan a program to help Nick make a successful transition. She shares information about Nick with them. They also discuss and compare the essential components that students need to succeed in their respective classrooms. Based on these similarities and differences, they identify skills and information that Nick will need to make a smooth adjustment to these classes.

Although Nick will not enter these classes for several weeks, the teachers agree that they should begin the transition program immediately. Ms. Thomas introduces Nick to the textbooks, note taking, technology, and assignments he will encounter in his new classes, and she teaches him some learning strategies that can help him succeed with these materials and tasks. She also begins to give Nick homework assignments and tests that parallel those given by his new teachers.

Nick also visits his new classes, and Ms. Thomas makes videos of parts of several class sessions. She reviews these visits and videos with him to discuss classroom procedures and other critical elements of the classroom environment. In addition to introducing Nick to the routines and expectations of these classrooms, Ms. Thomas uses the video to encourage Nick to discuss any questions and concerns he has about the new settings.

Ms. Thomas also uses the video to teach Nick appropriate note-taking skills. At first, they watch a video of a classmate taking notes while Ms. Thomas shows how to take notes. To make sure Nick understands the different note-taking techniques and when to apply them, Ms. Thomas stops the video and reviews with Nick when certain information is or is not

Creating Successful Transitions to Inclusive Settings

recorded and why a specific format is used. Next, Ms. Thomas and Nick review video of Nick taking notes during class.

Upon entering his new classes, Nick's teachers meet with him to discuss his transition. They ask Nick to discuss how things are going for him and what they can do to assist him. They also share their feelings about Nick's progress and make suggestions that can help him. They agree that Ms. Thomas should work with Nick more on his note-taking and organizational skills. To help him improve his note-taking skills, she also taught him to use the learning strategy, *CALL UP* (Czarnecki, Rosko, & Fine, 1998, p. 14), which involves the following steps:

Copy from board.

Add details.

Listen and write the question.

Listen and write the answer.

Utilize the text.

Put it in your own words.

Ms. Thomas and Nick also used *Kidtools* to access a range of online organizational resources for students and teachers.

What other factors should you consider when planning a transitional program to prepare students such as Nick for success in a general education classroom? What other transitions do students make? How can you help them make these transitions? After reading this chapter, you should have the knowledge, skills, and dispositions to answer these as well as the following questions:

- How can I help students make the transition to general education classrooms?

- How can I help students make the transitions to new schools?
- How can I help students from culturally and linguistically diverse backgrounds make the transition to inclusive settings?
- How can I help students make the transition from school to adulthood?
- How can I help students develop self-determination?

Throughout their lives, *all students* make many beginnings and transitions. Placement in inclusive settings involves beginnings and transitions for students like Nick (Turnbull et al., 2010). Moving from one setting to another, students must learn to adjust to different curriculum demands, teaching styles, behavioral expectations, classroom designs, and student socialization patterns (Roberts, Keane, & Clark, 2008). Students moving from preschool to kindergarten, elementary to middle and high school settings, a special day school to a new school, or leaving school to search for work or to enter a postsecondary program, will encounter new expectations, rules, choices, extracurricular activities, and personnel (Downing, 2008).

Ultimately, as all of your students graduate from school, you want to help them transition to lives that offer them these positive features:

- Accessibility: They can get to where they want to go.
- Accommodation: They can do what they want to do.
- Resource availability: They can access the resources they need to succeed.
- Social support: They are accepted by others.
- Equality: They are treated with respect and equally with others (Smith et al., 2009).

To foster these positive outcomes for students, it is essential for you to work collaboratively with other professionals, family members, and students help prepare students to function independently and for the many transitions they face (Flexer, Baer, Luft, & Simmons, 2008; Sitlington, Neubert, & Clark, 2010). It is also crucial to view transition as an ongoing process to teach students the skills that will help them succeed in inclusive classrooms and society. This chapter offers a variety of strategies for helping students make the transition to inclusive settings. These strategies are appropriate for students with disabilities, but they also can be used to help *all students* function in inclusive settings and make transitions to new school environments.

TRANSITIONING TO GENERAL EDUCATION CLASSROOMS

HOW CAN I HELP STUDENTS MAKE THE TRANSITION TO GENERAL EDUCATION CLASSROOMS? Some of your students may be transitioning to your inclusive classroom from special education classrooms or other schools. You foster their transition by understanding their unique abilities and challenges, using transenvironmental programming, identifying and teaching essential classroom procedures and behaviors and learning strategies, and helping students to apply their learning in different classroom environment.

Understand Students' Unique Abilities and Challenges

As Ms. Thomas did in the chapter-opening vignette, general education teachers can be given information about students before they are placed in inclusive settings (Downing, 2008). Families and the students' current teachers can create a folder or technology-based profile containing text, video and audio files, and photos that present students' strengths, challenges, ability levels, social and behavioral skills, preferences, interests, as well as successful instructional strategies and background information to guide the team in developing a program that will help students make the transition to inclusive settings (Thompson, Meadan, Fansler, Alber, & Balogh, 2007). For example, McKinley and Stormont (2008) developed a schools support checklist that helps teachers identify and provide successful strategies for teaching students with disabilities in inclusive settings. Figure 6.1 presents questions that can guide the information-sharing process.

Additional information regarding students can supplement the information-sharing process. For students with sensory disabilities, their general education teachers can receive information on the nature of the sensory loss, as well as the amount of residual hearing or vision. For deaf and hard of hearing students and those with significant cognitive disabilities, teachers also can be informed of the students' communication abilities and the ways in which they communicate. For students who are English language learners, teachers should be apprised of their language abilities and the best approaches for helping them learn English. Finally, for students with special physical and health needs, teachers need information about health and medical issues and concerns, assistive devices, social skill development, and teaching and physical design accommodations.

Use Transenvironmental Programming

A four-step **transenvironmental programming** model can serve as a framework for developing a program to prepare students for success in inclusive settings. The four steps in the model are (a) environmental assessment, (b) intervention and preparation, (c) generalization to the new setting, and (d) evaluation in the new

FIGURE 6.1 Sample information-sharing questions

What are the student's academic strengths? Academic challenges?

What instructional approaches, arrangements, and materials have been effective with the student? Which have not been effective?

What adaptive devices and technology does the student require?

What instructional and testing accommodations does the student require?

What type and amount of adult and peer support does the student need?

What factors and variables motivate the student?

What instructional activities are appropriate for use with the student?

What cultural factors should be considered in designing an educational program for the student? For involving the family in the educational program?

What language(s) does the student speak? What language(s) does the family speak?

What social and behavioral skills does the student possess and need to develop?

What are the student's hobbies and interests?

Who are the student's friends?

In what school clubs or extracurricular activities does/could the student participate?

How does the student get along with her or his peers?

How does the student feel about her or his disability?

What school personnel and community agencies will be working with the student? What services will they provide?

To what extent will the student's family be involved in the planning process?

What communication system will be used to communicate between professionals? With family members?

What are the student's medical and medication needs?

Has the student been prepared to enter the inclusive setting?

What are the student's educational, social, cultural, linguistic, medical, and physical strengths and challenges?

What classroom management strategies and classroom design adaptations have been successful?

What alternative assessment strategies and procedures have been used with the student?

What school-based supportive and community-based services have been used with the student? What are the outcomes of these services?

TABLE 6.1 Sample transenvironmental programming model

General Education Class	Special Education Class
Ms. G. uses textbooks, computers, and other instructional technology.	Mr. K. can teach the student to use textbooks, computers, and other instructional technology.
Students interact with each other during recess.	Mr. K. can teach the student to initiate and engage in play with others.
Ms. G. expects students to raise their hands before speaking.	Mr. K. can teach the student to follow the rules of the general education classroom.
Ms. G. gives an hour of homework three times per week.	Mr. K. can give the student an hour of homework three times per week.
Ms. G. presents information through lectures and expects students to take notes.	Mr. K. can teach the student listening and note-taking skills.

REFLECTIVE

Think about your transition to college. What challenges did you experience? How did you address them? Who helped you with the transition?

Teachers can help students transition to inclusive settings by teaching them about their surroundings. What aspect of your classroom and school would help students transition to their new surroundings?

environment. A sample transenvironmental programming model for a student is presented in Table 6.1.

Environmental Assessment The content and goals of the transitional program are developed from an **environmental assessment**. This assessment involves analyzing the critical features of the new learning environment and the key skills that affect student performance (see Figure 6.2) and interviewing teachers and students (Lane, Wehby, & Cooley, 2006). In addition, you can assess other features of the general education program, such as routines in the cafeteria and at assemblies; movement between classes; and expectations in physical education, art, and music classes. After information on the inclusive settings is collected, you and your colleagues can meet to analyze the differences between the two settings, identify areas where teaching will be needed to help students succeed in the inclusive setting, and plan strategies to address these areas. In planning the transitional program, you also may need to determine the order in which skills will be taught, as well as which skills will be taught before and after students have been placed in inclusive settings.

Some schools include a classmate on the placement team to help identify the content of the transitional program. The student can provide input in such areas as books and materials needed, social interaction patterns, class routines, and student dress. Peers also can help welcome and orient students to their new environment and teach them about classroom- and school-related routines.

Intervention and Preparation In the intervention and preparation phase of the transenvironmental model, a variety of teaching strategies are used to prepare students to succeed in the new learning environment.

Teach Classroom and School Procedures and Successful Behaviors. As students move to inclusive classrooms or make the transition from elementary to secondary educational settings, they need to be taught the procedures, stated rules, and routines

FIGURE 6.2 Sample environmental assessment form

Teacher: **Subject:**

Grade: **Date:**   **Teacher Completing the Observation:**

A. TEACHING MATERIALS AND SUPPORT PERSONNEL
1. What textbooks and teaching materials are used in the class? How difficult are these texts and teaching materials?
2. What supplementary materials are used in the class? How difficult are these materials? What are their unique features?
3. What types of media and technology are often used in the classroom?
4. What type(s) of support personnel are available in the classroom? How often are they available?
5. What teaching accommodations does the teacher employ?

B. PRESENTATION OF SUBJECT MATTER
1. How does the teacher present information to students (e.g., lecture, small groups, cooperative learning groups, learning centers)?
2. What is the language and vocabulary level used by the teacher?

C. LEARNER RESPONSE VARIABLES
1. How do students respond in the class (e.g., take notes, read aloud, participate in class, copy from the board)?
2. In what ways can a student request help in the classroom?
3. How are directions given to students? How many directions are given at one time?

D. STUDENT EVALUATION
1. How often and in what ways does the teacher evaluate student progress?
2. How are grades determined?
3. What types of tests are given?
4. What test accommodations does the teacher use for students?
5. Does the teacher assign homework? (What type? How much? How often?)
6. Does the teacher assign special projects or extra-credit work? Please explain.

E. CLASSROOM MANAGEMENT
1. What is the teacher's management system?
2. What are the stated rules in the classroom?
3. What are the unstated rules in the classroom?
4. What are the consequences of following the rules? What are the consequences of not following the rules?
5. In what ways and how often does the teacher reinforce the students?
6. Does the teacher follow any special routines? What are they?

F. SOCIAL INTERACTIONS
1. How would you describe the social interactions inside and outside the classroom (e.g., individualistic, cooperative, competitive)?
2. What are the student norms in this class concerning dress, appearance, and interests?
3. What are the students' attitudes toward individual differences?
4. What is the language and vocabulary level of the students?
5. In what locations and ways do students interact in the classroom and the school?
6. What strategies does the teacher employ to promote friendships among students?
7. What personality variables does the teacher exhibit that seem to affect the class?

G. PHYSICAL DESIGN
1. What, if any, architectural barriers exist in the classroom?
2. How does the classroom's design affect the students' academic performance and social interactions?

Source: Adapted from "Preparing Secondary Students for the Mainstream," by S. J. Salend and D. Viglianti, 1982, *Teaching Exceptional Children, 14*, pp. 138–139. Copyright 1982 by The Council for Exceptional Children. Reprinted by permission.

REFLECTIVE

What skills make up the hidden curriculum in schools? In your inclusive classroom?

of the new setting (Carter et al., 2005; Roberts, Keane, et al., 2008). In addition, students, particularly those from culturally diverse backgrounds and those with social and behavioral skills challenges, should be introduced to and explicitly taught the **hidden curriculum**, the unstated culturally based social skills and rules that are essential to successful functioning in classrooms, schools, and social situations (Myles, 2008). You can explicitly teach these stated and unstated skills using the guidelines presented in the UDL and You feature in this chapter.

Students can be introduced to several aspects of the new classroom setting, such as the teacher's style, class rules, class jobs, and special events, as well as schoolwide routines such as lunch count, changing classes, using combination locks, homework, attendance, and the like. The class schedule can be reviewed, and necessary materials and supplies for specific classes can be identified. You can explain procedures for storing materials; using learning centers, technology, materials, and other equipment; working on seat work activities and in small groups; getting help; handing in completed assignments; seeking permission to leave the room; and making transitions to activities and classes. You can also tour the classroom to show students the design of the room and the layout of the school, the behaviors that they will need to succeed, and the location of teaching materials. Once new students move into inclusive classrooms, classmates can be peer mentors to assist them in learning about the class and school routines.

Use Preteaching. **Preteaching** can be used to prepare students like Nick for the academic, behavioral, and social expectations of the inclusive setting (LaCava, 2005; Roberts, Keane, et al., 2008). In preteaching, the special educator uses the curriculum, teaching style, and instructional format of the teacher in the general education classroom. For example, Ms. Thomas used preteaching to introduce Nick to the textbooks, note-taking requirements, assignments, homework, and tests he will encounter in his new classes.

Teach Students to Take on Independent Assignments. Because students also have to complete many assignments on their own, you can teach them to work on them independently. Using a *job* or *travel card*, students interact with their teacher(s) to determine what the assignment is, what directions they should follow for completing it, what materials they need to do the assignment, the best ways to obtain the materials, where to complete the assignment, the amount of time needed to finish it, and the procedures for handing in their work and finishing assignments early (Cahill, 2008; Griffin et al., 2006). Students also can learn to use TRICK BAG, a learning strategy to assist them in remembering assignments and organizing their materials (Scott & Compton, 2007).

Develop Students' Organizational Skills. You also can encourage students to work independently by helping them develop their organizational skills (Anderson, Munk, Young, Conley, & Caldarella, 2008; Finstein, Yao Yang, & Jones, 2006). Following are several strategies that can help students become more organized.

- *Assignment notebooks:* In many general education classrooms, students take notes and record information in their notebooks according to the specifications of their teacher(s). Students can be taught to color code their notebooks by content area, listing assignments in the notebook including page numbers, dates when the assignments are due, and relevant information needed to complete the task (Cahill, 2008; Joseph & Konrad, 2009). Periodically check students' notebooks for neatness, organization, completeness, and currency, and remind them to use the notebooks for important assignments, projects, and tests. You also can have students

An important transitional skill for success in inclusive settings is the ability to work independently. How do you help your students learn to work independently?

UDL and YOU

Explicitly Teaching Students to Use Learning Strategies

As Ms. Thomas did with Nick, you can incorporate the principles of UDL to help your students succeed in inclusive settings by teaching them to use a range of learning strategies (Strichart & Mangrum, 2010). **Learning strategies** are techniques that teach students how to learn, behave, and succeed in academic and social situations (Graham & Harris, 2009; Schumaker & Deshler, 2009). Learning strategy instruction teaches students ways to effectively and efficiently organize, remember and retrieve important content, solve problems, and complete tasks independently (Lenz, 2006; Meltzer, Katzir, Miller, Reddy, & Roditi, 2004). In determining whether a specific learning strategy should be taught, address the following questions:

- Is the strategy critical for success in inclusive settings?
- Is the strategy required in many settings?
- Is the strategy age-appropriate?
- Does the student have the prerequisite skills to learn and apply the strategy?
- Does the strategy enable the student to solve problems independently?

Once you identify appropriate learning strategies, you can use the following steps to explicitly teach your students to use in a variety of settings.

1. Select a strategy that is appropriate for the tasks or the setting and that will improve students' performance.
2. Allow students to perform a task to determine what strategy they now use and how effectively they use it.
3. Help students understand the problems caused by their current strategy, and get them interested in learning the new strategy.
4. Explain and describe the new strategy, its application, and its advantages compared with those of the old strategy.
5. Obtain a commitment from students to learn the new strategy.
6. Describe and model the new strategy for students, including a description of each step as you demonstrate it.
7. Teach students to rehearse the strategy verbally.
8. Give students opportunities to practice the strategy with materials written at their level and then with materials used in the general education classroom.
9. Develop an understanding of when to use the strategy.
10. Offer feedback on the students' use of the strategy.
11. Assess students' mastery of the strategy.
12. Develop systems to help students remember the steps of the strategy, such as self-monitoring checklists.
13. Collect data on the effectiveness of the strategy and help students understand the connection between the strategy and their school success (Holzer, Madaus, Bray, & Kehle, 2009; Lenz, 2006; Meadan & Mason, 2007; Rogevich & Perin, 2009; Scott & Compton, 2007).

Once students learn the strategy, it is important for you to promote independent use and generalization of the strategy so that students know when and where to use a strategy across many different situations and settings (Hart & Whalon, 2008). Visually, you can prompt students to use the strategy by using graphic organizers and checklists, posting it in your classroom, or giving students strategy cue cards with pictorial demonstrations of the steps in the strategy (Joseph & Konrad, 2009; Meadan & Mason, 2007). You also can verbally prompt students to use the strategy by asking them to use it, and encourage your students to verbalize the steps they are taking in performing a task. Collaborate with others so that they are aware of the strategy, and model, prompt, and reinforce its use across subject areas to help students apply the strategy in different settings (Fenty et al., 2008).

A variety of learning strategies for helping students succeed in elementary and secondary inclusive setting are possible (Allsopp, Minskoff, & Bolt, 2005; Babkie & Provost, 2002; Combes, Walker, Esprivalo Harrell, & Tyler-Wood, 2008; Dieker & Little, 2005; Graham & Harris, 2009; Lenz, 2006; Lenz et al., 2004; Schumaker & Deshler, 2009; Schumaker et al., 2006; Scott & Compton, 2007; Strichart & Mangrum, 2010). In later chapters, we will discuss other learning strategies that students can be taught as part of your efforts to differentiate instruction to promote their learning abilities and mastery of particular types of material.

You and your colleagues also can design learning strategies for students (Keller, Bucholz, & Brady, 2007). First, identify the learning outcome and sequence the key parts of the task or process. To make it easier for students to remember and use the strategy, try to limit the number of steps to no more than seven. Each step should be briefly stated and should begin with a verb. Next, find an action word or a synonym relating to each part of the task or process that will trigger a memory of that part. The words are then used to create a mnemonic that will help students remember the steps, such as an acronym using the first letter of each word. STRATEGY and CREATE and are mnemonic learning strategies that can help you develop mnemonic learning strategies for use by your students (Heaton & O'Shea, 1995; Keller et al., 2007). As students develop skill in using learning strategies, they can be taught to develop their own learning strategies.

Teaching Students to Use Learning Strategies

Ms. Washington, one of Nick's general education teachers, has noticed that several of her students including Nick are not prepared for class physically and mentally. She observes the students closely for several days to determine which skills and strategies they use successfully and which ones they seem to lack. She then meets with the students to talk about her concerns and how their current approaches are affecting their performance. Though initially reluctant, the students indicate that they aren't pleased with their classroom performance and would like to do better. She discusses a learning strategy called PREP and explains how it might help them. PREP involves four stages:

Prepare materials

- Get the notebook, study guide, pencil, and textbook ready for class.
- Mark difficult-to-understand parts of notes, the study guide, and textbook.

Review what you know

- Read notes, study guide, and textbook cues.
- Relate cues to what you already know about the topic.
- List at least three things you already know about the topic.

Establish a positive mind-set

- Tell yourself to learn.
- Suppress put-downs.
- Make a positive statement.

Pinpoint goals

- Decide what you want to find out.
- Note participation goals. (Ellis, 1989, p. 36)

After reviewing the strategy and briefly explaining each step, Ms. Washington asks the students to decide whether they are willing to make a commitment to learning this strategy. One student says, "No," and Ms. Washington tells her that she does not have to learn it, but if she changes her mind, she can learn it at another time. Nick and the other students indicate that they are willing to try to learn the strategy. To increase their motivation and reinforce their commitment, Ms. Washington has the students set goals.

Ms. Washington begins by modeling and demonstrating the strategy by verbalizing and "thinking out loud" so that students can experience the thinking processes they will need when using the strategy. She models the procedure several times, using a variety of materials from the class, and reviews how she uses the PREP acronym to remember the steps in the strategy. Students discuss how the PREP strategy compares with their current approaches to learning, as well as the overt and covert behaviors necessary to implement the strategy.

Next, Ms. Washington has the students attempt to learn the steps of the strategy. She divides them into teams and has each team rehearse and memorize the strategy and its proper sequence. To help some students learn the strategy, she gives them cue cards. As students memorize the steps, Ms. Washington gives them cue cards containing less information. When the students can give the steps in the correct sequence, she has them apply the strategy with materials from the classroom. Students work in cooperative learning groups to practice the strategy and receive feedback from their peers. Ms. Washington circulates around the room, observes students using the strategy, and provides feedback. She encourages the students to concentrate on becoming skilled in using the strategy and not to be concerned about the accuracy of the content. As students become adept in using the strategy, Ms. Washington gives them other materials so that they can apply the strategy in many different situations. When students are able to do this, she gives them a test to check their mastery of the material.

Once students master the strategy, Ms. Washington encourages them to use it in her class. She observes them to see whether they are employing the strategy and keeps records of their academic performance. Periodically, Ms. Washington reviews the strategy procedures. She cues students to use the strategy through verbal reminders, cue cards, listing the strategy on the board, and reviewing its components. Because the strategy has greatly improved the students' performance, Ms. Washington is working with some of the other teachers to help students use it in their classrooms.

- Why did Ms. Washington decide to teach her students to use learning strategies?
- What methods did she use to teach her students to use learning strategies?
- What did Ms. Washington do to involve her students in mastering learning strategies?
- What did she do to help her students use the learning strategies in her class and in their other classes?
- How would you teach your students to use learning strategies?

use a homework buddy, a peer who can be contacted for missed assignments and further clarification. To help prevent the loss of notebooks, encourage students to use folders to carry assignments and other relevant materials and information. Finally, remind students to put their names in all textbooks and cover them.

- *Assignment logs:* Your students can be taught to use an assignment log to keep track of assignments (Anderson et al., 2008; Cahill, 2008). The log can consist of two pocket folders with built-in space to store assignment sheets that contain the name of the assignment, a description of it, the dates the assignment was given and is due, and a place for a family member's signature. When assignments are given, students complete the information on the assignment sheet and place the sheet in the pocket folder labeled "To Be Completed." When the assignment is completed, the assignment sheet is updated (signed by a family member) and put in the "Completed Work" pocket folder. A sample assignment log is presented in Figure 6.3.
- *Sticky notes and highlighters:* Teach your students to use sticky notes and highlighters to record and highlight directions, mark where they left off on an assignment, remind them of important steps in a sequence, and remember important events in the day (Stormont, 2008). They also can use sticky notes to list the assignments given and to check off those completed.

Help Students Develop Daily and Weekly Schedules. A transitional program also can help students learn how to manage their time and keep track of the many activities that occur in inclusive settings (Carter et al., 2005). Students can become more productive by developing a schedule charting their daily activities, including the time of day and the activity that should and did occur during that time period. At the beginning, you can help students plan their schedules. Later on, as they develop skill in planning and following their schedules, they can plan their own schedules and record the obstacles they encounter in following them. In developing their schedules, students can be taught to do the following:

- Identify specific goals to be accomplished.
- Consider and allot time for all types of activities, including studying, social activities, relaxation, and personal responsibilities.
- Consider the times of the day at which they are most alert and least likely to be interrupted.
- Avoid studying material from one class for long periods of time.
- Divide study time into several short periods rather than one long period.

REFLECTIVE

What learning strategies do you use? Are they successful? How did you learn them? What other learning strategies might be helpful to you?

FIGURE 6.3 Sample assignment log

Date	Date Due	Class/ Subject	Materials and Technology Needed	Assignment	Date Completed

- Be aware of their attention span when planning study periods.
- Arrange school tasks based on due dates, importance of tasks, and time demands.
- Group similar tasks together.
- Schedule time for relaxation.
- Reward studying by planning other activities (Salend, 2009).

A sample weekly planning schedule is presented in Figure 6.4.

Generalization   Once a transitional skill has been learned in one setting, you can take steps to promote **generalization**, the transfer of training to the inclusive setting (McIntosh & MacKay, 2008). In planning for generalization, you should consider the student's abilities, as well as the nature of the general education classroom, including academic and social content, activities, and teaching style. Because transfer of training to other settings does not occur spontaneously, you should have a systematic plan to promote it (Bellini, Peters, Benner, & Hopf, 2007; Shaw, 2008).

You can use a variety of strategies to plan for generalization (Konrad & Test, 2007; McIntosh & MacKay, 2008), offering many adult and peer models so that students see how the skill or strategy is used appropriately in many different settings and conditions. Generalization also can be fostered by providing them with multiple opportunities to perform under the varied conditions and expectations they will encounter in different settings. This can be done by giving students the opportunity to experience various aspects of the inclusive classroom, involving others who work with students, and providing them with immediate and specific feedback regarding their performance. You also can provide students with incentives by collaborating with them to prepare a contract that outlines the skills they

IDEAs to Implement Inclusion

Teaching Organizational Skills

Josh is having a tough time adjusting to high school. When he does an assignment, he usually receives a good grade. However, far too often, his notebook is messy and incomplete, and he forgets to do his assignments and to study for tests. In addition to his classes, Josh participates in extracurricular activities and occasionally works at a local restaurant.

His family and teachers, frustrated by his erratic performance, decide that a weekly schedule will help Josh organize his activities and complete his schoolwork. At first, each Monday, Josh meets with one of his teachers, Ms. Gates, to plan his schedule. They divide each day into hourly time slots, list class assignments and tests, and outline after-school and home activities as well as job-related commitments. They then determine which activities have specific time commitments and record them in the schedule. Next, they list Josh's weekly assignments and due dates and estimate the amount of time needed to complete them. Josh and Ms. Gates then establish priorities and enter the items in the schedule. Finally, they review the schedule to ensure that all activities have been given sufficient time and that there is a balance among activities. Throughout the week, Ms. Gates checks Josh's progress in following the schedule. As Josh masters the steps in planning and implementing his schedule, Ms. Gates encourages him to develop his own schedule and monitor his own performance.

Here are some other strategies you can use to implement the IDEA in your inclusive classroom and help students develop their organizational skills:

- Teach students to use calendars on which they list their homework, exams, long-term assignments, and classroom and school activities.
- Use class time to review schedules, notebooks, folders, and desks to reorganize them and throw out unnecessary materials.
- Give students space and materials in which to store items such as cartons or desk organizers.
- Teach students to use sticky pads to record self-reminders.
- Mark a notebook page that is 20 pages from the last sheet to remind students to purchase a new notebook.
- Conduct a scavenger hunt using students' desks and lockers that causes students to clean these areas up.

Sources: Anderson et al. (2008); Cahill (2008); Finstein et al. (2006); Stormont (2008).

FIGURE 6.4 Sample weekly planning schedule

Tasks for week of _____ (date)   **Student name _____**

Schoolwork	Day to do by	Time required
Essay	Thursday	3 hours
Homework	Tuesday & Friday	2 hours
Math quiz prep	Quiz Wednesday	1 hour
Plan for next week	Monday	15 min.

Chores

Clean room	Saturday	3 hours
Trash out	Friday evening	10 min

Work

Baby-sit	Wednesday & Saturday	7 hours

	Monday	Tuesday	Wednesday	Thursday	Friday	Saturday	Sunday
Schedule:							
	7:30 a.m. bus	7:30 a.m. bus	7:30 a.m. bus	7:30 a.m. bus	7:30 a.m. bus	9:00 a.m. breakfast	9:00 a.m. 9:15 Plan
	8–2:30 school	8–2:30 school	8–2:30 school	8–2:30 school	8–2:30 school		
	3:00–4:00 Social studies and math homework	3:00–4:00 Work on essay	4:00–5:00 Finalize essay	3:00–4 Science and English homework	3:00–3:10 Take out the trash	10:00–12:00 Finish cleaning room	
	4:00–5:00 Work on essay	4:00–5:00 Study for math quiz	7:00–9:00 p.m. Baby-sit		3:30–4:30 Clean room	4:00–9:00 p.m. Baby-sit	
Tasks:							
	Homework: 1 hour	Essay:1 hour	Essay:1 hour	Homework: 1 hour	Trash:10 min	Clean room: 2 hours	Family/me time
	Essay:1 hour	Study for math quiz:1 hour	Work:2 hours		Start on Cleaning room:1 hour	Work:5 hours	Fill out planning table for next week:15 min.
Notes:		Call Stan for help with #6 on the practice quiz			Bring home list of next week's assignments		

Source: Shields and Heron (1989).

must demonstrate in order to receive specific student identified rewards. Students also can be encouraged to self-monitor and maintain a journal to reflect on their own performance and to assume greater control over their learning (Joseph & Konrad, 2009). You also can teach for generalization by using several strategies to prepare students for the demands of the general education classroom, including changing the

- types, amount, and frequency of reinforcement;
- directions and examples you give to students and the supports and cues you use to help students understand and follow them;
- resources, technologies and materials and response modes used by students to complete learning activities;

Making Connections
Find out more about using contracting and self-monitoring with your students in Chapter 7.

Promoting Generalization

Diana is having difficulty in her science and social studies classes, which present information through textbooks. Her social studies, science, and resource room teachers meet to discuss Diana's performance and agree that she would benefit from learning SQ3R, a text comprehension strategy. Her resource room teacher introduces the strategy and helps her learn it in that setting. However, her other teachers notice that Diana often fails to apply the strategy in their classrooms. To help her do so, they give her the following self-monitoring checklist, which presents the skills Diana should demonstrate when using the strategy in social studies and science:

Steps	Yes	No
1. Did I survey the chapter?		
a. Headings and titles		
b. First paragraph		
c. Visual aids		
d. Summary paragraphs		
2. Did I ask questions?		
3. Did I read the selection?		
4. Did I recite the main points?		
5. Did I produce a summary of the main points?		

Diana's use of the strategy increases, and her performance in science and social studies improves. Here are some other strategies you can use to implement the IDEA in your inclusive classroom and promote generalization:

- Discuss with students other settings in which they could use the strategies and skills.
- Provide examples and nonexamples of behaviors and skills as well as the settings and conditions associated with using the strategies and skills.
- Work with students to identify similarities and differences among settings.
- Practice and role-play the use of the strategies and skills in multiple situations.
- Ask other teachers to help and prompt students to use the strategies and skills.
- Help students see the link between the strategies and skills and improved performance.

Sources: Combes et al. (2008); Fenty et al. (2008); Hart and Whalon (2008); McIntosh and MacKay (2008).

- groupings and locations in which students work; and
- teachers and peers with whom students work (Hart & Whalon, 2008; Vaughn, Bos, & Lund, 1986; Shaw, 2008)

TRANSITIONING TO NEW SCHOOLS

HOW CAN I HELP STUDENTS MAKE THE TRANSITION TO NEW SCHOOLS?
Students moving to new schools and from special day schools and between schooling levels (transitions to elementary, middle, and high school settings) or returning to their schools after an injury or hospitalization also need transitional programs to prepare them for success in their new educational settings (Arroyos-Jurado & Savage, 2008; Downing, 2008). Such a transitional program can introduce students to the new school's personnel and describe their roles; to the school's physical design, including the location of the cafeteria, gymnasium, and auditorium; and to important rules, procedures, locations (e.g., classrooms, lockers, elevators, bathrooms, etc.), and extracurricular activities (Spencer, 2005). You can orient students to the new setting by giving them a tour of the school that introduces them to key areas and suggested routes, assigning a reliable student to help the new students learn about your class and school, and color-coding students' schedules (Frasier, 2007).

Collaborate and Communicate with Professionals and Families

In planning and implementing a transitional program for these students, you need to collaborate with other professionals and with students' families to identify the transitional skills that will be taught, develop a transition time line, prepare students for the transition, determine effective instructional strategies and supports, collect data on students' performance, establish communication procedures, and evaluate the transition process (Arroyos-Jurado & Savage, 2008). Since ongoing communication once students attend their new school also is essential, you can provide them with feedback on the effectiveness of the transition plan, solicit their suggestions, and address their concerns and questions.

Adapt Transitional Models, and Foster Collaboration Across Schools

You can adapt models for helping students transition to schools and classes (Brandes, Ormsbee, & Haring, 2007; Carter et al., 2005; Downing, 2008; Frasier, 2007; Roberts, Keane, et al., 2008). The models involve the following elements:

1. *Deciding on placement:* At first, a team determines which community school is appropriate based on location, attitudes of school personnel, availability of services, and needs of the students. They identify key personnel in the sending and receiving schools and programs, and they gather and share information about the students who will be moving from one setting to another.

2. *Approximating the new environment:* Teachers in the sending school help students adjust to the new school by trying to duplicate the demands, conditions, and teaching methods of the new setting.

3. *Leveling of academic skills:* Students are prepared for the academic requirements of the new setting and start using the new school's textbooks, teaching materials, and assignments.

4. *Building skills in the new school:* Staff from the sending school meet with teachers, administrators, and support staff from the new school to discuss strategies that have been used successfully with the students. Educational goals are developed and shared with teachers at the new school. The support needs of students and their teachers at the new school are identified, and appropriate strategies are instituted.

5. *Visiting the school:* Students visit and tour the new school to get a picture of the important aspects of the school and its physical design.

6. *Starting with small units of time:* At first, students may attend the new school for a brief period to help them adjust gradually. As students become comfortable in the new school, the attendance period increases until the students spend the whole school day in the new setting.

7. *Accompanying and advocating for the student:* At first, a staff member from the sending school may accompany the students to the new school to serve as a resource for the students and the staff. At the same time, a staff member from the receiving school serves as an advocate to assist the students in the new setting.

8. *Promoting social acceptance and academic success:* Teachers in the new school promote the social acceptance of the new students by locating their work area near class leaders or assigning them an important class job. Teachers also teach peers about individual differences and friendships. In addition, they use appropriate teaching accommodations and monitor their effectiveness.

9. *Opening lines of communication:* Ongoing communication systems between personnel from the sending and receiving schools and between the receiving school and the home are established.

10. *Scheduling follow-up:* As part of the communication system, follow-up meetings are held to discuss the students' progress and to resolve conflicts.

Brandes et al. (2007) provides a form for planning and implementing transitions to early childhood programs; Carter et al. (2005), Frasier (2007), Lambert (2005), Mizelle (2005), and Spencer (2005) offer guidelines, strategies, and resources that you can use to help students transition to middle and high schools.

Offer Student and Family Orientations and Student Visiting, Shadowing, and Mentoring Programs

Transitions to new schools also can be fostered by offering student and family orientations and student visiting, shadowing, and mentoring programs. Student and family orientations can be scheduled at the new school to introduce students and their families to their new school including the available academic and supportive programs, student and extracurricular activities, policies and procedures, and the professionals and the services they provide. Orientations also can be scheduled at students' sending schools by having professionals and students from the new school speak to students about the new school.

In addition to visiting the school for a period of time, students also can learn about their new school by shadowing another student for a school day. Once students attend their new school, they can be assigned a student mentor for an extended period of time to assist them in making the transition to their new school.

TRANSITIONING STUDENTS FROM CULTURALLY AND LINGUISTICALLY DIVERSE BACKGROUNDS

HOW CAN I HELP STUDENTS FROM CULTURALLY AND LINGUISTICALLY DIVERSE BACKGROUNDS MAKE THE TRANSITION TO INCLUSIVE SETTINGS?
Many of the transitional strategies previously discussed are appropriate for students from linguistically and culturally diverse backgrounds. However, a transitional program for these students can also include teaching cultural norms, language, and socialization skills, as well as the terminology related to each content area (Rance-Roney, 2009). A good transitional program for these students also will help them master the hidden curriculum and the language skills necessary for academic learning, such as listening, reading, speaking, and writing (Brice et al., 2007). It will also teach students **pragmatics**, the functional and cultural aspects of language.

Teach Cultural Norms

A transitional program for students from diverse backgrounds can teach them the cultural norms and communication skills that guide social and academic classroom life. For example, although most teachers may expect students to raise their hands to ask for help, some students, because of their cultural backgrounds, may hesitate to seek assistance in that way because they are taught not to draw attention to themselves. A transitional program should also help make students aware of the culture of the school, including explicit and unstated skills, rules, routines, language, and customs (West et al., 2007). You can help students learn these different cultural behaviors by (a) respecting and understanding their cultural perspectives; (b) explaining to the students the new perspectives and the environmental conditions associated with them; (c) using modeling, role playing, prompting, and scripting to teach new behaviors; and (d) understanding that it may take some time for these students to develop competence in the new culture. You also can help students make the transition to your class and school by assigning them class jobs and leadership roles, giving them peer helpers, following classroom and instructional routines, and labeling objects in the classroom in their native language (Smith, 2009).

Orient Students to the School

Several activities help orient students to their new school. When students arrive, give them a list of common school vocabulary words and concepts. You also can pair these students with a peer (a bilingual one if necessary and available) who can serve as a host until they are acclimated. In addition, you can give students a tour of the school and photos labeled with the names of important locations and school personnel.

Teach Basic Interpersonal Communication and Social Skills

Many English language learners also need help in developing the *basic interpersonal communication skills (BICS)* needed to be successful in general education settings (Lopez Estrada, Gomez, & Ruiz-Escalante, 2009). BICS and other social skills can be taught using many strategies that give students valuable experiences. Some of these strategies, which you can use to teach social skills to *all students,* are described here. They are most effective when you use them in some combination, in natural settings, with pictorial prompts and feedback, and on a frequent basis (Angell et al., 2008; Fenty et al., 2008; Ganz, Kaylor, Bourgeois, & Hadden, 2008).

Modeling   Modeling allows students to view language and social interaction patterns. For example, students can observe peers in the inclusive classroom during a social interaction activity or view a video of such an activity. You can then review these observations with students, emphasizing language, behaviors, and cues that promote social interactions—specifically, strategies and language for beginning and maintaining social interactions. Like Nick and Ms. Thomas, you also can use video modeling and video self-modeling, where students view others or themselves successfully performing a series of behaviors (Mechling, Gast, & Gustafson, 2009; Taber-Doughty, Patton, & Brennan, 2008).

Role Playing   Students can develop BICS and social skills by role-playing social interaction situations (Kuhn et al., 2008). Where possible, the role play should take place in the environment in which the behavior is to be used. After the role play, you can give students feedback on their performance.

Prompting   Prompting helps *all students* learn relevant cues for using appropriate interpersonal skills. In prompting, students are taught to use the environment to learn new skills. For example, students and teachers can visit social settings (e.g., playground, cafeteria, etc.), identify stimuli, and discuss how these stimuli can be used to promote socialization.

Scripting   Because much of the dialogue in social conversation is predictable and often redundant, you can show students the language and structure of social interactions via scripts that present text of conversations that might occur in a specific setting (Ganz et al., 2008). For example, a typical conversation at lunchtime can be scripted to include questions and responses relating to the day's events ("How are you doing today?"), menus ("Are you buying lunch today?"), and school or class events ("Are you going to the game after school?"). You can enhance the effectiveness of scripting by pairing them with videos, icons, and photos depicting and prompting the language presented (Charlop, Gilmore, & Chang, 2008).

Teach Cognitive Academic Language Proficiency Skills

The strategies for teaching BICS also can be used to teach *cognitive academic language proficiency (CALP)*. CALP is taught by giving students techniques for understanding the important vocabulary and concepts that guide instruction in inclusive settings (Levine & McCloskey, 2009). You can help students learn them by preteaching them prior to using them in lessons and reading activities, and using concrete objects, visuals and gestures to introduce, explain and reinforce their meaning.

Making Connections
This discussion of teaching basic interpersonal communication and cognitive language proficiency builds on what we discussed in Chapter 3.

Making Connections
This discussion of these strategies for helping students develop the social skills that support friendships builds on what we discussed in Chapter 5.

Why is it important that a transitional program for students from linguistically and culturally diverse backgrounds helps students develop an awareness of routines, language, and customs?

Creating Successful Transitions to Inclusive Settings

Students can be encouraged to list words and concepts used in the classroom discussions, textbooks, and assignments in a word file for retrieval as needed. For quick retrieval, the file can be organized alphabetically or by content area. As students master specific terms, those terms can be deleted or moved to an inactive section of the file. Students can also keep a record of key words and concepts by using the *divided page* method. Students divide a page into three columns. In column 1, they list the term, phrase, or concept. The context in which it is used is given in column 2, and the word is defined briefly in column 3. Students can then keep a separate list for each new chapter or by subject area. These methods of listing difficult terms can be adapted for students who are learning English by recording information in their dominant language. For example, the primary language equivalent of words and phrases can be included in a word list or as separate sections of the divided page.

You also can post in your classroom a glossary of content-area terms that are important for students to know in order to learn (Palinscar, Magnusson, Cutter, & Vincent, 2002). The glossary should include technical vocabulary that is related to the topic your class is studying, synonyms and common terms for these vocabulary words, and examples of these terms.

Making Connections
Find out more about how you can differentiate your instruction for students from culturally and linguistically diverse backgrounds in Chapter 8.

Offer Newcomer Programs

To help immigrant students adjust, many school districts have developed **newcomer programs**, which offer students academic and support services to help them learn English and academic content, and make the transition to and succeed in inclusive classrooms and society. After spending time in a newcomer program, students transfer to bilingual/ESL or general education classrooms where they receive content area instruction using effective ESL strategies (Rance-Roney, 2009).

TRANSITIONING FROM SCHOOL TO ADULTHOOD

HOW CAN I HELP STUDENTS MAKE THE TRANSITION FROM SCHOOL TO ADULT-HOOD? Prior to graduation, your students may need your assistance in making the transition to adulthood (Flexer, Baer, Luft, & Simmons, 2008). You can help them make this transition by developing a Summary of Performance (SOP) and implementing an Individualized Transition Plan (ITP) that addresses the areas of employment, independent living arrangements, leisure, and postsecondary education (Sitlington et al., 2010). Successful transitions in these areas can enhance your students' **quality of life**—which refers to their feelings of well-being, social involvement, and opportunities to achieve their potential (Elhoweris et al., 2007)—and reduce the likelihood that they will leave school before graduating.

Develop a Summary of Performance, and Implement an Individualized Transition Plan

As students graduate or exceed the age for special education services, comprehensive planning teams need to develop a SOP that addresses students' academic achievement and functional performance and includes suggestions for achieving their postsecondary goals (Kochhar-Bryant & Shaw, 2009). Comprehensive teams also need to implement ITPs that contain the transition services to help them prepare for and make the transition from school to adult life (Inge & Moon, 2006; Mazzotti et al., 2009). *Transition services* are coordinated services and activities and the interagency agreements and linkages that foster the transition to postschool activities. Postschool activities include postsecondary education, vocational education, integrated employment, continuing and adult education, adult services, independent living, and community participation. The SOP and ITP also outline instructional activities and community experiences that help students develop the skills to obtain employment, live independently, and participate in postsecondary education.

In designing SOPs and ITPs, planning teams should use person-/student-centered planning processes that focus on the strengths, preferences, and cultural and gender-related perspectives of students and their families (Flexer et al., 2008; Trainor, 2008). For example, while the dominant culture places an emphasis on achieving independence, some cultures do not view independence from the family as a desirable goal of a transitional program. Students and their families should be actively involved in the process to create a plan aligning the transitional program to state and district learning standards, using problem- and community-based learning, and focusing on enhancing students' self-determination and quality of life (Ankey, Wilkins, & Spain, 2009; Sitlington et al., 2010). The process should include the following:

- An assessment of students' career goals and interests, strengths, dreams, independence, social skills, hobbies, interpersonal relations, self-determination, decision-making skills, self-advocacy, and communication levels
- An assessment of students' current and desired skill levels, interests, and challenges and their cultural and gender related perspectives and their families' viewpoints regarding making the transition to postsecondary education, employment, community participation, and/or adult living
- An identification of transition placements and programs that match assessment data
- An assessment of the new environment(s) to identify the physical, social, emotional, and cognitive skills necessary to perform effectively in the new setting
- A list of the related services, functional supports, accommodations, and assistive devices that can affect success in the new environment(s), as well as any potential barriers such as transportation problems
- A statement of and time lines for the goals and objectives of the transitional program, including those related to student empowerment, self-determination, self-advocacy, and decision-making skills
- A list of the academic, vocational, social, and adult living skills necessary to achieve the transition goals
- A list of teaching strategies, approaches, materials, technologies, accommodations, and experiences, as well as the supportive and community-based services and supports necessary to achieve the stated goals of the transitional program and link them to statewide learning standards
- A statement of each individual's and participating agency's role and responsibilities, including interagency collaborations
- A description of the communication systems that will be used to share information among professionals, among community agencies, and between school and family members
- A system for evaluating the success of the transition program on a regular basis (Flexer et al., 2008; Hogansen, Powers, Geenen, Gil-Kashiwabara, & Powers, 2008; Hendricks & Wehman, 2009; Mazzotti et al., 2009; Sitlington et al., 2010; Trainor, 2008).

A component of a sample transitional plan is presented in Figure 6.5. Transitional programming for students who are leaving school is designed to prepare them to participate actively in their communities and to become self-sufficient and independent. It also is designed to address the poor postschool outcomes that students with disabilities experience, including low participation in postsecondary education programs, low employment rates, and low satisfaction with their adult lives. Therefore, transitional programming often addresses four areas related to one's quality of life: employment, living arrangements, leisure, and postsecondary education.

PEARSON
myeducationlab

Go to the Assignments and Activities section of the Topic *Transition Planning* in the MyEducationLab for your course and complete the activity entitled *The Transition Plan Document* to learn more about developing the ITP.

FIGURE 6.5 Sample component of an ITP

INDIVIDUALIZED TRANSITION PLAN

Planning Meeting Date _____

Name of Student   Alan _____   Date of Birth   16 years old at time of meeting _____

Planning Team   Alan, Alan's mother, Mrs. Thomas (classroom teacher), Jeff R.

(job coach), Mr. Jones (school administrator) and John M. (paraprofessional)

Transition Options	Goal	School Representatives and Responsibilities	Parent/Family Responsibilities	Agencies Involved Responsibilities and Contact Person	Supportive IEP Goal(s)/Objective(s)

Vocational Placements
  Competitive
  Supportive
  Sheltered
  Specify the above or other
It is unclear whether Alan will be better able to perform in a competitive or supportive work environment 5 years from now, but both options are being explored.
Identify current and past vocational experiences.   Alan currently spends 2 hours each week working at a local nursery.
	X
	X
	___
	X
		1. Teacher will increase from 2 hrs. weekly to 5 hrs. weekly the time Alan spends working at the nursery.
		2. Job coach will expand the types of jobs Alan performs from maintenance tasks to more nursery trade related tasks.
		3. Job coach will introduce two additional vocational experiences for Alan each of the next 3 years so that Alan can, in his last 2 years of school, choose a vocational area of preference and refine his skills in these.
			1. Alan's mother will begin to give Alan a regular, weekly allowance.
			2. Mother will begin to explore vocational options/interests by: a) checking with friends who own businesses to see if any have training opportunities for Alan; and b) spending time with Alan visiting different places and talking with Alan about the different jobs observed on these "exploration trips."
			3. Mother will assign Alan some household "jobs" so Alan has the opportunity to be responsible for chores.
				1. Job coach/teacher will arrange Alan's schedule next year to include more community-based vocational experiences.
				2. School administrator will initiate canvass of local businesses to explore potential vocational training sites for Alan including:
				  a) local automotive parts refurbishing site
				  b) local shipping company
				  c) local supermarket chain
				  d) local restaurant
				3. Contact at local VESID office will visit school to provide overview training to staff re: job-related skills development.
				4. Job coach/teacher will perform functional assessment at each worksite to identify areas in which Alan needs support.
					—communication
					—identify job(s) he likes
					—behavior relaxation, identification of feelings
					—money management
					—skill mastery in designated tasks/jobs
					—rooming via uniform care and laundry, etc.
					—functional time telling
					—learning how to use staff lounge for break/meal times
					—social skills training (co-workers)

Source: From *Supplement for Transition Coordinators: A Curricular Approach to Support the Transition to Adulthood of Adolescents with Visual or Dual Sensory Impairments and Cognitive Disabilities,* by J. O'Neil, G. Gothelf, S. Cohen, L. Lehman, and S. B. Woolf, 1990, New York: Hunter College of the City University of New York and the Jewish Guild for the Blind; ERIC Documentation Reproduction Service No. EC 300 449–453.

Prepare Students for Employment

An important outcome for many young people leaving high school is employment so that they can earn money, interact with others, and advance in their careers. Working allows one to move toward financial independence, contribute to the community, and develop self-confidence. Unfortunately, the unemployment rate for non-college-bound young people and those with disabilities is still quite high, and these groups are less likely to aspire to high-status occupations. Most students with disabilities who find employment often work in part-time, unskilled positions that pay at or below the minimum wage and offer few opportunities for advancement. These low-wage positions limit the opportunities for self-sufficiency and a reasonable quality of life.

Several models are available to address the difficulties that students with disabilities and other special needs experience in finding a job (Flexer et al., 2008; Sitlington et al., 2010).

Competitive Employment Young people who are leaving school need help in making the transition to competitive and supported employment. **Competitive employment** involves working as a regular employee in an integrated setting with coworkers who do not have disabilities and being paid at least the minimum wage (Brooke, Revell, & Wehman, 2009). Individuals usually find competitive employment through a job training program, with the help of family and friends, or through a rehabilitation agency.

Supported Employment Whereas some individuals with disabilities may find competitive employment, many others, particularly those with significant disabilities, benefit from supported employment. **Supported employment** provides ongoing assistance and services as individuals learn how to obtain competitive employment, perform and hold a job, travel to and from work, interact with coworkers, work successfully in integrated community settings, and receive a salary that reflects the prevailing wage rate.

Job Coach Because a key component of all supportive employment models is a job coach, case manager, school counselor, or a supported employment specialist, you may be asked to work collaboratively with these professionals, families, and employers (Targett, Young, Revell, Williams, & Wehman, 2007). Although the functions of the **job coach** depend on the supported employment model, this person may perform many different functions including assessing employment and vocational skills, and offering job training and placement services. Once individuals are placed on the job, the job coach also can help them learn how to communicate and maintain social relationships with supervisors and other employees, identify and implement job-related accommodations, and evaluate and improve their job performance.

Career Education Programs A good career education program should offer a range of services and activities and begin in elementary school and occur throughout schooling to help *all students* make the transition to work and postsecondary education (Flexer et al., 2008; Sitlington et al., 2010). Because the employment outcomes of students with disabilities also are related to gender and ethnicity, career education programs and curricula should address these important variables (Hogansen et al., 2008). Therefore, although career education programs should include career awareness, orientation, exploration, preparation, and placement (Targett et al., 2007), they also should address self-determination, independence, self-awareness, disability awareness, cultural and gender issues, and career planning (Johnson, Mellard, & Lancaster, 2007; Lindstrom et al., 2008). You also can collaborate with others to show *all students* the importance of work inside and outside the home, the range of jobs that people perform, and the preparation for these jobs, and help them understand how the fear-of-success syndrome, and sex roles and cultural factors can impact their career choices.

Elementary School Years. In elementary school, career education programs usually focus on *career awareness*, an understanding of the various occupations and jobs available, the importance of work, and an initial self-awareness of career interests. These programs also introduce students to daily living and social skills, attitudes, values, and concepts related to work through classroom jobs, homework, chores at home, money, and hobbies.

PEARSON
myeducationlab

Go to the Assignments and Activities section of the Topic *Transition Planning* in the MyEducationLab for your course and complete the activity entitled *Vocational Training*. As you watch the video and complete the accompanying questions, note the help vocational training can be for students transitioning to post-school life.

REFLECTIVE

How did you become interested in teaching? What career education programs helped you to make that decision? What job-related and interpersonal skills do you need to be an effective teacher? What career education experiences helped you develop those skills? How did your cultural background and gender affect your career choice?

Middle School/Junior High Years. In middle school/junior high school, career education programs usually focus on *career orientation,* an identification of career interests through practical experience and exposure to a variety of occupations. Through field trips, speakers, special vocational classes, small job tryouts, and integrated curricula, students become familiar with work settings, attitudes, and job-related and interpersonal skills. They also develop an appreciation of the values associated with working.

High School Years. In high school, career education programs often focus on career exploration, preparation, and placement. *Career exploration* activities give students simulated and direct experiences with many occupations to help them determine their career goals and interests. For example, students can visit work settings and observe workers as they perform their jobs. Vocational guidance and counseling also help students obtain information about a variety of jobs. *Career preparation* helps students adjust to work by offering teaching, support, and work experiences through vocational education programs. A career preparation program includes training in specific job-related skills and the opportunity to use these skills in simulated or real work settings. *Career placement,* the placement of students in jobs or other postsecondary settings, often occurs around the time of graduation from high school.

Functional Curriculum and Community-Based Learning Career education and other transitional skills can be fostered via use of a **functional curriculum** and **community-based learning programs** (Bambara et al., 2006; Bouck, 2009). In a functional curriculum, goals and methods tailored to individual students prepare them for a successful transition to adult living, including living, working, and socializing in their communities. When determining the individualized goals of a functional curriculum, teachers examine the importance of each goal to students' current and future needs. They also consider the relevance of each goal to the student's age and current level of performance. In community-based learning programs, students are placed in community settings that offer them opportunities to learn a range of functional skills, including community-related skills (e.g., shopping, using public transportation), vocational skills, domestic skills (e.g., cooking, cleaning), and functional academic skills (e.g., reading signs, using money).

Community-based learning programs also include cooperative work education or work-study programs, where students may attend school and work part-time to blend their academic, functional and vocational skills development (Westling & Fox, 2009). Through an agreement between schools and employers, students' educational and work experiences are coordinated. Students are encouraged to complete school while getting the training and experiences needed for future employment. Community-based learning programs give students financial aid and the opportunity to learn job-related skills and experiences.

Service Learning Programs One type of inclusive community-based learning program is **service learning,** where *all students* perform and reflect on experiential activities that foster their learning and benefit the community (Dymond, Renzaglia & Chun, 2008; O'Connor, 2009). These programs provide real-life experiences that are linked to the curriculum to foster academic learning and teach students about their communities, civic responsibility, and the world of work and career choices (David, 2009). They also help students develop academic, communication, social, problem-solving, motivation, empathy, and self-determination skills (Olnes, 2008). Typically, such programs involve projects related to advocacy and community involvement (e.g., creating a play area), environmental issues (e.g., enhancing a local wetlands), social concerns (e.g., working in a homeless shelter or in a program for elderly persons), and cultural and historical issues (e.g., supporting local cultural and historical sites (O'Connor, 2009). Dymond et al. (2008), O'Connor (2009), and Olnes (2008) offer guidelines and resources for implementing inclusive secondary and elementary service learning programs.

PEARSON
myeducationlab

Go to the Assignments and Activities section of the Topic *Transition Planning* in the MyEducationLab for your course and complete the activity entitled *Functional Life Skills Training.* As you watch the video and complete the accompanying questions, consider the importance of preparing students for life after the classroom.

REFLECTIVE

Have you participated in a service learning program? What activities did you perform? How did your participation impact you and your community?

Foster Independent Living Arrangements

As students leave school, they also may need help in learning to live in community-based living arrangements (Flexer et al., 2008; Hendricks & Wehman, 2009). To make a successful transition, students need training to overcome negative attitudes, environmental constraints (e.g., the availability of transportation, shopping, and leisure activities), and socioeconomic barriers. In addition, students can learn how to be self-sufficient and take care of their needs, maintain the property, and seek help from others when necessary.

Promote Students' Participation in Leisure Activities

Although often overlooked, leisure is an important quality-of-life issue and a key component for students who are leaving school (Hendricks & Wehman, 2009). Through after-school, leisure and recreational activities, individuals increase their psychological, physical, and personal well-being; their development of friendships and cognitive and noncognitive skills; and their integration into inclusive community settings (Schwartz & Pace, 2008). Unfortunately, studies of the leisure activities of individuals with disabilities reveal that they are less likely to belong to school or community groups and participate in recreational activities than their peers who are not disabled (Rose, McDonnell, & Ellis, 2007). You can foster your students' participation in leisure activities by exposing them to a range of leisure activities and encouraging them to share their leisure activities with others. Ault and Collins (2009), Collins, Epstein, Reiss, and Lowe (2001), Kleinert et al. (2007), Roth, Pyfer, and Huettig (2007), Schwartz and Pace (2008), and Westling and Fox (2009) offer guidelines for supporting the participation of students with disabilities in community-based after-school, sports, recreation, religious, and leisure activities.

Leisure Education Because leisure is important for everyone, more and more leisure education services are being provided to students so that they can interact with others in community-based leisure activities throughout life. **Leisure education** teaches students to function independently during free-time activities at school, at home, and in the community; decide which leisure activities they enjoy; participate in leisure and recreational activities with others; and engage in useful free-time activities (Westling & Fox, 2009).

Explore Postsecondary Education Opportunities

A growing number of students with disabilities and students who are immigrants are exploring a range of postsecondary education opportunities (Gregg, 2007) and going to college (Holzer et al., 2009; Jewell, 2009). In addition to programs that make them aware of and encourage them to pursue postsecondary education opportunities, and help them prepare to take required entrance exams, these students will benefit from transitional and support programs that help them assess their readiness for and succeed in postsecondary education (Kochhar-Bryant, Bassett, & Webb, 2009; Sitlington et al., 2010). A postsecondary education transition program also should help them select and apply to appropriate colleges, which often entails frequent contacts and visits to identify and understand the available academic, financial aid, and support programs as well as the admission requirements (Oesterreich & Knight, 2008). It also should help students and their families complete the application procedures; provide required documentation; check eligibility for supportive services and financial support; and understand the disability-related laws that

All students should be encouraged to participate in leisure and after-school activities. What leisure and after-school activities are available for your students?

REFLECTIVE

Research suggests that students with disabilities attending colleges are reluctant to disclose their disabilities and ask for the accommodations to which they are entitled (Denhart, 2008). Why do you think this is the case? What can be done to help them overcome this reluctance?

impact admissions, accommodations, and dismissals (Hughes & Weiss, 2008; Lindstrom, 2007; Shaw, Madaus, & Banerjee, 2009).

The postsecondary education transition program also should help students develop the skills necessary to succeed academically and socially, including engaging in self-advocacy and understanding and informing others of their disability, their strengths, challenges, and goals, and the accommodations, support services, and assistive technology they will need (Garner, 2008; Shaw et al., 2009). A transitional program also can address students' attitudes and help them develop the learning strategies needed for succeeding with large classes and online courses, as well as reading, note taking, writing, studying, test taking, time management, and course load demands (Kirby, Silvestri, Allingham, Parrila, & La Fave, 2008; Strichart & Mangrum, 2010). The transition plan may involve teaching college-bound students with disabilities the goal-setting, social, and self-advocacy skills they need to be successful, including how to communicate with others and their professors and access college supportive services and resources (Adreon & Durocher, 2007; Gil, 2007; Hong, Ivy, Gonzalez, & Ehrensberger, 2007; Hughes & Weiss, 2008).

A growing number of community colleges and colleges are also providing programs for students with significant cognitive disabilities (Alpern & Zager, 2007). Although these programs differ from a traditional college curriculum, they offer students with significant disabilities access to a range of educational, life skills, vocational activities, and social interactions that can increase their employment, independent living, and recreational opportunities and foster their independence and inclusion into society (Stodden & Whelley, 2004). These postsecondary education programs employ a range of models that vary based on the services they provide and the level of inclusiveness they foster (Hart, Mele-McCarthy, Pasternak, Zimbrich, & Parker, 2004). A *substantially separate program model* focuses on offering life skills and community-based instruction; participating students have limited interactions with the general student population and curriculum. In addition to offering a life skills curriculum, a *mixed program model* provides participating students with opportunities to follow the typical campus schedule, interact with the general student population during social and recreational events, and attend selected classes. The *inclusive, individual support model* offers individualized accommodations, resources, assistive devices, and services to participating students so that they can participate in various campus courses, certificate programs, internships and activities.

DEVELOPING STUDENTS' SELF-DETERMINATION SKILLS

HOW CAN I HELP STUDENTS DEVELOP SELF-DETERMINATION? An important quality-of-life issue and an aspect of success in inclusive settings and society is the development of **self-determination**, an individual's ability to identify and take actions to achieve one's goals in life (Smith et al., 2009; Trainor, 2008). Whether moving to a general education setting or to adulthood, self-determination skills can help empower students to gain control over their lives and adjust to the independence and choices associated with inclusive settings and adulthood (Sitlington et al., 2010).

Self-determination development occurs throughout one's schooling and should begin when students start school. Because it involves lifelong experiences and opportunities, you can collaborate with other teachers and family members to include goals related to self-determination on students' IEPs, 504 plans, and ITPs, and use the strategies described here to help students develop independence and self-determination within your inclusive classroom (Konrad, Walker, Fowler, Test, & Wood, 2008). It also is important for you to adjust your goals and strategies related to teaching self-determination to accommodate the cultural perspectives of your students and their families (Trainor, 2008).

Using Technology to Promote Inclusion
SUPPORTING SUCCESSFUL TRANSITIONS

As we saw in the chapter-opening vignette, videos of inclusive settings can help introduce students to the important factors that affect academic performance and social interactions in inclusive settings, and promote the use of already-learned skills in the new setting (Ayres & Langone, 2008). Videos also can be used to prepare students to function in community-based settings (Mechling et al., 2009). Like Nick, your students can use video self-modeling to learn and practice skills by viewing videos of activities and their behaviors in inclusive settings (Cihak & Schrader, 2008; Cummings et al., 2008). Students can then reflect on their behaviors and practice appropriate responses to many general education classroom situations. Videos also can be used to create a tour of the new school and the new classroom that students can view before they enter the new setting. Here are some other ways you can use technology to help students make successful transitions:

- Teach students to use technology to foster their organizational and transition-related skills and their use of learning strategies (Wexler, 2009). Students can use handheld devices such as personal digital assistants (PDAs), portable video-based devices, and digital recording devices to electronically create, store, and access specific features of assignments, jobs or other transitional tasks; a "to do" list; and daily, weekly, and monthly calendars (Taber-Doughty et al., 2008). These devices and resources also can be programmed to record and play back audio and video messages, pictures and photos, directions, and reminders and to prompt and guide students to use appropriate social skills, learning strategies and to engage in independent behaviors related to a transition-related task (Cihak, Kessler, & Alberto, 2008; Mechling, 2008). For example, students can listen to and view (a) a prerecorded script that contains step-by-step instructions using video, understandable language and icons and in a familiar voice; (b) individualized prompts spaced at appropriate intervals that remind students to engage in specific behaviors; and (c) statements of encouragement praise ("You are doing a good job"), and evaluation ("Did you finish the job?").

- Access Web resources to support your students' organizational and self-determination skills and use of learning strategies, and to promote the generalization of skills and strategies (Joseph & Konrad, 2009). For example, eKidTools, KidTools, and StrategyTools offer a range of templates supporting the acquisition of learning strategies and self-determination skills in elementary and secondary students (Miller, Fitzgerald, Koury, Mitchem, & Hollingsead, 2007), and the instructional strategies online database provides a listing of research-based learning strategies (Hodges, Higbee Mandlebaum, Boff, & Miller, 2007).

  - Use technology to involve students in the transitional process and to develop their self-determination skills (Schaffer & Marks, 2008)

and to teach transitional skills (Hansen & Morgan, 2008).

- Use presentation software such as PowerPoint to prepare a digital task analysis to teach students transitional and functional skills (Ayres & Langone, 2005) and to create community-based digital stories (Schleibaum, 2007). This involves taking digital images (video or pictures) of each step in a task analysis or story, and converting the digital images into PowerPoint slides that include brief written and oral descriptions of each step in the task analysis, or aspect of the story.

- Support students' self-awareness and self-advocacy skills by having them create digital video stories to learn about themselves and to share information about themselves with others including their strengths, challenges, accommodations, interests, career preferences and transitional goals (Skouge, Kelly, Roberts, Leake, & Stodden, 2007; Thompson et al., 2007).

- Teach English language learners to use Web-based translation systems so that they can receive prompt translations of blocks of English text in their native languages (Berlin, 2009).

- Provide students with online mentors. Students and mentors can be matched and communicate electronically. Webcameras (webcams) also can allow students to have online "face-to-face" interactions with individuals with a range of disabilities. Guidelines and etiquette for communicating online can be established such as the time commitment required, the nature of the messages to be sent, the approximate time period within which a response may be expected, and the type of mentoring.

- Use virtual reality software and online virtual reality experiences to provide students with opportunities to learn and practice transitional and social skills in a safe environment, and simulated community settings (Ayres & Langone, 2008; Cummins, 2007). For example, via virtual reality, students can take a virtual ride on public transportation, go shopping at a virtual supermarket, perform a virtual job, interact socially with others in a virtual community, or respond to a virtual job- or post-secondary education–related interview (Cafiero, 2008).

- Provide students with technology that fosters their independence and leisure. For example, two-way text-message pagers are used by deaf and hard of hearing students to communicate with others, weighted utensils and button hookers promote eating and dressing, and adaptive play and recreational devices facilitate participation in leisure activities (Wolfe Poel, 2007).

- Use the Internet to provide students with access to mainstream media and communications and affinity support groups and networks that focus on disability issues, interests, and experiences (Cafiero, 2008; Wexler, 2009). News segments, commentaries, and documentaries from professional organizations, individuals with disabilities, advocacy groups, and television and radio stations can be accessed via web sites (Bromley, 2008).

Teach Goal Setting and Problem Solving

Teaching students to become actively involved in setting and problem solving ways to attain their educational, social-emotional, and transitional goals are important aspects of helping them become self-determined individuals (Lee, Palmer, & Wehmeyer, 2009). Students will need to receive instruction in how to set and prioritize reasonable, concrete, and specific goals, and establish strategies and time lines for achieving them. To do this, you can help your students create, implement and evaluate action plans to achieve their identified goals by teaching them to

- reflect on who they are ("Who am I?" "What do I want?" "What things are keeping me from achieving what I want?");
- develop goal statements including desired behaviors and levels of performance (e.g., "What are my goals?");
- understand the dimensions associated with their goals ("What factors do I need to consider in planning to achieve my goals?");
- identify possible steps for and barriers to achieving their goals (e.g., "What can I do to achieve my goals?" "What are the best ways to achieve my goals? What barriers are in my way and keep me from achieving my goals?" "How can I remove the barriers to achieving my goals?");
- select the best actions to take and create and implement a plan for attaining their goals (e.g., "How can I best achieve my goals?" "Who can help me achieve my goals?" "When should I start my plan?"); and
- evaluate their success at achieving their goals (e.g., "Did I meet my goal?" "Did I follow my plan?" "Did my actions help me achieve my goals?" and "What should I do next?") (Devlin, 2008; Lee et al., 2009).

You also can use your students' responses to these questions to develop self-determination contracts, self-monitoring systems, and graphic organizers with them to guide the implementation of their action plans (Guerra, 2009; Joseph & Konrad, 2009). For example, Rock (2004) offers guidelines and strategies for teaching goal setting to students including the learning strategy, ACT-REACT, and Guerra (2009) provides guidelines for using a LIBRE stick figure as a graphic organizer to guide students in problem solving. Periodically remind students of their goals and strategies for achieving them by asking them to state their goals, and identify what they can do to achieve their goals. You also can have them use I WILL cards containing first-person statements that prompt students to focus on the behaviors that will help them meet their goals (see Figure 6.6) (Boutot, 2009). Students also can complete a Think Sheet that asks them to identify "What is up?" "Why am I feeling this way?" and "What can I do to feel better?" (Kolb & Stevens Griffith, 2009).

Offer Choices

Goal setting is related to allowing students to make choices, which also can promote self-determination, independence, socialization, positive behavior, and improved academic performance (Hong et al., 2007). You can foster choice making by teaching students how to make and express their choices and helping them understand the consequences of their choices (Guskey & Anderman, 2008). Because the school day involves a series of choices, you also can integrate activities involving choices into both teaching and nonteaching parts of the daily schedule by conducting a preference inventory and then tailoring your activities and schedule to incorporate your students' choices (Guskey & Anderman, 2008; Kern & State, 2009). During academic tasks, students can be given a menu of choices regarding the assignments they complete, the time and order in which they begin and complete tasks, the learning materials they will use, the location in the room in which they prefer to work, and the individuals with whom they would like to collaborate (Goodman & Williams, 2007;

FIGURE 6.6 Sample I WILL card

When the teacher gives directions for an assignment, I will:

Look at and listen to the teacher

Write down important things

Ask questions if I'm unsure

Start working

FIGURE 6.7 Sample assignment interest preference survey

SOCIAL STUDIES
Mrs. Bowman
Ninth Grade

Please indicate your order of preference, beginning with "1" to indicate the most interesting assignment you would like to complete:

☐ Explain the importance and consequences of civil right movements in America.

☐ Explain the contributions different social movements have made to our democracy.

☐ Conduct independent research to identify resources relevant to civil rights.

☐ Explain how lessons learned from historic struggles apply to emerging civil rights challenges that face our country.

☐ Provide examples of civil rights outstanding political figures and summarize their achievements.

Source: From "Incorporating Choice and Preferred Activities into Classwide Instruction," by L. Kern and T. M. State, *Beyond Behavior, 18,* 2009, p. 8. Copyright (2009) by the Council for Children with Behavioral Disorders. Reprinted with permission.

Kern & State, 2009). For example, you can give them a list of tiered assignments that differ in terms of learning styles or levels of difficulty and allow them to choose the assignments that best match their learning preferences and skill levels (Painter, 2009). Figure 6.7 contains a sample assignment interest preference survey, and Figure 9.5 later in the book presents an example of a lesson incorporating student choice and preferences.

Making Connections
Find out more about ways for giving students choices in Chapter 9.

If students have difficulty making choices, you can start by providing them with options, giving them choice boards and yes/no or sticky-note prompts, assessing their preferences concerning items presented to them, or allowing them to make some choices during nonacademic activities (Jaime & Knowlton, 2007; Ryan, Pierce, & Mooney, 2008). Cooperative learning arrangements, student-selected projects and rewards, self-management techniques, and learning strategies also allow students to assume more responsibility and control over their own learning.

Foster Self-Awareness

Self-determined individuals are also **self-aware** individuals, who can identify and express their preferences, strengths, and challenges and advocate for themselves (Merlone & Moran, 2008). A variety of strategies can help you involve students in understanding and assessing their learning preferences, strengths, challenges, and styles (Schreiner, 2007). For example, Campbell-Whatley (2006), Eisenman and Tascione (2002), Lindstrom et al. (2008), Merlone and Moran (2008), and Schreiner (2007) present effective strategies and resources for fostering the self-awareness of students by teaching them about disabilities, special education, accommodations, and federal and state laws, and having them identify what they know about their individual differences and challenges, how their individual differences and challenges affect them and their views of themselves, and how they could use this information in the future.

Develop Self-Advocacy and Leadership Skills

Self-determined individuals use their self-awareness and strengths to plan strategies to advocate for themselves, to overcome their challenges, to achieve their goals, and to assume leadership positions (Meadan & Monda-Amaya, 2008; Merlone & Moran, 2008). You can use a range of resources and collaborate with others to enhance your students' self-advocacy and leadership skills and show them how to achieve their goals (Campbell-Whatley, 2006; Schreiner, 2007; Smith, et al., 2009). You also can make sure that *all students* assume leadership roles in your school and your classroom (Smith, 2009).

Your students' self-advocacy and empowerment also can be fostered by teaching them to use assertive communication strategies (Kolb & Stevens Griffith, 2009). These strategies include learning to (a) be calm and direct in expressing feelings and desires; (b) employ "I statements"; (c) explain reactions to and feelings about others' behavior; and (d) state preferences and ways to deal with future situations.

Fostering your students' active participation in the IEP and transitional planning processes and other decisions that affect them also helps them develop their self-advocacy and leadership skills (Konrad, 2008). For example, you can teach them to use I-PLAN, a self-advocacy strategy:

Inventory your strengths, areas to improve, goals, needed accommodations, and choices for learning.

Provide your inventory information.

Listen and respond.

Ask questions.

Name your goals (Van Reusen & Bos, 1994).

PROACT (Ellis, 1998) and ASSERT (Kling, 2000) are additional learning strategies that help students develop effective self-advocacy skills. You can also use peer mentors, guest speakers, role plays, and books and videos about the lives of individuals with special needs to help students learn about self-advocacy and leadership (Campbell-Whatley, 2006; Lindstrom et al., 2008; Merlone & Moran, 2008).

Making Connections
This discussion on self-advocacy builds on the roles you can assume as an advocate for your students and their families discussed in Chapter 4.

Making Connections
This discussion builds on the strategies for involving students in developing their IEPs discussed in Chapter 2.

Promote Self-Esteem

Promoting **self-esteem** in students and their own sense of self-efficacy can improve their learning and ability to advocate for themselves (Merlone & Moran, 2008; Smith et al., 2009). Students with low self-esteem often make negative statements about themselves that hinder their performance, such as "I'm not good at this, and I'll never complete it." You can promote self-esteem by helping students understand the harmful effects of low self-esteem, and by structuring academic activities and social situations so that students succeed and reflect on the factors that help them to be successful. Other methods include recognizing students' achievements and talents, giving them moderately challenging tasks, focusing on their recent successes, teaching them to use self-management techniques and learning strategies, asking them to perform meaningful classroom and school-based jobs and leadership positions, and posting their work in the classroom and throughout the school (Margolis & McCabe, 2006; Meadan & Monda-Amaya, 2008; Sagor, 2008; Smith, 2009).

Making Connections
Find out more about how you can foster your students' self-esteem in Chapter 7.

Provide Attribution Training

Students' self-determination and self-esteem can be fostered by helping them develop an internal locus of control, the belief that their actions affect their success (Hong et al., 2007; Merlone & Moran, 2008). An internal locus of control can be fostered via **attribution training**, which involves teaching students to analyze the events and actions that lead to success and failure. Students who understand positive attributions recognize and acknowledge that their successful performance is due to effort ("I spent a lot of time studying for this test"), ability ("I'm good at social studies"), and other factors within themselves. Students who fail to understand attribution often attribute their poor performance to bad luck ("I got the hardest test"), teacher error ("The teacher didn't teach that"), lack of ability ("I'm not good at math"), or other external factors. Sample formats that you can use to assess and improve your students' attributions is presented in Figure 6.8.

Work with students to help them learn to use positive attributions by teaching them to (a) understand how attributions and effort affect performance, (b) view failure as the first part of learning and a sign of the need to work harder, (c) focus on improvement and analyze past successes, (d) talk about mistakes, and (e) assume responsibility for successful outcomes (Eisenman, 2007). You also can encourage students to use positive attributions by modeling them, and having students self-record them. Help them focus on their progress by responding to students' correct responses with specific feedback regarding their effort ("You're really working hard" or "You have really learned to do this") and ability ("You have the skill to do this"), and by responding to students' incorrect responses with a strategy or informational feedback ("Try another way of doing this") (Joseph & Konrad, 2009; Margolis & McCabe, 2006; Siegle & McCoach, 2005). A learning strategy called *BELIEF* (Duchardt, Deshler, & Schumaker, 1995) can help students learn to change their ineffective attributions. You also can foster a learning environment that allows and encourages students to take risks and greater control over their learning. When possible, it is also a good idea to use intrinsic motivation rather than external motivation and rewards.

Making Connections
Find out more about ways to motivate your students instrinsically in Chapter 9.

Provide Access to Positive Role Models

Access to positive role models such as self-determined individuals with disabilities can promote self-determination in students (Lee, Palmer, Turnbull, & Wehmeyer, 2006). These role models can be found in affinity support groups and mentors that focus on the strengths needs, interests, and experiences of students.

Affinity Support Groups You can foster self-determination by promoting positive group and individual identities in students (Wexler, 2009). This can be done by introducing students to **affinity support groups** of peers with common traits. For

FIGURE 6.8 Sample attribution assessments

Attribution Assignment Self-Report

Name: Assignment: Date:

I did well on this assignment because (check all that apply)

☐ It was easy.
☐ I worked hard on it.
☐ I was lucky.
☐ I am good at it.

I did not do well on this assignment because (check all that apply)

☐ It was too hard.
☐ I didn't try my best.
☐ I was unlucky.
☐ I am not good at it.

Weekly Attribution Reflection

Name: Class: Date:

1. How did I do in class in this week?
2. What did I do well in class this week?
3. What things did I do that helped me do well?
4. What did I not do well in class this week?
5. Why did I not do well?
6. What things can I do to be more successful?

Comments:

Student:

Teacher:

Sources: Corral and Antia (1997); Kozminsky and Kozminsky (2002).

Mentors can help students make transitions to adulthood and can help them develop self-determination. How have mentors helped you?

example, you and your colleagues at school can establish an affinity support group of students with disabilities. Like other school groups made up of individuals with similar characteristics (e.g., sports teams, performing arts groups, academic clubs), this affinity support group can help students understand and value the skills and qualities they bring to school and learn to respect the individuality of others. The group can define their goals and activities: sharing experiences, expressing strengths, challenges and interests, planning school activities, performing community service, and serving as an advocacy group to support each other.

Mentors **Mentors**, self-determined, successful adults who guide and assist younger individuals, can be valuable in helping students improve their learning and make the transition to adulthood and develop self-determination (Grandin, 2007; Osborn, Freeman, Burley, Wilson, Jones, & Rychener, 2007). Mentoring programs match mentors and protégés on the basis of shared strengths, interests, needs, goals, and personalities and provide them with oppor-

A GUIDE TO ACTION
Promoting Students' Self-Determination

A very important part of your inclusive classroom is promoting students' self-determination. To create a classroom that promotes students' self-determination, consider the following points:

- Teach students how to set and attain their goals.
- Integrate into the daily schedule activities that encourage students to make choices.
- Be aware of students' preferences.
- Show that you respect students' choices and decisions.
- Include students in planning, implementing, and evaluating instructional activities, and fostering their prosocial behavior.
- Encourage students to take responsibility for their decisions and learning.
- Encourage IEP teams to consider students' self-determination skills.
- Make it easy for students to attend and participate in IEP meetings.
- Teach students to advocate for themselves.

- Create a learning environment that helps students feel good about themselves.
- Encourage students to analyze how their actions contribute to success and failure.
- Give students opportunities to have positive role models, and to participate in service learning and community-based programs.
- Provide students with access to resources that focus on their strengths, needs, interests, and experiences.
- Use curricula and teaching materials and activities to foster students' self-determination.
- Encourage *all students* to assume leadership positions.
- Understand the impact of students' cultural backgrounds on their self-determination.
- Model self-determination for students.

How would you rate the extent to which you promote self-determination in your students? ( ) Excellent ( ) Good ( ) Needs Improvement ( ) Needs Much Improvement

Create a plan of action for promoting your students' self-determination that includes your goals, the actions you will take and the resources you will need to achieve them, and the ways you will evaluate your success.

tunities to have an ongoing, reciprocal one-to-one relationship and shared experiences (Koch, 2006). Mentors serve as models of appropriate qualities and behaviors; teach and share knowledge; listen to the thoughts and feelings of **protégés**; offer advice, support, and encouragement; and promote protégés to others (Converse & Lingugaris Kraft, 2009). For example, by sharing their experiences and meeting regularly with protégés, mentors serve as role models for students attending colleges and universities, working in competitive employment situations, living independently, participating in community recreation activities, and having a family life. Mentors also can help protégés understand their talents and develop confidence in their abilities.

Same-race and same-language mentors, and personnel who understand the students' language and culture, also can help students from different cultural and language backgrounds make the many school- and society-based transitions they face (Wilder, Ashbaker, Obiakor, & Rotz, 2006). Mentors from the community can help culturally and linguistically diverse students with various aspects of schooling, as well as helping them continue to value their cultural and linguistic identities. For example, same-language mentors can share their past and current experiences as English language learners. This allows them to relate to students and their experiences in learning a new language, and helps students to make school- and society-based transitions.

Use Self-Determination Curricula and Teaching Resources

In addition to the strategies we have discussed, curricula and teaching resources to help students develop the attitudes, knowledge, and skills to act with self-determination within the general education curriculum also are available (Flexer et al., 2008; Wehmeyer & Field, 2007). These curricula provide a variety of instructional and assessment strategies and resources to teach self-determination skill and foster access and success within the general education curriculum (Eisenman, 2007; Lee, Wehmeyer, Palmer, Soukup, & Little, 2008). For example, Konrad et al. (2008) offer a model for teaching a range of self-determination skills linked to learning standards within the general education curriculum. Eisenman (2007), Konrad et al. (2007, 2008), and Schaffer and Marks (2008) provide a listing of curricula, children's and young adult books, online resources, and films that can be used to teach a range of self-determination skills; and Test, Browder, Karvonen, Wood, and Algozzine (2002) offer guidelines for writing lesson plans for promoting self-determination.

SUMMARY

This chapter offered guidelines for planning and using transitional programs to prepare students for success in inclusive settings. As you review the questions posed in this chapter, remember the following points.

How Can I Help Students Make the Transition to General Education Classrooms?

CEC 4, 5, 8, 9, 10; PRAXIS 3; INTASC 8, 9

You can help students make this transition by understanding their unique abilities and challenges, using transenvironmental programming, identifying and teaching essential classroom procedures and behaviors, and helping students to use their skills in different settings. You can help students succeed by teaching them to use learning strategies that can improve their independent work and organizational skills.

How Can I Help Students Make the Transition to New Schools?

CEC 4, 5, 7, 9, 10; PRAXIS 3; INTASC 9

You can work with families and others to develop a transitional plan; adapt a variety of transitional models; foster collaboration across schools; and offer student and family orientations and student visiting, shadowing, and mentoring programs.

How Can I Help Students from Culturally and Linguistically Diverse Backgrounds Make the Transition to Inclusive Settings?

CEC 2, 3, 4, 5, 6, 9, 10; PRAXIS 2, 3; INTASC 3, 9

You can teach students the accepted cultural norms; orient them to the new school; help them develop social skills, and basic communication and cognitive academic language proficiency skills; and offer newcomer programs.

How Can I Help Students Make the Transition from School to Adulthood?

CEC 2, 4, 5, 7, 9, 10; PRAXIS 2, 3; INTASC 4, 9

You can develop an SOP and implement an ITP that addresses students' needs in the areas of employment, independent living arrangements, leisure, and postsecondary education and enhances their quality of life.

How Can I Help Students Develop Self-Determination?

CEC 2, 4, 5, 7, 9, 10; PRAXIS 2, 3; INTASC 4, 5, 9

You can teach students to set and problem-solve strategies to attain their goals, offer students choices, foster their self-awareness, help them develop self-advocacy and leadership skills and self-esteem, provide attribution training and access to positive role models, and use self-determination curricula and teaching resources.

MATTHEW

Just as Ms. McLeod is beginning a lesson, Matthew approaches her with a question. She tells him that she cannot answer it now and asks him to return to his seat. On the way to his seat, Matthew stops to joke around with his classmates, and Ms. McLeod again asks him to sit in his seat. Matthew walks halfway to his desk and then turns to ask one of his classmates if he can borrow a piece of paper. Again, Ms. McLeod asks him to find his seat, and he complies.

The class begins the lesson, with Ms. McLeod asking the students various questions. Matthew calls out the answers to several questions, and Ms. McLeod reminds him to raise his hand. As the lesson continues, Matthew touches another student, and the student swats Matthew's hand away. He then makes faces at Maria, who is sitting next to him. Maria laughs and starts sticking her tongue out at Matthew. Matthew raises his hand to respond to a question but cannot remember what he wants to say when Ms. McLeod calls on him, and starts telling a story and jokes. The class laughs, and Ms. McLeod tells Matthew to pay attention.

As Ms. McLeod begins to give directions for independent work, Matthew stares out the window. Ms. McLeod asks him to stop and get to work. He works on the assignment for 2 minutes and then "trips" on his way to the wastepaper basket. The class laughs, and Ms. McLeod tells Matthew to return to his seat and get to work. When he reaches his desk, he begins to search for a book, and makes a joke about himself. His classmates laugh, and Ms. McLeod reminds Matthew to work on the assignment. At the end of the period, Ms. McLeod collects the students' work, and notes that Matthew and many of his classmates have only completed a small part of the assignment.

7

Creating a Classroom Environment That Promotes Positive Behavior

What strategies could Ms. McLeod use to help Matthew improve his learning and behavior? After reading this chapter, you should have the knowledge, skills, and dispositions to answer that as well as the following questions:

- How can I collaborate with others to develop and implement school-wide positive behavioral interventions and supports and to conduct functional behavioral assessments?

- How can I promote positive classroom behavior in students?

- How can I prevent students from harming others?

- How can I adapt the classroom design to accommodate students' learning, behavioral, social, and physical strengths and challenges?

For students to be successful in inclusive settings, their classroom behavior must be consistent with teachers' expectations and must promote their learning and socialization with peers. Appropriate academic, social, and behavioral skills allow students to become part of the class, the school, and the community. Unfortunately, for reasons both inside and outside the classroom, the behavior of some students like Matthew may interfere with their learning and socialization as well as that of their classmates. Therefore, you will need to have a comprehensive and balanced classroom management plan. This involves using many of the different strategies and physical design changes discussed in this chapter to help your students engage in behaviors that support their learning and socializing with others. A good classroom management system recognizes the close relationship between positive behavior and effective instruction (Preciado, Horner, & Baker, 2009). Therefore, an integral part of a classroom management system includes your use of such effective instructional practices as understanding students' learning and social strengths and challenges; providing students with access to an engaging and appropriate curriculum; and using innovative, motivating, culturally responsive, differentiated teaching practices and instructional accommodations (Sutherland et al., 2008), which are discussed in greater detail in other chapters. As we learned in Chapters 4 and 5, it is also important to foster communication and collaboration with other professionals and families and to create a welcoming and comfortable learning environment, as well as to communicate with students, respect them, and build relationships with them. If students are classified as having a disability, your schoolwide and classroom policies and practices need to be consistent with certain rules and guidelines for disciplining them (Katsiyannis, Conroy, & Zhang, 2008).

SCHOOLWIDE POSITIVE BEHAVIORAL INTERVENTIONS AND SUPPORTS

HOW CAN I COLLABORATE WITH OTHERS TO DEVELOP AND IMPLEMENT SCHOOLWIDE POSITIVE BEHAVIORAL INTERVENTION AND SUPPORTS AND TO CONDUCT FUNCTIONAL BEHAVIORAL ASSESSMENTS? It is important for you to collaborate with others to develop your school's *schoolwide positive behavioral intervention and supports* (SWPBIS), a collaborative data-based decision-making process for establishing and implementing a continuum of schoolwide and individualized instructional and behavioral strategies and services that are available and used to support the learning and positive behavior of *all students* (Sugai, Simononsen, & Horner, 2008). Collaboration also can help you make sure that your expertise, goals, and concerns are reflected in the SWPBIS and that your classroom management plan and practices are consistent with it.

SWPBIS systems are proactive and culturally responsive. They seek to prevent students from engaging in problem behaviors by changing your teaching practices and the environment in which the behaviors occur to help students acquire the academic, behavioral and social skills that they will need to succeed in inclusive classrooms (Coyne, Simonsen, & Faggella-Luby, 2008; Preciado et al., 2009). They are sensitive to students' strengths and challenges and students' cultural and linguistic backgrounds. SWPBIS systems are implemented in tiers that provide a continuum of academic, behavioral, and social interventions and supports based on data related to students' responses to them (Chitiyo & Wheeler, 2009; Coyne et al., 2008; Fairbanks, Simonsen, & Sugai, 2008; Simonsen, Sugai, & Negron, 2008). Tier 1, primary prevention, includes universal interventions and supports that are used with *all students* by all educators in all settings. Students whose behavior does not improve as a result of primary preventive measures and who do not harm themselves or others move up the continuum and receive more specialized tier 2 secondary prevention interventions and supports. These are targeted to subgroups of students who are considered

REFLECTIVE

What social and behavioral skills are important for success in your inclusive classrooms?

FIGURE 7.1 Sample SWPBIS tiers

Tier 1: Primary Prevention via Universal Interventions and Supports

- ☐ Promote active family involvement
- ☐ Create a positive, accepting, caring, and safe school and classroom environment (foster students' friendships and self-esteem; establish positive relationships with students; employ classroom designs that support learning, socialization, and prosocial behavior).
- ☐ Establish, teach, and enforce positively stated, culturally sensitive, uniform rules, routines, procedures, and expectations for the school and classroom.
- ☐ Supervise classrooms and school-based locations (monitor hallways, playgrounds, cafeterias), and use teacher proximity.
- ☐ Use schoolwide and classwide interventions (acknowledging and praising; using cues, class meetings, dialoguing, affective education, and group-oriented interventions).
- ☐ Teach social skills, learning strategies, and acceptance of individual differences.
- ☐ Use a challenging, relevant, interactive, and multicultural curriculum and effective, motivating, and culturally responsive teaching practices and technologies.
- ☐ Implement a continuum of techniques for responding to positive behaviors and inappropriate behaviors.
- ☐ Use peer-mediated instruction and behavioral support and leadership and community building strategies (use peer mediation and conflict resolution programs, cooperative learning; and assign classroom jobs and leadership roles to all students).
- ☐ Implement antibullying programs

Tier 2: Secondary Prevention via Specialized Interventions and Supports Targeted to Specific Groups of Students

- ☐ Use more structured positive reinforcement systems that involve individualized reinforcement surveys and more frequent delivery of reinforcement.
- ☐ Increase collaboration and communication with families (implementing a two-way notebook, daily/weekly progress reports, home–school contracts).
- ☐ Increase supervision, structure, praise, and prompts.
- ☐ Use more individualized behavioral interventions (self-management techniques, contracting, token/point systems) and classroom design accommodations.
- ☐ Employ a more individualized continuum of behavior reduction strategies and use the fair-pair rule to teach positive alternative behaviors (consider using the fair-pair rule and redirection, precision requests, choice statements, interspersed requests, planned ignoring, and careful reprimands).
- ☐ Provide more intensive social skills, learning strategy, and academic instruction.
- ☐ Offer peer and adult mentoring.

Tier 3: Tertiary Prevention via More Individualized and Intensive Interventions and Supports

- ☐ Conduct a functional behavioral assessment, and develop a behavioral intervention plan.
- ☐ Use more intensive individualized behavioral interventions, and deliver more frequent incentives.
- ☐ Provide more intensive academic and social skills instruction.
- ☐ Use the wraparound process to plan, deliver, and evaluate a range of individualized school-, class-, home-, and community-based interventions, supports, and services (consider providing culturally appropriate academic, health, psychological, counseling, and family education services).

Sources: Chitiyo and Wheeler (2009); Conroy, Sutherland, Snyder, and Marsh (2008); Coyne et al., (2008); Eber et al. (2008); Fairbanks et al. (2008); Meadan and Monda-Amaya (2008); Simonsen, Sugai, and Negron (2008).

Making Connections
The use of data-based decisions and a continuum of tiered intervention and supports builds on our earlier discussion of RTI in Chapter 2.

Making Connections
Find out more about progress monitoring and other ways to assess the effectiveness of your teaching practices in Chapter 12.

vulnerable to developing more chronic behavioral difficulties. The third tier in the continuum involves use of more highly individualized prevention interventions and supports for students who do not respond tier 2 interventions or whose behavior requires immediate and more intensive interventions and services. Determinations about the effectiveness of your SWPBIS system and corresponding decisions about moving students up and down the continuum are based on data collected via progress monitoring observational data (which we will discuss later in this chapter); feedback from educators, students, families and community members; and class- and schoolwide data related to students' academic and behavioral performance (e.g., grades, test scores, discipline referrals, etc.). A sample three-tier SWPBIS system is outlined in Figure 7.1. Additional information to guide your implementation of these interventions and supports are provided in the rest of this chapter.

CONDUCTING FUNCTIONAL BEHAVIORAL ASSESSMENTS

Integral aspects of schoolwide positive behavioral support systems also may include a functional behavioral assessment and a behavioral intervention plan, especially for students who require tier 3 tertiary interventions (Chitiyo & Wheeler, 2009). In the following sections, you will learn how to collaborate with others to conduct functional behavioral assessments and how to implement specific positive behavioral interventions and supports.

A *functional behavioral assessment (FBA)* is a person-centered, multi-method, problem-solving process that involves gathering information to

- measure student behaviors;
- determine why, where, and when a student uses these behaviors;
- identify the academic, instructional, social, affective, cultural, environmental, and contextual variables that appear to lead to and maintain the behaviors; and
- plan appropriate interventions that address the purposes the behaviors serve for students (Chandler & Dahlquist, 2010; Kerr & Nelson, 2010; Trussell, Lewis, & Stichter, 2008).

Although an FBA is only one aspect of a comprehensive behavior support planning process (e.g., medical factors and systems of care and wraparound processes should also be considered), it helps educators and family members develop a plan to change student behavior by (a) examining the causes and functions of the student's behavior, including the student' academic skills, and (b) identifying strategies that address the conditions in which the behavior is most likely and least likely to occur (McIntosh, 2008; Umbreit, Ferro, Liaupsin, & Lane, 2007). Guidelines for conducting an FBA and examples relating to the chapter-opening vignette of Matthew and Ms. McLeod are presented here.

Create a Diverse Multidisciplinary Team

As with the comprehensive planning team, in conducting an FBA, you will collaborate with a diverse team that includes the student's teachers and educators with expertise in developing FBAs and behavioral intervention plans (Park, 2007; Umbreit et al., 2007). The inclusion of family and community members also can provide important information about the student's history, cultural perspectives, experiential and linguistic background, and home-based events that may affect the student and the family. In the case of Matthew, the team was composed of two of his teachers, his mother and brother, a school psychologist who had experience with the FBA process, the principal at his school, and a representative from a community group.

Identify the Problematic Behaviors

First, the team identifies the behavior that will be examined by the FBA by considering the following questions: (a) What does the student do or fail to do that causes a problem? (b) How often, for how long, and in what settings does the behavior occur? (c) How do the student's academic, social, cognitive, language, physical, and sensory abilities affect the behavior? (d) How does the behavior affect the student's learning, socialization, and self-concept, as well as classmates and adults? For example, in the chapter-opening vignette, Matthew's poor on-task behavior seems to be undermining both his learning and the classroom environment. When several behaviors are identified as problematic, it is recommended that they be prioritized based on their level of interference.

The team also needs to examine the relationship, if any, between the behavior and the student's cultural and language background (Rothstein-Fisch &

FIGURE 7.2 Example of observational recording strategies

Date	Length of Sessions	Number of Events
9/11	30 minutes	ⅢⅠ
9/15	30 minutes	ⅢⅠ ⅢⅠ Ⅰ
9/20	30 minutes	ⅠⅠⅠ

(a) Event Recording of Call-outs

Date	Occurrence Number	Time Start	Time End	Total Duration
5/8	1	9:20	9:25	5 minutes
	2	9:27	9:30	3 minutes
5/9	1	10:01	10:03	2 minutes
	2	10:05	10:06	1 minute
	3	10:10	10:14	4 minutes

(b) Duration Recording of Out-of-seat Behavior

15 Sec	15 Sec	15 Sec	15 Sec
+	−	−	+
+	+	−	−
+	−	−	−
−	+	+	+
+	+	−	+

(c) Interval Recording of On-task Behavior

Trumbull, 2008; Taylor & Whittaker, 2009). Some students from diverse backgrounds may have different cultural perspectives than their teachers, and communication problems between students and teachers often are interpreted as behavioral problems. For example, a student may appear passive in class, which may be interpreted as evidence of immaturity and lack of interest. However, in the student's culture, the behavior may be considered a mark of respect for the teacher as an authority figure.

Define the Behavior

Next, the behavior is defined in observable and measurable terms by listing its characteristics (Trussell et al., 2008). For example, Matthew's off-task behavior can be defined in terms of his calling out and extraneous comments, his extensive comments related to teacher questions, his ability to remain in his work area, his interactions with classmates, and the amount of work he completed.

Observe and Record the Behavior

After the behavior has been defined, the team selects an appropriate observational recording method and uses it during times that are representative of typical classroom activities (Alberto & Troutman, 2009). These systems also can be used to monitor the success of the interventions and supports you use as part of your SWPBIS. Examples of different observational recording systems are presented in Figure 7.2.

Observing students and recording their behavior can provide valuable information and help you evaluate the effectiveness of your SWPBIS. What types of information can observations give you about your students?

Event Recording   If the behavior to be observed has a definite beginning and end and occurs for brief time periods, event recording is a good choice. In **event recording**, the observer counts the number of behaviors that occur during the observation period, as shown in Figure 7.2a. For example, event recording can be used to count the number of times Matthew was on task during a typical 30-minute teacher-directed activity. Data collected using event recording are displayed as either a frequency (number of times the behavior occurred) or a rate (number of times it occurred per length of observation).

You can use a range of devices for event recording such as handheld counter (Parette et al., 2007). If a mechanical counter is not available, make marks on a pad, an index card, a chalkboard, or a piece of paper taped to your wrist. You also can use a transfer system in which you place small objects (e.g., poker chips, paper clips) in one pocket and transfer an object to another pocket each time the behavior occurs. The number of objects transferred to the second pocket gives an accurate measure of the behavior.

Duration and Latency Recording   If time is an important factor in the observed behavior, a good recording strategy would be either duration or latency recording. In **duration recording**, shown in Figure 7.2b, the observer records how long a behavior lasts. **Latency recording** is used to determine the delay between receiving instructions and beginning a task. For example, duration recording can be used to find out how much time Matthew spends on task. Latency recording would be used to assess how long it took Matthew to begin an assignment after the directions were given. The findings of both recording systems can be presented as the total length of time or as an average. Duration recording data also can be summarized as the percentage of time the student engaged in the behavior by dividing the amount of time the behavior lasts by the length of the observation period and multiplying by 100.

Interval Recording or Time Sampling   With **interval recording** or *time sampling*, the observation period is divided into equal intervals, and the observer notes whether the behavior occurred during each interval; a plus (+) indicates occurrence and a minus (−) indicates nonoccurrence. A + does not indicate how many times the behavior occurred in that interval, only that it did occur. Therefore, this system shows the percentage of intervals in which the behavior occurred rather than how often it occurred.

The interval percentage is calculated by dividing the number of intervals in which the behavior occurred by the total number of intervals in the observation period and then multiplying by 100. For example, you might use interval recording to record Matthew's on-task behavior. After defining the behavior, you would divide the observation period into intervals and construct a corresponding interval score sheet, as shown in Figure 7.2c. You would then record whether Matthew was on task during each interval. The number of intervals in which the behavior occurred would be divided by the total number of intervals to determine the percentage of intervals in which he was on task.

Anecdotal Records   An anecdotal record, also known as a *narrative log* or *continuous recording*, is often useful in reporting the results of an observation (Salend, 2009). An **anecdotal record** is a narrative of the events that took place

REFLECTIVE

How would you define, in observable and measurable terms, and what recording strategies would you use to assess out-of-seat, inattentive, aggressive, tardy, noisy, and disruptive behavior?

during the observation; it helps you understand the academic context in which student behavior occurs, and the environmental factors that influence student behavior. Use the following suggestions to write narrative anecdotal reports:

- Give the date, time, and length of the observation.
- Describe the activities, classroom design, individuals, and their relationships to the setting in which the observation occurred.
- Report in observable terms all of the student's verbal and nonverbal behaviors, as well as the responses of others to these behaviors.
- Avoid interpretations as well as using adjectives and adverbs.
- Indicate the sequence and duration of events.
- Vary the times and setting of the observations.

The chapter-opening vignette contains a sample anecdotal record relating to an observation of Matthew.

Obtain Additional Information About the Student and the Behavior

An important part of an FBA is obtaining information regarding the student and the behavior (Kerr & Nelson, 2010; Umbreit et al., 2007). Using multiple sources and methods, the team gathers information to determine the student's skills, strengths, challenges, interests, hobbies, preferences, self-concept, attitudes, health, culture, language, and experiences (Chandler & Dahlquist, 2010). Data regarding successful and ineffective interventions used in the past with the student also can be collected. Often this information is obtained by reviewing student records and by interviewing the student, teachers, family members, ancillary support personnel, and peers or having these individuals complete a checklist or rating scale concerning the behavior (Trussell et al., 2008; Underwood, Umbreit, & Liaupsin, 2009). For example, Ms. McLeod asked Matthew to respond to the following questions: (a) What do I expect you to do during class time? (b) How did the activities and assignments make you feel? (c) Can you tell me why you didn't complete your work? (d) What usually happens when you disturb other students? Additional information about Matthew and the data collection strategies used by the team as part of the functional behavioral assessment process are summarized in Table 7.1.

Perform an Antecedents-Behavior-Consequences(A-B-C) Analysis

While recording behavior, you may use an A-B-C analysis to collect data to identify the possible antecedents and consequences associated with the student's behavior (Chandler & Dahlquist, 2010; Underwood et al., 2009). ***Antecedents*** and ***consequences*** are the events, stimuli, objects, actions, and activities that precede and trigger the behavior, and follow and maintain the behavior, respectively. A sample functional behavioral assessment for Matthew that contains an A-B-C analysis of his off-task behavior is presented in Table 7.1.

Analyze the Data

The A-B-C data are then analyzed and summarized to identify when, where, with whom, and under what conditions the behavior is most likely and least likely to occur (see Figure 7.3 for questions that can guide you in analyzing the behavior's antecedents and consequences in settings in which the behavior is displayed and not displayed) (Arter, 2007; Chandler & Dahlquist, 2010; Underwood et al., 2009). The A-B-C analysis data are also analyzed to try to determine why the student uses the behavior, also referred to as the ***perceived function*** of the behavior. The team can

TABLE 7.1 Sample functional behavioral assessment for Matthew

Behavior: Off-task			
What Are the Antecedents of the Behavior?	**What Is the Behavior?**	**What Are the Consequences of the Behavior?**	**What Are the Functions of the Behavior?**
• Teacher-directed activity • Content of the activity • Individualized nature of the activity • Duration of the activity • Location of Matthew's work area • Placement of peers' work areas • Proximity of the teacher • Teacher comment or question • Availability of other activities	Matthew calls out, makes extraneous comments in response to teacher questions or comments, distracts others, leaves his work area, and completes a limited amount of work.	• Receives teacher attention • Receives peer attention • Avoids unmotivating activity • Performs a pleasant activity (e.g., interacting with peers) • Receives reprimands • Leaves seat	• To avoid or express his disappointment with the instructional activity • To receive attention from adults and peers
Data Collection Strategies:	Observations, student, family and teacher interviews, behavior checklists, and standardized testing		
Additional Information			
Academic:	• Matthew has scored significantly above grade level on standardized tests in reading and mathematics.		
Social/Peer:	• Matthew spends time alone after school because there are few activities available for him. • Matthew's peers describe him as the class clown. • Matthew likes to talk with and work with others.		
Family:	• Matthew likes to interact with others in social situations and community events. • Matthew does his homework while interacting with others.		

attempt to identify the perceived function of the behavior by considering the following questions:

1. What does the student appear to be communicating via the behavior?
2. How does the behavior benefit the student (e.g., getting attention or help from others; avoiding a difficult or unappealing activity; gaining access to a desired activity or peers; receiving increased status and self-concept, affiliation with others, sense of power and control, sensory stimulation or feedback, basic needs, satisfaction)?
3. What setting events contribute to the problem behavior (e.g., the content area and instructional strategies; the student being tired, hungry, ill, or on medication; the occurrence of social conflicts, schedule changes, or academic difficulties; the staffing patterns and interactions)?
4. How does the behavior relate to the student's culture, experiential and language background, interests, sensory and basic needs, and academic and social skills?

FIGURE 7.3 A-B-C analysis questions

In analyzing the antecedents of student behavior, consider if the behavior is related to the following:

- Physiological factors such as medications, allergies, hunger/thirst, odors, temperature levels, or lighting
- Home factors or the student's cultural perspective
- Student's learning, motivation, communication, and physical abilities
- The physical design of the classroom, such as the seating arrangement, the student's proximity to the teacher and peers, classroom areas, transitions, scheduling changes, noise levels, size of the classroom, and auditory and visual stimuli in the room
- The presence and behavior of peers and/or adults
- Certain days, the time of day, the length of the activity, the activities or events preceding or following the behavior or events outside the classroom
- The way the material is presented or the way the student responds
- The curriculum and the teaching activities, such as certain content areas and instructional activities, or the task's directions, difficulty and staff support
- Group size and/or composition or the presence and behavior of peers and adults

In analyzing the consequences of student behavior, consider the following:

- What are the behaviors and reactions of specific peers and/or adults?
- What is the effect of the behavior on the classroom atmosphere?
- How does the behavior affect progress on the activity or the assigned task?
- How does the behavior relate to and affect the student's cultural perspective and interests?
- What encourages or discourages the behavior?

Possible antecedents for Matthew's behavior include the content, type, duration, and level of difficulty of the instructional activity; the extent to which the activity allows him to work with others; and the location of the teacher. Possible consequences for Matthew's behavior may include getting teacher and peer attention, and avoiding an unmotivating task.

Develop Hypothesis Statements

Next, the prior information collected and the A-B-C analysis data are used to develop specific and global statements, also referred to as *summary statements*, concerning the student and the behavior hypotheses about the student and the behavior, which are verified (Kerr & Nelson, 2010; Preciado et al., 2009). **Specific hypotheses** address the reasons why the behavior occurs and the conditions related to the behavior including the possible antecedents and consequences. For example, a specific hypothesis related to Matthew's behavior would be that when Matthew is given a teacher-directed or independent academic activity, he will use many off-task behaviors to gain attention from peers and the teacher. **Global hypotheses** address how factors in the student's life in school, at home, and in the community impact on the behavior. In Matthew's case, a possible global hypothesis can address the possibility that his seeking attention is related to his limited opportunities to interact with peers after school. After hypothesis statements are developed, direct observation is used to collect data to validate their accuracy (Trussell et al., 2008).

Consider Sociocultural Factors

When analyzing the A-B-C information to determine hypotheses, the team should consider the impact of cultural perspectives and experiential and language background on the student's behavior and communication (Gollnick & Chinn, 2009; Obiakor et al., 2007). Behavioral differences in students related to their learning histories and behaviors, family's cultural perspectives, preference for working on several tasks at once, listening and responding styles, peer interaction patterns, responses to authority, verbal and nonverbal communication, speaking in class, turn-taking sequences, physical space, eye contact, and student–teacher interactions can be attributed to their cultural backgrounds (Cartledge & Kourea, 2008; West et al., 2007).

To do this, behavior and communication must be examined in a social/cultural context (Rothstein-Fisch & Trumbull, 2008). For example, four cultural factors that may affect students' behavior in school are outlined here: time, movement, respect for elders, and individual versus group performance. However, although this framework for comparing students may be useful in understanding certain cognitive, movement, and interaction styles and associated behaviors, you should be careful in generalizing a specific behavior to any cultural group. Thus, rather than considering these behaviors as characteristic of the group as a whole, you should view them as attitudes or behaviors that an individual may consider in learning and interacting with others.

Time   Different cultural groups have different concepts of time. Some cultures view timeliness as essential and as a key characteristic in judging competence. Students are expected to be on time and to complete assignments on time. Other cultures may also view time as important, but as secondary to relationships and performance (Cloud & Landurand, n.d.). For some students, helping a friend with a problem may be considered more important than completing an assignment by the deadline. Students who have different concepts of time may also have difficulties on timed tests or assignments.

Movement   Different cultural groups also have different movement styles, which can affect how others perceive them and interpret their behaviors. Different movement styles can affect the ways students walk, talk, and learn. For example, some students may prefer to get ready to perform an activity by moving around to organize themselves. Other students may need periodic movement breaks to support their learning.

Respect for Elders   Cultures, and therefore individuals, have different ways to show respect for elders and authority figures such as teachers. In most cultures, teachers and other school personnel are viewed as prestigious and valued individuals who are worthy of respect. However, respect may be demonstrated in many different ways, such as not making eye contact with adults, not speaking to adults unless spoken to first, not asking questions, and using formal titles. Mainstream culture in the United States does not always show respect for elders and teachers in these ways. Therefore, the behaviors mentioned may be interpreted as communication or behavior problems rather than as cultural marks of respect.

Individual Versus Group Performance   Whereas some cultures prize individualism and working independently, other cultures view group cooperation as more important. For students from these cultures, responsibility to society is seen as an essential aspect of competence, and their classroom performance is shaped by their commitment to the group and the community rather than to individual success. As a result, for some African American, Native American, and Latino/a students who are brought up to believe in a group solidarity orientation, their behavior may be designed to avoid being viewed as "acting white" or "acting Anglo" (Duda & Utley, 2005).

Humility is important in cultures that value group solidarity. By contrast, cultures that emphasize individuality award status based on individual achievement. Students from cultures that view achievement as contributing to the success of the group may perform better on tasks perceived as benefiting a group. They may avoid situations that bring attention to themselves, such as reading out loud, answering questions, gaining the teacher's praise, disclosing themselves, revealing problems, or demonstrating expertise (Bui & Turnbull, 2003).

Develop a Behavioral Intervention Plan

Based on its information and hypotheses, the team collaboratively develops a **behavioral intervention plan** focusing on the use of function-based interventions designed to address the student's learning and behavior by changing the classroom environment to better accommodate the student's characteristics, strengths, interests, relationships, and challenges (Chandler & Dahlquist, 2010; Trussell et al., 2008; Underwood et al., 2009). The plan should identify specific measurable goals for academic skills and appropriate behaviors, and the individuals and services responsible for helping the student achieve these goals (Killu, 2008). It also should outline the positive, age-appropriate, culturally appropriate teaching, and function-based behavioral supports and strategies and school and community resources that change the antecedent events and consequences by addressing the following issues: (a) What antecedents and consequences can be changed to increase appropriate behavior and decrease inappropriate behavior? (b) What teaching strategies, curricular accommodations, classroom management strategies, motivational techniques, social skills and learning strategy instruction, classroom design modifications, and schoolwide and community-based services can be used to increase appropriate behavior and decrease inappropriate behavior? (c) Which of these changes are most likely to be effective, acceptable, easy to use, culturally sensitive, least intrusive, and beneficial to others and the learning environment? (Arter, 2007; Kerr & Nelson, 2010; Park, 2007).

A sample behavioral intervention plan for Matthew is presented in Table 7.2. Additional strategies for increasing appropriate behavior and decreasing inappropriate behavior and modifying the classroom environment that Ms. McLeod can use are discussed later in this chapter.

Evaluate the Plan

Once the plan has been implemented, the team continues to collect data to examine how effectively the plan is influencing the student's behavior, learning, and socialization (Chandler & Dahlquist, 2010; Killu, 2008; Park, 2007). The extent to which the plan was age-, culturally-, and gender-appropriate, implemented as intended, as well as the impact of the plan on the classroom environment and the student's peers, teachers, and family, also should be assessed. Based on these data and feedback from others, the team revises the plan, changes the interventions, and collects additional data if necessary.

PROMOTING POSITIVE CLASSROOM BEHAVIOR

HOW CAN I PROMOTE POSITIVE CLASSROOM BEHAVIOR IN STUDENTS? Many supports and strategies to promote good classroom behavior exist (Alberto & Troutman, 2009; Henley, 2010; Kerr & Nelson, 2010; Wheeler & Richey, 2010). They include relationship-building strategies, social skills instruction, antecedents-based interventions, consequences-based interventions, self-management techniques, group-oriented management systems, and behavior reduction techniques.

Employ Relationship-Building Strategies

Building meaningful and genuine caring relationships with and among your students is an essential aspect of creating a learning environment that supports their learning, motivation, and promotes their positive classroom behavior (Learned et al., 2009; Mihalas et al., 2009). You also can establish a classroom environment that is based on mutual respect and show your students that you are an open, empathetic, welcoming, respectful, culturally sensitive, understanding, nonjudgmental, and honest person whom they can trust by using the strategies described here (Regan, 2009; Smith et al., 2009). It also means using age-appropriate strategies to teach them, discipline them, and interact with them.

Get to Know and Demonstrate a Personal Interest in Students An essential aspect of building relationships with students is getting to know them and demonstrating a personal interest in them (Mihalas et al., 2009; Regan, 2009). To do this, you need to learn about what is important to them, which can be accomplished by

REFLECTIVE

Perform an FBA on one of your behaviors, such as studying or eating. How could you use the results to change your behavior?

Making Connections
This discussion of ways to establish caring and respectful relationships with your students builds on our earlier discussion of promoting acceptance and friendships in Chapter 5.

TABLE 7.2 Behavioral intervention plan for Matthew

Goals	Interventions	Individuals	Evaluation
1. To decrease Matthew's call-outs and extraneous comments	• Teach Matthew to use a self-management system that employs culturally appropriate reinforcers selected by Matthew	• Matthew • Teachers • Family members • School psychologist	• Data on Matthew's call-outs and extraneous comments • Teachers, student, and family interview data
2. To increase Matthew's work completion	• Relate the content of the instructional activity to Matthew's experiential background and interests • Use cooperative learning groups. • Promote active student responding via response cards and group physical responses. • Provide Matthew with choices in terms of the content and process of the instructional activities. • Solicit feedback from students concerning the ways to demonstrate mastery. • Use culturally relevant materials. • Personalize instruction by using students' names, interests, and experiences. • Use suspense, games, technology, role plays, and simulations. • Teach learning strategies.	• Matthew • Teachers • Family members • Principal	• Data on Matthew's work completion and accuracy • Teacher, student, and family interview data
3. To increase Matthew's in-seat behavior	• Use cooperative learning groups. • Use group-oriented response-cost system. • Establish a classwide peer-mediation system. • Place Matthew's desk near the teacher's work area.	• Matthew • Teachers • Peers • Family members • School psychologist • Principal	• Data on Matthew's in-seat behavior • Observation data • Teacher, student, and family interview data
4. To increase Matthew's involvement in after-school activities	• Teach social skills. • Pair Matthew with peers who participate in after-school activities. • Invite community groups and school-based groups to talk to the class about their after-school activities. • Share and read in class materials about community and leisure activities. • Take field trips to community facilities and after-school activities in the community. • Work with school and community groups to increase the availability of after-school activities.	• Matthew • Teachers • Peers • Family members • Community members • School counselor • Principal	• Data on after-school activities attended by Matthew • Teachers, student, family, school counselor, and community member interview data

interacting with them informally, observing them in various situations and settings, and using journals to solicit information from them. For example, some teachers find time each school day or during a class period to have a brief personal conversation with their students about nonacademic subjects (Smith & Lambert, 2008). You can ask students to talk in class or write about their interests, hobbies, families, and extracurricular activities. You can then use this information to plan instructional activities, interact with them, and comment on important achievements and events in their lives. For example, include references to students' skills, achievements, and contributions in your instructional presentations and examples. You can also show your interest in students by attending extracurricular events, greeting them by name, and welcoming them to your class (Landsman, Moore, & Simmons, 2008).

Your personal interest in students also can be demonstrated by establishing and maintaining rapport with them. Rapport can be established by

- listening actively,
- talking to students about topics that interest them,
- showing an interest in students' personal lives,
- letting them know you missed them when they are absent and welcoming them back,
- sharing your own interests and stories,
- displaying empathy and giving emotional support,
- letting them perform activities in which they excel,
- scheduling surprises for them and recognizing special events in students' lives such as birthdays,
- doing favors for them and allowing them to do things for you,
- participating in after-school activities and spending informal time with them,
- complimenting them and celebrating their successes (Mihalas et al., 2009; Price & Nelson, 2007; Regan, 2009; Smith, 2009).

Building meaningful relationships with and among your students is an essential aspect of supporting their learning and promoting their positive classroom behavior. How do you establish meaningful relationships with your students?

Develop Students' Self-Esteem

You can build relationships with students and establish a good learning environment by helping them develop their self-esteem (Smith et al., 2009). This can be done by providing students with opportunities to show their competence to others and to perform skills, roles, and jobs that are valued by others (Regan, 2009; Smith, 2009). You also can foster their self-esteem by listening to them and showing them that you value their ideas, opinions, feedback, and skills by involving them in the decision-making process and giving them choices (Mihalas et al., 2009; Kern & State, 2009).

Use Humor   In addition to defusing difficult classroom situations, humor can help you and your students develop a good relationship and a positive classroom atmosphere (Franklin, 2006). Your effective use of humor can help you put students at ease, gain their attention, and help them see you as a person. When using humor with your students, make sure that you have a good relationship with students and that they understand and are receptive to humor; the situation warrants its use; it is targeted at yourself or a situation; and it fosters empathy, understanding, and relationships (Frenette, 2007; Smith & Shapon-Shevin, 2009). You need to be careful using humor: Make sure that it is not directed toward students as ridicule or sarcasm; is not misinterpreted; and is free of ability, racial, ethnic, socioeconomic religious, sexual, and gender bias stereotypes and connotations. You also need to be aware of events in the students' lives, your school, and the world when using humor appropriately and strategically.

Making Connections
This discussion of ways to develop students' self-esteem builds on our earlier discussion of self-esteem in Chapter 6.

Acknowledge and Praise Students   Acknowledging positive aspects of your students' behavior can promote self-esteem in students, and strengthen the bond between you and your students. One effective way of acknowledging students is to praise them, which can create a positive environment in your classroom and encourage prosocial behavior (Kennedy & Jolivette, 2008). You can follow

Creating a Classroom Environment That Promotes Positive Behavior

Promoting Students' Self-Esteem

Ms. Vang noticed that several of her students often made negative comments about themselves and seemed reluctant to volunteer and participate in classroom activities. Concerned about their attitude, Ms. Vang decided to develop some activities to help her students feel better about themselves and her classroom. To make students aware of their strengths, she posted their work on bulletin boards and acknowledged their contributions. She also set up a rotating system so that all students could perform jobs and act as classroom leaders.

Here are some other strategies you can use to implement the IDEA in your inclusive classroom and promote students' self-esteem:

- Build students' confidence by complimenting them, focusing on positive aspects and improvements, showing

faith in their abilities, and acknowledging the difficulty of tasks.

- Give students learning activities that they can succeed at.

- Recognize and show appreciation for students' interests, hobbies, and cultural and language backgrounds.

- Make teaching personal by relating it to students' experiences.

- Use facial expressions and eye contact to show interest, concern, and warmth.

Sources: Denton (2008); Learned et al. (2009); Margolis and McCabe (2006); Regan (2009).

---

several guidelines to make your praise more effective (Conroy, Sutherland, Snyder, AL-Hendawi, & Vo, 2009; Gable, Hester, Rock, & Hughes, 2009; Lam, Yim, & Ng, 2008; Willingham, 2008). Your praise statements should be directed toward the praiseworthy behaviors of *all students* and delivered immediately in a noncontrolling, positive, and natural way. It also should describe the specific behavior that is being praised (rather than saying, "This is a good paper," say, "You did a really good job of using topic sentences to begin your paragraphs in this paper"), and be paired with student names. Your praise should be sincere; focus on students' current successes rather than their past failures; relate to attributes of the behavior rather than your students; and be personalized to the students' age, skill level, and cultural background. When using praise, consider whether students prefer to be praised in front of their classmates or in private. Keep in mind that some students may not want to receive praise as it may be interpreted by them and their peers as signs of their "selling out" or "acting white" (Duda & Utley, 2005).

It also is important to use praise to acknowledge effort and improvement as well as specific behaviors and outcomes ("You worked hard on this and it really helped you improve") rather than praising students for specific abilities such as their intelligence ("You are smart at solving problems") (Dweck, 2007). You also should individualize praise so that your students' achievements are evaluated in comparison with their own performance rather than in competition with the performance of others.

You also should examine your *praise or reinforcement ratio*, which refers to the ratio between the number of positive and negative statements you direct toward your students. Try to achieve a ratio of four to five positive comments to one reprimand/corrective comment (Conroy et al., 2008; Simpson & Allday, 2008). You can increase the frequency and credibility of praise by establishing a plan of where, when, and how to deliver praise; using diverse and spontaneous statements that do not distract students or interrupt the flow of the lesson; posting an icon in your classroom that prompts you to praise students; and establishing goals, recording, and self-evaluating your use of praise. For example, you can maintain a chart that lists the time, statements, recipients, and behaviors associated with your praise statements (Stormont & Reinke, 2009).

Praise notes also acknowledge students (Mitchem, Young, & West, 2000). These are written statements that acknowledge what students did and why it was important ("I like how you. . . ."; "It was helpful because. . . ."). In addition to giving them

Making Connections
Find out more about guidelines for using praise and feedback to support your students' academic performance in Chapter 9.

REFLECTIVE

What is your praise or reinforcement ratio? What can you do to increase or maintain it?

to students, share these notes with others or post them in your classroom. You also can teach your students to write praise notes to their classmates for engaging in prosocial behaviors (Fenty, Miller, & Lampi, 2008; Peterson Nelson et al., 2008).

Conduct Meetings and Use Dialoguing   Individual and class meetings are designed to help students understand the perspectives of others, an essential ingredient of building relationships and resolving classroom-related conflicts (Mihalis et al., 2009). With you and other professionals such as the school counselor, students as a group can share their opinions and brainstorm solutions to classroom conflicts, class behavior problems, concerns about schoolwork, and general topics that concern students during *class meetings* (Jones & Jones, 2007). Promote discussion by presenting open-ended topics using *defining* questions ("What does it mean to interrupt the class?"), *personalizing* questions ("How do you feel when someone interrupts the class?"), and *creative thinking* questions ("How can we stop others from interrupting the class?"). In class discussions, *all students* have a right to share their opinions without being criticized by others, and only positive, constructive suggestions should be presented.

Classroom problems and tensions between students can be identified and handled by placing a box in the classroom where students and adults submit compliments and descriptions of problems and situations that made them feel upset, sad, annoyed, or angry. Compliments and concerns can be shared with the class, and *all students* can brainstorm possible solutions to concerns.

You can also use dialoguing such as problem-solving conferences to build relationships with students and help them understand their behavior and problem-solve alternatives to inappropriate behaviors as well as solutions to problematic situations (Crowe, 2008). This process involves (a) meeting with students to discover their view of a situation or issue ("What happened?" "Why did it happen?"), (b) helping students reevaluate the situation to identify the real issues and difficulties ("How do you view the situation now?"), (c) phrasing the issues in the students' words ("Is _____ what you are saying?"), (d) helping them identify solutions to the issues and difficulties ("What do you think should be done to address the situation?"), and (e) discussing their solutions ("What do you think of the plan? What do we need to do to make it successful?") (Crowe, 2008; Dwairy, 2005).

Be Aware of Nonverbal Communication   Your relationship with your students also will be affected by nonverbal communication, which includes physical distance and personal space, eye contact and facial expressions, and gestures and body movements (Banks, Bacon, Young, & Jackson, 2007; Learned et al., 2009). When nonverbal communication is not understood, the result can be miscommunication and conflicts between students and teachers. Therefore, your nonverbal messages should promote positive interactions, be consistent with students' behavioral expectations, and communicate attitudes.

Nonverbal behaviors also should be consistent with students' and teachers' cultural backgrounds. For example, individuals from some cultures may feel comfortable standing close to persons they are talking to, while those from other cultures may view such closeness as a sign of aggressiveness. Because physical gestures may also have different meanings in different cultures, make sure that they are not misinterpreted by your students and their families.

Use Affective Education Techniques   Affective education strategies and programs help build relationships with and among students and assist them in understanding their feelings, attitudes, and values. These strategies and programs involve students in resolving conflicts. They also try to promote students' emotional, behavioral, and social development by increasing their self-esteem and their ability to express emotions effectively. Students who feel good about themselves and know how to express their feelings build positive relationships with others and tend not to have behavior problems.

REFLECTIVE

Observe several individuals with whom you deal regularly. How do they interact nonverbally with others? Are their nonverbal and verbal behaviors congruent? When these behaviors are incongruent, on which type of behavior do you rely?

Use Conflict Resolution and Peer Mediation Programs   Because conflicts often serve as a barrier to building relationships, classroom- and school-related conflicts, particularly those based on age and cultural differences, can be handled through use of conflict resolution programs such as **peer mediation** (Duda & Utley, 2005). Peer mediation involves students trained to serve as peer mediators using communication, problem solving, and critical thinking to help students who have conflicts meet face to face to discuss and resolve disagreements. Johnson and Johnson (1996) have developed a peer mediation and conflict resolution program called Teaching Students to Be Peacemakers.

Include Social Skills Instruction

An important component of an effective classroom management plan is social skills instruction. With social skills teaching, students like Matthew can discover how to learn and socialize with others. Social skills instruction also can help students learn how to work in groups; make friends; recognize and respond appropriately to the feelings of others; resolve conflicts; understand their strengths, challenges, and emotions; and deal with frustration and anger (Bardon, Dona, & Symons, 2008).

You can help students develop their social skills by clearly explaining the behavior, its importance, and when it should be used. Demonstrate, explain, role-play, and practice using the behavior in person or via videos, as well as provide students with numerous opportunities to use it in natural settings with peers. You also can integrate social skills instruction across your curriculum by embedding social skills into academic learning activities and having students maintain reflective journals of their social skills.

Use Antecedent-Based Interventions

Antecedent-based interventions are changes in classroom events, environment, and stimuli that precede behavior (Simpson & Allday, 2008). They allow you to try to take actions to encourage positive behavior and minimize the likelihood of inappropriate behaviors occurring. They also include teacher behaviors such as using curricular and teaching accommodations (see Chapters 8–11), and classroom design changes (discussed later in this chapter).

Give Clear and Direct Directions

Your verbal communications with your students play an important role in helping them behave appropriately. Compliance with your requests can be fostered by speaking to students in a respectful, firm, and calm manner (Smith & Lambert, 2008). You also can phrase your statements to them so that they are

- stated in positive terms and focus on what students should do rather than what they should not do,
- presented to students in an appropriate sequence of steps when giving multiple commands, and
- phrased directly rather than indirectly and tell students what to do rather than asking them to do something (Herschell, Greco, Filcheck, & McNeil, 2002; Stormont & Reinke, 2009).

Use Teacher Proximity and Movement   Your proximity and movement can promote positive behavior (Mulrine et al., 2008; Simpson & Allday, 2008). This can be done by (a) standing near students who have behavior problems and room locations where problems typically occur; (b) placing students' desks near you; (c) talking briefly with students while walking around the room; (d) delivering praise, feedback, and consequences while standing close to students; and (e) monitoring your movement patterns to ensure you move around the room in unpredictable ways and that *all students* receive attention and interact with you (Conroy et al., 2008). When using

Making Connections
This discussion of social skills builds on the discussion of strategies for fostering students' social skills in Chapters 5 and 6.

Making Connections
Find out more about how to use effective strategies to help students understand and follow directions for assignments in Chapter 9.

proximity, you should be aware of its effects on students. For example, the proximity of adults can prevent students from interacting with classmates and developing independent behaviors. Because some students may view your proximity as a sign that you do not trust them, it is important for you to use this technique judiciously and unintrusively (Duda & Utley, 2005). To avoid the possible stigma of moving a student's desk near you, move around the classroom so that you periodically position yourself near *all students*.

REFLECTIVE

How do your students view teacher proximity?

Use Cues Cues can be used to promote good classroom behavior. You and your students can create prearranged cues that you deliver to them to prompt them to engage in positive behaviors. Cues provided via color wheels or number-based behavioral rubrics also can indicate acceptable or unacceptable behavioral levels in the classroom for different activities (Fudge & Skinner, 2007; Li, 2009). For example, red or 1 can signal no talking, yellow or 2 that soft voices are appropriate, and green or 3 that typical classroom voices should be used.

Verbal and nonverbal cues such as physical gestures can be used to prompt group or individual responses. These cues also can establish routines, remind students of appropriate behaviors, or signal to students that their behavior is unacceptable and should be changed. For example, individualized eye contact, hand signals, and head movements can be used to indicate affirmation, correction, or the need to refocus on appropriate behavior, and verbal reminders can be used to alert students to the need for them to engage in appropriate behavior. When using cues, make sure they are culturally appropriate.

Follow Routines

Because unexpected changes in classroom routines can cause students like Matthew to act out and respond inappropriately, it is important to follow consistent and predictable routines and foster transitions from one activity to another (Gable et al., 2009; Li, 2009). When students know what routines and activities to expect in the classroom each day, they are more likely to feel that they are in control of their environment, which can reduce instances of misbehavior in the classroom.

Consider Scheduling Alternatives Establishing and maintaining a regular schedule is an important way to follow ongoing classroom routines (Li, 2009; Trussell, 2008). Good scheduling (see Figure 7.4) also can improve student learning and behavior. A regular schedule with ongoing classroom routines helps students understand the day's events. Many students with disabilities also receive instruction and services from support personnel, so you may need to coordinate their schedules with other professionals. Also, because these students may miss work and assignments while outside the room, you need to establish procedures for making up these assignments. Some students may benefit from object and visual schedules, which pair specific activities with concrete items and pictorials depicting the activities (Banda, Grimmett, & Hart, 2009; Li, 2009). Marks et al. (2006) and Downing and Eichinger (2003) offer guidelines for designing and using schedules with students with autism spectrum disorders and moderate and severe disabilities, respectively. Important factors in scheduling and ways to help your students learn the schedule are presented in Figure 7.4.

Help Students Make Transitions Transitions from one period to the next, and from one activity to the next within a class period, are a significant part of the school day. For many of your students, these transitions can lead to behaviors that interfere with student learning. You can minimize problems with transitions by allowing students to practice making transitions and by making accommodations in the classroom routine (Banda et al., 2009; Price & Nelson, 2007). You can review the day's schedule and directions for transitioning to activities with students, alert them to

FIGURE 7.4 Classroom scheduling guidelines

CONSIDER STUDENT CHARACTERISTICS AND CHALLENGES

- Consider students' physical, sensory, and cognitive abilities and chronological ages.
- Examine the objectives, activities, and priorities in students' IEPs.
- Adapt the schedule and the length of activities based on students' ages and attention spans.
- Involve students in planning the schedule for negotiable events such as free-time activities.
- Begin with a lesson or activity that is motivating and interesting to students.
- Plan activities so that less popular activities are followed by activities that students enjoy.
- Teach difficult material and concepts when students are most alert.
- Alternate movement and discussion activities with passive and quiet activities, and alternate small-group and large-group activities.
- Work with individual students during activities that require limited supervision.
- Give students breaks that allow them to move around and interact socially.
- Give students several alternatives when they complete an assigned activity early.

HELP STUDENTS LEARN THE SCHEDULE

- Post the schedule in a prominent location using an appropriate format for the students' ages.
- Review the schedule periodically with students.
- Record the schedule on loop tapes that automatically rewind and then repeat the same message.
- Avoid frequently changing the schedule.
- Share the schedule with families and other professionals.

Sources: Li (2009); Trussell (2008).

PEARSON
myeducationlab

Go to the Assignments and Activities section of the Topic *Classroom/Behavior Management* in the MyEducationLab for your course and complete the activity entitled *Transitions Within the Classroom*. As you watch the video and answer the accompanying questions, note the importance of clear expectations and specific direction when it comes to transitions within the classroom.

---

upcoming transitions ("You have 2 minutes to get ready for the next activity"), and pair them with other students who efficiently transition to new activities. You can use verbal, visual, musical, or physical cues to signal students that it is time to get ready for a new activity and that they need to complete their work (Fudge & Skinner, 2007). In addition, you can use schedules containing visual representations of classroom activities, and pictorial cue cards that prompt students to (a) listen to directions, (b) put their materials away, and (c) get ready for the next activity. You also can use learning strategies that teach students to make successful transitions and reward groups or individual students for making an orderly and smooth transition, pair students to help each other finish an activity, and review several motivating aspects of the next activity. Babkie (2006), for instance, has developed a learning strategy called CHANGE to assist students in learning to make transitions.

Having clear expectations, coordinating with your paraeducators, and giving students specific directions on moving to the next activity can help them make the transition (Simpson & Allday, 2008). For example, rather than telling students, "Get ready for social studies class," say, "Finish working on your assignment, put all your materials away, and line up quietly." When students come from a less structured social activity like lunch or recess to a setting that requires quiet and attention, a transitional activity is important. For example, following recess, have students write in a journal one thing that was discussed in class the previous day. This can help prepare them for the day's lesson and smooth the transition.

Establish, Teach, and Enforce Rules   To create an effective, efficient, and pleasant learning environment, it is important to establish, teach, and enforce culturally sensitive and developmentally appropriate classroom rules that promote your students' learning, socialization, behavior, and safety using the following guidelines (Gable et al., 2009; Kostewicz, Ruhl, & Kubina, 2008). When students are involved in developing the rules, they learn that they are also responsible for their actions, and they are more likely to follow the rules (Landsman et al., 2008). Therefore, you can work with students to develop reasonable and attainable rules that address cooperative and productive learning behaviors, guide classroom interactions, and are acceptable both to them and to you (Guskey & Anderman, 2008). Ask students what rules they think the class needs, present classroom problems and ask students to brainstorm solutions and rules to address these problems, or have students create a classroom constitution or mission statement. You also can have students work in groups to suggest rules for specific classroom activities (e.g., rules during teacher-directed instruction, free time, transitions, etc.). Students also can help determine the consequences for following rules and the violations for breaking them. This process should have some flexibility based on students' individual differences and circumstances (Simpson & Allday, 2008).

Several guidelines will make your rules meaningful to students (Gable et al., 2009; Kostewicz et al., 2008). Phrase rules so that they are concise, stated in the students' language, easily understood, and usable in many situations and settings. Each rule should begin with an action verb. It should include a behavioral expectation that is defined in observable terms and the benefits of following the rule. Your rules also should be respectful of your students' cultural, linguistic, and experiential backgrounds. When exceptions to rules exist, identify the exceptions and discuss them in advance.

Whenever possible, state rules in positive terms (Simonsen et al., 2008). For example, a rule for in-seat behavior can be stated as "Work at your desk" rather than "Don't get out of your seat." Rules also can be stated in terms of students' responsibilities such as "Show respect for yourself by doing your best." Rules also may be needed and phrased to help students respect *all students*. For example, you may want to introduce rules related to teasing and name-calling such as "Be polite, show respect for others, and treat others safely and fairly."

It also is important that you help students learn the rules (Gable et al., 2009; Kostewicz et al., 2008; Simonsen et al., 2008). You can do this by describing and demonstrating the observable behaviors that make up the rules, giving examples of rule violations and behaviors related to the rules, and role-playing rule-following and rule-violating behaviors. You and your students also can create T-charts that list what appropriate behaviors associated with the rules would look like and sound like. You can discuss the rationale for the rules, the contexts in which rules apply, and the need for and benefits of each rule. At the beginning, review the rules frequently with the class, asking students periodically to recite them or practice one of them. It also is important to praise students for following the rules and to offer positive and corrective feedback to students who initially fail to comply so that they can succeed in the future. For example, when a student breaks a rule, you can state the rule, request compliance, and offer options for complying with it.

Posting the rules on a neat, colorful sign in an easy-to-see location in the room also can help students remember them (Trussell, 2008). Some students with disabilities and younger students may have difficulty reading, so pictures representing the rules are often helpful. You also can personalize this method by taking and posting photographs of students acting out the rules, labeling the photos, and using them as prompts for appropriate behavior. Additionally, you can help students understand the rules and commit to following them by enforcing the rules immediately and consistently and by reminding students of the rules when a class member complies with them.

Use Consequence-Based Interventions

Consequence-based interventions are changes in the classroom events and stimuli that follow a behavior (Alberto & Troutman, 2009; Henley, 2010; Kerr & Nelson, 2010; Wheeler & Richey, 2010). Several consequence-based interventions will now be described.

PEARSON **myeducationlab**

Go to the Building Teaching Skills and Dispositions section of the Topic *Classroom/Behavior Management* in the MyEducationLab for your course and complete the activity entitled *Establishing Classroom Rules and Routines*. As you work through the learning unit, consider the importance of culturally sensitive, developmentally appropriate classroom rules.

Use Positive Reinforcement   A widely used, highly effective method for motivating students to engage in positive behaviors is **positive reinforcement**. With this method, an action is taken or stimulus is given after a behavior occurs. The action or stimulus increases the rate of the behavior or makes it more likely that the behavior will occur again. Actions or stimuli that increase the probability of a repeated behavior are called **positive reinforcers**. For example, you can use verbal and physical (e.g., smiling, signaling OK, giving a thumbs-up) praise as a positive reinforcer to increase a variety of classroom behaviors such as Matthew's on-task behavior.

When using positive reinforcement, you need to consider several things. First, it is critical to be consistent and make sure that reinforcers desired by students are delivered after the behavior occurs, especially when the behavior is being learned. As the student becomes successful, gradually deliver the reinforcement less often and less quickly and raise the standards that students must meet to receive reinforcement.

One type of positive reinforcement used by many classroom teachers is based on "Grandma's rule": **Premack's principle**. According to this rule, students can do something they like if they complete a less popular task first. For example, a student who works on an assignment for a while can earn an opportunity to work on the computer.

Another positive reinforcement system that can promote good behavior is the *classroom lottery,* in which you write students' names on "lottery" tickets after they demonstrate appropriate behavior and place the tickets in a jar in full view of the class. At the end of the class or at various times during the day, you or a designated student draws names from the jar, and those selected receive reinforcement. The lottery system can be modified by having the class earn a group reward when the number of tickets accumulated exceeds a preestablished number.

Select Appropriate Reinforcers   Key components of positive reinforcement are the reinforcers or rewards that students receive. You can use a variety of culturally relevant edible, tangible, activity, social, and group reinforcers. However, you should be careful in using reinforcers because their impact can be short-lived and tied to the availability of the rewards (Willingham, 2008). They also can have negative effects on student motivation and performance such as causing students to cheat and not take control of their own learning (Guernsey, 2009; Kohn, 2003). You can address this problem by using reinforcers only when necessary and for a limited amount of time, and carefully examining their impact on your students. You also can embed rewards in the activity, make rewards more subtle, use rewards equitably and for improved performance, combine rewards with praise, fade out the use of rewards, and encourage students to reinforce themselves via self-statements.

Making Connections
Find out more about guidelines for motivating students in Chapter 9.

Many food reinforcers have little nutritional value and can cause health problems, so you should work with family members and health professionals to evaluate them with respect to students' health needs and allergic reactions. Tangible reinforcers involve students earning a desired object as a result of their positive behaviors. Activity reinforcers, which allow students to perform an enjoyable task or activity that interests them, are highly motivating alternatives. One flexible activity reinforcer is free time. It can be varied to allow students to work alone, with a peer, or with adults. Students also can be given break cards which they can use at selected time periods (Cihak & Gama, 2008). Class jobs also can motivate students (Smith, 2009). At first, you may assign class jobs. When students perform these jobs well, they can be given jobs that require more responsibility.

Some teachers use a reinforcement hierarchy to delineate levels of reinforcement based on how naturally occurring the reinforcer is (Boutot, 2008). As students become more proficient, you can move away from using contrived reinforcers such as edibles and tangibles and use more naturally occurring reinforcers such as activities, free time and praise.

Administer Reinforcement and Preference Surveys   Many classroom management systems fail because the reinforcers are not appropriate, not desired by students, or ineffective. One way to solve this problem is to ask for students' preferences via a **reinforcement or preference survey** (Alberto & Troutman, 2009). You also can identify student preferences by observing students and interviewing others who know the student well (Boyd, Alter, & Conroy, 2005).

Teachers typically use three formats for reinforcement surveys: open-ended, multiple-choice, and rank order (Fenty et al., 2008). The *open-ended* format asks students to identify reinforcers by completing statements about their preferences ("If I could choose the game we will play the next time we go to recess, it would be"). The *multiple-choice* format allows students to select one or more choices from a list of potential reinforcers ("If I had 15 minutes of free time in class, I'd like to (a) work on the computer, (b) play a game with a friend, or (c) listen to music on the headphones"). For the *rank order* format, students grade their preferences from strong to weak using a number system.

You can consider several factors when developing reinforcement or preference surveys. Items can be phrased using student language rather than professional jargon (*reward* rather than *reinforcer*) and can reflect a range of reinforcement. In addition, keep in mind the reinforcer's effectiveness ("Do students like the reinforcers and engage in the activities?"), availability ("Will I be able to give the reinforcer at the appropriate times?"), practicality ("Is the reinforcer consistent with the class and school rules?"), cultural relevance ("Is the reinforcer consistent with the students' cultural backgrounds?"), and cost ("Will the reinforcer prove too expensive to maintain?"). Finally, because students may have reading and/or writing difficulties, you may need to read items for students as well as record their responses. Alberto and Troutman (2009) provide examples of reinforcement surveys; and Lee, Nguyen, Yu, Thorsteinsson, Martin, and Martin (2008), Reid and Green (2006), and Stafford (2005) offer guidelines for using preference surveys with students with developmental disabilities.

Use Contracting   You and your students may work together to develop a **contract**, a written agreement that outlines the behaviors and results of a specific behavior management system. Contracts should give immediate and frequent reinforcement. They should be structured for success by calling at first for small changes in behavior. Both parties must consider the contract fair, and it must be stated in language that the students can read and understand.

FIGURE 7.5 **Sample contract outline**

This is a contract between _____ and
Student's or class's name

_____ . The contract starts on _____ and ends
Teacher's name

on _____ . We will renegotiate it on _____ .

During _____

Environmental conditions (times, classes, activities)

I (we) agree to _____ .

Behavior student(s) will demonstrate

If I (we) do, I (we) will _____ .

Reinforcers to be delivered

The teacher will help by _____ .

I (we) will help by _____ .

_____
Teacher's Signature

_____
Student or Class Representative's Signature

_____
Date

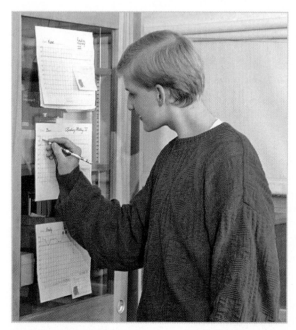

Students can use self-management strategies to monitor and change their behavior. How could you help your students use self-management?

A contract should be developed by you with your students. Family members and other professionals also can be involved in formulating the contract when they have specific roles in implementing it. Generally, contracts include the following elements:

- A statement of the specific behavior(s) the student(s) is to increase/decrease in observable terms
- A statement of the environment in which the contract will be used
- A list of the types and amounts of reinforcers and who will provide them
- A schedule for the delivery of reinforcers
- A list of the things the teacher and student(s) can do to increase the success of the system
- A time frame for the contract, including a date for renegotiation
- Signatures of the student(s) and teacher

Figure 7.5 presents an outline of a sample contract.

Use Group-Oriented Management Systems

Group influence can be used to promote good behavior and decrease misbehavior by using *group-oriented systems*. Group-oriented management systems have several advantages over traditional methods: They foster cooperation among members; they teach responsibility to the group and enlist the class in solving classroom problems; they are adaptable to a variety of behaviors and classrooms; and they give students a positive method of dealing with the problems of peers.

UDL and You

Teaching Students to Use Self-Management Interventions

You can incorporate the principles of UDL to help your students develop successful behaviors that support their learning and socialization by teaching them to use *self-management interventions.* These strategies, also called *cognitive behavioral interventions,* actively involve students in monitoring and changing their behaviors and increasing their independence. Students can be taught to use them by introducing the expected behavior(s) and the self-management strategies, having them observe models using them, and giving them opportunities to practice and master them in a variety of settings (Wilkinson, 2008). A variety of self-managed interventions are available, and you may want to want to make them as inconspicuous and age-appropriate as possible and teach your students to use combinations of them (Menzies, Lane, & Lee, 2009; Ryan, Pierce, et al., 2008). You also can improve their effectiveness by teaching your students how to use the data to analyze and improve their behavior (Hudson, Shupe, Vasquez, & Miller, 2008).

Self-Monitoring In **self-monitoring,** often called *self-recording,* students measure their behaviors by using a data collection system. Sample self-recording systems are presented in Figure 7.6. For example, your students can be taught to increase their on-task behavior during class by placing a 1 in a box when they pay attention for several minutes and a 2 if they do not.

You can increase your students' ability to record their own behavior by using a *countoon,* a recording sheet with a picture of the behavior and space for students to record each occurrence (Whitby & Miller, 2009). A countoon for in-seat behavior, for example, would include a drawing of a desk. Students also can use sticky notes and highlighters to keep track of their behavior, assignments, and work completion, and write reminders to themselves (Stormont, 2008).

Self-Evaluation In **self-evaluation** or *self-assessment,* students are taught to evaluate their behavior according to some standard or scale. For example, they can rate their on-task and disruptive behavior using a 0-to-5-point (unacceptable to excellent) rating scale. Students then earn points, which they exchange for reinforcers, based on both their behavior and the accuracy of their rating.

Students also can be asked to respond to a series of questions that prompt them to evaluate their behavior. For example, they can respond to the following:

- How would you describe your behavior in class today?
- What positive behaviors did you use? What happened as a result of these behaviors?
- Which of your behaviors were problems? Why were these behaviors a problem?

- What are some things you could do to continue to use positive behaviors? To improve your behavior?

Students also can use a self-evaluation checklist or cue card listing behaviors paired with icons or pictorial demonstrations, to prompt and assess their behavior (Hart & Whalon, 2008; Joseph & Konrad, 2009). For example, a yes/no checklist can include the following behaviors:

- I raised my hand to answer questions.
- I paid attention to the teacher.
- I stayed in my seat.
- I began my work on time.
- I finished my work.

Self-Reinforcement In **self-reinforcement,** students are taught to evaluate their behavior and then deliver self-selected rewards if appropriate. For example, after showing the correct behavior, students reinforce themselves by working for 15 minutes on the computer.

Self-Managed Free-Token Response-Cost In a *student-managed free-token response-cost* system, you give the student a card with a certain number of symbols. The symbols represent the number of inappropriate behaviors the student may exhibit before losing the agreed-on reinforcement. After each inappropriate behavior, the student crosses out one of the symbols on the card. If any symbols remain at the end of the class time, the student receives the agreed-on reinforcement.

Self-Instruction **Self-instruction** teaches students to regulate their behaviors and problem solve by verbalizing to themselves the questions and responses necessary to (a) identify problems ("What am I being asked to do?"), (b) generate potential solutions ("What are the ways to do it?"), (c) evaluate solutions ("What is the best way?"), (d) use appropriate solutions ("Did I do it?"), and (e) determine whether the solutions were effective ("Did it work?") (Robinson, 2007). To help them do this, you can use *cueing cards,* index cards with pictures of the self-teaching steps for following directions ("stop, look, listen" and "think") that are placed on the students' desks to guide them.

Self-Managing Peer Interactions A self-management system that students can use to deal with the inappropriate behavior of their peers is *3-Steps* (Schmid, 1998). When students are being bothered by peers, they use 3-Steps by (a) telling peers, "Stop! I don't like that"; (b) ignoring or walking away from peers if they do not stop; and (c) informing the teacher that they told them to stop, tried to ignore them, and are now seeking the teacher's help.

FIGURE 7.6 Examples of self-recording systems

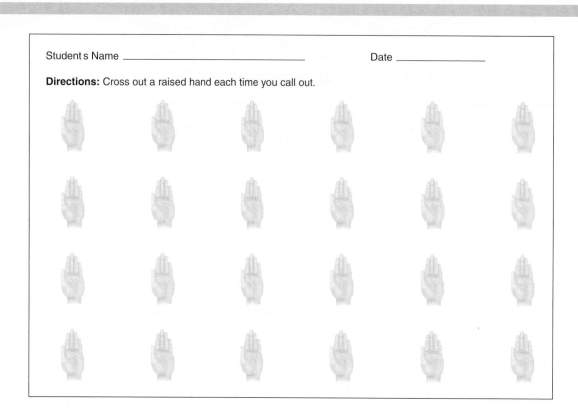

Student's Name _____   Date _____

Directions: Cross out a raised hand each time you call out.

Student's Name _____   Date _____

Directions: At different times throughout class, place a check in the box if you are sitting in your seat.

REFLECTIVE

Choose a behavior you would like to increase or decrease. Select one of the self-management strategies and keep track of your progress. Were you successful? If so, why? If not, why?

You can increase the likelihood that group-oriented systems will be successful by

- teaching students how the system works,
- clarifying the behavior so everyone understands it,
- setting reasonable goals and increasing them gradually, and
- monitoring the system and providing students with ongoing feedback (Babyak, Luze, & Kamps, 2000).

Several problems are possible with using group-oriented management systems. Because the success of these systems depends on the behavior of the whole group or class, a single disruptive individual can prevent the class from achieving its goals. If this happens, the offender can be removed from the group system and dealt with individually. Group-oriented management systems also can result in peer pressure

Using Self-Management Strategies

Matthew is having difficulty completing assignments because he is frequently off task—leaving his seat, talking to classmates, playing with objects, and looking around the room. Matthew's teacher, Ms. McLeod, is concerned about this behavior and decides that Matthew could benefit from a strategy that increases his awareness of it. Ms. McLeod meets with Matthew. They discuss his behavior and the use of a self-management strategy, which Matthew agrees to try. Before starting, they meet again to discuss the system and the behavior. At first, they talk about the importance of Matthew paying attention. Ms. McLeod explains that on-task behavior means eyes on the materials and/or on the teacher. Next, she demonstrates specific, observable examples of on-task and off-task behaviors, emphasizing the features of each. Afterward, she asks Matthew to show examples and nonexamples of on-task behavior.

Ms. McLeod and Matthew then discuss the self-management system and its benefit. Next, Ms. McLeod demonstrates the system for Matthew and thinks out loud as she uses it, which prompts a discussion about the actual conditions in which the system will be used. Before using the system in class, they role-play it. Ms. McLeod assesses Matthew's use of the system and gives him feedback.

Ms. McLeod and Matthew meet again, and this time she asks him to complete a reinforcement survey. The survey includes the following completion items:

The things I like to do at school are _____.

I am proudest in this class when I _____.

When I have free time in class, I like to _____.

The best reward the teacher could give me is _____.

Something that I would work hard for is _____.

Ms. McLeod is surprised by Matthew's responses. Rather than wanting tangible items, Matthew states that he would prefer a class job and extra time to spend with the teacher or his friends. Ms. McLeod and Matthew agree that if he succeeds in changing his behavior, he may choose a reward from among a class job, free time with a friend or Ms. McLeod, and the opportunity to work with a friend.

Next, they try the system in class. It involves placing on Matthew's desk a 4-by-6-inch card that contains 10 drawings of eyes. When Matthew fails to engage in on-task behavior, he crosses out one of the eyes. If any eyes remain at the end of the class period, Matthew can choose one of the activities they discussed. With this system, Matthew is able to increase his on-task behavior, and Ms. McLeod notices that Matthew is doing more assignments and completing them more accurately.

- Why did Ms. McLeod use a self-management system with Matthew?
- What did she do to promote the success of the system? What steps did Ms. McLeod use to teach Matthew to use the system?
- How could you use self-management strategies in your class? What benefits would they have for you and your students?

and scapegoating, so you must carefully observe the impact of these systems on your students. You can attempt to minimize problems by establishing behavioral levels that *all students and groups* can achieve. Choose target behaviors that benefit *all students,* allowing those who do not want to participate in a group to opt out. You also can use heterogeneous groups and limit the competition between groups so that groups compete against a criterion level rather than against other groups.

Use Interdependent Group Systems   When several students in a class have a behavior problem, a good strategy is an *interdependent* group system. The system is applied to the entire group, and its success depends on the behavior of the group. Popular reinforcers for groups of students are free time, a class trip, a party for the class, time to play a group game, or a special privilege.

Group Free-Token Response-Cost System.   One effective interdependent group system is a *group response-cost* system with free tokens. The group is given a certain number of tokens, which are placed in full view of the students and in easy reach of the teacher (e.g., paper strips on an easel or marks on the chalkboard). A token is removed each time a class member misbehaves. If any tokens remain at the end of the time period, the agreed-on reinforcement is given to the whole group. As the group becomes successful, the number of tokens given can gradually be decreased. Adaptations of this system include allowing students to be responsible for removing the tokens, and making each token worth a set amount. An illustration of the group response-cost system is presented in Figure 7.7a.

myeducationlab

Go to the Assignments and Activities section of the Topic *Classroom/Behavior Management* in the MyEducationLab for your course and complete the activity entitled *Self-Monitoring.*

myeducationlab

To reflect on and enhance your understanding how to help your students learn to use self-management strategies in your inclusive classroom, go to the IRIS Center Resources section of the Topic *Classroom/Behavior Management* in the MyEducationLab for your course, and complete the module entitled *SOS: Helping Students Become Independent Learners.*

FIGURE 7.7 Illustrations of group-oriented management strategies

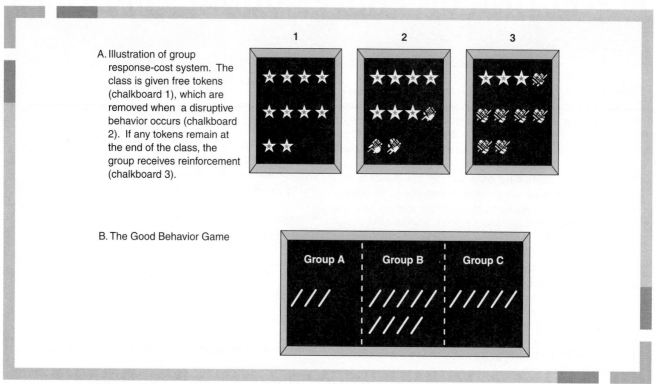

A. Illustration of group response-cost system. The class is given free tokens (chalkboard 1), which are removed when a disruptive behavior occurs (chalkboard 2). If any tokens remain at the end of the class, the group receives reinforcement (chalkboard 3).

B. The Good Behavior Game

Good Behavior Game. The *Good Behavior Game* is an interdependent group system whereby the class is divided into two or more groups (Conroy et al., 2008). Each group's inappropriate behaviors are recorded by a slash on the blackboard (see Figure 7.7b). If the total number of slashes is less than the number specified by the teacher, the groups earn special privileges.

You can modify the Good Behavior Game to account for different types and frequencies of misbehaviors. The system can be tailored to the students by having different groups work on different target behaviors and with different criterion levels. To minimize the competition between groups, each group can earn the reinforcement if the number of misbehaviors is less than the group's own frequency level. For example, one group may work on decreasing calling out and have a criterion level of 25, and another group may work on reducing negative comments and have a criterion level of 8. Rather than competing, each group earns reinforcement if its number of slashes is less than its own criterion level. You also can modify the Good Behavior Game by giving groups merit cards for positive behaviors of the group or of individual members. These merit cards are then used to remove slashes that the group has previously earned.

Group Evaluation. A variety of group evaluation systems promote good classroom behavior. Two examples are the group average group evaluation system and the consensus-based group evaluation system. In the *group average system,* you give an evaluation form to each student in the group and ask each student to rate the group's behavior. You then determine a group rating by computing an average of the students' ratings. You also rate the group's behavior using the same form, and the group rating is compared with your rating. The group earns points, which are exchanged for reinforcers, based on their behavior and accuracy in rating their behavior.

The *consensus-based system* consists of (a) dividing the class into teams and giving each team an evaluation form, (b) having each team use a consensus method for determining the team's ratings of the class's behavior, (c) having the teacher rate the class's behavior using the same evaluation form, (d) comparing each team's ratings with the teacher's rating, and (e) giving reinforcement to each team based on the behavior of the class and the team's accuracy in rating that behavior.

Group evaluation also can be adapted so that one student's evaluation of the behavior of the whole group determines the reinforcement for the whole class. In this system, you and your students rate the class's behavior using the same evaluation form. You then randomly select a student whose rating represents the class's rating. Your rating is compared with this student's rating, and the group receives reinforcement based on the class's behavior and the student's agreement with your rating.

Teachers have different views of the effectiveness of token/point systems. What are your feelings about using them?

Use Dependent Group Systems A *dependent group system* is used when a student's behavior problem is reinforced by peers. In this system, the contingency is applied to the whole class, depending on the behavior of one member (Hansen & Lignugaris/Kraft, 2005). For example, you can use this system by randomly selecting several of your students who can earn free time for the whole class based on their achieving a specific level of appropriate behavior. When using a dependent group system, you need to be careful to assess the reactions of your students to their classmates who engage in behaviors that prevent the class from earning the desired reinforcers.

Use Independent Group Systems In an *independent group system,* individual students are reinforced based on their own performance or behavior. Thus, reinforcement is available to each student, depending on that student's behavior.

Token Economy/Point Systems. One independent group system that works well is a **token economy or point system** (Austin & Sciarra, 2010; Fairbanks et al., 2008; Ryan et al., 2008). Students earn tokens or points for showing appropriate behavior and can redeem these tokens for social, activity, tangible, and edible reinforcers. The steps of token economy or point systems are as follows:

Step 1. Collaborate with students and their families to determine the rules and behaviors that students must use to receive tokens.

Step 2. Choose tokens that are safe, attractive, durable, inexpensive, easy to handle and dispense, and controllable by the teacher. In selecting tokens, consider the age and cognitive abilities of students and the number of tokens needed per student.

Step 3. Identify the reinforcers that students want and determine how many tokens each item is worth. You can establish a store where students may go to buy items with their tokens and allow students to work in the store on a rotating basis. Keep a record of what items students buy, and stock the store with those items. Consider using an auction system in which students bid for available items.

Step 4. Collect other materials needed for the token economy system, such as a container for students to store their tokens and a chart to keep a tally of

REFLECTIVE

What types of group-oriented management systems do you use? How successful are they?

students' tokens. You also can establish a bank where students can store their tokens, and earn interest when saving them for a period of time.

Step 5. Arrange the room for effective and efficient use of the system. For example, desks can be arranged so that you have easy access to all students when dispensing tokens.

Step 6. Introduce and explain the token system to students.

Step 7. Use the token system. At first, give large numbers of tokens to students by catching students behaving appropriately, and allow students to exchange their tokens for reinforcers on a regular basis to show that the tokens have real value. Pair the delivery of tokens with praise and tell the students exactly which appropriate behavior(s) was exhibited. Use a timer to remind you to dispense tokens.

Step 8. Determine how to handle incorrect behavior. You can use a time-out card, which is placed on students' desks for a brief period to indicate that no tokens can be earned. When students behave appropriately for a brief, specified time period, the time-out card is removed and students can earn tokens. Avoid taking away tokens when students do not have enough tokens.

Step 9. Revise the system to correct any problems. For example, if a student is suspected of stealing tokens from others, give the student tokens that are unique in shape or color.

Step 10. Begin to phase out the token system. You can do this by increasing the number of appropriate responses necessary to earn a token, increasing the number of tokens needed for a specific reinforcer, giving tokens on an intermittent schedule, using fewer verbal prompts, giving students fewer chances to exchange tokens for reinforcers, and using a graduated reinforcement system that moves toward the use of naturally occurring reinforcers.

Employ Behavior Reduction Interventions

Teachers also are concerned about misbehavior and its impact on the learning environment and other students. When students misbehave, try to deal with it in a calm, matter-of-fact and private manner without holding grudges (Landsman et al., 2008; Rock & Thead, 2009). There are many ways of decreasing misbehavior, and try to use the most positive ways first. With these strategies, it is important to use the *fair-pair rule*, which means you make sure to teach positive replacement behaviors that can serve as appropriate alternatives to the misbehaviors that are being reduced (Gable et al., 2009; Underwood et al., 2009). For example, while using strategies to decrease Matthew's calling out, Ms. McLeod also would use interventions that help Matthew learn to raise his hand to speak. You also want to make sure that your response to student behavior doesn't escalate it or embarrass or isolate the student (Shukla-Mehta & Albin, 2003). Therefore, when selecting a procedure, carefully consider the following questions:

REFLECTIVE

What are some behaviors that may serve as positive alternatives to such misbehaviors as calling out, being off-task, being out of one's seat, and swearing?

- Is the strategy aversive?
- Does it produce bad side effects?
- Is it effective?
- Does it allow me to teach another behavior to replace the undesirable one?

Another issue to consider is the *least restrictive alternative* principle, also referred to as the *least intrusive alternative.* Use this principle as a guide in selecting methods that reduce the problem behavior without limiting a student's freedom more than necessary and without being physically or psychologically unappealing. Several methods for decreasing misbehavior are presented here.

Use Redirection, Precision Requests, and Choice Statements **Redirection** involves making comments or using behaviors designed to interrupt the misbehavior and prompt students to use appropriate behavior and work on the activity at hand (Babkie, 2006; Landsman et al., 2008). Redirection is most effective when it is done unobtrusively and early in the behavioral sequence. Typically, this starts with your stopping and looking at the students. If that is not successful, consider removing the individuals, objects, or stimuli that appear to be causing the misbehavior, and stating clearly what you want students to do. Other redirection strategies include

- introducing a new stimulus to recapture the student's attention;
- signaling the student verbally and nonverbally to stop a behavior;
- offering to help the student with a task;
- engaging the student in conversation;
- reminding the student to focus on the assignment;
- changing the activity or some aspect of it;
- giving the student a choice between positive behavior and a minor punishment, such as a loss of recess;
- modeling calm and controlled behavior, and using humor (Bucalos & Lingo, 2005).

Teachers also use precision requests to redirect students. **Precision requests** involve your directing a student to engage in positive behavior by using a polite and calm voice to state the student's name, and a concise description of the desired behavior, and then waiting 5 seconds for the student to respond appropriately (Gable et al., 2009).

You also can redirect students by using **choice statements**, which prompt students to choose between engaging in positive behavior and accepting the consequences associated with continued misbehavior. Based on the age of your students and the nature of the behavior, the following choice statements will be appropriate:

- When-then: "When you _____, then you can _____."
- If-then: "If you _____, then I will/you can _____."
- Either-or: "Either you _____, or you will _____."
- Here are your choices: "We need to _____; here are your choices: _____." (Herschell et al., 2002)

Employ Interspersed Requests Interspersed requests, also known as *preferenced-based teaching, pretask requests, high-probability request sequences,* and *behavioral momentum,* can be used to decrease students' avoidance and challenging behaviors and to help students make transitions, and avoid a series of escalating misbehaviors (Banda et al., 2009). Interspersed requests motivate students to do a difficult or unpleasant task by first asking them to perform several easier or preferred tasks that they can complete successfully in a short period of time. You do this by asking students to do two to four easy, preferred, or enjoyable tasks before giving them a task that they might resist, find difficult, or refuse to perform (Lee, Belfiore, & Gormley Budin, 2008). After the learning activity is completed, you also can have students engage in a preferred activity.

Use Planned Ignoring   In **planned ignoring**, also called *extinction,* the positive reinforcers of a behavior are withheld or ended, and students receive praise or positive reinforcement for demonstrating appropriate behaviors (Gable et al., 2009). When this happens, the inappropriate behavior decreases, and the prosocial behaviors increase. For example, Matthew's teachers might be inadvertently maintaining his habit of calling out by reminding him to raise his hand and by responding to his off-task comments. Rather than giving him attention through these reminders, you could decrease the behavior by ignoring his calling out and praising him when he raises his hand.

Planned ignoring takes time to be effective and often initially increases the rate and/or intensity of misbehavior. Therefore, you should use it only for behaviors that can be changed gradually and when you can identify and withhold all reinforcers that are maintaining these behaviors. You can speed up the effectiveness of planned ignoring by combining it with reinforcement of appropriate alternative behaviors. Planned ignoring should not be used for behaviors maintained by reinforcers that are difficult to withdraw, such as peer attention. Finally, planned ignoring might increase aggressive behavior.

PEARSON
myeducationlab

To enhance your understanding of interventions to decrease inappropriate and noncompliant behaviors and increase positive behaviors, go to the IRIS Center Resources section of the Topic *Classroom/Behavior Management* in the MyEducationLab for your course, and complete the modules entitled *Addressing Disruptive and Noncompliant Behaviors (Part 1)*, *Understanding the Acting-Out Cycle*, and *Addressing Disruptive and Noncompliant Behaviors (Part 2): Behavioral Interventions*.

Consider Careful Reprimands   Occasionally, you may need to use reprimands to deal with misbehavior. You can make these reprimands more effective by using them carefully and infrequently, by making them brief, firm, and matter-of-fact, and by delivering them immediately after the misbehavior occurs and in close contact to the student (Gable et al., 2009). Reprimands are specific statements delivered in an assertive tone of voice that direct students to engage in an appropriate alternative behavior ("Stop now, and do your work") rather than questions ("Why aren't you doing your work?"). Reprimands should be focused on the behavior rather than the student. You also should combine reprimands with appropriate nonverbal behaviors such as eye contact, gestures and facial expressions, and avoid the use of sarcasm and judgmental language, which can harm students' self-esteem and cause negative comments from peers.

Rather than use a public verbal reprimand, you can speak to students privately about behavior problems. During these interactions, you can briefly and succinctly tell them what you think, ask probing questions such as "Are you having problems with the assignment?" and discuss a plan for acting appropriately.

PREVENTING STUDENTS FROM HARMING OTHERS

HOW CAN I PREVENT STUDENTS FROM HARMING OTHERS? As reflections of society, schools, unfortunately, are dealing with a growing number of incidents where students are threatening or harming each other. Therefore, your school will need to establish schoolwide programs and strategies for situations that involve bullying, harassment, and other violent acts (Wessler, 2008). You also can work with students and their families and professionals to create a safe, caring school environment that does not tolerate bullying, harassment, or violent acts and that fosters and acknowledges acceptance of individual differences and the development of friendships.

Students Who Are Bullies

You will probably need to deal with bullying or peer harassment that has a negative academic, psychological, behavioral, and physical effect on bullies, their victims, and bystanders (Olweus, 2003; San Antonio & Salzfass, 2007; Wessler, 2008). Bullying reflects a power imbalance in social relationships that results in repeated and intentional instances of peer harassment that cause harm (CEC, 2008; Crothers & Kolbert, 2008). Bullying and peer harassment may take different forms:

- *Verbal and written:* name-calling, taunting, and negative and threatening comments, phone calls, or e-mails
- *Physical:* hitting; pushing; scratching; unwanted sexual touching; damaging personal property; extorting money; and gestures that imply disapproval, intimidation, or derogatory comments
- *Social:* spreading false rumors, excluding from a group, or sharing personal information
- *Sexual:* sexually harassing and/or abusing others, and engaging in exhibitionism or voyeurism.

With the growing use of the technology, cyberbullying has become a major form of bullying that you and your students may encounter (CEC, 2008). Cyberbullying can occur via harmful, inappropriate, threatening, embarrassing, and hurtful e-mails, text messages, blogs, and text, images, and photos postings on the Internet. You and your colleagues at school can counter cyberbullying by making sure that schoolwide antibullying policies and programs address this form of bullying and teaching your students to use technology in appropriate, safe and respectful ways (Mustacchi, 2009).

As Table 7.3 indicates, bullies tend to be physically stronger and more aggressive, impulsive, and defiant than their classmates. Male bullies are more likely to engage in physical bullying (Olweus, 2003), whereas female students are more likely to bully by exclusion, manipulation of friendships, gossiping, and other forms of social bullying (Brown, 2005). Although all students may be targeted by bullies, as Table 7.3 suggests, some students are particularly likely to be victimized by bullies,

Making Connections
Find out more about how to teach your students to be good digital citizens who use technology in safe and appropriate ways in Chapter 8.

TABLE 7.3 **Possible characteristics of bullies and their victims**

Bullies	Victims
Physical development and coordination exceeds peers'.	Physical development and coordination lags behind peers'
Aggressive, impulsive, defiant, dominant, oppositional, and hot-tempered	Nonassertive, shy, quiet, passive, and cautious
Easily upset, angered, and frustrated	Anxious, nervous, immature, insecure, and depressed
Average to above-average self-esteem	Low self-esteem
Confident, secure, athletic, and viewed by some as popular	Limited social skills and few friendships
Friendships with others who are likely to support or engage in bullying	May get along better with adults than peers
Doesn't comply with rules and expects to get own way	Frequently absent, late, or reluctant to come to school
Nonempathetic and brags	Sudden decline in school performance
Views violence and aggression positively	Avoids parts of school that are unsupervised
Exhibits antisocial and violent behaviors such as fighting, vandalizing property, substance abuse, truancy, smoking, and carrying a weapon	Viewed as not fitting in, an easy target, vulnerable, and being physically, psychologically, emotionally, culturally, socially, and experientially different (e.g., overweight, small, disabled, gay/lesbian, or from a different race, ethnic, or language background)
May come from families characterized by a lack of warmth, supervision, and school involvement and the use of physical and corporal discipline and bullying	

Sources: Heinrichs (2003); National Youth Violence Prevention Resource Center (2009); Stop Bullying Now (2009).

including students with disabilities, students identified as gifted and talented, students who are GBLT, students from culturally and linguistically diverse backgrounds, and those with other individual differences (e.g., overweight, small) (CEC, 2008; Young, Allen Heath, Ashbaker, & Smith, 2008).

A range of bullying prevention programs and resources that can be used with elementary-secondary-level students are available (Beaudoin & Taylor, 2009; Crothers & Kolbert, 2008; Mah, 2009). You can collaborate with students, families, professionals, and other interested parties to develop, implement, and evaluate your school's bullying prevention program (San Antonio & Salzfass, 2007). Such a program should provide information to educators and families about the warning signs that a student is being bullied, which may include

- an avoidance of school;
- a sudden decrease in academic performance;
- an increase in being late to class without a plausible explanation;
- difficulty sleeping and frequent nightmares, headaches, and stomachaches;
- torn clothing and/or unexplained bruises;
- frequent requests for additional money;
- belongings being lost;
- a nervousness around specific class-/schoolmates;
- a withdrawal from others; and
- a reluctance to try new things.

As part of your school's antibullying efforts, you can work with your colleagues to teach students the different types of behaviors that constitute bullying and to encourage them to report instances of it to their teachers. It also helps to teach students the difference between reporting behaviors that safeguard themselves and others and reporting behaviors for the sole purpose of getting a classmate in trouble.

The school's bullying prevention program should help students, professionals, and family members understand their roles and responsibilities in addressing peer harassment, and provide them with preventive and proactive strategies and policies to deal with bullying (Young et al., 2008). Bullying prevention strategies and policies include the following:

- Conducting a survey to determine the extent of bullying by examining where, when, and how students are bullied and which students and groups of students are most vulnerable to being bullies and bullied
- Observing students in many different activities and settings
- Establishing school rules that prevent all types of bullying, such as students in this school will not bully others, will treat everyone with respect, and will help others who are bullied; and consequences when these rules are not followed
- Using a confidential message box that allows students to report incidents of bullying
- Holding meetings with students to discuss bullying incidents
- Identifying locations where bullying is most likely to occur and increasing supervision of those places
- Teaching and modeling respectful behaviors toward others
- Creating a school environment that does not tolerate bullying by forming friendship groups and having students make No Bullying Zone posters
- Confronting and disciplining bullies quickly and firmly by addressing their inappropriate behavior and using the situation as an opportunity to teach prosocial behaviors (e.g., "What you did to Juan was wrong, mean, and hurtful"; "I don't know where you learned that type of behavior, but we don't act that

way in this school"; "Is there anything you wish to say to me?"; "What are we going to do to make sure it doesn't happen again?")

- Addressing victims of bullying by being supportive, refuting the actions of bullies, and informing them that you will take action to address the situation (e.g., "I'm sorry that John did that to you. He was wrong and it was not fair to you. I don't know where he learned that, but I talked with him about this.")
- Referring bullies and their victims for counseling and other appropriate services
- Fostering communication among and between teachers and families (CEC, 2008; Crothers & Kolbert, 2008; Heinrichs, 2003; San Antonio & Salzfass, 2007).

The use of a social-emotional learning curriculum and the teaching of social skills are also important aspects of bullying prevention (Crothers & Kolbert, 2008; Heinrichs, 2003; San Antonio & Salzfass, 2007). Help bullies develop empathy for others (Hu, 2009), and teach them self-management and anger management skills. Try using CALM, a mnemonic-based learning strategy that prompts students to manage their anger and give them a "cool card" that reminds them to take a deep breath, count backward from 10, and think of something relaxing (Anderson, Fisher, Marchant, Young, & Smith, 2006; Williams & Reisberg, 2003). You also can have bullies engage in acts that benefit and show respect for others. For example, students who have used bullying can be asked to apologize and do something nice for their victims, clean up part of the school, reflect on how harassment makes their victims feel, or keep a journal of their acts of kindness.

Victims of bullying need to learn how to develop self-esteem, understand social cues to avoid being a victim and to respond in an assertive way that does not make the situation worse (Crothers & Kolbert, 2008; Kolb & Stevens Griffith, 2009). They must also understand when and how to get help from adults. Students who are neither bullies nor victims need to learn how to actively support victims and how to counteract bullies and their harassing acts (CEC, 2008).

Students with Aggressive and Violent Behaviors

As we have seen in our nation's schools, all segments of society and all parts of the country are encountering violence. By being aware of the warning signs, you may be able to prevent aggressive and violent acts from occurring. The early warning signs include social withdrawal, feelings of isolation, persecution or rejection, low motivation, poor school performance, anger, frequent discipline problems, fights with others, intolerance of individual differences, substance abuse, and membership in gangs. Although the signs vary, some of the common indicators of an escalating situation are verbal abuse (e.g., cursing and threats), shouting, body tenseness, destruction of property, self-injurious actions, threatening verbal statements and physical gestures, and possession of weapons. If you encounter a violent incident, you should attempt to follow the school policies for dealing with such situations.

ADAPTING THE CLASSROOM DESIGN

HOW CAN I ADAPT THE CLASSROOM DESIGN TO ACCOMMODATE STUDENTS' LEARNING, BEHAVIORAL, SOCIAL, AND PHYSICAL STRENGTHS AND CHALLENGES? The design of the classroom environment can complement your teaching style and help students learn, behave well, and develop social skills (Emmer & Everston, 2009; Evertson & Emmer, 2009). You can affirm students and the value of education by creating an aesthetically pleasing, cheerful, and inviting classroom that is clean, well lit, odor-free, colorful, and respectful of your students' unique identities and challenges. For example, quiet areas for reflection can establish a classroom environment that

Making Connections
This discussion on strategies for preventing bullying and harassment builds on the specific behaviors for acting promptly and decisively to respond to intolerant and insensitive acts that were discussed earlier in Chapter 5.

REFLECTIVE
Does your school have policies for dealing with bullying, intolerant behaviors, and derogatory language? What procedures and practices are addressed in the policy? How effective is the policy?

Making Connections
Specific strategies you can engage in when encountering violent incidents were discussed earlier in Chapter 2.

values learning and individuality (Nielsen & Higgins, 2005). Your classroom can also be designed to ensure student safety if you check to make sure that high-traffic locations and important classroom materials and technology are accessible to *all students* and free of congestion, electrical wires are anchored and covered, decorations and plants are nontoxic, dangerous materials and equipment are locked in cabinets, sharp edges and broken furniture are removed, and walls, floors, and equipment are in good condition (Trussell, 2008).

Seating Arrangements

Generally, students are seated in areas that allow them to see clearly all presentations and displays. These locations also allow you to see and reach your students. When small-group teacher-directed instruction is used, students can be seated in a semicircle facing you. In a larger-group teacher-directed activity, it may be better for *all students* to face you sitting in a row, circular, or horseshoe arrangement. When students work in groups, they can arrange their desks so that they face each other, allowing them to share information efficiently and quietly. You also can encourage students to personalize their work area.

Each student's desk should be of the right size and placed so as to include the student in all classroom activities and maintain good posture and body alignment. The space around students' desks should be large enough to give you easy access to students in order to monitor performance and distribute papers. Putting tennis balls on the legs of desks and chairs can help minimize noise and make it easier to move them (Rock & Thead, 2009). Students also need a place to store their materials so that they are readily available to students when they need them. If students' desks are not large enough, tote trays can be used to store their supplies.

Teacher's Desk

The location of your desk allows you to monitor behavior and progress and to move quickly if a problem occurs. For monitoring students, your desk can be placed in an area that provides a view of the whole classroom. Any obstacles that prevent you from scanning different parts of the room can be removed. When you are working with students in other parts of the room, you can sit facing the other students in the class.

Posting students' work can make the classroom more attractive and can motivate students. How do your students feel when you post their work?

Bulletin Boards and Walls

Bulletin boards can help you create a pleasant, attractive environment that promotes learning and class pride. *Decorative* bulletin boards make the room attractive and interesting and often relate to a theme. *Motivational* bulletin boards encourage students by showing progress and publicly displaying their work. *Instructional* bulletin boards, or *teaching walls,* often include an acquisition wall, which introduces new concepts and material, and a maintenance wall, which reviews previously learned concepts. *Manipulative* bulletin boards use materials that students can manipulate to learn new skills.

Displays should be planned so that they are at the students' eye level. Whenever possible, involve students in decorating areas of the room so that the walls and ceiling of the classroom are colorful and attractive.

You also can include a space for displaying student assignments, as well as pictures, posters, and art forms that reflect the students' families, homes, neighborhoods, and other cultural groups that may not otherwise be represented in the classroom (Trussel, 2008). Posting the daily assignment schedule and examples of products on part of the bulletin board or wall can help students remember to perform all assigned tasks. Wall displays can include a clock, a list of class rules, and a calendar large enough to be seen from all parts of the classroom.

Learning Centers and Specialized Areas

Learning centers can help students develop independent and problem-solving skills and learn to work collaboratively. You can use a variety of centers such as skill centers that provide students with opportunities to practice skills they have learned and discovery centers which allow students to explore new skills. You can increase the effectiveness of your learning centers by (a) including activities at each center geared to a range of student academic levels, interests, and needs; (b) organizing materials so that students can easily locate, select, and return them; (c) making self-correction an integral part of centers; (d) addressing the technological and furniture needs of students with disabilities; and (e) teaching students how to use them independently and to work in small groups (King-Sears, 2006).

Classroom Design Accommodations

Many students, especially those with disabilities, need specific classroom design accommodations in order to perform as well as possible. Guidelines for physical accommodations of general education classrooms are outlined here.

Students from Diverse Cultural and Language Backgrounds   You can arrange the classroom environment to support the language learning of your students by making language part of all classroom activities and routines (Levine & McCloskey, 2009). For instance, label work areas and objects in the classroom in multiple languages. You also can give students access to materials and learning activities; set up social and work areas, listening areas, and meeting areas; and allow students to sit and work with peer models.

Deaf and Hard of Hearing Students   Classroom design accommodations should help deaf and hard of hearing students gain information from teachers and interact with peers (Howell, 2008; Roberts, 2010; Taylor, Smiley, & Richards, 2009). To make it easier to use lip reading and residual hearing, place the desks of these students in a central location, about two rows from the front, where students can see your and other students' lips. Hearing and lip reading also can be fostered by having the students sit in swivel chairs on casters. This makes it easy for them to move and to follow conversations. If students cannot see the speaker's lips, they can be allowed to change their seats. During teacher-directed activities, these students can be seated near the teacher and to one side of the room, where they have a direct line of sight to the lips of peers and teachers. A staggered seating arrangement also can help students have a direct view of speakers (Dodd-Murphy & Mamlin, 2002). A semicircular seating arrangement can promote lip reading during small-group instruction, and it is recommended that you position yourself in front of the student when delivering one-on-one instruction.

It also is important to consider lighting and noise levels when setting up work areas for these students (Haller & Montgomery, 2004). Glaring light can hinder lip reading; therefore, the source of information should not be in a poorly lighted area or one where the light is behind the speaker. Structural noises such as those of heating and cooling units; furniture movements; and external airborne noises, such as cars or construction outside the school, can be reduced by using carpets and acoustic tiles on the floor, drapes on windows, and sound-absorbent room dividers. Also, classes containing these students can be placed in rooms in quiet locations and away from noise centers such as gymnasiums, cafeterias, and busy hallways and corridors. The acoustical environment and the noise level in the classroom also can be improved by placing fabrics on desks and tables, cork protectors on the edges of desks to reduce the sounds of desks closing, rubber tips or tennis balls on the ends of the legs of chairs and desks, and absorbent materials on the walls (Dodd-Murphy & Mamlin, 2002).

Deaf and hard of hearing students may benefit from sitting next to an alert and responsible peer who can help them follow along during verbal conversations by indicating changes in the speaker. A peer also can be assigned to give these students information conveyed on the intercom system. Peers also can help these students react to fire drills (flashing lights for fire alarms also can be located throughout the school). However, as they adjust to the general education classroom, the help they receive from peers should be phased out.

Students with Visual Impairments   Several classroom design accommodations can help students with visual impairments function successfully in inclusive settings (Brody, 2006; Heward, 2009; Lewis, 2010). In particular, these students will benefit from a structured and predictable learning environment, which you can establish by following specific routines for classroom designs and activities (Li, 2009). You also can try to simplify the visual environment, by limiting the visual stimuli in the room and around these students' work areas (Swift et al., 2008).

Encourage them to use their residual vision by providing a glare-free and well-lighted work area, having adjustable lighting, and locating their work space so they don't face the windows. You also can reduce problems associated with glare by painting mild colors on walls, covering shiny surfaces with small rugs or sheets, using a gray-green chalkboard, placing adjustable translucent shades or blinds on windows, installing furniture and equipment with matte finishes, and positioning desks so that the light comes over the shoulder of the student's nondominant hand. During teacher-directed activities, the student should not have to look directly into the light to see the teacher. To reduce the fatigue associated with bending over, desks should have adjustable tops.

The work area for students with visual impairments should offer an unobstructed view of instructional activities, easy access to materials and assistive devices, and a direct trail to the major parts of the room (Li, 2009). When these students first come to your classroom, they can be taught how to move around the room and from their desk to the major classroom locations. These students can learn to navigate the classroom and the school by using **trace trailing**, directing them to the routes between their desks and major classroom and school landmarks by having them touch the surfaces of objects on the path. Visual descriptions of the room and routes can supplement trace trailing and help students develop a mental picture of the room. If you must rearrange the room, provide time so that these students can learn to adjust to the new arrangement. Students with visual disabilities also may benefit from color contrasts so they can identify and access important areas, materials and objects in the classroom (Brody, 2006). It also is important for you to use tactile symbols and signs in Braille placed in important locations in the classroom, and contrasting strips on the floors of areas to delineate dangerous areas of the room or school that require extra caution (e.g., the edges of steps, the floor near the radiator). These students' work areas should be in a quiet place, away from potentially harmful objects such as hot radiators, half-open doors, and paper cutters. Pathways throughout the room should be free of objects, and all students should be reminded not to leave things in pathways.

To help students compensate for their visual impairment by increased attention to verbal information, they should be seated where they can hear others well. Masking tape markers on the floor can help students with visual impairments keep their desks properly aligned. Because students with visual impairments may need devices and optical aids, you also should consider providing them with a sufficient, convenient, safe space to store this equipment. For example, a music stand or drafting table can be placed next to the students' work areas to reduce the problems of using large-print books.

Students with Health and Physical Disabilities   Students with health and physical disabilities may encounter a variety of environmental barriers that limit their access to inclusive settings (Wolfe Poel, 2007). These barriers include doors, hallways, stairs,

PEARSON
myeducationlab

To enhance your understanding of how to design your inclusive classroom to accommodate the strengths and challenge of your students, go to the IRIS Center Resources section of the Topic *Classroom/Behavior Management* in the MyEducationLab for your course, and complete the module entitled *Accommodations to the Physical Environment: Setting up a Classroom for Students with Visual Disabilities;* and examine the challenging cases by completing the case entitled *Effective Room Arrangement.*

Using Technology to Promote Inclusion
SUPPORTING STUDENT LEARNING AND BEHAVIOR

Many classrooms contain background noises from the street, the hallways, and the ventilation and lighting systems. These background noises can interfere with student learning and behavior, especially for students with learning, attention, and hearing difficulties. Carpets and drapes improve the acoustics in your classroom, as does technology such as sound-field amplification systems (Hu, 2008). Without having to raise your voice, sound-field amplification systems use FM and wireless technology to increase the sound of your voice and focus student attention on verbal information (Maag & Anderson, 2007). They serve to decrease the distance between you and your students and lessen the background noises that prevent students from hearing you.

There are two types of sound-field amplification systems: sound-field and personal FM. In both systems, you wear a small, lightweight wireless microphone, which allows you to move around the classroom. In the sound-field system, your speech is amplified for *all students* via a loudspeaker installed in your classroom. In the personal FM system, selected students wear headphones with a receiver that allows them to hear you more clearly.

Although these systems improve the performance of *all students* who use them, you need to remember to turn off the systems when you are directing comments to specific students or other professionals and to adjust the volume (Hu, 2008). You also should be aware that sound-field systems have several advantages over personal FM systems. They are less costly and are used by *all students*. Because individual students do not have to wear headsets, there is no stigma associated with their use. When using these systems, it is important to note that they do not lessen the negative impacts of noisy classrooms.

Here are some other ways you can use technology to create inclusive classroom environments that support student learning and behavior:

- Use software and Web resources such as eKidTools and StrategyTools, which provide templates to foster the creation of materials for use by students and teachers to support the implementation of contracts, classroom rules, self-management techniques, and token economy and point systems (e.g., checklists with pictorials, recording sheets with countoons, graphs, etc.) (Mitchem, Kight, Fitgerald, Koury, & Boonseng, 2007; Whitby & Miller, 2009).

- Use handheld computers or personal digital assistants (PDAs) to make digital recordings and graph real-time data related to observations of student behavior and to send text messages to students about their behavior (Edyburn & Basham, 2008; Salend, 2009).

- Foster students' use of self-management techniques by teaching them to use PDAs with visual, tactile and auditory prompts to demonstrate, self-record, self-evaluate, and self-reinforce their prosocial behaviors (Mitchem et al., 2007; Parette et al., 2007). For example, students can use audio recorders to create, store, and hear brief prompts and reminders related to their behavior.

- Use and teach your students to use various high and low technologies and software packages to record, graph, store, access, and reflect on data regarding their learning and behavior (Parette et al., 2007; Salend, 2009) and to create a behavior matrix to problem solve and evaluate interventions to teach prosocial behaviors (Hung & Lockard, 2007).

- Use software and Web-based resources to identify, create and administer reinforcement and preference surveys (Mitchem et al., 2007; Salend, 2009). Students also can indicate their preferences for reinforcers and activities via multimedia-based formats (Lee et al., 2008).

- Use software and PDAs to create visual activity schedules and choice boards, which employ combinations of pictures, graphics, symbols, words, sounds, and voices to prompt students to engage in appropriate behaviors and to help them make transitions from one scheduled activity to another and choices and to communicate their preferences (Banda et al., 2009; Cafiero, 2008).

- Use electronic and nonelectronic audio, visual, or vibrating display systems such as kitchen timers, alarm clocks, or vibrating devices set at varying intervals to prompt students to engage in prosocial behavior, to use self-management techniques, to make transitions, and to signal you to provide students with feedback on their behavior (Joseph & Konrad, 2009). For example, you can help students make transitions by using an electronic device that provides a visual record of the amount of time allotted for an activity and signals when one activity is over and another is about to begin (Mainzer, Castellani, Lowry, & Nunn, 2006).

- Allow students to earn opportunities to use technology such as playing educational technology-based games by demonstrating appropriate behavior (Salend, 2009).

- Use on-line antibullying and violence prevention programs and resources (CEC, 2008; San Antonio & Salzfass, 2007). For example, *Stop Bullying Now* (stopbullyingnow.hrsa.gov) is a website that uses resources and novel ways such as animated games to provide information to students, families, and professionals about bullying and ways to prevent it.

(Continued)

- Provide students with visual impairments with illuminated magnifiers that allow them to coordinate the distance from the light source to the text, and the magnification of the print, and specially designed high-wattage, low-glare lightbulbs (Griffin et al., 2002).

- Use technology to facilitate the movement of students throughout the school and your class. Students with visual impairments can carry a small Global Positioning System (GPS) receiver offering orally or Braille presented step-by-step directions that can guide them in moving around schools and classrooms and finding locations, objects and materials (Noonan, 2006). Braille and audible buttons can be installed in important school locations and on signs, maps, and elevators. Barcode scanners with multilingual speech can be used to help students with visual impairments and English language learners identify important bar-coded objects and places located around the classroom and school (Wolfe Poel, 2007).

- Incorporate the principles of universal design by having motion sensors, automatic buttons, keypad entry, and voice recognition to activate doors, lights, lockers, elevators, sinks, and toilets; or using keypad entry of fingerprints (Pivik et al., 2002; Wehmeyer et al., 2004).

steep or unusable ramps, and inaccessible bathrooms, lockers, water fountains, recreation areas, and elevators. You can help students avoid these barriers by placing signs around your school to direct individuals to the most accessible routes to important locations in your school.

Students who use wheelchairs or prostheses will need aisles and doorways at least 32 inches wide so that they can maneuver easily and safely in the classroom (Heller et al., 2009). If possible, arrange desks and classroom furniture with aisles that can accommodate their assistive devices, and have turning space for wheelchairs. Some students may also need space to recline during the school day.

For students who use wheelchairs, the floor coverings in the classroom are important. Floors should have a nonslip surface; deep pile, shag, or sculptured rugs can limit mobility. Floors should be covered with tightly looped, commercial-grade carpet smooth enough to allow wheelchairs to move easily and strong enough to withstand frequent use. To keep the rug from fraying or rippling, tape it down from wall to wall without placing padding underneath it.

Ergonomic furniture that is rounded, with padding on the edges and with no protrusions, is appropriate for many students with physical disabilities. Work areas should be at least 28 inches high to allow students who use wheelchairs to get close to them. Because the reach of students who use wheelchairs is restricted, work tables should not be wider than 42 inches. For comfortable seating, chairs can be curvilinear, have seat heights at least 16 inches above the ground, and be strong enough to support students who wish to pull up on and out of the chairs. Work areas for students with physical disabilities can include space for computers or other assistive devices that they may need.

Although students with physical disabilities should have the same type of furniture as their peers, some students may need specialized chairs to help them sit independently and maintain an upright position (Best & Bigge, 2005; Wolfe Poel, 2007). For example, some students may need corner chairs, floor sitters, or chairs with arm and foot rests (Best, Reed, & Bigge, 2005). The chairs and wheel chairs of some students also may be adapted by inserting foam, towels, wood, and cushions or installing shoulder and chest straps and belts. Some students also may use special chairs with abductors or adductors to support them in aligning their legs.

Students with physical disabilities also may need the height and slant of their work areas to be adjusted to accommodate their needs and wheelchairs or prostheses (Best et al., 2005; Wolfe Poel, 2007). Therefore, you may want to request that your classroom include desks with adjustable-slant tops and adjustable-height workstations. Some students may need stand-up desks; others may use a desktop or lap board and book support placed on their wheelchairs. These desks can have a cork surface to hold students' work with pushpins.

Transferring Students Who Use Wheelchairs

When Ms. Wade felt a twinge in her back as she helped transfer Mickey from his wheelchair to his seat, she knew she had to talk with Mr. Roman, the occupational therapist. When she caught up with Mr. Roman, he smiled and said, "Welcome to the club. Luckily, there are some things that you can do so that you won't hurt your back. Before you move Mickey, loosen up so that your muscles are ready to be exerted, tell Mickey what is going to happen, and encourage him to help you in the transfer. Then, approach him directly so that you can square up, lift him with your legs, not your back, and keep your back straight. Try to maintain a smooth, steady movement and a wide base of support by placing one foot in front of the other and getting as close as possible to Mickey. As you move, take short steps and avoid becoming twisted when changing directions." The next time Ms. Wade saw Mr. Roman, she thanked him and said, "It's a piece of cake."

Here are some other strategies you can use to implement the IDEA in your inclusive classroom and transfer students who use wheelchairs:

- Wear comfortable footwear that minimizes the likelihood of slipping.
- Encourage students who are able to bear some weight by standing to wear slip-resistant footwear and sturdy belts.
- Use walls or sturdy objects to assist in maintaining balance.
- Ask for assistance from others when necessary as it is easier for two people to transfer students who are difficult to lift.
- Consult with a physical or occupational therapist (Best & Bigge, 2005).

Because students with physical disabilities may have to work at the chalkboard, at least one chalkboard in the classroom can be lowered to 24 inches from the floor. To help students work at the chalkboard, attach a sturdy vertical bar as a handrail, and provide them with a sit/stand stool.

Teachers must understand the importance of body positioning and know how to reposition students and move and transfer students who use wheelchairs (Heller et al., 2009). To prevent pressure sores and help students maintain proper positioning, their position should be changed every 20 to 30 minutes. Posting photographs and descriptions of suggested positions for students with physical disabilities can remind you and others to use the right positioning and transferring techniques. Equipment such as side-lying frames, walkers, crawling assists, floor sitters, chair inserts, straps, standing aids, and beanbag chairs also can help students maintain or change positions.

Several classroom accommodations can help students whose movements are limited. Buddies can be assigned to bring assignments and materials to the students' desks. Boxes or containers can be attached to students' work areas to provide them with access to and storage for their work materials. You can allow these students to leave class early to get to their next class and avoid the rush in the hallway. Securing papers by taping them to the students' desks, and using clipboards or metal cookie sheets and magnets, can help with writing assignments. Similarly, connecting writing utensils to strings taped to students' desks can help students retrieve them when dropped. Desks with textured surfaces or with a barrier around the edge also can help prevent papers, books, and writing utensils from falling. Built-up utensils, Velcro fasteners, cut-out cups, switches, and nonslip placemats can be used for students with physical disabilities.

Students with Behavior and Attention Disorders   You can organize your classroom to support the positive behavior of students with behavior and attention disorders (Mulrine et al., 2008; Zentall, 2006). Since it is easier for you to observe students, monitor performance, and deliver cues and nonverbal feedback when students are sitting nearby, you may want to locate the work areas of students with behavior and attention disorders near you (Conroy et al., 2008). Placing these students near good peer models with whom they feel comfortable can also help them learn appropriate classroom behaviors. To make peer models more effective, you can praise them.

It is important for you to try to minimize visual and auditory distractions for students with behavior and attention disorders, build movement into your learning environment, and establish physical and visual boundaries for them (Koenig et al., 2009; Mulrine et al., 2008). For example, some teachers place tape or a carpet square to delineate students' work areas. Examine the movement patterns in the classroom when determining the work areas, and avoid putting the desks of these students in parts of the room that are cluttered, have a lot of activity or visually loaded areas of the room. You also can decrease visual distractions by placing a cloth over them when they are not important for learning, and decrease auditory distractions by giving students earplugs or headphones.

You also can foster the learning and positive behavior of these students by tailoring their work spaces to their strengths and challenges. For example, they may benefit from use of adjustable-height work spaces that allow them to vary the height of their stool so that they can work sitting down or standing up with swinging foot rests (Saulny, 2009). Some teachers use a study carrel for students with attention problems. However, study carrels and specialized desks should not be used often because they may isolate or stigmatize these students. You can reduce the potential problems associated with using specialized work settings by discussing how individuals learn and function best in different ways, allowing *all students* to use them, referring to it in a positive way, and using them for several purposes, such as a relaxation area and a technology or media center.

What Would You Do in Today's Diverse Classroom?

★ Victor, one of your students, is misbehaving. During teaching activities, he often calls out answers without your permission, talks to other students, and makes inappropriate comments. When this happens, you reprimand Victor and remind him to raise his hand. He rarely completes his assignments, and several of your students have complained that he bothers them.

★ It is nearing the beginning of the school year, and your class of 23 students will include 1 student with a physical disability, 3 students with learning disabilities, 1 student with attention difficulties, and 2 students who are learning English. You are concerned about how to design your classroom to accommodate their strengths and challenges.

★ You and several other teachers have noticed that some students are afraid to go to certain parts of your school and believe that it is because they are being bullied. You contacted your principal who has called a meeting to discuss ways to prevent bullying.

1. What factors do you need to consider in addressing these situations?
2. What would be your goals, and what actions would you take to achieve them?
3. What knowledge, skills, dispositions, strategies, resources, and supports do you need to address these situations?
4. How would you evaluate the success of your efforts?

PEARSON
myeducationlab Watch a teacher conducting a lesson with her students about bullying and how to prevent it by visiting the MyEducationLab for this course. Go to the *Assignments and Activities* section under the topic *Classroom/Behavior Management* and complete the activity entitled *Schoolwide Response to Bullying* to answer questions about preventing bullying.

Summary

This chapter offered guidelines for helping students learn in inclusive classrooms by promoting good classroom behavior and modifying the classroom design for various types of students. As you review the chapter, consider the following questions and remember the following points.

How Can I Collaborate with Others to Develop and Implement Schoolwide Positive Behavioral Interventions and Supports and to Conduct Functional Behavioral Assessments?

CEC 1, 2, 3, 5, 6, 7, 8, 9, 10; PRAXIS 3; INTASC 8, 9, 10

SWPBIS is a collaborative data-based decision-making process for establishing and implementing a continuum of schoolwide and individualized instructional and behavioral strategies and services that are available and used to support the learning and positive behavior of *all students*. An FBA involves collaborating with others to identify and define the problem behavior, record the behavior using an observational recording system, obtain more information about the student and the behavior, perform an A-B-C analysis, analyze the data and develop hypothesis statements, consider sociocultural factors, and develop and evaluate a behavioral intervention plan. Collaboration can help you make sure that your expertise, goals, and concerns are reflected in your school's SWPBIS and your students' FBAs and that your classroom management plan and practices are consistent with them.

How Can I Promote Positive Classroom Behavior in Students?

CEC 1, 2, 3, 4, 5, 6, 9; PRAXIS 3; INTASC 5, 6, 9

You can use relationship-building strategies, social skills instruction, antecedents-based interventions, consequences-based interventions, self-management techniques, group-oriented management systems, and behavior reduction techniques.

How Can I Prevent Students from Harming Others?

CEC 5, 9; PRAXIS 3; INTASC 9

You can work with students and their families and professionals to create a safe, caring school environment that does not tolerate bullying, harassment, or violence of any kind. This collaboration should also foster and acknowledge acceptance of individual differences and the development of friendships. You should be aware of the warning signs of violence and of the steps to take when violence occurs.

How Can I Adapt the Classroom Design to Accommodate Students' Learning, Behavioral, Social, and Physical Strengths and Challenges?

CEC 2, 3, 5, 9; PRAXIS 3; INTASC 5, 9

You can consider such factors as seating arrangements; positioning the teacher's desk; designing bulletin boards, walls, specialized areas, and learning centers; and using classroom design accommodations.

Part III

Differentiating Instruction for All Students

Part III of the book—which includes Chapters 8, 9, 10, and 11—is designed to help you vary your teaching to promote the learning of *all students* by addressing their individual strengths and challenges in inclusive classrooms. It offers information, strategies, and resources to help *all students* access and succeed in the general education curriculum.

Chapter 8 introduces the concept of differentiating instruction for *all students*, as well as how to use a variety of curricular and instructional accommodations and instructional technology and assistive devices for this purpose. Chapter 9 provides strategies for fostering learning when using large- and small-group instruction for *all students*, including how to use the principles of effective teaching and cooperative learning. Chapter 10 offers guidelines for teaching and differentiating instruction so that you can help *all students* learn to read, write, and spell. Chapter 11 presents ways to vary content area instruction to help *all students* learn by providing guidelines for differentiating mathematics, science, and social studies instruction.

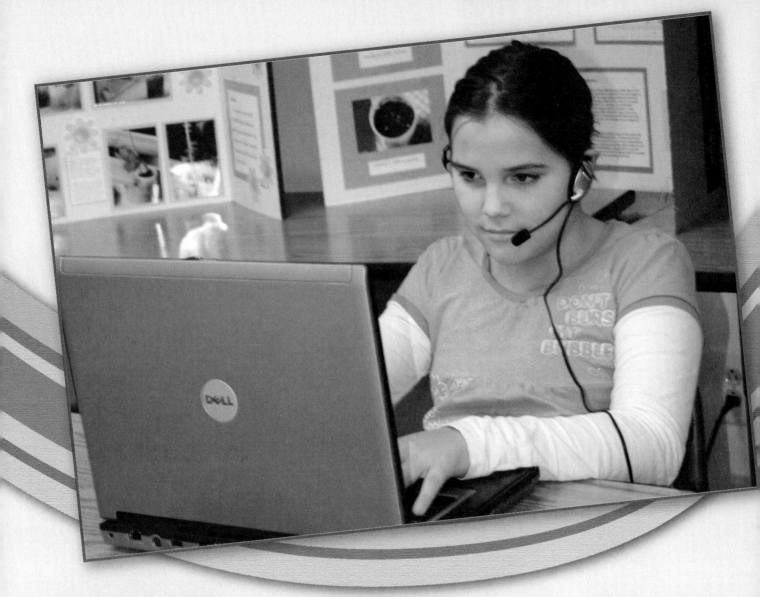

JULIA AND TOM

In addition to several students with learning disabilities, Ms. Taravella's inclusion class included Julia, a student with a visual disability, and Tom, a student with significant cognitive disabilities. To assist Ms. Taravella in teaching her students, her teaching team included Ms. Stoudamire, a special education teacher, and Mr. Howry, a paraeducator. Ms. Steckler, a vision specialist, also was available periodically to help the team teach Julia, and Ms. Camac, the school's technology specialist, also helped Ms. Taravella use technology to teach her students.

As part of the districtwide curriculum related to the study of the solar system, the class was working on a unit about the sun, the moon, and the planets. Before implementing the unit, Ms. Taravella and her teaching team collaborated to plan it. They began by discussing the essential information they wanted their students to learn and agreeing on their curricular goals. They consulted assessment information and IEPs, and determined individualized goals for

their students. Whereas all of their students' curricular goals were aligned to the districtwide curriculum, Tom's goals also reflected several of the functional goals in his IEP. Because of their prior knowledge and level of mastery, the goals for Julia and several other students were enhanced to include learning about the derivation and meaning of the planets' names.

The team then used these curricular goals to create a menu of student products that varied in both difficulty and learning style to assess student mastery. The activities included creating a new planet; making visual displays and dioramas; giving oral or PowerPoint/Keynote presentations; writing a paper, a blog, or a wiki highlighting the unique characteristics of the sun, the moon, or a planet; and creating a podcast or a digital video about life on the sun, the moon, or a planet. The team then outlined their learning activities and the teaching strategies, student groupings, and resources they needed to use to support the participation and learning of their students.

8

Differentiating Instruction for Diverse Learners

Ms. Taravella, Ms. Camac, and Ms. Stoudamire led the students in performing a variety of individualized large- and small-group learning activities. The teachers presented a series of digital videos on the solar system to show colorful and animated video segments of the sun, the moon, and the different planets. Occasionally, they repeated segments or paused the presentation to highlight different features. Ms. Camac helped Ms. Steckler obtain a wireless headphone system so that Julia could hear a running description of the visual material being presented. To help students identify, organize, and remember the important points of the presentation, the teachers used an interactive white-smartboard to lead the class in creating a graphic organizer and playing a game (Name That Planet) comparing the planets. The students were particularly excited about using the white-smartboard to view Web sites that offered webcams of different planets.

The team also implemented instructional accommodations and arrangements for the students, including Julia and Tom, which were consistent with their IEPs. To support the learning of Julia and several of her classmates, the

teachers and their colleagues paired visually presented information with tactile/kinesthetic- and auditory-based learning activities. They gave these students opportunities to learn by using hands-on replicas of the sun, the moon, and the different planets. Ms. Steckler used a software program to prepare enlarged handouts for Julia and collaborated with Mr. Howry to create charts of the sun, the moon, and the planets with string so that Julia and her classmates could access visual information through tactile experiences.

Ms. Taravella and Ms. Stoudamire used many of the same materials in different ways to support Tom's learning. While Ms. Taravella worked with students classifying and comparing the planets, Tom worked with Ms. Stoudamire sorting replicas of the planets by size and color. Tom also used the tactile planet chart to compare the sizes of the planets and to count the number of planets. Under the guidance of Ms. Taravella, Tom, Julia, and their classmates who have difficulty accessing text used digital teaching materials to have text highlighted, defined, enlarged, or read aloud by the computer. These materials also allowed the students to record their responses by typing text, drawing, speaking, or entering words from a list. Marta, an English language learner, used these materials in both English and Spanish.

The educators also created a webquest designed to guide the students in learning about the early study of and beliefs about the solar system by cultures around the world. Students worked in collaborative groups to access Web-based information related to early explorations of the sun, the moon, and the planets and the different cultural meanings regarding them. They learned about the different early observatories that had been set up throughout the world, and the various tools that the early astronomers used to observe and calculate the movements in the solar system. They also learned how different calendars and rituals were established based on these movement patterns. The groups then shared their findings with their classmates and others by postings on the class's website.

After completing the unit of instruction, the students chose a strategy for sharing their learning from the list of activities that the teachers had created. To make sure that students selected appropriate activities, Ms. Taravella and Ms. Stoudamire focused their choices. They also kept a record of students' choices and encouraged them to try new activities. Julia and Tom chose to work with several other students to create a web page about Saturn. Julia volunteered to design and create the Web page, and Tom worked with Mr. Howry to draw pictures and reproduce pictures of Saturn, which were then added to the group's Web page via use of a digital camera. The group's Web page and the other products students completed were then posted on the class's Web site, which also included a weblog of the class's learning activities and digital pictures of the students' assignments with accompanying narration.

What other strategies could Ms. Taravella and Ms. Stoudamire and their colleagues use to differentiate instruction for Julia, Tom, and the other students? After reading this chapter, you will have the knowledge, skills, and dispositions to answer this as well as the following questions:

- How can I differentiate instruction for students?

- How can I differentiate instruction for students who have difficulty reading and gaining information from print materials?

- How can I differentiate instruction for students from diverse cultural and language backgrounds?

- How can I use instructional technology and assistive devices to differentiate instruction for students?

Julia, Tom, and the other students were successful learners because Ms. Taravella and her colleagues used a variety of curricular and teaching accommodations to differentiate instruction for their students. To accommodate the diverse learners in their classrooms, educators differentiate

- *content* (what they teach),
- *process* (how they teach),
- *product* (how students demonstrate content mastery),
- *affect* (how students connect their thinking and feelings), and
- *learning environment* (how the classroom is designed and what instructional groupings they use) (Price & Nelson, 2007; Tomlinson et al., 2008).

They use varied curricula and instructional arrangements, strategies, resources, materials, and technology to address their students' individual learning strengths and challenges, preferences, and styles, as well as their developmental levels, interests, and experiential, cultural, and language backgrounds (van Garderen & Whittaker, 2006). This chapter describes proven strategies for differentiating instruction to address the many unique learning strengths and challenges of students. While these strategies can be used to help various types of students learn, they also can be used to differentiate instruction for *all students*. For example, Ms. Taravella and her colleagues used instructional accommodations not only to differentiate instruction for Julia and Tom but also to ensure the learning of *all* of their students.

DIFFERENTIATING INSTRUCTION

HOW CAN I DIFFERENTIATE INSTRUCTION FOR STUDENTS? Like Ms. Taravella and Ms. Stoudamire, you can engage in a variety of professional practices to differentiate instruction for your students so that they can succeed in the general education curriculum (see Figure 8.1). These effective practices are discussed in the following sections and in other chapters of this book. In reflecting on their use, consider their potential impact; prior effectiveness; and the skills, resources, support, and time requirements you need to implement them.

Tailor Curricular Goals and Teaching Strategies to Your Students and Your Learning Environment

As we saw in the chapter-opening vignette, the types of curricular goals and teaching strategies used to differentiate your instruction should be tailored to your students and your local and statewide learning standards, and your learning environment (Childre, Sands, & Tanner Pope, 2009; Parish & Stodden, 2009). Therefore, you need to consider your students' strengths and challenges and the variables you control in your classroom (Lee et al., 2009).

myeducationlab

Go to the Assignments and Activities section of the Topic *Instructional Practices and Learning Strategies* in the MyEducationLab for your course and complete the activity entitled *Differentiating Instruction*. As you watch the video and answer the accompanying questions, consider how differentiating instruction benefits *all students* in your classroom.

FIGURE 8.1 **Differentiated instruction practices**

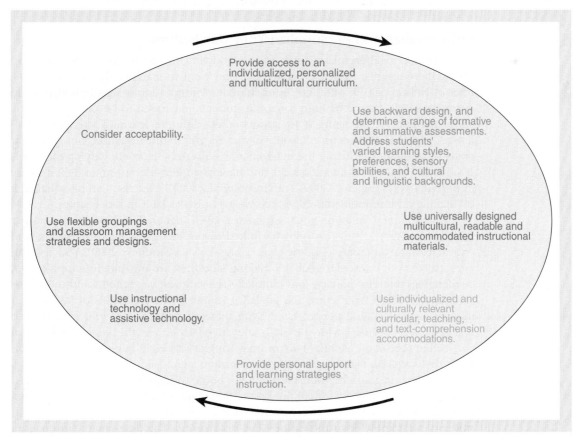

In planning lessons and units of instruction that are tailored to your students and your classroom, you and your colleagues can consider the following issues:

- What are the themes, goals, and objectives of the lesson/activity?
- What teaching materials and arrangements will be used in the lesson/activity?
- When, where, and how long will this lesson/activity occur?
- Will all students be able to participate in this lesson/activity in the same ways as their classmates?
- What supports, personal assistance, learning strategies, instructional accommodations, and/or instructional technology/assistive devices are needed to help students participate fully?
- How can the curriculum and student assessment be supplemented or changed to address the different learning styles and challenges of students?
- How can the lesson/activity be differentiated to reflect students' learning styles, language, culture, experiences, behavioral needs, motivation, interests, talents, strengths, challenges, and IEPs?
- How can the lesson/activity be differentiated in terms of the complexity of the content, type and amount of work, teaching materials used, grouping patterns, support needed, location, pace and time, and the products produced?
- Can students participate in the activity but work on other skills or work with others on an activity that has different goals?
- How can the lesson/activity be differentiated to motivate and engage students and provide them with choices?
- What materials will be needed to engage students in the lesson/activity?
- How can the classroom environment be differentiated to engage students in the lesson/activity?
- How can student mastery of the content of the lesson/activity be assessed throughout and at the end of the lesson/activity?

Individualize and Personalize Your Curriculum

An initial step in differentiating instruction is individualizing your curriculum by identifying the concepts, principles, and skills you want to teach (Fisher & Frey, 2008; Price & Nelson, 2007). Although most students will not require accommodations in curricular goals, the curriculum for some students may need to be personalized by supplementing or changing it to address their different learning strengths, challenges, and styles (Thompson, 2008; Voltz et al., 2005). Individualize your curricular goals by adding or reducing the material and skills to be learned, varying the levels of difficulty of the content addressed, and having students demonstrate their mastery in different ways (Salend, 2009; Tomlinson et al., 2008). You also can personalize it by making it more multicultural, which we will discuss later in this chapter.

In addition to aligning your curricular goals to national, statewide, and district standards, your goals also should be linked to big ideas, essential questions, and critical learning outcomes (Childre et al., 2009; Parish & Stodden, 2009). You also can personalize your curricular goals by making sure they are meaningful, appropriate, challenging, interdisciplinary, and culturally relevant for *all students* and their lives (Thompson, 2008). Your curricular goals for students who have IEPs or 504 accommodation plans should be consistent with these documents and individualized so that they are provided with the skills they need to access the general education curriculum (Lee et al., 2009). Many of your students also will benefit from curricular goals that focus on teaching them to use learning strategies.

Curriculum goals for your students also should relate to your assessment of their existing levels of mastery. Therefore, at the beginning of a lesson or unit of instruction you can use a variety of classroom-based assessment techniques to assess your students' prior knowledge and various levels of mastery. This assessment information, combined with your examination of your curriculum, can help you individualize your curricular goals for your students by determining the following:

- What levels of content mastery and skills do my students have?
- What content and skills do I expect *all* my students to learn?
- What content and skills do I expect *most* of my students to learn?
- What content and skills do I expect *some* students to learn? (Lenz, Bulgren, Kissam, & Taymans, 2004)

Use Backward Design, and Determine a Range of Formative and Summative Assessments

Prior to planning your instructional activities, use **backward design**, a process for planning units of instruction and individual lessons by which you first determine the assessments you will use to evaluate your students' learning (Childre et al., 2009). Once you determine these assessments, you use them to guide you in designing and sequencing the instructional activities that your students will engage in to achieve your learning outcomes (Parrish & Stodden, 2009).

In planning and implementing your assessments, consider using both *formative* and *summative* assessment to evaluate your students' learning and your teaching (Salend, 2009). **Formative assessment** relates to your use of assessment strategies during instruction to monitor your students' learning progress and to use this information to make ongoing decisions about the effectiveness of your teaching and ways you can improve it (Brookhart, Moss, & Long, 2008; Tomlinson, 2008b). **Summative assessment** focuses on your use of assessments at the end of instruction to assess student mastery of specific content, topics, concepts and skills taught, and to communicate this information to others (Chappuis & Chappuis, 2008).

Tiered assignments during and at the end of instructional units allow you to differentiate your assessments to meet the strengths and challenges of individual students (Painter, 2009). In this method, you identify concepts that need to be learned, delineate multiple ways in which students can show mastery that differ in complexity and learning style, and allow students to select how they want to demonstrate their learning (Salend, 2009). For example, at the end of the unit, Ms. Taravella and Ms. Stoudamire identified and gave their students a menu of choices about how they could demonstrate their learning. They also made sure that students selected appropriate activities, and tried new activities.

> **Making Connections**
> Find out more about a range of assessment techniques and accommodations that you can use in your inclusive classroom in Chapter 12.

Use Curricular Accommodations

Once the curricular goals and assessment strategies are delineated, you can use curricular accommodations to help a diverse group of students access and master them (Lee et al., 2009; McKinley & Stormont, 2008). Some individualized curricular accommodations that you may consider include

- giving students choices about what they learn and how they learn it;
- collaborating with students to create learning contracts that specify learning goals, activities, and products;
- altering the instructional content, tasks, and pace;
- enhancing the multicultural aspects of the content;
- designing alternative projects to allow students to demonstrate mastery;
- focusing on fewer or different objectives; and
- modifying students' requirements and assessments.

Your lessons and curricular areas can be differentiated for academically diverse students by using multilevel teaching and curriculum overlapping (Downing, 2008; Giangreco, 2007; Lee et al., 2009). In **multilevel teaching**, students are given lessons in the same curricular areas as their peers but at varying levels of difficulty. Some students may work on a reduced or increased number of items or more or less complex

UDL and YOU
Using Universally Designed Curriculum and Teaching Materials

An essential aspect of differentiating instruction for your students is the use of universally designed curriculum and teaching materials (Metcalf & Evans, 2009). This use of universally designed curriculum and teaching materials provide you with ways to differentiate your instruction based on your students' learning styles and cognitive, physical, sensory, motivational, cultural, and language characteristics (Dukes & Lamar-Dukes, 2009). They also allow you to offer a wide range of flexible options that so that your students can select to access and respond to information of varying levels of difficulty in a variety of formats (Kurtts, Matthews, & Smallwood, 2009). Thus, directions, content, and learning activities are clearly presented in multiple formats, and learners choose the appropriate formats that fit their learning styles and preferences (Sopko, 2008). In addition, assessment, motivation, prompting, and feedback are available throughout the learning experience.

One example of UDL curriculum and teaching materials that Ms. Taravella and her colleagues used involved providing their students with digitally presented, interactive teaching activities. Digitally presented learning activities such as electronic books foster reading fluency and text comprehension for a broad range of students through help menus that connect them to

- *text-to-speech capabilities and translation resources* that offer help through the use of digitized reading in multiple languages and definitions of words or video clips of sign language translations;

- *teaching resources and/or strategy prompts* that are embedded in the selection to allow students to review

material, understand context cues, look ahead to preview material, respond to questions, ask questions about the material, engage in games and simulations, pay attention to underlined or highlighted information, receive corrective feedback, and construct mental pictures;

- *reader-friendly resources* that allow readers to select the text size, the language read, and the page display, add color highlights, and note where the reader last read;

- *illustrative resources* that offer students access to examples; comparisons; and visuals of concepts through the use of graphics, animation, and sound;

- *informational or supplementary resources* that provide additional information and enrichment via access to multimedia presentations, electronic encyclopedias, dictionaries, and databases;

- *summarizing resources* that offer students graphics, outlines, and overviews of the structure, content, and major features of the text;

- *collaborative resources* that allow students to work together;

- *notational resources* that allow students to take notes, construct sticky notes, summarize main points, add color, and highlight text electronically as they read; and

- *assessment resources* that record ongoing data on student performance and make it readily available to students and teachers. (Anderson-Inman, 2009; Douglas, Ayres, Langone, Bell, & Meade, 2009)

REFLECTIVE

REFLECTIVE

Think about a lesson you recently taught or are planning to teach. How did/could you use multilevel teaching to adapt the lesson to the needs of a student with a significant disability? A student with a mild disability? A student who is gifted and talented? An English language learner?

learning objectives. For example, while other students were classifying and comparing the planets, Tom was sorting replicas of the planets by size and color. Similarly, because of her advanced level of mastery, Julia's instructional program was supplemented so that she was learning about the derivation and meaning of the planets' names.

Curriculum overlapping involves teaching a diverse group of students individualized skills from different curricular areas. In this method, teaching of a practical, functional, specific skill related to the student's academic program is embedded in learning activities across the curriculum. For example, when the class was working on science, Tom also worked on counting the planets.

Use Individualized Teaching/Instructional Accommodations

The use of *individualized teaching/instructional accommodations*—changes in the ways information is presented or the ways students respond—are essential aspects of differentiated instruction (Byrnes, 2008; McKinley & Stormont, 2008). Rather than being disability specific, teaching accommodations for students should be individually determined based on students' individual characteristics, including their cultural, linguistic and experiential backgrounds. They also should be consistent with research and districtwide policies, appropriate for the content to be learned, and acceptable to students, educators, and families. They should be selected and implemented to help students access their learning strengths, overcome their learning challenges, and demonstrate their mastery of content being taught (Bianco et al., 2009). Finally, it is essential that the effectiveness of teaching accommodations in fostering student learning be evaluated (Salend, 2009).

Stough (2002) offers a continuum for delineating differentiation techniques based on their impact on the individual profiles of students and the level of curriculum mastery expected of students. The first level of the continuum refers to *access differentiation techniques*. These techniques provide students with access to the curriculum and do not affect the level of mastery expected of students. They help students like Julia participate at the same level as others and do not require adjustments in the structure or content of the curriculum. Examples of *access differentiation techniques* include Braille, sign language, bilingual dictionaries, and instructional and assistive technology.

The second level of the continuum relates to *low-impact differentiation techniques*. Although these techniques involve adjustments in teaching methods, they have minimal to no impact on the level of curricular mastery expected of students. These instructional techniques alter the ways students are taught, but do not require significant adjustments in the structure or content of the curriculum. Examples of these types of techniques include content enhancements, word processing and spell checkers, learning strategies instruction, and peer-mediated instruction.

The third level of the continuum addresses *high-impact differentiation techniques* that affect curricular expectations. These instructional techniques, sometimes referred to as *modifications*, alter the content of the curriculum, as well as the ways students are taught, and require adjustments in the structure and content of the educational program that affect the level of curricular mastery expected of students. Examples of this level of the continuum include some of the accommodations used to teach Tom, such as the use of multilevel teaching and curriculum overlapping.

Decisions about individualized teaching accommodations for students are made based on data to determine whether and how students' disabilities affect their educational performance, and whether and to what extent individual students will need teaching accommodations to access the general education curriculum (Byrnes, 2008). You and your colleagues can use a variety of methods and sources to collect data concerning students' skills, strengths, challenges, learning and testing styles and preferences, self-concept, attitudes, and health (Salend, 2009). Sample questions that can guide you and your colleagues in analyzing student information to determine appropriate teaching accommodations for individual students include the following:

- Does the student exhibit academic and social behaviors that interfere with his or her learning or the learning of others? If so, what are these behaviors and what strategies and resources are needed to address them?
- What instructional methods, approaches, strategies, specialized equipment, technology, materials, and/or classroom designs have been successful in supporting the student's learning?
- What strategies and resources are needed to help the student understand directions and respond to classroom activities?
- What are the student's learning and testing style preferences?
- Does the student have sensory, medical, and/or attention conditions that affect his or her classroom performance?
- Does the student require more time and or additional motivation to complete assignments?

Making Connections
Find out more about how this continuum applies to grading students in inclusive classrooms in Chapter 12.

Use Instructional Materials Accommodations

Varying the instructional materials to accommodate your students and their varied academic abilities, interests, experiential and cultural backgrounds, and learning preferences is another way you can differentiate instruction (McKinley & Stormont, 2008). In addition to many of the strategies presented in this book, you can use the following instructional materials accommodations:

- Vary the amount of the material that students are exposed to and asked to complete (e.g., students read half the assignment and complete only the first three questions).
- Vary the format of the materials (e.g., have Julia, Tom, and other students access the materials digitally and via other forms of technology).
- Supplement the materials (e.g., provide Julia, Tom, and other students with manipulatives, replicas, visuals, graphic organizers, cues, and prompts).
- Use materials that present similar content at lower readability levels.
- Use alternative materials (e.g., create a chart with string so that Julia, Tom, and their classmates can tactilely access visual information).

Provide Personal Supports

Making Connections
This discussion of the roles of paraeducators builds on what we discussed earlier in Chapter 4.

As was evident in the chapter-opening vignette, you can differentiate your instruction for students by providing them with personal supports from other professionals, paraeducators, and peers. In addition to using a variety of cooperative-teaching instructional formats and consultation with specialists like Ms. Steckler, personal supports can be provided by using paraeducators like Mr. Howry and grouping arrangements where students learn in cooperative learning groups. Paraeducators also may be asked to provide physical supports so students with physical, sensory, or cognitive disabilities can access all aspects of the learning environment (Suter & Giangreco, 2009).

Paraeducators can be invaluable in helping you and your students, but if used improperly, they can hinder the school performance and independence of students (Giangreco & Broer, 2007). When paraeducators work too closely with specific students (sometimes called the Velcro effect), it is important for you to make sure that they don't impede effective inclusion programs by

- allowing general educators to avoid assuming responsibility for educating students with disabilities (e.g., saying, "She is so good with Mitchell that I just let her handle it");
- fostering the separation of students with disabilities from the rest of the class (e.g., working with a student with disabilities in a separate location);
- creating dependence on adults (e.g., prompting and assisting students when it is not necessary);
- limiting interactions with peers (e.g., being near the student can intimidate peers and reduce socialization);
- teaching ineffectively (e.g., not adjusting an unsuccessful activity);
- causing the loss of personal control (e.g., making decisions for students with significant communication, physical, and/or sensory difficulties);
- causing the loss of gender identity (e.g., taking students to the bathroom based on the gender of the paraeducator, not the student);
- interfering with the teaching of other students (e.g., using behaviors that distract other students) (Causton-Theoharris, 2009; Giangreco & Broer, 2007; Liston et al., 2009).

To prevent these situations from occurring, clarify their roles and make sure they are performing duties that are commensurate with their job descriptions (Carnahan et al., 2009; Causton-Theoharis, 2009). It also is essential for you to collaborate and communicate with paraeducators to differentiate instruction and deliver appropriate services to support the learning of *all students*. Also, take actions to help them perform the job and address their concerns (Devlin, 2008; Liston et al., 2009). For example, orient them by sharing your teaching philosophy, providing a tour of the school, introducing them to key school personnel, describing relevant programs and daily routines, and reviewing the dress code and other standards of decorum. In the orientation program, you can also explain the need for and rules on confidentiality, and discuss scheduling, handling emergencies, and other school procedures.

In addition, you can offer paraeducators an education program so that they understand and have the skills to perform their roles (Carnahan et al., 2009; Causton-Theoharis, 2009; Devlin, 2008). Such a program includes many types of information. It explains the roles of paraeducators inside and outside the classroom, as well as their legal and ethical responsibilities. It identifies the special medical, social, and academic strengths and challenges of students and the technology they use. It provides an overview of the curriculum, teaching, and behavior management techniques and reviews the communication system you will be using.

Because it is your job to make curriculum decisions and to supervise paraeducators when they provide instruction, it is important to monitor their actions and communicate regularly with them (Causton-Theoharis, 2009; Liston et al., 2009; Maggin et al., 2009). Collaborate with them to jointly plan and coordinate activities, monitor student performance, and deal with problems and conflicts. It is also important to treat them respectfully, give them feedback on their performance, solicit their point of view about their roles, strengths, and challenges and acknowledge their contributions (Carnahan et al., 2009; Devlin, 2008).

Address Students' Learning Styles and Preferences

When choosing methods to differentiate instruction, you should address students' learning styles and preferences (Tomlinson, 2008). Use learning style assessments, and note the situations and conditions that appear to influence individual students, and then adjust learning and assessment activities to accommodate students' learning styles and preferences (Beam, 2009; Servilio, 2009). You can use different types of reinforcement and feedback to increase students' motivation and acknowledge their performance. You also can structure the classroom so that noise levels, students' nearness to others, distractions, movement, and desk arrangements are acceptable to students and consistent with their preferences. For example, you can let students choose whether to work at their desks or in some other place. Finally, when planning the length and nature of learning activities and daily and weekly schedules, you can think about the various learning style and preferences of students such as attention span, ability to move while learning, time of day, and grouping considerations such as learning alone or in groups and with or without adults present.

Learning and teaching styles also are classified as either *field independent* or *field dependent* (Levine & McCloskey, 2009). Field-independent students appear to work best on individual tasks such as independent projects and relate formally to teachers; field-dependent students prefer to work in groups and establish personal relationships with others, including teachers. Field-independent teachers foster learning through competition and independent assignments; field-dependent teachers use personal and conversational teaching techniques.

Learning styles can be affected in other ways by cultural factors. For example, some cultures emphasize learning through verbal rather than visual descriptions; other cultures emphasize physical modeling over pictorials. Students' socioeconomic status can also influence their learning and cognitive styles.

Address Students' Sensory Abilities

Students with sensory disabilities have unique challenges, which you need to address when differentiating your instruction for them. For students like Julia, who have visual disabilities, you must present information orally; for students who are deaf and hard of hearing, you should use visual forms. At all times, you should encourage independence. Because the sensory functioning of students with sensory

PEARSON

Go to the Assignments and Activities section of the Topic *Instructional Practices and Learning Strategies* in the MyEducationLab for your course and complete the activity entitled *Accommodating Varied Levels of Readiness, Ability, and Learning Styles*. As you watch the video and answer the accompanying questions, think about the ways that student learning styles can be addressed through instruction.

REFLECTIVE

How do you prefer to learn and teach? How do you adapt when the teaching strategy and environment are different from the way you prefer to learn? Should teachers match students' learning styles all the time? Should students be taught to adapt their learning styles to the various teaching styles they will encounter in schools?

disabilities varies tremendously, you need to consider their unique needs and abilities when modifying your teaching methods, and the learning environment.

Differentiating Instruction for Students with Visual Disabilities As the teachers did in the chapter-opening vignette, you can collaborate with vision and mobility specialists to design and implement many strategies to differentiate instruction for students with visual disabilities (Li, 2009; Taylor et al., 2009). Many of these strategies also can be used for students who are visual learners. Help them; follow along in class by giving important directions verbally or recording them; phrasing questions and comments so that they include students' names; and using peers to read directions and materials, describe events in the classroom, and take notes.

You also can help these students learn by giving them opportunities to learn by doing, and by providing with physical prompts and pairing verbal and tactile cues (Bruce, Randall, & Birge, 2008; Lewis, 2010; Swift et al., 2008). It also is suggested that you use real objects and manipulatives that are familiar, meaningful, and motivating to students and provide them with large-print books, photo-enlarged handouts and tests, tactile books, Braille reference books and dictionaries, adaptive computer software, and audio-based materials (Howell, 2008; Spungin & Ferrell, 2007). However, understand that as students grow older, they may be reluctant to use special materials in the presence of their peers. When providing students with tactile learning experiences or asking them to respond orally, it is important to give students sufficient time to interact with all aspects of the learning materials or answer, and provide the supports students need to benefit from the tactile representations. You also might find it helpful to experiment with the materials yourself by using them with your eyes closed.

You also can use technology to produce large, clear typewritten materials with high contrasts (i.e., black type on a white background) (Swift et al., 2008). Tracing over the letters, numerals, and pictorials with a black felt-tip marker or black ballpoint pen makes it easier to see them, and placing a piece of yellow acetate over a page of print enhances the contrast and darkens the print. Students with visual impairments may experience visual fatigue during activities that require continuous use of visual skills. In these situations, it may be helpful to present one visual item at a time, to give students additional time to complete assignments and tests or to reduce the number and length of activities that call for visual concentration.

Student learning can also be promoted by using several strategies to help students locate learning materials and move around the classroom and the school (Heward, 2009). You can use *o'clock* directions to describe the location of an object on a flat surface (e.g., "Your book is at three o'clock, and your pencil is at nine o'clock"). If an object is nearby and in danger of being knocked over, guide the student's hand to the object or hand the student the object by gently touching his or her hand with the object. When giving directions to specific places in the classroom or school, use nonvisual statements and remember that directions for going left and right should be in relation to the student's body rather than yours.

Differentiating Instruction for Deaf and Hard-of-Hearing Students Many strategies are available for differentiating instruction for deaf and hard-of-hearing students, which also can be used for students who are auditory learners (Howell, 2008; Taylor et al., 2009). These strategies include using good communication techniques, which are (a) standing still and facing the person when speaking; (b) speaking clearly, at a moderate pace, and using short sentences; (c) speaking in a normal voice; (d) maintaining a proper speaking distance; (e) keeping the mouth area clear; (f) using facial and body gestures; (g) speaking in an area where the light is on your lips and face; and (h) providing transitions to indicate a change in the subject. Try to limit movement and unnecessary gestures, and present all spelling and vocabulary words in sentences (context), as many words presented in isolation look alike to lip readers. In addition, you can use visual signals to gain the student's attention, and use instructional technology such as interactive white-smartboards to present material so that the student can view the material and your lips simultaneously. If necessary,

Making Connections
This discussion of ways to differentiate your instruction for students with visual disabilities builds on what we discussed earlier in Chapters 2 and 7.

PEARSON
myeducationlab

To enhance your understanding of instructional accommodations that can support the performance of students with visual disabilities in your inclusive classroom, go to the IRIS Center Resources section of the Topic *Visual Impairment* in the MyEducationLab for your course, and complete the modules entitled *Instructional Accommodations: Making the Learning Environment Accessible to Students with Visual Disabilities* and *Accommodations to the Physical Environment: Setting up a Classroom for Students with Visual Disabilities.*

rephrase, repeat, summarize, or simplify your comments and questions, as well as those of other students, to make them more understandable, and ask questions to check understanding of orally presented directions and content. When using multimedia, shine a light on the speaker's face when the room is darkened for films or slides, and give the student the script of a video, or a recording to help the student follow along.

You also can use visually oriented techniques such as experiential and hands-on learning to help students learn (Roberts, 2010; Wurst et al., 2005). Offer demonstrations and provide examples. Create a visually rich learning environment and use written materials, visual aids such as graphic organizers to present content and summarize the main points of lessons, and cues to support instruction. Supplement information presented orally with real objects, manipulatives, and concrete visual aids (e.g., maps, globes). Write daily assignments, the schedule, important directions and information, technical terms, and new vocabulary on the board, and give students test directions, assignments, vocabulary lists, models, feedback, and lecture outlines in writing. Teach students to look up difficult-to-pronounce words in the dictionary.

Deaf and hard-of-hearing students may need the service of an educational interpreter. What have been your experiences working with educational interpreters?

Using Educational Interpreters Effectively. An *educational interpreter*, a professional who helps transfer information between individuals who do not communicate in the same way, can assist you in differentiating instruction for deaf and hard-of-hearing students. Depending on the student's preference, many educational interpreting methods exist. Early in the school year, you and the interpreter can meet to agree on the responsibilities of both persons. The teacher has primary responsibility and the interpreter aids communication. To help teachers and interpreters communicate, planning meetings can be scheduled on a regular basis.

Because interpreters may not know the content and teaching strategies used in the classroom, it is helpful to orient them to the curriculum and to give them copies of textbooks and other relevant materials. A knowledge of class routines, projects, and long-term assignments can assist interpreters in helping students understand assignments. With a difficult unit, including technical vocabulary and other content that may be hard to explain by alternative means, you and the interpreter can meet to discuss key terms. For example, when teaching about the geological history of the earth, you could give the interpreter a list of key terms and copies of lesson plans so that the interpreter can plan in advance how to translate and explain terms such as *Paleozoic era*, *Oligocene epoch*, and *Jurassic period*.

To maximize the effectiveness of the interpreter in your classroom, try these tips:

- Be sensitive to the time delays caused by interpreting.
- Talk to the students, not to the interpreter.
- Avoid directing comments to the interpreter during class time. Signals can be used to indicate the need for discussion after class.
- Encourage the interpreter to seek help when communication problems arise during class that affect the translation process.
- Avoid involving the interpreter in disciplining the student for misbehavior unless this misbehavior is directed at the interpreter. When the interpreter is involved in disciplinary actions, help students understand the roles and perspectives of the persons involved.
- Place the interpreter in a position that makes interpretation easy.

Making Connections
This discussion of ways to differentiate your instruction for students who are deaf and hard of hearing builds on what we discussed earlier in Chapters 2 and 7.

Differentiating Instruction for Diverse Learners

Consider Acceptability

When selecting strategies to differentiate instruction, another important factor to consider is **acceptability**, the extent to which you and your colleagues view a specific assessment, curricular and teaching practice as easy to use, effective, appropriate for the setting, fair, and reasonable (Carter, 2008). Reasonableness can be assessed by examining your practices in terms of

- which individuals will be responsible for implementing it;
- how much extra time and what materials, resources and technology are needed to implement it;
- whether it will require important changes in your teaching style;
- whether it is consistent with your philosophy;
- whether it requires preparation and practice for students and educators to implement;
- whether it is intrusive;
- how it will affect others; and
- how much it will cost.

An important aspect of treatment acceptability is the impact of your practices and accommodations on specific students and their peers (Salend, 2009). You are more likely to use strategies you perceive as fair and benefiting *all students*. Other factors related to students include age appropriateness, risks such as student embarrassment or isolation, intrusiveness into the student's personal space, and student cooperation. For example, giving a student a math assignment while the other students are working on social studies can isolate the student. Make sure that the accommodation does not adversely affect either the students or their classmates.

When adapting your curricular and teaching practices, you also need to consider students' reactions to and perceptions of these changes. In general, students prefer teachers who adapt their methods and believe that *all students* benefit from these accommodations. Some students, however, particularly those with disabilities, are concerned that accommodations in tests, textbooks, and homework may isolate them from their general education peers.

DIFFERENTIATING INSTRUCTION FOR STUDENTS WHO HAVE DIFFICULTY READING AND GAINING INFORMATION FROM PRINT MATERIALS

HOW CAN I DIFFERENTIATE INSTRUCTION FOR STUDENTS WHO HAVE DIFFICULTY READING AND GAINING INFORMATION FROM PRINT MATERIALS? You probably present a lot of content to your students using print materials. However, because many students have difficulty reading and gaining information from print materials, you may need to use the teacher- and student-directed strategies presented here as well as the strategies presented in Chapters 10 and 11 and elsewhere in this book. When selecting and using these methods, it is important for you to teach your students about the different types of text structures and how to use learning strategies to support their text comprehension (Englert, 2009; Faggella-Luby & Deshler, 2008). It also is important for you to collaborate with your school's literacy specialist and provide *all students* with numerous opportunities to develop their decoding skills and vocabulary and to read selections across the curriculum that they find motivating and that relate to their prior knowledge and experiential backgrounds (Ebbers & Denton, 2008).

Use Teacher-Directed Text Comprehension Strategies

Previewing Before assigning a reading selection, you can use prereading activities to preview new vocabulary and word pronunciation, text structures, motivate students, and activate their prior knowledge (Roberts, Torgesen, Boardman, &

Scammacca, 2008; Williams, 2005). Scanning the selection and discussing the meaning of boldfaced or italicized terms is helpful. New vocabulary words can be placed in a word file of index cards by chapter. English language learners also may find it helpful for you to write critical vocabulary in their native language and link new vocabulary to visuals and cognates in their native languages (Denton, Wexler, Vaughn, & Bryan, 2008; Dong, 2009).

Previews, structured overviews, self-monitoring checklists, and prereading organizers can help students understand the purpose of the reading selection, identify the text structures employed, and direct their attention to the relevant information in the selection (Faggella-Luby & Deshler, 2008; Roberts et al., 2008; Whalon & Hanline, 2008). For example, you can give students an outline of the selection's main points and discuss them before reading or have students complete an outline as they read the selection. As students read the assignment, emphasize key points by underlining and highlighting them; repeating, discussing, and summarizing them; and questioning students about graphs, pictures, and diagrams.

You also can use cues to help students identify and understand essential information presented in print. Prompt students to focus on important content by highlighting it or labeling it as important in the margins. Margin notes, like the ones in this book, can be written on textbook pages that include definitions, statements, questions, notes, and activities that help students understand and interact with the material. You also can teach your students to understand and use text features such as headings, visuals, and highlighted words to support their ability to focus on and understand important text (Fisher & Frey, 2008).

Activating or priming students' prior knowledge before reading the selection also can help them understand the new material and vocabulary (Englert, 2009; Gately, 2008; Vacca & Vacca, 2008). This can be done by using brainstorming, and discussing and predicting text structures and components of the story. You and your students also can learn to use different types of graphic organizers based on the nature of information being presented (Whalon, Al Otaiba, & Delano, 2009) (see Figure 8.2b on page 302). You can introduce your students to important background information by displaying and reviewing some of the key and motivating illustrations in the reading selection. You also can use a *K-W-L* strategy: *K* (students identify what they **K**now about the reading selection and the topic), *W* (students create questions or statements related to what they **W**ant to learn from reading about the topic), and *L* (students discuss what they have **L**earned from reading about the topic).

You can improve students' comprehension skills by asking them to do a writing activity related to the assignment before they read the selection (Roberts et al., 2008). Learning logs, study guides, written summaries, and questions related to readings can be used to help students understand the material by allowing them to organize their thoughts.

Questioning A popular strategy for guiding text comprehension—having students individually or in groups respond to or generate questions about the text before, during, and after reading—can focus attention on the purpose of the assignment (Falk-Ross et al., 2009; Fink Chorzempa & Lapidus, 2009; Whalon et al., 2009). You can use

- *literal questions*, which ask about the facts presented in the selection (who, what, where, when, why, and how);
- *literacy-based questions*, which are related to the written and oral language components of the selection;
- *inferential questions*, which cause students to make interpretations about and reflect on the material;
- *ponderable questions*, which present dilemmas or situations that have no right or wrong answer;
- *elaborative questions*, which ask students to incorporate their prior knowledge into information presented in the selection.

You can help students answer questions by teaching them about the different kinds of questions and by modifying the language, type, and timing of the questions (Fink Chorzempa & Lapidus, 2009; Sanacore, 2005). At first, present literal questions that deal with factual information in the reading selection. Then move to those that require inference and evaluation on the part of students and more complex skills. You also should try to phrase your questions so that *all* students feel comfortable responding. Open-ended questions can be used so that different students can provide different responses and insights to questions. When students have difficulty responding to open-ended questions, you can rephrase them, using simpler language or a multiple-choice format. You can help students gain information from books by using *prequestions* posed before the selection is read and *postquestions* posed afterward. Postquestions are particularly effective in promoting recall by establishing the need for review. Be careful in using prequestions; they can cause students to focus too much on information related to the answers while ignoring other content. You can help students develop text comprehension skills by asking them to generate their own questions and summarize a selection's content in their own words.

One questioning strategy that teachers and students can learn is Question the Author (QtA) (Salinger & Fleischman, 2005). When using this strategy with your students, you ask them questions to guide and assess their text comprehension and reading strategies. For example, as students read text, you can ask them to identify important information ("What is the important information in that paragraph? Why is it important?"), understand key terminology ("Why did the author choose this word? What does it mean in the context of the sentence?"), and question content ("Do you agree with the author? Why or why not?").

Another effective text comprehension strategy that involves students responding to questions about the text and story structure (e.g., who, what, where, when and how questions about the story) is Reread-Adapt and Answer-Comprehend (RAAC) (Therrien, Gormley, & Kubina, 2006). You implement RAAC by (a) prompting students to read the selection as fast as they can and to pay attention to what they have read so that they can answer questions about the story; (b) having students read who, what, where, when, and how questions about the story; (c) asking students to reread the story aloud while you correct their errors and praise their improvements; (d) having students adapt and answer questions about the story while you prompt them if they make errors; and (e) evaluating student progress and making decisions about future reading selections based on their progress.

Reciprocal Teaching   Text comprehension skills also can be improved by *reciprocal teaching*, which involves a dialogue between you and your students (Ash, Kuhn, & Walpole, 2009; Gately, 2008). Here you ask students to read a selection silently, summarize it, discuss and clarify problem areas and unclear vocabulary, use questions to check understanding, and give students the opportunity to predict future content. After you model these strategies, students take the role of the teacher while you provide help through prompting ("What type of question would a teacher ask in this situation?"), instructing ("A summary is a short statement that includes only essential information"), modifying the activity ("If you can't predict what's going to happen, summarize the information again"), praising students ("That was a good prediction"), and offering corrective feedback ("What information could help you make your prediction?").

Collaborative Strategic Reading   A multicomponent reading comprehension strategy that is based on reciprocal teaching is Collaborative Strategic Reading (CSR) (Brigham, Berkley, Simpkins, & Brigham, 2007; Vaughn & Edmonds, 2006). In CSR, teachers use modeling and talking aloud to teach students why, when, and how to use the following strategic reading comprehension strategies:

- *Previewing:* Students read the selection, recall what they know about it, and predict what it is about.
- *Click and clunk:* Students identify difficult parts of the selection and create fix-up sentences to make the sentences understandable.

- *Get the gist:* Students read and restate the important aspects of the selection.
- *Wrap-up:* Students summarize the important aspects of the selection and generate easy, harder and hardest questions that might be on a test. *Easy questions* are those whose one or two word answers are in the text. *Harder questions* are those that involve one or two sentences combining information presented in the text. The *hardest questions* are those that require students to use prior knowledge and information from the selection.

Once students learn the strategic reading strategies, three to five students work collaboratively to read the text and apply the strategic strategies. To assist each group, ask them to maintain a log of their activities, progress, and use of the strategies or assign students to perform roles (e.g., group leader, the click and clunk or gist experts, recorder, timekeeper). You also can implement technology-based collaborative strategic reading (Kim, Vaughn, Klingner, Woodruff, Reutebuch, & Kouzekanani, 2006).

Collaborative Reading Groups   Your students also can work in collaborative reading groups to foster their text comprehension (Chiang & Lin, 2007; Fisher & Frey, 2008; Guthrie et al., 2009). In collaborative reading groups, students share responsibility for reading the text and making sure that all group members comprehend it. You can foster the success of these groups by teaching your students how to work collaboratively and assigning them different roles to support the success of the group. Possible roles include the *questioner* (who prompts the group to generate questions), *page master* (who identifies special text features and important sections and prompts the group to summarize them), *vocabulary enricher* (who helps the group identify and define important and difficult vocabulary), *connector* (who assists the group in making connections between the text and their lives and learning), and *illustrator* (who guides the group in creating pictures or graphic organizers depicting the key elements and information from the selection) (O'Brien, 2007). When using collaborative reading groups, try make sure that *all students* have the opportunity to perform a range of the roles within the group.

Story/Text Mapping   Some students may benefit from *story/text mapping*, in which you help them identify the major elements of a story or passage using a visual representation (see Figure 8.2a on page 301) (Gately, 2008; Stone, Boon, Fore, Bender, & Spencer, 2008). Give students story/text maps that contain pictorial prompts paired with text and spaces for them to list the key elements of the story or passage such as the setting (characters, time, and place), the plot or problem, the goal, the action, the outcome, and the characters' reactions (e.g., graphics of individuals paired with "Who are the characters?") (Whalon & Hanline, 2008). As students read information on the components-of-the-story/text map, ask them to discuss the information and write the correct response on their map. As students learn to do this, they can complete the story/text map independently. Boyle and Weishaar (1997) have developed TRAVEL, a type of map that helps students create cognitive organizers to help them understand text.

Communicative Reading Strategies   Communicative reading strategies offer students corrective feedback designed to support their independent use of text

PEARSON
myeducationlab
To enhance your understanding of how to use collaborative strategic reading strategies to foster your students' text comprehension, go to the IRIS Center Resources section of the Topic *Instructional Practices and Learning Strategies* in the MyEducationLab for your course, and complete the module entitled *CSR: A Reading Comprehension Strategy.*

Making Connections
Find out more about how you can have your students work in cooperative learning groups in Chapter 9.

Story and text maps can facilitate students' text comprehension. What strategies do you use to foster your students' reading comprehension?

comprehension strategies (Fisher & Frey, 2008). This involves your monitoring students' text comprehension as they read, and intervening to assist them by engaging them in conversations about the text, offering prompts and cues to help them focus and understand the topic, simplifying sentences, defining and explaining new vocabulary, summarizing passages, highlighting and explaining pronoun references, and linking ideas and words, and text across passages and chapters.

Teach Student-Directed Text Comprehension Strategies

Students may learn to use a variety of student-directed comprehension strategies (Englert, 2009; Faggella-Luby & Deshler, 2008; Schumaker et al., 2006). You can help your students learn to employ these strategies by modeling and role-playing their use, thinking aloud as you use them, and offering opportunities for guided/collaborative and independent practice (Fink Chorzempa & Lapidus, 2009; Servilio, 2009). You can foster their use of these strategies by providing them with or posting pictorial prompts and self-monitoring checklists such as the ones presented in Figure 8.2 (Guthrie et al., 2009). You also can give them sticky notes and ask students to use them to summarize text, list main ideas, supporting details, and specific story elements, and prompt students to ask questions or make comments (Stormont, 2008).

Finding the Main Idea   Students can learn to identify the main idea of a paragraph, which is usually embedded in the topic sentence (Coyne, Zipoli, & Ruby, 2006; Guthrie et al., 2009).Therefore, you can teach your students how and where to find topic sentences. For example, you can display a paragraph on a PowerPoint slide and model and prompt students in identifying the main idea (Kroeger, Burton, & Preston, 2009). Students also can be taught how to identify main points by looking for repetition of the same word or words throughout the paragraph, examining headings and subheadings, and delineating major and supporting ideas (Anderson, 2006). They also can be taught to ask who, what, where, when, and how questions to identify the main ideas in paragraphs.

Predicting   A good reading comprehension strategy for students to use is predicting (Englert, 2009). Individually or in pairs or small groups, students can read sections of a selection and make predictions about it (Alber-Morgan, Matheson Ramp, Anderson, & Martin, 2007; Whalon & Haline, 2008). As students continue to read, they check their predictions and reflect on why their predictions were correct or incorrect. When students finish reading, they summarize the selection using no more than 10 words and discuss and receive feedback on their predictions.

Surveying   Students can be taught to survey reading assignments through use of *SQ3R*, a technique that consists of the following steps:

Step 1. Survey. Surveying allows students to look for clues to the content of the chapter. In surveying, students can do the following: (a) examine the title of the chapter and try to anticipate what information will be presented; (b) read the first paragraph to try to determine the objectives of the chapter; (c) review the headings and subheadings to identify main points; (d) analyze visual aids to find relevant supporting information and related details; and (e) read the final paragraph to summarize the main points.

Step 2. Question. Questioning helps students identify important content by formulating questions based on restating headings and subheadings and their own reactions to the material.

Step 3. Read. Reading enables students to examine sections more closely and answer the questions raised in the questioning phase.

Step 4. Recite. Reciting helps students recall the information for further use. In this step, students can be encouraged to study the information they have just covered.

Step 5. Review. Reviewing also helps students remember the content. This can be done by having them prepare an oral or written summary of the main topics.

PEARSON
myeducationlab

Go to the Assignments and Activities section of the Topic *Reading Instruction* in the MyEducationLab for your course and complete the activity entitled *Reading Instruction that Reaches All Students.* As you watch the video and answer the accompanying questions, note the importance of differentiating instruction to best meet the needs of all students.

(a) Story/Text Mapping
(Use to identify the major elements of the story/passage.)

Setting

Where and when does
the story occur?

Characters

Who is in the story? What
are their characteristics?

Actions

What happens in the story?
What does each character do?

Conflicts/Problems

What conflicts and or problems
are presented?

Solution

What happens to the characters?
How are the problems solved?

Ending

How does the story end?

(Continued)

FIGURE 8.2 Continued

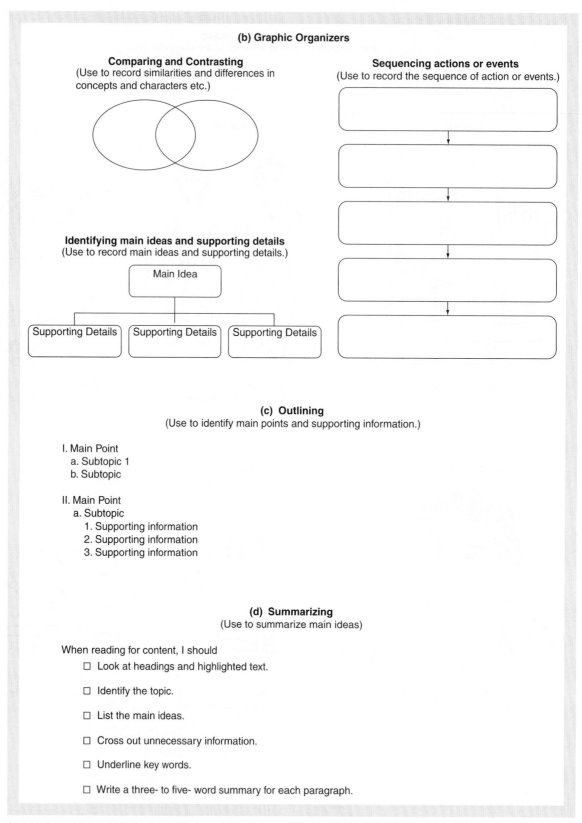

(b) Graphic Organizers

Comparing and Contrasting
(Use to record similarities and differences in concepts and characters etc.)

Sequencing actions or events
(Use to record the sequence of action or events.)

Identifying main ideas and supporting details
(Use to record main ideas and supporting details.)

Main Idea

Supporting Details   Supporting Details   Supporting Details

(c) Outlining
(Use to identify main points and supporting information.)

I. Main Point
  a. Subtopic 1
  b. Subtopic

II. Main Point
  a. Subtopic
    1. Supporting information
    2. Supporting information
    3. Supporting information

(d) Summarizing
(Use to summarize main ideas)

When reading for content, I should
  ☐ Look at headings and highlighted text.

  ☐ Identify the topic.

  ☐ List the main ideas.

  ☐ Cross out unnecessary information.

  ☐ Underline key words.

  ☐ Write a three- to five- word summary for each paragraph.

Sources: Casteel, Isom and Jordan (2000); Whalon and Hanline (2008).

A modified version of SQ3R is *multipass*, in which students review the content of a reading selection three times. In the first pass, or *survey*, students become familiar with the structure and organization of the selection. The second review, the *size-up* pass, helps students identify the main points of the chapter. In the final or *sort-out* pass, students read the selection again and answer the accompanying questions.

Other similar techniques—such as *SOS* (Schumaker, Deshler, Alley, & Warner, 1983), *OK5R* (Pauk, 1984), *PQST* (Pauk, 1984), *PARTS* (Ellis, 1996), and *SCROL* (Grant, 1993)—also can be selected based on students' ability levels.

Self-Questioning   Students can be taught to use several self-questioning procedures to improve their text comprehension skills (Englert, 2009; Faggella-Luby & Deshler, 2008; Roberts et al., 2008). In one self-questioning technique, students determine the reasons for studying the passage, identify the passage's main ideas by underlining them, generate a question associated with each main idea and write it in the margin, find the answer to the question and write it in the margin, and review all the questions and answers. Students also can use self-questioning to deconstruct sentences to determine their meaning. For example, students can ask themselves, "What is this sentence about? What is the subject? The verb?" (Anderson, 2006).

You can teach your students to use the learning strategies to generate questions. The Self-Questioning Strategy involves students composing questions addressing the selection they are reading, predicting answers to their questions, and locating and discussing the answers as they read the selection (Schumaker et al., 2006). You also can teach them to use the mnemonic RAM to: (1) **R**ead the passage and ask yourself who, what, where and why questions; (2) **A**nswer the questions while you read the text; and (3) **M**ark your answers with a meaningful symbol (Brigham et al., 2007).

Your students also can work in groups to pose and discuss text comprehension questions by using Socratic discussions (Fink Chorzempa & Lapidus, 2009) and reciprocal questioning (Whalon & Hanline, 2008). You can implement *Socratic discussions* by having your students generate questions after reading text, which are then discussed by the class to identify, examine, and reflect on the information presented in the reading selection. *Reciprocal questioning* involves your students working in collaborative pairs to generate text questions.

Paraphrasing   Paraphrasing requires students to read text, ask questions about it to determine the main idea and other relevant information, and paraphrase the answers to these questions (Dieker & Little, 2005). Paraphrased statements should consist of a complete sentence, be correct and logical, and provide new and useful information. Students can learn to use *RAP*, a learning strategy that involves **R**eading the paragraph, **A**sking yourself what was the main idea and the important supporting details, and **P**utting the main idea and details in your own words (Hagaman & Reid, 2008).

Outlining   Outlining chapters allows students to identify, sequence, and group main and secondary points so that they can better understand what they have read (Joseph & Konrad, 2009; Margolis & McCabe, 2006; Siegle & McCoach, 2005) (see Figure 8.2c). Students can learn to use a separate outline for each topic, identify essential parts of a topic using Roman numerals, present subtopics by subdividing each main heading using capital letters, and group information within a subdivision in a sequence using Arabic numerals.

Summarizing   Another approach to teaching text comprehension skills is *summarization* (Englert, 2009; Faggella-Luby & Deshler, 2008; Whalon et al., 2009) (see Figure 8.2d). The five basic summarization rules students can employ are (a) identify and group main points, (b) eliminate information that is repeated or unnecessary, (c) find the topic sentence, (d) devise topic sentences for paragraphs that have none, and (e) delete phrases and sentences that fail to present new or relevant information (Anderson, 2006). You can foster your students' summarization skills by having them read paragraphs and underline key words and phrases, and write three- to five-word summaries in the margins (Nilson, 2007).

Paragraph Restatements and Paragraph Shrinking   *Paragraph restatements* help students actively process reading material by encouraging them to create original sentences that summarize the main points of the selection. The sentences should include the fewest possible words. They can be written in the textbook, recorded as notes on a separate sheet, or constructed mentally. In *paragraph shrinking*, students read a paragraph orally and then state its main idea in 10 words or less by identifying the most important information about who or what the paragraph is about (Kroeger et al., 2009).

Visual Imagery   Visual imagery or visualizing requires students to read a section of a book, create an image for every sentence read or paragraph, contrast each new image with the prior one, and evaluate the images to make sure they are complete (Anderson, 2006). You can teach students to use visual imagery by asking them to create visual images for concrete objects, having them visualize familiar objects and settings, asking them to create images while listening to high-imagery stories, and having them devise images as they read (Hart & Whalon, 2008). You also can teach them to use *SCENE*, a learning strategy that involves **S**earching for picture words, **C**reating or changing the scene, **E**ntering details, **N**aming the parts, and **E**valuating your picture.

Verbal Rehearsal   In verbal rehearsal, students pause after reading several sentences to themselves and verbalize to themselves the selection's content. At the beginning, you can cue students to use verbal rehearsal by placing red dots at various points in the selection.

Combinations of Student-Directed Comprehension Strategies.   In addition to learning the previously discussed student-directed text comprehension strategies, students also may benefit from learning how to combine these strategies (Faggella-Luby & Deshler, 2008; Roberts et al., 2008; Whalon et al., 2009). One such strategy is *TWA*, which involves the following:

> **T** (Think Before Reading): Think about (a) the author's purpose, (b) what you know, and (c) what you want to learn.
>
> **W** (While Reading): Think about (a) reading speed, (b) linking knowledge, and (c) rereading parts.
>
> **A** (After Reading): Think about (a) the main idea, (b) summarizing information, and (c) what you learned (Mason, Meadan, Hedin, & Corso, 2006; Rogevich & Perin, 2009).

Enhance the Readability of Materials

Students with reading and learning difficulties must often use commercially produced and teacher-developed print materials whose readability levels are too high for them. You can increase students' understanding of reading matter by modifying the material, making the text less complex, and using instructional technology.

Highlight Essential Information   Highlighting helps students identify main points and locate essential information. Cues linking questions with the location of the answers in the selection can help students learn how to find the answers. For example, you can color-code study questions and their answers in the text. Pairing questions with the numbers of the pages containing the answers, simplifying vocabulary by paraphrasing questions, defining important and difficult terms, breaking multiple-part questions into separate questions, or recording questions on digital recorders and including the pages where the answers occur are other helpful methods.

Use Instructional Technology   The use of instructional technology also can foster text comprehension. As we saw earlier in this chapter, you can use a variety of digital materials which read text to students and offer a variety of supports including access to dictionaries and thesauri and pronunciation guides (Izzo, Yurik, & McArrell, 2009). Many of these materials also have multiple highlighters that allow for *dynamic and dual highlighting*. Whereas *dynamic highlighting* helps students focus their attention

Try the various comprehension strategies using material in this textbook or in a textbook for the grade you would like to teach. Which were easiest? Which were most effective?

on important text by simultaneously color coding and reading it, *dual highlighting*, also called *masking*, uses two colors so that one color highlights the text and another color highlights the text that is being read (Silver-Pacuilla et al., 2004).

You also can use software and web-based programs to offer students access to self-paced, interactive activities to develop their comprehension of written text (Hasselbring & Bausch, 2006; Zorfass & Clay, 2008). Many of these programs include visual and auditory cues designed to assist students in decoding the material and using effective text comprehension strategies such as highlighting main ideas and other important information, summarization, questioning, and story grammars. For example, many digital, software, and Web-based materials include *rebus prompts*, which assist students in comprehending written text by pairing important words with their pictures. Software programs that allow teachers and students to create graphic organizers and cognitive maps also can improve students' text comprehension (Reeves & Stanford, 2009). You also can use Microsoft Word AutoSummarize to condense and summarize longer text selections into shorter versions.

Readability software programs also are available to help you prepare readable materials for your students (Salend, 2009). In addition to computing the readability of your materials, many of these programs guide you in making them more readable. For instance, these programs can identify difficult words that can then be replaced with more readable alternatives such as synonyms that are more appropriate for your students. When using these programs, keep in mind that the content-based terms that are essential to student learning cannot and should not be simplified.

Audio- and video-based materials also can be used by students. Audio recordings of text-based materials that are available in digital formats have the added advantages of allowing users to determine the playback rate, and to set bookmarks.

Teachers can use the principles of typographic design to produce highly readable and legible materials for use with students. How successful are you at using these principles?

IDEAs to Implement Inclusion

Adjusting the Complexity of Text Language

Ms. Mantel's class had several students whose reading abilities varied widely. Sometimes they were able to read the material and understand it. At other times, they struggled. Ms. Mantel noticed that her students' reading abilities appeared to be related to the linguistic complexity of the text. She decided to break up the reading selections that caused her students the most trouble into several smaller sections and began to simplify the choice and arrangements of words and sentences in the selections. First, she examined the length of sentences and shortened them. She broke long sentences into two or three shorter sentences. Second, she highlighted main ideas, concepts, and words, and introduced only one idea at a time. Third, she helped her students understand the order of the concepts presented by using signal words such as *first, second*, and *third*. Fourth, because her students had difficulty understanding the relationship between concepts, she used words that show relationships, such as *because, after*, and *since*.

Here are some other strategies you can use to implement the IDEA in your inclusive classroom and reduce the linguistic complexity of text:

- Eliminate unnecessary words and sections that may distract students.

- Use easy-to-understand language and words with which students are familiar rather than uncommon or unusual words (e.g., *use* rather than *utilize*).

- Refrain from using proper names, irregularly spelled words, ambiguous terms, and use of multiple terms for the same word or concepts as well as double negatives, abbreviations, contractions, acronyms, quotations, and parentheses.

- Use clear pronoun references and word substitution to clarify relationships.

- Rephrase paragraphs so that they begin with a topic sentence followed by supporting details.

- Present a series of events or actions in chronological order, and cluster information that is related.

- Embed definitions and examples of new words and concepts, and avoid using different words that have identical meanings.

- Insert text and examples to clarify main points.

- Present text in the present tense and avoid use of the passive voice.

- Create visual aids that present content and depict processes.

Sources: Kozen, Murray, and Windell (2006); Salend (2009).

Using Technology to Promote Inclusion
PREPARING READABLE AND LEGIBLE MATERIALS

An important factor in differentiating instruction for your students is providing them with access to high-quality instructional materials that support their learning. The visual look of text affects its readability and legibility. Technology—including the use of word processing programs, scanners, laser printers, and digital cameras—offers you access to various dimensions of typographic design that can help you produce universally designed text-based instructional materials for students that promote speed, clarity, and understanding (Ferreri, 2009; Salend, 2009). These dimensions, which are outlined here, also can be used to prepare all the materials you use to teach and assess your students and to communicate with families and colleagues. It is also important to include page numbers when preparing materials that have multiple pages, to use bullets to present essential information that does not have a numerical or hierarchical sequence, to display significant information in text blocks with an appropriate border, and to date materials when the date is an important factor.

Type Size

Type that is too small is difficult to decipher, and type that is too large requires excessive eye movements to follow the text and can cause the reader to pause more often while reading a line.

In terms of type size, 12- to 14-point type is easier to read than smaller or larger print at typical reading distances. However, larger type of at least 18-point may be more appropriate for young students who are beginning to read and for students who have visual difficulties (Ferreri, 2009). Larger type can reduce eye fatigue. Larger type also should be used when preparing materials that students will view at a distance of greater than 10 feet such as PowerPoint presentations.

Typefaces/Fonts

You can make material more readable by using typefaces, also referred to as *fonts*, with simple designs, as well as those familiar to students. Most printed materials use a serif font such as Times Roman, which promotes the reading of text via the use of small lines that are part of the serif strokes to align the text on the line. However, students who struggle with reading may benefit from materials that are prepared using sans serif fonts such as Arial, which can make letter and word identification a little easier because the text will resemble hand lettering. It also is important not to mix fonts as it can make text more difficult to read.

Case

Lowercase letters provide cues that help readers perceive, discriminate, and remember differences in letters and word shapes. For this reason, text should be printed in lowercase and capital letters where grammatically appropriate. ALL-CAPITAL PRINTING CAN SLOW DOWN THE READING PROCESS, and its use should be limited to short, noncontinuous important text that needs to be HIGHLIGHTED, such as headings and subheadings, or an essential word or phrase in a sentence or paragraph.

Style

Style refers to variants such as *italics* and **boldface.** *The use of italics or boldface variants slows reading of continuous text* and should be used only to **emphasize** and *highlight* small amounts of text embedded in sentences and paragraphs or to make headings stand out. Italics and boldface are preferable to underlining to highlight important material; underlining can distract the reader and make it harder to discriminate letters. For example, underlining can cause students to perceive *y* as *v* or *u* and *g* as *a*. Excessive boldface can make the page appear darker and more dense, which makes it more difficult and less motivating to read. Furthermore, readers also may find boldface used in the middle of sentences to be distracting as it tends to focus their attention on the highlighted words.

Proportional and Monospaced Type

Monospaced or fixed type uses the same horizontal space for all letters, whereas proportionally spaced type varies the horizontal space of letters, depending on their form. Although proportionally spaced type makes reading easier by providing additional perceptual cues for letter recognition and enhancing the flow of the text, some learners may prefer monospaced type.

Line Length

Line length refers to the number of characters and spaces in a line. Material that is printed in long lines may cause fatigue by making it difficult to find the next line to read, whereas text that is printed in short lines
demands that students' eyes
change lines frequently.

You can use several strategies to design materials that have an appropriate line length of about 4 inches. One method is to count characters and spaces and to maintain a line length and character count of between 40 and 70. Another method is to structure the material by using line lengths of 7 to 12 words. This method adjusts the line length to the linguistic complexity of the material and therefore the reading skill of students.

Another factor to consider is whether the material has word clusters, a series of words that need to be presented together in order to provide the context for understanding the material. Where possible, word clusters should be presented on the same line.

Spacing

When designing print materials, it is useful to view space as a hierarchy that proceeds from smallest to largest, as follows: (a) space between letters, (b) space between words, (c) space between lines, (d) space between paragraphs, (e) space between columns, (f) space between sections, and (g) space from the text area to the edge of the page. Failure to follow these spatial relationships can confuse and frustrate readers. For

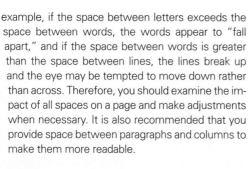

example, if the space between letters exceeds the space between words, the words appear to "fall apart," and if the space between words is greater than the space between lines, the lines break up and the eye may be tempted to move down rather than across. Therefore, you should examine the impact of all spaces on a page and make adjustments when necessary. It is also recommended that you provide space between paragraphs and columns to make them more readable.

Leading

The vertical space between lines, referred to as *leading*, can be adjusted to make materials more readable. In general, you can increase the readability of your materials by making the leading 25% to 30% of the point size. For students with low vision, it is important to increase the leading so that the space between lines of text is greater.

Justification

Justification refers to the alignment of the edges of text. Left-justified or aligned text and staggered right margins are the best choices for readability at all reading levels, as it makes it easier for the reader to see and track the text. Right-justified text results in uneven word and letter spacing of text and can cause students with and without reading difficulties to experience problems tracking the flow of text.

Centered text slows the reading process and is best used for special purposes like titles or lists.

Right-aligned text disturbs the flow of reading because the eye does not know where to go to begin reading the next line.

It is important to read through materials you develop from left to right and top to bottom to make sure that the organization and spacing are consistent and provide a logical structure for the reader to follow. When preparing materials that are to be stored in notebooks, it is important to use a wider left margin so that there is sufficient space for punch holes.

Background and Contrast

Students' ability and motivation to read, and eye strain also can be affected by the color contrast between the text and the background. Contrast also can attract or distract the reader to the critical content being presented. Therefore, the color of the text and background should differ so that it is easier for students to locate important information. When selecting colors, choose those whose lightness differs as much as possible. While using colored type can help highlight text, it should be used carefully. It is suggested that materials consist of black or blue text on an off-white, pale, or matte pastel background. It is also important to avoid gray backgrounds, especially when essential information is presented. In addition to increasing the expense of producing materials, specific colors such as yellow or light green may be difficult for students to read.

Varying the contrast also can help focus the readers' attention to important content. Important content can be made to stand out by surrounding it with white space and/or by embedding it in thick and dark borders. For example, important directions for an assignment or test items can be placed in boxes that are bordered by white space.

Visuals

Visuals can enhance the reading process and make materials more understandable and motivating. When using visuals, make sure they are necessary by determining whether they (a) support the reading process and are linked to the text, (b) help students understand and identify important information, (c) enhance the visual presentation of the material and do not distract the students' attention, and (d) are integrated and labeled appropriately, current, age-appropriate, and culturally sensitive.

Sources: Acrey, Johnstone, and Milligan (2005); Beddow, Kettler, and Elliott (2008); Rotter (2006); Salend (2009); Voss (2005).

Many of these audio recordings are becoming available electronically via Recordings for the Blind and Dyslexic (www.rfbd.org), the Internet, and electronic libraries (e-libraries). For example, Bookshare (www.bookshare.org) allows individuals with visual, learning and physical disabilities that hinder their ability to read print to download digital books and textbooks and software that reads text aloud, or displays it on a Braille device or a computer screen (Harrison, 2009). Through LibriVox (www.librivox.org), you and your students can volunteer to read and create audiofiles of text-based materials which can then be downloaded by others. Dyck and Pemberton (2002) offer guidelines for preparing audio-presented text-based materials.

Video of content that is related to or parallels the material presented in textbooks and other print materials also can orient students to content in these materials. Video also provides direct visual experience with the material that can improve students' understanding and memory of the content to be mastered.

DIFFERENTIATING INSTRUCTION FOR STUDENTS FROM DIVERSE CULTURAL AND LANGUAGE BACKGROUNDS

HOW CAN I DIFFERENTIATE INSTRUCTION FOR STUDENTS FROM DIVERSE CULTURAL AND LANGUAGE BACKGROUNDS? In addition to using cooperative learning (which we will learn more about in Chapter 9) and the other strategies presented in this book, you can consider the following guidelines when adjusting your curriculum and teaching methods for students from diverse cultural and language backgrounds. Again, these guidelines can be used to enhance instruction for *all students*.

Use a Multicultural Curriculum

As Ms. Taravella and her colleagues did in the chapter-opening vignette, one means of making learning relevant, interdisciplinary, and challenging for *all students* is by using a *multicultural curriculum*, which acknowledges the voices, histories, experiences, and contributions of all ethnic and cultural groups (Banks, 2009; Gollnick & Chinn, 2009; Taylor & Whittaker, 2009). The goal of a multicultural curriculum is to help *all students* do the following: (a) understand, view, and appreciate events from various cultural perspectives; (b) understand and function in their own and other cultures; (c) take personal actions to promote racial and ethnic harmony and to counter racism and discrimination; (d) understand various cultural and ethnic alternatives;

A GUIDE TO ACTION
Creating Readable and Legible Materials

You can foster your students' learning by providing them with readable and legible materials. To create effective readable and legible classroom materials and tests, consider the following points:

- Make sure your materials are not too wordy.
- Highlight key terms and concepts.
- Use words that students can read and understand.
- Embed definitions and examples of new and difficult words and concepts in the text.
- Make sure the lengths of sentences and paragraphs and sentence structures are appropriate.
- Make sure that sentences contain no more than one complex idea.
- Avoid using double negatives, abbreviations, contractions, acronyms, quotations, and parentheses.
- Refer directly to important points, objects, or events rather than using pronouns.
- Begin paragraphs with a topic sentence and present information and events logically and in chronological order.
- Number or letter directions, lists, and steps.
- Establish clear transitions to and connections between concepts.
- Make sure that the graphics are necessary, current, age-appropriate, culturally sensitive, placed in the right locations; and that they explain, highlight, or summarize the material.
- Avoid overuse of visuals and unnecessary stimuli or text.
- Check to see that the materials are grammatically correct and presented in a tense and voice your students can understand.

- Use type sizes and typefaces (fonts) that are appropriate for and familiar to students.
- Present text in lowercase and capital letters when grammatically appropriate.
- Use brief, highlighted headings.
- Use boldface and italics sparingly and only to highlight headings or small amounts of text within sentences or paragraphs.
- Use appropriate spaced type, line lengths, spacing, and leading.
- Use left-justified margins, staggered right margins, and wider margins at the bottom of the page.
- Make the overall spacing consistent so it provides a logical structure for students to follow.
- Make sure that the length of the materials are appropriate, and number the pages.
- Create an appropriate contrast between lettering color and background color.
- Make important content stand out by surrounding it with white space and/or by embedding it in thick and dark borders.
- Use bullets to present essential information that does not have a numerical or hierarchical sequence.
- Present important information in text blocks with an appropriate border and surrounding.
- Date materials when the date is an important factor.

How would you rate the readability and legibility of your classroom materials? ( ) Excellent ( ) Good ( ) Need Improvement ( ) Need Much Improvement

Create a plan of action for improving the readability and legibility of your classroom materials that includes your goals, the actions you will take and the resources you will need to achieve them, and the ways you will evaluate your success.

(e) develop their academic skills; and (f) improve their ability to make reflective personal and public decisions and to choose actions that contribute to enhancing and changing society (Banks, 2008).

Multicultural education is often seen as focusing on the needs of students of color and students who speak languages other than English. However, a true multicultural curriculum should teach information about *all groups* and should be directed at *all students* (Gollnick & Chinn, 2009; Nieto & Bode, 2008). A multicultural curriculum also should address content integration and the knowledge construction process, use an equity pedagogy, and foster prejudice reduction and an empowering school culture and social structure (Banks, 2008; Taylor & Whittaker, 2009). Figure 8.3 provides definitions and examples of these dimensions of multicultural education.

A multicultural curriculum should teach information about *all groups* and should be directed at *all students*. How could you make your curriculum more multicultural?

The multicultural curriculum should address all content areas. For example, a science lesson on plants can include a discussion of plants in other countries and in various regions of the United States. The Native American counting technique that uses knots in a rope can be taught as part of a math lesson.

Four hierarchical methods for incorporating multicultural information into the curriculum have been identified (Banks, 2008, 2009). In the *contributions* approach, various ethnic heroes, highlights, holidays, and cultural events are included to the curriculum. In the *additive* approach, content, concepts, themes, and issues related to various cultures are added to the curriculum. In both of these approaches, no substantive changes are made in the organization or goals of the curriculum. As a result, while students are introduced to the contributions of various cultural groups, they are often given little information about various cultural groups, and fail to understand the social and political realities behind the experiences of these groups (Taylor & Whittaker, 2009).

The *transformation* approach to multicultural curriculum reform tries to enhance the curriculum by encouraging students to examine and explore content, concepts, themes, issues, problems, and concerns from various cultural perspectives. In this approach, students learn to think critically and reflect on the viewpoints of different cultural, gender, and social class groups. For example, a lesson on the impact of the North American Free Trade Agreement (NAFTA) can compare its impact from the perspectives of groups in all countries of North America.

The *social action* approach, although similar to the transformation approach, encourages and teaches students to identify social problems and take action to solve them. Students are given opportunities to challenge and change practices that they consider unfair. For example, as part of their unit, Ms. Taravella's and Ms. Stoudamire's class might analyze data on the number of people of color and females working as scientists studying the solar system. They can then propose and evaluate actions to address the problems that discourage people of color and females from becoming scientists.

Parallel lessons, which allow students to learn about individuals and content from both the mainstream culture and other cultures, also help make a curriculum multicultural. For example, a lesson on Abraham Lincoln could be paired with lessons on a comparable historical figure in other countries.

Use Multicultural Teaching Materials

A multicultural curriculum should contain teaching materials that reflect a wide range of experiences and aspirations (Gollnick & Chinn, 2009; Taylor & Whittaker, 2009).

REFLECTIVE
REFLECTIVE

How has your cultural background influenced your perspectives? How are your cultural perspectives similar to and different from those of others? How would multicultural education influence your cultural perspectives?

FIGURE 8.3 Dimensions and examples of multicultural education

Category	Definition	Examples
Content Integration	Content integration deals with the extent to which teachers use examples and content from a variety of cultures and groups to illustrate key concepts, principles, generalizations, and theories in their subject area or discipline.	• Biographies of women or persons of color who are scientists and mathematicians • Learning about demographics of diverse groups in mathematics • Using primary documents about the history of non-Anglo European peoples • Reading and creating multicultural literature • Including images of many kinds of families in the curriculum
The Knowledge Construction Process	The knowledge construction process relates to the extent to which teachers help students to understand, investigate, and determine how the implicit cultural assumptions, frames of references, perspectives, and biases within a discipline influence the ways in which knowledge is constructed within it.	• Examine the degree to which authors who are female or people of color are included in the curriculum • Including the perspectives of both the dominant and nondominant cultures in any description of historical conflict • Examining labels applied to persons with disabilities from the perspective of the person • Validating the importance of languages other than English • Discussing the difference between Western and non-Western views on science • Interviewing community elders about their immigration experiences
An Equity Pedagogy	An equity pedagogy exists when teachers modify their teaching in ways that will facilitate the academic achievement of students from diverse racial, cultural, and social-class groups. This includes using a variety of teaching styles that are consistent with the wide range of learning styles within various cultural and ethnic groups.	• Knowing the cultural background of students and incorporating them into classroom instruction and procedures • Using cooperative learning or group experiences with students who learn best collaboratively • Placing students in pairs to encourage question and answer exchanges
Prejudice Reduction	This dimension focuses on the characteristics of students' racial attitudes and how they can be modified by teaching methods and materials.	• Using heterogeneous groups by gender, race, and language in cooperative learning groups • Developing racial identity (e.g., through a family tree) • Teaching the concept of race as a social, not biological, construct • Studying various religions in the context of a winter holiday season or historical event
An Empowering School Culture and Social Structure	Grouping and labeling practices, sports participation, disproportionality in achievement, and the interaction of the staff and the students across ethnic and racial lines are among the components of the school culture that must be examined to create a school culture that empowers students from diverse racial, ethnic, and cultural groups.	• Including students in determining classroom rules or allowing them choice of assignment • Including students with disabilities or all students who try out for a performance • Actively recruiting and hiring teachers of color • Reducing the numbers of African Americans and Hispanics who are inappropriately placed in special education programs • Working with community groups to provide mentoring and tutoring programs • Involving families in school decision-making bodies

Source: From "Planning Differentiated Multicultural Instruction for Secondary Inclusive Classrooms," by D. van Garderen and C. Whittaker, 2006, *Teaching Exceptional Children*, 38(3), pp. 12–20. Copyright 2006 by The Council for Exceptional Children. Reprinted with permission.

Therefore, materials that reflect cultural, ethnic, linguistic, and gender diversity should be used frequently and should be fully integrated into the curriculum (Banks, 2008; Nieto & Bode, 2008). Guidelines for evaluating multicultural teaching materials are presented in Figure 8.4.

FIGURE 8.4 Guidelines for evaluating multicultural teaching materials

To what extent do the materials include the various groups in U.S. society?

How are various groups portrayed in the materials?

Are the viewpoints, attitudes, reactions, experiences, and feelings of various groups accurately presented?

Do the materials present a varied group of credible individuals to whom students can relate in terms of lifestyle, values, speech and language, and actions?

Are individuals from diverse backgrounds depicted in a wide range of social and professional activities?

Do the materials show a variety of situations, conflicts, issues, and problems as experienced by different groups?

Are a wide range of perspectives on situations and issues offered?

Does the material incorporate the history, heritage, experiences, language, and traditions of various groups?

Are the experiences of and issues important to various groups presented in a realistic manner that allows students to recognize and understand their complexities?

Are culturally diverse examples, situations, experiences, and anecdotes included throughout the materials?

Are the materials factually correct?

Are the experiences, contributions, and content of various groups fully integrated into the materials and the curriculum?

Are graphics accurate, inclusive, and ethnically sensitive?

Do the materials avoid stereotypes and generalizations about groups?

Are members of various groups presented as having a range of physical features (e.g., hair texture, skin color, facial features)?

Is the language of the materials inclusive, and does it reflect various groups?

Do the materials include learning activities that help students develop a multicultural perspective?

Use Culturally Relevant and Responsive Teaching Strategies

Teaching strategies should be relevant and responsive to your students' experiences, cultural perspectives, language backgrounds, and developmental ages (Diaz-Rico & Weed, 2010; Gollnick & Chinn, 2009). They should reflect and be aligned with your students' cultural and linguistic backgrounds and preferred learning styles, which in turn requires you to be aware of your students' cultural values (Banks, 2008). It also means that you teach in a way that helps your students find relevant connections between themselves and the subject matter, the instructional strategies used, and the tasks they are asked to perform (Cartledge & Kourea, 2008; Nieto & Bode, 2008).

Research has identified effective strategies for teaching students from diverse cultural and language backgrounds, and other groups of students:

Making Connections
This discussion of a multicultural curriculum and teaching materials and the use of culturally relevant and responsive teaching strategies builds on what we discussed in Chapters 3 and 5.

- *Emphasizing verbal interactions:* Use activities that encourage students to respond verbally to the material in creative ways such as group discussions, role plays, storytelling, group recitations, choral and responsive reading, and rap.

- *Teaching students to use self-talk:* Encourage and teach students to learn new material by verbalizing it to themselves, such as thinking aloud.

- *Facilitating divergent thinking:* Encourage students to explore and devise unique solutions to issues and problems through activities such as brainstorming, group discussions, debates, and responding to open-ended questions.

- *Using small-group instruction and cooperative learning:* Allow students to work in small groups, and use cooperative learning arrangements including peer tutoring and cross-age tutoring.

- *Employing verve in the classroom:* Introduce *verve*, a high level of energy, exuberance, and action, into the classroom by displaying enthusiasm for teaching and learning, using choral responding, moving around the classroom, varying your voice quality, snapping your fingers, using facial expressions, and encouraging students to use their bodies to act out and demonstrate content.

- *Focusing on real-world tasks:* Introduce content, language, and learning by relating them to students' home, school, and community life, and to their cultures and experiences.

- *Promoting teacher–student interactions:* Use teaching methods based on exchanges between students and teachers. Ask frequent questions, affirm students' responses, give feedback, offer demonstrations and explanations, and rephrase, review, and summarize material (Gay, 2004; Goldenberg, 2008; Obiakor, 2007; Shealey & Callins, 2007).

Use Reciprocal Interaction Teaching Approaches

You can supplement teaching activities that emphasize the development of skills with *reciprocal interaction teaching approaches (RITA)* that foster learning through verbal and written dialogues between students and teachers and among students. In using reciprocal interaction, you use students' prior knowledge and experiences to add a context that promotes comprehension and incorporates language development and use. The curriculum and teaching focus on meaningful, authentic activities related to students' lives, and they target higher-level critical thinking skills rather than basic skills.

When implementing RITA, you also use student–centered teaching and dialogues, student–student interactions, problem-solving situations, and guided questioning to help students control their learning. Higher-level thinking is promoted through teacher modeling and thinking aloud, presenting new information as collaborative problems to be solved, posing open-ended questions, asking students to justify their responses and explain their reasoning, helping students explore alternative perspectives, encouraging students to evaluate and monitor their thinking and that of others, and viewing students' miscues as opportunities to discuss new information.

You also can employ **scaffolding**, breaking down comments and concepts students don't understand or a task students have difficulty performing into smaller components that promote understanding or mastery (Echevarria, Vogt, & Short, 2010). Scaffolding methods include relating the task to students' prior knowledge, using visual and language cues, modeling effective strategies, and highlighting the key parts of the task (Levine & McCloskey, 2009; Paxton-Buursma & Walker, 2008). As students gain skill or mastery, scaffolding supports are gradually removed so that students function independently to understand, apply, and integrate their new learning.

When using RITA, you also can promote teacher–student interactions through the use of confirmation checks ("Are you saying . . . ?"), comprehension checks ("Do you understand what I just said?" "Tell me in your own words what I'm saying"), clarification requests ("Can you explain that again?" "In a different way?"), repetitions, and expansions. Conversational interactions also can be fostered by you and your students asking questions related to who, where, why, when, and what.

Use Effective ESL and Dual-Language Approaches and Techniques

Instruction for English language learners can be differentiated by using effective ESL and dual-language approaches and techniques such as total physical response, sheltered English, natural language approaches, and new vocabulary and concept instructional techniques (Diaz-Rico & Weed, 2010; Echevarria et al., 2010; Lessow-Hurley, 2009; Levine & McCloskey, 2009; Whelan Ariza, 2010).

Total Physical Response   *Total physical response (TPR)* improves students' vocabulary through modeling, repeated practice, and movement. In TPR, you model the message by emphasizing physical gestures and objects. (You state the message, model, and physically emphasize movements related to the concept of, say, sharpening a pencil.) Next, the class as a group responds to your directions. (You ask the students to sharpen their pencils and the students, as a group, make the appropriate motion.) Finally, individual students respond to verbal commands given by you and their peers. (Individual students are asked by you and their peers to sharpen a pencil.) As students develop skills, the complexity of the language skills taught increases.

Sheltered English   **Sheltered English**, or *content-based instruction*, uses cues, gestures, technology, manipulatives, drama, and visual stimuli and aids to teach new vocabulary and concepts. As part of your use of sheltered English, you need to simplify your vocabulary and grammar. When using a sheltered English approach, present lessons that cover grade-level content and teach students the terminology needed to understand the concepts in specific content areas. Create a context; present information orally and visually; use hands-on activities and media; and help students learn by restating, paraphrasing, simplifying, and expanding the material. It is also important to connect the curriculum to students' culture, experiences, and language and to promote interactions among students.

Lessons using a sheltered English approach typically are organized in the following sequence:

1. Identify, define, and teach terminology that is essential to understanding the lesson and related to the curriculum. Key terms are posted as a visual reference for students and are added to students' word banks.

2. Select and explain the main academic vocabulary and concepts to students.

3. Help students learn and understand the main concepts by presenting content using visual aids, objects, physical gestures, facial expressions, manipulatives, and technology. Where possible, allow students to experience the concepts.

4. Make instruction meaningful by giving students opportunities to relate the concepts to their prior knowledge and experiential background.

5. Check students' understanding, encourage them to seek clarification, and offer feedback.

6. Encourage students to work and interact with their peers (Freeman & Crawford, 2008; Short & Echevarria, 2005).

Natural Language Techniques   You also can help students develop language by using and prompting your students to use natural language techniques: expansion, expatiation, parallel talk, and self-talk (Paxton-Buursma & Walker, 2008). **Expansion** allows you to present a language model by expanding on students' incomplete sentences or thoughts or ask your students to expand on a classmate's statement. **Expatiation** occurs when you or one of your students adds new information to the comments of others. **Parallel talk** involves describing an event that students are seeing or doing. **Self-talk** consists of talking about one's actions, experiences, or feelings.

New Vocabulary and Concept Teaching Techniques   Effective teaching for English language learners requires you to help them learn new vocabulary and concepts. To aid these students, focus on essential vocabulary key words and concepts that students use often, and are related to their lives and the material they are learning. In addition, teach vocabulary in context rather than in isolation; teach related words and concepts together; and teach using concrete examples, visuals, pictorials, and physical movements to highlight the important features of new vocabulary words when possible (Denton et al., 2008). For example, you can teach words like *cold* or *frigid* by pretending to shiver. When introducing new vocabulary and concepts, you can consider the following sequence:

Step 1. Analyze the concept to be taught and identify its key features, including the concept's structure and characteristics. Determine whether the context is important for understanding the concept.

Step 2. Introduce and label the concept in a variety of situations. If possible, present the concept using clear, consistent language, concrete materials, manipulatives, and visuals.

Step 3. Show and discuss examples and nonexamples of the concept, moving from easy to difficult. Present and use the concept in many naturally occurring situations, and elaborate on the characteristics that define the concept and distinguish it from others.

Making Connections
Find out more about strategies for developing your students' vocabulary in Chapter 10.

REFLECTIVE

Watch a television show or film in a new language. What factors helped you understand the content?

Differentiating Instruction for English Language Learners

Ms. Phalen's class included several English language learners. The class was learning about the cycle of the butterfly. First, Ms. Phalen read and discussed a book on this topic with her students. They talked about such terms as *caterpillar, cocoon*, and *butterfly*. Then Ms. Phalen had the students reenact the cycle of the butterfly. She told them to roll themselves into a little ball. Then she asked them to pretend they were caterpillars. They acted like caterpillars, and then became a cocoon and broke out of the cocoon as butterflies. With their arms outstretched like butterflies, the students then "flew" around the room. After this activity, Ms. Phalen had her students work in small groups to draw pictures of the cycle of the butterfly.

Here are some other strategies you can use to implement the IDEA in your inclusive classroom and differentiate instruction for English language learners:

- Establish a relaxed learning environment that encourages students to take risks and attempt to use both languages, and emphasize communication rather than language form. For example, correct students indirectly by restating their incorrect comments in correct form. (If the student says "My notebook home," you say, "I see—your notebook is at home.")

- Make it easier for students to understand and respond by articulating clearly in a normal tone of voice; pausing often; limiting the use of idiomatic expressions, slang, and pronouns; highlighting key words through increased volume and slight exaggeration; using rephrasing, simple vocabulary, and shorter complete sentences; and giving students enough wait time.

- Begin new lessons with reviews of relevant previously learned concepts, and show the relationships between previously learned concepts and new material.

- Relate material and examples to students' experiences, use cultural referents, and use real-world language and meaningful, functional activities.

- Be consistent in your use of language, and use repetition to help students acquire the rhythm, pitch, volume, and tone of their new language.

- Use gestures, facial expressions, voice changes, pantomimes, demonstrations, rephrasing, visuals, props, manipulatives, and other cues to provide a context that conveys the meaning of new terms and concepts.

- Introduce new material in context, discussing changes in the context while it is occurring. Talk about what has occurred in context so that ambiguities are reduced.

- Develop students' language competence by using modeling, questioning, art forms, drama, simulations, role plays, storytelling, music, and games.

- Supplement oral instruction and descriptions with demonstrations; hands-on activities; and visual materials such as charts, maps, graphs, pictures, graphic organizers, and chalkboard writing.

- Allow students to express their knowledge, understanding, and intended meaning nonverbally. For example, rather than asking a student to define a word or concept, ask the student to draw a picture depicting it.

- Encourage and show students how to use bilingual dictionaries, pictionaries, and glossaries.

- Offer regular summaries of important content, and check students' understanding frequently.

Sources: Diaz-Rico and Weed (2010); Dong (2009); Echevarria et al. (2010); Goldenberg (2008); Lessow-Hurley (2009); Levine and McCloskey (2009); Whelan Ariza (2010).

Step 4. Contrast the concept with other related concepts.

Step 5. Allow students to practice using the concept in functional activities related to their interests and learning levels.

Encourage Students to Respond

You may need to encourage English language learners and students with speech and language difficulties to respond verbally (Goldenberg, 2008; Zwiers & Crawford, 2009). You can promote student responding by using open-ended questions, allowing students to use gestures until they develop language competence, and praising and expanding on students' contributions and seeking more information when necessary. Give students enough time to interact with and discuss material before responding, and encourage students to share their opinions, ask questions, and expand on the comments of others. You also can stimulate the use of language by providing experiences that encourage discussion, such as introducing new objects into the classroom; changing the classroom environment; allowing students to work and play together; sending students on errands; creating situations in which students need to ask for help; asking students to recount events or talk about doing something while doing it; and using visuals that display pictorial absurdities.

USING INSTRUCTIONAL TECHNOLOGIES AND ASSISTIVE DEVICES

HOW CAN I USE INSTRUCTIONAL TECHNOLOGY AND ASSISTIVE DEVICES TO DIFFERENTIATE INSTRUCTION FOR MY STUDENTS? You can employ a range of instructional technologies and assistive devices to support your use of differentiated instruction and UDL (Wissick, Gardner, & Dempsey, 2009). In choosing which technologies to use, consider whether they match your curricular and instructional goals and educational philosophy and your students' strengths and challenges (King-Sears & Evmenova, 2007). Also, evaluate their impact on your students' learning and including whether they are age-appropriate and your students feel comfortable using them.

Instructional Technology

Recent technological developments allow you to use a wide range of instructional technologies and interactive multimedia to present content in multiple modalities and to create motivating and contextualized learning environments and ways for *all students* to show their learning (Dell et al., 2008; Rao, Dowrick, Yuen, & Boisvert, 2009). Interactive multimedia can link text, sound, animation, video, and graphics to present information to students in a nonlinear, instantaneous fashion that promotes critical thinking skills and social interactions. These technologies can be integrated across the curriculum to differentiate instruction so that you address students' diversities and varied learning strengths and challenges, and allow students to be more actively engaged in directing and showcasing their learning (Mulrine, 2008; Salend, 2009).

Computer-Based Instruction   You can supplement and individualize teaching by using *computer-based instruction* (Campbell & Mechling, 2008). Computers can help you individualize your instruction and assessment by directing students to items related to their skill levels and allowing students to work at their own pace. Through the use of computers, you can differentiate your instruction by providing your students with access to drill-and-practice, instructional games, tutorials, simulations, and problem-solving programs (Parette & Peterson-Karlan, 2007). For example, software tutorial programs can monitor students as they use the program, analyze students' errors, and offer individualized feedback prompts (e.g., "Did you look at the signs for all the numbers?"), and additional items to foster student learning. Technology also can be used by students to demonstrate their mastery of content and present their work to others (Salend, 2009).

However, the effectiveness of computer-based instruction depends on the software program used. Many programs are open to criticism; you should carefully evaluate the ones you use (Boone & Higgins, 2007). A form for evaluating software programs is presented in Figure 8.5.

Video-Based Digital Materials

Video-based digital materials have many multimedia features that can help you differentiate your instruction. As we saw in the chapter-opening vignette, you can present content via video-based digital materials containing sequential or nonlinear frames of realistic graphic displays, video segments, slides, motion pictures, audio information, text, and animation and sound effects. With remote control, you can quickly access high-quality visual and auditory information randomly or continuously, and you can halt the presentation to highlight critical information or to ask students questions. Thus, digitally based teaching allows students to hear explanations in various languages, and view colorful, animated, and expressive visual displays and demonstrations, computer graphics, and sound effects that accurately depict concepts and material in a gradual and systematic way.

Digital materials also have the added advantages of allowing content to be presented through the use of music, speech, and dynamic illustrations to motivate students and promote concept and vocabulary development across content areas, as well as reading and listening comprehension. These materials can present text and

Making Connections
Find out more about how you can use technology to assess student learning in Chapter 12.

Making Connections
Find out more about using interactive boards in Chapter 9.

FIGURE 8.5 Sample educational software evaluation form

Software Features	Yes	No	Comments
Content and Instructional Considerations			
Curricular and instructional goals are identified and appropriate.			
Content is up-to-date, valid, relevant, unbiased and supported by references.			
Content and visual images are developmentally and age appropriate and can be presented in multiple formats.			
Instructional activities are appropriate, varied, and motivating.			
Content can be differentiated based on levels of difficulty and complexity.			
Content can be differentiated based on students' responses.			
Many opportunities to respond to and interact with similar and differentiated content are provided.			
Ease of Use Considerations			
Program loads easily, quickly, and reliably.			
Program is welcoming and user friendly and can be used independently by students.			
Language is age-appropriate and free of biases.			
Menus and navigational features are easy to access and use, logical, and presented in multiple formats (text, icons, and audio).			
Relevant features are easily identified and clearly labeled.			
Prerequisite educational and technological skills students need to use are identified.			
Tutorials and opportunities to practice related to how to use the program and its features are available.			
Help and search features are readily available and helpful.			
Page layouts present directions and content in an organized, predictable, nondistracting, sequential, and logical manner.			
Directions are easy to understand and follow, available in multiple formats (text, audio, video), and can be presented on demand.			
Content and directions are presented in readable and legible text.			
Formats for responding are differentiated, intuitive, and easy to use.			
Limited keyboarding skills are necessary for use.			
Error minimization techniques are provided.			
Links are identified, appropriate, active, and helpful.			
Individualization Considerations			
Options to revise content are provided.			
Options to provide access to students with a range of disabilities and English language learners are available, intuitive, and easy to use.			
Alternate input devices and other technologies for students with special needs easily interface with the program.			
Options to access digital speech of text and audio descriptions of visual images are provided.			
Adjustments can be easily made in text size, font, color, style variants, spacing, and backgrounds.			
Adjustments in the speed, amount, time, and sequence of the presentation of and response to content can be easily made.			
Strategies for highlighting important content can be easily accessed (e.g., color cuing, bold, italics).			
Animation and sound features can be used, turned off, and individualized.			
Personalized visual and auditory cues, prompts, reminders and reinforcement are available and foster student performance, attention, and motivation.			
Feedback and Assessment Considerations			
Options to provide individualized and personalized informative and corrective feedback are available.			
Feedback provided to students is immediate, positive, and consistent.			

(Continued)

FIGURE 8.5 **Continued**

Software Features	Yes	No	Comments
Feedback and Assessment Considerations			
Opportunities for students and teachers to review individual and cumulative responses are provided.			
Student responses can be easily retrieved and revised.			
Student responses are recorded automatically and reliably.			
Valid student performance data are provided and accessed easily in varied understandable formats for students and teachers.			
Support and Documentation Considerations			
Hardware and software requirements are listed.			
Information about the credentials of the program developer is provided and establishes the developer's credibility.			
Documentation and research to demonstrate effectiveness are provided.			
Contact information is presented.			
Follow-up support is readily available and helpful.			
Cost is reasonable.			
Comments:			

Sources: Boone & Higgins (2007); Salend (2009).

illustrations using different voices and languages for the various characters, including sign language. Individual words and text can be repeated, defined, presented in sign language, or translated into another language by highlighting the text to be pronounced or pressing a button. Digital technology also allows you and your students to adjust the pace of the oral reading, magnify the text, vary the colors of the illustrations, and compare their reading with the oral reading.

Video-based digital materials are also being used to make teaching and reference materials more accessible and understandable to students (Anderson-Inman, Terrazas-Arellanes, & Slabin, 2009). Because this technology integrates graphics, spoken text, captioning, video segments, animation, and sound effects, information presented in digital encyclopedias and dictionaries can become more meaningful and motivating to students.

Digital equipment that allows you and your students to develop materials and products also is available. For example, you and your students can use technologies such as presentation software and digital stories to foster and showcase student learning.

Presentation Software You and your students can use presentation software such as PowerPoint and Keynote to make classroom presentations more effective, motivating and interactive (Doyle & Giangreco, 2009; Salend, 2009). PowerPoint presentations are especially helpful for your deaf and hard-of-hearing students and English language learners as they allow you to present material so that students can view the material, visuals, and your lips simultaneously. Using presentation software you can prepare a digital task analysis that demonstrates to your students how to perform specific academic, social, behavioral, transitional, and functional skills (Schleibaum, 2007). This involves taking digital images (video or pictures) of each step in a task analysis and converting the digital images into presentation software slides that include brief written and oral descriptions of each step in the task analysis.

Making Connections
Find out more on how to use presentation software effectively in Chapter 9.

Digital Videos/Stories Your instruction and student learning also can be enhanced by use of digital videos and stories (Rao et al., 2009). Digital videos or stories created

Making Connections
Find out more about how to teach your students to create digital videos and stories in Chapter 10.

by you and your students presenting role plays, documentaries, narratives, news reports, essays, poems, book reports, interviews, and skill demonstrations can be integrated into your instructional program across the curriculum (Sprankle, 2008). These programs allow your students to record narrations to describe learning products, processes, and outcomes and to integrate music and artwork.

Digital, Document, and Web Cameras   Digital cameras give you and your students access to digital technology in order to create video-based teaching and learning projects and increase visual literacy skills (Sopko, 2008). Users can immediately see the recorded image, store it in memory, delete it, or download it so that it can be edited, enlarged, e-mailed, embedded in Web pages, imported to other documents, added to student products or learning materials, or printed. Digital cameras are particularly useful for visually presenting learning tasks that are completed in a series of sequential steps. Document cameras are replacing overheads in classrooms as they allow teachers to display text, images, documents, three-dimensional objects, and Web sites. Web cameras (webcams) allow you and your students to view live events. When using webcams, it is important for you to preview the sites to make sure they are appropriate for your students.

Captioning Television, Interactive White-Smartboards, and Liquid Crystal Display Computer Projection Panels   Captioning and liquid crystal display (LCD) computer projection panels are other valuable teaching methods, particularly for deaf and hard-of-hearing students and English language learners (Sopko, 2008). The dialogue that accompanies closed-caption materials can be presented on the screen in real time via a device that receives closed-caption signals connected to the screen. Real-time closed-captioning can be used with a wide variety of students, including those with reading difficulties and those who speak different languages; it provides an auditory and a visual context for learning new vocabulary and information (Anderson-Inman, et al., 2009). For example, set-top television translators can convert closed captions from one language into another. As we saw in the chapter-opening vignette, students with visual disabilities like Julia benefit from descriptive video services, a specialized sound track system that enhances television and CD/DVD viewing by providing a running description of the images, events, characters' actions and body language, and scenes.

Via an Internet connection and a special slate and stylus and/or remote control device, interactive white-smartboards can help you differentiate your instruction across the curriculum for students by accessing and displaying information and images from the Internet or software programs; presenting digital graphics, text, video clips, and stereo sound; playing educational games; and recording, storing, and sending notes, handouts, and assignments to students (Mounce, 2008). For example, you can pair text with visual cues such as icons and pictorials to help students read words and understand information. You and your students can access the boards by touching the screen and icons displayed on the screen, or from anywhere in the room by writing on them electronically using a slate and a special stylus, or wireless and remote control devices such as handheld devices (Auchincloss & McIntyre, 2008).

LCD computer projection panels promote information sharing by interfacing a computer with a digital projector so that students can view more easily the information displayed on the monitor. With LCD projection, you can display images from multimedia sources with more colors and sharper resolution. You can also teach content in ways that are interesting, multidimensional, motivating, and tailored to students' needs.

Technology-Based Simulations and Virtual Reality   Technology-based simulations and virtual reality systems allow students to engage in a range of learning experiences that present digitally generated images and accompanying text depicting real or imaginary interactive and three-dimensional learning environments (Gee & Levine, 2009; Sayeski, 2008). Via problem-solving, simulation, and virtual learning software programs and Web sites, your student can have access to a range of learning experiences and multidimensional dilemmas and situations across the curriculum that can foster their academic, critical thinking, social, and metacognitive skills (Okolo, Englert, Bouck, & Heutsche, 2007; Salend, 2009). Virtual reality systems, which are available via software programs and the Internet, range from relatively simple simulations to more sophisticated lifelike learning, social and community-based environments (Cafiero, 2008; Cote, 2007; Cummings, 2007). For example, virtual reality can provide students with a safe environment to learn and practice how to cross the street or to conduct scientific experiments.

Internet   The Internet provides you and your students with access to information, as well as many exploratory and discovery-based learning and communication experiences (Richardson, 2009). It allows you to access national, state, and district learning standards, as well as digital instructional activities and materials aligned with the standards. It allows students to control their learning more effectively, and it offers them options related to what and how they learn.

Some of the ways you and your students can use the Internet to differentiate instruction to support learning are presented here. When using the Internet as an instructional tool, keep in mind that it is essential for you to address issues of accessibility and to teach students how to be good digital citizens who use technology safely, appropriately, and respectfully.

Address Accessibility Issues   When using the Internet with students, you need to make sure that *all students* can use Web sites and Web-based and digital materials by examining them in terms of their success at incorporating the principles of universal design (Krach & Jelenic, 2009). To do this, you can use Web accessibility software tools that guide you in evaluating and enhancing the accessibility of Web-based content and digital materials (Skylar, 2007). For example, these resources and materials can be made more accessible for *all students* by pairing graphic images with text and audio descriptions; using appropriate typeface and fonts, style variants, colors, and contrasts; and making sure that the site is easy to navigate, allows adjustments in timed responses, and is not visually distracting (Hartley & Boone, 2005).

Software programs are available that help students with a range of disabilities access the Internet (Dell et al., 2008). These programs, which are available in several languages, allow individuals with visual, dexterity-based, cognitive, and reading disabilities to tailor their browsing and navigating the Internet by using audio descriptors and prompting, closed captioning and text labels, error minimization strategies, and mouse and keyboard accommodations, reducing and reorganizing the visuals presented on the screen, presenting text and images that are read aloud, or enlarging text, graphics, browser controls, mouse pointers, and busy indicators (the hourglass). These programs also provide users with choices related to the text, images and backgrounds in terms of colors, fonts, spacing, and layout (presenting text in a single column) and whether to eliminate backgrounds, animations, time requirements, and images.

> **Making Connections**
> This discussion about accessible technology builds on our earlier discussion of the digital divide in Chapter 3.

Teach Students to Be Good Digital Citizens Who Use Technology Safely, Respectfully and Appropriately   Students need to learn how to be good digital citizens who use technology in a safe, respectful, and appropriate manner (Mustacchi, 2009; November, 2008; Richardson, 2009). When using technology, it is vital that you establish and teach rules, etiquette, and common sense for using the Internet and protecting privacy. As part of this instruction, you need to teach your students to avoid inappropriate Web sites and to refrain from posting or giving out personal information and pictures. They should be taught about viruses and spam and how to avoid them. Your students should learn how to conduct searches, identify the most appropriate links, and interact with others as well as what constitutes and how to avoid plagiarism (Moore Howard & Davies, 2009) and cyberbullying (Mustacchi, 2009). It is important that you teach your students how to evaluate Web sites and Web-based information (Badke, 2009; Richardson, 2009) (see Figure 8.6). Monitor your students' use of technology during instruction to

FIGURE 8.6 Guidelines for evaluating Web sites and Web-based information

- Who produced the site? When and why did they produce it?
- Does the title of the site reflect the content presented?
- Is contact information for the site available?
- Is the site produced by a credible individual, organization, or group?
- What are the goals and purposes of the site?
- Does the site have a specific agenda and any biases?
- Is the information provided current, accurate, helpful, and detailed?
- Is the information presented free of opinions, errors, emotional appeals, and biases?
- Are useful supporting visuals provided?
- Who provided the information for the site?
- Are the credentials of the author(s) of the information provided? Appropriate?
- Are sources of the information provided, relevant, and cited correctly?
- Are relevant links to other sites provided? Are these links active, up-to-date, appropriate, and useful?
- Is the site frequently updated?
- When was the site last updated?

Source: From Salend, S. J. (2009). *Classroom testing and assessment for all students: Beyond standardization.* Thousands Oaks, CA: Corwin Press. Reprinted with permission.

make sure students are using it appropriately (e.g., not e-mailing others or playing video games).

If you share your students' work with others using online formats, take precautions. Therefore, prior to posting student work electronically, you should

- obtain permission from students, their families, and your school district;
- delete confidential and personally identifying information from students' work;
- check to see that your students used pseudonyms and numbers instead of their real names;
- make sure that visuals of students are blocked out;
- evaluate the content and visuals to make sure they are appropriate for viewing by others;
- use password protection to control who can post and view student work; and
- limit access so that only your students and their families can view their work (November, 2008).

Use the Internet to Have Students Communicate with Others   The Internet allows students to learn and communicate with others. Bulletin board folders, e-mail, video- and Web conferencing, and chat groups offer students opportunities to talk to, share information and experiences with, and learn from others (Richardson, 2009). Internet bulletin boards allow students to locate and meet others with whom they may want to interact. E-mail gives them the chance to send private messages to and receive them from other individuals. Videoconferencing and chat groups offer students a forum to talk with others. Through the Internet, students and classes can have digital pals from other schools in the district, geographic region, country, and world with whom they communicate and learn. These interactions give students direct opportunities to learn about and with others, to experience different ways of life, and to learn and use a new language.

Use the Internet to Access Electronic Resources   The Internet provides you and your students with access to an enormous electronic library of lesson plans, learning activities, videos, resources, pictorials, videos, wikis, podcasts, encyclopedias, webcams, and databases containing information about virtually every subject and content area and in every language (Richardson, 2009). For example, you can locate and share classroom-appropriate video clips by using video sharing and streaming video sites such as TeacherTube (*www.teachertube.com*) and SchoolTube (*www .schooltube.com*). When using these video sharing sites, preview the videos to make sure that they are appropriate for your students and align with your instructional goals. Internet connections allow you and your students to examine and browse through these electronic documents and resources. You and your students also can visit and access information from museums and webcams via the Internet.

Your students also can access information, and share their learning by using **wikis**, which are Web sites that offer content on a range of topics created and edited by users. Thus, your students can learn about or demonstrate what they know about a specific topic by creating a new wiki or editing an existing wiki (Knobel & Wilber, 2009; Schweder & Wissick, 2009). They also can receive feedback on their wiki entries by periodically viewing the wiki to see the comments and changes made by others. Because wikis are edited by users, it is important to teach students to carefully evaluate and verify the information obtained from wikis (Badke, 2009) (see Figure 8.6).

Podcasts available via the Internet allow your students to watch or hear live or prerecorded events and learning activities occurring throughout the world. They also can be made by you to present information that your students can view at their convenience and by your students to showcase their work (Langhorst, 2007; Williams, 2007). For example, video and audio-podcasts can consist of you reviewing key terminology prior to a test, or students reading, giving presentations, discussing issues, or solving problems. When creating podcasts to share with others, it is helpful to include markers, which allow others to easily locate or access specific parts of the podcast.

You and your students can access electronic resources by using **RSS Site Summary (RSS)**, which is also referred to as *Really Simple Syndication* (Richardson, 2009). RSS compiles brief summaries of the content on particular topics available at various Web sites so that users can identify relevant online content without having to access multiple sites.

Use the Internet to Create Web Sites, Weblogs, Webquests, and Tracks

You also can use the Internet to create accessible, easy-to-use classroom Web sites, weblogs, webquests, and tracks. Creating a Web site or page for your class is a good way to involve students in learning about the Internet and communicating with other students, families, and individuals throughout the world. For example, your class can work as a group to plan, design, and create a classroom Web page relating to important aspects of your class. Like Ms. Taravella and Ms. Stoudamire, you also can post students' work on your class's Web page, and students can receive and respond to inquiries from others about their Web page. You also can use your Web site to make important learning materials available to students.

You and your students also can create *weblogs* (or *blogs*), online diaries that are easily and continuously updated to present information about your class's activities (Davis & McGrail, 2009). Teachers also use blogs as a way to extend classroom discussions or question and answer sessions beyond the confines of their classrooms. Individual and groups of students also can maintain blogs to share information about things they are learning, to comment on their experiences and events around the world, and to interact with others (Knobel & Wilber, 2009). For example, your students can maintain blogs to present their assignments and to share their knowledge of a specific topic and across the curriculum (Schweder & Wissick, 2007). In addition to text, blogs can include **video blogs**, **vlogs**, as well as audio files such as music or narrations, and links to other related websites.

Another type of Internet-based instructional activity that is becoming more common in classrooms is a **webquest** (Skylar, Higgins, & Boone, 2007). This is an inquiry-oriented, cooperatively structured group activity in which some or all of the information and content that your students use comes from resources on the Internet or videoconferencing. For example, Ms. Taravella and her colleagues had students work in collaborative groups to complete webquests that asked them to use the Internet to gather and present information on the early explorations of the solar system and the corresponding cultural beliefs of different groups. Webquests can be structured in a variety of ways, including as Internet hunts, puzzles, projects, and study guides.

Tracks are online lessons that guide student learning related to a specific topic by directing them to a variety of instructional activities presented by accessing a series of teacher-specified Web sites. Students then visit these sites to engage in learning activities which include producing products that demonstrate their learning or completing an online quiz of material presented via the track.

Assistive Technology

Technology has been used to develop many assistive devices to promote the learning, independence and communication abilities of students with various disabilities like Julia and Tom. These devices are an integral part of students' IEPs. They also can be used to create assistive technology toolkits, a list of technology devices and services that teachers and students can use to support the learning and socialization of students in inclusive classrooms.

Devices for Students with Physical Disabilities For students who have difficulty speaking intelligibly, augmentative and alternative communication systems devices are invaluable. Low-technology devices, such as communication boards with pictures/words/objects, which are nonelectric and tend to be homemade by clinicians, also are useful. Some students may benefit from use of a Picture Exchange Communication System (PECS) that allows them to communicate via use of a pictorial-based system (Beck, Stoner, Bock, & Parton, 2008; Sulzer-Azaroff, Hoffman, Horton, Bondy, & Frost, 2009).

High-technology augmentative communication systems, sometimes referred to as speech-generating devices or voice output communication aides, based on computer hardware and software and output devices transform strokes and/or word input into speech can increase communication and student learning (Thunberg, Ahlsen, & Dahlgren Sandberg, 2009; Wilkins & Ratajczak, 2009). Students can input a phrase or press a key or icon that activates the technology's speech capabilities. Specific vocabulary sets can be programmed based on students' educational and communicative needs, as well as the setting in which they need to communicate. As the technology evolves, these devices are being made smaller and more portable and with digitized speech that sounds more natural.

Some students, including those with physical disabilities, also may have problems inputting information into technology in traditional ways (e.g., pressing more than one key at a time). To meet their needs, alternative methods have been developed (see Figure 8.7). These students also may benefit from accommodations to the standard keyboard such as keyboard overlays or larger, ergonomic and alternative keyboards that can be placed at different angles and have different letter/key and spacing arrangements. Other alternatives are auditory keys that offer oral feedback when they are accessed, keyguards, stickers to signify keys, key locks, and word prediction and speech recognition programs. They also may need to use specialized keys that increase the accessibility of the keyboard (see Figure 8.8). Students with tremors and/or uncontrolled hand or finger movements may need to use an adapted more accessible mouse, joystick, trackball or touchpad that can adjust for extraneous movements (Lotempio, 2008). Some students also may benefit from other built-in accessibility features including on-screen keyboarding, screen magnification, visual and auditory warnings, text-to-speech recognition, text narration, and enhanced mouse visibility and movement. Students also may benefit from mouse and typing echo systems that orally describe cursor and keyboard movements.

Voice/speech recognition and voice-activated systems are allowing students with a range of disabilities to use technology, access and browse the Internet, and interact and share their ideas with others (Fitzgerald, 2008; MacArthur, 2009). These

Making Connections
This discussion of assistive devices builds on our earlier discussion of an individualized technology asessment in Chapter 2.

REFLECTIVE

What instructional technologies and assistive devices did you use as a student? As a teacher? What were the positive and negative effects of these technologies on your learning and your students' learning?

FIGURE 8.7 Alternative methods of inputting information into computers

1. *Voice recognition:* The computer recognizes the user's speech and converts it into action
2. *Key guard:* A device that modifies the traditional keyboard to change the size and spacing of the keys. It may include a key lock that automatically toggles specialty keys
3. *Keyboard alteration programs:* Programs that modify the keyboard in terms of key accept time and key repeating
4. *Graphics tablet:* A small slate that may be covered by templates of words, pictures, numerals, and letters that are input when touched by a special stylus
5. *Adapted switches:* Switches controlled by pressure or body movements. They can be activated by foot, head, cheek, chin, tongue, or eye movements
6. *Scanning systems:* An array of letters, phrases, and numerals displayed on the screen at a rate that is adjusted to the student's need. The student selects the message from the scanner by using the keyboard or a switch
7. *Touch screens/on-screen keyboards/light pens:* Devices that allow the student to activate the computer by touching or writing on the screen
8. *Joystick:* A stick that is moved in different directions, controlling the movement of the cursor
9. *Vocal joystick:* A microphone-like device that is connected with a sound card that allows cursor movements to be controlled by auditory sounds made by users
10. *Mouthstick:* A tool that is placed in the mouth and used to press buttons and activate switches
11. *Headband:* A headband-like device that is worn by the student to control the computer through head or eye movements
12. *Sip and puff systems:* A long command tube attached to a computer or wheelchair on which the student sucks
13. *Skateboard:* A block of wood on rollers attached to the student's arm that is moved in different directions to control cursor movements
14. *Mouse:* A mouselike object that is moved in different directions to control the computer. Adaptations of the mouse can be controlled by using the numeric pad of the keyboard (keyboard mouse) or by a headsetlike device, such as a headband, that conveys directions to the computer via head movements
15. *Eye gaze:* Use of eye gazes and scanning to select stimuli that appear on the computer screen
16. *Sensors:* Sensors are attached to the user and the computer and activated by facial movements or physical gestures

FIGURE 8.8 Specialized keys for using technology

- *StickyKeys,* which results in one key press taking the actions associated with multiple keys being pressed simultaneously
- *MouseKeys,* which allows movement of the mouse pointer through use of the numeric keypad
- *ToggleKeys,* which activates an auditory sound when specific features are activated, such as the lock keys NUM LOCK, CAPS LOCK, or SCROLL LOCK
- *FilterKeys,* which contains a range of features that vary the keyboard response time and address the inadvertent pressing of keys
- *RepeatKeys,* which provides users with control over whether repeated key strokes are converted into actions and allow users to set the repeat start time and rate
- *BounceKeys,* which allow users who tend to bounce when activating or releasing a key to access only one action or keyboard character at a time

Source: Salend (2009).

systems, which are also available on many devices, can convert spoken words into text or into actions that activate technology (Parette et al., 2007). For example, students can access menus or Web site links by stating an action or a name/number or write papers by dictating their ideas and then editing them via use of word processing (Zhao, 2007). These systems continue to have improved accuracy rates and can recognize the different accents of students from different regions in the United States (e.g., Great Lakes, southern United States, etc.) and students from other parts of the world (e.g., Australia, Britain, Southeast Asian, India, Mexico, Spain, etc.) (Pogue, 2008b). However, keep in mind that these systems are still being perfected; the programs will need to be taught to recognize a student's voice and students will need training to use them effectively.

Assistive devices also help individuals with disabilities organize and take notes in class. Some students use tablet personal computers (tablet PCs) and laptop computers with word processing programs and lightweight, voice-activated digital recorders or digital dictation systems for note taking. Portable devices including PDAs and wireless tablet PCs allow students to access online material, to receive motivational prompts and organizational reminders, to take notes that include illustrations and to receive and send notes and class and homework assignments to and from teachers and classmates (Bouck et al., 2007; Smith Myles, Ferguson, & Hagiwara, 2007). They also allow teachers to monitor students' understanding of instruction and provide feedback to students on their performance via active responding systems. These devices provide access to information and resources available through other technologies such as the Internet. PDAs and paging systems also can help students engage in appropriate social skills, recall and access information, and remember to use the correct sequence of tasks and routines, as well as organize schedules, information, and events (Taber-Doughty et al., 2008). These devices can be programmed to deliver reminders to students via pictures, speech, audio, video, and text (Cihak et al., 2008; Mechling, 2008).

Making Connections
Find out more about active responding systems in Chapter 9.

Scanning and form-typing software is available to help students complete forms and worksheets (Thompson, Bakken, Fulk, & Peterson-Karlan, 2005). Using this technology, hard copies of forms or assignments are scanned into a digital format and then completed by students using their computers.

Computer technology including advances in design, sensors, and robotics has also helped increase the independence of individuals with physical disabilities (Lotempio, 2008). The Independence Enhanced Wheelchair is a robotic wheelchair that uses computer and GPS technology to allow individuals to input where they want to go, which is then processed by the device to plan and execute the most effective path to get there including ways to get around barriers such as furniture and other individuals. Robotic devices and computerized systems and sensors in the home can be programmed to turn on the oven, reconnect a phone left off the hook, shut off lights, lock doors, and adjust the sound of the television so that these individuals can live on their own. Infrared remote control systems and voice activation also allow individuals to control and operate learning and independent living devices and appliances.

Instructional and assistive devices are helping students succeed in inclusive settings. What technologies help your students?

Devices for Students with Visual and Reading Disabilities   Several assistive devices have been developed to help use print materials. Various lightweight text scanners and optical character-reading systems with speech synthesis recognize letters, group letters into words, read words, and provide the correct pronunciation of words in a sentence in several languages. Printed materials are scanned and stored in memory. Students can then view the printed page, hear the text being read aloud, look up the meaning of unfamiliar words, highlight important content, and insert bookmarks. When selecting a scanning-based reading adaptive device, you should consider the ability of the scanner to scan accurately and the availability of an automatic document/page feeder.

Making Connections
Find out more about technologies that can support your students' reading and writing in Chapter 10.

Technology-based screen- and text-reading programs read text aloud by word, letters or by phonetic markers; or convert words, sentences, and paragraphs into fluent speech (Auchincloss & McIntyre, 2008; Izzo et al., 2009). Using these programs, students can hear text read aloud as they read along (as the text read is digitally highlighted) (Harrison, 2009). These programs, which can read in different voices and languages, allow users to search for or highlight words, sentences, and paragraphs that can be read aloud. These programs also can be customized to create pronunciation dictionaries and to control the speed, pitch, and volume of the speech.

Screen- and text-reading technologies also are available on many devices (Parette et al, 2007). For instance, the "Save as DAISY XML" feature can convert text-based Word documents, such as your tests and other print materials, into Digital Accessible Information SYstem (DAISY) files, accessible formats that can be orally presented to your students with visual impairments and students with reading difficulties.

Also available are smaller and more portable optical character reading systems such as the Kurzweil-National Federation of the Blind Reader Mobile (KNFB Reader Mobile), the ReadingPen, and the C-pen. These devices allow users to scan printed materials, which are then read aloud to them; they are also useful for your students who are learning English. When considering using these devices, it is important to remember that they are most helpful for reading words or sentences rather than paragraphs or pages.

Low-tech devices can be used to assist students with reading (Ferreri, 2009; Higbee Mandlebaum, Hodges, & Messenheimer, 2007). Line guides or masks such as reading rulers, windows, or index cards can assist students who have difficulty tracking and maintaining their place on a line. Some students also may benefit from placing color acetate overlays on their reading materials to help them adjust the contrast in the text.

As we discussed earlier in this chapter, digitized books help students use printed materials, including textbooks. Talking calculators, globes, and other devices are available to support the learning of these students. For example, electronic dictionaries with digitized speech help students define unfamiliar words. Screen magnification programs enlarge text and graphics to an appropriate size and adjust the colors on the screen to offer users the best contrast (Swift et al., 2008). Many of these programs contain zoom features that allow users to zoom in on specific areas of the screen. Font enlargement features also allow users to adjust the size of the fonts in which text is presented (Ferreri, 2009). Students with visual difficulties can benefit from use of Braille, larger keys, flicker-free monitors that have a higher resolution and contrast, and external magnification devices that are placed over the existing monitor.

Technology also is available to help students like Julia access information media and technology presented information (Ely et al., 2006). An eDescription, like the descriptive video system used by Julia, can provide access by offering a description of visually presented images and text. Students with visual disabilities also may use a tactile graphics display (TGD), so they can tactilely access electronic images and text.

Technology also is available to assist students and professionals in converting electronic files and print materials into audio, large-print, or Braille formats (Dell & Newton, 2008), and to assist students with visual disabilities in taking

Braille-based notes (Hopkins, 2006). Technology allows you and your students and colleagues to scan print materials, and then enlarge or enhance them or translate and convert them into Braille materials for use by students. For example, Visiprint (www.visiprintsoftware.com) provides software that can help you prepare large-print documents that can be tailored to the different needs and preferences of your students. You also can label items in your classroom with a Braille labeler or via a talking bar-code scanner and reader, and provide these students with access to a handheld color identifier that verbally identifies colors of objects (Wolfe Poel, 2007). Students with visual disabilities also may benefit from using a refreshable Braille note taker, a portable assistive device that converts electronically produced text into Braille or speech.

A variety of optical aids to help students with low vision access visual images and text are available (Eisenberg, 2008). In addition to goggles, handheld pocket magnifiers, magnifiers mounted on a base, and magnifiers attached to eyeglass frames or incorporated in the lenses to magnify printed materials for individuals with visual disabilities, lightweight and portable electronic optical devices have been developed. Electronic optical devices are also available to make reading and seeing easier by allowing individuals to make choices about the size, contrast, and colors of text/images and their backgrounds. During reading activities, typoscopes can be used with these students to direct and focus their attention on specific words (Wolfe Poel, 2007).

Communication systems for individuals with visual disabilities also exist. Tele-Braille helps deaf and blind individuals communicate by converting a message typed on a Braille keyboard into print on a video monitor, which is read by a sighted person. The sighted person then types a response, which is converted into a Braille display. Devices with large-print, Braille, and voice output capabilities also allow students with visual disabilities to communicate. These students also may benefit from the use of Braille printers, refreshable Braille displays, and Braille note takers.

Electronic travel aids can increase the independent movement of students with visual disabilities. These students can use a handheld electronic device that vibrates to alert students to barriers in their path and to indicate the distance to obstacles. The Laser Cane emits three laser beams that provide a sound signaling objects, dropoffs, or low-hanging obstacles in the user's path. Students with visual impairments as well as those with other disabilities can carry a cell phone or PDA with small GPS receiver offering orally or Braille presented step-by-step directions that can guide them in moving around schools and classrooms and finding locations, objects and materials (Bouck et al., 2007).

Devices for Deaf and Hard-of-Hearing Students Technology is making a profound improvement in assistive devices for deaf and hard-of-hearing students. New types of hearing aids based on digital technology contain smaller and more powerful computer chips that recognize and selectively amplify human speech, filter out background noises, deliver more realistic sound, and tailor the sound to the individual's needs and acoustic setting. Technologies are fostering communication between individuals with and without hearing. IP-RELAY (*www.ip-relay.com*) uses Internet telephony to allow deaf and hard-of-hearing individuals to communicate with others. Using this technology, a confidential operator fosters telephone conversations by converting speech to text for deaf and hard-of-hearing individuals and text to speech for individuals who have hearing.

PDAS, cell phones and two-way pagers with amplification, text messaging and video features allow deaf and hard of hearing individuals to communicate, develop their independence, and foster learning. Speech-to-text translation systems provide these students access to oral presentations by viewing a monitor that presents the speaker's comments (Hopkins, 2006).

PEARSON
myeducationlab

To enhance your understanding of assistive technology devices that can support the performance of students with visual disbilities in your inclusive classroom, go to the IRIS Center Resources section of the Topic *Visual Impairment* in the MyEducationLab for your course, and complete the module entitled *Accommodations to the Physical Environment: Setting Up a Classroom for Students with Visual Disabilities.*

These students also can access technology-based information via systems with closed-captioning and where the text and graphics appear on the video monitor accompanied by a video of a signer who signs the text. For students who have some hearing, a digitized voice can read the text as it is presented via closed-captioning or as the signer signs it. Some students who rely on speechreading may benefit from a classroom speechreading technology system that involves a live video transmission of the speaker's lips to a desktop monitor located on students' desks.

Making Connections
Find out more about using technology to help students access oral presentations and take notes in Chapter 9.

Devices for Students from English Language Backgrounds   The academic performance and language learning of students who are English language learners can be enhanced through many of the instructional technology and assistive devices previously discussed, which they can access using their preferred language. They also may benefit from technology that provides meaningful, active, and motivating learning experiences, sensory-based support, and captioning and translating in their primary and new languages (Lowdermilk et al., 2008). Using the Internet, they can access authentic text, audio and video resources, and media sites in multiple languages (e.g., online radio and television broadcasts). They also can use the Internet to read, hear, and write in multiple languages and communicate with native speakers of many languages via Web sites, e-mail, chat rooms, and blogs.

Translation software can be used to foster language development and communication with individuals who speak other languages. English language learners can use translation software and handheld talking translators that can convert verbal statements or text from one language into another. When using these programs, it is important for you and your students to understand that they may at times provide inaccurate translations and may not cover the range of dialects associated with specific languages.

Technology also is available that promotes English language acquisition (Lowdermilk et al. 2008; Mulholland, Pete, & Popeson, 2008). Programs that build on students' prior linguistic and cultural knowledge and employ colors, 3-D visuals, videos, vignettes, audio, sounds, and animation to present the meanings and pronunciation of words and sentences and their semantic relationships can be particularly helpful for your students who are English language learners. Effective software programs for these students also should provide them with numerous opportunities to practice labeling and requesting items; repeating words, phrases, and sentences; identifying things and their related features; understanding gestures; and engaging in reading and writing.

Bilingual software programs, Web sites, translation, and word processing provide bilingual online assistance with content presentation, dictionaries, thesauruses, and spelling and grammar checkers. Interactive programs offer access to bilingual glossaries, captioning, visual presentations, and many opportunities for students to develop their vocabulary, word recognition, and reading and listening comprehension skills. PowerPoint presentations and videos of visuals paired with text of key words and questions also can be used with these students to develop their vocabulary and expressive language skills (Reagon, Higbee, & Endicott, 2007). Technology can be used to help students learn their new language by allowing them to see mouth movements associated with sounds, hear the pronunciation of words and sentences, and then record and receive feedback on their own attempts to speak.

The Language Master is a handheld device that contains electronic dictionary, thesaurus, and grammar and spell checker that pronounces words, gives definitions and synonyms, corrects the spelling of phonetic words, and offers educational games involving targeted vocabulary words (Lindsey-Glenn & Gentry, 2008). The Language Master allows you and your students to develop their vocabulary by playing, recording, and erasing oral material on stimulus cards and writing on the stimulus cards to provide visual cues.

PEARSON
myeducationlab
To reflect on and enhance your understanding of how you can differentiate your curriculum and instruction to plan and implement lessons that foster your students' access to the general education curriculum, go to the IRIS Center Resources section of the Topic *Instructional Practices and Learning Strategies* in the MyEducationLab for your course, and complete the module entitled *Content Standards: Connecting Standards-Based Curriculum to Instructional Planning.*

REFLECTING ON PROFESSIONAL PRACTICES

Using Instructional and Assistive Technology to Differentiate Instruction

Ms. Taravella and Ms. Camac, the school's technology specialist, were excited about developing and teaching a unit on the Vietnam War using instructional technology. They started to develop the unit by searching the Internet for content, online lesson plans, and teaching resources about Vietnam and the war. They also participated in a chat room related to teaching and technology, which also provided suggestions for the unit. Then they identified and reviewed interesting and relevant Web sites and resources and created their unit. They also visited the sites, which provided help in designing various Web-based activities.

Because their students' experience with the Internet varied, Ms. Taravella and Ms. Camac began by teaching students about the Internet and how to use it appropriately. They modeled and provided an overview of how to access and navigate the Internet and evaluate sites and Web-based information. They paired experienced users with novices to perform a World Wide Web scavenger hunt that required them to conduct searches for various topics. They had students go online to access activities that taught them how to use the Internet safely, responsibly, efficiently, and effectively. They brainstormed with students and framed rules for use of the Internet by having students respond to such questions as "What would you do if you were asked for personal information or your password?" "What would you do if someone wanted to meet you or sell you something?" and "What would you do if you received or encountered offensive material?" They also told students not to believe everything they read or heard via the Internet. They gave students guidelines for examining and verifying sites and information, which included identifying the individuals who created the site, the dates on which it was created and updated, the location and organizational affiliation of the site, and the content of the site.

Once they were convinced that students could use the technology appropriately, Ms. Taravella and Ms. Camac assigned students to work in groups. Each group selected a variety of learning activities from a menu that included

- gathering information about the war from Web sites and wikis;

- viewing a video that portrayed actual battles and presented interviews with soldiers;

- taking a three-dimensional panoramic tour of the Vietnam Memorial through pictures that Ms. Camac had taken the previous summer with a digital camera;

- watching videos of news reports from the 1960s and 1970s and documentaries about the Vietnam War and antiwar activities throughout the United States and the world;

- exchanging e-mail messages with military experts and leaders of the antiwar movement;

- examining primary-source documents online;

- viewing and listening to podcasts that contained discussions about the war, including eyewitness accounts of the war from the viewpoint of soldiers, protestors, and Vietnamese citizens;

- making a virtual visit to an exhibition on the Vietnam War at the Smithsonian Museum; and

- establishing a keypal online relationship with Vietnamese and U.S. students and their families.

While the groups worked, the teachers and the other professionals in the room helped them. When computers froze because students tried to download too much information, they helped students reboot them. They also aided students who had difficulty accessing information from websites (like Julia) by using an Internet screen reading program that read the text and images aloud and reformatting the text and images so that they were easier for students with reading difficulties to read.

Ms. Taravella and Ms. Camac also allowed each group to choose its own final product. Group projects included writing and making a video and podcast of a play about the Vietnam War, completing a webquest, wiki, or a track about the war, preparing a presentation about the war using presentation software and digital photos, conducting an online survey of the community's knowledge of the Vietnam War, and creating a memorial to Vietnam Veterans and the peace movement. All students helped develop their group's project. Tom, a student with a severe disability, used his assistive communication system to speak lines in his group's play, and Marta, an English language learner, helped her group translate their community survey into Spanish.

The teachers and their students used the class's Web page to create a weblog that provided an ongoing summary of the class's learning activities that also included digital photos of the groups' projects with accompanying narration. They were pleased when they received e-mail messages from other teachers and their students' families commenting on the students' products and requesting to use activities from their unit.

- What strategies did Ms. Taravella and Ms. Camac use to differentiate instruction for their students?

- What process and resources did they use to create and implement their technology-based unit?

- What do you think the students and their families thought about this unit?

- What difficulties might you encounter in using instructional technology activities in your classroom?

- How could you attempt to solve these difficulties?

SUMMARY

This chapter offered guidelines for differentiating instruction to address the diverse learning strengths and challenges of your students. As you review the questions posed in this chapter, remember the following points:

How Can I Differentiate Instruction for Students?
CEC 2, 3, 4, 5, 7, 9, 10; PRAXIS 3; INTASC 1, 2, 3, 4, 5, 6, 7, 9

You can tailor your curricular goals and teaching strategies to the individual strengths and challenges of your students and your learning environment. It is also important to use backward design to determine a range of formative and summative assessments; individualized curricular, teaching, and instructional materials and accommodations; and universally designed materials. You also can provide personal support; address students' learning styles, preferences, and sensory abilities; and consider acceptability.

How Can I Differentiate Instruction for Students Who Have Difficulty Reading and Gaining Information from Print Materials?
CEC 2, 4, 7, 9; PRAXIS 3; INTASC 2, 3, 4, 7, 9

You can use a variety of teacher- and student-directed text comprehension strategies. In addition, you can make materials more readable by modifying them, reducing their linguistic complexity, incorporating the principles of typographical design, and using instructional technology.

How Can I Differentiate Instruction for Students from Diverse Cultural and Language Backgrounds?

CEC 1, 3, 4, 5, 6, 7, 9, 10; PRAXIS 3; INTASC 1, 2, 3, 4, 5, 6, 7, 8, 9, 10

You can use a multicultural curriculum, multicultural instructional materials, culturally relevant and responsive teaching strategies, reciprocal interaction, and effective ESL and dual-language approaches and techniques. You can also encourage students to respond.

How Can I Use Instructional Technology and Assistive Devices to Differentiate Instruction for Students?

CEC 6, 7, 9; PRAXIS 3; INTASC 4, 6, 7, 9

Recent developments in instructional technology allow you to create differentiated, interactive, motivating, and contextualized learning environments for students by using computer-based instruction, video-based digital materials, presentation software, digital videos/stories, digital, document, Web cameras, captioning interactive white-smartboards, liquid crystal display projection panels, and technology-based simulations. The Internet provides you and your students with access to information, as well as many learning and communication experiences. You also can use a wide variety of assistive devices to help students learn, communicate with others, use technology, be organized, take notes, increase their range of movements and mobility, read text, hear sounds, and learn a new language. When using these technologies, make sure you address accessibility issues, and teach your students to be good digital citizens who use technology safely, appropriately, and respectfully.

MS. ANDERSON

Ms. Anderson begins her lesson by reminding students, "We have been learning about poetic elements and devices." She then tells them, "One of the most popular types of poetry is song. Yes, when each of you listens to your favorite songs, you're actually attending a poetry reading of sorts. For homework, I asked you to bring the lyrics of your favorite song to class. Who would like to share their favorite song with us? And what you like about it?" Ms. Anderson pauses for several seconds before randomly picking a student to respond. After students identify their favorite songs, she chooses one of the songs and plays it via the interactive smart-whiteboard. She tells the students that later on they will be working with their songs/poems.

Ms. Anderson tells the students, "We are going to learn about several new poetic devices." Using a Power-Point presentation displayed on the interactive board, she reviews the poetic devices they have learned and then identifies and defines several new ones. She then plays her favorite song, "A Hard Days Night by the Beatles," and discusses what she likes about it. She displays the words of her favorite song on the interactive board and discusses the different poetic elements in the song, focusing on the new poetic devices she wants them to learn. She periodically uses a stylus to highlight poetic elements in different colors, and then asks students to identify the poetic element highlighted and justify their responses. For example, she highlights the words "It has been a hard day's night and I've been working like a dog" and asks, "Is it a metaphor or a simile? Why?" Students respond to her questions using clickers, a handheld wireless active responding device, which allows her to quickly assess student understanding and provide feedback or offer additional instruction to individual students. Sometimes she

9

Differentiating Large- and Small-Group Instruction

asks another student if he or she agrees with a student's response. The students also used their clickers to play a game, Name That Poetic Device, which asked them to identify specific poetic devices used in the students' favorite songs.

Next, Ms. Anderson has students work in think-pair-share groups to identify poetic devices by visiting poetry Web sites and reading or listening to poems. Students independently think about the poems and devices, discuss their answers with their partners, and then share their responses with the class. She then gives students an independent assignment that involves identifying the various poetic elements they have been learning about. She describes the assignment to students, explains what she wants them to do, and does an example with the students. She differentiates the assignment for students in several ways. Some students respond to true/false statements,

while others match poetic devices to their corresponding statements. Some students are asked to identify poetic devices in various statements, while others are given a list of poetic elements and asked to compose statements that reflect them. As students work on the assignment, Ms. Anderson circulates around the room, acknowledging and assisting them. She also solicits feedback from students by asking them to complete a feedback form to identify things that are still confusing to them and what she can do to help them understand the material better (see Figure 9.6). For homework, she asks students to identify the poetic devices used in their favorite songs. She also tells the students that tomorrow they will be working in cooperative learning groups to analyze their favorite songs and the poetic devices used.

What other ways could Ms. Anderson use to differentiate instruction for her students? After reading this chapter, you should have the knowledge, skills, and dispositions to answer this as well as the following questions:

- How can I differentiate large-group instruction for students?
- How can I use effective teacher-centered instruction?
- How can I successfully use cooperative learning arrangements with students?

Like Ms. Anderson, you teach in many different ways. You use presentations and teacher-centered instruction, and cooperative learning to help students learn. These different instructional formats also mean that you need to use flexible instructional groupings that include large and small groups. While the size and composition of your groups will be related to your instructional goals and activities as well as the content you plan to teach, try to vary grouping arrangements based on your students' academic skills and readiness; interest in and knowledge of the content; learning strengths, challenges, styles, and preferences; and socialization. Smaller groups of students with diverse strengths and challenges are particularly appropriate for inclusive classrooms as they help you teach effectively and promote interactions among your students. Whole-group instruction is most appropriate when you want to introduce content to *all students* or maintain a sense of classroom community. When it is essential to focus instruction on the learning of a smaller number of students, it may be necessary to group students by their levels of mastery of the material. Sometimes, you can also assign them to groups randomly or allow them to choose their groups. In grouping students, make sure that they get to work with *all of their classmates* and that students are not grouped solely based on their learning ability or success. This chapter offers strategies that you can use to differentiate large- and small-group instruction for *all students*.

DIFFERENTIATING LARGE-GROUP INSTRUCTION

HOW CAN I DIFFERENTIATE LARGE-GROUP INSTRUCTION FOR STUDENTS? You can use the following strategies to differentiate your instruction and foster student learning when you are teaching large groups of students.

Have Students Work Collaboratively

The amount of information students gain from teacher-directed presentations can be increased by using a variety of learning arrangements in which students work collaboratively, such as collaborative discussion teams, Send a Problem, Numbered Heads Together, and think-pair-share (Gersten, Baker, Smith-Johnson, Dimino, & Peterson, 2006; Harper & Maheady, 2007).

Collaborative Discussion Teams   **Collaborative discussion teams** can be used throughout the presentation. After a certain amount of time, usually 10 to 15 minutes, teams can respond to discussion questions, react to material presented, or predict what will happen or be discussed next. Teams can then be called on to share their responses. At the end of the presentations, teams can summarize the main points and check each other's comprehension.

Send a Problem   In the **Send a Problem** technique, groups make up questions that are answered by other groups. This is done by developing a list of questions related to material being presented in class, recording the answers to each question, and passing the questions from group to group.

Numbered Heads Together **Numbered Heads Together** can be used to help students review and check their understanding of orally presented information. You can use this method by doing the following:

1. Assign students to mixed-ability groups of three or four.
2. Assign a number (1, 2, 3, or 4) to each student in each group.
3. Break up the oral presentation by periodically asking the class a question and telling each group, "Put your heads together and make sure that everyone in your group knows the answer."
4. Tell the groups to end their discussion, call a number, ask all students with that number to raise their hands, select one of the students with that number to answer, and ask the other students with that number to agree with or expand on the answer.

Think-Pair-Share **Think-pair-share**, another cooperative learning strategy that Ms. Anderson used in the chapter-opening vignette, can help students reflect on and master content. The process is as follows:

1. Pair students randomly.
2. Give students a question, problem, or situation.
3. Ask individual students to think about the question.
4. Have students discuss their responses with their partners.
5. Select several pairs to share their thoughts and responses with the class.

Encourage Students to Participate and Ask Questions

To benefit from oral instruction and to understand assignments and directions, students need to be active participants who share their perspectives and experiences and ask questions. However, many students may be reluctant to do so. To help these students overcome their lack of participation, you can praise them for speaking and asking questions, ask them open-ended questions, give them time to write down their thoughts and questions during class, give students the correct answer and ask them to state the corresponding question, and teach students when and how to share information and ask questions. You also can teach them how to follow up on the statements of others and to use the SLANT learning strategy (see Paxton-Buursma & Walker, 2008).

Help Students Take Notes

The amount of information gained from the teacher's oral presentations also depends on the students' ability to take notes, which can help students stay engaged. A variety of strategies for improving students' note-taking skills are presented here (Connor & Lagares, 2007; Strichart & Mangrum, 2010).

Teachers can use a variety of strategies to help students take notes. What strategies do your teachers use to promote your note taking in class?

Outlines You can give students a framework for note taking and recording information. A **strategic note-taking form** contains teacher-prepared cues that guide students in taking notes and prompts them to use effective note-taking skills during oral presentations (Boyle & Weishaar, 2001) (see Figure 9.1). While a strategic note-taking form can be used repeatedly regardless of the content of the class, listening guides and skeleton/slot/frame outlines are tailored to the unique content of a specific class. A **listening guide** is a list of important terms and concepts that parallels the order in which they will be presented in class (see Figure 9.2). Students add to this list by writing supplemental information and supportive details. A **skeleton/slot/frame outline** or *guided notes* (Musti-Rao, Kroeger, & Schumacher-Dyke, 2008) present a sequential overview of

FIGURE 9.1 Sample strategic note-taking format

Name: Class: Date:

Complete Before the Class

What topic is going to be discussed in class?

-
-
-

What do I know about the topic?

-
-
-

Complete During the First Half of the Class

What does the teacher say is the topic?

-
-
-

What are three to seven main ideas and supporting details related to the topic being discussed?

-
-
-
-
-
-
-

How can I briefly and quickly summarize the main ideas and supporting details that were discussed?

What new vocabulary and terminology do I need to review?

-                         •   •
-                         •   •

Complete During the Second Half of the Class

What are three to seven main ideas and supporting details related to the topic being discussed?

-
-
-
-
-
-
-

How can I briefly and quickly summarize the main ideas and supporting details that were discussed?

What new vocabulary and terminology do I need to review?

-                         •   •
-                         •   •

Complete at the End of the Class

What are the five main points? How can I briefly summarize them?

-
-
-
-
-

Source: Boyle (2001).

FIGURE 9.2 **Sample listening guide**

Civil War

A. The sides
   1. The Union:

   2. The Confederacy:

   3. The Border States:
     a.   c.
     b.   d.

B. Advantages of each side
   1. The Union:
     a.   c.
     b.   d.
   2. The Confederacy:
     a.   c.
     b.   d.

C. The strategy of each side:
   1. The Union:
     a.
     b.
     c.
   2. The Confederacy:
     a.
     b.
     c.

D. Key individuals to know
   1. Abraham Lincoln
   2. Jefferson Davis
   3. Stonewall Jackson
   4. Robert E. Lee
   5. Ulysses S. Grant
   6. Clara Barton

Source: Developed by Peter Goss, social studies teacher, New Paltz Central Schools, New Paltz, New York.

the key terms and main points as an outline made up of incomplete statements with visual cues such as spaces, letters, and labels that can help students determine the amount and type of information to be recorded. Students listen to the lecture or read the textbook chapter and fill in the blanks to complete the outline, which then serves as the students' notes. You can encourage students to use outlines by periodically pairing students to check each other's outlines and sometimes collecting them.

If giving students outlines is not feasible, you can teach students to use a two-column note-taking system by

1. placing a vertical line in the middle of a page and labeling the left side of the page "Main Ideas" and the right side of the page "Supporting Information";

2. recording key points and words under the "Main Ideas" column;

3. listing supporting details related to the key points and words to the right, under the Supporting Information column; and

4. creating a box near the bottom of the page to record key vocabulary and summarize the critical ideas from the lesson, and to jot down questions you have (Strichart & Mangrum, 2010).

You can foster note taking by listing the major points. Also, structure students' notes at the beginning of class by listing questions relating to the day's work and then discussing answers to them at the end of class.

Highlighting Main Points   To help students determine important points to include in their notes, you can emphasize these points by adjusting your pace and rate of speaking, pausing for attention, using introductory phrases (e.g., *an important point, remember that, it is especially important*), and changing inflection (Boyle, 2001). Throughout your presentation, reiterate the main points and concepts by restating them, and citing examples or asking questions related to them (Blythe & Sweet, 2008). You also can present them visually to your students paired with an oral summary before you move on to the next part of your presentation. Near the end of your presentation, summarize your main points.

Another method that can help students identify important points is **oral quizzing**, in which the teacher allots time at the end of the class to respond to students' questions and to ask questions based on the material presented. End-of-class time can also be devoted to summarizing and reviewing notes and main points and discussing what points should be in the students' notes. Pairing students to check each other's notes after class also ensures that students' notes are in the desired format and include relevant content. In addition, you can check the student notes by regularly collecting and reviewing them.

Peer Note Takers and Digital Recorders   For students who have difficulty taking notes, peer note takers can be used (Stinson, Elliot, Kelly, & Liu, 2009). When selecting peer note takers, you should consider their mastery of the content, sensitivity to students who need help with note taking, and ability to take legible and organized notes. Students also can record class sessions and then replay them after class using a digital recorder that allows them to listen to notes at their own pace. Whether students are using peer note takers or technology, they can be required to take notes during class. This allows them to practice their note taking skills and keep alert in class. It also helps prevent resentment from other students who may think that students with peer note takers or digital recorders have to do less work. You also can foster the note-taking process by providing students with time at the end of the class to compare their notes with their peers.

Teach Note-Taking Skills and Strategies

REFLECTIVE

What skills and strategies do you use to pay attention and take notes in class? Are they successful? How do they compare with the strategies presented in this book?

Students can improve their note-taking skills by using several behaviors before, during, and after the class (Strichart & Mangrum, 2010). These behaviors and note-taking skills are presented in Figure 9.3. You also can help students learn to use a variety of note-taking skills and strategies—for example, CALL UP and "A" NOTES (Czarnecki, Rosko, & Fine, 1998) and LINKS and AWARE (Suritsky & Hughes, 1996). Because the note-taking strategy selected depends on the content, students also can be taught to match their strategy to the material. A *chart* is used when the speaker is contrasting information. When information is ordered by the date of occurrence, students can use a *timeline,* which involves making a horizontal line across the page and recording the events and dates in sequence. If the material is presented in steps, then *stepwise,* or numerical, note taking is best. Examples of these three systems are presented in Figure 9.4.

Foster Students' Listening Skills

Because listening is critical to learning from teacher-directed presentations, you can foster students' listening skills. Try to identify your students who struggle with listening by noting those who ask you to repeat directions and those who fail to complete their work. You also can look to see what barriers to listening exist in your classroom such as aural and visual distractions and try to address them. To increase listening, you can also provide visual aids, vary the pace of the oral presentation to emphasize critical points, move around the room, place the student near the speaker, and minimize unimportant and distracting noises and activities. Periodically, you can ask questions about critical content and have students try to predict what will be discussed next.

Using Cues   Both nonverbal and verbal cues can help students listen. *Nonverbal* cues, such as eye contact and gestures, as well as awareness of the reactions of their peers, can increase a student's listening skills. For example, if a student observes others in the class looking intently at the teacher, it can indicate the need to listen carefully. Some students may benefit from using a cue card that lists the guidelines for listening.

Students can be taught how to respond to *verbal* cues such as pacing, inflection, and loudness. They can also learn the words and statements that teachers use to highlight and organize key points.

FIGURE 9.3 Recommended student note-taking skills

Before the Class

- Try to anticipate what the teacher will cover by reading the assigned material, completing assigned activities and homework, and reviewing notes from previous classes.
- Bring writing utensils, notebooks, and a digital recorder if necessary.
- Come to class mentally and physically prepared.
- Select a seat near the speaker, and take a good listening posture.
- List the name of the class, page number, and date on each page to ensure continuity.
- Organize notebook pages into two columns, one on the left for checking understanding and the other on the right for recording notes.

During the Class

- Pay attention, and avoid being distracted by outside stimuli.
- Listen to and watch for verbal and nonverbal cues from the speaker and the audience.
- Write legibly, and record notes in your own words.
- Jot down only critical points and essential details.
- Write complete statements rather than unconnected words or phrases.
- Record the teacher's examples to clarify information.
- Listen for signal words and key phrases that indicate important information and transitions from one point to another.
- Highlight important ideas through highlighting, underlining, extra spacing, and boxing.
- Skip a line to indicate transitions between material.
- Draw diagrams and sketches to help you understand key points and concepts.
- Use symbols. For example, a ? can indicate missed information, and an = can indicate a relationship between two concepts.
- Use shorthand and abbreviations.
- Be brief and concise.
- Record relevant information and points that the teacher presents visually.
- Identify words you do not understand.

Near the End of Class

- Add any missing words, incomplete thoughts, related details, or original ideas.
- Summarize the main points using a *noteshrink* technique, which involves surveying the notes, identifying and highlighting main points, and listing these points in the quiz column.

After the Class

- Review and edit notes, and rewrite them (if necessary).
- Identify important points and information that needs further clarification, and then seek additional explanations from teachers and/or peers.
- Ask the teacher or a peer to provide missed information.
- Indicate an overlap between the textbook and the teacher's comments.
- Record the length of time spent on a topic.
- Look up the meanings of words identified as those you do not understand, and record their definitions in your notes.
- Replace abbreviations, shorthand, and symbols with the full word(s) they represent.
- Compare your notes with your classmates' notes.

Sources: Boyle (2001); Connor and Lagares (2007); Strichart and Mangrum (2010).

Listening Materials Many materials that help teach listening skills have been developed for elementary and secondary students (Swain, Friehe, & Harrington, 2004; Tilley-Gregory, 2004). These materials teach a variety of listening skills, including identifying and paying attention to auditory stimuli; using memory strategies such as visualization, rehearsal, and grouping; following directions; determining the sequence, main ideas, and details of the information; identifying supporting information; and making inferences and predicting outcomes.

Listening Learning Strategies You can help your students enhance their listening skills by teaching them to use listening learning strategies (Swain et al., 2004). For

FIGURE 9.4 Three methods of note taking

Chart Method

	Hamilton	*Jefferson*
Cabinet Position	Secretary of the Treasury	Secretary of State
Political Party	Federalist	Republican
Constitutional	Supported England	Supported France

Timeline Method

Archduke Ferdinand Assassinated		Germany Declares War on France		U.S. Declares War on Germany
	1914		1915	
1914		1914		1917
	Germany Declares War on Russia		Germany Sinks *Lusitania*	

Stepwise Method

The three principles underlying Roosevelt's "Good Neighbor" Policy:
1. Noninterference in affairs of independent countries
2. Concern for economic policies of Latin American countries
3. Establishment of inter-American cooperation

example, teach them to use TALS, a strategy that prompts active listening by encouraging students to **T**hink, **A**sk Why, **L**isten for What, and **S**ay to Self. You also can teach students to use the Give Me Five strategy, which can be reinforced with a hand in the high-five position posted in the room with each finger containing one of the following: Eyes on Speaker, Mouth Quiet, Body Still, Ears Listening, and Hands Free.

Teachers may need to modify the ways they give directions to students. How do you modify directions for your students?

Gain and Maintain Students' Attention

An important aspect of listening to and following directions is paying attention. However, many students have difficulty focusing their attention. You may have to use several attention-getting strategies, such as

- directing them to listen carefully ("Listen carefully to what I say");
- giving clear, emphatic instructions ("Take out your books and open to page 24");
- pausing before speaking to make sure that all students are paying attention;
- limiting distractions.

You also can use age-appropriate cues, such as a verbal statement or physical gesture (raising a hand, blinking the lights), to alert students to the need to pay attention.

Once you have gained students' attention, you can use several methods to maintain it. First, you can present material rapidly and have students respond often.

A GUIDE TO ACTION
Enhancing Oral Presentations

While you use a range of techniques to deliver instruction in your inclusive classroom, a very important teaching strategy involves presenting information orally to your students. To enhance your oral presentations, consider the following points:

- State your objectives, purpose, and the focal point and relevance of the topic at the beginning of your presentation.
- Before you begin, review and explain all prerequisite information and key terms so that students understand them.
- Establish the relationship between new material and previously covered material.
- Make sure that the pace and sequence of the presentation is appropriate for your students.
- Maintain student interest by using changes in voice level, stories to make a point, jokes, and humorous anecdotes.
- Provide students with opportunities to participate and ask questions throughout your presentation.
- Use ordinal numbers and time cues (*first, second, finally*) to organize information for students.
- Emphasize important concepts and critical points by varying voice quality and by using cues (e.g., "It is important that you remember"). Present important points visually, and repeat them as necessary.
- Use examples, illustrations, charts, diagrams, advance organizers, maps, and multimedia to make the material more concrete for students.
- Refer to individuals, places, or things by nouns rather than pronouns, and by using specific numerals instead of ambiguous ones (use *two* instead of *a couple*).
- Avoid vague terms and phrases (i.e., "these kinds of things," "somewhere," "to make a long story short," "as you all know," etc.).
- Ask questions that require students to think about the information presented and that assess understanding and recall.
- Reiterate the main points and concepts at different points throughout the presentation by restating them, and citing examples or asking questions related to them.
- Pause periodically during your presentation to give your students the opportunity to answer questions (a wait time of at least 3 to 5 seconds is recommended), discuss and review new content and their notes, jot down questions, and rehearse important points.
- Give students the opportunity to ask questions during and after the class.
- Provide a summary of the main points presented prior to the end of the class.
- Give students time at the end of class to review, discuss, summarize, and organize the main points and their notes.
- Whenever possible, use technology to support your presentations.

How would you rate your oral presentations? ( ) Excellent ( ) Good ( ) Need Improvement ( ) Need Much Improvement

Create a plan of action for enhancing your oral presentations that includes your goals, the actions you will take and the resources you will need to achieve them, and the ways you will evaluate your success.

For example, like Ms. Anderson, you can select students randomly to respond, remind students that they may be called on next, ask students to add information to or explain an answer given by a peer, and use repetition. You also can group students with peers who can stay attentive, maintain eye contact with *all students*, create suspense, change activities, and vary the ways of presenting material and asking students to respond.

Motivate Students

Motivation is an important aspect of learning, listening, and following directions. Motivation is often categorized as *extrinsic* or *intrinsic*. **Extrinsic motivation** relates to taking actions as a result of external consequences such as tangible rewards and approval from others. **Intrinsic motivation** refers to taking actions as a result of internally based consequences (e.g., sense of mastery and accomplishment) and is viewed as a higher level of motivation than extrinsic motivation. Therefore, when possible, it is also a good idea to use intrinsic motivation rather than external motivation and rewards.

Because of their past history of struggle or failure, some students with special needs temporarily may lack the motivation necessary to be successful learners. Because

REFLECTIVE

How do you help your students become intrinsically motivated?

UDL and YOU
Giving Clear, Explicit, and Complete Directions

Students will perform better during large- and small-group instruction if you use the principles of UDL to give clear, explicit, and complete directions using multiple formats and strategies. When explaining assignments, make certain that *all students* are attentive, pausing when they are not. Communicate by speaking slowly and clearly, using a voice that your students can hear and language they can understand. Try to keep your statements as brief as possible, and emphasize key words and statements.

Start by describing the assignment and the reasons for working on it ("This assignment will help us remember the parts and functions of plants, which will be on your test next week") and highlighting the motivating aspects of the assignment ("You are going to work in groups to compare the different plants we have around our school"). Next, give directions visually and review them orally. When giving directions orally, you can simplify the vocabulary, cut down on unnecessary words and information, and use consistent terms from assignment to assignment. Ensure that students copy the directions in their notebooks or sticky notes (Stormont, 2008), or embed them in the activity (Hume, 2007). For students who have difficulty copying from the blackboard or writing, a teacher-prepared handout can be given, using the writing style to which the students are accustomed. Students can then use a highlighter to highlight important details they need to remember. Directions for completing assignments can also be recorded digitally for use by students.

In presenting directions that have several steps, you can number and list the steps in order and provide visual prompts via use of pictorials and symbols. You can also use software, PDAs, and digital cameras to create technology-based activity directions, which employ combinations of pictures, graphics, symbols, words, sounds, and voices to help students understand and follow sequential directions (Banda, Grimmett, & Hart, 2009; Cafiero, 2008). For example, an assignment using dictionary skills can be presented by listing and using visuals to depict the steps:

1. Use the dictionary guide words.
2. Check the pronunciation of each word.
3. Write the definition.

Students will also understand directions more clearly if you provide a model of the assignment and describe the qualities you will use in evaluating it. It helps to encourage students to ask questions about the assignment, and have students paraphrase and explain the directions to the rest of the class (McKinley & Stormont, 2008). Question students to see how well they understand the

- instructions ("What am I asking you to do?" "What steps are you required to follow in doing this assignment?" "Can you anticipate any problems in doing this assignment?");
- materials they need to complete the assignment ("What materials do you need?");
- ways they can get help ("If you have a problem, whom should you ask for help?");
- time frame for completing the assignment ("How long do you have to work on the assignment?");
- things they can do if they finish the assignment ("What can you do if you finish early?");
- questions they have about the assignment ("Do you have any questions about the assignment?").

Finally, to ensure understanding, students can underline important directions before beginning, and complete several problems from the assignment under your supervision before beginning to work independently.

For students who continue to have problems in following directions, you can break directions into shorter, more meaningful statements. When possible, give no more than two instructions at a time. These students can work on one part of the assignment at a time and can check with an adult before advancing to the next part. Long assignments can be divided into several shorter ones, with students completing one part before working on the next.

Another way to help students follow directions is to allow time for students to receive teacher or peer assistance (Rock & Thead, 2009). You can move around the room to monitor students and provide assistance to those who need it. You can also teach them to use a signup sheet to schedule teacher–student meetings. The times when adults are available to provide help can be listed, and students can sign their names next to the desired time. You also can set up a signal system so that students can unobtrusively alert you to their need for assistance. They also can place a color-coded card on their desks to indicate the urgency with which they need your assistance, with red meaning they need your assistance as soon as possible.

motivation is dependent on a range of factors, you may need to employ a variety of instructional techniques and curriculum accommodations to motivate your students. As Ms. Anderson did in the chapter-opening vignette, you also can motivate your students by integrating technology into your curriculum (Lemke & Coughlin, 2009).

Create a Supportive and Rewarding Learning Environment   One of the most important motivational strategies for students is providing them with a supportive learning environment that includes positive interactions with their teachers that build students' self-efficacy and confidence as well as their sense of belonging and usefulness (Learned et al., 2009; Mihalas et al., 2009). You can create a positive learning environment for students by displaying enthusiasm for teaching and learning and building and maintaining rapport with them (Regan, 2009; Smith, 2009). Rapport can be established by talking with students about topics that interest them, participating in after-school activities with them, and recognizing their unique talents and important events in their lives.

You also can display verbal and nonverbal behaviors that let your students know that you believe they can succeed. For example, you can verbally encourage students to try and remind them of their recent achievements.

Offer a Meaningful, Interesting, Age-Appropriate, Creative, Interdisciplinary, and Appropriately Challenging Curriculum and Instructional Program   Providing students with access to a meaningful, interesting, interdisciplinary, and appropriately challenging curriculum and an age-appropriate and creative instructional program are also critical factors in establishing a learning environment that motivates students to succeed (Bartholomew, 2008; McLean, 2009). Student motivation can be built by using a curriculum that is related to essential questions and big ideas; high-interest activities that provide students with opportunities to apply concepts, and express their opinions; and community-based and culturally relevant topics and instructional materials that relate to students' lives, skill levels, and prior knowledge, as Anderson did in linking poetry to students' favorite songs (Childre et al., 2009). You also can plan your schedule so that you alternate low- and high-interest learning activities and assignments and use high-preference activities to motivate students to work on low-preference activities (Banda, Matuszny, & Therrien, 2009; McKinley & Stormont, 2008).

You also can enhance the motivational aspects of your curriculum by using problem-based learning. **Problem-based learning** involves students working collaboratively to create and examine solutions to real-life and community-based situations and problems (David, 2008). In particular, your students may find problem-based learning software and Web sites especially motivating as they allow them to simultaneously learn, problem-solve, and develop their academic choice-making and technology skills (Cote, 2007; Gee & Levine, 2009; Salend, 2009).

You also can share with students why the content, process, and learning activities and products are worthwhile to them (Nilson, 2007). For instance, you can help them see and understand how the content they are learning relates to their current and future interests, needs, and goals.

Use Novelty, Curiosity, and Movement   Students also may benefit from learning activities that are enjoyable and pique their curiosity via use of novelty and movement (McKinley & Stormont, 2008; Mulrine et al., 2008). Novelty can be integrated into lessons by using suspense, fantasy, color, sensory experiences, technology, and other innovative ways to arouse student interest, and keep them engaged in the learning process. Novelty also can be fostered by using students' interests and experiences and popular characters, items and trends in classroom examples and assignments and academic learning games (discussed later in this chapter).

Involve Students in the Instructional Process   Involving students in the instructional process so that they have a greater commitment to and control over their learning also can increase their motivation (Guskey & Anderman, 2008; McLean, 2009). Therefore, provide students with numerous opportunities to select personally important goals,

Making Connections
This discussion of creating a supportive and rewarding learning environment and building positive relationships with and among students builds on what we discussed earlier in Chapters 5 and 7.

Making Connections
Find out more about problem-based learning in Chapter 11.

participate in instructional planning and evaluation, and respond and make choices during instructional activities (Kern & State, 2009; Margolis & McCabe, 2006). At the beginning of a lesson, work with your students to solicit their preferences, to set learning goals, and to make choices about the learning activities that will help them achieve their goals (see Figure 6.7). During academic tasks, students can be given choices related to the time and order in which they begin and complete tasks, the learning materials they will use, the location in the room in which they prefer to work, and the individuals with whom they would like to collaborate. You also can give them a menu of tiered assignments that differ in terms of learning styles or levels of difficulty and allow them to choose the assignments that best match their learning preferences and skill levels (Painter, 2009). At the end of the lesson, they can self-correct their work to evaluate whether they achieved their goals, and reflect on their success. Figure 9.5 presents an example of a lesson incorporating student choice and preferences.

FIGURE 9.5 **Sample lesson incorporating student choice and preferences**

Mr. Franklin wanted to incorporate student choice and preference in his Science lesson on recycling. In order to do so, he followed the steps below:

BEFORE THE LESSON

- Before planning his lesson on recycling, Mr. Franklin conducted a survey with his students and asked them what they would be interested to learn more about.
- Based on his prior observations and interactions with his students, he knew that his students enjoyed hands-on experiments, and activities that relate to their everyday lives.
- He also knew of students who loved using technology rather than paper and pencil tasks.
- He considered his material resources (e.g., available computers, physical space, staff, and time) and developed his lesson accordingly.

DURING THE LESSON

- At the onset of the lesson on recycling, he presented students with a choice of two different activities (i.e., develop a recycling survey, plan a recycling program).
- He then had the students vote as a class on what activity they wanted to pursue that day. The option receiving the majority of votes could be conducted that day. Another option could have been to divide the students in two groups according to their preference.
- He made the content relevant to the students by giving them the option of writing a recycling plan for their classroom or neighborhood, developing their own questions for the survey or browsing the Internet to search for other surveys available to use as an example.
- He further allowed the students to choose to work into groups, pairs, or individually on the voted activity.
- After the students decided on the activity and the working formation, he encouraged them to choose the manner of completion and the materials needed. For example, the students could handwrite the survey/recycling plan on recycled paper or type it on the computer.

END OF LESSON

- He asked the students to select one take-home project to be completed by the end of the unit (i.e., creating and monitoring a compost pile, creating a resource notebook with domestic recycling materials and local units that recycle them, or write a persuasive speech to promote the establishment of a recycling program in their school or community).
- He asked students to anonymously write on a piece of paper what parts of the lesson they enjoyed the most and why.

Source: From "Incorporating Choice and Preferred Activities into Classwide Instruction," by L. Kern and T. M. State, *Beyond Behavior*, 18, 2009, p. 9. Copyright by the Council for Children with Behavioral Disorders. Reprinted with permission.

Student involvement and motivation also can be promoted by **attribution training**, which involves teaching them to analyze the events and actions that lead to their success and failure (Hong et al., 2007; Merlone & Moran, 2008). Thus, at the end of an activity, your students can complete the attribution assessments presented in Figure 6.8 to examine the extent to which their effort and motivation affected their learning. Encourage students to use positive attributions by modeling them and having students self-record them. You also can help them focus on their progress by responding to students' correct responses with specific feedback regarding their effort ("You're really working hard. You have really learned to do this"), and ability ("You have the skill to do this"), and by responding to students' incorrect responses with a strategy or informational feedback ("Try another way of doing this") (Joseph & Konrad, 2009; Margolis & McCabe, 2006).

Give and Solicit Feedback   Giving students feedback and soliciting feedback from them and their classmates involves and motivates students and builds academic relationships with them to support their learning (Carr, 2008; Conroy et al, 2009). Like Ms. Anderson, you can regularly give them feedback on their performance (we will learn how to use feedback to support student learning later in this chapter), and ask your students to provide information on their educational challenges, progress in and questions about learning new material, reactions to instructional activities, situations that are affecting their learning, and strategies for completing a task. You can ask students to identify the things they did well and the things they can do better. Your students also can respond to the following prompts: " I understand . . ."; "I don't understand . . ."; "I am not sure how to . . ."; "I would like to improve and have additional practice with and examples of . . ."; "I would like you to review . . ."; "It would help me learn better if you . . ." (Lenz, Graner, & Adams, 2003). You can incorporate these prompts into learning logs that students maintain or self-evaluation interviews. You also can provide students with a feedback form such as the one in Figure 9.6 that Ms. Anderson's student completed, which allows students and teachers to communicate to support teaching and learning. You also can work with your students to help them recognize their learning progress by

- making and reviewing video recordings of students during learning activities and analyzing them with students;
- reviewing work samples collected over time;
- having students complete learning logs regarding what they learned, how they learned it and what they assistance they need;
- asking students to summarize what they learned on exit tickets that they complete near the end of class; and
- having students set goals and self-monitor and chart their progress toward meeting them (Menzies et al., 2009; Salend, 2009).

Making Connections
Find out more about assessment strategies to solicit information from and involve students in reflecting on their own learning in Chapter 12.

ELEMENTS OF EFFECTIVE TEACHER-CENTERED INSTRUCTION

HOW CAN I USE EFFECTIVE TEACHER-CENTERED INSTRUCTION? Elements of effective teacher-centered lessons can be used for both large- and small-group instruction to explicitly teach content and skills from across the curriculum to your students (Burns & Ysseldyke, 2009; Harper & Maheady, 2007; Rupley, Blair, &

FIGURE 9.6 **Sample student feedback form**

Class: <u>English 89</u>   Student: _____   Teacher: <u>Ms. Anderson</u>   Week: _____

Directions: Please give me feedback on our class using the following:

Day	Student Feedback	Teacher Comments
	How did things go for you in class today?	
Monday	1 2 3 4 ⑤ Not so well OK Great day	
What did you like? ⇨ What don't you understand? ⇨ What can I do to help you understand? ⇨	*I liked hearing everyone's favorite songs (poems). It was interesting to see the different songs people like.*	I did, too, glad you enjoyed it.
Tuesday	1 2 3 4 5 Not so well OK Great day	
What did you like? ⇨ What don't you understand? ⇨ What can I do to help you understand? ⇨		
Wednesday	1 2 ③ 4 5 Not so well OK Great day	
What did you like? ⇨ What don't you understand? ⇨ What can I do to help you understand? ⇨	*It was fun to use the clickers and to play the game.* *I still don't understand the difference between a metaphor and a simile.*	I don't think you are the only one who is confused. I'll go over it again and teach it in a different way.
Thursday	1 2 3 4 5 Not so well OK Great day	
What did you like? ⇨ What don't you understand? ⇨ What can I do to help you understand? ⇨		
Friday	1 2 3 ④ 5 Not so well OK Great day	
What did you like? ⇨ What don't you understand? ⇨ What can I do to help you understand? ⇨	*I think I understand the difference now working in a group was helpful.*	Good, we will be doing more group work. If you use the words like or as to make a comparison, it is a simile.

Source: Lenz, Graner, and Adams (2003).

Motivating Students

Ms. Wilhem notices that her students are not as enthusiastic as they were earlier in the school year. Some students are not completing their assignments, and fewer students are participating in class. The number of yawns and notes passed in class seems to be increasing.

To reverse this cycle, Ms. Wilhem decides to change the major assignment for her upcoming unit on spreadsheets. Noticing that her students spend a lot of time talking about getting jobs and buying a car and clothes, she decides to have them research a career and develop a spreadsheet that outlines their expenditures during the first year of employment. She also asks them to access Web sites related to their job preferences and to write a narrative answering the following questions: Why did you choose this career? What education or training do you need? What is the anticipated demand for this career? What is the beginning salary?

She asks students to share their spreadsheets and narratives with the class. All the students complete the assignment and seem to enjoy sharing their findings. Here are some strategies you can use to implement the IDEA in your inclusive classroom and motivate students:

- Observe students, interview them and others who know them to learn about their preferences, interests, hobbies and what motivates them.
- Survey students at the beginning of a unit to determine what they already know about it and what questions they have.
- Use activities, materials, and examples that are interesting, creative, challenging, and relevant to students' lives, academic abilities, learning styles, and cultural perspectives.
- Display enthusiasm for teaching and for the material being presented.
- Vary the teaching format, grouping arrangements, and student products, and incorporate group work, self-correction and self-reinforcement into learning activities.

Sources: Connor and Lagares (2007); Margolis and McCabe (2006); Ryan et al., (2008).

Nichols, 2009; Seo, Brownell, Bishop, & Dingle, 2008). These elements include an instructional sequence that involves

- the identification of the goals of your lesson that relate to big ideas and important concepts and why they are important to students;
- the review of prerequisite skills and knowledge, the use of task analysis, conspicuous teaching behaviors and scaffolding such as explanations, examples, visual representations, demonstrations and feedback;
- the use of judicious review via the provision of ongoing and numerous opportunities for students to respond and to engage in guided and independent practice; and
- ongoing assessment to guide your teaching and evaluate your students/mastery, generalization and maintenance.

When using these techniques with your students, particularly those who are English language learners, provide contextual cues and integrate tasks into a meaningful whole (Goldenberg, 2008; Levine & McCloskey, 2009). You may also need to use other teaching frameworks and formats to promote learning and the development of higher-order thinking and problem-solving abilities.

Element 1: Establish the Lesson's Purpose by Explaining Its Goals and Objectives

As Ms. Anderson did in the chapter-opening vignette, you can begin a lesson by identifying its goals and objectives and their purpose and emphasizing how the lesson's objectives relate to students' lives (Goldenberg, 2008; Payne, Marks, & Bogan, 2007). This helps to focus their attention on the new information and motivate them. When students know the lesson's purpose, they will understand your goals and the importance of the content. You can share the goals and objectives of your lessons with your students by

- presenting them to students explicitly ("We are going to learn to . . ."),
- listing them and asking students to read them and ask questions about them, and
- telling students why the goals/objectives are important to learn and connecting them to past and future learning.

You also can start the lesson with an **anticipatory set**, a statement or an enjoyable activity that introduces the material and motivates students to learn it by relating the goals of the lesson to their prior knowledge, interests, strengths, and future life events (Huber, 2005). Some teachers use a visual or oral device as part of their anticipatory set. For example, in the chapter-opening vignette, Ms. Anderson used an anticipatory set that asked students to identify and share their favorite songs.

Element 2: Review Prerequisite Skills, and Activate Prior Knowledge

After clarifying the lesson's purpose, it is important for you to review previously learned relevant skills and activate students' prior knowledge about the new material (Price & Nelson, 2007; Shaw, 2008). For example, before introducing new poetic devices, Ms. Anderson reviewed the ones students had already learned. You can review prerequisite skills by correcting and discussing homework, asking students to define key terms, having them apply concepts, or assigning an activity requiring mastery of prior relevant material.

Element 3: Use Task Analysis, and Introduce Content in Separate Steps Followed by Practice

Next, specific points are presented to students in small, sequential steps. Task analysis can help you identify the steps used to master a skill and individualize the lesson matching the level of difficulty of the task to the various skill levels of students and the skills your students need to practice (Kubina & Yurich, 2009). **Task analysis** is a systematic process of stating and sequencing the parts of a task to determine what subtasks must be performed to master the task (Rao & Kane, 2009). For example, Ms. Anderson used task analysis to sequence the level of difficulty of her assignments to differentiate them for her students so that some students answered true/false statements, some matched poetic devices to their corresponding statements, some identified poetic devices in statements, and others composed statements that reflected the various types of poetic devices.

Element 4: Give Clear, Specific, and Complete Directions, Explanations, and Relevant Examples

Remember the guidelines for giving directions and gaining and maintaining students' attention and enhancing motivation presented earlier in this chapter, and give students detailed explanations and examples of content using clear, complete, specific, explicit statements. Try to avoid using confusing wording ("you know," "a lot," "these things"), and use terms that students understand. While the rate of presentation will depend on the students' skills and the complexity of the material, you should maintain a swift pace (Cartledge, & Kourea, 2008; Shaw, 2008). However, to ensure understanding, you can repeat key points, terms, questions, directions, and concepts, use visual and contextual supports, and adjust the pace of the lesson to allow for reteaching and repetition (Goldenberg, 2008).

Element 5: Provide Time for Active and Guided Practice

Practice activities provide *all students* with numerous opportunities to respond so that you can ensure that they have mastered the skill (Harper & Maheady, 2007; Kubina & Yurich, 2009). It is often best to structure time for practice after you introduce small amounts of difficult or new material. Because success during practice helps students learn, you should strive for a practice success rate of at least 75% to 80% and prepare practice activities that require students to respond to both easier and harder items. Good practice activities are varied and related to the content and students' strengths, challenges, and experiential backgrounds and include responding to the teacher's questions, summarizing major points, and using peer tutoring (Rupley et al., 2009).

Academic games should promote the involvement of all participants. How do you structure your academic games to help all your students learn?

Academic Learning Games   **Academic learning games** can motivate students to practice skills and concepts learned in lessons (Connor & Lagares, 2007). Academic games may take several forms including technology-based games, board games, movement-oriented games, simulations, and role plays (Lerner & Johns, 2007; Salend, 2009).

In academic games, the academic component is controlled by the teacher, who can vary the level of the skill, the presentation, and the response modes to match the needs and levels of many different students. Thus, students of varying abilities can interact within the same teaching format yet use skills that differ in complexity.

When using academic games, you should make sure your students understand the rules and don't get overly competitive or stimulated. Games can stress cooperation rather than competition. One cooperative strategy requires players to strive for a common goal. In this technique, winning occurs when the whole group achieves the goal. Devising game pawns as puzzle pieces also fosters cooperation in an academic game. For example, each player's pawn can be part of a puzzle that is completed when each player reaches a specified goal. Competition with oneself can be built into common-goal games by setting individualized time limits or by increasing the difficulty of the content. The time limits and content levels can be based on a previously established standard or a prior level of performance. You also can help players cooperate by phrasing questions so that they require the input of more than one player to be answered correctly.

Rules, too, can be designed to optimize cooperation. A rule that requires players to change teams or movers periodically during the game can promote cooperation. A rule that requires one player to move toward the goal, depending on the academic performance of another player, also fosters a coalition of game players. Another cooperative rule allows a player who has reached the goal to aid the other players by helping to answer questions put to them.

Element 6: Promote Active Responding, and Check for Understanding

It is important that you provide students with numerous opportunities to actively respond and check for understanding after presenting key points (Cartledge, & Kourea, 2008; Haydon, Borders, Embury, & Clarke, 2009). When checking for

Identify a game you or your students like to play. How can you apply the principles presented here to make this game cooperative?

understanding, you can have all students respond actively and identify main points or state agreement or disagreement with the comments and responses of their peers. You also can check for understanding by involving students in the instructional process. For example, you can give them red, yellow, and green cards, which students display to demonstrate their varying levels of understanding (green indicates students understand, yellow indicates students have some understanding, and red indicates students have limited or no understanding) (Leahy, Lyon, Thompson, & William, 2005).

Questioning Like Ms. Anderson, you can promote active student responding and check for understanding by asking questions (Fisher & Frey, 2008; Trussell, 2008). Questions can be stated clearly, at the language and ability levels of various students, and distributed fairly so that *all students* must respond openly. Thus, rather than targeting a question to a specific student ("Jack, what is the difference between a metaphor and a simile?"), you can phrase questions using comments such as "Everyone listen and then tell me" or "I want you all to think before you answer." Also, you can randomly select students to respond, give them a sufficient amount of time to formulate their answers (at least 3 to 5 seconds), and then ask other students to respond to these answers. Questions also can be directed to students so that they expand on their first answers or those of others. If students fail to respond to the question, you can ask them if they know the answer, ask them about related knowledge, direct the question to another student, or provide the correct answer. When questioning students, avoid promoting inattention by repeating questions, answering questions for them, or supplementing incomplete answers.

Questions can be adjusted to the difficulty of the content and the skill levels of the students. To check understanding of simple facts or basic rules, use product questions that ask students to give the answer or to restate information and procedures, such as "What is alliteration?" To check students' ability to use complex skills, ask questions that require them to apply basic rules or generalizations. For example, Ms. Anderson asked her students to apply their knowledge of poetic devices by writing statements depicting them. You also can use process questions that ask students to discuss how they arrived at an answer.

Questioning techniques can be adapted for students who are English language learners. You can encourage these students to answer questions by providing visual supports and clues such as pictures, gestures, and words; initially asking students questions that require only one- or two-word answers; rephrasing questions when necessary; asking complex questions that can be answered in many different ways; probing responses such as "I don't know"; and repeating and elaborating on students' answers.

Making Connections
Find out more about using questioning effectively in Chapter 11.

Active Student Responding To encourage active student responding and the review of content that needs to be overlearned, you can use *choral responding,* in which students answer simultaneously on a cue from the teacher, or have students tell their classmates the answer, or have students write down their answer and then check each student's response (Haydon et al., 2009). Group responses that allow each member of the group to respond with a physical gesture also are desirable. For example, students can respond to a question with a yes or no answer by placing their thumbs up or down and indicate their agreement or disagreement with an OK sign.

Response cards and write-on boards also help students respond and stay engaged (Haydon et al., 2009; Musti-Rao et al., 2008). **Response cards** take the form of items that are displayed by students in class to demonstrate their answers to questions or problems posed by their teacher. Preprinted response cards containing typical answers (Yes, No, Agree, Disagree, or specific numerals for math) are given to students so that they can select the cards that give their responses. These cards are appropriate for content that has a limited number of answers, such as true/false questions or questions that require agreement or disagreement. Write-on dry erase boards allow students to record their answers on blank cards or boards and then erase them. While these boards are typically used when teachers want students to recall information, they also can be used to have students to respond to open-ended questions and to solve problems.

As we saw in the chapter opening vignette, interactive real-time technology-based active responding systems, also called *clickers* or *classroom response systems*, are being used to make classroom presentations more interactive, motivating, and effective (Salend, 2009). These systems allow you to assess your students' learning by having them periodically respond electronically to factual, computational, conceptual, and comprehension questions; probes and quizzes; interactive activities; and polls, play learning games, and review questions. Thus, you can use these systems to have all of your students, not just the ones who raise their hands, respond in your inclusive classroom. For example, during her lessons on poetic elements, Ms. Anderson monitored her students' understanding of key points by asking them to use their clickers to answer her questions. She then used their responses, which were immediately tabulated and displayed on her computer, to determine which students were ready to proceed to the next activity and to target her teaching for students who needed additional instruction. You can use these systems to make choices about whether to make the results available to students to provide them with prompt feedback. These systems have the added advantage of providing your students, especially those who are quiet or shy, with a way to "silently" ask questions and lets you unobtrusively send responses or provide feedback to individuals or groups of students.

Effective teachers use a variety of different ways to foster active student responding. How do you provide your students with opportunities to respond actively?

Making Connections
Find out more about how you can use active responding systems to monitor your students' learning progress in Chapter 12.

Element 7: Give Frequent, Prompt, and Specific Feedback

You can foster the teaching and learning process in your inclusive classroom by making sure that students' responses are followed by frequent, timely, clear, descriptive, positive, constructive and specific feedback from you, classmates, and other professionals (Brookhart, 2008; Cartledge & Kourea, 2008). Make sure that feedback from you is not viewed by your students as criticism or ridicule. Therefore, make sure that your feedback does not come across to your students as being judgmental or accusatory or as lectures, teasing, advice, demands, or ultimatums (Tugend, 2009). Rather, your feedback, which can be delivered verbally or visually (e.g., hand signals, gestures, computer graphics), should be focused and understandable so that it tells students why their response or product is correct, incorrect, or needs additional work or effort and motivates and guides them how to improve their learning (Conroy et al., 2009).

The type of feedback should be differentiated based on the nature of the response. Therefore, in determining what type of feedback to use, you can categorize students' responses as *correct and confident, correct but unsure, partly correct,* or *incorrect.* If the answer is correct and confident, you can confirm it with a short statement or praise and ask additional questions at the same or a more difficult level. Incorrect answers that are the result of careless errors on the part of students can be responded to by giving the correct answer and encouragement to use the correct process. Student responses that are *correct but unsure, partly correct,* or *incorrect* can be responded to using one of the types of feedback presented next.

Process Feedback   Students who are unsure of their correct responses may need **process feedback**, in which you praise students and reinforce their answer by restating why it was correct. Besides responding to correct answers, it is important to provide feedback to students whose answers are partly correct. You can confirm the part of the answer that is correct and then restate or simplify the question to address the incorrect part.

Corrective Feedback   **Corrective feedback**, also referred to as *error correction*, involves your identifying errors, showing students how to correct them, giving students opportunities to engage in the correct response and acknowledging them for it. For example, you can model the correct response and ask the students to imitate you or you can guide students in performing the behavior or skill (Kubina & Yurich, 2009). Corrective feedback is more effective in promoting learning than **general feedback**, in which responses are identified simply as correct or incorrect; **right-only feedback**, in which only correct responses are identified; or **wrong-only feedback**, in which only incorrect responses are identified.

Instructive Feedback   **Instructive feedback** promotes learning by giving students extra information and teaching on the task or content. After students answer, you offer instructive feedback by acknowledging what students have done well and giving additional information that

- expands on the target skills being taught (e.g., defining a sight word or giving a word's antonym),
- parallels the skills being taught (e.g., linking a numeral with its corresponding number word or a mathematical/scientific symbol with its meaning), or
- offers new information (e.g., describing the color of something or an additional property) or the next steps that they need to engage in to expand their learning or make it more efficient.

Prompting   You can foster student learning and help correct students' errors related to a lack of understanding by using a variety of visual, auditory, or tactile **prompts** (Fisher & Frey, 2008; Trussell, 2008). Prompts can be categorized from most to least intrusive, including *manual prompts,* in which the student is physically guided through the task; *modeling prompts,* in which the student observes someone else perform the task; *oral prompts* that describe how to perform the task; and *visual prompts* that show the student the correct process or answer in a graphic presentation. Prompts can be used sequentially or simultaneously, depending on the skills of the students and the complexity of the task.

Praising   Praise coupled with comments about strengths and challenges can provide valuable feedback to students and improve their work (Conroy et al., 2009). Because some studies have shown that frequent praise can reduce students' independence, self-confidence, and creativity (Dweck, 2007), you should distribute praise evenly and examine its effect on students (Willingham, 2008). Rather than just praising on-task behavior and task correctness, use praise to encourage independence, effort, determination, and creativity. Your praise statements should be delivered in a noncontrolling way and tailored to the age, skill level, and cultural background of the students (Gable et al., 2009; Lam et al., 2008). It also is important to individualize praise so that the students' achievements are evaluated in comparison with their own performance rather than the performance of others.

Making Connections
This discussion on praise builds on what we discussed earlier in Chapter 7.

Student-Directed Feedback   Students can be a valuable source of feedback (Carr, 2008; Menzies et al., 2009). They can be encouraged and taught to use self-monitoring and self-correction techniques to record and analyze their own progress. They can chart their mastery of a specific skill by graphing their percentage or number correct every day. Students can also be given answer keys to correct their own work, or they can exchange work with peers and offer feedback to peers on their work.

Element 8: Offer Time for Independent Activities

You can end successful lessons by giving students independent activities that allow them to demonstrate mastery of the material (Rupley et al., 2009). Independent work also can be directed at fostering the maintenance and generalization of new skills by providing students with multiple opportunities to perform overtime and under the varied conditions and expectations they will encounter in different settings (Hart & Whalon, 2008; McIntosh & MacKay, 2008). Make sure that the activities fit the students' instructional levels and needs, and try to give them numerous opportunities to make correct responses. As they work on the assignment, move around the room to monitor their performance and offer prompt feedback. If completed assignments do not meet your expectations, students can be asked to revise or redo them until the product meets your standards.

You can modify independent assignments by providing help or access to peer tutors (Rock & Thead, 2009). Students can ask for help by placing a help sign or card on their desks, raising their hands, or signing a list. At first, provide help by asking questions and making statements that help students assume responsibility for figuring out answers, such as "What things can help you figure out the answer?" and "Have you asked three of your classmates for help before asking me?"

Although it is appropriate to individualize the tasks, do not have students work in a different content area from the rest of the class since this might isolate them. Also, when possible, students should complete assignments and work with materials similar to those that other students are using.

You can use teacher-created graphic templates, forms, and cues that are stamped on student assignments to individualize them. These templates allow all students to work on the same assignments by using visual prompts that adjust the workload of students, inform students how to complete assignments, adapt the ways in which students respond to items, and vary the time students have to complete the assignment. Sample stamps are presented in Figure 9.7.

Element 9: Summarize Main Points, and Evaluate Mastery, Maintenance, and Generalization

At the end of the lesson, summarize the main points and evaluate students' understanding and mastery of the content, maintenance and generalization. You can use progress monitoring and assess students' mastery of content in a 1- to 5-minute probe. You also can ask your students to complete a learning log indicating what they learned, how they learned it, what they are confused about, and what additional information they would like to learn. It is recommended your students be able to demonstrate mastery by completing independent work at an accuracy level of at least 90% (Trussell, 2008). Because maintenance and generalization are critical for building a foundation for learning new skills, weekly and monthly maintenance and generalization probes also are desirable. The results of these assessments can be recorded and used to make teaching decisions. The results also can be shared with students so they can evaluate and reflect on their learning and effort. For example, students can be asked to examine their work and effort to identify the aspects that contributed to and hindered their success as well as actions they can take to improve their learning.

Homework Homework can be useful in fostering and evaluating student mastery of content. Although homework has the potential to be a valuable tool for supporting and supplementing in-class instruction, many students often experience great difficulty completing their homework assignments (Christopher, 2008; Markow, Kim, & Liebman, 2007). To address these homework difficulties, you can use a variety of practices to make it a process that supports student learning (Biddulph, Hess, & Humes, 2006; Darling-Hammond & Ifill-Lynch, 2006; Margolis, 2005; Marzano & Pickering, 2007; Vatterott, 2009).

PEARSON myeducationlab

To enhance your understanding of the different ways you use scaffolding to differentiate your instruction, go to the IRIS Center Resources section of the Topic *Inclusive Practices* in the MyEducationLab for your course, and complete the module entitled *Providing Instructional Supports: Facilitating Mastery of New Skills.*

Making Connections
Find out more about progress monitoring and other ways to assess student learning in Chapter 12.

FIGURE 9.7 Sample stamps to differentiate student assignments

Stamps to Differentiate the Student Response Required

Assignment can be completed
_____ orally with the teacher
_____ with an adult
_____ as we discussed

Allows the teacher to alter the method of student response. Excellent for students who have difficulty organizing thoughts and ideas in writing or those with handwriting/graphomotor deficits. Teacher can specify that the student complete the assignment a certain way (e.g., dictated to a parent, using a tape recorder, in note form, etc.).

Do the ★ items orally with the teacher.

Allows the teacher to alter the method of student response on selected items. Useful on quizzes or tests with students who need more time to complete written work. For example, essay questions could be completed orally with the teacher during class testing time rather than making arrangements for additional time to complete the item(s) in writing.

Complete:
_____ independently
_____ with a learning buddy
_____ in a cooperative group
of _____

This stamp allows the teacher to adjust how students work within the classroom—alone or in some type of cooperative group.

Stamps for Providing Additional Time to Complete Assignments

Do you need additional time to complete this assignment?

YES   NO

If yes, see the teacher to make arrangements.

Allows the student to inform the teacher of the need for additional time in a private and unobtrusive way. Arrangements for additional time can then be made. Excellent for quizzes and tests and other tasks where time is often limited.

Incomplete — Complete by

_____

Direct students to complete or redo their work by a time/date specified by the teacher.

Stamps for Adjusting Workload

Complete the following:
_____ All
_____ All Odd
_____ All Even
_____ Every Third
_____ First Five
_____ First Ten

This stamp is effective when an assignment has several of the same type of questions/problems (e.g., math worksheet). The teacher can select all or a portion of the items for the student to complete.

Select
_____ ● items
_____ ▲ items
_____ ★ items
to complete

Teacher codes questions by importance, type, or level using the symbols and then writes down how many of each type the student should complete. The student then self-selects from the questions on the page. This provides the student control in work completion—the teacher sets clear expectations while the student is still allowed some choice.

Complete all circled items.

Allows the teacher to select specific items to be completed by the student.

Stamps for Setting Clear Expectations for Written Assignments

Remember:
_____ . ? !
_____ complete sentences
_____ capital letters

Prompts students to pay attention to certain aspects of writing as they complete a writing assignment.

To be graded for:
_____ content/organization
_____ sentence structure
_____ capitalization/punctuation
_____ spelling
_____ form
_____ neatness
_____ all of the above

Teacher checks off what the student is to focus attention on when completing the written assignment. One or more things can be checked off.

Source: From *Using Stamps to Differentiate Student Assignments*, by M. M. Boyer, 1995, Phoenix, AZ: Author. Reprinted by permission.

Helping Students Complete Independent Assignments

Ms. Maphis's class included a wide range of students. Some students completed independent assignments quickly; others took more time. Concerned about student frustration and the need to avoid isolating students, Ms. Maphis decided to modify her independent assignments. First, rather than having students work on one long assignment, she decided to give several shorter assignments that covered the same content. She also prepared different versions of assignments that modified their content to meet students' skill levels by decreasing the number and types of items students had to answer, by interspersing items on previously mastered content with items on new material, and by placing the most important items to be completed at the beginning of the assignment. She also built in opportunities for students to receive feedback by asking students to correct their own work, to seek feedback after completing a specific number of items tailored to the students' skill levels, and to use a prearranged signal to indicate that they need assistance.

Here are some other strategies you can use to implement the IDEA in your inclusive classroom and help students complete independent assignments:

- Give clear and concise directions in a list of steps.
- Have students work on one assignment or worksheet at a time.

- Provide cues to highlight key parts of directions, details of items, and changes in item types.
- Offer examples of correct response formats and provide self-correcting materials.
- Divide assignments into sections by folding, drawing lines, cutting off parts of the page, boxing, and blocking out with an index card or a heavy crayon; then give students one section at a time.
- Teach students to use sticky notes and highlighters to support their independent work. For example, they can use sticky notes to record the sequence and time periods in which they need to do things, and to mark the questions they have for the teacher and the last thing they worked on before taking a break.
- Provide enough space for students to record their answers, and limit the amount of distracting visual stimuli.
- Scan assignments into a computer and allow students to complete the assignment using a computer that provides feedback and guidance on their responses.

Sources: Griffin et al. (2006); Rock and Thead (2009); Stormont (2008).

Adjust the Amount and Type of Homework. Assigning a reasonable amount of homework that is moderately challenging and doable for students and in smaller units can increase the probability that your students will complete it. You also can help students who struggle with homework to complete it by linking it to their real-life experiences, shortening assignments, extending deadlines, using other evaluation strategies, and modifying the types of assignments and the responses required. It is also important to coordinate homework assignments with others—particularly for secondary-level students who have different teachers in each content area.

While you should try to create homework assignments that are interesting and challenging, the type of homework will depend on the instructional purpose. If the goal of homework is to practice material learned in class, it may be appropriate to assign some type of drill-oriented assignment. When the purpose of homework is to prepare students for upcoming lessons, assignments can be structured to expose them to the information necessary to perform successfully in class. Finally, when you want students to apply and integrate what they have learned, you can use long-term assignments that require the integration of many skills and processes.

Establish and Follow Homework Routines. You can teach and follow regular routines for assigning, collecting, evaluating, and returning homework. When assigning homework, use the guidelines previously discussed in this chapter for giving clear, explicit, and complete directions, and monitor students' understanding of their assignments and the guidelines for completing them. Make sure that *all students* have a copy of the assignment and the necessary materials to take home by posting them online or making photocopy of assignments for students who need help recording assignments. You can help students record, keep track of, and complete their homework by teaching them to maintain an agenda book via the use of the learning strategy TRICK BAG (see Scott & Compton, 2007).

It also is important for you to give guidance regarding how long the assignment should take as well as how you are going to evaluate it. You also should inform your students and their families of your policies for missed or late assignments, extra credit, and homework accommodations. An important part of your homework routine that can motivate students to complete their homework is evaluating it frequently and immediately and giving students feedback. You also motivate your students by periodically interviewing randomly selected students concerning their homework and assigning them a homework grade (Stern & Avigliano, 2008).

Teach Study and Organizational Skills   Teaching your students study and organizational skills also can help students complete their homework. Therefore, you can teach your students skills related to goal setting, task planning, and using a homework notebook and a monthly and weekly planner. Your students also may benefit from instruction in how to schedule and budget their time, select an environment conducive to completing their homework (remember this may not be possible for some of your students), and organize their materials. You can help your students who struggle with homework acquire these skills by having them work with peers who have well-developed study and organizational skills.

Collaborate with Families   Because family members play an important role in the homework process, your homework practices should promote collaboration with them. Make families an important part of the homework process by asking them to sign homework, and contacting them about the purpose of homework and the amount and type of homework given. Offer them suggestions on how to help their children complete their homework by establishing effective homework routines such as setting a time and schedule for doing homework, creating a location to do homework that supports its completion, making sure the required materials are available, motivating homework completion, and dealing with frustration. You also should provide families with information about the quality of their children's homework as well as their children's efforts.

Your homework practices also should recognize the unique strengths and challenges of your students' families. It is also important to make sure that your homework practices do not (a) create disharmony in family–child relationships and interactions; (b) deny students and their families access to leisure time; (c) conflict with the families' economic needs and cultural perspectives; and (d) confuse, frustrate, or embarrass students and their families. Therefore, it is important for you to periodically query families regarding homework. For example, you can ask them to respond to the following:

- How long did it take for your child to complete the homework?
- Did your child understand the homework?
- Was the homework too difficult?
- Did your child have all the materials to complete the homework?
- What can I do to make homework a better learning experience for your child? (Margolis, 2005)

> **Making Connections**
> This discussion of organizational skills relates to what we discussed earlier in Chapter 6.

> **Making Connections**
> Find out more about study skills in Chapter 12.

COOPERATIVE LEARNING ARRANGEMENTS

HOW CAN I SUCCESSFULLY USE COOPERATIVE LEARNING ARRANGEMENTS WITH STUDENTS? In addition to structuring learning so that students work individually, or in teacher-centered small and large groups, effective teachers like Ms. Anderson differentiate instruction by having their students work in **cooperative learning** arrangements (Johnson & Johnson, 2009; Sapon-Shevin, 2008). In cooperative learning arrangements, students work with their peers to achieve a shared academic goal rather than competing against or working separately from their classmates. You structure the learning environment so that each class member contributes to the

Helping Students Complete Homework

Ms. Rios felt strongly about the value of homework and assigned it 4 days a week. She checked her students' assignments regularly and noticed that Matt often failed to complete his homework. When questioned about his homework, Matt said, "It was too hard," "I did not know what to do," or simply "I can't do this." Recognizing Matt's difficulties, Ms. Rios approached Matt's friend, Jamal, who completed his homework, to see whether he would be willing to work with Matt. Jamal agreed and Ms. Rios spoke to Matt, who also was interested in working with Jamal. Both Matt and Jamal were responsible for making sure that their partners had recorded the assignment in their assignment notebooks. Before starting their homework, Matt and Jamal spoke over the phone or worked at each other's home to make sure that they both understood the material presented in class and the homework assignment. As they worked on their homework assignments, they monitored each other's work, offered feedback, and discussed any difficulties.

Here are some other strategies you can use to implement the IDEA in your inclusive classroom and help students complete homework:

- Individualize assignments for students by using short- and long-term assignments and by relating assignments

to students' experiences, interests, career goals, and IEPs.

- Encourage students who have difficulty with homework to access assignments online, record assignments in their notebooks or PDAs, to use homework planners, and to use a daily or weekly teacher-prepared homework assignment sheet or checklist. Encourage students to check with a classmate about homework assignments.

- Give students opportunities to begin their homework in class.

- Create authentic and innovative homework assignments that make homework a more enjoyable, motivating, and meaningful experience for students and their families. For example, Internet-based homework assignments can be structured so that students and their families take "virtual field trips" to museums and scientific and historical sites, or play online academically integrated games.

- Create a homework club to provide after school homework assistance and tutoring for students.

Sources: Biddulph et al. (2006); Darling-Hammond and Ifill-Lynch (2006); Margolis (2005); Marzano and Pickering (2007); Smith Myles et al. (2007).

Students benefit academically and socially from working in cooperative learning groups. How has working in cooperative groups affected you academically and socially?

group's goal. When learning is structured cooperatively, students are accountable not only for their own achievement but also for those of other group members. Cooperative learning is especially worthwhile for heterogeneous student populations as it helps students actively participate and stay engaged in the learning process. It promotes friendships and encourages mutual respect, self-esteem, and learning among students of various academic abilities and different language, racial, and ethnic backgrounds (Goldenberg, 2008; Rothstein-Fisch & Trumbull, 2008).

Cooperative learning activities have five important components different from group work: positive interdependence, individual accountability, face-to-face interactions, interpersonal skills, and group processing (Johnson & Johnson, 2009; O'Brien, 2007). **Positive interdependence** is established when students understand that they must work together to achieve their goal. You can promote positive interdependence by using cooperative learning activities with mutual goals, role interdependence and specialization, resource sharing, and group rewards. **Individual accountability** is understanding that each group member is responsible for contributing to the group and learning the material. This is often established by giving individualized tests or probes, adding group members' scores together, assigning specific parts of an assignment to different group members, randomly selecting group members to respond for the group, asking all members of the group to present part of the project, asking students to keep a journal of their contributions to the group, or tailoring roles to the ability levels of students (Fisher & Frey, 2008). For example, you can make sure all group members contribute to a project by using individually assigned colors so that each student's contributions are visually represented by their assigned colors (e.g., different-colored type or different-colored markers, crayons, or pencils). Building individual accountability into cooperative learning groups helps reduce the **free-rider effect**, in which some members fail to contribute and allow others to do the majority of the work. *Face-to-face interactions* and the use of *interpersonal skills* occur when students encourage and help each other learn the material. Group processing is often achieved by having groups reflect on the learning products they created and the processes they used to produce them.

PEARSON
myeducationlab

To examine challenging cases related to helping students be successful in your inclusive classroom during small- and large-group instruction, go to the IRIS Center Resources section of the Topic *Instructional Practices and Learning Strategies* in the MyEducationLab for your course, and complete the case entitled *Fostering Student Accountability for Classroom Work.*

Select an Appropriate Cooperative Learning Format

Cooperative learning begins by selecting an appropriate format. The format you choose will depend on the characteristics of your students, as well as their experiences in working cooperatively. Generally, it is wise to start by having students work in pairs before they work in groups.

The cooperative learning format selected also will depend on the content, objectives, and mastery levels of the assignment. According to Maheady, Harper, and Mallette (1991), peer tutoring and classwide peer tutoring (CWPT) are best for teaching basic skills and factual knowledge in content areas; jigsaw is appropriate for text mastery; and the learning together approach is the desired format for teaching higher-level cognitive material and having students learn how to work together and reach a consensus on controversial material.

Peer Tutoring   In **peer tutoring**, one student tutors and assists another in learning a new skill. Peer tutoring increases student learning across a range of content areas and fosters positive attitudes toward school for tutors and tutees (Fuchs et al., 2008; McDuffie, Mastropieri, & Scruggs, 2009; Musti-Rao & Cartledge, 2007; Stenhoff & Lignugaris/Kraft, 2007). It also promotes a greater sense of responsibility and an improved self-concept, as well as increased academic and social skills. When using peer tutoring, you can do the following:

- Establish specific goals within your curriculum for the sessions.
- Plan particular learning activities and select appropriate materials to meet the identified goals.
- Select tutors who have mastered the content to be taught.
- Teach students to be successful tutors, including how to establish rapport, respect and maintain confidentiality, present the material and tasks, record tutees' responses, use prompts, correct errors, and offer praise and feedback. Some teachers schedule a tutor huddle, where tutors get together to learn and practice the content they will be teaching and the instructional strategies they will be using. You also can provide tutors with cue cards that prompt and remind them of the behaviors they should engage in to tutor and praise and record tutee performance.
- Provide information to tutees so that they understand the peer tutoring process and are willing to work with a tutor.
- Match tutors and tutees based on such factors as strengths, challenges, and personalities.
- Schedule sessions for no longer than 30 minutes and no more than three times per week.

- Monitor and evaluate the tutoring process and program periodically, provide feedback to both members of the dyad, and assess student learning.
- Allay families' potential concerns by explaining to them the role and value of peer tutoring (Herring-Harrison, Gardner, & Lovelack, 2007; Kourea, Cartledge, & Musti-Rao, 2007; Ramsey, Jolivette, & Patton, 2007; Van Norman, 2007).

It is important that you use reciprocal peer tutoring so that *all students* have opportunities to serve as tutors and tutees (Sutherland & Snyder, 2007). For example, a student who performs well in math could teach math to a student who tutored him or her in reading. Students who are not proficient at teaching academic skills can teach nonacademic skills related to their hobbies or interests.

It is also important for you to give peer tutors feedback and to have them reflect on their success. For example, following a peer tutoring session, tutors can reflect on the lesson by responding to the following:

- I think the lesson went well because _____.
- The things I liked about teaching this lesson were _____.
- During this lesson, my classmate learned _____.
- My classmate still needs to work on _____.
- Next time I teach this lesson, I will _____.

Classwide Peer Tutoring   **Classwide peer tutoring (CWPT)** is effective in teaching reading, spelling, vocabulary, math, and social studies to a wide range of students educated in a variety of settings (Bowman-Perrott, 2009; Harper & Maheady, 2007). You can implement CWPT by following these steps:

1. Divide the class into groups of three to four students with each group containing one high-, midrange-, and low-performing student.
2. Encourage groups to choose a name for their team and to personalize their work folders.
3. Let students know that they are responsible for helping their teammates learn what has been taught.
4. Develop study guides addressing weekly content that contain 10 to 30 questions and their answers.
5. Give each group a work folder that consists of a study guide, the numbered cards relating to the study guide questions, and blank sheets of writing paper.
6. Set a timer for 30 minutes.
7. Direct groups to begin by having a student from each group choose the top card and the team member seated to left of the selector serve as the tutor by reading the question to the team.
8. Have each group member, except the tutor, write their answer to the question on a piece of paper and showing their response to the tutor. A correct response earns five points for the individual student. An incorrect response prompts tutors to offer the correct response, ask tutees to write this response one or two times, and award two points to teammates for correcting their errors. No points are given to teammates who do not attempt to correct their errors or who do so incorrectly.
9. Have groups continue to rotate tutor responsibilities and repeat the process of selecting a card, reading the question, and awarding points.
10. Circulate around the classroom to give bonus points for appropriate tutee and tutor behavior.
11. Alert students that CWPT is over and that they should compute their individual points. Individual points are then recorded on a large poster and added together to compute the team total.

After this procedure is repeated throughout the week, students take individual tests and receive points for each correct response. All points earned by the groups are totaled at the end of the week, and the group with the most points is acknowledged through badges, stickers, certificates, public posting of names, free time, or an agreed upon reward. You can make this system less competitive by giving all groups a chance to earn rewards and acknowledgment if they achieve their goals or exceed a previously established point total.

Jigsaw   The **jigsaw** format divides students into groups, with each student assigned a task that is essential in reaching the group's goal (Ash et al., 2009). Every member makes a contribution that is integrated with the work of others to produce the group's product. When teams work on the same task, expert groups can be formed by having a member of each group meet with peers from other groups who have been assigned the same subtask. The expert group members work together to complete their assignment and then share the results with their original jigsaw groups.

You can structure the students' assignment so that each group member can succeed. For example, a lesson about Martin Luther King Jr. can be structured by giving each student one segment of King's life to learn about and teach to others in their group. Students who were assigned the same aspect of King's life meet in expert groups to complete their part; then the original group answers questions on all segments of King's life.

Learning Together   A cooperative learning format that places more responsibility on group members is the **learning together approach** (Johnson & Johnson, 2009). In this format, students are assigned to teams, and each team is given an assignment. Teams decide whether to divide the task into its components or approach the task as a whole group. All group members are involved in the team's decisions by offering their knowledge and skills and by seeking help and clarification from others. Every group produces one product, which represents the combined contributions of all group members. You then grade this product, with each student in the group receiving the group grade. For example, you could use learning together to teach students about mammals by dividing the class into groups and having each group develop part of a bulletin board display with information and artwork about a particular mammal. The students in each group then would contribute to the group's display by reporting information, doing artwork, or dictating material about mammals.

Establish Guidelines for Working Cooperatively

You and your students can establish guidelines for working cooperatively. Some guidelines that can foster cooperation include the following:

- Each group will produce one product.
- Each group member will help other group members understand the material.
- Each group member will seek help from her or his peers.
- Each group member will stay in his or her group.
- No group member will change her or his ideas unless logically persuaded to do so.
- Each group member will indicate acceptance of the group's product by signing his or her name.

Keep in mind that some problems might occur in cooperative learning arrangements: increased noise, complaints about partners, and equitable contributions. Noise can be minimized by developing and posting rules, developing signals that make students aware of their noise levels, assigning a student to monitor the group's noise level, providing rewards for groups that follow the rules, and teaching students to use their quiet voices. Complaints can be discussed with the group and students who work collaboratively can be reinforced.

The issue of equitable contributions of each member to the group can be addressed in a variety of ways. One way is via a group journal, a process log of the group's activities, including a description of each student's contribution and effort (see Figure 9.8c). Individual group members can also keep a journal of their participation and contributions. You can help *all students* participate and share their learning by conducting debriefing, rehearsing, and revoicing sessions that allow individual students to examine their learning and prepare to share it with their classmates.

Form Heterogeneous Cooperative Groups

Assign students to cooperative, heterogeneous groups by considering their sex, race, ethnicity, language ability, disability, and academic and social skill levels. You also can consider characteristics such as motivation, personality, interests, and communication skills. For example, students who sit quietly and do not participate could be assigned to a highly supportive team.

Another factor to consider in forming groups is the students' ability to work together. You can get this information through observation and/or by administering a sociogram. While groups can be changed for each cooperative lesson, keeping the students in the same group for several weeks provides continuity that is helpful in developing cooperative skills. How long a group remains together can depend on the students' ages, the nature of the task, and the group's interpersonal skills. At the beginning, you can use small groups of two or three students, increasing them to five when students become accustomed to cooperative learning. When forming new groups, start with activities that help students get acquainted.

Arrange the Classroom for Cooperative Learning

To structure your classroom for cooperative work, arrange the students' desks or tables in clusters, place individual desks in pairs for peer tutoring, or block off a carpeted corner of the room. For larger groups, desks can be placed in circles to foster eye contact and communication. The time needed to complete cooperative projects may vary, so give groups a safe area to store in-progress projects and other materials. To help *all students* succeed in cooperative learning arrangements, it is important for you to design your classroom to complement your differentiation techniques and your use of universal design to help students learn, behave well, and develop social skills.

Another way to promote cooperative work is to post group reminders. For example, you can post a chart with strategies for respecting the individuality of each group member. These strategies include referring to each group member by name, speaking quietly, and encouraging all members to participate.

PEARSON
myeducationlab

Go to the Assignments and Activities section of the Topic *Instructional Practices and Learning Strategies* in the MyEducationLab for your course and complete the activity entitled *Small Group Instruction*. As you watch the video and answer the accompanying questions, consider how small group instruction helps develop students' cooperative learning skills.

Develop Students' Cooperative Skills

Cooperative learning depends on the quality of the interactions of group members. Because many students have little experience with this arrangement, you may have to devote some time to helping students learn to work together effectively (Johnson & Johnson, 2009). Interpersonal and group processing skills that students must develop to work well together include getting to know and trust peers, communicating directly and clearly, listening actively, seeking assistance, supporting, encouraging and complimenting others, accepting differences, managing resources, balancing personal and group goals, building consensus, making decisions, and resolving conflicts.

You can use a **T-chart** to help your students develop cooperative skills (Stanford & Reeves, 2005). This involves (a) drawing a horizontal line and writing the cooperative skill on the line, (b) drawing a vertical line from the middle

FIGURE 9.8 Sample formats for evaluating cooperative learning groups

(a) Sample Cooperative Learning Self-Monitoring Form

Group Members: **Group Name:**

Activity: **Date:**

Directions: Make a mark each time you or a team member uses a cooperative behavior that helped your group.

Collaborative Behaviors	Student 1	Student 2	Student 3	Student 4	Student 5
Shared ideas, comments, and reactions					
Helped and encouraged others					
Listened to others					
Showed empathy and respect for others					
Complimented and gave feedback to others					
Helped our group build consensus and resolve conflicts					
Asked for assistance from others					
Performed a role to help our group					

Comments:

(Continued)

FIGURE 9.8 Continued

(b) Sample Cooperative Learning Group Survey

Group Members: **Group Name:**

Activity: **Date:**

Directions: Use the following rating scale to evaluate your group's success at working cooperatively.

Rating:

1 = We struggled
2 = We need some improvement
3 = We were good
4 = We were excellent

Cooperative Behaviors	Rating			
Our group worked quietly and efficiently.	1	2	3	4
Our group developed and agreed on a plan.	1	2	3	4
Our group listened to and discussed everyone's ideas and questions.	1	2	3	4
Our group shared roles and responsibilities.	1	2	3	4
Our group shared resources.	1	2	3	4
Our group made sure everyone understood and contributed to our assignment.	1	2	3	4
Our group helped and encouraged each other.	1	2	3	4
Our group treated everyone with respect.	1	2	3	4

What things did our group do well?

How can our group improve?

(c) Sample Cooperative Learning Journal or Reflective Questions

Group Members: Group Name:

Activity: Date:

Directions: Answer the following questions; make sure you give examples to support your answers.

1.   How well did your group work together?

2.   What did you learn in your group today?

3.   What did you do that contributed to the group's work?

4.   What did you do to encourage others to participate and contribute?

5.   What did others do to support you and the work of the group?

6.   What things surprised you the most about your group?

7.   What did you or other members of your group do that interfered with your group's success?

8.   What things could your group do to improve?

Source: Gut (2000).

Using Cooperative Learning

Ms. Anderson decided to try using cooperative learning with her students after reading about and attending several professional development sessions on cooperative learning. The first time she tried it, she divided the students into groups and gave each group an assignment to work on together. She then circulated throughout the room and observed the groups. In one group, Luis, an English language learner, sat quietly and did not participate in his group's project. Luis did not speak throughout the activity, and no one spoke to him. In another group, students relied on Maria to do the assignment while they talked about an upcoming school event. In still another group, students disagreed over who would do what to complete the group's project.

Frustrated but not about to give up, Ms. Anderson realized that she needed to help her students learn to work collaboratively. She started by having pairs of students study for a quiz together and receive their average grade score. Next, she had students work together in peer tutoring dyads; she arranged it so that all students served as both tutors and tutees.

She also taught her students how to develop specific collaborative skills. For example, she had them discuss the need to encourage all group members to participate. They then brainstormed, role-played, and practiced ways to encourage others to contribute to the group. Another lesson focused on the need for and use of developing consensus.

After several lessons on collaborative skills, Ms. Anderson asked her students to write a report while working in cooperative learning groups. She told them that they would be working cooperatively and asked, "How will I know if you're cooperating?" The students' responses were listed on the blackboard and discussed.

To ensure the participation of all students, Ms. Anderson assigned shy or quiet students like Luis to groups with supportive peers. To make sure that all students contributed to and understood the group's project, she told the class that she would randomly select group members to explain parts of the group's report. To help groups work efficiently, she assigned one student in each group to be the group's recorder and another student to make sure that each member of the group participated.

As the groups worked on their projects, Ms. Anderson monitored their progress and observed their use of collaborative skills. When students demonstrated such skills, she acknowledged them. Periodically, she asked groups to model various collaborative skills. She also asked each group to keep a record of the skills they used. At the end of the class session, she and the students discussed and reflected on their collaborative skills.

- Why do you think Ms. Anderson wanted her students to use cooperative learning?
- What problems did she encounter initially?
- How did she attempt to solve these problems?
- What other problems might arise in using cooperative learning? How can teachers address these problems?
- What have been your experiences in using cooperative learning as a teacher? As a student?

of the horizontal line, (c) listing students' responses to the question "What would the skill look like?" on one side of the vertical line, and (d) listing students' responses to the question "What would the skill sound like?" on the other side of the vertical line.

You also teach students to use TARGET, a learning strategy designed to facilitate their ability to work cooperatively. TARGET involves the following steps:

1. **T**hink and talk about learning.
2. **A**im for team goals.
3. **R**eview team roles and responsibilities.
4. **G**et materials, supplies, and technology resources.
5. **E**nergize team for learning.
6. **T**ell other teams about your performance. (Mainzer, Castellani, Lowry, & Nunn, 2006, p. 3)

In addition, the round robin, the round table, and the paraphrase passport promote team-building and communication skills. **Round robin** gives each student a chance to participate and to share comments and reactions with others.

Using Technology to Promote Inclusion

MAKING LARGE- AND SMALL-GROUP INSTRUCTION ACCESSIBLE TO ALL STUDENTS

As we saw in the chapter-opening vignette, technology is available to help you differentiate your large- and small-group instruction to make it accessible to *all students*. Technologies such as using presentation software including PowerPoint and Keynote can support student learning by providing visual and audio support and computer-generated text and graphics. They also allow you to present content and highlight main points and key vocabulary while maintaining eye contact with students, and adjusting the pace of instruction. With these technologies, you can also model and provide students with high-quality notes. Presentation software can help you gain and maintain student attention and foster your students' motivation by using color, animation, sound, visuals, video, easy-to-read color combinations, and the principles of graphic design.

If slides contain a great deal of text and factual information that is read verbatim to students, student engagement and motivation can be hindered. Therefore, when using presentation software, make sure that your presentation doesn't limit student participation and become too scripted, and be prepared to deviate from the presentation based on students' responses and questions. You also should design your presentations so that you encourage students to react to the information presented and use slides to prompt and guide students in engaging in active learning experiences. You also can make them more effective by (a) limiting the text presented on each slide so that each slide contains six or fewer words per line and no more than six lines; (b) focusing the slides on big ideas and key points; (c) pairing text with motivating and appropriate visuals, links, and short audio and video segments; and (d) avoiding the overuse of animation features (Doyle & Giangreco, 2009).

You also can differentiate your large- and small-group instruction by using interactive smart-whiteboards, which provide a touch screen surface to help you present current and pertinent information, learning activities, educational games, and multimedia programs and Web sites that contain video, graphics, sound, and animation (Campbell & Mechling, 2008; Mounce, 2008). Supplement your use of interactive boards by using technology that that allows you and your students to write on or highlight computer-displayed material and images from anywhere in your room. For example, via various technologies (laptops, electronic pens, clickers), *all students* can work on an assignment, example, or problem displayed on the interactive board. Interactive boards also can help students with visual disabilities or students who have difficulty copying from the board access notes. In this system, handwriting, text, and graphics displayed on the board are sent to a computer and then printed out in either standard or Braille formats.

Here are some other ways you can use technology to create inclusive classrooms that support student learning in large- and small-group instruction:

- Supplement your technology-based presentations and your lessons by using relevant videos and images. You can search for them online using search engines that have image/video searching features or specialized image/video search sites.

- Record classroom instructional activities, class discussions, minilessons, and teacher-directed presentations and make them available to students via audio and video podcasts. Students can then download them to review material and take notes at their convenience.

- Allow your students to take notes using laptops, hand-held devices, software or digital recorders. Software can facilitate note taking by allowing your students to create bulleted lists, paste and make illustrations, and record audio-based notes (Horney et al., 2009; Manjoo, 2009).

- Motivate students to take notes by using digital pens that save and then transmit handwritten text and drawings to computers (Pogue, 2008b). Once their notes are digitized, students can edit and organize them and share them with others.

- Provide students, particularly those who are deaf or hard of hearing and those who are English language learners, with access to lectures and notes by using technology-based note-taking systems (Stinson et al., 2009). These systems provide real-time speech-to-text transcription through use of speech-to-text software, Communication Access Realtime Translation (CART), and C-Print. CART involves a note-taker taking notes that are made immediately available to students via technology. C-Print is a computerized abbreviation and phonetic system to record comments of teachers and students, which are then displayed as text for others via a computer. At the end of class sessions, text files are edited to provide students with notes (Hopkins, 2006).

- Provide students with access to notes and handouts by scanning these materials and printing them or converting them to Braille (Hopkins, 2006). Students with visual disabilities also can use *Braille Lite,* a personal digital assistant that allows students to take and retrieve notes in Braille and store books and other important documents and files. Similarly, *Braille and Speak,* a handheld note taker, allows students to record notes in class in Braille and then read the notes back using a speech synthesizer.

- Create a class Web site that allows students to access teacher- or peer-prepared class notes and outlines, assignments and their directions, and independent and guided practice activities. Your Web site also can

(Continued)

include a page called the Homework Assistance Center, which provides access to homework assignments and due dates, your homework policies, and suggestions to guide families in helping their children complete their homework. You also provide students with a list of homework assistance Web sites and other resources (e.g., sites, search tools, virtual trips, books, and articles) that can be used in completing the homework assignments (Bouck et al., 2007), and allow them to submit their homework electronically.

- Structure in-class and homework assignments so they provide students with the opportunity to use educational game software programs and play Internet-based academically integrated games that are linked to your curriculum and learning standards (Bouck et al., 2007; Salend, 2009). Using software programs and Web sites, you can create or have students access novel and motivating learning activities and problem solving experiences across the curriculum

that are presented via video, interactive smart-whiteboard, PowerPoint, or collaborative game formats (Barab, Gresalfi, & Arici, 2009; Cote, 2007; Gee & Levine, 2009; Mounce, 2008).

- Use technology to provide students with opportunities to work collaboratively. Software is available that allows you and your students to engage in online, real-time, and interactive learning collaborations including text/audio/video and closed-captioning communications, synchronized notes, and work sharing. Software programs also are available that facilitate text editing collaborations by maintaining backups of all revisions to products, and allowing all group members to make, view, and track changes and cursor movements from anywhere and at anytime.

- Use technology to foster your use of peer tutoring and classwide peer tutoring systems (Van Norman & Wood, 2008; Wood, Mackiewicz, Van Norman, & Cooke, 2007). These technologies can assist you and your students in creating peer-tutoring content and materials, providing feedback and support to tutors and tutees, and monitoring and assessing student performance.

Whereas round robin involves oral sharing, **round table** involves passing a pencil and paper around so that each student can contribute to the group's response. The **paraphrase passport** requires students to paraphrase the statements of their teammate who has just spoken and then share their own ideas and perspectives.

Communication and consensus skills can be fostered by such strategies as *talking chips* and *spend-a-buck*. **Talking chips** helps students participate equally by giving each of them a set number of talking chips, which are placed in the middle of the work area each time a student speaks. Once students use up all their chips, they cannot speak until all group members have used all their chips. **Spend-a-buck** helps groups reach a consensus by giving each group member four quarters, which are then spent on the group's options.

Another method of teaching cooperative learning skills is **role delineation**, in which each member of the group is given a specific role (O'Brien, 2007). For example, to produce a written product, a team might need a reader, a group facilitator to promote brainstorming and decision making, a recorder to record all contributions, a writer to edit the product, and a reporter to share information about the group's process and product. Other students might be assigned the roles of keeping the group on task, keeping track of time, explaining word meanings, managing materials, monitoring the group's noise level, operating technology, encouraging all group members to participate and help others, and providing positive comments. Periodically, students can complete evaluation sheets that ask them to react to the roles and contributions of group members, as well as suggest what the group could do to improve.

Monitoring groups and providing feedback can build cooperative skills. Therefore, it is important for you to observe groups, model cooperative skills, intervene when necessary, and provide feedback on group processing skills. It also is important for you to involve students in reflecting on their cooperative behaviors and experiences. Students can give feedback on their own collaborative skills by self-monitoring their individual or their group's collaborative skills (see Figure 9.8a) or completing a brief survey (see Figure 9.8b). After students complete a cooperative lesson, they can be encouraged to reflect on their experience and comment on how well the group is working collaboratively by keeping a journal or responding to reflective questions (see Figure 9.8c). You also can use sentence completion questions to prompt students to reflect on their group's collaborative efforts. For example, after working collaboratively, students can be asked to respond to these statements:

- Our group was good at _____.
- Our group needs to work on _____.

You also can adapt these formats to guide your observations and reflections of your students' cooperative behaviors.

Evaluate Cooperative Learning

In addition to evaluating your students' ability to work together, you can evaluate groups based on their mastery of subject matter. To promote peer support and group accountability, students are evaluated as a group, and each student's learning contributes to the group's evaluation. A popular method for evaluating cooperative learning is the *group project/group grade* format. The group submits for evaluation one final product (a report, an oral presentation) that represents all members' contributions. You then evaluate the product and give each group member the same grade.

In another evaluation format, *contract grading,* groups contract for a grade based on the amount of work they agree to do according to a set of criteria. Thus, group members who have different skill levels can perform different parts of the task according to their ability. For example, a cooperative lesson might contain five activities, some more difficult than others, with each activity worth 10 points. The contract between you and the groups might then specify the criteria the groups must meet to achieve an A (50 points), a B (40 points), or a C (30 points).

> **Making Connections**
> Find out more about grading alternatives in Chapter 12.

Some teachers use the *group average method,* where individual grades on a quiz or part of a project are averaged into a group grade that each group member receives. Each group member receives the average grade. For example, each group member could be given an individualized test tailored to his or her abilities in math. During the week, group members help each other master their assignments and prepare for their tests.

When using group average method, you should be aware of some situations that you may need to address. At first, some students may resist the concept of group grades. You can minimize this resistance by assuring students that group members will be assigned only work that they can complete. Inform students that if all group members do their best and help others, they will all receive good grades. Although the group average grade can give students strong incentives to help others learn the material, it can serve to punish good students and rewards free-riders. If you find that is the case, you should consider using other grading alternatives. For instance, some teachers modify the group average by using improvement scores. In this system, students are assigned a base score, depending on their prior performance, and earn points for their teams by improving on their base score.

SUMMARY

This chapter offered guidelines for differentiating large- and small-group instruction to meet the unique learning needs of students. As you review the questions posed in this chapter, remember the following points.

How Can I Differentiate Large-Group Instruction for Students?
CEC 3, 4, 5, 6, 7, 9; PRAXIS 3; INTASC 2, 3, 4, 5, 6, 7, 9

You can have students work collaboratively, use presentation software and interactive boards, encourage students to participate and ask questions, help students take notes, teach note-taking skills and strategies, foster students' listening skills, gain and maintain students' attention, and motivate students.

How Can I Use Effective Teacher-Centered Instruction?
CEC 3, 4, 5, 6, 7, 9; PRAXIS 3; INTASC 2, 3, 4, 5, 6, 7, 9

To teach effectively, you should establish the lesson's purpose; review prerequisite skills; give clear, explicit, and complete directions, explanations, and relevant examples; provide time for active and guided practice; promote active responding and check for comprehension; give frequent, prompt, and specific feedback; offer time for independent activities; summarize main points; and evaluate mastery, maintenance, and generalization.

How Can I Successfully Use Cooperative Learning Arrangements With Students?
CEC 3, 4, 5, 6, 7, 9; 10, PRAXIS 3; INTASC 2, 3, 4, 5, 6, 7, 9

You can select an appropriate cooperative learning format, establish guidelines for working collaboratively, form heterogeneous cooperative groups, arrange the classroom for cooperative learning, develop students' cooperative skills, and evaluate cooperative learning.

MR. PIKE

As Mr. Pike's students enter his classroom, they start working on either independent reading or journal writing. Mr. Pike then shares a book with them. He is reading an African folktale, which is part of a theme on understanding people from diverse cultures. Before reading the story, Mr. Pike discusses the African reverence for nature and the use of animals in folktales to represent human traits.

As a follow-up activity to his lesson on folktales, Mr. Pike asks his students to work in groups to write and illustrate a short folktale using animals as the characters in the story, to be read to or performed for the class in a week. Before assigning students to groups, Mr. Pike conducts a lesson and discussion on folktales. While the students work, Mr. Pike circulates around the room to observe and meet with individual students and groups. One group conference focuses on why that group selected a camel to be

its main character; another conference deals with creating a storyline.

The group activity is followed by individualized reading. Students independently read books about individuals from various cultures that they have selected from a list prepared and previewed by Mr. Pike and the class. When students come across a word they don't know, Mr. Pike prompts them to figure it out by asking what words make sense or encouraging them to sound it out. Students who select the same book to read are grouped together in literature circles, and they meet with Mr. Pike to discuss the book and work on group projects. Steven, a student with a severe cognitive disability, chooses a picture book to read with another student. Occasionally, Mr. Pike teaches a minilesson to help his students learn new vocabulary, spelling, and strategies for

Differentiating Reading, Writing, and Spelling Instruction

reading fluently. While Mr. Pike teaches his minilesson, his paraeducator works with Steven and several other students on phonemic awareness, word identification skills, and vocabulary.

The students and Mr. Pike also read these books during sustained silent reading. Students react to what they have read by making entries in their literature response journals. Mr. Pike periodically collects and reads the journals and responds to students' entries via written comments or individual conferences.

What strategies does Mr. Pike use to promote the literacy skills of his students? After reading this chapter, you

should have the knowledge, skills, and dispositions to answer this as well as the following questions:

- How can I help my students learn to read?
- How can I help my students learn to write?
- How can I help my students learn to spell?

In addition to differentiating instruction for diverse learners and teaching with large and small groups, teachers like Mr. Pike also need to help students develop literacy skills. This chapter offers guidelines for differentiating instruction so that you can help your students learn to read, write, and spell.

HELPING STUDENTS LEARN TO READ

HOW CAN I HELP STUDENTS LEARN TO READ? You can support students' reading by using the principles of effective early reading interventions, offering specialized interventions to supplement instruction for students, and focusing your instruction on developing and promoting their phonemic awareness, reading fluency, text comprehension, and vocabulary.

Offer Early Identification and Intervention

Early identification and intervention are critical aspects in teaching students who have reading difficulties (Bailet, Repper, Piasta, & Murphy, 2009; Burke, Hagen-Burke, Kwok, & Parker, 2009; Lo, Wang, & Haskell, 2009). Research indicates that students who experience reading difficulties have problems with **reading fluency**, which refers to the speed and accuracy with which they read orally. Reading fluency also includes **prosody**, a student's ability to read smoothly with proper levels of stress, pauses, volume, and intonation (Hudson, Pullen, Lane, & Torgesen, 2009). In addition to reading in a slow and halting way, mixing letters and words up, losing their place, and not remember what they read (Mercer & Pullen, 2009), they exhibit difficulties in the areas of phonemic awareness, vocabulary development, memory, decoding, word recognition, reading comprehension, and using clues to help them read. These students also are characterized by their failure to respond to instructional strategies that are usually effective in teaching students to read. Because reading is an integral aspect of many learning activities, their challenges in learning to read also may increase the likelihood that they may experience behavioral difficulties (McIntosh, Horner, Chard, Dickey, & Braun, 2008).

Students identified as having reading difficulties are not likely to outgrow them; therefore, it is important to recognize and address their special challenges early and comprehensively (Phillips, Lonigan, & Wyatt, 2009; Rader, 2008). You also can support their literacy development by collaborating with other teachers, literacy specialists, librarians, speech and language teachers, paraeducators, and family members to implement the principles of effective early reading interventions (see Figure 10.1) as well as the following guidelines for developing their phonemic awareness, phonics skills, reading fluency, vocabulary, and text comprehension (Falk-Ross et al., 2009). Because literacy instruction should be sequential, specific, and intensive, it is important for you to identify students' frustration, instructional,

FIGURE 10.1 Principles of effective early reading interventions

1. Recognize that reading is a developmental process.
2. Use an instructional sequence that gradually moves from easy to more difficult tasks.
3. Promote students' phonetic awareness, print awareness, oral language, alphabetic understanding and decoding.
4. Provide instructional supports in the initial stages of reading instruction and gradually remove them.
5. Offer direct and explicit instruction to help students develop accurate and fluent word analysis skills.
6. Emphasize use of language and teach vocabulary in a systematic and integrative way.
7. Structure learning activities so that students have numerous opportunities to respond, practice and receive feedback.
8. Activate students' prior knowledge.
9. Incorporate students' experiences, ideas, and referents into instructional activities.
10. Provide students with meaningful interactions with text.
11. Begin to develop students' comprehension skills by exposing them to a variety of texts.
12. Assess student progress on a regular basis.

Sources: Lo et al. (2009); Menzies et al. (2008); Seo et al. (2008); Whalon et al. (2009).

and independent levels and make sure instruction begins and proceeds at an appropriate place and pace (Harn, Linan-Thompson, & Roberts, 2008). As we will discuss, no one approach or program will meet the needs of *all students*, so it also is important for you to employ a balanced approach to teaching reading and supplement your instruction with specialized reading programs, strategies, and materials (Menzies, Mahdavi, & Lewis, 2008; Seo et al., 2008). It also is essential that you use ongoing assessments of student progress to evaluate and inform your teaching (Jenkins, Graff, & Miglioretti, 2009; Roehrig, Walton Duggar, Moats, Glover, & Mincey, 2008). As you plan your literacy instruction, remember to use your school and community's library as a valuable resource.

Making Connections
Find out more about ways to monitor your students' learning progress in Chapter 12.

Offer Specialized Interventions to Supplement Instruction for Diverse Students

Although the effective strategies that are presented in this chapter are relevant for *all students*, it is also important for you to offer specialized interventions to supplement your reading instruction for some of your students (Johnston, McDonnell, & Hawken, 2008; Kostewicz & Kubina, 2008). Because of syntactical, representational, and phonological variations across languages and limited literacy in their first language and vocabulary development in their second language, you may need to employ specialized interventions to help English language learners read in their new language (Lovett et al., 2008; Pilonieta & Medina, 2009). For example, because some phonemes may not occur in students' native language or letters may have different sounds in different languages, some of your English language learners may need additional assistance to benefit from phonemic awareness and phonics instruction. Similarly, students whose first language does not use an alphabetic script (e.g., Chinese and Japanese) or has regular phoneme/grapheme correspondence (e.g., Spanish, Italian, Turkish), may experience difficulties connecting regular and irregular letters and sounds in English (Guajardo Alvarado, 2007). Thus, for some English language learners, it may be effective to initially teach them to read using instruction and interventions in their native language, to employ phonemic awareness and phonics instruction that includes variations in the order of the sounds that you teach, to explain the cultural meanings of words and phrases, and to use a range of techniques to foster their vocabulary development (Denton et al., 2008; Goldenberg, 2008). It also is important to try to distinguish whether their reading miscues and reading fluency difficulties are a result of decoding, vocabulary or pronunciation difficulties and to respond accordingly.

The success of your literacy instruction for these students also can be enhanced by providing them with opportunities to read multicultural and bilingual challenging and readable materials that relate to their experiential, linguistic, and cultural backgrounds (Levine & McCloskey, 2009). When the students' native and second languages share similarities and cognates, you can help students develop their vocabulary by making these commonalities explicit (Agirdag, 2009; Dong, 2009). For example, you can point out to your Spanish-speaking students that the English word *community* is *communidad* in Spanish. You also can pair vocabulary words with visuals depicting them, act out vocabulary for them, and give them bilingual dictionaries and thesauri (Goldenberg, 2008). It is also important for you to use effective text comprehension strategies and ESL techniques and review and practice to make sure your students develop basic vocabulary in their new language.

Students with moderate and significant intellectual disabilities also need specialized interventions to support their reading development (Allor, Mathes, Champlin, & Cheatham, 2009; Browder, Ahlgrim-Delzell, Courtade, Gibbs, & Flowers, 2008). For these students, supplement your reading instruction by providing them with systematic and repeated phonemic awareness, phonics, vocabulary, and word recognition instruction accompanied by ongoing practice, prompting and feedback. You can foster

Making Connections
This discussion of effective text comprehension and ESL techniques relates to what we discussed earlier in Chapter 8.

the reading skills of these students by using read-alouds and reading games; pairing vocabulary with student-friendly language and pictorials, digital books, videos, and gestures; and focusing instruction on high-frequency sight words (Douglas et al., 2009). These students may benefit from your varying your instructional sequence by using model-lead-test, time delay, and the system of least prompts. **Model-lead-test** involves your modeling and orally presenting the material to be learned, helping students understand it through prompts and practice, and testing students' mastery. **Time delay** is a procedure designed to foster student learning by delivering prompts that limit the likelihood that students will make errors (Browder, Ahlgrim-Delzell, Spooner, Mimis, & Baker, 2009). It can be implemented as progressive time delay where you gradually increase the time between presentation of a word and the corresponding prompt via use of the following steps:

1. Present a flash card and ask students to identify the word.
2. Prompt students immediately (0-second delay) by providing the answer during several trials.
3. Show students flash cards, and they respond and receive feedback from you.
4. Repeat these steps and increase the amount of time between the presentation of the flash card and your statement of the answer.
5. Gradually fade out your assistance so that students can respond quickly and independently.

You also can use a constant time delay system where the time between the presentation of the word and the delivery of the assistance remains the same throughout your instruction (Tucker Cohen, Wolff Heller, Alberto, & Fredrick, 2008), or you can vary the number of words you teach (Pruitt & Cooper, 2008).

The **system of least prompts** involves (a) giving students the opportunity to respond without assistance, (b) providing assistance (if needed) by modeling the correct response and having students imitate it, and (c) physically guiding students in making the correct response (if needed). Because many of these students may have difficulties responding verbally, you also may need to foster their responses by pointing to the correct response or via the use of augmentative communication systems.

Promote Phonemic Awareness

Effective early reading intervention programs promote students' **phonemic awareness**, also called *phonological awareness*, the processing and manipulation of the different sounds that make up words and the understanding that spoken and written language are linked (Burke et al., 2009; Lo et al., 2009). Phonemic awareness, which is different from phonics instruction, is critical to the development of the *alphabetic principle*, the ability to associate letters with their corresponding sounds, which serves as the foundation for decoding words and learning to read (Cheesman, McGuire, Shankweiler, & Coyne, 2009; Hudson et al., 2009). Phonemic awareness instruction usually includes activities to develop students' ability to hear rhymes, identify sounds, blend sounds into words, segment or break words into sounds, and manipulate or delete sounds (Cunningham & Hall, 2009; Fox, 2010; Groves Scott, 2009; Pullen & Lloyd, 2007). Phonemic awareness provides students with the skills necessary to benefit from a phonetic-based approach to learning to read (which we will discuss later in this chapter) (Bailet et al., 2009; Johnston, et al., 2008; Menzies et al., 2008).

Motivate Students to Read   Because students develop their phonemic awareness and reading proficiency by reading regularly, it is important to motivate *all students* to read (Dunston & Gambrell, 2009; Seo et al., 2008). You can do this by

- modeling the enjoyment of reading and demonstrating that reading can be fun;
- using reading materials that are well written, easy to comprehend, challenging, and interesting to students and related to their lives;

- giving students a range of reading choices including stories and information books;
- creating a relaxed and safe learning and reading environment;
- allowing students to read with other students;
- playing recordings of selections and students' favorite stories and singing songs;
- using games, technology, and the Internet;
- giving students a variety of ways to express their reactions to material they have read;
- acknowledging students' efforts, persistence, and attempts to read as well as their progress (Rasinski et al., 2009; Sanacore, 2005; Seo et al., 2008; Tatum, 2006; Vacca et al., 2009).

Making Connections
You can use many of the motivation enhancing strategies we discussed earlier in Chapter 9 to encourage your students to read.

As Mr. Pike did in the chapter-opening vignette, you can motivate students to read by choosing reading selections that relate to students' experiences and cultures.

Reading Aloud to Students.   Reading aloud to students can motivate them by introducing them to the enjoyment and excitement of reading. Reading aloud to students also allows you to model good oral reading, promote phonological awareness, vocabulary development and comprehension, and offer background knowledge in such areas as story structure and content (Allor et al., 2009; Verden & Hickman, 2009). When reading to students, introduce the selection by discussing the title and cover of the book and asking students to make predictions about the book. You also can introduce the author and illustrator and talk with students about other books they have read by the author or on a similar topic or theme. As you read to students, promote their interest and understanding by using animated expressions; displaying illustrations so that all students can see and react to them; relating the book to students' experiences; discussing the book in a lively, inviting, and thought-provoking manner; and offering students a variety of learning activities (i.e., writing, drama, art) to respond to and express their feelings about the selection.

Picture and Patterned Books.   You can motivate students to read and write through the use of picture and patterned books. Whereas **picture books** are short books that use pictures and illustrations to enhance the reader's understanding of the meaning and content of the story (Martinez, Roser, & Harmon, 2009; Zambo, 2007), **patterned books** use a predictable and repeated linguistic and/or story pattern (Zipprich, Grace, & Grote-Garcia, 2009). Although they are appropriate for *all students,* they are particularly effective in helping students with reading difficulties and English language learners learn a wide range of reading strategies including decoding, predicting, and using context, semantics and syntactical cues.

Involve Families   The active involvement of families also can motivate students and help them develop their reading and phonemic awareness skills (Rasinski, Homan, Biggs, 2009). Family members can serve as role models by reading a variety of materials, showing their children that reading is useful, fun, interesting, and informative. You can support the involvement of families by providing them with copies and lists of age- and reading level–appropriate books, sharing effective reading instructional strategies with them, and communicating regularly with them about their child's reading progress.

Family members can promote literacy by showing that reading is fun, interesting, and informative. How do you collaborate with family members to promote literacy?

Promote Reading Fluency

Reading fluency is an essential skill for you to promote (Hudson et al., 2009). It is an especially important reading goal for students whose reading difficulties make them reluctant to read, especially in front of others. You can address their reluctance and develop their reading fluency skills in several ways (Bender & Larkin, 2009). You can use choral or echo reading, also called duolog or paired reading, which involves you and your students reading selections, stories, poems, books, and student-authored materials together, paired reading, where they read simultaneously with you or classmate (Rasinski et al., 2009; Whalon et al., 2009). Rather than calling on them, you can solicit their permission to be called on to read aloud.

You also can prepare them to read a specific selection fluently in class by preteaching high-frequency and difficult-to-read words and vocabulary, modeling fluent reading for them, and using repeated reading and previewing of easily readable text (Ferreri, 2009; Rasinski et al., 2009; Vadasy & Sanders, 2008). In **repeated reading**, students are given numerous opportunities to practice reading short (between 50 and 200 words), appropriate, and relevant materials at their independent or instructional level until they can read them fluently. Repeated reading typically involves students reading passages aloud to an educator or a classmate who also maintains a record of the student's reading, receiving corrective feedback on errors and performance feedback on their accuracy, speed, expression, volume, and smoothness, and continuing to read the selection until they can read it fluently (Alber-Morgan et al., 2007). You also can use timed readings where students work toward reaching a fluency goal by reading different passages at a specific reading level before moving to passages at the next level (Pruitt & Cooper, 2008), or read lyrics of songs (Patel & Laud, 2007). You also can motivate them to do repeated readings by varying what students read (e.g., sometimes you can have them read cartoons or sentence strips), where they read (e.g., sometimes have them read in different locations in your classroom or the school), who they read with (e.g., sometimes have them read with you, classmates, other adults, etc.), and what devices they use while reading (e.g., sometimes have them read with special pointers and highlighters, digital recorders, swimming goggles, binoculars, etc.) (Higbee Mandlebaum, Hodges, & Messenheimer, 2007).

Because repeated reading is most effective when students have a model so they can hear fluent reading, you can use various previewing techniques to enhance its effectiveness (Welsch, 2006). **Previewing** refers to methods that give a student opportunities to read or listen to text prior to reading (Kubina & Hughes, 2007). Listening previewing involves a student listening and following along as an adult or peer reads the selection aloud or having the student read along with a classmate or adult. Other previewing strategies include oral previewing, where the students read the passage aloud prior to the whole-class reading session; and silent previewing, where students read the passage silently before the reading session.

You can engage in several other teaching practices to foster your students' reading fluency (Guthrie et al., 2009; Seo et al., 2008). Offer them opportunities to read each day, give them reading materials that interest them and allow them to be successful, use speed-based drill-and-practice activities, and have them set goals and record and graph their progress. You can emphasize fluency by prompting them to try to make their eyes go faster, combine several words together at the same time, pair words like *a* and *the* with words that follow them, and ask themselves if the word makes sense. You can teach and model reading at an appropriate pace and with expression, tracking with fingers, and encourage students to do the same (Peia Oakes, Harris, & Churley Barr, 2009). As students read and encounter difficulty in decoding words, you also can offer immediate and specific corrective feedback including encouraging them to sound the word out, to reread it and use word structure cues, and to relate it to their background knowledge about the text. You also can assist them by modeling and teaching them how to break the word into syllables giving them the phonetic rule, supplying them with the correct reading of the word, defining and explaining unfamiliar words, and using a variety of prompts and cues (which we will discuss later in this chapter) (Knight-McKenna, 2008).

You also can teach them to use a variety of fluency-enhancing reading strategies, including

- using root words and affixes to decode unknown words,
- pausing appropriately based on the punctuation,
- using semantic and syntactic cues to read with expression,
- self-correcting errors, and
- limiting omissions by using a finger to trace the print.

You also can record students during reading activities and have them analyze and reflect on their reading.

Foster Word Identification You can promote reading fluency by fostering your students' word identification skills (Bender & Larkin, 2009; Boyle, 2008; Ferreri, 2009). One way to do that is to teach your students to use strategies for identifying unfamiliar words. Several word recognition strategies that can help your students decode unfamiliar words, including the following:

- *Rhyming keywords:* Students read unfamiliar words by comparing them with rhymes of familiar or keywords that they already know (e.g., using the keyword *time* as a rhyme or prompt to read *crime*).
- *Vowel alert:* Students read unfamiliar words by identifying the vowel sound after examining the letters that precede and follow the vowels.
- *Seek the part you know:* Students read unfamiliar words by identifying the parts of the unfamiliar words they know (e.g., dividing *rainbow* into *rain* and *bow*).
- *Peeling off:* Students read unfamiliar words by using affixes at the beginnings and endings of words and then focusing on the root word (e.g., peeling off the affixes *un* and *ing* to facilitate reading of *unlocking*) (Ehri, Satlow, & Gaskins, 2009; Lovett, Lacerenza, & Borden, 2000; Rupley et al., 2009).

Your students can learn to use learning strategies to help them learn to read unknown words (Boyle, 2008; Ehri et al., 2009). You can help students read unknown words by teaching them to use their knowledge of the initial consonant or consonants (*s* in *sat*), referred to as the *onsets,* and the vowels that follow the consonant(s) to create the rest of the syllable (*at* in *sat*), referred to as the *rimes* (Ehri et al., 2009; Rupley et al., 2009). You can facilitate this by using color coding to teach onsets and rimes (Hines, 2009), and by teaching your students to use the FISH strategy, which involves:

Find the rime (the first vowel and the rest of the word)

Identify the rime or a word you know that ends like that

Say the rime (the word you know without the first sound)

Hook the new onset (beginning sound) to the rime (Whitaker, Harvey, Hassell, Linder, & Tutterrow, 2006, p. 15).

Students also can use the STOP strategy, which involves **S**taring at the unknown word, **T**elling yourself each letter sound, **O**pening your mouth and saying each letter, and **P**utting the letters together to say the word. They can use DISSECT or WIST, too (Boyle, 2008; Ehri et al., 2009).

You also can foster students' word identification skills by teaching them to use syllable-based reading strategies, which help them learn how to break difficult to read words into syllables or recognizable chunks (Bhattacharya, 2006; Boyle, 2008; Knight-McKenna, 2008; Rupley et al., 2009). For example, first teach students to identify the different syllable types and then (a) divide words into their syllable segments, (b) highlight each segment by underlining or circling it, (c) pronounce each segment, and (d) decode the whole word. You also can prompt them to isolate difficult sounds

REFLECTIVE

What strategies do you use to identify unfamiliar words? How did you learn these strategies?

in words, to focus their attention on familiar letter combinations and beginning and ending sounds, to use context clues, and to finger-point words while reading (Vadasy, Sanders, & Peyton, 2005).

Students can also be taught to use an *integrated processing* strategy to help them read unknown words. Students implement this strategy by making a line below each part of an unknown word, verbalizing each part of the word without raising their writing instrument, and attempting to quickly reread the word. The student then rereads the sentence, and makes sure that the word makes sense in the context of the sentence.

Repeated reading practice, word flashcard, and technology-presented drills can be used to provide the repetition that some students need to identify words. You can modify these drills by using interspersal of known items, a technique that involves adjusting the percentage of unknown and known words. For example, an interspersed word sequence of 30% unknown words and 70% known words has been successful in helping students with reading difficulties recognize words.

Environmental Print.   Environmental print—that is, materials that are found in students' natural environments—can help *all students*, particularly those who are learning English, develop their reading fluency and give meaning to printed symbols (Seo et al., 2008). You prompt students to interact with environmental print by posting important words and vocabulary in different locations in your classroom (e.g., walls, posters, sheets on students' desks) as well as signs, labels, posters, calendars, advertisements, menus, and wall charts (Cunningham, 2008). You also can provide them with opportunities to read online, magazines and newspapers written at different levels of difficulty (Weigel & Gardner, 2009; Wolf & Barzillai, 2009).

Support Older Struggling Readers   You need to understand and be particularly sensitive to older students who struggle with reading (Joseph & Schisler, 2009; Roberts et al., 2008; Rupley et al., 2009). In addition to motivating these students to read using the strategies we discussed, you can make reading an integral part of content area instruction.

REFLECTIVE

What types of cues do you use to prompt your students' reading?

It is also important for you to be aware of students' frustration, instructional, and independent instructional reading levels (Vacca et al., 2009). You can use this information to plan instruction so that students are working on learning activities and using reading materials that challenge and interest them and are not asked to perform tasks that cause them to become frustrated and anxious (Joseph & Schisler, 2009).

You also can offer specialized instruction to address their needs by

- using high-interest, easy-to-read, multicultural, age- and curriculum-appropriate print and online materials and popular culture and young adult novels and books that address themes that are interesting and beneficial to students;
- delivering nonintrusive and age-appropriate prompts, error correction techniques, and instructional feedback;
- teaching phonemic awareness and skills via multisyllable age-appropriate words and lyrics from popular songs and poetry;
- teaching visual and media literacy;
- using videos to supplement print materials;
- developing word recognition and phonetic skills and fluency via reading games;
- reading aloud to students and providing them with time for independent reading;
- expanding their vocabulary knowledge;
- having them work collaboratively with their classmates;
- providing tutoring to develop and support specific reading skills;
- assessing and acknowledging their progress (Bruce, 2008; Dunston & Gambrell, 2009; Guthrie et al., 2009; Heron-Hruby & Alvermann, 2009; Joseph & Schisler, 2009;

UDL and YOU
Using Prompting and Cuing Strategies

Like Mr. Pike, you can incorporate UDL into your literacy instruction by using prompting and cuing strategies to help your students read difficult or unfamiliar words (Ferreri, 2009; Seo et al., 2008; Zipprich et al., 2009). *Reading prompts* refer to cues and reminders that assist students in reading successfully and allow you to guide and correct them in a respectful and supportive way. They can be divided into two types: teacher prompting and student prompting. Teacher prompting is used by the teacher to help students make the correct response and guide them to use effective cues. Student prompting is used by students to determine the correct response and includes configuration and context cues.

Both teacher and student prompting should be natural and age- and culturally appropriate, and should be faded out as students progress. For example, it is often more appropriate to teach secondary students to use configuration, context, syntactic, semantic, and syntactic cues than to deliver language, visual, and physical prompts to them.

Language Prompts Language cues use the students' language skills as the basis for triggering the correct response. For example, if a student had difficulty decoding the word *store,* a vocabulary cue such as "You buy things at a . . ." might elicit the correct response. Other language-oriented cues include rhyming ("It rhymes with *door*"), word associations ("Choo! Choo!" to cue the word *train*), analogies ("Light is to day as dark is to night"), antonyms ("It's the opposite of . . ."), and binary choices ("Is the trip long or short?"). Language cues also include phonemic cues, which entail prompting students to read a word by sounding it out, by providing them with the initial sound or syllable, and by giving them the phonetic rule (e.g., "This word follows the short 'a' rule").

Visual Prompts Visual prompts can help students focus on certain aspects of words. For instance, attention to medial vowels can be fostered visually by color cues (make the medial vowel a different color than the other letters), size cues (enlarge the medial vowel while keeping the other letters constant, such as *cAt*), or graphic cues (accentuate the medial vowel by underlining or circling it, such as *cat*). Visual prompts are valuable in correcting reversals. For example, difficulty discriminating *b* and *d* can be reduced by cuing one of the letters graphically.

Pictorial prompting, in which words and their pictures are linked, is a good strategy for helping deaf and hard-of-hearing students and students with intellectual disabilities read words. It is especially helpful in reading nouns and prepositions. These students also may benefit from picture reading, which involves students responding to teachers asking questions about characters, objects, topics, and sequences in wordless books.

Pictorial cues can also be helpful to students who reverse words or confuse homophones. For example, if a student typically reads the word *saw* as *was,* a drawing of a saw above the word *saw* would help the student make this distinction. Similarly, homophones like *sea* and *see* can be differentiated for students by drawings of waves and eyes, respectively (Seo et al., 2008). Finally, visual cues, such as pointing to an object in the classroom or showing a numeral, can be used to prompt the reading of words that correspond, respectively, to objects in the classroom and number words.

Physical Prompts Physical prompts are most effective in communicating words or concepts with perceptually salient features (Johnston et al., 2008). These words can be cued by miming the distinct qualities or actions associated with them. In addition to miming, you can use finger spelling or pointing as a cue to elicit a correct response.

Configuration Cues Configuration cues relate to the outline of the word and can be useful when there are noticeable differences in the shape and length of words. Students use configuration cues when they note the length of the words and the size and graphic characteristics of the letters. While research on the effectiveness of configuration cues is inconclusive, it appears that they are most effective when used with context cues and other prompting strategies.

Context Cues The context in which the word is presented can provide useful cues for determining the pronunciation of unknown words. Potential context cues that students can use include syntactic, semantic, and picture features of the text. Context cues are best suited for words that occur near the middle or the end of the sentence.

Syntactic Cues Syntactic cues deal with the grammatical structure of the sentence containing the word. The syntactic structure of English dictates that only certain words can fit into a particular part of a sentence or statement. Thus, students can be taught to use parts of sentences to figure out difficult words.

Semantic Cues Semantic cues, available by examining the meanings of the text, can help students improve their word identification skills. Semantic cues can be taught by having students closely examine the sentence containing the unknown word, as well as the entire reading selection in which the word appears. These cues are particularly appropriate when students are learning to read abstract words.

Pictorial Cues Many reading passages contain illustrations to promote fluency, comprehension, and motivation. These pictorial cues also can help students recognize new words by helping them establish the context of the story. To maximize the effects of illustrations on word recognition, the students' attention can be directed to the word and the illustration.

Making Connections
Effective strategies to develop students' text comprehension were discussed earlier in Chapter 8.

PEARSON
myeducationlab

Go to the Assignments and Activities section of the Topic *Reading Instruction* in the MyEducationLab for your course and complete the activity entitled *Context Clues*.

Konrad et al., 2007; Lewis & Ketter, 2008; Slavin, Chamberlain, & Daniels, 2007; Vacca et al., 2009).

You can support the reading of *all of your students*, especially those who struggle with reading, by allowing them to select the books they want to read (Rich, 2009). You can encourage choice by exposing them to a range of books and genres, and teaching them how to choose reading materials that are appropriate for them (Sanacore, 2005). One way to do that is to teach students to use the *Five Finger Test*, which involves students

- choosing a book that they might want to read,
- reading a page in the middle of the book,
- holding up a finger each time they encounter a word they don't know, and
- selecting another book if they hold up at least five fingers before completing the page.

You also can provide your students with a rubric for self-selecting reading material (see Table 10.1) and teach them how to use it.

Enhance Students' Text Comprehension

In addition to promoting students' phonemic awareness and reading fluency, an effective reading program also focuses on developing students' comprehension. In addition to using and teaching your students to use a variety of text comprehension strategies, you can support their text comprehension by helping them develop their vocabulary.

Develop Students' Vocabulary

Developing your students' vocabulary is a good way to enhance their reading fluency and comprehension (Ebbers & Denton, 2008; Taylor, Mraz, Nichols, Rickelman, & Wood, 2009). You can identify, preview, activate students' prior knowledge, and teach new vocabulary presented in reading selections and during academic instruction, and use effective ESL approaches and new vocabulary and concept instructional techniques with *all students* (Johnson, 2009). Some teachers use a "word of the day" technique, where they focus teaching and student attention on a word from a vocabulary list by having students engage in a variety of learning activities related to the word that provide students with numerous opportunities to see, copy, examine, say, define, use, and engage it during instruction (Vesely & Gryder, 2009).

It is important to make sure that your vocabulary instruction is relevant to your students' learning and experiences (Allor et al., 2009; Roberts et al., 2008). Therefore, focus vocabulary instruction on words that students will encounter frequently in literacy activities and content instruction, that have meaningful connections to students' lives and that are critical to them understanding the content in the instructional materials they will be reading (Ebbers & Denton, 2008; Swanson & Howerton, 2007). You can have students work in groups or individually to identify and define important vocabulary words in instructional materials and to create the following:

- Vocabulary cards with the name, picture, and definition of the term on the front of the card and the term's relationship to important content and other vocabulary on the back (see Figure 10.2 on page 385)

Teachers can promote students' reading skills by allowing them to select interesting and appropriate reading materials. How do you help students select reading materials and what types of reading materials do your students find most interesting?

TABLE 10.1 Rubric for self-selecting appropriate reading material

Book/Story/Chapter/Article Title: _____

Author(s): _____

	Score			
Readability Factors	**1**	**2**	**3**	**4**
Vocabulary • Score	• There are 10 or more words I do not know.	• There are 7–9 words I do not know.	• There are 4–6 words I do not know.	• There are 3 or fewer words I do not know.
Sentences • Score	• Almost all of the sentences are long and complex.	• A few sentences are easy but most are long and complex.	• A few sentences are long and complex but most are easy.	• Almost all of the sentences are short and easy.
Topic and Concepts • Score	• I am unfamiliar with the topic and most of the concepts are new to me.	• I know a little about the topic and concepts.	• I know much about the topic and concepts.	• I am highly familiar with the topic and none of the concepts are new to me.
Clarity of Ideas • Score	• The ideas are presented unclearly and are difficult to understand.	• A few of the ideas are presented clearly enough to understand without difficulty.	• Most of the ideas are presented clearly enough to understand easily.	• The ideas are presented very clearly and are easy to understand.
Level of Abstraction (includes figurative language, metaphors, similes, slang, symbols, theories) • Score	• The author uses language and/or presents ideas that are highly abstract.	• The author uses many abstract words and phrases and/or presents more than one abstract idea.	• The author uses a few abstract words and phrases and/or presents an abstract idea.	• The author uses language and/or presents ideas that are concrete
Organization • Score	• I cannot figure out the organization.	• It is difficult to follow the organization.	• I can follow the organization but I have to concentrate.	• I can follow the organization easily.
Design and Format (includes font, print the size, paragraph length, use of columns, use of illustrations and other visuals, and other design issues) • Score	• The material is poorly designed and the format impedes reading.	• The design and format create some problems for me.	• The design and format create no serious problems for me.	• The material is well designed and format facilitates reading.
Genre • Score	• I am not familiar with the writing form and style.	• I have only read this kind of writing once or twice.	• I have read this kind of writing a few times.	• I am very familiar with the writing form and style.

(Continued)

TABLE 10.1 **Continued**

Book/Story/Chapter/Article Title: _____

Author(s): _____

Readability Factors	Score			
	1	**2**	**3**	**4**
Interest and Motivation • Score	• I am not interested in the topic and don't have any particular motivation or reason to read this material.	• I am slightly interested in the topic and would have difficulty explaining why I want to read this material.	• I am somewhat interested in the topic and have a couple of ideas about why I want to read this material.	• I am extremely interested in the topic, highly motivated, and have a definite reason to read this material.
Pacing and Fluency • Score	• If others watched and heard me read, they would describe me as tense and my reading as choppy.	• If others watched and heard me read, they would describe me as uneasy and my reading as frequently hesitant.	• If others watched and heard me read, they would describe me as comfortable but my reading as sometimes unsure.	• If others watched and heard me read, they would describe me as relaxed and my reading as fluent.
• Total Score				

Directions:
1. Read the first page of the book. If the first page is not a full page, read the next page also.
2. Check the box of the score most appropriate for each readability factor.
3. Write the score in the box under each readability factor.
4. Total the scores.
5. Determine if you can read the material independently.
- If the total score is 30–40, the material can be read independently. If the score is 38–40, perhaps this material is too easy for you.
- If the total score is 20–29, the material is challenging. Decide which factors are most important to you. If you scored 3 or 4 on each of these factors, the material can be read independently. If you scored 1 or 2 on the most important factors, the material should be read only with assistance.
- If the total score is < 20, the material is too difficult to read without assistance.

Sources: From "How Do I Find a Book to Read? Middle and High School Students Use a Rubric for Self-Selecting Material for Independent Reading," by B. R. Schirmer and A. S. Lockman, 2001, *Teaching Exceptional Children, 34*(1), pp. 36–42. Copyright 2001 by The Council for Exceptional Children. Reprinted with permission.

- Vocabulary self-awareness charts that contain a listing of key vocabulary words, their definitions and examples, and rating by students of the extent to which they know the words well (+), somewhat (?), or not very well (–)
- Vocabulary picture dictionaries that present vocabulary words, their definitions, and student drawings depicting the major elements of the words
- Word maps that present the vocabulary word with its meaning, related key words, synonyms, antonyms, as well as drawing of the word and a sentence using it
- Personal vocabulary journals that contain various entries related to vocabulary words they are learning and hints for learning and remembering

FIGURE 10.2 Sample vocabulary card

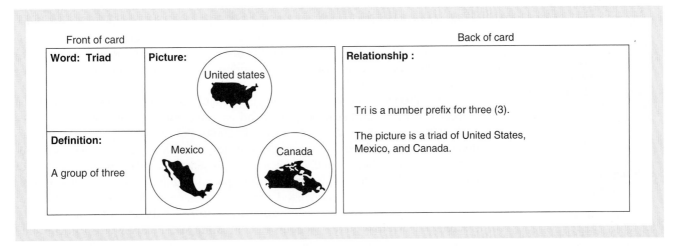

Source: Taylor, Mraz, et al. (2009).

definitions (Lee & Herner-Patnod, 2007; Swanson & Howerton, 2007; Taylor, Mraz, et al., 2009)

These products also can be digitalized so that all students can access them when they need them (Skylar et al., 2007).

You can help students develop their vocabulary by providing them with repeated opportunities to learn about and use vocabulary words in a variety of contexts, especially those words that have multiple meanings (Roberts et al., 2008; Swanson & Howerton, 2007). For example, Alber and Foil (2003) suggest that teachers use the following instructional sequence to introduce vocabulary to students:

- Visually display the word, pronounce it, and ask students to say it.
- Discuss the word's meaning(s), display pictures illustrating the word, and give students multiple examples of the word's usage in context.
- Link the word and its meanings to students' prior knowledge and prompt students to describe their experiences with the word.
- Provide students with multiple opportunities to use the word in context and different situations and offer specific feedback.
- Promote generalization by teaching multiple examples and uses of the word, helping students understand slight differences in words that have similar meanings (e.g., integrate and incorporate), prompting and reinforcing students' use of new vocabulary, and having students self-record their use of vocabulary words.

You can introduce and then review new and critical vocabulary throughout your lessons by pairing it with pictorials and videos, linking words and their meanings to kinesthetic and sensory experiences such as gestures, and encouraging students to use visual imagery to picture the words in their heads (Allor et al., 2009; Whalon et al., 2009). You also can create a memorable event or physically act out with your students the important attributes of vocabulary words (Alber & Foil, 2003). For example, dress up in a memorable way to depict the word *garish,* or you and your students can spin around to introduce them to the salient features of the word *pirouette.* In addition, explain new vocabulary after it is encountered in a reading selection, use them frequently, and have students maintain a file or notebook containing new vocabulary words, their definitions, and drawings depicting them. Other vocabulary development strategies include using repetition, modeling, games, and drama and a cloze strategy, posting words throughout your classroom, and teaching students to use print and online versions of dictionaries and thesauruses (Falk-Ross et al., 2009; Morgan & Moni, 2007; Roberts et al., 2008).

Making Connections
This discussion of strategies for teaching vocabulary builds on our earlier discussion of effective ESL and dual language teaching techniques discussed earlier in Chapter 8.

Making Connections
Find out more about graphic organizers, semantic webs, mnemonic devices, and memory-enhancing strategies in Chapter 11.

PEARSON
myeducationlab
Go to the Assignments and Activities section of the Topic *Reading Instruction* in the MyEducationLab for your course and complete the activity entitled *Vocabulary and Fluency*.

Making Connections
This discussion relates to the use of peer tutoring and classwide peer tutoring discussed earlier in Chapter 9.

You also can help your students foster their vocabulary by teaching them how to use context clues, cognates, and key morphemes, affixes, and root words to determine meanings; discussing the origins of words; explaining idiomatic expressions, synonyms, and antonymns; and teaching students to use mnemonic devices to foster their memory skills (Dong, 2009; Ebbers & Denton, 2008; Reed, 2008; Taylor et al., 2009). For example, you can teach students that *alt* means *high* and *anti* means *against.*

You also can visually present the critical features of new vocabulary words via graphic organizers and semantic webs and use mnemonic and key word strategies (Swanson & Howerton, 2007; Taylor et al., 2009). For example, you and your students can create semantic word maps depicting the connections between vocabulary words and other related concepts. Or present vocabulary words via use of concept wheels, circles divided into sections presenting the word, its picture, its definition, and other words associated with it. Another visually oriented method of teaching new vocabulary words is **semantic feature analysis (SFA)**. SFA involves creating a visual that guides students in comparing vocabulary words to determine the ways they are similar and different. Video with captioning and audio also can be used to teach vocabulary (Anderson-Inman, Terrazas-Arrellanes, & Slabin, 2009).

Students may use learning strategies that help them develop their vocabulary. Schumaker et al. (2006) developed the LINCS Vocabulary Strategy, which is designed to help students learn new vocabulary words by developing their skills at using key words, important phrases and sentences, and mental images.

Story Grammars and Frames. Story grammars and frames can support your students' vocabulary and comprehension of text. **Story grammars** are outlines of the ways stories are organized. They often involve identifying and articulating a reading selection's main characters, story lines, conflicts, and ending.

Frames outline important components of stories and provide cues to help students understand text in a variety of genres. One effective frame is the circle story, which is developed by plotting a story's important components in a clockwise sequence on a circle diagram.

Storytelling and Drama. Storytelling and drama can help students construct meaning from text, and promote listening comprehension, vocabulary, and writing skills (Ohler, 2006). Although *all students* benefit from storytelling and drama, they are particularly good teaching techniques for students whose cultures have an oral tradition and for those who are English language learners (Campano, 2007). Students can act out and retell stories through miming, gestures, role playing, and the use of props.

Use Peer-Based Instruction Reading instruction in inclusive settings can be supplemented by using peer-based instruction (Ash et al., 2009; O'Brien, 2007). Peer tutoring and classwide peer tutoring programs help your students improve their reading fluency, word identification, vocabulary, and reading comprehension (Bowman-Perrott, 2009; Harper & Maheady, 2007; Sutherland & Snyder, 2007).

Peer/Partner Reading Programs. You can help develop your students' reading skills by using same or cross-age peer reading or partner reading programs (Guthrie et al., 2009; Saddler & Staulters, 2008). In these programs, students read together with either their classmates or younger or older students.

Peer-Assisted Learning Strategies. One peer-mediated system that has been effective in promoting the reading fluency, vocabulary, and text comprehension of kindergarten, elementary and secondary students and English language learners is peer-assisted learning strategies (PALS) (Joseph & Schisler, 2009; Kroeger et al., 2009; McMaster, Kung, Han, & Cao, 2008). Students work with peers in partner reading, paragraph shrinking, and prediction relay. *Partner reading* involves students taking turns reading aloud for 5 minutes, with the more proficient student reading first.

Paragraph shrinking involves students reading orally and then asking each other questions designed to identify the main idea of each paragraph. In the *prediction relay,* students work in dyads with one student making a prediction about a half page of text, orally reading the text, and then summarizing the main idea.

Literature Circles and Literature Response Journals.   Like Mr. Pike, you can use **literature circles**, or *literature discussion groups or book clubs*, small groups of students who work collaboratively to share their reactions to and discuss various aspects of books that all group members have decided to read (Anderson & Corbett, 2008; Berkeley, 2007). Some teachers adapt literature circles by providing students with digitized books and by assigning specific roles to students such as discussion leader (monitors and fosters the discussion), passage reader (reads key passages aloud), connector (links content to students' experiences), definer (looks up and explains key vocabulary), summarizer (reviews key points and the sequence of action), and illustrator (develops corresponding graphics) (O'Brien, 2007; Powell-Brown, 2006). You also can teach them the skills they need to ask questions, respond to the comments and questions of others, and agree and disagree respectfully (Paxton-Buursma & Walker, 2008). Students also can work in literature response groups to read different genres and respond to them in various ways.

Literature response journals can be used as a follow-up to sustained silent reading periods or literature circles (Roessing, 2009). In these journals, students describe their reactions to and thoughts about the material they have been reading, as well as any questions they have. Students also are encouraged to write about their opinions and emotional responses to the book, relate the book to their own experiences, and make predictions about the book and its characters. You can read students' journals and offer comments that encourage students to redirect, expand, and refocus their reactions and questions.

One type of literature response journal is the *character study journal,* in which students make entries related to an interesting character. While reading the selection, students react to and write about their character, including the character's dilemmas, feelings, and responses.

Shared Book Reading.   You and your students can share in reading a variety of materials. In **shared book reading**, you read a new or familiar story together, discussing aspects of the story as you read it (Bellon-Harn & Harn, 2008). Students also can react to it through arts and crafts, drama, reading, or writing; and students then reread the story on their own. Big books with large print and pictures and storybooks are particularly appropriate for shared book reading for younger students and struggling readers, as they allow you to display the words the students are reading.

Students also can share their reactions and learning through use of readers' theater, dinner party, Socratic discussions, and book or author talks (Berkeley, 2007; Fink Chorzempa & Lapidus, 2009; Keehn, Harmon, & Shoho, 2008). In readers' theater, students give a dramatic reading of key passages, which are then discussed by a group of students. In the dinner party, students role-play characters from the book, who are interviewed by a commentator. You can implement Socratic discussions by having your students generate questions after reading text, which are then discussed by the class to identify, examine, and reflect on the information presented in the reading selection. Students also can give book or author talks with and without props or read their favorite parts to the class.

Guided Reading.   Guided reading involves working with students in small groups to explore books and ideas (Guthrie et al., 2009; Menzies et al., 2008). Guided reading usually starts with you introducing the story and fostering students' interest in reading it. Next, the students read the text to themselves as you observe them and listen to note their reading behaviors. After reading the story, you talk with your students about it to have them make predictions about and personal connections to the

PEARSON
myeducationlab

To enhance your understanding of ways to use peer-assisted learning strategies (PALS) to foster your students' reading, go to the IRIS Center Resources section of the Topic *Reading Instruction* in the MyEducationLab for your course, and complete the modules entitled *PALS: A Reading Strategy for Grades K–1, PALS: A Reading Strategy for Grades 2–6,* and *PALS: A Reading Strategy for High School.*

story. You also may have them reread parts of the story, and demonstrate reading strategies and help students learn how to use them.

An important component of guided reading is the group reading conference, a time when groups discuss books or selections that they have been reading independently. Structure the conference by asking open-ended questions that require students to think, express an opinion, and relate the selection to their own experiences.

Sustained Silent Reading.   A group-oriented reading technique that teachers like Mr. Pike employ is *sustained silent reading*. During **sustained silent reading**, you, your students, and other members of the class read self-selected materials for an extended period of time (Hartley, 2008). Typically, the rules for sustained silent reading are (a) read silently, (b) do not interrupt others, and (c) do not change books.

Use a Balanced Approach

Most reading programs are based on a particular teaching philosophy, and therefore they differ in their instructional approach. In planning reading instruction for your students, select approaches that are appropriate to your students' individual learning characteristics. In addition, examine the impact of these approaches on your students' rate of learning and emotional responsiveness. Although some students may benefit from one specific reading approach, no one approach will meet the needs of *all students*. Most students, however, perform best if you use a balanced approach that combines elements of the various approaches described in the following sections (Tompkins, 2010).

Phonetic-Based Approaches   **Phonetic-based reading approaches** teach students to recognize and understand the phonological features of language and of individual words and letters (Tompkins, 2010; Vaughn & Roberts, 2007). These approaches focus on teaching students to master the connection between graphemes (letters) and their corresponding sounds (phonemes) and to use strategies for decoding or "sounding out" new and unknown words (Fox, 2010). Therefore, phonics instruction is geared to teaching students the relationship between letters and sounds, and it focuses on helping students learn to blend and segment sounds within words. The effectiveness of phonics instruction is increased when it is combined with phonemic awareness, fluency, vocabulary, and comprehension instruction.

Phonetic approaches are categorized as synthetic or analytic (Ehri et al., 2009; Hines, 2009). The synthetic approach develops phonetic skills by teaching students the specific symbol–grapheme (e.g., *g*) to sound–phoneme (e.g., *guh*) correspondence rules. Once students learn the sound and symbol rules, they are taught to synthesize the sounds into words through blending.

In the analytic approach to phonetics instruction, the phoneme–grapheme correspondence is learned by teaching students to analyze words. These word analysis skills help students understand that letters within words sound alike and are written the same way.

Another analytic method uses a linguistic approach to teach reading. Students learn to read and spell words within word families that have the same phonetic patterns. Through repeated presentations of these word families, students learn the rules of sound–symbol correspondence. For example, the *at* family would be introduced together, using words such as *bat, cat, fat, hat, rat,* and *sat*.

PEARSON
myeducationlab

Go to the Assignments and Activities section of the Topic *Reading Instruction* in the MyEducationLab for your course and complete the activity entitled *Effective Reading Instruction*. As you watch the video and answer the accompanying questions, consider the ways in which a balanced approach to literacy instruction can benefit *all students*.

Most students will benefit from a balanced approach to teaching reading. How do you balance your approaches to teaching reading?

Phonetic approaches might present some problems for students with disabilities. Students taught using these phonetic approaches tend to not guess words that do not follow phonetic rules, read more regular words than irregular words, and pronounce words based on graphic and phonetic cues rather than semantic and syntactic cues. Students may have difficulty in identifying words that do not follow phonetic patterns and in isolating and blending sounds, so you may need to supplement phonetics instruction with other approaches (Joseph & Seery, 2004).

Whole-Word Approaches **Whole-word reading approaches** help students make the link between whole words and their oral counterparts (Vacca et al., 2009). In the whole-word approach, meaning also is emphasized. New words are taught within sentences and passages or in isolation. Students taught through whole-word methods tend to attempt to read unfamiliar words, use context cues rather than graphic cues, and substitute familiar words for new words. You can modify these approaches by decreasing the number of words to be learned, using flash cards that contain the word and a pictorial of the word, offering spaced practice sessions, providing opportunities for overlearning, and delivering more frequent reinforcement.

Language Experience Approach A **language experience reading approach** is based on the belief that what students think about, they can talk about; what students can say, they can write or have someone write for them; and what students can write, they can read (Falk-Ross et al., 2009; Tompkins, 2010). Language experience approaches are highly individualized; they use the students' interests, hobbies, and experiences as the basis for creating reading materials that are highly motivating and that foster creativity.

Whole Language Approach A balanced reading program also can include many of the elements and strategies associated with a **whole language approach**. This approach uses students' natural language and experiences in and out of school to immerse them in a supportive, stimulating, natural learning environment that promotes their literacy. Reading, writing, listening, speaking, and thinking are integrated into each lesson and activity, and learning is viewed as proceeding from the whole to the part rather than the reverse.

The whole language curriculum is developmental and often organized around themes and units that increase language and reading skills. Students are motivated to read and improve their reading by reading authentic, relevant, and functional materials that make sense to them and relate to their experiences. At first, students read meaningful, predictable whole texts. Next, they use the familiar words in these texts to learn new words and phrases. While learning to read, students also learn to write. They are encouraged to write about their experiences by composing letters, maintaining journals, making lists, labeling objects in the classroom, and keeping records.

Use Remedial Reading Programs, Strategies, and Materials

Because many students, particularly those with disabilities, have difficulty reading, you may need to supplement your reading instruction with some of the remedial reading programs, strategies, and materials described here.

Multisensory Strategies Multisensory strategies teach letters and words using combinations of visual, auditory, kinesthetic, and tactile modalities. Several multisensory strategies are available, including writing the word in chalk, spelling the word after saying it, tracing three-dimensional letters with students' eyes shut, and tracing letters on the students' backs.

Fernald Method. A multisensory, whole-word, language experience strategy that was developed for students with learning problems is the Fernald method, which involves four steps: tracing, writing without tracing, recognition in print, and word analysis.

Orton-Gillingham-Stillman Strategy. The Orton-Gillingham-Stillman Strategy uses a multisensory synthetic phonics approach to teaching reading (Ritchey & Goeke, 2006). At first, students are taught letter–sound symbol correspondence by viewing the letters, hearing the sounds they make, linking the letters to their sounds, and writing the letters. Once 10 letters (*a, b, f, h, i, j, k, m, p, t*) are mastered, blending of the sounds is taught. Blending is followed by story writing, syllabification, dictionary skills, and instruction in spelling rules.

Wilson Reading Wilson Reading is a program that uses explicit and systematic instruction, visual-auditory-kinesthetic/tactile multisensory strategies, and frequent reviews and repetition to teach reading and writing. The program offers a series of sequenced lessons to develop students' fluency in sound–symbol correspondence and phoneme–grapheme correspondence, to teach alphabetic coding and phonological skills, and to foster students' word recognition, vocabulary, expressive language and text comprehension.

Programmed Reading Materials Some students may benefit from a highly structured approach to the teaching of reading that involves use of programmed materials such as *Reading Mastery, Reading Excellence: Word Attack and Rate Development Strategies* (*REWARDS*), *Horizons Fast Track A-B*, and *Corrective Reading* (Mooney, Benner, Nelson, Lane, & Beckers, 2007). These programs teach reading via fast-paced, scripted lessons that present information in small, focused, and discrete steps that follow a planned sequence of skills. Each skill within the sequence is presented so that teachers model and lead students in developing the skill, and provide students with opportunities to review, practice, overlearn, and apply the skill while receiving feedback. Student progress is continually assessed, and errors are corrected before students can proceed to the next skill. You follow the presentation sequence by adhering to the directions outlined in the manual. Because these programs are highly scripted, concerns have been raised about their use including being overly rigid, stifling creativity, viewing students as passive learners, and failing to help students develop higher-level reading skills.

HELPING STUDENTS LEARN TO WRITE

HOW CAN I HELP MY STUDENTS LEARN TO WRITE? One content area directly related to reading that occurs throughout the school curriculum is written language. However, many of your students, particularly those with disabilities and those who are English language learners, may struggle with writing (Bender, 2008). An examination of their writing may reveal problems in the areas of idea generation, text organization, sentence structure, vocabulary usage, spelling, punctuation, and grammar and a general lack of knowledge about what constitutes good writing, which can affect their performance across the curriculum (Dockrell et al., 2009; Graham & Harris, 2009). Research indicates that you can address these difficulties and enhance your students' writing by making writing a meaningful and authentic, integral part of the curriculum, using a process-oriented approach to writing instruction, teaching students to use learning strategies, and employing technology-supported applications (Baker, Chard, Ketterlin-Geller, Apichatabutra, & Doabler, 2009; Englert, 2009; Graham & Harris, 2009). As with all of your instruction, it also is critical that you use a range of assessment strategies to monitor your students' writing progress and use this information to inform your instructional planning and teaching (Hessler, Konrad, & Alber-Morgan, 2009; McMaster, Du, & Petursdottir, 2009; Romeo, 2008).

Make Writing Meaningful, Authentic, and an Integral Part of the Curriculum

Instruction in writing should be meaningful, and it should allow students to write for social, creative, recreational, and occupational purposes as well as to express opinions and share information. Students also should be allowed to perform genuine

A GUIDE TO ACTION
Creating a Balanced and Literacy-Rich Learning Environment

It is important for you to use a range of approaches and techniques to foster your students' literacy skills. To ensure an effective inclusive classroom that promotes your students' literacy skills, consider the following points as you work toward creating a balanced and literacy-rich learning environment:

- Select and use reading approaches that are appropriate to your students' individual learning characteristics.
- Use a range of activities to develop your students' phonemic awareness.
- Maintain a classroom environment that is print-rich through the use of charts, mobiles, logos, signs, flash cards, and posters, as well as the labeling of objects and areas in the classroom.
- Help students develop reading fluency and use a variety of strategies to foster their word identification skills.
- Create opportunities for students to interact verbally with their peers, talk about their ideas and reactions, and participate actively in reading and writing activities.
- Give students access to a variety of high-quality literature genres.
- Provide students with choices concerning the books they read, the topics they write about, and the projects they complete.
- Teach students how to use context and root words, dictionaries, and thesauri to determine word meanings.
- Use visuals, memorable events, physical exaggerations, story grammars, repetition, modeling, and drama to foster students' vocabulary and text comprehension.

- Focus reading and writing activities on students' experiences, interests, and background knowledge.
- Model reading and writing by demonstrating and sharing your ongoing efforts in these areas.
- Make areas for reading, writing, speaking, listening, and content-area learning available to students.
- Display work on bulletin boards, blackboards, doors, and walls that has been written and read by students.
- Create a comfortable physical environment for learning, and involve families in literacy development.
- Maintain a classroom library of digital and print books and reading materials related to students' reading levels, interests, and cultural backgrounds.
- Stock your classroom with books that contain repetitive language, an interesting storyline, pictures related to the text, and a predictable structure.
- Whenever possible, use technology to support your students' reading and writing.
- Have students maintain personal and dialogue journals and logs of books read.
- Supplement your reading instruction by using remedial reading programs, strategies, and materials.

How would you rate your ability to create a balanced and literacy-rich learning environment? ( ) Excellent ( ) Good ( ) Needs Improvement ( ) Needs Much Improvement.

Create a plan of action for enhancing your ability to create a balanced and literacy-rich learning environment that includes your goals, the actions you will take and the resources you will need to achieve them, and the ways you will evaluate your success.

---

writing tasks that have an authentic audience, are motivating and of interest to them, and serve a real purpose (Danoff, 2008; Graham & Harris, 2009; Levy, 2008).

Rather than assume that students are improving their writing skills during writing instruction, opportunities to write and the teaching of written expression should be an ongoing part of the students' instructional program across the curriculum (Graham & Harris, 2009; Walling, 2009). For example, writing can be incorporated into content-area instruction and assessment by using the following instructional techniques:

- *Sentence synthesis:* Students are given several key words from a lesson and asked to use them in writing meaningful sentences related to the main points of the lesson ("Write two meaningful sentences about virus, bacteria, and fungus").
- *Question all-write:* Students respond in writing to questions posed by their teachers ("What is the difference between weathering and erosion?").

- *Outcome sentences:* Students respond in writing to teacher-directed prompts during the lesson ("I learned that _____"; "I am not sure why _____").
- *Frames:* Students are asked to complete skeletal paragraphs that include important information and ideas and transition words related to the lesson.
- *Short statements:* Students are asked to write short statements describing people, places, and things covered in lessons, comparing concepts, or outlining the process they used to solve a problem or perform an experiment (e.g., "Write a short statement outlining how you solved the problems we discussed in class").

Use Journals

As we saw in the chapter-opening vignette, journals, in which students write about their personal reactions to events and their experiences, are a good way to make writing meaningful (Fink-Chorzempa et al., 2005; Grande, 2008; Reeves & Standard, 2009). For example, students can maintain a personal journal or a dialogue journal. In the personal journal, students write about their own lives, including such topics as family members, friends, feelings, hobbies, and personal events. The dialogue journal, in which you and your students write confidential responses to each other, can motivate students to write while promoting a good relationship between you and your students. As students become comfortable with writing in their journals, you can probe the meaning of their statements and seek more in-depth responses by using probing questions, making comments, sharing observations, responding to students' questions, and asking for more detail. Students also can be asked to maintain simulated journals in which they take and write about the perspective of another person, or a buddy journal in which they maintain a written conversation with one of their classmates.

Students also can be encouraged to write by linking writing to content-area instruction, and their culture and experiences. All students can be given opportunities to write poems, essays, and short stories related to content-area learning that express their ideas and cultural experiences. As they write about their cultural backgrounds, students also learn about and understand the cultural experiences of their classmates.

Use Technology-Based Writing Activities

The use of technology is an excellent way to provide your students with meaningful and motivating writing experiences (Brozo & Puckett, 2009). Digital storytelling is a particularly good format for your students to develop and demonstrate their writing skills and share information about themselves with others (Kaylor, 2008; Rao et al., 2009). For example, your students can use a range of technologies to create digital stories and storybooks that include text, narration, video clips, scanned photographs and artwork, and background music and sounds that present the story, titles, and credits. Your students also can create digital stories presenting role plays, documentaries, narratives, news reports, essays, poems, book reports, interviews, and skill demonstrations (Sprankle, 2008). Technologies like digital stories can be used to motivate and foster the writing of *all of your students*, but they are particularly useful for students who are reluctant to write, students who are English language learners, and students with disabilities (Rance Roney, 2009; Skouge et al., 2007).

In addition to developing your students' writing skills and motivating them to write, technology-based writing activities allow you and your students to share and promote your students' technology skills (MacArthur, 2009; Wissick et al., 2009). Technologies such as blogs, Web pages, digital stories, and wikis have the added advantage of making student work more authentic because it can be shared with and used by others easily (Brozo & Puckett, 2009; Salend, 2009). However, it is critical that you exercise caution and take safeguards when sharing students' work with others (November, 2008). Because many students learn to use different and unconventional writing techniques for communicating with their friends via e-mail and text messaging (e.g., no spacing between words, punctuation ["Hello!!!!!"] and uppercase to emphasize a point, symbols to display emotions [smiley faces], acronyms and abbreviations [LOL]), teach students the difference between social and other forms of written communications, and make sure that they understand that they need to use appropriate spelling, grammar, capitalization, and punctuation. Also, you should consider whether use of technology facilitates the writing process without altering the goals and purpose of your students' writing. For instance, whereas writing a blog about a specific topic might be an appropriate writing activity for developing students' narrative writing skills, using Twitter or PowerPoint might not be an appropriate way to foster students' narrative writing.

Making Connections
The use of technology-based writing activities relates to our earlier discussion in Chapter 8 of instructional and assistive technologies and teaching your students to use technology in safe and responsible ways.

Use a Process-Oriented Approach to Writing Instruction

Although there is considerable overlap in the stages of writing, many advocate a process-oriented approach in teaching writing (Guzel-Ozmen, 2009; Santangelo, Harris, & Graham, 2008). A process-oriented approach to writing is viewed as consisting of holistic subprocesses: planning/prewriting, drafting, editing, revising, and publishing (Englert, 2009; see also Figure 10.3). These subprocesses lead to writing

FIGURE 10.3 Stages of the writing process

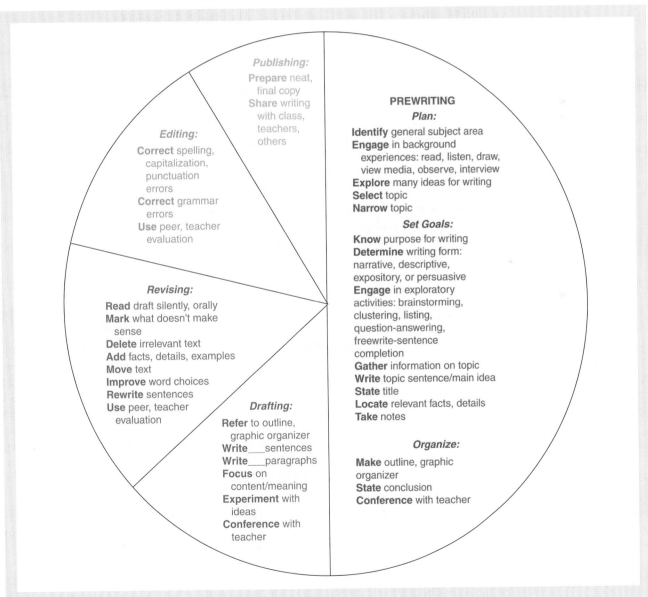

Source: "Teaching the writing process to students with LD," by B. J. Scott and M. R. Vitale, 2003, *Intervention in School and Clinic, 38,* pp. 220–225. Copyright 2003 by Sage Publications. Reprinted with permission.

Differentiating Reading, Writing, and Spelling Instruction

activities that have a real purpose and a real audience. The subprocesses and writing strategies, together with technology-supported writing applications, are presented in the following sections.

Planning/Prewriting   During the planning or prewriting phase, students determine the purpose and audience of the writing task, activate their relevant prior knowledge, generate and group ideas, and plan how to present the content to the reader (Santangelo et al., 2008). You can facilitate the planning process by providing students with engaging and varied experiences to write about, making writing relevant to their lives, helping them generate and organize their ideas, and assisting them in developing a plan (Harris et al., 2008). For example, you can use digital pictures of school- and community-based events and locations to encourage students to write. Prewriting activities to help students with the planning process are discussed here.

Idea Generation.   Allowing students to work on topics they themselves have chosen can foster idea generation. When students select their own topics and make decisions about content, they have a personal connection to their work and develop a sense of ownership toward writing. Multimedia, software, online experiences, simulations, trips, interviews, graphic and pictorial representations, music, sensory explorations, creative and visual imagery, speakers, demonstrations, interviews, brainstorming, and researching all help students select topics. Having students talk about or draw their stories also helps them generate ideas for writing (Fink-Chorzempa et al., 2005).

Because writing is linked to reading, students can obtain ideas for writing from reading. Reading and discussing passages before writing can help students select topics and add details to their writing. Students can write stories by changing the characters or action in a story they have just listened to or read. Predictable books can stimulate such story writing because they often follow repetitive storylines (Zipprich et al., 2009). Students also can be given books containing pictures that tell a story and asked to write the text that tells the story (Zambo, 2007).

Story Starters/Enders.   Some students may benefit from the use of writing prompts such as **story starters/enders**, in which they are given the first or last paragraph of a story or the initial or ending sentence of a paragraph, and are asked to complete the story or paragraph (Goddard & Sendi, 2008). Music, pictures, and videos also can prompt students to write by serving as starters. Similarly, you can use story frames in which students complete blank frames by writing in information related to the frame. In addition, use paragraph organization worksheets and paragraph draft outlines to help students plan and organize their writing.

Outlines and Semantic Maps.   Ideas generated by students can be organized by helping students develop an outline or graphic organizer, which includes the main topics and supporting ideas grouped together, as well as the order in which the ideas will be presented (Englert, 2009; Guzel-Ozmen, 2009; Sundeen, 2007). Students also can be taught to organize their writing by developing a **semantic map**—a diagram or map of the key ideas and words that make up the topic (Figure 10.4). Mapping allows students to identify main points and to plan the interrelationship between them. In introducing semantic maps, you can ask questions that help students understand their own decision-making processes and learn from others.

Making Connections
Find out more about using semantic maps in Chapter 11.

Models and Prompts.   Models and prompts also can facilitate the planning process. You or your students who write well can serve as models for others by verbalizing the process used to plan writing projects. You also can help students plan their writing by giving them a planning think sheet, which contains a series of questions that prompt them in planning their writing (Englert, 2009). For example, you can give students a think sheet that asks them to respond to such questions as (a) Why am I writing? (b) What am I writing about? (c) What do I know about the topic? (d) Who is my audience? and (e) What do they need to know about the topic? (Guzel-Ozmen, 2009).

FIGURE 10.4 **A sample writing semantic map**

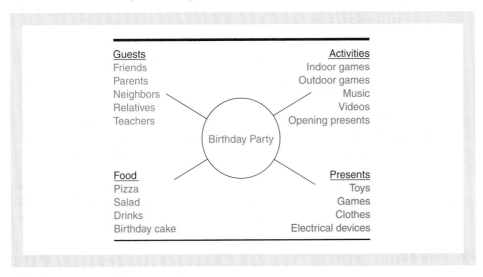

FIGURE 10.5 **Sample writing self-evaluation questions**

Does each paragraph start with a topic sentence?
Does each paragraph include relevant supporting information?
Are the paragraphs organized appropriately?
Are the main characters introduced and described?
Is the location of the story presented and described?
Is the time of the story introduced?
Does the story include a starting event?
Does the story include the main characters' reactions to the starting event?
Does the story present actions to resolve conflicts?
Does the story have an ending?
Does the ending include the outcome's effects on the main characters?

Drafting   In the drafting phase, writers transform their ideas and plans into sentences and paragraphs. They attempt to establish a relationship and an order between sentences and paragraphs and make appropriate word choices. Although it should not be emphasized in the drafting stage, some attention to the rules of grammar, punctuation, and spelling may be appropriate. In a writing process approach, these skills are taught using the students' own writing through individualized or group lessons. During this step, encourage students to plan their draft, and provide time to revise it.

You can help students prepare the draft in several ways. These include asking questions to help students explore alternatives, offering suggestions, giving them exemplary evaluative and instructional models, encouraging them, and focusing attention on the writing task. Throughout the writing process, give students self-evaluation questions, and encourage them to use the self-evaluation guidelines. For example, some teachers and students use a six-traits model to evaluate student written work based on their ideas, organization, voice word choice, sentence fluency, and conventions (mechanical correctness) (Perchemlides & Coutant, 2004). Sample self-evaluation questions for writing stories are presented in Figure 10.5. Giving your students instructional rubrics can help them in drafting, editing, and revising processes. Some of your students may benefit from the opportunity to use individualized word banks containing words they often use in writing and to record their words via technology, or dictate to a scribe, which can be gradually reduced as students learn to write independently.

Making Connections
Find out more about instructional rubrics in Chapter 12.

Editing and Revising In this phase, students edit their drafts by making revisions to ensure that their products achieve their writing goals (Englert, 2009; Santangelo et al., 2008). You can introduce students to revision by reviewing a sample paper as a group. The class can identify the positive aspects of the paper, as well as the problems a reader would have in reading it. The discussion should focus on the content, organization, and word choices rather than on mechanical errors. The class can then complete the revision by correcting the problems identified in the paper as a group. For example, you and your students can help classmates generate a list of synonyms to replace nondescriptive words (such as *nice, great, fine,* and *good*) that have been used repeatedly. The Find (Search) and Replace functions of many word processing programs can then be used to locate the nondescriptive word and replace it with the new words.

Students also can be taught to correct their own papers and to do content, organizational, and mechanical editing by maintaining an editing log (see Figure 10.6). The editing log includes the date, the error, the correction, and the rule being applied.

Proofreading. Proofreading is an important part of the editing and revising processes. Students can be taught to review their written products to check for misspelled words, sentence fragments, and errors in punctuation, capitalization, and grammar. You can help students proofread their work by giving them a proofreading checklist or teaching them to use COPS, a learning strategy for fostering proofreading skills (see Figure 10.8).

Students can improve their proofreading skills by using proofreader's marks. You can train students to use these marks by teaching them the system and modeling its use when giving feedback on written assignments. Additionally, you can give students a handout of editing symbols paired with examples of their use.

Models. You can foster the editing process by giving students writing sample models that show the correct format, writing style, and organization of content. The value of the model can be increased by reviewing it with students and marking it with comments highlighting the qualities that help to make it an excellent product.

FIGURE 10.6 **Sample editing log**

Name _____

Date	Error and Correction	Rule
1/25/2008	*Error:* The student suddenly jumped out of his seat, however, the teacher ignored him. *Correction:* The student suddenly jumped out of his seat; however, the teacher ignored him. or The student suddenly jumped out of his seat. However, the teacher ignored him.	This is called a comma splice or run-on sentence. It can be corrected by replacing the first comma with a semicolon or with a period and a capital letter to start a new sentence.
1/25/2008	*Error:* The boys father met them at school. *Correction:* The boys' father met them at school.	The father "belongs" to the boys, so *boys* should be possessive. The apostrophe comes after the *s* because the word *boys* is plural.

Source: Prepared by Catharine Whittaker.

For example, you can emphasize the topic sentence by circling it and writing "This is a good topic sentence. It introduces the reader to the content in the paragraph." Similarly, the inclusion of specific sections in the written product can be noted to ensure that the student's paper includes all the necessary sections.

In addition to providing students with a model, teachers can promote writing and editing by providing a checklist of items, an instructional rubric, or a listing of questions they can use in evaluating their work and editing the work of others (Englert, 2009; Guzel-Ozmen, 2009). The evaluation guidelines, questions, or rubric can then guide students in evaluating their papers before handing them in. You also can create an evaluation form or self-monitoring system that guides students in evaluating the mechanical aspects of their work such as their punctuation, capitalization, grammar, and spelling (Goddard & Sendi, 2008). For example, you can use colored dots or labels paired with specific codes or symbols placed on students' products to denote that they have used a specific skill correctly.

Collaborative Writing Groups. Collaborative writing groups can promote a positive environment for writing and improving the writing skills of students (Englert, 2009; Fink-Chorzempa et al., 2005; Ruckdeschel, 2009). Students can work in collaboration by reading their products to the group or to individual group members, editing the products of group members, brainstorming ideas for writing, developing outlines as a group, and producing a group product such as a class newsletter or a digital story (Rao et al., 2009).

Collaborative groups can be particularly helpful in editing and revising written assignments. One collaborative strategy is the **author's chair**. In this technique, once their product has been completed, students read it aloud to their peers, who discuss its positive features and ask questions about strategy use, meaning, and writing style.

Students can work in groups to offer feedback and to edit drafts. You can establish guidelines for peer writing groups, including focusing on feedback that emphasizes the positive aspects of the product, being specific, directing feedback at the work rather than the author, phrasing negative reactions as questions, giving reactions orally or in writing, and offering writers time to respond to the reactions of their peers. Enhance the value of the peer editing process by providing students with evaluation guidelines such as the ones in Figure 10.5 or by giving students forms that can guide the editing and feedback process (see Figure 10.7).

In addition, to help students receive feedback from others, establish rules for accepting reactions from others, including the following:

- Listen carefully to all comments from others.
- Ask for feedback from as many people as possible.
- Do not dispute or dismiss feedback from others.
- Seek clarification or examples when you don't understand another person's reaction.
- Check your understanding of another person's reaction by paraphrasing the statements in your own words.

Writers' Workshop. Another collaborative writing strategy designed to create a community of writers is the **writers' workshop**, where students write and receive feedback from peers and teachers on topics they select (Tompkins, 2010; Wright, Drewniak, & O'Dell, 2009). The workshop is divided into four parts: *status of the class, minilessons, workshop proper,* and *sharing.* In the status component, you conference with individual students to identify the project(s) on which they are working, the help they will need, and the progress they are making. Minilessons, approximately 5 minutes long, offer students direct and explicit instruction on specific skills such as process skills (e.g., idea generation), grammar and spelling skills, writing skills (e.g., paragraph development), and classroom routines. The majority of the writers' workshop consists of the workshop proper, during which you and

Making Connections
This use of collaborative writing groups and writers' workshop relates to our earlier discussion of cooperative learning arrangements in Chapter 9.

FIGURE 10.7 Sample peer editing forms

SAMPLE PEER EDITOR FEEDBACK FORM

Author:

Editor:

Title of Piece:

1. The things I like about this piece are:

2. The things you need to improve about this piece are:

3. The ways you could improve this piece are:

SAMPLE AUTHOR FORM

Author:

Editor:

Title of Piece:

1. The positive things about my piece are:

2. The things I need to improve about my piece are:

3. The ways I could improve my piece are:

your students actively write. In addition to writing, you circulate around the room to monitor student progress, help students hear their own voices and solve minor problems, and confer with individual students. In the final component, students share their work with others, receive feedback, and publish their work.

Publishing   Publishing students' written products presents an excellent opportunity for sharing their work with others and for receiving feedback. For example, students can publish their work in books that they design, submit work to magazines and newspapers, and create newsletters. Technology also can be a valuable resource in the fourth stage of the writing process: publishing and sharing it with others (Brozo & Puckett, 2009). As we discussed earlier, students also can "publish" and share their work by posting it online via blogs, Web pages, wikis, and digital stories (Salend, 2009).

Provide Feedback

Feedback should facilitate, not frustrate, the writing process (Santangelo et al., 2008). A teacher conference is an excellent means of providing feedback and encouraging students to reflect on their writing. By meeting individually with students, you serve as both reader and coach, helping students learn to examine their writing.

Initially, you can focus on the positive aspects of the students' writing, and acknowledge and encourage them to write by praising them and their accomplishments and effort, sharing their stories with others by reading them in class, and posting their writing in the room or elsewhere in the school. Because identifying all errors can frustrate students, especially when it is highlighted in red, corrective feedback should focus on no more than two writing problems at a time. You can initially pinpoint errors that interfere with the writer's ability to make the product understandable to the reader and then emphasize grammar, punctuation, spelling, and usage errors. Instruction to correct grammatical and spelling errors can focus on skills that are within the student's repertoire and occur within the context of the student's writing.

Teach Students to Use Learning Strategies

You can help students improve their writing by teaching them to use learning strategies (Schumaker & Deshler, 2009). These written language learning strategies are part of the *Self-Regulated Strategy Development* (*SRSD*) model, which refers to an explicit instructional model for teaching students to use a variety of learning strategies and related acronyms designed to enhance their self-regulation skills and attitudes across a range of writing genres (Harris, Graham, Mason, & Friedlander, 2008). In the SRSD model, you teach specific writing strategies by using the following steps:

> *Step 1. Develop and activate background knowledge.* You set the stage for learning the strategy by helping students learn and understand the knowledge and skills they need to apply the strategy.
>
> *Step 2. Discuss the strategy.* You and your students discuss each step of the strategy as well as the goals, benefits, and mnemonics associated with its use.
>
> *Step 3. Model use of the strategy.* You overtly model use of the strategy including verbalizing the steps, processes and questions you engage in to implement it. Following modeling, you discuss with students the advantages and challenges associated with using the strategy and ways to make it more effective and efficient for them to use.
>
> *Step 4. Memorize the strategy.* You teach your students to use a variety of activities to remember the strategy and its mnemonic.
>
> *Step 5. Support use of the strategy.* You provide a range of supports and prompts to encourage your students to use the strategy. As they develop proficiency in using the strategy, you gradually fade out your supports.
>
> *Step 6. Foster independent use of the strategy.* You help students internalize use of the strategy so they can apply it independently across the different writing assignments and learning situations they will encounter (Graham & Harris, 2009).

Another set of writing and reading learning strategy interventions are referred to as *Cognitive Strategy Instruction in Writing* (*CSIW*) (Englert, 2009). Like SRSD, CSIW is an intervention that incorporates an instructional sequence involving teacher and student dialogues, prompting and other scaffolding strategies, collaborative student groups, and modeling and guided practice to teach students to independently use a range of learning strategies designed to improve their reading and writing. As part of CSIW, students also are provided with Think Sheets or cue cards, which contain prompts and self-questions to guide them in using the strategy. Examples of some of the different writing learning strategies, their acronymns, and their instructional goals are presented in Figure 10.8.

Use Technology-Supported Writing Applications

Students can improve their writing skills and the writing products they produce by using technology-supported writing applications (Brozo & Puckett, 2009; Lange, Mulhern, & Wylie, 2009; MacArthur, 2009; Wissick et al., 2009). These technological applications, which can support communication and collaboration and the subprocesses in the writing process, should be selected based on your students' strengths and challenges (Cullen, Richards, & Frank, 2008). Therefore, English language learners can use multilingual versions of these technologies.

Making Connections
This discussion of feedback relates to our earlier discussion in Chapter 9 of how to give effective feedback to support student learning.

PEARSON
myeducationlab

To enhance your understanding of the writing process and the use of learning strategies to help your students learn to write persuasive essays, go to the IRIS Center Resources section of the Topic *Instructional Practices and Learning Strategies* in the MyEducationLab for your course, and complete the module entitled *Improving Writing Performance: A Strategy for Writing Expository Essays.*

PEARSON
myeducationlab

To reflect on and enhance your understanding of the Self-Regulated Strategy Development model and your teaching of a range of self-regulated learning strategies to improve your students' writing, go to the IRIS Center Resources section of the Topic *Instructional Practices and Learning Strategies* in the MyEducationLab for your course, and complete the module entitled *Using Learning Strategies: Instruction to Enhance Student Learning.*

Making Connections
This use of learning strategies to foster student writing relates to our earlier discussion in Chapter 6 of learning strategies and how to teach students to use them.

FIGURE 10.8 Sample writing learning strategies

Instructional Goal	Acronym	Strategic Steps
To foster proofreading	COPS (Schumaker & Deshler, 2009)	**C**: Have I capitalized letters that need to be capitalized? **O**: What is the overall appearance of my paper? **P**: Have I used proper punctuation? **S**: Are the words I used spelled correctly?
To foster planning	P(paw)LANS (Patel & Laud, 2009)	**P**: Purpose of writing (Pick topic, Audience, Why am I writing?) **L**ist goals **A**nd make . . . **N**otes **S**equence Notes
To foster paragraph writing	GO 4 IT . . . NOW (Konrad & Test, 2007)	**G**: Goal statement (topic sentence) **O**: Objectives (4 of them, supporting details) **I**: Identify a **T**: Timeline **N**: Name topic **O**: Order details **W**: Wrap it up
To foster transitions between paragraphs	UNITE (Laud & Patel, 2008)	**U**: Unload all you know in note form. **N**: Note categories and arrange facts into each. **I**: Identify categories in your topic sentence. **T**: Tie detailed sentences together with transitions. **E**: End with an exciting conclusion.
To foster revision	SCAN (Harris et al., 2008)	**S**: Does it make sense to me? **C**: Is it connected to my beliefs? **A**: Can I add more? **N**: Note my errors.
To foster the writing process	POWER (Englert, 2009)	**P**: Plan (What am I writing about? Who is my audience? Why am I writing? What do I know about the topic? Brainstorm) **O**: Organize (How can I group my ideas? What can I call them?) **W**: Write (Write main idea sentences for my different groups, add details, evidence, and examples and use keywords) **E**: Edit (Does it make sense? What questions will readers have? Did I implement my plan? Place * next to the parts I like the best. Place ? next to the parts that are confusing.) **R**: Revise (What should I add or delete? Should I rearrange my ideas?)

FIGURE 10.8 **Continued**

To foster opinion/argumentative writing	POW + TREE (Ferretti, Andrews-Weckerly, & Lewis, 2007; Harris, Graham, & Mason, 2002; Ortiz Lienemann & Reid, 2008)	**P**: Pick my idea. **O**: Organize my notes. **W**: Write and say more. **T**: Topic sentence. Tell what you believe! **R**: Reasons (three or more). Why do I believe this? **E**: Explain reasons (or Examine the reasons from the audience's point of view). Say more about it. **E**: Ending. Wrap it up right!
To foster opinion/argumentative writing	STOP + DARE (Ferretti et al., 2007)	**S**: Suspend judgment. **T**: Take a side. **O**: Organize my ideas. **P**: Plan more as I write. **D**: Develop a topic sentence. **A**: Add supporting ideas. **R**: Reject possible arguments from the other side. **E**: End with a conclusion.
To foster story grammar writing	POW, WWW, What = 2, How = 2 (Asaro & Saddler, 2009)	**POW** and **W**: Who are the main characters? **W**: When does the story take place? **W**: Where does the story take place? **W**: What do the main characters do? **W**: What happens when the main characters try to do it? **H**: How does the story end? **H**: How do the characters feel?

Word Processing   Word processing can foster students' writing (Cullen et al., 2008; MacArthur, 2009). It can help students focus on the writing process; minimize spelling and grammatical errors; facilitate publication; eliminate handwriting problems so that all students produce a neat, clean copy; provide students with a novel experience that motivates them to write; make text revision easy; eliminate the tedious process of copying; and allow students to insert graphics that illustrate and support written text.

Enlarged print systems and talking word processors that "read" the text on the computer screen can enhance the writing capabilities of students with visual and reading disabilities (Brozo & Puckett, 2009). Talking word processors allow students to detect syntax errors, receive feedback on spelling as they enter words, and hear their text read. Word processors that have voice output systems can provide immediate auditory and visual feedback to users concerning keystrokes and various commands as they type, as well as orally reviewing individual letters and words, sentences, paragraphs, highlighted text, and whole documents after the text has been typed. These applications can be combined with *text windowing*, the simultaneous visual highlighting of text as it is read to help students focus on, monitor, and proofread their writing. Because most talking word processors pronounce words

REFLECTIVE

How did you learn to write? When you write a paper for class or a letter to a friend, what processes do you use? How does the use of technology affect your writing?

REFLECTING ON PROFESSIONAL PRACTICES

Using a Process Approach to Teaching Writing

Mr. Pike notices that many of his students are having difficulty with writing assignments. A review of their written products reveals that they are extremely short and disorganized, lack important elements, and include irrelevant information. To correct these problems, Mr. Pike decides to try a different approach to teaching students to write.

Mr. Pike begins by writing a description of himself, reading it to his students, and asking them to guess who is being described. After the students guess correctly, Mr. Pike explains how he wrote it. He draws a semantic map on the board and demonstrates how he used it to list the important characteristics he wanted to mention in his description. He then gives the students a semantic map outline and asks them to complete it using the characteristics that best describe themselves.

The next day, Mr. Pike asks the students to use their semantic maps to write a draft that describes themselves. After the drafts are completed, he collects them, selects students to read them to the class, and has the class guess who wrote each piece. He concludes the day's writing lesson by telling students that tomorrow they will work on revising their descriptions.

Mr. Pike begins the next day's lesson by explaining the purpose of revising a draft. Using his description of himself, Mr. Pike asks students to identify things they liked about it. After this is done, he asks them to identify ways in which the description could be improved. Following this discussion, he reviews several guidelines for giving and accepting feedback. He then selects a student's draft and role-plays giving feedback with the student.

Mr. Pike then places students in dyads, gives each group member a checklist to guide the feedback process, and asks members to read each other's papers and share their reactions. While students work collaboratively, Mr. Pike monitors their progress and assists them in developing collaborative skills. During the last 15 minutes of the period, Mr. Pike and the whole class discuss how it feels to give and receive feedback.

The next day's writing period is devoted to revising students' drafts based on the feedback they have received. Mr. Pike works on his draft and circulates around the room to monitor student progress and to confer with individual students. After students revise their writing, they type their product on the computer using a range of writing assistance software and share their printout with their dyad partner. They then make final revisions, and a copy of each student's description is printed out and compiled into a class book called *Who's Who,* which is shared with students' families, other teachers, and the principal and is posted on the class's web page.

- Why did Mr. Pike decide to use a process approach to teach writing?
- What procedures and strategies did he use to implement a writing process approach?
- What are the advantages of using a process approach to teach writing?
- What are the potential problems with this approach?
- What resources would you need to implement a process approach to teach writing?

based on phonetic spellings, some word processing programs include pronunciation editing, which allows students to adjust the speech of the program so that words that are not phonetically based are pronounced correctly. A variety of special monitors and print enlargement programs also are available for students who can benefit from word processing through the use of enlarged print.

Talk-type or voice-activated word processing programs based on computerized speech recognition can help students improve their writing and overcome their spelling difficulties (Cullen et al., 2008). They are especially appropriate for students who struggle with written communication but have strong verbal communication skills. In these programs, the individual talks into a headphone-mounted microphone, pausing briefly after each word. The individual's comments then appear as electronic text on a video monitor and may be revised via word processing. While researchers are developing voice recognition systems that are not speaker-dependent, require little pretraining to use, process a large vocabulary accurately, screen background noises, and recognize continuous speech, students need to learn how to use the system. They also need to speak clearly, refrain from making extraneous sounds, articulate punctuation, and correct errors.

Some of your students may experience difficulties using word processing such as having difficulty remembering functions that require multiple key presses or syntax codes, using inefficient cursor movements, and using deletion procedures inappropriately. Therefore, some students may need to use word processing programs that have safeguards to prevent the loss of documents, offer easy-to-read manuals and directions for use, and contain pictures and cues as prompts. Students also may benefit from word processing programs that use simple keystrokes to delete and insert text and move the cursor, offer prompting and verification to help students save documents and load features, include easy-to-use menus, and use language that students can understand.

Students also may prefer to use portable word processing systems, which are lighter than laptops and therefore easier for students to transport from location to location (Parette et al., 2005). Some of your students with writing and motor difficulties may benefit from use of word processing programs with abbreviation expanders (Lindstrom, 2007). These word processing programs convert abbreviations for commonly used words, phrases, and sentences into full text.

To benefit from word processing, students might need specialized keyboards and alternate ways to use technology and instruction in keyboarding skills and the word processing program (Heller, Mezei, & Thompson Avant, 2008). Keyboarding skills also can be taught to students through the use of typing programs that accept only correct responses, provide numerous practice activities, introduce skills gradually, contain graphics for finger positions, and offer frequent feedback (Brown, 2009). Prompt cards that display the keys and their functions help students to remember key functions and patterns of multiple-key pressing. Typing teaching programs that analyze students' typing patterns, including strengths and challenges, and plan customized programs tailored to students' unique learning styles also are available.

Making Connections
The use of specialized keyboards and alternate ways to use technology relates to what we discussed earlier in Chapter 8.

Spell Checkers Word processing programs come with a spell checker, which helps students with spelling difficulties in revising their writing (MacArthur, 2009; Moats, 2006). Spell checkers review written text and identify spelling errors and other words that do not match the program's dictionary. Students then correct the spelling errors by typing in the correct spelling or by choosing from a list of alternatives presented by the spell checker. Students can add words to the spell checker's dictionary to tailor it to their unique spelling needs. Those with reading disabilities may benefit from programs that use talking spell checkers to read word choices to them, while other students may prefer a program that offers a definition of each word presented as an alternative. Students also may benefit from using spell checkers that identify homonyms and prompt students to check them by providing them with a pop-up box containing the different homophones and their definitions (Lange et al., 2009), pair visuals with typed text, and orally present words in the correct list or present word choices in short lists (MacArthur, 2009).

However, spell checkers have several limitations that especially affect students who struggle with spelling (Cullen et al., 2008; Moats, 2006). In particular, they cannot suggest the correct spelling of words when the student's version does not resemble the correct spelling. They often cannot identify words that are spelled correctly but used in the wrong context, such as homonyms. Spell checkers often identify correctly spelled words as errors if these words are not available in their dictionaries, such as proper nouns, uncommon words, and specialized vocabulary. Spell checkers also may not be able to provide the correct spelling of every word that has been misspelled. Ashton (1999) developed the CHECK procedure, a mnemonic learning strategy you can teach to your students who use spell checkers; and McNaughton, Hughes, and Ofiesh (1997) developed INSPECT, a learning strategy to teach students to use a spell checker.

Word Cueing and Prediction Word cueing and prediction programs offer students choices of words and phrases as they compose text and are helpful for students who have difficulty recalling words (Cullen et al., 2008; Hasselbring & Bausch, 2006; MacArthur, 2009). Whereas **word cueing programs** offer choices based on the first letters typed by students, **word prediction programs** offer word and phrase options

You can use collaborative writing groups and technology-supported writing applications to foster students' writing. How do you use peer groups and technology to support your students' writing?

based on context, word frequency (i.e., how frequently the word is used in English), word recency (i.e., how recently the word has been used by the writer), grammatical correctness, and commonly associated words and phrases. As students type text, a changing list of predicted words and phrases appears on the screen. Students can then decide to select the predicted words and insert them into their written products or to continue typing. The word and phrase banks that are integral parts of these programs can be tailored for students based on their needs and the topic and content of their written product. Thus, when students are writing about science, the word bank can be customized by including words from the science content being studied.

Electronic Dictionaries, Glossaries, and Thesauri

Your students may benefit from using electronic dictionaries, glossaries, and thesauri which can help them understand and define words, identify synonyms, limit word repetition, and increase the variety of words they use when writing (Zorfass, Fideler, Clay, & Brann, 2007). Because many of these programs use multimedia such as animations, 3-D visuals, colorful graphics, and audio pronunciations to help students understand and learn word meanings and determine appropriate alternative words and phrases, these programs are particularly helpful for your students who are English language learners. However, when using these programs, you should consider whether they serve to inadvertently overstimulate your students and interfere with their writing.

Text Organization, Usage, Grammar, and Punctuation Assistance   Technologies that use visual and auditory prompts, graphic organizers and semantic mapping to help students to generate text ideas, to remember important information and terminology to include when writing, and to organize the text and check text for word usage, syntax, punctuation, capitalization, and style can be useful (MacArthur, 2009; Wissick et al., 2009). For example, some word processing programs have interactive prompting capabilities that help students write effectively. These programs provide prompts and guidelines that appear on the screen to guide development of the student's product. You can tailor these and create your own prompts to adapt to the different types of writing assignments and challenges of students. Some programs offer students assistance in generating ideas to write about, selecting a writing style, and conforming to the writing style selected. Graphics-based writing software programs, which offer storyboarding and framing, pictures, video, sound, animation, and voice recording, can motivate students and assist them in planning, organizing, and composing text.

Word usage and grammar checkers and punctuation assistance programs identify inappropriate word choices and grammatical and punctuation errors and present alternatives to address them. Students then examine the alternatives and select the option that they believe best corrects the error. Many of these programs guide students in selecting an appropriate alternative by offering prompts, as well as reviews and explanations of the different selections and their corresponding word meanings and grammatical applications. Features such as automatic correction, available in many word processing programs (e.g., AutoCorrect in Microsoft Word), can be employed by your students to guide them in producing grammatically correct essay responses. For instance, these programs can be set to automatically capitalize proper nouns and the first words of sentences.

You also can provide your students with access to writing grading and feedback resources. Using these programs, your students (a) submit their essays electronically;

Teaching Handwriting

Although Ms. Stepanovich had her students write using computers, she also wanted them to develop the legibility and fluency of their handwriting so that they could express themselves in writing. During handwriting activities, she noticed that several students had poor writing posture that interfered with the size, slant, proportion, alignment, and spacing of letters. Therefore, Ms. Stepanovich used modeling to teach her students proper posture and paper positioning. She asked students to watch her as she wrote at her desk and told them, "Look at me when I write. I sit upright, with my back against the back seat of my chair and both of my feet on the floor. As I write, I lean my shoulders and upper back forward in a straight line, place my elbows extended slightly at the edge of my desk, and use my forearms as a pivot for my movements. I hold my pen lightly between the index finger and the middle finger, with the thumb to the side and the index finger on top. My thumb is bent to hold the pen high in the hand, and the utensil rests near the knuckle of the index finger, and my pinky and ring fingers touch the paper."

Ms. Stepanovich also created and posted charts that showed students how to position their paper when writing. For manuscript writing, a chart demonstrated how to hold the paper perpendicular to the front of the body, with the left side placed so that it is aligned with the center of the body. For cursive writing, the charts showed right-handers slanting the paper counterclockwise and left-handers slanting it clockwise. As students wrote, Ms. Stepanovich guided them physically, encouraged them to look at the charts, and gave them feedback on their posture and ability to hold the pen correctly.

Here are some other strategies you can use to implement the IDEA in your inclusive classroom and improve your students' handwriting:

- Focus initial instruction on helping students develop the prerequisite fine motor, visual motor, and visual discrimination skills and wrist stability needed for handwriting by using activities such as cutting, tracing, coloring, fingerpainting, discriminating, and copying shapes.
- Teach the meaning of the directional concepts that guide letter formation instruction such as up, down, top, center, bottom, around, left, right, across, middle, and diagonal.

- Use a combination of procedures that includes modeling, self-instruction, copying, cueing, and teaching the basic strokes.
- Teach letters that have similar stroke movements together.
- Organize instruction so that the easiest letters to learn and the letters that appear most often in reading materials are taught first.
- Model and verbalize how to form letters and discuss the similarities and differences among letters.
- Teach students to use proper writing postures and appropriate ways to hold their writing instruments and position their papers when writing. For example, mark students' writing utensils with dots to teach them where to hold them, and tap on students' work areas to teach them how to align their papers.
- Use supplemental handwriting programs and provide students with writing instruments that have a greater diameter.
- Use paper with colored, solid, and dashed lines to help students learn correct letter heights and paper with perpendicular lines to teach proper spacing. Adapt writing paper by emphasizing the base lines and marking the starting and end points with green and red dots, respectively.
- Offer left-handed students left-handed models, group them together, teach them to write letters vertically or with a slight backward slant, have them write on the left side of the blackboard, and provide them with left-handed desks.
- Post writing models and place a chart presenting lowercase and uppercase letters, the numerals 1 through 10, and numbered arrow cues indicating the corresponding stroke directions in a location that all students can see.
- Provide students with opportunities to evaluate and self-correct their handwriting.
- Monitor students' handwriting legibility and fluency and offer them corrective feedback.

Sources: Cahill (2009); Crouch and Jakubecy (2007); Graham and Harris (2005, 2006); Ritchey (2006).

(b) receive immediate detailed feedback concerning their essays' content, style, word choices, organization, mechanics, and conventions; and (c) use the feedback to revise their essay responses (MacArthur, 2009).

HELPING STUDENTS LEARN TO SPELL

HOW CAN I HELP MY STUDENTS LEARN TO SPELL? A skill area that can affect both writing and reading is spelling (Santoro, Coyne, & Simmons, 2006; Savage, Pillay, & Melidona, 2008). Reading is a decoding process; spelling is an encoding process. Consequently, many students who experience difficulties in reading also are likely to have problems with spelling, which hinders their writing (Graham & Harris, 2006; Howard, DaDeppo, & De La Paz, 2008). For instance, to avoid frequent spelling errors, students who struggle with spelling may use less sophisticated and varied vocabulary in their written products. You can help students learn to spell by employing a combination of approaches and by using a variety of strategies to adapt spelling instruction.

Use a Combination of Approaches

Your students may benefit from a spelling program that combines several approaches (Graham & Harris, 2005; Graham, Harris, & Fink-Chorzempa, 2003; Howard et al., 2008). These combinations mean you need to consider using a range of rule-governed and whole-word approaches to teaching spelling.

Rule-Governed Approaches **Rule-governed spelling approaches** promote spelling skills by teaching students to use morphemic and phonemic analysis and basic spelling rules (Amtmann, Abbott, & Berninger, 2008; Reed, 2008). In using rule-governed approaches, you help students learn spelling rules and patterns by asking them to analyze words that follow the same grapheme–phoneme correspondence, to discuss similarities and differences in words, to identify the rules that apply, to practice the use of the rule with unfamiliar words, and to learn exceptions to the rule (Harris, 2007; Larkin & Snowling, 2008).

Moats (2006) identifies the following five principles that can help guide spelling instruction:

1. The language of origin and history of use of specific words can explain their spelling.
2. The meaning and part of speech of specific words can determine their spelling.
3. The specific sounds within words are spelled using single letters and/or multiple letter combinations.
4. The positions of sounds within words can affect their spelling.
5. The spellings of certain sounds are based on established rules for letter sequences and patterns.

Therefore, as part of your spelling instruction, use the strategies discussed earlier in this chapter to foster students' phonemic awareness and vocabulary development. You also can teach students the ways in which spelling is predictable and how to use Latin-based prefixes, suffixes and Greek-based words, and parts of speech to determine the spelling of specific words. Students can learn how to spell irregular words that do not follow predictable phoneme–grapheme correspondence by grouping them with similar regular words (e.g., teaching *two* with *twin* and *twice*) and by highlighting their irregular features to assist students in memorizing them (e.g., friend) and using mnemonic associations (e.g., *A rat* is found in sep*arat*e, Your princi*pal* is your *pal*) (Carreker, 2005; Willingham, 2009).

One rule-governed model for teaching spelling is the **linguistic spelling approach**, in which spelling instruction focuses on the rules of spelling and patterns related to whole words (Gentry, 2005). Once the students learn a series of words with similar spelling, opportunities to generalize the rule to other words in the family arise. For example, students are taught the *oat* family using the words *boat* and *coat*. Later, they apply the pattern to other words from that family such as *goat, moat,* and *float.*

Whereas the linguistic approach is based on learning spelling patterns within whole words, the **phonetic spelling approach** is based on learning to apply phoneme–grapheme correspondence within parts of words. Thus, a phonetic approach to spelling involves teaching students the sound–symbol correspondence for individual letters and combinations of letters (e.g., digraphs and diphthongs). Students then apply these rules by breaking words into syllables, pronouncing each syllable, and writing the letter(s) that correspond to each sound. Although phonetic approaches to teaching spelling have been successful, words that represent irregularities in the English language, including multiple-letter sounds, word pronunciations, and unstressed syllables, are deterrents to phonetic spelling.

Whole-Word Approaches   Whole-word approaches help students focus on the whole word through a variety of multisensory activities. They include test-study-test procedures, corrected-test methods, and word study techniques.

Test-Study-Test Procedures.   Perhaps the most frequently used method of spelling instruction is the test-study-test method. In this method, students take a pretest on a fixed list of words, study the words they misspell, and take a posttest to assess mastery. You also can use a study-test procedure in which students study all the week's spelling words and then take a test. When posttesting students with these procedures, it is recommended that teachers intersperse known and unknown words in the test.

You can adapt test-study-test procedures by decreasing the number of spelling words given to students from five to three to increase their spelling performance. Thus, rather than having students try to master a large list of words each week, you can break down the list so that students study and are tested on three words each day. Also, use a flow word list rather than a fixed list. Flow lists can help you individualize spelling by allowing students who master spelling words to delete those words from the list and replace them with new words. Whether using a fixed or flow list of spelling words, give students time to work at their own rate, and require them to demonstrate mastery over a period of time.

Corrected-Test Methods.   The corrected-test method allows you to guide students in correcting their spelling errors by spelling words orally while students correct them; spelling words and accentuating each letter as students simultaneously point to each letter in the word; spelling words while students write the correct letter above the crossed-out, incorrect letter; writing the correct spelling on students' papers near the incorrectly spelled word, which students then correct; and copying students' errors, modeling the correct spelling, and observing students as they write the word correctly.

Word Study Techniques.   Word study techniques include a wide range of activities designed to help students systematically study and remember spelling words (Baer, Invernizzi, Johnston, & Templeton, 2010; Graham & Harris, 2006). A multistep word study procedure can include verbalizing the word, writing and saying the word, comparing the written word with a model, tracing and saying the word, writing the word from memory and checking it, and repeating prior steps as necessary. You also can use word study methods that encourage students to close their eyes and visualize the spelling word, verbalize the word while writing it, or finger-spell or write words in the air (Graham et al., 2003). Another word study strategy you can use is *word sort*, which involves having students engage in a variety of activities that require them to group and regroup words based on their shared spelling features (Harris, 2007; Invernizzi, Johnston, Baer, & Templeton, 2009). Rasinski and Oswald (2005) describe Making Words and Making and Writing Words, word study techniques that use a variety of word-building strategies to teach about the characteristics of words and how to spell them.

Adapt Spelling Instruction

Many students, including those with disabilities, may exhibit problems in spelling. You can adapt spelling instruction for them in the following ways.

Explain the Importance of Spelling   Explaining the importance and relevance of spelling can motivate students to improve their spelling skills. You can emphasize

REFLECTIVE

What approaches were used by your teachers to teach you spelling? What were the strengths of these approaches? What were their weaknesses?

Teaching Spelling

Ms. Sylvestre noticed that Ricardo, an English language learner, was struggling with his spelling. She observed that many of the vocabulary words that Ricardo chose to use in writing assignments were misspelled. Analyzing his errors, she noticed several patterns. Ricardo often left off the -ed when writing words in the past tense. For example, he wrote *encourage* instead of *encouraged.* She also noticed that he had difficulty spelling words with a double consonant in the middle such as *putting, happen,* and *pressure.*

Ms. Sylvestre used this information to help Ricardo improve his spelling. She started by teaching him to hear and add the -ed to words in the past tense. First, she explained past tense to him and then articulated words in the past tense and asked Ricardo to repeat them. Then, she presented him with a series of words and asked him to identify those that were in the past tense. When she felt confident that Ricardo understood past tense and could hear the "ed" sound, she introduced a mnemonic device to help him remember to add the -ed ending to regular verbs that are past tense. She told Ricardo to "think of a person named Ed who did everything yesterday. Ed will often be at the end of the verb because everything he does has happened already. Remember if the verb ends with a consonant, that consonant is doubled before the -ed is added." She then had Ricardo practice this skill using regular verbs and verbs that ended in a consonant.

When Ricardo demonstrated mastery on several spelling activities involving -ed words, Ms. Sylvestre focused instruction on helping him to spell words with the double consonant in the middle. She used a phonetic approach with Ricardo that involved her modeling how to look at the words, sound them out, and break them apart to analyze the spelling. After she modeled doing it, she and Ricardo did it together. Eventually, she had Ricardo do it without her assistance. As Ricardo became successful in spelling these words, Ms. Sylvestre identified a new set of words to teach him to spell.

Here are some other strategies you can use to implement the IDEA in your inclusive classroom and improve your students' spelling:

- Teach spelling daily for 15–20 minutes or for 30 minutes three times per week, and make spelling an ongoing part of reading and writing instruction.
- Encourage students to visualize spelling words.
- Have students use spelling words in sentences.
- Teach students to use visual representation to help them remember the spelling of words. For example, students can visually represent the spelling of the word *handle* by drawing a picture of a hand with an *L* shaped out of the index finger and the thumb and the letter *E* connected to it.
- Use peer tutoring systems such as classwide peer tutoring to help students improve their spelling.

Sources: Graham and Harris (2006); Harris (2007); Howard et al. (2008); Moats (2006).

the relevance of spelling by helping students see the connection among spelling, reading, and writing.

Analyze Students' Spelling Errors   You can observe students while they spell and their spelling products to note the progress and the types of errors they make (Harris, 2007; Howard et al., 2008). For example, some of your students may use invented spelling where they spell non-phonetic words phonetically, and many English language learners may engage in cross-linguistically developed spelling, spelling words incorrectly by mixing elements from their first and second languages. Appropriate spelling instruction can be based on the students' error patterns.

Choose Personalized and Relevant Spelling Words   You can motivate students and improve their spelling by personalizing their spelling words and focusing initially on a core of frequently used words, as well as on words that are part of the student's listening, writing, and spelling vocabulary (Corcos & Willows, 2009). Students' spelling words can be selected by both you and your students and be those that frequently appear in students' writing products, used in students' textbooks and reading materials, or relate to students' lives and interests (Harris, 2007). Also focus instruction on some of the spelling words that are particularly difficult for your students to remember (Howard et al., 2008).

Provide Time to Review Words Previously Learned   Students with disabilities may experience difficulty remembering words previously mastered. Therefore, you can provide time to review and study previously learned words and use spelling words in other situations (Graham & Harris, 2006).

Teach Students to Use Cues and Learning Strategies   Meaning and sound-alike cues, mnemonic devices, and configuration clues help students figure out correct spellings (Loeffler, 2005). For example, some students may benefit from drawing blocks around the outline of the word to remember its configuration. Students can be encouraged to select cues that make sense to them and relate to their experiences and culture.

Classroom posters can provide students with spelling cues. For example, you can post spelling strategy charts to give students a range of spelling techniques. Students can be taught learning strategies that prompt them to use effective spelling techniques and cues (Howard et al., 2008). For example, Keller (2002) created SPELLER Steps, a learning strategy that prompts students to spell words, and Howard et al. (2008) describe the use of PESTS to help students learn to spell words that bug them.

Teach Dictionary Skills   Spelling problems can be minimized by encouraging students to use the dictionary to confirm the spelling of unknown or irregular words, spelling demons, confusing rules, and difficult word combinations (Moats, 2006). Therefore, students need to learn print and online dictionary skills, including alphabetizing, locating words, using guide words, and understanding syllabification and pronunciation. Students in primary grades can use a picture dictionary until they learn the skills needed to use a regular dictionary.

You can have students make personal dictionaries or word banks of the words that are difficult for them to spell (Gipe, 2006). As students write, they consult their personal dictionaries to help them with word choice and spelling. Personal dictionaries also can be developed for math, science, and social studies words. Students, including English language learners, also can create word books that include pages for each letter of the alphabet, with weekly entries of spelling words in sentences and their definitions on the appropriate page.

Teach Students to Proofread and to Correct Spelling Errors   Spelling can be enhanced by having students proofread their work and correct their spelling errors (Moats, 2006). You can encourage students to proofread for spelling errors by

- checking with a list, word wall, or classmate;
- giving them a list of words and having them identify and correct the misspellings;
- assigning them to find the spelling errors in the assignments of their peers;
- listing the number of errors in a student's assignment and having students locate and correct the errors;
- marking words that may be incorrectly spelled and having students check them;
- teaching them to use a spelling rubric (Cunningham, 2008; Loeffler, 2005).

Students also can be encouraged and taught to correct their own spelling errors. Students correct their spelling by (a) comparing their spelling of words with a correct spelling model; (b) noting incorrect letter(s) by crossing them out, boxing them, or circling them; (c) writing the correct letters above the incorrect letters; and (d) writing the correct spelling on a line next to the incorrect spelling.

Model Appropriate Spelling Techniques   You can improve the spelling skills of students by giving them oral and written models to imitate. When writing on the blackboard or interactive board, periodically emphasize the spelling of words, and occasionally spell words or interactive board peers spell them for the class. You also can model a positive attitude toward spelling by teaching spelling with enthusiasm and encouraging positive attributions regarding the use of spelling strategies.

Teach Students to Use the Spell Checker   As we discussed earlier in this chapter, you can help students with spelling by teaching them to use spell checkers (MacArthur, 2009).

Teach Useful Prefixes, Suffixes, and Root Words   Teaching students useful prefixes, suffixes, and root words can help them spell and define new multisyllabic words (Harris, 2007; Moats, 2006).

Use Technology   Technology can be used to improve students' spelling (Amtmann et al., 2008; Harris, 2007). Software programs offer students opportunities to practice their spelling skills within individualized teaching formats and instructional learning games.

Use Spelling Games   Teacher-made and technology-based spelling games can motivate students and give them the opportunity to practice spelling skills in a nonthreatening environment (Harris, 2007). Commercially produced games include Scrabble, Spello, and Boggle.

Making Connections
Find out more about effective memory skills and strategies that you can teach your students to use in Chapter 11.

Foster Spelling Fluency   Foster spelling fluency by providing your students with many opportunities to practice spelling and write (Savage et al., 2008; Vaughn & Roberts, 2007). For example, have them look at a word, cover it with a sticky note or index card, and write and compare it to the correct spelling of the word (Stormont, 2008). You also can foster spelling fluency by teaching your students to use effective memory enhancing strategies (Bouck, Bassette, Taber-Doughty, Flanagan, & Szwed, 2009; Howard et al., 2008).

Provide Feedback to Students   As students practice their spelling, you can provide them with prompt and specific feedback regarding their accuracy and ability to apply spelling strategies and rules taught. You also can deliver feedback to help them correct their spelling errors by modeling the correct spelling of words and giving them opportunities to practice writing the words correctly (Santoro et al., 2006).

Using Technology to Promote Inclusion
MAKING LITERACY INSTRUCTION ACCESSIBLE TO ALL STUDENTS

In addition to the hardware resources and software applications already discussed in this chapter and other chapters, there are other technologies you can integrate into your inclusive classroom to differentiate literacy instruction (Brozo & Puckett, 2009; Wissick et al., 2009). Enhance the effectiveness of these technologies by motivating students to use them, teaching students how to use them, and recognizing their limitations. It also is important for you to use these technologies to supplement your providing high-quality reading and writing instruction to your students, which includes giving them numerous opportunities to read and write under your supervision.

You can use a variety of hardware and software resources to help your students to develop their reading skills (Anderson-Inman, 2009; Dell et al., 2008). Some teachers use text-to-speech and optical character recognition systems to help their students with fluency difficulties access reading materials and decode unknown words. They use an optical scanner to convert print materials to electronic text, which is then converted into speech by a talking word processor. Students then select and highlight sections, sentences,

words, or syllables, which are then pronounced by the computer. Students also can use a digital highlighter that moves from word to word; use pronunciation dictionaries; and control the speed, pitch, and volume of the speech used to read the text. Different students use the system in different ways. Some students use it to read the whole text, while other students use it only when they encounter an unknown word. The system also can be adapted for English language learners by including digital talking dictionary that pronounces and defines highlighted English words in the students' native languages. A digital American Sign Language dictionary can be used to help deaf and hard-of-hearing students.

Lightweight and portable optical character recognition systems, which have headphone connections so that they can be used without disturbing others, are also available. These devices allow users to scan printed materials, which are then read aloud to them are also useful for your students who are learning English. When considering using these devices, it is important to remember that they are most useful for reading words or sentences rather than paragraphs or pages.

Here are some other ways you can use technology to create inclusive classrooms that support students' literacy development:

- Use a variety of types of software programs and speech generating augmentative communication

(Continued)

devices to teach phonemic awareness and phonics to students, and to promote students' reading fluency, vocabulary and comprehension and their word recognition, decoding and spelling skills (Blachowicz & Fisher, 2006; Hasselbring & Bausch, 2006; Ogura, Coco, & Bulat, 2007; Sopko, 2008; Wilkins & Ratajczak, 2009). For example, your students can use digital flashcards to learn reading and spelling words (Doyle & Giangreco, 2009).

- Use technology-based literacy curriculum materials. Audio recordings of text-based materials that are available in digital formats are available electronically via Recordings for the Blind and Dyslexic (*www.rfbd.org*), Bookshare (*www.bookshare.org*), the Internet, and electronic libraries (e-libraries) (Harrison, 2009).

- Provide students with access to online reading materials such as magazines and articles that relate to their interests (Weigel & Gardner, 2009; Wolf & Barzillai, 2009).

- Use software programs to create high-interest books, digital stories, and picture books with prompts for students or to work with students to create digital reading materials for others (Wissick et al., 2009) and to determine the readability of print materials (Salend, 2009).

- Make digital recordings of individual students reading, and provide students with access to reading models, listening previews, and repeated reading via use of audible books or multimedia, software programs, or computerized models of others reading (Rasinski et al., 2009). You can have students read chorally with a recorded model fluently reading the same text at different speeds (Sorrell, Mee Bell, & McCallum, 2007).

- Pair pictures, symbols, video, and animations with text to prompt students' reading, writing and vocabulary development and to assist them in using word processing and other software programs (Parette & Peterson-Karlan, 2007).

- Use technology to simultaneously display words, and sentences and their prerecorded readings (Van Norman & Wood, 2008) and to present flash cards of letters, sight words, sentences, and vocabulary at varying rates or time delay prompts and to have students play reading, vocabulary, and spelling games (Campbell & Mechling, 2009; Corcos & Willows, 2009).

- Use presentation software slides with audio to teach word recognition and phonics (Coleman-Martin, Heller, Cihak, & Irvine,

2005). Create a sequence of slides with corresponding audio for each word so that students see and hear the word (slide 1), view and hear the first phoneme highlighted in a dark color (slide 2), view and hear the second phoneme highlighted in a dark color while the first phoneme is presented in a lighter color (slide 3), and repeat this process until each phoneme in the word has been presented. Following the presentation of each slide, students are presented with the whole word and asked to try to sound it out. At the end of the session, students are presented with a slide of the word in a darker color and larger font and asked to read the word.

- Foster students' reading and motivation to read by making and showing them video or audio recordings of themselves reading successfully.

- Use low-tech devices to assist students with reading (Ferreri, 2009). Line guides, windows, or masks such as reading rulers or index cards can assist students who have difficulty tracking and maintaining their place on a line. Placing color acetate overlays on their reading materials to help them adjust the contrast in the text. Students who speak softly when they read may benefit from using commercial or teacher-made devices that provide them with auditory feedback while they read (Higbee Mandlebaum et al., 2007).

- Facilitate students' ability to plan and compose written text by using visual and auditory prompts, outlining, semantic mapping, and graphics-based writing programs and multimedia and digital journals (Reeves & Standard, 2009; Wissick et al., 2009).

- Have students collaborate with online peers on writing projects and peer revision or write to online pen pals via e-mail.

- Teach students to use handheld reference devices that contain electronic dictionaries, thesauri, and grammar and spell checkers that pronounce words, give definitions and synonyms, correct the spelling of phonetic words, and offer educational games involving targeted vocabulary words (Lindsey-Glenn & Gentry, 2008).

- Use digital devices to teach handwriting and spelling. For example, students can practice their handwriting and spelling skills with auditory prompts using digital pens and computers and via smart-whiteboards with wireless pads and electronic pens, spelling, sight, and vocabulary words can be displayed and handwriting can be modeled for students (Bouck et al., 2009; Pogue, 2008a).

- Help students hold their writing utensils by using such low-technology devices as tape, wrist weights, foam rubber bands, a triangle or grips to slip over the writing utensil, or specialized writing utensils that allow for adapted grips such as large-diameter pencils, crayons, holders, Wiggle pens, weighted holders, and writing frames (Thompson et al., 2005).

- Provide students with slantboards and Velcro to help them see and stabilize literacy materials and templates and adapted paper such as Right Line writing paper, which has raised green lines that provide students with visual and tactile handwriting writing cues (Johnston et al., 2008; Thompson et al., 2005).

Assess Progress Continuously   Use a variety of strategies to assess your students' spelling progress continuously (McLoughlin & Lewis, 2008; Overton, 2009). Rather than giving a spelling test at the end of the week including all of their spelling words, consider giving daily spelling assessments that focus on words students misspelled in prior assessments (Amtmann et al., 2008).

Have Students Record Their Progress   Self-recording motivates students by giving them a visual representation of their progress. Students also can set spelling goals for themselves based on their prior performance and chart their success in achieving their goals. For example, students can keep a cumulative chart or graph of words spelled correctly, maintain weekly graphs that measure performance on pretests and posttests, or self-correct and track their spelling performance on writing tasks. They also can maintain a spelling journal with entries related to the spelling words and patterns they have learned (Harris, 2007).

What Would You Do in Today's Diverse Classroom?

★ Richard is having difficulty with reading. He reads haltingly and stiffly and often has to read words several times as he attempts to sound them out. He is reluctant to read aloud and makes excuses to avoid doing it.

★ Robin has good ideas but struggles with writing and spelling. Her writing, which is limited, contains repetitive words and irrelevant information, misspellings, and grammatical errors, and it is very difficult to follow. As a result, she dislikes writing and views it as a tedious way to communicate.

★ Rosibel is an English language learner whose reading and writing continue to improve. However, her work often consists of many sentences that are disorganized and lacking in terms of capitalization, and punctuation.

1. How would Richard, Robin, and Rosibel's difficulties impact their performance in your inclusive classroom?

2. What would you do to help them?

3. What knowledge, skills, dispositions, resources, and support from others would be useful in helping them learn to read, write, and spell?

PEARSON myeducationlab   Watch a teacher present an interactive writing lesson designed to support and differentiate the reading and writing development of students who are English language learners by visiting the MyEducationLab for this course. Go to the *Assignments and Activities* section under the topic *Cultural and Linguistic Diversity* and complete the activity entitled *Writing Strategies That Support English Language Learners in the Inclusive Classroom* to answer questions about differentiating reading, writing and spelling instruction for *all students*.

Summary

This chapter presented guidelines and strategies for differentiating reading, writing, and spelling instruction. As you review the questions posed in this chapter, remember the following points.

How Can I Help My Students Learn to Read?
CEC 3, 4, 5, 6, 7, 8, 9; PRAXIS 3; INTASC 1, 2, 3, 4, 5, 6, 7, 9
You can support students' reading by using the principles of effective early reading interventions, offering specialized interventions to supplement instruction for

students, and focusing your instruction on developing and promoting their phonemic awareness, reading fluency, vocabulary, and text comprehension. You can do this by motivating students to read; involving their families; fostering their word identification skills; using prompting and cuing strategies; supporting older struggling readers; developing their vocabulary; and using peer-based instruction. It also is important for you to employ a balanced approach to teaching reading and supplement your instruction by using remedial reading programs, strategies, and materials.

How Can I Help My Students Learn to Write?

CEC 3, 4, 5, 6, 7, 8, 9; PRAXIS 3; INTASC 1, 2, 3, 4, 5, 6, 7, 9

You can make writing a meaningful, authentic, and integral part of the curriculum; use a process-oriented approach to writing instruction; teach students to use learning strategies; and employ technology-supported writing applications.

How Can I Help My Students Learn to Spell?

CEC 3, 4, 5, 6, 7, 8, 9; PRAXIS 3; INTASC 2, 3, 4, 5, 6, 7, 9

You can help students learn to spell by employing a combination of approaches and by using a variety of strategies to adapt spelling instruction.

MS. RIVLIN

Ms. Rivlin and her students are studying geometry, including the perimeter and area of various geometric shapes. To help motivate her students and develop their appreciation of geometry as a factor in their lives, she begins by reading a selection to her students from a book where the characters use geometry. She then asks her students to identify shapes in their environment, and write journal entries describing them. For homework, students are asked to find pictures of two-dimensional figures and write about and orally describe these shapes. Ms. Rivlin uses students' homework in class by having them exchange their geometric shapes so they can describe the figures their classmates have collected.

The students experiment with shapes by performing various geoboard activities. Using tangrams, they investigate the properties of shapes, discuss the similarities and differences among the shapes, and create new shapes.

Ms. Rivlin uses an interactive white-smartboard to display various geometry shapes she found at the MathMol Library of Geometric Images, and to introduce the various concepts related to geometric shapes, area, and perimeter. She also has her students electronically construct and experiment with various shapes with Geometer's Sketchpad and perform exercises using online manipulatives, which they access from the National Library of Virtual Manipulatives.

In addition, Ms. Rivlin has students work in cooperative learning groups to experiment with, brainstorm about, and solve problems. In their groups, students research and write about the cultural origins and meanings of geometric shapes. One group reports about the Egyptian pyramids, including information about the area and perimeter of these structures, while another group uses the Internet to gather and present information about Mayan ruins and geometric shapes. As a

Differentiating Mathematics, Science, and Social Studies Instruction

culminating activity, Ms. Rivlin asks each group to design a community-based recreational area. Groups begin by collecting data about the various dimensions of the area and the different types of recreational areas. One group chooses to design a skateboarding area, while other groups design a park, a series of gardens, athletic fields, and an art and music center. They then create and draw their recreational area, and share their designs with the whole class. At the end of the unit, Ms. Rivlin works with her students to create portfolios that demonstrate their knowledge and mastery of geometry.

What additional strategies can Ms. Rivlin use to promote the mathematics skills of her students? After reading this chapter, you should have the knowledge, skills, and dispositions to answer this as well as the following questions.

- How can I differentiate mathematics instruction?
- How can I differentiate science and social studies instruction?

Many strategies for differentiating classroom instruction to enhance learning, motivation, and literacy development can be used across academic disciplines (see Chapters 8, 9, and 10). However, like Ms. Rivlin, you may find that you need to make accommodations to a specific content area to promote learning for students. This chapter offers guidelines for differentiating mathematics, science, and social studies instruction. It is important to remember that many of these instructional strategies can be used across the different content areas. Also, keep in mind that no one curriculum and approach will meet the needs of *all students*. Most students, however, perform best if you use a balanced curriculum and approach that combines elements discussed in this chapter.

Because students look up to you, you can serve as a positive role model to promote their attitudes and confidence in learning all subjects. Although it is important for you to convey a positive and enthusiastic attitude toward teaching and learning all subjects through your language and teaching behaviors, it is especially important in helping *all of your students* learn mathematics and science.

DIFFERENTIATING MATHEMATICS INSTRUCTION

HOW CAN I DIFFERENTIATE MATHEMATICS INSTRUCTION? Many students, particularly those with disabilities, experience problems in learning mathematics (Fuchs & Fuchs, 2008; Lembke & Foegen, 2009; Morgan, Farkas, & Wu, 2009). Figure 11.1 presents some of the common characteristics displayed by students who have difficulties with mathematics. As a result, they struggle with understanding numbers and counting and number relationships, patterns, and operations (this is called *number sense*); learning and retrieving math facts; performing computations; estimating plausible answers; and solving word problems, which also can hinder their attitudes toward mathematics (Bryant, Bryant, Gersten, Scammacca, & Chavez, 2008; Faulkner, 2009; Hopkins & Egeberg, 2009; Locuniak & Jordan, 2008; Powell, Fuchs, Fuchs, Cirino, & Fletcher, 2009; Raghubar et al., 2009; Rousselle & Noel, 2008).

However, these students can improve their computational and mathematics reasoning skills when they are taught using a focused, hands-on, engaging, and interactive curriculum that allows them to develop number sense, and the mathematical understanding and skills that serve as a foundation for them learning how to experience, think about, and solve meaningful mathematical problems (Faulkner, 2009; Gurganus, 2007; Sherman, Richardson, Yard, 2009). You can help these students benefit from and succeed with this curriculum and approach by planning

Go to the Assignments and Activities section of the Topic *Content Area Teaching* in the MyEducationLab for your course and complete the activity entitled *Mathematical Concepts*. As you watch the video and answer the accompanying questions, think about the ways you can differentiate mathematics instruction to benefit *all students*.

FIGURE 11.1 Common characteristics of students with mathematics difficulties

Students with mathematics problems may have difficulty with

- recognizing and writing numerals and other mathematics symbols;
- counting without using fingers;
- ordering, aligning and spacing numbers;
- understanding numbers and number relationships, patterns and operations;
- recalling number facts and counting quickly;
- understanding mathematics vocabulary;
- performing operations and multidigit calculations;
- changing from one operation to another;
- estimating and making approximate calculations;
- using effective and efficient mathematical strategies;
- solving problems.

Sources: Bryant, Bryant, Gersten, Scammacca, and Chavez (2008); Fuchs and Fuchs (2008); Gersten et al. (2005); Hopkins and Egeberg (2009); Lembke and Foegen (2009); Locuniak and Jordan (2008); Morgan, Farkas, and Wu (2009); Raghubar et al. (2009); Rousselle and Noel (2008).

and organizing instruction according to the following principles, many of which also can be used to structure your teaching of science and social studies.

Focus Instruction, and Use a Problem-Solving Approach

The National Council of Teachers of Mathematics (NCTM) established guidelines that promote five general mathematical goals for *all students:* (a) learning to value mathematics, (b) developing confidence in one's mathematical ability, (c) becoming mathematical problem solvers, (d) learning to communicate mathematically, and (e) learning to reason mathematically (Van de Walle, Karp, & Bay-Williams, 2010). The NCTM endorsed a problem-solving and discovery learning approach to the teaching and assessment of principles and processes in mathematics that gives *all students* opportunities to use mathematics to solve meaningful problems and apply mathematics to real-world issues (Freeman & Crawford, 2008). The NCTM's (2007) *Curriculum Focal Points for Prekindergarten Through Grade 8 Mathematics* called for curricular changes that focus on teaching the most important mathematical concepts and skills in prekindergarten through eighth grade. The NCTM encourages educators to use these focal points to plan a range of learning activities that foster the development of the basic mathematical understandings and skills students need to learn to reason and communicate mathematically and become confident mathematical problem solvers.

Help Students Develop Their Math Facts and Computation Skills

You can promote the success of your mathematics instructional program by offering instruction that helps students develop their math facts and computation skills (Hopkins & Egeberg, 2009; Riccomini, & Witzel, 2010; Sherman et al., 2009). A *demonstration plus model* strategy has been successful in helping students with learning problems develop computational skills. The strategy involves these steps:

Step 1. You demonstrate the procedures for solving a specific type of computation problem while presenting the key words for each step.

Step 2. Students view your example and perform the steps in the computation while giving the key words for each step.

Step 3. Students complete additional problems, referring to your example if necessary.

You also can teach students to use mental calculation shortcuts (Gurganus, 2007; Hopkins & Egeberg, 2009). For example, you can help them learn to use number combinations that they know (3 + 3 = 6) to figure out other number combinations (4 + 3 = 7) as well as using relations among operations (7 + 2 = 9, which means 9 − 2 = 7). You also can develop math facts by posting fact charts in your classroom (Fashl, 2007). To discourage students from relying on the chart unnecessarily, some teachers blacken out the math facts student have mastered.

Your students with moderate and significant intellectual disabilities may need specialized interventions to support their learning of a range of mathematical skills and concepts, which may help other students as well (Browder, Spooner, Ahlgrim-Delzell, Harris, & Wakeman, 2008; Cihak & Foust, 2008; Jimenez, Browder, & Courtade, 2008; Rao & Kane, 2009). For these students, you can supplement your mathematics instruction by providing them with systematic and repeated instruction that focuses on real-life applications of mathematics in authentic settings. Thus, you teach money skills with respect to making purchases of items that are of interest to them, and teach computation skills in terms of the number or value of stamps needed to mail a letter. This real-life instruction should be accompanied by use of task analysis to break down the skills into smaller sequential steps that you teach by providing these students with ongoing practice, prompting and feedback via use of model-lead-test, time delay, and the system of least prompts. You also can use concrete materials such as number lines and numerals linked to their corresponding number of dots to help them develop mathematical skills.

Making Connections
The use of model-lead-test, time delay and the system of least prompts was discussed earlier in Chapter 10.

Differentiating Mathematics, Science, and Social Studies Instruction

Vary the Instructional Sequence Some students who are having difficulty learning math facts and computation skills may benefit from adjustments in the teaching sequence (Riccomini & Witzel, 2010; Sherman et al., 2009). For example, while the traditional teaching sequence for addition computation skills is based on the numeric value of the sum, some teachers use a teaching sequence that progresses from count-ons (e.g., +1, +2, + 3) to zero facts (3 + 0, 7 + 0) to doubles (3 + 3, 8 + 8) to 10 sums (4 + 6, 3 + 7).

Varying the teaching sequence to cluster math facts can make it easier to remember them. Rather than teaching math facts in isolation, you can present related math facts together. For example, students can learn the cluster of multiplying by 2 together. As students demonstrate mastery, they can practice mixed groups of math facts. Students also can be taught to use *doubling* (e.g., learning 7 × 4 by doubling 7 × 2) and *helping* or *near facts* (e.g., learning 5 × 6 by adding 5 to 5 × 5) to multiply.

Promote Mastery and Automaticity An important goal of math instruction in basic facts is to have students respond quickly and accurately (Fuchs & Fuchs, 2008; Hopkins & Egeberg, 2009). You can offer students a variety of activities that promote mastery and automaticity, such as using peer-directed and technology-assisted systems that provide students with numerous opportunities to respond (Powell et al., 2009). You also can foster students' math fluency by using appropriate specialized mathematics curriculum and teaching materials (Gurganus, 2007; Riccomini & Witzel, 2010; Sherman et al., 2009; Sood & Jitendra, 2007). For example, *Knowing Math* is a mathematics intervention program designed for small groups that combines effective practices from the United States and East Asia such as mathematical conversations between students and teachers that foster students' mastery of mathematical knowledge and skills (Ketterlin-Geller, Chard, & Fien, 2008).

Match Instruction to Students' Error Types The instructional strategy selected often will depend on the types of errors that students make (Allsopp, Kyger, Lovin, Gerretson, Carson, & Ray, 2008). You can use the principle of the *least error correction*, which involves identifying the nature of students' errors by analyzing their performance on items between the last correct item and the first item failed, and then planning instruction to address the common and significant errors (Cawley, Parmar, Foley, Salmon, & Roy, 2001). You also can ask students to think aloud by verbalizing how they approached a task.

Present Mathematics Appropriately

Organize Instruction to Follow a Developmental Instructional Sequence You can follow a developmental instructional sequence that involves three stages: (1) concrete, (2) semiconcrete or representational, and (3) abstract and teacher modeling followed by student practice (Bryant et al., 2008; Ketterlin-Geller, Chard, & Fien, 2008; Miller & Hudson, 2007; Riccomini & Witzel, 2010). First, introduce and illustrate new mathematical skills and concepts by using three-dimensional objects such as concrete aids and manipulatives, and then provide opportunities for students to use these concrete materials to practice the new skills and concepts (Gurganus, 2007). Next, semiconcrete aids such as demonstrations or illustrations via drawings, technology, or textbooks are presented to students to represent concepts and to offer additional learning activities to develop their proficiency. Finally, promote understanding, speed, and accuracy by using abstract strategies such as mathematical symbols and oral and written language rather than manipulatives or pictorials. Following this developmental approach, you foster generalization through a graduated word problems sequence in which students first work on word problems without irrelevant information, then progress to word problems with irrelevant information, and finally create their own word problems.

Introduce Concepts and Present Problems Through Everyday Situations You can promote learning, motivate students, and help them learn to value mathematics by connecting mathematics to situations and problems that are familiar and meaningful to them (Browder et al., 2008; Hudson & Miller, 2006; Van de Walle et al., 2010). As Ms. Rivlin did in the chapter-opening vignette, present math problems by anchoring them to real-life situations and issues, and discuss the relevance of learning a new skill and the situations in which the skill can be applied. For example, students can investigate problems by gathering data related to employment, social and environmental issues, friends, health, sports, music, and art. By linking mathematical problems to other subject areas such as reading and science, you can make mathematical connections to the practical, recreational, and cultural aspects of students' lives. A good way to introduce mathematical concepts and connect mathematics to students' lives is by using literature (Hyde, 2007; Lott Adams & McKoy Lowery, 2007).

You also can connect mathematics to students' cultural backgrounds and world cultures, which is referred to as **ethnomathematics** (Barta & Pleasant-Jetté, 2005). Materials that explore the different cultural origins of mathematics, discuss mathematical solutions and practices developed and used in all parts of the world, present the achievements of mathematicians from various language and cultural backgrounds, and offer various culturally diverse, practical applications of mathematics can be used to relate students' experiences to mathematics. For example, students can be taught number sense by learning about and comparing our number system with the hieroglyphic numerals of Egypt, Chinese rod numerals, and ancient Mayan numerals, and about elements of probability by playing such games of chance as dreidel (a game played during Hannukah) and *toma-todo* (a Mexican game) (Zaslavsky, 2002). Connections to students' lives and cultures also can be established by using rhythms, songs, raps, and chants that teach mathematics, as well as by employing strategies that were used to teach mathematics in students' native countries. You also can frame word problems using familiar community and multicultural and nonsexist references so that students conduct problem-solving activities focused on challenges in the community.

Teach the Language of Mathematics   Learning the language (vocabulary and symbols) of mathematics can promote mathematical literacy and proficiency, communication, and reasoning and give students a framework for solving problems (Lee & Herner-Patnode, 2007; Freeman & Crawford, 2008; Van de Walle et al., 2010). Although it is essential for you to identify, teach, and consistently use important mathematics vocabulary and symbols to all of your students, it is especially important for your students with disabilities and your students who are English language learners (Dong, 2009). Therefore, it is important for you to identify and teach important mathematics vocabulary (e.g., *numerator, divisor, sum, square root, surface area*, etc.) and symbols (e.g., <, >, %). It also is important for you to teach technical, subtechnical, general, and symbolic mathematics vocabulary, especially those terms that they will encounter frequently during instruction and when using content-based materials (Schleppegrell, 2007). Whereas **technical math vocabulary** refers to terms that have one meaning (e.g., *square* or *rational number*), **subtechnical math vocabulary** (e.g., *area, degrees, value, product, chance*) refers to terms that have multiple meanings across different contexts and content areas. **General math vocabulary** includes those mathematical terms that have different meanings outside the world of mathematics (e.g., *negative numbers*), and **symbolic math vocabulary** relates to abstract numbers and abbreviations that are hard to define and understand (e.g., *infinity*).

You can help students learn math (science and social studies) vocabulary by using the vocabulary and concept development strategies and approaches we learned about in prior chapters. For example, you can teach them roots, suffixes, and prefixes for mathematical terms such as *tri-, -meter, -graph*, and *octo-* (Thompson & Chappell, 2007). Use them frequently, restate them in different ways using language students understand, and present them in multiple visual formats. You also can provide your students with access to technology such as HELP Math, a Web-based curriculum that provides students with a range of interactive multimedia learning activities based on effective ESL teaching principles to foster understanding of mathematical language, symbols, and concepts (Freeman & Crawford, 2008). You also can assign and teach math terms as vocabulary words, use math terms as part of academic games, and post math terms and their definitions and visual representations in your classroom. You also can color-code words related to their mathematical categories (e.g., geometry, algebra, patterns), and have students act out math terms (e.g., different angle types) (Lee & Herner-Patnode, 2007).

You and your students can develop and maintain a multilingual math notebook, dictionary, or glossary that contains definitions, visual explanations, examples, and graphics of frequently used mathematical terminology (Dong, 2009) (see Figure 11.2). For example, the dictionary/glossary can contain multilingual presentations of the term, definitions, and examples of math terms such as *sums, quotients, proper fractions, prime number, binomial, quadrilateral,* and *reciprocals.* Students having difficulty with the term *denominator,* for example, can locate its definition and view examples—"The denominator is the bottom part of a fraction that indicates the number of parts. In this fraction, the 6 is the denominator." In addition, students can write in their notebooks definitions for mathematical terms using their own words. They also can create a mathematical operations chart that lists various mathematical symbols, terms, and the words that refer to similar (tens column and tens place) and different mathematical operations and terms (Miller & Hudson, 2006).

Making Connections
This discussion of teaching the language of mathematics relates to the earlier discussion of ways to foster students' vocabulary development in Chapter 10.

Use a Variety of Teaching Aids

Teach Students to Use Manipulatives and Concrete Teaching Aids Like Ms. Rivlin, you can use manipulatives and concrete teaching aids to promote students' number sense and understanding of basic, abstract, and symbolic concepts by introducing these concepts in a nonthreatening way that makes the connection between mathematics and students' lives (Donabella & Rule, 2008; Faulkner, 2009; Miller & Hudson, 2007). These tools offer students opportunities to explore concepts before learning standard math terms and notation. Manipulatives are particularly valuable in helping English language learners and students with language difficulties learn math concepts.

A range of manipulatives are available to teach a variety of concepts (Fashl, 2007; Posamentier, Smith, & Stepelman, 2010; Van de Walle et al., 2010). Make sure that the ones you use are age and culturally appropriate for your students and are easy and safe for your students to use (students with fine motor difficulties may need larger manipulatives). Software programs and Web sites that allow students to manipulate virtual objects also can be used to foster your students' mathematical problem-solving abilities (Murray, Silver-Pacuilla, & Innes Helsel, 2007a).

When using manipulatives and concrete teaching aids to teach math concepts, the following guidelines are helpful (Donabella & Rule, 2008; Gurganus, 2007; Miller & Hudson, 2007). At first, introduce them by modeling their use and explaining the concepts illustrated. Next, allow students to experiment with the materials, to solve

FIGURE 11.2 **Sample visual and bilingual mathematics language dictionary**

Mathematical Terms (English)	Mathematical Terms (Spanish)	Definition	Graphic Example
Equilateral Triangle	Triángulo ēquilátero	A triangle in which all three sides are equal and each angle measures 60 degrees.	
Congruent Angles	Ángulos congruentes	Angles that have the same angle measure in degrees.	

Sources: Dong (2009); Taylor et al. (2009).

problems independently and in groups, and to describe their actions. You can structure students' use of the materials by asking questions that guide their experimentation. To promote generalization, give students opportunities to use a variety of manipulatives. When using manipulatives with students who have behavioral difficulties, you may need to remind them of the classroom rules and reinforce them for complying with the procedures for using and handling the materials.

Use Visuals to Illustrate Concepts, Problems, Solutions, and Interrelationships Oral and textbook-based math instruction can be supplemented by the use of visuals and graphics (Ketterlin-Geller, et al., 2008; Miller & Hudson, 2007; Van de Walle et al., 2010). Drawings, diagrams, and graphic organizers of new concepts, patterns, equations, and interrelationships can help students discuss and visualize mathematical computations, ideas, concepts, and solutions

Problem solving can be aided by using manipulatives and other teaching aids. What manipulatives do your students like to use?

(Ives, 2007; van Garderen, 2008). Students gain a visual, concrete framework for understanding the foundations of the process, as well as the steps necessary to solve problems. Because material used to present mathematics can be difficult to read, misunderstandings related to reading mathematical language can be minimized by using drawings and diagrams that depict difficult content. Graphing calculators and personal digital assistants also can provide students with opportunities to learn mathematics visually, explore different concepts, and develop their problem-solving skills (Bouck, 2009; Kortering, McClannon, & Braziel, 2008; Posamentier et al., 2010).

When offering depictions of math concepts and problem-solving techniques, you can discuss patterns and relationships, highlight essential information, and focus students' attention by using colored chalk, marking pens, or technology-based graphics. For example, when introducing students to the definitions of and differences among equilateral, isosceles, and scalene triangles, you can record the definitions and present examples of each type of triangle, and then highlight key words in the definition and shade key sides and angles.

To further help them solve problems, encourage students to visualize solutions to math problems, draw pictures, illustrate and translate findings, and record notes (Montague, 2007; Van de Walle et al., 2010). Students also can learn to solve problems by using graphs. Teach them how and when to create different types of graphs (e.g., circle, bar, line, histogram) to help them visualize and present solutions to problems.

Use Instructional Technology, and Teach Students to Use It Like Ms. Rivlin, you can use instructional technology to enhance and support mathematics instruction, which also is consistent with the NCTM standards that view technology as an essential aspect of teaching mathematics (Bouck & Flanagan, 2009; Freeman & Crawford, 2008; Murray et al., 2007a; Van de Walle et al., 2010). Instructional technology can offer you and your students visual and auditory stimuli and interactive activities and simulations that can make mathematics come alive for students and help them collect real data and explore solutions to problems (Kortering et al., 2008). These technologies—including software programs; spreadsheets; databases; technology-based academic games, simulations, and drill-and-practice programs; tutorials; graphics programs; and graphing calculators—help students develop number sense, math facts, mathematical language, and solve math problems (Bouck, 2009a; Fuchs, Fuchs & Hollenbeck, 2007; Kortering et al., 2008; Mancil & Maynard, 2007; Posamentier et al., 2010). The Internet and multimedia programs allow students to access real data that can be used in solving meaningful problems. Via technology, teachers and students can access **applets**, brief online interactive demonstrations and manipulatives that offer animated and visual presentations of a range of mathematical content (Zorfass, Follansbee, & Weagle, 2006). Technology also can provide your students with numerous opportunities to practice math facts and receive prompt corrective feedback (Bouck & Flanagan, 2009; Powell et al., 2009). For example, via digital pens linked to computers, students can practice a range of calculation skills, receive auditory prompts to guide them in performing multistep computations, and play math games (Bouck et al., 2009).

Instructional technology can provide you with opportunities to differentiate mathematics instruction for a wide range of students (Kortering et al., 2008; Murray, Silver-Pacuilla, & Innes Helsel, 2007a). *My Math* is a mathematics software program that contains three components: Computation Problems, Word Problems, and Story Problems (Cawley, Foley, & Doan, 2003). Students and teachers can choose the level of difficulty of the content to be used in each of the three components. For example, the Word Problems component allows students to choose from word problems that are of varying structures and lengths, and to access questions that prompt students. *GO Solve Word Problems* is a software program designed to improve the problem-solving skills of students by providing them with graphic organizers that assist them in identifying and organizing the critical information needed to solve the problems (Hasselbring, Lott, & Zydney, 2005). *HELP Math* is a Web-based curriculum that provides students with a range of interactive multimedia learning activities based on effective ESL teaching principles to foster understanding of mathematical language, symbols, and concepts (Freeman & Crawford, 2008).

Problem-based learning presented via multimedia and hands-on collaborative group formats can help you structure lessons so that students with different learning abilities can work together to solve mathematical problems (Bottge, Rueda, Serlin, Hung, & Kwon, 2007; Bouck & Flanagan, 2009). For example, *The Adventures of Jasper Woodbury*, *Kim's Komet*, *Fraction of the Cost*, and *Bart's Pet Project* use a multimedia format to present stories and math problems. These problems, designed for students with different reading and mathematical abilities, serve as springboards or anchors for hands-on projects that have students work cooperatively to use their mathematical skills to solve problems of interest to them.

Provide and Teach Students to Use Calculators Calculators can help students develop their mathematical literacy and solve problems (Bouck & Bouck, 2008; Fashl, 2007). Once students know how and why to perform an algorithm, calculators can give them the ability to learn, retrieve, and self-check computation facts, thus promoting their independence and their exploration of math problems, and increasing their speed in solving problems (Murray, Silver-Pacuilla, & Innes Helsel, 2007b). For these reasons, the NCTM has called for teachers to provide students with calculators.

Some students may have difficulty using calculators, such as those who reverse numbers, and may benefit from calculators with special features such as a talking calculator, which states the numerals entered and computed (Parette, Wojcik, Peterson-Karlan, & Hourcade, 2005). Talking calculators can help students perform addition, subtraction, multiplication, division, square root, and percentage calculations by stating the function or name of each key as it is pressed (Osterhaus, 2007). Calculators that provide a printout or display of all numerals and operations entered may be helpful for students with motor, memory, or attention difficulties because they offer products that can be checked for memory and accuracy. Some students may need to use calculators with fewer or larger keys and displays or those that allow on-screen entry of numbers; others may need calculators that provide graphic displays and information about numbers including their type (e.g., odd or even, prime or composite) and their multiples and factors.

Students also may benefit from using calculators designed for specific mathematical tasks (Parette et al., 2007). For example, the *Coin-u-Lator* is designed to assist students in performing calculations involving monetary values, the proportions calculator provides visual presentations (shading of fractional parts of geometric shapes), decimal equivalents, and the steps in solving problems related to proportions, and the algebra calculator performs several functions related to algebraic expressions.

REFLECTIVE

What is your view of calculators? Should students be allowed or encouraged to use them?

Use a Variety of Instructional Approaches

Use Peer-Mediated Instruction   As Ms. Rivlin did in the chapter-opening vignette, you can use peer-mediated instruction such as peer tutoring and cooperative learning groups so that your students work in groups to learn math facts and to communicate about and experiment with solutions to mathematical problems (Bryant et al., 2008; Fuchs et al., 2008; Ketterlin-Geller et al., 2008; Kunsch, Jitendra, & Sood, 2007). Peer-mediated instruction allows students to work in groups to ask questions, share ideas, clarify thoughts, experiment, brainstorm, and present solutions with their classmates. Students can understand many perspectives and solutions to mathematical problems and appreciate that math problems can be approached and solved in a variety of ways.

Making Connections
This use of peer-mediated instruction relates to our earlier discussion of cooperative learning arrangements in Chapter 9.

Offer Students Specialized Instruction in Solving Word Problems   Although many students have difficulty solving mathematics word problems, students with learning difficulties may experience particular difficulties (Powell et al., 2009; Sherman et al., 2009). Therefore, these students will need specialized instruction in approaching and solving word problems. Specialized instruction can be tailored to address the individual needs of students by examining students' error patterns when solving word problems with respect to the following:

- Problem recognition: Does the student recognize a representation of a mathematical question in word problems?
- Problem definition: Does the student know what mathematical processes to use to solve word problems?
- Problem comprehension: Does the student understand the mathematical language in word problems?

Such factors as length, problem type, syntactic complexity, vocabulary level, context, amount of nonessential information and irrelevant numbers, sequence and number of ideas presented, and mathematical steps required can make it difficult to solve word problems (Garcia, Jimenez, & Hess, 2006; Powell et al., 2009a). Therefore, you can improve your students' problem-solving abilities by

- simplifying the syntax,
- using vocabulary students understand,
- deleting irrelevant or ambiguous information,
- limiting the number of ideas presented,
- rearranging the information and presenting it in the order students can follow in solving the problem, and
- using word problems that depict situations that relate to students' lives.

Students also can be taught to identify the problem type, critical elements of word problems, and irrelevant details, and to sequence information in the order in which it will be needed (Bryant et al., 2008; Fuchs et al., 2008). These skills can be developed by teaching students to underline the question and circle the given parts of the problem, by providing practice items in which students identify the problem type and restate the specifics of the problem in their own words, and by having students act out the problem.

In addition, try using a schema-based instructional model where you teach your students to distinguish and understand the mathematical structures related to different types of mathematical word problems and to create appropriate graphic representations or diagrams that organize and facilitate the information in the problem type and guide students in solving it (Fuchs et al., 2008; Jitendra, Griffin, Haria, Leh, Adams, & Kaduvetoor, 2007; Xin & Jitendra, 2006). Four types of diagrams were identified by van Garderen (2006) that can be used to graphically represent mathematical problems: networks, matrices/tables, hierarchies, and part-whole diagrams. **Networks**, also called *line diagrams*, involve points connected via lines and are most appropriate for word problems that ask students to put objects in a specific order. When word problems require students to combine information and compare relationships between more than one set of information, *matrices/tables* are particularly useful. Whereas *hierarchies* are often used to represent problems that contain similar and different information, *part-whole diagrams* depict the relationships between the part and the whole. Sample graphic representations are presented in Figure 11.3.

You also can teach your students to use story grammars to guide them in solving different types of word problems (Fuchs et al., 2008; Xin et al., 2008). This involves teaching your students to identify the problem type or structure and to then create a visual story grammar or map of the major elements of the word problem. Teach your students about and how to differentiate the different types of word problems (e.g.,

FIGURE 11.3 **Sample graphic representations**

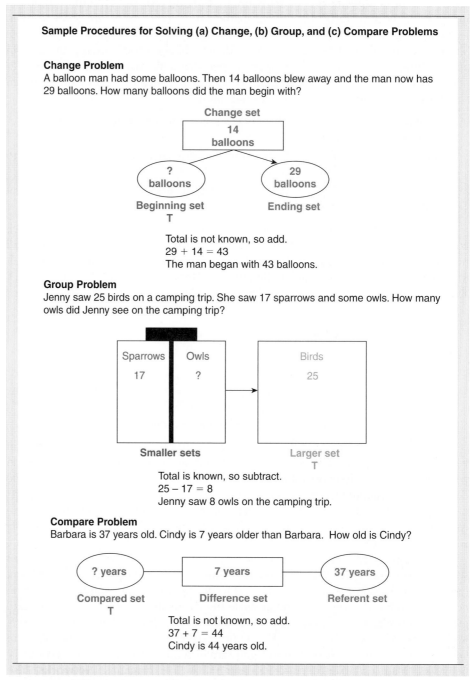

Sample Procedures for Solving (a) Change, (b) Group, and (c) Compare Problems

Change Problem
A balloon man had some balloons. Then 14 balloons blew away and the man now has 29 balloons. How many balloons did the man begin with?

Change set
14 balloons

? balloons — Beginning set T

29 balloons — Ending set

Total is not known, so add.
29 + 14 = 43
The man began with 43 balloons.

Group Problem
Jenny saw 25 birds on a camping trip. She saw 17 sparrows and some owls. How many owls did Jenny see on the camping trip?

Sparrows 17 | Owls ?
Smaller sets

Birds 25
Larger set T

Total is known, so subtract.
25 – 17 = 8
Jenny saw 8 owls on the camping trip.

Compare Problem
Barbara is 37 years old. Cindy is 7 years older than Barbara. How old is Cindy?

? years — Compared set T

7 years — Difference set

37 years — Referent set

Total is not known, so add.
37 + 7 = 44
Cindy is 44 years old.

Source: From "Teaching Students Math Problem-Solving Through Graphic Representations," by A. K. Jitendra, 2002, *Teaching Exceptional Children 34*(4), pp. 34–39. Copyright 2002 by The Council for Exceptional Children. Reprinted with permission.

part-part-whole, additive compare, equal group, multiplicative compare, total, difference, and change), and then give them word problem story grammar prompt cards that contain a definition of and visual associated with the problem type and self-questions to guide students in identifying the relevant story elements presented in the word problem. For example, to guide students in solving part-part-whole word problems, that involve the combination of two or more parts into a whole, you can give them the following (Xin et al., 2008);

Making Connections
This discussion of using story grammars to foster students' word problem–solving skills relates to our earlier discussion of text comprehension strategies in Chapter 8.

Part 1	Part 2	Whole
☐	+ ☐	= ☐

☐	Identify the part of the problem that tells you about the whole or combined amount. Write that number in the big box, labeled Whole.
☐	Identify the part of the problem that tells you about one of the parts that makes up the whole. Write that number in the first small box, labeled Part 1.
☐	Identify the part of the problem that tells you about another part that makes up the whole. Write that number in the second small box, labeled Part 2.

Initially, you can help students understand that a diagram is a visual representation depicting the key parts of a problem and the relationships among these parts. You can motivate students to use diagrams by explaining how their use benefits students, and teach students to use graphic codes (e.g., numbers and letters) and symbols (? represents unknown information) to represent the key parts of the problem (e.g., objects and individuals in the problem). Then verbally explain and visually model how to identify the type of problem pattern and visually represent relevant information in word problems. Next, teach students to identify and highlight important information in the problem that can be added to teacher-prepared visuals provided for them, and indicate unknown information through use of a question mark. Finally, students can be taught to independently identify essential information, use codes and symbols to denote essential information, create visuals that depict the essential information presented in the word problems and how they are related, and solve the problem. This instructional sequence can be used to teach students to visually represent the key features in the different types of word problems they will encounter (van Garderen, 2007).

Because many students who find mathematics difficult may often come up with unreasonable answers and settle for their first answer, your students' ability to solve word problems also can be enhanced by teaching them to estimate and check their answers (Van de Walle et al., 2010). You can do this by helping them understand the importance of estimation and verification, and the relationship between estimates and answers. You also can model, teach, and prompt students to use the different ways to estimate and check answers. For instance, students can learn to estimate calculations by rounding numbers to their closest tens/hundreds/thousands or by creating a series of subproblems (Rousselle & Noel, 2008).

The problem-solving skills of students can be enhanced by incorporating speaking and writing tasks into mathematics instruction (Faulkner, 2009; Thompson & Chappell, 2007; van Garderen, 2008). Model and encourage students to think aloud and talk mathematically by asking them to describe the processes and procedures they are using to solve problems and to explain and justify their answers (Allsopp et al., 2008). Students also can keep a math journal that relates to mathematical content they are learning about. Their journals also can contain reactions to and notes on mathematics issues, topics, activities, and teaching, as well as explanations, clarifications, diagrams, and applications of math problems (Posamentier et al., 2010). Students also can write their story problems; write letters to others outlining a mathematical solution, rule, or concept; translate visual representations into text; and describe and reflect on their problem-solving strategies. They also can design, implement, and write up a math project that requires them to collect data, compute results, develop graphs and other pictorials, and share conclusions.

Teach Students to Use Self-Management Techniques and Learning Strategies
Students who struggle with mathematics often have difficulties with multistep tasks and problems. Self-management techniques and learning strategies can be taught to help students follow sequential steps and solve problems involving a variety of mathematical procedures (Alter, Wyrick, Brown, & Lingo, 2008; Fuchs, Fuchs & Hollenbeck, 2007; Miller & Hudson, 2007; Montague, 2007). Techniques such as self-monitoring checklists prompt students to remember and engage in the multiple steps necessary to complete a task (Gagnon & Maccini, 2007) or to check their work (Fuchs et al., 2008). For instance, you can post or give students a cue card that prompts them to check their work by asking themselves:

- Does my answer make sense?
- Are my numbers lined up correctly?
- Are my computations correct?
- Did I use appropriate symbols?
- Did I use the correct signs? (Fuchs et al., 2008)

Self-management also can be effective in helping students learn the math facts and computation skills needed to solve problems that require multistep math operations (Maccini, Mulcahy, & Wilson, 2007). For example, self-instruction teaches students to perform computations by describing to themselves the steps and questions necessary to identify and perform the calculations. Successful self-instructional techniques for teaching computation skills include 4 B's, equal additions, count-bys, touch math, count-ons, count-all, maximum and minimum addend, zero facts, doubles, and turn-around, and decomposition strategies that involve using a known fact to compute the correct answer (Bryant et al., 2008; Hopkins & Egeberg, 2009; Miller & Hudson, 2007; Tournaki, 2003). Students also can be taught to use a Copy, Cover, and Compare technique to learn math facts (Maccini et al., 2007).

Several learning strategies have been developed to help students solve mathematical problems (Miller & Hudson, 2007), including *Solve It!* (Montague, 2006). In general, the steps in *Solve It!* include the following:

> *Step 1. Read the problem for understanding.* Students read the problem to understand it and to determine the question and to find any unknown words and clue words. Clue words are those words that indicate the correct operation to be used. For example, the words *all together, both, together, in all, and, plus*, and *sum* suggest that the problem involves addition; words like *left, lost, spend*, and *remain* indicate that the correct operation is subtraction. However, you need to be aware that clue words do not always cue the appropriate operation. When students encounter unknown words, they can ask you to pronounce and define them.
>
> *Step 2. Reread and paraphrase the problem.* Read the problem a second time to identify and paraphrase relevant information, which can be highlighted by underlining, while deleting irrelevant information and facts. Focus on determining what mathematical process and unit can be used to express the answer.
>
> *Step 3. Visualize and draw the problem.* Students visualize the problem and draw a representation of the information given.
>
> *Step 4. Hypothesize a plan and write the problem.* Students hypothesize and write the steps in solving the problem in order with the appropriate signs.
>
> *Step 5. Estimate the answer.* Before solving the problem, students estimate the answer. The estimate provides a framework for determining the reasonableness of their response.

Step 6. Compute and solve the problem. Students solve the problem, as outlined in step 4, by calculating each step in the process, giving attention to the correctness of the calculations, the order of the operations, and the unit used to express the answer.

Step 7. Check the answer. Students check their work to make sure it makes sense and compare their answer with their estimate. They examine each step in terms of necessity, order, operation selected, and correctness of calculations.

The steps in other mathematics learning strategies, their acronymns, and their instructional goals are presented in Figure 11.4.

Making Connections
This use of learning strategies to foster students' mathematics skills relates to our earlier discussion in Chapter 6 of learning strategies and how to teach students to use them.

FIGURE 11.4 Sample mathematics learning strategies

Instructional Goal	Acronym	Strategic Steps
To foster solving two-digit plus two-digit problems that do not require regrouping	SAW (Hudson & Miller, 2006)	**S**: Set up to solve. Read the problem and identify the sign. **A**: Attack the problem. Add the ones column and write the answer in the ones column. Add the tens column and write the answer in the tens column. **W**: Wrap it up. Check the addition.
To foster adding and subtracting fractions	LAP (Test & Ellis, 2005)	**L**: Look at the denominator and sign. **A**: Ask yourself, will the smallest denominator divide into the largest denominator an even number of times? **P**: Pick your fraction type.
To foster word problem type identification	RUN Fuchs et al. (2008)	**R**: Read the problem. **U**: Underline the questions. **N**: Name the problem type.
To foster word problem solving	DOTS Xin, Wiles, & Lin (2008)	**D**: Detect the problem type. **O**: Organize the information, using the word problem conceptual model diagrams. **T**: Transform the diagram into a meaningful math equation. **S**: Solve for the unknown quantity or variable in the equation and check your answer.
To foster algebraic word problem solving	STAR Maccini & Ruhl (2000)	**S**: Search the word problem (Read and ask yourself, "What facts do I know? What do I need to find?" Write down facts.) **T**: Translate the problem (Choose a variable: identify the operations and represent the problem concretely, semiconcretely, and abstractly.) **A**: Answer the problem (Use cues and a work mat.) **R**: Review the solution (Reread the problem and ask yourself, "Does my answer make sense? Why or why not?" Check your answer.)
To foster vary word problem solving	FOPS (Montague, 2007)	**F**: Find the problem type (Ask yourself, "Did I read and retell the problem to ask if it is a vary problem? Did I look for a rate or ratio type of association between two dimensions?") **O**: Organize the information using the vary diagram. "Did I write the labels for the two dimensions of the diagram? Did I write the numbers given for the two pairs of associations in the diagram? Did I write a '?' for the missing number?" **P**: Plan to solve the problem. "Did I transform the information in the diagram into a math sentence or an equation?" **S**: Solve the problem. "Did I solve for the missing number in the math sentence or equation? Did I write the complete answer? Did I check if the answer makes sense?"

Developing Students' Word Problem–Solving Skills

Although Ms. Ventnor's students were making progress in developing their computation skills, she was concerned about the difficulties they were having with word problems. To help them, she decided to focus on developing their problem-solving skills. She started by presenting word problems through the use of pictorials, highlighting important words in problems, and having students write or state math problems without computing the answers. She also began to personalize problems by using students' names and relating problems to their interests, cultures, experiences, and classroom or current events. When presenting these problems, she asked students to paraphrase the problems in their own words, and had them work in groups to act out word problems, create drawings of the problems, and compose problems to be solved by their classmates. As her students began to develop their problem-solving skills, she asked them to solve problems and minimized the complexity of the calculations by using easier and smaller numbers. To guide them in solving problems, she posted charts around the room that prompted them to use the word problem–solving skills she taught them. She also prompted them to explain their reasoning by asking them to respond to questions such as "Why did you do it that way?" Here are some other strategies you can use to implement the IDEA in your inclusive classroom and develop your students' word problem–solving skills:

- Teach students how to differentiate between relevant and irrelevant information by presenting problems that have too little or too much information.

- Teach students the unique features of the various problem types, and then have them sort different problems based on their distinguishing features.

- Write number cues above specific parts of word problems to show the steps students can follow to solve the problems.

- Encourage students to estimate answers, think aloud, and brainstorm solutions to word problems.

- Teach students to look for patterns in problems, use charts and graphs to organize data, and relate solutions to previous problems.

- Give students diagrams and teach them to draw diagrams to identify the important features of word problems.

- Give students numerous opportunities to engage in simple and familiar problems followed by more complex problem situations so that they get to apply and generalize their word problem–solving skills and strategies across a range of problem situations.

- Have students create their own problems.

- Give students problems that have more than one answer and problems that can be solved in several ways.

- Encourage and recognize multiple solution strategies to solve problems.

Sources: Hudson and Miller (2006); Fuchs et al. (2008); Jitendra et al. (2007); Van de Walle et al. (2010); van Garderen (2008); Xin and Jitendra (2006).

Give Students Models, Cues, and Prompts Some students may understand the processes used to solve problems involving several operations executed in a particular sequence, but they may need models, cues, and prompts to guide them in organizing performing these operations and paying attention to important details such as signs, symbols, and directions (Fahsl, 2007; Fuchs et al., 2008; Raghubar et al., 2009). Problem-solving assignments can be coded so that they include a model for calculating the answer or paired with cuing forms that prompt students to use specific strategies to solve problems. The model can vary, depending on students' skill levels and needs. Sample models are presented in Figure 11.5.

Flip charts and cue cards can offer students a model of the correct format and order in approaching a task and guide students in taking notes (Kortering et al., 2008; Montague, 2007). Each page of the flip chart represents a step accompanied by an example that guides students in solving problems and performing computations. A sample flip chart for division of fractions is presented in Figure 11.6.

Charts also can be placed in the room to help students. These charts can present math terms, facts, and symbols (*subtract* = *take away* = −), as well as the steps to follow for a specific type of problem, such as the steps in dividing fractions. For example, a fraction strip chart presenting strips divided into halves, thirds, fourths, and so on, can be posted to help students learn the concepts associated with fractions. Charts also can be posted to guide them in solving word problems. For example, you can guide them in solving problems that require them to add two or more quantities by posting a chart that prompts them to determine the following:

1. How many for part 1?
2. How many for part 2?

FIGURE 11.5 Algorithm models

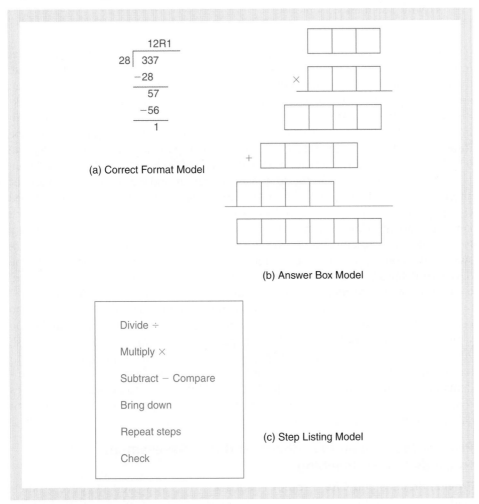

(a) Correct Format Model

(b) Answer Box Model

Divide ÷

Multiply ×

Subtract − Compare

Bring down

Repeat steps

Check

(c) Step Listing Model

FIGURE 11.6 Flip chart for dividing fractions

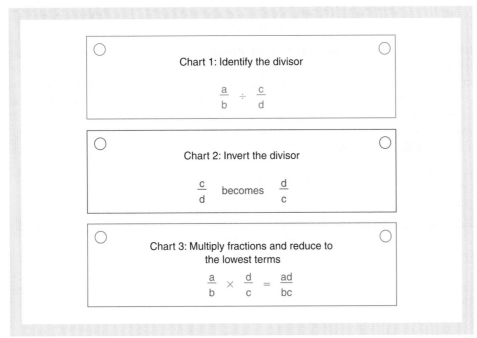

Chart 1: Identify the divisor

$$\frac{a}{b} \div \frac{c}{d}$$

Chart 2: Invert the divisor

$$\frac{c}{d} \quad \text{becomes} \quad \frac{d}{c}$$

Chart 3: Multiply fractions and reduce to the lowest terms

$$\frac{a}{b} \times \frac{d}{c} = \frac{ad}{bc}$$

3. What is the total?

4. Write the number sentence.

5. Find *X*. (Fuchs et al., 2008, p. 163)

Cues also can be used with students who have difficulty remembering the order in which to solve computation items (Fahsl, 2007). Arrows can be drawn to indicate the direction in which students should proceed. Cues such as green and red dots, go and stop signs, and answer boxes tell students when to proceed or stop when working on a specific item. Attention to signs (+, −, ×) can be emphasized by color coding, boldfacing, circling and underlining. The skill of noticing signs can also be fostered by listing the sign and its operation at the top of each worksheet (+ = add: 6 + 3 = 9) and teaching students to trace the sign before beginning the computation.

Another type of cue, *boxing*, or placing boxes around items, can focus students' attention on specific problems within a group (Fahsl, 2007). When boxing items, you should leave enough space within the box to do the calculations needed to solve the item. As students' skills increase, they can be encouraged to assume responsibility for boxing items. Boxing also can aid students who have problems placing their answer in the correct column. A color-coded or shaded box or a broken line can be drawn to delineate columns so that students place their answers appropriately and to prompt students to remember to regroup when necessary (see Figure 11.7).

Problems with aligning answers also can be minimized by having students use centimeter graph paper (rather than lined paper), on which only one digit can be written in each box, or by turning lined paper so that the lines run vertically (Fahsl, 2007). You also can enlarge graph paper for your students, especially those with handwriting difficulties. Alignment problems also can be reduced by teaching students to estimate the answer and check its reasonableness. An answer that deviates significantly from the estimate may indicate an alignment problem, and students can check their work accordingly.

Provide Practice and Feedback, and Use Assessment to Guide Future Teaching

Provide Practice and Offer Prompt Feedback Help your students develop their mathematical skills by providing them with numerous opportunities to practice using them and by offering prompt feedback (Fuchs & Fuchs, 2008; Hopkins & Egeberg, 2009). You can use corrective feedback to tell students that their response is correct or incorrect, identify which part is correct or incorrect, and offer students a strategy to obtain the correct response (Powell et al., 2009).

Involve Students in the Assessment Process The NCTM calls for involving students in the assessment process to help them gain insight into their knowledge of math and the ways in which they think about math. Therefore, you can consider using student-centered strategies that involve students in setting goals, choosing appropriate assessment techniques, and identifying helpful teaching strategies and materials such as portfolio assessment, and student interviews (Allsopp et al., 2008; Van de Walle et al., 2010).

Making Connections
This discussion of practice and feedback relates to our earlier discussion in Chapter 9.

FIGURE 11.7 **Examples of cues to prompt students to regroup**

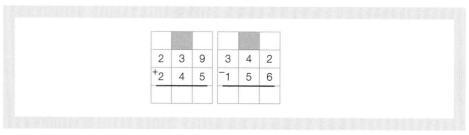

Source: Fahsl (2007).

As part of the self-assessment process, students can think aloud to share with you how they approached a task (Ketterlin-Geller et al., 2008). They also can reflect on, locate, and correct their errors. In addition to giving their answers to problems, students also can be asked to talk about or write their explanations of the ways they solved problems. Student reflection also can be fostered by asking them to discuss or write about the following:

- What they were supposed to do
- How they approached the problem(s)
- Why they approached the problem(s) in that way
- Whether their approach was successful or unsuccessful
- What was successful about their approach
- How they would approach the problem(s) differently (Butler et al., 2005)

Students also can be taught to evaluate their mastery of concepts by graphing their performance. You also can provide an error analysis and correction sheet that asks students to list the problem, the steps in solving the problem, the correct answer(s), the errors made, and the reason for the errors. A checking center equipped with answer keys, teacher's guides, supplementary materials, peer tutors, and recordings of potential solutions can promote self-checking and minimize the demands on your time.

Assess Mastery and Progress over Time   Maintaining skills is important for students with disabilities, so you can conduct ongoing progress monitoring assessments via curriculum-based measurement probes to assess their mastery and retention of previously learned skills (Foegen, 2008; Fuchs & Fuchs, 2008). You also can observe your students and ask them questions to identify the strategies they use to perform computations and solve problems (Salend, 2009). You can use this information to give students feedback on their performance and encourage them to record their own progress over time.

DIFFERENTIATING SCIENCE AND SOCIAL STUDIES INSTRUCTION

HOW CAN I DIFFERENTIATE SCIENCE AND SOCIAL STUDIES INSTRUCTION? In addition to the strategies for differentiating instruction presented in this section, many of the suggestions for teaching mathematics outlined in the previous section also apply to teaching science and social studies.

Choose and Use Appropriate Instructional Materials

Although the specific content in each area is different, science and social studies share several teaching methods. Both areas are often taught using content-oriented approaches that rely on oral presentations and text-based instructional materials such as textbooks. Because some students, including students with disabilities, may sometimes have difficulty learning information from oral presentations and textbooks, science, social studies, and content-area teaching should be differentiated by using appropriate instructional materials.

Choose Textbooks and Other Text-Based Materials Carefully   Much of the content in science and social studies is presented via textbooks and other text-based materials that are often difficult for students, particularly those with learning difficulties, to use (Espin, Cevasco, van den Broek, Baker, & Gersten, 2007; Harniss, Caros, & Gersten, 2007). It is important to determine the readability level of textbooks and text-based materials and to use the teacher- and student-directed text comprehension strategies to help students gain information from textbooks. In addition, textbooks and text-based materials for students should be chosen carefully in terms of structure, organization, coherence, content, ongoing and interspersed opportunities for review and practice, and audience appropriateness (Beal, Mason-Bolick, & Martorella, 2009; Dimino, 2007; Harniss et al., 2007).

Making Connections
Find out more about student-centered assessment strategies in Chapter 12.

PEARSON
myeducationlab

To reflect on and enhance your understanding of strategies you can use to differentiate your mathematics instruction, go to the IRIS Center Resources section of the Topic *Content Area Teaching* in the MyEducationLab for your course, and examine the challenging cases by completing the cases entitled *Algebra (Part 1): Applying Learning Strategies to Beginning Algebra*, and *Algebra (Part 2): Applying Learning Strategies to Intermediate Algebra*.

Making Connections
Find out more about progress monitoring and curriculum-based measurement in Chapter 12.

Making Connections
Ways to determine and enhance the readability of text-based materials and the use of teacher and student-directed text comprehension strategies were discussed earlier in Chapter 8.

Choosing appropriate textbooks is a crucial part of successful content-area instruction. What guidelines do you use in selecting textbooks?

Textbooks and other materials also should relate to students' background knowledge, provide students with real-world applications, and give them multiple opportunities to think about and reflect on foundational concepts in the discipline (Noddings, 2008). Unfortunately, many textbooks and instructional materials do not include the accomplishments or perspectives of individuals from diverse cultural and language backgrounds. Many of them ignore other cultures and female students, engage in stereotyping, offer only one interpretation of issues, avoid important issues, and present information about certain groups in isolation (Alter, 2009). Because of the bias and gaps in many textbooks and text-based materials, many teachers rely on hands-on, activity-based teaching approaches instead and use supplementary materials. You also can supplement text-based instruction and motivate your students via use of collaborative reading groups, and instructional technology and Internet-based learning experiences that pair text with graphics and pictures.

Teach Students How to Use Textbooks and Instructional Materials   Students can be taught how to use and obtain information from the textbooks and instructional materials used in inclusive classrooms (Carroll, 2007; Conderman & Elf, 2007). Examine the vocabulary and concept development that students will need to use the book, and teach students how to identify and define these terms (Ebbers & Denton, 2008; Roberts, Torgeson, et al. 2008). For example, you and your students can review chapters from the book, selecting key terms and concepts that they can define by using the book's glossary or another resource, such as a dictionary or an encyclopedia. When students become adept at this task, they can be encouraged to perform the steps alone. You also can post important content vocabulary on a community chart in your classroom.

Because information is usually presented in a similar way from chapter to chapter in textbooks and instructional materials, reviewing the organization of the materials is also helpful (Carroll, 2007; Dimino, 2007; Nilson, 2007). This involves reviewing and explaining the functions of and interrelationships among the material's components (table of contents, text, glossary, index, appendices) and the elements of the book's chapters (titles, objectives, abstract, headings, summary, study guides, follow-up questions, references, alternative learning activities).

You also can help students use learning strategies to access and evaluate information from textbooks and instructional materials (Nilson, 2007). For example, they can learn to use text headings to enhance their reading and learning from text-based materials through learning strategies such as *SCROL* (Grant, 1993). The SCROL strategy involves the following:

Survey: Students read the headings and subheadings and ask themselves, "What do I know about this topic?" and "What information is going to be presented?"

Connect: Students ask, "How do the headings and subheadings relate to each other?" and list key words that provide connections.

Read: Students read the headings and outline the major ideas and supporting details without looking back at the text.

Outline: Students record the headings and outline the major ideas and supporting details without looking back at the text.

Look back: Students look back at the heading and subheadings, and then check and correct their outlines.

In addition, students can be taught to evaluate the information presented in texts and other instructional materials. For example, De La Paz, Morales, and Winston (2007) developed a historical reasoning learning strategies that students can learn to evaluate text by (a) identifying the author's purpose, (b) examining the extent to which the supporting reasons and explanations make sense, and (c) determining if there is evidence of bias.

When teaching about textbooks and instructional materials, it may be helpful to teach students the strategies and text structures and styles used by the author(s) to present content (Carroll, 2007; Williams et al., 2007). Students can learn to identify five patterns that are typically used by authors: enumeration, time order, compare-contrast, cause-effect, and problem solution. These strategies are often repeated throughout the book, so students can be taught to analyze a book by examining

- the numbering (*1, 2, 3*), lettering (*a, b, c*), or word (*first, second, third*) system used to show the relative importance of information, as well as the order of ideas;
- the typographic signs (boldfacing, underlining, color cueing, boxing) used to highlight critical information;
- the word signals that indicate the equal importance of information (*furthermore, likewise*), elaboration (*moreover*), rebuttal and clarification (*nevertheless, however, but*), summarization (*therefore, consequently*), and termination (*finally, in conclusion*).

For example, you can teach students to look for and understand that the clue words *because, since, therefore,* and *thus* introduce cause-effect information (Williams et al., 2007). They also can learn that once they encounter these words, they can ask themselves, "What is the cause?" and "What is the effect?"

You can also help students by showing them how to gain information from visual displays. Prompt them to examine illustrations and to preview the graphics to get a general idea of their purpose. Teach them to read the title, captions, and headings to determine relevant information from the graphic; identify the units of measurement; and discuss, relate, and generalize graphic information to the text.

Many textbooks and instructional materials often come with supplemental materials such as student activity worksheets and overviews and opportunities to practice and review important content (Harniss et al., 2007). Therefore, students can receive some training in understanding the importance of these activities and strategies for successfully completing them. For example, you can help students learn to complete interspersed and end-of-chapter questions by teaching them to do the following:

- Read each question to determine what is being asked.
- Identify words in the question that can guide the reader to the correct answer.
- Determine the requirement of the question and the format of the answer.
- Convert appropriate parts of the question into part of the answer.
- Identify the paragraphs of the chapter that relate to the question.
- Locate the answer to the question by reading the chapter.
- Write the answer to the question.
- Check the answer for accuracy and form.

Learning to look for highlighted information that is usually italicized or boldfaced also can help students identify main points that often contain answers to study questions.

Note Taking from Textbooks. Good note-taking skills are invaluable in learning from textbooks and other text-based materials (Coutant & Perchemlides, 2005). A useful method to teach students involves setting up a margin, about 2 inches from the left side

REFLECTIVE

How is this book organized to present information? What strategies are used to highlight information? What aspects of the book help promote your learning?

To enhance your understanding of how to foster your students' comprehension of textbook and other print materials, go to the IRIS Center Resources section of the Topic *Instructional Practices and Learning Strategies* in the MyEducationLab for your course, and complete the module entitled *CSR: A Reading Comprehension Strategy.*

of the paper, where students can jot down questions based on the information presented in the chapter, on chapter subheadings, and on discussion/study questions. Students also can use this column to list vocabulary words and their definitions. They can use the rest of the page to record answers to the questions and other critical information from the chapter.

If the school allows it, highlighting information in a textbook can help students identify parts of a chapter that are critical for class discussions and can assist them in studying for exams. When marking text-based materials, <u>students can be taught to use double lines to delineate text that denotes main ideas</u> and <u>single lines to identify supporting ideas</u>. [When several continuous lines present essential content, students can use a vertical bracket in the margin rather than underlining.]

A GUIDE TO ACTION
Selecting Textbooks and Other Text-Based Materials

Textbooks and text-based materials should be chosen carefully so they support your instructional program and foster student learning. To select challenging but understandable textbooks and text-based materials for use with your students, consider the following questions:

- Is the content appropriate, multidimensional, correct, up-to-date, and interesting to students?
- Is the content organized around important concepts and big ideas?
- Are the objectives clear and related to the curriculum?
- Are the language and vocabulary appropriate for students and clearly defined in language that students can understand?
- Are there informative headings and subheadings that provide readers with accurate previews of what will be presented?
- Does the material provide signals to highlight (e.g., boldface, italics) and clarify main points and key vocabulary (marginal definitions and notations, definitions embedded in sentences, examples, graphic aids, pointer words and phrases)?
- Is information presented in an organized fashion (using preview or introductory statements, topic sentences, summary statements, lists, enumeration words)?
- Does the material offer clear and logical transitions that help the reader adjust to changes in topics and understand the connections between topics?
- Does the material come with support materials to help students learn, such as study guides, graphic organizers, concept maps, illustrations, pictorials, supplemental learning activities, self-assessment probes, a table of contents, an index, a glossary, appendices, and software programs?

- Does the material provide ongoing and interspersed opportunities for students to review and practice critical aspects of the content presented?
- Are the pictorial and graphic aids appropriate and easy to read and interpret?
- Do the illustrations provide a visual framework for understanding the material and supplementing the text?
- Are illustrations referred to and explained?
- Are chronological sequences or events presented in order of occurrence?
- Is the content balanced and integrated, as well as sufficiently broad and deep?
- Does the content provide students with multiple opportunities to think about and reflect on foundational concepts in the discipline?
- Does the textbook clearly establish and highlight the relationships among important facts, concepts, and roles?
- Does the material address cultural universals and include information about and the perspectives of individuals from diverse cultural backgrounds, as well as their contributions?
- Is the material free of stereotyping and linguistic bias (e.g., exclusive use of masculine terms)?
- Does the material include real-life applications, learning activities, and strategies to check for student understanding, such as interspersed reviews, questions, and activities that help students identify, understand, apply, relate to, and assess their mastery of critical information?
- Is the layout appropriate and well-organized?
- Is the material interesting looking, and does it make good use of space and colors?

How would you rate your selection of textbooks and other text-based materials? ( ) Excellent ( ) Good ( ) Needs Improvement ( ) Needs Much Improvement

Create a plan of action for improving your selection of textbooks and other text-based materials that includes your goals, the actions you will take and the resources you will need to achieve them, and the ways you will evaluate your success.

Coding by using symbols in margins and in the text are also helpful (Coutant & Perchemlides, 2005). Asterisks in the margins can be used to identify and rate important content, and question marks in the margins can prompt students to seek clarification for material that they do not agree with or do not understand. Students also can be taught to circle key and transition words, highlight important words that are repeated, and box words that indicate enumeration and transition. After reading important sections, students also can be taught to write a brief summary of the important content presented.

Use Study Guides   You can prepare **study guides** to help students identify the critical information in assignments and provide activities to help students master it (Salend, 2009). Study guides contain a series of statements, questions, and/or activities that help students identify and learn critical information from textbooks, instructional materials, and oral presentations. They can be used to teach content-specific vocabulary, structure content-specific readings, practice and review previously learned material, and introduce new material.

Although study guides vary, they often include the reading assignment, objectives, rationale, text references, a chapter summary, an outline, study questions, activities, definitions of key terms, and student evaluation probes. Study guides also can take the form of a **framed outline**, an ordered list of the chapter's main points with key words blanked out. The students fill in the blanks while reading the selection or listening to a lecture in class. You also can use hypertext to develop digital study guides for students, so that key words can be highlighted and clicked on to link students to related text and visual content (Skylar et al., 2007).

Wood (1995) identified five types of study guides that can be used to assist students in reading informational text: the (a) point-of-view reading guide, (b) interactive reading guide, (c) learning-from-text guide, (d) textbook activity guide, and (e) reading road map.

The *point-of-view reading guide* uses an interview format to prompt students to see events and material from multiple viewpoints. This guide requires students to assume the roles and perspectives of the individuals depicted in the text. For example, when reading about the abolition of slavery, students can be asked to provide text and reader-based information by responding to the question "As an abolitionist, how did you feel about slavery?"

The *interactive reading guide* is designed so that students can collaborate to complete it. This reading guide asks students "to predict, develop associations, write, chart, outline, or re-tell information in their own words to a partner or a group" (Wood, 1995, p. 138). Once groups or pairs complete the guide, they discuss their responses with the whole class.

The *learning-from-text guide* is structured so that students progress by answering questions about the textbook that proceed from a literal level ("What is erosion?") to an inferential level ("How does erosion affect people?") to a generalization or evaluative level ("If you were on a committee to minimize the effects of erosion in your community, what things would you want the committee to do?").

The *textbook activity guide* provides students with a study guide that prompts them to use self-monitoring and metacognitive strategies as they read the textbook. For example, as students read textbooks, they are guided to assess their understanding of the material by responding to self-monitoring statements such as "I understand this information," "I don't think I understand this information," and "I don't understand this information and need help." Metacognitive strategy codes also direct students to use various metacognitive strategies to enhance their understanding of the textbook material. For example, metacognitive strategy codes can prompt students to predict information, paraphrase information in their own words, survey material, create a chart, and use self-questioning.

The *reading road map* gives students a time frame for adjusting their reading rate based on the importance of the textbook material. A reading road map "includes missions

REFLECTIVE

Look back at the notes you have taken for this book. What note-taking strategies did you use? How well do you use them? Which strategies do you find to be most efficient?

Making Connections
This use of framed outlines relates to our earlier discussion of note taking in Chapter 9.

(interspersed questions and activities), road signs (indicating the speed or rate of reading), and location signs (headings and page or paragraph numbers)" (Wood, 1995, p. 141).

In developing and using study guides, consider the following:

- Create separate study guides for each chapter, unit of content, or class presentation.
- Identify the key words, main points, and important concepts to be highlighted.
- Adjust the readability of the study guide, highlight critical vocabulary and points, and give students cues to indicate the pages and paragraphs, or Web sites, where answers and relevant information to complete the study guides are located.
- Be creative: use pictures, drawings, and digital activities that engage students' attention and provide motivation.
- Devise interspersed questions, brief sentences, and multimodality activities focusing on the critical components of the material so that they are consistent with the order of the information presented in the textbook or in class. Also, vary the format and structure of the study guide to accommodate different types of questions and activities.
- Give students enough space to write their answers on the study guide and add relevant, appropriate, and motivating graphics and visuals.
- Distribute the study guides, explain their purpose, and model how to use and complete them.
- Have students complete the study guides individually or in groups.
- Discuss and review the answers, and offer students feedback on their performance.

You also can teach your students to work together to develop their own study guides.

Use Adapted Textbooks and a Parallel Alternative Curriculum

Some of your students may have difficulty reading on-grade science and social studies textbooks. For these students, it may be appropriate to use **adapted textbooks**, which present the same content as the on-grade textbook but at a lower readability level. You can find appropriate adapted textbooks corresponding to on-grade textbooks by contacting representatives from book companies.

In addition to adapted textbooks, **parallel alternative curriculum (PAC) materials** have been developed to address students' unique strengths and challenges (Kaplan, Guzman, & Tomlinson, 2009). These materials supplement the textbook by providing students with alternative ways to master critical information.

Use Content Enhancements

Content enhancements are strategies that help students identify, organize, understand, and remember important content and generalize their learning to a range of situations (Bulgren, Deshler, & Lenz, 2007). They help students understand abstract information and see the relationship between different pieces or types of information. Bulgren et al. (2007), Bulgren (2006), and Boudah, Lenz, Bulgren, Schumaker, and Deshler (2000) offer guidelines for using a unit organizer, an interactive content enhancement technique. A variety of other content enhancements are presented next.

Advance and Post Organizers   Advance and post organizers are written or oral statements, activities, technology-based tasks, and/or illustrations that offer students a framework for determining and understanding the essential information in a learning activity. Advance organizers are used at the beginning of a lesson to orient students to the content to be presented. Post organizers are used at the end of the lesson to help students review and remember the content that has been

Graphic organizers help students make comparisons, clarify relationships, formulate inferences, and draw conclusions. What types of graphic organizers help you learn?

UDL and YOU
Using Graphic Organizers

Many teachers incorporate the principles of UDL into their instruction by using graphic organizers which can serve as advance or post organizers (Connor & Lagares, 2007; Reeves & Standard, 2009). A **graphic organizer**, also called a *structured overview*, explicitly identifies and presents key terms before or after students encounter them in class and textbooks. This is a visual-spatial illustration made up of lines and geometric shapes (circles, rectangles, squares, triangles, etc.) of the key terms that comprise concepts and topics and their interrelationships or organization (Ellis & Howard, 2007). It presents information through the use of webs, matrices, time lines, process chains, cycles, Venn diagrams, and networks. Graphic organizers help students identify and organize important information about a topic so that they can activate prior knowledge and link it to new concepts. They also help students see the big picture and the relationships between main points and supporting details, make comparisons, clarify relationships, develop inferences, and draw conclusions (Gajria, Mullane, Sharp, & Heim, 2003).

There are several types of graphic organizers: central and hierarchical, directional, and comparative (Ellis & Howard, 2007; Gajria et al., 2003). *Central* and *hierarchical* graphic organizers are structured around one central topic (i.e., an idea or a concept) and are typically used to depict concepts and the elements that describe them. In a central graphic organizer, important information related to the central topic is depicted visually as radiating outward from the central topic. In a hierarchical graphic organizer, supporting information is presented in order of importance, with items being supraordinate to other items. *Directional* graphic organizers present information in a linear or cyclical sequence and are often used to depict cause-effect information or content that can be presented in a sequential pattern such as a cycle, continuum, time line, or flowchart. Directional organizers are often used to present processes, procedures, sequences of events, and time lines (see Figure 11.8A). *Comparative* graphic organizers are used to compare/contrast two or more concepts and typically include information presented in a matrix, Venn diagram, or chart (see Figure 11.8B).

You can develop graphic organizers by doing the following:

- Preview and analyze the curriculum area, Web site, or textbook to identify key information, concepts, and terms.
- Construct an outline of the main information. Arrange the information, concepts, and terms students are to learn based on their interrelationships.
- Select a graphic organizer format that coincides with the organization of the information to be learned.
- Label important ideas and concepts clearly.
- Delete information you want students to contribute, as well as information that is distracting or irrelevant.
- Include additional terms that are important for students to know.
- Add graphics to motivate students and promote mastery of the information.
- Assess the graphic organizer for completeness, clarity, and organization.
- Prepare three versions of the graphic organizer: a completed version, a semicompleted version, and a blank version. Use the blank version with students who write quickly. Use the semicompleted version with students who have some difficulty copying and organizing information. Use the completed version with students who have significant difficulties copying and organizing information.
- Introduce the graphic organizer to the students so that they know its purpose, and understand how they can use it to help them learn.
- Include additional information relevant to the overview (Ellis & Howard, 2007; Gajria et al., 2003; Skylar et al., 2007).

presented. For example, when assigning a reading selection in a science textbook, you can focus students' reading via an advance organizer such as "Read pages 65 to 68, visit the Web site (Name/URL) on mirrors, and find out and watch the video of how a mirror works. Pay careful attention to such terms as *plane mirror, virtual image, parabolic mirror, principal axis, principal focus*, and *focal length*." Similarly, a class-developed outline that summarizes the main points of a presentation on the

FIGURE 11.8A Sample directional graphic organizers

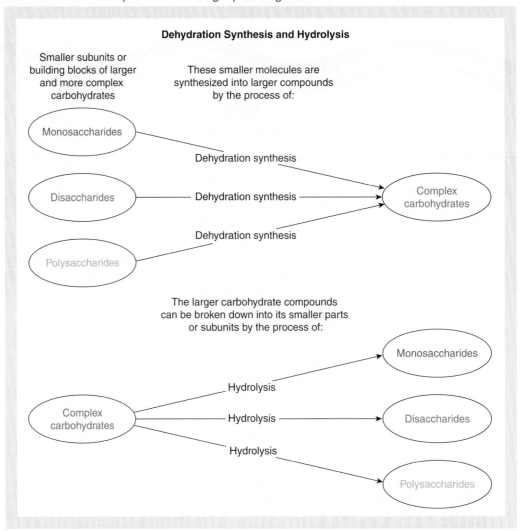

FIGURE 11.8B Sample comparative graphic organizers

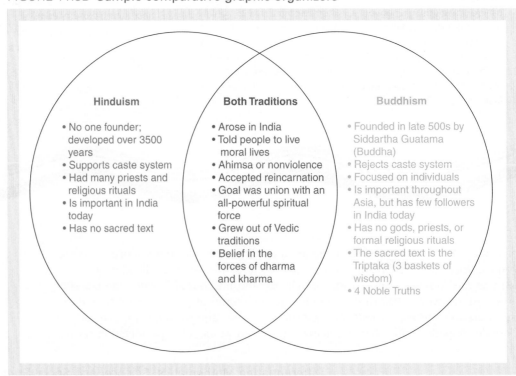

geography of your state could serve as a post organizer. In addition to social studies and science, advance and post organizers can be used to teach in all content areas. Several types of advance and post organizers are described next.

As students become accustomed to using graphic organizers, they can be encouraged to develop their own. Scanlon, Deshler, and Schumaker (1996) developed a learning strategy called ORDER to help students develop their own graphic organizers.

Semantic Webs. **Semantic webs**, also called *semantic maps*, like graphic organizers, provide a visual depiction of important points and concepts, as well as the relationships between these points and concepts, and can be developed by students (Vaughn & Edmonds, 2006). They can be used to introduce, review, and clarify new and previously learned material. A semantic web includes a key word or phrase that relates to the main point of the content, which serves as the focal point of the web; web strands, which are subordinate ideas related to the key word; strand supports, which include details and information related to each web strand; and strand ties, which establish the interrelationships among different strands. Semantic webs may take other shapes as well (see Figure 11.9).

Anticipation Guides. The **anticipation guide** is an advance organizer that introduces students to new content by having them respond to several teacher-generated oral or written statements or questions concerning the material (Brozo & Puckett, 2009). For example, an anticipation guide might include a series of true/false statements that the students answer and discuss before reading a chapter in the textbook (see Figure 11.10). An anticipation guide also could include asking students to write

myeducationlab

Go to the Assignments and Activities section of the Topic *Content Area Teaching* in the MyEducationLab for your course and complete the activity entitled *Collaboration to Support Social Studies Goals*.

FIGURE 11.9 **Semantic web of the three branches of government**

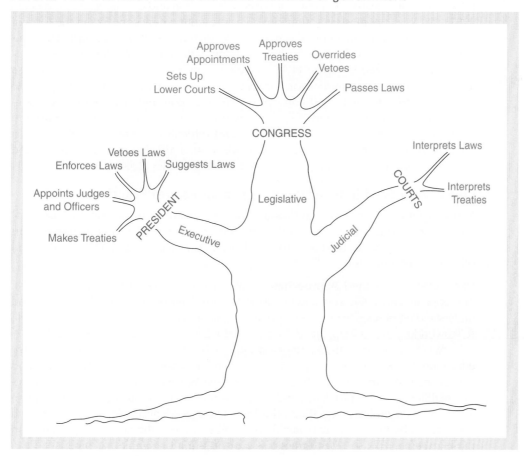

FIGURE 11.10 Anticipation guide on energy resources

Working as a group, read the statements and place a *T* next to those that are true and an *F* next to those that are false. Be prepared to explain the reasons for rating a statement as true or false.

- Ninety-five percent of the energy needs of the United States are provided by fossil fuels.
- Spacecraft and many homes use solar energy.
- Hydroelectric power has no negative effects on the environment.
- Fossil fuels produce more energy per gram than nonfossil fuels.
- Before the radiation decays, radioactive wastes must be stored for a thousand years.

questions about the title or headings of a specific selection. The steps in constructing anticipation guides are as follows:

1. Analyze the text and determine the main points.
2. Convert main points into short, declarative, concrete statements that students can understand.
3. Present statements to students in a way that leads to anticipation and prediction.
4. Have students discuss their predictions and responses to the statements.
5. Discuss the students' reading of the text selection, and then compare and evaluate their responses with the information presented in the text.

Concept Mastery Routines.   Many science and social studies concepts can be taught using a *concept mastery routine*, which is a set of instructional strategies for fostering student learning of content-based information and concepts (Bulgren et al., 2007). The concept mastery routine involves presenting new concepts in the form of a concept diagram containing the relevant characteristics of the concept. The concept diagram can also be used to help students review for tests. A sample concept diagram is presented in Figure 11.11. Once concepts are mastered, teachers can use a concept comparison routine or concept anchoring routine. In the *concept comparison routine*, the mastered concept is explored more fully by comparing examples from the same category (e.g., comparing two types of diseases). Mastered concepts are used to teach students new and difficult concepts through use of a *concept anchoring routine*, where characteristics that are shared by the known and new concepts are listed and examined in a table (Bulgren, 2006).

Use a Variety of Instructional Approaches and Practices

You can differentiate social studies and science instruction by using a variety of approaches and practices such as the ones described here. Again, it is important to remember that you can use these approaches and practices to teach mathematics and other content areas, too.

Use Activities-Oriented Approaches   You can use an activities-oriented approach. This approach uses discovery and inquiry to help students develop their knowledge and understanding of science and social studies based on their experiences (Bybee, Powell, & Trowbridge, 2008; Chiappetta & Koballa, 2010; Lynch, et al., 2007; Maxim, 2010).

When using an activities-oriented approach, offer students a variety of active educational experiences that provide engagement, exploration, development, and extension. The learning cycle begins with the *engagement phase*, in which challenging, real-life activities, problems, and questions are used to motivate students to learn about the topic and to assess their prior knowledge. Students explore the content and phenomena by manipulating materials and start to address the questions presented in the engagement phase. For example, as part of a unit on simple machines, you can

REFLECTIVE

Develop a graphic organizer, concept teaching routine, anticipation guide, or semantic web for the content presented in this chapter. Did they help you identify and master the content? What was challenging about creating them?

FIGURE 11.11 Sample concept diagram

Concept Name: Democracy

Definitions: A democracy is a form of government in which the people hold the ruling power, citizens are equal, the individual is valued, and compromise is necessary.

Characteristics Present in the Concept:

Always	Sometimes	Never
form of government	direct representation	king rules
people hold power	indirect representation	dictator rules
individual is valued		
citizens equal		
compromise necessary		

Example:

(Germany today)

(Athens (about 500 B.C.))

Nonexample:

(Germany under Hitler)

(Macedonia (under Alexander))

Source: From "Effectiveness of a Concept Teaching Routine in Enhancing the Performance of LD Students in Secondary-Level Mainstream Classes," by J. Bulgren, J. B. Schumaker, and D. Deshler, 1988, *Learning Disability Quarterly, 11.* Copyright 1988. Reprinted by permission.

ask students to identify simple machines that they use and have them take apart broken household appliances. During the *exploration phase*, students formulate new ideas and questions to be developed in the later phases. For example, you can have students explore how the household appliances work, identify their components, and develop hypotheses about how to fix them. In the *development phase*, students investigate and add to their understanding by gathering more information and drawing conclusions about the concepts, the phenomena, and the questions previously generated. Using our example, students can access the Internet to learn more about the appliances and to draw conclusions about how they work. The final stage, *extension or elaboration*, gives students opportunities to apply their learning to new and different situations as well as to their own experiences. They also often report their learning to others. In our example, students can hypothesize how other machines and household appliances that they use work, and report on their findings to their classmates.

An effective activities-oriented approach provides students with hands-on and multisensory experiences and materials (Kottler & Costa, 2009; Kortering et al., 2008; Kurtts et al., 2009). Hands-on learning offers students concrete experiences that establish a foundation for learning abstract concepts. Hands-on and multisensory activities also allow students to explore and discover content. In addition, these activities reduce the language and literacy demands that may interfere with the learning of students with disabilities and students who are English language learners. For example, students can learn about electricity by building electric circuits and can become familiar with the geography of a region by making a topographical map out of papier-mâché.

Using Semantic Webs

Ms. Rivlin collects and grades students' notebooks at the end of each unit of instruction. She notices that her students are handing in notebooks that lack many pieces of information from classes and textbook readings that she thinks are important. As a result, many students are having difficulty in class and are doing poorly on tests.

To help her students identify and retain information, Ms. Rivlin decides to use semantic webs to help them review and organize material relating to the unit they are studying on the federal government.

After asking students to read and showing brief video clips about the roles of the three branches of government, Ms. Rivlin writes the key words *executive, legislative*, and *judicial* on the board. She asks students what these words mean and then asks them to brainstorm related ideas and concepts. As students present their ideas, Ms. Rivlin asks the class to determine whether the ideas are new and relevant and should be listed on the board or whether they are not relevant or overlap with the ideas already on the board. She then asks the students to work in groups to examine the relationships between the concepts listed on the board and group the related concepts together under the key words.

After reviewing their groupings, Ms. Rivlin and her students create a treelike semantic web that contains the branches of the government and the duties performed by the president, Congress, and the courts (see Figure 11.9). The students then review the web, add new material based on texts and classroom discussions, and copy it in their notebooks. To further reinforce the concept of checks and balances, Ms. Rivlin draws a picture of a seesaw balanced by an equal number of checkmarks on both sides. Before the unit ends, Ms. Rivlin collects students' notebooks and is pleased to see that they have copied the webs and pictorials. She also is pleased when she sees that students' knowledge of the material has improved.

- Why did Ms. Rivlin decide to use semantic webs?
- How do content enhancements like semantic webs benefit students?
- What steps and strategies did Ms. Rivlin follow in using semantic webs?
- What other strategies could she use to help her students learn the material?

Organize Instruction Around Big Ideas and Interdisciplinary Themes Activities-oriented approaches focus on depth of understanding rather than broad coverage of science, social studies, and other content areas. Coyne, Kame'enui, and Carnine (2007) suggest that you organize science, social studies, and content-area instruction around **big ideas**: critical topics, concepts, issues, problems, experiences, or principles that assist students in organizing, interrelating, and applying information so that meaning-

IDEAs to Implement Inclusion

Ensuring Safety in Laboratory Settings

Ms. Castro's chemistry class included several students with sensory and physical disabilities. She was concerned about their ability to safely use and learn from the frequent laboratory experiments that students performed. Her principal and several of her colleagues suggested that she purchase specialized equipment such as spoons with sliding covers, glassware with raised letters and numbers, lightweight fire extinguishers, and devices with visual and auditory on/off indicators and warnings. They also recommended that she label important areas, material, and substances in the room and assign students to work with lab partners.

Here are some other strategies you can use to implement the IDEA in your inclusive classroom and ensure safety in the laboratory:

- Post, discuss, and distribute to students the rules, safety considerations, and evacuation procedures before beginning an experiment.

- Make sure that students wear safety equipment such as splashproof goggles and rubber gloves and aprons.
- Use plastic items (e.g., beakers) instead of breakable ones.
- Use print and sandpaper labeling for hazardous materials, and make sure that combustible gas supplies contain odorants.
- Provide adapted laboratory stations for students who need them. An adapted station may include a work surface 30 inches from the floor, accessible and modified equipment controls, appropriate space for clearance, and wider-than-usual aisles.
- Equip the laboratory with adjustable-height storage units, pull-out or drop-leaf shelves and countertops, single-action lever controls and blade-type handles, and flexible connections to water, electrical, and gaslines.

Sources: Bargerhuff and Wheatly (2004); Chiappetta and Koballa (2010).

ful links can be established between the content and students' lives. Organizing instruction through big ideas also gives students a framework for learning "smaller ideas" such as facts related to the broader concepts and big ideas being studied.

You can translate the big ideas from your curriculum into essential questions, which guides lesson planning and instruction and motivates and fosters student understanding of meaningful concepts (Bulgren et al., 2007; Childre et al., 2009; Wiggins & McTighe, 2008). Essential questions

- are challenging, open ended, inquiry-based and have no obvious "right" answer;
- address broad, relevant, and foundational concepts rather than memorization of facts;
- are presented to stimulate and maintain student exploration and reflection;
- engage students in reading, writing, listening, and discussing to formulate their thinking and responses; and
- offer multiple levels of student engagement based on their developmental levels and understanding of the content (Farber, 2009; Noddings, 2008).

For example, "What makes a president great?" is an essential question that can be discussed from multiple perspectives and developmental levels and allows teachers to introduce students to a variety of foundational social studies concepts.

Student learning can also be promoted by linking instruction to important broad, common, and interdisciplinary themes that can accommodate the diverse learning abilities of students (Savage & Armstrong, 2008). Interdisciplinary themes can link the various science and social studies disciplines, as well as relate them to other subject areas. For example, an integrated unit on the Incas of Peru could include a social studies investigation of the geographic area affected by the Incas, Incan cultural traditions, and Incan religious beliefs. In science class, students could study the scientific, medical, and agricultural methods of the Incas. In math, they could learn about the Incan system of record keeping based on different colored cords and knots. For art, students could learn about cultural symbols associated with the Incas and produce art forms that reflect these traditional symbols. Throughout this unit, students can read and write about the Incas.

Use Problem-Based Learning to Relate Instruction to Students' Lives and General Societal Issues Relating science and social studies to practical, recreational, and cultural events and problems that are familiar and relevant to students can promote learning, increase motivation, and help students learn to value science and social studies (Bybee et al., 2008; Chiappetta & Koballa, 2010; Kortering et al., 2008; Maxim, 2010). In using problem-based learning, you present students with background information and open-ended issues and problems related to real-life situations and discuss with students the relevance of these problems to their lives, as well as the situations in which this content can be applied (Bianco et al., 2009). Students then gather additional information using a range of resources and propose and evaluate solutions to the problems posed. For example, students can investigate important social problems and issues such as immigration, discrimination, water supply, weather, pollution, nutrition, and solar energy.

Science, social studies, and other content-area instruction can also be connected to students' cultural backgrounds and communities. You can try to link your curriculum to **cultural universals**, which are needs and experiences that exist in all cultures, albeit in different ways, including such topics as food, shelter, clothing, and transportation (Alleman, Knighton, & Brophy, 2007). You also can use learning activities and materials that explore the different cultural and historical origins of science, discuss scientific solutions and practices developed and used in all parts of the world, highlight the achievements of scientists and historians from various cultural and language backgrounds, and present a range of culturally diverse practical applications of science to help students understand the multicultural aspects of science. Connections to students' lives and cultures also can be established by having students perform activities that

PEARSON
myeducationlab

Go to the Assignments and Activities section of the Topic *Content Area Teaching* in the MyEducationLab for your course and complete the activity entitled *Science Instruction Using Concepts of Universal Design for Learning.*

address community problems; use artifacts, buildings, geographical sites, museums, and other resources in the students' community; and interview community members to illustrate and reinforce concepts, issues, phenomena, and events.

Instruction also can foster the development of **social responsibility**, an interest in and concern for the well-being of others and the environment (Beal et al., 2009; Schmidt, 2009; Weilbacher, 2009). Social responsibility encourages the development of social consciousness, which helps students explore their hopes for the future and the impact of their actions on others. A curriculum to teach students social responsibility can help them develop an understanding of our social and ecological interdependence, a sense of what it means to be part of a community, a sense of history, and basic social skills including communication, conflict management, and perspective taking. Social responsibility can be taught throughout the curriculum by examining real-world issues. For example, mathematics classes can explore the impact of math (such as statistics) on the political process; science classes can address the relationship between science, technology, and the world; and social studies classes can examine racism in society.

Making Connections
This discussion of effective questions techniques builds on the earlier discussion of questioning in Chapter 9.

Use Effective Questioning Techniques   Another way to foster, direct, and assess student learning is by using effective questioning strategies that guide learning and promote critical thinking and reflection (Bybee et al., 2008; Posamentier et al., 2010). Effective questioning also can help you assess whether your students are learning the material and identify misconceptions students have that need to be addressed (Beal et al., 2009). Maxim (2010) identified three types of questions teachers typically ask: literal, inferential, and critical. **Literal questions** focus on content derived from class presentations and instructional materials and ask students to recall, name, list, or describe information presented. **Inferential questions** require students to provide answers that are not explicitly stated in the presentation and instructional materials and ask students to analyze, compare, and synthesize information presented. **Critical questions** ask students to provide personal judgments and reactions to the content and to apply and evaluate the information presented to other situations.

Questions can also differentiate your instruction and motivate. For example, use literal questions to help students who are in the process of learning new material and employ inferential and critical questions to enrich the learning of students who have already demonstrated mastery of the material.

Use Specially Designed Programs and Curricula   Specially designed programs and curricula are available and can be integrated into existing science and social studies instructional programs (Lynch et al., 2007). Hapgood and Sullivan Palinscar (2007) note that inquiry-based programs like *Science IDEAS* and *Guide Inquiry Supporting Multiple Literacies* can be used to integrate the teaching of science and literacy. Educators have developed activity-based science programs for students with visual disabilities called *Science Activities for the Visually Impaired* (SAVI) and programs for students with physical disabilities called *Science Enrichment Learning for Learners with Physical Handicaps* (SELPH). These programs use a laboratory approach to teaching science that stresses observations, manipulation of materials, and the development of scientific language. *Project MAVIS (Materials Adaptations for Visually Impaired Students)* has adapted social studies

Relating science, social studies, and mathematics to practical problems that are relevant to students can promote learning and motivation. What practical problems relating to your students' lives may interest them in science, social studies, and mathematics?

materials for students with visual and physical disabilities, but these materials also can be used with other students. A laboratory-based curriculum model is *Science for All Children* (SAC) (Cawley, Foley, & Miller, 2003).

Enhance Students' Memory Because content-oriented approaches to teaching science and social studies require students to retain large amounts of information and many new terms, helping students enhance and develop their memory skills and strategies is important for success in inclusive classrooms. These skills and strategies also can be used by students across the curriculum to minimize errors and speed their recall. You can improve your students' memory by providing them with access to or encouraging them to create

- visual representations of the words or content to be remembered,
- conceptual representations of what the words or content to be remembered does, and
- linguistic representations of the sounds of the words and content to be remembered as well as how they fit into sentences (Connor & Lagares, 2007).

You can introduce new words and content by creating a memorable event or physically presenting the important attributes of the material to be remembered (Alber & Foil, 2003).

A variety of methods and mnemonic devices can be used to help students remember content, including pictures, acronyms, acrostics, and rhymes (Rotter, 2009; Strichart & Mangrum, 2010; Willingham, 2009). Whereas **acronyms**, or *first-letter mnemonics*, foster memory by creating a meaningful word or phrase using the first letter of the words or phrases to be remembered, **acrostics** trigger recall by employing a sentence based on the first letter of the words to be memorized. For example, your students can learn the acronym HOMES to prompt their memory of the Great Lakes and the acrostic **M**y **V**ery **E**nergetic **M**om **J**ust **S**erved **U**s **N**achos to remember the planets in their order from the sun. Your students also can learn to use mnemonic associations by linking the information to be remembered with a part of the information that is difficult to remember. Although mnemonic associations are particularly helpful in remembering difficult spelling words (e.g., *A rat* is found in sep*arat*e, they also can be used to remember other types of material (e.g., stala**g**mites grow from the **g**round and stala**c**tites from the **c**eiling (Willingham, 2009). You can encourage your students to use mnemonics by teaching them to use such learning strategies as the FIRST-Letter Mnemonic Strategy and LISTS (Nagel, Schumaker, & Deshler, 1986) and the Paired Associates Strategy (Bulgren, Schumaker, & Deshler, cited in Bulgren, Hock, Schumaker, & Deshler, 1995).

Another mnemonic device your students can use is the keyword method (Fontana, Scruggs, & Mastropieri, 2007; Wolgemuth, Cobb, & Alwell, 2008). This method involves your students associating the new vocabulary word or concept with a word that sounds similar to an easy-to-remember illustration using the following steps:

1. *Recoding.* The new vocabulary word or concept is recoded into a concrete key word that sounds similar and is familiar to the student. The key word should be one that students can easily picture. For example, the key word for the word *sauro* might be a *saw*.
2. *Relating.* An *interactive illustration*—a mental picture or drawing of the key word interacting with the definition of the vocabulary word—is created. A sentence describing the interaction also is developed. For example, the definition of *sauro* and the key word *saw* can be depicted using the sentence "A lizard is sawing."
3. *Retrieving.* On hearing the new vocabulary word, students retrieve its definition by thinking of the key word, creating the interactive illustration and/or its corresponding sentence, and stating the definition.

REFLECTIVE

Select a content area and create literal, inferential, and critical questions. Share and critique your questions with a partner. What things were good about your questions? How could your questions be improved?

PEARSON
myeducationlab

Go to the Building Teaching Skills and Dispositions section of the Topic *Content Area Instruction* in the MyEducationLab for your course and complete the activity entitled *Facilitating Learners' Knowledge Construction.* As you watch the video and answer the accompanying questions, consider how memory and knowledge construction work together.

You can plan your lessons so that they foster student memory of new content (Connor & Lagares, 2007; Rotter, 2009). Link new content to material your students already know, making it personally relevant to them. Give students opportunities to review small amounts of material frequently rather than trying to memorize large amounts of information at once. Use creative repetition by using a variety of motivating instructional formats that prompt your students to practice their new learning throughout the lesson. Additionally, structure your lessons so that you (a) present new material at the beginning of your lessons and review it at the end of your lessons, (b) use graphic organizers and visuals and incorporate novelty and humor into learning activities, and (c) have students work with partners to rehearse and check each other's memory of critical information. You also can use technology to provide your students with access to visual and auditory cues and practice opportunities that can foster their memory of academic content (Perez Sanchez & Beltran Liera, 2007).

You also can teach your students to use the following strategies (Mind Tools, 2008; Rotter, 2009; Salend, 2009; Strichart & Mangrum, 2010; Willingham, 2009).

Mental Visualization.   Your students can remember important concepts and terms by associating them with a mental image or symbol of the content. When using visualization, your students should be encouraged to create positive, pleasant, colorful, and three-dimensional images, as these qualities make the images more realistic and memorable. Memory of images can be enhanced by adding movement, appropriate humor, smells and sound, and exaggerating important parts. For example, to remember the definition of *stalactite*, they can visualize a three-dimensional, limestone-colored stalactite dripping from the ceiling of a cave.

Visual Associations.   Your students can remember related words and concepts by using visual associations depicting these relationships, such as having two or more conflicting concepts collide, viewing similar concepts as joined together, placing sequentially related concepts in a staircase or their proper sequence, or linking related concepts by having them rotate around each other on a merry-go-round.

Stories.   Your students can create brief stories with words and images that trigger their memory of sequential lists of related information or important concepts.

Loci.   Your students can employ images of familiar places to trigger their memory of specific information or events. For example, they can foster their memory of George Washington Carver, who discovered over 300 uses of peanuts, by imagining him eating peanuts in Washington, DC.

Categorizing.   Your students can prompt their memory of a series of key terms or information by sorting them into groups based on common traits and then memorizing each group. For example, to foster memory of the 50 different states, your students can create groups based on geographical locations and then focus their studying on each geographic category.

Rhyming and Music.   Your students can create rhymes and music to aid their memory of specific content. For example, they can memorize the spelling rule rhyme "*i* before *e* except after *c*" or the rule "30 days has September. . . ."

Games.   Your students can play a variety of online and face-to-face games such as Concentration using flash cards related to the content that they need to memorize.

Use Instructional Technology and Multimedia   Instructional technology and multimedia can enhance science and social studies instruction and play a key role in activities-based approaches (Beal et al., 2009; Kortering et al., 2008; Kurtts et al., 2009). Instructional technology and multimedia can be used to introduce, review, and virtually apply science and social studies concepts. Using these devices, students can experience events, places, and phenomena such as scientific experiments, geographic locations around the world, or historical events. For example, multimedia applications allow students to perform complicated scientific experiments, such

Making Connections
These techniques for enhancing students' memory relate to teaching students' study skills, which we will discuss in Chapter 12.

REFLECTIVE

What strategies do you use to enhance and develop your memory? How did you learn them?

as those involving chemical reactions, on the computer. In addition to providing an opportunity to obtain and observe unique aspects of the content, these instructional delivery systems can motivate students and stimulate their curiosity. Through the Internet and telecommunications, students also can learn science, social studies, and mathematics by being linked to data and educational resources, problem-solving experiences, and interactions with students and professionals around the world (Bybee et al., 2008; Chiappetta & Koballa, 2010; Cote, 2007).

Take Students on Field Trips   Field trips also can make learning more meaningful and real for students and connect learning to community-based situations. In particular, visits to historical and science museums, as well as ecological and historical sites, allow students to experience what they hear and read about (Maxim, 2010). Many museums and sites offer students hands-on experiences that promote learning and provide information as well as after-school learning opportunities for students. Museums also can provide students with access to authentic and primary sources, artifacts, documents, and photos, which can add to the excitement of learning. To help you and your students benefit from field trips, many museums and sites provide

Making Connections
Resources for providing your students with digital books were presented earlier in Chapter 8.

REFLECTIVE

Have you used a digital textbook or book? What were its advantages and disadvantages?

Using Technology to Promote Inclusion
MAKING MATHEMATICS, SCIENCE, AND SOCIAL STUDIES INSTRUCTION ACCESSIBLE TO ALL STUDENTS

Technological advances are resulting in innovative ways that can help you differentiate mathematics, science, and social studies instruction. One such technological innovation is the **digital textbook**, or *electronic textbook* (e-textbook), which is the electronic version of textbooks that can be accessed by students in a variety of ways including computers, flashdrives, and handheld devices (Harrison, 2009; Trotter, 2008). E-textbooks have several advantages over traditional textbooks (Lewin, 2009; Wissick et al., 2009). Because digital texts can be read to students via text-to-speech programs, they help students with visual and reading difficulties access textbook content (Anderson-Inman, 2009). Other features that help students identify key topics, vocabulary, and text structures (e.g., variable text size, highlighting, multicolored headings, bookmarking) also assist them in accessing content and taking notes. Digital textbooks also help students understand the material by listening to descriptions of graphics and allowing them to use on-line resources such as abridged editions, graphics, outlines, animation, pictures, audio, and video. You also can embed prompts into digital materials that guide your students in comprehending what they read and in using strategic learning strategies and staying motivated and engaged (Zorfass & Clay, 2008). They also have built-in dictionaries and glossaries, and allow students to conduct word searches to help them understand and view animated presentations of unfamiliar concepts and vocabulary (see Figure 11.12). Digital textbooks can extend and motivate student learning by providing links that allow students to access content-related podcasts, blogs, wikis, videos, videoconferences, recorded classroom presentations, PowerPoint/Keynote presentations, simulation activities, academic games and real-time data, self-paced tutorials, and various self-assessment formats. In addition, e-textbooks have capabilities that allow students to highlight content and take notes, bookmark important material, vary the rate at which the text is read, and move easily by chapter, page, heading and subsections (Horney et al., 2009).

Here are some other ways you can use technology to create inclusive classrooms that support student learning in the areas of mathematics, science, and social studies:

- Take your students on "virtual field trips" to various museums and scientific, mathematical and historical sites via the Internet (Okolo et al., 2007; Chiappetta & Koballa, 2010). You and your students also can watch or hear live or prerecorded **podcasts** of events and learning activities occurring throughout the world or create your own podcasts (Salend, 2009).

- Provide students with access to primary sources, artifacts, online picture dictionaries, electronic libraries, databases, and journals through use of the Internet and multimedia (Beuck, Courtad, Heutsche, Okolo, & Englert, 2009; Connor & Lagares, 2007; Doyle & Giangreco, 2009).

- Teach students to use multimedia, programs, and handheld references devices such as electronic dictionaries, thesauri, and encyclopedias to access references and resources and obtain information about specific topics. **Wikitextbooks**, collaboratively developed and editable online textbooks, are also becoming available. By subscribing to a **RSS Site Summary (RSS)**, students can receive brief summaries of the content on particular topics available at various Web sites so that they can identify relevant online content without having to access multiple sites (Richardson, 2009).

(Continued)

Differentiating Mathematics, Science, and Social Studies Instruction

- Use online problem-based learning, computer-assisted instruction, virtual manipulatives and reality, educational games, and simulation multimedia packages that ask students to respond collaboratively and individually to authentic and multidimensional dilemmas and situations in mathematics, science and social studies (Bottge et al., 2007; Bouck & Flanagan, 2009; Chiappetta & Koballa, 2010; Cote, 2007; Gee & Levine, 2009; Kurtts et al., 2009; Maxim, 2010; Murray et al., 2007a; Wissick et al., 2009). For example, students can perform software simulations of various types of science experiments and social studies activities and virtually manipulate objects to solve math problems.

- Access online resources related to using a concrete-representational-abstract instructional sequence for teaching a range of mathematical concepts and skills (Witzel, Riccomini, & Schneider, 2008).

- Integrate into instructional activities Web sites that offer access to information presented via webcameras (webcams) that allow students to view live events related to your curriculum. Prior to using webcam sites, check to make sure that they are appropriate for your students.

- Use technology to condense and highlight material from textbooks and make it more accessible to students. For example, you can create PowerPoint presentations of key concepts and important vocabulary from textbooks and embed pictorials, video clips, and bulleted flashing text to make them more accessible for students. You also can use Microsoft Word AutoSummarize to condense and summarize longer selections from textbooks and other print materials into shorter versions.

- Identify relevant streaming video and audio, pictures, graphics, and images via the Internet and incorporate them into lessons and technology-based presentations (Okolo, 2006; Wissick et al., 2009). You can enhance the effectiveness of these clips by interspersing them with questions and brief discussions and pairing them with written materials (Gersten et al., 2006).

- Use software to convert calculations, symbols, and unusual alignments in complex mathematical and scientific text documents into electronic files that can be more easily accessed by students using technology.

- Use the Internet and software programs to access and create interactive and technology-based graphic organizers, study guides, webquests, and tracks across the curriculum that have links to digital resources (Boon, Fore, Blankenship, & Chalk, 2007; Ellis & Howard, 2007; Skylar et al., 2007) and to design a range of graphic organizers for use with students (Parette, Crowley, & Wojcik, 2007; Reeves & Standard, 2009; Wissick et al., 2009).

- Use specialized technology to support the learning of students with sensory disabilities (Osterhaus, 2007). For example, you can teach your students with visual disabilities to use Nemeth Braille, a technology for coding mathematical and scientific notation that employs Braille, or you and your students can use embossing technologies to create tactile graphics such as graphs, maps, charts, study guides. These students also can use raised line paper and rubberized graph boards and adapted rulers, compasses and protractors.

It is important for all students to have role models who have been successful in math and science. Do your students have diverse role models?

teacher training programs, model curricula and teaching strategies, special tours, exhibits, and materials for school groups, as well as traveling exhibits that prepare students for and build upon experiences at the museum.

Address the Challenges of Diverse Learners

Female students, students from various cultural and language backgrounds, and students with disabilities are often underrepresented in advanced math and science classes and in careers in these fields (Huebner, 2009). This underrepresentation is often attributed to math/science anxiety, as well as to societal expectations and norms that make it acceptable for these students to ignore or question their abilities in science and math. Evidence indicates that teachers treat male and female students differently, encouraging males to achieve in math and science and discouraging females. Therefore, you need to be aware of your behavior, and of societal pressures, so that you can change any such tendencies and create a classroom that encourages math and science competence in *all students*.

FIGURE 11.12 Online electronic-textbook dictionary

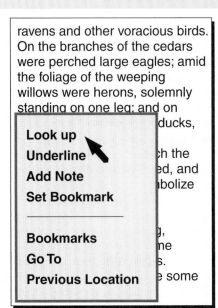

ravens and other voracious birds. On the branches of the cedars were perched large eagles; amid the foliage of the weeping willows were herons, solemnly standing on one leg; and on ...... ducks,

Look up
Underline
Add Note
Set Bookmark

Bookmarks
Go To
Previous Location

ravens and other voracious birds. On the branches of the cedars were perched large eagles; amid the foliage of the weeping willows were herons, solemnly standing on one leg; and on every hand were crows, ducks, hawks, wild birds, and a multitude of cranes, which the Japanese consider sacred, and which to their minds symbolise long life and prosperity.

As he was strolling along, Passepartout espied some violets among the shrubs. "Good!" said he; "I'll have some supper."

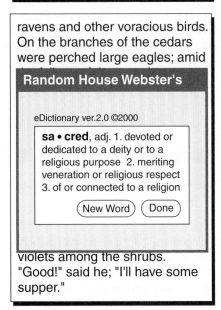

ravens and other voracious birds. On the branches of the cedars were perched large eagles; amid

Random House Webster's

eDictionary ver.2.0 ©2000

sa • cred, adj. 1. devoted or dedicated to a deity or to a religious purpose 2. meriting veneration or religious respect 3. of or connected to a religion

(New Word)   (Done)

violets among the shrubs. "Good!" said he; "I'll have some supper."

An online companion dictionary provides quick access to new or difficult vocabulary with immediacy and within a meaningful context. The user chooses the "Look up" function, then clicks on an unfamiliar word. The appropriate entry from a built-in dictionary is shown in a pop-up window. Text is from Jules Verne's *Around the World in Eighty Days*, which is no longer under copyright. Facsimile screens are based on the RCA eBook layout.

Source: From "Reading, Writing, and Publishing Digital Text," by R. Boone and K. Higgins, 2003, *Remedial and Special Education*, 24. pp. 132–140. Copyright 2003 by SAGE Publications. Reprinted with permission.

Promoting Math and Science Education for All Students

The teachers in the Madison School were shocked and disappointed at the small number of female students who had enrolled in their after-school science and math program. Unsure of the reasons for the low turnout, the teachers spoke to several of their female students, who said that they didn't sign up for the program because "Science is for nerds," "My friends will think I'm weird," and "I'm not good at science and math." Struck by these comments, the teachers decided to revamp their math and science teaching so that it appealed to *all students*. First, they shared studies with students that showed the relationships among gender and math, science, and technology. They also had their students analyze textbooks, instructional materials, and activities that presented females in nonstereotypical science and math roles. They then developed and taught an interdisciplinary unit about scientists and mathematicians who are female, who are from culturally and linguistically diverse backgrounds, or who have disabilities. They invited several local scientists and mathematicians from these diverse groups to speak about their jobs and education. As a culminating activity, students worked in cooperative learning groups to study why females, individuals from diverse backgrounds, and people with disabilities are underrepresented in science and mathematics.

Here are some other strategies you can use to implement the IDEA in your inclusive classroom and promote math and science education for *all students:*

- Model and encourage *all students* to have a positive attitude toward math and science and take intellectual risks.

- Establish a learning environment that fosters high expectations for *all students* and allows them to be active, inquiring participants.

- Provide students with a historical and multicultural understanding of math and science, and infuse math and science into other subject areas.

- Present problems and situations so that *all students* are depicted in active, nonstereotypical ways, and avoid using statements, materials, and pictorials that suggest that certain groups of students are not skilled in math and science.

- Emphasize the problem-solving aspects of math and science rather than speed and competition, and encourage students to use a variety of verbal and visual problem-solving techniques.

- Teach math and science using real-life situations, hands-on materials, cooperative learning groups, projects, and games. For example, as part of a unit on pollution, students can work in cooperative learning groups to study water, air, and noise pollution in their own communities.

- Communicate and demonstrate to students, their families, and other teachers the importance of seeking advanced training and pursuing careers in math and science.

- Contact a diverse group of scientists and mathematicians in your community to serve as mentors for your students.

- Assign class and school jobs to *all students* that require them to solve problems and use their math and science skills.

Sources: Bybee et al. (2008); Furner, Yahya, and Duffy (2005); Huebner (2009); Koch (2005).

What Would You Do in Today's Diverse Classroom?

★ Fred has a good understanding of numbers and their relationships, patterns, and operations. However, he struggles performing multistep operations and solving word problems.

★ Felicia's struggles with reading affect her confidence and learning in social studies and science. As a result, she does not identify important information from textbooks and teacher-directed lessons, and fails to complete her assignments.

1. How would Fred and Felicia's difficulties impact their performance in your inclusive classroom?

2. What would you do to help Fred and Felicia overcome their challenges?

3. What knowledge, skills, dispositions, resources, and support from others would be useful in helping them learn mathematics, science, and social studies?

myeducationlab Watch two teachers discuss and demonstrate the use of technology to differentiate social studies instruction for students who struggle with reading and writing by visiting the MyEducationLab for this course. Go to the *Assignments and Activities* section under the topic *Content Area Teaching*, and complete the activity entitled *Using Technology to Support Literacy in the Content Areas* to answer questions about differentiating social studies, science, and mathematics instruction for students in inclusive classrooms.

Summary

This chapter presented guidelines and strategies for differentiating mathematics, science, and social studies instruction. As you review the questions posed in this chapter, remember the following points.

How Can I Differentiate Mathematics Instruction?
CEC 3, 4, 5, 7, 9; PRAXIS 3; INTASC 1, 2, 3, 4, 5, 6, 7, 9

Focus mathematics instruction and use a problem-solving approach to foster the development of the basic mathematical understandings and skills students need to learn to reason and communicate mathematically and become confident mathematical problem solvers. This involves helping students develop their math facts and computation skills and teaching them mathematics by experiencing and thinking about meaningful problems related to their lives. In addition, present mathematics appropriately, use a developmental instructional sequence, a variety of teaching aids and instructional approaches, provide practice and feedback, and use assessment to guide future teaching.

How Can I Differentiate Science and Social Studies Instruction?
CEC 3, 4, 5, 7, 9; PRAXIS 3; INTASC 1, 2, 3, 4, 5, 6, 7, 9

Choose textbooks and other text-based materials carefully and teach students how to use them, and use study guides, adapted textbooks, a parallel alternative curriculum, and content enhancements. In addition, you can promote students' memory, use activities-oriented approaches, organize instruction around big ideas and interdisciplinary themes, and employ problem-based learning to relate instruction to students' lives and social problems. You also can use effective questioning techniques, instructional technology and multimedia, and specially designed programs and curricula, take students on field trips, and address the challenges of diverse learners.

Part
IV
Evaluating Individual and Programmatic Progress

You have learned about the fundamentals of inclusion, the need to create a school and classroom environment that supports learning for *all students,* and strategies for differentiating instruction to accommodate *all students.* With these components in place, it is essential for you to learn how to evaluate the effectiveness of your inclusion program. This evaluation can help you assess the impact of your program on *all students,* family members, and teachers, including yourself. It also can aid you in documenting the strengths of your inclusion program and pinpointing areas in need of revision.

Part IV, which consists of Chapter 12, provides a framework and specific strategies and resources for evaluating inclusive classrooms and programs. Specifically, it presents guidelines for determining whether your inclusive classroom is resulting in positive educational, social, behavioral, and self-concept outcomes for *all students.* It also provides guidelines for grading your students and techniques for examining students', as well as family members' and educators', perceptions of and experiences with inclusion that can help you assess your students' progress and evaluate various programmatic components of your inclusive classroom and your school's inclusion program.

THE MADISON SCHOOL DISTRICT

For several years, the Madison School District had implemented inclusion programs in all its schools. Although things seemed to be going well, the district was faced with the question of whether its inclusion programs were benefiting students. The topic first came up at a meeting with the students' families. Some families of students without disabilities expressed concerns about whether the needs of the students with disabilities were interfering with the education of other students. A few of the families of students with disabilities also were worried about their children being ridiculed by others and about losing individualized services. As a result, the school board asked the superintendent of schools to provide data on the program.

The superintendent created a committee to evaluate the school district's inclusion programs. The committee included a diverse group of students, family members, educators, administrators, and community members. The committee began by identifying ways to examine the impact of the program on students' academic, social, and behavioral performance by reviewing the results of standardized tests, report card grades, and the findings of alternative assessments. They also discussed other data sources including attendance patterns, participation in after-school programs, behavioral referrals, and observations of student interaction patterns. For secondary-level students, they considered such factors as the types of diplomas students received as well as their success in attending college and finding jobs.

The committee also thought the perceptions and experiences of students, educators, and family members should be an important part of the evaluation process. They created interviews and surveys for these different groups designed to identify successful inclusive educational policies as well as issues that needed to be addressed or revised. For example, students, educators, and family members expressed some concerns about

Evaluating Student Progress and the Effectiveness of Your Inclusion Program

the school district's testing accommodations and report card grading policies and made recommendations for improving them. During interviews, several students noted that some of the testing and grading accommodations they received were embarrassing because leaving the classroom to take tests made them feel different. They also indicated that it is distracting when someone is reading a test to another student. One parent stated, "I am very disappointed, confused, and angry. I worked with the IEP team to identify the testing accommodations my son should receive. We listed them in the IEP, and I assumed he would receive them, especially for the state tests. Then, they told me the state says he can only use state-approved testing accommodations when taking the state tests. What about the other testing accommodations he's supposed to receive? He uses them to take his teachers' tests. Why can't he use them for the state test?" A teacher said, "While I understand the need for some instructional and testing accommodations, many of them are inappropriate and unfair. They change the nature of my grading and

give students with disabilities an advantage over other students. I wish they would consult me and consider the other students when making decisions about accommodations."

How can school districts evaluate the effectiveness of their inclusion programs on an ongoing basis? After reading this chapter, you should have the knowledge, skills, and dispositions to answer this as well as the following questions:

- How can I evaluate the academic performance of my students?
- How can I grade my students in inclusive settings?
- How can I evaluate the social and behavioral performance of my students?
- How can I measure perceptions of my inclusive classroom?
- How can I improve the effectiveness of my inclusive classroom?

Like the Madison School District, it is important for you to evaluate the effectiveness of your inclusion classroom by examining its impact on *all students,* on yourself and other professionals, and on students' families (see Table 12.1). An evaluation can help you monitor your students' academic, social, and behavioral progress; inform your teaching; and assess and improve all aspects of your inclusive classroom. It can also allay the concern that the academic and behavioral needs of students with disabilities will require excessive school resources and teacher attention and therefore jeopardize the education of students without disabilities. Information on the perceptions of students, teachers, and family members is also helpful in examining what these groups think about your inclusive classroom. This information can validate successful programmatic factors and inclusive educational policies that should be continued, as well as pinpoint procedures that need to be revised.

EVALUATING THE ACADEMIC PERFORMANCE OF STUDENTS

HOW CAN I EVALUATE THE ACADEMIC PERFORMANCE OF MY STUDENTS? An important goal of your inclusive classroom is to enhance the academic performance of *all students.* Therefore, effective and reflective teachers engage in *formative assessments* to monitor and support teaching and learning and examine and inform their instruction and *summative assessments* to document student learning and the outcomes associated with their teaching (Salend, 2009). Using both forms of assessment, they make students active participants in evaluating their learning and connect instruction and assessment to determine what students have learned and what material they need to reteach to some students, as well as how their students learn best and how they need to adjust their teaching strategies. A variety of summative and formative assessment strategies for monitoring your students' academic progress and guiding your teaching are presented next. These strategies also can used to identify students' strengths and challenges so that you design and deliver an educational program that builds on their strengths and helps them overcome the things with which they struggle (Bianco et al., 2009).

Making Connections
This use of formative and summative assessment relates to what we discussed earlier in Chapter 8.

TABLE 12.1 **Evaluating inclusive classrooms**

Students	Educators	Families
Evaluation Variables		
• Student's academic, social, and behavioral performance • Student's perceptions and experiences • Programmatic factors	• Student performance measures • Perceptions and experiences • Programmatic factors • Cooperative teaching experiences	• Child performance measures • Perceptions and experiences • Programmatic factors
Data Collection Strategies	**Data Collection Strategies**	**Data Collection Strategies**
• Test scores and participation rates • Classroom-based alternatives to standardized testing (e.g., curriculum-based measurement, portfolio assessment, instructional rubrics, dynamic assessment, observations, teacher-made tests, etc.) • Mastery of IEP goals, promotion and graduation rates, and report card grades • Observational, sociometric, and self-concept measures; participation in extracurricular activities; attendance records; and discipline reports, etc. • Postschool outcomes • Interviews and questionnaires	• Interviews and questionnaires • Observations	• Interviews and questionnaires • Observations

Standardized and High-Stakes Testing

Federal requirements mandate that *all students,* including those with disabilities, are expected to participate in standardized testing programs. These tests are often referred to as **high-stakes testing** because important decisions about students' educational programs are made based on their results, including grade-level promotion and graduation. Therefore, because most students with disabilities are participating in state and federal testing programs, student performance on these standardized tests also can be used to examine the impact of your inclusion program on your students' academic performance (Salisbury, Brookfield, & Odom, 2005). Your school also can use these data to compare the scores of students educated in inclusion classes with the scores of their counterparts who are not taught in inclusion classes.

Concerns About High-Stakes Testing   The use of high-stakes testing has raised concerns about the reliance on one exam as the measure of student learning (Farley, 2009; Nichols & Berliner, 2008). Many students report that standardized testing puts an enormous amount of pressure on them, hinders their motivation and learning, and minimizes the effort that they have put in throughout the school year. Several teachers also report concerns about the quality of the tests and the ways they are used because many states have opted to replace existing tests that assess problem-solving skills tested via essays with multiple-choice tests that assess recall of facts in order to reduce the time and money devoted to scoring tests (Winerip, 2006). The pressure to judge student learning and teacher effectiveness based on the results of standardized tests can result in educators teaching to the test at the expense of other important aspects of the curriculum. For example, concerns have been raised about school districts narrowing the curriculum by eliminating or significantly reducing the instructional time devoted to subjects that are not the focus of standardized testing. Family members report that they often do not understand what the tests measure, how to interpret the results, and why their child's test scores differ from their report card grades.

The concerns of students, families, and educators can be addressed by using multiple ways to assess student learning, including classroom-based assessment strategies (Overton, 2009; Salend, 2009), which we will discuss later in this chapter. The usefulness of standardized testing also can be enhanced by educators analyzing the data to identify the content and skills mastered by students as well as changes to the curriculum and instructional strategies that need to be implemented to support student learning.

Determining Valid, Appropriate, and Individualized Testing Accommodations for Diverse Learners   Recognizing that some students with special needs will need testing accommodations in order to take high-stakes tests, with only students with more significant cognitive disabilities taking alternate assessments, the IDEA requires that students' IEPs contain statements related to testing accommodations. Valid **testing accommodations** are variations in testing administration, environment, equipment, technology, and procedures that allow students to access tests and accurately demonstrate their competence, knowledge, and abilities without altering the integrity of the tests (Byrnes, 2008; Lazarus et al., 2009). Testing accommodations are designed to remove disability-related barriers that are not relevant to the validity of the test (e.g., the ability to see test items or to hear oral directions) without changing the nature or results of the test or giving students an advantage over others so that tests provide an accurate measure of students' skills (Fletcher et al., 2009; Ketterlin-Geller, Yovanoff, et al., 2007). For example, having a proctor read test items would not be a valid testing accommodation on a reading test as it changes the nature of the test from reading to listening comprehension. However, it might be an appropriate testing accommodation for use on a mathematics test that is not designed to assess reading.

Rather than being disability-specific, testing accommodations should be individually determined based on students' unique characteristics and learning strengths and challenges. Therefore, whether your students are taking statewide, districtwide,

PEARSON
myeducationlab

Go to the Assignments and Activities section of the Topic *Assessment* in the MyEducationLab for your course and complete the activity entitled *High-Stakes Testing.*

PEARSON
myeducationlab

To enhance your understanding of high-stakes testing, go to the IRIS Center Resources section of the Topic *Assessment* in the MyEducationLab for your course, and complete the module entitled *Accountability: High-Stakes Testing for Students with Disabilities.*

PEARSON
myeducationlab

To hear an expert discuss concerns about using standardized testing with English language learners, go to the IRIS Center Resources section of the Topic *Assessment* in the MyEducationLab for your course, and listen to the podcast entitled *Episode 3: Alfredo Artiles on Testing Culturally and Linguistically Diverse Learners.*

REFLECTIVE

What has been the effect of high-stakes testing on you, your students and their families, and your school district?

or teacher-made tests, you and your colleagues on IEP/504 teams can use the following guidelines for determining valid, appropriate and individualized testing accommodations for your students for use during high-stakes and classroom-based assessments (Salend, 2009).

Consider a Range of Testing Accommodations. Because of the varied purposes of testing and the unique qualities of your students, it is important for you and your colleagues to consider a range of possible testing accommodations (see Figure 12.1). Testing accommodations are usually categorized as relating to presentation and response mode formats, to timing, scheduling, and setting alternatives, and to linguistically based factors (Salend, 2009). It also is important to be aware that students also may benefit from more than one type of testing accommodation and may therefore need packages of different types of testing accommodations (Fletcher et al., 2009).

Presentation mode testing accommodations include changes in the way test questions and directions are presented to students (see Figure 12.1a). They include reading tests to students, formatting the test's questions, and using cues such as highlighting, text boxes, and models so that the directions, organization, and layout are easy for your students to understand and follow.

Response mode testing accommodations involve making changes in the way students respond to test items or determine their answers (see Figure 12.1b). For example, some students may need to indicate their responses by providing oral responses, pointing or through eye movements, and deaf and hard-of-hearing students may need to respond via sign language.

Testing accommodations include changes in the manner in which test questions and directions are presented to students. Do testing accommodations give students with disabilities an advantage over other students or violate the integrity of your tests?

It was my first high school final. I studied more than I ever had and thought I had a good chance of getting an A or B. I . . . took my regular seat at the large table by the window. During the teacher's directions, I forced myself to listen. I was doing good. Then I noticed this squirrel outside in the tree. . . . I watched the squirrel for 20 minutes. My teacher walked over and asked when I was going to start my exam. I looked away from the squirrel, but then I noticed this girl snapping her gum. . . . It was driving me crazy. I couldn't think. . . . She finally spit her gum out, but by that time it was too late. I didn't have enough time to finish now that I didn't even start the exam. . . . I felt sick to my stomach. I knew my mom would be mad. (Yehle & Wambold, 1998, p. 8)

Some students like this one require **timing, scheduling,** and **setting testing accommodations,** which are adjustments with respect to where, when, with whom, and for how long and often students take tests and include giving students extended time or allowing them to take tests in a more private location (see Figure 12.1c). These types of accommodations are particularly appropriate for students who (a) have problems with processing information and being on task, (b) require additional time to use specialized testing techniques (e.g., dictating answers or reading test items aloud), (c) need specialized testing conditions (e.g., special lighting or acoustics) or equipment/furniture, (d) have physical conditions that cause them to tire easily, (e) experience test anxiety, and (f) take medications that are only effective for a limited amount of time or have side effects that affect test performance. For example, students who need motivation to start and sustain their attention or effort may benefit from a private testing location that provides them with access to verbal praise or some type of reinforcement.

FIGURE 12.1 Possible testing accommodations

(a) Presentation Mode Accommodations

- Reading directions and items aloud
- Clarifying or simplifying language
- Repeating directions as necessary
- Listing directions in sequential order
- Providing a sample of each item type
- Highlighting changes in the directions
- Presenting only one sentence per line
- Using markers or masks to maintain place
- Using reminders
- Highlighting <u>KEY</u> words or phrases
- Organizing or sequencing items appropriately and logically
- Increasing the spacing between items
- Placing fewer items on a page
- Providing a proctor
- Offering aid in turning pages and maintaining place
- Presenting tests via signing or Braille

(b) Response Mode Accommodations

- Responding via native language or preferred mode of communication
- Providing extra space
- Using lined or grid paper
- Using enlarged answer bubbles or blocks
- Providing check sheets, graphic organizers, and outlines
- Providing a proctor to monitor place and the recording of answers
- Answering on the test
- Allowing students to dictate answers
- Fewer items per page
- Using multiple-choice items
- Giving oral exams, open-book tests, and take-home tests
- Providing a scribe

(c) Timing, Scheduling, and Setting Accommodations

- Giving more time or untimed tests
- Providing shorter versions of tests
- Allowing breaks as needed
- Adjusting the testing order
- Taking tests in small groups or individually in separate locations
- Allowing movement and background sounds
- Providing preferential seating arrangements (carrels)
- Providing adaptive furniture or equipment
- Eliminating items or sections
- Varying the times of the testing sessions
- Scheduling shorter testing sessions
- Administering tests over several days
- Eliminating visual and auditory distractions
- Delivering reinforcement
- Providing specific environmental arrangements (lighting, acoustics, sound amplification)

(d) Linguistically Based Accommodations

- Using understandable and familiar language
- Repeating orally based directions or items
- Teaching the language of academic testing
- Pairing items or directions with graphics or pictures
- Translating tests
- Allowing responses in native language or dialects
- Offering review sheets and lists of important vocabulary
- Allowing use of bilingual materials (bilingual glossaries or dictionaries)
- Providing context clues
- Providing alternate ways to demonstrate mastery of test material
- Providing translators to administer tests

Source: From "Determining Appropriate Testing Accommodations: Complying with NCLB and IDEIA," by S. J. Salend, *Teaching Exceptional Children, 40*(4), 2008, p. 17, Copyright 2008 by the Council for Exceptional Children. Reprinted with permission.

Linguistically based testing accommodations, which are typically used with English language learners, are designed to minimize the extent to which students' language proficiency affects their test performance. They include ways to adjust the language and readability of test items and directions so that they are appropriate for students' varying language and reading levels such as reducing the number of words or sentences, using synonyms to replace longer words, and modifying the sequence of the information presented (Herrera, Murry, & Cabral, 2007; Ketterlin-Geller, et al., 2007; Yovanoff, et al., 2007) (see Figure 12.1d). They also include the use of a translator or bilingual materials such as giving students both English and their native language versions of tests or bilingual glossaries or allowing them to respond in their native language (Saunders, 2008). When allowing students to use bilingual glossaries it is important that these materials only include direct translations of words and do not offer students assistance by providing them with definitions, explanations or clarifications. They also allow students to demonstrate mastery of test material in alternative ways, such as

UDL and YOU
Using Proctors, Readers, Scribes, and Interpreters

Testing accommodations allow for the incorporation of the principles of UDL into testing and assessment practices. One frequently used testing accommodation is the use of a proctor or reader who orally presents the test directions and items to students by reading them aloud to students (Elbaum, 2007; Fletcher et al., 2009). This person also can monitor students for signs of fatigue and adjust the testing schedule and administration accordingly. Proctors also can help students during the test by answering student questions about the test, turning pages for them, making sure they record answers in the correct space and follow the correct sequence, checking to see that the question numbers correspond to the numbers on the answer sheet, providing a copy of the text to avoid having to flip between the text and the items, delivering on-task and focusing prompts, and motivating students to sustain their effort.

Some of your students may need the services of a scribe to record their dictated responses to test questions. To facilitate the efficiency of the process and integrity of the answers, the scribe should

- inform students that they, not scribes, are responsible for reading all parts of the question to themselves;
- maintain a verbatim record of students' dictated responses, beginning each sentence with a capital and ending each sentence with a period;
- hide a copy of the response until students indicate that they are finished dictating their response;
- avoid editing students' responses and questioning, correcting, and coaching students; and
- employ a system of index cards marked with letters or numbers to allow students to indicate their choices on objective tests such as multiple-choice and true/false questions (Clapper, Morse, Thurlow, & Thompson, 2006).

Scribes may want to make a digital recording of the session to ensure that student responses were written as dictated and that no assistance or prompting was provided to students.

Deaf and hard-of-hearing students may benefit from a trained professional who can sign and interpret oral directions and translate their answers. When appropriate, English language learners can also take translated tests, be provided with translators to administer tests, and be allowed to respond in their native language or dialect. However, keep in mind that translations do not remove the cultural bias in tests that are related to content, item, picture, and task selection. Some concepts in English, referred to as **empty concepts** (e.g., certain time and color concepts), may not exist in other cultures and languages. In addition, because words may have different levels of difficulty across languages and dialects, test translations may change the psychometric properties of the original test. Additionally, translation does not account for experiences and words that have different or multiple meanings in different cultures. Thus, despite the translation, the constructs underlying the test items still reflect the dominant culture and may not be appropriate for students from other cultures.

When using proctors, readers, scribes, and translators, you need to be aware of several cautions. Their use can slow down the testing process, embarrass students who use them, and serve as a distraction for other students taking the test. Also, to be effective, educators providing these services and students receiving them need to receive training. For example, proctors, readers, scribes, and interpreters must be careful not to give students cues and additional information that may affect students' test performance or alter the test (Clapper et al., 2006). Guidelines that readers can follow to improve their effectiveness and maintain the test's integrity, which also are appropriate for scribes, translators, and interpreters, are provided in Figure 12.2.

with projects developed by cooperative learning groups or through the use of drawings, charts, manipulatives, demonstrations, or drama (Spinelli, 2008).

Match Testing Accommodations to Effective Teaching Accommodations. The testing accommodations provided to your students should match the effective teaching accommodations you use within your daily classroom instruction to support student learning. For instance, the instructional accommodations you use to help a student understand classroom directions also should be used to help the student understand test directions and items.

FIGURE 12.2 Guidelines for reading tests to students

Prior to the Test Administration

- Read and review the test and learn the definitions and pronunciations of unfamiliar terms and mathematical and scientific expressions and formulas
- Eliminate generic directions if they are not appropriate for the testing situation
- Make sure that testing materials are organized and presented in a way that makes it easy for you to access and follow
- Review testing materials to understand all of the administration conditions associated with the test (i.e., allowable and prohibited test administration actions)
- Distribute testing materials to students in accordance with the test's directions

During the Test Administration

- Refrain from alerting students to their errors and confirming correct responses
- Avoid providing assistance, cueing, and engaging in actions that impact the student's answers such as
  - Reminding, prompting, coaching, and teaching students
  - Unnecessarily highlighting or paraphrasing important information
  - Changing your voice
  - Explaining vocabulary, concepts, and visuals
  - Clarifying and elaborating on parts of the test
- Read only approved parts of the test (e.g., reading passages and questions assessing reading comprehension can impact the validity of those items by making them into measures of listening comprehension)
- Read all of the text on the test including directions, examples, and items
- Establish an appropriate pace that includes reading all parts of the question before soliciting and acknowledging the student's answer(s)
- Reread the entire question when asked to repeat a question to make sure that critical parts of questions are not inadvertently highlighted
- Consider facilitating the validity of the test administration and the rereading process by making a digital recording of the test administration (e.g., replaying questions that have been asked to be repeated)
- Use your voice to highlight key parts of questions that are printed in boldface, italics, or capitals
- Spell synonyms and other words requested by the student (if permissible)
- Redirect off-task comments from the student
- Observe students for signs of fatigue as reading tests tends to make the testing experience longer and more tiring

Source: From Salend, S. J. (2009). *Classroom testing and assessment for all students: Beyond standardization*. Thousand Oaks, CA: Corwin Press. Reprinted with permission.

Be Consistent with State and Districtwide Policies, and Differentiate Between Classroom-Based and High-Stakes Assessments. To avoid the confusion, disappointment, and anger experienced by the parent at the beginning of this chapter, it is important for teams to differentiate between testing accommodations that are used during the administration of statewide, districtwide, and classroom-based assessments, and to make this distinction explicit when listing testing accommodations on students' IEPs and 504 accommodation plans. As a result, the testing accommodations related to high-stakes testing should be consistent with state and districtwide policies on approved testing accommodations and should be provided under certain testing situations (Elliott & Thurlow, 2006). Because policies related to testing accommodations are changing and vary from state to state (Lazarus et al., 2009), you and your colleagues should obtain information about your state's testing accommodations policies by contacting your state education department or visiting its Web site.

You and your colleagues have more flexibility when selecting testing accommodations for districtwide and classroom-based assessments (keep in mind that your district may have districtwide testing policies that must be followed). For example, while use of a thesaurus for a statewide writing test may not be approved, teams may determine that it is an appropriate testing accommodation for classroom-based writing assessments in English, science, and social studies classes. However, even during classroom-based testing, accommodations should not alter the integrity of tests, and they should be consistent with the purpose of the tests and the nature of the items.

REFLECTIVE

Research reveals that students with disabilities who attend private and public schools in the wealthiest communities were more likely to receive testing accommodations than students with disabilities who attend schools in less affluent communities (Lewin, 2003). Why do you think this is the case?

Evaluating Student Progress and the Effectiveness of Your Inclusion Program

When possible, it is beneficial for the testing accommodations used for teacher-made tests and high-stakes tests to match each other. That way, students can become more familiar with the conditions they will encounter when taking high-stakes tests, and you can assess student performance with respect to how students are tested on high-stakes assessments.

Consider the Perspectives of Students and Teachers. When selecting testing accommodations, another important factor to consider is the perspectives of students and teachers. With respect to your students, it is essential to make sure that testing accommodations are fair and do not have a negative impact on your students who receive them or their classmates. For example, many students might feel similar to the student quoted at the beginning of this chapter who felt that taking tests in separate locations was embarrassing, isolating, and stigmatizing. Additionally, it is important that the testing accommodations you use with your students are age appropriate.

Although testing accommodations should not give students an advantage over their classmates, testing accommodations selected for your students should address their disabilities so that they give them a *differential boost* (Fletcher et al., 2009; Fuchs, Fuchs, & Capizzi, 2005). This means that the testing accommodations selected for your students with disabilities should boost their performance and, if used by their classmates, should have a minimal impact on their classmates' test performance (Bouck & Bouck, 2008). For example, while taking a large-print test can help students with visual difficulties, other students may find that it makes the test more difficult and causes the testing session to be longer. If a testing accommodation benefits both your students with and without disabilities, you need to be careful to make sure it is not changing the nature of your test. If it doesn't undermine the integrity of your test, consider if it is a good testing practice that you should make available to *all students*.

You and your colleagues' perspectives also are important in choosing testing accommodations (Salend, 2009). Therefore, you and your colleagues need to reflect on whether they are valid, effective, and appropriate by determining if they impact the integrity of the tests and their administration. In addition, information about ease of implementation of the testing accommodations should be considered including the extent to which you and your colleagues have the materials, time, resources, technology, equipment, and preparation and training to implement the testing accommodations consistently and effectively.

Teaching Study and Test-Taking Skills. Many of your students may not perform well on tests because they do not use effective study and test-taking skills. Therefore, while *all students* may benefit from receiving instruction in how to study for and take tests, the teaching of effective study and test-taking skills and strategies is especially useful for your students with special needs as well as your students who do well on classroom-based activities and assignments yet perform poorly on tests (Holzer et al., 2009; Meltzer, Roditi, Stein, Krishnan, & Sales Pollica, 2008). Some school districts list these skills as instructional goals on students' IEPs and 504 accommodation plans (Strichart & Mangrum, 2010). Rather than teaching to the test, instruction in study and test-taking skills provide students with the strategies they need to prepare for and succeed on tests.

You can use a variety of assessment strategies to identify which study and test-taking skills and strategies your students need to develop (Kirby et al., 2008). You can observe them during testing, interview them after testing (e.g., "How did you answer these questions?"), and examine their answer sheets to identify the effective strategies they used and need to learn (Songlee et al., 2008). You also can use different surveys that assess students' knowledge and use of study and test-taking strategies or create your own survey (Salend, 2009).

Because an important essential aspect of studying is being aware of what to study, you can help your students learn how to prepare to study by learning about

PEARSON
myeducationlab

Go to the Assignments and Activities section of the Topic *Assessment* in the MyEducationLab for your course and complete the activity entitled *Accommodations for Standardized Tests* to examine ways to determine appropriate accommodations for diverse learners.

and anticipating the content that most likely will be assessed on tests as well as the types of items that will comprise the tests. For example:

- Give them an overview of the purpose, content, and format of the test and study guides, review sheets, vocabulary lists, and outlines that highlight the material to be included on the test, the format of the test, the types of questions that will be on the test, and the resources students can use to help them study. A study guide template that you can tailor to your students and your tests is provided in Figure 12.3.
- Schedule time in class for students to review their notes, assignments, textbooks, reference materials, and past tests and quizzes, to practice with sample test items, to identify and predict important terminology and topics that are likely to appear on the test, and to ask questions about the content likely to be on the test.

FIGURE 12.3 **Sample study guide template**

When is the test?

The date of the test is _____.

How much time should I spend studying for the test?

You should study at least _____ minutes/hours each day beginning on
_____.

How many and what types of questions will be on the test?
How many points are sections worth?

The test will be made up of
_____ Multiple-choice questions worth _____ points
_____ Matching questions worth _____ points
_____ True-false questions worth _____ points
_____ Sentence-completion (fill in the blank) questions worth _____ points
_____ Essay questions worth _____ points
_____ Other types of questions worth _____ points

What topics will be covered on the test?

The test will cover the following topics:

❑   ❑
❑   ❑
❑   ❑

What vocabulary words should I know?

You should study and know the following vocabulary words:

❑   ❑
❑   ❑
❑   ❑

What concepts should I know?

You should study and know the following concepts:

❑   ❑
❑   ❑
❑   ❑

(*Continued*)

FIGURE 12.3 **Continued**

What materials should I study?

When studying for the test, make sure you review:

Textbook Chapters and Other Readings

Class Notes

Class Assignments

Homework Assignments

Web Sites and Online Information

How can I practice for the test?

Here are some practice questions:

1.

2.

3.

4.

What else can I do to prepare for the test?

Here are some other things you can do to prepare for the test:

☐

☐

☐

☐

Source: From Salend, S. J. (2009). *Classroom testing and assessment for all students: Beyond standardization.* Thousand Oaks, CA: Corwin Press. Reprinted with permission.

- Teach students to listen for cues from their teachers that indicate important content that may appear on tests such as when their teachers review or ask questions about certain topics, or mention content in the days before the test.
- Work with them to develop visuals that highlight and depict the relationship between important terms, concepts, and topics.
- Provide them with time to work in collaborative groups to review notes and textbooks, predict possible questions, teach and quiz each other, and create study and memory aids.
- Assign homework prior to tests that requires them to identify, review, and practice test content.
- Play educational games using review questions that parallel the content and questions types that will be on the test.
- Provide students with a list of possible test questions (usually essay questions) that they should be prepared to answer, and then make sure that some of those questions do appear on the test (Fisher & Frey, 2008; Meltzer et al., 2008; Rozalski, 2007; Salend, 2009; Strichart & Mangrum, 2010; Walker & Schmidt, 2004).

In addition to preparing to study, you also can teach your students to use effective study and test-taking skills (see Figure 12.4) (Denstaedt et al., 2009; Lagares & Connor, 2009). Students can be taught to use a range of test-taking learning strategies (see Figure 12.5) and a variety of effective methods and mnemonic devices to develop their memory of test content.

Making Connections
The use of effective methods and mnemonic devices to foster your students' memory skills was discussed earlier in Chapter 11.

FIGURE 12.4 Recommended study and test-taking skills and strategies

Studying for Tests

- Estimate the amount of time needed to study, and create a checklist that addresses the duration of study sessions and the content to be reviewed including its priority and level of difficulty. Use this information to develop a reasonable study schedule of spaced, and focused sessions that cover manageable chunks of content and provides for short breaks away from the study area.
- Begin to study early with short review sessions. Schedule a major study session early enough to obtain clarification and assistance about difficult material from teachers.
- Don't cram; try to finish studying the day before the test.
- Don't schedule study sessions too close to meals or bedtime.
- Determine the specific objectives of each study session.
- Study the most difficult content areas first.
- Try to study in a distraction-free, uncluttered, quiet, comfortable environment.
- Gather and organize all the materials needed in studying (e.g., notes, textbooks, assignments, handouts, readings, quizzes, reference books, paper, writing utensils, highlighters, and technology).
- Create an outline of important topics, including main ideas and secondary supporting points, and key questions and their corresponding data sources (e.g., pages from textbooks, dates of class notes).
- Create summaries and visual aids of key concepts and topics and their relationships.
- Play games and use flash cards that prompt the memory, review, and practice of important content such as terminology, formulas, and lists and mnemonic devices you have created.
- Plan study sessions with others and try to explain content to a classmate, a friend, or a relative.
- End study sessions with summaries of the key points to be remembered.
- Sleep and eat well before the test.

Taking Tests

- Remain calm.
- Write your name on the test and any other required personally identifying information.
- Listen carefully to the teacher's introduction of the test and explanations of the instructions and directions.
- Read all parts of the directions and items carefully to identify the (a) specific details (e.g., "*Answer two out of the three essay questions*"); (b) types of answers they are asked to provide; (c) aids, resources, and assistance you can use; and (d) time, length, and space constraints. Strategically highlight critical parts of test directions and items and pay close attention to parts of tests that have been highlighted for you by your teachers via use of *italics*, **boldface**, and CAPITALIZATION.
- Ask questions about and seek clarification regarding things you do not understand or questions that can be interpreted in different ways.
- Preview the test to identify the number and types of questions on the test as well as the point values and weights associated with each item and section. Use this information and the time allotted to complete the test to create a plan that includes the order and time line for working on the test. In devising your plan, keep in mind that it is usually most efficient to start with easier questions and sections that are worth the most points and to try not to spend too much time on any single question (unless it is worth a significant number of points).
- Perform a *memory dump* to jot down on the test paper or scrap paper essential facts, definitions, formulas, dates, and names that you are likely to use on the test and mnemonics and drawings to foster your memory.
- Make three passes through the test based on levels of difficulty. In the first pass, read all questions and respond to those you know how to answer, using a symbol to note those that are somewhat difficult (?) and very difficult (??). During the second pass, respond to those questions you marked as somewhat difficult. Answer all unanswered questions during the third pass.
- Write notes in the margins to guide your answers as well as explanations for answers for your teachers (e.g., "I selected choice (c) because . . ."). Additionally, use margin notes to alert yourself that an item or page has been checked so that you do not have to use additional time reviewing it again.
- Identify and analyze critical words and phrases, and look for and use word, grammatical, pictorial, and content clues. Be aware that word clues such as *always* and *never* suggest extremes and often indicate incorrect answers and that grammatical correctness such as subject-verb agreement, verb tense, and modifiers can aid you in identifying the correct response. Also remember that sometimes content from one test question can help you figure out the correct answer to another one.

(Continued)

FIGURE 12.4 Continued

- Use self-talk and scrap paper to figure out and plan responses.
- Stay with your first choice when you are unsure of the answer and change answers only if you misread the questions or obtained new information about the question elsewhere on the test. When changing answers, make sure that you erase your previous answers completely.
- Answer all questions including extra-credit and bonus questions, even if it means writing partial answers or guessing. However, when you lose additional points for incorrect answers, answer only those questions that have a high probability of being correct.
- Review questions and check your answers to make sure they are correct, complete, easy to read, and marked appropriately. Prior to handing in your test, check to make sure that you have not inadvertently skipped questions, steps, or parts of answers or mismarked your answer sheet. Proofread your written answers to make sure that they are logical and sound correct, and that you correctly wrote answers that you originally drafted on scrap paper. Determine if you need to provide more information or revise your answers, and check your spelling, grammar, punctuation, and mathematical calculations.

Completing Multiple-Choice Items

- Paraphrase the item's stem or view each choice as a true/false statement if you are not sure of which choice is correct.
- Examine each response alternative, select the one that is most complete and inclusive, and eliminate choices that are obviously false or incorrect, that contain absolute words (i.e., *always, all, never*), that are not related to content covered in class, or that are absurd or deal with nonsense or irrelevant information.
- Be aware that the choices *all of the above* or *none of the above* (especially when two or more choices seem correct or incorrect) and numbers that represent the middle range are often correct, as are alternatives that are unusually long and detailed, much shorter that the others, or contain language that is found in the stem or wording that is similar to the language used by teachers or in the textbook are usually correct.
- Understand that when alternative answers are contradictory, one of them is likely to be correct, and when two options provide similar information, neither of them should be considered.
- Use clues such as subject-verb agreement, verb tense, modifiers such as *a* or *an*, and other information from the stem to help determine the correct response.

Completing Matching Items

- Survey both columns to get an idea of the choices, to identify their relationships, to note if each column has an equal number of items, and to determine if an alternative can be used more than once.
- Read the initial pair in the left-hand column first and then read the choices in the right-hand column before answering
- Work on the easiest pairs first and skip pairs that are difficult.
- Record the correct answer if you know it immediately, and high choices in the right-hand column that have been used.
- Avoid guessing until all other pairs have been answered, as an incorrect match can multiply the number of errors.

Completing True/False Items

- Determine the type of true/false items on the test before beginning.
- Read all parts of the statement and mark the statement as *False* if any part of the statement is not true or correct.
- Look for *specific determiners* within true/false items, which are words that vary, qualify, limit, or provide the conditions and context associated with statements. When statements contain absolute words that imply that the statement is extreme or true 100% of the time, such as *no, never, none, every, always, every, entirely, only, all, best, worst, absolutely,* and *certainly,* the statement is usually false. Conversely, the use of qualifiers that moderate statements, such as *sometimes, generally, often, frequently, ordinarily,* and *usually,* often indicate that a statement is true.
- Recognize that longer statements that contain specific details tend to indicate that a statement is true and statements that include a justification or a reason usually are false.
- Highlight negative words and prefixes and examine their impact on the meaning and truthfulness of statements. When statements contain negatives, eliminate the negatives, assess whether the revised statement is true or false, and then determine whether the original statement is true or false.
- Guess true if you do not know the answer and there is no penalty for incorrect answers, as teachers tend to include more true statements than false statements on their tests.

Completing Sentence Completion Items

- Begin by reading the statement, identifying possible responses, and selecting the best answer.
- Try to answer sentence completion items by converting them into questions.
- Try to prompt your memory by converting the sentence into a question.
- Use the grammatical structure of the item to help you formulate the answer. If the stem ends in *a* or *an*, the correct answer probably starts with a consonant or a vowel, respectively.

(Continued)

FIGURE 12.4 **Continued**

- Use the number and length of the blanks provided as a clue. Often two blanks with no words between them indicate that a two-word response, such as an individual's name, is the answer. Two blanks separated by words should be approached as two separate statements. A long blank tends to suggest that the correct answer is a phrase or a sentence.
- Jot down a descriptive answer or use synonyms when you don't know the exact word or phrase (this might help you receive partial credit).

Completing Essay Questions

- Determine if each question must be answered or if there are choices in answering questions.
- Read the questions, determine what you are being asked to do, and quickly and briefly record relevant points to be mentioned next to each question.
- Highlight key words related to the directions and important information to be addressed.
- Make a plan for answering all questions that includes working on the easiest questions first and allotting an appropriate amount of time to respond to all questions. Provide more time for more difficult questions and write the amount of time allotted next to each question.
- Reread the question, and jot down new points, and highlight important terminology and concepts and make drawings to show relationships among concepts and topics to be used in answering each question. Delete unnecessary points and information that you previously recorded.
- Create an outline before writing by identifying the important topics and key words and the sequence of their main points.
- Use your outline as a guide for composing your answer by (a) paraphrasing the essay question or subquestions as the topic sentence of your introductory paragraph to present the main point(s) and an overview of your answer, (b) organizing your essay in a logical sequence so that each paragraph addresses main points and supporting details, (c) establishing clear transitions from sentence to sentence and paragraph to paragraph, (d) giving examples and citing specific information to support your perspectives and statements, and (e) concluding your essay with a summary of the main points and why they are important.
- Consider if it is appropriate to present related points as bulleted or numbered lists or to highlight key information in your essay.
- Provide a general statement that qualifies your answer when you are not exactly sure of specific facts (e.g., use the general phrase "*during the early 20th century*" instead of listing a specific year).
- Proofread your essay for clarity, organization, completeness, legibility, spelling, punctuation, and grammar.
- Try to answer each question in some way since the scoring of most essay questions allows for the awarding of partial credit. Write down your outline and a list of key points rather than leaving a question blank if you are running out of time. You also can note how you could have elaborated on your answer if you had more time.
- Remember to show your work, especially on math and science tests.

Sources: Educational Testing Service (2005); Kretlow et al. (2008); Meltzer, Roditi, Stein, Krishman, and Sales Pollica (2008); Salend (2009); Strichart and Mangrum (2010); Therrien, Hughes, Kapelski, and Mokhtari (2009); Walker and Schmidt (2004).

Your teaching of effective study and test-taking skills and strategies can be enhanced by involving your students' families (Meltzer et al., 2008; Songlee et al., 2008). Families can be an excellent resource for helping their children develop the skills they need to be successful on your tests, so collaborate and communicate with them by soliciting feedback from them about their children's study habits and providing them with information about your testing and assessment practices as well as guidelines and resources for fostering their children's use of effective study and test-taking skills and strategies (Salend, 2009).

Addressing Test Anxiety   Some of your students, particularly those with special needs, may suffer from test anxiety, which can interfere with their ability to concentrate and perform in testing situations. In addition to using scheduling, timing and setting testing accommodations, instruction in the use of effective study and test-taking skills and strategies can help reduce some of the anxiety about testing that these students experience and can help them feel comfortable with the test format (Berendt & Koski, 1999; Salend, 2009). You also can minimize their test anxiety by

- focusing on the importance of being on time and taking a few minutes to relax and focus, rather than arriving too early, so that they avoid interactions with other students, which may intensify their anxiety (e.g., other students asking questions about what they studied, or spreading false rumors about tests);
- teaching and prompting them to use relaxation techniques such mediation, headphones with calming music, visualization, and movement (Lytle & Todd, 2009);

REFLECTIVE

What study and test-taking strategies do you use? Are they successful? How did you learn these strategies?

Evaluating Student Progress and the Effectiveness of Your Inclusion Program

FIGURE 12.5 Sample test-taking learning strategies

Instructional Goal	Acronym	Strategic Steps
To foster students' general test-taking skills	PIRATES (Holzer, Madaus, Bray, & Kehle, 2009)	**P**repare to Succeed • Put your name and write PIRATES on the test. • Allot time and determine an order for completing the parts of the test. • Say something positive to yourself about the test and your performance. • Start as quickly as possible and within 2 minutes. **I**nspect the Test's Directions • Read the directions very carefully. • Highlight key words that tell you what to do, and where to do it. • Notice special requirements you need to follow. **R**ead, Remember, and Reduce to Answer the Test's Questions • Read all parts of each question. • Remember what we have been learning about. • Reduce your answer choices by eliminating those that you know are incorrect. **A**nswer or Abandon • Answer all questions you are sure of. • Abandon those questions you are unsure of and mark them so you can turn back to them later. **T**urn Back • Turn back to all questions that were not answered. **E**stimate When You Are Unsure of the Answer • Avoid choices that contain absolute words. • Choose the longest and most detailed choice. • Eliminate choices that present similar information. **S**urvey the Test Before Handing It In • Make sure you answered all of the questions. • Stay with your first choice.
To foster students' essay test–taking skills	ANSWER (Therrien et al., 2009)	**A**nalyze the action words: Read the question very carefully and highlight the key words. **N**otice requirements: Highlight and mark the important requirements of the essay and rephrase the question in your own words. **S**et up an outline: List the main points of the essay in an outline. **W**ork in details: Add important details and supporting points to your outline. **E**ngineer your answer: Write your essay by starting with introductory sentence followed by supporting sentences related to the main points in your outline. **R**eview your answer: Check your essay to make sure that you have answered all parts of the question and edit your essay.
To foster students' ability to answer objective test items	DREAMS (Yell & Rozalski, 2008)	**D**irections must be read carefully. Look for keywords related to what you are being asked to do. Keywords include *best, none, never, all,* and *always.* **R**ead all answers before choosing your answer. **E**asy questions should be answered first. Skip the hard questions until you finish answering the easy ones. **A**bsolute qualifiers are usually false. Absolute qualifiers include *no, none, never, only, every, all,* and *always.* **M**ark questions as you read them. Cross out the ones you have answered. Place a star next to the questions that are difficult for you, and return to them after you have answered all of the easier questions. **S**imilar and absurd options can usually be eliminated.

(*Continued*)

FIGURE 12.5 **Continued**

Instructional Goal	Acronym	Strategic Steps
To foster students' general test-taking skills	SEWERS (Rozalski, 2007)	**S**ign your name to the test. **E**xamine the test and estimate how long you think it will take you to complete it. **W**rite down any mnemonics, memory aids, and important content that you have memorized. **E**xhale and focus. **R**ead the instructions carefully. Highlight important parts of the directions. **S**urvey the whole test before turning it in.
To foster students' general test-taking skills	DETER (Strichart & Mangrum, 2010)	**D:** Read the **Directions**. Ask for explanations of the directions or words you do not understand **E:** **Examine** the whole test to see how much you have to do. **T:** Decide how much **Time** you should allot to each test question. **E:** Answer the **Easiest** questions first. **R:** **R**eview your answers to make sure you did your best and answered all required questions.

- encouraging them to think about their past success and efforts and to occasionally praise themselves during testing;
- fostering their understanding that an appropriate level of nervousness may be helpful in enhancing their test performance;
- teaching them to work on one question at a time rather than being preoccupied with the entire test and to start with easier test items first so they can build their confidence, rather than becoming unnecessarily nervous about difficult items;
- incorporating motivating and encouraging words and icons throughout the test as well as those that remind them to relax (e.g., "You are halfway done. Relax, take a deep breath, and continue working.");
- asking them how you can make the testing situation more pleasant and comfortable for them;
- using humor and minimizing competition;
- asking them to reflect on their use of successful anxiety reducing strategies as well as other techniques they need to consider;
- informing them that tests are only one way that you assess their academic performance and determine their grades;
- avoiding timed tests; and
- using alternative assessment activities to allow them to demonstrate mastery (Educational Testing Service, 2005; Tennessee Department of Education, 2008; Salend, 2009; Strichart & Mangrum, 2010; Walker & Schmidt, 2004).

Creating Valid and Accessible Teacher-Made Tests   Teacher-made tests are often used to evaluate students' performance in general education classrooms. High-quality teacher-made tests can aid you and your students in several ways. They can help you communicate to your students and their families important aspects of your curriculum and motivate your students to learn the concepts and skills you have taught. Your tests also can guide your teaching by identifying curricular areas mastered by your students as well as those that require additional or modified instruction. Test performance can be used to provide feedback to your students about their learning.

Creating a good test is not easy. When designing tests and using testing accommodations discussed earlier in this chapter, you must be careful to make sure they

Making Connections
Make sure your tests are presented using the guidelines for enhancing the legibility and readability of text-based materials which was discussed earlier in Chapter 8.

are valid and do not compromise the integrity of the test, course, or curriculum. You should design your tests with *all students* in mind and incorporate the principles of UDL so that they are accessible to *all students* and that you minimize the need for specialized testing accommodations (Ketterlin-Geller et al., 2007; Lazarus et al., 2009).

Test Content.   To foster the validity of your tests, the number of items should be sufficient and the content of the items on your tests should be directly related to the objectives of your curriculum and assess the most important topics, concepts, and skills you have taught. The tests should reflect not only *what* but also *how* content has been taught. Content taught via analysis, synthesis, or problem-solving techniques is best tested through essay questions, whereas factual and rote memory material may be tested by objective items. Additionally, the language and terminology used in both test directions and items should be consistent with those used in class.

Weigh the content of your tests to reflect the complexity of the concepts you taught and the amount of instructional time you devoted to teaching them. This means that the percentage of test questions related to specific content areas should reflect the amount of time your class spent on these topics. For example, on a test following a unit in which 30% of class time was spent on the U.S. Constitution, approximately 30% of the test items should focus on material related to the Constitution. Shorter and more frequent tests of specific content rather than fewer, longer, and more comprehensive tests can help your students who have difficulty remembering large amounts of information.

Test Format.   Even though many of your students can master the content necessary to perform well on a test, they may have difficulty with the test's format. Tests that cause confusion and distraction because of poor appearance or spatial design can defeat students before they begin. Therefore, items should be clearly and darkly printed on a solid, nondistracting background. Ideally, tests should be typed. If they must be written, the writing should be in the style (manuscript or cursive) familiar to the student.

Confusion can be minimized by proper presentation, organization, spacing, and sequencing of items. Presenting items in a fixed, predictable, symmetrical, and numbered sequence that emphasizes the transition from one item to another can help ensure that your students do not skip lines or fail to complete test items. Many students will find it helpful if you limit the number of items on a page and group similar item types together or surround them in text boxes. It also is helpful if you organize the presentation of items so that they are sequenced from easiest to hardest.

Allowing students to write on the test itself rather than transferring answers to a separate page can reduce confusion for students with organizational difficulties. Providing enough space for responses allows students to complete an answer without continuing on another page and can structure the length of responses. Some students may benefit from you providing them with space between items so that they can provide a rationale for their responses to short-answer items. Including page numbers on test pages also can help you give directions to students and guide students in locating or asking questions about specific items.

Test Directions.   Make sure that your directions are presented in language students understand and that you include directions for each section of the test that contains different types of items. Try to avoid vague terms that may confuse students or be misinterpreted by them (e.g., *frequently*, *usually*, etc.), and eliminate unnecessary information. Items and the directions for completing them should appear on the same page so that students do not have to turn back and forth.

Your directions should be complete and guide students in answering the questions. Therefore, they should clearly and concisely present what you are asking them to do, specify the precision you expect in their answers (angle measurements must be within a specific number of degrees), contain the point totals associated with items and sections in a prominent location, and provide formulas and other relevant information needed to answer (unless memorization of these are essential and what you are testing). It also helps your students to understand the test directions if you

- present sequenced information in chronological order through use of numerals or the number words (e.g., *first, second,* and *third*) and
- use bullets to present essential information that does not have a numerical or hierarchical order.

Cues can be embedded into your tests to help students pay attention to important aspects of the directions and test items. You can use

- stylistic variants such as circling, underlining, boldfacing, or enlarging to highlight critical information;
- text boxes surrounded by white space to focus attention on important directions and to present a correct model of each type;
- direction reminder prompts placed at important locations throughout the test (e.g., *"Remember to write clearly and in complete sentences"*); and
- symbols, icons, and pictorials to prompt students to the directions for a new set of test items (e.g., color-coded arrows pointing to directions for specific item types).

In composing your directions and items, be careful to avoid clues that can unintentionally guide students to the correct response. Therefore, you should proofread your tests to make sure that they do not include grammatical cues (e.g., the articles *a* and *an,* plurals), word cues (e.g., the same words appear in the question and answer), and similarity cues (e.g., the information in one question leads to the answers in other questions).

Enhancing Engagement, Motivation, and Strategy Use.   Embedding motivating and encouraging words and accompanying visuals and reminders to use effective test-taking strategies can prompt students to engage in behaviors that help them succeed on your tests. At the beginning of the test, you can include a statement and graphic icon that encourages students to do well and to work hard. Throughout the test, you can periodically place prompts to remind students to pay attention, ask questions, maintain their effort, be motivated, and to engage in self-reinforcement (see Figure 12.6). For example, at the end of the test, you can place statements and visuals that congratulate them (e.g., *"Way to go. Congratulations on finishing the test"*), and remind them to review each question before handing their test in to you.

You also can motivate students by using test questions that are related to their lives and appropriate for their academic abilities. When possible, try to personalize your tests by phrasing items using the students' and teachers' names (make sure that individuals will not be embarrassed or object to having their names used in questions) and incorporating students' interests and experiences as well as integrating popular characters, items, and trends in test items. For instance, items can be phrased using names and persons, places, and things associated with their community. You can use creative test items that incorporate suspense, fantasy, curiosity, uncertainty, and novelty.

You also need to make sure that your questions are inclusive, respectful and reflective of your students' individual differences. This means that your questions should have a multicultural perspective and present individuals and groups in realistic, factually correct, and nonstereotypical ways and that you should use a variety of appropriate cultural referents and terms.

FIGURE 12.6 Sample engagement, motivation, and strategy use prompts

Prompting Students to Ask Questions or Seek Clarification

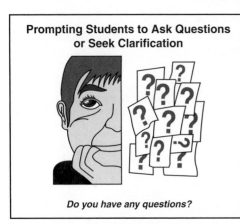

Do you have any questions?

Prompting Students to Relax

Relax, Take a deep breath.

Smile. You are halfway through the test.

Prompting Review of Answers

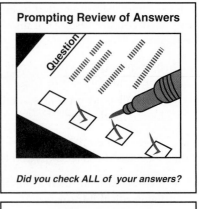

Did you check ALL of your answers?

Prompting Students to Use a Test-Taking Strategy

Remember to use the PIRATES strategy.

Prompting Students to Engage in Self-Reinforcement

Working hard? Give yourself a high-five.

Test Items. You will need to consider several factors in determining and writing your test items. One important factor is whether you should align the content and format of your test items with the high-stakes tests your students will take. While you don't want to teach to the high-stakes test, doing so helps your students become more familiar with the conditions they will encounter when taking such tests. Also try to avoid **hinging,** which refers to the use of test items whose correct answers require students to answer preceding questions correctly. Additional effective practices and guidelines you can use in writing different types of test items are discussed here (Badgett & Christmann, 2009a, 2009b; Brookhart & Nitko, 2008; Hogan, 2007; Salend, 2009).

Multiple-Choice Items. Students' performance on multiple-choice items can be improved by composing well-written, grammatically correct items that students can read and understand—using language free of double negatives. The stem, which presents a question, statement, paragraph, or visual (e.g., chart, map), should provide a context for answering the item, contain only one major point and only relevant information, and be longer than the answer alternatives. The three to five choices should be feasible and of the same length and specificity, should be presented vertically, and should not contain key words or phrases from the stem or categorical words such as *always, all, only,* or *never.* Choices should share common elements (if the correct choice is a specific continent, then all of the alternative should be continents), be presented in the same format (e.g., all nouns, plurals, percentages), and be arranged in a logical sequence such as by alphabetical, numerical, or chronological order.

Multiple-choice items can be tailored to the needs of students by highlighting keywords, reducing the number of choices, and eliminating more difficult choices, such as having to select *all of the above* or *none of the above*. Finally, allowing students to circle the answer they choose can alleviate problems in recording answers. An example of a multiple-choice item is as follows:

Directions: (Circle) the letter of the choice that best answers the ques-tion. Each multiple-choice item is worth 3 points.

In which court case did the Supreme Court decide that *segregating students by race* was *unconstitutional?*

(a) *Plessy v. Ferguson School System*

(b) *Baker v. Carr Unified School District*

(c) *Newkirk v. Phalen School District*

(d) *Brown v. Board of Education of Topeka*

Matching Items. When writing matching items, you should consider several variables that can affect students' performance. Use matching items when you can create homogeneous lists of corresponding premises and responses that relate to a single theme or concept. Each matching section of the test should contain a maximum of 10 grammatically similar and concise item pairs. When more than 10 items are needed, group the additional items by topic in a separate matching section. There should be 25% more items in one column than in the other and only one correct response for each pair. Because students usually approach matching items by reading an item in the left-hand column and then reading all the available choices in the right-hand column, you can help your students save time and work in a coordinated fashion by listing the longer items in the left-hand column. For example, a matching item designed to assess mastery of vocabulary would have the definitions in the left-hand column and the vocabulary words in the right-hand column.

Place clear, unambiguous directions that clearly state the basis for matching the item pairs and both columns on the same page and label the items in one column with numbers and the items in the other column with letters. This prevents the frustration some students encounter when matching questions are presented on more than one page. To avoid the disorganization that can occur when students respond by drawing lines connecting their choices from both columns, direct students to record the letter or number of their selection in the blank provided. You also can improve student performance on this type of test question by giving choices that are clear and concise, embedding an example in the matching question, informing students whether items from columns can be used more than once, labeling both columns, and organizing columns in a sensible and logical fashion. A sample matching item is as follows:

Directions: Match each definition in column 1 with its geographic term in column 2 by:

1. Reading the definition in Column 1

2. Finding its matching geographic term in Column 2

3. Writing the letter of the geographic term in the Column 2 in the blank next to its definition in Column 1.

- The first one is done for you as an example.

- Remember that each geographic term may be selected either once or not at all.

- Each correct match is worth 2 points.

Column 1: Definition	Column 2: Geographic Term
__E__ 1. A small, raised part of the land, lower than a mountain	A. Peninsula
_____ 2. Land surrounded by water on three sides	B. Plateau
_____ 3. An area of high, flat land	C. Reservoir
_____ 4. A lake where a large water supply is stored	D. Valley
_____ 5. Low land between mountains or hills	E. Hill
_____ 6. Low and wet land	F. Swamp
	G. Isthmus
	H. Island

True/False Items.   Many of your students may have difficulty responding to the true/false part of a test. Although these items typically are presented as statements that students identify as *true* or *false,* they also take the form of questions for which the response is *yes* or *no* (e.g., "Is it possible for a naturalized citizen to become president of the United States? Yes or No").

In particular, students may have problems responding to items that require them to correct all false choices. To eliminate problems, phrase questions concisely so they are clearly either true or false, highlighting critical parts of the statements. Eliminate items that assess trivial information, opinions, or values or that mislead students, and avoid stating items negatively. Focus each item on only one point, avoid items that ask students to change false statements into true statements, and limit the number of true/false questions per test. Make all true/false items of the same length, if possible, and group them by content assessed. Phrase items so that they do not provide students with cues by avoiding the use of vague statements, terms, and phrases (e.g., *usually, probably, rarely, frequently, is useful for*), which can be interpreted differently by your students; qualifying words (e.g., *often, may, can, sometimes, usually, frequently, generally*), which cue students that a statement is true; and absolute words (e.g., *always, all, every, entirely, only, never, none*), which indicate that a statement is false. Avoid predictable answer patterns (e.g., TTFF or FTFT) by randomizing the sequence of true and false statements so that there are no obvious patterns and including a similar number of statements that are true and false. Students who fail to discriminate the *T* and the *F,* or who write *T*s that look like *F*s and vice versa, should be allowed to record their response by circling either *True* or *False.* A true/false question is as follows:

Directions:

1. Read each statement.

2. If the statement is **true**, circle (True.)

3. If the statement is **false**, circle (False.)

- Each true/false item is worth 1 point.

True False 1. The bee that lays eggs in the colony is the *queen*.

Sentence Completion Items. Sentence completion items can be difficult for students. You can increase the usefulness of these items by making sure that they assess critical information and that the omitted word is relevant. Because statements to be completed that come directly from print materials such as textbooks can be too vague when taken out of context, you should clearly phrase sentence completion items so that students can understand them. Additionally, word blanks should be placed near the end of items, be of the same length to avoid hints about the length of the answer, kept to a minimum in each sentence, and require a one-word response. If word blanks must contain more than one word, limit the length to a short phrase. Avoid giving grammatical cues. For example, use *a(n)* before a blank that is answered with a noun (e.g., "A narrow section of land that connects two larger portions of land is a(n) *isthmus*."). Determine if you will accept specific synonyms, abbreviations, and other possible variations as correct responses as well as misspellings and let students know this in advance.

You also can adjust the items for your students by providing several response choices or a text box containing a word bank that includes a list of choices from which

Directions:

1. Read the sentence.

2. Look at the *word bank*.

3. Choose the word from the word bank that correctly completes the sententce.

- Each word in the word bank can be used only once.

4. Write the correct word on the blank at the end of the sentence.

5. Write clearly so I can read it.

- Each correctly completed sentence is worth 1 point.

1. The subatomic particles inside an atom that have a **positive** charge are_____.

2. Isotopes are atoms of the **same** element that have **different** *numbers* of_____.

Word Bank	
Compounds	Ions
Deuterons	Neutrons
Electrons	Protons

students select to complete the statement. Words in the word bank should share similar grammatical features (e.g., similar parts of speech, capitalization, etc.), be presented in a logical order (e.g., alphabetical, numerical order), and have proper spacing. You should inform students if words from the word bank may be used more than once. A sample sentence completion item with a word bank is at the bottom of p. 475 (Salend, 2009, p. 37).

Essay Questions.   Essay questions present unique problems for many students because of the numerous skills needed to answer them. Make sure that your essay questions are focused, appropriate, and understandable in terms of readability and level of difficulty. Specify the desired length of their response, any time limits associated with writing their essay(s), and your basis for evaluating it. When essays ask students to present their opinions, make sure that your students understand that they will be judged on their ability to support their opinion rather than the position they express. Key words that guide students in analyzing and writing the essay can be highlighted and defined or students can be allowed to use a word list or dictionary. You also can consider allowing students to use their books and notes to answer essay questions. It is also important to make sure that students, especially those with writing difficulties, have sufficient time to draft and write their answers.

You also can help your students interpret essay questions correctly and guide their essays in several ways. Provide check sheets or outlines listing the components that can help them organize their response. Rather than using a single open-ended essay question, direct the organization and ensure the completeness of the response by using subquestions that divide the open-ended question into smaller sequential questions that can elicit all the parts of an accurate, well-structured, detailed answer. Similarly, important concepts that students should include in their essays can be listed, highlighted, and located in a prominent place so that students will read them before writing their essays. For example, an essay question on meteors can be presented as follows:

As the student representative for your community's local planetarium, you have been asked to contribute to development of the new exhibit on meteors. Write a 300 to 400-word essay, describing what should be included in the exhibit relating to the *occurrence* of meteors and *why* we see them. In writing your answer, discuss the following:

* What are meteors made of?

* Why do we see meteors at certain predictable times of the year?

* Why do predictable meteor showers always seem to begin at the same place?

* What are we actually seeing when we see a bright meteor streak through the night sky?

> REMEMBER

° Use and discuss such terms as *comets, dust, orbits, atmosphere, radiant, velocity, vaporize,* and *composition.*

° Provide evidence and examples to support your statements and positions.

° Use correct grammar, punctuation, spelling, and paragraph organization.

° Use the **ANSWER** strategy to prepare your essay.

° Your essay is worth 25 points.

Scoring Alternatives.   When scoring your students' tests, it is preferable to avoid using an X, slash, or a red-colored pen to mark incorrect answers as these indicators often have negative connotations for students. Therefore, you can use a more neutral symbol to note incorrect answers such as a question mark (?), place a check mark next to the correct answer alternative in multiple-choice and true/false items, and write the correct words for sentence completion items and correct letters for matching items. Another alternative is to leave incorrect answers blank and to award points only for correct answers. You also can write a rationale for your scoring that includes brief comments related to correct and incorrect parts of answers.

You also can consider whether to use a variety of scoring alternatives, which should be used cautiously and only occasionally to motivate *all of your students* and to reinforce their efforts to succeed on your tests. These alternatives include (a) not counting items that you and your students find confusing, tricky, or overly difficult; (b) giving partial credit for parts of their answers and displaying correct work; (c) providing extra-credit options; (d) awarding bonus points for specific items; (e) letting students earn back points by revising incorrect answers or retaking different test questions that test similar content. When grammar, spelling, and punctuation are not the elements being tested, you can consider not penalizing students for these errors or giving students separate grades for content and mechanics. On essay tests, students initially can be given credit for an outline, web, diagram, or chart in place of a lengthy response.

To limit the use of these alternatives, you also can establish guidelines addressing the number of times students can use these options, the maximum grade a student can receive for a test that was originally below a certain level (e.g., grades on retakes cannot exceed 80%), and the types of items that cannot be retaken (e.g., extra-credit items cannot be retaken). To discourage guessing, you also can deduct points for incorrect answers.

Alternatives to Working Independently.   Although students usually take tests individually, you also can use a range of alternatives that provide students with opportunities to work collaboratively with others.

In **cooperative group testing**, students work collaboratively on open-ended tasks that have nonroutine solutions (Michaelsen & Sweet, 2008). You can then evaluate each group's product and cooperative behavior. Students also can be asked to respond individually to questions about their group's project.

A variation of cooperative group testing is a **two-tiered testing system**. In this system, students working in collaborative groups take a test, and each student receives the group grade. After the group test, students work individually on a second test that covers similar material. Students can be given two separate grades, their two grades can be averaged together into one grade, or they can be allowed to select the higher grade.

Some teachers use a format that involves students (a) working on a test independently for a specified amount of time; (b) being allowed to access relevant resources (textbooks, notes, online resources) for a specified amount of time; and (c) working on the test with a classmate for a specified period time (Edyburn, 2009). During each of these conditions, students record their answers using a different-colored pen. You can then grade their test as a whole or award different grades for the three different conditions.

In cooperative group testing, students work collaboratively on open-ended tasks that have nonroutine solutions. What are some tasks that you could use to assess your students using cooperative group testing?

Student Involvement.   Your tests can be made fairer by involving students in the testing process. Incorporate students' suggestions in writing and scoring tests. Ask them to submit possible test questions. Students also can be allowed to choose the type of test they take. For example, you can create three versions of a test: multiple-choice, essay, and sentence completion. Your students can then select the test that best fits their response style and study habits.

You can structure your tests to also give students some choice in responding to items. For example, a test can consist of 20 items with varying formats, and students can be directed to respond to any 15 of them; you can give them a series of open-ended questions presented in a tic-tac-toe format and ask them to select any three questions to answer, or you can specify that they choose three questions that give them tic-tac-toe (Edyburn, 2009).

Making Connections
The use of cooperative group testing relates to our earlier discussion of cooperative learning arrangements in Chapter 9.

A GUIDE TO ACTION
Creating Valid and Accessible Teacher-Made Tests

Your teacher-made tests should be created carefully so they align with your instructional program and accurately and fairly assess your students' learning. To develop appropriate teacher-made tests, consider the following questions:

Content

- Do test items measure important objectives related to the curriculum and the topics, concepts, and skills objectives taught?
- Are there a sufficient number of test items?
- Does the test require students to apply skills that they have not been specifically taught?
- Are the types of questions consistent with the strategies used to help students learn the content?
- Are the language and terms used in test directions and items consistent with those used in class?
- Does the percentage of items devoted to specific content areas reflect the amount of class time spent on those areas and the level of difficulty of the material?
- Is the scope of the material being tested too broad? Too narrow?

Format, Readability, and Legibility

- Is the readability of the test appropriate?
- Are similar item types grouped together and/or surrounded by text boxes?
- Are items organized within each section based on their level of difficulty?
- Is the length of the test reasonable?
- Is there a reasonable number of items per page?
- Do items on a page have proper organization, symmetry, and spacing, and are they numbered and ordered correctly?
- Are students allowed to write their answers on the test rather than having to transfer their responses to a separate answer sheet?
- Do students have enough space to record their responses?
- Is space provided for students to write justifications for their responses to short-answer items?
- Are page numbers provided on test pages?
- Is the test legible, neat, and free of distracting features?

Test Directions

- Are directions and items presented in language students can understand, on the same page, in text boxes, and for all sections of the test that contain different types of items?
- Are directions free of vague terms and unnecessary information?
- Are directions complete and do they provide students with the relevant information they need to answer the questions?
- Do directions present sequenced information in chronological order through use of numerals or the number words and use bullets to present essential information that does not have an established order?
- Are cues provided to alert students to specifics of directions and items? Changes in directions and item types?
- Is the test free of clues that can unintentionally guide students to the correct response?

Motivation, Engagement, and Strategy Use

- Are test-based and visual prompts embedded into the test to encourage students to be motivated and engaged and to use effective test-taking behaviors?
- Are test items personalized for students and inclusive, respectful and reflective of students' individual differences?

Multiple-Choice Items

- Does the stem provide a context for answering the item, and is it longer than the answer alternatives?
- Does the stem relate to only one point and include only relevant information?
- Are items grammatically correct and free of double negatives, grammatical cues, and categorical words?
- Are all the choices feasible, of the same length, specificity, element and format, free of key words or phrases from the stem, and presented vertically in a logical order?
- Is the correct choice clearly the best answer?

Matching Items

- Does the content to be assessed relate to homogeneous lists of corresponding premises and responses that address one concept?
- Does the matching section include no more than 10 grammatically similar and concise item pairs?
- Are there 25% more choices in one column than in the other?
- Is an example embedded?
- Is there only one correct response for each pair?
- Are the directions and the columns presented on the same page?

- Are columns labeled and organized in a sensible, logical manner?
- Do students respond by writing the letter or number in a blank rather than drawing lines from column to column?
- Are the longer item statements listed in the left-hand column and the shorter statements in the right-hand column?

True/False Questions

- Are questions phrased clearly, without double negatives, vague terms, qualifying words, and absolute words?
- Do items relate to relevant information?
- Are critical parts of statements highlighted?
- Are items focused on only one point, of the same length, and grouped by content assessed?
- Do students respond by circling their choice of *True* or *False* rather than writing out their response or changing false statements into true statements?
- Are items unequivocally true or false?
- Are predictable answer patterns avoided?

Sentence Completion Items

- Do items relate to meaningful information?
- Are items understandable to students, and do they have only one answer?
- Do items provide students with a sufficient context for answering?

- Do word blanks require a one-word response?
- Are word blanks placed at the end of the item, of the same length, and kept to a minimum?
- Are grammatical cues avoided?
- Are response choices or text boxes with word banks provided?
- Are students informed of whether synonyms, abbreviations, and other possible variations as correct responses as well as misspellings and multiple uses of words in the word bank are allowed?

Essay Questions

- Are the readability and level of difficulty of the question appropriate?
- Are key words highlighted?
- Are open-ended questions divided into smaller sequential questions?
- Are students provided with a list of important concepts that should be discussed, and aware of the time limits and the criteria to be used to evaluate their essays?

How would you rate your teacher-made tests? ( ) Excellent ( ) Good ( ) Needs Improvement ( ) Needs Much Improvement

Create a plan of action for improving your teacher-made tests that includes your goals, the actions you will take and the resources you will need to achieve them, and the ways you will evaluate your success.

Alternatives to Standardized and Teacher-Made Testing

Most students with disabilities should be able to take tests with appropriate testing accommodations. However, for some students, particularly those with the most significant cognitive disabilities, it may not be practical or appropriate to take part in statewide assessments (see your state's guidelines for determining student eligibility for alternate assessments). These students must participate in an alternate assessment system developed by your state and aligned with state standards (Parrish & Stodden, 2009; Spooner et al., 2008, Towles-Reeves et al., 2009). Although many states use a portfolio assessment system for these students, which we will discuss later in this chapter, you and your colleagues may want to use a range of classroom-based assessment strategies as part of or to supplement your state's alternative assessment system. These assessment alternatives to standardized and teacher-made testing, which involve the use of learning products associated with daily classroom instruction, also are very useful in helping you monitor the learning progress of *all students* and making decisions about how to improve your teaching and instructional program (Salend, 2009; Tomlinson, 2008b).

Progress Monitoring. **Progress monitoring** refers to your conducting ongoing assessments to examine your students' learning progress and the effectiveness of your teaching practices and instructional program. Thus, assessment data are continuously collected over time and promptly reviewed to identify students who are progressing and ready for new instruction as well as those students who have not yet demonstrated mastery and need additional or revised instruction (Yell, Busch, & Rogers, 2007). In addition to examining student learning, an integral part of progress

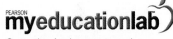

Go to the Assignments and Activities section of the Topic *Assessment* in the MyEducationLab for your course and complete the activity entitled *Authentic Assessment* to examine alternatives to standardized and teacher-made testing.

monitoring is a continuous examination of your teaching effectiveness. Thus, you also look at the data you have collected to inform your teaching and make any necessary adjustments that will help your students to learn better.

A variety of classroom assessment strategies that you can use to monitor the learning progress of *all students* and to inform your teaching are discussed in the following sections. In selecting appropriate classroom-based assessment techniques for use with your students, you can consider the following:

- Will the assessment technique measure meaningful skills and content?
- Will the assessment technique help me plan, deliver, and evaluate my instructional program?
- Will the assessment technique take away time from my instructional program?

Curriculum-Based Measurement   **Curriculum-based measurement (CBM)** provides individualized, direct, and repeated measures of students' proficiency and progress across the curriculum (Espin et al., 2008; Foegen, 2008; Jenkins et al., 2009). Because CBM is an ongoing, dynamic process involving content derived directly from students' instructional programs, it allows for continuous measurements of your students' progress and your teaching effectiveness (Capizzi & Barton-Arwood, 2009; Kritikos, 2010). CBM is an integral part of the *Response-to-Intervention* (RTI) process; and when it is used formally to identify students in need of special education, it requires the use of systematic policies, practices, and procedures related to delivering research-based instruction, establishing aimlines related to norms for growth rates at various grade levels, and monitoring student progress. However, you can use it more informally across the curriculum. For example, you can use a CBM to assess your students' progress in defining key vocabulary terms and the success of your instructional practices by conducting ongoing assessments of your students' ability to define the key terms (see Figure 12.7).

You can use the following guidelines for conducting a CBM:

1. *Identify the content area(s) to be assessed.* CBM begins by examining and determining the content areas to be assessed.

Making Connections

This discussion of progress monitoring and curriculum-based measurement builds on our earlier discussion of the Response-to-Intervention model in Chapter 2.

FIGURE 12.7 **Sample curriculum-based measurement graph**

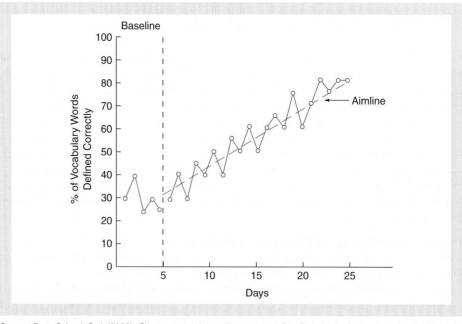

Source: From Salend, S. J. (2009). *Classroom testing and assessment for all students: Beyond standardization.* Thousand Oaks, CA: Corwin Press. Reprinted with permission.

2. *Define the school-related tasks that will constitute the assessment probe and the sample duration.* Identify and select meaningful learning activities and tasks that are directly related to your curriculum to be your assessment probe. Also specify the sample duration by establishing the amount of time your students will have to complete the assessment probe. For example, you can measure writing with an assessment probe of the number of words written during a sample duration of 5 minutes and assess mastery of social studies vocabulary by asking students to define specific key terms during a sample duration of 10 minutes.

3. *Determine whether performance or progress measurement will be used.* Performance measurement involves changes on a specific task that remains constant throughout the CBM. Progress measurement evaluates student progress on sequentially ordered levels/objectives within the curriculum.

4. *Prepare and organize the necessary materials.* Select material from the curriculum related to the assessment tasks in advance.

5. *Administer the CBM.* Take several measures of your students' performance on the assessment probe prior to your teaching, which is called a **baseline**. The baseline offers a standard that allows you to assess student learning and the success of your teaching.

6. *Establish an aimline.* Determine an aimline, which is a diagonal broken line starting at the left side of your CBM graph with a student's initial performance levels and ending on the right side of your CBM graph with your final goal for the student (see Figure 12.7). It establishes the expected rate of student learning and provides an actual and visual reference point for judging students' progress and making decisions about their instructional program.

7. *Teach and administer the assessment probe.* Teach your students and then assess their learning progress by giving them the assessment probe.

8. *Record and graph students' performance over time.* Determine and graph student performance on the assessment probe (see Figure 12.7). The vertical axis measures the student's performance on the school-related task (e.g., the percentage of vocabulary words defined correctly). The horizontal axis indicates the days on which the CBM is given.

9. *Analyze the results to determine students' progress.* You can use the data to determine student progress and identify the students who have mastered the skills and are ready for new instructional objectives, those who are progressing but need additional time or teaching to demonstrate mastery of skills, and those who have not progressed and need changes in their instructional goals and program.

10. *Examine and compare the efficacy of different instructional strategies.* You can examine the data to assess and compare the efficacy of different teaching methods and make decisions about your teaching practices. Thus, you can determine whether to continue to use certain teaching strategies, how to improve your current practices and what new strategies you need to implement.

Dynamic Assessment **Dynamic assessment** is another way to monitor your students' learning progress and to inform your instruction, by examining how students react to and benefit from instruction by using a test-teach-retest model (Macrine & Sabbatino, 2008; Grigorenko, 2009). While your students work on a task, you observe how they learn and offer help and feedback to improve their performance and skills to see how they respond to instruction (Allsopp et al., 2008). As students master skills, you offer less help and feedback and try to improve students' problem-solving abilities.

Learning Journals/Logs Student learning progress also can be assessed through the use of **learning journals** or *learning logs*. Periodically, you can ask students to write comments in their journals on what they learned, how they learned it, what they do not understand, why they are confused, and what help they would like to receive (Carr, 2008; Salend, 2009). Students who have difficulty writing can maintain an audio log or complete sentence prompts (e.g., "I learned . . ."; "The strategies that I used to learn were . . ."; "I still don't understand . . ."; "You can help me by . . ."). You and the students can then examine the logs to identify instructional goals and accommodations.

Students also can make journal entries on specific information covered in classes, attitudes toward a content area, how material covered in class relates to their lives, and additional questions that need to be studied. For example, after learning about fractions, students can be asked to respond to the following questions: (a) What are fractions, and why do we use them? (b) What part of learning about fractions do you find easy? Hard? (c) Write a story to go with the problem $3/4 + 1/4 = 1$.

Some teachers modify the learning log/journal process by having students complete exit tickets. At the end of class, they ask their students to write down their answer(s) to questions related to the content and skills taught that day and to list some things that are still confusing to them.

Think-Aloud Techniques   Information about student learning and the ways students approach a task can be assessed via use of **think-aloud techniques**, in which students state the processes they are using and describe their thoughts while working on a task (Falk-Ross et al., 2009; Learned et al., 2009). You can encourage students to think aloud by modeling the procedure and talking as you work through tasks and situations. You can also prompt students to think aloud by asking probing questions such as "What are you doing now?" "What are you thinking about?" "What do you mean by?" "Can you tell me more about how you did this?" and "How did you come up with that answer?"

Self-Evaluation Questionnaires/Interviews/Checklists   *Self-evaluation questionnaires, interviews,* or *checklists* can provide information on students' perceptions of their educational challenges, progress in learning new material, and strategies for completing a task (Carr, 2008). For example, a questionnaire or interview might focus on asking students to respond to the following questions: "What are some things you do well when you read?" "What are some areas in reading that cause you difficulty?" "In what ways is your reading improving?" and "What areas of your reading would you like to improve?"

Observations   Although observational techniques are typically used to record students' social behaviors, you also can use them to monitor and document your students' academic performance and academic-related behaviors (Painter, 2009; Swedeen, 2009). You can maintain observation journals of student actions during learning activities or anecdotal records of students performing various content area activities, as well as observing students' products and/or the processes or strategies they use. Some teachers structure their observations by using teacher-made rating scales and checklists.

Observational techniques can be used to collect data on the amount of time planned for teaching, time actually spent teaching, and time spent by students on teaching activities in class, as well as the rates and sources of interruptions to planned teaching. These data also can be used to help determine whether the presence of students with disabilities in general education classrooms reduces the teacher's attention and instructional time devoted to their classmates without disabilities.

Active Responding Systems   Many teachers use active responding systems to conduct real-time assessment of their students' learning progress (Haydon, Borders, Embury, & Clarke, 2009; Musti-Rao, Kroeger, & Schumacher-Dyke, 2008; Salend, 2009). During instruction, they use these systems to check student understanding of the content and skills they have just taught and then use the data to continue their lesson as planned or to modify it to help students learn. You can use active responding to assess student learning by having students

- display colored cards to indicate their levels of understanding (e.g., a green card can indicate a good understanding, a yellow card can indicate some understanding, and a red card can indicate limited or no understanding);

Making Connections
The use of self-evaluation questionnaires and interviews relates to the strategies for soliciting feedback from students about their learning and reactions to your instructional program presented earlier in Chapter 9.

Making Connections
This discussion of active responding systems builds on our earlier discussion in Chapter 9.

- respond chorally or in unison with gestures (thumbs-up or -down, OK sign, etc.) to short-answer or true/false questions or stating their agreement or disagreement with specific statements and examples;
- write answers on dry erase boards to questions or problems; and
- use technology-based active responding systems whereby you monitor student learning and understanding by having them respond electronically via handheld devices to factual, comprehension, and review questions and activities.

Educational Games   A novel and motivating way to conduct real-time assessments of your students' learning is through the use of educational games. Educational games allow you to monitor your students' learning progress by examining their responses to questions or activities that allow them to progress through the game. Using software programs and Web sites, your students can play technology-based educational games across the curriculum that are presented via video, interactive whiteboard, PowerPoint, virtual reality, or collaborative game formats (Barab, Gresalfi, & Arici, 2009; Mounce, 2008; Salend, 2009).

Error Analysis   You can increase the amount of information obtained from formal and informal assessment procedures by using **error analysis**. This method is used to examine students' responses to identify areas of difficulty and patterns in the ways students approach a task (Allsopp et al., 2008). Error analysis usually focuses on identifying errors related to inappropriate use of rules and concepts, rather than careless random errors or those caused by lack of instruction. Based on this information, you can plan instruction to correct error patterns.

Authentic/Performance Assessment   You also can use **authentic assessment** (also called *performance assessment*) to monitor student learning progress and measure the impact of your instructional programs on your students' academic performance (Darling-Hammond & Friedlaender, 2008; Spinelli, 2008). In this type of assessment, students work on meaningful, complex, relevant, open-ended learning activities that are incorporated into the assessment process and linked to your curriculum and learning standards (Bianco et al., 2009; Burke, 2009). The results of these activities are authentic products that reveal their ability to apply the knowledge and skills they have learned to contextualized problems and real-life settings. For example, for an authentic assessment at the elementary level related to a unit on the plant life cycle, your students could create a book explaining this topic to others. At the secondary level, your students can develop and disseminate a brochure on election issues as an authentic assessment for a unit on the electoral process.

Portfolio Assessment   Authentic/performance assessment is closely related to **portfolio assessment**, which involves teachers, students, and family members working together to create a continuous and purposeful collection of various authentic student products across a range of content areas throughout the school year that show the process and products associated with student learning (Cohen & Spenciner, 2007). Student centered and archival in nature, portfolios allow students to set goals and have more control over their learning. They contain samples over time that are periodically reviewed to reflect on and document progress, effort, attitudes, achievement, development, and the strategies students use to learn.

Although portfolios are useful for documenting the learning progress of *all students*, they are particularly useful in complying with the assessment mandates for

PEARSON
myeducationlab
Go to the Building Teaching Skills and Dispositions section of the Topic *Assessment* in the MyEducationLab for your course and complete the activity entitled *Assessing Students' Written Work.*

REFLECTIVE

What performance/authentic assessment tasks might be appropriate for measuring your understanding of the material presented in this course and book?

In authentic/performance assessment, students apply the knowledge and skills they have learned to contextualized problems and real-life settings. How can you use authentic assessment with your students?

Using Student Portfolios

James moved into the Madison School District in November and was placed in Ms. Feld's class. To prepare an educational program for James, Ms. Feld examined his performance on several norm-referenced tests administered while he attended his prior school. The test results indicated that James's reading and writing skills were significantly below his classmates. However, they provided little information about his strengths and challenges and the teaching strategies that could be used to help him. Therefore, Ms. Feld decided to work with James to develop a reading and writing portfolio.

Throughout the school year, James and Ms. Feld selected a variety of items for his portfolio, including a recording of James reading, a collection of pieces that he wrote based on a single theme using a process approach to writing, written summaries of books he read, and a self-recording graph of James's daily reading. The items were stored electronically in a digital portfolio by date and subject area, which was easily shared with James' parents and other teachers. When James and Ms. Feld selected an item for the portfolio, they discussed what it revealed about James's progress in reading and writing. After discussing the item's significance, each of them wrote a caption statement that was attached to the item.

During several family–teacher conferences throughout the school year, Ms. Feld and James shared his portfolio with his family. Before these meetings, James and Ms. Feld examined the whole portfolio and summarized what it demonstrated about James's progress in reading and writing. James began the conference by presenting his portfolio. First, he mentioned the goals and purpose of the portfolio and how it was organized. He then spoke about the content and special items in the port-

folio, discussing why items were selected and what they showed about his learning. Ms. Feld spoke about James's progress by citing various portfolio items. James's family gave their reactions to his portfolio and asked questions about it. James, his family, and Ms. Feld discussed how his reading and writing had changed, the patterns that were evident in his reading and writing, the strategies he was using in these areas, and the changes in his attitude and motivation. They also talked about the skills and learning strategies that needed to be developed, as well as goals and plans for future work to address his instructional needs.

At the end of the meetings, Ms. Feld, James, and James's family wrote notes summarizing their reactions to the portfolio, which then were added in the digital portfolio. James's family was proud of him, and pleased to see real and understandable signs that James was learning. James's notes indicated that he was feeling good about himself and that he liked having some control over his learning. Ms. Feld felt much better knowing that her instructional program was helping James make progress in reading and writing.

- Why did Ms. Feld decide to work with James to develop a portfolio?
- What roles did James perform in the portfolio process?
- What roles did James's family perform?
- How did Ms. Feld involve James and his family in the portfolio process?
- What was the effect of the portfolio on James, his family, and Ms. Feld?
- How could you use portfolios with your students?

students with significant cognitive disabilities. Therefore, instead of taking high-stakes grade-level tests based on statewide learning standards, your students with significant cognitive disabilities can complete alternative assessments aligned to *alternate achievement standards* that are not as complex as grade-level achievement standards (Towles-Reeves, Kleinert, & Muhomba, 2009; Spooner et al., 2008). These modified assessments are designed for your students who

- take a general education class for reasons other than mastery of the general education curriculum,
- require extensive instructional modifications, and
- are not able to participate in high-stakes testing even with testing accommodations.

In many states, modified assessments involve the use of portfolios to compare student work over time and to link student learning products to statewide standards.

Here are some guidelines for using portfolio assessment that you may want to consider:

1. *Identify the goals of the portfolio.* Typically, the goals of students' portfolios are individualized, broadly stated, related directly to the curriculum, and cover an extended period of time. For students with disabilities, portfolio goals also can be linked to their IEPs.

2. *Determine the type of portfolio.* There are different types of portfolios: showcase, reflective, cumulative, and goal based. A *showcase portfolio* presents the student's best work and is often used to help students enter a specialized program or school or apply for employment. A *reflective portfolio* helps teachers, students, and family members reflect on students' learning, including attitudes, strategies, and knowledge. A *cumulative portfolio* shows changes in the products and process associated with students' learning throughout the school year. A *goal-based portfolio* has preset goals; items are selected to fit those goals, such as goals from a student's IEP. A *process portfolio* documents the steps and processes a student has used to complete a piece of work.

3. *Select a variety of real classroom products that address the goals of the portfolio.* Students, teachers, and family members can jointly select a range of authentic classroom products related to the goals of the portfolio. You and your students also can use video and audio recordings to document students' accomplishments (Skouge et al., 2007). In selecting items to be part of a portfolio consider the following questions:
   - What classroom products should be included in the portfolio that show the student has made progress learning?
   - What classroom learning products should be included in the portfolio that show the processes and learning strategies the student employs?

   Some teachers schedule a selection day on which students choose items for their portfolios; others encourage students to select items that are in progress or completed. You can help students select portfolio items by offering models, allowing students to learn from each other by sharing their portfolios, and creating and sharing evaluation criteria with students. You also can assist students in selecting items by asking them to select an assignment that (a) was their favorite, (b) was initially difficult for them, (c) shows their understanding or mastery of specific skills, and (d) shows their creative abilities and problem-solving skills.

4. *Establish procedures for collecting, storing, organizing, and noting the significance of students' products.* Portfolio items are usually stored in individualized folders such as file folders, binders, and boxes with dividers organized in a variety of ways: chronologically (e.g., early/intermediate/later works) or according to students' IEPs, academic or content-area subjects, student interests, or thematic units. You can ask your students to personalize their portfolios by covering them with photographs, pictures, and logos.

   Technology and multimedia can be used to create electronic or digital portfolios (Romeo, 2008; White Englund, 2009; Zuger, 2008). Software programs offer ways to scan audio and video clips of students and student-produced projects; import external files containing student work from other programs (e.g., word processing and presentation software); organize portfolios by subject, theme, or project; and link students' work to national, statewide, and districtwide standards, instructional rubrics, and individualized lesson plans; and facilitate the ease with which portfolios can be shared with others (Salend, 2009). A sample electronic portfolio is presented in Figure 12.8.

5. *Record the significance of items included in students' portfolios and help students reflect on them.* When selecting products for a portfolio, teachers and students write **caption statements**, brief descriptions that identify the item, provide the context in which it was produced, and reflect on why it was selected. A sample caption statement is presented in Figure 12.9.

   Help your students reflect on their portfolios by asking them to discuss why they selected a particular piece. They can respond to questions that relate to
   - *learning outcomes* (e.g., "What did you learn from working on this project?" or "What did you do well on this project?");
   - *improvement* (e.g., "If you could redo this, how would you improve it?" or "How is this piece different from your other pieces?");

Evaluating Student Progress and the Effectiveness of Your Inclusion Program

FIGURE 12.8 **Sample digital portfolio**

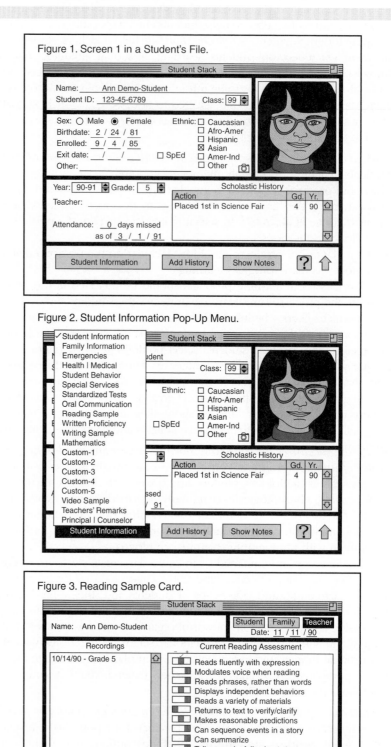

Figure 1. Screen 1 in a Student's File.

Figure 2. Student Information Pop-Up Menu.

Figure 3. Reading Sample Card.

Source: From "An Equation to Consider: The Portfolio Assessment Knowledge Base + Technology = The Grady Profile," by D. L. Edyburn, 1994, *LD Forum*, 19, 1994, pp. 36, 37. Copyright 1994 by *LD Forum*. Reprinted with permission.

FIGURE 12.9 Sample caption statement

Date: 12/18/2010

Teacher Comments: This piece demonstrates James's ability to engage in the writing process and use story elements. James was given a choice of several themes and selected a theme relating to Thanksgiving. James completed the piece using a checklist that guided him in creating and organizing the elements of the story. When James first discussed the piece with me, I encouraged him to elaborate on his story.

Student Comments: I have been working on a story about Thanksgiving. I feel good about this item because I made up the story. In working on this story, I used a checklist that Ms. Feld gave me. The checklist asked me: What is the title of the story? Who are the characters? Where does the story take place? What happens in the story? and How does the story end?

- *process* (e.g., "What process did you go through to complete this assignment?");
- *strategy use* (e.g., "What strategies did you use to work on this piece?" "Were they effective?"), as well as other aspects of student learning.

You also can ask your students to respond to questions such as the following:

a. What was the assignment? (Describe the assignment.)
b. What things did I do well on this assignment?
c. What things did I learn from working on this assignment?
d. What strategies and techniques did I use to work on the assignment?
e. How could I improve this assignment?

Another way to promote reflection is by asking students to compare a recently completed item with an earlier work, by having students reflect on each other's work, by asking them to write letters for their portfolios explaining why a specific item was chosen, or by writing a portfolio introduction that compares items, identifies patterns, and interprets the meaning of the whole portfolio.

Because some of your students may experience difficulty reflecting, scribes or audio and video recordings can be employed to facilitate their participation in the self-reflection process. Reetz (1995) and Countryman and Schroeder (1996) identify the following prompts, which can be used to help students compose caption statements:

Improvements

This piece shows my improvement in _____. I used to _____, but now I _____.

Pride

I am proud of this work because _____. In this piece, notice how I _____.

Special Efforts

This piece shows something that is hard for me. As you can see, I have worked hard to _____.

IEP Objectives

This work shows my progress on _____. I have learned to _____. I will continue to _____.

Content Areas

In (content area) I have been working on _____. My goal is to _____.

Thematic Units

I have been working on a unit relating to the theme of _____. As part of this unit, I selected the following pieces: _____. These pieces show that I _____.

Projects

I have been working on a project about _____. I learned _____. The project shows I can _____.

Difficulties

This piece shows the trouble I have with _____.

Strategy Use

This piece shows that I used the following method: _____. The steps I used were _____ and _____.

You also can ask students to respond to a series of yes or no questions about items (e.g., "Are you proud of this work? Does this item show that you . . . ? Would you like this to be in your portfolio?") or to point to items they like and to specify parts of assignments that show their learning.

Making Connections
You can help prepare students to discuss their portfolios with others by using the guidelines for involving students in their IEPs that were discussed earlier in Chapter 2.

6. *Review and evaluate portfolios, and share them with others.* Portfolios should be reviewed and evaluated periodically by teachers, students, family members, and administrators throughout the school year during conferences. Students can share their portfolios with others and portfolios can then be examined to assess students' educational, behavioral, language, and social-emotional performance and skills. Near the end of the conference, participants can be asked to write or dictate a note or letter to the portfolio stating what they think is the most meaningful information in the portfolio, as well as what the portfolio indicates about the student's progress and educational program.

Instructional Rubrics   Authentic/performance assessment and portfolio assessment often include the use of **instructional rubrics** (or simply *rubrics*), statements specifying the criteria associated with different levels of proficiency for evaluating student performance (Painter, 2009; Romeo, 2008). Educators using instructional rubrics assess process, performance, and progress by delineating the various categories associated with assessment tasks and learning activities, the different levels of performance, and the indicators describing each level and then rating student performance on products that show their learning (Andrade, 2008). A writing rubric developed by Ms. Cheryl Ebert, an English teacher at the Johnson City (New York) High School, is presented in Figure 12.10.

You can choose to use holistic or analytic rubrics (Spinelli, 2006). Holistic rubrics require teachers to select one level of performance or rating that best represents the quality of the learning product and are used most frequently with comprehensive assessments related to district, state or national standards. Conversely, analytic rubrics have several categories of indicators, which are rated separately, allowing teachers to differentiate levels of performance within and among the categories. Analytic rubrics typically are used to provide specific feedback to students to support their learning.

Rubrics can help you promote student learning and clarify and communicate your expectations (Andrade, 2008; Stevens & Levi, 2009). They also make grading and

Advances in technology and multimedia are providing authentic ways to assess student learning. How do you use technology to assess your students?

FIGURE 12.10 Sample writing rubric

Name: | Assignment:

Narrative/Descriptive Writing Scoring Guide | Date:

Course Outcome: Students will be able to internalize a writing process which includes planning, composing, revising, and self-evaluating.

Criteria Quality	Focus on and Organization of Task	Narrative	Descriptive	Style and Diction	Grammar, Usage, and Mechanics
Excellent 90+ (A)	• Topic is approached in a unique and imaginative way. • Attitude and point of view remain the same for entire paper. • Paragraphs and sentences are organized and make sense.	• Opening situation is clearly established. • Characters are effectively introduced and developed. • Description is original and vivid. • Conflict is clearly developed. • Conflict is logically and completely solved.	• Very descriptive words or phrases are used. • Details are chosen to create a very clear picture or image for the reader throughout the writing.	• Uses well-chosen and appropriate words all of the time. • Expresses ideas in an imaginative and creative way. • Effective paragraphing. • Varies sentence structure.	• Can correctly use certain parts of speech, ending punctuation, and indentation at all times. • Correctly uses comma and quotations at all times. • Uses proper tense throughout. • Few or no spelling errors. • Capitalization correct throughout.
Quality 80+ (B)	• Topic is understood. • Attitude and point of view are clear, but not used throughout the paper. • Paragraphs are not always organized, but sentences are organized in a pattern.	• Opening situation is established. • Characters are adequately introduced and developed. • Includes some description. • A conflict is developed. • Conflict is solved.	• Descriptive words or phrases are used. • Details are chosen to create a good picture or image for the reader throughout the writing.	• Generally chooses appropriate words. • Expresses ideas clearly. • Some sentence structures are repetitious. • Some errors in sentences. • Correct paragraphing.	• Can correctly use certain parts of speech, ending punctuation, and indentation in most cases. • Correctly uses commas and quotations most of the time. • Uses proper tense throughout. • Minor spelling errors. • Capitalization appropriate.
Acceptable 70+ (C)	• Topic is understood, but ideas are not developed enough. • Attitude and point of view change throughout the writing. • Paragraphs are not always organized, and sentence order does not make sense.	• Opening situation is not appropriate or established. • Characters are not well developed. • Conflict is not established or does not make sense. • Conflict is not completely solved.	• Few descriptive words or phrases are used. • There are not enough details to keep the picture or image in the reader's mind.	• Sometimes chooses inappropriate words. • Meaning is clear, but word choice is not varied. • Some sentences are choppy. • Fragments/run-ons. • Errors in paragraphing.	• Word usage is limited. • Errors or omissions in the use of commas or quotations. • Errors in verb tense, but meaning is clear. • Several spelling errors, but meaning is clear.
Below Expectations	• Topic is not understood. • Attitude, point of view are unclear. • Paragraphs are not organized, nor do the sentences make sense.	• Lacking major elements of narrative structure.	• Almost no descriptive words or phrases are used. • Details, if any, do not create a picture for the reader.	• Chooses incorrect or inappropriate words. • Meaning is unclear or confusing, point is not made. • Many fragments and/or run-ons. • Incorrect or no paragraphing.	• Little or no knowledge of use of parts of speech or ending punctuation. • Commas, quotes, capitalization, punctuation errors throughout the paper. • Spelling errors interfere with understanding. • Constant shifting of verb tenses.

Notes:

Source: Developed by Cheryl Ebert, English teacher, Johnson City High School, Johnson City Central School District, Johnson City, NY.

FIGURE 12.11 Guidelines for creating instructional rubrics

Step 1. Determine whether to use instructional rubrics to assess student learning. Consider the different ways to assess student learning, and determine if the use of an instructional rubric is the best format for evaluating the assignment and mastery of the targeted learning standards.

Step 2. Examine examples of the assignment to identify important features and relevant categories. Look at samples of the assignment completed by your students in the past to determine the important features that make the assignments excellent, good, and in need of improvement. Use these important features to identify the relevant categories that the instructional rubric will address.

Step 3. Determine the levels of performance. Devise an age-appropriate scale reflecting the instructional rubric's three or four levels of performance, such as Beginning (1), Developing (2), Accomplished (3), and Exemplary (4). Determine whether to assign points to each level and to weight different categories based on their importance. Solicit feedback from students to help name the performance levels.

Step 4. Write indicators that guide you and your students in using the instructional rubric. Compose a set of indicators, which are brief statements that clearly present the specific features related to your instructional rubric's identified categories and different performance levels. Indicators are typically number based (three or more, at least two, fewer than three, many, some, few, no), time based (all of the time, most of the time, some of the time), or descriptive (clearly established, established, unclear). Examine indicators to delete irrelevant ones, combine those that overlap, and add important ones that are missing.

Step 5. Review the rubric. Examine the rubric to make sure the instructional rubric is positive, understandable, unbiased, and doesn't stifle your students' creativity.

Step 6. Teach and encourage students to use the instructional rubric. Help your students learn to use the rubric by clearly explaining it to them, demonstrating how and reminding them to use it, and conducting conferences with them to discuss their use of it.

Step 7. Evaluate students' assignments using the instructional rubric, and revise it accordingly. Reflect on the impact of the rubric on your students' learning and grades and your teaching and grading; revise it based on your reflections.

Sources: Salend (2009); Stevens and Levi (2009); Whittaker, Salend, Duhaney (2001).

feedback more objective and consistent, which in turn helps students understand the qualities associated with assignments and aids them in monitoring and self-evaluating their own work.

Instructional rubrics are most effective when you create them with your students and teach them to use them (see Figure 12.11 for guidelines for creating instructional rubrics). You also can post your instructional rubrics online so your students and their families can access them at their convenience.

IEPs   Students' academic performance in inclusive settings also can be determined by examining their IEPs. For example, you can assess their progress by examining their success in attaining the goals outlined in their IEPs. If specific goals have not been achieved, the evaluation can attempt to explain why and whether these goals are still appropriate.

Promotion and Graduation Rates   Promotion and graduation from high school rates are important indicators of success of inclusive classrooms. However, because many states have adopted promotion and graduation requirements that are tied to students' performance on high-stakes testing, many students, particularly students with special needs, are not being promoted or graduating. Some states employ some type of diploma alternatives to acknowledge students' efforts and motivate them to stay in school, including (a) an IEP-based diploma based on mastery of their IEP goals, (b) a certificate of completion or attendance based on completion of a course of study or attendance

REFLECTIVE
REFLECTIVE

Have you taken a technology-based test? How did it affect your performance? What was helpful for you? Difficult for you?

Using Technology to Promote Inclusion

USING TECHNOLOGY-BASED TESTING AND ASSESSMENT

Technology allows you to differentiate your testing and assessment practices based on your students' strengths and challenges and your curriculum goals (Bouck, 2009b; Salend, 2009). Advances in technology-based testing provide alternatives to traditional testing formats and offer novel ways to assess student learning (Beddow et al., 2008). Because technology-based testing can be based on the principles of universal design it allows tests to be administered in individualized ways so that testing accommodations are embedded and students are offered choices concerning a test's presentation and response mode formats and the testing accommodations they want to use (Lazarus et al., 2009; Russell, Hoffmann, & Higgins, 2009). Your students can decide whether they want to have test directions and items presented in verbal or written or video/pictorial or masked formats; or via Braille, text/screen readers, and enlargers, captioning, sign or simplified language; or in multiple formats; (Vreeburg, Izzo, Yarick, & McArrell, 2009). They can select whether they want to respond via voice recognition technology; word processor; Brailler; digital recorder, talking calculator; touch screens; mouse clicks; or adapted switches, devices, and keyboards. Students also can make choices to repeat directions; highlight text; access strategy reminders; eliminate distracting backgrounds, sounds, animations, and images; and adjust the font, print size, color, spacing, and background of the test. Via technology, your students who are English language learners can choose to take tests administered in their preferred language, and access bilingual dictionaries/glossaries and pop-up translations.

Your students also can determine the pace of the test administration, the sequence in which items are presented, and the number of items that appear on the screen at a time. As they take a test, they can access the items they have completed as well as those they would like to review again, and view an on-screen clock and indicator that informs them of the time and the amount of time left to complete the test (Beddow et al., 2008). Students also can periodically receive reinforcement and encouragement (e.g., "Congratulations, you are finished with the multiple-choice questions") and prompts to remind them to stay focused and motivated and to engage in self-reinforcement (e.g., "Keep working hard. Give yourself a thumbs-up"). By embedding error minimization techniques such as making sure that students respond to an item before allowing them to move to the next item, or pairing responses to multiple-choice or true/false items with videos and pictorials and an automated oral recording stating the answer option (e.g., A, B, C, or D, or Yes, No, Sometimes, etc.), technology-based testing also can limit students' test-taking errors.

Technology-based testing also allows you to tailor the administration of tests to the skill levels and scheduling preferences of your students. For example, a technology-administered exam can be structured so that the difficulty of each question depends on how the student performed on the prior question(s). If the student answers a question correctly, the computer can branch to a more difficult item; if he or she answers a question incorrectly, the computer can branch to an easier item. Student performance on these exams is then based on their correct responses and the level of difficulty. The flexibility associated with technology-based testing also can address students' varied scheduling needs by allowing for individualized and group administrations in various locations, extended time, breaks, multiple testing sessions, time of day considerations, and variations in the sequence in which subtests are administered. Technology-based testing also can foster student learning by facilitating the speed at which test results are shared with others, linked to statewide learning standards, used to make curricular and instructional changes, and employed to examine student progress over an extended period of time (Bouck, 2006).

It is important to be aware of concerns about technology-based testing. In addition to the digital divide, these concerns include making the test taking process longer and more tiring, especially for students who may not be comfortable reading larger amounts of text on screen or who are required to use malfunctioning or dated hardware and software (e.g., small screens with low resolution). Additionally, technology-based testing may require students to use a different set of test taking skills. High-tech cheating also has been a growing concern associated with technology-based testing, which usually involves accessing unauthorized information and resources such as notes, online resources, or spellcheckers via use of some type of technology. To address high-tech cheating, some educators are taking actions to prevent students from having access to devices, the Internet, and wireless networks and using classroom management software, which allows them to monitor students' use of technology during testing and ensuring that each student's computer only presents the test.

Here are some other ways you can use technology to assess student learning and the effectiveness of your inclusive classroom:

- Convert tests into PDF files so that students can complete them using technology (Hoffman, Hartley, & Boone, 2005), and obtain guidelines for designing and evaluating the accessibility of tests online (Beddow et al., 2008).

- Use software programs and Web sites to prepare, administer, and score tests, quizzes, and surveys electronically, and prepare reports on the results (Salend, 2009).

- Teach your students the skills they need to take technology-based tests, and give them practice in taking tests via technology.

- Use technology to help students prepare and study for tests. For example, you can make review materials,

(Continued)

study guides, important notes, practice tests, and digital recordings of important instructional activities and teacher-directed presentations and instruction and models of effective study and test-taking skills available online (Lancaster, Lancaster, Schumaker, & Deshler, 2006; Saavedra, 2008). You also can have students create digital flash cards and study materials and provide them with links to Web sites that offer information and resources about study and test-taking skills (Doyle & Giancreco, 2009; Salend, 2009).

- Employ technology to facilitate the implementation of progress monitoring and to create CBM assessment probes and to record, graph, analyze, and share CBM data and observations of student behaviors and interactions (Capizzi & Barton-Arwood, 2009; Edyburn & Basham, 2008; Parette, Peterson-Karlan, Wojcik, & Bardi, 2007).

- Have students maintain a learning blog containing periodic entries related to their performance on classroom instructional activities (Davis & McGrail, 2009). You can then access and comment on their learning blog and provide them with appropriate instructional feedback based on their entries and share them with your students' families.

- Provide students with opportunities to demonstrate their learning by engaging in technology-based performance assessments (Salend, 2009; Wissick et al., 2009). For example, students can showcase their learning outcomes by creating Web pages and sites, blogs, podcasts, and digital presentations, movies, or stories, engaging in technology-based simulations and virtual learning experiences, and completing webquests and tracks, and using wikis.

- Use technology to assess students' responses to authentic situations and give students opportunities to use, develop, and assess their critical thinking, social, and metacognitive skills (Salend, 2009). For example, your students can be given audio and video clips of academic and social situations and asked to respond to them in a` variety of ways.

- Use the Internet to access and edit a bank of instructional rubrics developed by others and to create and post your own rubrics for use by students and other teachers (Salend, 2009).

- Maintain an electronic grade book by using a Web-based system or spreadsheet that stores and computes grades and test scores, and make them available to students and their families via password protection.

- Create visual and audio digital diaries that can serve as observations of students in a range of classroom situations and activities to assess their academic, language, social, and behavioral development over time (Cox Suarez & Daniels, 2008; Sprankle, 2008).

for a specified period of time, and (c) a work-study diploma based on their work in community-based settings. In using these alternatives, you should be careful that they do not demean students, lessen the availability of services for them, or limit their postsecondary options and opportunities. It is particularly important to provide these students with a comprehensive transition plan.

GRADING STUDENTS

HOW CAN I GRADE MY STUDENTS IN INCLUSIVE SETTINGS?

Mr. Jones, a general educator, and Ms. Gold, a special education teacher, worked as a cooperative teaching team in the Madison School District. While they had worked well together to design and implement a variety of differentiation techniques to support student learning, their different perspectives on grading became evident when they started to work on students' report cards. Mr. Jones considered it his responsibility to grade all the students. He also felt that it was only fair to grade all students in the same way, as their averages and class ranking would determine their eligibility for honors, awards and admission to

Many states have changed their graduation requirements and the types of diplomas they offer. Has this occurred in your state? What is its impact on your students and their families?

college. Although he recognized the importance of classroom-based assignments, he thought students' grades should be based mostly on tests because all students would ultimately have to pass the statewide assessments. He also thought that some of the students had received special help from Ms. Gold, and that students who did not use differentiation techniques should receive higher grades. He also was concerned that the students' families get a true picture of their children's learning in relation to others.

Ms. Gold agreed with Mr. Jones about the need to communicate accurate and realistic information about their children's learning to families. However, Ms. Gold believed that she should collaborate with Mr. Jones in grading students and that grades should be based on multiple assessment measures and not just tests. She thought that students with special needs should not be penalized for using differentiation techniques that allowed them to learn and demonstrate their mastery of the class content and did not violate the integrity of the curriculum and standards.

Report Card Grading

Report card grades are another indicator of student progress in inclusive classrooms. As the conflict between Mr. Jones and Ms. Gold reveals, major challenges of grading students in inclusive classrooms include

- determining the purposes of grading,
- considering and communicating the impact of differentiated instruction and the use of differentiation techniques to support student learning,
- determining the roles of different professionals and legal mandates in the grading process, and
- fostering equity and fairness.

Thus, like many teachers in inclusive classrooms, Mr. Jones and Ms. Gold need help addressing these issues by implementing equitable and legally sound districtwide report card systems that allow all students to achieve meaningful grades that reflect their classroom experience, individual achievements and challenges, and the learning standards in your curriculum (Brookhart & Nitko, 2008; Guskey & Bailey, 2009; Jung & Guskey, 2007; Munk, 2008; K. O'Connor, 2009). Guidelines and models for grading students that promote individualization, fairness, and communication and support the use of differentiated instruction in inclusive classrooms are presented next.

Consider and Address the Legal Guidelines for Grading   Section 504 and Title II of the ADA, which are under the supervision of the Office of Civil Rights (OCR), have led to specific legal interpretations that guide the grading of *all students* in inclusive settings. These OCR guidelines mandate that

- *all students* must be treated similarly in terms of grades, class ranking, honors, awards, graduation, and diplomas;
- a modified grading system can be employed if it is available to *all students;*
- *all students* who take a general education class for no credit or reasons other than mastery of the curriculum can be provided with grading procedures that are different from the rest of the class;
- guidelines and criteria for ranking *all students* or granting awards cannot arbitrarily lessen or exclude the grades of students with disabilities;
- the weighting of grades and awarding of honors are allowable if they are based on objective criteria and courses that are open and available to *all students;*
- report card or transcript designations, symbols, or terminology that indicate participation in special education or that a student received pedagogical accommodations or a modified curriculum in general education classes are not permissible unless the grades and courses of *all students* are treated in the same manner.

Identify the Purpose of Report Card Grades   The grading of *all students* should be compatible with the district's preferences regarding the purposes of grading. Whereas report cards should be aligned to curricular standards, different grading systems may be appropriate for different grades as the purposes of grading may change as students progress through school. At the elementary level, an anecdotal grading system can be used to communicate academic gains as well as social and developmental accomplishments. In high schools where grading is used to rank students to determine their eligibility for programs and awards, a grading system that compares students based mostly on their academic performance is often used.

Making Connections
The continuum of differentiation techniques was discussed earlier in Chapter 8.

Agree on the Nature and Impact of Differentiated Instruction Techniques   Teachers like Mr. Jones and Ms. Gold can use the continuum for differentiation techniques to resolve their differences regarding the nature and impact of differentiated instruction. The continuum delineates three levels of differentiation techniques that are based on their impact on the curriculum mastery expected of students: access, low-impact, and high-impact differentiation techniques (Stough, 2002).

Select Grading Systems That Support Differentiated Instruction and Communication   After agreeing on the nature and impact of the differentiation techniques, educators can select appropriate report card alternatives that provide information about individual growth and support differentiation and communication. For example, educators can use report card instructional and testing differentiation techniques cover sheets for *all students* (see Figure 12.12) to communicate the instructional and testing differentiation strategies that were provided and are associated with students' grades. As described next, a range of norm-referenced, criterion-referenced, or self-referenced grading systems or a combination of these types of referent grading systems can be used in inclusive settings to support and communicate your use of differentiated instruction (Brookhart & Nitko, 2008).

Norm-Referenced Grading Systems   **Norm-referenced grading systems** involve giving numerical or letter grades to compare students using the same academic standards. They can be tailored to inclusive classrooms to foster communication and differentiation in a variety of ways.

As in a figure skating competition where a skater's score is based on the quality and level of difficulty of the routine, numerical grades for specific assignments or courses can be computed based on preestablished difficulty levels. For example, you can give *all students* a list of differentiated assignments and their corresponding levels of difficulty. They can choose which assignment(s) to complete and receive grades that reflect the quality and level of difficulty of the assignment. For example, a student who completes an assignment of an average level of difficulty with a quality grade of 90 could have that grade multiplied by 1 to compute a final grade (e.g., 90 × 1.0 = 90), while a student who completes a more difficult assignment with a quality grade of 90 could have the grade multiplied by a factor of 1.05 to compute a final grade (e.g., 90 × 1.05 = 94.5).

You also can use **multiple grading** to adjust your numerical/letter grades by grading students on multiple factors: achievement, effort, and level of curriculum difficulty. Grades for these factors can then be averaged or weighted to produce a composite final grade. For example, a student who was assigned an achievement grade of 95, an effort grade of 90, and a level-of-curriculum-difficulty grade of 85 could have these grades averaged into a final grade of 90. Additionally, based on their importance, you can weight the various factors used to grade your students. For example, a formula that gives a double weighting to students' achievement grade could be used to compute the same student's final grade as follows:

$$\frac{2 \times \text{Achievement grade (95)} + \text{effort grade (90)} + \text{level-of-curriculum-difficulty grade (85)}}{4} = 91.25$$

Student's name: _____

Grade: _____

Teacher(s): _____

INSTRUCTIONAL DIFFERENTIATION TECHNIQUES

Check all the instructional differentiation techniques used

☐ Word processor/spell checker
☐ Note-taking assistance
☐ Use of technology (please specify)
☐ Learning strategies instruction
☐ Specialized seating arrangements
☐ Study skills instruction
☐ Memory aids and strategies
☐ Additional time to complete tasks
☐ Manipulatives
☐ Electronic textbooks
☐ Frequent comprehension checks
☐ Daily/weekly planner
☐ Redirection
☐ Tiered assignments
☐ Adapted directions
☐ Shorter assignments
☐ Scheduling accommodations
☐ Frequent reinforcement
☐ Modeling
☐ Adapted textbooks
☐ Visuals to support instruction

☐ Adapted materials
☐ Adult assistance
☐ Peer-mediated instruction
☐ Verbal prompts
☐ Curriculum overlapping
☐ Self-correcting materials
☐ Cues to highlight information
☐ Adapted homework
☐ Calculators
☐ Graphic organizers
☐ Frequent communication with families
☐ Generalization strategies
☐ Listening/note-taking guides
☐ Frequent feedback
☐ Examples/models of correct response formats
☐ Prompting
☐ Concrete teaching aids
☐ Limited distractions
☐ Study guides

☐ Other (please specify) _____
_____

TESTING DIFFERENTIATION TECHNIQUES

Check all the testing differentiation techniques used

☐ Items omitted
☐ Extended time
☐ Individual administration
☐ Directions/items read
☐ Adapted directions
☐ Word processor/spell check
☐ Adapted multiple-choice items
☐ Calculator
☐ Increased space in between items
☐ Fewer items
☐ Adapted matching items
☐ Adapted true/false items
☐ Adapted sentence completion items
☐ Adapted essay questions

☐ Proctor
☐ Scribe
☐ Separate location
☐ Breaks
☐ Alternate response mode
☐ Administration over several sessions
☐ Cues to highlight information
☐ Oral test
☐ Cooperative group testing
☐ Extra-credit options
☐ Bonus points
☐ Writing mechanics waived
☐ Use of technology (please specify)

☐ Other (please specify) _____
_____

Level grading can help you individualize your grading by using a numerical or letter subscript to indicate your use of differentiated instruction techniques to help your students achieve a specific level of curriculum mastery. For example, a B_3 grade can indicate that a student is performing in the B range on a 3rd-grade level of curriculum mastery, and a C_{10a} grade can indicate that a student is performing in the C range on a 10th-grade level of curriculum mastery with the use of differentiation techniques.

You also can supplement your use of numeric or letter grades by communicating the differentiation techniques that support student learning. For example, you list the instructional and testing differentiation techniques associated with students' grades as follows:

Grade	Differentiation Techniques
89	Peer note taker, individualized homework, extended time on assignments and tests

Criterion-Referenced Grading Systems   Rather than comparing your students based on their numerical or letter grades, **criterion-referenced grading systems** allow you to report on your students' mastery within the curriculum. You can modify these grading systems to promote communication and differentiation in several ways.

You can report on your students' levels of curriculum mastery and the differentiation techniques used by completing a series of predetermined, open-ended statements addressing important aspects of your curriculum. Examples of open-ended question prompts across a variety of academic and social domains and grade levels are as follows:

- Pays attention for _____ minutes.
- Recognizes numbers up to _____.
- Solves algebraic equations up to _____.
- Identifies _____ letters of the alphabet.
- Reads _____ words.
- Writes a paragraph of _____ sentences.
- Writes using the following conventions: _____.
- Uses the following learning strategies: _____.
- Understands the following forms of poetry: _____.
- Successfully performs the following experiments: _____.

To help students' families interpret this information, you can share normative data regarding a student's relative standing with them. You can do this by giving them a listing of age-appropriate curricular expectations or embedding this information within each item. For example, the context for judging the report card statement "defines *30* scientific terms" can be provided by placing the age-appropriate expectations for students in terms of numbers recognized in parentheses—for example, "Defines 30 (50) scientific terms." Open-ended sentences also can be phrased so that they provide a list of the differentiation techniques used. For example, the sentence completion statement "solves the following types of word problems" can be revised to add differentiation techniques used so that it reads, "solves the following types of word problems, with _____ (list differentiation techniques)."

Rating scales and checklists can also be used to present information related to criterion-referenced grading and differentiation techniques to others. You do this by linking items to benchmarks associated with the curriculum and evaluating your students according to their mastery of these benchmarks. For example, you can grade your students on the their mastery of your curriculum by using the following scale: **S** (strong performance), **M** (meeting expectations), **P** (progressing toward meeting expectations), **NI** (needs improvement) and **NA** (not addressed). As presented in Figure 12.13,

FIGURE 12.13 Sample checklist and rating scale items addressing the use of instructional differentiation techniques

SAMPLE CHECKLIST ITEMS

1. Performs computations with a calculator _____.
2. Maintains place when reading using a mask or marker _____.
3. Writes using a teacher-produced word bank _____.

SAMPLE RATING SCALE ITEMS

1. Writes a complete paragraph:

_____	_____	_____	_____	_____
Performs independently	Performs mostly independently	Performs with some assistance	Performs with some differentiation techniques	Performs with considerable differentiation techniques and assistance

2. Takes notes:

_____	_____	_____
independently	with a teacher-prepared outline	with the aid of peer note-takers

3. Completes assignments and exams:

_____	_____	_____	_____	_____
independently	with step-by-step instructions	with a reduced number of items	with extended time	with peer or adult assistance

4. Spells:

_____	_____	_____	_____
independently	with a spell checker	with a dictionary or pictionary	with a word bank

checklist and rating scale items can include information on the nature and degree of the differentiation techniques used to promote student mastery.

You also can individualize criterion-referenced grading systems by using mastery-level grading and contract grading. **Mastery-level grading** involves you and your students dividing course content into a hierarchy of skills and determining appropriate learning activities and differentiation techniques based on an initial assessment of your students' individual needs. After your students complete these learning activities and receive the appropriate differentiation techniques, they demonstrate their mastery of the content by performing an activity or taking a test. This process is repeated until all skills are mastered. Similarly, in **contract grading**, you and your students develop a contract outlining the learning goals/objectives, the amount and nature of the learning activities and differentiation techniques, and the products your students must complete as well as the procedures for evaluating learning products and assigning grades.

Self-Referenced Grading Systems **Self-referenced grading systems** are often used to communicate your students' progress over a period of time. In self-referenced grading systems, *all students* are graded based on their progress in comparison with their past performance, ability levels, effort, and special needs. One type of self-referenced grading you can use is **descriptive grading**, which involves your writing comments that address your students' academic progress, learning styles, effort, attitudes, behavior, socialization, strengths, and challenges and the instructional accommodations that support their learning.

You also can use **progressive improvement grading**, which involves your providing your students with feedback and differentiation techniques as they work on a range of individualized assessment and learning activities throughout the grading period. However, you only use their performance on assessment and learning activities during the final weeks of the grading period to assess their growth and determine grades.

Address the Special Challenges and Situations of Students and Teachers District policies also can offer teachers guidance on the

- types of grading systems to be used;
- the factors to be considered in determining students' grades (i.e., whether report card grades should also reflect students' effort, behavior, work habits, and attitude and whether these factors should be graded separately from grades based solely on academic achievement);
- the weighting of final exams and other grading activities;
- the level for passing a class; and
- the computation of grades, grade-point averages, and class ranks.

Issues related to collaborative grading should be addressed to minimize the confusion that teachers like Mr. Jones and Ms. Gold experience by clarifying each team member's role and responsibility in grading students so that grading students is a collaborative process based on the input of all educators who work with students (Murawski & Dieker, 2004). The district's policies can also cover the assignment of incomplete grades.

The district's policy also should address procedures for determining grading adaptations for students who need them. Jung and Guskey (2007) and Silva, Munk, and Bursuck (2005) developed models that can be used to determine grading accommodations that involves selecting, implementing and evaluating grading alternatives that address specific grading purposes and the individualized challenges of students. For example, some students might benefit from use of an **IEP grading system**, in which the individualized goals, differentiation techniques, and performance criteria on students' IEPs serve as the reference point for judging student progress and assigning grades.

Use Effective Practices That Support the Teaching, Learning, and Grading Processes
You will need to use practices that foster the use of differentiated instruction, enhance student learning, and facilitate the grading process (Brookhart & Nitko, 2008; O'Connor, 2009; Reeves, 2008; Zapf, 2008). Effective practices that support the teaching, learning, and grading processes include the following:

- *Communicating expectations and grading guidelines to your students and their families*
- *Informing students and families regarding grading progress on a regular basis*
- *Reviewing exemplary models of classroom assignments*
- *Using a range of assignments that address students' varied learning strengths, challenges and styles*
- *Employing classroom-based assessment alternatives to traditional testing*
- *Providing feedback on assignments and grading students after they have learned something rather than while they are learning it*
- *Involving students in the grading process*
- *Avoiding competition and promoting collaboration*
- *Giving separate grades for content and style*
- *Designing valid tests and providing students with appropriate testing accommodations*
- *Using extra credit judiciously.* Use extra credit to motivate students to expand their understanding of concepts, and assist those students who need additional points to raise their grades from one level to another (e.g., moving from a 75 to an 80). However, because extra credit should not be used to help students compensate near the end of the grading period for work they failed to do, use it judiciously.

REFLECTIVE

Do grading alternatives and accommodations compromise standards and reduce course integrity? Should grades be assigned only by the general education classroom teacher or through collaboration with others?

- *Establish a Do It Over policy.* Use a do it over policy, which helps avoid problems with extra credit, that requires *all students* to continue to work on their assignments until they receive a specific grade such as a C.
- *Using median scores to compute grades.* Averaging tends to accentuate the effect of a poor score or a missing assignment (a zero grade is especially devastating for students when you average their grades), and makes it difficult for students to receive a good grade, which can be discouraging for them. Therefore, consider using the median to determine students' grades and creating procedures that allow students to receive incomplete grades if they need more time to submit work.

EVALUATING SOCIAL AND BEHAVIORAL PERFORMANCE

HOW CAN I EVALUATE THE SOCIAL AND BEHAVIORAL PERFORMANCE OF MY STUDENTS? One premise of inclusive classrooms is that they will have a positive effect on students' social and behavioral development. For students with disabilities, desired social and behavioral outcomes include being on task, making friends, increasing their social and behavioral skills, and improving their self-concepts. For students without disabilities, social and behavioral outcomes include becoming more accepting and understanding of individual differences, more aware of and sensitive to the needs of others, and more willing to make friends with students with disabilities.

Observational and Sociometric Techniques

You can use observational and sociometric techniques to gain insights into students' interaction and friendship patterns and to learn about their social and behavioral competence (Estell et al., 2008; Salisbury et al., 2005). Observations of students' behavioral and social skills also can be recorded on checklists and rating scales. These scales provide a list of behavioral and social skills that guide your observations of your students, and help you identify their strengths and challenges. To ensure that the results are accurate and representative of student behavior, you may want to ask several different individuals to rate your students in various settings. A sample rating scale based on the social and behavioral skills that some teachers believe are important for success in inclusive classrooms is presented in Figure 12.14.

Data collected via observation can be supplemented by interviews with family members, other teachers, and students. Still other information sources are documents revealing the number and types of discipline reports, behavioral incidents, interruptions caused, bullying and teasing behaviors, suspension/expulsions, and referrals to special education. Changes in students' attendance patterns and friendships also can be examined to assess their social and behavioral development.

Self-Concept and Attitudinal Measures

Many strategies have been developed to assess students' self-concepts and attitudes, which you can use as part of your evaluation of your inclusive classroom (Popham, 2009). You can use a variety of assessment instruments including interviews to measure your students' academic and social self-concepts, attitudes, and their perceptions of how they learn and view themselves and their skills and competency levels (McLoughlin & Lewis, 2008; Wagner, Newman, Cameto, Levine, & Marder, 2007).

MEASURING PERCEPTIONS OF INCLUSIVE CLASSROOMS

HOW CAN I MEASURE PERCEPTIONS OF MY INCLUSIVE CLASSROOM? An evaluation of inclusive classrooms should include an examination of the perceptions and experiences of students, teachers, and family members. This information can help you analyze the effectiveness of your inclusive classroom, document changes over time, validate successful inclusive programmatic factors and educational policies that should be continued, and pinpoint procedures that need to be revised.

PEARSON
myeducationlab

Go to the Assignments and Activities section of the Topic *Assessment* in the MyEducationLab for your course and complete the activity entitled *Grading Criteria*. As you watch the video and answer the accompanying questions, think about the impact the criteria have on helping you monitor student progress.

Making Connections
Strategies for assessing your students' friendships and prosocial behaviors were discussed earlier in Chapters 5 and 7.

Please rate each skill using the following scale:

| Always (1) | Usually (2) | Sometimes (3) | Rarely (4) | Never (5) |

Behavioral and Social Skills	Always (1)	Usually (2)	Sometimes (3)	Rarely (4)	Never (5)
1. Follows directions	1	2	3	4	5
2. Asks for help when it's appropriate	1	2	3	4	5
3. Begins an assignment after teacher gives assignment to class	1	2	3	4	5
4. Complies with class rules	1	2	3	4	5
5. Doesn't speak when others are talking	1	2	3	4	5
6. Works well with others	1	2	3	4	5
7. Interacts cooperatively with others	1	2	3	4	5
8. Shares with others	1	2	3	4	5
9. Attends class regularly	1	2	3	4	5
10. Seeks teacher's permission before speaking	1	2	3	4	5
11. Works independently on assignments	1	2	3	4	5
12. Seeks teacher's permission before leaving seat	1	2	3	4	5
13. Brings necessary materials to class	1	2	3	4	5
14. Participates in class	1	2	3	4	5
15. Makes friends	1	2	3	4	5
16. Has a sense of humor	1	2	3	4	5

All students can benefit from inclusive teaching practices. How do your students benefit from your inclusive teaching practices?

Students' Perceptions

Your students' perceptions including their attitudes are crucial in evaluating your inclusive classroom (Popham, 2009; Wagner et al., 2007). Interviews and questionnaires can be used to collect information from students on the academic and social benefits of your inclusive classroom, as well as their insights, experiences, and attitudes. When using interviews and questionnaires, be sure items and directions are clearly stated and phrased using students' language rather than professional jargon. When professional terms like *inclusion* must be used, they should be defined so that your students can understand them.

You also need to consider whether it is appropriate to use phrases such as *students with and without disabilities* and to tailor specific items for both types of students. Because interviews and questionnaires may take a long time to complete, you may choose to administer them over several days. Interviews are particularly appropriate for younger students and those who have difficulty reading and writing. A list of potential interview questions is presented in Figure 12.15.

Questionnaires also allow you to investigate your students' feelings about and reactions to various aspects of inclusive classrooms. It is best to use a closed-form questionnaire that is easy for them to complete. This type of questionnaire has a yes-no or true/false format or asks students to mark a number or a statement that best indicates their response. For students who have reading and/or writing difficulties, you may need to read items for them as well as record their responses. A sample questionnaire is presented in Figure 12.16.

FIGURE 12.15 Sample inclusion student interview

Others sometimes call your class an inclusion classroom. This means that students who learn, act, look, and speak in different ways are learning together in the same class. It also means that other teachers work with students in this classroom rather than taking them to another classroom.

I am going to ask you some questions about your class.

1. Do you think that all types of students learning in the same class is a good idea? Why or why not?
2. What things do you like about being in this class?
3. What things don't you like about being in this class?
4. What have you learned from being in this class?
5. In what areas are you doing well? Having difficulty?
6. Are you completing all your schoolwork and homework? If so, what things are helping you to complete your work? If not, what things are keeping you from completing your work?
7. What are your teachers doing to help you in your class?
8. How do you get along with other students in this class? How has being in this class affected your friendships and popularity?
9. In what afterschool activities do you participate? If none, why?
10. How do you think your classmates feel about being in this class?
11. What do you think your classmates learned from being in this class?
12. What changes have you observed in your classmates since being in this class?
13. What parts of being in this class have been hard for you? For your classmates? For your teacher(s)? Why?
14. What would you tell other students about being in this class?
15. What ways can you think of to make this class work better?

FIGURE 12.16 Sample student inclusion survey

Please circle the word that best describes your feelings about your class:

1. I like being in a class with different types of students.	Yes	Sometimes	No
2. I learned a lot, and so did others.	Yes	Sometimes	No
3. I am more likely to help other students.	Yes	Sometimes	No
4. I saw other students making fun of their classmates.	Yes	Sometimes	No
5. I have improved at teaching others.	Yes	Sometimes	No
6. I am more understanding of the behaviors and feelings of others.	Yes	Sometimes	No
7. I was made fun of by my classmates.	Yes	Sometimes	No
8. I feel better about myself.	Yes	Sometimes	No
9. I feel that I belong in this class.	Yes	Sometimes	No
10. I improved my schoolwork and grades.	Yes	Sometimes	No
11. I am better at making friends.	Yes	Sometimes	No
12. I improved at learning from others.	Yes	Sometimes	No
13. I am less likely to make fun of others.	Yes	Sometimes	No
14. I felt the same as the other students in my class.	Yes	Sometimes	No
15. I received help from my teacher(s) when I needed it.	Yes	Sometimes	No
16. I did most of my schoolwork without help.	Yes	Sometimes	No
17. I liked having several teachers in the classroom.	Yes	Sometimes	No
18. I liked working with other students.	Yes	Sometimes	No
19. I enjoyed being in this classroom.	Yes	Sometimes	No
20. I would like to be in a class like this next year.	Yes	Sometimes	No

Teachers' Perceptions

Teachers are vital to the success of inclusion. Therefore, in evaluating inclusion programs, their perceptions of and experiences with inclusion are very important. This information can help school districts assess the impact of their inclusion programs on students, evaluate various aspects of these programs, and design and implement effective inclusion programs.

Questionnaires   Questionnaires and interviews can be used to elicit teachers' feelings about and reactions to their inclusive classrooms, including their beliefs and concerns, as well as their feelings about the impact of their classrooms and programs. Questionnaires and interviews also can address teachers' satisfaction with (a) their roles in implementing inclusion programs, (b) the quality of the resources they have received to implement inclusion, (c) their experiences in collaborating and communicating with others, (d) their skills and preparation to implement inclusion successfully, and (e) the policies and practices concerning inclusion of the school and the district. A sample questionnaire designed to assess teachers' perceptions of and experiences with inclusive education is presented in Figure 12.17.

Interviews   Interviews give teachers the opportunity to provide rich and descriptive examples, insights, and suggestions that can be valuable in evaluating inclusive educational programs. In addition to individual interviews, focus group interviews can be used. Potential interview questions that can be used to examine teachers' experiences in inclusion programs are presented in Figure 12.18.

Interviews with teachers also can provide valuable information that can pinpoint students' strengths and existing or potential problems in their academic, behavioral, and social-emotional performance by addressing the following questions:

- How is the student performing academically, socially, and behaviorally in your class?
- To what extent has the student achieved the goals listed in the IEP? If the goals have not been achieved, what is an explanation?
- Does the student complete classwork, homework, and other assigned projects?
- What methods, materials, instructional and testing accommodations, and alternative grading techniques have been successful? Unsuccessful?
- What accommodations have been provided to meet the student's cultural and language needs? How effective have these accommodations been?
- How does the student get along with classmates?
- In what extracurricular activities does the student participate?
- Is the student receiving the necessary supportive services?
- How is the communication system with other personnel and the student's family working?

Teachers also can provide feedback on students' progress and performance within inclusive classrooms by periodically completing a student progress form such as the one presented in Figure 12.19.

Cooperative Teaching Experiences   Many school districts like the Madison School District employ cooperative teaching arrangements as part of their efforts to implement inclusion programs. Therefore, an ongoing evaluation of inclusion programs also should include an examination of the experiences and perceptions of cooperative teaching teams and their impact on student learning (Hang & Rabren, 2009). Such information can help validate successful collaborative practices and identify those practices in need of revision. Sample surveys and interviews to solicit feedback from teachers concerning their efforts to work collaboratively have been presented in Figures 4.5 and 4.6.

FIGURE 12.17 Sample teacher's inclusion survey

Please indicate your feelings about and experiences with inclusion using the following scale:

Strongly Disagree (SD)	Disagree (D)	Neutral (N)	Agree (A)	Strongly Agree (SA)
1	2	3	4	5

	SD	D	N	A	SA
1. I feel that inclusion is a good idea.	1	2	3	4	5
2. I feel that I have the time and the training to implement inclusion successfully.	1	2	3	4	5
3. I feel that inclusion helps students develop friendships.	1	2	3	4	5
4. I feel that inclusion is working well in my class.	1	2	3	4	5
5. I feel that I receive the necessary support and assistance to implement inclusion successfully.	1	2	3	4	5
6. I feel that it is difficult to modify instruction and my teaching style to meet the needs of students with disabilities.	1	2	3	4	5
7. I feel that inclusion helps students academically.	1	2	3	4	5
8. I feel that having other adults in the classroom is an asset.	1	2	3	4	5
9. I feel that the demands of the curriculum make it difficult to implement inclusion.	1	2	3	4	5
10. I feel that I have been sufficiently involved in the inclusion process in my school.	1	2	3	4	5
11. I feel that I perform a subordinate role as a result of inclusion.	1	2	3	4	5
12. I feel that I do not have enough time to communicate and collaborate with others.	1	2	3	4	5
13. My students' academic performance has been negatively affected.	1	2	3	4	5
14. My students have become more accepting of individual differences.	1	2	3	4	5
15. My students feel better about themselves.	1	2	3	4	5
16. My students have picked up undesirable behaviors from their classmates.	1	2	3	4	5
17. My students have received less teacher attention.	1	2	3	4	5
18. My students have been teased by their classmates.	1	2	3	4	5
19. My students have grown socially and emotionally.	1	2	3	4	5
20. My students feel that they belong in my class.	1	2	3	4	5
21. My students feel positive about my class.	1	2	3	4	5
22. My students show pride in their work.	1	2	3	4	5

Use of Universal Design for Learning (UDL)

As part of your evaluation of your inclusive classroom, you also can examine your use of the principles of universal design for learning (Sopko, 2008). This can involve reflecting on the extent to which you incorporate the principles of UDL to make your curriculum, instruction, classroom management and design, and assessment accessible to and usable by *all students*. It also involves an assessment of the support you receive to learn about UDL and obtain the resources you need to implement it.

Family Members' Perceptions

Family members are particularly affected by the impact of inclusion programs on their children. Therefore, they too can provide feedback on their children's academic, social, and behavioral development (Swedeen, 2009). They can also

REFLECTIVE

How would you describe your understanding and use of UDL?

1. How is inclusion working in your class? Your school? What is working well? What is not working well?

2. What factors have contributed to the success of inclusion in your class? At your school?

3. What factors have prevented inclusion from working in your class? At your school?

4. What are your biggest concerns about and frustrations with inclusion?

5. What things do you enjoy most about inclusion?

6. Do you have difficulty meeting the needs of students with certain types of disabilities? If so, what types of disabilities do these students have and what problems are you experiencing?

7. Do you feel that you have the support, resources, and time to implement inclusion effectively? If not, what support, resources, and scheduling arrangements would be helpful to you?

8. Do you feel that you have the skills and training to implement inclusion effectively? If not, what skills would you like to develop and what training would you like to receive?

9. Which individuals (give titles, not names) have been most helpful in assisting you to implement inclusion? How have these individuals assisted you? What additional assistance would you like to receive?

10. How has inclusion affected your students with disabilities? Please describe any benefits and/or negative consequences you have observed in these students.

11. What accommodations have been provided to meet the cultural and linguistic needs of your students? How effective have these accommodations been?

12. Have your students participated in the statewide testing program? If yes, what were the results? What, if any, alternative testing techniques were employed? Were they effective? If no, why not and what alternative assessment strategies have been employed?

13. How has inclusion affected your students without disabilities? Please describe any benefits and/or negative consequences you have observed for these students.

14. How has inclusion affected you as a professional and a person? Please describe any benefits and/or any negative consequences for you.

15. In what ways has your role changed as a result of your school's effort to implement inclusion? What do you enjoy about your new roles? What concerns do you have about your new roles?

16. How did it feel to collaborate with another professional? What was most difficult? Most enjoyable? Most surprising?

17. How did the collaboration process change throughout the school year?

18. What did you learn from collaborating with another professional?

19. What suggestions would you have for other professionals who are planning to work collaboratively?

20. If another professional asked you for advice about inclusion, what advice would you give?

21. What things has your school district done to facilitate inclusion in your school? To hinder inclusion in your school?

22. What schoolwide and districtwide inclusion practices would you like to see retained? What practices would you like to see revised?

23. What additional information would you like to have about inclusion?

assess the effectiveness of the school district's inclusion practices and policies, as well as identify and make recommendations about programmatic policies and practices that need revision. A sample interview and a questionnaire on the perceptions and experiences of families concerning inclusion programs are provided in Figures 12.20 and 12.21, respectively.

IMPROVING THE EFFECTIVENESS OF INCLUSIVE CLASSROOMS AND PROGRAMS

HOW CAN I IMPROVE THE EFFECTIVENESS OF MY INCLUSIVE CLASSROOM? After you have collected data on students' progress and on students', teachers', and family members' perceptions of your inclusion program, members of the school or school district's comprehensive planning team or inclusive educational program planning committee can analyze them. The data can be used to examine the effect of the program and develop an action plan to improve the program's effectiveness and to advocate for inclusive programs.

FIGURE 12.19 Sample student progress form

Teacher(s):   Class: Date:

How are things going with _____?
    (student's name)

Areas	How are things going?					Comments
Academic progress	1 *We need to talk*	2	3 *OK*	4	5 *Very well*	
Mastery of IEP goals	1 *We need to talk*	2	3 *OK*	4	5 *Very well*	
Classroom participation	1 *We need to talk*	2	3 *OK*	4	5 *Very well*	
Class work completion	1 *We need to talk*	2	3 *OK*	4	5 *Very well*	
Homework completion	1 *We need to talk*	2	3 *OK*	4	5 *Very well*	
Accommodations	1 *We need to talk*	2	3 *OK*	4	5 *Very well*	
Collaboration	1 *We need to talk*	2	3 *OK*	4	5 *Very well*	
Supportive services	1 *We need to talk*	2	3 *OK*	4	5 *Very well*	
Family communication	1 *We need to talk*	2	3 *OK*	4	5 *Very well*	
In-class behavior	1 *We need to talk*	2	3 *OK*	4	5 *Very well*	
Peer relationships	1 *We need to talk*	2	3 *OK*	4	5 *Very well*	
Student effort and motivation	1 *We need to talk*	2	3 *OK*	4	5 *Very well*	
Other (please list)	1 *We need to talk*	2	3 *OK*	4	5 *Very well*	

- What things are working well?
- What concerns do we need to address?
- How can we address these concerns?
- When should we talk?

Source: Prom (1999).

Examine the Impact on Student Performance

First, the committee can examine the effect of your inclusion program on the academic, social, and behavioral performance of your students by reviewing the results of standardized tests and the findings of alternative assessments. This information can be supplemented by an examination of other indicators of student progress and program effectiveness. Such indicators include data on graduation rates, participation in and performance on statewide tests, attendance patterns, participation in extracurricular activities, behavioral referrals, suspensions, course failures, and accrual of credits (Idol, 2006).

1. Do you think that placing students with disabilities in general education classrooms with their peers who do not have disabilities is a good idea? Why or why not?

2. What things do you like about your child being in an inclusion classroom?

3. What concerns do (did) you have about your child being in an inclusion classroom? Do you still have these concerns?

4. How does your child feel about being in an inclusion classroom? What things does your child like about being in an inclusion classroom? What concerns, if any, does your child have about being in an inclusion classroom? How could these concerns be addressed?

5. How do you feel about the educational program your child is receiving in his or her inclusion classroom?

6. How do you feel about the special education and supportive services your child is receiving in his or her inclusion classroom?

7. How has being in an inclusion classroom affected your child academically, socially, and behaviorally? Please describe any benefits and/or negative consequences you have observed in your child. What factors led to these changes?

8. How has your child's placement in an inclusion classroom affected other students? His or her teachers? Other families? Other professionals who work with your child? Please describe any benefits and/or any negative consequences for these individuals.

9. How has your child's placement in an inclusion classroom affected you? Please describe any benefits and/or any negative consequences for you.

10. Have your goals for your child's future changed as a result of your child's being placed in an inclusion classroom? If yes, in what ways?

11. What roles have you performed in the inclusion process? Are you satisfied with your roles in the inclusion process? If so, what roles have been particularly important and satisfying? If not, why not, and what roles would you like to perform?

12. What things seem to make inclusion work well at your child's school? What things seem to prevent inclusion from working well at your child's school? In what ways can inclusion be improved in your child's class and school?

13. What schoolwide and districtwide inclusion practices would you like to see retained? What practices would you like to see revised?

14. What do you think of the access to, timeliness, and coordination of the services your child is receiving?

15. How is the communication system between you and the school working?

16. What additional information would you like to have about inclusion and your child's class?

FIGURE 12.21 Sample family inclusion survey

Please indicate your feelings about and experiences with inclusion using the following scale:

Strongly Disagree (SD)	Disagree (D)	Neutral (N)	Agree (A)	Strongly Agree (SA)
1	2	3	4	5

	SD	D	N	A	SA
1. I feel satisfied with the educational and supportive services my child is receiving.	1	2	3	4	5
2. I feel satisfied with the school's communication with families.	1	2	3	4	5
3. I feel that being in an inclusion class has been positive for my child.	1	2	3	4	5
4. I feel that inclusion helps children academically and socially.	1	2	3	4	5
5. I feel that families are adequately involved in the inclusion process.	1	2	3	4	5
6. I feel that the school district did a good job of explaining the inclusion program to me.	1	2	3	4	5
7. My child learned a lot.	1	2	3	4	5
8. My child talks positively about school.	1	2	3	4	5
9. My child feels proud of his/her classwork.	1	2	3	4	5
10. My child has learned to feel comfortable interacting with other students.	1	2	3	4	5
11. My child has grown socially and emotionally.	1	2	3	4	5
12. My child's education has been negatively affected.	1	2	3	4	5
13. My child has received fewer services.	1	2	3	4	5
14. My child has made more friends.	1	2	3	4	5
15. My child has become more confident and outgoing.	1	2	3	4	5
16. My child has become more accepting of individual differences.	1	2	3	4	5
17. My child has picked up undesirable behavior from classmates.	1	2	3	4	5
18. My child has been teased by classmates.	1	2	3	4	5
19. My child has teased classmates.	1	2	3	4	5
20. My child would like to be in an inclusion class next year.	1	2	3	4	5

For secondary students, data on the types of diplomas students are receiving, as well as their success in attending college, finding a job, living independently, and being socially integrated into their communities can be measures of the ability of the inclusion program to help students make the transition from school to adulthood.

To reflect and enhance your understanding of ways to evaluate and improve the impact of your inclusive classroom on your students with disabilities, go to the IRIS Center Resources section of the Topic *Inclusive Practices* in the MyEducationLab for your course, and complete the module entitled *Accessing the General Education Curriculum: Inclusion Considerations for Students with Disabilities.*

Determine Program Strengths, Concerns, and Possible Solutions

The data on the perceptions of students, teachers, and family members regarding your inclusion program also can be analyzed to determine the strengths of the program and validate aspects of it that appear to be working well. In addition, these data can be used to identify components of the program that need revision, as well as develop an action plan to implement potential solutions. Possible concerns associated with inclusion programs and potential solutions to address these concerns are presented in Table 12.2.

What Would You Do in Today's Diverse Classroom?

1. Your inclusion classroom includes some of the students we met earlier in this book:

   ★ Marty knows a lot about a variety of different topics and likes to share his knowledge with others. However, he struggles to complete his assignments and has difficulties with reading, writing, and math. Marty likes to interact with others but sometimes gets carried away, which bothers some of his friends (see Chapter 2).

   ★ Halee has had a difficult time adjusting to her new culture and language. She appears to be shy and withdrawn and has had some difficulties completing her assignments. Her difficulties in school appear to be having a negative effect on her self-esteem (see Chapter 3).

   ★ Tom's abilities and skills are significantly below those of his peers. He speaks in one-, two-, or three-word sentences and often has difficulty understanding others. It takes him a while to learn things and generalize his new learning to new situations (see Chapter 8).

      a. What would be the goals of your inclusive classroom for these students?

      b. How would you evaluate the effectiveness of your inclusive classroom based on the academic, behavioral, and social performance and progress of these students?

      c. What roles would the perceptions of students, other teachers, and family members play in your evaluation of your inclusion program? How would you gather information from these groups about the program?

      d. What knowledge, skills, dispositions, resources, and supports do you need to evaluate your inclusive classroom?

      e. What difficulties might arise in educating these students in your inclusion program? How could you address these difficulties to improve the effectiveness of the program?

2. Your principal asks you to reflect on the impact of your inclusive classroom on your students and your teaching and the ways it can be improved. What types of things would you reflect on?

myeducationlab Watch a teacher reflect on his experiences teaching in an inclusive classroom by visiting the MyEducationLab for this course. Go to the *Assignments and Activities* section under the topic *Inclusive Practices,* and complete the activity entitled *Description of an Inclusive Classroom* to answer questions about reflecting on your inclusive classroom.

TABLE 12.2 Possible concerns about inclusion and potential solutions

Possible Concerns	Potential Solutions
Students are not benefiting academically, socially, and behaviorally.	• Collect and examine data on the impact of the program on students (see Chapter 12). • Meet with families (see Chapter 4). • Revise students' IEPs (see Chapter 2). • Use strategies to promote the academic development of students, such as differentiating instruction, teaching students to use learning strategies, adapting large- and small-group instruction, modifying instructional materials and techniques, employing technology, and using culturally relevant instructional strategies (see Chapters 2, 3, 6, and 8–11). • Incorporate the principles of universal design into your inclusive classroom (see all chapters). • Use strategies to promote acceptance of individual differences and friendships and to foster students' social skills and self-determination (see Chapters 5 and 6). • Use strategies to foster positive classroom behavior (see Chapter 7). • Modify the classroom environment to promote students' academic, social, and behavioral development (see Chapter 7).
Students with disabilities are having a difficult time adjusting to inclusive classrooms.	• Help students with disabilities make the transition to inclusive settings (see Chapter 6). • Learn about the strengths and challenges of students with disabilities (see Chapter 2).
Students with disabilities are not participating in statewide and districtwide assessments.	• Use a range of testing and assessment practices to monitor the academic, social, and behavioral progress of students and to inform teaching (see Chapter 12). • Incorporate the principles of universal design into your assessment practices including the use of valid and appropriate testing accommodations, the creation of valid and accessible teacher-made tests, and the use of appropriate report card grading practices (see Chapter 12). • Differentiate instruction to promote the learning of all students (see Chapters 8–11).
Students from various cultural and language backgrounds are having difficulties in inclusive settings and are disproportionately represented in special education.	• Learn more about the unique strengths and challenges of students from various cultural and language backgrounds (see Chapter 3) and about disproportionate representation (see Chapter 1). • Promote interactions among students (see Chapters 5 and 9). • Use differentiated instruction, culturally relevant instructional strategies and instructional materials, cooperative learning, and a multicultural curriculum (see Chapters 8–11). • Communicate and collaborate with families and community organizations (see Chapter 4).
Teachers express negative attitudes about working in inclusion programs.	• Give teachers information and research about inclusion programs (see Chapter 1). • Identify the sources of teachers' negative attitudes, and plan activities to address these concerns (see Chapters 1, 4, and 12). • Provide opportunities to talk with teachers, family members, and students who have experience with successful inclusion programs and to design and engage in meaningful professional development (see Chapters 1 and 4). • Involve teachers in planning and evaluating all aspects of inclusion programs (see Chapters 1, 4, and 12).
Family and community members have negative attitudes about inclusion programs.	• Give family and community members information and research about inclusion programs (see Chapter 1). • Identify the sources of these negative attitudes, and plan activities to address these concerns (see Chapters 1, 4, and 12). • Invite family members, other professionals, and community members to visit inclusion programs (see Chapters 1 and 4). • Offer family and community members data on the impact of the inclusion program (see Chapters 1 and 12). • Involve family and community members in planning and evaluating all aspects of the inclusion program (see Chapters 1, 4, and 12).

(Continued)

Possible Concerns	Potential Solutions
General education teachers report that they are not receiving enough support from others.	• Examine existing arrangements for providing teaching support (see Chapter 4). • Provide general education teachers with greater support from special educators, paraeducators, and ancillary support personnel (see Chapters 4 and 8) and the resources they need to incorporate UDL into their inclusive classrooms (see all chapters).
Teachers report difficulty meeting the requirements of the general education curriculum.	• Give teachers appropriate curriculum materials, technology, and equipment (see Chapters 8–11). • Help teachers explore ways to differentiate instruction, and diversify and modify the curriculum (see Chapters 2, 3, and 7–11) and to incorporate UDL into all aspects of their inclusive classrooms (see all chapters).
Teachers indicate that the large class size reduces the success of the program and their ability to meet the needs of students.	• Make sure that the class size is appropriate (see Chapters 1 and 4). • Encourage teachers to differentiate instruction, and use cooperative learning arrangements and peer-mediated instruction, instructional technology, and behavior management techniques (see Chapters 7–11).
Teachers express concerns about educating students with certain types of disabilities in inclusive settings.	• Identify teachers' specific concerns (see Chapters 1 and 12). • Provide teachers with education and information to understand and address the educational, social, medical, physical, cognitive, and behavioral strengths and challenges of students (see Chapters 2 and 3). • Make sure that teachers and students are receiving the necessary assistance and resources to differentiate their instruction and incorporate the principles of UDL (see all chapters).
Teachers report that they do not have the expertise and knowledge and skills to implement inclusion effectively.	• Conduct a needs assessment to identify teachers' professional development needs (see Chapter 12). • Offer systematic, ongoing, coordinated, and well-planned staff development activities (see Chapter 4). • Encourage teachers to visit model programs and attend professional conferences (see Chapter 4). • Provide teachers with access to professional journals and other resources addressing current trends, models, research, and strategies (see all chapters).
Teachers report that there is not enough time for collaboration and communication among staff members.	• Use flexible scheduling to give teachers the time to collaborate and communicate (see Chapter 4). • Maintain appropriate caseloads for teachers (see Chapters 1 and 4). • Schedule regular meetings (see Chapter 4).
Cooperative teaching teams report that they are having problems resolving problems involving teaching style, personality, and philosophical differences.	• Examine the mechanism and variables used for matching teachers in cooperative teaching teams (see Chapter 4). • Offer education to help teachers work collaboratively (see Chapter 4). • Provide mechanisms for resolving disagreements among teachers working in teaching teams (see Chapter 4). • Establish mechanisms for ensuring equal-status, cooperative teaching relationships among teachers and for sharing accountability for educational outcomes for all students (see Chapter 4). • Provide time for teachers to collaborate and coordinate instructional activities and supportive services (see Chapter 4).

SUMMARY

This chapter offered a variety of strategies for evaluating the progress of students and the effectiveness of inclusion programs. As you review the questions posed in this chapter, remember the following points.

How Can I Evaluate the Academic Performance of My Students?

CEC 5, 7, 8, 9; PRAXIS 3; INTASC 8, 9, 10

You can use standardized high-stakes testing, valid, appropriate and individualized testing accommodations, teacher-made tests, and technology-based testing and assessments. You also can gather information about students' academic progress and inform your teaching by using curriculum-based measurement, dynamic assessment, learning journals/logs, think-aloud techniques, and self-evaluation questionnaires/interviews/checklists, observations, active responding systems, educational games, and error analysis. Students' learning progress also can be assessed by using authentic/performance assessment, portfolio assessment, and instructional rubrics and by examining their IEPs and promotion and graduation rates.

How Can I Grade My Students in Inclusive Settings?

CEC 1, 5, 7, 8, 9; PRAXIS 3; INTASC 8, 9, 10

You can grade students in your inclusive classroom by considering and addressing legal issues; identifying the purpose of grades; agreeing on the nature and impact of differentiated instruction techniques; selecting grading systems that support differentiated instruction and communication; addressing the special challenges and situations of students and teachers; and using effective practices that support the teaching, learning, and grading processes.

How Can I Evaluate the Social and Behavioral Performance of My Students?

CEC 5, 7, 8, 9;` PRAXIS 3; INTASC 8, 9, 10

You can evaluate the impact of your inclusion program on your students' social and behavioral performance by using observational and sociometric techniques, and self-concept and attitudinal measures.

How Can I Measure Perceptions of My Inclusive Classroom?

CEC 1, 4, 5, 8, 9, 10; PRAXIS 3; INTASC 8, 9, 10

You can measure students', teachers', and family members' perceptions of your inclusive classroom program by using questionnaires and interviews.

How Can I Improve the Effectiveness of My Inclusive Classroom?

CEC 1, 4, 5, 8, 9, 10; PRAXIS 3; INTASC 8, 9, 10

You can work with others to analyze data on the impact of your inclusive classroom to validate program strengths, identify program components that need revision, and determine strategies for improving the program.

Glossary

Abandonment   An individual's decision not to use an educational service or device (e.g., students not using a specific assistive technology device because it makes them feel different from their peers).

Ableism   The belief that individuals with disabilities are in need of assistance, fixing, and pity.

Absence seizure   (also referred to as *petit mal*) A type of seizure characterized by a brief period in which the individual loses consciousness, appears to be daydreaming, looks pale, and drops any objects he or she is holding.

Academic learning games   Games that motivate students to practice skills and concepts learned in lessons.

Acceptability   The extent to which professionals view a specific curricular and teaching accommodation as easy to use, effective, appropriate for the setting, fair, and reasonable.

Accommodation   Changes in curriculum, instruction, and assessment that allow students to participate in and access all aspects of inclusive classrooms and schools without significantly altering the nature of the activity.

Acculturation   The extent to which members of one culture adapt to a new culture.

Acquired condition   A condition due to an illness or accident.

Acquired Immune Deficiency Syndrome (AIDS)   A viral condition that destroys an individual's defenses against infections.

Acronyms   (also referred to as *first-letter mnemonics*) A mnemonic device that fosters memory by creating a meaningful word or phrase using the first letter of the words or phrases to be remembered.

Acrostics   A mnemonic device that triggers recall by employing a sentence based on the first letter of the words to be memorized.

Adapted textbook   A textbook that presents the same content as the on-grade textbook but at a lower readability level.

Advance and post organizers   Written or oral statements, activities, and/or illustrations that offer students a framework for determining and understanding the essential information in a learning activity.

Affinity support groups   Groups made up of individuals who share common traits.

Aimline   The diagonal broken line starting at the left and ending on the right side of a graph depicting data from a curriculum-based measurement that establishes the expected rate of student learning and provides a reference point for judging students' progress and making decisions about their instructional program.

Alphabetic principle   The ability to associate letters with their corresponding sounds.

Alternative teaching   A co-teaching instructional arrangement where one teacher works with a smaller group or individual students while the other teacher works with a larger group. This arrangement is used to individualize instruction, remediate skills, promote mastery, or offer enrichment based on students' needs.

Anecdotal record   (also referred to as a *narrative log* or *continuous recording*) A narrative of the events that took place during an observation.

Anorexia   (also referred to as *anorexia nervosa*) A refusal to eat and a disturbed sense of one's body shape or size, which results in a skeletal thinness and loss of weight that is denied by the individual.

Antecedents   The events, stimuli, objects, actions, and activities that precede and trigger the behavior.

Anticipation guide   An advance organizer that introduces students to new content by having them respond to several teacher-generated oral or written statements or questions concerning the material.

Anticipatory set   A statement or an enjoyable activity that introduces the material in a lesson and motivates students to learn it by relating the goals of the lesson to their prior knowledge, interests, strengths, and future life events.

Applets   Brief online interactive demonstrations and manipulatives that offer animated and visual presentations of a range of mathematical content.

A priori model   A model for coordinating a student's instructional program whereby supportive services educators introduce and teach content that supports the content to be learned in the general education classroom.

Articulation disorders   Disorders that are characterized by omissions, substitutions, distortions, and additions of sounds.

Asperger syndrome   A condition characterized by being literal and fact oriented, having rigid verbal skills and a narrow range of interests, and adhering strictly to routines, which weakens one's social functioning and ability to understand the viewpoints of others.

Assistive technology device An item, piece of equipment, or product system—whether bought, modified, or customized—that is used to increase, maintain, or improve the functional capabilities of an individual with a disability.

Assistive technology service Any service that directly assists an individual with a disability to select, acquire, or use an assistive technology device, including physical, occupational, and speech therapy.

Asthma A respiratory ailment causing difficulty in breathing due to constriction and inflammation of the airways.

Ataxia A type of cerebral palsy characterized by difficulties in balancing and using the hands.

Athetosis (also referred to as *dyskinetic*) A type of cerebral palsy characterized by uncontrolled and irregular movements usually occurring in the arms, hands, or face.

Attention deficit disorder (ADD) A psychiatric condition characterized by a persistent pattern of inattention, impulsivity, and/or hyperactivity-impulsivity that is more frequent and severe than is typically observed in individuals at a comparable level of development.

Attribution training Technique for teaching students to analyze the events and actions that lead to success and failure.

Audiometric test A test that measures the intensity and frequency of sounds one can hear.

Aura (also called *prodrome*) A sensation and a symptom indicating that a seizure is imminent.

Authentic assessment (also referred to as *performance assessment*) A type of assessment where students work on meaningful, complex, relevant, open-ended learning activities that reveal their ability to apply the knowledge and skills they have learned to contextualized problems and real-life settings.

Author's chair A collaborative group writing technique where students read aloud their completed written products to their peers, who discuss its positive features and ask questions about strategy, meaning, and writing style.

Autism (also referred to as *pervasive developmental disorder* [PDD]) A condition marked by significant difficulties in verbal and nonverbal communication, socialization, and behavior that typically occurs at birth or within the first 3 years of life.

Autism spectrum disorder (ASD) A broad continuum of cognitive and neurobehavioral conditions that typically include impairments in socialization and communication coupled with repetitive patterns of behavior.

Backward design A process for planning units of instruction and individual lessons by which assessments are first determined and then used to guide the design and sequence of the instructional activities students will engage in to achieve mastery of the identified learning outcomes.

Baseline A measurement of students' performance or behavior prior to the initiation of an intervention.

Basic interpersonal communication skills (BICS) The social language skills that guide students in developing of social relationships and engaging in casual face-to-face conversations (e.g., "Good morning. How are you?").

Research indicates that students typically take up to 2 years to develop BICS in a second language.

Behavioral Intervention Plan (BIP) A plan focusing on how the learning environment will change to address a student's behavior, characteristics, strengths, and challenges that includes specific measurable goals for appropriate behaviors, and the individuals, interventions, supports, and services responsible for helping the student achieve these goals.

Belief systems The values and perspectives that inform a family's world view, way of life, priorities, and decision making.

Big ideas Critical topics, concepts, issues, problems, experiences, or principles that assist students in organizing, interrelating, and applying information so that meaningful links can be established between the content and students' lives.

Bilingual education An educational program that uses both the students' native and the new language and the culture of students to teach them.

Binge eating disorder A condition that typically involves repeated instances of secretive binge eating that lead to feelings of guilt.

Bipolar disorder A persistent condition resulting in individuals having fluctuating moods that vary from depression to a mania that may be characterized by grandiose, provocative, or aggressive thoughts and actions; recklessness; increased energy, distractibility, and activity levels; and a reduced need for sleep.

Bridge system An approach where students are encouraged to be bidialectical and to understand that different dialects are used in different situations.

Bulimia (also referred to as *bulima nervosa*) A binging on food followed by repeated attempts to purge oneself of the excess calories by vomiting, taking medications or laxatives, fasting, or exercising.

Caption statements Brief descriptions that identify portfolio items, provide the context in which they were produced, and reflect on why they were selected.

Cerebral palsy A condition caused by damage to the central nervous system before birth or during one's early years that affects voluntary motor functions and muscle tension or tone.

Childhood disintegrative disorder A condition associated with a loss of speech and other previously learned skills and the presence of other autistic-like behaviors following an initial period of normal development.

Choice statements Comments that prompt students to choose between engaging in positive behavior and accepting the consequences associated with continued misbehavior.

Classwide peer tutoring A type of cooperative learning arrangement that involves randomly dividing the class into two groups and setting up tutoring dyads within both groups. During the first 10 to 15 minutes of the period, one student tutors the other. The members of each dyad then reverse their roles and continue for another equal time period. After this procedure is repeated throughout the week, students take individual tests and receive points for each correct response. All points earned by the groups are totaled at the end of the week, and the group with the most points is acknowledged through badges, stickers, certificates, public posting of names, or additional free time.

Code switching   A phenomenon commonly observed in individuals learning a second language that is characterized by using words, phrases, expressions, and sentences from one language while speaking another language.

Cognitive/academic language proficiency (CALP)   The language skills that relate to literacy, cognitive development, and academic development in the classroom (e.g., photosynthesis, onomatopoeia, and least common denominator). Research indicates that it often takes students up to 7 years to develop and use these language skills.

Cognitive Strategy Instruction in Writing (CSIW)   An intervention that incorporates an instructional sequence involving teacher and student dialogues, prompting and other scaffolding strategies, collaborative student groups, and modeling and guided practice to teach students to independently use a range of learning strategies designed to improve their reading and writing.

Collaborative consultation   (also referred to as *collaborative problem solving*) A process involving professionals working together to problem-solve and implement mutually agreed-on solutions to prevent and address students' learning and behavioral difficulties and to coordinate instructional programs.

Collaborative discussion teams   A cooperative technique used during teacher-directed presentations where students work in groups to periodically respond to discussion questions, react to material presented, or predict what will happen or be discussed next. Groups also are asked to share their responses and summarize the main points and check each other's comprehension at the end of presentations.

Comic strip conversations   A variation of social story that only uses pictorials to depict events and prosocial behavioral responses.

Community-based learning programs   Programs where students are placed in community-based settings that offer them opportunities to learn a range of functional skills, including community-related skills (e.g., shopping, using public transportation), vocational skills, domestic skills (e.g., cooking, cleaning), and functional academic skills (e.g., reading signs, using money).

Competency-oriented approach   A way of viewing and dealing with students that focuses on their strengths and what they can do rather than seeing them in terms of their challenges and what they cannot do.

Competitive employment   Employment that involves working as a regular employee in an integrated setting with co-workers who do not have disabilities and being paid at least the minimum wage.

Comprehensive planning team   A group made up of professionals and family members, with the student when appropriate, that makes important decisions regarding the education of students with disabilities.

Conduct disorders   "A repetitive and persistent pattern of behavior in which the basic rights of others or major age-appropriate societal norms or rules are violated" (American Psychiatric Association, 2000, p. 93).

Congenital condition   A condition present at birth.

Congruence   A logical relationship among the curriculum, learning goals, teaching materials, and strategies used in the general education classroom, and supportive services programs.

Consequences   The events, stimuli, objects, actions, and activities that follow and maintain the behavior.

Contract   A written agreement between teachers and students that outlines the behaviors students will demonstrate and the consequences that the teacher will provide.

Contract grading   A grading system that involves teachers and students developing a contract outlining the learning goals/objectives, the amount and nature of the learning activities and differentiation techniques, and the products students must complete, as well as the procedures for evaluating learning products and assigning grades.

Cooperative group testing   A testing system that involves students working collaboratively on open-ended tasks that have nonroutine solutions.

Cooperative learning   An instructional arrangement where students work with their peers to achieve a shared academic goal rather than competing against or working separately from their classmates.

Corrective feedback   A type of feedback often used to show students how to work more effectively that involves identifying errors and showing students how to correct them.

Co-teaching   (also called *cooperative* or *collaborative teaching*) A teaching arrangement whereby teachers and ancillary support personnel work together to educate all students in a general education classroom. Educators involved in co-teaching share responsibility and accountability for planning and delivering instruction, evaluating, grading, and disciplining all of their students.

Criterion-referenced grading systems   Grading systems that involve reporting on students' mastery within the curriculum.

Criterion-referenced testing   Tests that allow teachers to compare student's performance with a specific level of skill mastery.

Critical questions   Questions that ask students to provide personal judgments and reactions to the content and to apply and evaluate the information presented to other situations.

Cultural universals   Needs and experiences that exist in all cultures, albeit in different ways.

Curriculum-based measurement   A type of assessment that provides individualized, direct, and repeated measures of students' proficiency and progress in content derived directly from students' instructional programs and the curriculum.

Curriculum compacting   Allowing students who demonstrate mastery at the beginning of a unit of study to work on new and more challenging material or student-selected topics via alternate learning activities.

Curriculum overlapping   A curricular accommodation that involves teaching a diverse group of students individualized skills from different curricular areas.

Daily/weekly note   A brief note that alerts families to the accomplishments and improvements in their children and other issues of interest or concern.

Daily/weekly progress reports   A written record of a student's performance in school.

Deaf   Students who have a hearing loss that is so severe (70 to 90 decibels or greater) that they are not able to process linguistic information through hearing, with or without amplification, which adversely affects educational performance.

Deinstitutionalization   The movement of individuals with special needs from institutional settings to community-based settings.

Depression   A persistent condition characterized by an overwhelming sadness, apathy, irritability, and hopelessness, along with a persistent loss of interest and enjoyment in everyday pleasurable activities.

Descriptive grading   A grading system that involves teachers writing comments related to students' academic progress in terms of mastery of the curriculum.

Diabetes   A chronic metabolic condition where the body does not produce enough insulin, resulting in such symptoms as frequent requests for liquids, repeated trips to the bathroom, unhealthy skin color, headaches, vomiting and nausea, failure of cuts and sores to heal, loss of weight despite adequate food intake, poor circulation as indicated by complaints about cold hands and feet, and abdominal pain.

Digital divide   The phenomena associated with the barriers that students from culturally and linguistically diverse backgrounds, students living in poverty, students with disabilities, and female students may encounter that limit their access to and use of technology in their homes and schools.

Digital textbooks   (also referred to as *electronic textbooks* or *e-textbooks*) Electronic versions of textbooks that can be read aloud via computers or handheld devices.

Disability simulations   Activities in which students experience how it feels to have a disability.

Disordered eating   A generalized condition that refers to individuals who are preoccupied by the size and/or shape of their bodies and limit their eating and engage in compulsive exercise.

Disparate impact   Examines the extent to which treating all students the same way has differential outcomes for members of different groups (e.g., letters written in English are sent home to all families inviting them to attend a meeting, and a smaller percentage of families from linguistically diverse backgrounds attend the meeting).

Disparate treatment   Treating students differently because of their characteristics and membership in a group (e.g., students from culturally and linguistically diverse backgrounds are disciplined differently than others for the same offense).

Disproportionate representation   (also called *disproportionality*) The presence of students from a specific group in an educational program that is higher or lower than one would expect based on their representation in the general population of students.

Down syndrome   A condition associated with difficulties in learning and expressive and receptive language development and relative strengths in visual short-term memory.

Duration recording   An observational recording system where the observer notes how long the behavior occurred.

Dynamic assessment   A type of assessment that involves examining how students react to and benefit from instruction by using a test-teach-retest model.

Empty concepts   A term used to refer to concepts that may not exist in other cultures and languages (e.g., certain time and color concepts).

English as a Second Language (ESL)   (also referred to as *English to Speakers of Other Languages* [ESOL]) Usually a pull-out program where content instruction and communication occur only in English, and the students' native culture and language are used to develop their skills in understanding, speaking, reading, and writing English.

Environmental assessment   A process that involves analyzing the critical features of learning environments that affect student performance.

Epilepsy   A condition characterized by seizures that occur on a regular basis.

Error analysis   A method used to examine students' responses to identify areas of difficulty and patterns in the ways students approach a task. Error analysis usually focuses on identifying errors related to inappropriate use of rules and concepts, rather than careless random errors or those caused by lack of training.

Ethnomathematics   The connection between mathematics and students' cultural backgrounds and world cultures.

Event recording   An observational recording system where the observer records the number of behaviors that occur during the observation period.

Expansion   A natural language technique where teachers present a language model by expanding on a student's incomplete sentences or thoughts.

Expatiation   A natural language technique where teachers add new information to the comments of students.

Expressive language   The ability to express one's ideas in words and sentences.

Extended families   Households where children live that are headed by family members or individuals other than their parents.

Extrinsic motivation   Refers to one taking actions as a result of external consequences such as tangible rewards and approval from others.

Fluency disorders   Difficulties associated with the rate and rhythm of an individual's speech. Stuttering is the most prevalent fluency disorder.

Formative assessment   The use of assessment strategies during instruction to monitor students' learning progress and to use this information to make ongoing decisions about teaching effectiveness and ways to improve it.

Fragile X syndrome   A condition associated with learning, speech, and language difficulties, and autistic-like behaviors.

Framed outline   A type of study guide that consists of an ordered list of the main points with key words blanked out, which are then filled in by students while reading the selection or listening to a lecture in class.

Free-rider effect   A consequence that sometimes occurs when using cooperative learning where some group members fail to contribute and allow others to do the majority of the work.

Functional behavioral assessment (FBA) A person-centered, multimethod, problem-solving process that involves gathering information to determine why, where, and when a student uses behaviors and identifying the variables that appear to lead to and maintain the behaviors and planning appropriate interventions that address the purposes the behaviors serve for students.

Functional curriculum A curriculum that focuses on skills that students need to function independently.

General feedback A type of feedback in which responses are identified as correct or incorrect.

General math vocabulary Mathematical terms that have different meanings outside the world of mathematics (e.g., negative numbers).

Generalization The transfer of training and use of skills across a variety of settings and situations.

Generalized anxiety disorder A anxiety disorder characterized by chronically worrying, difficulty relaxing, and frequent complaints of physical ailments such as stomachaches and headaches.

Global hypotheses Statements that address how factors in the student's life in school, at home, and in the community have an impact on a behavior.

Graphic organizer (also referred to as a *structured overview*) A visual-spatial illustration (i.e., webs, matrices, time lines, process chains, cycles, and networks) of the key terms that comprise concepts and their interrelationships.

Hard of hearing Students with mild or severe hearing losses (20 to 70 decibels) who are often able to use some spoken language to communicate.

Hidden curriculum The unstated, culturally based social skills and rules that are essential to successful functioning in classrooms, schools, and social situations.

High-incidence disabilities Refers to learning disabilities, mild intellectual disabilities, mild emotional/behavioral disorders, and speech/language impairments that make up the vast majority of disabilities experienced by students. These disability conditions also are sometimes referred to as *mild disabilities.*

High-stakes assessment Assessments, typically involving standardized testing, whereby the results are used to make extremely important decisions about students and their educational programs.

High-stakes testing A term used to refer to tests whose results are used to make important decisions about students' educational programs, including grade-level promotion and graduation.

High-technology devices Assistive technology devices that are usually electronic, costly, and commercially produced and that may require some training to use them effectively, such as electronic communication systems, and motorized wheelchairs.

Hinging The use of items whose correct answers require students to answer preceding questions correctly.

Homebound instruction An arrangement for students who cannot attend school whereby a teacher delivers instruction in the student's home.

Homeless children Children who do not have a regular and adequate residence and may be living with others, in cars, motels, bus or train stations, campgrounds, or shelters.

Human immunodeficiency virus (HIV) A virus that causes AIDS that is passed from one person to another through the exchange of infected body fluids.

Hyperglycemia A condition characterized by high blood sugar levels that can cause one to be thirsty, tired, and lethargic and have dry, hot skin, loss of appetite, difficulty breathing, and breath that has a sweet, fruity odor.

Hyperlexia A condition characterized by advanced reading abilities and significant difficulties in comprehending what is read, using expressive language, and socializing with others.

Hypertext (also referred to as *hypermedia*) A computerized teaching system that provides alternative nonsequential and nonlinear formats for mastering content, including additional text, specialized graphics, audio, digital video clips, animated presentations, and computer-produced speech and sound effects.

Hypertonia A type of cerebral palsy characterized by movements that are jerky, exaggerated, and poorly coordinated.

Hypoglycemia A condition characterized by low blood sugar levels that can cause one to be confused, drowsy, inattentive, irritable, dizzy, perspiring, shaking, and hungry, with headaches and a pale complexion.

Hypotonia A type of cerebral palsy characterized by loose, flaccid musculature and difficulty sometimes maintaining balance.

IEP grading system A grading system in which the individualized goals, differentiation techniques, and performance criteria on students' IEPs serve as the reference point for judging student progress and assigning grades.

Impartial hearing officer An individual, selected by the school district from a list of approved persons, who hears disputes between families and school districts regarding the education of students with disabilities.

Inclusion An educational philosophy for structuring schools so that all students are educated together in general education classrooms.

Individual accountability A component of cooperative learning that involves group members understanding that each group member is responsible for contributing to the group and learning the material. It is often established by giving individualized tests or probes, adding group members' scores together, assigning specific parts of an assignment to different group members, randomly selecting group members to respond for the group, asking all members of the group to present part of the project, asking students to keep a journal of their contributions to the group, or tailoring roles to the ability levels of students.

Individualized Education Program (IEP) A written, individualized plan listing the special education and related services students with disabilities will receive to address their unique strengths and challenges.

Individualized technology assessment A process for determining the assistive technology devices and services that students with disabilities should receive.

Inferential questions Questions that require students to provide answers that are not explicitly stated in the presentation and instructional materials and that ask students to analyze, compare, and synthesize information presented.

Instructional rubrics (also referred to as *rubrics*) Statements specifying the criteria associated with different levels of proficiency for evaluating student performance. *Holistic* rubrics require teachers to select one level of performance or rating that best represents the quality of the learning product. *Analytic* rubrics have several categories of indicators, which are rated separately, allowing teachers to differentiate levels of performance within and among the categories.

Instructive feedback A type of feedback designed to promote learning by giving students extra information and teaching on the task or content.

Intellectual disabilities A term used to replace *mental retardation* that refers to a condition that occurs prior to age 18 that involves significant limitations both in intellectual functioning and in adaptive behavior as expressed in conceptual, social, and practical adaptive skills.

Interspersed requests (also referred to as *preferenced-based teaching, pretask requests, high-probability request sequences,* and *behavioral momentum*) A technique to decrease students' avoidance and challenging behaviors by asking them to perform several easier or preferred tasks that they can complete in a short period of time.

Interval recording (also referred to as *time sampling*) An observational recording system where the observation period is divided into equal intervals, and the observer records whether the behavior occurred during each interval.

Intrinsic motivation Refers to one taking actions as a result of internally based consequences such as a sense of mastery and accomplishment.

IQ-Achievement Discrepancy Model A process for identifying students with learning disabilities by determining whether there is a significant gap between their learning potential and academic achievement.

I WILL cards Index cards containing first-person statements that prompt students to engage in appropriate behavior (e.g., "When someone says hello, I will . . .").

Jigsaw A type of cooperative learning arrangement that involves dividing students into groups, with each student assigned a task that is essential in reaching the group's goal. Every member makes a contribution that is integrated with the work of others to produce the group's product.

Keyword method A mnemonic device that associates the new vocabulary word with a word that sounds similar to an easy-to-remember illustration.

Language dominance The language in which the student is most fluent.

Language experience reading approach An instructional approach to teaching reading that is based on the belief that what students think about, they can talk about; what students can say, they can write or have someone write for them; and what students can write, they can read.

Language preference The language in which the student prefers to communicate, which can vary depending on the setting.

Language proficiency The degree of skill in speaking the language(s); includes receptive and expressive language skills.

Language-related disorders Disorders related to one's ability to understand and communicate meaning.

Latency recording An observational recording system where the observer records how long it takes an individual or individuals to begin a task after receiving instructions to begin.

Learning journals (also referred to as *learning logs*) An assessment technique that involves students writing comments in their journals/logs related to what they learned, how they learned it, what they do not understand, why they are confused, and what help they would like to receive.

Learning strategies Techniques that teach students how to learn, behave, and succeed in academic and social situations and ways to effectively and efficiently organize, remember, and retrieve important content; solve problems; and complete tasks independently.

Learning together approach A type of cooperative learning arrangement that involves teams determining how they will approach a task. All group members are involved in the team's decisions, and each group produces one product, which represents the combined contributions of all group members, with each student in the group receiving the group grade.

Least restrictive environment (LRE) An individually based principle that calls for schools to educate students with disabilities as much as possible with their peers who do not have disabilities.

Leisure education Educational experiences that teach students to function independently during free-time activities at school, at home, and in the community; decide which leisure activities they enjoy; participate in leisure and recreational activities with others; and engage in useful free-time activities.

Level grading A grading system that involves using a numeric or letter subscript to indicate a specific level of curriculum mastery. For example, a B_3 grade can indicate that a student is performing in the B range on a third-grade level of curriculum mastery.

Linguistic approach A rule-governed spelling approach in which instruction focuses on the rules of spelling and patterns related to whole words.

Linguistically based testing accommodations Testing accommodations designed to minimize the extent to which students' language proficiency affects their test performance, including ways to adjust the language and readability of test items and directions so that they are appropriate for students' varying language and reading levels.

Listening guide A type of teacher-prepared note-taking form that contains a list of important terms and concepts that parallels the order in which they will be presented in class.

Literal questions Questions that focus on content derived from class presentations and instructional materials and ask students to recall, name, list, or describe information presented.

Literature circles (also referred to as *literature discussion groups or book clubs*) Small groups of students who work collaboratively to share their reactions to and discuss various aspects of books that all group members have decided to read.

Literature response journals Journals where students describe their reactions to and thoughts about the material they have been reading, as well as any questions they have.

Low-incidence disabilities   Refers to physical, sensory, and more significant disabilities that make up a small percentage of the disabilities experienced by students.

Low-technology devices   Assistive technology devices that are usually nonelectronic, inexpensive, homemade, readily available, and easy to use, such as pencil holders and strings attached to objects.

Mainstreaming   The partial or full-time programs that educate students with disabilities with their general education peers.

Map Action Planning System (MAPS)   A person-centered planning strategy used to develop IEPs and inclusion plans.

Mastery-level grading   A grading system that involves teachers and students dividing course content into a hierarchy of skills and determining appropriate learning activities and differentiation techniques based on an initial assessment of students' individual needs. After students complete these learning activities and receive the appropriate differentiation techniques, they demonstrate their mastery of the content by performing an activity or taking a test. This process is repeated until all skills are mastered.

Mediation   A process whereby families and school districts meet to attempt to resolve differences regarding the education of students with disabilities.

Medically fragile   A term used to describe students with chronic and progressive conditions who require the use of specialized technological health care procedures to maintain their health and/or provide life support.

Mental retardation   A disability condition whereby students demonstrate significantly subaverage general intellectual functioning, existing concurrently with deficits in adaptive behavior and manifested during the developmental period, which adversely affects their educational performance. Although the term *mental retardation* continues to be used in the IDEA, the field of special education uses the term *intellectual disabilities* to refer to individuals previously identified as having mental retardation (see the glossary definition of *intellectual disabilities*).

Mentors   Successful individuals who guide and assist others in being successful by modeling appropriate qualities and behaviors; teaching and sharing knowledge; listening to the thoughts and feelings of protégés; offering advice, support, and encouragement; and promoting protégés to others.

Migrant students   Students whose parents or guardians are migratory agricultural workers (including dairy and fishing workers) and who, in the preceding 36 months, have moved from one school district to another to accompany their parents or guardians.

Model-lead-test   An instructional sequence that involves teachers modeling and orally presenting the material to be learned, helping students understand it through prompts and practice, and testing students' mastery.

Multicultural education   An educational philosophy that seeks to help teachers acknowledge and understand the increasing diversity in society and in the classroom, and to see their students' diverse backgrounds as assets that can support student learning and the learning of others.

Multilevel teaching   A curricular accommodation where students are given lessons in the same curricular areas as their peers but at varying levels of difficulty.

Multiple grading   A grading system where numeric/letter numerical grades are based on multiple factors: achievement, effort, and level of curriculum difficulty. Grades for these factors can then be averaged or weighted to produce a composite final grade.

Networks   (also called *line diagrams*) Diagrams involving points connected via lines that are most appropriate for word problems that ask students to put objects in a specific order.

Newcomer programs   Programs designed to help immigrant students adjust that offer students academic and support services to help them make the transition to and succeed in general education classrooms.

Noise-induced hearing loss   A gradual hearing loss resulting from repeated exposure to loud noises.

Nonverbal learning disabilities   A type of learning disability that is characterized by difficulties processing nonverbal, visual-spatial information, and communications such as body language, gestures, and the context of linguistic interactions.

Normalization   A principle for structuring society so that the opportunities, social interactions, and experiences of individuals with disabilities parallel those of adults and children without disabilities.

Norm-referenced grading systems   Grading systems that involve giving numeric or letter grades to compare students using the same academic standards.

Norm-referenced testing   Tests that provide measures of performance that allow teachers to compare a student's score with the scores of others.

Number sense   The understanding of numbers and counting and number relationships, patterns, and operations.

Numbered Heads Together   A cooperative technique used to review and check student understanding of orally presented information that involves (a) assigning students to mixed-ability groups of three or four; (b) giving each student in each group a number (1, 2, 3, 4); (3) breaking up the oral presentation by periodically asking the class a question and telling each group, "Put your heads together and make sure that everyone in your group knows the answer"; and (d) having the groups end their discussion, calling a number and selecting one of the students with that number to answer, and asking the other students with that number to agree with or expand on the answer.

Occupational therapist   A licensed professional who deals with the upper extremities and fine motor abilities; works with students to prevent, restore, or adapt to impaired or lost motor functions; and helps students develop the necessary fine motor skills to perform everyday actions independently.

Ocular motility   The ability to track stationary and moving visual stimuli.

One teaching/one helping   A co-teaching instructional arrangement where one teacher instructs the whole class while the other teacher circulates to collect information on students' performance or to offer help to students. This arrangement is used to take advantage of the expertise of one teacher in a specific subject area, while allowing the other teacher to monitor and assist students.

Oral quizzing   A technique in which the teacher allots time at the end of the class to respond to students' questions and to ask questions based on the material presented.

Otherwise qualified   Extent to which an individual can do something regardless of the presence of a disability.

Overrepresentation   The presence of students from a specific group in an educational program being higher than one would expect based on their representation in the general population of students.

Panic disorder   An anxiety disorder where specific types of events cause one to become fearful and to experience emotional discomfort and a variety of physical symptoms such as shortness of breath, heart palpitations, and excessive sweating and fainting.

Parallel alternative curriculum (PAC) materials   Materials that supplement the textbook by providing students with alternative ways to master critical information.

Parallel talk   A natural language technique that involves describing an event that students are seeing or doing.

Parallel teaching   A co-teaching instructional arrangement where both teachers teach the same material at the same time to two equal groups of students. This arrangement is used to lower the student–teacher ratio to teach new material, to review and practice material previously taught, or to encourage student discussions and participation.

Paraphrase passport   A technique used to give each student in a group a chance to participate and to share comments and reactions with others that involves asking students to paraphrase the statements of their teammate who has just spoken and then share their own ideas and perspectives.

Partial seizure   A seizure that affects only a limited part of the brain.

Patterned book   A book that uses a predictable and repeated linguistic and/or story pattern.

Peer mediation   Programs that train students to use communication, problem-solving, and critical thinking skills to mediate conflicts between students.

Peer tutoring   A type of cooperative learning arrangement where one student tutors and assists another in learning a new skill.

Perceived function   The purposes or reasons why a student engages in a specific behavior.

Person-centered planning   (also referred to as *student-centered planning*) A process that guides the delivery of services that recognizes the importance of the roles that students and their families play as advocates in identifying meaningful goals and appropriate strategies and services for meeting them. Person-/student-centered planning also employs a variety of assessment procedures to identify the strengths, preferences, personal characteristics, cultural, linguistic, and experiential backgrounds and challenges of students and their families.

Pervasive developmental disorder—not otherwise specified (PDD-NOS)   (also referred to as *atypical autism*) A condition that resembles autism but is usually not as severe or extensive.

Phonemic awareness   (also referred to as phonological awareness) The processing and manipulation of the different sounds that make up words and the understanding that spoken and written language are linked.

Phonetic spelling approach   A rule-governed spelling approach based on learning to apply phoneme–grapheme correspondence within parts of words.

Phonetic-based reading approaches   An instructional approach to teaching reading that is based on helping students recognize and understand the phonological features of language and of individual words to use strategies for decoding or "sounding out" new and unknown words.

Physical therapist   A licensed professional who focuses on the assessment and training of the lower extremities and large muscles and helps students strengthen muscles, improve posture, and increase motor function and range.

Picture book   Short books that use pictures and illustrations to enhance the reader's understanding of the meaning and content of the story.

Planned ignoring   (also referred to as *extinction*) A technique for reducing inappropriate behavior that involves withholding positive reinforcers such as teacher attention.

Podcast   Audio- and video-based broadcasts available via the Internet that present information about a specific topic or allow viewing of a recorded event or learning activity.

Portfolio assessment   A type of assessment that involves teachers, students, and family members working together to create a continuous and purposeful collection of various authentic student products across a range of content areas throughout the school year that show the process and products associated with student learning. A *showcase* portfolio presents the student's best work and is often used to help students enter a specialized program or school or apply for employment. A *reflective* portfolio helps teachers, students, and family members reflect on students' learning, including attitudes, strategies, and knowledge. A *cumulative* portfolio shows changes in the products and process associated with students' learning throughout the school year. A *goal-based* portfolio has preset goals and items are selected to fit those goals, such as goals from a student's IEP. A *process* portfolio documents the steps and processes a student has used to complete a piece of work.

Positive interdependence   A component of cooperative learning that involves students understanding that they must work together to achieve their goal. It is usually fostered by using cooperative learning activities with mutual goals, role interdependence and specialization, resource sharing, and group rewards.

Positive peer reporting   A procedure that involves students publicly praising their classmates for engaging in prosocial behaviors.

Positive reductive procedures   (also referred to as *differential reinforcement techniques*) A technique for reducing inappropriate behavior that involves reinforcing and increasing a positive behavior that cannot coexist with the misbehavior.

Positive reinforcement   An action taken or a stimulus is given after a behavior occurs that increases the rate of the behavior or makes it more likely that the behavior will occur again.

Positive reinforcers   Actions or stimuli that increase the probability of a repeated behavior.

Post hoc model   A model for coordinating a student's instructional program whereby supportive instruction reinforces skills previously introduced and taught in the general education classroom.

Power cards   An adaptation of social stories that links the prosocial behaviors to be fostered to the student's special interests.

Prader-Willi syndrome   A condition associated with cognitive and sequential processing difficulties, obsessive-compulsive behaviors, and relative strengths in integrating stimuli into a unified whole.

Pragmatics   The functional and cultural rules that guide communication and language usage.

Praise or reinforcement ratio   The ratio between the number of positive and negative statements you direct toward your students.

Precision requests   A technique that involves directing a student to engage in positive behavior by using a polite and calm voice to state the student's name, and a concise description of the desired behavior, and then waiting 5 seconds for the student to respond appropriately.

Premack's principle   (also referred to as *Grandma's rule*) Allowing students to do something they like if they complete a less popular task first.

Prereferral system   A problem-solving process whereby a team of educators assist teachers in addressing individual students that occurs prior to considering students for placement in a special education program.

Presentation mode testing accommodations   Testing accommodations that change the way test questions and directions are presented to students.

Preteaching   A technique used to prepare students for the academic, behavioral, and social expectations of a new classroom that involves introducing them to the curriculum, teaching style, and instructional format they will encounter in the new class.

Previewing   Methods that give students opportunities to read or listen to text prior to reading. *Listening* previewing involves students listening and following along as an adult or peer reads the selection aloud or having them read along with a classmate or adult. Other previewing strategies include *oral* previewing, where the students read the passage aloud prior to the whole-class reading session; and *silent* previewing, where students read the passage silently before the reading session.

Priming   A technique that involves familiarizing students with new activities, information, routines, and materials prior to introducing them in class.

Problem-based learning   (also referred to as *discovery learning*) Learning approaches that allow students to work on complex open-ended problems and issues that have multifaceted solutions. The technique involves having students work collaboratively to create and examine solutions to real-life and community-based situations and problems.

Process feedback   A type of feedback often used with students who are unsure of their correct responses that involves praising students and reinforcing their answer by restating why it was correct.

Progress monitoring   A process of conducting ongoing assessments to examine students' learning progress and the effectiveness of teaching practices and the instructional program.

Progressive improvement grading   A grading system that involves teachers providing students with feedback and differentiation techniques as they work on a range of individualized assessment and learning activities throughout the grading period, with only their performance on assessment and learning activities during the final weeks of the grading period being used to assess their growth and determine grades.

Prompts   Visual, auditory, or tactile cues used by teachers to foster student learning and help correct students' errors related to a lack of understanding. Prompts can include *manual* prompts, in which the student is physically guided through the task; *modeling* prompts, in which the student observes someone else perform the task; and *oral* prompts that describe how to perform the task and that show the student the correct process or answer in a graphic presentation.

Prosody   An aspect of reading fluency that relates to a student's ability to read smoothly with proper levels of stress, pauses, volume, and intonation.

Protégés   Individuals who receive mentoring.

Psychomotor seizure   A seizure characterized by a short period in which the individual remains conscious and engages in inappropriate and bizarre behaviors.

Quality of life   One's feelings of well-being, social involvement, and opportunities to achieve one's potential.

Reading fluency   The speed and accuracy with which one reads orally.

Receptive language   The ability to understand spoken language.

Redirection   Making comments or using behaviors designed to interrupt the misbehavior and prompt students to use appropriate behavior and work on the activity at hand.

Reinforcement or preference survey   A technique that asks students to identify the reinforcers they prefer.

Related services   A range of services and aids available to students with disabilities that are selected to help them benefit from a special education program (e.g., speech and language therapy, counseling, school health and social work services, occupational and physical therapy, etc.).

Repeated reading   A technique where students are given numerous opportunities to practice reading short (between 50 and 200 words), appropriate, and relevant materials at the reader's independent or instructional level until they can read them fluently.

Residential school   A school where students live and participate in a 24-hour program.

Resource room   A classroom where students go to receive individualized remedial instruction, usually in small groups.

Response cards   "Cards, signs, or items that are simultaneously held up by students in the class to display their responses to questions or problems presented by the teacher" (Heward et al., 1996, p. 5).

Response mode testing accommodations   Testing accommodations that involve making changes in the way students respond to test items or determine their answers.

Response to intervention (RTI)   A multitiered identification and instructional model for assessing the extent to which students respond to a series of more intensive research-based interventions.

Rett syndrome   A progressive genetic disorder found in girls that affects one's neurological development and often includes a loss of previously learned skills, repetitive hand movements, and a loss of functional use of one's hands.

Right-only feedback   A type of feedback in which only correct responses are identified.

Role delineation   A technique used to give each student in a group a chance to participate that involves assigning a specific role to each member of the group.

Round robin   A technique used to give each student in a group a chance to participate and to share comments and reactions with others that involves asking each student to orally share their contributions to the group's response.

Round table   A technique used to give each student in a group a chance to participate and to share comments and reactions with others that involves passing a pencil and paper around so that each student can contribute to the group's response.

RSS Site Summary (RSS)   (also referred to as *Really Simple Syndication*) A technology-based service that compiles and sends brief summaries of the content on particular topics available at various Web sites so that users can identify relevant online content without having to access multiple Web sites.

Rubrics   See *Instructional rubrics.*

Rule-governed spelling approaches   An instructional approach to teaching spelling based on helping students learn to use morphemic and phonemic analysis and basic spelling rules.

Scaffolding   Techniques for breaking down comments students don't understand or a task students have difficulty performing into smaller components that promote understanding or mastery. Scaffolding methods include relating the task to students' prior knowledge, using visual and language cues, modeling effective strategies, and highlighting the key parts of the task.

Schoolwide positive behavioral interventions and supports   A collaborative data-based decision-making process for establishing and implementing a continuum of schoolwide and individualized instructional and behavioral strategies and services that are available and used to support the learning and positive behavior of all students.

Selective mutism   A condition whereby children avoid communication in selective social situations or environments, despite possessing the ability to speak and communicate.

Self-awareness   The ability of individuals to identify and express their preferences, strengths, and challenges.

Self-determination   One's ability to identify and take actions to achieve one's goals in life.

Self-esteem   An individual's sense of self-efficacy.

Self-evaluation   (also referred to as *self-assessment*) A type of self-management intervention strategy where students evaluate their behavior according to a standard or scale.

Self-instruction   A type of self-management intervention strategy where students regulate their behaviors by verbalizing to themselves the questions necessary to identify problems and generate and evaluate appropriate solutions.

Self-management intervention strategies   (also referred to as *cognitive-behavioral interventions*) Techniques where students are actively involved in monitoring and changing their behaviors.

Self-monitoring   (also referred to as *self-recording*) A type of self-management intervention strategy where measures record their behaviors using a data collection system.

Self-referenced grading systems   Grading systems that involve students being graded based on their progress in comparison with their past performance, ability levels, effort, and special needs.

Self-Regulated Strategy Development (SRSD) model   An explicit instructional model for teaching students to use a variety of learning strategies and related acronyms designed to enhance their self-regulation skills and attitudes across a range of writing genres.

Self-reinforcement   A type of self-management intervention strategy where students evaluate their behavior and then deliver self-selected reinforcers.

Self-talk   A natural language technique that consists of talking out loud about your actions, experiences, or feelings.

Semantic feature analysis (SFA)   A technique for teaching vocabulary that involves creating a visual that guides students in comparing vocabulary words to determine the ways they are similar and different.

Semantic map   A diagram or map of the key ideas and words that make up the topic.

Semantic web   (also referred to as *semantic map*) A visual depiction of important points and concepts, as well as the relationships between these points and concepts.

Send a Problem   A cooperative technique used during teacher-directed presentations where students work in groups to periodically make up questions that are sent to and answered by other groups.

Separation anxiety disorder   An anxiety disorder that is triggered by separation from one's primary caregivers.

Service learning   A type of community-based learning program where students perform and reflect on experiential activities that foster their learning and benefit the community. These programs provide real-life experiences that teach students about their communities, civic responsibility, and the world of work and career choices (e.g., working in a program for elderly persons or preschoolers).

Shared book reading   A technique where students and teachers read a new or familiar story together, discussing aspects of the story as they read it.

Sheltered English   (also referred to as *content-based instruction*) An ESL technique that uses cues, gestures, technology, manipulatives, drama, and visual stimuli and aids to teach new vocabulary and concepts.

Silent period   A process often observed in individuals learning a second language that is marked by a focus on processing language and an avoidance of speaking.

Skeleton/slot/frame outline   (also referred to as *guided notes*) A type of teacher-prepared note-taking form that presents a sequential overview of the key terms and main points as an outline made up of incomplete statements with visual cues such as spaces, letters, and labels that can help students determine the amount and type of information to be recorded.

Social phobia   An anxiety disorder related to interactions in public settings.

Social responsibility   An interest in and concern for the well-being of others and the environment.

Social stories   A technique for teaching social skills that involves use of individualized, brief, easy-to-follow stories written from students' viewpoints that describe social situations, the perspectives of others, relevant social cues, appropriate social behaviors, and ways to engage in and the consequences for demonstrating appropriate behaviors.

Sociometric techniques   Techniques that involve students responding confidentially to a series of questions that identify the social relationships they prefer and their friendships.

Special day school   A school solely for students with special needs.

Special education   An integral part of the educational system that involves delivering and monitoring a specially designed and coordinated set of comprehensive, research-based instructional and assessment practices and related services to students with learning, behavioral, emotional, physical, health, or sensory disabilities. These instructional practices and services are tailored to identify and address the individual challenges and strengths of students; to enhance their educational, social, behavioral, and physical development; and to foster equity and access to all aspects of society.

Specific hypotheses   Statements that address the reasons why a behavior occurs and the conditions related to the behavior, including the possible antecedents and consequences.

Specific learning disability   A disorder in one or more of the basic psychological processes involved in understanding or using spoken or written language, which may appear as an impaired ability to listen, think, speak, read, write, spell, or do mathematical calculations. The term *learning disability* includes such conditions as perceptual handicaps, brain injury, minimal brain dysfunction, dyslexia, and developmental aphasia. It does not include learning problems that are primarily the result of visual, hearing, or motor handicaps; mental retardation; emotional disturbance; or environmental, cultural, or economic disadvantage.

Speech and language impairment   A communication disorder such as stuttering, impaired articulation, a language impairment, or a voice impairment that adversely affects educational performance.

Speech-related disorders   Disorders related to the verbal aspects of communicating and conveying meaning.

Spend-a-buck   A technique that helps groups reach a consensus by giving each group member four quarters, which are then spent on the group's options.

Spina bifida   A condition caused by the failure of the vertebrae of the spinal cord to close properly, which usually results in paralysis of the lower limbs, as well as loss of control over bladder function.

Station teaching   A co-teaching instructional arrangement where both teachers teach different or review content at the same time to two equal groups of students, and then switch groups and repeat the lesson. This arrangement is used when teaching material that is difficult but not sequential, when several different topics are important,

or when reviewing material is an important objective of the lesson.

Story grammars   Outlines of the ways stories are organized that often identify the main characters, storylines, and conflicts, and end in a reading selection.

Story starters/enders   A type of writing prompt in which students are given the first or last paragraph of a story or the initial or ending sentence of a paragraph, and then are asked to complete the story or paragraph.

Strategic note-taking form   A type of teacher-prepared note-taking form that contains teacher-prepared cues designed to guide students in taking notes and prompt them to use effective note-taking skills during oral presentations.

Student with a visual disability   An impairment in vision that, even with correction, adversely affects educational performance. The term includes both partial sight and blindness.

Students who are functionally blind   Students who require Braille for effective reading and writing; they can use their vision to move through the classroom and classify objects by color.

Students who are gifted and talented   Students who give evidence of high performance capability in areas such as intellectual, creative, artistic, or leadership capacity, or in specific academic fields, and who require special services or activities not ordinarily provided by the school.

Students who are totally blind   Students who have no vision or limited light perception and do not respond to visual input.

Students who have low vision   Students who can see nearby objects but have trouble seeing them at a distance.

Students with emotional disturbance   Students who exhibit one or more of the following characteristics over a long period of time and to a marked degree, which adversely affects their educational performance: (a) inability to learn that cannot be explained by intellectual, sensory, or health factors; (b) inability to build or maintain good relationships with peers and teachers; (c) inappropriate behaviors or feelings under normal circumstances; (d) a general, pervasive mood of unhappiness or depression; (e) a tendency to develop physical symptoms or fears associated with personal or school problems. The term includes students who have schizophrenia. It does not include students who are socially maladjusted unless they are emotionally disturbed.

Students with interrupted formal education (SIFE)   Students who have encountered circumstances causing them to have limited, erratic, or nonexistent access to schooling.

Students with obsessive and compulsive disorders (OCD)   Students who feel compelled to think about or perform repeatedly an action that appears to be meaningless and irrational and is against their own will.

Students with oppositional and defiant behaviors   Students who engage in a variety of behaviors designed to resist the requests of authority figures.

Students with orthopedic impairments   Students who have a severe orthopedic impairment that adversely affects educational performance. The term includes impairments caused by congenital anomaly (e.g., clubfoot, absence of some member, etc.), impairments caused by disease (e.g., poliomyelitis, bone tuberculosis, etc.), and impairments from other causes (e.g., cerebral palsy, amputations, and fractures or burns that cause contractures).

Students with other health impairments   Students who have limited strength, vitality, or alertness—including a heightened alertness to environmental stimuli that results in limited alertness with respect to the educational environment—that is due to chronic or acute health problems such as attention deficit disorder, a heart condition, tuberculosis, rheumatic fever, nephritis, asthma, sickle-cell anemia, epilepsy, lead poisoning, leukemia, diabetes, or Tourette's syndrome, which adversely affects educational performance. The term *other health impaired* can also include students who are medically fragile or those who may be dependent on technological devices for ventilation, oxygen, and tube feeding.

Study guides   Guides that contain a series of statements, questions, and/or activities that help students identify and learn critical information from textbooks, instructional materials, and oral presentations.

Subtechnical math vocabulary   Mathematical terms that have multiple meanings across different contexts and content areas (e.g., area and degrees).

Summary of Performance (SOP)   A statement provided to students with disabilities when they graduate or exceed the age for receiving special education services that addresses their academic achievement and functional performance and includes suggestions for achieving their postsecondary goals.

Summative assessment   The use of assessments at the end of instruction to assess student mastery of specific content, topics, concepts and skills taught, and to communicate this information to others.

Supported employment   Employment that involves providing ongoing assistance and services as individuals learn how to obtain competitive employment, perform and hold a job, travel to and from work, interact with co-workers, work successfully in integrated community settings, and receive a salary that reflects the prevailing wage rate.

Sustained silent reading   A group-oriented reading technique that involves students and teachers silently reading self-selected materials for an extended period of time.

Symbolic math vocabulary   Mathematical terms that relate to abstract numbers and abbreviations that are hard to define and understand.

System of least prompts   An instructional sequence that involves (a) giving students the opportunity to respond without assistance, (b) providing assistance (if needed) by modeling the correct response and having students imitate it, and (c) physically guiding students in making the correct response (if needed).

Talking chips   A technique that helps students in a group participate equally that involves giving each of them a set number of chips, which are placed in the middle of the work area each time a student speaks. Once students use up all their chips, they cannot speak until all group members have used all their chips.

Task analysis   A systematic process of stating and sequencing the parts of a task to determine what subtasks must be performed to master the task.

T-chart   A technique designed to teach social and cooperative skills that involves (a) drawing a horizontal line and writing the skill on the line; (b) drawing a vertical line from the middle of the horizontal line; (c) listing students' responses to the question "What would the skill look like?" on one side of the vertical line; and (d) listing students' responses to the question "What would the skill sound like?" on the other side of the vertical line.

Teacher mentoring   Frequent collaborative interactions between experienced, effective teachers and new teachers to address the challenges that new teachers encounter.

Team-teaching   A co-teaching instructional arrangement where both teachers plan and teach a lesson together. This arrangement is used when it is important to blend the talents and expertise of teachers or to foster interactions with students.

Technical math vocabulary   Mathematical terms that have one meaning (e.g., *square* or *rational number*).

Testing accommodation   Variations in testing administration, environment, equipment, technology, and procedures that allow students to access testing programs and accurately demonstrate their competence, knowledge, and abilities without altering the nature and integrity of the tests and the results or giving students an advantage over others.

Text windowing   The simultaneous visual highlighting of text as it is read to help students focus on, monitor, and proofread their writing.

Think-aloud techniques   Techniques in which students state the processes they are using and describe their thoughts while working on a task.

Think-pair-share   A cooperative technique used to help students reflect on and master content that involves (a) pairing students randomly; (b) giving students a question, problem, or situation; (c) asking individual students to think about the question; (d) having students discuss their responses with their partners; and (e) selecting several pairs to share their thoughts and responses with the class.

Tiered assignments   A curricular accommodation involving teachers identifying the concepts that need to be learned and allowing students to choose to respond in alternative ways that differ in complexity and learning style.

Time delay   An instructional sequence that involves teachers varying and gradually fading out the length of time in which they present a task and prompt students so that students learn to respond quickly and independently.

Timing, scheduling, and setting testing accommodations   Adjustments with respect to where, when, with whom, and for how long and often students take tests.

Token or point economy system   A classroom management system where students earn tokens for showing appropriate behavior and redeem these tokens for reinforcers.

Tonic seizure   A type of seizure marked by sudden stiffening of the muscles.

Tonic-clonic seizure   (also referred to as *grand mal*) A type of seizure marked by loss of consciousness and bladder control, stiff muscles, saliva drooling out of the mouth, and violent body shaking. After a brief period, the individual may fall asleep or regain consciousness and experience confusion.

Total physical response (TPR)   A technique for teaching vocabulary concepts through modeling, repeated practice, and movement. In TPR, teachers state and model the concept and physically emphasize movements related to the concept.

Tourette's syndrome   An inherited neurological condition whose symptoms include involuntary multiple muscle movements and tics, and uncontrolled, repeated verbal responses such as noises (laughing, coughing, throat clearing), words, or phrases.

Trace trailing   A technique used by individuals with visual impairments to move around a classroom-, school-, or community-based location that involves touching the surfaces of objects on the path.

Track   Online lessons that guide student learning related to a specific topic by directing them to a variety of instructional activities presented by accessing a series of teacher-specified Web sites.

Transenvironmental programming   A four-step model for preparing students to transition to inclusive classrooms.

Transgendered   Individuals who do not identify themselves as either of the two sexes.

Transition services   A set of coordinated activities to improve students' academic and functional achievement and to address postsecondary goals in the areas of training, education, employment, community participation, and, where appropriate, independent living skills.

Traumatic brain injury (TBI)   An acquired injury to the brain caused by an external physical force, resulting in total or partial functional disability or psychosocial impairment, or both, that adversely affects educational performance. The term applies to open or closed head injuries resulting in impairments in one or more areas, such as cognition; language; memory; attention; reasoning; abstract thinking; judgment; problem solving; sensory, perceptual, and motor abilities; psychosocial behavior; physical functions; information processing; and speech. The term does not apply to brain injuries that are congenital or degenerative, or brain injuries induced by birth trauma.

Twice exceptional students   Students with disabilities who also are gifted and talented.

Two-tiered testing   A testing system that involves students working in collaborative groups and taking a test, with each student receiving the group grade. After the group test, students work individually on a second test that covers similar material. Students can be given two separate grades, their two grades can be averaged together into one grade, or they can be allowed to select the higher grade.

Two-way bilingual program   (also referred to as a *dual language program*) An integrated bilingual educational program that mixes students who speak languages other than English with students who speak English and offers content in each language approximately 50% of the time.

Two-way notebooks   Notebooks carried to and from school by students that allow educators and family members to exchange comments and information, ask questions, and brainstorm solutions.

Underrepresentation   The presence of students from a specific group in an educational program being lower than one would expect based on their representation in the general population of students.

Universal design   A set of principles that guide the design and delivery of products and services so that they are usable by individuals with a wide range of functional capabilities.

Universal design for learning (UDL)   An approach that guides the designing and implementation of flexible curriculum and teaching and assessment materials and strategies, learning environments, and interactions with others so that they are inclusive of all students, families, and professionals.

Verbalisms   Words or phrases that are inconsistent with sensory experiences.

Video blogs   (also referred to as *vlogs*) Blogs that contain video clips as well as text, audio files such as music or narrations, and links to other related Web sites.

Virtual reality   A technology-based application that allows individuals to experience what it feels like to see, touch, smell, and move through artificial, three-dimensional, interactive environments that present computer-generated images and accompanying text depicting real or imaginary environments.

Visual acuity   The ability to see details.

Visual field   The area one sees when viewing something straight ahead.

Voice disorders   Deviations in the pitch, volume, and quality of sounds produced.

Voice recognition systems   (also referred to as *voice-activated systems*) Computerized software systems that convert spoken words into text or into actions that activate computers and computer menus.

Weblogs   (also referred to as *blogs*) Online diaries that are easily updated regularly to present information about a topic or a group or one's activities.

Webquest   An inquiry-oriented, cooperatively structured group activity in which some or all of the information that learners interact with comes from resources on the Internet or videoconferencing.

Whole language approach   An instructional approach to teaching reading that is based on using students' natural language and experiences to foster their literacy, viewing learning as proceeding from the whole to the part, and integrating reading, writing, listening, speaking, and thinking into each lesson and activity.

Whole-word reading approaches   An instructional approach to teaching reading that is based on helping students make the link between whole words and their oral counterparts and their meaning.

Wikis   Web sites that offer content on a range of topics created and edited by users.

Wikitextbooks   Collaboratively developed and editable online textbooks.

Williams syndrome   A condition associated with anxieties and fears; heart and health problems; hypersensitivity to sound; difficulty with visual-spatial tasks; and relative strengths and talents in terms of language, sociability, verbal processing, and music.

Word cueing programs Types of software programs that offer students choices of words and phrases based on the first letters typed by students.

Word prediction programs Types of software programs that offer students choices of words and phrases based on context, word frequency (i.e., how frequently the word is used in English), word recency (i.e., how recently the word has been used by the writer), grammatical correctness, and commonly associated words and phrases.

Wraparound process A multidisciplinary, interagency, strength-based, and student- and family-focused process for collaboratively designing and delivering individualized, culturally sensitive, school- and community-based educational, counseling, medical, and vocational services to address the unique strengths, challenges, and behaviors of students and their families.

Writers' Workshop A collaborative group writing technique where students write and receive feedback from peers and teachers on topics they select. The workshop is divided into four parts: status of the class, minilessons, workshop proper, and sharing.

Wrong-only feedback A type of feedback in which only incorrect responses are identified.

References

Acrey, C., Johstone, C., & Milligan, C. (2005). Using universal design to unlock the potential for academic achievement of at-risk learners. *Teaching Exceptional Children, 35*(2), 22–31.

Adams, D. C., & Carson, E. S. (2006). Gay-straight alliances: One teacher's experience. *Journal of Poverty, 10*(2), 103–111.

Adger, C. T., Wolfram, W., & Christian, D. (2007). *Dialects in schools and communities.* Mahwah, NJ: Erlbaum.

Adreon, D., & Durocher, J. S. (2007). Evaluating the college transition needs of individuals with high-functioning autism spectrum disorders. *Intervention in School and Clinic, 42*(5), 271–279.

Agirdag, O. (2009). All languages welcomed here. *Educational Leadership, 66*(7), 20–24.

Agostino v. Felton, 117 S. Ct. (1997).

Ainscow, M. (2008). Making sure that every child matters: Towards a methodology for enhancing equity within educational systems. In C. Forlin (Ed.), *Catering for learners with diverse needs: An Asia-Pacific focus* (pp. 11–29). Hong Kong: Hong Kong Institute of Education.

Alber, S. R. (1996). Sustained silent reading: Practical suggestions for successful implementation. *Reading and Writing Quarterly: Overcoming Learning Difficulties, 12*(4), 403–406.

Alber, S. R., & Foil, C. R. (2003). Drama activities that promote and extend your students' vocabulary proficiency. *Intervention in School and Clinic, 39,* 22–29.

Alber-Morgan, S. R., Matheson Ramp, E., Anderson, L. L., & Martin, C. M. (2007). Effects of repeated readings, error correction, and performance feedback on the fluency and comprehension of middle school students with behavior problems. *The Journal of Special Education, 41*(1), 17–31.

Alberto, P. A., & Frederick, L. D. (2000). Teaching picture reading as an enabling skill. *Teaching Exceptional Children, 33*(1), 60–64.

Alberto, P. A., & Troutman, A. C. (2009). *Applied behavior analysis for teachers* (8th ed.). Upper Saddle River, NJ: Merrill/Pearson Education.

Alleman, J., Knighton, B., & Brophy, J. (2007). Social studies: Incorporating all children using community and cultural universals as the centerpiece. *Journal of Learning Disabilities, 40*(2), 166–173.

Allor, J. H., Mathes, P. G., Champlin, T., & Cheatham, J. P. (2009). Research-based techniques for teaching early reading skills to students with intellectual disabilities. *Education and Training in Developmental Disabilities, 44*(3), 356–366.

Allor, J. H., & McCathren, R. B. (2003). Developing emergent literacy skills through storybook reading. *Intervention in School and Clinic, 39,* 72–79.

Allsopp, D. H. (1999). Using modeling, manipulatives, and mnemonics with eighth-grade math students. *Teaching Exceptional Children, 32*(2), 46–54.

Allsopp, D. H., Kyger, M. M., Lovin, L., Gerretson, H., Carson, K. L., & Ray, S. (2008). Mathematics dynamic assessment: Informal assessment that responds to the needs of struggling learners in mathematics. *Teaching Exceptional Children, 40*(3), 6–17.

Allsopp, D. H., Minskoff, E. H., & Bolt, L. (2005). Individualized course-specific strategy instruction for college students with learning disabilities and ADHD: Lessons learned from a model demonstration project. *Learning Disabilities Research and Practice, 20,* 103–118.

Almodovar, A., Tomaka, J., Thompson, S., Mckinnon, S., & O'Rourke, K. (2006). Risk and protective factors among high school students on the US/Mexico border. *American Journal of Health Behavior, 30,* 745–752.

Al Otaiba, S. (2005). How effective is code-based reading tutoring in English for English learners and preservice teacher-tutors? *Remedial and Special Education, 26,* 245–254.

Al Otaiba, S., & Fuchs, D. (2002). Characteristics of children who are unresponsive to early literacy intervention: A review of the literature. *Remedial and Special Education, 23,* 300–316.

Al Otaiba, S., & Pappamihiel, N. E. (2005). Guidelines for using volunteer literacy tutors to support reading instruction for English language learners. *Teaching Exceptional Children, 37*(6), 6–11.

Al Otaiba, S., & Rivera, M. O. (2006). Individualizing guided oral reading fluency instruction for students with emotional and behavioral disorders. *Intervention in School and Clinic, 41,* 144–149.

Al Otaiba, S., & Smartt, S. (2003). Summer sound camp: Involving parents in early literacy intervention for children with speech and language delays. *Teaching Exceptional Children, 35*(3), 30–35.

Alper, S., Schloss, P. J., & Schloss, C. N. (1996). Families of children with disabilities in elementary and middle school: Advocacy models and strategies. *Exceptional Children, 62*(3), 261–270.

Alpern, C. S., & Zager, D. (2007). Addressing communication needs of young adults with autism in a college-based inclusion program. *Education and Training in Developmental Disabilities, 42*(4), 428–437.

Alter, G. T. (2009). Challenging the textbook. *Educational Leadership, 66*(8), 72–75.

Alter, P. J., Wyrick, A., Brown E. T., & Lingo, A. (2008). Improving mathematics problem solving skills for students with challenging behavior. *Beyond Behavior, 17*(3), 2–7.

Altieri, J. L. (2008). Fictional characters with dyslexia: What are we seeing in books? *Teaching Exceptional Children, 41*(1), 48–57.

Alvarez McHatton, P. (2007). Listening and learning from Mexican and Puerto Rican single mothers of children with disabilities. *Teacher Education and Special Education, 30*(4), 237–248.

Alvarez McHatton, P., & Daniel, P. L. (2009). Co-teaching at the pre-service level: Special education majors collaborate with English education majors. *Teacher Education and Special Education, 31*(2), 118–131.

American Council for Drug Education. (2009). *Signs and symptoms of drug use*. Retrieved July 22, 2009, from http://www.acde.org/parent/signs.htm.

American Psychiatric Association. (2000). *Diagnostic and statistical manual of mental disorders* (4th ed., text rev.). Washington, DC: Author.

Amtmann, D., Abbott, R. D., & Berninger, V. W. (2008). Identifying and predicting classes of response to explicit phonological spelling instruction during independent composing. *Journal of Learning Disabilities, 41*(3), 218–234.

Anderson, D. (2006). In and out surprises in reading comprehension instruction. *Intervention in School and Clinic, 41,* 175–179.

Anderson, D. H., Fisher, A., Marchant, M., Young, K. R., & Smith, J. A. (2006). The cool-card intervention: A positive support strategy for managing anger. *Beyond Behavior, 16*(1), 3–13.

Anderson, D. H., Munk, J. H., Young, K. R., Conley, L., & Caldarella, P. (2008). Teaching organizational skills to promote academic achievement in behaviorally challenged students. *Teaching Exceptional Children, 40*(4), 6–13.

Anderson, P. L. (2000). Using literature to teach social skills to adolescents with LD. *Intervention in School and Clinic, 35*(5), 271–279.

Anderson, P. L., & Corbett, L. (2008). Literature circles for students with learning disabilities. *Intervention in School and Clinic, 44*(1), 25–33.

Anderson-Inman, L. (2009). Supported eText: Literacy scaffolding for students with disabilities. *Journal of Special Education Technology, 24*(3), 1–8.

Anderson-Inman, L., Terrazas-Arellanes, F., & Slabin, U. (2009). Supported eText in captioned videos: A comparison of expanded versus standard captions on student comprehension of educational content. *Journal of Special Education Technology, 24*(3), 21–34.

Andrade, H. G. (2000). Using rubrics to promote thinking and learning. *Educational Leadership, 57*(5), 13–18.

Angell, M. E., Bailey, R. L., & Larson, L. (2008). Systematic instruction for social-pragmatic language skills in lunchroom settings. *Education Training in Developmental Disabilities, 43*(3), 342–359.

Angell, M. E., Stoner, J. B., & Shelden, D. L. (2009). Trust in education professionals: Perspectives of mothers of children with disabilities. *Remedial and Special Education, 30*(3), 160–176.

Ankey, E. A., & Wilkins, J., & Spain, J. (2009). Mothers' experiences of transition planning for their children with disabilities. *Teaching Exceptional Children, 41*(6), 28–36.

Antshel, K. M., & Joseph, G. R. (2006). Maternal stress in nonverbal learning disorder: A comparison with reading disorder. *Journal of Learning Disabilities, 39,* 194–205.

Araujo, B. E. (2009). Best practices in working with linguistically diverse families. *Intervention in School and Clinic, 45*(2), 116–123.

Armstrong, T. (2009). Multiple intelligences in the classroom (3rd ed.). Alexandria, VA: ASCD.

Arroyos-Jurado, E., & Savage, T. A. (2008). Intervention strategies for serving students with traumatic brain injury. *Intervention in School and Clinic, 43*(4), 252–254.

Arter, P. S. (2007). The positive alternative learning supports program: Collaborating to improve student success. *Teaching Exceptional Children, 40*(2), 38–47.

Arthaud, T. J., Aram, R. J., Breck, S. E., Doelling, J. E., & Bushrow, K. M. (2007). Developing collaboration skills in pre-service teachers: A partnership between general and special education, *Teacher Education and Special Education, 30*(1), 1–12.

Artiles, A. J., & Bal, A. (2008). The next generation of disproportionality research: Toward a comparative model in the study of equity in ability differences. *The Journal of Special Education, 42*(1), 4–11.

Artiles, A. J., Rueda, R., Salazar, J. J., & Higareda, I. (2005). Within-group diversity in minority disproportionate representation: English language learners in urban school districts. *Exceptional Children, 71,* 283–300.

Artiles, A. J., & Zamora-Duran, G. (1997). *Reducing disproportionate representation of culturally and linguistically diverse students in special and gifted education*. Reston, VA: Council for Exceptional Children.

Asaro, K., & Saddler, B. (2009). Effects planning instruction on a young writer with Asperger syndrome. *44*(5), 268–275.

Ash, G. E., Kuhn, M. R., & Walpole, S. (2009). Analyzing "inconsistencies" in practice: Teachers' continued use of round robin reading. *Reading and Writing Quarterly, 25*(1), 87–103.

Ashton, T. M. (1999). Spell checking: Making writing meaningful in the inclusive classroom. *Teaching Exceptional Children, 32*(2), 24–27.

Auchincloss, C., & McIntyre, T. (2008). iPod "teach": Increased access to technological learning supports through use of the iPod touch. *Journal of Special Education Technology, 23*(2), 45–49.

August, D., Calderon, M., Carlo, M., & Nuttall, M. (2006). Developing literacy in English-language learners: An examination of the impact of English-only versus bilingual instruction. In P. D. McCardle, & E. Hoff (Eds.), *Childhood bilingualism: Research on infancy through school age* (pp. 91–106). Cleveland, UK: Multilingual Matters.

August, D., Carlo, M., Dressler, C., & Snow, C. (2005). The critical role of vocabulary development in English language learners. *Learning Disabilities Research and Practice, 20,* 50–57.

Ault, M. J., & Collins, B. C. (2009, April). *Inclusion of persons with disabilities and their families in faith-based communities.* Presentation at the annual meeting of the Council for Exceptional Children, Seattle.

Austin, V. L., & Sciarra, D. T. (2010). *Children and adolescents with emotional and behavioral disorders.* Upper Saddle River, NJ: Merrill/Pearson Education.

Ayres, K. M., & Langone, J. (2005). Evaluation of software for functional skills instruction: Blending best practice with technology. *Technology in Action, 1*(5), 1–8.

Ayres, K. M., & Langone, J. (2008). Video supports for teaching students with developmental disabilities and autism: Twenty-five years of research and development. *Journal of Special Education Technology, 23*(3), 1–8.

Azzam, A. M. (2008). Left behind-By design. *Educational Leadership, 65*(4), 91–92.

Babkie, A. M. (2006). 20 ways to be proactive in managing classroom behavior. *Intervention in School and Clinic, 41,* 184–187.

Babkie, A. M., & Provost, M. C. (2002). Select, write, and use metacognitive strategies in the classroom. *Intervention in School and Clinic, 37,* 173–177.

Baca, L. M. (2008, April). *Special education and Ells.* Presentation at the Bilingual Education Technological Assistance Center conference, Albany, NY.

Baca, L. M., & Baca, E. (2004). Bilingual special education: A judicial perspective. In L. M. Baca, & H. T. Cervantes (Eds.), *The bilingual special education interface* (4th ed., pp. 76–99). Upper Saddle River, NJ: Merrill/Pearson Education.

Baca, L. M., & Cervantes, H. T. (2004). *The bilingual special education interface* (4th ed.) Upper Saddle River, NJ: Merrill/Pearson Education.

Badgett, J. L., & Christmann, E. P. (2009a). *Designing elementary instruction and assessment: Using the cognitive domain.* Thousand Oaks, CA: Corwin Press.

Badgett, J. L., & Christmann, E. P. (2009b). *Designing middle and high school instruction and assessment: Using the cognitive domain.* Thousand Oaks, CA: Corwin Press.

Badke, W. (2009). Stepping beyond Wikipedia. *Educational Leadership, 66*(6), 54–55.

Baer, D. R., Invernizzi, M., & Johnston, F. (2006). *Words their way: Letter and picture sorts for emergent spellers.* Upper Saddle River, NJ: Merrill/Pearson Education.

Baer, D. R., Invernizzi, M., Johnston, F., & Templeton (2010). *Words their way: Letter and picture sorts for emergent spellers* (2nd ed.). Upper Saddle River, NJ: Pearson Education.

Bailet, L. L., Repper, K. K., Piasta, S. B., & Murphy, S. P. (2009). Emergent literacy intervention for prekindergarteners at risk of reading failure. *Journal of Learning Disabilities, 42*(4), 336–355.

Baker, S. K., Chard, D. J., Ketterlin-Geller, L. R., Apichatabutra, C., & Doabler, C. (2009). Teaching writing to at-risk students: The quality of evidence for self-regulated strategy development. *Exceptional Children, 75*(3), 303–320.

Baker, S., Gersten, R., & Graham, S. (2003). Teaching expressive writing to students with learning disabilities: Research-based applications and examples. *Journal of Learning Disabilities, 36,* 109–123.

Baker, S., Gersten, R., & Scanlon, D. (2002). Procedural facilitators and cognitive strategies: Tools for unraveling the mysteries of comprehension and the writing process, and for providing meaningful access to the general curriculum. *Learning Disabilities Research and Practice, 17,* 65–77.

Bambara, L. M., Browder, D. M., & Koger, F. (2006). Home and community. In M. E. Snell & F. Brown (Eds.), *Instruction of students with severe disabilities* (6th ed., pp. 526–568). Upper Saddle River, NJ: Merrill/Pearson Education.

Banda, D. R., Grimmett, E., & Hart, S. L. (2009). Activity schedules: Helping students with autism spectrum disorders in general education classrooms manage transition issues. *Teaching Exceptional Children, 41*(4), 16–21.

Banda, D. R., Matuszny, R. M., & Therrien, W. J. (2009). Enhancing motivation to complete math tasks using high-preference strategy. *Intervention in School and Clinic, 44*(3), 146–150.

Banks, E., Bacon, J., Young, K., & Jackson, F. R. (2007). Perceptions of African American and European American teachers on the education of African American boys. *Multiple Voices, 10*(1 & 2), 94–106.

Banks, J. A. (2008). *An introduction to multicultural education* (4th ed.). Boston: Allyn & Bacon.

Banks, J. A. (2009). *Teaching strategies for ethnic studies* (8th ed.). Boston: Allyn & Bacon.

Banks, S., (2004). Voices of tribal parents and caregivers of children with special needs. *Multiple Voices, 7*(1), 33–47.

Barab, S. A., Gresalfi, M., & Arici, A. (2009). Why educators should care about games. *Educational Leadership, 67*(1), 76–80.

Bardon, L. A., Dona, D. P., & Symons, F. J. (2008). Extending classwide social skills interventions to at-risk minority students: A preliminary application of randomization tests combined with single-subject design methodology. *Behavioral Disorders, 33*(3), 141–152.

Bargerhuff, M. E., & Wheatly, M. (2004). Teach with CLASS: Creating laboratory access for science students with disabilities. *Teacher Education and Special Education, 27,* 318–321.

Barta, J. J., & Pleasant-Jetté, C. M. (2005). Integrating anti-bias education. In D. A. Byrnes & G. Kiger (Eds.), *Common bonds: Anti-bias teaching in a diverse society* (3rd ed., pp. 119–134). Olney, MD: Association of Childhood Education International.

Bartholomew, B. (2008). Sustaining the fire. *Educational Leadership, 65*(6), 55–60.

Bartlett, L. D., Etscheidt, S., & Weisenstein, G. R. (2007). *Special education law and practice in public schools* (2nd ed.). Upper Saddle River, NJ: Merrill/Pearson Education.

Barton, P. E. (2004). Why does the gap persist? *Educational Leadership, 62*(3), 9–13.

Barton-Arwood, S. M., Wehby, J. H., & Falk, K. B. (2005). Reading instruction for elementary-age students with emotional and behavioral disorders: Academic and behavioral outcomes. *Exceptional Children, 72*, 7–27.

Battle, D. A., Dickens-Wright, L. L., & Murphy, S. (1998). How to empower adolescents: Guidelines for effective self-advocacy. *Teaching Exceptional Children, 30*(3), 28–32.

Bausch, M. E., & Ault, M. J. (2008). Assistive technology implementation plan: A tool for improving outcomes. *Teaching Exceptional Children, 41*(1), 6–17.

Bay, M., & Parker-Katz, M. (2009). Perspectives on induction of beginning special educators: Research summary, key program features, and the state of state-level policies. *Teacher Education and Special Education, 32*(1), 17–32.

Beal, C., Mason-Bolick, C. M., & Martorella, P. (2009). *Teaching social studies in middle and secondary schools* (5th. ed.). Upper Saddle River, NJ: Pearson Education.

Beam, A. P. (2009). Standards-based differentiation: Identifying the concept of multiple intelligence for use with students with disabilities. *TEACHING Exceptional Children Plus, 5*(4) Article 1. Retrieved [July 26, 2009] from http://escholarship.bc.edu/education/tecplus/vol5/iss4/art1.

Beck, A. R., Stoner, J. B., Bock, S. J., & Parton, T. (2008). Comparison of PECS and the use of a VOCA: A replication. *Education and Training in Developmental Disabilties, 43*(2), 198–216.

Beddow, P. A., Kettler, R. J., & Elliott, S. N. (2008). TAMI: Test accessibility and modification inventory. Retrieved September 22, 2008, from http://peabody.vanderbilt.edu/TAMI.xml.

Begeny, J. C., & Martens, B. K. (2007). Inclusionary education in Italy: A literature review and call for more empirical research. *Remedial and Special Education, 28*(2), 80–94.

Beland, K. (2007). Teaching social and emotional confidence. *Educational Leadership, 64*(7), 68–71.

Bellini, S., Peters, J. K., Benner, L., & Hopf, A. (2007). A meta-analysis of school-based social skills interventions for children with autism spectrum disorders. *Remedial and Special Education, 28*(3), 153–162.

Bellon-Harn, M. L., & Harn, W. E. (2008). Scaffolding strategies during repeated storybook reading: An extension using a voice output communication aid. *Focus on Autism and Other Developmental Disabilities, 23*(2), 112–124.

Bender, W. N. (1997). *Understanding ADHD: A practical guide for teachers and parents* Upper Saddle River, NJ: Merrill/Pearson Education.

Bender, W. N. (2008). *Learning disabilities: Characteristics, identification, and teaching strategies* (6th ed.). Upper Saddle River, NJ: Merrill/Pearson Education.

Bender, W. N., & Larkin, M. J. (2009). *Reading strategies for elementary students with learning difficulties: Strategies for RTI* (2nd ed.). Thousand Oaks, CA: Corwin Press.

Bender, W. N., & McLaughlin, P. J. (1997). Weapons violence in schools: Strategies for teachers confronting violence and hostage situations. *Intervention in School and Clinic, 32*(4), 211–216.

Bender, W. N., Shubert, T. H., & McLaughlin, P. J. (2001). Invisible kids: Preventing school violence by identifying kids in trouble. *Intervention in School and Clinic, 37*, 105–111.

Berendt, P. R., & Koski, B. (1999). No shortcuts to success. *Educational Leadership, 56*(6), 45–47.

Berger, G. W., Bartley, D. L., Armstrong, N. Kaatz, D. & Benson, D. (2007). The importance of a team approach in working effectively with selective mutism: A case study. *Teaching Exceptional Children Plus, 4*(2) Article 1. Retrieved February 14, 2009, from http://escholarship.bc.edu/tecplus/vol4/iss2/art1.

Berkeley, S. (2007). Middle schoolers with reading disabilities in book club? *TEACHING Exceptional Children Plus, 3*(6) Article 5. Retrieved [August 17, 2009] from http://escholarship.bc.edu/education/tecplus/vol3/iss6/art5.

Berkeley, S., Bender, W. M., Peaster, L. G., & Saunders, L. (2009). Implementation of response to intervention: A snapshot of progress. *Journal of Learning Disabilities, 42*(1), 85–95.

Berlin, L. (2009, May 17). A web that speaks your language. *New York Times*, BU 4.

Bernad-Ripoll, S. (2007). Using a self-as-model video combined with social stories to help a child with Asperger syndrome understand emotions. *Focus on Autism and Other Developmental Disabilities, 22*(2), 100–106.

Best, S. J. (2005a). Definitions, supports, issues, and services in schools and communities. In S. J. Best, K. W. Heller, & J. L. Bigge, (Eds.), *Teaching individuals with physical, health, or multiple disabilities* (5th ed., pp. 3–29). Upper Saddle River, NJ: Merrill/Pearson Education.

Best, S. J. (2005b). Health impairments and infectious diseases. In S. J. Best, K. W. Heller, & J. L. Bigge (Eds.), *Teaching individuals with physical, health, or multiple disabilities* (5th ed., pp. 59–85). Upper Saddle River, NJ: Merrill/Pearson Education.

Best, S. J. (2005c). Physical disabilities. In S. J. Best, K. W. Heller, & J. L. Bigge (Eds.), *Teaching individuals with physical, health, or multiple disabilities* (5th ed., pp. 31–58). Upper Saddle River, NJ: Merrill/Pearson Education.

Best, S. J. (2009). Universal precautions. In K. W. Heller, P. E. Forney, P. A. Alberto, S. Best, S., & M. N. Schwartzman (Eds.), *Understanding physical, health, and multiple disabilities* (2nd ed., pp. 399–405.). Upper Saddle River, NJ: Merrill/Pearson Education.

Best, S. J., & Bigge, J. L. (2005). Cerebral palsy. In S. J. Best, K. W. Heller, & J. L. Bigge (Eds.), *Teaching individuals with physical, health, or multiple disabilities* (5th ed., pp. 87–109). Upper Saddle River, NJ: Merrill/Pearson Education.

Best, S. J., & Heller, K. W. (2009a). Acquired infections and AIDs. In K. W. Heller, P. E. Forney, P. A. Alberto, S. Best, & M. N. Schwartzman (Eds.), *Understanding physical, health, and multiple disabilities* (2nd ed., pp. 368–386.). Upper Saddle River, NJ: Merrill/Pearson Education.

Best, S. J., & Heller, K. W. (2009b). Congenital infections. In K. W. Heller, P. E., Forney, P. A., Alberto, S. Best, S., & M. N. Schwartzman (Eds.), *Understanding physical, health, and multiple disabilities* (2nd ed., pp. 387–398.). Upper Saddle River, NJ: Merrill/Pearson Education.

Best, S. J., Reed, P., & Bigge, J. L. (2005). Assistive technology. In S. J. Best, K. W. Heller, & J. L. Bigge (Eds.), *Teaching individuals with physical, health, or multiple disabilities* (5th ed., pp. 179–226). Upper Saddle River, NJ: Merrill/Pearson Education.

Bhattacharya, A. (2006). Syllable-based reading strategy for mastery of scientific information. *Remedial and Special Education, 27,* 116–123.

Bianco, M., Carothers, D. E., & Smiley, L. R. (2009). Gifted students with Asperger Syndrome: Strategies for strength-based programming. *Intervention in School and Clinic, 44*(4), 206–215.

Biddulph, G., Hess, P., & Humes, R. (2006). Help a child with learning challenges be successful in the general education classroom. *Intervention in School and Clinic, 41,* 315–316.

Billingsley, F., & Albertson, L. R. (1999). Finding the future for functional skills. *Journal of The Association for Persons with Severe Handicaps, 24,* 298–302.

Blachowicz, C., & Fisher, P. J. (2006). *Teaching vocabulary in all classrooms* (3rd ed.). Upper Saddle River, NJ: Merrill/Pearson Education.

Black, R. S., & Pretes, L. (2007). Victims and victors: Representation of physical disability on the silver screen. *Research & Practice for Persons with Severe Disabilities, 32*(1), 66–83.

Black-Hawkins, K., Florian, L., & Rouse, M. (2007). *Achievement and inclusion in schools.* London: Routledge.

Blair, C., & Scott, K. G. (2002). Proportion of LD placements associated with low socioeconomic status: Evidence for a gradient? *The Journal of Special Education, 39,* 14–22.

Blythe, H., & Sweet, C. (2008). Keeping your classroom C.R.I.S.P. *Thriving in Academe, 26*(2), 5–8.

Board of Education of the Hendrick Hudson Central School District v. Rowley, 102 S. Ct. 3034 (1982).

Bock, M. A. (2007). The impact of social-behavioral learning strategy training on the social interaction skills of four students with Asperger syndrome. *Focus on Autism and Other Developmental Disabilities, 22*(2), 88–95.

Bomer, R., Dworin, J. E., May, L., & Semingson, P. (2008). *Miseducating teachers about the poor: A critical analysis of Ruby Payne's claim's about poverty.* Retrieved March 15, 2009, from http://www.tcrecord.org/Content.asp?ContentId=14591.

Boon, R. T., Fore, C., Blankenship, T., & Chalk, J. (2007). Technology-based pratices in social studies instruction for students with high-incidence disabilities: A review of the literature. *Journal of Special Education Technology, 22*(4), 41–56.

Boone, R., & Higgins, K. (2003). Reading, writing, and publishing digital text. *Remedial and Special Education, 24,* 132–140.

Boone, R., & Higgins, K. (2007). The software check-list: Evaluating educational software for use by students with disabilities. *Technology in Action, 3*(1), 1–16.

Boone, R., Wolfe, P. S., & Schaufler, J. H. (1999). Written communication in special education: Meeting the needs of culturally and linguistically diverse families. *Multiple Voices, 3*(1), 25–36.

Bottge, B. A. (1999). Effects of contextualized math instruction on problem solving of average and below-average achieving students. *Journal of Special Education, 33*(2), 81–92.

Bottge, B. A. (2001). Building ramps and hovercrafts and improving math skills. *Teaching Exceptional Children, 34*(1), 16–23.

Bottge, B. A., & Hasselbring, T. S. (1999). Teaching mathematics to adolescents with disabilities in a multimedia environment. *Intervention in School and Clinic, 35*(2), 113–116.

Bottge, B. A., Heinrichs, M., Mehta, Z. D., & Hung, Y. (2002). Weighing the benefits of anchored math instruction for students with disabilities in general education classes. *Journal of Special Education, 35,* 186–200.

Bottge, B. A., Rueda, E., Serlin, R. C., Hung, Y., & Kwon, J. M. (2007). Shrinking achievement differences with anchored math problems: Challenges and possibilities. *The Journal of Special Education, 41*(1), 31–49.

Bottge, B., Rueda, E., & Skivington, M. (2006). Situating math instruction in rich problem-solving contexts: Effects on adolescents with challenging behaviors. *Behavioral Disorders, 31,* 394–407.

Bouck, E. C. (2006). Online assessments in the content areas: What are they good for? *Journal of Special Education Technology, 21*(2), 67–73.

Bouck, E. C. (2009). No Child Left Behind, the Individuals with Disabilities Education Act and functional curricula: A conflict of interest. *Education and Training in Developmental Disabilities, 44*(1), 3–13.

Bouck, E. C., Bassette, L., Taber-Doughty, T. Flanagan, S. M., & Szwed, K. (2009). Pentop computers as tools for teaching multiplication to students with mild intellectual disabilities. *Education and Training in Developmental Disabilities, 44*(3), 367–380.

Bouck, E. C., & Bouck, M. K. (2008). Does it add up? Calculators as accommodations for sixth grade students with disabilities, *Journal of Special Education Technology, 23*(2), 17–32.

Bouck, E. C., Courtad, C. A., Heutsche, A., Okolo, C. M., & Englert, C. S. (2009). The virtual history museum: A universally designed approach to social studies instruction. *Teaching Exceptional Children, 42*(2), 14–20.

Bouck, E. C., & Flanagan, S. (2009). Assistive technology and mathematics: What is there and where can we go in special education? *Journal of Special Education Technology, 24*(2), 17–30.

Bouck, E. C., Okolo, C. M., & Courtad, C. A. (2007). Technology at home: Implications for children with disabilities. *Journal of Special Education Technology, 22*(3), 43–56.

Boudah, D. J., Knight, S. L., Kostobryz, C., Welch, N., Laughter, D., & Branch, R. (2000). Collaborative research in inclusive classrooms: An investigation with reflections by teachers and researchers. *Teacher Education and Special Education, 23,* 241–252.

Boudah, D. J., Lenz, B. K., Bulgren, J. A., Schumaker, J. B., & Deshler, D. D. (2000). Don't water down: Enhance content learning through the unit organizer routine. *Teaching Exceptional Children, 32*(3), 48–56.

Boutot, E. A. (2006). Fitting in: Tips for promoting acceptance and friendships for students with autism spectrum disorders in inclusive classrooms. *Intervention in School and Clinic, 42,* 156–161.

Boutot, E. A. (2008). Using a reinforcement hierarchy to reduce prompt-dependency. *DDD Express, 19*(1), 1, 8.

Boutot, E. A. (2009). Using "I will" cards and social coaches to improve social behaviors of students with Asperger syndrome. *Intervention in School and Clinic, 44*(5), 276–281.

Boutot, E. A., & Bryant, D. P. (2005). Social integration of students with autism in inclusive settings. *Education and Training in Developmental Disabilities, 40,* 14–23.

Bowman-Perrott, L. (2009). Classwide peer tutoring: An effective strategy for students with emotional and behavioral disorders. *Intervention in School and Clinic, 44*(5), 259–267.

Boyd, B. A., Alter, P. J., & Conroy, M. A. (2005). Using their restricted interests: A novel strategy for increasing the social behaviors of children with autism. *Beyond Behavior, 14*(3), 3–9.

Boyd, B. A., Alter, P. J., & Conroy, M. A. (2005). Using their restricted interests: A novel strategy for increasing the social behaviors of children with autism. *Beyond Behavior, 14*(3), 3–9.

Boyer, M. (1998, April). *Using stamps to differentiate student assignments.* Presentation at the annual meeting of the Council for Exceptional Children, Minneapolis, MN.

Boyle, A. R., Washburn, S. G., Rosenberg, M. S., Connelly, V. J., Brinckerhoff, L. C., & Banerjee, M. (2002). Reading SLICK with new audio texts and strategies. *Teaching Exceptional Children, 35*(2), 50–55.

Boyle, J. R. (2001). Enhancing the note-taking skills of students with mild disabilities. *Intervention in School and Clinic, 36,* 221–224.

Boyle, J. R. (2008). Reading strategies for students with mild disabilities. *Intervention in School and Clinic, 44*(1), 3–9.

Boyle, J. R., & Weishaar, M. (1997). The effects of expert-generated versus student-generated cognitive organizers on the reading comprehension of students with learning disabilities. *Learning Disabilities Research and Practice, 12*(4), 228–235.

Boyle, J. R., & Weishaar, M. (2001). The effects of strategic notetaking on the recall and comprehension of lecture information for high school students with learning disabilities. *Learning Disabilities Research and Practice, 16,* 133–141.

Boyle, J. R., & Yeager, N. (1997). Blueprints for learning: Using frameworks for understanding. *Teaching Exceptional Children, 29*(4), 26–31.

Bradley, J. F., & Monda-Amaya, L. E. (2005). Conflict resolution: Preparing preservice special educators to work in collaborative settings. *Teacher Education and Special Education, 28,* 171–184.

Brady, M. P., & Rosenberg, H. (2002). Job observation and behavior scale: A supported employment assessment instrument. *Education and Training in Mental Retardation and Developmental Disabilities, 37,* 427–433.

Brandes, J. A., Ormsbee, C. K., & Haring, K. A. (2007). From early intervention to early childhood programs: Timeline for early successful transitions (TEST). *Intervention in School and Clinic, 42*(4), 204–211.

Brandon, R. R. (2007). African American parents: Improving connections with their child's educational environment. *Intervention in School and Clinic, 43*(2), 116–120.

Brandon, R., & Brown, M. R. (2009). African American families in the special education process: Increasing their level of involvement. *Intervention in School and Clinic, 45*(2), 85–90.

Brice, A. (2001, November). *Children with communication disorders: Update 2001.* Arlington, VA: ERIC Clearinghouse on Disabilities and Gifted Education.

Brice, A., & Roseberry-McKibbin, C. (2001). Choice of languages in instruction: One language or two? *Teaching Exceptional Children, 33*(4), 10–17.

Brice, A., Miller, K., & Brice, R. G. (2007). A study of English as a second language in general education classrooms. *Multiple Voices, 10*(1 & 2), 82–93.

Brigham, R., Berkley, S., Simpkins, P., & Brigham, M. (2007, Winter). Reading comprehension strategy instruction. *Current Practice Alerts, 12,* 1–4.

Brigharm, N., Morocco, C. C., Clay, K., & Zigmond, N. (2006). What makes a high school a good high school for students with disabilities. *Learning Disabilities Research and Practice, 21,* 184–190.

Bromley, B. E. (2008). Broadcasting disability: An exploration of the educational potential of a video sharing web site. *Journal of Special Education Technology, 23*(4), 1–14.

Brooke, V. A., Revell, G., & Wehman, P. (2009). Quality indicators for competitive employment outcomes: What special education teachers need to know about transition planning. *Teaching Exceptional Children, 41*(4), 58–66.

Brookhart, S. M. (2004). *Grading.* Upper Saddle River, NJ: Merrill/Pearson Education.

Brookhart, S. M. (2008). *How to give effective feedback to your students.* Alexandria, VA: Association for Supervision and Curriculum Development.

Brookhart, S. M., Moss, C., & Long, B. (2008). Formative assessment that empowers. *Educational Leadership, 66*(3), 52–57.

Brookhart, S. M., & Nitko, A. J. (2008). *Assessment and grading in classrooms.* Upper Saddle River, NJ: Merrill/Pearson Education.

Browder, D. M., Ahlgrim-Delzell, L., Courtade, G., Gibbs, S. L., & Flowers, C. (2008). Evaluation of the effectiveness of an early literacy program for students with significant developmental disabilities, *Exceptional Children, 75*(1), 33–54.

Browder, D. M., Ahlgrim-Delzell, L., Courtade-Little, G., & Snell, M. E. (2006). General curriculum access. In M. E. Snell & F. Brown (Eds.), *Instruction of students with severe disabilities* (6th ed., pp. 489–525). Upper Saddle River, NJ: Merrill/Pearson Education.

Browder, D. M., Ahlgrim-Delzell, L., Spooner, F., Mimis, P. J., & Baker, J. N. (2009). Using time delay to teach literacy to students with severe developmental disabilities. *Exceptional Children, 75*(3), 343–364.

Browder, D. M., Fallin, K., Davis, S., & Karvonen, M. (2003). Consideration of what may influence student outcomes on alternate assessment. *Education and Training in Developmental Disabilities, 38,* 255–270.

Browder, D. M., Spooner, S., Ahlgrim-Delzell, L., Harris, A. A., & Wakeman, S. (2008). A meta-analysis on teaching mathematics to students with significant cognitive disabilities. *Exceptional Children, 74*(4), 407–432.

Browder, D. M., Wakeman, S. Y., Flowers, C., Rickelman, R. J., Pugalee, D., & Karvonen, M. (2007). Creating access to the general curriculum with links to grade-level content for students with significant cognitive disabilities: An explication of the concept. *The Journal of Special Education, 41*(1), 2–16.

Brown v. Board of Education of Topeka, 347 U.S. 483 (1954).

Brown, L. M. (2005). *Girlfighting: Betrayal and rejection among girls.* New York: New York University Press.

Brown, M. R. (2009). A new multicultural population: Creating effective partnerships with multiracial families. *Intervention in School and Clinic, 45*(2), 124–131.

Brownell, M. T., & Walther-Thomas, C. (2000). An interview with Dr. Angelita Felix. *Intervention in School and Clinic, 35,* 290–293.

Brownell, M. T., Yeager, E., Rennells, M. S., & Riley, T. (1997). Teachers working together: What teacher educators and researchers should know. *Teacher Education and Special Education, 20*(4), 340–359.

Brozo, W. G. (2006). Bridges to literacy for boys. *Educational Leadership, 64*(1), 71–74.

Brozo, W. G., & Hargis, C. (2003). Using low-stakes reading assessment. *Educational Leadership, 61*(3), 60–64.

Brozo, W. G., & Puckett, K. S. (2009). *Supporting content area literacy with technology.* Upper Saddle River, NJ: Pearson Education.

Brozo, W. G., & Simpson, M. (2003). *Readers, teachers, learners: Expanding literacy across the content areas* (4th ed.). Upper Saddle River, NJ: Merrill/Pearson Education.

Bruce, S., Randall, A., & Birge, B. (2008). Colby's growth to language and literacy: The achievements of a child who is congenitally deafblind. *TEACHING Exceptional Children Plus,* 5(2) Article 6. Retrieved [July 27, 2009] from http://escholarship.bc.edu/education/tecplus/vol5/iss2/art6.

Bryant, D. P. (2005). Commentary on early identification and intervention for students with mathematics difficulties. *Journal of Learning Disabilities, 38,* 340–345.

Bryant, D. P., Bryant, B. R., Gersten, R., Scammacca, N., & Chavez, M. M. (2008). Mathematics intervention for first- and second-grade students with mathematics difficulties. The effects of tier 2 intervention delivered as booster lessons. *Remedial and Special Education, 29*(1), 20–32.

Bryant, D. P., Bryant, B. R., & Hammill, D. D. (2000). Characteristic behaviors of students with LD who have teacher-identified math weaknesses. *Journal of Learning Disabilities, 33,* 168–177, 199.

Bryant, D. P., Bryant, B. R., & Raskind, M. H. (1998). Using assistive technology to enhance the skills of students with learning disabilities. *Intervention in School and Clinic, 34*(1), 53–58.

Bryant, D. P., Kim, S. A., Hartman, P., & Bryant, B. R. (2006). Standards-based mathematics instruction and teaching

middle school students with mathematical disabilities. In M. Montague and A. K. Jitendra (Eds.), *Teaching mathematics to middle school students with learning difficulties* (pp. 7–28). New York: Guilford.

Bryant, D. P., Ugel, N., Thompson, S., & Hamff, A. (1999). Instructional strategies for content-area reading instruction. *Intervention in School and Clinic, 34*(5), 293–302.

Bucalos, A. B., & Lingo, A. S. (2005). What kind of "managers" do adolescents really need? Helping middle and secondary teachers manage classrooms effectively. *Beyond Behavior, 14*(2), 9–14.

Bucholz, J. L., Keller, C. L., & Brady, M. P. (2007). Teachers' ethical dilemmas: What would you do? *Teaching Exceptional Children, 40*(2), 60–64.

Bui, Y. N., & Turnbull, A. (2003). East meets West: Analysis of person-centered planning in the context of Asian American values. *Education and Training in Developmental Disabilities, 38,* 18–31.

Bulgren, J. A. (2006). Integrated content enhancement routines: Responding to the needs of adolescents with disabilities in rigorous inclusive secondary content classes. *Teaching Exceptional Children, 38*(6), 54–58.

Bulgren, J. A., Deshler, D. D., & Lenz, B. K. (2007). Engaging adolescents with LD in high order thinking about history concepts using integrated content enhancement routines. *Journal of Learning Disabilities, 40,* 121–133.

Bulgren, J. A., Deshler, D. D., & Schumaker, J. B. (1997). Use of a recall enhancement routine and strategies in inclusive secondary classes. *Learning Disabilities Research and Practice, 12*(4), 198–208.

Bulgren, J. A., Hock, M. F., Schumaker, J. B., & Deshler, D. D. (1995). The effects of instruction in a paired associates strategy on the information mastery performance of students with learning disabilities. *Learning Disabilities Research and Practice, 10*(1), 22–37.

Bunch, G., & Valeo, A. (2004). Student attitudes toward peers with disabilities in inclusive and special education schools. *Disability and Society, 19*(1), 61–76.

Burke, K. (2009). *How to assess authentic learning* (5th ed.). Thousand Oaks, CA: Corwin Press.

Burke, M. D., Hagan-Burke, S. Kwok, O., & Parker, R. (2009). Predictive validity of early literacy indicators from the middle of kindergarten to second grade. *The Journal of Special Education, 42*(4), 209–226.

Burns, M. K. (2002). Comprehensive system of assessment to intervention using curriculum-based assessments. *Intervention in School and Clinic, 38,* 8–13.

Burns, M. K., & Ysseldyke, J. E. (2009). Reported prevalence of evidence-based instructional practices in special education. *The Journal of Special Education, 43*(1), 3–11.

Burstein, N., Sears, S. Wilcoxen, A., Cabello, B., & Spagna, M. (2004). Moving toward inclusive practices. *Remedial and Special Education, 25,* 104–116.

Butler, D. L., Beckingham, B., & Lauscher, H. J. N. (2005). Promoting strategic learning by eighth-grade students struggling in mathematics: A report of three case studies. *Learning Disabilities Research and Practice, 20,* 156–174.

Bybee, R. W., Powell, J. C., & Trowbridge, L. W. (2008). *Teaching secondary school science: Strategies for developing scientific literacy* (9th ed.). Boston: Allyn & Bacon/Pearson Education.

Byrnes, D. A. (2005b). Sexual diversity issues in schools. In D. A. Byrnes & G. Kiger (Eds.), *Common bonds: Anti-bias teaching in a diverse society* (3rd ed., pp. 105–117). Olney, MD: Association of Childhood Education International.

Byrnes, D. A., Pray, L., & Cortez, D. (2005). Language diversity in the classroom. In D. A. Byrnes & G. Kiger (Eds.), *Common bonds: Anti-bias teaching in a diverse society* (3rd ed., pp. 75–90). Olney, MD: Association of Childhood Education International.

Byrnes, M. (2004). Alternate assessment FAQs (and Answers). *Teaching Exceptional Children, 36*(6), 58–62.

Byrnes, M. (2008). Writing explicit, unambiguous accommodations: A team effort. *Intervention in School and Clinic, 44*(1), 18–24.

Cafiero, J. M. (2008). Technology supports for individuals with autism spectrum disorders. *Technology in Action, 3*(3), 1–12.

Cahill, S. M. (2008). Teaching organizational skills through self-regulated learning strategies. *TEACHING Exceptional Children Plus,* 5(1) Article 3. Retrieved [June 19, 2009] from http://escholarship.bc.edu/education/tecplus/vol5/iss1/art3.

Calderon, M. E., & Minaya-Rowe, L. (2003). *Designing and implementing two-way bilingual programs: A step-by-step guide for administrators, teachers, and parents.* Thousand Oaks, CA: Corwin.

Callins, T. (2006). Culturally responsive literacy instruction. *Teaching Exceptional Children, 39*(2), 62–65.

Cameron, D. L., & Cook, B. G. (2007). Attitudes of preservice teachers enrolled in an infusion preparation program regarding planning and accommodations for included students with mental retardation. *Education and Training in Developmental Disabilities, 42*(3), 353–363.

Campano, G. (2007). Honoring students stories. *Educational Leadership, 65*(2), 48–55.

Campbell, M. L., & Mechling, L. C. (2009). Small group computer-assisted instruction with SMART Board technology: An investigation of observational and incidental learning of nontarget information. *Remedial and Special Education, 30*(1), 47–57.

Campbell, P. H. (2006). Addressing motor disabilities. In M. E. Snell & F. Brown (Eds.), *Instruction of students with severe disabilities* (6th ed., pp. 291–327). Upper Saddle River, NJ: Merrill/Pearson Education.

Campbell-Whatley, G. (2006). Why am I in special education and what can I do about it?: Helping students develop self-determination. *TEACHING Exceptional Children Plus,* 3(2) Article 4. Retrieved [June 20, 2009] from http://escholarship.bc.edu/education/tecplus/vol3/iss2/art4

Cancio, E. J., & Conderman, G. (2008). Promoting longevity: Strategies for teachers of students with emotional and behavioral disorders. *Beyond Behavior, 17*(3), 30–36.

Capizzi, A. M. (2008). From assessment to annual goal: Engaging a decision-making process in writing measurable IEPs. *Teaching Exceptional Children, 41*(1), 18–25.

Capizzi, A. M., & Barton-Arwood, S. M. (2009). Using curriculum-based measurement graphic organizer to facilitate collaboration in reading. *Intervention in School and Clinic, 45*(1), 14–23.

Capizzi, A. M., & Fuchs, L. S. (2005). Effects of curriculum-based measurement with and without diagnostic feedback on teacher planning. *Remedial and Special Education, 26,* 159–174.

Capper, C. A., & Pickett, R. S. (1994). The relationship between school structure and culture and student views of diversity and inclusive education. *The Special Education Leadership Review, 2*(1), 102–122.

Carnahan, C. R., Williamson, P., Clarke, L., & Sorensen, R. (2009). A systematic approach for supporting paraeducators in educational settings: A guide for teachers. *Teaching Exceptional Children, 41*(5), 34–45.

Carnine, D. W., Silbert, J., Kame'enui, E. J., Tarver, S. G., & Jungohann, K. (2006). *Teaching struggling and at-risk readers: A direct instruction approach.* Upper Saddle River, NJ: Merrill/Pearson Education.

Carr, S. C. (2002). Assessing learning processes: Useful information for teachers and students. *Intervention in School and Clinic, 37,* 156–162.

Carr, S. C. (2008). Student and peer evaluation: Feedback for all learners. *Teaching Exceptional Children, 40*(5), 24–31.

Carreker, S. (2005). Teaching spelling. In J. Birsh (Ed.), *Multisensory teaching of basic language skills* (2nd ed., pp. 257–295). Baltimore: Brookes.

Carroll, C. J. (2001). Teacher-friendly curriculum-based assessment in spelling. *Teaching Exceptional Children, 34*(2), 32–39.

Carter, E. W., Clark, N. M., Cushing, L. S., & Kennedy, C. H. (2005). Moving from elementary to middle school: Supporting a smooth transition for students with severe disabilities, *Teaching Exceptional Children, 37*(3), 32–37.

Carter, G. R. (2008). Teaching about religions and beliefs in public schools. *Education Update, 50*(8), 3.

Carter, S. L. (2008). Further conceptualization of treatment acceptability. *Education and Training in Developmental Disabilities, 43*(2), 135–143.

Cartledge, G. (1999). African-American males and serious emotional disturbance: Some personal perspectives. *Behavioral Disorders, 25,* 76–79.

Cartledge, G., & Kourea, L. (2008). Culturally responsive classrooms for culturally diverse students with and at risk for disabilities. *Exceptional Children, 74*(3), 351–371.

Cartledge, G., Kea, C. D., & Ida, D. J. (2000). Anticipating differences—Celebrating strengths: Providing culturally competent services for students with serious emotional disturbance. *Teaching Exceptional Children, 32*(3), 30–37.

Cartledge, G., Wang, W., Blake, C., & Lambert, M. C. (2002). Middle school students with behavior disorders acting as social skill trainers for peers. *Beyond Behavior, 11*(3), 14–18.

Casteel, C. P., Isom, B. A., & Jordan, K. F. (2000). Creating confident and competent readers. *Intervention in School and Clinic, 36,* 67–74.

Castellani, J., & Jeffs, T. (2001). Emerging reading and writing strategies using technology. *Teaching Exceptional Children, 33*(5), 60–67.

Causton-Theoharis, J. N. (2009). *The paraprofessional's handbook for effective support in inclusive classrooms.* Baltimore: Brookes.

Causton-Theoharis, J. N., & Malmgren, K. W. (2005). Increasing peer interactions for students with severe disabilities via paraprofessional training. *Exceptional Children, 71,* 431–444.

Cawley, J. F. (2001). Perspectives: Mathematics interventions and students with high-incidence disabilities. *Remedial and Special Education, 23,* 2–6.

Cawley, J. F., Fitzmaurice, A. M., Sedlak, R., & Althaus, V. (1976). *Project math.* Tulsa, OK: Educational Progress.

Cawley, J. F., & Foley, T. E. (2002). Connecting math and science for all students. *Teaching Exceptional Children, 34*(4), 14–19.

Cawley, J. F., Foley, T. E., & Doan, T. (2003). Giving students with disabilities a voice in the selection of arithmetical content. *Teaching Exceptional Children, 36*(1), 8–16.

Cawley, J. F., Foley, T. E., & Miller, J. (2003). Science and students with mild disabilities: Principles of universal design. *Intervention in School and Clinic, 38,* 160–171.

Cawley, J. F., Hayden, S., Cade, E., & Baker-Kroczynski, S. (2002). Including students with disabilities into the general education science classroom. *Exceptional Children, 68,* 423–435.

Cawley, J. F., Parmar, R. S., Foley, T. E., Salmon, S., & Roy, S. (2001). Arithmetic performance of students: Implications for standards and programming. *Exceptional Children, 67,* 311–328.

Cedar Rapids Community School District v. Garret F. 96–1793 S. Ct. (1999).

Center for Applied Linguistics. (2005). *Guiding principles for dual language education.* Washington, DC: Author.

Cerve, K. (2008, October 26). *Elementary schoolchildren learn being disabled isn't so easy.* Retrieved October 31, 2008, from http://www.beaufortgazette.com/local/v-print/story/596833.html.

Chadsey, J., & Gun Han, K. (2005). Friendship-facilitation strategies: What do students in middle school tell us? *Teaching Exceptional Children, 38*(2), 52–57.

Chandler, L. K., & Dahlquist, C. M. (2010). *Functional assessment: Strategies to prevent and remediate challenging behavior in school settings* (3rd ed.). Upper Saddle River, NJ: Merrill/Pearson Education.

Chappuis, S. & Chappuis, J. (2008). The best value in formative assessment. *Educational Leadership, 65*(4), 14–18.

Chard, D. J., & Osborn, J. (1999). Word recognition instruction: Paving the road to successful reading. *Intervention in School and Clinic, 34*(5), 271–277.

Chard, D. J., Vaughn, S., & Tyler, B. (2002). A synthesis of research on effective interventions for building fluency with elementary students with learning disabilities. *Journal of Learning Disabilities, 35,* 386–406.

Charlop, M. H., Gilmore, L., & Chang, G. T. (2008). Using video modeling to increase variation in the conversation of children with autism. *Journal of Special Education Technology, 23*(3), 47–66.

Chau, M., & Douglas-Hall, A. (2008). *Low-Income Children in the United States National and State Trend Data, 1997–2007.* Retrieved March 2, 2009, from http://www.nccp.org/publications/pub_851.html.

Checkley, K. (2008). Tapping parent and community support to improve student learning. *Education Update, 50*(4), 1–2, 4.

Cheesman, E. A., McGuire, J. M., Shankweiler, D., & Coyne, M. (2009). First-year teacher knowledge of phonemic awareness and its instruction. *Teacher Education and Special Education, 32*(3), 270–289.

Chiang, H., & Lin, Y. (2007). Reading comprehension instruction for students with autism spectrum disorders: A review of the literature. *Focus on Autism and Other Developmental Disabilities, 22*(4), 259–267.

Chiappetta, E. L., & Koballa, T. R. (2006). *Science instruction in the middle and secondary schools: Developing fundamental knowledge and skills for teaching* (6th ed.). Upper Saddle River, NJ: Merrill/Pearson Education.

Childre, A., Sands, J. R., & Tanner Pope, S. (2009). Backward design: Targeting depth of understanding for all learners. *Teaching Exceptional Children, 41*(5), 6–14.

Chitiyo, M., & Wheeler, J. J. (2009). Challenges faced by school teachers in implementing postive behavioral support in their school systems. *Remedial and Special Education, 30*(1), 58–63.

Christensen, L. (2008). Welcoming all languages. *Educational Leadership, 66*(1), 59-62.

Christner, B., & Dieker, L. A. (2008). Tourette syndrome: A collaborative approach focused on empowering students, families, and taxpayers. *Teaching Exceptional Children, 40*(5), 44–51.

Christopher, S. (2008). Homework: A few practice arrows. *Educational Leadership, 65*(4), 74–76.

Church, K., Gottschalk, C. M., & Leddy, J. N. (2003). 20 ways to enhance social and friendship skills. *Intervention in School and Clinic, 38,* 307–310.

Cihak, D. F., & Foust, J. L. (2008). Comparing number lines and touch points to teach addition facts to students with autism. *Focus on Autism and Other Developmental Disabilities, 23*(3), 131–137.

Cihak, D. F., & Gama, R. I. (2008). Noncontingent escape access to self-reinforcement to increase task engagement for students with moderate to severe disabilities. *Education and Training in Developmental Disabilities, 43*(4), 556–568.

Cihak, D. F., Kessler, K., & Alberto, P. A.. (2008). Use a handheld prompting system to transition independently through vocational tasks for students with moderate and severe intellectual disabilities. *Education and Training in Developmental Disabilities, 43*(1), 102–110.

Cihak, D. F., & Schrader, L. (2008). Does the model matter? Comparing video self-monitoring and video adult modeling for task acquisitioin and maintenance by adolescents with autism spectrum disorders. *Journal of Special Education Technology, 23*(3), 9–20.

Clapper, A. T., Morse, A. B., Thurlow, M. L., & Thompson, S. J. (2006). *How to develop state guidelines for access assistants: Scribes, readers, and sign language interpreters.* Minneapolis, MN: University of Minnesota, National Center on Educational Outcomes.

Clark, B. (2008). *Growing up gifted: Developing the potential of children at home and at school* (7th ed.). Upper Saddle River, NJ: Merrill/Pearson Education.

Clayton, J., Burdge, M., Denham, A., Kleinert, H. L., & Kearns, J. (2006). A four-step process for accessing the general curriculum for students with significant cognitive disabilities. *Teaching Exceptional Children, 38*(5), 20–27.

Cloud, N. (2008, May). *English language learners with interrupted formal education (SIFEs): Issues and strategies.* Presentation at the conference on English language learners with interrupted formal education. New Paltz, NY: Ulster BOCES.

Cloud, N., & Landurand, P. M. (n.d.). *Multisystem: Training program for special educators.* New York: Teachers College Press.

Clyde K. and Sheila K. v. Puyallup School District, 35 F.3d 1396, 9th Circuit, 1994.

Cohen, A. S., Gregg, N., & Deng, M. (2005). The role of extended time and item content on a high-stakes mathematics test. *Learning Disabilities Research and Practice, 20,* 225–233.

Cohen, L. G., & Spenciner, L. J. (2007). *Assessment of children and youth with special needs* (3rd ed.). Boston: Allyn & Bacon.

Cole v. Greenfield-Central Community Schools, 657 F. Supp. 56 (S.D. Ind. 1986).

Coleman-Martin, M. B., Heller, K. W., Cihak, D. F., & Irvine, K. L. (2005). Using computer-assisted instruction and the nonverbal reading approach to teach word identification. *Focus on Autism and Other Developmental Disabilities, 20,* 80–90.

Collier, V. P., & Thomas, W. P. (2004). The astounding effectiveness of dual language education for all. *NABE Journal of Research and Practice, 2*(1), 1–20.

Collins, B. C., Epstein, A., Reiss, T., & Lowe, V. (2001). Including children with mental retardation in the religious community. *Teaching Exceptional Children, 33*(5), 53–59.

Collins, R. R. (2009). Taking care of one another. *Educational Leadership, 66*(8), 81–82.

Combes, B. H., Walker, M., Esprivalo Harrell, P., & Tyler-Wood, T. (2008). PAVES: A presentation strategy for beginning presenters in inclusive environments. *Teaching Exceptional Children, 41*(1), 42–47.

Conderman, G., & Elf, N. (2007). What's in this book? Engaging students through a textbook exploration activity. *Reading and Writing Quarterly: Overcoming Learning Difficulties, 23*(1), 111–116.

Conderman, G., Ikan, P. A., & Hatcher, R. E. (2000). Student-led conferences in inclusive settings. *Intervention in School and Clinic, 36,* 22–26.

Conderman, G., Johnston-Rodriguez, S., & Hartman, P. (2009). Communicating and collaborating in co-taught classrooms. *TEACHING Exceptional Children Plus, 5*(5) Article 3. Retrieved [July 27, 2009] from http://escholarship.bc.edu/education/tecplus/vol5/iss5/art3.

Conderman, G., & Koroghlanian, C. (2002). Writing test questions like a pro. *Intervention in School and Clinic, 38,* 67–74.

Conderman, G., & Stephens, J. T. (2000). Voices from the field: Reflections from beginning special educators. *Teaching Exceptional Children, 33*(1), 16–21.

Conderman, G., & Strobel, D. (2006). Problem solving with guided repeated oral reading instruction. *Intervention in School and Clinic, 42,* 34–39.

Connor, D. J., & Bejoian, L. M. (2006). Pigs, pirates, and pills: Using film to teach the social context of disability. *Teaching Exceptional Children, 39*(2), 52–60.

Connor, D. J., & Lagares, C. (2007). Facing high stakes in high school. 25 successful strategies for an inclusive social studies classroom. *Teaching Exceptional Children, 40*(2), 18–27.

Conroy, M. A., Brown, W. H., & Davis, C. (2001). Applying the IDEA 1997 disciplinary provisions to preschoolers with challenging behaviors. *Beyond Behavior, 11*(1), 23–26.

Conroy, M. A., & Stichter, J. P. (2003). The application of antecedents in the functional assessment process: Existing research, issues and recommendations. *Journal of Special Education, 37,* 15–25.

Conroy, M. A., Sutherland, K. S., Snyder, A., AL-Hendawi, M. & Vo, A. (2009). Creating a positive classroom atmosphere: Teachers's use of effective praise and feedback. *Beyond Behavior, 18*(2), 18–26.

Conroy, M. A., Sutherland, K. S., Snyder, A., Marsh, S. (2008). Classwide interventions: Effective instruction makes a difference. *Teaching Exceptional Children, 40*(6), 24–30.

Contopidis, E., LeRoux, J. M., & Halpern, D. (2007). A closer look: Disproportionality among rural school districts. *Multiple Voices, 10*(1 & 2), 147–159.

Converse, N., & Lingugaris Kraft, B. (2009). Evaluation of a school-based mentoring program for at-risk middle school youth. *Remedial and Special Education, 30*(1), 33–46.

Cook, G. (2006, April 4). Siblings of disabled have their own troubles. *New York Times,* F5.

Cook-Sather, A. (2003). Listening to students about learning differences. *Teaching Exceptional Children, 35*(4), 22–27.

Copeland, S. R., Hughes, C., Carter, E. W., Guth, C., Presley, J. A., Williams, C. R., & Fowler, S. E. (2004). Increasing access to general education: Perspectives of participants in a high school peer support program. *Remedial and Special Education, 25,* 342–352.

Corcos, E., & Willows, D. M. (2009). Processing words varying in personal familiarity (based on reading and spelling) by poor readers and age-matched and reading-matched controls. *Remedial and Special Education, 30*(4), 195–206.

Corral, N., & Antia, S. D. (1997). Self-task: Strategies for success in math. *Teaching Exceptional Children, 29*(4), 42–45.

Coster, W. J., & Haltiwanger, J. T. (2004). Social-behavioral skills of elementary students with physical disabilities included in general education classrooms. *Remedial and Special Education, 25,* 95–103.

Cote, D. (2007). Problem-based learning software for students with disabilities. *Intervention in School and Clinic, 43*(1), 29–37.

Council for Exceptional Children. (2001). Virtual reality, brain imaging, the LD debate and more to impact special education. *CEC Today 8*(3), 1, 9–10, 14–15.

Council for Exceptional Children. (2002). Help students cope with chronic fear. *CEC Today 8*(6), 1, 9, 12, 14.

Council for Exceptional Children. (2007). *CEC's position on response to intervention (RtI).* Arlington, VA: Council for Exceptional Children.

Council for Exceptional Children. (2008). *New diversity terminology.* Arlington, VA: Council for Exceptional Children.

Council for Exceptional Children. (2008). *Addressing bumps in the collaboration road*. Retrieved April 16, 2009, from http://www.cec.sped.org/AM/PrinterTemplate.cfm?Section=CEC_Today1&TEMPLATE.

Council for Exceptional Children. (2008). *Bullying of children with exceptionalities: Tackling it in your school and classroom*. Retrieved July 1, 2009, from http://www.cec.sped.org/AM/PrinterTemplate.cfm?Section=Home&TEMPLATE=/CM/Content.

Council for Exceptional Children. (2009). *Best practices for administering medications in school*. Retrieved March 2, 2009, from http://www.cec.sped.org/AM/PrinterTemplate.cfm?Section=Home&CONTENTID=11752.

Countryman, L. L., & Schroeder, M. (1996). When students lead parent–teacher conferences. *Educational Leadership, 53*(7), 64–68.

Coutant, C., & Perchemlides, N. (2005). Strategies for teen readers. *Educational Leadership, 63*(2), 42–47.

Coutinho, M. J., & Oswald, D. P. (2005). State variation in gender disproportionality in special education. Findings and recommendations. *Remedial and Special Education, 26*, 7–15.

Coutinho, M. J., Oswald, D. P., & Best, A. M. (2002). The influence of sociodemographics and gender on the disproportionate identification of minority students as having learning disabilities. *Remedial and Special Education, 23*, 49–59.

Cox Suarez, S., & Daniels, K. J. (2008). Listening for competence through documentation: Assessing children with language delays using digital video. *Remedial and Special Education*.

Coyne, M. D., Kame'enui, E. J., & Carnine, D. (2007). *Effective teaching* strategies that accommodate diverse learners (3rd ed.). Upper Saddle River, NJ: Merrill/Pearson Education.

Coyne, M. D., Kame'enui, E. J., & Simmons, D. C. (2001). Prevention and intervention in beginning reading: Two complex systems. *Learning Disabilities Research and Practice, 16*, 62–73.

Coyne, M. D., Simonsen, B., & Faggella-Luby, M. (2008). Cooperating initiatives: Supporting behavioral and academic improvement through a systems approach. *Teaching Exceptional Children, 40*(6), 54–59.

Coyne, M. D., Zipoli, R. P., & Ruby, M. F. (2006). Beginning reading instruction for students at risk for reading disabilities: What, how, and when. *Intervention in School and Clinic, 41*, 161–168.

Cramer, S., Erzkus, A., Mayweather, K., Pope, K., Roeder, J., & Tone, T. (1997). Connecting with siblings. *Teaching Exceptional Children, 30*(1), 46–51.

Cramer, S., & Stivers, J. (2007). Don't give up! Practical strategies for challenging collaborations. *Teaching Exceptional Children, 39*(6), 6–11.

Crews, S. D., Bender, H., Vanderwood, M., Cook, C. R., Gresham, F. M. & Kern, L. (2008). Risk and protective factors of emotional and/or behavioral disorders in children and adolescents: A mega-analytic synthesis. *Behavioral Disorders, 32*(2), 64–77.

Crothers, L. M., & Kolbert, J. B. (2008). Tackling a problematic behavior management issue: Teachers' intervention in childhood bullying problems. *Intervention in School and Clinic, 43*(3), 132–139.

Crouch, A. L., & Jakubecy, J. J. (2007). Dysgraphia: How it affects a student's performance and what can be done about it. *TEACHING Exceptional Children Plus, 3*(3) Article 5. Retrieved [August 24, 2009] from http://escholarship.bc.edu/education/tecplus/vol3/iss3/art5.

Crowe, C. (2008). Solving behavior problems together. *Education Leadership, 66*(3), 44–47.

Crundwell, A., & Killu, K. (2007). Understanding and accommodating students with depression in the classroom. *Teaching Exceptional Children, 40*(1), 48–55.

Crundwell, A., & Marc, R. (2006). Identifying and teaching children with selective mutism. *Teaching Exceptional Children, 38*(3), 48–54.

Cullen, J., Richards, S. B., & Frank, C. L. (2008). Using software to enhance the writing skills of students with special needs. *Journal of Special Education Technology, 23*(2), 33–43.

Cullinan, D. (2007). *Students with emotional and behavioral disorders: An introduction for teachers and other helping professionals* (2nd ed.). Upper Saddle River, NJ: Merrill/Pearson Education.

Cullotta, K. A. (2008, December 28). The parent-teacher talk gains a new participant. *New York Times,* 23.

Cummings, T. M. (2007). Virtual reality as assistive technology. *Journal of Special Education Technology, 22*(2), 55–64.

Cummings, T. M., Higgins, K., Pierce, T., Miller, S., Boone, R., & Tandy, R. (2008). Social skills instruction for adolescents with emotional disabilities: A technology-based intervention. *Journal of Special Education Technology, 23*(1), 19–33.

Cummins, J. (2000). *Language, power, and pedagogy: Bilingual children in the crossfire*. Clevedon, UK: Multilingual Matters.

Cunningham, P. M. (1998). The multisyllabic word dilemma: Helping students build meaning, spell, and read "big" words. *Reading and Writing Quarterly: Overcoming Learning Difficulties, 14*(2), 189–218.

Cunningham, P. M. (2008). *Phonics they use: Words for reading and writing*. New York: Harper Collins.

Cunningham, P. M., & Hall, D. (2009). *Making words first grade: 100 hands-on lessons for phonemic awareness, phonics and spelling*. Boston: Allyn & Bacon/Pearson Education.

Cushing, L. S., Carter, E. W., Clark, N., Wallis, T. & Kennedy, C. H. (2009). Evaluating inclusive educational practices for students with severe disabilities using the program quality measurement tool. *The Journal of Special Education, 42*(4), 195–208.

Cushing, L. S., & Kennedy, C. H. (1997). Academic effects of providing peer support in general education classrooms on students without disabilities. *Journal of Applied Behavior Analysis, 30*, 139–151.

Cutshall, S. (2005). Why we need "the year of languages." *Educational Leadership, 62*(4), 20–23.

Czarnecki, E., Rosko, D., & Fine, E. (1998). How to call up notetaking skills. *Teaching Exceptional Children, 30*(6), 14–19.

Damico, J. S. (1991). Descriptive assessment of communicative ability in limited English proficient students. In E. Hamayan & J. S. Damico (Eds.), *Limiting bias in the assessment of bilingual students* (pp. 157–218). Austin, TX: PRO-ED.

Daniel, P. L. (2007). Invitation to all: Welcoming gays and lesbians into my classroom and curriculum. *English Journal, 96*(5), 75–80.

Daniel, R. R. v. State Board of Education, 874 F.2d 1036, 5th Circuit, 1989.

Daniels, V. I. (2007). Working with multicultural learners with gifts and talents. In F. E. Obiakor, (Ed.), *Multicultural special education: Culturally responsive teaching* (pp. 110–125). Upper Saddle River, NJ: Merrill/Pearson Education.

Danoff, S. (2008). Life ain't no crystal stair. *Educational Leadership, 65*(6), 76–79.

Dardig, J. C. (2005). The McClurg monthly magazine and 14 more practical ways to involve parents. *Teaching Exceptional Children, 38*(2), 46–51.

Darling-Hammond, L., & Friedlander, D. (2008). Creating excellent and equitable schools. *Educational Leadership, 65*(8), 14–21.

Darling-Hammond, L., & Ifill-Lynch, O. (2006). If they'd only do their work. *Educational Leadership, 63*(5), 8–13.

Darling-Hammond, L., & Richardson, N. (2009). Teacher learning: What matters? *Educational Leadership, 66*(5), 46–55.

Davern, L. (2004). School-to-home notebooks. *Teaching Exceptional Children, 36*(5), 22–27.

David, J. L. (2008). Project-based learning. *Educational Leadership, 65*(5), 80–84.

David, J. L. (2009). Service learning and civic participation. *Educational Leadership, 66*(8), 83–84.

Davidson, E., & Schniedewind, N. (2005). Class differences: Economic inequality in the classroom. In D. A. Byrnes & G. Kiger (Eds.), *Common bonds: Anti-bias teaching in a diverse society* (3rd ed., pp. 53–73). Olney, MD: Association of Childhood Education International.

Davies, D. K., Stock, S. E., & Wehmeyer, M. L. (2001). Enhancing independent Internet access for individuals with mental retardation through use of a specialized web browser: A pilot study. *Education and Training in Mental Retardation and Developmental Disabilities, 36,* 107–113.

Davies, D. K., Stock, S. E., & Wehmeyer, M. L. (2002). Enhancing independent task performance through use of a handheld self-directed visual and audio prompting system. *Education and Training in Mental Retardation and Developmental Disabilities, 37,* 209–218.

Davis, A. P., & McGrail, E. (2009). The joy of blogging. *Educational Leadership, 66*(6), 74–77.

Davis, B. M. (2009). *The biracial and multiracial student experience: A journey to racial literacy.* Thousand Oaks, CA: Corwin Press.

DeCapua, A., Smathers, W., Tang, L. M. (2007). Schooling interrupted. *Educational Leadership, 64*(6), 40–46.

Delano, M. E., & Stone, L. (2008). Extending the use of social stories to young children with emotional and behavioral disabilities. *Beyond Behavior 18*(1), 2–8.

De La Paz, S. (2001). STOP and DARE: A persuasive writing strategy. *Intervention in School and Clinic, 36,* 234–243.

De La Paz, S., Morales, P., & Winston, P. N. (2007). Source interpretation: Teaching students with and without LD to read and write historically. *Journal of Learning Disabilities, 40*(2), 134–144.

De La Paz, S., Owen, B., Harris, K. R., & Graham, S. (2000). Riding Elvis's motorcycle: Using self-regulated strategy development to PLAN and WRITE for a state writing exam. *Learning Disabilities Research and Practice, 15,* 101–109.

Dell, A. G., & Newton, D. (2008). Easy converter v.3.01. *Journal of Special Education Technology, 23*(4), 66–68.

Dell, A. G. Newton, D., & Petroff, J. (2008). *Assistive technology in the classroom: Enhancing the school experiences of students with disabilities.* Upper Saddle River, NJ: Merrill/Pearson Education.

Deming, A. M., & Lochman, J. E. (2008). The relation of locus of control, anger, and impulsivity to boys' aggressive behavior. *Behavioral Disorders, 33*(2), 108–119.

Demmert, W. G. (2005). The influences of culture on learning and assessment among Native American students. *Learning Disabilities Research and Practice, 20,* 16–23.

Denham, A., & Lahm, E. A. (2001). Using technology to construct alternate portfolios of students with moderate and severe disabilities. *Teaching Exceptional Children, 33*(5), 10–17.

Denhart, H. (2008). Deconstructing barriers: Perceptions of students labeled with learning disabilities in higher education. *Journal of Learning Disabilities, 41*(6), 483–497.

Denning, C. B. (2007). Social skills interventions for students with Asperger Syndrome and high-functioning autism: Research findings and implications for teachers. *Beyond Behavior, 16*(3), 16–23.

Denstaedt, L., Kelly, J. C., & Kryza, K. (2009). *Winning strategies for test taking, grades 3–8: A practical guide for teaching test preparation.* Thousand Oaks, CA: Corwin Press.

Denton, C. A., Wexler, J., Vaughn, S., & Bryan, D. (2008). Intervention provided to linguistically diverse middle school students with severe reading disabilities. *Learning Disabilities Research and Practice, 23*(2), 29–89.

Denton, P. (2008). The power of words. *Educational Leadership, 66*(1), 28–31.

Deshler, D. D., Schumaker, J. B., Lenz, B. K., Bulgren, J. A., Hock, M. F., Knight, J., & Ehren, B. J. (2001). Ensuring content-area learning by secondary students with learning disabilities. *Learning Disabilities Research and Practice, 16,* 96–108.

DeSimone, J. R., & Parmar, R. S. (2006). Middle school mathematics teachers' beliefs about inclusion of students with learning disabilities. *Learning Disabilties Research and Practice, 21,* 98–110.

Dettmer, P., Thurston, L. P., Knackendoffel, A., & Dyck, N. J. (2009). Collaboration, consultation, and teamwork for students with special needs (6th ed.). Upper Saddle River, NJ: Merrill/Pearson Education.

de Vise, D. (2008, March 17). *In the mainstream but isolated: Montgomery's integration of special-needs students angers some parents.* Retrieved April 12, 2009, from http://www.washingtonpost.com/wp-dyn/content/article/2008/03/16/AR2008031602435_p.

Devlin, P. (2008). Create effective teacher-paraprofessional teams. *Intervention in School and Clinic, 44*(1), 41–44.

Devlin, P. (2008). Enhancing the job performance of employees with disabilities using the self-determined career development model. *Education and Training in Developmental Disabilities, 43*(4), 502–513.

Diament, M. (2009). *Scoop essentials: Inside the world of siblings.* Retrieved April 26, 2009, from http://www.disabilityscoop.com/2009/04/21/inside-the-world-of-siblings/2940.

Diana v. California State Board of Education, No. C-70–37, RFP, (N.D. Cal., 1970).

Diaz-Rico, L. T., & Weed, K. Z. (2010). *Crosscultural, language, and academic development handbook: The Complete K-12 Reference Guide* (4th ed.). Boston: Allyn & Bacon.

Dieker, L., & Little, M. (2005). Secondary reading: Not just for reading teacher anymore. *Intervention in School and Clinic, 40,* 276–283.

Dillon, S. (2006, March 26). Schools cut back subjects to push reading and math. *New York Times,* A1, A22.

Dimino, J. A. (2007). Bridging the gap between research and practice. *Journal of Learning Disabilities, 40*(2), 183–189.

Doan, K. (2006). A sociocultural perspective on at-risk Asian-American students. *Teacher Education and Special Education, 29*(3), 157–167.

Dockrell, J. E., Lindsay, G., & Connelly, V. (2009). The impact of specific language impairment on adolescents' written text. *Exceptional Children, 75*(4), 427–446.

Dodd-Murphy, J., & Mamlin, N. (2002). Minimizing minimal hearing loss in the schools: What every classroom teacher should know. *Preventing School Failure, 46,* 86–92.

Doelling, J. E., & Bryde, S. (1995). School reentry and educational planning for the individual with traumatic brain injury. *Intervention in School and Clinic, 31*(2), 101–107.

Doelling, J. E., Bryde, S., & Parette, H. P. (1997). What are multidisciplinary and ecobehavioral approaches and how can they make a difference for students with traumatic brain injuries? *Teaching Exceptional Children, 30*(1), 56–60.

Dole, S., & McMahan, J. (2005). Using videotherapy to help adolescents cope with social and emotional problems. *Intervention in School and Clinic, 40,* 151–155.

Donabella, M. A., & Rule, A. C. (2008). Four seventh grade students who qualify for academic intervention services in mathematics learning multi-digit multiplication with the Montessori Checkerboard. *TEACHING Exceptional Children Plus, 4*(3) Article 2. Retrieved [September 3, 2009] from http://escholarship.bc.edu/education/tecplus/vol4/iss3/art2.

Dong, Y. R. (2005). Getting at the content. *Educational Leadership, 62*(4), 14–19.

Dong, Y. R. (2009). Linking to prior learning. *Educational Leadership, 66*(7), 26–31.

Donnelly, J. A. (2002). Guidelines for respectful support of individuals on the autism spectrum. *DDD Express, 13*(1), 1, 11.

Dore, R., Dion, E., Wagner, S., & Brunet, J. P. (2002). High school inclusion of adolescents with mental retardation: A multiple case study. *Education and Training in Mental Retardation and Developmental Disabilities, 37,* 253–261.

Douglas, K. H., Ayres, K. M., Langone, J., Bell, V., & Meade, C. (2009). Expanding literacy for learners with intellectual disabilities: The role of supported eText. *Journal of Special Education Technology, 24*(3), 35–44.

Downing, J. E. (2008). Including students with severe and multiple disabilities in typical classrooms (3rd ed.). Baltimore, MD: Brookes.

Downing, J. E., & Eichinger, J. (2003). Creating learning opportunities for students with severe disabilities in inclusive classrooms. *Teaching Exceptional Children, 36* (1), 26–31.

Downing, J. E., & Peckham-Hardin, K. D. (2007). Inclusive education: What makes it a good education for students with moderate to severe disabilities? *Research and Practice for Persons with Severe Disabilities, 32*(1), 16–30.

Dowrick, P. W., Kim-Rupnow, W. S., & Power, T. J. (2006). Video feedforward for reading. *Journal of Special Education, 39,* 194–207.

Doyle, M. B. (2000). Transition plans for students with disabilities. *Educational Leadership, 58*(1), 46–48.

Doyle, M. B. (2002). *The paraprofessional's guide to the inclusive classroom: Working as a team* (2nd ed.). Baltimore: Brookes.

Doyle, M. B., & Giangreco, M. F. (2009). Making presentation software accessible to high school students with intellectual disabilities. *Teaching Exceptional Children, 41*(3), 24–31.

Dozor, A. (2009, April, 22). Allergy season can be tough on kids. *Times Herald Record,* 3B.

Drasgow, E., Yell, M. L. & Robinson, T. R. (2001). Developing legally correct and educationally appropriate IEPs. *Remedial and Special Education, 22,* 359–373.

Drew, C. J., & Hardman, M. L. (2007). *Intellectual disabilties across the lifespan* (9th ed.). Upper Saddle River, NJ: Merrill/Pearson Education.

Dryfoos, J. G. (2008). Centers of hope. *Educational Leadership, 65*(7), 38–43.

Duchardt, B. A., Deshler, D. D., & Schumaker, J. B. (1995). A strategic intervention for enabling students with learning disabilities to identify and change their ineffective beliefs. *Learning Disability Quarterly, 18*(3), 186–201.

Duda, M. A., & Utley, C. A. (2005). Positive behavioral support for at-risk students: Promoting social competence in at-risk culturally diverse learners in urban schools. *Multiple Voices, 8*(1), 128–143.

Dukes C., & Lamar-Dukes, P. (2009). Inclusion by design: Engineering inclusive practices in secondary schools. *Teaching Exceptional Children, 41*(3), 16–23.

Dwairy, M. (2005). Using problem-solving conversations with students. *Intervention in School and Clinic, 40,* 144–151.

Dweck, C. S. (2007). The perils and promises of praise. *Educational Leadership, 65*(2), 34–39.

Dyches, T. T., Hobbs, K., Wilder, L. K., Sudweeks, R. R., Obiakor, F. E., & Algozzine, B. (2005). Multicultural representation in autism. *Linking Research and Practice in Special Education: An international perspective, 1*(1), 1–15.

Dyches, T. T., Prater, M. A. & Jenson, J. (2006). Portrayal of disabilities in Caldecott books. *Teaching Exceptional Children Plus, 2*(5) Article 2. Retrieved August 2, 2006, from http://escholarship.bc.edu/tecplus/vol2/iss5/art32.

Dyck, N., & Pemberton, J. (2002). A model for making decisions about text adaptations. *Intervention in School and Clinic, 38,* 28–35.

Dymond, S. K., Renzaglia, A., & Chun, E. J. (2008). Inclusive high school servive learning programs: Methods for and barriers to including students with disabilities. *Education and Training in Developmental Disabilities, 43*(1), 20–36.

Dymond, S. K., & Russell, D. L. (2004). Impact of grade and disability on the instructional context of inclusive classrooms. *Education and Training in Developmental Disabilities, 39,* 127–140.

Eber, L., Breen, K., Rose, J., Unizycki, R. M., & London, T. H. (2008). Wraparound as a tertiary level intervention for students with emotional/behavioral needs. *Teaching Exceptional Children, 40*(6), 6–15.

Ebbers, S. M., & Denton, C. A. (2008). A root awakening: Vocabulary instruction for older students with reading difficulties. *Learning Disabilities Research and Practice, 23*(2), 90–102.

Echevarria, J. (1995). Sheltered instruction for students with learning disabilities who have limited English proficiency. *Intervention in School and Clinic, 30*(5), 302–305.

Echevarria, J., & McDonough, R. (1995). An alternative reading approach: Instructional conversations in a bilingual special education setting. *Learning Disabilities Research and Practice, 10*(2), 108–119.

Echevarria, J. A., Vogt, M. J., & Short, D. J. (2010). *Making content comprehensible for secondary English learners: The SIOP model.* Boston: Allyn & Bacon.

Edyburn, D., & Basham, J. (2008). Collecting and coding observational data. *Journal of Special Education Technology, 23*(2), 56–60.

Egan, J. (2008, September 14). The bipolar kid: What does it mean to be a manic-depressive child?. *New York Times Magazine,* 66–75, 88, 92, 94–95.

Ehri, L. C., Satlow, E., & Gaskins, I. (2009). Grapho-phonemic enrichment strengthens keyword analogy instruction for struggling young readers. *Reading and Writing Quarterly: Overcoming Learning Difficulties, 25*(2–3), 162–191.

Eisenberg, A. (2008, May 25). The magnifying glass gets an electronic twist. *New York Times,* BU4.

Eisenman, L. T. (2007). Self-determination interventions: Building a foundation for school completion. *Remedial and Special Education, 28*(1), 2–8.

Eisenman, L. T., & Tascione, L. (2002). "How come nobody told me?" Fostering self-realization through a high school English curriculum. *Learning Disabilities Research and Practice, 17,* 35–46.

Elbaum, B. (2002). The self-concept of students with learning disabilities: A meta-analysis of comparisons across different placements. *Learning Disabilities Research and Practice, 17,* 216–226.

Elbaum, B. (2007). Effects of an oral testing accommodation on the mathematics performance of secondary students with and without learning disabilities. *Journal of Special Education, 40,* 218–229.

Elhoweris, H., & Alsheikh, N. (2006). Teachers' attitudes toward inclusion. *International Journal of Special Education, 21*(1), 115–118.

Elhoweris, H., Whittaker, C., & Salend, S. J. (2007). Addressing the religious and spiritual diversity of students with disabilities and their families. *Multiple Voices, 10*(1 & 2), 1–7.

Elliott, S. N., Kratochwill, T. R., & Schulte, T. R. (1998). The assessment accommodation checklist. *Teaching Exceptional Children, 31*(2), 10–14.

Elliott, S. N., & Marquart, A. (2004). Extended time as a testing accommodation: Its effects and perceived consequences. *Exceptional Children, 70,* 349–367.

Elliott, J. L., & Thurlow, M. L. (2006). *Improving test performance of students with disabilities . . . on district and state assessments* (2nd ed.). Thousand Oaks, CA: Corwin Press.

Ellis, E. S. (1989). A metacognitive intervention for increasing class participation. *Learning Disabilities Focus, 5*(1), 36–46.

Ellis, E. S. (1994). Integrating writing strategy instruction with content-area instruction: Part 1—Orienting students to organizational strategies. *Intervention in School and Clinic, 29*(3), 169–179.

Ellis, E. S. (1996). Reading strategy instruction. In D. D. Deshler, E. S. Ellis, & B. K. Lenz (Eds.), *Teaching adolescents with learning disabilities: Strategies and methods* (2nd ed., pp. 61–125). Denver: Love.

Ellis, E. S. (1997). Watering up the curriculum for adolescents with learning disabilities. *Remedial and Special Education, 18*(6), 326–346.

Ellis, E. S. (1998). Watering up the curriculum for adolescents with learning disabilities—Part 2. *Remedial and Special Education, 19*(2), 91–105.

Ellis, E. S., & Covert, G. (1996). Writing strategy instruction. In D. D. Deshler, E. S. Ellis, & B. K. Lenz (Eds.), *Teaching adolescents with learning disabilities: Strategies and methods* (2nd ed., pp. 127–207). Denver: Love.

Ellis, E. S., & Howard, P. W. (2007, Spring). Graphic organizer. *Current Practice Alerts, 13,* 1–4.

Ely, R., Emerson, R. W., Maggiore, T., Rothberg, M., O'Connell, T., & Hudson, L. (2006). Increased content knowledge of students with visual impairments as a result of extended descriptions. *Journal of Special Education Technology, 21*(3), 31–43.

Emerson, J., & Lovitt, T. (2003). Perspective: The educational plight of foster children in schools and what can be done about it. *Remedial and Special Education, 24,* 199–203.

Englert, C. S. (2009). Connecting the dots in a research program to develop, implement, and evaluate strategic literacy interventions for struggling readers and writers. *Learning Disabilities Research and Practice, 24*(2), 93–103.

Englert, C. S., Berry, R., & Dunsmore, K. (2001). A case study of the apprenticeship process: Another perspective on the apprentice and the scaffolding metaphor. *Journal of Learning Disabilities, 34,* 152–171.

Englert, C. S., & Mariage, T. V. (1991). Making students partners in the comprehension process: Send for the reading POSSE. *Learning Disability Quarterly, 14,* 123–138.

Englert, C. S., Wu, X., & Zhao, Y. (2005). Cognitive tools for writing: Scaffolding the performance of students through technology. *Learning Disabilities Research and Practice, 20,* 184–198.

Englert, C. S., Zhao, Y., Collings, N., & Romig, N. (2005). Learning to read words: The effects of internet-based software in the improvement of reading performance. *Remedial and Special Education, 26,* 357–371.

Esparza Brown, J., & Doolittle, J. (2008). A cultural, linguistic, ecological framework for response to intervention with English language learner. *Teaching Exceptional Children, 40*(5), 66–72.

Espin, C. A., Cevasco, J., van den Broek, P., Baker, S., & Gersten, R. (2007). History as narrative: The nature and quality of historical understanding for students with LD. *Journal of Learning Disabilities, 40*(2), 174–182.

Espin, C. A., De La Paz, S., Scierka, B. J., & Roelofs, L. (2005). The relationship between curriculum-based measures in written expression and quality and completeness of expository writing for middle school students. *Journal of Special Education, 38,* 208–217.

Espin, C. A., Wallace, T., Campbell, H., Lembke, E. S., Long, J. D., & Ticha, R. (2008). Curriculum-based measurement in writing: Predicting the success of high-school students on state standard tests. *Exceptional Children, 74*(2), 174–193.

Estell, D. B., Jones, M. H., Pearl, R., Van Acker, R., Farmer, T. W., & Rodkin, P. C. (2008). Peer groups, popularity, and social preference: Trajectories of social functioning among students with and without learning disabilities. *Journal of Learning Disabilities, 41*(1), 5–14.

Etscheidt, S. K. (2002). Discipline provisions of IDEA: Misguided policy or tacit reform intiatives? *Behavioral Disorders, 27,* 408–422.

Etscheidt, S. K., & Bartlett, L. (1999). The IDEA amendments: A four-step approach for determining supplementary aids and services. *Exceptional Children, 65*(2), 163–174.

Everston, C. M., & Emmer, E. T. (2009). *Classroom management for elementary teachers* (8th ed.). Upper Saddle River, NJ: Merrill/Pearson Education.

Everston, C. M., & Emmer, E. T. (2009). *Classroom management for middle and high school* (8th ed.). Upper Saddle River, NJ: Merrill/Pearson Education.

Fabel, L. (2009). *Report: Special education integration fails expectations.* Retrieved on March 2, 2009, from http://www.dcexaminer.com/local/Report-Special-ed-integration-fails-expectations_02_27-40396677.html.

Faggella-Luby, M. N., & Deshler, D. D. (2008). Reading comprehension in adolescents with LD: What we know; What we need to learn. *Learning Disabilities Research and Practice, 23*(2), 70–78.

Fairbanks, S., Simonsen, B., & Sugai, G. (2008). Classwide secondary and tertiary tier practices and systems. *Teaching Exceptional Children, 40*(6), 44–52.

Falk-Ross, F., Watman, L., Kokesh, K., Iverson, M., Williams, E., & Wallace, A. (2009). Natural complements: Collaborative approaches for educators to support students with learning difficulties and literacy difficulties. *Reading and Writing Quarterly: Overcoming Learning Difficulties, 25*(1), 104–117.

Faltis, C. J. (2006). *Teaching English language learners in elementary school communities: A joinfostering approach* (4th ed.). Upper Saddle River, NJ: Merrill/Pearson.

Farber, S. (2009). *Learning experience guidelines.* New Paltz, NY: Ulster BOCES Teaching American History Project.

Fashl, A. J. (2007). Mathematics accommodations for all students. *Intervention in School and Clinic, 42*(4), 198–203.

Faulkner, V. N. (2009). The components of number sense: An instructional model for teachers. *Teaching Exceptional Children, 41*(5), 24–30.

Fenty, N. S., Miller, M. A., & Lampi, A. (2008). Embed social skills instruction in inclusive settings. *Intervention in School and Clinic, 43*(3), 186–192.

Ferguson, P. M. (2002). A place in the family: An historical interpretation of research on parental reactions to having a child with a disability. *Journal of Special Education, 36,* 124–130.

Ferreri, A. J. (2009). Including Matthew: Assessment-guided differentiated literacy instruction. *TEACHING Exceptional Children Plus, 5*(3) Article 3. Retrieved [August 16, 2009] http://escholarship.bc.edu/education/tecplus/vol5/iss3/art3.

Ferretti, R. P., Andrews-Weckerly, S., & Lewis, W. E. (2007). Improving argumentative writing of students with learning disabilities: Descriptive and normative considerations. *Reading and Writing Quarterly, 23*(3), 267–285.

Ferretti, R. P., MacArthur, C. D., & Okolo, C. M. (2002). Teaching effectively about historical things. *Teaching Exceptional Children, 34*(6), 66–69.

Ferri, B. A., & Connor, D. J. (2005). In the shadow of *Brown*: Special education and overrepresentation of students of color. *Remedial and Special Education, 26,* 93–100.

Ferri, B. A., Keefe, C. H., & Gregg, N. (2001). Teachers with learning disabilities: A view from both sides of the desk. *Journal of Learning Disabilities, 34,* 22–31.

Ferriter, B. (2009). Learning with blogs and wikis. *Educational Leadership, 66*(5), 34–39.

Fielder, C. R., Chiang, B., Van Haren, B. Jorgensen, J., Halberg, S., & Boreson, L. (2008). Culturally responsive practices in schools: A checklist to address disproportionality in special education. *Teaching Exceptional Children, 40*(5), 52–59.

Figueroa, R. A., & Newsome, P. (2006). The diagnosis of LD in English learners: Is it nondiscriminatory? *Journal of Learning Disabilities, 39,* 206–214.

Fink Chorzempa, B., Graham, S., & Harris, K. R. (2005). What can I do to help young children who struggle with writing? *Teaching Exceptional Children, 37*(5), 64–66.

Fink Chorzempa, B., & Lapidus, L. (2009). "To find yourself, think for yourself": Using Socratic discussions in inclusive classrooms. *Teaching Exceptional Children, 41*(3), 54–59.

Finstein, R. F., Yao Yang, F., & Jones, R. (2006). Build organizational skills in students with learning disabilities. *Intervention in School and Clinic, 42,* 174–178.

Fisher, D., & Frey, N. (2001). Access to the core curriculum: Critical ingredients for student success. *Remedial and Special Education, 22,* 148–157.

Fisher, D., & Frey, N. (2008). Releasing responsibility. *Educational Leadership, 66*(3), 32–37.

Fisher, D., Frey, N., & Thousand, J. (2003). What do special educators need to know and be prepared to do for inclusive schooling to work? *Teacher Education and Special Education, 26,* 42–50.

Fisher, D., Pumpian, I., & Sax, C. (1998). Parent and caregiver impressions of different educational models. *Remedial and Special Education, 19,* 173–180.

Fitzgerald, J. L., & Watkins, H. W. (2006). Parents' rights in special education: The readability of procedural safeguards. *Exceptional Children, 72,* 497–510.

Fitzgerald, M. (2008, January 27). The coming wave of gadgets that listen and obey. *New York Times*, BU 4.

Fitzpatrick, M., & Brown, M. R. (2008). Assistive technology access and use: Considerations for culturally and linguistically diverse students and their families. *Journal of Special Education Technology, 23*(4), 47–52.

Fleming, J. L., & Monda-Amaya, L. E. (2001). Process variables critical for team effectiveness. *Remedial and Special Education, 22,* 158–171.

Fletcher, J. M., Francis, D. J., Boudousquie, A., Copeland, K., Young, V., Kalinowski, S., & Vaughn, S. (2006). Effects of accommodations on high-stakes testing for students with reading disabilities. *Exceptional Children, 72,* 136–150.

Fletcher, J. M., Francis, D. J., O'Malley, K., Copeland, K., Mehta, P., Caldwell, C. J., Kalinowski, S., Young, V., & Vaughn, S. (2009). Effects of a bundled accommodations package on high-stakes testing for middle school students with reading disabilities. *Exceptional Children, 75(4),* 447–463.

Flexer, R. W, Baer, R. M., Luft, P., & Simmons, T. J. (2008). *Transition planning for secondary students with disabilities* (3rd ed.). Upper Saddle River, NJ: Merrill/Pearson Education.

Flower, A., Burns, M. K., & Bottsford-Miller, N. A. (2007). Meta-analysis of disability simulation research. *Remedial and Special Education, 28*(2), 72–77.

Floyd, L. O., & Vernon-Dotson, L. (2008). Using home learning tool kits to facilitate family involvement. *Intervention in School and Clinic, 44*(3), 160–166.

Foegen, A. (2006). Evaluating instructional effectiveness: Tools and strategies for monitoring student progress. In M. Montague and A. K. Jitendra (eds.), *Teaching mathematics to middle school students with learning difficulties* (pp. 108–132). New York, NY: Guilford.

Foegen, A., & Deno, S. L. (2001). Identifying growth indicators for low-achieving students in middle school mathematics. *The Journal of Special Education, 35,* 4–16.

Fontana, J. L., Scruggs, T. E., & Mastropieri, M. A. (2007). Mnemonic strategy instruction in inclusive secondary social studies. *Remedial and Special Education, 28*(6), 345–355.

Ford, D. Y., Grantham, T. C., & Whiting, G. W. (2008). Culturally and linguistically diverse students in gifted education: Recruitment and retention issues. *Exceptional Children, 74*(3), 289–308.

Forgan, J. W., & Gonzalez-DeHass, A. (2004). How to infuse social skills training into literacy instruction. *Teaching Exceptional Children, 36* (6), 24–30.

Forgan, J. W., & Vaughn, S. (2000). Adolescents with and without LD make the transition to middle school. *Journal of Learning Disabilities, 33,* 33–43.

Forgan, J. W., & Weber, R. K. (2001). Selecting software for students with high incidence disabilities. *Intervention in School and Clinic, 37,* 40–47.

Forlin, C. (2008). Educational reform to include all learners in the Asia-Pacific region. In C. Forlin (Ed.), *Catering for learners with diverse needs: An Asia-Pacific focus.* (pp. 3–10). Hong Kong: Hong Kong Institute of Education.

Fox, B. J. (2006). *Phonics for the teacher of reading* (9th ed.). Upper Saddle River, NJ: Merrill/Pearson Education.

Fox, B. J. (2010). *Phonics and structural analysis for the teacher of reading: Programmed for self-instruction* (10th ed.). Boston: Allyn & Bacon/Pearson Education.

Fradd, S. H., & Weismantel, M. J. (1989). *Meeting the needs of culturally and linguistically different students: A handbook for educators.* Austin, TX: PRO-ED.

Franklin, J. (2005). Redefining rural schools: Sudden population shifts stretch educators and resources. *Education Update, 47*(4), 4–5, 7.

Franklin, J. (2006). The essential ounce of prevention: Effective classroom management means more than intervention. *Education Update, 48*(3), 3–7.

Frattura, E., & Capper, C. A. (2006). Segregated programs versus integrated comprehensive service delivery for all learners: Assessing the differences. *Remedial and Special Education, 27*(6), 355–364.

Frederickson, N., & Turner, J. (2003). Utilizing the classroom peer group to address children's social needs: An evaluation of the circle of friends intervention approach. *Journal of Special Education, 36,* 234–245.

Freeman, B., & Crawford, L. (2008). Creating a middle school mathematics curriculum for English-language learners. *Remedial and Special Education, 29*(1), 9–19.

Freeman, S. F. N., Alkin, M. C., & Kasari, C. L. (1999). Satisfaction and desire for change in educational placement for children with Down syndrome: Perceptions of parents. *Remedial and Special Education, 20*(3), 143–151.

Freire, P. (1970). *Pedagogy of the oppressed.* New York: Continuum.

Frenette, L. (2006, April 27). When kids are on chemo. *New York Teacher,* 24.

Frenette, L. (2007, December 6). School psychologists learn healing humor. *New York Teacher,* 16.

Frenette, L. (2009, February 5). Dealing with death, grief. *New York Teacher,* 9.

Frey, T. J. (2009). An analysis of online professional development and outcomes for students with disabilities. *Teacher Education and Special Education, 32*(1), 83–96.

Friend, M., & Cook, L. (2010). *Interactions: Collaborative skills for school professionals* (6th ed.). Upper Saddle River, NJ: Pearson Education.

Froschl, M., & Gropper, N. (1999). Fostering friendships, curbing bullying. *Educational Leadership, 56*(8), 72–75.

Fuchs, D., Deshler, D., & Zigmond, N. (1994, March). *How expendable is general education? How expendable is special education?* Paper presented at the meeting of the Learning Disabilities Association of America, Washington, DC.

Fuchs, D., Fernstrom, P., Scott, S., Fuchs, L., & Vandermeer, L. (1994). A process for mainstreaming: Classroom ecological inventory. *Teaching Exceptional Children, 26*(3), 11–15.

Fuchs, D., Fuchs, L. S., Mathes, P. G., Lipsey, M. E., & Eaton, S. (2000). A meta-analysis of reading differences with and without the disabilities label: A brief report. *Learning Disabilities: A Multidisciplinary Journal, 10,* 1–3.

Fuchs, D., Fuchs, L. S., Thompson, A., Svenson, E., Yan, L., Al Otaiba, S., Yang, N., McMater, K. N., Prentice, K.,

Kazdan, S., & Saenz, L. (2001). Peer-assisted learning strategies in reading: Extensions for kindergarten, first grade, and high school. *Remedial and Special Education, 22,* 15–21.

Fuchs, L. S., & Fuchs, D. (2001). Helping teachers formulate sound test accommodation decisions for students with learning disabilities. *Learning Disabilities Research and Practice, 16,* 174–181.

Fuchs, L. S., & Fuchs, D. (2002). Mathematical problem-solving profiles of students with mathematical disabilities with and without comorbid reading difficulties. *Journal of Learning Disabilities, 35,* 563–573.

Fuchs, L. S., & Fuchs, D. (2005). Enhancing mathematical problem solving for students with disabilities. *Journal of Special Education, 39,* 45–57.

Fuchs, L. S., & Fuchs, D. (2007). A model for implementing responsiveness to intervention. *Teaching Exceptional Children, 39*(5), 14–23.

Fuchs, L. S., & Fuchs, D. (2008). Mathematics disabilities in the primary grades: Seven principles of effective practice. *New Times for Division of Learning Disabilities (DLD), 26*(1), 1–2.

Fuchs, L. S., Fuchs, D., & Capizzi, A. M. (2005). Identifying appropriate test accommodations for students with learning disabilities. *Focus on Exceptional Children, 37,* 1–8.

Fuchs, L. S., Fuchs, D., Hamlet, C. L., Powell, S. R., Capizzi, A. M., & Seethaler, P. M. (2006). The effects of computer-assisted instruction on number combination skill in at-risk first graders. *Journal of Learning Disabilities, 39,* 467–475.

Fuchs, L. S. Fuchs, D., & Hollebeck, K. N. (2007). Extending responsiveness to intervention to mathematics at first and third grades. *Learning Disabilities Research and Practice, 22*(1), 13–24.

Fuchs, L. S., Fuchs, D., & Kazdan, S. (1999). Effects of peer-assisted learning strategies on high school students with serious reading problems. *Remedial and Special Education, 20*(5), 309–318.

Fuchs, L. S., Fuchs, D., Prentice, K., Burch, M., & Paulsen, K. (2002). Hot math: Promoting mathematical problem solving among third-grade students with disabilities. *Teaching Exceptional Children, 35*(1), 70–73.

Fuchs, L. S., Seethaler, P. M., Powell, S. R., Fuchs, D., Hamlett, C. L., & Fletcher, J. M. (2008). Effects of preventative tutoring on the mathematical problem solving of third-grade students with math and reading difficulties. *Exceptional Children, 74*(2), 155–173.

Fudge, D. L., & Skinner, C. H. (2007, March). *Taming the terrible transitions: Effective class-wide behavior management.* Presentation at the annual meeting of National Association of School Psychologists, New York.

Fulk, B. M. (1997). Think while you spell: A cognitive motivational approach to spelling instruction. *Teaching Exceptional Children, 29*(4), 70–71.

Fulk, B. M., & King, K. (2001). Classwide peer tutoring at work. *Teaching Exceptional Children, 34*(2), 48–53.

Fulk, B. M., & Stormont-Spurgin, M. (1995). Fourteen spelling strategies for students with learning disabilities. *Intervention in School and Clinic, 31*(1), 16–20.

Furner, J. M., Yahya, N., & Duffy, M. L. (2005) 20 ways to teach mathematics: Strategies to reach all students. *Intervention in School and Clinic, 41,* 16–23.

Futrell, M. H., & Gomez, J. (2008). How tracking creates a poverty of learning. *Educational Leadership, 65*(8), 74–79.

Gable, R. A., Arllen, N. L., Evans, W. H., & Whinnery, K. M. (1997). Strategies for evaluating collaborative mainstream instruction: "Let the data be our guide." *Preventing School Failure, 41*(4), 153–158.

Gable, R. A., Hester, P. H., Rock, M. L., & Hughes, K. G. (2009). Rules, praise, ignoring and reprimands revisited. *Intervention in School and Clinic, 44*(4), 195–295.

Gagnon, J. C., & Maccini, P. (2001). Preparing students with disabilities for algebra. *Teaching Exceptional Children, 34*(1), 8–15.

Gajria, M., Mullane, T., Sharp, E. R., & Heim, T. (2003, April). *Concept mapping: Improving content area comprehension for secondary students with learning disabilities.* Presentation at the annual meeting of the Council for Exceptional Children, Seattle.

Ganz, J. B., Kaylor, M., Bourgeois, B., & Hadden, K. (2008). The impact of social scripts and visual cues on verbal communication in three children with autism spectrum disorders. *Focus on Autism and Other Developmental Disabilities, 23*(2), 79–94.

Garcia, A. I., Jimenez, J. E., & Hess, S. (2006). Solving arithmetic word problems: An analysis of classification as a function of difficulty in children with and without arithmetic LD. *Journal of Learning Disabilities, 39,* 270–281.

Garcia, E. (2002). *Student cultural diversity: Understanding and meeting the challenge* (3rd ed.). Boston: Houghton Mifflin.

Garcia, E. E., & Jensen, B. T. (2007). Helping young Hispanic learners. *Educational Leadership, 64*(6), 34–39.

Garcia, E. E., Jensen, B. T., & Scribner, K. P. (2009). The demographic imperative. *Educational Leadership, 66*(7), 8–13.

Garcia, E. E., & Cuellar, D. (2006). Who are these linguistically and culturally diverse students? *Teachers College Record, 108*(11), 2220–2246.

Garcia, S. B., & Ortiz, A. A. (2006). Preventing disproportionate representation: Culturally and linguistically responsive prereferral interventions. *Teaching Exceptional Children, 38*(4), 64–67.

Gardner, H. (2006). *Multiple intelligences: New horizons.* New York: Basic Books.

Garmston, R., & Wellman, B. (1998). Teacher talk that makes a difference. *Educational Leadership, 55*(7), 30–34.

Garner, D. B. (2008). Postsecondary education success: Stories of three students with learning disabilities. *TEACHING Exceptional Children Plus, 4*(4) Article 4. Retrieved [June 19, 2009] from http://escholarship.bc.edu/education/tecplus/vol4/iss4/art4.

Garrick Duhaney, L. M. (2005). Fostering equity curriculum and pedagogy: Educating students with dialectical variations. In R. Hoosain & F. Salili (Eds.), *Language in multicultural education.* (pp. 95–114). Greenwich, CT: Information Age.

Garrick Duhaney, L. M., & Whittington-Couse, M. (1998, April). *Using learning styles and strategies to enhance academic learning for linguistically and culturally diverse students.* Presentation at the Conference on Providing

Appropriate Instruction and Services to Culturally and Linguistically Diverse Learners, Fishkill, NY.

Gately, S. E. (2004). Developing concept of word: The work of emergent readers. *Teaching Exceptional Children, 36*(6), 16–22.

Gately, S. E. (2005). Help your students deal with tragedy. *Intervention in School and Clinic, 41*(1), 5–8.

Gately, S. E. (2004). Facilitating reading comprehension for students on the autism spectrum. *Teaching Exceptional Children, 40*(3), 40–45.

Gay, G. (2004). Beyond *Brown*: Promoting equality through multicultural education. *Journal of Curriculum and Supervision, 19,* 193–217.

Gay, Lesbian, Straight Education Network. (2002a). *Curricular inclusion of LGBT content.* New York: Author.

Gay, Lesbian, Straight Education Network. (2002b). *Selected bibliography of books for children and young adults with LGBT characters and themes.* New York: Author.

Gee, J. P., & Levine, M. H. (2009). Welcome to our virtual worlds. *Educational Leadership, 66*(6), 48–52.

Gentry, J. R. (2005). Instructional techniques for emerging writers and special needs students at kindergarten and grade 1 levels. *Reading and Writing Quarterly: Overcoming Learning Difficulties, 21,* 113–134.

Gerber, P. J., & Price, L. A. (2003). Persons with learning disabilities in the workplace: What we know so far in the Americans with Disabilities Act era. *Learning Disabilities Research & Practice, 18*(2), 132.

Gersten, R. (1999). The changing face of bilingual education. *Educational Leadership, 56*(7), 41–45.

Gersten, R., & Baker, S. K., Smith-Johnson, J., Dimino, J., & Peterson, A. (2006). Eyes on the prize: Teaching complex historical content to middle school students with learning disabilities. *Exceptional Children, 72,* 264–280.

Gersten, R., & Chard, D. (1999). Number sense: Rethinking arithmetic instruction for students with mathematical disabilities. *Journal of Special Education, 33,* 18–28.

Gersten, R., Jordan, N. C., & Flojo, J. R. (2005). Early identification and interventions for students with mathematics difficulties. *Journal of Learning Disabilities, 38,* 293–304.

Gersten, R., & Geva, E. (2003). Teaching reading to early language learners. *Educational Leadership, 60*(7), 44–49.

Getch, Y., Bhukhanwala, F., & Neuharth-Pritchett, S. (2007). Strategies for helping children with diabetes in elementary and middle schools. *Teaching Exceptional Children, 39*(3), 46–51.

Giangreco, M. F. (2006). Foundational concepts and practices for educating students with severe disabilities. In M. E. Snell & F. Brown (Eds.), *Instruction of students with severe disabilities* (6th ed., pp. 1–27). Upper Saddle River, NJ: Merrill/Pearson Education.

Giangreco, M. F. (2007). Extending inclusive opportunities. *Educational Leadership, 64*(5), 34–38.

Giangreco, M. F., Baumgart, M. J., & Doyle, M. B. (1995). How inclusion can facilitate teaching and learning. *Intervention in School and Clinic, 30*(5), 273–278.

Giangreco, M. F., & Broer, S. M. (2007). School based screening to determine overreliance on paraprofessionals. *Focus on Autism and Other Developmental Disabilities, 22*(3), 149–159.

Giangreco, M. F., Dennis, R., Cloninger, C., Edelman, S., & Schattman, R. (1993). "I've counted Jon": Transformational experiences of teachers educating students with disabilities. *Exceptional Children, 59,* 359–372.

Giangreco, M. F., Edelman, S. W., & Broer, S. M. (2003). Schoolwide planning to improve paraeducator supports. *Exceptional Children, 70,* 63–79.

Giangreco, M. F., Yuan, S., McKenzie, B., Cameron, P., & Fialka, J. (2005). "Be careful what you wish for . . .": Five reasons to be concerned about the assignment of individual paraprofessionals. *Teaching Exceptional Children, 37*(5), 28–34.

Gibb, G. S., & Taylor Dyches, T. (2007). *Guide to writing quality individualized education programs.* Boston: Allyn & Bacon.

Gil, L. A. (2007). Bridging the transition gap from high school to college: Preparing high school students with disabilities for a successful postsecondary experience. *Teaching Exceptional Children, 40*(2), 12–17.

Ginsberg, M. B. (2007). Lessons at the kitchen table. *Educational Leadership, 64*(6), 56–61.

Gipe, J. P. (2006). *Multiple paths to literacy: Classroom techniques for struggling readers* (6th ed.). Upper Saddle River, NJ: Merrill/Pearson Education.

Goddard, Y. L., & Heron, T. E. (1998). Pleaze, teacher, help me learn to spFell better: Teach me self-correction. *Teaching Exceptional Children, 30*(6), 38–43.

Goddard, Y. L., & Sendi, C. (2008). Effects of self-monitoring on the narrative and expository writing of four fourth-grade students with learning disabilities. *Reading and Writing Quarterly: Overcoming Learning Difficulties, 24*(4), 408–433.

Goetz Ruffino, A., Mistrett, S. G., Tomita, M., & Hajare, P. (2006). The universal design for play tool: Establishing validity and reliability. Journal of Special Education Technology, *21*(4),

Goldenberg, C. (2008). Teaching English language learners: What the research does-does not-say. *American Educator, 32*(2), 8–23, 42–43.

Gollnick, D. M., & Chinn, P. C. (2009). *Multicultural education in a pluralistic society* (8th ed.). Upper Saddle River, NJ: Merrill/Pearson Education.

Goodwin, M. S. (2008). Enhancing and accelerating the pace of autism research and treatment: The promise of developing innovative technology. *Focus on Autism and Other Developmental Disabilities, 23*(2), 125–128.

Gordon, P. A., Feldman, D., & Chiriboga, J. (2005). Helping children with disabilities develop and maintain friendships. *Teacher Education and Special Education, 28,* 1–9.

Gormley, S., & Ruhl, K. L. (2005). Dialogic shared storybook reading: An instructional technique for use with young students in inclusive settings. *Reading and Writing Quarterly: Overcoming Learning Difficulties, 21,* 307–313.

Gorski, P. (2008). The myth of the "culture of poverty." *Educational Leadership, 65*(7), 32–37.

Gosselin, K. (1996). *Taking epilepsy to school.* Valley Park, MO: JayJo Books.

Graham, S. (1992). Helping students with LD progress as writers. *Intervention in School and Clinic, 27*(3), 134–144.

Graham, S., & Harris, K. R. (1992). Cognitive strategy instruction in written language for learning disabled students. In S. Vogel (Ed.), *Educational alternatives for teaching students with learning disabilities* (pp. 95–115). New York: Springer.

Graham, S., & Harris, K. R. (2005). Improving the writing performance of young struggling writers: Theoretical and programmatic research from the Center on Accelerating Student Learning. *Journal of Special Education, 39,* 19–33.

Graham, S., & Harris, K. R. (2006). Preventing writing difficulties: Providing additional handwriting and spelling instruction to at-risk children in first grade. *Teaching Exceptional Children, 38*(5), 64–66.

Graham, S., Harris, K. R., & Fink, B. (2000). Extra handwriting instruction: Prevent writing difficulties right from the start. *Teaching Exceptional Children, 33*(2), 88–91.

Graham, S., Harris, K. R., & Fink-Chorzempa, B. (2003). Extra spelling instruction: Promoting better spelling, writing and reading performance right from the start. *Teaching Exceptional Children, 35*(6), 66–68.

Graham, S., Harris, K. R., & Larsen, L. (2001). Prevention and intervention of writing difficulties for students with learning disabilities. *Learning Disabilities Research and Practice, 16,* 74–84.

Graham, S., Harris, K. R., & Loynachan, C. (1996). The directed spelling thinking activity: Application with high-frequency words. *Learning Disabilities Research and Practice, 11*(1), 34–40.

Graham, S., & Harris, K. R., & MacArthur, C. (2006). Explicitly teaching struggling writers: Strategies for mastering the writing process. *Intervention in School and Clinic, 41,* 290–294.

Grande, M. (2008). Using dialogue journals and interest inventories with classroom volunteers. *Teaching Exceptional Children, 41*(2), 56–65.

Grandin, T. (2007). Autism from the inside. *Educational Leadership, 64*(5), 29–32.

Grant, R. (1993). Strategic training for using text headings to improve students' processing of content. *Journal of Reading, 36,* 482–488.

Graves, B., Leiva, P., & Sparaco, J. (2005, November). *HEP Oneonta/Camp Oneonta-Making a huge difference.* Presentation at the New York State Migrant Education Training, Syracuse, NY.

Gravois, T. A., & Rosenfeld, S. A. (2006). Impact of instructional consultation teams on disproportionate referral and placement of minority students in special education. *Remedial and Special Education, 27,* 42–52.

Green, P. (2009, January 15, 2009). Your mother is moving in? That's great. *New York Times,* DI, D4.

Greer, C., & Oldendorf, S. (2005). Teaching religious diversity through children's literature. *Childhood Education, 81,* 209–218.

Gregg, N. (2007). Underserved and unprepared: Postsecondary learning disabilities. *Learning Disabilities Research and Practice, 22*(4), 219–228.

Gregg, N., & Mather, N. (2002). School is fun at recess: Informal analyses of written language for students with learning disabilities. *Journal of Learning Disabilities, 35,* 7–22.

Griffin, H. C., Griffin, L. W., Fitch, C. W., Albera, V., & Gingras, H. (2006). Educational interventions for individuals with Asperger syndrome. *Intervention in School and Clinic, 41,* 150–155.

Griffin, H. C., Williams, S. C., Davis, M. L., & Engleman, M. (2002). Using technology to enhance cues for children with low vision. *Teaching Exceptional Children, 35*(2), 36–42.

Grigorenko, E. L. (2009). Dynamic assessment and response to intervention: Two sides of one coin. *Journal of Learning Disabilities, 42*(2), 111–132.

Groves Scott, V. (2009). *Phonemic awareness: Ready-to-use lessons, activities, and games* (2nd ed.). Thousand Oaks, CA: Corwin Press.

Guajardo Alvarado, C. (2007, November/December). Dyslexia and the Spanish-speaking and bilingual student. *NABE News,* 5–8, 28.

Guernsey, L. (2003, August 23). Fishing for information? Try better bait. *New York Times,* G8.

Guernsey, L. (2009, March 23). Rewards for students under a microscope. *New York Times,* D1, D6.

Guerra, N. S. (2009). LIBRE stick figure tool: A graphic organizer to foster self-regulated social cognitive problem solving. *Intervention in School and Clinic, 44*(4), 229–233.

Gun Han, K., & Chadsey, J. G. (2004). The influence of gender patterns and grade level on friendship expectations of middle school students toward peers with severe disabilities. *Focus on Autism and Other Developmental Disabilities, 19,* 205–214.

Gunter, P. L., Shores, R. E., Jack, S. L., Rasmussen, S. K., & Flowers, J. (1995). On the move: Using teacher/student proximity to improve students' behavior. *Teaching Exceptional Children, 28*(1), 12–14.

Gurganus, S. (2004). 20 ways to promote number sense. *Intervention in School and Clinic, 40,* 55–58.

Guskey, T. R. (2001). Helping standards make the grade. *Educational Leadership, 59*(1), 20–27.

Guskey, T. R. (2002). Critical friends. *Educational Leadership, 59*(6), 45–51.

Guskey, T. R. (2003). How classroom assessments improve learning. *Educational Leadership, 60*(5), 6–11.

Guskey, T. R., & Anderman, E. M. (2008). Students at bat. *Educational Leadership, 66*(3), 8–15.

Guskey, T. R., & Bailey, J. M. (2009). *Developing standards-based report cards.* Thousand Oaks, CA: Corwin Press.

Gut, D. M. (2000). We are social beings: Learning how to learn cooperatively. *Teaching Exceptional Children, 32*(5), 46–53.

Gut, D. M., & Safran, S. P. (2002). Cooperative learning and social stories: Effective social skills strategies for reading teachers. *Reading and Writing Quarterly: Overcoming Learning Difficulties, 18*(1), 87–91.

Guthrie, J. T., & Davis, M. H. (2003). Motivating struggling readers in middle school through an engagement model of classroom practice. *Reading and Writing Quarterly: Overcoming Learning Difficulties, 19,* 59–85.

Gutierrez, M. (2007). *Addressing the needs of LEP/ELL students.* New Paltz, NY: Mid-Hudson Migrant Education Outreach Program.

Guzel-Ozmen, R. (2006). The effectiveness of modified cognitive strategy instruction in writing with mildly mentally retarded Turkish students. *Exceptional Children, 72,* 281–297.

Hadden, S., & Fowler, S. A. (1997). Preschool: A new beginning for children and parents. *Teaching Exceptional Children, 30*(1), 36–39.

Hagaman, J. L., & Reid, R. (2008). The effects of the paraphrasing strategy on the reading comprehension of middle school students at risk for failure in reading. *Remedial and Special Education, 29*(4), 222–234.

Hagan-Burke, S., & Jefferson, G. L. (2002). Using data to promote academic benefit for included students with mild disabilities. *Preventing School Failure, 46*, 113–117.

Hagiwara, T. (1998). Introduce multiculturalism in your classroom. *Intervention in School and Clinic, 34*(1), 43–44.

Hall, J. (2008). *Childhood cancer survivors face more hurdles.* The Edmonton Journal. Retrieved May 27, 2008, from http://Canada.com/components.

Hall, L. J. (2009). *Autism spectrum disorders: From theory to practice.* Upper Saddle River, NJ: Merrill/Pearson Education.

Hall, L. J., & McGregor, J. A. (2000). A follow-up study of the peer relationships of children with disabilities in an inclusive school. *Journal of Special Education, 34*, 114–126, 153.

Haller, A. K., & Montgomery, J. K. (2004). Noise-induced hearing loss in children: What educators need to know. *Teaching Exceptional Children, 36*(4), 22–27.

Hanc, J. (2008). *Finding similarities among the differences.* Retrieved [December 12, 2008] from http://www.nytimes.com/2008/11/11/giving/11SERVE.html?

Hang, Q., & Rabren, K. (2009). An examination of co-teaching: Perspectives and efficacy indictors. *Remedial and Special Education, 30*(5), 259–268.

Hansen, D. L., & Morgan, R. L. (2008). Teaching grocery store purchasing skills to students with intellectual disabilities using a computer-based instruction program. *Education and Training in Developmental Disabilities, 43*(4), 431–442.

Hansen, S. D., & Lignugaris/Kraft, B. (2005). Effects of a dependent group contingency on the verbal interactions of middle school students with emotional disturbance. *Behavioral Disorders, 30*, 170–184.

Hapgood, S., & Sullivan Palinscar, A. (2007). Where literacy and science intersect. *Educational Leadership, 64*(4), 56–61.

Hapner, A., & Imel, B. (2002). The students' voices: "Teachers started to listen and show respect." *Remedial and Special Education, 23*, 122–126.

Harbort, G., Gunter, P. L., Hull, K., Brown, Q., Venn, M. L., Wiley, L. P., & Wiley, E. W. (2007). Behaviors of teachers in co-taught classes in a secondary school. *Teacher Education and Special Education, 30*(1), 13–23.

Harmon, J. M. Hedrick, W. B., & Wood, K. D. (2005). Research on vocabulary instruction in content areas: Implications for struggling readers. *Reading and Writing Quarterly: Overcoming Learning Difficulties, 21*, 261–280.

Harn, B. A., Linan-Thompson, S., & Roberts, G. (2008). Intensifying instruction: Does additional instructional time make a difference for the most at-risk first graders? *Journal of Learning Disabilities, 41*(2), 115–125.

Harn, W. E., Bradshaw, M. L., & Ogletree, B. T. (1999). The speech-language pathologist in the schools: Changing roles. *Intervention in School and Clinic, 34*(3), 163–169.

Harniss, M. K., Caros, J., & Gersten, R. (2007). Impact on the design of U.S. history textbooks on content acquisition and academic engagement of special education. *Journal of Learning Disabilities, 40*(2), 100–110.

Harper, G. F., & Maheady, L. (2007). Peer-mediated teaching and students with learning disabilities. *Intervention in School and Clinic, 43*(2), 101–107.

Harris, C. R. (1991). Identifying and serving the gifted new immigrant. *Teaching Exceptional Children, 23*, 26–30.

Harris, K. R., Graham, S., & Mason, L. (2002). POW plus TREE equals powerful opinion essays. *Teaching Exceptional Children, 34*(5), 74–77.

Harris, K. R., Graham, S., Mason, L. H., & Friedlander, B. (2008). *POWERFUL writing strategies for all students.* Baltimore, MD: Brookes.

Harris, L.A. (2007). Adolescent literacy: Wordy study with middle and high school students. *TEACHING Exceptional Children Plus, 3*(4) Article 4. Retrieved [August 23, 2009] from http://escholarship.bc.edu/education/tecplus/vol3/iss4/art4.

Harrison, A. (2009). Bookshare.org: Accessible texts for students with print disabilities. *Journal of Special Education Technology, 24*(2), 38–41.

Harry, B. (1995). African American families. In B. A. Ford, F. E. Obiakor, & J. M. Patton (Eds.), *Effective education of African American exceptional learners* (pp. 211–233). Austin, TX: Pro-ED.

Harry, B. (2008). Collaboration with culturally and linguistically diverse families: Ideal versus reality. *Exceptional Children, 74*(3), 372–388.

Harry, B., Allen, N., & McLaughlin, M. (1995). Communication versus compliance: African-American parents' involvement in special education. *Exceptional Children, 61*(4), 364–377.

Harry, B., Arnaiz, P., Klingner, J., & Sturges, K. (2008). Schooling and construction of identity among minority students in Spain and the United States. *The Journal of Special Education, 42*(1), 5–14.

Harry, B., & Klingner, J. K. (2007). Discarding the deficit model. *Educational Leadership, 64*(5), 16–21.

Hart, D., Mele-McCarthy, J., Pasternack, R. H., Zimbrich, K., & Parker, D. R. (2004). Community college: A pathway to success for youth with learning, cognitive, and intellectual disabilities in secondary settings. *Education and Training in Developmental Disabilities, 3*, 54–66.

Hart, J. E., & Whalon, K. J. (2008). Promote academic engagement and communication of students with autism spectrum disorder in inclusive settings. *Intervention in School and Clinic, 44*(2), 116–120.

Hartley, J. (2008). "You should read this book." *Educational Leadership, 65*(6), 73–75.

Hartman, C. (2006). Students on the move. *Educational Leadership, 63*(5), 20–24.

Hasselbring, T. S., & Bausch, M. E. (2006). Assistive technologies for reading. *Educational Leadership, 63*(4), 72–75.

Hasselbring, T. S., & Goin, L. I. (2004). Literacy instruction for older struggling readers: What is the role of technology. *Reading and Writing Quarterly: Overcoming Learning Difficulties, 20*, 123–144.

Hasselbring, T. S., Lott, A., & Zydney, J. (2005). *Technology-supported math instruction for students with disabilities: Two decades of research and development.* Washington,

DC: Center for Implementing Technology in Education. Available at http://www.citeducation.org/mathmatrix/#.

Hawbaker, B. W. (2007). Student-led IEP meetings: Planning and implementation strategies. *Teaching Exceptional Children Plus*, 3(5) Article 4. Retrieved February 22, 2009 from http://escholarship.bc.edu/education/tecplus/vol3/iss5/art4.

Haydon, T., Borders, C., Embury, D., & Clarke, L. (2009). Using effective instructional devilery as a classwide management tool. *Beyond Behavior, 18*(2), 12–17.

Haynes, C. C. (2005). Living with our deepest differences: Religious diversity in the classroom. In D. A. Byrnes & G. Kiger (Eds.), *Common bonds: Anti-bias teaching in a diverse society* (3rd ed., pp. 25–35). Olney, MD: Association of Childhood Education International.

Heath, M. A., Leavy, D., Hansen, K., Ryan, K., Lawrence, L., & Sonntag, A. G. (2008). Coping with grief: Guidelines and resources for assisting children. *Intervention in School and Clinic, 43*(5), 259–269.

Heaton, S., & O'Shea, D. J. (1995). Using mnemonics to make mnemonics. *Teaching Exceptional Children, 28*(1), 34–36.

Hehir, T. (2005). New directions in special education: Eliminating ableism in policy and practice. Cambridge, MA: Harvard Educational Publishing Group.

Hehir, T. (2007). Confronting ableism. *Educational Leadership, 64*(5), 8–14.

Heinrichs, R. R. (2003). A whole-school approach to bullying: Special considerations for children with exceptionalities. *Intervention in School and Clinic, 38,* 195–204.

Heller, K. W. (2009a). Traumatic spinal cord injury and spina bifida. In K. W. Heller, P. E. Forney, P. A. Alberto, S. Best, & M. N. Schwartzman (Eds.), *Understanding physical, health, and multiple disabilities* (2nd ed., pp. 94–117.). Upper Saddle River, NJ: Merrill/Pearson Education.

Heller, K. W. (2009b). Diabetes. In K. W. Heller, P. E. Forney, P. A. Alberto, S. Best, & M. N. Schwartzman (Eds.), *Understanding physical, health, and multiple disabilities* (2nd ed., pp. 333–348.). Upper Saddle River, NJ: Merrill/Pearson Education.

Heller, K. W. (2009c). Monitoring students' disabilities and individualized health care. In K. W. Heller, P. E. Forney, P. A. Alberto, S. Best, & M. N. Schwartzman (Eds.), *Understanding physical, health, and multiple disabilities* (2nd ed., pp. 349–366.). Upper Saddle River, NJ: Merrill/Pearson Education.

Heller, K. W., Eastbrooks, S., McJannet, D., & Swinehart-Jones, D. (2009). Vision loss, hearing loss, and deaf-blindness. In K. W. Heller, P. E. Forney, P. A. Alberto, S. Best, & M. N. Schwartzman (Eds.), *Understanding physical, health, and multiple disabilities* (2nd ed., pp. 191–218.). Upper Saddle River, NJ: Merrill/Pearson Education.

Heller, K. W., & Cohen, E. T. (2009). Seizures and epilepsy. In K. W. Heller, P. E. Forney, P. A. Alberto, S. Best, & M. N. Schwartzman (Eds.), *Understanding physical, health, and multiple disabilities* (2nd ed., pp. 294–315.). Upper Saddle River, NJ: Merrill/Pearson Education.

Heller, K. W., Forney, P. E., Alberto, P. A., Best, S., & Schwartzman, M. N. (2009). *Understanding physical, health, and multiple disabilities* (2nd ed.). Upper Saddle River, NJ: Merrill/Pearson Education.

Heller, K. W., & Garrett, J. T. (2009). Cerebral palsy. In K. W. Heller, P. E. Forney, P. A. Alberto, S. Best, & M. N. Schwartzman (Eds.), *Understanding physical, health, and multiple disabilities* (2nd ed., pp. 72–93). Upper Saddle River, NJ: Merrill/Pearson Education.

Heller, K. W., Mezei, P., & Schwartzman, M. (2009). Muscular dystrophies. In K. W. Heller, P. E. Forney, P. A. Alberto, S. Best, & M. N. Schwartzman (Eds.), *Understanding physical, health, and multiple disabilities* (2nd ed., pp. 232–260). Upper Saddle River, NJ: Merrill/Pearson Education.

Heller, K. W., & Schwarzman, M. (2009). Cystic Fibrosis. In K. W. Heller, P. E. Forney, P. A. Alberto, S. Best, & M. N. Schwartzman (Eds.), *Understanding physical, health, and multiple disabilities* (2nd ed., pp. 261–279). Upper Saddle River, NJ: Merrill/Pearson Education.

Heller, K. W., Schwarzman, M., & Fowler, L. (2009). Asthma. In K. W. Heller, P. E. Forney, P. A. Alberto, S. Best, & M. N. Schwartzman (Eds.), *Understanding physical, health, and multiple disabilities* (2nd ed., pp. 316–332). Upper Saddle River, NJ: Merrill/Pearson Education.

Heller, K. W, Mezei, P. J., & Thompson Avant, M. J. (2008). Meeting the assistive technology needs of students with Duchenne Muscular Dystrophy. *Journal of Special Education Technology, 23*(4), 15–30.

Hendricks, D. R., & Wehman, P. (2009). Transition from school to adulthood for youth with autism spectrum disorders: Review and recommendations. *Focus on Autism and Other Developmental Disabilities, 24*(2), 77–88.

Henfield, M. S., Moore, J. L., & Wood, C. (2008). Inside and outside gifted education programming: Hidden challenges of African American students. *Exceptional Children, 74*(4), 433–452.

Henley, M. (2010). *Classroom management: A proactive approach* (2nd ed.). Upper Saddle River, NJ: Merrill/Pearson Education.

Herrera, S. G., Murry, K. G., & Cabral, R. M. (2007). *Assessment accommodations for classroom teachers of culturally and ligustically diverse students*. Boston: Allyn & Bacon.

Herring-Harrison, T. J., Gardner, R., & Lovelack, T. S. (2007). Adapting peer tutoring for learners who are deaf or hard of hearing. *Intervention in School and Clinic, 43*(2), 82–87.

Herschell, A. D., Greco, L. A., Filcheck, H. A., & McNeil, C. B. (2002). Who is testing whom? Ten suggestions for managing the disruptive behavior of young children during testing. *Intervention in School and Clinic, 37,* 140–148.

Hershey, S., & Reilly, V. (2009). "Hobo" is not a respectful word. *Educational Leadership, 66*(8), 64–67.

Hessler, T., & Konrad, M. (2008). Using curriculum-based measurement to drive IEPs and instruction in written expression. *Teaching Exceptional Children, 41*(2), 28–39.

Hessler, T., Konrad, M., & Alber-Morgan, S. (2009). Assess student writing. *Intervention in School and Clinic, 45*(1), 68–71.

Hester, P. (2002). What teachers can do to prevent behavior problems in schools. *Preventing School Failure, 47,* 33–38.

Hetherington, E. M., & Kelly, J. (2000). *For better or for worse: Divorce reconsidered*. New York: Norton.

Heward, W. L. (2009). *Exceptional children: An introduction to special education* (9th ed.). Upper Saddle River, NJ: Merrill/Pearson Education.

Higbee Mandlebaum, L., Hodges, D., & Messenheimer, T. (2007). Get students to read it again. *Intervention in School and Clinic, 42*(6), 295–299.

Higgins, K., Boone, R., & Lovitt, T. C. (1996). Hypertext support for remedial students and students with learning disabilities. *Journal of Learning Disabilities, 29*(4), 402–412.

Higgins, K., Boone, R., & Williams, D. L. (2000). Evaluating educational software for special education. *Intervention in School and Clinic, 36,* 109–115.

Hines, J. T., (2008). Making collaboration work in inclusive high school classrooms: Recommendations for principals. *Intervention in School and Clinic, 43*(5) 277–282.

Hines, R. A. (2001, December). *Inclusion in middle schools.* Champaign, IL: ERIC Clearinghouse on Elemenentary and Early Childhood Education.

Hobbs, T., Bruch, L., Sanko, J., & Astolfi, C. (2001). Friendship on the inclusive electronic playground. *Teaching Exceptional Children, 33*(6), 46–51.

Hobson v. Hansen, 269 F. Supp. 401 (1967) (D.C.C., 1967).

Hodges, D., Higbee Mandlebaum, L., Boff, C., & Miller, M. (2007). Instructional strategies online database (ISOD). *Intervention in School and Clinic, 42*(4), 219–224.

Hoerr, T. R. (2009). The rule of six. *Educational Leadership, 66*(7), 83–84.

Hogan, T. P. (2007). *Educational assessment: A practical introduction.* Hoboken, NJ: John Wiley & Sons.

Hogansen, J. M., Powers, K., Geenen, S., Gil-Kashiwabara, E., & Powers, L. (2008). Transition goals and experiences of females with disabilities: Youth, parents, and professionals. *Exceptional Children, 74*(2), 215–234.

Hollenbeck, K., Rozek-Tedesco, M. A., Tindal, G., & Glasgow, A. (2000). An exploratory study of student-paced versus teacher-paced accommodations for large-scale math tests. *Journal of Special Education Technology, 15*(2), 27–38.

Holzer, M. F., Madaus, J. W., Bray, M. A., & Kehle, T. J. (2009). The test-taking strategy intervention for college students with learning disabilities. *Learning Disabilities Research and Practice, 24,* 44–56.

Hong, B. S. S. Ivy, W. F., Gonzalez, H. R., & Ehrensberger, W. (2007). Preparing students for postsecondary education. *Teaching Exceptional Children, 40*(1), 32–39.

Hooper, S. R., & Umansky, W. (2009). *Young children with special needs* (5th ed.). Upper Saddle River, NJ: Merrill/Pearson Education.

Hoover, J. J. Baca, L., Smith-Davis, J., & Wexler Love, E. (2007). Preparing masters teachers for educating immigrant students with special needs: A summary of research. *NABE News, 30*(2), 11–13, 26.

Hoover, J. J., Klingner, J. K., Baca, L., & Patton, J. M. (2008). *Methods for teaching culturally and linguistically diverse exceptional learners.* Upper Saddle River, NJ: Merrill/Pearson Education.

Hoover, J. J., & Patton, J. R. (2008). The role of special educators in a multitiered instructional system. *Intervention in School and Clinic, 43*(4), 195–202.

Hopkins, J. (2006). All students being equal. *Technology and Learning, 26*(10), 26–28.

Hopkins, S., & Egeberg, H. (2009). Retrieval of simple addition facts: Complexities involved in addressing a commonly identified mathematical learning difficulty. *Journal of Learning Disabilties, 42*(3), 215–229.

Horne, J. (1998). Rising to the challenge. *Teaching Tolerance, 7*(1), 26–31.

Horney, M. A., Anderson-Inman, L., Terrazas-Arellanes, F., Schulte, W., Mundorf, J., Smolkowski, K., Katz-Buonincontro, J., & Frisbee, M. L. (2009). Exploring the effects of digital note taking on student comprehension of science texts. *Journal of Special Education Technology, 24*(3), 45–61.

Hourcade, J., Parette, P., & Anderson, H. (2003). Accountability in collaboration: A framework for evaluation. *Education and Training in Developmental Disabilities, 38,* 398–404.

Howard, L., Grogan Dresser, S., & Dunklee, D. R. (2009). *Poverty is not a learning disability: Equalizing opportunities for low SES students.* Thousand Oaks, CA: Corwin Press.

Howard, L., & Potts, E. A. (2009). Using co-planning time: Strategies for a successful co-teaching marriage. *Teaching Exceptional Children Plus, 5*(4) Article 2. Retrieved May 19, 2009, from http://escholarship.bc.edu/tecplus/vol5/iss4/art2.

Howard, S., DaDeppo, L. M. W., & De La Paz, S. (2008). Getting the bugs out with PESTS: A mnemonic approach to spelling sight words for students with learning disabilities. *TEACHING Exceptional Children Plus, 4*(5) Article 3. Retrieved [August 23, 2009] from http:// escholarship.bc.edu/education/tecplus/vol4/iss5/art3.

Howell, J. (2008). Sensory impairments. In M. S. Rosenberg, D. L. Westling, & J. McLeskey (Eds.), *Special education for today's teachers: An introduction* (pp. 346–373). Upper Saddle River, NJ: Merrill/Pearson Education.

Hu, W. (2008, March 16). In a time of distracted ears, teachers ensure they're loud and clear. *New York Times,* 37.

Hu, W. (2009, April 5). Schools' gossip girls and boys get some lessons in empathy. *New York Times,* 1, 26.

Huber, J. J. (2005). Collaborative units for addressing multiple grade levels. *Intervention in School and Clinic, 40,* 301–308.

Hudson, P. (1996). Using a learning set to increase the test performance of students with learning disabilities in social studies classes. *Learning Disabilities Research and Practice, 11*(2), 78–85.

Hudson, P., & Miller, S. P. (2006). *Designing and implementing mathematics instruction for students with diverse learning needs.* Boston: Allyn & Bacon.

Hudson, P. J., Shupe, M., Vasquez, E., & Miller, S. P. (2008). Teaching data analysis to elementary students with mild disabilities. *TEACHING Exceptional Children Plus, 4*(3) Article 5. Retrieved [July 2, 2009] from http://escholarship. bc.edu/education/tecplus/vol4/iss3/art5.

Hudson, R. F., Pullen, P. C., Lane, H. B., & Torgesen, J. K. (2009). The complex nature of reading fluency: A multidimensional view. *Reading and Writing Quarterly: Overcoming Learning Difficulties, 25*(1), 4–32.

Hudson, R. F., & Smith, S. W. (2001). Effective reading instruction for struggling Spanish-speaking readers:

A combination of two literatures. *Intervention in School and Clinic, 37,* 36–39.

Huebner, T. A. (2009). Encouraging girls to pursue math and science. *Educational Leadership, 67*(1), 90–91.

Hughes, C., Carter, E. W., Hughes, T., Bradford, E., & Copeland, S. R. (2002). Effects of instructional versus non-instructional roles on the social interactions of high school students. *Education and Training in Mental Retardation and Developmental Disabilities, 37,* 146–162.

Hughes, C., Copeland, S. R., Agran, M., Wehmeyer, M., Rodi, M. S., & Presley, J. A. (2002). Using self-monitoring to improve performance in general education high school classes. *Education and Training in Mental Retardation and Developmental Disabilities, 37,* 262–272.

Hughes, C., Copeland, S. R., Guth, C., Rung, L. L., Hwang, B., Kleeb, G., & Strong, M. (2001). General education students' perspectives on their involvement in a high school peer buddy program. *Education and Training in Mental Retardation and Developmental Disabilities, 36,* 343–356.

Hughes, C., Guth, C., Hall, S., Presley, J., Dye, M., & Byers, C. (1999). "They are my best friends": Peer buddies promote inclusion in high school. *Teaching Exceptional Children, 31*(5), 32–37.

Hughes, C., Pitkin, S. E., & Lorden, S. W. (1998). Assessing preferences and choices of persons with severe and profound mental retardation. *Education and Training in Mental Retardation and Developmental Disabilities, 33*(4), 299–316.

Hughes, C., Rung, L. L., Wehmeyer, M. L., Agran, M., Copeland, S. R., & Hwang, B. (2000). Self-prompted communication book use to increase social interactions among high school students. *Journal of the Association for Persons with Severe Handicaps, 25,* 153–166.

Hughes, C., & Weiss, M. P. (2008). Making the transition to college for students with learning disabilities. *New Times for DLD, 26*(3), 1–2.

Hughes, C. A., Ruhl, K. L., Schumaker, J. B., & Deshler, D. D. (2002). Effects of instruction in an assignment completion strategy on the homework performance of students with learning disabilities in general education classes. *Learning Disabilities Research and Practice, 17,* 1–18.

Hughes, C. A., Deshler, D. D., Ruhl, K. L., & Schumaker, J. B. (1993). Test-taking strategy instruction for adolescents with emotional and behavioral disorders. *Journal of Emotional and Behavioral Disorders, 1*(3), 189–198.

Hughes, C. A., & Weiss, M. P. (2008). Making the transition to college for students with learning disabilities. *New Times for DLD, 26*(3), 1–2, 4.

Hughes, C. A. (1996). Memory and test-taking strategies. In D. D. Deshler, E. S. Ellis, & B. K. Lenz (Eds.), *Teaching adolescents with learning disabilities: Strategies and methods* (2nd ed., pp. 209–266). Denver: Love.

Huguelet, J. (2007). No more haves and have nots. *Educational Leadership, 64*(8), 45–47.

Hulett, K. E. (2009). *Legal aspects of special education.* Upper Saddle River, NJ: Merrill/Pearson Education.

Hume, K. (2007). Practical strategies to increase active involvement in students with developmental disabilities, *DDD Express, 18*(2), 1, 12.

Hung, W., & Lockard, J. (2007). Using an advance organizer guided behavior matrix to support teachers' problem solving in classroom behavior management. *Journal of Special Education Technology, 22*(1), 21–36.

Hunt, P., Alwell, M., Farron-Davis, F., & Goetz, L. (1996). Creating socially supportive environments for fully included students who experience multiple disabilities. *Journal of the Association for Persons with Severe Handicaps, 21,* 53–71.

Hunt, P., Farron-Davis, F., Beckstead, S., Curtis, D., & Goetz, L. (1994). Evaluating the effects of placement of students with severe disabilities in general education versus special class. *Journal of the Association for Persons with Severe Handicaps, 19*(3), 200–214.

Hunt, P., Hirose-Hatae, A., Doering, K., Karasoff, P., & Goetz, L. (2000). "Community" is what I think everyone is talking about. *Remedial and Special Education, 21,* 305–317.

Hunt, P., Soto, G., Maier, J., & Doering, K. (2003). Collaborative teaming to support students at risk and students with severe disabilities in general education classrooms. *Exceptional Children, 69,* 315–332.

Hyde, A. (2007). Mathematics and cognition. *Educational Leadership, 65*(3), 43–47.

Idol, L. (1987). Group story mapping: A comprehension strategy for both skilled and unskilled readers. *Journal of Learning Disabilities, 20,* 196–205.

Idol, L. (1997). Key questions related to building collaborative and inclusive schools. *Journal of Learning Disabilities, 30*(4), 384–394.

Idol, L. (2006). Toward inclusion of special education students in general education: A program evaluation of eight schools. *Remedial and Special Education, 27,* 77–94.

Idol, L., Nevin, A., & Paolucci-Whitcomb, P. (1999). *Models for curriculum-based assessment: A blueprint for learning.* Austin, TX: PRO-ED.

Igoa, C. (1995). *The inner world of the immigrant child.* New York: St. Martin's.

Inge, K. J., & Moon, M. S. (2006). Vocational prepartation and transition. In M. E. Snell & F. Brown (Eds.), *Instruction of students with severe disabilities* (6th ed., pp. 569–609). Upper Saddle River, NJ: Merrill/Pearson Education.

Invernizzi, M., Johnston, F., Baer, D. H., & Templeton, S. (2009). *Words their way: Word sorts for within word pattern spellers* (2nd ed.). Upper Saddle River, NJ: Pearson Education.

Irvine, J. J. (1991, May). *Multicultural education: The promises and obstacles.* Paper presented at the Sixth Annual Benjamin Matteson Invitational Conference of the State University of New York at New Paltz, New Paltz.

Irving Independent School District v. Tatro, 104 S. Ct. 3371, 82 L.Ed. 2d 664 (1984).

Israel, S. (2009, March 8). For many homeless students, schools substitute for homes. *Times Herald Record,* 6–7.

Ives, B. (2007). Graphic organizers applied to secondary algebra instruction for students with learning disabilties. *Learning Disabilities Research and Practice, 22*(2), 110–118.

Izzo, M. V., Yurick, A., & McArrell, B. (2009). Supported eText: Effects of text-to-speech on access and achievement for high school students with disabilities. *Journal of Special Education Technology, 24*(3), 9–20.

Jackson, A. (2007). High schools in the global age. *Educational Leadership, 65*(8), 58–61.

Jackson, F. B. (2002). Crossing content: A strategy for students with learning disabilities. *Intervention in School and Clinic, 37,* 279–282.

Jaime, K., & Knowlton, E. (2007). Visual supports for students with behavior and cognitive challenges. *Intervention in School and Clinic, 42*(5), 259–270.

Jellinek, M., Bostic, J. Q., & Schlozman, S. C. (2007). When a student dies. *Educational Leadership, 65*(3), 78–82.

Jenkins, J. R., Graff, J. J., & Miglioretti, D. L. (2009). Estimating reading growth using intermittent CBM progress monitoring. *Exceptional Children, 75*(2), 151–164.

Jewell, M. (2009). Undocumented—with college dreams. *Educational Leadership, 66*(7), 48–52.

Jik Bae, S., & Clark, G. M. (2005). Incorporate diversity awareness in the classroom: What teachers can do. *Intervention in School and Clinic, 41,* 49–51.

Jimenez, B. A., Browder, D. M., & Courtade, G. R. (2008). Teaching an algebraic equation to high school students with moderate developmental disabilities. *Education and Training in Developmental Disabilties, 43*(2), 266–274.

Jimenez, J. E., del Rosario Ortiz, M., Rodrigo, M., Hernandez-Valle, I., Ramirez, G., Estevez, A., O'Shanahan, I., & de la Luz Trabue, M. (2003). Do the effects of computer-assisted practice differ for children with reading disabilities with and without IQ-achievement discrepancy? *Journal of Learning Disabilities, 36,* 34–47.

Jitendra, A. K. (2002). Teaching students math problem-solving through graphic representations. *Teaching Exceptional Children, 34*(4), 34–39.

Jitendra, A. K., DiPipi, C. M., & Perron-Jones, N. (2002). An exploratory study of schema-based word-problem-solving instruction for middle school students with learning disabilities: An emphasis on conceptual and procedural understanding. *Journal of Special Education, 36,* 23–38.

Jitendra, A. K., Edwards, L. L., Sacks, G., & Jacobson, L. A. (2004). What research says about vocabulary instruction for students with learning disabilities. *Exceptional Children, 70,* 299–322.

Jitendra, A. K., Griffin, C., Deatline-Buchman, A., Dipipi-Hoy, C., Scesniak, E., Sokol, N. G., & Xin, Y. P. (2005). Adherence to mathematics professional standards and instructional criteria for problem-solving in mathematics. *Exceptional Children, 71,* 319–338.

Jitendra, A. K., Griffin, C., Haria, P. Leh, J. Adams, A., & Kaduvetoor, A. (2007). A comparison of single and multiple strategy instruction on third grade students' mathematical problem solving. *Journal of Educational Psychology, 99,* 115–127.

Johns, B. H., & Carr, V. G. (1995). *Techniques for managing verbally and physically aggressive students.* Denver: Love.

Johnson, D. R., & Johnson, F. P. (2009). *Joining together: Group theory and group skills* (10th ed.). Upper Saddle River, NJ: Merrill/Pearson Education.

Johnson, D. R., Mellard, D. F., & Lancaster, P. (2007). Road to success: Helping young adults with learning disabilities plan and prepare for employment. *Teaching Exceptional Children, 39*(6), 26–32.

Johnson, D. R., Stodden, R. A., Emanuel, E. J., Luecking, R., & Mack, M. (2002). Current challenges facing secondary education and transition services: What research tells us. *Exceptional Children, 68,* 519–531.

Johnson, D. W., Johnson, R. T. (1996). Peacemakers: Teaching students to resolve their own and schoolmates' conflicts. In E. L. Meyen, G. A. Vergason, & R. J. Whelan (Eds.), *Strategies for teaching exceptional children in inclusive settings* (pp. 311–329). Denver: Love.

Johnson, D. W., Johnson, R. T., & Holubec, E. (2002). *Circles of learning* (5th ed.). Edina, MN: Interaction.

Johnson, E. R. (2009). *Academic language! Academic literacy!* Thousand Oaks, CA: Corwin Press.

Johnson, E. S., & Smith, L. (2008). Implementation of response to intervention at middle school: Challenges and potential benefits. *Teaching Exceptional Children, 40*(3), 46–52.

Johnson, G., Johnson, R. L., & Jefferson-Aker, C. R. (2001). HIV/AIDS prevention: Effective instructional strategies for adolescents with mild mental retardation. *Teaching Exceptional Children, 33* (6), 28–33.

Johnson, J. R., & McIntosh, A. S. (2009). Toward a cultural perspective and understanding of disability and deaf experience in special and multicultural education. *Remedial and Special Education, 30*(2), 67–83.

Johnston, F., Baer, D. R., & Invernizzi, M. (2006). *Words their way: Word sorts for derivational and relations spellers.* Upper Saddle River, NJ: Merrill/Pearson Education.

Johnston, S. S., McDonnell, A. P., & Hawken, L. S. (2008). Enhancing outcomes in early literacy for young children with disabilities: Strategies for success. *Intervention in School and Clinic, 43*(4), 210–217.

Jolivette, K., Lingo, A. S., Houchins, D. E., Barton-Arwood, S. M. & Shippen, M. E. (2006). Building math fluency for students with developmental disabilities and attentional difficults using Great Leaps Math. *Education and Training in Developmental Disabilities, 41,* 392–400.

Jones, E. D., Southern, W. T., & Brigham, F. J. (1998). Curriculum-based assessment: Testing what is taught and teaching what is tested. *Intervention in School and Clinic, 33*(4), 239–249.

Jones, T. (2005). Incorporate diversity into your classroom. *Intervention in School and Clinic, 41,* 9–12.

Jones, V. (2002). Creating communities of support: The missing link in dealing with student behavior problems and reducing violence in schools. *Beyond Behavior, 11*(2), 16–23.

Jones, V., & Jones, L. (2007). *Comprehensive classroom management* (8th ed.). Boston: Allyn & Bacon.

Jordan, A. (2008, December 5). *Making a difference: Northborough fourth-graders get a lesson in learning disabilities.* Retrieved December 12, 2008, from http://www.metrowestdailynews.com/news/x1755422375/Making-a-difference-Northbor.

Jordan, N. C., & Hanich, L. B. (2000). Mathematical thinking in second-grade children with different forms of LD. *Journal of Learning Disabilities, 33,* 567–579.

Joseph, L. M. (2000). Student as a strategic participant in collaborative problem-solving teams: An alternative model for middle and secondary schools. *Intervention in School and Clinic, 36,* 47–53.

Joseph, L. M. (2002). Helping children link sound to print: Phonics procedures for small-group or whole-class settings. *Intervention in School and Clinic, 37,* 217–221.

Joseph, L. M., & Konrad, M. (2009). 20 ways to have students self-manage their academic performance. *Intervention in School and Clinic, 44*(4), 246–249.

Joseph, L. M., & Schisler, R. (2009). Should adolescents go back to the basics? A review of teaching word reading skills and high school students. *Remedial and Special Education, 30*(3), 131–147.

Joseph, L. M., & Seery, M. E. (2004). Where is the phonics? A review of the literature on the use of phonetic analysis with students with mental retardation. *Remedial and Special Education, 25,* 88–94.

Jung, L. A., Gomez, C., Baird, S. M., & Galyon Keramidas, C. L. (2008). Designing intervention plans: Bridging the gap between individualized education programs and implementation. *Teaching Exceptional Children, 40*(1), 26–35.

Jung, L. A., & Guskey, T. R. (2007). Standards-based grading and reporting: A model for special education. *Teaching Exceptional Children, 40*(2), 48–53.

Kamens, M. W. (2007). Learning about co-teaching: A collaborative student teaching experience for preservice teachers. *Teacher Education and Special Education, 30*(3), 155–166.

Kaplan, N., Guzman, I., & Tomlinson, C. A. (2009). *Using the parallel curriculum model in urban settings, Grades K–8.* Thousand Oaks, CA: Corwin Press.

Karnes, F. A, & Stephens, K. R. (2008). *Achieving excellence: Educating the gifted and talented.* Upper Saddle River, NJ: Merrill/Pearson Education.

Karp, K. S., & Voltz, D. L. (2000). Weaving mathematical instructional strategies into inclusive settings. *Intervention in School and Clinic, 35,* 206–215.

Katsiyannis, A., Ellenburg, J. S., Acton, O. M., & Torrey, G. (2001). Addressing the needs of students with Rett syndrome. *Teaching Exceptional Children, 33*(5), 74–78.

Katsiyannis, A., Conroy, M., & Zhang, D. (2008). District-level administrators's perspectives on the implementation of functional behavior assessment in schools. *Behavioral Disorders, 34*(1), 14–26.

Katsiyannis, A., Landrum,T.J., & Reid, R. (2002). Rights and responsibilities under Section 504. *Beyond Behavior, 11* (2), 9–15.

Katsiyannis, A., Landrum, T. J., & Vinton, L. (1997). Practical guidelines for monitoring treatment of attention-deficit/hyperactivity disorder. *Preventing School Failure, 41*(3), 131–136.

Katsiyannis, A., & Maag, J. W. (2001). Manifestation determination as a golden fleece. *Exceptional Children, 68,* 85–96.

Katsiyannis, A., Yell, M. L., & Bradley, R. (2001). Reflections on the 25th anniversary of the Individuals with Disabilities Education Act. *Remedial and Special Education, 22,* 324–334.

Kauffman, J. M., & Landrum, T. (2009). *Characteristics of emotional and behavioral disorders of children and youth* (9th ed.). Upper Saddle River, NJ: Merrill/Pearson Education.

Kauffman, J. M., Mock, D. R., & Simpson, R. L. (2007). Problems related to underservice of students with emotional or behavioral disorders. *Behavioral Disorders, 33*(1), 43–57.

Kavale, K. A., & Forness, S. A. (2000). History, rhetoric, and reality: Analysis of the inclusion debate. *Remedial and Special Education, 21,* 279–296.

Kavale, K. A., Hirshoren, A., & Forness, S. R. (1998). Meta-analytic validation of the Dunn and Dunn model of learning style preferences: A critique of what was Dunn. *Learning Disabilities Research and Practice, 13*(2), 75–80.

Kavale, K. A., & Spaulding, L. S. (2008). Is response to intervention good policy for specific learning disability? *Learning Disabilities Research and Practice, 23*(4), 169–179.

Kaylor, M. (2008). Use digital storytelling to improve your students' writing skills. *CEC Today,* Retrieved [December 16, 2008] from http://www.cec.sped.org/AM/PrinterTemplate.cfm?Section=CEC_Today1&TEMPLATE

Kea, C. D., & Utley, C. A. (1998). To teach me is to know me. *The Journal of Special Education, 32,* 44–47.

Kearns, J. F., Kleinert, H. L., Clayton, J., Burdge, M., & Williams, R. (1998). Principal supports for inclusive assessment: A Kentucky story. *Teaching Exceptional Children, 31*(2), 16–23.

Kearns, J. F., Kleinert, H. L., & Kennedy, S. (1999). We need not exclude anyone. *Educational Leadership, 56*(6), 33–38.

Keefe, C. H., & Spence, C. D. (2003, August). Successful transition into kindergarten. *CEC Today, 10*(2), 12.

Keehn, S., Harmon, J., & Shoho, A. (2008). A study of readers theater in eighth grade: Issues of fluency, comprehension and vocabulary. *Reading and Writing Quarterly: Overcoming Learning Difficulties, 24*(4), 335–362.

Keller, C. L. (2002). A new twist on spelling instruction for elementary school teachers. *Intervention in School and Clinic, 38,* 3–7.

Keller, C. L., Bucholz, J., & Brady, M. P. (2007). Yes, I can! Empowering paraprofessionals to teach learning strategies. *Teaching Exceptional Children, 39*(3), 18–23.

Kelly, R. (2000). Working with webquests: Making the web accessible to students with disabilities. *Teaching Exceptional Children, 32*(6), 4–13.

Kennedy, C., & Jolivette, K. (2008). The effects of positive verbal reinforcement on the time spent outside the classroom for students with emotional and behavioral disorders in residential settings. *Behavioral Disorders, 33*(4), 211–221.

Kennedy, C. H., Shukla, S., & Fryxell, D. (1997). Comparing the effects of educational placement on the social relationships of intermediate school students with severe disabilities. *Exceptional Children, 64,* 31–47.

Kent, E. G., & Aala, B. (2005). *I have Tourette's but Tourette's doesn't have me.* Los Angeles: HBO Films.

Kern, L., Bambara, L., & Fogt, J. (2002). Class-wide curricular modifications to improve the behavior of students with emotional and behavioral disorders. *Behavioral Disorders, 27,* 317–326.

Kern, L., Starosta, K. M., Bambara, L. M., Cook, C. R., & Gresham, F. R. (2007). Functional assessment-based intervention for selective mutism. *Behavioral Disorders, 32*(2), 94–108.

Kern, L., & State, T. M. (2009). Incorporating choice and preferred activities into classwide instruction. *Beyond Behavior, 18*(2), 3–11.

Kerr, M. M., & Nelson, C. M. (2001). *Strategies for addressing behavior problems in the classroom* (6th ed.). Upper Saddle River, NJ: Merrill/Pearson Education.

Kershaw, S. (2003, January 18). Freud meets Buddha: Therapy for immigrants. *New York Times,* B1–B2.

Ketterlin-Geller, L. R., Alonzo, J., Braun-Monegan, J. & Tindal, G. (2007). Recommendations for accommodations: Implications of (In)consistency. *Remedial and Special Education, 28,* 194–206.

Ketterlin-Geller, L. R., Chard, D. J., & Fien, H. (2008). Making connections in mathematics: Conceptual mathematics intervention for low-performing students. *Remedial and Special Education, 29*(1), 33–45.

Ketterlin-Geller, L. R., Yovanoff, P., & Tindal, G. (2007). Developing a new paradigm for conducting research on accommodations in mathematics testing. *Exceptional Children, 73,* 331–347.

Killeen, W. (2009, January 11, 2009). *In his shoes: Sixth-graders get lessons on what it's like to go through life with a brain injury.* Retrieved February 7, 2009, from http://www.boston.com/news/local/massachusetts/articles/2009/01/11/in_his_shoes?mode=PF.

Killu, K. (2008). Developing effective behavior intervention plans. *Intervention in School and Clinic, 43*(3), 140–146.

Killu, K., & Crundwell, R. M. A. (2008). Understanding and developing academic and behavioral interventions for students with bipolar disorder. *Intervention in School and Clinic, 43*(4), 244–251.

Kim, A. Vaughn, S. Klingner, J. K., Woodruff, A. L., Reutebuch, C. K., & Kouzekanani, K. (2006). Improving the reading comprehension of middle school students with disabilities through computer-assisted collaborative strategic reading. *Remedial and Special Education, 27,* 235–249.

King, E. W. (2005). Addressing the social and emotional needs of twice-exceptional students. *Teaching Exceptional Children, 38*(1), 16–20.

King, G., Baxter, D., Rosenbaum, P., Zwaigenbaum, L., & Bates, A. (2009). Belief systems of families of children with autism spectrum disorders or Down syndrome. *Focus on Autism and Other Developmental Disabilities, 24*(1), 50–64.

King, K., & Gurian, M. (2006). Teaching to the minds of boys. *Educational Leadership, 64*(1).

King-Sears, M. E. (1999). Teacher and researcher co-design self-management content for an inclusive setting: Research training, intervention, and generalization effects on student performance. *Education and Training in Mental Retardation and Developmental Disabilities 34*(2), 134–156.

King-Sears, M. E. (2006). Designing and delivering learning center instruction. *Intervention in School and Clinic, 42,* 137–147.

King-Sears. M. E., & Evmenova, A. S. (2007). Premises, principles, and processes for integrating TECHnology into instruction. *Teaching Exceptional Children, 40*(1), 6–15.

Kingsley, K. V. (2007). 20 ways to empower diverse learners with educational technology and digital media. *Intervention in School and Clinic, 43*(1), 52–56.

Kirby, J. R., Silvestri, R., Allingham, B. H., Parrila, R., & La Fave, C. B. (2008). Learning strategies and study approaches of postsecondary students with dyslexia. *Journal of Learning Disabilities, 41*(1), 85–96.

Kleinert, H., Green, P., Hurte, M., Clayton, J., & Oetinger, C. (2002). Creating and using meaningful alternate assessments. *Teaching Exceptional Children, 34*(4), 40–49.

Kleinert, H. L., Miracle, S. A., & Sheppard-Jones, K. (2007). Including students with moderate and severe disabilities in extracurricular and community recreation activities: Steps to success. *Teaching Exceptional Children, 39*(6), 33–38.

Kling, B. (2000). ASSERT yourself: Helping students of all ages develop self-advocacy skills. *Teaching Exceptional Children, 32*(3), 66–70.

Klingner, J. K., Artiles, A. J., & Mendez Barletta, L. (2006). English language learners who struggle with reading: Language acquisition or LD? *Journal of Learning Disabilities, 39,* 108–128.

Klingner, J. K., & Edwards, P. A. (2006). Cultural considerations with response to intervention models, *Reading Research Quarterly, 41*(1), 108–115.

Klingner, J. K., Hoover, J. J., & Baca, L. M. (2008). *Why do English language learners struggle with reading? Distinguishing language acquisition from learning disabilities.* Thousand Oaks, CA: Corwin Press.

Klingner, J. K., Vaughn, S., Hughes, M. T., Schumm, J. S., & Elbaum, B. (1998). Outcomes for students with and without learning disabilities in inclusive classrooms. *Learning Disabilities Research and Practice, 13*(3), 153–161.

Klingner, J. K., Vaughn, S., Schumm, J. S., Cohen, P., & Forgan, J. W. (1998). Inclusion or pull-out: Which do students prefer? *Journal of Learning Disabilities, 31*(2), 148–158.

Knight, M. G., Ross, D. E., Taylor, R. L., & Ramasamy, R. (2003). Constant time delay and interspersal of known items to teach sight words to students with mental retardation and learning disabilties. *Education and Training in Developmental Disabilities, 38,* 179–191.

Knight-McKenna, M. (2008). Syllable types: A strategy for reading multisyllabic words. *Teaching Exceptional Children, 40*(3), 18–27.

Knobel, M., & Wilber, D. (2009). Let's talk 2.0. *Educational Leadership, 66*(6), 20–24.

Koch, J. (2005). Creating gender equitable classroom environments. In D. A. Byrnes & G. Kiger (Eds.), *Common bonds: Anti-bias teaching in a diverse society* (3rd ed., pp. 91–104). Olney, MD: Association of Childhood Education International.

Koch, K. R. (2006). Learning to learn and teach despite LD. *Teaching Exceptional Children Plus, 2*(3)Article 4. Retrieved April, 2, 2006, from http://escholarship.bc.edu/education/tecplus/vol2/iss3/art4.

Kochhar-Bryant, C. A., & Shaw, S. (2009). *What every teacher needs to know about: Transition and IDEA 2004.* Upper Saddle River, NJ: Merrill/Pearson Education.

Kohn, A. (2003). Almost there, but not quite. *Educational Leadership, 60*(6), 27–29.

Kolb, S. M., & Stevens Griffith, A. C. (2009). "I'll repeat myself, again?!" Empowering students through assertive communication strategies. *Teaching Exceptional Children, 41*(3), 32–36.

Konrad, M. (2008). Involve students in the IEP process. *Intervention in School and Clinic, 43*(4), 236–239.

Konrad, M., Helf, S., & Itoi, M. (2007). More bang for the book: Using children's literature to promote self-determination and literacy skills. *Teaching Exceptional Children, 40*(1), 64–71.

Konrad, M., & Test, D. W. (2007). Effects of GO 4 IT . . . NOW! Strategy instruction on written IEP goal articulation and paragraph-writing skills of middle school students with disabilities. *Remedial and Special Education, 28*(5), 277–291.

Konrad, M., Walker, A. R., Fowler, C. H., Test, D. W., & Wood, W. M. (2008). A model for aligning self-determination and general curriculum standards. *Teaching Exceptional Children, 40*(3), 53-64.

Kortering, L. J., & Braziel, P. M. (1999). Staying in school: The perspective of ninth-grade students. *Remedial and Special Education, 20*(2), 106–113.

Kortering, L. J., McClannon, T. W., & Braziel, P. M. (2008). Universal design for learning: A look at what algebra and biology students with and without high incidence conditions are saying. *Remedial and Special Education, 29*(6), 352–363.

Kostewicz, D. E., & Kubina, R. M. (2008). The national reading panel guidepost: A review of reading outcome measures for students with emotional and behavioral disorders. *Behavioral Disorders, 33*(2), 62–74.

Kostewicz, D. E., Ruhl, K. L., & Kubina, R. M. (2008). Creating classroom rules for students with emotional and behavioral disorders: A decision-making guide. *Beyond Behavior, 17*(3), 14–21.

Kottler, E., & Costa, V. B. (2009). *Secrets to success for science teachers*. Thousand Oaks, CA: Corwin Press.

Kourea, L., Cartledge, G., & Musti-Rao, S. (2007). Improving the reading skills of urban elementary students through total class peer tutoring. *Remedial and Special Education, 28*(2), 95–107.

Kozen, A. A., Murray, R. K., & Windell, I. (2006). Increasing all students' chance to achieve: Using and adapting anticipation guides with middle school learners. *Intervention in School and Clinic, 41*, 195–200.

Kozleski, E. B., Engelbrecht, P., Hess, R., Swart, E., Eloff, I., Oswald, M., Molina, A., & Jain, S. (2008). Where differences matter: A cross-cultural analysis of family voice in special education. *The Journal of Special Education, 42*(1), 26–35.

Kozminsky, E., & Kozminsky, L. (2002). The dialogue page: Teacher and student dialogues to improve learning motivation. *Intervention in School and Clinic, 39*, 88–95.

Kozol, J. (1991). *Savage inequalities: Children in American schools*. NewYork: Crown.

Krach, S., K., & Jelenic, M. (2009). The other technological divide: K–12 web accessibility. *Journal of Special Education Technology, 24*(2), 31-37.

Krajewski, J. J., & Hyde, M. S. (2000). Comparison of teen attitudes toward individuals with mental retardation between 1987 and 1998: Has inclusion made a difference? *Education and Training in Mental Retardation and Developmental Disabilities, 35*, 284–293.

Krashen, S. (2005). Skyrocketing scores: An urban legend. *Educational Leadership, 62*(4), 37–39.

Kretlow, A. G., Lo, Y., White, R. B., & Jordan, L. (2008). Teaching test-taking strategies to improve the academic achievement of students with mild mental disabilities. *Education and Training in Developmental Disabilities, 43*(3), 397–408.

Kritikos, E. P. (2010). *Special education assessment: Issues and strategies affecting today's classrooms*. Upper Saddle River, NJ: Merrill/Pearson Education.

Kroeger, S. D., Burton, C., & Preston, C. (2009). Integrating evidence-based practices in middle science reading. *Teaching Exceptional Children, 41*(3), 6–15.

Kroeger, S. D., & Kouche, B. (2006). Using peer-assisted learning strategies to increase response to intervention in inclusive middle math settings. *Teaching Exceptional Children, 38*(5), 6–13.

Kubina, R. M. (2005). Developing reading fluency through a systematic practice procedure. *Reading and Writing Quarterly: Overcoming Learning Difficulties, 21*, 185–192.

Kubina, R. M., & Hughes, C. A. (2007, Fall). Fluency instruction. *Current Practice Alerts, 15*, 1–4.

Kubina, R. M., & Yurich, K. K. L. (2009). Developing behavioral fluency for students with autism: A guide for parents and teachers. *Intervention in School and Clinic, 44*(3), 131–138.

Kuder, S. J. (2008). *Teaching students with language and communication disabilities* (3rd ed.). Boston: Allyn & Bacon.

Kuhn, B. R., Allen, K. D., & Shriver, M. D. (1995). Behavioral management of children's seizure activity: Intervention guidelines for primary-care providers. *Clinical Pediatrics, 34*, 570–575.

Kuhn, L. R., Bodkin, A. E., Devlin, S. D., & Doggett, R. A. (2008). Using pivotal response training with peers in special education to facilitate play in two children with autism. *Education and Training in Developmental Disabilities, 43*(1), 37–45.

Kunsch, C. A., Jitendra, A. K., & Sood, S. (2007). The effects of peer-mediated instruction in mathematics for students with learning problems: A research synthesis. *Learning Disabilities Research and Practice, 22*(1), 1–12.

Kurtts, S. A., & Gavigan, K. W. (2008). Understanding (dis)Abilities through children's literature. *Children's Literature, 31*(1), 23–31.

Kurtts, S. A., Matthews, C. E., & Smallwood, T. (2009). (Dis)solving the differences: A physical science lesson using universal design. *Intervention in School and Clinic, 44*(3), 151–159.

LaCava, P. G. (2005). Facilitate transitions. *Intervention in School and Clinic, 41*, 46–48.

Lacava, P. G., Golan, O., Baron-Cohen, S., & Smith Myles, B. (2007). Using assistive technology to teach emotion recognition to students with Asperger syndrome: A pilot study. *Remedial and Special Education, 28*, 174–181.

Lackaye, T., Margalit, M., Ziv, O., & Ziman, T. (2006). Comparisons of self-efficacy, mood, effort, and hope between students with learning disabilities and their non-LD-matched peers. *Learning Disabilities Research and Practice, 21,* 111–121.

Lackaye, T., & Rublin, H. (2001). Lots of pain, little gain: Five problems with homework in the elementary school. *New York Exceptional Individuals, 26*(4), 8–9.

Lagares, L., & Connor, D. J. (2009). Help students prepare for high school examinations. *Intervention in School and Clinic, 45*(1), 63–67.

Lam, S., Yim, P., & Ng. Y. (2008). Is effort praise worthy? The role of beliefs in the effort-ability relationship. *Contemporary Educational Psychology, 33,* 694–710.

Lambert, J. (2005). Easing the transition to high school. *Educational Leadership, 62*(7), 61–63.

Lambert, M. A., & Nowacek, J. (2006). Help high school students improve their study skills. *Intervention in School and Clinic, 41,* 241–243.

Lamme, L. L., & Lamme, L. A. (2002). Welcoming children from gay families into our schools. *Educational Leadership, 59*(4), 65–69.

Lancaster, P. E., Lancaster, S. J. C., Schumaker, J. B., & Deshler, D. D. (2006). The efficacy of an interactive hypermedia program for teaching a test-taking strategy to students with high-incidence disabilities. *Journal of Special Education Technology, 21*(2), 17–30.

Landsman, J. (2006). Bearers of hope. *Educational Leadership, 63*(5), 26–32.

Landsman, J., Moore, T., & Simmons, R. (2008). Reluctant teachers reluctant learners. *Educational Leadership, 65*(6), 62–66.

Lane, H. B., & Pullen, P. C. (2004). *Phonological awareness assessment and instruction.* Needham Heights, MA: Allyn & Bacon.

Lane, H. B., Pullen, P. C., Eisele, M. R., & Jordan, L. (2002). Preventing reading failure: Phonological awareness assessment and instruction. *Preventing School Failure, 46,* 101–111.

Lane, K. L., Mahdavi, J. N., & Borthwick-Duffy, S. (2003). Teacher perceptions of the prereferral intervention process: A call for assistance with school-based interventions. *Preventing School Failure, 47,* 148–155.

Lane, K. L., Wehby, J. H., & Cooley, C. (2006).Teacher expectations of students' classroom behavior across the grade span: Which social skills are necessary for success? *Exceptional Children, 72,* 153–167.

Langdon, T. (2004). DIBELS: A teacher friendly basic literacy accountability tool for primary classroom. *Teaching Exceptional Children, 37*(2), 54–58.

Langhorst, E. (2007). After the bell, beyond the walls. *Educational Leadership, 64* (8), 74–77.

Lang Rong, X., & Preissle, J. (2009). *Educating immigrant students in the 21st century: What every educator needs to know.* Thousand Oaks, CA: Corwin Press.

Lange, A. A., Mulhern, G., & Wylie, J. (2009). Proofreading using an assistive software homophone tool: Compensatory and remedial effects on the literacy skills of students with reading difficulties. *Journal of Learning Disabilities, 42*(4), 322–335.

Lapkoff, S., & Li, R. M. (2007). Five trends for schools. *Educational Leadership, 64*(6), 8–15.

Larkin, R. F., & Snowling, M. J. (2008). Morphological spelling development. *Reading and Writing Quarterly, 24*(4), 363–376.

Larry P. v. Riles, 495 F. Supp. 926 (N.D. Cal. 1979).

Lau v. Nichols, 414 U.S. 563 (1974).

Laud, L. E., & Patel, P. (2008). Teach struggling writers to unite their paragraphs. *TEACHING Exceptional Children Plus,* 5(1) Article 4. Retrieved [August 24, 2009] from http://escholarship.bc.edu/education/tecplus/vol5/iss1/art4.

Lava, V. F., & Lehman, L. R. (2007). The power of autobiography: Rethinking disability, rethinking teaching. *Excelsior: Leadership in Teaching and Learning, 1*(2), 19–32.

Lazarus, B. D. (1998). Say cheese: Using personal photographs as prompts. *Teaching Exceptional Children, 30*(6), 4–7.

Lazarus, S. S., Thurlow, M. L., Lail, K. E., & Christensen, L. (2009). A longitudinal analysis of state accommodations policies: Twelve years of change, 1993–2005. *The Journal of Special Education, 43*(2), 67–80.

Leahy, S., Lyon, C., Thompson, M., & William, D. (2005). Classroom assessment: Minute by minute, day by day. *Educational Leadership, 63*(3), 18–24.

Learned, J. E., Dowd, M. V., & Jenkins, J. R. (2009). Instructional conferencing: Helping students succeed on independent assignments in inclusive settings. *Teaching Exceptional Children, 41*(5), 46–51.

Lechtenberger, D., Mullins, F. E., & Greenwood, D. (2008). Achieving the promise: The significant role of schools in transforming children's mental health in America. *Teaching Exceptional Children, 40*(4), 56–64.

Lee, D. H., Oakland, T., Jackson, G., & Glutting, J. (2008). Estimated prevalence of attention-deficit/hyperactivity disorder symptoms among college freshman: Gender, race, and rater effects. *Journal of Learning Disabilities, 41*(4), 371–384.

Lee, D. L., Belfiore, P. J., & Gormley Budin, S. (2008). Riding the wave: Creating a momentum of school success. *Teaching Exceptional Children, 40*(3), 65–70.

Lee, H., & Herner-Patnod, L. (2007). Teaching mathematics vocabulary to diverse groups. *Intervention in School and Clinic, 13*(2), 121–126.

Lee, S., Palmer, S. B., Turnbull, A. P., & Wehmeyer, M. L. (2006). A model for parent-teacher collaboration to promote self-determination in young children with disabilities. *Teaching Exceptional Children, 38*(3), 36–41.

Lee, S., Palmer, S. B., & Wehmeyer, M. L. (2009). Goal setting and self-monitoring for students with disabilities: Practical tips and ideas for teachers. *Intervention in School and Clinic, 44*(3), 139–145.

Lee, S., Soukup, J. H., Little, T. D., & Wehmeyer, M. L. (2009). Student and teacher variables contributing to access to the general education curriculum for students with intellectual and developmental disabilities, *The Journal of Special Education, 43*(1), 29–44.

Lee, S., &, Turnbull, A. P., & Zan, F. (2009). Family perspectives: Using a cultural prism to understand families from Asian cultural backgrounds. *Intervention in School and Clinic, 45*(2), 99–108.

Lee, S., Yoo, S., & Bak, S. (2003). Characteristics of friendships between children with and without disabilities.

Education and Training in Developmental Disabilities, 38, 157–166.

Lee, S., Wehmeyer, M. L., Palmer, S. B., Soukup, J. H., & Little, T. D. (2008). Self-determination and access to the general education curriculum. *Journal of Special Education, 42,* 91–107.

Lembke, E., & Foegen, A. (2009). Identifying early numeracy indicators for kindergarten and first-grade students. *Learning and Disabilities Research and Practice, 24*(1), 12–20.

Lenz, B. K. (2006). Creating school-wide conditions for high-quality learning classroom instruction. *Intervention in School and Clinic, 41,* 261–266.

Lenz, B. K., Bulgren, J. A., Kissam, B. R., & Taymans, J. (2004). Smarter planning for academic diversity. In B. K. Lenz, D. D. Deshler, & B. R. Kissam (Eds.), *Teaching content to all: Evidence-based inclusive practices in middle and secondary schools* (pp. 47–77). Boston: Allyn & Bacon.

Lenz, B. K., Deshler, D. D., & Kissam, B. R. (2004). *Teaching content to all: Evidence-based inclusive practices in middle and secondary schools.* Boston: Allyn & Bacon.

Lenz, K., Graner, P., & Adams, G. (2003). Learning express-ways: Building academic relationships to improve learning. *Teaching Exceptional Children, 35*(3), 70–73.

Lerner, J., & Johns, B. (2007, November). *Creative and motivating strategies to prepare teachers for making adaptations for students with special needs.* Presentation at the annual meeting of the Teacher Education Division (TED) of the Council for Exceptional Children, Milwaukee.

Lessow-Hurley, J. (2009). *The foundations of dual language instruction* (5th ed.). Boston: Allyn & Bacon.

Levine, L. N., & McCloskey, M. L. (2009). *Teaching learners of English in mainstream classrooms.* Upper Saddle River, NJ: Pearson Education.

Levine, M. (2003). Celebrating diverse minds. *Educational Leadership, 61*(2), 12–18.

Levine, P., & Nourse, S. W. (1998). What follow-up studies say about postschool life for young men and women with learning disabilities: A critical look at the literature. *Journal of Learning Disabilities, 31*(3), 212–233.

Levy, M. (2006). Online games lift spirits of seriously ill kids. Retrieved [November 11, 2006] from http://usatoday.com/tech/gaming/2006-11-06-starlight-games_x.htm.

Levy, S. (1999). The end of the never-ending line. *Educational Leadership, 56*(6), 74–77.

Levy, S. (2008). The power of audience. *Educational Leadership, 66* (3), 75–79.

Levy, S., Coleman, M., & Alsman, B. (2002). Reading instruction for elementary students with emotional/behavioral disorders: What's a teacher to do? *Beyond Behavior, 11*(3), 3–10.

Lewin, T. (2001, July 19). Child well-being improves, U.S. says. *New York Times,* 14.

Lewin, T. (2003, November 8). Change in SAT procedure echoes in disability realm: Looking closer at requests for more time. *New York Times,* A10.

Lewin, T. (2009, August, 9). *Moving into a digital future where textbooks are history.* The New York Times, A1, A15.

Lewis, C., & Ketter, J. (2008). Encoding youth: Popular culture and multicultural literature. *Reading and Writing Quarterly: Overcoming Learning Difficulties, 24*(3), 283–310.

Lewis, S. (2007). Understanding students with visual impairments. In A. Turnbull, R. Turnbull, & M. L. Wehmeyer (Eds.), *Exceptional lives: Special education in today's schools* (5th ed., pp. 429–459). Upper Saddle River, NJ: Merrill/Pearson Education.

Lewis, S. (2010). Understanding students with visual impairments. In A. Turnbull, R. Turnbull, & M. L. Wehmeyer (Eds.), *Exceptional lives: Special education in today's schools* (6th ed., pp. 368–396). Upper Saddle River, NJ: Merrill/Pearson Education.

Lewis, T. J. (2001). Building infrastructure to enhance schoolwide systems of positive behavioral support: Essential features of technical assistance. *Beyond Behavior, 11*(1), 10–12.

Leyser, Y., & Kirk, R. (2004). Evaluating inclusion: An examination of parent views and factors influencing their perspectives. *International Journal of Disability, Development, and Education, 51,* 271–285.

Li, A. (2004). Classroom strategies for improving and enhancing visual skills in students with disabilities. *Teaching Exceptional Children, 36*(6), 38–46.

Li, A. (2009). Identification and intervention for students who are visually impaired and who have autism spectrum disorders. *Teaching Exceptional Children, 41*(4), 22–35.

Lienemann, T. O., Graham, S., Leader-Janssen, B., & Reid, R. (2006). Improving the writing performance of struggling writers in second grade. *Journal of Special Education, 40,* 66–78.

Linan-Thompson, S., Bryant, D. P., Dickson, S. V., & Kouzekanani, K. (2005). Spanish literacy instruction for at-risk kindergarten students. *Remedial and Special Education, 26,* 236–244.

Lindsey-Glenn, P. F., & Gentry, J. E. (2008). Improving vocabulary skills through assistive technology: Rick's story. *TEACHING Exceptional Children Plus,* 5(2) Article 1. Retrieved [July 27, 2009] from http://escholarship.bc.edu/education/tecplus/vol5/iss2/art1.

Lindstrom, J. H. (2007). Determining appropriate accommodations for postsecondary students with reading and written expression disorders. *Learning Disabilities Reseach and Practice, 22*(4), 229–236.

Lindstrom, L., Johnson, P., Doren, B., Zane, C., Post, C., & Harley, E. (2008). Career connections: Building opportunities for young women with disabilities. *Teaching Exceptional Children, 40*(4), 66–71.

Lingnugaris/Kraft, B., Marchand-Martella, N., & Martella, R. C. (2001). Strategies for writing better goals and short-term objectives or benchmarks. *Teaching Exceptional Children, 34*(1), 52–58.

Linn, A., & Smith Myles, B. (2004). Asperger syndrome and six strategies for success. *Beyond Behavior, 14*(1), 3–9.

Liston, A. G., Nevin, A., & Malian, I. (2009). What do paraeducators in inclusive classrooms say about their work? Analysis of national survey data and follow-up interviews in California. *TEACHING Exceptional Children Plus,* 5(5), Article 1. Retrieved [July 27, 2009] from http://escholarship.bc.edu/education/tecplus/vol5/iss5/art1.

Lloyd, C., Wilton, K., & Townsend, M. (2000). Children at high-risk for mild intellectual disability in regular classrooms: Six New Zealand case studies. *Education and Training in Mental Retardation and Developmental Disabilities, 35,* 44–54.

Lloyd, J. W., Saltzman, N. J., & Kauffman, J. M. (1981). Predictable generalization in academic learning as a result of preskills and strategy training. *Learning Disability Quarterly, 4,* 203–216.

Lo, L. (2005). Barriers to successful partnerships with Chinese-speaking parents of children with disabilities in urban schools. *Multiple Voices, 8*(1), 84–95.

Lo, Y., Wang, C., & Haskell, S. (2009). Examining the impact of early reading intervention on the growth rates in basic literacy skills of at-risk urban kindergarteners. *The Journal of Special Education, 43*(1), 12–28.

Lo, Y., & Cartledge, G. (2006). FBA and BIP: Increasing the behavior adjustment of African American boys in schools. *Behavioral Disorders, 31,* 147–161.

Locuniak, M. N., & Jordan, N. C. (2008). Using kindergarten number sense to predict calculation fluency in second grade. *Journal of Learning Disabilties, 41*(5), 451–459.

Lodato Wilson, G. (2008). 20 ways to be an active co-teacher. *Intervention in School and Clinic, 43*(4), 240–243.

Loeffler, K. A. (2005). No more Friday spelling tests? An alternative spelling assessment for students with learning disabilities. *Teaching Exceptional Children, 37*(4), 24–27.

Lopez Estrada, V., Gomez, L, & Ruiz-Escalante, J. A. (2009). Let's make dual language the norm. *Educational Leadership, 66*(7), 54–58.

Lotempio, S. M. (2008, Fall). Need any help with that? *UB Today,* 22–26.

Lott Adams, T., & McKoy Lowery, R. (2007). An analysis of children's strategies for reading mathematics. *Reading and Writing Quarterly: Overcoming Learning Difficulties, 23*(2), 161–178.

Lovett, M. W., De Palma, M., Fritjers, J., Steinbach, K., Temple, M., Benson, N., & Lacerenza, L. (2008). Interventions for reading difficulties: A comparison of response to intervention by ELL and EFL struggling readers. *Journal of Learning Disabilities, 41*(4), 333–352.

Lovett, M. W., Lacerenza, L., & Borden, S. L. (2000). Putting struggling readers on the PHAST track: A program to integrate phonological and strategy-based remedial reading instruction and maximize outcomes. *Journal of Learning Disabilities, 33,* 409–504.

Lovin, L., Kyger, M., & Allsopp, D. (2004). Differentiation for special needs learners. *Teaching Children Mathematics, 11,* 158–167.

Lovitt, T. C., & Cushing, S. (1999). Parents of youth with disabilities: Their perceptions of school programs. *Remedial and Special Education, 20*(3), 134–142.

Lovitt, T. C., Emerson, J. & Sorensen, P. (2005). Listening to and raising the voices of at-risk and culturally and linguistically diverse children in foster care. *Multiple Voices, 8*(1), 36–44.

Lovitt, T. C., Plavins, M., & Cushing, S. (1999). What do pupils with disabilities have to say about their experience in high school? *Remedial and Special Education, 20*(2), 67–76, 83.

Lowenthal, B. (2001). *Abuse and neglect: The educator's guide to the identification and prevention of child maltreatment.* Baltimore: Brookes.

Lynch, S., & Adams, P. (2008). Developing standards-based individualized education program objectives for students with significant needs. *Teaching Exceptional Children, 40*(3), 36–39.

Lynch, S., Taymans, J., Watson, W. A., Ochsendorf, R. J., Pyke, C., & Szesze, M. J. (2007). Effectiveness of a highly rated science curriculum unit for students with disabilities in general education classrooms. *Exceptional Children, 73,* 202–223.

Lytle, R., & Todd, T. (2009). Stress and the student with autism spectrum disorders: Strategies for stress reduction and enhanced learning. *Teaching Exceptional Children, 41*(4), 36–42.

Mabbot, D. J., & Bisanz, J. (2008). Computational skills, working memory, and conceptual knowledge in older children with mathematics learning disabilities. Journal of Learning Disabilities, *Journal of Learning Disabilities, 41*(1), 15–28.

MacArthur, C. A, (2009). Reflections on research on writing and technology for struggling writers. *Learning Disabilities Research and Practice, 24*(2), 93–103.

MacArthur, C. A., & Cavalier, A. R. (2004). Dictation and speech recognition technology as test accommodations. *Exceptional Children, 71,* 43–58.

Maccini, P., & Gagnon, J. C. (2006). Mathematics instructional practices and assessment accommodations by secondary special and general educators. *Exceptional Children, 72,* 217–234.

Maccini, P., & Hughes, C. A. (1997). Mathematics interventions for adolescents with learning disabilities. *Learning Disabilities Research and Practice, 12*(3), 168–176.

Maccini, P., Mulcahy, C. A., & Wilson, M. G. (2007). A follow-up of mathematics interventions for secondary students with learning disabilities. *Learning Disabilities Research and Practice, 22*(1), 58–74.

Macrine, S. L., & Sabbatino, E. D. (2008). Dynamic assessment and remediation approach: Using the DARA approach to assist struggling readers. *Reading and Writing Quarterly: Overcoming Learning Difficulties, 24*(1), 52–76.

Madaus, J. W. (2008). Employment self-disclosure rates and rationales of university graduates with learning disabilities. *Journal of Learning Disabilities, 41*(4), 291–299.

Magiera, K., Simmons, R. J., & Crandall, L. (2005, April). *Implemementing co-teaching effectively: One school district's experience.* Presentation at the annual meeting of the Council for Exceptional Children, Baltimore.

Maheady, L., Harper, G. F., & Mallette, B. (1991). Peer-mediated instruction: A review of potential applications for special education. *Reading, Writing, and Learning Disabilities International, 7,* 75–103.

Maheady, L., Harper, G. F., & Mallette, B. (2001). Peer-mediated instruction and interventions and students with mild disabilities. *Remedial and Special Education, 22,* 4–14.

Mainzer, L., Castellani, J., Lowry, B., & Nunn, J. (2006). GLOBE tech: Using technology to maximize classroom performance with team-based instruction. *Technology in Action, 2*(1), 1–12.

Makkonen, R. (2004, January). Teaching math to migrant students: Lessons from successful districts. *Harvard Education Letter,* 5.

Maldonado-Colon, E. (1991). Development of second language learners' linguistic and cognitive abilities.

The Journal of Educational Issues of Language Minority Students, 9, 37–48.

Maldonado-Colon, E. (1995, April). *Second language learners in special education: Language framework for inclusive classrooms.* Paper presented at the international meeting of the Council for Exceptional Children, Indianapolis.

Malian, I. M., & Love, L. (1998). Leaving high school: An ongoing transition study. *Teaching Exceptional Children, 30*(3), 4–10.

Malian, I. M., & Nevin, A. (2002). A review of self-determination literature: Implications for practitioners. *Remedial and Special Education, 23,* 68–74.

Mancil, G. R., & Maynard, K. L. (2007). Mathematics instruction and behavior problems: Making the connection. *Beyond Behavior, 16*(3), 24–28.

Mancil, G. R., & Pearl C. (2008). Restricted interests as motivators: Improving academic engagement and outcomes of children on the autism spectrum. *Teaching Exceptional Children Plus, 4*(6) Article 7. Retrieved February 17, 2009 from http://escholarship.bc.edu/education/tecplus/vol4/iss6/art7.

Manjoo, F. (2009, May 28). Bringing order to chaos of notes. *New York Times,* 9..

Manley, R. S., Rickson, H., & Standeven, B. (2000). Children and adolescents with eating disorders: Strategies for teachers and school counselors. *Intervention in School and Clinic, 35,* 228–231.

Manning, M. L., & Baruth, L. G. (2009). *Multicultural education of children and adolescents* (5th ed.). Boston: Allyn & Bacon.

Manset, G., & Semmel, M. I. (1997). Are inclusive programs for students with mild disabilities effective? A comparative review of model programs. *Journal of Special Education, 31,* 155–180.

Manwaring, J. S. (2008). Wendy or Tinkerbell? How the underrepresentation of girls impacts gender roles in preschool special education. *Teaching Exceptional Children, 40*(5), 60-65.

Margalit, M., & Raskind, M. H. (2009). Mothers of children with LD and ADHD: Empowerment through online communication. *Journal of Special Education Technology, 24*(1), 39-49.

Margolis, H. (1999). Lack of student motivation: A problem solving focus. *Channels, 13,* 18–19.

Margolis, H. (2005). Resolving struggling learners' homework difficulties: Working with elementary school learners and parents. *Preventing School Failure, 50*(1), 5–12.

Margolis, H., & McCabe, P. P. (2006). Improving self-efficacy and motivation: What to do, what to say. *Intervention in School and Clinic, 41,* 218–227.

Markow, D., Kim, A., & Liebman, M. (2007). *The homework experience: A survey of students, teachers, and parents.* New York: MetLife.

Marks, S. U., Hudson, J., Schrader, C., Longaker, T., & Levine, M. (2006). Reconsidering behavior management with autism spectrum disorders. *Beyond Behavior, 15*(2), 7–12.

Marks, S. U., Schrader, C., & Levine, M. (1999). Paraeducator experiences in inclusive settings: Helping, hovering, or holding their own? *Exceptional Children, 65*(3), 315–328.

Marquardt, E. (2005). *Between two worlds: The inner lives of children of divorce.* New York: Random House.

Marston, D. (1996). A comparison of inclusion only, pull-out only, and combined service models for students with mild disabilities. *Journal of Special Education, 30*(2), 121–132.

Martorella, P. H., & Beal, C. (2002). *Social studies for elementary school classrooms: Preparing children to be global citizens* (3rd ed.). Upper Saddle River, NJ: Merrill/Pearson Education.

Martorella, P., Beal, C. & Bolick, C. M. (2005). *Teaching social studies in middle and secondary schools* (4th. ed.). Upper Saddle River, NJ: Merrill/Pearson Education.

Marzano, R. J., & Marzano, J. S. (2003). The key to classroom management. *Educational Leadership, 61*(1), 6–13.

Marzano, R. J., & Pickering, D. J. (2007). The case for and against homework. *Educational Leadership, 64*(6), 74–79.

Mason, L. H., Harris, K. R., & Graham, S. (2004). POW + WWW, What = 2, How = 2 equals fun and exciting stories. *Teaching Exceptional Children, 36*(6), 70–73.

Mason, L. H., Meadan, H., Hedin, L., & Corso, L. (2006). Self-regulated strategy development instruction for expository text comprehension. *Teaching Exceptional Children, 38*(4), 47–52.

Masood, A. E., Turner, L. A., & Baxter, A. (2007). Casual attributions and parental attitudes toward children with disabilities in the United States and Pakistan. *Exceptional Children, 73*(4), 475-487.

Mathes, P. G., Grek, M. L., Howard, J. K., Babyak, A. E., & Allen, S. H. (1999). Peer-assisted learning strategies for first-grade readers: A tool for preventing early reading failure. *Learning Disabilities Research and Practice, 14*(1), 50–60.

Mattison, R. E. (2008). Characteristics of reading disability types in middle school students classified ED. *Behavioral Disorders, 34*(1), 27–41.

Matuszny, R. M., Banda, D. R., & Coleman, T. J. (2007). A progressive plan for building collaborative relationships with parents from diverse backgrounds. *Teaching Exceptional Children, 39*(4), 24-33.

Maxim, G. W. (2003). *Dynamic social studies for constructivist classroom: Inspiring tomorrow's social scientists.* (8th ed.). Upper Saddle River, NJ: Merrill/Pearson Education.

Maxim, G. W. (2010). *Dynamic social studies for constructivist classroom: Inspiring tomorrow's social scientists* (9th ed.). Upper Saddle River, NJ: Pearson Education.

Mazzotti, V. L., Rowe, D. A., Kelley, K. R., Test, D. W., Fowler, C. H., Kohler, P. D., & Kortering, L. J. (2009). Linking transition assessment and postsecondary goals: Key elements in the secondary planning process. *Teaching Exceptional Children, 42*(2), 44–51.

McCabe, H. (2008). Effective teacher training at the autism institute in the People's Republic of China. *Teacher Education and Special Education, 31*(2), 103–117.

McCracken, H. (2006). *That's what different about me! Helping children understand autism spectrum disorders.* Shawnee Mission, KS: Autism Aspergere Publishing.

McCrystal, P., Higgins, K., & Percy, A. (2006). Brief report: School exclusion drug use and delinquency in adolescence. *Journal of Adolescence, 29,* 829-836.

McDonnell, J., Johnson, J. W., Polychronis, S., & Risen, T. (2002). Effects of embedded instruction on students with moderate disabilities enrolled in general education classes.

Education and Training in Mental Retardation and Developmental Disabilities, 37, 363–377.

McDonnell, J., Thorson, N., McQuivey, C., & Kiefer-O'Donnell, R. (1997). The academic engaged time of students with low incidence disabilities in general education classes. *Mental Retardation, 35,* 18–26.

McDuffie, K. A., Mastropieri, M. A., & Scruggs, T. E. (2009). Differential effects of peer tutoring in co-taught and non-co-taught classes: Results for content learning and student-teacher interactions. *Exceptional Children, 75*(4), 493–512.

McGrath, D. (2008, November 20). A growing season for learning. Teaching migrant children sows challenges, reaps, rewards. *New York Teacher,* 14–16.

McGuire, J. M., Scott, S. S., & Shaw, S. F. (2006). Universal design and its applications in educational environments. *Remedial and Special Education, 27,* 166–175.

McIntosh, A. S. (2008, Winter). A focus on functional behavioral assessment. *Current Practices Alerts, 16,* 1–4.

McIntosh, K., & MacKay, L. D. (2008). Enhancing the generalization of social skills: Making social skills curricula effective after the lesson. *Beyond Behavior, 18*(1), 18–25.

McIntosh, K., Horner, R. H., Chard, D. J., Dickey, C. R., & Braun, D. H. (2008). Reading skills and function of problem behavior in typical school settings. *The Journal of Special Education, 42*(3), 131–147.

McKinley, L. A., & Stormont, M. A. (2008). The school supports checklist: Identifying support needs and barriers for children with ADHD. *Teaching Exceptional Children, 41*(2), 14–21.

McLeskey, J. (2007). Reflections on inclusion: Classic articles that shaped our thinking. In J. McLeskey (Ed.), *Reflections on inclusion: Classic articles that shaped our thinking* (pp. v–xii). Arlington, VA: Council for Exceptional Children.

McLeskey, J., Henry, D., & Hodges, D. (1999). Inclusion: What progress is being made across disability categories? *Teaching Exceptional Children, 31*(3), 60–64.

McLeskey, J., & Waldron, N. L. (2002). Inclusion and school change: Teacher perceptions regarding curricular and instructional adaptations. *Teacher Education and Special Education, 25,* 41–54.

McLoughlin, J. A., & Lewis, R. B. (2005). *Assessing students with special needs* (6th ed.). Upper Saddle River, NJ: Merrill/Pearson Education.

McLoughlin, J. A., & Nall, M. (1995). Allergies and learning/behavioral disorders. *Intervention in School and Clinic, 29,* 198–207.

McMaster, K. L., Du, X., & Petursdottir, A. (2009). Technical features of curriculum-based measures for beginning writers. *Journal of Learning Disabilities, 42*(1), 41–60.

McMaster, K. L., Kung, S. Han, I., & Cao, M. (2008). Peer-assisted learning strategies: A "tier 1" approach to promoting English language learners response to instruction. Exceptional Children, 74(2), 194–214.

McNaughton, D., Hughes, C. A., & Clark, K. (1997). The effects of five proofreading conditions on the spelling performance of college students with learning disabilities. *Journal of Learning Disabilities, 30*(6), 643–651.

McNaughton, D., Hughes, C. A., & Ofiesh, N. (1997). Proofreading for students with learning disabilities:

Integrating computer with strategy use. *Learning Disabilities Research and Practice, 12*(1), 16–28.

McTighe, J., & Thomas, R. S. (2003). Backward design for forward action. *Educational Leadership, 60*(5), 52–55.

Meadan, H., & Halle, J. W. (2004). Social perceptions of students with learning disabilities who differ in social status. *Learning Disabilities Research and Practice, 19,* 71–82.

Meadan, H., & Mason, L. H. (2007). Reading instruction for a student with emotional disturbance: Facilitating understanding of expository text. *Beyond Behavior, 16*(2), 18–26.

Meadan, H., & Monda-Amaya, (2008). Collaboration to promote social competence for students with mild disabilities in the general classroom: A structure for providing social support. *Intervention in School and Clinic, 43*(3), 158–167.

Mechling, L. C. (2008). High tech cooking: A literature review of evolving technologies for teaching a functional skill. *Education and Training in Developmental Disabilities, 43*(4), 474–485.

Mechling, L. C., & Gast, D. L. (2003). Multi-media instruction to teach grocery word associations and store locations: A study of generalization. *Education and Training in Developmental Disabilities, 38,* 62–76.

Mechling, L. C., Gast, D. L., & Gustafson, M. R. (2009). Using video modeling to teach extinguishing of cooking related fires to individuals with moderate intellectual disabilities. *Education and Training in Developmental Disabilities, 44*(1), 67–79.

Medicinenet.com (2009). Anorexia nervosa. Retrieved [July 21, 2009] from http://www.medicinenet.com/anorexia_nervosa/article.htm.

Meese, R. L. (1999). Teaching adopted students with disabilities: What teachers need to know. *Intervention in School and Clinic, 34*(4), 232–235.

Meese, R. L. (2005). A few new children: Postinstitutionalized children of intercounty adoption. *Journal of Special Education, 39,* 157–167.

Meltzer, L., Roditi, B., Stein, J., Krishnan, K., & Sales Pollica, M. A. (2008). Effective study and test-taking strategies for kids with learning difficulties. Retrieved [June 19, 2008] from http://www.greatschools.net/cgi-bin/showarticle/1160.

Meltzer, L. J., Katzir, T., Miller, L., Reddy, R., & Roditi, B. (2004). Academic self-perceptions, effort, and strategy use in students with learning disabilities: Changes over time. Learning Disabilities Research and Practice, 19, 99–108.

Meltzer, L. J., & Roditi, B. (1994). *The student observation system.* Chelmsford, MA: Research ILD.

Menear, K. S., & Smith, S. (2008). Physical education for students with autism: Teaching tips and strategies. *Teaching Exceptional Children, 40*(5), 32–39.

Menzies, H. M., Lane, K., & Lee, J. M. (2009). Self-monitoring strategies for use in the classroom: A promising practice to support productive behavior for students with emotional or behavioral disorders. *Beyond Behavior, 18*(2), 27–35.

Menzies, H. M., Mahdavi, J. N., & Lewis, J. L. (2008). Early intervention in reading: From research to practice. *Remedial and Special Education, 29*(2), 67–77.

Mercer, C. D., Campbell, K. U., Miller, M. D., Mercer, K. D., & Lane, H. B. (2000). Effects of a reading fluency intervention for middle schoolers with specific learning disabilities. *Learning Disabilities Research and Practice, 15,* 179–189.

Mercer, C. D., & Miller, S. P. (1992). Teaching students with learning problems in math to acquire, understand, and apply basic math facts. *Remedial and Special Education, 13*(3), 19–35, 61.

Mercer, C. D., & Pullen, P. C. (2009). *Teaching students with learning disabilities* (7th ed.). Upper Saddle River, NJ: Merrill/Pearson Education.

Merlone, L. & Moran, D. (2008). Transition works: Self-awareness and self-advocacy skills for students in the elementary learning center. *TEACHING Exceptional Children Plus, 4*(4) Article 1. Retrieved [June 19, 2009] from http://escholarship.bc.edu/education/tecplus/vol4/iss4/art1.

Mesibov, G. B. (2008). Using TEACCH to facilitate inclusion of students with ASD. In C. Forlin (Ed.), *Catering for learners with diverse needs: An Asia-Pacific focus.* (pp. 54–60). Hong Kong: Hong Kong Institute of Education.

Metcalf, D., & Evans, C. (2009, April). *Goof-proof lesson planning: DI + UDL = Access for all learners.* Presentation at the annual meeting of the Council for Exceptional Children, Seattle.

Michael, R. J. (1992). Seizures: Teacher observations and record keeping. *Intervention in School and Clinic, 27*(4), 211–214.

Michael, R. J. (1995). *The educator's guide to students with epilepsy.* Springfield, IL: Thomas.

Michaelsen, L., & Sweet, M. (2008). Team-based learning. *NEA Higher Education Advocate, 25*(6), 5–8.

Midgley, C. (2008, June 25). *Disability dolls become more popular.* Retreived June 26, 2008, from http://www.timesonline.co.uk/tol/life_and_style/health/article4206469.ece?.

Mihalas, S., Morse, W. C., Allsopp, D. H., & Alvarez McHatton, P. (2009). Cultivating caring relationships between teachers and secondary students with emotional and behavioral disorders: Implications for research and practice. *Remedial and Special Education, 30*(2), 108–125.

Miller, K. J., Fitzgerald, G. E., Koury, K. A., Mitchem, K. J., & Hollingsead, C. (2007). Kidtools: Self-management, problem-solving, organizational and planning software for children and teachers. *Intervention in School and Clinic, 43*(1), 12–19.

Miller, L. L., & Felton, R. H. (2001). "It's one of them . . . I don't know": Case study of a student with phonological, rapid naming, and word-finding deficits. *Journal of Special Education, 35,* 125–133.

Miller, M., Miller, S. R., Wheeler, J., & Selinger, J. (1989). Can a single-classroom treatment approach change academic performance and behavioral characteristics in severely behaviorally disordered adolescents? An experimental inquiry. *Behavioral Disorders, 14*(4), 215–225.

Miller, S. P., & Hudson, P. J. (2006). Helping students with disabilities understand what mathematics means. *Teaching Exceptional Children, 39*(1), 28–35.

Miller, S. P., Strawser, S., & Mercer, C. D. (1996). Promoting strategic math performance among students with learning disabilities. *LD Forum, 21*(2), 34–40.

Mills v. Board of Education of the District of Columbia, 348 F. Supp. 866 (D.D.C., 1972).

Mills, P. E., Cole, K. N., Jenkins, J. R., & Dale, P. S. (1998). Effects of differing levels of inclusion on preschoolers with disabilities. *Exceptional Children, 65*(1), 79–90.

Mitchem, K., Kight, J., Fitgerald, G., Koury, K., & Boonseng, T. (2007). Electronic performance support systems: An assistive technology tool for secondary students with mild disabilities. *Journal of Special Education Technology, 22*(2), 1–14.

Mitchem, K. J., & Young, K. R. (2001). Adapting self-management programs for classroom use: Acceptability, feasibility, and effectiveness. *Remedial and Special Education, 22,* 75–88.

Mitchem, K. J., Young, K. R., & West, R. P. (2000). Changing student, parent, and faculty perceptions: School is a positive place. *Intervention in School and Clinic, 35,* 248–252.

Mizelle, N. B. (2005). Moving out of middle school. *Educational Leadership, 62*(7), 56–59.

Moats, L. C. (2001). When older students can't read. *Educational Leadership, 58*(6), 36–40.

Moats, L. C. (2004). Efficacy of a structured, systematic language curriculum for adolescent poor readers. *Reading and Writing Quarterly: Overcoming Learning Difficulties, 20,* 145–159.

Moats, L. C. (2006, Winter). How spelling supports reading and why it is more regular and predictable than you may think. *American Educator,* 12–22, 42–43.

Monda-Amaya, L. E., Dieker, L., & Reed, F. (1998). Preparing students with learning disabilities to participate in inclusive classrooms. *Learning Disabilities Research and Practice, 13*(3), 171–182.

Montague, M. (1997). Cognitive strategy instruction in mathematics for students with learning disabilities. *Journal of Learning Disabilities, 30*(2), 164–177.

Montague, M. (2006). Self-regulation strategies for better math performance in middle school. In M. Montague & A. K. Jitendra (Eds.), *Teaching mathematics to middle school students with learning difficulties* (pp. 89–107). New York: Guilford.

Montague, M. (2007). Self-regulation and mathematics instruction. *Learning Disabilities Research and Practice, 22*(1), 75–83.

Montague, M., Enders, C., Dietz, S., Dixon, J., & Cavendish, W. M. (2008). A longitudinal study of depressive symptomology and self-concept in adolescents. *The Journal of Special Education, 42*(2), 67–78.

Montague, M., & van Garderen, D. (2003). A cross-sectional study of mathematics achievement, estimation skills, and academic self-perception in students with varying ability. *Journal of Learning Disabilities, 36,* 437–448.

Montague, M., Warger, C., & Morgan, T. H. (2000). Solve it! Strategy instruction to improve mathematical problem solving. *Learning Disabilities Research and Practice, 15,* 110–116.

Montgomery, D. (2005). Communicating without harm: Strategies to enhance parent-teacher communication. *Teaching Exceptional Children, 37*(5), 50–55.

Mooney, P., Benner, G. J., Nelson, J. R., Lane, K. L. & Beckers, G. (2007). Standard protocol and individualized remedial reading interventions for secondary students with emotional and behavioral disorders. *Beyond Behavior, 17*(1), 3–10.

Moore Howard, R., & Davies, L. J. (2009). Plagiarism in the internet age. *Educational Leadership, 66*(6), 64–67.

More, C. (2008). Digital stories targeting social skills for children with disabilities: Multidimensional learning. *Intervention in School and Clinic, 43*(3), 168–177.

Moreno, J., Aguilera, A., & Saldana, D. (2008). Do Spanish parents prefer special schools for their children with autism? *Education and Training in Developmental Disabilities, 43*(2), 162–173.

Morgan, P. L., Farkas, G., & Wu, Q. (2009). Five-year growth trajectories of kindergarten children with learning difficulties in mathematics. *Journal of Learning Disabilities, 42*(4), 306–321.

Morgan, M., & Moni, K. B. (2007). 20 ways to motivate students with disabilities using sight-vocabulary activities. *Intervention in School and Clinic, 42(4)*, 42–45.

Morgan, R. L., Ellerd, D. A., Gerity, B. P., & Blair, R. J. (2000). That's the job I want! How technology helps young people in transition. *Teaching Exceptional Children, 32*(4), 44–49.

Morocco, C. C., & Hindin, A. (2002). The role of conversation in a thematic understanding of literature. *Learning Disabilities Research and Practice, 17*, 144–159.

Morrison, R. S., & Blackburn, A. M. (2008). Take the challenge: Building social competency in adolescents with Asberger's syndrome. *TEACHING Exceptional Children Plus, 5*(2) Article 5. Retrieved [June 16, 2009] from http://escholarship.bc.edu/education/tecplus/vol5/iss2/art5.

Mounce, A. B. (2008). Teaching content with interactive whiteboards. *Journal of Special Education Technology, 23*(1), 54–58.

Mu, K., Siegel, E. B., & Allinder, R. M. (2000). Peer interactions and sociometric status of high school students with moderate or severe disabilities in general education classrooms. *Journal of the Association for Persons with Severe Handicaps, 25*, 142–152.

Mueller, T. G. (2009). IEP facilitation: A promising approach to resolving conflicts between families and schools. *Teaching Exceptional Children, 41*(3), 60–67.

Mulholland, R., Pete, A. M., & Popeson, J. (2008). Using animated language software with children diagnosed with autism spectrum disorders. *TEACHING Exceptional Children Plus, 4*(6) Article 3. Retrieved [August 2, 2008] from http://escholarship.bc.edu/education/tecplus/vol4/iss6/art3.

Mullins, F., McKnab, P. A., & Dempsey, S. D. (2002). 20 ways to make the most of a conference experience. *Intervention in School and Clinic, 38*, 113–116.

Mulrine, C. F. (2008). *How to create online learning environments for gifted and talented learners.* Retrieved December, 5, 2008, from http://www.cec.sped.org/AM/PrinterTemplate.cfm?Section=Home&CONTENTID=10669

Mulrine, C. F., Prater, M. A., & Jenkins, A. (2008). The active classroom: Supporting students with attention deficit hyperactivity disorder through exercise. *Teaching Exceptional Children, 40*(5), 16–23.

Munk, D. D. (2008). *Individualizing a grading system for a student with LD and an IEP.* Retrieved February 7, 2008, from http://www.greatschools.net/LD/school-learning/grading-system-for-a-student-with-ld-and-an-iep.gs?content=1019.

Munk, D. D., Bruckert, J., Call, D. T., Stoehrmann, T., & Randandt, E. (1998). Strategies for enhancing the performance of students with LD in inclusive science classes. *Intervention in School and Clinic, 34*(2), 73–78.

Munk, D. D., & Bursuck, W. D. (2001). Preliminary findings on personalized grading plans for middle school students with learning disabilities. *Exceptional Children, 67*, 211–234.

Murawski, W. W. (2006). Student outcomes in co-taught secondary English classes: How can we improve? *Reading and Writing Quarterly: Overcoming Learning Difficulties, 22*, 227–247.

Murawski, W. W., & Dieker, L. (2008). 50 ways to keep your co-teacher: Strategies for before, during, and after co-teaching. *Teaching Exceptional Children, 40*(4), 40–48.

Murdick, N. L., Gartin, B. C., & Crabtree, T. L. (2007). *Special education law* (2nd ed.). Upper Saddle River, NJ: Merrill/Pearson Education.

Murdick, N. L., Gartin, B. C., & Rao, S. M. (2005). Teaching children with hyperlexia. *Teaching Exceptional Children, 36*(4), 56–59.

Murdick, N. L., & Petch-Hogan, B. (1996). Inclusive classroom management: Using preintervention strategies. *Intervention in School and Clinic, 31*(3), 172–176.

Murphy, M. M., & Mazzocco, M. M. M. (2008). Mathematics learning disabilities in girls with Fragile X or Turner syndrome during late elementary school. *Journal of Learning Disabilities, 41*(1), 29–46.

Murray, B., Silver-Pacuilla, H., & Innes Helsel, F. (2007a). Improving basic mathematics instruction: Promising technology resources for students with special needs. *Technology in Action, 2*(5), 1–6, 8.

Murray, C., & Greenberg, M. T. (2006). Examining the importance of social relationships and social contexts in the lives of children with high-incidence disabilities. *Journal of Special Education, 39*, 220–233.

Murray, C. & Naranjo, J. (2008). Poor, black, learning disabled, and graduating: An investigation of factors and processes associated with school completion among high-risk urban youth. *Remedial and Special Education, 29*(3), 145–160.

Murray, C., & Wren, C. T. (2003). Cognitive, academic, and attitudinal predictors of the grade point averages of college students with learning disabilities. *Journal of Learning Disabilities, 36*, 407–415.

Murray, T., & Taylor, L. S. (2009). Gender. In L. S. Taylor & C. R. Whittaker (Eds.), *Bridging multiple worlds: Case studies of diverse educational* (2nd ed.) (pp. 194–222). Boston: Allyn & Bacon.

Muscott, H. S., Szczesiul, S., Berk, B., Staub, K., Hoover, J., & Perry-Chisholm, P. (2008). Creating home-school partnerships by engaging families in schoolwide positive behavior supports. *Teaching Exceptional Children, 40*(6), 6–14.

Mustacchi, J. (2009). R U safe? *Educational Leadership, 66*(6), 78–82.

Musti-Rao, S., & Cartledge, G. (2007). Delivering what urban readers need. *Educational Leadership, 65*(2), 56–62.

Musti-Rao, S., Kroeger, S. D., & Schumacher-Dyke, K. (2008). Using guided notes and response cards at the postsecondary level. *Teacher Education and Special Education, 31*(3), 149–163.

Myers, A., & Eisenman, L. (2005). Student-led IEPs: Take the first steps. *Teaching Exceptional Children, 37*(4), 52–58.

Myles, B. (2008). The hidden curriculum-unwritten rules that students with disabilities often miss. Retrieved February 12, 2008, from http://www.cec.sped.org/AM/Templatecfm?TEMPLATE=%2FCContentDisplay.cf.

Nagel, D. R., Schumaker, J. B., & Deshler, D. D. (1986). *The FIRST-Letter mnemonic strategy.* Lawrence: University of Kansas Institute for Research in Learning Disabilities.

Narr, R. A. F. (2006). Teaching phonological awareness with deaf and hard-of-hearing students. *Teaching Exceptional Children, 38*(4), 53–58.

National Law Center on Homelessness and Poverty. (2009). Homelessness and poverty in America. Retrieved March 2, 2009, from http://www.nlchp.org/hapia.cfm.

National Council for the Accreditation of Teacher Education. (2009). *Professional standards for the accreditation of schools, colleges, and departments of education.* Retrieved May 8, 2009, from http://www.ncate.org.

National Council of Teachers of Mathematics. (2007). *Curriculum focal points for prekindergarten through grade 8 mathematics: A quest for coherence.* Retrieved November 25, 2006, from http://www.nctm.org/focalpoints/intro.asp.

National Youth Violence Prevention Resource Center. (2009). *Bullying facts and statistics.* Retrieved August 15, 2009, from http://www.safeyouth.org/scripts/faq/bullying.asp.

Nelson, J. R., & Roberts, M. L. (2000). Ongoing reciprocal teacher-student interactions involving disruptive behaviors in general education classrooms. *Journal of Emotional and Behavioral Disorders, 8,* 27–37.

Nelson, J. R., Stage, S. A., Epstein, M. H., & Pierce, C. D. (2005). Effects of prereading intervention on the literacy and socialskills of children. *Exceptional Children, 72,* 29–45.

Nevin, A. I., Cramer, E., Voigt, J., & Salazar, L. (2008). Instructional modifications, adaptations, and accommodations of coteachers who loop. *Teacher Education and Special Education, 31*(4), 283–297.

Nevin, A., Malian, I., & Williams, L. (2002). Perspectives on self-determination across the curriculum: Report of a preservice special education teacher preparation program. *Remedial and Special Education, 23,* 75–81.

Newton, D. A., & Dell, A. G. (2009). Issues in assistive technology implementation: Resolving AT/IT conflicts. *Journal of Special Education Technology, 24*(1), 51–56.

New York State Education Department. (n.d.). *The identification and reporting of child abuse and maltreatment.* Albany: Author.

Nichols, S. L., & Berliner, D. C. (2008). Testing the joy out of learning. *Educational Leadership, 65*(6), 14–19.

Nielsen, M. E., & Higgins, L. D. (2005). The eye of the storm: Services and programs for twice-exceptional learners. *Teaching Exceptional Children, 38*(1), 8–15.

Nieto, S. (2009). From surviving to thriving. *Educational Leadership, 66*(5), 8–13.

Nieto, S., & Bode, P. (2008) *Affirming diversity: The sociopolitical context of multicultural education* (5th ed.). Boston: Allyn & Bacon.

Nilson, L. (2007). Getting students to do the readings. *NEA Higher Education Advocate, 25*(2), 6–7.

Noddings, N. (2008). All our students thinking. *Educational Leadership, 65*(5), 8–13.

Noonan, E. (2006). *GPS is giving directions to people who never drive.* Retrieved March 25, 2006, from http://chron.com/disp/story.mpl/tech/news/3747453.html

November, A. *Web literacy for educators.* Thousand Oaks, CA: Corwin Press.

Oberti v. Board of Education of the Borough of Clementon School District, 995 F.2d, 1009, 3rd Circuit, 1993.

Obiakor, F. E. (1999). Teacher expectations of minority exceptional learners: Impact on accuracy of self-concepts. *Exceptional Children, 66*(1), 39–53.

Obiakor, F. E. (2001b). Multicultural education: Powerful tool for preparing future general and special educators. *Teacher Education and Special Education, 24,* 241–253.

Obiakor, F. E. (2007). *Multicultural special education: Culturally responsive teaching.* Upper Saddle River, NJ: Merrill/Pearson Education.

Obiakor, F. E., Alogizzine, R., Bakken, J. P. (2007). Challenging the "good" school myth to work with multicultural exceptional learners. *Multiple Voices, 10*(1 & 2), 17–27.

Obiakor, F. E., & Ford, B. A. (2002). Educational reform and accountability: Implications for African Americans with exceptionalities. *Multiple Voices, 5*(1), 83–93.

O'Brien, C. (2007). Using collaborative reading groups to accommodate diverse learning and behavior needs in the general education classroom. *Beyond Behavior, 16*(3), 7–15.

O'Connor, M. P. (2009). Service works! Promoting transition success for students with disabilities through participation in service learning. *Teaching Exceptional Children, 41*(6), 13–17.

ODIHR Advisory Council on Freedom of Religion or Belief (2007). *Toledo guiding principles on teaching about religions and beliefs in public schools.* Warsaw, Poland: Author.

Oesterreich, H. A., & Knight, M. G. (2008). Facilitating transitions to college for students from culturally and linguistically diverse backgrounds. *Interventions in School and Clinic, 43*(5), 300–304.

Ogura, P., Coco, L., Bulat, J. (2007). Using innovative technology to foster reading development among young children with severe cognitive impairments. *TEACHING Exceptional Children Plus, 4*(1) Article 3. Retrieved [September 7, 2009] from http://escholarship.bc.edu/education/tecplus/vol4/iss1/art3.

Ohler, J. (2006). The world of digital storytelling. *Educational Leadership, 63*(4), 44–47.

Okada, S., Ohtake, Y., & Yanagihara, M. (2008). Effects of perspective sentences in social stories on improving the adaptive behaviors of students with autism spectrum disorders and related disabilities. *Education and Training in Developmental Disabilities, 43*(1), 46–60.

Okolo, C. M. (2006). Using video to teach content-area information: How can the web help teachers. *Journal of Special Education Technology, 21*(3), 48–51.

Okolo, C. M., Englert, C. S., Bouck, E. C., & Heutsche, A. M. (2007). Web-based history learning environments: Helping all students learn and like history. *Intervention in School and Clinic, 43*(1), 3–11.

Olivos, E. M. (2009). Collaboration with Latino families: A critical perspective of home-school interactions. I*ntervention in School and Clinic, 45*(2), 109–115.

Olnes, L. (2008). Special projects for special people: Students with disabilities serve others through service-learning projects. *TEACHING Exceptional Children Plus, 5*(2) Article 4. Retrieved [June 23, 2009] from http:// escholarship.bc.edu/education/tecplus/vol5/iss2/ art4.

Olweus, D. (2003). A profile of bullying at school. *Educational Leadership, 60*(6), 12–17.

O'Malley, J. M., & Valdez Pierce, L. (1996). *Authentic assessment for English language learners: Practical approaches for teachers.* New York: Addison-Wesley.

Ormsbee, C. K. (2001). Effective preassessment team procedures: Making the process work for teachers and students. *Intervention in School and Clinic, 36,* 146–153.

Ormsbee, C. K., & Finson, K. D. (2000). Modifying science activities and materials to enhance instruction for students with learning and behavioral problems. *Intervention in School and Clinic, 36,* 10–13.

Ortiz, A. A., & Wilkinson, C. Y. (1989). Adapting IEPs for limited English proficient students. *Academic Therapy, 24,* 555–568.

Ortiz, A. A., & Wilkinson, C. Y. (1991). Assessment and intervention model for bilingual exceptional student (Aim for the Best). *Teacher Education and Special Education, 14*(1), 35–42.

Ortiz Lienemann, T., & Reid, T. (2008). Using self-regulated strategy development to improve expository writing with students with attention deficit hyperactivity disorder. *Exceptional Children, 74*(4), 471–486.

Osborn, J., Freeman, A., Burley, M., Wilson, R., Jones, E., & Rychener, S. (2007). Effects of tutoring on reading achievement of students with cognitive disabilities, specific learning disabilities, and students receiving Title 1 services. *Education and Training in Developmental Disabilities, 42*(4), 467–475.

Osterhaus, S. (2007). Technology for students with visual impairments. *Technology in Action, 2*(5), 7.

Otis-Wilborn, A., Winn, J., Griffin, C., & Kilgore, K. (2005). Beginning special educators' forays into general education. *Teacher Education and Special Education, 28,* 143–152.

Overton, T. (2006). *Assessing learners with special needs: An applied approach* (5th ed.). Upper Saddle River, NJ: Merrill/Pearson Education.

Owens, R. E. (2001). *Language development: An introduction* (5th ed.). Needham Heights, MA: Allyn & Bacon.

Owens, R. E. (2010). *Language disorders: A functional approach to assessment and instruction* (5th ed.). Boston: Allyn & Bacon.

Owen-DeSchryver, J. S., Carr, E. G., Cale, S. I., & Blakely-Smith, A. (2008). Promoting social interactions between students with autism spectrum disorders and their peers in inclusive school settings. *Focus on Autism and Other Developmental Disabilities, 23*(1), 15–28.

Painter, D. D. (2009). Providing differentiated learning experiences through multigenre projects. *Intervention in School and Clinic, 44*(5), 288–293.

Palincsar, A. S., Magnusson, S. J., Cutter, J., & Vincent, M. (2002). Supporting guided-inquiry instruction. *Teaching Exceptional Children, 34* (3), 88–91.

Palmer, D. S., Fuller, K., Aurora, T., & Nelson, M. (2001). Taking sides: Parent views on inclusion for their children with severe disabilities. *Exceptional Children, 67,* 467–484.

Parette, Jr., H. P., Crowley, E. P., & Wojcik, B. W. (2007). Reducing overload in students with learning and behavioral disorders: The role of assistive technology. *TEACHING Exceptional Children Plus, 4*(1) Article 4. Retrieved [July 4, 2009] from http://escholarship.bc.edu/ education/tecplus/vol4/iss1/art4.

Parette, H. P., & McMahan, G. A. (2002). What should we expect of assistive technology? Being sensitive to family goals. *Teaching Exceptional Children, 35*(1), 56–61.

Parette, H. P., & Petch-Hogan, B. (2000). Approaching families: Facilitating culturally/linguistically diverse family involvement. *Teaching Exceptional Children, 33*(2), 4–11.

Parette, H. P., & Peterson-Karlan, G. R. (2007). Facilitating student achievement with assistive technology, *Education and Training in Developmental Disabilities, 42*(4), 387–397.

Parette, H. P., Peterson-Karlan, G. R., Wojcik, B. W., & Bardi, N. (2007). Monitor that progress! Interpreting data trends for assistive technology decision making. *Teaching Exceptional Children, 40*(1), 22–29.

Parette, H. P., Wojcik, B. W., Peterson-Karlan, G., & Hourcade, J. J. (2005). Assistive technology for students with mild disabilities: What's cool and what's not. *Education and Training in Developmental Disabilities, 40,* 320–331.

Park, K. L. (2007). Facilitating effective team-based functional behavior assessments in typical school settings. *Beyond Behavior, 17*(1), 21–31.

Parker, R., Hasbrouck, J. E., & Denton, C. (2002a). How to tutor students with reading comprehension problems. *Preventing School Failure, 47,* 45–47.

Parker, R., Hasbrouck, J. E., & Denton, C. (2002b). Tips for teaching. How to tutor students with reading problems. *Preventing School Failure, 47,* 42–44.

Parker Adams, E., & Adams, A. A. (2008). Reality lessons in traumatic brain injury. *Teaching Exceptional Children Plus, 4*(3)Article 1. Retrieved February 7, 2009, from http://escholarship.bc.edu/education/tecplus/ vol4iss3/1.

Parker-Pope, T. (2009, February 3). Telling food allergies from false alarms. *New York Times.* Retrieved March 1, 2009, from http://www.nytimes/2009/02/03/health/ 03well.html?_r=2&ref=science&pagewanted=p.

Parmar, R. S., & Cawley, J. F. (1991). Challenging the routines and passivity that characterize instruction for children with mild handicaps. *Remedial and Special Education, 12*(5), 23–32, 43.

Parmar, R. S., Cawley, J. F., & Frazita, R. R. (1996). Word problem-solving by students with and without mild disabilities. *Teaching Exceptional Children, 26*(4), 16–21.

Parrish, P. R., & Stodden, R. A. (2009). Aligning assessment and instruction with state standards for children with significant disabilities. *Teaching Exceptional Children, 41*(4), 46-57.

Patel, P., & Laud, L. E. (2007). Using songs to strengthen reading fluency. *TEACHING Exceptional Children Plus, 4*(2) Article 4. Retrieved [August 18, 2009] from http://escholarship.bc.edu/education/tecplus/vol4/iss2/art4.

Paterson, D. (2007). Teachers' in-flight thinking in inclusive classrooms. *Journal of Learning Disabilities, 40*(5), 427–435.

Patterson, P. P., Petit, C., & Williams, S. (2007). Conducting telephone conference IEPs. *TEACHING Exceptional Children Plus, 3*(5) Article 3. Retrieved [June 3, 2009] from http://escholarship.bc.edu/education/tecplus/vol3/iss5/art3.

Patton, J. M., & Townsend, B. L. (1999). Ethics, power, and privilege: Neglected considerations in the education of African American learners with special needs. *Teacher Education and Special Education, 22,* 276–286.

Patton, J. R., Cronin, M. E., Bassett, D. S., & Koppel, A. E. (1997). A life skills approach to mathematics instruction: Preparing students with learning disabilities for the real-life math demands of adulthood. *Journal of Learning Disabilities, 30*(2), 178–187.

Pauk, W. (1984). *How to study in college.* Boston: Houghton Mifflin.

Paulsen, K. J. (2005). Infusing evidence-based practices into the special education preparation curriculum. *Teacher Education and Special Education, 28,* 21–28.

Paulsen, K. J. (2008). School-based collaboration. *Intervention in School and Clinic, 43*(5), 313–315.

Pavri., S., & Luftig, R. (2000). The social face of inclusive education: Are students with learning disabilities really included in the classroom? *Preventing School Failure, 45*(1), 8–14.

Pavri, S., & Monda-Amaya, L. (2000). Loneliness and students with learning disabilities in inclusive classrooms: Self-perceptions, coping strategies, and preferred interventions. *Learning Disabilities Research and Practice, 15,* 22–33.

Pavri, S., & Monda-Amaya, L. (2001). Social support in inclusive schools: Student and teacher perspectives. *Exceptional Children, 67,* 391–411.

Paxton-Buursma, D., & Walker, M. (2008). Piggybacking: A strategy to increase participation in classroom discussions by students with learning disabilities. *Teaching Exceptional Children, 40*(3), 28–34.

Payne, L. D., Marks, L. J., & Bogan, B. L. (2007). Using curriculum-based assessment to address the academic and behavioral deficits of students with emotional and behavioral disorders. *Beyond Behavior, 16*(3), 3–6.

Payne, R. (2008). Nine powerful practices. *Educational Leadership, 65*(7), 48–53.

Peck, C. A., Carlson, P., & Helmstetter, E. (1992). Parent and teacher perceptions of outcomes for typically developing children enrolled in integrated early childhood programs: A statewide survey. *Journal of Early Intervention, 16,* 53–63.

Peck, C. A., Donaldson, J., & Pezzoli, M. (1990). Some benefits non-handicapped adolescents perceive for themselves from their social relationships with peers who have severe disabilities. *Journal of the Association for Persons with Severe Handicaps, 15*(4), 241–249.

Peck, S. (2004). Communication made easier: Facilitating transitions for students with multiple disabilities. *Teaching Exceptional Children, 36* (5), 60–63.

Peetsma, T. (2001). Inclusion in education: Comparing pupils' development in special and regular education. *Educational Review, 53,* 125–136.

Peia Oakes, W., Harris, P. J., & Churley Barr, L. (2009). A model for supplementing reading instruction for young children with behavioral risk factors. *Beyond Behavior, 18*(3), 10–18.

Pellitteri, J., Dealy, M., Fasano, C., & Kugler, J. (2006). Emotionally intelligent interventions for students with reading disabilities. *Reading and Writing Quarterly: Overcoming Learning Difficulties, 22,* 155–171.

Pemberton, J. B. (2003). Integrated processing: A strategy for working on unknown words. *Intervention in School and Clinic, 38,* 247–250.

Pemberton, J. B., Rademacher, J. A., Tyler-Wood, T., & Cereijo, M. V. P. (2006). Aligning assessments with state curriculum standards and teaching strategies. *Intervention in School and Clinic, 41,* 283–289.

Pennsylvania Association for Retarded Children v. Commonwealth of Pennsylvania, 343 F. Supp. 279 (E.D. Pa., 1972).

Perchemlides, N., & Coutant, C. (2004). Growing beyond grades. *Educational Leadership, 62*(2), 53–56.

Perez Sanchez, L. F., & Beltran Liera, J. A. (2007). Memory strategy training in Spanish people with moderate intellectual disabilities in a technological setting. *Journal of Special Education Technology, 22*(2), 45–54.

Perkins-Gough, D. (2006). Do we really have a "boy crisis"? *Educational Leadership, 64*(1), 93–94.

Peterson Nelson, J. A., Caldarella, P., Young, K. R., & Webb, N. (2008). Using peer praise notes to increase the social involvement of withdrawn adolescents. *Teaching Exceptional Children, 41*(2), 6–13.

Pewewardy, C., & Fitzpatrick, M. (2009). Working with American Indian students and families: Disabilities, issues, and interventions. *Intervention in School and Clinic, 45*(2), 91–98.

Phillips, B. M., Lonigan, C. J., & Wyatt, M. A. (2009). Predictive validity of the Get Ready to Read! Screener: Concurrent and long-term relations with reading-related skills. *Journal of Learning Disabilities, 42*(2), 133–147.

Phillips, L., Sapona, R. H., & Lubic, B. L. (1995). Developing partnerships in inclusive education: One school's approach. *Intervention in School and Clinic, 30*(5), 262–272.

Pierson, M. R., & Glaeser, B. C. (2007). Using comic strip conversations to increase social satisfaction and loneliness in students with autism spectrum disorder. *Education and Training in Developmental Disabilities, 42*(4), 460–466.

Pivik, J., McComas, J., & Laflamme, M., (2002). Barriers and facilitators to inclusive education. *Exceptional Children, 69,* 97–107.

Plyler v. Doe, 457 U.S. 202 (1982).

Pogue, D. (2008a, August 7). Speak up, a computer is listening. *New York Times,* BU 1, 8.

Pogue, D. (2008b, May 8). Gadget fanatics, take note. *New York Times*, BU 1, 9.

Poolaw v. Bishop, 23IDELR 406, 9th Circuit, 1995.

Popham, W. J. (2003). The seductive allure of data. *Educational Leadership, 60*(5), 48–51.

Popham, W. J. (2005). Students' attitudes count. *Educational Leadership, 63*(8), 85–86.

Popham, W. J. (2006). Those [fill-in-the-blank] tests! *Educational Leadership, 62*(5), 84–85.

Posamentier, A. S., Smith, B., & Stepelman, J. (2006). *Teaching secondary mathematics: Techniques and enrichment units* (7th ed.). Upper Saddle River, NJ: Merrill/Pearson Education.

Powell, S. R., Fuchs, L. S., Fuchs, D., Cirino, P. T., & Fletcher, J. M. (2009). Effects of fact retrieval tutoring on third-grade students with math difficulties with and without reading difficulties. *Learning Disabilities Research and Practice, 24*(1), 1–11.

Powell-Brown, A. (2006). Why can't I just see the movie? Fostering motivation in children who struggle with reading. *Intervention in School and Clinic, 42,* 84–90.

Praisner, C. L. (2003). Attitudes of elementary school principals toward the inclusion of students with disabilities. *Exceptional Children, 69,* 135–145.

Pransky, K. (2009). There's more to see. *Educational Leadership, 66*(7), 74–78.

Prater, M. A. (2003). She will succeed: Strategies for success in inclusive classrooms. *Teaching Exceptional Children, 35*(5), 58–64.

Prater, M. A., Bruhl, S., & Serna, L. A. (1998). Acquiring social skills through cooperative learning and teacher-directed instruction. *Remedial and Special Education, 19*(3), 160–172.

Prater, M. A., & Dyches, T. T. (2008). Books that portray characters with disabilities: A top 25 list for children and young adults. *Teaching Exceptional Children, 40*(4), 32–39.

Prater, M. A., Dyches, T. T., & Johnstun, M. (2006). Teaching students about learning disabilities through children's literature. *Intervention in School and Clinic, 42,* 14–24.

Prater, M. A., & Sileo, N. M. (2001). Using juvenile literature about HIV/AIDS: Ideas and precautions for the classroom. *Teaching Exceptional Children, 33*(6), 34–45.

Preciado, J. A., Horner, R. H., & Baker, S. K. (2009). Using a function-based approach to decrease problem behaviors and increase academic engagement for Latino English language learners. *The Journal of Special Education, 42*(4), 209–226.

Premack, D. (1959). Toward empirical behavior laws. *Psychological Review, 66*(4), 219–233.

Prensky, M. (2008). Turning on the lights. *Educational Leadership, 65*(6), 40–45.

Presley, J. A., & Hughes, C. (2000). Peers as teachers of anger management to high school students with behavioral disorders. *Behavioral Disorders, 25,* 114–130.

Prestia, K. (2003). Tourette's syndrome: Characteristics and interventions. *Intervention in School and Clinic, 39,* 67–71.

Preston, A. S., Heaton, S. C., McCann, S. J., Watson, W. D., & Selke, G. (2009). The role of multidimensional attentional abilities in academic skills of children with ADHD. *Journal of Learning Disabilities, 42*(3), 240–249.

Price, K. M., & Nelson, K. L. (2007). *Planning effective instruction: Diversity responsive methods and management* (3rd ed.). Belmont, CA: Thomson/Wadsworth.

Price, L. A., Gerber, P. J., & Mulligan, R. (2007). Adults with learning disabilities and the underutilization of the Americans with Disabilities Act. *Remedial and Special Education, 28*(6), 340—344.

Prom, M. (1999). Measuring perceptions about inclusion. *Teaching Exceptional Children, 31*(5), 38–42.

Provost, M. C., Rullo, A., & Buechner, M. (2000). 20 ways to make spelling sizzle. *Intervention in School and Clinic, 39,* 87–98

Pruitt, B. A., & Cooper, J. T. (2008). Ready, set, go: Three strategies to build reading fluency. *Beyond Behavior, 17*(3), 8–15.

Pullen, P. C., & Justice, L. M. (2003). Enhancing phonological awareness, print awareness, and oral language skills in preschool children. *Intervention in School and Clinic, 39,* 87–98.

Pullen, P.C., & Lloyd, J. W. (2007, Summer). Phonics instruction. *Current Practice Alerts, 14,* 1–4.

Quart, A. (March 16, 2008). When girls will be boys. *New York Times Magazine,* 32–37.

Rafferty, Y., Piscitelli, V., & Boettcher, C. (2003). The impact of inclusion on language development and social competence among preschoolers with disabilities. *Exceptional Children, 69,* 467–480.

Raghubar, K., Cirino, P., Barnes, M., Ewing-Cobbs, L., Fletcher, J., & Fuchs, L. (2009). Errors in multi-digit arithmetic and behavioral inattention in children with math difficulties. *Journal of Learning Disabilities, 42*(4), 356–371.

Ramirez, A. Y., & Soto-Hinman, I. (2009). A place for all families. *Educational Leadership, 66*(7), 79–82.

Ramsey, M. L., Jolivette, K., & Patton, B. (2007). Peer-assisted learning strategies (PALS) for reading in the EBD classroom. *Beyond Behavior, 17*(1), 2–7.

Rance-Roney, J. (2009). Best practices for adolescent ELLs. *Educational Leadership, 66*(7), 32–57.

Rao, K., Dowrick, P. W., Yuen, J. W. L., & Boisvert, P. C. (2009). Writing in a multimedia environment: Pilot outcomes for high school students in special education. *Journal of Special Education Technology, 24*(1), 39–49.

Rao, S., & Gagie, B. (2006). Learning through seeing and doing: Visual supports for children with autism. *Teaching Exceptional Children, 38*(6), 26–33.

Rao, S., & Kane, M. T. (2009). Teaching students with cognitive impairment chained mathematical task of decimal subtraction using simultaneous prompting. *Education and Training in Developmental Disabilities, 44*(2), 244–256.

Rasinski, T. (2004). Creating fluent readers. *Educational Leadership, 61*(6), 46–51.

Rasinski, T., Homan, S., & Biggs, M. (2009). Teaching reading fluency to struggling readers: Methods, materials, and evidence. *Reading and Writing Quarterly: Overcoming Learning Difficulties, 25*(2–3), 192–204.

Rasinski, T., & Oswald, R. (2005). Making and writing words: Constructivist word learning in a second-grade classroom.

Reading and Writing Quarterly: Overcoming Learning Difficulties, 21, 151–163.

Rasinski, T., & Padak, N. (2004). Beyond consensus—Beyond balance: Toward a comprehensive literacy curriculum. *Reading and Writing Quarterly: Overcoming Learning Difficulties, 20,* 91–102.

Raskind, M. H., & Higgins, E. L. (1998). Assistive technology for postsecondary students with learning disabilities: An overview. *Journal of Learning Disabilities, 31*(1), 27–40.

Raver, S. A. (2009). *Early childhood special education—0–8 years: Strategies for positive outcomes.* Upper Saddle River, NJ: Merrill/Pearson Education.

Raymond, E. B. (1997, November). *Accommodating diversity, combating homophobia.* Presentation at the annual meeting of the New York Federation of Chapters of the Council for Exceptional Children, New York.

Raymond, E. B. (2008). *Learners with mild disabilities: A characteristics approach* (3rd ed.). Upper Saddle River, NJ: Merrill/Pearson Education.

Rea, P. J., McLaughlin, V. L., & Walther-Thomas, C. (2002). Outcomes for students with learning disabilities in inclusive and pullout programs. *Exceptional Children, 68,* 203–222.

Reagon, K. A., Higbee, T. S., & Endicott, K. (2007). Using video instruction procedures with and without embedded text to teach object labeling to preschoolers with Autism: A preliminary investigation. *Journal of Special Education Technology, 22*(1), 13–20.

Reasoner Jones, L. (2008). *Teaching secrets: Bridging the gender gap.* Teacher Magazine. Retrieved September 8, 2008, from http://www.teachermagainze.org/tm/articles/2008/09/0301tln_jones.h20.html?print11.

Reed, D. K. (2008). A synthesis of morphology interventions and effects on reading outcomes for students in grades K-12. *Learning Disabilities Research and Practice, 23*(1), 36–49.

Reetz, L. J. (1995, April). *Portfolio assessment in inclusion settings: A shared responsibility.* Presentation at the annual meeting of the Council for Exceptional Children, Indianapolis.

Reeves, D. B. (2008). Effective grading. *Educational Leadership, 65*(5), 85–87.

Reeves, S., & Standford, P. (2009). Blending technology and literacy strategies: Engaging learners with emotional and behavioral disorders. *Journal of Special Education Technology, 24*(2), 42–45.

Regan, K. S. (2003). Using dialogue journals in the classroom: Forming relationships with students with emotional disturbance. *Teaching Exceptional Children, 36*(2), 34–39.

Regan, K. S. (2009). Improving the way we think about students with emotional and/or behavioral disorders. *Teaching Exceptional Children, 41*(5), 60–65.

Reid, D., & Green, C. (2006). Preference-based teaching: Helping students with severe disabilities enjoy learning without problem behavior. *Teaching Exceptional Children Plus, 2*(3) Article 2. Retrieved April 2, 2006, from http://escholarship.bc.edu/education/tecplus/vol2/iss3/art12.

Reid, D. K., & Button, L. J. (1995). Anna's story: Narratives of personal experience about being labeled learning disabled. *Journal of Learning Disabilities, 28*(10), 602–614.

Reid, R., & Nelson, J. R. (2002). The utility, acceptability, and practically of functional behavioral assessment for students with high-incidence problem behaviors. *Remedial and Special Education, 23,* 15–23.

Reyes, I. (2004). Functions of codeswitching in schoolchildren's conversation. *Bilingual Research Journal, 28*(1), 77–98.

Reynhout, G., & Carter, M. (2007). Social story efficacy with a child with autism spectrum disorder and moderate intellectual disability. *Focus on Autism and Other Developmental Disabilties, 22*(3), 173–182.

Riccomini, P. J., & Witzel, B. S. (2010). *Computation of integers: Math intervention for elementary and middle grades students.* Upper Saddle River, NJ: Merrill/Pearson Education.

Rice, N., Drame, E., Owens, L., & Frattura, E. M. (2007). Co-instructing at the secondary level: Strategies for success. *Teaching Exceptional Children, 39*(6), 12–18.

Rich, M. (2009, August 30). Students get new reading assignment: Pick books you like. *New York Times, 1,* 18–19.

Richards, H. V., Brown, A. F., & Forde, T. B. (2007). Addressing diversity in schools: Culturally responsive pedagogy. *Teaching Exceptional Children, 39*(3), 64–68.

Richardson, W. (2009). Becoming network-wise. *Educational Leadership, 66*(6), 26–31.

Rinaldi, C., & Samson, J. (2008). English language learners and response to intervention: Referral considerations. *Teaching Exceptional Children, 40*(5), 6–15.

Ritchey, K. D. (2006). Learning to write: Progress-monitoring tools for beginning and at-risk writers. *Teaching Exceptional Children, 39*(2), 22–26.

Ritchey, K. D. & Goeke, J. L. (2006). Orton-Gillingham and Orton-Gillingham-based reading instruction: A review of the literature. *Journal of Special Education, 40,* 171–183.

Rizza, M. G., & Morrison, W. F. (2007). Identifying twice exceptional students: A toolkit for success. *Teaching Exceptional Children Plus, 3*(3) Article 3. Retrieved February 17, 2009, from http://escholarship.bc.edu/education/tecplus/vol3/iss3/art3.

Roberts, G., Torgesen, J. K., Boardman, A., & Scammacca, N. (2008). Evidence-based strategies for reading instruction of older students with learning disabilities. *Learning Disabilities Research and Practice, 23*(2), 63–69.

Roberts, J. M. A., Keane, E., & Clark, T. R. (2008). Making inclusion work: Autism spectrum Australia satellite class project. *Teaching Exceptional Children, 41*(2), 22–27.

Roberts, S. (2008a, August 7). Census data show minorities often a majority of the population under 20. *New York Times,* A15.

Roberts, S. (2008b, Decemeber 9). In biggest U.S. cities, minorities are at 50%. *New York Times,* A28.

Roberts, S. (2009, May 14). Asian and Hispanic minorities growing, but more slowly. *New York Times,* A24.

Roberts, S. (2010). Understanding students with hearing loss. In A. Turnbull, R. Turnbull, & M. L. Wehmeyer (Eds.), *Exceptional lives: Special education in today's schools* (6th ed., pp. 392–426). Upper Saddle River, NJ: Merrill/Pearson Education.

Robinson, L., & Kelley, B. (2007). Developing reflective thought in preservice educators: Utilizing role-plays and digital video. *Journal of Special Education Technology, 22*(2), 31–44.

Robinson, S. M. (1999). Meeting the needs of students who are gifted and have learning disabilities. *Intervention in School and Clinic, 34*(4), 195–204.

Robinson, T. R. (2007). Cognitive behavioral interventions: Strategies to help students make wise behavioral choices. *Beyond Behavior, 17*(1), 7–13.

Rock, M. L. (2004). Transfiguring it out: Converting disengaged learners to active participants. *Teaching Exceptional Children, 36*(5), 64–72.

Rock, M. L., & Thead, B. K. (2009). 20 ways to promote student success during independent seatwork. *Intervention in School and Clinic, 44*(3), 179–184.

Rodriguez, C. D., & Higgins, K. (2005). Preschool children with developmental delays and limited English proficiency. *Intervention in School and Clinic, 40,* 236–242.

Roehrig, A. D., Walton Duggar, S., Moats, L., Glover, M., & Mincey, B. (2008). When teachers work to use progress monitoring data to inform literacy instruction: Identifying potential supports and challenges. *Remedial and Special Education, 29*(6), 364–382.

Roessing, L. (2009). *The write to read: Response journals that increase comprehension.* Thousand Oaks, CA: Corwin Press.

Rogevich, M. E., & Perin, D. (2009). Effects of science summarization of a reading comprehension intervention for adolescents with behavior and attention disorders. *Exceptional Children, 74*(2), 135–154.

Rollock, N. (2007). Why black girls don't matter: Exploring how race and gender shape academic success in an inner city school. *Support for Learning, 22*(4), 197–203.

Roll-Pettersson, L. (2001). Teacher perceptions of supports and resources needed in regard to pupils with special needs in Sweden. *Education and Training in Mental Retardation and Developmental Disabilities, 36,* 42–54.

Roll-Pettersson, L. (2008). Teacher perceived efficacy and the inclusion of a pupil with dyslexia or mild mental retardation: Findings from Sweden. *Education and Training in Mental Retardation and Developmental Disabilities, 43*(2), 42–54.

Rolstad, K., Mahoney, K., & Glass, G. V. (2005). The big picture: A meta-analysis of program effectiveness research on English language learners. *Educational Policy, 19*(4), 572–594.

Romeo, L. (2008). Informal writing assessment linked to instruction: A continuous process for teachers, students, and parents. *Reading and Writing Quarterly: Overcoming Learning Difficulties, 24*(1), 25–52.

Romero, M., & Parirno, A. (1994). Planned alternation of languages (PAL): Language use and distribution in bilingual classrooms. *Journal of Educational Issues of Language Minority Students, 13,* 137–161.

Roopnarine, J., Bynoe, P., Singh, R., & Simon, R. (2005). Caribbean families in English speaking countries: A rather complex mosaic. In J. Roopnarine & U. Gielen (Eds.), *Families in global perspective* (pp. 311–329). Boston, MA: Allyn & Bacon.

Rose, R. (2008). Promoting inclusion by addressing the needs of local communities: Working together to promote social and educational conhesion. In C. Forlin (Ed.), *Catering for learners with diverse needs: An Asia-Pacific focus.* (pp. 30–53). Hong Kong: Hong Kong Institute of Education.

Rose, T. E., McDonnell, J., & Ellis, G. (2007). The impact of teacher beliefs on the provision of leisure and physical activity education curriculum decisions. *Teacher Education and Special Education, 30*(3), 183–198.

Roseberry-McKibbin, C. (2007). *Language disorders in children: A multicultural and case perspective.* Boston: Allyn & Bacon.

Rosenberg, M. S., & Jackman, L. A. (2003). Development, implementation, and sustainability of comprehensive school-wide behavior management systems. *Intervention in School and Clinic, 39,* 10–21.

Rosenberg, M. S., Westling, D. L., & McLeskey, J. (2008). *Special education for today's teachers: An introduction.* Upper Saddle River, NJ: Merrill/Pearson Education.

Roth, K., Pyfer, J., and Huettig, C. (2007). Transition in physical recreation and students with cognitive disabilities: Graduate and parent perspectives. *Education and Training in Developmental Disabilities, 42*(1), 94–106.

Rothstein, R. (2009). Equalizing opportunity: Dramatic differences in children's home life and health mean that schools can't do it alone. American Educator, 33(2), 4–7, 45–47.

Rothstein-Fisch, C., & Trumbull, E. (2008). *Managing diverse classrooms: How to build on students' cultural strengths.* Alexandria, VA: Association for Supervision and Curriculum Development.

Rotter, K. (2006). Creating instructional materials for all pupils. Try COLA. *Intervention in School and Clinic, 41,* 273–282.

Rotter, K. M. (2009). Enhancing memory in your students: COMPOSE yourself. *TEACHING Exceptional Children Plus, 5*(3) Article 4. Retrieved [September 10, 2009] from http://escholarship.bc.edu/education/tecplus/vol5/iss3/art4.

Rousselle, L., & Noel, M. P. (2008). Mental arithmetic in children with mathematics learning disabilities: The adaptive use of approximate calculation in an addition verification task. *Journal of Learning Disabilties, 41*(6), 498–513.

Rozalski, M. E. (2007). Practice, practice, practice: How to improve students' study skills. *Beyond Behavior, 17*(1), 17–23.

Rubinstein-Avila, E. (2006). Connecting with Latino learners. *Educational Leadership, 63*(5), 38–43.

Ruckdeschel, S. (2009). *Peer coaching for adolescent writers.* Thousand Oaks, CA: Corwin Press.

Rueda, R., & Garcia, E. (1997). Do portfolios make a difference for diverse students? The influence of type of data on making instructional decisions. *Learning Disabilities Research and Practice, 12*(2), 114–122.

Rueda, R., Jin Lim, H., & Velasco, A. (2007). Cultural accommodations in the classroom: An instructional perspective. *Multiple Voices, 10*(1 & 2), 61–72.

Rues, J. P. Graff, J. C., Ault, M. M., & Holvoet, J. (2006). Special health care procedures. In M. E. Snell & F. Brown (Eds.), *Instruction of students with severe disabilities* (6th ed., pp. 251–290). Upper Saddle River, NJ: Merrill/Pearson Education.

Rupley, W. H., Blair, T. R., & Nichols, W. D. (2009). Effective reading instruction for struggling readers: The role of direct/explicit teaching. *Reading and Writing Quarterly: Overcoming Learning Difficulties, 25*(2–3), 239–260.

Rupley, W. H., & Nichols, W. D. (2005). Vocabulary instruction for the struggling reader. *Reading and Writing Quarterly: Overcoming Learning Difficulties, 21,* 239–260.

Russell, C. L. (2008). How are your person first skills?: A self-assessment. *Teaching Exceptional Children, 40*(5), 40–43.

Russell, M., Hoffmann, T., & Higgins, J. (2009). NimbleTools: A universally designed test delivery system. *Teaching Exceptional Children, 42*(2), 6–12.

Ryan, J. B., Pierce, C. D., & Mooney, P. (2008). Evidence-based teaching strategies for students with EBD. *Beyond Behavior, 17*(3), 8–13.

Ryan, J. B., Reid, R., & Ellis, C. (2008). Special educators' knowledge regarding psychotropic interventions for students with emotional and behavioral disorders. *Remedial and Special Education, 29*(5), 269–279.

Saavedra, S. (2009). Reviewing for a test could be just a click away on your iPod. Retrieved [March 3, 2008] from http://www.signonsandiego.com/news/education/20080304-9999-1n4ipods.html.

Sacramento City Unified School District, Board of Education v. Holland, 14F.3d, 1398, 9th Circuit, 1994.

Saddler, B. (2004). 20 ways to improve writing ability. *Intervention in School and Clinic, 39,* 310–314.

Saddler, B., & Andrade, H. (2004). The writing rubric. *Educational Leadership, 62*(2), 48–52.

Saddler, B., & Staulters, M. (2008). Beyond tutoring: After-school literacy instruction. *Intervention in School and Clinic, 43*(4), 203–209.

Safran, S. P. (1998). Disability portrayal in film: Reflecting the past, directing the future. *Exceptional Children, 64*(2), 227–238.

Safran, S. P. (2000). Using movies to teach students about disabilities. *Teaching Exceptional Children, 32*(3), 44–47.

Safran, S. P. (2001). Asperger syndrome: The emerging challenge to special education. *Exceptional Children, 67,* 151–160.

Safran, S. P., & Oswald, K. (2003). Positive behavior supports: Can schools reshape disciplinary practices? *Exceptional Children, 69,* 361–373.

Sagor, R. (2008). Cultivating optism in the classroom. *Educational Leadership, 65*(6), 26–31.

Salend, S. J. (2001). Creating your own professional portfolio. *Intervention in School and Clinic, 36,* 195–201.

Salend, S. J. (2004). Fostering inclusive values in children: What families can do. *Teaching Exceptional Children, 37*(1), 64–69.

Salend, S. J. (2009). *Classroom testing and assessment for all students: Beyond standardization.* Thousand Oaks, CA: Corwin Press.

Salend, S. J., & Duhaney, L. M. (2002a). Grading students in inclusive settings. *Teaching Exceptional Children, 34*(3), 8–15.

Salend, S. J., & Garrick Duhaney, L. M. (2002b). What do families have to say about inclusion? How to pay attention and get results. *Teaching Exceptional Children, 35*(1), 62–66.

Salend, S. J., & Garrick Duhaney, L. M. (2007). Research related to inclusion and program Effectiveness: Yesterday, today, and tomorrow. In J. McLeskey (Ed.), *Reflections on inclusion: Classic articles that shaped our thinking* (pp. 127–129, 147–159). Arlington, VA: Council for Exceptional Children.

Salend, S. J., Garrick Duhaney, L. M., & Montgomery, W. (2002). A comprehensive approach to identifying and addressing issues of disproportionate representation. *Remedial and Special Education, 23,* 289–299.

Salend, S. J., & Sylvestre, S. (2005). Understanding and addressing oppositional and defiant classroom behaviors. *Teaching Exceptional Children, 37*(6), 32–39.

Salinger, T. (2003). Helping older, struggling readers. *Preventing School Failure, 47,* 79–85.

Salinger, T., & Fleischman, S. (2005). Teaching students to interact with text. *Educational Leadership, 63*(2), 90–92.

Salisbury, C. L., & McGregor, G. (2002). The administrative climate and context of inclusive elementary schools. *Exceptional Children, 68,* 259–274.

Salisbury, C. L., Brookfield, J., & Odom, S. (2005, April). *Effects of inclusive class membership on students without disabilities.* Presentation at the international convention of the Council for Exceptional Children, Baltimore.

Salpeter, J. (2006). Inside the divide. *Technology and Learning, 26*(8), 22–28.

Samson, J. F., & Lesaux, N. K. (2009). Language-minority learners in special education: Rates and predictors of identification for services. *Journal of Learning Disabilities, 42*(2), 148–162.

Sanacore, J. (1999). Encouraging children to make choices about their literacy learning. *Intervention in School and Clinic, 35*(1), 38–42.

Sanacore, J. (2002). Questions often asked about promoting lifetime literacy efforts. *Intervention in School and Clinic, 37,* 163–167.

Sanacore, J. (2005). Increasing student participation in the language arts. *Intervention in School and Clinic, 41,* 99–104.

San Antonio, D. M. (2008). Understanding students and struggles. *Educational Leadership, 65*(7), 74–79.

San Antonio, D. M., & Salzfass, E. A. (2007). How we treat one another in school. *Educational Leadership, 64*(8), 32–39.

Sanders, J., & Cotton Nelson, S. (2004). Closing gender gaps in science. *Educational Leadership, 62*(3), 74–77.

Santangelo, T. (2009). Collaborative problem solving effectively implemented, but not sustained: A case for aligning the sun, the moon, and the stars. *Exceptional Children, 75*(2), 185–209.

Santangelo, T., Harris, K. R., & Graham, S. (2008). Using self-regulated strategy development to support students who have "trubol giting thangs into werds." *Remedial and Special Education, 29*(2), 78–89.

Santoro, L. E., Coyne, M. D., & Simmons, D. C. (2006). The reading-spelling connection: Developing and evaluating a beginning spelling intervention for children at risk of reading disability. *Learning Disabilities Research and Practice, 21,* 122–133.

Santoro, L. E., Jitendra, A. K., Starosta, K., & Sacks, G. (2006). Reading well with Read Well: Enhancing the reading performance of English language learners. *Remedial and Special Education, 27,* 105–115.

Sapon-Shevin, M. (2001). Schools fit for all. *Educational Leadership, 58*(4), 34–39.

Sapon-Shevin, M. (2008). Learning in an inclusive community. *Educational Leadership, 66*(1), 49–53.

Saulny, S. (2009). Students stand when called upon, and when not. *New York Times,* Article 5. Retrieved [June 30, 2009] from http://www.nytimes.com/2009/02/25/us/25desks.html.

Saunders, M. D. (2001). Who's getting the message? Helping your students understand in a verbal world. *Teaching Exceptional Children, 33*(4), 70–75.

Savage, R., Pillay, V., & Melidona, S. (2008). Rapid serial naming is a unique predictor of spelling in children. *Journal of Learning Disabilities, 41*(3), 235–250.

Savage, T. V., & Armstrong, D. G. (2008). *Effective teaching in elementary social studies* (6th ed.). Boston: Allyn & Bacon.

Savage, T. V., Savage, K., & Armstrong, D. G. (2006). *Teaching in the secondary school.* (6th ed.). Upper Saddle River, NJ: Merrill/Pearson Education.

Sayeski, K. L. (2008). Virtual manipulatives as an assistive technology support for students with high-incidence disabilities. *Journal of Special Education Technology, 23*(1), 47–53.

Scanlon, D. (2002). Proving what they know: Using a learning strategy in an inclusive classroom. *Teaching Exceptional Children, 34*(4), 50–54.

Scanlon, D., & Mellard, D. F. (2002). Academic and participation profiles of school-age dropouts with and without disabilities. *Exceptional Children, 68,* 239–258.

Scanlon, D. J., Deshler, D. D., & Schumaker, J. B. (1996). Can a strategy be taught and learned in secondary inclusive classrooms? *Learning Disabilities Research and Practice, 11*(1), 41–57.

Schaffer v. Weast, 126 S. Ct. 528 (2005).

Schaffer, J. & Marks, S. U. (2008). Promoting self-determination through a movie project. *TEACHING Exceptional Children Plus, 4*(6) Article 5. Retrieved [June 19, 2009] from http://escholarship.bc.edu/education/tecplus/vol4/iss6/art5.

Schalock, R., Luckasson, R., Shogren, K., Bradley, V. Borthwick-Duffy, S., Buntix, W., et al. (2007). The renaming of mental retardation: Understanding the change to the term intellectual disability. *Intellectual and Developmental Disabilities, 45,* 116–124.

Schiff, R., Bauminger, N., & Toledo, I. (2009). Analogical problem solving in children with verbal and nonverbal learning disabilities. *Journal of Learning Disabilities, 42*(1), 3–13.

Schirmer, B. R., & Bailey, J. (2000). Writing assessment rubric: An instructional approach with struggling writers. *Teaching Exceptional Children, 33*(1), 52–58.

Schirmer, B. R., & Lockman, A. S. (2001). How do I find a book to read? Middle and high school students use a rubric for self-selecting material for independent reading. *Teaching Exceptional Children, 34*(1), 36–42.

Schleibaum, K. M. (2007). Using community-based social stories to enhance instruction for high school students with moderate disabilities. *Journal of Special Education Technology, 22*(2), 59–63.

Schleppegrell, M. J. (2007). The linguistic challenges of mathematics teaching and learning: A research review. *Reading and Writing Quarterly: Overcoming Learning Difficulties, 23*(2), 139–160.

Schmid, R. E. (1998). Three steps to self-discipline. *Teaching Exceptional Children, 30*(4), 36–39.

Schmidt, L. (2009). Stirring up justice. *Educational Leadership, 66*(8), 32–37.

Schniedewind, N., & Davidson, E. (2006). *Open minds to equality: A sourcebook of learning activities to affirm diversity and promote equity* (3rd ed.). Williston, VT: Rethinking Schools.

Schoenfeld, N. A., & Konopasek, D. (2007). Medicine in the classroom: A review of psychiatric medications for students with emotional or behavioral disorders. *Beyond Behavior, 17*(1), 14–20.

School Board of Nassau County, Florida et al. v. Arline, 480 U.S. 273 (1987).

Schreiner, M. B. (2007). Effective self-advocacy: What students and special educators need to know. *Intervention in School and Clinic, 42*(5), 300–304.

Schroeder, J. L., & Johnson, G. E., (2009). Accessing substance abuse prevention programs for schools. *Intervention in School and Clinic, 44*(4), 234–240.

Schuck, S. E. B., & Crinella, F. M. (2005). Why children with ADHD do not have low IQs. *Journal of Learning Disabilities, 38,* 262–280.

Schumaker, J. B., Deshler, D. D. (2009). Adolescents with learning disabilities as writers: Are we selling them short? *Learning Disabilities Research and Practice, 24*(2), 69–80.

Schumaker, J. B., Deshler, D. D., Alley, G. R., & Warner, M. M. (1983). Toward the development of an intervention model for learning disabled adolescents: The University of Kansas Institute. *Exceptional Education Quarterly, 4,* 45–74.

Schumaker, J. B., Deshler, D. D., Nolan, S. M., & Alley, G. R. (1994). *The self-questioning strategy.* Lawrence: University of Kansas Press.

Schumaker, J. B., Deshler, D. D., Woodruff, S., Hock, M. F., Bulgren, J. A., & Lenz, B. K. (2006). Reading strategy interventions: Can literacy outcomes be enhanced for at-risk adolescents? *Teaching Exceptional Children, 38*(3), 64–68.

Schumaker, J. B., Nolan, S. M., & Deshler, D. (1985). *Learning strategies curriculum: The error monitoring strategy.* Lawrence: University of Kansas Press.

Schwartz, D. C., & Pace, D. (2008). Students create art: Expanding an after-school program. *Teaching Exceptional Children, 40*(4), 50–55.

Schwartz, I. S., Staub, D., Peck, C. A., & Chrysan, G. (2006). Peer relationships. In M. E. Snell & F. Brown (Eds.), *Instruction of students with severe disabilities* (6th ed., pp. 375–404). Upper Saddle River, NJ: Merrill/Pearson Education.

Schwarz. P. A. (2007). Special education: A service, not a sentence. *64*(5), 39–42.

Schweder, W., & Wissick, C. A. (2009). The power of wikis. *Journal of Special Education Technology, 24*(1), 57–60.

Scott, B. J., & Vitale, M. R. (2003). Teaching the writing process to students with LD. *Intervention in School and Clinic, 38,* 220–225.

Scott, V. G., & Compton, L. (2007). A new TRICK for the trade: A strategy for keeping an agenda book for secondary students. *Intervention in School and Clinic, 42*(5), 280–284.

Scott, V. G., & Weishaar, M. K. (2003). Curriculum-based measurement for reading progress. *Intervention in School and Clinic, 38,* 153–159.

Seattle School District No 1 v. B. S., 82 F.3d 1493 (9th Cir. 1996).

Scruggs, S. (2008, October, 29). "I don't feel so left out anymore'. *Times Herald Record,* 5B.

Scruggs, T. E., Mastropieri, M. A., & McDuffie, K. A. (2007). Co-teaching in inclusive classrooms: A metasynthesis of qualitative research. *Exceptional Children, 73*(4), 392–416.

Sebald, A., & Luckner, J. (2007). Successful partnerships with families of children who are deaf. *Teaching Exceptional Children, 39*(3), 54–60.

Seethaler, P. M., & Fuchs, L. S. (2006). The cognitive correlates of computational estimation skill among third-grade students. *Learning Disabilities Research and Practice, 21*(4), 233–243.

Seider, S. (2009). Social justice in the suburbs. *Educational Leadership, 66*(8), 54–58.

Seo, S., Brownell, M. T., Bishop, A. G., & Dingle, M. (2008). Beginning special education teachers's classroom reading instruction: Practices that engage elementary students with learning disabilities, *Exceptional Children, 75*(1), 97–122.

Serfass, C., & Peterson, R. L. (2007). A guide to computer-managed IEP record systems. *Teaching Exceptional Children, 40*(1), 16–21.

Servilio, K. L. (2009). You get to choose! Motivating students to read through differentiated instruction. *TEACHING Exceptional Children Plus, 5*(5) Article 5. Retrieved [July 26, 2009] from http://escholarship.bc.edu/education/tecplus/vol5/iss5/art5.

Shapiro, A. (1999). *Everyone belongs: Changing negative attitudes toward classmates with disabilities.* New York: RoutledgeFalmer.

Shaw, S. F., & Madaus, J. W. (2008). Policy and law briefs: Preparing school personnel to implement section 504. *Intervention in School and Clinic, 43*(4), 226–230.

Shaw, S. F., Madaus, J. W., & Banerjee, M. (2009). Enhance access to postsecondary education for students with disabilities. *Intervention in School and Clinic, 44*(3), 185–190.

Shaw, S. R. (2008). An educational programming framework for a subset of students with diverse learning needs: Borderline intellectual functioning. *Intervention in School and Clinic, 43*(5), 291–299.

Shealey, M. W., & Callins, T. (2007). Creating culturally responsive literacy programs in inclusive classrooms. *Intervention in School and Clinic, 42*(4), 195–197.

Sheehey, P., Ornelles, C., & Noonan, M. J. (2009). Biculturalization: Developing culturally responsive approaches to family participation. *Intervention in School and Clinic, 45*(2), 132–139.

Sheehey, P. H., & Sheehey, P. E. (2007). Elements for successful parent-professional collaboration: The fundamental things apply as time goes by. *TEACHING Exceptional Children Plus, 4*(2) Article 3. Retrieved [June 1, 2009] from http://escholarship.bc.edu/education/tecplus/vol4/iss2/art3.

Shepherd, T. L. (2007). Infinite diversity in infinite combinations: Portraits of individuals with disabilities in Star Trek. *TEACHING Exceptional Children Plus, 3*(6) Article 1. Retrieved [June 10, 2009] from http://escholarship.bc.edu/education/tecplus/vol3/iss6/art1.

Sherman, H. J., Richardson, L. I., & Yard, G. J. (2009). *Teaching learners who struggle with mathematics: Systematic intervention and remediation* (2nd ed.). Upper Saddle River, NJ: Pearson Education.

Short, D., & Echevarria, J. (2005). Teacher skills to support English language learners. *Educational Leadership, 62*(4), 9–13.

Shriner, J. G. (2000). Legal perspectives on school outcomes assessment for students with disabilities. *Journal of Special Education, 33,* 232–239.

Shriner, J. G., & DeStefano, L. (2003). Participation and accommodation in state assessment: The role of individualized education programs. *Exceptional Children, 69,* 147–162.

Sideridis, G. D. (2007). Why are students with LD depressed? A goal orientation model of depression vulnerability. *Journal of Learning Disabilities, 40*(6), 526–539.

Siegel, E., & Allinder, R. M. (2005). Review of assessment procedures for students with moderate and severe disabilities. *Education and Training in Developmental Disabilities, 40,* 343–351.

Siegle, D., & McCoach, D. B. (2005). Making the difference: Motivating gifted students who are not achieving. *Teaching Exceptional Children, 38*(1), 22–27.

Sileo, J. M., & Whittaker, C. R. (2009). Sexual orientation. In L. S. Taylor & C. R. Whittaker (Eds.), *Bridging multiple worlds: Case studies of diverse educational* (2nd ed.) (pp. 194–222). Boston: Allyn & Bacon.

Sileo, N. (2005). Design HIV/AIDS prevention education: What are the roles and responsibilities of classroom teachers? *Intervention in School and Clinic, 40,* 177–181.

Silva, M., Munk, D. D., & Bursuck, W. M. (2005). Grading adaptations for students with disabilities. *Intervention in School and Clinic, 41,* 87–98.

Silver-Pacuilla, H., Ruedel, K., & Mistrett, S. (2004). *A review of technology-based approaches for reading instruction: Tools for researchers and vendors.* Washington, DC: National Center for Technology Integration.

Silver-Pacuilla, H., & Fleischman, S. (2006). Technology to help struggling students. *Educational Leadership, 63*(5), 84–85.

Silverman, J. C. (2007). Epistemological beliefs and attitudes toward inclusion in pre-service teachers. *Teacher Education and Special Education, 30*(1), 42–51.

Silverman, F. L., & Millspaugh, R. (2006). Physical proximity of occupational therapy and learning support instruction: How room sharing can promote collaboration for professionals and success for students. *Teaching Exceptional Children Plus, 2*(4) Article 2. Retrieved April 2, 2006, from http://escholarship.bc.edu/education/tecplus/vol2/iss4/art2.

Simmons, R. J. & Magiera, K. (2007). Evaluation of co-teaching in three high schools within one school district: How do you know when you are TRULY co-teaching? TEACHING Exceptional Children Plus, 3(3) Article 4. Retrieved [June 3, 2009] from http://escholarship.bc.edu/education/tecplus/vol3/iss3/art4.

Simonsen, B., Sugai, G., & Negron, M. (2008). Schoolwide positive behavior supports: Primary systems and practices. *Teaching Exceptional Children, 40*(6), 32–40.

Simpson, C. G., Swicegood, P. R., & Gaus, M. D. (2006). Nutrition and fitness curriculum: Designing instructional interventions for children with developmental disabilities, *Teaching Exceptional Children, 38*(6), 50–53.

Simpson, R. G., & Allday, R. A. (2008). PIE-R2: The area of a circle and good behavior management. *TEACHING Exceptional Children Plus, 4*(4) Article 5. Retrieved [July 1, 2009] from http://escholarship.bc.edu/education/tecplus/vol4/iss4/art5.

Simpson, R. L., (2004). Inclusion of students with behavior disorders in general education settings: Research and measurement issues. *Behavioral Disorders, 30,* 19–31.

Sindelar, P. T., Shearer, D. K., Yendol-Hoppey, D., & Liebert, T. W. (2006). The sustainability of inclusive school reform. *Exceptional Children, 72,* 317–331.

Singer, G. H. S. (2002). Suggestions for a programatic program of research on families and disability. *Journal of Special Education, 36,* 148–154.

Siperstein, G. N., & Leffert, J. S. (1999). Managing limited resources: Do children with learning problems share? *Exceptional Children, 65*(2), 187–199.

Siperstein, G. N., Parker, R. C., Bardon, J. N., & Widaman, K. F. (2007). A national study of youth attitudes toward the inclusion of students with intellectual disabilities. *Exceptional Children, 73*(4), 435–455.

Sitlington, P. L., & Neubert, D. A., & Clark, G. M. (2010). *Transition education and services for students with disabilities* (5th ed.). Upper Saddle River, NJ: Merrill/Pearson Education.

Skiba, R. J., Simmons, A. B., Ritter, S., Gibb, A. C., Rausch, M. K., Cuadrado, J., & Chung, C. (2008). Achieving equity in special education: History, status, and current challenges. *Exceptional Children, 74*(3), 264–288.

Skouge, J. R., Kelly, M., Roberts, K. D., Leake, D. W., & Stodden, R. A. (2007). Technologies for self-determination for youth with developmental disabilities. *Education and Training in Developmental Disabilities, 42*(4), 475–482.

Skowronek, J. S., Leichtman, M. D., & Pillemer, D. B. (2008). Long-term episodic memory in children with attention-deficit/hyperactivity disorder. *Learning Disabilities Research and Practice, 23*(1), 25–35.

Skylar, A. A. (2007). Section 508: Web accessibility for people with disabilities. *Journal of Special Education Technology, 22*(4), 57–62.

Skylar, A. A., Higgins, K., & Boone, R. (2007). Strategies for adapting webQuests for students with learning disabilities. *Intervention in School and Clinic, 43*(1), 20–28.

Slavin, R. E. (1990). *Cooperative learning: Theory, research, and practice.* Upper Saddle River, NJ: Pearson Education.

Slavin, R. E. (1998). Can education reduce social inequity? *Educational Leadership, 55*(4), 6–10.

Slavin, R. E., Chamberlain, A., & Daniels, C. (2007). Preventing reading failure. *Educational Leadership, 65*(2), 22–27.

Slavin, R. E, & Cheung, A. (2005). A synthesis of research on language of reading instruction for English language learners. *Review of Education Research, 75*(2), 247–284.

Sloan, W. M. (2008). Celebrating students' diverse strengths. *Educational Update, 50*(2), 4–5.

Sloan, W. M. (2009). Creating global classrooms. *Educational Update, 51*(1), 1, 4–7.

Smith, J., L. M., Fien, H., & Paine, S. C. (2008). When mobility disrupts learning. *Educational Leadership, 65*(7), 59–63.

Smith, R., & Lambert, M. (2008). Assuming the best. *Educational Leadership, 66*(1), 16–20.

Smith, R. M. (2002). Inscrutable or meaningful? Understanding and supporting your inarticulate students. *Teaching Exceptional Children, 34*(4), 28–33.

Smith, R. M. (2009). Front and center: Contradicting isolation by supporting leadership and service by students with disabilities. *TEACHING Exceptional Children Plus, 5*(5) Article 4. Retrieved [July 4, 2009] from http://escholarship.bc.edu/education/tecplus/vol5/iss5/art4.

Smith, R. M., Gallagher, D., Owen, V., & Skrtic, T. M. (2009). Disability studies in education: Guidelines and ethical practice for educators. In J. Andrzejewski, M. P., Baltodano, & L. Symcox (Eds.), *Social justice, peace, and environmental education* (pp. 235–251). New York: Routledge.

Smith, R. M., & Sapon-Shevin, M. (2009). *Disability humor, insults, and inclusive practice.* Retrieved June 15, 2009, from http://cortland.edu/ids/sasc/.

Smith, R. M., Salend, S. J., & Ryan, S. (2001). Watch your language: Closing or opening the special education curtain. *Teaching Exceptional Children, 33*(4), 18–23.

Smith, S., Boone, R., & Higgins, K. (1998). Expanding the writing process to the Web. *Teaching Exceptional Children, 30*(5), 22–26.

Smith, S. J., & Smith, S. B. (2002). On the right track: Technology for organizing and presenting digital information. *Intervention in School and Clinic, 37,* 304–311.

Smith, T. E. C., Gartin, B. C., Murdick, N. L., & Hilton, A. (2006). *Families and children with special needs: Professionals and family partnerships.* Upper Saddle River, NJ: Merrill/Pearson Education.

Smith-Davis, J. (2002). World initiatives for inclusive education. *Teaching Exceptional Children, 35*(1), 77.

Smith Myles, B. (2006). *Children and youth with Asperger Syndrome: Strategies for success in inclusive settings.* Beverly Hills, CA: Sage.

Smith Myles, B., Ferguson, H., Hagiwara, T. (2007). Using a personal digital assistant to improve the recording of homework assignments by an adolescent with Asperger Syndrome. *Focus on Autism and Other Developmental Disabilities, 22*(2), 96–99.

Smith Myles, B., Lee, H. J., Smith, S. M., Kai-Chien, T., Chou, Y., Cooper Swanson, T., & Hudson, J. (2007). A large-scale study of the characteristics of Asperger Syndrome. *Education and Training in Developmental Disabilities, 42*(4), 448–459.

Snell, M. E., & Brown, F. (2006). *Instruction of students with severe disabilities* (6th ed.). Upper Saddle River, NJ: Merrill/Pearson Education.

Snell, M. E., & Janney, R, E. (2000). Teachers' problem-solving about children with moderate and severe disabilities in elementary classrooms. *Exceptional Children, 66,* 472–490.

Snow, C. (2009). To ensure inclusion, freedom, and respect for all, we must use PEOPLE FIRST LANGUAGE. Retrieved June 15, 2009, from http://www.disabilityisnatural.com/images/stories/freearticlespdf/pfl9.pdf.

Sober, T. (2009, November). *How economic class impacts teaching and learning*. Presentation at the annual meeting of the Multicultural Education Conference, New Paltz, NY.

Soenksen, D., & Alper, S. (2006). Teaching a young child to appropriately gain attention of peers using a social story intervention. *Focus on Autism and Other Developmental Disabilities, 21,* 36–44.

Songlee, D., Miller, S. P., Tincani, M., Sileo, N. M., & Perkins, P. G. (2008). Effects of test-taking strategy instruction on high-functioning adolescents with autism spectrum disorders. *Focus on Autism and Other Developmental Disabilities, 23*(4), 217–228.

Sood, S., & Jitendra, A. K. (2007). A comparative analysis of number sense instruction in reform-based and traditional mathematics textbooks. *The Journal of Special Education, 41*(3), 145–158.

Sopko, K. M. (2008). *Universal design for learning: Implementation in six local education agencies.* Alexandria, VA: National Association of State Directors of Special Education.

Sorrell, C. A., Mee Bell, S., & McCallum, R. S. (2007). Reading rate and comprehension as a function of computerized versus traditional presentation mode: A preliminary study. *Journal of Special Education Technology, 22*(1), 1–12.

Sotto, C. D., & Ball, A. L. (2006). Dynamic characters with communication disorders in children's literature. *Intervention in School and Clinic, 42,* 40–45.

Soukup, J. H., Wehmeyer, M. L., Bashinski, S. M., & Bovaird, J. A. (2007). Classroom variables and access to the general curriculum for students with disabilities. *Exceptional Children, 74*(1), 101–120.

Sparks, S. (2000a). Classroom and curriculum accommodations for Native American students. *Intervention in School and Clinic, 35,* 259–263.

Sparks, S. (2000b). Utilize native American elders in the classroom and school. *Intervention in School and Clinic, 35,* 306–307.

Spears, E. H. (2006). Students with HIV/AIDS and school consideration. *Teacher Education and Special Education, 29*(4), 213–224.

Spencer, V. G. (2005). Crossing over. *Intervention in School and Clinic, 40,* 247–249.

Spencer, V. G., & Balboni, G. (2003). Can students with mental retardation teach their peers? *Education and Training in Developmental Disabilities, 38,* 32–61.

Spencer, V. G., Simpson, C. G., Day, M. & Buster, E. (2008). Using the power card strategy to teach social skills to a child with autism. *TEACHING Exceptional Children Plus,* 5(1) Article 2. Retrieved [June 15, 2009] from http://escholarship.bc.edu/education/tecplus/vol5/iss1/art2.

Spencer, V. G., Simpson, C. G., & Lynch, S. A. (2008). Using social stories to increase positive behaviors for children with autism spectrum disorders. *Intervention in School and Clinic, 44*(1), 58–61.

Spiegel, G. L., Cutler, S. K., & Yetter, C. E. (1996). What every teacher should know about epilepsy. *Intervention in School and Clinic, 32*(1), 34–38.

Spinelli, C. G. (2004). Dealing with cancer in the classroom: The teacher's role and responsibilities. *Teaching Exceptional Children, 36*(4), 14–21.

Spinelli, C. G. (2006). *Classroom assessment for students in special and general educa*tion (2nd ed.). Upper Saddle River, NJ: Merrill/Pearson Education.

Spinelli, C. G. (2008). Addressing the issue of cultural and linguistic diversity and assessment: Informal evaluation measures for English language learners. *Reading and Writing Quarterly: Overcoming Learning Difficulties, 24*(1), 101–118.

Spooner, F., Ahlgrim-Delzell, L., Kohprasert, K., Baker, J., & Courtade, G. (2008). Content analysis of science performance indicators in alternate assessment. *Remedial and Special Education, 29*(6), 343–351.

Sprankle, B. (2008). Action: Caught on video. *Technology and Learning, 28*(9), 29–32.

Spungin, S. J. & Ferrell, K. A. (2007). *The role and function of the teacher of students with blindness or low vision.* Retrieved September 4, 2008, from http://cecdvi.org/Position%20Papers/RevisedRole&FunctionofTVI2006.doc.

Stafford, A. M. (2005). Choice making: A strategy for students with severe disabilities. *Teaching Exceptional Children, 37*(6), 12–17.

Stafford, A. M., Alberto, P. A., Fredrick, L. D., Heflin, L. J., & Heller, K. W. (2002). Preference variability and the instruction of choice making with students with severe intellectual disabilities. *Education and Training in Mental Retardation and Developmental Disabilities, 37,* 70–88.

Stanford, P., & Reeves, S. (2005). Assessment that drives instruction. *Teaching Exceptional Children, 37*(4), 18–22.

Stanford, P., & Siders, J. A. (2001). E-pal writing. *Teaching Exceptional Children, 34*(2), 21–25.

Stang, K. K., & Lyons, B. M. (2008). Effects of modeling collaborative teaching for pre-service teachers. *Teacher Education and Special Education, 31*(3), 182–194.

Staub, D. (1998). *Delicate threads: Friendships between children with and without special needs in inclusive settings.* Bethesda, MD: Woodbine House.

Staub, D., Schwartz, I. S., Galluci, C., & Peck, C. A. (1994). Four portraits of friendship at an inclusive school. *Journal of the Association for Persons with Severe Handicaps, 19*(4), 314–325.

Stecker, P. M. (2006). Using curriculum-based measurement to monitor reading progress in inclusive elementary settings. *Reading and Writing Quarterly: Overcoming Learning Difficulties, 22,* 91–97.

Stecker, P. M. (2007). Tertiary intervention: Using progressive monitoring with intensive services. *Teaching Exceptional Children, 39*(5), 50–57.

Stecker, P. M., & Fuchs, L. S. (2000). Effecting superior achievement using curriculum-based measurement: The importance of individual progress monitoring. *Learning Disabilities Research and Practice, 15,* 128–134.

Stenhoff, D. M., & Lignugaris/Kraft, B. (2007). A review of the effects of peer tutoring on students with mild disabilities in secondary settings. *Exceptional Children, 74*(1), 8–30.

Stephens, K. R., & Karnes, F. A. (2000). State definitions for the gifted and talented revisited. *Exceptional Children, 66*(2), 219–238.

Stern, J., & Avigliano, J. (2008, November). *Differentiated team teaching.* Presentation at the State University of New York at New Paltz. New Paltz, NY.

Stevens, D. D., & Levi, A. (2009). Too much time grading papers? *NEA Higher Education Advocate, 26*(6), 5–8.

Stinson, M. S., Elliot, L. B., Kelly, R. R., & Liu, Y. (2009). Deaf and hard-of-hearing students' memory of lectures with speech-to-text and interpreting/note taking services, *The Journal of Special Education, 43*(1), 52–64.

Stivers, J. (2008). Strengthen your coteaching relationship. *Intervention in School and Clinic, 44*(2), 121–125.

Stivers, J., Francis-Cropper, & Straus, M. (2008). Educating families about inclusive education: A month-by-month guide for teachers of inclusive classes. *Intervention in School and Clinic, 44*(1), 10–17.

Stodden, R. A., & Whelley, T. (2004). Postsecondary education and persons with intellectual disabilities: An introduction. *Education and Training in Developmental Disabilities, 39,* 6–15.

Stone, R. H., Boon, R. T., Fore, C., Bender, W. N., & Spencer, V. (2008). Use of text maps to improve the reading comprehension skills among students in high school with emotional and behavioral disorders. *Behavioral Disorders, 33*(2), 87–98.

Stoner, J. B., Jones Bock, S. J., Thompson, J. R., Angell, M. E., Heyl, B. S., & Crowley, E. P. (2005). Welcome to our world: Parent perspectives of interactions between parents of young children with ASD and education professionals. *Focus on Autism and Other Developmental Disabilities, 20,* 39–51.

Stop Bullying Now. (2009). *Children who bully.* Retrieved August 15, 2009, from http://stopbullyingnow.hrsa.gov/HHS_PSA/pdfs/SBN_Tip_1.pdf.

Stormont, M. (2008). Increase academic success for children with ADHD using sticky notes and highlighters. *Intervention in School and Clinic, 43*(5), 305–308.

Stough, L. M. (2002). Teaching special education in Costa Rica: Using a learning strategy in an inclusive classroom. *Teaching Exceptional Children, 34*(5), 34–39.

Stough, L. M., & Baker, L. (1999). Identifying depression in students with mental retardation. *Teaching Exceptional Children, 31*(4), 62–66.

Strichart, S. S., & Mangrum, C. T. (2010). *Study skills for learning disabled and struggling students* (4th ed.). Saddle River, NJ: Merrill/Pearson Education.

Students for Social Justice. (n.d.). Being gay at Greeley. *Left Is Right, 2*(1), 1–4.

Sturm, J. M., Rankin, J. L., Beukelman, D. R., & Schutz-Muehling, L. (1997). How to select appropriate software for computer-assisted writing. *Intervention in School and Clinic, 32*(3), 148–161.

Suarez-Orozco, M. M., & Sattin, C. (2007). Wanted: Global citizens. *Educational Leadership, 64*(7), 58–62.

Sugai, S., Simonsen, B., & Horner, R. H. (2008). Schoolwide positive behavior supports: A continuum of positive behavior supports for all students. *Teaching Exceptional Children, 40*(6), 5–6.

Sugai, G., & Smith, P. (1986). The equal additions method of subtraction taught with a modeling technique. *Remedial and Special Education, 7,* 40–48.

Sulzer-Azaroff, B., Hoffman, A. O., Horton, C. B., Bondy, A. & Frost, L. (2009). The picture exchange communication system (PECS): What does the research say? *Focus on Autism and Other Developmental Disabilities, 24*(2), 89–103.

Sundeen, T. H. (2007). So what's the big idea? Using graphic organizers to guide writing for secondary students with learning and behavioral issues. *Beyond Behavior, 16*(3), 29–34.

Suritsky, S. K., & Hughes, C. A. (1996). Notetaking strategy instruction. In D. D. Deshler, E. S. Ellis, & B. K. Lenz (Eds.), *Teaching adolescents with learning disabilities: Strategies and methods* (2nd ed., pp. 267–312). Denver: Love.

Suter, J. C., & Giangreco, M. F. (2009). Numbers that count: Exploring special education and paraprofessional service delivery in inclusion-oriented schools. *The Journal of Special Education, 43*(2), 67–80.

Sutherland, K. S., Lewis-Palmer, T., Stichter, J. P., & Morgan, P. L. (2008). Examining the influence of teacher behavior and classroom context on the behavioral and academic outcomes of students with emotional or behavioral disorders. *The Journal of Special Education, 41*(4), 223–233.

Sutherland, K. S., & Snyder, A. (2007). Effects of reciprocal peer tutoring and self-graphing on reading fluency and classroom behavior of middle school students with emotional or behavioral disorders. *Journal of Emotional and Behavioral Disorders, 15*(2), 103–118.

Sutherland, K. S., & Wehby, J. A. (2001). Exploring the relationship between increased opportunities to respond to academic requests and the academic and behavioral outcomes of students with EBD: A review. *Remedial and Special Education, 22,* 113–121.

Sutherland, K. S., Wehby, J. A., & Yoder, P. J. (2002). Examination of the relationship between teacher praise and opportunities for students with EBD to respond to academic requests. *Journal of Emotional and Behavioral Disorders, 10,* 5–13.

Swain, K. D., Friehe, M., & Harrington, J. M. (2004). Teaching listening strategies in the inclusive classroom. *Intervention in School and Clinic, 40,* 48–54.

Swanson, E. A., & Howerton, D. (2007). *Intervention in School and Clinic, 42*(5), 290–294.

Swedeen, B. L. (2009). Signs of an inclusive school: A parent's perspective on the meaning and value of authentic inclusion. *TEACHING Exceptional Children Plus, 5*(3) Article 1. Retrieved [June 1, 2009] from http://escholarship.bc.edu/education/tecplus/vol5/iss3/art1.

Swicegood, P. R. (1994). Portfolio-based assessment practices. *Intervention in School and Clinic, 30*(1), 6–15.

Swift, S. H., Davidson, C. R., & Weems, L. J. (2008). Cortical impairment in children: Presentation, intervention, and prognosis in educational settings. *Teaching Exceptional Children Plus, 4*(5) Article 4. Retrieved [February 12, 2009] from http://escholarship.bc.edu/education/tecplus/vol4/iss5/art4.

Symons, F. J., Clark, R. D., Roberts, J. P., & Bailey, D. B. (2001). Classroom behavior of elementary school-age boys with fragile X syndrome. *Journal of Special Education, 34,* 194–202.

Taber-Doughty, T., Patton, S. E., & Brennan, S. (2008). Simultaneous and delayed video modeling: An examination of system effectiveness and student preferences. *Journal of Special Education Technology, 23*(1), 1–18.

Tankersley, M. (1995). A group-contingency management program: A review of research on the good behavior game and implications for teachers. *Preventing School Failure, 40*(1), 19–24.

Tannock, M. T. (2009). Tangible and intangible elements of collaborative teaching. *Intervention in School and Clinic, 44*(3), 173–178.

Targett, P., Young, C., Revell, G., Williams, S. & Wehman, P. (2007). Customized employment in the one stop career centers. *Teaching Exceptional Children, 40*(2), 6–11.

Tatum, A. W. (2006). Engaging African American males in reading. *Educational Leadership, 63*(5), 44–49.

Taunt, H. M., & Hastings, R. P. (2002). Positive impact of children with developmental disabilities on their families. *Education and Training in Mental Retardation and Developmental Disabilities, 37,* 399–410.

Taylor, D. B., Mraz, M., Nichols, W. D., Rickelman, R. J., & Wood, K. D. (2009). Using explicit instruction to promote vocabulary learning for struggling readers. *Reading and Writing Quarterly, 25*(2–3), 205–220.

Taylor, L. S., & Whittaker, C. R. (2009). *Bridging multiple worlds: Case studies of diverse educational communities (2nd ed.).* Boston: Allyn & Bacon.

Taylor, R. L., & Smiley, L. R., & Richards, S. B. (2009). *Exceptional students: Preparing teachers for the 21st century.* Boston: McGraw-Hill.

Taymans, J. M., & West, L. L. (2001, December). *Selecting a college for students with learning disabilities or attention deficit hyperactivity disorder (ADHD).* Arlington, VA: ERIC Clearinghouse on Disabilities and Gifted Education.

Test, D. W., Aspel, N. P., & Everson, J. M. (2006). *Transition methods for youth with disabilities.* Upper Saddle River, NJ: Merrill/Pearson Education.

Test, D. W., Browder, D. M., Karvonen, M., Wood, W., & Algozzine, B. (2002). Writing lesson plans for promoting self-determination. *Teaching Exceptional Children, 35*(1), 8–15.

Test, D. W., & Ellis, M. F. (2005). The effects of LAP fractions on addition and subtraction of fractions with students with mild disabilities. *Education and Treatment of Children, 28*(1), 11–24.

Therrien, W. J., Gormley, S., & Kubina, R. M. (2006). Boosting fluency and comprehension to improve reading achievement. *Teaching Exceptional Children, 38*(3), 22–26.

Therrien, W. J., Hughes, C. Kapelski, C. & Mokhtari, K. (2009). Effectiveness of a test-taking strategy on achievement in essay tests for students with learning disabilities. *Journal of Learning Disabilities, 42*(1), 14–23.

Therrien, W. J., & Kubina, R. M. (2006). Developing reading fluency with repeated reading. *Intervention in School and Clinic, 41*(3), 156–190.

Thomas, W. P., & Collier, V. P. (1997). *School effectiveness for language minority students.* Washington, DC: National Clearinghouse for Bilingual Education.

Thomas, W. P., & Collier, V. P. (2003). The mutual benefits of dual language. *Educational Leadership, 61*(2), 61–64.

Thompson, D. R., & Chappell, M. F. (2007). Communication and representation as elements in mathematical literacy. *Reading and Writing Quarterly: Overcoming Learning Difficulties, 23*(2), 179–196.

Thompson, G. (2008). Beneath the apathy. *Educational Leadership, 65*(6), 50–54.

Thompson, G. (2009, March 15). Where education and assimilation collide. *New York Times,* 1, 17–18.

Thompson, J. R., Bakken, J. P., Fulk, B. M., & Peterson-Karlan, G. (2005). *Using technology to improve the literacy skills of students with disabilities.* Naperville, IL: Learning Point Associates.

Thompson, J. R., Meadan, H., Fansler, K. W., Alber, S. B., & Balogh, P. A. (2007). Family assessment portfolios: A new way to jumpstart family/school collaboration. *Teaching Exceptional Children, 39*(6), 19–25.

Thompson, S. J., Quenemoen, R. F., & Thurlow, M. L. (2006). Factors to consider in the design of inclusive online assessments. In M. Hricko & S. L. Howell (Eds.), *Online assessment and measurement: Foundations and challenges* (pp. 102–117). Hershey, PA: Information Sciences Publishing.

Thompson, S. J., Thurlow, M. L., Quenemoen, R. F., & Lehr, C. A. (2002). *Access to computer-based testing for students with disabilities (Synthesis Report 45).* Minneapolis University of Minnesota, National Center on Educational Outcomes.

Thousand, J. S., Rosenberg, R. L., Bishop, K. D., & Villa, R. A. (1997). The evolution of secondary inclusion. *Remedial and Special Education, 18*(5), 270–284, 306.

Thunberg, G., Ahlsen, E., & Dahlgren Sandberg, A. (2009). Interaction and use of speech-generating devices in the homes of children with autism spectrum disorders: An analysis of conversational topics. *Journal of Special Education Technology, 24*(2), 1–16.

Thurlow, M. L. (2002). Positive educational results for all students: The promise of standards-based reform. *Remedial and Special Education, 23,* 195–202.

Thurlow, M. L., Elliott, J. L., & Ysseldyke, J. E. (2003). *Testing students with disabilities: Practical strategies for complying with district and state requirements.* Thousand Oaks, CA: Corwin.

Thurlow, M. L., House, A. L., Scott, D. L., & Ysseldyke, J. E. (2000). Students with disabilities in large-scale assessments: State participation and accommodation policies. *Journal of Special Education, 34,* 154–163.

Thurlow, M. L., Lazarus, S. S., Thompson, S. J., & Morse, A. B. (2005). State policies on assessment participation and accommodations for students with disabilities. *Journal of Special Education, 38,* 232–241.

Tilley-Gregory, D. (2004). How to improve your students' auditory processing skills. *CEC Today, 10*(5), 16.

Timothy W. v. Rochester, N.H. Sch. Dist., 875 F.2d 954, 1st Circuit, 1989.

Tindal, G., Heath, B., Hollenbeck, K., Almond, P., & Harniss, M. (1998). Accommodating students with disabilities on large-scale tests: An experimental study. *Exceptional Children, 64*(4), 439–450.

Tomlinson, C. A. (2008a). The goals of differentiation. *Educational Leadership, 66*(3), 26–31.

Tomlinson, C. A. (2008b). Learning to love assessment. *Educational Leadership, 65*(4), 8–13.

Tomlinson, C. A., Brimijoin, K., & Narvaez, L. (2008). *The differentiated school: Making revolutionary changes in teaching and learning.* Alexandria, VA: ASCD.

Tompkins, G. E. (2002). Struggling readers are struggling writers, too. *Reading and Writing Quarterly: Overcoming Learning Difficulties, 18,* 175–194.

Tompkins, G. E. (2006). *Literacy for the 21st century: A balanced approach* (4th ed.). Upper Saddle River, NJ: Merrill/Pearson Education.

Tompkins, G. E. (2010). *Literacy for the 21st century: A balanced approach* (5th ed.). Upper Saddle River, NJ: Merrill/Pearson Education.

Torgesen, J. K. (2000). Individual differences in response to early interventions in reading: The lingering problem of treatment resisters. *Learning Disabilities Research and Practice, 15*(1), 55–64.

Tournaki, N. (2003). The differential effects of teaching addition through strategy instruction versus drill and practice to students with and without learning disabilities. *Journal of Learning Disabilities, 36,* 449–458.

Towles-Reeves, E., Kleinert, H., & Muhomba, M. (2009). Alternate assessment: Have we learned anything new. *Exceptional Children, 75*(2), 233–252.

Trainor, A. A. (2008). Using cultural and social capital to improve postsecondary outcomes and expand transition models for youth with disabilities. *The Journal of Special Education, 42*(3), 148–162.

Trent, S. C., Kea, C. D., & Oh, K. (2008). Preparing preservice educators for cultural diversity: How far have we come? *Exceptional Children, 74*(3), 328–350.

Trotter, A. (2008, October 20). Math study evaluates digital aids. *Education Week.* Retrieved September 10, 2009, from http://http://www.edweek.org/ew/articles/2008/10/22/09software.h28.html?print=1.

Trout, A, L., Lienemann, T. O., Reid, R., & Epstein, M. H. (2007). A review of non-medication interventions to improve the academic performance of children and youth with ADHD. *Remedial and Special Education, 28*(4), 207–226.

Trussell, R. P. (2008). Classroom universals to prevent problem behaviors. *Intervention in School and Clinic, 43*(3), 179–185.

Trussell, R. P., Lewis, T. J., & Stichter, J. P. (2008). The impact of targeted classroom interventions and function-based behavior interventions on problem behaviors of students with emotional/behavioral disorders. *Behavioral Disorders, 33*(3), 153–166.

Tucker Cohen, E., Wolff Heller, K., Alberto, P., & Fredrick, L. D. (2008). Using a three-step decoding strategy with constant time delay to teach word reading to students with mild and moderate mental retardation. *Focus on Autism and Other Developmental Disabilities, 23*(2), 67–78.

Tugend, A. (2009, August 29). For the best results, take the sting out of criticism. *New York Times,* B6.

Turnbull, A., Edmonson, H., Griggs, P., Wickham, D., Sailor, W., Freeman, R., Guess, D., Lassen, S., McCart, A., Park, J., Riffel, L., Turnbull, R., & Warren, J. (2002). A blueprint for schoolwide positive behavior support: Implementation of three components. *Exceptional Children, 68,* 377–402.

Turnbull, A., Turnbull, R., & Wehmeyer, M. L. (2010). *Exceptional lives: Special education in today's schools* (6th ed.). Upper Saddle River, NJ: Merrill/Pearson Education.

Turnbull, R., Turnbull, A., Wehmeyer, M. L., & Park, J. (2003). A quality of life framework for special education outcomes. *Remedial and Special Education, 24,* 67–74.

Umbreit, J., Ferro, B., Liaupsin, C., & Lane, K. L. (2007). *Functional behavioral assessment.* Upper Saddle River, NJ: Merrill/Pearson Education.

Underwood, M. A., Umbreit, J., & Liaupsin, C. (2009). Efficacy of a systematic process for designing function-based interventions for adults in a community setting. *Education and Training in Developmental Disabilities, 44*(1), 25–38.

United States Census Bureau (2007). *Poverty.* Retrieved March 2, 2009, from http://www.census.gov/hhes/www/poverty.

Uphold, N., Walker, A., & Test, D. W. (2007). Resources for involving students in their IEP process. *Teaching Exceptional Children Plus, 3*(4) Article 1. Retrieved February 25, 2009, from http://escholarship.bc.edu/tecplus/vol3/iss4/art1.

U.S. House of Representatives. *Report* 103–208. (1993). Washington, DC: Author.

Vacca, J. L., Vacca, R. T., Gove, M. K., Burkey, L. C., Lenhart, L. A., & McKeon, C. A. (2009). *Reading and learning to read* (7th ed.). Upper Saddle River, NJ: Pearson Education.

Vacca, R. T. (2002). From efficient decoders to strategic readers. *Educational Leadership, 60*(3), 6–11.

Vacca, R. T., & Vacca, J. L. (2008). *Content area reading: Literacy and learning across the curriculum* (9th ed.). Boston: Allyn & Bacon.

Vadasy, P. F., Sanders, E. A. (2008). Benefits of repeated reading intervention for low-achieving fourth- and fifth-grade students. *Remedial and Special Education, 29*(4), 235–249.

Vadasy, P. F., Sanders, E. A., & Peyton, J. A. (2005). Relative effectiveness of reading practice or word-level instruction in supplemental tutoring: How text matters. *Journal of Learning Disabilities, 38,* 364–380.

Vadasy, P. F., Sanders, E. A., Peyton, J. A., & Jenkins, J. R. (2002). Timing and intensity of tutoring: A closer look at the conditions for effective early literacy training. *Learning Disabilities Research and Practice, 17,* 227–241.

Van de Walle, J. A., Karp, K. S., & Bay-Williams, J. M. (2010). *Elementary and middle school mathematics: Teaching developmentally* (7th ed.). Upper Saddle River, NJ: Pearson Education.

Van Dycke, J. L., Martin, J. E., & Lovett, D. L. (2006). Why is this cake on fire? Inviting students into the IEP process. *Teaching Exceptional Children, 38*(3), 42–47.

Van Dycke, J. L., & Peterson, L. Y. (2003). Eight steps to help students develop IEP goals. *CEC Today, 10*(4), 13.

van Garderen, D. (2004). Reciprocal teaching as a comprehension strategy for understanding mathematical word problems. *Reading and Writing Quarterly: Overcoming Learning Difficulties, 20,* 225–229.

van Garderen, D. (2006). Teaching visual representation for mathematics problem solving. In M. Montague & A. K. Jitendra (Eds.), *Teaching mathematics to middle school students with learning difficulties* (pp. 72–88). New York: Guilford.

van Garderen, D., & Montague, M. (2003). Visual-spatial representation, mathematical problem solving, and students of varying abilities. *Learning Disabilities Research and Practice, 18,* 246–254.

van Garderen, D., & Whittaker, C. (2006). Planning differentiated multicultural instruction for secondary inclusive classrooms. *Teaching Exceptional Children, 38*(3), 12–20.

Van Haren, B., & Fieldler, C. R. (2008). 20 ways to support and empower families of children with disabilities. *Intervention in School and Clinic, 43*(6), 231–235.

Van Norman, R. K. (2007). "Who's on first?" Using sports trivia peer tutoring to increase conversational language. *Intervention in School and Clinic, 43*(2), 88–100.

Van Norman, R. K., & Wood, C. L. (2008). Effects of prerecorded sight words on the accuracy of tutor feedback. *Remedial and Special Education, 29*(2), 96–107.

Van Reusen, A. K., Bos, C. S. (1994). Facilitating student participation in individualized education programs through motivation strategy instruction. *Exceptional Children, 60,* 466–475.

VanTassel-Baska, J., & Stambaugh, T. (2006). *Comprehensive curriculum for gifted learners* (3rd ed.). Boston: Allyn & Bacon.

Varlas, L. (2005, August). Bridging the widest gap: Raising the achievement of black boys. *Education Update, 47*(8), 1–3, 8.

Vatterott, C. (2009). Rethinking homework: Best practices that support diverse needs. Alexandria, VA: Association for Supervison and Curriculum Development.

Vaughn, S., Bos, C. S., & Lund, K. A. (1986). . . . But they can do it in my room: Strategies for promoting generalization. *Teaching Exceptional Children, 18,* 176–180.

Vaughn, S., & Edmonds, M. (2006). Reading comprehension for older students. *Intervention in School and Clinic, 41*(3), 131–137.

Vaughn, S., Elbaum, B. E., & Schumm, J. S. (1996). The effects of inclusion on the social functioning of students with learning disabilities. *Journal of Learning Disabilities, 29,* 598–608.

Vaughn, S., & Klingner, J. K. (1998). Students' perceptions of inclusion and resource room settings. *Journal of Special Education, 32*(2), 79–88.

Vaughn, S., Linan-Thompson, S., Mathes, P. G., Cirino, P. T., Carlson, C. D., Pollard-Durodola, S. D., Cardenas-Hagan, E., & Francis, D. J. (2006). Effectiveness of Spanish intervention for first-grade English language learners at risk for reading difficulties. *Journal of Learning Disabilities, 39,* 56–73.

Vaughn, S., Mathes, P. G., Linan-Thompson, S., & Francis, D. J. (2005). Teaching English language learners at risk for reading disabilities to read: Putting research into

practice. *Learning Disabilities Research and Practice, 20,* 58–67.

Vaughn, S., & Roberts, G. (2007). Secondary interventions in reading: Providing additional instruction for students at risk. *Teaching Exceptional Children, 39*(5), 40–49.

Verden, C. E., & Hickman, P. (2009). "Teacher, it's just like what happens at my house." *TEACHING Exceptional Children Plus,* 5(6) Article 5. Retrieved [September 18, 2009] from http://escholarship.bc.edu/education/tecplus/vol5/iss6/art5.

Vesely, P. J., & Gryder, N. L. (2009). Word of the day improves and redirects student attention while supporting vocabulary development. *Intervention in School and Clinic, 44*(5), 282–287.

Villa, R. A., & Thousand, J. S. (2000). Setting the context: History of and rationales for inclusive schooling. In R. A. Villa & J. S. Thousand (Eds.), *Restructuring for caring and effective education: Piecing the puzzle together* (pp. 7–37). Baltimore: Brookes.

Villa, R. A., Thousand, J. S., Meyers, H., & Nevin, A. (1996). Teacher and administrator perceptions of heterogeneous education. *Exceptional Children, 63*(1), 29–45.

Villa, R. A., Thousand, J. S., & Nevin, A. I. (2008). *A guide to co-teaching: Practical tips for facilitating student learning* (2nd ed.). Thousand Oaks, CA: Corwin Press.

Villegas, A. M., & Lucas, T. (2007). The culturally responsive teacher. *Educational Leadership, 64*(6), 28–33.

Voltz, D. L. (1998). Cultural diversity and special education teacher preparation: Critical issues confronting the field. *Teacher Education and Special Education, 21,* 63–70.

Voltz, D. L., Brazil, N., & Ford, A. (2001). What matters most in inclusive education: A practical guide for moving forward. *Intervention in School and Clinic, 37,* 23–30.

Voltz, D. L., Sims, M. J., Nelson, B., & Bivens, C. (2005). MECCA: A framework for inclusion in the context of standards-based reform. *Teaching Exceptional Children, 37(5),* 14–19.

Voss, K. S. (2005). *Teaching by design: Using your computer to create materials for students with learning differences.* Bethesda, MD: Woodbine House.

Wachter, C. A., & Bouck, E. C. (2008). Suicide and students with high-incidence disabilities: What special educators need to know. *Teaching Exceptional Children, 41*(1), 66–72.

Wadsworth, D., & Remaley, M. H. (2007). What families want. *Educational Leadership, 64*(6), 23–27.

Wadsworth, D. E., & Knight, D. (1999). Preparing the inclusion classroom for students with special physical and health needs. *Intervention in School and Clinic, 34*(3), 170–175.

Wagner, M., Newman, L., Cameto, R., Garza, N., & Levine, P. (2005). *After high school: A first look at the postschool experiences of youth with disabilities.* Menlo Park, CA: SRI International.

Wagner, M., Newman, L., Cameto, R., Levine, P., & Marder, C. (2007). *Perceptions and expectations of youth with disabilities.* Retrieved [September 17, 2009] from http://ies.ed.gov/pubsearch/pubsinfo.asp?pubid=NCSER20073006.

Waldron, N. (2007). Reflecting on teacher attitudes. In J. McLeskey (Ed.), *Reflections on inclusion: Classic articles that shaped our thinking* (pp. 183–187). Arlington, VA: Council for Exceptional Children.

Walker C., & Schmidt, E. (2004). *Smart tests: Teacher-made tests that help students learn*. Portland, ME: Stenhouse Publishers.

Walker, L. (2009). Nine reasons to Twitter in schools. *Tech & Learning, 29*(10), 50.

Walker Tileston, D., & Darling, S. K. (2009). *Teaching students of poverty and diverse cultures*. Thousand Oaks, CA: Corwin Press.

Wallace, T., Anderson, A. R., Bartholomay, T., & Hupp, S. (2002). An ecobehavioral examination of high school classrooms that include students with disabilities. *Exceptional Children, 68*, 345–359.

Wallerstein, J. S., Lewis, J. A., & Blakeslee, S. (2000). *The unexpected legacy of divorce: A 25-year landmark study*. New York: Hyperion.

Walling, D. R. (2009). *Writing for understanding: Strategies to increase content learning*. Thousand Oaks, CA: Corwin Press

Walther-Thomas, C., & Brownell, M. (2000). An interview with Dr. Janis Bulgren. *Intervention in School and Clinic, 35*, 232–236.

Walther-Thomas, C., & Brownell, M. (2001). An interview with Bonnie Jones: Using student portfolios effectively. *Intervention in School and Clinic, 36*, 225–229.

Webb, J. T. (1995). Nurturing the social-emotional development of gifted children. *Teaching Exceptional Children, 27*(2), 76–77.

Wegner, J. R., & Edmister, E. (2007). Understanding students with communication disorders. In A. Turnbull, R. Turnbull, & M. L. Wehmeyer (Eds.), *Exceptional lives: Special education in today's schools* (5th ed., pp. 130–154). Upper Saddle River, NJ: Merrill/Pearson Education.

Wehmeyer, M. L., Smith, S. J., Palmer, S. B., & Davies, D. K. (2004). Technology use by students with intellectual disabilities: An overview. *Journal of Special Education Technology, 19*(4), 7–21.

Wehmeyer, M. L., & Agran, M. (2006). *Mental retardation and intellectual disabilities: Teaching students with innovative and research-based strategies*. Upper Saddle River, NJ: Merrill/Pearson Education.

Wehmeyer, M. L., Palmer, S. B., Agran, M., Mithaug, D. E., & Martin, J. E. (2000). Promoting causal agency: The self-determined learning model of instruction. *Exceptional Children, 66*, 439–453.

Weigel, M., & Gardner, H. (2009). The best of both literacies. *Educational Leadership, 66*(6), 38–41.

Weilbacher, M. (2009). The window into green. *Educational Leadership, 66*(8), 39–44.

Weiss, M. P., & Lloyd, J. W. (2003). Conditions for co-teaching: Lessons from a case study. *Teacher Education and Special Education, 26*, 27–41.

Welch, A. B. (2000). Responding to student concerns about fairness. *Teaching Exceptional Children, 33*(2), 36–40.

Welsch, R. G. (2006). 20 ways to increase oral reading fluency. *Intervention in School and Clinic, 41*(3), 180–183.

Wessler, S. L. (2008). Civility speaks up. *Educational Leadership, 66*(1), 44–48.

West, E., Leon-Guerrero, R., & Stevens, D. (2007). Establishing codes of acceptable schoolwide behavior in a multicultural society. *Beyond Behavior, 16*(2), 32–38.

West, R. P., Young, K. R., Callahan, K., Fister, S., Kemp, K., Freston, J., & Lovitt, T. C. (1995). The musical clocklight: Encouraging positive classroom behavior. *Teaching Exceptional Children, 27*(2), 46–51.

Westling, D. L., & Fox, L. (2009). *Teaching students with severe disabilities* (4th ed.). Upper Saddle River, NJ: Merrill/Pearson Education.

Westling, D. L., Herzog, M. J., Cooper-Duffy, K., Prohn, K., & Ray, M. (2006). The teacher support program: A proposed resource for the special education profession and an initial validation. *Remedial and Special Education, 27*, 136–147.

Wexler, L. (2009, May/June). Alien no more. *The Penn Stater, 96*(5), 44–49.

Whalon, K., Al Otaiba, S., & Delano, M. E. (2009). Evidence-based reading instruction for individuals with autism spectrum disorders. *Focus on Autism and Other Developmental Disabilities, 24*(1), 3–16.

Whalon, K., & Hanline, M. F. (2008). Effects of a reciprocal questioning intervention on the question generation and responding of children with autism spectrum disorder. *Education and Training in Developmental Disabilities, 43*(3), 367–387.

Wheeler, J. J., & Richey, D. D. (2010). *Behavior management: Principles and practices of positive behavior supports* (2nd ed.). Upper Saddle River, NJ: Merrill/Pearson Education.

Wheeler, R. S. (2008). Becoming adept at code-switching. *Educational Leadership, 65*(7), 54–58.

Whelan Ariza, E. N. (2010). *Not for ESOL Teachers: What every classroom teacher needs to know about the linguistically, culturally, and ethnically diverse student* (2nd ed.). Boston: Allyn & Bacon.

Whitbread, K. M., Bruder, M. B., Fleming, G., & Park, H. J. (2007). Collaboration in special education: Parent-professional training. *Teaching Exceptional Children, 39*(4), 6–15.

Whitby, P., & Miller, K. J. (2009). Using eKidtools software tools to provide behavior support in general education settings. *TEACHING Exceptional Children Plus, 5*(3) Article 5. Retrieved [July 1, 2009] from http://escholarship.bc.edu/education/tecplus/vol5/iss3/art5.

White, R., Algozzine, B., Audette, R., Marr, M. B., & Ellis, E. D. (2001). Unified discipline: A school-wide approach for managing problem behavior. *Intervention in School and Clinic, 37*, 3–8.

White Englund, L. (2009). Designing a web site to share information with parents. *Intervention in School and Clinic, 45*(1), 45–51.

Whittaker, C. R., Salend, S. J., & Duhaney, D. (2001). Creating instructional rubrics for inclusive classrooms. *Teaching Exceptional Children, 34*(2), 8–13.

Whittaker, C. R., Salend, S. J., & Elhoweris, H. (2009). Religious diversity in schools: Addressing the issues. *Intervention in School and Clinic, 44*(5), 314–319.

Wiener, J., & Tardif, C. Y. (2004). Social and emotional functioning of children with learning disabilities: Does special education placement make a difference? *Learning Disabilities Research and Practice, 19*(1), 20–32.

Wiggins, G., & McTighe, J. (2008). Put understanding first. *Educational Leadership, 65*(8), 36–41.

Wiggins, K. C., & Damore, S. J. (2006). "Survivors" or "Friends"? A framework for assessing effective collaboration. *Teaching Exceptional Children, 38*(5), 49–56.

Wilder, L. K., Ashbaker, B. Y., Obiakor, F. E., & Rotz, E. J. (2006). Building multicultural transitions for ethnically diverse learners with disabilities. *Multiple Voices, 9*(1), 22–33.

Wilder, L. K., Dyches, T. T., Obiakor, F. E., & Algozzine, B. (2004). Multicultural perspectives on teaching students with autism. *Autism and Other Developmental Disabilities, 19*, 105–113.

Wilkins, J., & Ratajczak, A. (2009). Developing students' literacy skills using high-tech speech-generating augmentative and alternative communication devices. *Intervention in School and Clinic, 44*(3), 167–172.

Wilkinson, L. A. (2008). Self-management for children with high-functioning autism spectrum disorders. *Intervention in School and Clinic, 43*(3), 150–157.

Williams, B. (2007). *Educator's podcast guide.* ISTE: Washington DC.

Williams, C. B., & Finnegan, M. (2003). From myth to reality: Sound information for teachers about students who are deaf. *Teaching Exceptional Children, 35*(3), 40–45.

Williams, G. J., & Reisberg, L. (2003). Successful inclusion: Teaching social skills through curriculum integration. *Intervention in School and Clinic, 38*, 193–210.

Williams, J. P. (2005). Instruction in reading comprehension for primary-grade students: A focus on text structure. *Journal of Special Education, 39*, 6–18.

Williams, J. P., Nubla-Kung, A. M., Pollini, S., Stafford, K. B., Garcia, A., & Snyder, A. G. (2007). Teaching cause-effect text structures through social studies content to at-risk second graders. *Journal of Learning Disabilities, 40*(2), 111–120.

Williams, S. C. (2002). How speech-feedback and word-prediction software can help students write. *Teaching Exceptional Children, 34*(3), 72–78.

Williams, V. I., & Cartledge, G. (1997). Passing notes—Parents. *Teaching Exceptional Children, 30*(1), 30–34.

Wilson, G. L. (2004). Using videotherapy to access curriculum and enhance growth. *Teaching Exceptional Children, 36*(6), 32–37.

Wilson, G. L. (2005). This doesn't look familiar: A supervisor's guide for observing co-teachers. *Intervention in School and Clinic, 40*, 271–275.

Wilson, G. L., & Michaels, C. A. (2006). General and special education students' perceptions of co-teaching: Implications for secondary-level literacy instruction. *Reading and Writing Quarterly: Overcoming Learning Difficulties, 22*, 205–225.

Winerip, M. (2006, March 22). Standardized tests face a crisis over standards. *New York Times,* B7.

Winter, S. M. (2007). *Inclusive early childhood education: A collaborative approach.* Upper Saddle River, NJ: Merrill/Pearson Education.

Winter-Messiers, M. A. (2007). From tarantulas to toilet brushes: Understanding the special interest areas of children and youth with Asperger syndrome. Remedial and Special Education, *Remedial and Special Education, 28*(3), 140-152.

Wissick, C. A., Gardner, J. E., & Dempsey, M. (2009, April). *Implementing universal design for learning and differentiated instruction with free web tools.* Presentation at the annual meeting of the Council for Exceptional Children, Seattle.

Witzel, B., Mercer, C. D., & Miller, M. D. (2003). Teaching algebra to students with learning difficulties: An investigation of an explicit instruction model. *Learning Disabilities Research and Practice, 18*, 121–131.

Witzel, B. S., Riccomini, P. J., & Schneider, E. (2008). Implementing CRA with secondary students with learning disabilities in mathematics. *Intervention in School and Clinic, 43*(5), 270–276.

Witzel, B., Smith, S. W., & Brownell, M. T. (2001). How can I help students with learning disabilities learn algebra? *Intervention in School and Clinic, 37*, 101–104.

Wolf, M., & Barzillai, M. (2009). The importance of deep reading. *Educational Leadership, 66*(6), 32–37.

Wolfe Poel, E. (2007). Enhancing what students can do. *Educational Leadership, 64*(5), 64–67.

Wolfensberger, W. (1972). *The principle of normalization in human services.* Toronto: National Institute on Mental Retardation.

Wolgemuth, J. R., Cobb, R. B., & Alwell, M. (2008). The effects of mnemonic interventions on academic outcomes for youth with disabilities: A systematic review. *Learning Disabilities Research and Practice, 23*(1), 1–10.

Wood, K. D. (1995). Guiding middle school students through expository text. *Reading and Writing Quarterly: Overcoming Learning Difficulties, 11*(2), 137–147.

Wright, E. R., Drewniak, L. M., & O'Dell, R. (2009). *After-school tutoring and students with learning disabilities: Impact on writing/attitude.* Presentation at the annual meeting of the Council for Exceptional Children, Seattle.

Wrigley, P. G. (2004, November). *Does this migrant child belong in special education?* Presentation at the New York State Migrant Education Conference, Syracuse.

Wurst, D., Jones, D., & Luckner, J. (2005). Promoting literacy development with students who are deaf, hard-of-hearing, and hearing. *Teaching Exceptional Children, 37*(5), 56–62.

Wyatt, E. (2000, April 5). More special education students taking and passing the Regents exam. *New York Times,* B6.

Xin, Y. P., & Jitendra, A. K. (1999). The effects of instruction on solving mathematical word problems for students with learning problems: A meta-analysis. *Journal of Learning Disabilities, 32*(4), 207–225.

Xin, Y. P., & Jitendra, A. K. (2006). Teaching problem-solving skills to middle school students with learning difficulties: Schema-based strategy instruction. In M. Montague & A. K. Jitendra (Eds.), *Teaching mathematics to middle school students with learning difficulties* (pp. 51–71). New York: Guilford.

Xin, Y. P., Jitendra, A. K., & Deatline-Buchman, A. (2005). Effects of mathematical word problem-solving instruction on middle school students with learning problems. *Journal of Special Education, 39*, 181–192.

Xin, Y. P., Wiles, B., & Lin, Y. (2008). Teaching conceptual model-based word problem story grammar to enhance mathematics problem solving. *The Journal of Special Education, 42*(3), 148–162.

Yehle, A. K., & Wambold, C. (1998). An ADHD success story: Strategies for teachers and students. *Teaching Exceptional Children, 30*(6), 8–13.

Yell, M. L. (1997). Teacher liability for student injury and misconduct. *Beyond Behavior, 8*(1), 4–9.

Yell, M. L. (2006). *The law and special education* (2nd ed.). Upper Saddle River, NJ: Merrill/Pearson Education.

Yell, M. L., Katsiyannis, A. Ryan, J. B., & McDuffie, K. A. (2009). Schaffer v. Weast: The Supreme Court on the burden of proof in special education due process hearings. *Intervention in School and Clinic, 44*(4), 241–245.

Yell, M. L., Busch, T. W., & Rogers, D. C. (2007. Planning instruction and monitoring student performance. *Beyond Behavior, 17*(1), 31–38.

Yell, M. L., Katsiyannis, A., Ryan, J. B., McDuffie, K. A., & Mattocks, L. (2008). 20 ways to ensure compliance with the individuals with disabilities education improvement act of 2004. *Intervention in School and Clinic, 44*(1), 45–51.

Yell, M. L., Katsiyannas, A., & Shiner, J. G. (2006). The No Child Left Behind Act, adequately yearly progress, and students with disabilities. *Teaching Exceptional Children, 38*(4), 32–39.

Yell, M. L., & Peterson, R. L. (1995). Disciplining students with disabilities and those at risk of school failure: Legal issues. *Preventing School Failure, 39*(2), 39–44.

Yell, M. L. & Rozalski, M. E. (2000). Searching for safe schools: Legal issues in the prevention of school violence. *Journal of Emotional and Behavioral Disorders, 8,* 187–196.

Yell, M. L., Shriner, J. G., Meadows, N. & Drasgow, E. (2009). *Evidence based practices for educating students with emotional and behavioral disorders.* Upper Saddle River, NJ: Merrill/Pearson Education.

Yell, M. M. (2002). Putting gel to pen to paper. *Educational Leadership, 60*(3), 63–66.

Young, E. L., Allen Heath, M., Ashbaker, B. Y., & Smith, B. (2008). Sexual harassment among students with educational disabilities: Perspectives of special educators. *Remedial and Special Education, 29*(4), 208–221.

Yssel, N., Engelbrecht, P., Oswald, M. M., Eloff, I., & Swart, E. (2007). Views of inclusion: A comparative study of parents' perceptions in South Africa and United States. *Remedial and Special Education, 28*(6), 356–365.

Ysseldyke, J., Lehr, C. A., & Stodolka Bulygo, A. (2008). Supplemental educational servies: Implications for students with disabilities. *Remedial and Special Education, 29*(6), 333–342.

Ysseldyke, J., Nelson, J. R., Christenson, S., Johnson, D. R., Dennison, A., Triezenberg, H., Sharpe, M., & Hawes, M. (2004). What we know and need to know about the consequences of high-stakes testing for students with disabilities. *Exceptional Children, 71,* 75–94.

Ysseldyke, J., Thurlow, M., Bielinski, J., House, A., Moody, M., & Haigh, J. (2001). The relationship between instructional and assessment accommodations in an inclusive state accountability system. *Journal of Learning Disabilities, 34,* 212–220.

Zambo, D. M. (2007). What can you learn from Bombaloo? Using picture books to help young students with special needs regulate their emotions. *Teaching Exceptional Children, 39*(3), 32–39.

Zambo, D. M. (2008). Looking at ADHD through multiple lenses: Identifying girls with the inattentive type. Intervention in School and Clinic, 44(1), 34-40.

Zambo, D. M. (2009). Using visual literacy to help adolescents understand how images influence their lives. *Teaching Exceptional Children, 41*(6), 60–67.

Zapf, S. (2008). Reaching the fragile student. *Educational Leadership, 66*(1), 67–71.

Zaslavsky, C. (2002). Exploring world cultures in math class. *Educational Leadership, 60*(2), 66–69.

Zentall, S. S. (2006). *ADHD and education: Foundations, characteristics, methods, and collaboration.* Upper Saddle River, NJ: Merrill/Pearson Education.

Zetlin, A. G., Weinberg, L. A., & Shea, N. M. (2006). Improving educational prospects for youth in foster care: The educational liaison model. *Intervention in School and Clinic, 41,* 267–272.

Zhang, D. (2001). Self-determination and inclusion: Are students with mild mental retardation more self-determined in regular classrooms? *Education and Training in Mental Retardation and Developmental Disabilities, 36,* 357–362.

Zhang, D., & Katsiyannis, A. (2002). Minority representation in special education: A persistent challenge. *Remedial and Special Education, 23,* 180–187.

Zhao, Y. (2007). Speech technology and its potential for special education. *Journal of Special Education Technology, 22*(3), 35-42.

Zigmond, N. (2006). Reading and writing in co-taught secondary school social studies classrooms: A reality check. *Reading and Writing Quarterly: Overcoming Learning Difficulties, 22,* 249–268.

Zigmond, N., Jenkins, J., Fuchs, L. S., Deno, S., Fuchs, D., Baker, J. N., Jenkins, L., & Couthino, M. (1995). Special education in restructured schools. Findings from three multi-year studies. *Phi Delta Kappan, 76,* 531–540.

Zipprich, M. A., Grace, M., & Grote-Garcia, S. A. (2009). Building story schema: Using patterned books as a means of instruction for students with disabilities. *Intervention in School and Clinic, 44*(5), 294-299.

Zorfass, J., & Clay, K. (2008). Biology, reading, comprehension, and technology: Tools for shaking it up. *Journal of Special Education Technology, 23*(4), 53–61.

Zorfass, J. M., Fideler, E. F., Clay, K., & Brann, A. (2007, May). Enhancing content literacy: Software tools help struggling students. *Technology in Action, 2*(6), 1–12.

Zorfass, J., Follansbee, R., & Weagle, V. (2006). Integrating applets into middle grades math: Improve conceptual understanding for students with math difficulties. *Technology in Action, 2*(2), 1–12.

Zuger, S. (2008). Build better eportfolios. *Technology and Learning, 29*(1), 46–37.

Zwiers, J. (2005). The third language of academic English. *Educational Leadership, 62*(4), 60–63.

Zwiers, J., & Crawford, M. (2009). How to start academic conversations. *Educational Leadership, 66*(7), 70–73.

Name Index

Subject Index

Abandonment, of assistive technology, 57–58
A-B-C (antecedents-behavior-consequences) analysis, 247–249
Ableism, 178
Absence seizure, 82
Abstract strategies, in mathematics instruction, 418
Academic difficulties, 64–65, 112
Academic learning games, 349
Academic performance
    impact of inclusion on, 31–32, 33–34, 510
    traumatic brain injury and, 85
Academic performance evaluation, 456–492. *See also* Assessment
    alternatives to standardized and teacher-made tests, 479–490, 492
    standardized testing, 457–462
    study and test-taking skills instruction, 462–467, 468–469, 491–492
    teacher-made tests, 469–479
    technology-based testing and assessment, 491–492
    test anxiety, 467, 469
Acceptability, of differentiated instruction strategies, 296
Acceptance, fostering, 199–200
Access differentiation techniques, 291
Accessibility, 319, 322, 323
Accommodation plans, Section 504, 29, 30
Accommodations. *See also* Testing accommodations
    classroom design, 275–276, 278–280
    curricular, 289–290
    in IEP, 57
    individualized teaching/instructional, 290–291
    instructional materials, 292
Accountability, individual, 358–359
Acculturation, 163
Achievement gap, 121
Achievement standards, alternate, 52
Acknowledging students, 253–254
Acquired conditions, 78
Acquired immune deficiency syndrome (AIDS), 123, 125, 196
Acronyms, 445
Acrostics, 445
Active responding, 350–351, 482–483
Activities-oriented approaches to science and social studies instruction, 440–441
Activity reinforcers, 261
ACT-REACT learning strategy, 232
Adapted physical educators, 141–142
Adapted switches, 323
Adapted textbooks, 436
ADD (attention deficit disorder), 70–72, 73
Additive approach to multicultural curriculum, 309
Administrators, school, 138
Adopted children, 126–127
Adulthood, transition to, 224–230
Advance organizers, 436-437
Adventures of Jasper Woodbury, The, 422
Advocacy, 157–158, 221, 231, 234
Advocacy groups, 20
Affective education, 255
Affinity support groups, 235–236

Affirmative sentences, 202
African Americans, 21, 121
Aggressive behaviors, 273
AIDS (acquired immune deficiency syndrome), 123, 125, 196
Aimline, 481
Algorithm models, 429
Aligned text, 307
All-capital printing, 306
Allergies, 79–80
All learners/students, as term, 1–2
Alphabetic principle, 376
Alternate achievement standards, 52
Alternative assessment, 115
Alternative teaching, 144, 145
American Foundation for the Blind, 199
Americans with Disabilities Act, 29, 493
Analytic approach to phonetics instruction, 380
Analytic rubrics, 488
Anecdotal records, 246–247
Anorexia nervosa, 121, 122
"A" NOTES strategy, 338
Answer box models, 423
ANSWER learning strategy, 468
Antecedent-based interventions, 256
Antecedents, 247
Antecedents-behavior-consequences (A-B-C) analysis, 247–249
Antibias curriculum, 189
Anticipation guides, 439, 440
Anticipatory sets, 348
Applets, 421–422
A priori model, 155
Articulation disorders, 74
Asian and Pacific Islanders, 107
Asperger syndrome, 87
ASSERT learning strategy, 234
Assessment. *See also* Academic performance evaluation; Functional behavioral assessment (FBA)
    alternative, 115
    attitudes toward differences, 176–178
    authentic, 483, 492
    concerns about, 508
    differentiated instruction, 289
    dynamic, 481
    English language learners, 112–113, 115, 116, 118
    environmental, 212, 213
    formative, 289, 456
    individualized technology, 52, 56, 58
    mathematics instruction, 430–431
    performance, 483, 492
    portfolio, 483–488
    self-assessment, 189, 263, 395, 430–431, 482
    spelling instruction, 412
    summative, 289, 456
    technology-based, 491–492
Assignment interest preference surveys, 233
Assignment logs, 216–217
Assignment notebooks, 214–216
Assistive technology
    attitude change strategies, 188–189
    deaf and hard of hearing students, 326–327

differentiated instruction, 322–327, 328
English language learners, 327
in IEP, 52, 56–58
for low-incidence disabilities, 76
physical disabilities, 322–324
reading disabilities, 324–326
types, 15–16
visual disabilities, 324–326
Assistive technology devices, 15–16
Assistive technology services, 16
Asthma, 79–80
Ataxia, 78
Athetosis, 78
Attention deficit disorder (ADD), 70–72, 73
Attention difficulties, 112, 279–280
Attention-getting strategies, 340–341
Attitude change strategies, 178–189
    assistive devices, teaching about, 188–189
    books, 187, 188
    checklist, 179
    curriculum guides and instructional materials, 187–188
    disabilities and individuals with disabilities, studying, 186
    disability simulations, 183–185
    fairness issues, 183
    films/videos, 187
    guest speakers, 186–187
    tips, 178–183
Attitudes
    assessment instruments, 176
    social and behavioral performance evaluation, 501
    toward differences, 176–178
    toward disability, 164
    toward inclusion, 35–36, 510
    toward placement, 31, 32–33
Attribution training, 235, 236, 345
Audio diaries, 492
Audiometric test, 90
Audio recordings, 305, 307
Augmentative communications systems, 322
Aura, 82
Authentic assessment, 483, 492
Author's chair, 397
Author talks, 387
Autism, 87
Autism spectrum disorder, 31, 86–89
Automaticity, in mathematics instruction, 418
AWARE strategy, 338

Background, in print materials, 307
Backward design, 289
Balancing (team member role), 143
Bart's Pet Project, 422
Baseline, in curriculum-based assessment, 481
Basic interpersonal communication skills (BICS), 113, 223
Beginning teachers, 155–156
Behavior. *See also* Functional behavioral assessment (FBA)
    antecedent-based interventions, 256
    behavior reduction interventions, 268–270
    consequence-based interventions, 259–262

Graph paper, 430
Graphs, in curriculum-based assessment, 480, 481
Group average evaluation, 266, 369–370
Group evaluation, 266–267
Group free-token response-cost system, 265–266
Group journals, 362, 365
Group-oriented management systems, 262, 264–268
Group processing, 359
Group project/group grade evaluation format, 369
Group *versus* individual performance, 250
Guest speakers, 186–187
Guided Inquiry Supporting Multiple Literacies, 444
Guided notes, 335, 337
Guided reading, 387–388
Guide to Action feature
  disproportionate representation, 23
  equity in the classroom, 123
  families, meeting with, 162
  individual differences, selecting materials about, 188
  learning environment, 391
  oral presentations, 341
  prereferral, 50
  readable/legible materials, creating, 308
  Response-to-Intervention, 50
  rules, 260
  self-determination, 237
  tests, teacher-made, 478–479
  textbook selection, 434

Hands-on learning, 441
Handwriting instruction, 405, 412
Harassment, peer, 270–273, 277
Harder questions, 299
Hardest questions, 299
Hard of hearing, defined, 90. *See also* Deaf and hard of hearing students
Harm, preventing, 270–273
Harmonizing and compromising (team member role), 143
Headbands (assistive device), 323
Hearing aids, 326
Hearing impairments. *See* Deaf and hard of hearing students
Hearing loss warning signs, 92
Hearing officers, impartial, 45
Helping facts, 418
HELP Math, 419, 422
Heterogeneous cooperative groups, 362
Hidden curriculum, 214, 215
Hierarchical graphic organizers, 437–438
Hierarchies, in mathematics instruction, 424
High-functioning autism, 87
High-impact differentiation techniques, 291
High-incidence disabilities, 62–64. *See also specific disabilities*
Highlighting, 217, 304–305, 337–338, 434–435
High-probability request sequences, 269
High-stakes testing, 22, 457, 461–462. *See also* Standardized testing
High-technology assistive devices, 16
Hinging, 474
Hispanics, 21, 107
HIV (human immunodeficiency virus), 123, 125, 196
Holidays, religious, 195
Holistic rubrics, 490
Homebound instruction, 14
Home experience factors, in assessing English language learners, 115, 116
Homelessness, 103, 196
Home-school contracts, 169
Homework, 353, 356–357, 358, 367–368

Horizons Fast Track A-B, 390
Hospitals, 14
Human immunodeficiency virus (HIV), 123, 125, 196
Humor, 182, 253
Hyperglycemia, 81
Hyperlexia, 95–96
Hypertonia, 78
Hypoglycemia, 81
Hypothesis statements, 249
Hypotonia, 78

IDEA. *See* Individuals with Disabilities Education Act (IDEA)
IDEA Amendments of 1997, 25, 26, 27
Idea generation, for writing, 394
IDEAs to Implement Inclusion feature
  AIDS, 125
  attention deficit disorder, 73
  cerebral palsy, 79
  differentiating instruction for English language learners, 314
  expressive language disorders, 76
  family changes, 128
  friendship skills, 203
  gender equity, 194
  generalization, 220
  handwriting instruction, 405
  homework, 358
  IEP meetings, 62
  independent assignments, 356
  laboratory safety, 442
  linguistic diversity, 193
  math and science education, promoting, 450
  mentoring beginning teachers, 156
  motivating students, 347
  oppositional and defiant behaviors, 68
  organizational skills, 218
  readability, enhancing, 305
  self-esteem, 254
  spelling instruction, 408
  Tourette's syndrome, 81
  wheelchairs, transferring students who use, 279
  word problem-solving skills, 428
IEP. *See* Individualized Education Program (IEP)
IFSP (Individualized Family Service Plan), 25
Ignoring, planned, 269–270
Imagery, visual, 304
Immigrants, 68, 100–101, 107–110. *See also* Culturally and linguistically diverse students
Impartial hearing officers, 45
Improving Access to Assistive Technology for Individuals with Disabilities Act, 15
Inclusion. *See also* IDEAs to Implement Inclusion feature
  attitudes toward, 35–36, 508
  concerns and solutions, 508–509
  defined, 7–8
  educators, impact on, 35–37
  factors contributing to, 14–23
  families, impact on, 37–39
  implementing, 9–10
  mainstreaming *versus,* 11
  principles, 8, 11
  students with disabilities, impact on, 29, 31–33
  students without disabilities, impact on, 33–35
  universal design for learning principles and, 17–18
  vignette, 4–6
Inclusion program
  evaluating, 456–458
  family member perceptions, 503–504, 506
  improving effectiveness of, 504–505, 507–509
  student perceptions, 500–501
  teacher perceptions, 502–503, 504, 505

Inclusive, individual support model, 230
Independence Enhanced Wheelchair, 324
Independent activities, 214, 353, 354–356
Independent group systems, 267–268
Independent learning period, of second language learning, 114
Independent living arrangements, 229
Individual accountability, 358–359
Individual differences probes, 177
Individualized Education Program (IEP)
  components, 50–52
  defined, 49–50
  in general education settings, 61–62
  grading, 498
  IDEA and, 24, 25–26
  meetings, 62
  sample, 53–56
  special considerations, 52
  standardized and teacher-made testing alternatives, 492
  student involvement, 59–60
  summary form, 61–62, 63
  transition services, 58–59
  universally designed accommodations and, 57
Individualized Family Service Plan (IFSP), 25
Individualized teaching/instructional accommodations, 290–291
Individualized technology assessment, 52, 56, 58. *See also* Assistive technology
Individualized Transition Plan (ITP), 59, 224–226
Individuals-first language, 24–25, 180
Individuals with Disabilities Education Act (IDEA)
  about, 24–25
  assistive technology, 15
  attention deficit disorder, 72
  confidentiality, 158
  IEP, student involvement in, 59
  impact of, 23
  medications, 90
  mental retardation, as term, 19–20
  Section 504 compared to, 27–29
  special education identification process, 26
Individuals with Disabilities Education Act (IDEA) Amendments of 1997, 25, 26, 27
Individuals with Disabilities Educational Improvement Act, 24, 25–27
Individual *versus* group performance, 250
Infants and Toddlers with Disabilities Act, 24
Inferential questions, 297, 444
Information gathering and sharing (team member role), 143
Information-sharing questions, 211
Information-sharing strategies, 178–183. *See also* Attitude change strategies
Informative notices, 168
Initiating (team member role), 143
INSPECT learning strategy, 403
Institutional placements, 14
Instructional bulletin boards, 274
Instructional materials
  accommodations, 292
  attitude change strategies, 187–188
  listening skills, 339
  mathematics instruction, 420–422
  multicultural, 190–191, 309–311
  science and social studies instruction, 431–439
  self-determination, 237–238
  universal design for learning, 290
Instructional rubrics, 383–384, 488–490, 492
Instructional support teams, 46, 47
Instructional technology. *See also* Technology
  captioned television, interactive white-smartboards, and liquid crystal display computer projection panels, 318